General Index for the Linguistic Atlas of the Gulf States

Linguistic Atlas of the Gulf States

Volume Two
General Index for the Linguistic Atlas of the Gulf States

Lee Pederson, Editor
Susan Leas McDaniel, Associate Editor
Carol M. Adams, Assistant Editor

The University of Georgia Press
Athens and London

The work of the LAGS Project and the publication of this book
were made possible through the generous assistance of the
Research Tools Program of the National Endowment for the Humanities
and Emory University.

The editors and the publisher express their grateful appreciation.

The paper in this book meets the guidelines for permanence and durability
of the Committee on Production Guidelines for Book Longevity
of the Council on Library Resources.

Printed in the United States of America
92 91 90 89 88   5 4 3 2 1

Library of Congress Cataloging in Publication Data
(Revised for vol. 2)

Linguistic atlas of the Gulf States.

    Vol. 2–   Carol M. Adams, assistant editor.
    Bibliography: v. 1, p. [315]–363.
    Includes index.
    Contents: v. 1. Handbook for the Linguistic atlas
of the Gulf States—v. 2. General index for the
Linguistic atlas of the Gulf States.
    1. English language—Dialects—Gulf States—Atlases.
I. Pederson, Lee, 1930–   .
PE2970.G85L56 1986   912'.142'0976   83-24139
ISBN 0-8203-0715-7 (v. 1 : alk. paper)
ISBN 0-8203-0972-9 (v. 2 : alk. paper)

British Library Cataloging in Publication Data available.

Linguistic Atlas of the Gulf States

Lee Pederson, Director

Concordance Editors

Lee Pederson
Susan Leas McDaniel
Marvin Bassett

Concordance Editorial and Research Assistants

Waqas Ahmed
Nora Pederson
Nancy-Laurel Pettersen
Dawn Sutton
Margaret Whittier

Foreign Language Consultants

Glen E. Lich, Schreiner College, Kerrville, TX (German)
John J. Nitti, University of Wisconsin, Madison (Spanish)
George F. Reinecke, University of New Orleans (French)

Computer Consultants

C.J. Harden, Computing Center, Emory University
William H. McDaniel, Southern Bell
John J. Nitti, University of Wisconsin
Ronald S. Wood, Computing Center, Emory University

Contents

Introduction   ix

    A Concordance of Basic Materials   ix

    A Matrix for World Geography   xvi

    The General Index   xviii

Abbreviations   xxi

The General Index   1

Introduction

This index reorganizes the entries of the LAGS Concordance in a word list. As the *Handbook* (1986) explained the contents of the *Basic Materials* (1981) and served as a reader's guide to the collection of phonetic notation, this index provides an initial interpretation of the concordance. Rewritten in modified orthographics—conventional spelling with a few editorial symbols—the concordance reports all phonetic texts of the protocols in a close approximation of ordinary writing. This index inventories those orthographic forms, laying a foundation for the analysis that will follow.

Published by University Microfilms International, the *Concordance to the Basic Materials of the Linguistic Atlas of the Gulf States* (1986) appears in 153 fiche. These include the working papers of the second series, as described in the Handbook (313), those of the third series, described below, the introduction to the concordance, and the concordance itself in 40,934 pages.

Because the concordance is a directory both to the phonetic texts of the Basic Materials and the orthographic texts of this index, its form and content require attention here. The introduction to the concordance is therefore reprinted below. Because the working papers of the third series outline LAGS work in progress, their contents are also summarized here as "A Matrix for Word Geography." A review of those preliminary considerations explains how phonetic strings are transliterated in both concordance and index. Like the concordance, however, this index is a research tool that can be used without editorial elaboration.

A Concordance of Basic Materials

The LAGS Concordance is an alphabetical finding list of every word and phrase from the narrow phonetic notations of the LAGS protocols, transliterated into conventional spelling. It serves as a companion to the protocols by presenting all of their phonetically transcribed data in an uncomplicated format to accommodate a wide variety of readers. The materials are the idiolects of 1,121 natives of 452 counties and parishes in Alabama, Arkansas, Florida, Georgia, Louisiana, Mississippi, Tennessee, and Texas, as preserved on magnetic tape. Following the principles of completeness, consistency, and simplicity, LAGS seeks to make the retrieval of its data as convenient as possible, not only to linguistic geographers but also to anyone interested in the heritage of the South.

The LAGS corpus consists of field records (tape-recorded interviews) and the corresponding transcriptions of selected items that make up the protocols. The protocol collection contains approximately 700 "complete" volumes (those with at least 80% of the work-sheet items recorded, without the urban supplement), 300 "incomplete" volumes (those with less than 80% of the basic work-sheet material), and 164 volumes with the urban supplement, some of which are complete and some

incomplete. Every entry from every protocol appears in the concordance, and each entry has in turn been parsed by computer so that every word appears in the alphabetical list.

The rules for converting the protocol entries to the concordance format are the product of experiments in the spring and summer of 1981. The editors first made handwritten reductions of the phonetics to conventional spellings, proofreading and commenting on each other's work. They discussed changes in the direction of simplicity and consistency. The implementation of the concordance program involved both the conversion of the entries and the proofreading of the daily printouts of converted protocols. Each of the printouts generated by the program was read by the converter; the majority had a second reading by one other editor. In addition, the concordance itself was proofread and corrected by all three editors.

Using *Webster's Third New International Dictionary of the English Language, Unabridged* as the principal authority, the editors attempted to maintain consistency in the spelling of concordance entries. In most instances, the first spelling from the dictionary was used in the conversion, though some exceptions permitted a limited number of dialect forms. The most common of these are the following:

chimley (for *chimney*)   overhauls (for *overalls*)
chitlins (for *chitterlings*)   sallet (for *salad*)
critter (for *creature*)   shivaree (for *charivari*)
flitter (for *fritter*)   spicket (for *spigot*)
frail (for *flail*)   stomp (for *stamp*)
lighterd (for *lightwood*)   wheelbarrel (for *wheelbarrow*)
mushmelon (for *muskmelon*)

In addition, dialect spellings of verb forms appearing in *Webster's Third*, such as *drownded* (for *drowned*) or *fout* (for *fought*) appear in the concordance. Infinitives, however, have standard spellings regardless of pronunciation. Forms without spellings in *Webster's Third*, including place-names, varieties of fruits and vegetables, trade names, nonce forms, and other dialectal peculiarities, were verified if possible in other written sources or through confirmation by consultants. Those for which no verified spelling could be found were transliterated according to the phonetic transcription. A future errata list will update any concordance spellings that are determined to be incorrect, as well as typographical and conversion errors.

The creation of the concordance was governed by nine basic conversion rules and four additional guidelines for the use of "Phantom Space" (an asterisk to indicate multiple free forms bound for the purpose of word counts but parsed individually):

RULE 1: Convert all uninflected phonetic strings according to the first spelling of *Webster's Third New International Dictionary of the English Language, Unabridged.*

RULE 2: Disregard all deleted or excrescent internal syllables in uninflected phonetic strings.

RULE 3: Record all deleted initial and final syllables of uninflected phonetic strings in parentheses except for derivational suffixes, which will be accepted as pronounced.

RULE 4: Use special spellings only for animal calls, nonce forms, corrupted forms, and dialect spellings recurrently used by American linguistic geographers.

RULE 5: Convert all inflected phonetic strings according to the first spelling of *Webster's Third.*

RULE 6: Mark all deleted or special inflections according to the conventions of LAGS Concordance abbreviations.

RULE 7: Mark all deleted morphological and syntactic grammatical units according to the conventions of LAGS Concordance abbreviations.

RULE 8: Observe LAGS conventions of textual abbreviations, remarks, and marginalia.

RULE 9: Observe LAGS conventions of Phantom Space.

> RULE A: Use Phantom Space to bind all multiword proper nouns.

> RULE B: Use Phantom Space in compound nouns, verbs with postpositionals, and other compounds.

> RULE C: Use Phantom Space in compounds and phrases that provide explicit synonyms for work-sheet items that seek such information.

> RULE D: Use Phantom Space in all structures that comprise *noun + noun.*

LAGS Concordance conventions include scribal and grammatical glosses, symbols for form-class and function words, and markers to show deletion. Other conventions allow for folk etymology and wordplay and for the inclusion of many explanations of lexical and semantic significance, as well as notes on phonology and paralanguage. A list of codes and glosses follows:

Scribal and Conversion Glosses

F   French

G   German

S   Spanish

a   probable scribal error of text or marginal gloss

b   variant (or inappropriate) line use

c   disambiguation of entry

d   false start or hesitation

e   vocal qualifiers, including contrastive / emphatic stress

f   usage and illustration

g   citation

Grammatical Glosses

h   singular number, pronoun and noun

i   plural number, pronoun and noun

j   nominative case, pronoun and noun

k   possessive case, pronoun and noun

l   objective case, pronoun and noun

m   pronoun

n   noun

o   infinitive form, verb

p   third person singular, present (tense) indicative (mood), verb

q   present tense, verb (excluding third singular)

r   preterit tense, verb

s   present participial form, verb

t   past participial form, verb

u   imperative mood, verb

v   verb

w   comparison

x   adjective

y   adverb

z   function word

Textual Codes

[ ] frame deleted grammatical forms and signals, syntactic and inflectional units

( ) frame deleted initial and final syllables, derivational units

< > frame *remarks*, either contexts in conventional orthography provided by the scribe or scribal explanations of entries

Symbols Appearing within Brackets

Form-Class Words	*Function Words*
N- for noun	P- for preposition
V- for verb	X- for verb auxiliary
M- for pronoun	D- for determiner (article)
C- for copula (linking verb)	J- for conjunction
A- for adjective	R- for relative pronoun
B- for adverb	T- for dummy subject (*there*)

Qualifying Symbols

-0 for any deleted form-class or function word

Symbols for deleted inflections of form-class words:

-i for deleted pronoun or noun plural marker

-k for deleted pronoun or noun possessive marker

-p for deleted verb / copula third singular, present indicative marker

-q for other deleted verb / copula present tense marker

-r for deleted verb / copula preterit marker

-s for deleted verb / copula present participial marker

-t for deleted verb / copula past participial marker

-w for deleted adjective or adverb comparison marker

! for *sic*

? for *query*

To locate a particular concordance entry in its protocol, consult the first three columns on the page, headed *BOOK, PAGE,* and *LINE.* The next two columns, *SG* for *Scribal Gloss* and *GG* for *Grammatical Gloss,* may be empty or may contain the appropriate letters from the above code. Additional material within carets following the entry is a context or remark by the scribe or converter, added for clarification. The following is an example:

0768 073 6 d   he just act[V-p] the same with everybody < =common >

This item comes from protocol 768, page 73, line 6. The *d* gloss indicates a false start or hesitation in the pronunciation. The bracketed form following the verb indicates that the third person singular, present indicative, tense marker was deleted by this informant. Finally, the gloss < =*common* > shows that this entry is the informant's definition of *common* as applied to a person.

Homophones, Homographs, and Linkage

Users of the concordance must keep the form, content, and plan in mind. The treatment of homophones and homographs offers one set of examples to illustrate the way the LAGS reference system works. Central to this and every other component of the atlas is linkage. The tape, fiche, book, and disk texts transmit information independently, but they are most effectively used with an eye to their interdependent characteristics as well. Each component was organized as a link in a descriptive chain that extends from the tape-recorded interviews (the tape / text) to the microcomputer files and programs (the disk / text). In an effort to realize maximum coverage, coherence, and efficiency, LAGS composition proceeds bidirectionally through the work, steadily looking back for textual vagaries that require clarification and forward to the complex tasks that might be picked up more efficiently in the future. Until the published disk / text signals the completion of the atlas, LAGS research will continue to seek resources for further improvement. Meanwhile, we will continue to exploit our tools, sharpening older ones and roughing out newer ones in a predetermined, self-directed operation.

As composed, the LAGS concordance could not conveniently distinguish homophonous and, less frequently, homographic forms or explain its own systematic function within the LAGS materials. Homophones require grammatical or semantic glosses; homographs require phonological glosses. The former might have conflicted with basic concordance notation; the latter was impossible prior to the phonological survey reported in Working Paper #2 of the third series, included in this publication. "A Survey in Deductive Phonetics" helped identify the phonic ranges of contrastive units and support the system described as the Automatic Book Code (ABC), a graphophonemic alphabet. The earliest version of that code appears in the first working paper of the same series, "An English Technical Alphabet." The introduction to that series, "A Matrix for Word Geography" explains the relationships among the components of the atlas and anticipates the linkage that unites the parts. The concordance is the central unit of linkage for the fiche / text

and shares an interdependent and parallel function with the index of the book / text, the protocols for the tape / text, and file of files for the disk / text.

Homophonous forms include three sets of data. The first consists of nouns, verbs, modifiers, and function words that carry self-evident explanations. For example, homophonous *brake / break, pin / pen, ten / tin, marry / Mary / merry, hoarse / horse, morning / mourning*, or *heard / herd* require no special notation in the word list. Such pairs are distinguished through spelling. Others, however, need to be disambiguated, including homophonous grammatical forms, such as *done* (preterit, past participle, verb auxiliary, and adverbial), and homophonous lexical forms, such as *pen* (enclosure or instrument) or *can* (noun or verb).

Homographic forms are fewer in number, but these require phonological explanations. Here, the graphophonemic ABC distinguishes forms. Some of these include *read* as infinitive < reed > and preterit < red >, *refuse* as verb < reefyuez > and noun < refyuez >, and *wound* as noun < wuend / wownd > and verb < wownd >. Ideally, this procedure would extend through all phonemic variants in the word list. For example, a reader would be well served with a fully articulated set of variants, as for *French harp*: < french horp / frinch horp / franch horp / fre[n]ch horp / frents horp / french (h)orp / french ho(r)p / french ho[r]p / french hawrp >, to list some of the recorded patterns under that word. However, such notation would delay index publication and obscure descriptive responsibility within the system.

Linkage aims to unite the four LAGS modes—tape, fiche, book, and disk— in an interdependent descriptive system. The tape / text concept was outlined in Pederson's "Tape / Text and Analogues," *American Speech* 49(1974), 5-23. The fiche / text proceeds from that same notion, as a practical method of transmitting more than 174,500 pages of information in a concise format. The Basic Materials, including 129,000 pages of protocol notation (Ann Arbor: University Microfilms International, 1981) and the concordance in 40,000 pages could reach readers in no other way. The book / text includes those volumes published by the University of Georgia Press, initiated by the *Linguistic Atlas of the Gulf States, Volume 1, Handbook* (1986). Plans for the disk / text are outlined in Pederson's "An Electronic Atlas in Microform," the fourth paper in the current series of working papers gathered in the present publication. Here, *linkage* is best understood in the context of the work at hand. We have tried to produce a concordance that is an independently useful research tool. That is to suggest that a student of American literature might find information about a word or phrase in the concordance without reference to any of the other three textual modes. Similarly, a student of lexicography might compare the word list published here with that recorded in *DARE* or other historical dictionaries of the English language. Or a grammarian, historian, cultural geographer, or geographic linguist might consult the pages of the concordance to confirm a hunch without further study.

We also recognize the practical realities of an extended research project. This program is not only "reader friendly," it is also "writer friendly." This characteristic

underscores our dependence upon all the modes of the atlas in the completion of the work. As working papers appear in successive fiche / text publications, so maps not ready for the handbook will appear later as graphic plotter grids. In the same way, descriptive work that would refine this concordance to a higher order of elegance might jeopardize the completion of other tasks. For that reason, we offer as much as we can along that line and use our collective energies here to produce a work with a minimum number of mistakes.

Readers will find descriptive elaboration of most concordance entries elsewhere in the collection. With the matrix design in mind, one may begin here and move through the fiche / text back to the tape / text or forward toward the book / text and the disk / text. That ultimate format, a linguistic atlas on a small number of 5.25 diskettes ("floppy disks"), will offer the best we can provide. That text will file materials and programs for sorting and mapping and will give readers the resources to map all indexed LAGS data in whatever ways the programs allow or they see fit. For workers in the LAGS Project, that is the last word in geographic linguistics.

A Matrix for Word Geography

LAGS Working Papers, Third Series, include seven essays that help explain a research matrix for word study, a formal approach to conventional linguistic geography. They frame the central editorial problems and summarize a descriptive method that extends from writing to mapping. From those perspectives, the papers restate familiar goals in the context of present-day technology. Without violation to the aims of Aasen, Wenker, Gilléron, Jaberg, Jud, and Kurath, the LAGS Project introduced the tape recorder, camera, and computer as essential tools of its research and used them in classical linguistic geography.

These papers extend the implications of those mechanical resources to a public data base—the field records that the protocols index in the Basic Materials (1981). Published with the LAGS Concordance, these papers offer a bridge between the basic and descriptive materials of the atlas. As the concordance records an exhaustive conversion of protocol data, from narrow phonetics to conventional orthographics, these essays explain the form and function of writing systems and the composition of computer mapping through a graphic plotter grid. These editorial issues put the descriptive work in focus and suggest the appropriate domain of traditional linguistic geography.

Although never explicitly stated by the pioneers of this discipline, their work invariably functioned with effectiveness at the level of the phonological word. Gilléron's method requires direct interviewing, without which the investigation could not reach illiterate folk speakers. But the field worker, asking the questions and recording responses on the spot, could elicit and transcribe little information beyond the practical limits of the phonological word. Experienced American atlas

field workers, for example, recognize the difficulties while investigating the usage of these dependent clauses:

> he's the man) who / that / what / 0 (owns the orchard;

> he's the boy) whose / that's / what's / 0 (father is rich.

Such items suggest the problem of gathering systematically contrastive syntactic information with that method. And, for those reasons, traditional atlas study has always focused on the words. In all of the American projects, phonology, morphology, and lexical interpretations begin and end with the phonological word. No one has yet produced a convincing regional or social isogloss based on syntactic data gathered through conventional atlas research.

During the past several decades, however, other American linguists have demonstrated ways to investigate syntax from tape-recorded texts. As suggested elsewhere, the newfound resource brings with it large editorial responsibilities and introduces philological problems that sociolinguists tend to overlook. Because the LAGS program is a transitional atlas, one that seeks traditional goals with the tools of modern technology, its method accepts the limitations of classical atlas research and takes the phonological word as its maximum unit of systematic analysis.

That restriction makes possible a descriptive chain that extends from the systematic (deductive) phonetics of distinctive features analysis through several phonic levels to conventional orthographics. Although other writing systems are occasionally used in LAGS description, the primary codes are these: systematic phonetics (S), impressionistic phonetics (I), unitary phonemics (U), automatics (A), and orthographics (O). In this research, these are understood as links in a bilateral, interdependent, descriptive chain:

$$O > < A > < U > < I > < S$$

Working Papers #1-2, "An English Technical Alphabet" and "A Survey in Deductive Phonetics," explain the interrelationships and implications of these five codes.

As a tool of analysis, that descriptive chain overlays an informational chain to form a matrix for word study. The data base extends from the tape / text (T), through the protocols (P), into the concordance (C), and finally to the maps (M) and legendry (L):

$$T > < P > < C > < M > < L$$

This figure suggests the relationships of study implicit in these chains:

DESCRIPTION

O

INFORMATION T ←———————→ L INFORMATION

S

DESCRIPTION

Working Papers #3-4, "A Graphic Plotter Grid" and "An Electronic Atlas in Microform," explain the composition and uses of the graphic plotter grid. This tool provides a technique for mapping every item recorded in files in any combination that might prove useful in the investigation of regional and social patterns. As an extension of the box grid of the Dialect Survey of Rural Georgia, the programs for the graphic plotter grid offer onscreen or printed maps, and these help to chart the course of the editorial work. Upon completion of LAGS research, the core materials will be reproduced on a set of diskettes. A single packet of 10 double-sided, double-density, 40 track, soft-sectored diskettes will accommodate all necessary personal data files, 225 linguistic files, and an operations disk. As an electronic atlas in microform, the tool has the capacity to produce hundreds of thousands of different maps in a simple and inexpensive program.

Working Papers #5-6, "Mapping Phonetics in the Gulf States" and "A Reference Tool for Southern Folklore Study," explain microcomputer programs for phonology and vocabulary in terms of legendry composition. The phonological evidence proceeds from the survey in deductive phonetics, where distinctive features are identified and where phonological units are classified according to those features. The description terminates in the contrastive orthography of the Automatic Book Code (ABC), where unitary phonemics are realized intuitively (automatically) in a code suitable for legendry (book) composition and where the conventional orthographics of that book are linked with phonic writing. The lexical evidence extends the generalizations of Working Paper #1 to the composition of legendry entries. As suggested in the discussion of ABC, the principal resource of the alphabet is its application to word geography. The code gives a phonological dimension to word geography and helps to distinguish social and regional distribution of a common lexical form, as, for example, in *French harp*, the incidence of <i> and <e> in the first element and of <o(r)>, <or>, <aw(r)> and <awr> in the second.

Working Paper #7, "Microcomputing: Files and Maps for the LAGS Project," summarizes the applications of the microcomputer in the LAGS editorial work. The composition of files, maps, and indexes suggests the range of the work. These include phonological, grammatical, and lexical features drawn from the protocols, the concordance, and the survey in deductive phonetics. Taken together, the examples illustrate the self-imposed limits of a research program that aims at complete, consistent, and simple description on its own terms.

The General Index

The *General Index for the Linguistic Atlas of the Gulf States* is based on the LAGS Concordance. Because the concordance was prepared completely by computer, and the general index has been manually edited, a few systematic differences exist between the two. The index is a summary of the concordance but

is not a substitute for it; the user should always consult the concordance for fuller information, just as the user of the concordance should consult the protocols for clarification or the tapes for ultimate verification.

The general index was initially prepared from the concordance by Emory computer programmer C. J. Harden. To simplify the computer-generated index and to add supplementary information, LAGS editors worked with files created from the original computer tapes by John J. Nitti of the University of Wisconsin. Additional assistance in handling the entries was provided by computer consultant William H. McDaniel.

Each index entry consists of a headword, followed by the total number of occurrences of this word in the concordance, in parentheses. Most totals are followed by the part(s) of speech, as the word is used in LAGS, and the protocol page and line number of the first or principal instance of the word. As in the concordance, homophonous and homographic forms are not separated. Thus, the entry line "desk (879) n / adj 083.8" shows that the headword *desk* occurs 879 times in the concordance, as a noun or adjective, principally on page 83, line 8. French, Spanish, and German words are marked F, S, and G, respectively, following the part of speech. In the case of place-names, two-letter abbreviations designating the state(s) replace the parts of speech, as in "Dadeville (1) AL 087.4." No part of speech appears for uppercase words unless the words are German nouns or in compounds that have lowercase components: e.g., "Danes (1) 128.8" but "Dick's hatband (1) n 042.8." Words that are spelled rather than pronounced by the informant are represented as entirely uppercase (e.g., "KNUKS (1) 059.4," *skunk* spelled backwards, facetiously). Grunts and other sounds are also uppercase.

Headwords that appear as the first element in phrases are followed by each phrase, on a separate line, with the headword replaced by a swung dash (˜). For example:

> dandelion (11) n / adj 055A.5
> ˜ digger (1) n 120.5
> ˜ greens (5) n 055A.5.

In all cases, the total for the headword includes the totals for all the phrases listed below the word, plus instances of the headword in other contexts. For a place-name, the headword alone might serve as a name, in which case it is followed by a state abbreviation. If the phrases are also place-names, each is followed by the state in which it occurs. An example is *Decatur*, which occurs as the name of a town in Alabama, Georgia, and Mississippi, and as a county in Georgia and Tennessee. The index entry appears as follows:

> Decatur (65) AL GA MS 087.6
> ˜ County (6) GA TN 087.6.

Since the index is based on the concordance, a place-name is not always followed by a designation of the type of place, such as *Creek* or *River*. The user of the index can assume that a place-name occurring on page 30, line 7, is a body of water, while those from pages 86 and 87 are likely to be localities or communities. For further information, he should consult the concordance. For many words and phrases, the page and line number indicate the probable meaning: e.g., an entry for 56.9 is probably a watermelon variety, and one for 59.9 is most likely a fish. For spare lines, those which are not designated for work-sheet items, there is usually no way to determine a meaning without using the concordance.

Lowercase headwords precede uppercase instances of the same words (e.g., *dairy* before *Dairy*). A headword partly in parentheses will follow the word without parentheses, but will precede all uppercase uses; that is, *dairy*, *dair(y)*, *dai(ry)*, and *Dairy*. Hyphenated constructions follow those without hyphens (e.g., *deep dish* before *deep-dish*). In the computerized concordance, animal calls and other interjections that occur in multiples, such as *chicky(x3)*, are alphabetized as if the "times" sign (*x*) is the letter *X*. In the edited index, the sign is ignored in the alphabetizing.

All words from the concordance are reproduced in the index with the exception of personal names. Omitted are surnames, given names, animal names, and nicknames, unless those refer to historical or popular figures, or are related to work-sheet items (such as *Bill*, *Billy*, *Will*, and other variants derived from *William*).

Also omitted from the index are contractions with nouns. Contractions with pronouns and verbs are retained, labeled *pron* and *v*, respectively. Nouns which occur in the concordance with contractions are included in the total for the noun without the contraction.

Phrases appear in the index only when they follow the rules for "Phantom Space" in the concordance: proper nouns, work-sheet items and their variants, noun plus noun structures, and verbs plus postpositionals. Generally, lengthy phrases and other syntactic structures are not included.

Some words and proper names, in both the concordance and general index, have not been verified by the editors. These include some foreign words, place-names, and various artifacts, flora, and fauna. Many of these are marked with the gloss *?* in the concordance to indicate uncertainty. Those that are found to be incorrect will be placed on an errata list in a future publication.

Other concordance conventions are reflected in the index. Deleted noun and pronoun plural and possessive markers and unmarked parts of verbs are indicated with the appropriate symbols (e.g., *dive[V-r]* and *dive[V-t]* for the unmarked preterit and past participle). Zero forms are not included in this index except as parts of phrases, but are dealt with in the technical index. See the list of abbreviations below for other conventions used here.

Abbreviations

Parts of Speech

adj	adjective
adv	adverb
conj	conjunction
interj	interjection
n	noun
prep	preposition
pron	pronoun
v	verb

Languages

F	French
G	German
S	Spanish

Sounds

CLICK	clucking to horses, etc.
GRUNT(A)	affirmation
GRUNT(C)	animal call
GRUNT(E)	"enty"
GRUNT(H)	hesitation
GRUNT(N)	negation
GRUNT(O)	oath
GRUNT(R)	request for repetition
TRILL	toad sound

Deletions

A-	adjective
B-	adverb
C-	copula
D-	determiner
J-	conjunction
M-	pronoun
N-	noun
P-	preposition
R-	relative pronoun
T-	dummy subject
V-	verb
X-	verb auxiliary
-0	deleted word
-i	noun / pronoun plural
-k	noun / pronoun possessive
-p	verb third singular, present
-r	verb preterit
-s	verb present participle
-t	verb past participle
-w	adjective / adverb comparison

States

AL	Alabama
AK	Alaska
AR	Arkansas
AZ	Arizona
CA	California
CO	Colorado
CT	Connecticut
DC	District of Columbia
DE	Delaware
FL	Florida
GA	Georgia
HI	Hawaii
IA	Iowa
ID	Idaho
IL	Illinois
IN	Indiana
KS	Kansas
KY	Kentucky
LA	Louisiana
MA	Massachusetts
MD	Maryland
ME	Maine
MI	Michigan
MN	Minnesota
MO	Missouri
MS	Mississippi
MT	Montana
NC	North Carolina
ND	North Dakota
NE	Nebraska
NH	New Hampshire
NJ	New Jersey
NM	New Mexico
NV	Nevada
NY	New York
OH	Ohio
OK	Oklahoma
OR	Oregon
PA	Pennsylvania
RI	Rhode Island
SC	South Carolina
SD	South Dakota
TN	Tennessee
TX	Texas
UT	Utah
VA	Virginia
VT	Vermont
WA	Washington
WI	Wisconsin
WV	West Virginia
WY	Wyoming

The General Index

A

a (46770) adj/prefix 051.8
~ -asking (1) v 057.4
~ -backing up (1) v 057.4
~ -balking (2) v 057.4
~ -barking (1) v 097.8
~ -batting (1) v 057.4
~ -bawling (6) v 036.2
~ -bearing (1) v 057.4
~ -beating (2) v 057.4
~ -being (3) v 057.4
~ -bellowing (2) v 036.3
~ -bird-hunting (1) v 057.4
~ -bleating (3) v 057.4
~ -bleeding (1) v 057.4
~ -bleeding like (1) v 057.4
~ -blowing (22) v 007.4
~ -blowing on (1) v 006.3
~ -blowing up (1) v 057.4
~ -boaring (1) v 035.5
~ -boiling (5) v 057.4
~ -boiling out (1) v 057.4
~ -bossing (1) v 053.7
~ -bothering (2) v 077.6
~ -braying (1) v 036.4
~ -breaking (3) v 057.4
~ -breezing up (1) v 007.2
~ -brewing (1) v 057.4
~ -bringing (1) v 065.4
~ -brooding (1) v 057.4
~ -building (6) v 057.4
~ -bulging (2) v 027.8
~ -bulging out (1) v 027.8
~ -bulging with (1) v 027.8

~ -burning (15) v 057.4
~ -butting (1) v 057.4
~ -buying (5) v 057.4
~ -cackling (1) v 057.4
~ -calculating (1) v 094.1
~ -called (1) v 057.4
~ -calling (4) v 057.4
~ -calming down (3) v 007.3
~ cappella (1) adj 089.5
~ -carpentering (1) v 067.8
~ -carrying (1) v 057.4
~ -carrying on (2) v 079.3
~ -catching (4) v 057.4
~ -ceasing (1) v 007.3
~ -changing (2) v 057.4
~ -chopping out (3) v 015.8
~ -clacking (1) v 057.4
~ -cleaning (3) v 010.4
~ -cleaning up (1) v 010.4
~ -clearing (2) v 057.4
~ -clearing off (1) v 005.7
~ -clearing up (2) v 005.7
~ -climbing (2) v 096.3
~ -coming (37) v 057.4
~ -coming back (2) v 057.4
~ -coming by (1) v 057.4
~ -coming down (1) v 057.4
~ -coming in (1) v 057.4
~ -coming on (1) v 057.4
~ -coming out (3) v 057.4
~ -coming out of (1) v 057.4
~ -coming to (1) v 057.4
~ -coming up (8) v 057.4
~ -cooing (1) v 057.4
~ -cooking (11) v 057.4
~ -coon hunting (1) v 057.4

~ -coughing (4) v 057.4
~ -courting (8) v 081.4
~ -courting a girl (1) v 081.4
~ -courting her (6) v 081.4
~ -courting pretty heavy (1) v 081.4
~ -crawling (1) v 096.2
~ -creeping (1) v 096.2
~ -crowing (1) v 057.4
~ -crying (4) v 057.4
~ -curing (1) v 057.4
~ -cursing (2) v 057.4
~ -cutting (5) v 057.4
~ -cutting away (1) v 057.4
~ -dancing (1) v 057.4
~ -dating (2) v 097.9
~ -delivering (1) v 057.4
~ -digging (1) v 057.4
~ -ditching (3) v 030.2
~ -diving (2) v 095.3
~ -doing (36) v 057.4
~ -doping (1) v 057.4
~ -dragging (2) v 057.4
~ -draining (2) v 030.1
~ -drawing (2) v 057.4
~ -dreaming (2) v 097.2
~ -drilling (3) v 057.4
~ -drinking (4) v 057.4
~ -dripping off of (1) v 057.4
~ -driving (7) v 011.3
~ -driving along (1) v 057.4
~ -drizzling (5) v 006.6
~ -dropping (1) v 006.6
~ -drove (1) v 011.3
~ -drownded (1) v 096.1
~ -drownding (1) v 096.1
~ -drying (1) v 057.4
~ -dying (4) v 007.3
~ -eating (3) v 057.4
~ -falling (6) v 057.4
~ -falling in (1) v 057.4
~ -falls (1) v 057.4
~ -fanning (1) v 057.4
~ -faring (1) v 057.4
~ -farming (3) v 057.4
~ -farming away (1) v 057.4

~ -feeding (4) v 057.4
~ -feeling (2) v 057.4
~ -feisting around (1) v 084.8
~ -fencing with (1) v 096.7
~ -fighting (6) v 104.2
~ -finding (1) v 057.8
~ -finish[V-t] (1) v 057.4
~ -firing (1) v 070.2
~ -fishing (26) v 057.4
~ -fixing (3) v 057.4
~ -fixing to (2) v 101.2
~ -flaring up (1) v 057.4
~ -flicking (1) v 057.4
~ -flirting with her (1) v 081.4
~ -flooding (1) v 057.4
~ -flopping (1) v 057.4
~ -fluttering (1) v 057.4
~ -flying (6) v 057.4
~ -freezing (1) v 058.1
~ -fried (1) v 057.4
~ -furnishing (1) v 057.4
~ -fussing (1) v 057.4
~ -gathering (2) v 005.6
~ -gawking (2) v 057.4
~ -getting (28) v 057.4
~ -getting in (2) v 057.4
~ -getting up (2) v 007.2
~ -giving (2) v 057.4
~ -going (124) v 057.4
~ -going around (3) v 057.4
~ -going down (1) v 077.6
~ -going in (1) v 057.4
~ -going on (1) v 057.4
~ -going out (2) v 057.4
~ -going through (2) v 057.4
~ -going to (73) v 057.4
~ -going with her (1) v 081.4
~ -going with this boy (1) v 081.4
~ -going [P-0] (9) v 057.4

~ -gossiping (1) v 057.4
~ -graded (1) v 057.4
~ -grieving (2) v 057.4
~ -gritting (1) v 060.3
~ -groaning (1) v 099.5
~ -growing (16) v 057.4
~ -growing out (1) v 057.4
~ -growing up (23) v 057.4
~ -growling (1) v 057.4
~ -grunting (1) v 057.4
~ -guessing (1) v 057.4
~ -gushing (1) v 057.4
~ -gusting (1) v 007.2
~ -hammering (1) v 020.7
~ -hanging (4) v 057.4
~ -hanging in (1) v 057.4
~ -hanging on (2) v 097.9
~ -hanging over (1) v 027.4
~ -hanging up (1) v 095.9
~ -hanging [P-0] (1) v 042.7
~ -hard (1) adj 053.4
~ -hatching (1) v 057.4
~ -hauling (8) v 021.4
~ -hauling for (1) v 021.4
~ -hauling with (1) v 021.4
~ -having (5) v 057.4
~ -having to (1) v 057.4
~ -healing (1) v 057.4
~ -hearing (2) v 057.4
~ -helping (3) v 057.4
~ -hemorrhaging (1) v 055.9
~ -hewing (1) v 057.4
~ -hiding (1) v 096.4
~ -hiking (1) v 057.4
~ -hiring (1) v 057.4
~ -hitting (3) v 057.4
~ -hoeing (2) v 057.4
~ -holding (3) v 096.8
~ -holding on (2) v 013.5
~ -hollering (13) v 057.4
~ -holping (1) v 049.5

~ -honing (1) v 023.4
~ -hooping (1) v 057.4
~ -hooting (2) v 057.4
~ -hoping (2) v 057.4
~ -housekeeping (2) v 057.4
~ -howling (1) v 057.4
~ -hugging (1) v 057.4
~ -hunting (19) v 057.4
~ -hunting for (2) v 057.4
~ -hurrying (1) v 097.8
~ -hurting (2) v 057.4
~ -ironing (1) v 057.4
~ -ironing with (1) v 095.9
~ -jaywalking (1) v 085.2
~ -joking (2) v 057.4
~ -joking with (2) v 026.1
~ -juking (2) v 057.4
~ -jumping (3) v 057.4
~ -keeping (2) v 057.4
~ -kicking (2) v 057.4
~ -kidding (3) v 057.4
~ -killing (3) v 057.4
~ -kissing (11) v 081.7
~ -knocking (2) v 057.4
~ -knowing (1) v 057.4
~ la mode (1) adj 123.6
~ -lagging (1) v 057.4
~ -laughing (17) v 057.4
~ -laying (19) v 057.4
~ -laying across (1) v 096.6
~ -laying down (2) v 057.4
~ -laying on (1) v 057.4
~ -laying out (3) v 057.4
~ -leading (1) v 039.4
~ -leaking (1) v 057.4
~ -leaning (1) v 057.4
~ -leaving (1) v 057.4
~ -licking (2) v 057.4
~ -liking (1) v 081.4
~ -listening at (1) v 057.4
~ -living (38) v 057.4
~ -logging (1) v 057.4
~ -looking (11) v 057.4

~ -looking for (1) v 095.8
~ -looking out (1) v 057.4
~ -loose (30) v 057.4
~ -losing (2) v 094.5
~ -loving (3) v 081.7
~ -lowing (5) v 036.3
~ -lying (2) v 007.3
~ -lying down (1) v 007.3
~ -making (19) v 057.4
~ -many (156) adj 040.5
~ -man(y) (3) adj 090.7
~ -marrying (2) v 053.5
~ -matching (1) v 057.4
~ -meddling (1) v 101.3
~ -meeting (1) v 057.4
~ -mending (1) v 057.4
~ -milking (2) v 057.4
~ -misering (1) v 073.5
~ -misting (2) v 006.6
~ -mixing up (1) v 057.4
~ -mizzling (2) v 057.4
~ -moaning (1) v 036.3
~ -molting (1) v 057.4
~ -mooing for (1) v 036.3
~ -mopping (1) v 057.4
~ -mourning (1) v 079.3
~ -moving (6) v 057.4
~ -moving around (1) v 057.4
~ -moving in (1) v 057.4
~ -mowing (1) v 057.4
~ -nabbing (1) v 057.4
~ -nailing (1) v 057.4
~ -naming (1) v 032.7
~ -necking (2) v 081.7
~ -needing (1) v 057.4
~ -nickering (3) v 036.4
~ -not (1) adv 057.4
~ -packing (2) v 098.1
~ -parching (1) v 048.8
~ -passing (2) v 023.6
~ -paying (2) v 057.4
~ -peddling (2) v 088.8
~ -picking (1) v 053.4
~ -picking up (1) v 007.2

~ -piling (1) v 014.6
~ -pimping on (1) v 101.3
~ -pinching (1) v 057.4
~ -pitching (2) v 057.4
~ -planning (1) v 057.5
~ -planning on (2) v 101.2
~ -planting (2) v 057.4
~ -playing (3) v 057.4
~ -playing with (1) v 057.4
~ -plowing (4) v 057.4
~ -pop (2) adv 101.2
~ -popping (1) v 057.4
~ -preaching (4) v 057.4
~ -primping (4) v 057.4
~ -puking (1) v 080.3
~ -puking like a horse (1) v 080.3
~ -pulling (9) v 057.4
~ -pushing (3) v 097.7
~ -putting (2) v 057.4
~ -quieting down (1) v 007.3
~ -quilting (1) v 057.4
~ -quitting (1) v 057.4
~ -raining (12) v 057.4
~ -raising (6) v 057.4
~ -raring (1) v 057.4
~ -rattling (3) v 057.4
~ -reading (2) v 057.4
~ -renting (2) v 057.4
~ -riding (5) v 057.4
~ -ringing (3) v 057.4
~ -rising (4) v 007.2
~ -roaming (1) v 097.8
~ -rolling (1) v 064.6
~ -rooting (1) v 057.4
~ -rottening down (1) v 053.6
~ -running (49) v 102.3
~ -running around (1) v 057.4
~ -running back (1) v 057.4
~ -running down (1) v 057.4
~ -running over (1) v 057.4
~ -sailing (1) v 057.4
~ -sailing out of (1) v 057.4
~ -sampling (1) v 057.4

~ -sawing (1) v 057.4
~ -saying (4) v 057.4
~ -scraping (2) v 057.4
~ -scratching (1) v 057.4
~ -screaming (2) v 057.4
~ -screwing (1) v 057.4
~ -seeing (1) v 002.4
~ -seeing after (1) v 075.6
~ -seesawing (2) v 022.8
~ -selling (5) v 057.4
~ -serenading (2) v 057.4
~ -setting (17) v 049.3
~ -setting on (1) v 049.3
~ -sewing (2) v 057.4
~ -shaking (3) v 057.4
~ -shaving (1) v 057.4
~ -shelling (1) v 055A.2
~ -shining (3) v 097.8
~ -shivareeing (1) v 082.5
~ -shooting (2) v 057.4
~ -shopping (2) v 094.2
~ -showering (1) v 006.6
~ -siccing (1) v 033.2
~ -silking (1) v 056.4
~ -singing (9) v 083.1
~ -sitting (4) v 057.4
~ -sitting in (1) v 057.4
~ -sitting up (1) v 057.4
~ -skipping (1) v 057.4
~ -slapping (1) v 096.8
~ -sleeting (2) v 057.4
~ -slipping (1) v 057.4
~ -slipping up (1) v 102.4
~ -smacking (1) v 081.7
~ -smoking (3) v 057.4
~ -smooching (4) v 081.7
~ -snacking (1) v 048.6
~ -snudging around (1) v 088.7
~ -sparking (1) v 081.4
~ -sparking her (1) v 081.4
~ -spend[V-s] (1) v 097.9

~ -spooning (1) v 081.7
~ -springing (2) v 033.9
~ -sprinkling (5) v 006.6
~ -squalling (1) v 095.8
~ -squatting (2) v 057.4
~ -squirrel hunting (1) v 098.7
~ -staggering (1) v 057.4
~ -standing (6) v 057.4
~ -sticking out (1) v 057.4
~ -stinging (1) v 057.4
~ -stirring (1) v 057.4
~ -stobbing (1) v 104.3
~ -stomping (1) v 097.4
~ -storing (2) v 057.4
~ -storming (1) v 006.2
~ -straightening up (1) v 010.4
~ -striving (1) v 057.4
~ -struggling (1) v 057.4
~ -strutting (1) v 057.4
~ -studying (3) v 088.8
~ -suffering (2) v 057.4
~ -swallowed (1) v 057.4
~ -swallowing (1) v 057.2
~ -sweating (3) v 057.4
~ -sweeping up (1) v 057.4
~ -swimming (9) v 095.6
~ -swinging from (1) v 057.4
~ -taking (1) v 057.4
~ -talking (19) v 057.4
~ -talking about (1) v 013.5
~ -talking (a)bout (3) v 057.4
~ -tattling (2) v 101.3
~ -TC-ing after (1) v 075.7
~ -teaching (2) v 057.4
~ -telling (1) v 057.4
~ -tested (1) v 057.4
~ -thinking (3) v 025.2
~ -thinking about (1) v 057.4
~ -thinning (1) v 057.4

~ -threatening (2) v 005.6
~ -tiling (2) v 030.1
~ -tiptoeing (1) v 057.4
~ -tomcatting (1) v 088.9
~ -toting (3) v 098.1
~ -touching (2) v 098.2
~ -towing (2) v 057.4
~ -tracking (1) v 057.4
~ -trailing (1) v 057.4
~ -training (1) v 057.4
~ -trapping (1) v 057.4
~ -traveling (4) v 057.4
~ -trotting (1) v 057.4
~ -trout fishing (1) v 057.4
~ -trying (4) v 057.4
~ -trying to (5) v 057.4
~ -twisting (1) v 095.9
~ -using (6) v 057.4
~ -visiting (2) v 057.4
~ -wading (1) v 057.4
~ -waiting (3) v 057.4
~ -waiting on (2) v 099.1
~ -walking (8) v 057.4
~ -wanting (5) v 057.4
~ -wanting to (2) v 057.4
~ -warming up (1) v 007.3
~ -washing (6) v 057.4
~ -wasting (1) v 092.8
~ -watching (7) v 057.4
~ -wearing out (1) v 057.4
~ -weaving (1) v 057.4
~ -whacking (1) v 057.4
~ -whinkering (2) v 036.4
~ -whipping (2) v 057.4
~ whipping on you (1) v 065.5
~ -whirling (2) v 057.4
~ -whistling (3) v 057.4
~ -whizzing (1) v 006.2
~ -whooping (1) v 057.4
~ -wiggling (1) v 057.4
~ -wishing (1) v 057.4
~ -wondering (2) v 057.4
~ -working (42) v 057.4

~ -working at (2) v 057.4
~ -working for (2) v 057.4
~ -working in (1) v 016.1
~ -working on (3) v 057.4
~ -worrying (1) v 057.4
~ -writing (2) v 025.3
~ -yawning (1) v 057.4
A (96) 107.6
~ -frame (34) n 022.1
~ -frame house (1) n 118.9
~ -frame houses (3) n 118.9
~ harrow (4) n 021.7
~ har(row) (1) n 021.7
~ harrows (3) n 021.7
~ -Model (1) 023.6
~ -Model Ford (3) 088.8
~ -Models (1) 109.1
~ -O (1) 021.6
~ -One-A (1) 107.6
~ -One Road (1) 031.6
~ roof (2) n 011.4
~ steak (1) n 121.1
~ student (2) n 068.7
~ subject (1) n 080.7
aa(x3) (1) interj 037.5
AAs (1) 069.3
abandon lot (1) n 108.7
abating (5) v 007.3
(a)bating down (1) v 007.3
Abba (3) GA 087.2
Abbeville (24) AL GA LA MS 087.4
Abbie (2) 030.7
Abbottsford (1) GA 087.2
Abby Thomas (1) 106.7
ABC (3) 083.7
~ class (1) n 083.7
~ house (1) n 012.1
abdomen (1) n 080.1
abdom(en) (1) n 075.9
abed (7) adv 097.1
Abeline (1) TX 087.7
Abeltown (1) TN 087.3
Abercorn (1) 107.6
Abercrombie (1) AL 087.1

Aberdeen (9) MS 087.8
~ Road (1) 107.8
Abernathy (3) VA 087.3
~ graveyard (1) n 078.8
abide (1) v 050.6
abiding (2) adj 085.7
Abilene (4) KS TX 087.4
Abingdon (3) VA 087.1
able (183) adj 073.1
~ -bodied (3) adj 073.1
aboard (1) adv 084.8
abortado (1) n S 061.4
about (1250) adv/prep 070.2
(a)bout (704) adv/prep 070.1
(a)bouts (1) adv 088.9
above (90) adv/prep 082.6
~ -the-ground grave (1) n 117.6
~ -the-ground sweet potato (1) n 055.5
(a)bove (6) prep 082.7
aboveground vaults (1) n 117.6
Abraham Lincoln fence (1) n 016.4
Abrams Falls (1) TN 031.5
abscess (19) n 077.4
abscessed (2) v 080.8
abscesses (1) n 077.4
absconded (2) v 100.2
~ with (1) v 100.2
absent (16) adj 083.4
absentminded (6) adj 073.4
absolute (1) adj 125.3
absolutely (26) adv 091.1
absolutes (1) n 089.2
absorb (1) v 057.6
Absorbine Junior (1) 078.3
absurd (1) adj 092.4
abuela (2) n S 064.2
Abuela (1) S 064.2
(a)buelita (1) n S 064.2
(ab)uelita (1) n S 064.2
(ab)uelito (1) n S 064.1
abuelo (3) n S 064.1
(a)buelo (1) n S 064.1
Abuelo (1) S 064.1
abundance (1) n 001A.4
abundant (1) adj 041.3

academies (2) n 080.6
academy (3) n 088.7
Academy (7) 065.9
~ Street (2) 107.7
~ Street High (1) 125.9
Acadia (4) LA 087.1
~ Parish (1) LA 087.1
Acadians (3) 069.8
acantha tree (1) n 061.8
Acapulco (8) 114.1
~ Gold (7) 114.1
~ Green (1) 114.1
accelerator (100) n/adj 110.6
~ pedal (1) n 110.6
(ac)celerator (14) n/adj 110.6
~ pedal (2) n 110.6
accelerators (1) n 065.9
accent (12) n 131.2
accents (1) n 131.2
accept (10) v 058.5
(ac)cept (2) v 097.8
acceptable (1) adj 053.5
accepted (3) v 065.8
access (34) n/adj 107.4
~ ramp (1) n 107.4
~ ramps (1) n 107.4
~ road (11) n 031.8
~ roads (3) n 031.8
accessories (1)˙n 009.4
accident (16) n 085.6
~ -investigation vehicles (1) n 111.8
~ -prone (2) adj 073.3
accidental (1) adv 005.8
accommodate (1) v 057.6
(ac)commodating (1) adj 070.8
accompany (16) v 097.5
(ac)company (2) v 097.5
accompanying (1) v 097.5
accomplish (1) v 040.6
accordeon (1) n F 083.1
according (4) prep 075.8
~ on (1) prep 075.8
~ to (3) prep 095.9
(ac)cording (2) n/prep 075.7
~ to (1) prep 075.2
accordion (7) n/adj 020.5
~ dance (1) n 083.1
~ music (1) n 089.5
(ac)cordion (2) n 020.5

account (156) n/prep 039.6
(ac)count (93) n/prep 039.7
(Ac)count (1) 080.6
(ac)counters (1) n 069.7
(ac)counts (1) n 069.7
(ac)cumulated (1) v 065.9
accumulates (1) v 039.6
(ac)cumulation (1) n 010.2
accurate (5) adj 074.6
(ac)cuse (1) v 013.7
accuse[V-r] (1) v 013.7
accused (2) v 013.7
~ of (1) v 131.2
accustomed to (2) adj 053.7
AC/DC (4) 124.4
ace (4) n/adj 129.4
~ boon coon (1) n 129.4
~ of spades (3) n 069.3
(a)cetylene (5) adj 070.7
~ gas (1) n 070.7
~ lamps (1) n 024.3
~ lights (2) n 070.7
~ torch (1) n 075.6
ache (4) n 079.6
aches (1) n 079.6
aching (1) adj 090.7
acid (52) n/adj 114.2
~ rock (9) n 130.9
~ rock music (1) n 130.8
~ soil (2) n 029.8
acid[N-i] (1) n 016.7
acidic (1) adj 029.8
acidosis (1) n 080.3
acidy (1) adj 029.9
Ackerman (1) MS 087.7
Acme (2) LA 087.7
~ harrow (1) n 021.7
acne (2) n 077.4
acolytes (1) n 070.6
acorn (76) n/adj 056.6
~ catcher (1) n 011.5
~ head (1) n 074.8
~ nut (1) n 054.7
~ squash (35) n 056.6
~ squashes (1) n 056.6
~ tomatoes (1) n 055.3
~ trees (4) n 061.9
Acorn (2) 107.7

~ Avenue (1) 107.7
acorns (55) n 054.8
Acosta (1) 106.4
acoustic (1) adj 130.8
acquaintance (6) n 092.6
acquainted (4) v 075.6
~ to (2) v 032.8
~ with (1) v 092.6
acre (76) n/adj 051.8
~ lot (1) n 016.1
acre[N-i] (6) n 088.1
acreage (13) n 090.7
acreages (1) n 041.9
acres (145) n 016.1
Acres (8) 106.4
across (913) adv/prep 028.9
~ the river (1) n 130.2
(a)cross (160) adv/prep 082.6
acrosswise (1) adv 085.2
act (50) n/v 073.4
~ like (26) v 065.3
~ [J-0] if (1) v 100.1
act[V-p] (20) v 100.1
~ like (13) v 100.1
act[V-r] (21) v 100.1
~ as if (1) v 100.1
~ like (18) v 100.1
acted (150) v 100.1
~ as (2) v 100.1
~ as if (27) v 100.1
~ as though (8) v 100.1
~ like (93) v 100.1
~ [J-0] if (2) v 100.1
acting (27) v/adj 100.1
~ bar (1) n 022.6
~ like (4) v 100.1
~ pole (1) n 022.9
~ rookie (1) v 083.4
~ up (1) v 005.6
action (3) n 073.6
actions (6) n 065.3
active (372) adj 074.1
activeful (1) adj 074.1
activity (1) n 081.2
actor (90) n/adj 069.1
~ lady (1) n 069.1
~ star (1) n 069.1
actors (5) n 069.1
actress (650) n 069.1
actresses (3) n 069.1
actress's wife (1) n 069.1
acts (159) v 065.3
~ as if (1) v 100.1

~ like (109) v 065.3
actually (7) adv 091.6
acute indigestion (2) n 076.1
Acworth (1) GA 087.3
ad alley (1) n 099.7
Ada (1) OK 087.4
adagio (1) n 065.8
Adair (1) 106.5
Adairsville (2) GA 087.5
Adam[N-k] (28) 071.7
  ~ apple (27) n 071.7
  ~ ap(ple) (1) n 071.7
adamant (3) adj 074.8
Adamo Drive (1) 105.7
Adam's apple (292) n 071.7
Adams (18) MS 087.7
  ~ County (3) MS 087.9
  ~ Field (1) 106.5
  ~ Hospital (1) 084.5
  ~ House (1) 106.4
  ~ Park (1) 106.7
  ~ Street (1) 107.7
Adamsville (4) TN 105.6
add (5) v 070.3
  ~ onto (1) v 027.2
  ~ to (1) v 071.2
  ~ up (1) v 013.1
added (6) v 057.9
  ~ to (4) v 089.2
adder (21) n 093.7
adders (6) n 089.9
addict (112) n 114.3
addicted (3) v/adj 114.3
addiction (1) n 114.3
addicts (11) n 114.3
Addie (3) 031.4
  ~ Boat Dock (1) 031.4
  ~ Landing (2) MS 031.4
adding (2) v 025.4
  ~ to (1) v 101.3
Addison (1) AL 087.1
addition (2) n 090.4
Addition (3) 087.3
Additions (1) 105.4
addle (1) v 090.4
addlebrained (1) adj 074.7
addled (1) adj 074.7
address (1462) n/v/adj 100.8
  ~ book (1) n 100.8
(ad)dress (9) v 100.7

address[V-r] (1) v 100.7
addressed (35) v 100.7
(ad)dressed (1) v 100.7
addresses (4) n 100.8
addressing (31) v 100.7
(ad)dressing (1) v 100.7
Adel (4) GA 087.8
Adele Street (1) 107.7
adequate (1) adj 070.7
Adger (1) AL 087.2
adios (1) interj S 002.4
adjacent (4) adj 085.2
adjoin[V-s] (1) v 089.2
(ad)joining (2) v 089.2
adjourn (2) v 083.2
adjourns (3) v 083.2
adjust (1) v 010.4
administration (2) n 070.6
Administration (1) 088.8
administrator (4) n 115.4
(ad)ministrator (5) n 066.4
admirable (2) adj 073.2
admiral (8) n 068.5
Admiral (2) 108.9
  ~ Semmes (1) 106.4
  ~ Semmes Hotel (1) 108.9
admire (3) v 028.1
admirer (1) n 081.5
admiring (1) v 028.1
admission (2) n 080.6
adobe (4) n/adj 081.8
  ~ -covered brick (1) n 119.7
  ~ houses (1) n 081.9
(a)dobe (5) n/adj 060A.7
  ~ brick (1) n 007A.3
  ~ roads (1) n 031.6
adolescent (1) n 065.8
Adonis (2) 125.3
adopted (15) v/adj 066.4
  ~ by (1) v 104.6
  ~ child (2) n 065.7
  ~ family (1) n 066.4
  ~ home (1) n 066.3
  ~ parent (1) n 066.4
  ~ parents (6) n 066.4
(a)dopted (3) v/adj 066.4
  ~ parents (2) n 066.4
(a)dorable (1) adj 073.2
Adrian (1) GA 087.1
adult (32) n/adj 065.8
  ~ center (1) n 114.9
  ~ cinema (2) n 114.9

~ film (1) n 114.9
~ movie houses (1) n 114.9
~ movie theater (2) n 114.9
~ movie theaters (1) n 114.9
~ movies (2) n 114.9
~ stores (1) n 114.9
~ theater (7) n 114.9
~ theaters (8) n 114.9
(a)dult theaters (1) n 114.9
(a)dulterated (2) v 033.3
  ~ up (1) v 069.5
advance car (1) n 111.6
advanced (2) v/adj 070.6
advancement (1) n 077.8
advantage (1) n 092.4
advantages (1) n 039.7
Advention (1) 002.2
Adventist (8) 089.1
Adventist[N-i] (1) 089.1
adversary (4) n 090.1
adversity (1) n 104.8
advertised (1) v 070.6
advertisement (1) n 070.6
advertisements (2) n 065.8
advertising (2) v 095.7
advice (2) n 039.8
adviser (1) n 129.5
advises (1) v 052.5
advocates (1) n 065.8
adz (9) n 020.7
AEDC Lake (1) TN 030.7
aerial (8) adj 111.4
  ~ fire-fighter truck (1) n 111.4
  ~ ladder (3) n 111.4
  ~ truck (2) n 111.3
  ~ trucks (1) n 111.3
Aerial (1) GA 087.4
afar (1) adv 052.2
afeard (8) adj 074.3
(a)feard (1) adj 074.3
affable (5) adj 073.2
affair (4) n 130A.7
affairs (3) n 130.7
affect (1) v 070.7
affectionate (12) adj 066.1
affiliated (1) v 089.2
afflicted with (1) v 078.7
affliction (1) n 052.6

affluent (2) adj 070.6
(af)fluent (1) adj 065.9
afford (31) v 053.4
  ~ to (5) v 057.7
(af)ford (2) v 012.5
  ~ to (1) v 053.1
afghan (8) n 029.1
afghans (5) n 029.1
afire (87) adj 103.5
afloat (2) adv 024.5
afoot (4) adv 072.6
afore (3) prep/conj 089.7
afoul of (1) prep 032.6
afraid (766) adj 074.3
  ~ -like (1) adj 074.3
(a)fraid (225) adj 074.3
Africa (5) 087.9
African (34) 069.3
  ~ invasion (1) n 025.6
  ~ lamp (1) n 024.3
  ~ Methodist (1) 089.1
  ~ red worm (1) n 060.5
  ~ type (1) n 035.9
  ~ violet (1) n 051.8
  ~ watermelon (1) n 056.9
  ~ worm (1) n 060.5
African[N-i] (1) 069.3
Africans (16) 069.3
Afro (124) 123.9
  ~ -American (10) 069.3
  ~ -American engineers (1) n 069.3
  ~ -American Sons and Daughters Hospital (1) 084.5
  ~ -Americans (7) 069.3
  ~ -Cuban white (1) n 069.5
  ~ hair (1) n 123.9
  ~ look (1) n 123.9
  ~ -Saxon (1) 099.5
  ~ style (1) n 123.9
  ~ wild (1) n 080.6
(A)fro (13) 123.9
after (1510) adj/adv/ prep/ conj 032.7
  ~ five (1) n 080.6
  ~ -hours dance (1) n 083.1
  ~ meal (4) n 048.6
  ~ -wedding party (1) n 082.5
aft(er) (12) prep/conj 032.8

af(ter) (2) prep 065.3
aftermath (11) n 041.5
afternoon (881) n/adj
  002.3
  ~ chores (1) n 037.4
  ~ day (1) n 002.3
  ~ shower (1) n 006.1
afternoons (16) n 002.3
afterwards (1) adv 003.7
Afton Oaks (1) 106.2
again (1433) adv 093.1
(a)gain (5) adv 093.1
Again (1) 093.1
against (69) prep 065.9
(a)gainst (7) prep 104.8
agarita (2) n 062.2
agate (1) n 130.6
agates (1) n 130.6
age (105) n 046.9
Age (1) 129.3
aged (5) v 047.5
  ~ out (1) v 046.9
agencies (1) n 085.6
agency (1) n 070.6
agen(cy) (1) n 085.6
agent (3) n 119.6
agents (1) n 114.4
ages (5) n 004.6
aggie (3) n 101.7
Aggie (3) 099.6
  ~ jokes (1) n 099.6
aggies (2) n 130.6
Aggies (1) 069.4
aggravate (6) v 088.9
aggravated (12) v/adj
  075.2
aggravates (2) v 079.5
aggravating (7) v/adj
  065.8
aggravatingest (1) adj
  060A.7
aggravation (2) n 066.8
aggravator (1) n 063.2
Aggression (9) 085.8
aggressive (5) adj 124.3
(ag)gressive (1) adj 124.6
agile (34) adj 074.1
agitate (1) v 075.2
agitator (1) n 066.7
Agnes (1) 115.9
agnostic (1) n 088.7
ago (1890) adj 005.2
(a)go (6) adj 003.8
agree (18) v 025.4
  ~ with (11) v 091.1

(a)gree with (1) v 073.2
agreeable (23) adj 073.2
(a)greeable (2) adj 073.2
agriculture (2) n 066.8
Agriculture Street (1)
  107.7
aground (3) adv 102.3
agua (1) n S 028.6
Agua Dulce Creek (1) TX
  030.7
aguardiente (1) n S 050.8
ague (3) n 077.8
agues (2) n 076.1
ah (16) interj 037.7
aha (1) interj 092.2
ahead (67) adv 040.1
(a)head (13) adv/prep
  049.2
ahold (29) n 066.8
aholt (10) n 095.9
ahorseback (4) adv 096.9
aid (6) n/adj 012.3
Aid (5) 093.2
aide (6) n 065.2
aides (2) n 084.6
Aiken Creek (1) TX
  030.7
Aikens Lake (1) AL
  030.7
ailed (1) v 076.1
Ailey (1) GA 087.2
ailing (5) v 072.9
ailment (1) n 075.6
ailments (1) n 060.5
ails (1) n 012.2
aim (36) v 101.2
  ~ to (33) v 101.2
aim[V-p] to love her (1)
  v 081.4
aim[V-s] to (1) v 101.2
aimed to (4) v 101.2
aiming (46) v 101.2
  ~ on (2) v 101.2
  ~ to (29) v 101.2
  ~ [P-0] (1) v 101.2
Aimwell (2) AL LA 087.1
ain't (3428) v 025.4
  ~ no boogers (1) n
    130.1
Ain't Dead Yet (1) 025.3
air (253) n/v/adj 065.9
  ~ brake (1) n 063.2
  ~ -condition (15) n/adj
    118.5

~ -condition bugs (1) n
  060A.4
~ -condition flies (1) n
  060A.5
~ -conditioned (1) adj
  065.9
~ -conditioner (12) n
  118.5
~ -conditioners (7) n
  118.5
~ conditioning (16) n
  118.5
~ -conditioning system
  (1) n 118.5
~ -conditioning unit (1)
  n 118.5
~ -conditioning units
  (1) n 118.5
~ -conditioning vents
  (1) n 118.5
~ -conditions (1) n
  088.7
~ corps (1) n 081.9
~ -dried (1) adj 091.8
~ duct (1) n 118.5
~ ducts (2) n 118.5
~ force (3) n 070.7
~ guns (1) n 039.7
~ handler (1) n 118.5
~ -logged (1) adj 090.8
~ mattress (1) n 029.2
~ out (1) v 064.5
~ pocket (1) n 031.3
~ sealer (1) n 020.3
~ space (1) n 009.8
~ terminal (2) n 106.5
~ vents (2) n 008.1
Air (5) 106A.1
airboats (4) n 024.6
aircraft inspector (1) n
  051.8
Airdome (1) 084.4
Airedales (1) 033.3
Aires (1) 087.6
airfield (26) n 106.5
Airfield (1) 106.5
airing (4) n 064.6
airish (99) adj 007.4
airline (2) adj 109.8
  ~ limousine (1) n 109.8
  ~ mosquitoes (1) n
    060A.8
Airline Highway (3) 031.6
airman (1) n 068.4
airplane (7) n/adj 109.5

~ decorator (1) n 053.8
~ sleeping porch (1) n
  010.8
airplanes (7) n 065.9
airport (104) n/adj 106.5
  ~ bus (5) n 109.8
  ~ limousine (17) n
    109.8
  ~ limousine service (1)
    n 109.8
  ~ limousines (1) n
    109.8
Airport (104) 106.5
  ~ Boulevard (3) 107.6
airports (2) n 106.5
airs (6) n 100.1
airstrip (1) n 106.5
airstrips (1) n 106.5
airtight (2) adj 011.2
  ~ heater (1) n 118.4
Airway (1) 116.7
Airways (2) 107.5
airy (5) adj 007.4
aisle (2) n 015.3
Ajax harrow (2) n 021.7
AK-ing (1) v 125.6
akin (5) adj 066.5
Akins Creek (1) AL
  030.7
Akison Creek (2) TN
  030.7
Akron (4) OH 087.9
Alabama (1109) 086.4
  ~ fools (2) n 069.4
  ~ ham (1) n 046.3
  ~ melon (1) n 056.9
  ~ number-one bean (1)
    n 055A.4
  ~ River (16) AL 030.7
  ~ road (1) n 086.4
  ~ State (2) 086.4
  ~ Striped Back (1)
    056.9
  ~ Sweets (1) 056.9
Alabam(a) (7) 086.4
(Ala)bama (1) 086.4
Alabamans (1) 090.9
alabaster (5) n/adj 017.1
  ~ eggs (1) n 017.1
Alachua County (1) FL
  087.2
(A)lachua (6) FL 087.8
  ~ County (3) FL 087.1
Aladdin (11) 024.2
  ~ lamp (9) n 024.2

~ lamps (1) n 088.7
~ lantern (1) n 024.3
(A)laddin (4) 024.2
~ lamp (1) n 024.2
~ lamps (3) n 024.3
Alafia River (1) FL 030.7
Alafi(a) River (1) FL 030.7
Alaga syrup (1) n 051.3
alamo (1) n 061.8
Alamo (21) 106.4
~ Dam Lake (1) TX 030.7
~ Heights (9) 106.1
~ Plaza (2) 106.6
Alapaha (3) GA 030.7
~ River (2) GA 030.7
(A)lapaha (7) GA 087.8
~ River (3) GA 030.7
(a)larm (2) v/adj 070.9
~ clock (1) n 039.6
(a)larmingitis (1) n 076.4
Alaska (9) 086.6
Alazan (2) TX 030.7
~ Creek (1) TX 030.7
Albany (69) GA 087.7
~ State (1) 097.4
~ Theater (1) 084.4
albatross (1) n 091.9
Albermarle (1) 107.7
Albert (5) 057.3
~ Woody (1) 106.6
Albertville (1) AL 087.3
albino (17) n/adj 069.5
~ squirrel (2) n 059.7
albinos (4) n 069.5
albumin (4) n 045.7
albums (1) n 130.8
Albuquerque (2) NM 087.3
Alcazar Yard (1) 066.9
Alcoa (6) TN 087.3
~ Highway (2) 107.5
alcohol (56) n/adj 050.8
~ rub (1) n 070.8
alcoholic (98) n/adj 113.6
~ beverages (2) n 050.8
~ (E)piscopalian (1) n 126.5
~ parties (1) n 130.7
~ -testing thing (1) n 111.8
alcoholics (14) n 113.6
Alcorn (2) MS 087.2
Alcorub (2) 078.4

alcove (8) n/adj 007A.3
~ thing (1) n 080.7
Alcovy River (1) GA 030.7
alder (7) n/adj 061.9
~ tags (1) n 061.6
alderman (3) n 069.1
aldermen (4) n 080.8
aldermens (2) n 065.8
alders (1) n 010.5
Aldrich (1) AL 087.3
ale (9) n 121.9
Alec Mountain (1) GA 031.1
aleck (24) n 100.1
aleckes (1) n 125.5
alecks (4) n 092.1
alecky (1) adj 125.6
alert (33) adj 074.1
Aleutian Field (1) 106.5
Alexander (6) AR 087.8
~ City (5) AL 087.4
Alex(ander) City (4) AL 087.4
Alexandria (31) KY LA VA 086.5
Alexandri(a) (19) LA 087.7
Alexandr(ia) (1) LA 087.8
Alexand(ria) (1) LA 087.2
Alex(andria) (1) LA 087.6
Alexis (1) AL 087.2
alfalfa (18) n/adj 066.8
~ hay (2) n 014.6
~ worm (1) n 060.5
alfia tree (1) n 061.9
alfias (1) n 061.9
algebra (3) n 070.8
Algiers (4) LA 086.7
Algoma (3) MS 087.4
Aliceville (1) AL 087.9
alien (28) n 066.7
aliens (4) n 066.7
(a)light (1) v 088.8
alike (34) adj 065.3
(a)like (1) adj 065.3
alina tree (1) n 061.5
alive (57) adj 074.1
(a)live (2) adj 025.8
alkali (2) n 070.6
alkaline (4) adj 029.8
~ sand (1) n 029.8

~ soil (1) n 029.8
alkies (3) n 113.6
alky (2) n 113.6
all (5185) adj/adv/pron 082.8
~ -American (2) adj 069.2
~ -American boy (1) n 069.2
~ -American city (1) n 069.2
~ -American dog (1) n 033.3
~ -American dogs (1) n 033.3
~ around the Maypole (1) n 092.7
~ -beef wieners (1) n 121.8
~ -black school (3) n 069.3
~ -day dinner (1) n 088.9
~ -day rain (4) n 006.6
~ -day sucker (1) n 080.8
~ -dirt roads (1) n 074.4
~ four[N-i] (3) n 072.8
~ fours (19) n 072.8
~ -night food store (1) n 116.2
~ -night grocery (2) n 116.2
~ -night-long torch (1) n 024.3
~ -night store (1) n 116.2
~ right (168) adj 079.4
~ r(ight) (3) adj/adv 066.8
~ righty (4) adv 091.3
~ the (2) adv 028.9
~ the way (575) adv 028.9
~ the [N-0] (1) adv 028.9
~ -weather fence (1) n 126.1
~ -weather road (2) n 031.6
~ -white church (1) n 088.7
~ -white community (1) n 088.8

~ -white country club (1) n 088.8
~ [D-0] way (31) adv 028.9
All (4) 055.5
~ Gold (1) 055.5
~ Heart (2) 056.9
~ Seasons (1) 055.3
all[M-k] (16) pron 043.7
Allan (3) 087.7
Allatoona (3) GA 030.7
~ River (1) GA 030.7
allee (1) n F 031.9
Alleghenies (1) 082.6
Allen (16) LA 055.5
~ Branch (1) TN 030.7
~ Homes (1) 105.4
~ Parish (2) LA 087.6
~ Parkway (3) 107.5
~ Theater (1) 106.7
~ Thompson Field (1) 106.5
Allendale (4) GA 087.3
Allenhurst (1) GA 087.1
Allens Landing (4) 106.4
Allensville (1) TN 087.2
allergic (3) adj 053.5
(al)lergic (2) adj 065.9
allergy (1) n 063.2
alleviate (1) v 099.4
alley (175) n/adj 108.6
~ cat (3) n 059.4
~ dog (6) n 033.3
~ lawyers (1) n 067.8
~ road (2) n 031.8
~ -type thing (1) n 030.5
Alley (8) 108.6
alleys (78) n 108.6
alleyway (6) n 108.6
alleyways (3) n 108.6
Alliance (1) 088.8
Allie T. Nesta School (1) 066.8
alligator (60) n/adj 060.6
~ bait (1) n 069.3
~ catchers (1) n 069.9
~ fleas (1) n 060.5
~ gar (8) n 059.9
~ gars (3) n 059.9
~ hunting (1) n 099.8
~ mushmelon (1) n 056.7
~ pole (1) n 089.8
~ skin (1) n 056.8

~ snapper (1) n 060.6
~ snapping turtles (1) n
  060.6
~ tail (1) n 080.6
~ terrapin (1) n 060.7
~ trails (1) n 031.8
~ turtle (14) n 060.6
~ turtles (5) n 060.6
(alli)gator (10) n/adj
066.9
~ bait (1) n 069.3
~ baits (1) n 069.3
~ holes (1) n 080.8
~ tail (1) n 060.6
~ -tail terrapins (1) n
  060.6
~ -tail turtle (1) n
  060.6
Alligator (4) 107A.5
~ Alley (1) 107A.5
~ Creek (1) FL 030.7
~ Gully (1) LA 030.7
~ Lake (1) FL 030.7
alligator[N-i] (1) n 024.9
alligators (20) n 059.8
(alli)gators (4) n 059.5
allotment (3) n 016.1
(al)lotment (3) n 016.1
allotments (1) n 016.1
(al)lotments (2) n 016.1
allover (2) adj 026.4
~ apron (1) n 026.4
~ suit (1) n 027.4
allow (1) v 039.8
(al)low (3) v 040.7
allowed (13) v 025.4
~ in (1) v 025.4
~ to (6) v 049.6
(al)lowed (5) v 088.2
~ to (1) v 039.6
(al)lows (1) v 065.8
all's (179) pron 043.7
all'ses (3) pron 043.6
alluvial (8) adj 029.9
~ clay (1) n 029.8
~ plain (1) n 029.4
~ soil (3) n 029.4
~ topsoil (1) n 029.8
alluvi(al) (1) adj 029.8
(al)luvial (de)posits (1) n
029.8
Alma (4) AR LA 087.9
almanac (1) n 070.7
Almeda (3) 105.1
almighty (3) adj 092.3

Almighty (48) 089.3
~ God (5) 089.3
Almighty[N-k] sake (1) n
092.2
almond (248) n/adj 054.9
~ Danish (1) n 122.2
~ groves (1) n 061.6
~ macaroons (1) n
  122.2
~ nut (3) n 054.9
~ nuts (6) n 054.9
~ paste (1) n 054.9
~ seed (1) n 054.9
~ -shaped (1) adj 054.9
~ tree (1) n 054.9
~ trees (2) n 064.9
Almond (11) 030.7
~ Bayou (1) TX 030.7
~ Joy (9) 054.9
~ Joys (1) 054.9
almond[N-i] (1) n 054.9
almonds (353) n 054.9
Almorgo(do) Avenue (1)
093.9
almost (900) adj/adv
070.1
(al)most (130) adj/adv
070.2
Almyra (1) AR 087.4
aloe (6) n/adj 061.4
~ lotion (1) n 061.4
~ plant (1) n 061.4
~ tree (1) n 061.4
~ vera (2) n 061.4
aloes (2) n 078.4
alone (14) adj/adv 044.2
along (213) adv/prep
057.4
(a)long (61) adv 093.2
alongside (2) prep 028.9
aloose (1) adv 091.9
Aloysius College (1)
070.6
alpaca suit (1) n 027.7
alphabet (2) n 083.7
Alpharetta (2) GA 086.4
Alpine (2) AL 087.3
already (291) adv 057.9
also (18) adv 053.8
Altamaha (13) GA 030.7
~ River (7) GA 030.7
altar (4) n 051.9
alter (32) v 036.1
alt(er) (2) v 036.1
alter[V-r] (1) v 036.1

alterate (1) v 036.1
alteration (2) n 036.1
altercation (1) n 104.2
altered (28) v 036.1
altering (5) v 036.1
alternate (2) v/adj 036.1
~ road (1) n 037.1
alternator (1) n 110.5
althea (1) n 061.8
Altheimer (2) AR 087.6
although (1) conj 066.8
Alto (2) GA 087.4
altogether (1) adv 074.4
Alton (3) IL 107.9
~ Park (1) 106.3
altos (1) n S 030.8
Alucha Hill (1) 106.4
alum (1) n 078.2
aluminum (108) n/adj
065.9
~ boat (6) n 024.6
~ boats (2) n 024.6
~ -bottom boat (1) n
  024.6
~ -bottom boats (1) n
  024.6
~ bucket (7) n 017.3
~ buckets (3) n 017.3
~ double boiler (1) n
  017.6
~ fishing boat (1) n
  024.6
~ fishing boats (1) n
  024.6
~ foil (1) n 065.9
~ kettle (1) n 017.6
~ milk bucket (1) n
  017.3
~ pail (2) n 017.3
~ pan (1) n 017.5
~ siding (13) n 011.2
~ skillet (2) n 017.5
~ water bucket (1) n
  017.3
alumin(um) (3) n/adj
066.9
~ boat (1) n 024.6
(a)luminum (52) n/adj
017.3
~ blinds (1) n 009.5
~ boats (6) n 024.6
~ boxes (1) n 079.1
~ bucket (6) n 017.3
~ buckets (5) n 017.3

~ doors (1) n 070.7
~ fishing boat (1) n
  024.6
~ flat-bottom boat (1)
  n 024.6
~ pails (1) n 017.3
~ plant (1) n 025.2
~ pot (1) n 017.6
~ siding (4) n 011.2
~ soil (1) n 029.8
(a)lumin(um) (1) n
070.8
(a)lumi(num) (3) n
017.4
alumni (1) n 070.6
(a)lumni parties (1) n
130.7
alumnus (1) n 068.7
Alvarado (1) TX 087.3
Alvaton (1) GA 087.4
Alvin (4) TX 087.7
alway (1) adv 103.4
always (1451) adv 103.4
am (1048) v 042.6
(a)m (3) v 024.8
AM (2) 002.2
A&M (2) 106.4
~ College (1) 083.6
Ama (1) LA 087.6
amapola (1) n S 070.9
Amarillo (7) TX 087.1
~ willow (1) n 061.8
amateur (3) n 067.8
amaze (1) v 049.8
amazed (1) v 013.5
amazing (4) adj 042.6
Amazon (1) 124.3
Amazons (1) 124.3
ambeer (1) n 088.7
amber (2) adj 080.7
amberjack (2) n 080.8
amberjacks (1) n 059.9
ambiance (1) n 080.6
ambitious (1) adj 074.1
amble irons (2) n 008.3
ambrosia (1) n 048.5
ambulance (108) n/adj
111.5
~ driver (1) n 070.9
~ truck (1) n 111.5
ambulances (8) n 111.5
AME (2) 089.1
~ Zion Methodist (1)
  089.1
amen (4) interj 091.1

amenable (1) adj 073.2
America (47) 069.2
(A)merica (2) 069.2
americain (1) adj F 069.2
(a)mericain (1) adj F 044.3
American (819) 069.2
~ army (1) n 069.2
~ Beauty buggy (1) n 093.6
~ -born citizen (2) n 069.2
~ -born man (1) n 069.4
~ Box (1) 069.2
~ Business School (1) 069.2
~ catsup (1) n 069.2
~ cheese (3) n 048.1
~ chestnut (3) n 061.9
~ citizen (21) n 069.2
~ citizens (2) n 069.2
~ citizenship (1) n 069.2
~ Civil War (2) 085.8
~ elms (1) n 061.8
~ engine (1) n 069.2
~ flag (1) n 069.2
~ government (1) n 069.2
~ grass (1) n 015.8
~ history (2) n 069.2
~ Indian (1) 069.2
~ Indians (3) 126.4
~ League (1) 069.2
~ League baseball (1) n 069.2
~ Legion (6) 069.2
~ Legion Hall (1) 069.2
~ Lutherans (1) 069.2
~ machoism (1) n 084.8
~ maps (1) n 069.2
~ name (1) n 069.2
~ National (1) 108.5
~ Negroes (1) 069.3
~ of France (1) 111.2
~ people (4) n 069.2
~ race (2) n 069.4
~ Revolution (2) 069.2
~ wire (3) n 016.3
~ woman (1) n 069.2
(A)merican (128) 069.2
~ -born (1) adj 069.2

~ -born citizen (1) n 069.2
~ bread (1) n 044.3
~ Can Company (1) 069.2
~ cheese (1) n 048.1
~ citizen (1) n 069.2
~ citizens (3) n 069.2
~ Family Life building (1) n 108.5
~ fence (2) n 016.3
~ kids (1) n 069.2
~ League (1) 069.2
~ Legion (1) 069.2
~ Legionnaire (1) 069.2
~ man (1) n 069.2
~ National Bank Building (1) n 108.5
~ people (3) n 069.2
~ wire (6) n 016.3
Americanese (1) 131.1
Americanized (1) 069.2
americano (1) n S 069.5
Americans (108) 069.2
(A)mericans (17) 069.2
Americus (15) GA 087.7
amesite (2) n/adj 031.7
amethyst (1) n 123.1
amiable (11) adj 073.2
Amicalola Falls (1) GA 087.7
amigo (1) n S 129.4
Amigoland (1) TX 086.5
amigos (1) n S 002.4
Amite (8) LA 086.5
~ River (7) LA MS 030.7
(A)mite County (1) MS 087.7
Amity (2) AR 087.5
Ammis Park (1) 085.1
ammoniated mercury (1) n 078.3
ammunition (21) n 022.4
ammunitions (2) n 022.4
among (3) prep 085.8
amongst (9) prep 065.8
Amory (1) MS 087.4
amount (35) n/v 090.8
~ to (1) v 013.1
(a)mount (4) n/v 053.5
~ to (2) v 104.6
amphetamine (2) n 114.2
amphetamines (29) n 114.2

(am)phetamines (1) n 114.2
ampmeter (1) n 110.1
Amsterdam Avenue (2) 107.7
Amtrak (1) 080.8
amused (1) v 013.8
amusement parks (1) n 106.5
Amy (1) 125.5
an (2306) adj 118.9
(a)n (23) adj 069.1
Anacoco (10) LA 087.4
~ Creek (3) LA 030.7
~ Lake (1) LA 030.7
Anadama bread (1) n 044.9
Anadarkos (1) 070.9
analyze (1) v 065.8
anaqua (7) n/adj 062.3
~ tree (1) n 080.6
~ trees (1) n 061.8
(a)naqua (2) n 061.8
anaquas (1) n 061.8
Anastasia (2) 087.7
~ Island (1) FL 087.7
~ State Park (1) 086.8
ancestor (2) n/adj 088.7
~ bugs (1) n 088.7
ancestors (5) n 066.5
ancestry (1) n 053.3
anchor (8) n/v/adj 016.3
~ chain (1) n 016.3
Anchor Lake (1) MS 030.7
Anchorage (2) AK 087.8
anchored down (1) v 075.7
and (10148) conj 051.8
(a)nd (37) conj 088.1
Andalusia (15) AL 087.4
Anderson (10) GA IN TN 087.3
~ County (4) SC TN TX 087.3
~ Hall (1) 106.4
~ Island (1) LA 087.5
Andersonville (3) GA TN 087.3
Andies (1) 048.3
andiron (27) n/adj 008.3
~ set (1) n 008.3
andiron[N-i] (3) n 008.3
andirons (394) n 008.3
and/or (1) conj 082.4

andouille (7) n F 037.3
Andrew (8) 030.7
~ Jackson (2) 106.6
~ Jackson Hotel (2) 108.5
~ Jackson's home (1) n 106.4
~ Johnson Highway (1) 107.5
Andrews (2) 106.1
andy over (1) n 084.8
Andy (2) 048.3
~ apple (1) n 048.3
~ Brown's Creek (1) GA 030.7
anemic (3) adj 072.9
anesthesia (1) n 070.9
angel (31) n/adj 090.2
~ biscuit (1) n 044.4
~ dust (13) n 114.2
~ food (2) n 122.2
~ food cake (1) n 122.3
~ food cakes (1) n 122.1
~ hair (1) n 056.4
~ mushroom (1) n 057.1
~ wing (1) n 123.9
~ wings (1) n 115.5
Angel Face (1) 064.4
Angeles (24) 087.3
Ang(eles) (1) 087.8
angelfish (2) n 059.9
Angelina (8) TX 030.7
~ River (6) LA TX 030.7
Angelo (4) 087.6
angels (3) n 114.2
Angels (1) 066.4
anger (3) n 075.2
Angie (1) LA 087.8
anglais (1) adj F 079.7
angle (66) n/v/adj 085.2
~ -bottom (1) adj 024.6
~ in (1) v 108.3
~ -in parking (1) n 108.3
~ park (1) v 108.3
~ parking (24) n 108.3
~ side (1) n 085.2
Angle (2) 082.7
~ Avenue (1) 082.7
angle[V-t] (1) v 085.2
angled (1) v 085.2

angles (1) n 060.5
angleworm (3) n 060.5
angleworms (8) n 060.5
Anglican (2) 089.1
angling (20) v/adj 085.2
   ~ across (3) v 085.2
   ~ worms (1) n 060.5
Anglo (41) 069.4
   ~ -American (2) 069.2
   ~ customs (1) n 069.4
   ~ -Saxon (10) 069.4
   ~ -Sax(on) (1) 069.4
   ~ -Saxon four-letter
     words (1) n 090.8
   ~ -Saxon race (2) n
     069.4
   ~ -Saxons (1) 069.4
Anglos (7) 069.4
angly (1) adj 085.2
Angola (5) LA 087.8
Angora goats (2) n 081.8
angry (299) adj 075.2
   ~ flesh (1) n 078.2
an(gry) (1) adj 075.2
anguish (1) n 070.7
angular (3) adj 085.2
   ~ parking (1) n 108.3
Angus (28) 033.6
   ~ cattle (1) n 081.9
animal (42) n/adj 059.5
   ~ barn (2) n 014.2
   ~ bitc (1) n 095.9
   ~ dips (1) n 045.2
   ~ heat (3) n 091.9
   ~ husbandry (1) n
     070.6
   ~ sheds (1) n 011.7
   ~ yard (1) n 015.6
animal[N-i] (6) n 036.5
animals (264) n 036.5
animated (1) adj 073.2
ankle (49) n/adj 072.7
   ~ boot (1) n 123.8
   ~ skinning (1) n 083.1
   ~ strap (1) n 123.8
   ~ wipers (1) n 123.3
ankles (1) n 070.1
anklet (1) n 123.1
anklets (1) n 028.4
Ankry (1) MS 087.6
Ann (2) 030.7
Anna (2) MS 087.7
Annapolis (5) MD 087.2
Annee (1) F 093.3

Annette River (1) LA
030.7
annex (1) n 106.9
Annie (4) 130.4
   ~ Annie over (1) n
     130.4
   ~ Green Springs (2)
     114.7
Anniston (21) AL 087.5
anniversaries (1) n 130.7
anniversary (9) n/adj
070.6
   ~ kings (1) n 088.8
   ~ parties (3) n 130.7
   ~ party (2) n 130.7
annoy (1) v 013.1
annoyed (1) v 075.2
annuity (1) n 066.8
Annunciation Square (1)
106.4
Ano (1) S 093.3
anopheline mosquito (1)
n 078.5
another (246) pron/adj
066.8
   ~ world (1) n 078.5
anoth(er) (5) adj 070.7
(a)nother (26) pron/adj
010.5
(a)no(ther) (1) pron
103.2
(A)nother Year (1) 093.3
Ansley (7) 087.9
   ~ Park (5) 106.2
answer (971) n/v 100.6
   ~ back (1) v 100.6
   ~ for (1) v 100.6
   ~ up (1) v 100.6
answer[V-r] for (1) v
096.7
answered (43) v 100.6
   ~ for (3) v 100.6
   ~ to (1) v 100.6
answering (15) n/v 100.6
answers (50) n/v 100.6
   ~ for (1) v 100.6
ant (38) n/adj 060A.7
   ~ bed (1) n 060A.8
   ~ bit (1) v 033.4
antebellum (13) adj 088.8
   ~ days (1) n 065.8
   ~ home (2) n 007A.2
   ~ homes (4) n 080.8
   ~ mansion (1) n 118.9
   ~ -type (1) adj 118.9

   ~ -type home (1) n
     118.9
antelope (1) n 081.8
Antelope Gap (1) TX
031.3
anteroom (6) n 010.3
anteworm (1) n 081.9
anthem (2) n 089.5
anthems (1) n 089.5
Anthony (2) FL 087.6
   ~ Ferry (1) LA 087.9
anthracite coal (1) n
088.9
anti-lynching law (1) n
070.7
antibiotics (1) n 065.9
antigens (1) n 079.9
antigodlin (90) adj/adv
085.2
antigod(lin) (1) adv
085.2
antihistamines (1) n 078.6
Antillean Creole (1) 080.9
Antioch (8) AR GA LA
MS TN 087.7
   ~ Baptist Church (1)
     089.1
   ~ Creek (1) GA 030.7
antiquated (1) adj 065.9
antique (38) n/adj 010.2
   ~ armoire (1) n 009.7
   ~ chest (1) n 009.2
   ~ couch (1) n 009.1
   ~ furniture (2) n 009.4
   ~ room (1) n 010.3
   ~ stuff (6) n 010.2
   ~ things (1) n 013.9
   ~ trash (1) n 010.2
antique[N-i] (1) n 010.2
antiques (39) n 010.2
antiquey-type (1) adj
065.8
antiquing (1) v 080.7
antiseptic (8) adj 078.3
Antoine (2) AR 087.3
Antonio (65) 082.7
Antoni(o) (1) 087.9
Anton(io) (10) 030.7
(An)tonio (6) 030.7
(An)ton(io) (1) 087.5
antony over (11) n 098.4
ants (87) n 060A.5
antses (10) n 016.7
antsy (1) adj 074.1
anvil (12) n/adj 039.3

   ~ hammer (1) n 020.7
   ~ -shooting (1) n 091.8
   ~ wheel (1) n 023.5
anvils (3) n 008.3
anxious (29) adj 074.2
any (1610) adj/pron
040.8
   ~ damn thing (2) pron
     092.2
   ~ old place (1) pron
     040.2
an(y) (4) pron 049.6
(a)ny (3) pron 012.5
anybody (98) pron 070.2
anybo(dy) (1) pron 057.5
anybody's (2) adj 102.7
anyhow (108) adv 040.7
anymore (164) adv 095.2
anyone (27) pron 040.7
anyplace (115) adv 040.2
(any)place (1) adv 040.2
anything (454) pron 040.6
anythings (1) pron 039.7
anytime (18) adv 040.2
anyway (526) adv 040.7
anyways (10) adv 040.7
anywhat (1) conj 042.7
anywhere (762) adv 040.2
(any)where (2) adv 040.2
anywheres (46) adv 040.2
Apalachee River (1) GA
030.7
Apalachicola (15) FL
087.5
   ~ Bay (1) FL 030.3
   ~ River (4) FL 030.7
apart (53) adv 070.6
(a)part (3) adv 070.4
apartment (180) n/adj
119.2
   ~ building (18) n 119.2
   ~ buildings (9) n 119.2
   ~ complex (17) n 108.5
   ~ complexes (4) n
     119.2
   ~ house (19) n 119.2
   ~ houses (25) n 119.2
   ~ maintenance (1) n
     119.5
   ~ manager (3) n 119.5
   ~ projects (1) n 119.2
(a)partment (29) n/adj
014.1
   ~ building (2) n 119.2
   ~ buildings (3) n 119.2

~ complex (6) n 119.2
~ complexes (1) n 119.2
~ floor (1) n 119.4
~ hotel (1) n 119.2
~ house (4) n 119.2
~ house[N-i] (1) n 119.2
~ houses (2) n 088.9
~ manager (1) n 119.5
apartments (72) n 119.2
(a)partments (4) n 119.2
Apartments (1) 030.6
ape (9) n 069.3
apes (5) n 069.3
apex (1) n 011.6
apiece (7) adv 045.4
aplenty (19) adv 096.9
apoints (1) v 066.4
apologize (1) v 090.6
apoplexy (1) n 079.6
Appalachian (8) 086.2
~ area (1) n 086.2
~ Highland (1) GA 031.3
~ Highway (1) 107.6
~ Mountains (2) GA 087.4
~ Trail (3) 107.9
Appaloosa (6) 059.9
~ cat (1) n 059.9
~ catfish (1) n 075.6
~ cats (1) n 059.9
apparel (2) n 085.6
apparition (1) n 090.2
apparitions (3) n 090.2
appeal to (2) v 013.1
appealing (2) adj 125.3
appeals to (1) v 053.5
appearance (2) n 065.4
appears (2) v 088.3
appendectomy (16) n 066.8
(ap)pendectomy (1) n 080.1
appendices (1) n 080.1
appendicitis (405) n 080.1
appendici(tis) (2) n 080.1
appendi(citis) (1) n 080.1
(ap)pendicitis (408) n/adj 080.1
~ operation (1) n 080.1
(ap)pendicit(is) (1) n 080.1

(ap)pendici(tis) (2) n 080.1
(ap)pendic(itis) (1) n 080.1
appendix (56) n/adj 080.1
~ attack (5) n 080.1
~ operation (3) n 080.1
(ap)pendix (58) n/adj 080.1
~ attack (1) n 080.1
~ operation (1) n 080.1
~ trouble (1) n 080.1
appetite (3) n 039.8
appetizer (1) n 048.3
appetizing (1) adj 051.1
apple (1766) n/adj 061.9
~ Betties (1) n 048.3
~ Betty (4) n 048.3
~ bread (1) n 044.3
~ brown Betty (1) n 048.3
~ butter (12) n 051.6
~ cake (6) n 048.3
~ cider (4) n 080.8
~ cobbler (122) n 048.3
~ cobbler pie (4) n 048.3
~ cobblers (6) n 048.3
~ core (11) n 054.5
~ country (1) n 025.2
~ crisp (3) n 048.3
~ crunch (2) n 048.3
~ dumpling (7) n 048.3
~ dumplings (12) n 048.3
~ float (1) n 048.3
~ fritters (2) n 044.9
~ fruitcake (1) n 048.3
~ grove (1) n 053.2
~ house (1) n 015.5
~ jam (2) n 051.6
~ jelly (13) n 051.6
~ knocker (1) n 071.7
~ leather (1) n 054.6
~ melon (1) n 056.7
~ orchard (14) n 053.2
~ orchards (2) n 053.2
~ pandandy (1) n 048.3
~ pandowdy (10) n 048.3
~ (pan)dowdy (1) n 048.3
~ parch (1) n 048.3
~ peeler (1) n 002.7
~ peelings (3) n 084.8

~ picking (1) n 083.1
~ pie (147) n 048.3
~ -pie cobbler (1) n 048.3
~ -pie dumplings (1) n 048.3
~ pies (9) n 048.3
~ -polisher (10) n 125.6
~ preserves (3) n 051.6
~ press (1) n 080.6
~ project (1) n 080.7
~ pudding (5) n 048.3
~ puffs (3) n 048.3
~ roll (3) n 048.3
~ rolls (1) n 048.3
~ room (1) n 007A.4
~ salad (1) n 048.3
~ Schnitts (2) n G 054.6
~ seed (2) n 054.5
~ seeds (1) n 054.5
~ slump (1) n 048.3
~ sonker (1) n 048.3
~ stew (1) n 048.3
~ strudel (7) n 048.3
~ tart (3) n 048.3
~ tarts (9) n 048.3
~ tree (27) n 061.8
~ tree[N-i] (2) n 061.8
~ trees (42) n 061.8
~ turnover (6) n 122.8
~ turnovers (4) n 048.3
~ wine (1) n 114.7
ap(ple) (4) n 071.7
Apple (10) 083.1
~ Festival (1) 080.8
~ Honey (1) 056.9
~ Queen (1) 080.8
apple[N-i] (7) n 054.6
appleberries (1) n 062.4
applejack (5) n 114.7
apples (415) n 061.8
applesauce (27) n 048.5
Appletown (1) AR 087.4
appley apple (1) n 071.7
applicable (2) adj 070.8
application (1) n 088.3
applied for (2) v 053.4
Appling (4) GA 087.1
~ County (2) GA 087.9
applique (1) n 081.8
apply (3) v 013.1
applying (1) v 013.5
appointee (1) n 115.4
appointment (2) n 070.6

(ap)pointment (2) n 066.8
appreciate (58) v 093.4
(ap)preciate (31) v 093.4
appreciation (12) n/adj 095.7
~ gift (2) n 095.7
(ap)preciation (7) n/adj 095.7
~ gift (2) n 095.7
appreciative (6) adj 093.4
appreciat(ive) (1) adj 093.4
(ap)preciative (1) adj 093.4
apprehension (1) n 074.2
apprehensive (11) adj 074.2
apprentice (4) n 067.8
(ap)prentices (1) n 060A.4
apprenticeship (2) n 088.7
(ap)prenticeship (1) n 065.8
approach (3) n/adj 107.4
~ ramp (1) n 107.4
approaches (1) n 107.4
approaching (3) v 070.1
(ap)propriate (1) adj 070.7
appropriated (1) v 066.9
approval (1) n 063.8
approve of (1) v 053.6
approved (1) v 088.2
Apps (1) 059.9
apricot (9) n/adj 055.2
~ leather (1) n 054.6
~ tree (1) n 061.9
~ trees (1) n 061.8
~ worms (1) n 060.5
apricots (11) n 056.8
April (991) 001A.6
~ fool (4) n 001A.8
~ Fools' Day (2) 001A.6
~ shower (1) n 006.6
~ showers (7) n 006.6
April's fools (1) n 073.4
apron (959) n/adj 026.4
~ overalls (1) n 027.4
aprons (57) n 026.4
apt (79) adj 041.1
apurpose (53) adv 103.6
Aqua (2) 087.3
Aqualand (1) 106.7

aquel (1) pron S 047.3
Aquilla (2) TX 087.8
~ Creek (1) TX 030.7
Arab (6) AL 087.1
~ nursery (1) n 087.7
Arabi (1) LA 087.5
Arabia (1) 086.6
Arabian oil (1) n 024.1
arable (1) adj 029.3
Arabs (4) 065.9
arado (2) n S 021.6
Aransas (1) 086.5
arbor (13) n/adj 061.6
~ roof (1) n 011.4
arbors (4) n 088.8
arborvitae (1) n 061.7
arbutus (1) n 062.6
arc (1) n 053.5
Arc (9) 030.3
Arcade (1) 106.4
Arcadia (6) FL LA 087.6
Arcadi(a) (1) FL 087.8
arch (6) n/adj 008.4
~ rock (4) n 008.4
Arch (2) 105.5
~ Creek (1) FL 105.5
~ Creek Elementary
   School (1) 128.7
Archey Creek (1) AR
   030.7
architect (2) n 101.7
architectural (1) adj 070.6
archives (2) n 106.9
Archy Gray (1) 056.9
Arctic (1) 070.6
Arden (4) AR 107.8
~ Road (1) 106.1
Ardmajay (1) 057.3
Ardoyne Plantation (1)
   LA 087.1
Ardsley Park (2) 106.1
are (2105) v 042.1
(a)re (1) v 025.2
area (267) n 065.8
are(a) (10) n 065.8
areas (56) n 015.2
(are)as (1) n 107.2
areaway (1) n 007A.5
areawise (1) adv 080.6
arena (1) n 116.5
Arena (1) 106.4
aren't (203) v 024.8
Argenta (1) AR 087.3
Argonne (1) 107.8
argue (4) v 104.2

~ with (1) v 074.8
arguing (3) v 104.2
argument (4) n 129.7
argument[N-i] (1) n
   042.4
argumentry (1) adj 074.8
arguments (1) n 085.6
arid (3) adj 029.8
arise (19) v 076.7
arisen (10) v 003.3
arising (7) v 007.2
aristocracy (1) n 075.8
aristocrat (2) n 088.9
(a)ristocrat (1) n 066.9
aristocratic (2) adj 065.8
aristocrats (1) n 069.4
arithmetic (1) n 070.6
(a)rithmetic (9) n 065.9
Arithmetic (1) 099.6
ariz (1) v 003.3
Arizona (34) 086.5
~ ash (3) n 061.9
ark (3) n 010.3
Arkabutla (2) MS 087.2
~ Dam (1) MS 086.4
Arkadelphia (10) AR
   087.8
Arkadelphi(a) (2) AR
   087.3
Arkansan (2) 069.5
Arkansas (1000) 086.7
~ Black (1) 056.9
~ buffaloes (1) n 059.9
~ chicken (1) n 046.3
~ City (4) AR 087.7
~ City Hunting Club
   (1) 104.6
~ hard stones (1) n
   023.4
~ Hoosier (3) 086.7
~ mosquito (1) n
   060A.8
~ people (1) n 011.7
~ Post (2) AR 087.3
~ razorback (2) n 035.9
~ razorback hog (2) n
   035.9
~ Razorback (1) 035.9
~ razorbacks (2) n
   035.9
~ Razorbacks (2) 035.9
~ River (22) AR 030.7
~ shiner (1) n 061.2
~ soft stone (1) n 023.4
~ State (1) 086.7

~ steam shovel (1) n
   023.3
~ stone (2) n 023.4
~ toothpick (2) n 104.3
~ Traveler (3) 086.7
~ wedding cake (1) n
   044.5
~ yam (1) n 055.5
~ Yellow (1) 055.5
Arkan(sas) (1) 086.7
Ark(ansas) (1) 086.7
Arkansawyan (1) 096.9
Arkansawyans (1) 069.4
Arkansawyer (1) 069.6
Arkansawyers (1) 090.8
Arklatex (2) 081.8
Arky (1) 069.6
Arlington (35) AL GA
   MS TX VA 087.2
~ Heights (1) 105.1
~ Park (1) 106.1
~ River (1) FL 030.7
arm (107) n/v/adj 072.3
~ shoulder (1) n 046.5
~ shoulders (1) n 072.4
~ up (1) v 069.7
arm[N-i] (2) n 013.8
armadillo (27) n 081.8
armadillo[N-i] (1) n
   060.6
armadillos (27) n 060.7
Armanville (1) 087.5
Armaugh (1) 087.9
armband (1) n 028.3
armchair (13) n 008.8
armchairs (2) n 008.8
armed forces (1) n 089.2
armful (311) n 019.8
(arm)ful (3) n 019.8
armfuls (2) n 019.7
Armistice Day (1) 065.9
armload (213) n 019.8
armload[N-i] (1) n 019.8
armloads (2) n 019.8
armoire (124) n 009.7
armoires (35) n 009.7
Armorel (2) AR 087.2
Armpit (2) 131.1
~ of the Mid South (1)
   131.1
~ of the Nation (1)
   075.8
arms (14) n 072.5
armsful (2) n 019.8
armstrong (1) n 120.1

Armstrong (3) AL 087.8
~ Cork (1) 020.4
~ Springs (1) 087.6
Armuchee (5) GA 087.5
~ Creek (2) GA 030.7
army (43) n/adj 130.5
~ boots (1) n 129.7
~ cut (1) n 123.9
~ ducks (1) n 070.9
~ truck (1) n 109.6
~ worm (2) n 060.5
~ worms (7) n 060.5
Army (13) 053.2
~ Transportation Corps
   (1) 068.9
Arnaudville (1) LA 087.5
Arno (5) FL TN 087.3
~ community (1) TN
   087.1
~ Creek (1) TN 030.7
~ Pike (1) 089.9
Arnold (2) 031.1
aro (1) n S 020.3
aroma (9) n 051.1
aromatic (1) adj 047.5
aronker (1) n 059.9
arose (18) v 003.3
arosen (1) v 003.3
around (792) adv/prep
   052.5
~ the mulberry bush
   (1) n 098.4
~ the world (2) n 130.6
(a)round (146) adv/prep
   032.1
~ the moon (1) n 130.6
arounds (1) n 022.7
(a)rounds (1) n 122.2
arouse (3) v 076.7
aroused (1) v 097.3
Arp (4) GA TN 087.3
arpent (1) n 081.9
arpents (1) n 084.8
arrangements (2) n 079.2
(ar)rangements (3) n
   085.5
arranging (2) n/v 101.4
~ to (1) v 101.2
arras (1) n S 084.9
(ar)rest[V-t] (1) v 082.8
arrested (2) v/adj 057.8
~ hog (1) n 035.5
(ar)rested (1) v 082.8
arrival (2) n 057.9
arrive (5) v 089.7

arrived (1) v 053.4
arrogant (1) adj 074.8
arrow (1) n 107.3
ar(row) (1) n 070.8
Arrow (2) 087.5
arrowroot (2) n/adj 061.4
~ tea (1) n 061.4
arrows (1) n 107.3
arroyo (13) n S 030.4
Arroyo (5) 030.7
~ Colorado (1) TX 030.7
~ Concepcion (1) TX 030.7
~ del Tigre (1) TX 030.7
~ Diablo (1) TX 030.7
~ Las Negros (1) TX 030.7
arroyos (5) n S 030.4
Arsenal (1) 106.4
arsenic dip (1) n 084.8
art (11) n/adj 065.9
~ academy (1) n 106.8
~ center (1) n 106.4
~ galleries (1) n 106.4
~ museum (1) n 106.4
~ museums (1) n 106.4
~ shows (1) n 131.1
~ student (1) n 068.7
~ theater (1) n 114.9
Art (4) 106.7
Arta community (1) AL 087.5
arteries (3) n 107.6
artery (2) n 107.6
Artesia (5) MS 087.7
artesian (10) adj 106.6
~ water (1) n 088.7
~ wat(er) (1) n 048.9
~ well (4) n 011.7
~ wells (3) n 030.4
Artesian Square (1) 106.4
arthritic doctor (1) n 090.8
arthritis (721) n/adj 079.6
~ patients (1) n 081.8
arthrit(is) (1) n 079.6
arthri(tis) (1) n 079.6
Arthritis (1) 079.6
Arthur (21) 087.4
~ City (1) TX 087.4
~ Murray School of Dance (1) 083.1
Arthurs (1) 079.6

artichoke (6) n 061.4
artichokes (12) n 054.7
article (5) n 070.9
articles (3) n 070.7
artifacts (1) n 088.9
artificial (82) adj 017.1
~ bait (2) n 060.5
~ breeding bulls (1) n 092.8
~ egg (48) n 017.1
~ eggs (18) n 017.1
~ flowers (2) n 101.4
~ gas (1) n 065.9
~ glass egg (1) n 017.1
~ logs (2) n 008.5
~ palms (1) n 072.1
~ ponds (1) n 030.5
artillery (2) n 017.9
artist (5) n 051.8
Arts (1) 108.5
arty (2) adj 097.8
~ darty (1) adj 097.8
~ darty farty (1) adj 097.8
ary (6) adj 040.5
ar(y) (1) adj 071.2
Aryan (4) 069.4
as (3237) prep/conj 077.2
~ if (69) conj 088.3
~ though (30) conj 088.3
(a)s (3) prep 041.1
asadera (1) n S 048.2
asafetida (17) n/adj 061.4
~ bags (1) n 088.8
~ ball (1) n 061.4
~ balls (1) n 061.4
~ water (1) n 075.7
asbestos (16) n/adj 011.2
~ road (1) n 031.6
~ shingles (2) n 011.2
~ siding (5) n 011.2
ascared (22) adj 074.3
Ascension (4) LA 087.2
~ Parish (1) LA 087.2
(As)cension Parish (1) LA 087.2
ash (224) n/adj 061.8
~ bread (12) n 044.6
~ bucket (4) n 023.1
~ -bucket girl (1) n 065.7
~ can (1) n 008.7
~ -cooked corn bread (1) n 044.7

~ hoecake (1) n 044.6
~ hopper (28) n 093.7
~ hoppers (4) n 080.9
~ logs (1) n 008.5
~ pile (2) n 080.6
~ pit (3) n 008.7
~ pone (2) n 044.7
~ pones (2) n 044.6
~ shovel (3) n 008.7
~ tree (7) n 061.9
~ trees (8) n 061.8
~ wood (1) n 061.8
Ash Flat (4) AR 086.2
ash[N-i] (4) n 008.7
(a)shame (1) adj 073.9
ashamed (3) adj 058.1
(a)shamed (3) adj 090.4
Ashburn (3) GA 087.6
Ashby Street (1) 107.6
ashcake (66) n/adj 044.6
~ corn bread (1) n 044.7
ashcakes (29) n 044.6
Ashdown (2) AR 087.4
ashen (1) adj 072.9
Asher (2) 107.6
~ Avenue (1) 107.6
ashes (1063) n/adj 008.7
~ cake (1) n 044.6
Asheville (470) NC 087.4
Ashe(ville) (2) NC 087.4
Ashford (1) AL 087.2
Ashland (15) AL GA TN 087.4
~ City (4) TN 087.1
~ Place (1) 106.9
Ashley (8) MS 087.6
~ County (1) AR 087.4
~ Street (5) 114.8
ashore (4) adv 057.7
Ashport (2) TN 087.2
ashtray (1) n 098.3
Ashview (1) 106.5
Ashville (1) AL 087.2
ashy (3) adj 008.9
~ cake (1) n 044.6
Asia (1) 126.4
Asian (3) 126.4
~ area (1) n 126.4
Asians (1) 126.4
aside (3) adv/prep 057.8
~ of (1) prep 053.5
ask (1148) v 104.1
~ about (1) v 104.1
~ away (1) v 104.1

~ for (15) v 104.1
~ of (1) v 088.9
~ to (1) v 027.5
ask[V-p] (3) v 104.1
ask[V-r] (488) v 104.1
~ for (5) v 104.1
~ of (1) v 104.1
ask[V-s] (1) v 104.1
ask[V-t] (298) v 104.1
~ about (1) v 104.1
~ for (1) v 104.1
~ to (3) v 104.1
asked (615) v 104.1
~ to (1) v 104.1
askes (1) v 104.1
askew (1) adv 085.2
asking (74) v 104.1
~ about (1) v 096.8
~ for (3) v 057.5
asks (4) v 104.1
asleep (3) adj 070.1
(a)sleep (3) adj 058.7
asp (1) n 060.4
asparagus (14) n 055.7
(a)sparagus (2) n 055.8
aspens (1) n 061.8
asphalt (529) n/adj 031.6
~ concrete (1) n 031.6
~ drive (1) n 031.8
~ pave (2) n 031.6
~ pavement (1) n 031.6
~ pavements (1) n 031.6
~ paving (1) n 031.6
~ road (16) n 031.6
~ roads (15) n 031.6
~ shingles (3) n 011.2
~ top (2) n 031.6
asphalted (3) v/adj 031.6
asphalting (2) n/v 031.6
asphalts (2) n 031.6
aspirin (5) n/adj 078.4
~ tablet (1) n 025.7
ass (135) n/adj 072.8
~ backwards (2) adv 040.3
~ face (1) n 096.9
~ kick (1) n 117.8
~ kiss (1) n 125.6
~ kisser (8) n 125.6
~ kissers (1) n 125.6
~ kissing (1) v 125.6
~ whipping (2) n 065.5
ass[N-i] (1) n 040.3

assassination site (1) n 106.5
assed (5) adj 067.8
assemblies (2) n 126.3
assembly (1) n 080.7
Assembly (15) 089.1
~ of God (13) 089.3
~ of God's (1) 089.3
(As)sembly of God (4) 089.3
asses (4) n 033.7
assessing (1) v 024.9
assessment dues (1) n 094.8
assessor (1) n 085.5
(as)sessor (2) n 068.4
asshole (5) n/adj 073.4
~ buddy (1) n 129.4
Asshole of the Mid South (1) 131.1
assignation house (2) n 113.4
assignments (1) n 001A.3
assist (2) v 097.5
assistance (1) n 058.7
assistant (6) n/adj 068.8
~ engineers (1) n 112.4
~ manager (2) n 119.5
~ minister (1) n 067.8
(as)sistant (1) n 067.8
associate (2) v 057.7
~ with (1) v 053.6
(as)sociate with (1) v 070.6
associated (2) v 053.4
associates (1) n 129.6
association (3) n 065.8
(as)sociation (3) n 065.8
Association (6) 080.7
(As)sociation (1) 086.5
assume (5) v 094.1
Assumption (5) LA 030.7
~ Parish (2) LA 087.4
assure (1) v 070.2
assured (1) adj 074.8
(as)sured (1) v 033.4
Asteroid community (1) n 106.1
Asteroth (1) 090.1
asthma (16) n/adj 079.7
~ dog (1) n 033.3
~ dogs (1) n 033.3
Astorbilt (1) 028.1
(a)straddle (1) adv 090.6
astray (1) adv 041.1

astride (2) adv 080.6
(a)stride (1) adv 039.3
Astrodome (1) 106.4
Astroworld (1) 119.6
asylum (3) n 066.3
at (3592) prep 094.5
~ -a-loss price (1) n 094.5
~ her stomach (1) adv 080.4
~ his stomach (101) adv 080.4
~ his tummy (1) adv 080.4
~ my stomach (23) adv 080.4
~ stomach (2) adv 080.4
~ the stomach (43) adv 080.4
~ their stomach[N-i] (10) adv 080.4
~ your stomach (4) v 080.4
~ [D-0] stomach (1) v 080.4
(a)t (16) prep 040.7
~ his stomach (1) adv 080.4
AT and N Railroad (1) 081.9
atcha (1) n 030.9
Atchafalaya (10) LA 030.7
~ Basin (2) LA 030.7
~ River (3) LA 030.7
~ Spillway (1) LA 030.7
(At)chafalaya (9) LA 030.7
~ River (6) LA 030.7
(At)chafalay(a) (5) LA 030.7
~ River (3) LA 030.7
ate (823) v 048.7
~ at (1) v 048.7
~ off (1) v 048.7
~ on (1) v 048.7
~ too much (1) v 065.1
~ up (3) v 048.7
Atebrin (5) 078.4
aten (13) v 048.7
atheism (1) n 090.1
atheist (2) n 088.7

Athens (62) AL GA LA TN TX 087.6
~ Highway (1) 087.4
athlete (4) n 065.9
athlete[N-k] foot (1) n 070.6
athlete's (8) adj 081.8
~ feet (2) n 081.8
~ foot (6) n 072.6
athletes (1) n 065.9
athletic (18) adj 074.1
~ building (1) n 126.2
~ complex (1) n 126.2
~ feet (1) n 065.9
~ field (1) n 126.2
~ foot (1) n 080.6
~ shoes (1) n 123.8
athletically (1) adv 066.8
athletics (3) n 070.7
atisket atasket (2) n 130.3
(a)tisket (4) n 130.3
~ ataket (1) n 130.3
~ (a)tasket (3) n 092.8
Atkinson (1) GA 087.2
Atkin(son) County (1) GA 087.7
Atlanta (1111) GA TX 087.6
~ Airport (3) 106.5
~ Avenue (1) 093.9
~ Braves (1) 087.6
~ City (1) NJ 082.6
~ Federal Pen (1) 106.4
~ Highway (3) 031.7
~ Stadium (1) 106.6
~ University area (1) n 105.4
~ University complex (1) n 106.4
(At)lanta (22) GA 087.6
~ Crackers (1) 087.6
Atlantic (16) GA 107.6
~ Boulevard (2) 107.5
~ City (1) NJ 087.8
~ Coast Line (1) 095.9
~ National Bank (1) 108.5
~ Ocean (2) 030.7
~ ridley turtle (1) n 060.6
Atlas (2) 073.1
atmosphere (1) n 065.8
Atoka (1) TN 087.4
atolillo (3) n S 050.6
atomic energy (1) n 104.7

atrium (4) n 118.1
atriums (2) n 118.1
(at)tach[V-t] to (2) v 025.7
attached housing (1) n 119.1
attack (41) n/v/adj 033.2
~ command (1) n 033.2
~ him (1) v 033.2
(at)tack (1) v 033.2
attacked (5) v 033.5
attacking (1) v 025.5
attacks (1) n 042.7
Attala (7) MS 087.5
~ County (2) MS 085.5
(At)tala County (1) MS 087.9
Attalla (3) AL 087.5
(at)tempt[V-r] to (1) v 052.7
attempted to (1) v 100.1
attend (1) v 053.4
attendant (4) n 082.3
attendants (12) n 082.4
attended (3) v 053.4
(at)tended (1) v 057.4
attention (29) n/adj 012.5
~ getter (2) n 125.6
~ seeker (1) n 125.6
(at)tention (17) n/adj 045.9
~ seeker (1) n 125.6
attic (908) n/adj 009.8
~ fan (4) n 118.5
~ fans (1) n 009.8
~ junk (1) n 010.2
~ -like (1) adj 014.5
~ porch (1) n 010.8
~ room (3) n 009.8
~ rooms (2) n 009.8
~ space (3) n 009.8
~ stairs (2) n 009.8
Attic (1) 010.2
attics (15) n 009.8
attitude (3) n 053.3
attitudes (1) n 071.2
attorney (3) n 068.6
~ at law (1) n 085.7
~ general (1) n 068.3
(at)torney (3) n 070.6
~ general (1) n 068.3
Attoyac (2) TX 030.7
(At)toyac (1) TX 030.7
(at)tract (1) v 028.1
attracted (1) v 076.3

attractive (30) adj 125.4
  ~ -looking (1) adj 090.7
  ~ nuisance (1) n 108.7
(at)tractive (2) adj 074.1
  ~ man (1) n 125.3
atween (1) prep 092.9
au (25) prep F 054.3
  ~ lait (2) adj 032.4
  ~ revoir (3) interj 002.4
AU Center (1) 106.5
Aubrey (1) TX 087.5
Auburn (44) AL MS 087.3
  ~ Avenue (12) 105.6
  ~ Park (1) 106.5
  ~ Universty (1) 083.6
Auburntown (1) TN 087.3
Aucilla (2) FL 087.9
  ~ River (1) FL 030.7
auction (2) n/adj 070.6
  ~ barn (1) n 014.2
audience (2) n 082.8
audio (1) n 051.8
audiovisual program (1) n 070.5
auditorium (21) n 084.4
Auditorium (7) 106.4
auditors (1) n 066.8
Audrey (5) 104.7
Audubon (15) 106.4
  ~ Lake (1) LA 030.7
  ~ Park (13) 106.6
Augberta (1) 054.3
auger (5) n 080.8
augers (1) n 080.8
aught (7) n 070.7
aughts (3) n 001.9
August (1009) 001A.8
Aug(ust) (1) 001A.7
Augusta (70) GA 087.7
(Au)gusta (1) GA 087.8
Augustine (39) 086.7
Augustinian (1) 080.7
Aulon (2) 105.8
aunt (1189) n 067.9
Aunt (150) 067.9
  ~ Jenny Johnson Gap (1) AL 031.3
  ~ so-and-so (1) n 129.5
aunt[N-i] (1) n 067.9
auntie (115) n 067.9
Auntie (19) 067.9

Auntie's house (1) n 067.9
aunties (6) n 069.3
aunt's (6) adj 067.9
  ~ house (1) n 014.1
aunts (61) n 067.9
auntses (1) n 016.7
austere (1) adj 073.5
Austin (59) MS TX 087.5
  ~ Branch (1) TN 030.7
  ~ County (1) TX 087.7
  ~ Highway (1) 107.1
  ~ Home[N-i] project (1) n 105.5
  ~ Homes (1) 106.3
Austin's Hotel (1) 084.3
Austins (1) 109.1
Australia (3) 087.9
  ~ Island (1) LA 087.5
Australian (2) 061.9
  ~ pine trees (1) n 061.9
  ~ pines (1) n 061.8
Autaud (1) 054.7
Autauga (10) AL 087.4
  ~ County (5) AL 087.1
  ~ Creek (2) AL 030.7
Autaug(a) County (1) AL 087.4
Autaugaville (2) AL 087.5
authentic (2) adj 051.4
authoring (1) n 081.8
authority (4) n 115.3
authori(ty) (1) n 115.3
auto (21) n/adj 023.6
  ~ buggy (2) n 023.6
Auto (1) 070.6
autograph tree (1) n 061.8
automatic (35) n/adj 110.7
  ~ gearshift (1) n 110.7
  ~ laundry (2) n 116.5
  ~ pistol (1) n 113.1
  ~ -press round baler (1) n 097.9
  ~ shift (1) n 110.7
  ~ shotgun (1) n 051.8
  ~ transmission (2) n 110.7
automatically (3) adv 025.8
automatics (1) n 113.1
automobile (369) n/adj 023.6

  ~ accident (1) n 023.6
  ~ business (1) n 023.6
  ~ engine (1) n 023.6
  ~ garage (1) n 023.6
  ~ garages (1) n 023.6
  ~ killers (1) n 110.8
  ~ mechanic (4) n 023.6
  ~ repair business (1) n 023.6
  ~ seat (1) n 023.6
  ~ tag (1) n 023.6
  ~ tank (1) n 080.7
  ~ times (1) n 023.6
  ~ tire (1) n 023.6
  ~ tires (4) n 023.6
  ~ wreck (2) n 023.6
automo(bile) (2) n/adj 023.6
  ~ wreck (1) n 023.6
automobiles (88) n 023.6
autopsy (2) n 078.7
(au)topsy (1) n 065.8
autos (6) n 023.6
Autreyville (1) GA 087.8
aux (1) prep F 091.8
auxiliary (3) n/adj 042.5
  ~ roads (1) n 031.7
available (3) adj 039.7
avait (1) v F 021.6
avalanches (1) n 075.8
Avalon (1) 106.1
avant (1) n F 007.8
avaricious (1) adj 073.5
avenue (50) n 031.8
Avenue (198) 107.5
  ~ E (1) 107.7
Av(enue) (1) 105.2
avenues (18) n 031.8
Avera (1) GA 087.9
average (13) adj 079.4
Avery (8) GA NC 087.3
  ~ plow (1) n 093.8
  ~ turning plow (1) n 021.6
Averys (1) 021.6
Aviation (1) 083.6
avid (1) adj 090.4
Avis Chapel (2) TN 087.2
avocado (12) n/adj 055.8
  ~ grove (1) n 061.9
  ~ tree (1) n 096.7
  ~ trees (4) n 061.8
avocados (1) n 070.7
avoir un veau (1) v F 033.9

Avon Park (1) FL 087.7
Avondale (13) GA LA 087.2
  ~ Estates (1) GA 087.5
  ~ Park (1) 106.6
  ~ Zoo (1) 106.3
Avoyelles (2) LA 087.2
aw (61) interj 092.2
await for (1) v 099.1
awake (64) v 097.3
  ~ up (2) v 076.7
awake[V-r] (2) v 097.3
awaked (7) v 097.3
awaken (16) v 076.8
awaken[V-r] (2) v 097.3
awakened (33) v 076.7
aware (2) adj 025.7
away (1162) adv 039.5
(a)way (12) adv 102.8
Away (1) 115.8
aways (1) n 122.2
awful (170) adj/adv 074.8
  ~ rain (1) n 005.6
aw(ful) (1) adj 048.7
awfullest (24) adj 064.7
  ~ -looking (2) adj 064.7
awfully (33) adv 091.7
awk (1) n 073.4
awkward (226) adj 073.3
  ~ -like (1) adj 073.3
  ~ -looking (2) adj 073.3
awkwardest (1) adj 026.3
awkwardness (3) n 073.3
awkwards (1) adj 073.3
awl (1) n 051.8
awn (2) n 056.3
awning (2) n 070.6
awnings (3) n 070.6
awoke (62) v 097.3
  ~ up (1) v 097.3
awoken (1) v 097.3
AWOL (1) 083.4
awry (1) adv 081.9
ax (155) n/v/adj 120.9
  ~ grinder (6) n 023.5
  ~ handles (1) n 080.6
  ~ sharpener (3) n 023.5
  ~ wheel (1) n 023.5
Ax (1) 080.7
ax[V-p] (2) v 100.1
ax[V-r] (16) v 104.1
  ~ for (1) v 104.1
ax[V-t] (9) v 104.1

axed (24) v 104.1
   ˜ him (1) v 082.1
   ˜ to (1) v 104.1
axes (7) n/v 080.8
axing (7) v 104.1
axis (1) n 021.8
axle (877) n/adj 021.8
   ˜ -deep (2) adj 021.8
   ˜ grease (123) n 023.7
   ˜ -grease (1) v 023.7
   ˜ part (1) n 021.8
ax(le) (3) n 021.8
axle[N-i] (1) n 021.8
axles (35) n 021.8
axletree (2) n 021.8
Axminster (1) 096.8
Axson (1) GA 087.1
Axtell (1) TX 087.3
Aycocks Creek (2) GA
030.7
aye (1) interj 098.8
Ayers (2) 106.6
   ˜ Hall (1) 106.6
azalea (22) n/adj 062.7
   ˜ bushes (1) n 061.9
   ˜ corn (1) n 056.2
(a)zalea (1) n 062.6
Azalea Trail (5) 107.3
azaleas (30) n 062.7
(a)zaleas (1) n 062.8
Aztec (1) 119.7
Azucar (1) 030.7

B

B (7) 088.8
  ~ -girl (1) n 113.3
  ~ -O (1) 021.6
baa (42) n/v 036.2
  ~ like (1) v 038.4
baa(x2) (2) interj 038.4
baa(x5) (1) interj 037.6
babbling (1) adj 073.4
babe (2) n 125.4
Babe (8) 063.7
babies (27) n 064.3
baboso (1) n S 073.4
baby (1133) n/adj 081.6
  ~ bed (3) n 064.5
  ~ beef (2) n 121.2
  ~ boy (5) n 064.7
  ~ brother (1) n 053.4
  ~ buggies (17) n 064.5
  ~ buggy (222) n 064.5
  ~ bull (1) n 033.8
  ~ calf (26) n 033.8
  ~ calves (2) n 033.8
  ~ carriage (250) n 064.5
  ~ car(riage) (3) n 064.5
  ~ carriages (12) n 064.5
  ~ cart (6) n 064.5
  ~ chair (1) n 008.8
  ~ chick (1) n 036.9
  ~ chickens (1) n 064.4
  ~ chicks (1) n 051.1
  ~ clip (1) n 110.4
  ~ colt (2) n 027.5
  ~ coop (2) n 064.5
  ~ cots (1) n 064.5
  ~ cow (3) n 033.8
  ~ crib (1) n 064.5
  ~ daughter (1) n 064.8
  ~ daughter's picture (1) n 064.8
  ~ doll (3) n 123.8
  ~ -doll log cart (1) n 084.8
  ~ dolls (1) n 101.5

  ~ food (1) n 048.4
  ~ frog (2) n 060.3
  ~ girl (1) n 064.9
  ~ hog (1) n 035.5
  ~ in the oven (1) n 065.1
  ~ lima (5) n 055A.3
  ~ lima beans (3) n 055A.3
  ~ limas (13) n 055A.3
  ~ link (1) n 121.6
  ~ lobsters (1) n 060.8
  ~ moo (1) n 036.2
  ~ name (3) n 064.4
  ~ Negroes (1) n 104.6
  ~ nurse (1) n 065.2
  ~ onion (1) n 055.7
  ~ owl (1) n 059.2
  ~ pig (6) n 035.5
  ~ pigs (7) n 035.5
  ~ pin (2) n 026.5
  ~ -sat (2) v 049.3
  ~ shower (1) n 130.7
  ~ showers (1) n 130.7
  ~ -sit (3) v 049.3
  ~ -sitter (2) n 066.5
  ~ -sitting (1) n 024.9
  ~ snatcher (1) n 065.2
  ~ stroller (5) n 064.5
  ~ tomato (2) n 055.3
  ~ tomatoes (7) n 055.3
  ~ toy (1) n 101.5
  ~ walker (1) n 064.5
  ~ wheelchair (1) n 064.5
  ~ without a father (1) n 065.7
Baby (41) 064.4
  ~ Doll (1) 064.4
  ~ Giant (1) 116.2
  ~ Grandpa (1) 064.1
  ~ John's (1) 116.2
  ~ Love (1) 081.6
  ~ Ray Primer (1) 089.8
  ~ Sister (1) 064.4
Bab(y) (1) 056.9
baby[N-i] (3) n 099.8
baby[N-k] (2) adj 043.9
  ~ diaper (1) n 043.9
  ~ dog (1) n 025.8
babyish (1) adj 090.4
baby's (3) adj 026.5
  ~ pin (1) n 026.5
  ~ play-pretty (2) n 101.5

Baby's truck (1) n 011.3
bach (4) n/v 069.9
Bach (1) 130.8
bached (4) v 080.6
bachelor (14) n/adj 066.7
  ~ button (1) n 089.8
  ~ parties (2) n 130.7
  ~ party (1) n 130.7
  ~ side (1) n 075.6
  ~ uncle (1) n 068.2
  ~ uncles (1) n 068.2
bachelor's chest (1) n 009.2
bachelors (1) n 104.6
bachelors' camp (1) n 088.7
Bach's dust (1) n 027.2
back (3885) n/v/adj/ adv/ prep 038.2
  ~ a leg (2) v 037.5
  ~ alley (1) n 108.6
  ~ -ass-wards (1) adv 040.3
  ~ -back-up(x2) (1) v 038.2
  ~ bay (3) n 030.3
  ~ bedroom (35) n 007A.6
  ~ breaker (1) n 095.4
  ~ chunk (4) n 008.5
  ~ dirt road (1) n 031.7
  ~ door (13) n 007A.1
  ~ -door garden (1) n 050.5
  ~ doorstep (1) n 010.7
  ~ doorsteps (1) n 010.7
  ~ feet (2) n 072.6
  ~ field (1) n 016.1
  ~ fire log (1) n 008.5
  ~ forty (1) n 016.7
  ~ furrow (1) n 041.2
  ~ gallery (15) n 010.8
  ~ grease (1) n 010.4
  ~ hall (12) n 007A.5
  ~ here (3) adv 038.2
  ~ -in-the-woods folks (1) n 069.9
  ~ it (1) v 037.5
  ~ lane (1) n 031.7
  ~ legs (3) n 072.6
  ~ levee (1) n 015.7
  ~ lot (5) n 015.6
  ~ main (1) n 038.7
  ~ of (161) prep 010.5
  ~ of town (2) n 084.8

  ~ over here (1) adv 038.2
  ~ pantry (1) n 010.1
  ~ parlor (1) n 007.8
  ~ part (1) n 110.5
  ~ patio (1) n 010.8
  ~ patting (1) n 115.3
  ~ piazza (2) n 010.8
  ~ piece (1) n 008.5
  ~ plows (1) n 021.6
  ~ porch (604) n 007A.6
  ~ porches (4) n 007A.5
  ~ rake (1) n 024.6
  ~ ridge (1) n 030.8
  ~ road (35) n 031.7
  ~ roads (4) n 031.7
  ~ room (48) n 009.3
  ~ rooms (2) n 007A.5
  ~ -seat baby (1) n 065.7
  ~ shed (1) n 010.8
  ~ stabbers (1) n 125.5
  ~ stairway (2) n 010.7
  ~ step (1) n 010.7
  ~ steps (8) n 010.7
  ~ stomp (1) n 011.7
  ~ stoop (3) n 007A.6
  ~ stop (1) n 008.5
  ~ street (3) n 108.6
  ~ -street pave road (1) n 031.7
  ~ streets (1) n 031.8
  ~ strip (1) n 046.5
  ~ talk (1) v 101.7
  ~ that leg (1) v 037.5
  ~ thigh (1) n 072.8
  ~ to the right (1) adv 038.2
  ~ trouble (1) n 012.2
  ~ trunk (1) n 110.5
  ~ up (188) v 038.2
  ~ up here (7) v 038.2
  ~ up in here (1) v 038.2
  ~ up now (2) v 038.2
  ~ up there (3) v 038.2
  ~ -up(x2) (8) v 038.2
  ~ your foot (9) v 037.5
  ~ your leg (53) v 037.5
  ~ your leg here (1) v 037.5
  ~ your leg up (1) v 037.5
  ~ -your-leg(x2) here (1) v 037.5

~ your legs (1) v 037.5
~ your legs up (1) v 037.5
~ [P-0] (1) prep 010.5
back(x2) (23) v 038.3
~ your leg (1) v 037.5
back(x3) (2) v 038.3
Back (4) 056.9
~ of McCall (1) LA 087.4
~ River (1) GA 030.7
backband (6) n 038.7
backbiters (1) n 101.3
backbone (38) n/adj 046.6
~ -and-rib pie (1) n 047.1
~ pie (1) n 046.4
~ stew (1) n 047.4
backbones (1) n 121.3
backcountry (4) adj 069.9
~ folks (1) n 069.9
~ man (1) n 069.9
~ nigger (1) n 069.9
~ road (1) n 031.7
backed (36) v 100.7
~ down (1) v 082.1
~ off (2) v 057.9
~ out (14) v 082.1
~ out of (1) v 082.1
~ out on him (3) v 082.1
backer (1) n 115.3
backfield (2) n/adj 088.8
~ coach (1) n 088.8
background (3) n 026.3
backheels (1) n 069.9
backhoe (2) n/adj 030.2
~ diggers (1) n 030.2
backhoes (1) n 030.2
backhouse (45) n 012.1
backhouses (5) n 012.1
backies (1) n 012.1
backing (33) v 100.7
~ off (2) v 007.3
backings (6) n 050.8
backlog (385) n/v 008.5
backlogs (26) n 008.5
backpacking (1) n 098.1
backs (9) n 126.5
backset (3) n 076.3
backside (4) n 040.3
~ of (1) prep 010.5
backslider (1) n 060.8
backslipped (1) v 090.4

backstabbing (1) v 101.3
backstage lobby (1) n 010.8
backstairs (4) n 010.7
backstand (1) n 008.5
backstick (144) n 008.5
backsticks (21) n 008.5
backtrailed (1) v 088.7
backup log (1) n 025.3
backward (255) adj/adv 040.3
~ folks (1) n 069.9
backwards (606) adj/adv 040.3
~ weather (1) n 005.5
backwash (1) n 018.1
backwater (16) n/adj 030.3
~ land (1) n 029.4
~ -like slough (1) n 030.3
backwaters (2) n 030.3
backways (2) adv 040.3
backwood (6) adj 069.9
~ countryman (1) n 069.9
~ crackers (1) n 069.7
~ folks (1) n 069.9
~ hoosier (1) n 069.9
~ hoosiers (1) n 069.9
~ people (1) n 069.9
backwoods (30) n/adj 069.9
~ cracker (4) n 069.9
~ fellow (1) n 069.9
~ hick (1) n 069.9
~ hoosier (1) n 069.9
~ people (1) n 069.9
~ preacher (2) n 069.8
~ square dancing (1) n 083.1
~ talk (1) n 052.2
backwoodser (3) n 069.9
backwoodsman (21) n 069.9
backwoodsmen (2) n 069.9
backwoodsy (11) adj 069.9
~ place (1) n 075.7
backy (2) adj 012.1
~ house (1) n 012.1
~ houses (1) n 012.1
backyard (31) n/adj 015.6

~ garden (2) n 050.5
~ parties (2) n 130.7
bacon (2007) n/adj 046.5
~ drippings (3) n 046.5
~ end (1) n 046.6
~ ends (2) n 046.6
~ fat (3) n 046.6
~ grease (8) n 023.7
~ hog (1) n 035.5
~ meat (6) n 046.7
~ middling (1) n 046.4
~ rind (42) n 046.6
~ rinds (3) n 046.6
~ salt (1) n 046.3
~ skin (8) n 046.6
~ skins (1) n 046.6
~ slab (1) n 046.4
~ slices (1) n 046.7
~ squares (2) n 046.5
~ strip (1) n 046.7
~ strips (1) n 046.7
~ -type strips (1) n 046.7
bac(on) (2) n/adj 046.7
~ fat (1) n 046.3
Bacon (1) 087.8
bacons (2) n 046.5
Baconton (1) GA 087.2
bacteria (1) n 070.6
bad (981) adj 072.9
~ -ass (1) adj 099.6
~ bird broad (2) n 113.3
~ boy (1) n 090.1
~ car (1) n 109.4
~ cloudy day (1) n 005.5
~ day (75) n 005.5
~ days (1) n 005.5
~ dude (1) n 125.3
~ flesh (1) n 078.2
~ freeze (1) n 007.5
~ frost (2) n 007.5
~ grass (1) n 015.9
~ hard freeze (1) n 007.5
~ land (2) n 029.8
~ -looking day (3) n 005.5
~ -looking girl (1) n 125.4
~ -looking weather (1) n 005.5
~ -luck person (1) n 090.6

~ man (122) n 090.1
~ -man's horse (1) n 060A.4
~ -mouthing (1) v 129.7
~ -natured (1) adj 073.2
~ -off (3) adv 075.6
~ piece (1) n 113.1
~ place (1) n 078.1
~ rags (4) n 123.6
~ rain (3) n 006.1
~ rainy days (1) n 005.5
~ ride (3) n 109.4
~ run (1) n 050.8
~ soil (2) n 029.8
~ spell (5) n 005.5
~ spirits (2) n 090.2
~ sport (1) n 075.1
~ spread of weather (1) n 005.6
~ storm (5) n 006.2
~ -tempered (5) adj 075.1
~ throat (1) n 071.7
~ thunderstorm (2) n 006.2
~ trip (1) n 088.8
~ weather (35) n 006.2
~ weather day (1) n 005.5
~ whiskey (1) n 050.8
~ woman (1) n 113.3
Bad (2) 030.7
~ Branch (1) MS 030.7
badder (4) adj 066.1
baddest (8) adj 064.7
Baden (2) 087.5
~ -Baden (1) 087.5
badger (3) n/adj 077.2
~ preacher (1) n 067.8
badgering (1) v 080.6
badly (4) adv 072.9
badminton (2) n 130.4
bag (1783) n/v/adj 019.5
~ boys (2) n 019.5
~ business (1) n 019.5
~ down (3) v 027.8
~ factories (1) n 092.9
~ out (2) v 027.8
~ plant (2) n 019.5
~ sacks (1) n 019.7
~ sausage (1) n 121.6
~ swing (7) n 022.9

~ swings (1) n 022.9
~ up (1) v 019.7
Bag (1) 087.1
bag[N-i] (2) n 041.8
bagasse (21) n F 051.3
Bagdad (2) FL TX 087.4
bagel (1) n 045.2
bagels (3) n 044.4
baggage (1) n 115.3
bagged out (1) v 027.8
baggies (1) n 114.2
bagging (16) n/adj 019.7
    ~ sack (7) n 019.7
    ~ sacks (3) n 019.7
baggings (2) n 051.3
baggy (8) adj 027.8
Bagley (2) 106.7
    ~ Park (1) 106.7
    ~ Road (1) 107.8
bags (477) n 019.5
Bahala (1) 030.7
Bahama Islands (2) 087.5
Bahamas (10) 087.5
Bahamian brogue (1) n
    092.7
Bahia (3) 015.9
Bahi(a) grass (1) n 015.9
bail (13) n/v/adj 020.3
    ~ bucket (1) n 017.3
baile (1) n S 083.1
bailed bucket (1) n 017.4
Bailey (4) 107.6
    ~ Avenue (2) 107.6
    ~ Branch (1) MS 087.8
    ~ Lake (1) MS 030.7
Baileys (1) 096.8
Baileyton (1) AL 087.6
bails (2) n 020.3
Bainbridge (14) GA 087.1
baiser (1) n F 081.7
bait (206) n/v/adj 060.5
    ~ bed (1) n 080.6
    ~ dealer (1) n 060.5
    ~ minnows (1) n 061.2
    ~ shop (1) n 060.5
    ~ shrimp (2) n 060.5
    ~ shrimp[N-i] (1) n
      060.9
    ~ with (1) v 061.2
    ~ worm (6) n 060.5
    ~ worms (8) n 060.5
baitfishes (1) n 016.7
baits (61) n 060.5
bake (33) v/adj 121.5
    ~ apples (1) n 048.3

~ bread (3) n 044.7
~ chicken (1) n 121.5
~ corn bread (1) n
  044.9
~ days (1) n 010.7
~ on (1) v 074.4
~ ovens (1) n 017.9
~ potato (5) n 055.4
~ potatoes (3) n 055.4
baked (22) v/adj 121.7
    ~ apples (1) n 048.3
    ~ bread (1) n 044.6
    ~ chicken (1) n 121.5
    ~ corn bread (1) n
      044.6
    ~ eggs (2) n 046.2
    ~ ham (2) n 121.3
    ~ potato (5) n 055.4
    ~ potatoes (1) n 055.4
    ~ with (1) v 044.3
    ~ yam (1) n 055.5
Bakelite (1) 088.7
baker (62) n/adj 017.5
    ~ shop (1) n 045.1
Baker (15) 107.7
    ~ County (6) GA 087.4
    ~ Hotel (1) 106.8
baker[N-k] bread (16) n
  044.8
Bakerhill (1) AL 087.2
bakeries (1) n 045.1
baker's (46) adj 045.1
    ~ bread (40) n 045.1
    ~ dozen (3) n 055A.8
    ~ skillet (1) n 017.5
bakers (18) n 017.5
Bakers (3) 030.7
    ~ Creek (1) MS 030.7
    ~ Gap (1) TN 087.7
    ~ Hall (1) 105.7
bakery (117) n/adj 045.1
    ~ bread (76) n 045.1
    ~ doughnuts (1) n
      122.5
    ~ -made (1) adj 045.1
    ~ products (1) n 045.1
    ~ shop (1) n 045.1
    ~ -shop bread (2) n
      045.1
    ~ -type bread (1) n
      045.1
bakes (2) n/v 056.5
baking (118) n/adj 121.5
    ~ chicken (4) n 121.5
    ~ ears (1) n 056.2

~ hen (4) n 121.5
~ hens (5) n 121.5
~ meat (1) n 046.3
~ oven (1) n 017.5
~ pan (1) n 017.5
~ potato (7) n 055.4
~ potatoes (4) n 055.4
~ powder (60) n 045.5
~ powders (11) n 045.5
~ shop (1) n 045.1
~ skillets (1) n 017.5
~ soda (10) n 045.5
~ squash (2) n 056.6
baklava (1) n 122.3
bal (3) n F 083.1
    ~ de maison (1) n F
      083.1
Bal Harbour (1) 106.1
balai (2) n F 082.2
balance (7) n/adj 022.9
    ~ beam (1) n 022.6
    ~ board (1) n 022.6
    ~ seesaw (1) n 022.5
balances (1) n 022.6
balancin (1) n S 021.2
balancing (4) v/adj 022.6
    ~ board (1) n 022.6
    ~ boards (1) n 022.6
Balboa (1) 123.9
Balch Springs (1) 131.1
balcon (2) n F/S 010.8
balconies (7) n 010.8
balcony (161) n/adj 010.8
    ~ porch (1) n 010.8
balcon(y) porch (1) n
  010.8
bald (11) adj 030.8
    ~ eagle (2) n 059.3
    ~ -face egg custard (1)
      n 048.3
    ~ hill (1) n 030.8
    ~ knob (5) n 030.8
Bald Knob (6) AR 030.8
baldhead (1) n 115.5
baldheaded (1) adj 024.7
Baldwin (16) GA 087.3
    ~ Avenue (1) 107.7
    ~ County (6) AL 087.3
    ~ Creek (1) TX 030.7
    ~ reader (1) n 080.7
Baldwyn (3) MS 087.6
bale (237) n/v/adj 014.7
    ~ buggy (1) n 014.9
    ~ sacks (1) n 019.6
bale[N-i] (3) n 041.8

Balearic slingers (1) n
    080.6
baled (33) v/adj 014.8
    ~ hay (1) n 014.9
    ~ up (1) v 014.8
baler (35) n 014.9
balers (12) n 014.8
bales (149) n/v 014.8
Bali Hai (3) 114.7
baling (26) v/adj 014.9
    ~ hay (1) n 014.9
    ~ machine (2) n 014.9
    ~ wire (5) n 016.3
balk (4) n/v 074.8
balking (3) v 034.3
balky (3) adj 074.8
ball (212) n/v/adj 101.5
    ~ and chain (6) n 063.2
    ~ -and-socket joint (1)
      n 072.3
    ~ bearing (1) n 096.8
    ~ cat (1) n 096.8
    ~ club (1) n 091.7
    ~ game (2) n 053.4
    ~ games (1) n 098.4
    ~ hammer (1) n 020.7
    ~ -less (1) adj 090.8
    ~ park (3) n 085.1
    ~ peen claw hammer
      (1) n 020.7
    ~ peen hammer (4) n
      020.7
    ~ peen hammers (2) n
      020.7
    ~ point pen (13) n
      026.5
    ~ points (1) n 074.5
    ~ sausage (1) n 121.7
    ~ team (3) n 055A.8
    ~ the jack (3) n 083.1
    ~ up (1) v 047.6
    ~ willow (1) n 061.8
Ball (12) 131.1
    ~ Ground (3) GA
      087.5
    ~ Ground Highway (1)
      031.7
    ~ Ground Militia
      District (1) GA
      087.5
    ~ potatoes (1) n 055.4
ball[V-r] (1) v 089.9
ballad (11) n 089.5
ballads (4) n 130.8
Ballard (2) 087.6

~ County (1) KY 087.6
~ Mountain (1) AR 031.1
Ballast Point Pier (1) 106.4
ballbat (1) n 092.7
balled up (4) v 080.6
ballerina (1) n 123.8
ballerinas (1) n 123.8
ballet (3) n/adj 083.1
~ dancing (2) n 083.1
~ -type (1) adj 123.8
balling the jack (2) n 083.1
balloon (2) n 065.8
ballot (1) n 089.7
ballroom (11) n/adj 083.1
~ dance (2) n 083.1
~ dancing (6) n 083.1
ballrooms (1) n 080.7
balls (35) n 083.1
ballyhoo (2) n 061.2
balmy (11) adj 007.4
~ day (3) n 005.4
~ days (1) n 005.4
~ weather (2) n 007.4
balsa wood (1) n 008.6
balsamberries (1) n 062.6
Baltimore (660) MD 087.1
~ bums (1) n 089.8
~ minnows (1) n 061.2
Bamanite (1) 106.3
bamboo (15) n/adj 061.8
~ briers (1) n 015.9
~ chairs (1) n 008.8
~ curtains (1) n 009.5
~ rake (2) n 120.7
~ rakes (1) n 120.7
~ shade (1) n 009.5
~ shades (1) n 009.5
bamboos (3) n 062.4
bamboozled (1) v 058.8
Bamford (1) AL 087.3
banana (61) n/adj 070.7
~ bread (9) n 044.4
~ cantaloupe (3) n 056.7
~ cantaloupes (1) n 056.7
~ flitters (1) n 044.9
~ fritters (2) n 044.8
~ melon (14) n 056.7
~ melons (3) n 056.7

~ mushmelon (5) n 056.7
~ muskmelon (1) n 056.7
~ nut bread (5) n 044.4
~ pepper (3) n 051.7
~ pudding (1) n 048.3
~ shortcakes (1) n 048.3
~ snakes (1) n 084.8
~ squash (1) n 056.6
~ tree (2) n 061.9
~ trees (4) n 061.9
bananas (5) n 055.1
banc (1) n F 008.8
banco (1) n 083.1
band (265) n/adj 020.3
~ parties (1) n 130.7
Band (1) 131.8
bandage (1) n 070.6
bande (1) n F 065.8
banded king snake (1) n 092.9
Bandera (1) TX 087.4
banding (1) n 020.3
bandit (1) n 088.7
Banditos (1) 129.6
bandoleros (1) n 128.7
bands (94) n 020.3
bandy billa (1) n 022.5
bane (3) n 071.7
bang (3) n 095.4
banged on (1) v 097.4
bangers (1) n 126.6
bangle (1) n 028.4
bangles (3) n 028.4
bangs (5) n 123.9
banister (9) n/adj 007A.3
~ preacher (2) n 067.8
~ thing (1) n 008.4
banisters (13) n 007A.6
banjo (12) n/adj 020.6
~ harp (1) n 020.6
~ pickers (1) n 065.9
ban(jo) (1) n 070.6
banjos (6) n 065.8
bank (265) n/v/adj 030.8
~ bag (1) n 019.6
~ building (3) n 108.5
~ buildings (1) n 108.5
~ hooks (1) n 088.9
Bank (56) 108.5
~ of Bay Biscayne (1) 105A.7

~ of Commerce (1) 108.5
~ of Georgia (1) 108.5
banked (9) v 015.5
Bankhead (6) 107.7
~ Highway (2) 107.6
~ National Forest (1) AL 087.4
~ section (1) n 106.3
~ Tunnel (1) 106.6
banking (9) v 080.8
banks (27) n 030.8
Banks (10) 094.9
~ Canal (1) MS 030.2
~ County (2) GA 087.3
Bankston (1) AL 087.8
banky (2) adj 022.8
~ -boating (1) v 022.8
~ bow (1) n 022.5
banners (1) n 064.4
banquet (1) n 083.1
banquets (3) n 130.7
banquette (40) n F 031.9
banquettes (3) n F 031.9
banshee (1) n 006.2
banshees (1) n 090.2
Bantam (7) 056.2
~ chickens (1) n 036.7
~ corn (3) n 056.2
Bantams (3) 036.9
Bantu (1) 092.8
banty rooster (1) n 121.5
banyan (1) n 061.9
baptism (3) n 089.1
baptisms (1) n 089.1
Baptist (1233) 089.1
~ area (1) n 089.1
~ church (137) n 089.1
~ churches (4) n 089.1
~ Creek (1) MS 030.7
~ Hospital (1) 089.1
~ ladies (1) n 089.1
~ minister (3) n 089.1
~ Missionar(y) (1) 089.1
~ pallet (5) n 029.2
~ pallets (4) n 029.2
~ people (1) n 089.1
~ preacher (11) n 089.1
~ preachers (3) n 060.8
~ school (1) n 089.1
~ Towers (1) 119.2
Baptist[N-i] (24) 089.1
Baptistes (5) 089.1
Baptists (6) 089.1

baptize (5) v 089.1
baptize[V-r] (1) v 053.4
baptized (26) v 089.1
baptizing (5) n/v/adj 089.1
~ pool (1) n 089.1
bar (57) n/v/adj 007A.3
~ fence (3) n 016.2
~ glasses (1) n 048.9
~ harrow (1) n 021.7
~ off (3) v 015.8
~ soap (1) n 090.9
~ thing (1) n 099.8
Bar (2) 015.5
bar[N-i] (1) n 020.9
Barataria (2) 030.7
~ Bayou (1) LA 030.7
barb (11) n/adj 016.3
~ fence (1) n 016.3
barbarians (1) n 069.3
barbaric (2) adj 070.6
barbarish (1) adj 070.9
barbe (2) n F 056.4
barbecue (33) n/v/adj 083.1
~ bread (1) n 044.3
~ chicken (1) n 121.5
~ meat (1) n 080.8
~ pit (1) n 009.8
~ rib[N-i] (1) n 024.7
~ ribs (1) n 121.3
~ sauce (12) n 048.5
~ sauces (1) n 048.5
~ sausages (1) n 121.6
barbecued (6) v/adj 121.5
~ lamb (1) n 121.4
~ ribs (1) n 043.9
~ sauce (2) n 048.5
barbecueing (2) n 121.5
barbecuer (1) n 048.6
barbed (181) adj 016.3
~ wire (137) n 016.3
~ -wire (11) adj 016.3
~ -wire fence (18) n 016.3
~ -wire fences (7) n 016.3
~ -wire fencing (1) n 016.3
barber (6) n/adj 081.8
~ college (1) n 083.6
Barber Creek (2) MS 030.7
barbering (2) n/v 101.1
barberries (1) n 062.4

barberry (1) n 062.7
barbershop (3) n 052.6
Barbie club (1) n 129.6
barbiturate (2) n 065.8
barbiturates (27) n 114.2
Barbour (3) 087.5
~ County (1) AL 087.1
Bar(bour) County (1) AL 087.3
barbs (9) n 016.3
barbwire (880) n/adj 016.3
~ fence (132) n 016.3
~ fences (59) n 016.3
~ fencing (3) n 016.3
barbwires (4) n 016.3
barcotics (1) n 114.2
bardeau (1) n F 011.4
Bardin (3) FL 087.1
Bardstown (4) KY 087.1
bare (6) adj 032.3
~ feet (1) n 072.6
~ hand (1) n 072.5
bareback (3) adv 070.9
barefeeted (2) adj 072.6
barefoot (32) adj 032.3
~ children (1) n 072.6
~ coffee (6) n 032.3
~ root (1) n 061.4
Barefoot Bay (2) FL 030.3
barefooted (75) adj 032.4
~ butler (1) n 089.8
~ coffee (1) n 032.3
bareheaded (2) adj 032.3
barely (12) adv 095.2
barf (27) v/adj 080.3
~ bag (1) n 080.3
barfed (5) v 080.2
Barfield (2) AR 087.2
~ Landing (1) AR 031.4
barfing (1) v 080.3
barfish (9) n 059.9
bargain (39) n/adj 094.5
~ day (1) n 094.5
~ price (2) n 094.5
barge (12) n/adj 024.6
~ canal (1) n 030.2
barges (9) n 024.6
Barham Township (1) AR 087.2
baritone (1) n 065.8
bark (77) n/v/adj 054.8
~ at (1) v 025.3

~ sack (1) n 019.7
bark[V-p] (1) v 013.6
barked (1) v 090.7
barker (1) n 033.3
barking (12) n/v/adj 059.6
~ at (1) v 053.5
~ dog (1) n 033.3
Barkman Creek (1) TX 030.7
barks (21) n/v 016.8
barley (8) n/adj 041.8
~ bread (1) n 044.4
~ sausage (2) n 047.1
barleys (1) n 041.6
Barling (2) AR 087.3
barlow (5) n/adj 017.8
~ knife (3) n 104.3
barlows (2) n 104.3
barmy (1) adj 074.7
barn (2413) n/adj 014.2
~ area (1) n 014.2
~ areas (1) n 015.2
~ building (2) n 014.2
~ chamber (2) n 014.5
~ dairy room (1) n 010.3
~ dance (10) n 083.1
~ dances (3) n 083.1
~ door (1) n 014.2
~ fence (3) n 016.2
~ house (3) n 014.2
~ liquor (1) n 050.8
~ loft (44) n 014.5
~ lot (86) n 015.6
~ lots (6) n 015.6
~ owl (70) n 059.1
~ owls (15) n 059.2
~ party (1) n 083.1
~ raisings (2) n 083.1
~ red (1) adj 014.2
~ shed (8) n 015.1
~ snake (1) n 081.9
~ stable (1) n 015.2
~ stall (1) n 015.2
~ stalls (2) n 015.2
~ swallow (2) n 060A.7
~ -type (1) adj 014.2
Barn (1) 014.2
barn[N-i] (2) n 014.2
barned owl (2) n 059.2
Barnesville (15) GA 087.8
Barnett (2) 108.5
~ Bank building (1) n 108.5

~ Reservoir (1) MS 030.7
Barnetts Creek (1) GA 030.7
barnful (1) n 014.6
barns (180) n 014.2
barny house (1) n 118.6
barnyard (288) n/adj 015.6
~ animals (2) n 036.5
~ fertilize (2) n 029.3
~ fertilizer (3) n 015.6
~ fowls (2) n 036.6
~ garb (1) n 015.6
~ gate (1) n 015.6
~ lot (2) n 015.6
~ manure (4) n 029.3
~ owl (1) n 059.2
~ owls (1) n 059.1
~ pimp (1) n 084.8
~ weeds (1) n 015.9
barnyards (4) n 015.6
Baron Carondelet (1) 065.9
Barons Crossroads (1) AL 031.7
baroque (1) adj 115.9
barouche (1) n 084.8
Barr Park (1) 085.1
barrack (6) n 014.7
barracks (3) n 115.5
Barracks (1) 106.4
barracks-looking building (1) n 075.8
barracuda (1) n 080.9
barracudas (1) n 059.9
Barre (3) 030.6
barred (6) v/adj 035.4
~ hog (1) n 035.4
~ owls (1) n 059.1
~ sow (2) n 035.5
~ woman (1) n 099.7
Barred Rock (1) 084.8
barrel (1226) n/adj 019.1
~ chair (2) n 008.8
~ churn (3) n 019.1
~ flour (1) n 019.1
~ hook (2) n 020.3
~ hooks (1) n 020.3
~ hoop (23) n 020.3
~ hoop[N-i] (1) n 020.3
~ hoops (38) n 020.3
~ maker (1) n 019.1
~ planter (1) n 092.7

~ rims (1) n 020.3
~ ring (1) n 020.3
~ rings (3) n 020.3
~ roll (1) n 095.5
~ stave (3) n 019.1
~ staves (7) n 020.3
bar(rel) (3) n 019.1
Barrel (2) 019.1
barrel[N-i] (4) n 016.7
barrelful (1) n 019.1
barreling (1) n 019.1
barrels (448) n 019.1
barren (3) adj 029.5
Barren (3) 030.7
barrera (1) n S 096.4
barricaded (1) adj 102.6
barriers (2) n 110.8
barrileros (1) n S 080.6
Barrineau Park (1) FL 087.3
barring (1) v 015.7
barrio (1) n S 029.4
barroom (1) n 116.2
barrow (399) n/adj 035.4
~ hog (5) n 035.4
~ pit (1) n 080.6
~ white (1) n 123.9
bar(row) (169) n/adj 035.4
~ hog (10) n 035.4
barrowing (1) v 036.1
barrows (39) n 035.4
bars (26) n 015.3
barstools (1) n 008.8
Barstow (2) LA TX 087.8
Bartee Branch (1) TN 030.7
barters (1) v 094.2
Bartholomew (2) 030.7
Bartlett (2) TN 087.4
Barton (8) AL AR 087.3
~ Academy (1) 065.9
~ Creek (2) TX 030.7
~ plow (1) n 021.6
~ Springs (1) TX 087.8
Bartow (20) FL GA 087.2
~ Cemetery (1) 078.8
~ County (1) GA 087.6
~ High School (1) 125.8
barytes mining (1) n 080.6
base (569) n/adj 098.4
~ dirt (1) n 031.6
~ log (1) n 008.5

Base (3) 106.5
baseball (102) n/adj 130.4
~ park (1) n 085.1
~ parks (1) n 106.7
~ shoe (1) n 125.1
~ shoes (1) n 123.8
~ team (1) n 055A.8
baseborn (2) adj 065.7
~ children (1) n 065.7
baseline highway (1) n 031.6
baseman (1) n 130.1
basement (74) n 015.5
basements (3) n 007A.8
bases (6) n 098.4
bash (5) n 083.1
~ meeting (1) n 083.1
bashful (3) adj 074.7
Bashi (2) AL 087.2
basic (4) adj 029.8
basics (1) n 070.6
Basie (1) 130.8
basil (1) n 051.9
Basil Canal (1) LA 030.7
Basile (1) LA 087.3
basin (26) n/adj 020.1
~ land (2) n 029.5
~ stand (3) n 009.3
Basin (9) 030.7
~ Canal (1) LA 030.7
~ Street (1) 107.6
basing down (1) v 007.3
Basinger (2) FL 087.2
Basins (1) 030.7
basis (1) n 080.6
basket (1028) n/adj 020.1
~ child (1) n 065.7
~ factory (1) n 020.1
~ -like (1) adj 020.1
~ name (2) n 064.4
~ names (1) n 064.4
~ -type (1) adj 020.1
~ weave (2) n 016.4
~ weaver (1) n 020.1
bask(et) (2) n 020.1
bas(ket) (1) n 020.1
Basket (1) 020.1
basket[N-i] (4) n 020.1
basketball (71) n/adj 130.4
~ court (2) n 126.2
~ games (1) n 126.2
~ parties (1) n 130.7
~ shoes (1) n 123.8

~ team (1) n 055A.8
basketful (2) n 020.1
baskets (90) n 064.6
bass (565) n/adj/adv 059.9
~ ackwards (2) adv 040.3
~ baits (1) n 091.8
~ boat (10) n 024.6
~ boats (10) n 024.6
~ bread (1) n 044.6
~ fish (4) n 059.9
~ fishing (5) n 059.9
~ tournament (1) n 065.9
~ trees (1) n 062.9
~ viol (1) n 083.1
Bass (2) 059.9
~ Fish (1) 059.9
~ Weejuns (1) 123.9
bass(x2) (1) interj 038.4
basse-cour (2) n F 015.6
Basser boat (1) n 024.6
basses (6) n 059.9
Bassett Creek (3) AL 030.7
bassin (1) n F 017.2
bassinet (14) n 064.5
bassinets (2) n 064.5
bastard (642) n/adj 065.7
~ baby (2) n 065.7
~ berry (1) n 062.5
~ cane (1) n 024.9
~ child (49) n 065.7
~ children (1) n 065.7
~ childrens (1) n 065.7
~ kid (1) n 065.7
~ nigger (1) n 069.5
~ perch (1) n 059.9
~ son (1) n 065.7
~ young one (3) n 065.7
~ young ones (1) n 065.7
bast(ard) (2) n 065.7
bas(tard) (1) n 065.7
Bastard (1) 065.7
bastard[N-i] (1) n 065.7
bastardess (1) n 065.7
bastardized (2) adj 088.8
bastardly (1) adv 065.7
bastard's (1) adj 065.7
bastards (82) n 065.7
baste (1) v 046.2
Bastogne Bulge (1) 087.8

Bastrop (6) LA TX 087.5
bat (29) n/v/adj 059.1
~ ball (1) n 130.9
~ squirrel (1) n 059.6
Bat (2) 087.1
~ Harbor community (1) TN 087.1
~ Harbor School (1) 102.4
batard (2) n F 065.7
batch (20) n 055A.8
bateau (134) n/adj 024.6
~ -size (1) adj 024.6
bateaux (31) n 024.6
Bateman Branch (1) TN 030.7
Bates Field (4) 106.5
Batesville (19) AR MS 087.4
bath (718) n/adj 007A.7
~ and a half (9) n 118.3
~ cloth (90) n 018.5
~ cloths (5) n 018.5
~ facilities (1) n 012.1
~ rag (29) n 018.5
~ rags (1) n 018.5
~ towel (194) n 018.6
~ to(wel) (1) n 018.6
~ towels (16) n 018.6
~ water (1) n 043.4
Bath (3) 087.5
~ Springs (1) TN 086.7
bath[N-i] (3) n 007A.4
bathe (3) v 070.7
bathes (1) n 041.8
bathhouse (2) n 114.9
Bathhouse Row (1) 080.7
bathhouses (2) n 014.1
bathing (6) n/v/adj 018.1
~ bath cloth (1) n 018.5
~ suit (1) n 080.6
bathrobe (1) n 026.4
bathroom (593) n/adj 007A.2
~ outside (1) n 012.1
~ towel (1) n 018.6
~ towels (1) n 018.6
bathroom[N-i] (1) n 055A.7
bathrooms (57) n 126.3
baths (24) n 007A.9
bathtub (13) n/adj 050.9
~ gin (12) n 050.9

~ whiskey (1) n 050.8
Batmobile (3) 111.8
baton (3) n 113.2
~ rouge (1) n F 005.9
Baton (743) 087.8
~ Rouge (736) LA 087.8
~ Rouge Parish (4) LA 087.8
~ Rouge Zoo (1) 075.9
Bat(on) Rouge (2) LA 087.8
(Baton) Rouge (1) LA 087.8
Batre (4) 087.3
bats (19) n 060A.1
Batson (1) TX 087.1
battalions (1) n 001A.4
batted (1) adj 092.9
batten (41) n/adj 011.2
~ board (3) n 011.2
~ boards (1) n 011.2
~ door (1) n 080.8
~ things (1) n 009.5
bat(ten)-and-board (2) n 007A.1
battening (1) n 011.2
battens (4) n 011.2
batter (15) n/adj 051.8
~ bread (9) n 044.5
~ corn bread (1) n 044.6
battercake (45) n/adj 045.3
~ syrup (1) n 051.3
battercakes (165) n 045.3
battered (2) adj 046.3
~ side meat (1) n 046.3
~ -up (1) adj 080.7
batterie (1) n F 051.3
batteries (1) n 081.9
battery (6) n/adj 010.1
~ acid (2) n 050.8
batting (4) n/v 029.2
battle (31) n/v/adj 085.8
~ -ax (9) n 063.2
~ ball (1) n 130.2
~ stick (3) n 080.7
Battle (15) 030.7
~ Creek (1) GA 030.7
~ House (1) 106.8
~ of Nashville (1) 106.8

~ of Nashville monument (1) n 106.4
~ of New Orleans (1) 087.8
~ of Pea Ridge (1) 088.8
~ of Sabine Pass (1) 070.7
~ of San Jacinto (1) 087.5
~ of Shiloh (3) 087.7
~ of the Chickamauga (1) 080.8
battled (2) v 093.5
Battlefield (1) 106.8
Battleground (2) 106.4
battler (1) n 010.6
battles (3) n 130.5
battleship (1) n 106.4
Battleship (3) 106.4
  ~ Alabama (1) 106.4
  ~ Park (1) 106.4
  ~ Texas (1) 106.4
battling (92) n/v/adj 010.6
  ~ beech (1) n 080.7
  ~ bench (11) n 010.6
  ~ block (28) n 010.6
  ~ blocks (2) n 010.6
  ~ board (5) n 010.6
  ~ stick (38) n 010.6
  ~ sticks (3) n 010.6
battoir (1) n F 010.6
batty (4) adj 074.7
batty(x4) (1) interj 038.4
baubles (1) n 123.1
Bavarian (2) 017.1
  ~ china (1) n 017.1
  ~ cream (1) n 122.6
Bavarians (1) 127.2
Bawcomville (1) LA 087.1
bawdy house (2) n 113.4
bawl (170) n/v 036.2
  ~ for (1) v 036.3
bawled (1) v 036.2
bawling (109) v 036.2
  ~ for (3) v 036.3
bawls (72) v 036.2
Baxley (4) GA 087.4
  ~ Street (1) 107.5
Baxter (4) AR LA 087.8
  ~ Bayou (1) LA 030.3

Baxters Creek (1) AL 030.7
Baxterville (1) MS 087.3
bay (164) n/adj 030.3
  ~ beans (1) n 062.7
  ~ boats (1) n 024.6
  ~ chicken (1) n 081.9
  ~ field (1) n 029.4
  ~ front (1) n 080.6
  ~ horse (2) n 034.2
  ~ laurel (1) n 062.7
  ~ leaf (1) n 062.7
  ~ -leaf laurel (1) n 062.7
  ~ -leaf tree (1) n 061.4
  ~ niggers (1) n 128.6
  ~ roots (1) n 061.4
  ~ side (1) n 030.7
  ~ tree (11) n 061.8
  ~ trees (15) n 061.8
  ~ water (1) n 030.3
  ~ window (4) n 088.9
  ~ -window houses (1) n 118.9
  ~ windows (2) n 014.6
Bay (122) AR 030.3
  ~ Branch (1) GA 030.7
  ~ City (7) TX 086.2
  ~ (City) (1) TX 082.6
  ~ County (4) FL 087.1
  ~ Creek (1) MS 030.7
  ~ Creek community (1) MS 087.5
  ~ Flats (1) 105.7
  ~ Manor (1) 106.1
  ~ Minette (5) AL 087.2
  ~ Minette Creek (1) AL 030.7
  ~ Point (1) 106.3
  ~ Pole (1) GA 087.7
  ~ Pole Branch (1) GA 030.7
  ~ Saint Louis (7) MS 030.7
  ~ Shore (2) 106.1
  ~ Shore Boulevard (2) 107.7
  ~ Springs (1) MS 087.3
  ~ Street (5) 114.8
  ~ Street cadets (1) n 113.6
  ~ View (2) 105.4
Bayette (1) AR 030.9
Bayfront (7) 106.4
  ~ Arena (1) 106.4

~ Park (4) 106.4
~ Towers (1) 108.5
baygall (6) n 029.6
bayhead (1) n 029.6
Bayhead (1) FL 087.4
baying (3) v 036.4
  ~ [P-0] (1) v 096.9
bayonet (7) n 104.3
bayonets (1) n 062.7
bayou (277) n/adj 030.3
  ~ bank (1) n 030.3
  ~ bridge (1) n 091.8
  ~ country (3) n 093.7
  ~ land (1) n 029.6
  ~ people (1) n 069.9
  ~ red-necks (1) n 069.9
  ~ streams (1) n 030.6
  ~ water (1) n 050.8
bay(ou) (11) n/adj 030.6
  ~ land (2) n 029.6
  ~ water (1) n 088.7
ba(you) (3) n 030.6
Bayou (281) 030.7
  ~ Barataria (1) LA 030.7
  ~ Bartholomew (2) AR LA 030.7
  ~ Basin (1) LA 030.7
  ~ Bend (2) 106.4
  ~ Bienvenue (2) LA 030.7
  ~ Black (2) LA 030.3
  ~ Black Road (1) 031.7
  ~ Blanc (1) LA 087.4
  ~ Blue (2) LA 030.7
  ~ Boeuf (3) LA 030.7
  ~ Bourbe (1) LA 030.7
  ~ Casotte (1) MS 030.3
  ~ Chene (5) LA 030.7
  ~ Chico (1) FL 030.3
  ~ Coastal Cemetery (1) 078.8
  ~ Cocodrie (1) LA 030.7
  ~ Courtableau (1) LA 030.3
  ~ Creek (1) AR 030.7
  ~ Cross (1) LA 030.7
  ~ de Chene (1) LA 030.7
  ~ de Siard (1) LA 030.7
  ~ Deduce (1) MS 030.3
  ~ des Cannes (1) LA 030.3

~ Dorcheat (1) AR 030.7
~ Doza (1) LA 030.7
~ Duquesne (1) LA 030.7
~ Goula (2) LA 087.5
~ Gou(la) (1) LA 087.3
~ Grande (1) AL 030.3
~ La Batre (4) AL 087.3
~ Lacombe (2) LA 030.7
~ Lafourche (10) LA 030.3
~ Lafourche area (1) LA 087.5
~ Lamourie (1) LA 087.5
~ Liberty (4) LA 030.7
~ Louise (1) LA 087.1
~ Lulu (1) MS 030.7
~ Macon (2) AR 030.7
~ Macon Ridge (1) AR 030.7
~ Mallet (2) LA 030.7
~ Metairie (2) LA 030.7
~ Nezpique (1) LA 030.3
~ Ouachita (1) AR 030.3
~ Patassa (1) LA 030.7
~ Philip (1) MS 062.4
~ Pierre (6) LA MS 030.7
~ Pierre Lake (1) LA 030.7
~ Pigeon (3) LA 030.7
~ Queue de Tortue (1) LA 030.7
~ Rapides (2) LA 030.3
~ (Ra)pides (2) LA 087.2
~ Rigaud (1) LA 030.3
~ Rouge (1) LA 030.7
~ Saint John (6) LA 030.7
~ Sara (2) LA 086.3
~ Sauvage (1) LA 030.7
~ Serpent (1) LA 030.3
~ Shreve (1) LA 030.7
~ Sorrel (6) LA 030.7
~ Talla (1) MS 030.3

~ Teche (4) LA 030.7
~ Terrebonne (1) LA 030.7
~ Texter (1) FL 030.3
~ Township (1) AR 086.3
~ View (1) 106.1
~ View Junior High (1) 125.8
~ Vincent (1) LA 030.7
Bay(ou) (25) 030.7
~ Bleu (1) LA 030.7
~ Blue (1) LA 030.3
~ Houdier (1) LA 030.7
~ Lamourie (2) LA 030.7
~ Marcus Creek (1) FL 030.7
~ Meto (3) AR 030.7
~ Meto bottoms (1) n 029.4
~ Pierre (1) MS 030.7
~ Rapides (1) LA 087.5
(Bayou) de Siard (1) LA 030.7
bayous (73) n 030.3
bays (18) n 030.6
Bayshore (1) 107.6
Baytown (2) TX 086.2
bazaar (1) n 083.1
bazooka (3) n 020.5
BB (5) 022.4
~ -gun battles (1) n 130.5
~ -gun wars (2) n 130.5
~ shot (1) n 022.4
BB[N-i] (1) 022.4
be (4595) v 077.1
~ easy (1) v 037.5
~ fresh (31) v 033.9
~ gentle (1) v 037.5
~ in presently (1) v 033.9
~ quiet (1) v 037.5
~ still (28) v 037.5
~ still now (1) v 037.5
be[V-p] (130) v 094.1
be[V-q] (144) v 026.1
be[V-r] (3) v 098.6
be[V-t] (2) v 026.1
beach (45) n/adj 029.7
~ area (2) n 106.4
~ house (3) n 118.9
~ houses (1) n 014.1

~ land (1) n 029.7
~ parties (2) n 130.7
~ rice (1) n 050.7
~ road (1) n 031.7
~ shoes (2) n 123.8
~ soil (1) n 029.8
~ towel (2) n 018.6
~ towels (1) n 018.6
Beach (123) 107.5
~ Boulevard (2) 107.5
~ Boys (1) 130.8
~ Creek (1) GA 030.7
~ Drive (1) 107.8
~ Park (2) 105A.7
~ Road (1) 107A.7
beached him (1) v 082.1
beaches (5) n 105.1
Beaches (1) 087.5
bead (12) n/adj 071.4
~ -chain necklace (1) n 028.4
~ feelers (1) n 126.5
~ necklace (3) n 028.4
~ rattler (1) n 126.5
bead[N-i] (8) n 028.4
beaded necklace (3) n 028.4
beads (837) n 028.4
beagle (6) n/adj 033.3
~ hound (1) n 033.3
beagles (3) n 033.1
Beale Street (5) 107.6
Bealsville (1) FL 087.3
beam (30) n 021.6
Beamons Creek (1) AL 030.7
beams (1) n 014.5
bean (741) n/adj 055A.3
~ beetles (2) n 080.9
~ cooking (1) n 101.8
~ crops (1) n 055A.4
~ field (2) n 016.1
~ fields (1) n 016.1
~ flip (1) n 089.8
~ gumbo (1) n 084.8
~ hay (1) n 088.9
~ house (2) n 011.7
~ hull (1) n 055A.2
~ -hulling (1) n 083.1
~ hulls (1) n 055A.2
~ patch (5) n 016.1
~ plates (1) n 042.2
~ pole (1) n 073.3
~ pot (4) n 017.6
~ pots (3) n 017.6

~ sack (1) n 019.7
~ shooters (1) n 093.6
~ soup (1) n 081.8
~ stringing (4) n 083.1
~ trees (1) n 061.8
~ truck (1) n 109.7
Bean (4) 030.7
~ Creek (2) AR TN 030.7
~ Saline (1) 063.8
bean[N-i] (28) n 055A.4
beanbag (1) n 080.7
beans (3252) n 055A.4
Beanstalk (1) 055A.4
bear (69) n/v/adj 059.6
~ a calf (2) v 033.9
~ claw (1) n 122.5
~ claws (3) n 122.2
~ -cub wood fern (1) n 080.6
~ dogs (2) n 033.3
~ grass (10) n 015.9
~ -hugging (1) v 089.8
~ -hunt (1) v 082.7
~ -hunted (2) v 080.7
~ hunting (1) n 059.4
~ rug (1) n 125.2
~ tick (1) n 060A.8
Bear (38) 030.7
~ Branch (2) AL TN 030.7
~ Creek (31) AL AR FL GA LA MS TN TX 030.7
~ Lake (1) LA 030.7
~ River (1) AL 030.7
~ Run Creek (1) AL 030.7
bear[N-i] (1) n 013.8
beard (830) n 071.4
Beard Creek (1) AL 030.7
bearded (1) adj 129.3
Bearden (1) AR 087.2
beards (36) n 071.4
beared (1) v 095.8
bearer (5) n 082.4
bearing (6) n/v/adj 057.4
~ of animals (1) v 033.9
~ sow (1) n 035.5
bearings (1) n 052.1
bears (15) n 065.8
Bears (1) 112.5

Beaslys Branch (1) GA 030.7
beast (19) n 125.2
beast[N-i] (1) n 125.2
beat (171) n/v/adj 075.4
~ down (1) v 075.4
~ on (2) v 098.6
~ out (4) v 072.9
~ out of (3) v 065.5
~ up (3) v 096.9
Beat (4) 080.8
~ Five (1) 080.8
~ Twelve (2) 087.1
beat[V-t] (10) v 075.5
~ out (4) v 042.1
beaten (8) v/adj 065.5
~ biscuit (2) n 044.4
~ by (1) v 125.2
~ egg (1) n 046.2
beater (4) n 073.5
beating (94) n/v/adj 065.5
~ block (2) n 010.6
~ rain (3) n 006.1
~ stick (2) n 010.6
~ up (1) v 131.2
beatingest (2) adj 002.7
Beatle (2) 115.5
~ cut (1) n 115.5
~ music (1) n 130.8
Beatles (1) 130.8
beatnik (2) n 129.3
beatniks (3) n 129.3
Beatrice (1) AL 087.8
beats (8) n/v 105.1
Beaty Creek (1) TN 030.7
beau (200) n 081.5
Beau Brummel (2) 028.1
Beauclerc section (1) n 105.7
beaucoup (2) adj F 090.8
beaucoups (4) adj 055A.9
Beaudry (1) AR 086.9
Beaufort (4) NC SC TX 087.3
Beaumont (39) AL TX 087.6
~ area (1) n 105.6
Beaumonter (1) 088.8
beaup(x3) (1) interj 038.3
Beauregard (4) LA 070.9
beaut (2) n 125.4
beautician (1) n 089.6
beautied up (1) v 028.1

Beauties (3) 114.2
beautiest (1) adj 064.7
beautified (1) adj 028.1
beautiful (1163) adj 089.6
  ~ day (304) n 089.6
  ~ doll (1) n 125.4
  ~ girl (3) n 064.9
  ~ ladies (1) n 089.6
  ~ morning (9) n 089.6
  ~ rags (1) n 123.6
  ~ sky (1) n 005.4
  ~ sun (1) n 005.4
  ~ sunshine day (2) n 005.4
  ~ weather (6) n 005.4
  ~ woman (3) n 125.4
  ~ women (1) n 089.6
beauti(ful) (1) adj 028.1
beautiful[A-w] (2) adj 064.7
beautifulest (15) adj 064.7
beautifully (9) adv 089.6
beautify (5) v 028.1
beautifying (8) v 028.1
beauty (17) n/v/adj 089.6
  ~ parlor (2) n 115.7
  ~ -parlor girl (1) n 099.8
  ~ shop (2) n 007A.2
  ~ up (2) v 028.1
Beauty (5) 114.3
beautying up (1) v 028.1
Beauvoir (1) MS 087.3
beaux (4) n 081.5
beaver (14) n/adj 059.8
  ~ dam (1) n 029.7
  ~ dams (2) n 030.6
  ~ hound (1) n 033.1
Beaver (17) OK 087.3
  ~ Bayou (1) LA 030.7
  ~ Creek (11) AL LA TN 030.7
  ~ Dam Creek (1) AL 030.7
  ~ Lake (1) AR 030.7
  ~ Pond (1) GA 030.7
  ~ Run Creek (1) GA 030.7
Beaverdale (1) GA 087.4
Beaverdam (4) TN 030.7
  ~ Creek (2) GA TN 030.7
beavers (13) n 059.8
bebop (3) n/adj 083.1

~ music (1) n 130.8
became (83) v 102.4
(be)came (3) v 076.1
because (1024) conj/prep 088.6
  ~ of (7) prep 088.6
(be)cause (462) conj/prep 088.6
  ~ of (1) prep 088.6
  ~ [P-0] (1) prep 088.6
Beck Avenue (1) 107.7
Beckley (1) 105.8
Beckville (2) MS TX 086.4
become (15) v 102.2
(be)come (1) v 096.7
become[V-r] (9) v 098.6
  ~ of (1) v 095.8
(be)come[V-r] (1) v 096.7
becomes (3) v 065.3
becoming (14) v/adj 026.3
(be)coming (2) v 007.2
bed (1350) n/v/adj 009.3
  ~ blankets (1) n 029.1
  ~ bolster (4) n 028.9
  ~ couch (2) n 009.1
  ~ covering (2) n 028.7
  ~ coverlet (1) n 028.7
  ~ down (1) n 029.2
  ~ harrow (1) n 021.7
  ~ har(row) (1) n 021.7
  ~ pad (1) n 029.2
  ~ pillow (1) n 028.8
  ~ quilt (1) n 029.1
  ~ rest (1) n 028.9
  ~ sofa (1) n 009.1
  ~ stand (1) n 009.2
  ~ stone (1) n 023.5
  ~ tick (1) n 080.8
  ~ up (1) v 041.2
Bed (8) 009.1
bed[N-i] (1) n 013.8
bedbug (6) n 060A.8
bedbugs (6) n 060A.9
bedchamber (1) n 009.3
bedclothes (4) n 028.7
bedcover (11) n 028.7
bedcovers (3) n 028.7
bedded (4) v/adj 015.6
  ~ up (1) v 075.9
bedder (7) n 021.6
bedding (9) n/v/adj 028.7
  ~ ground (1) n 088.7

~ out (1) v 088.9
~ up (1) v 007.2
bedfast (3) adj 097.1
Bedford (6) TN 087.3
  ~ County (2) TN 087.1
  ~ Lake (1) TN 030.7
  ~ -Stuyvesant section (1) n 086.2
Bedias Creek (1) TX 030.7
bedpost[N-i] (2) n 016.5
bedrock (1) n 029.8
bedroll (12) n 029.2
bedrolls (1) n 029.2
bedroom (2559) n/adj 009.3
  ~ area (1) n 009.3
  ~ community (1) n 091.9
  ~ furnishing (1) n 009.4
  ~ furniture (5) n 009.4
  ~ safe (1) n 009.2
  ~ set (2) n 009.4
  ~ shoes (5) n 123.8
  ~ slippers (6) n 123.8
  ~ suite (14) n 009.3
  ~ suites (2) n 009.3
bedroom[N-i] (27) n 009.3
bedrooms (503) n 007A.2
beds (74) n 015.7
Beds (1) 080.9
bedspread (522) n 028.7
bedspreads (48) n 028.7
bedsprings (1) n 021.7
bedstead (15) n 009.3
bedsteads (11) n 009.3
bedtick (1) n 028.7
bedticking (5) n 081.9
bedticks (1) n 097.8
bedtime (11) n 002.4
bee (127) n/adj 060A.5
  ~ bird (1) n 082.9
  ~ birds (2) n 081.8
  ~ gums (1) n 080.7
  ~ moth (1) n 060A.1
  ~ town (1) n 096.7
  ~ tree (2) n 060A.6
Bee (4) 030.7
  ~ Gap (1) FL 030.4
  ~ Gum Road (1) 031.9
  ~ Lake (1) MS 030.7
bee(x2) (1) interj 038.5
bee[N-i] (1) n 060A.5

Beebe (2) AR 087.6
beech (48) n/adj 061.8
  ~ framing (1) n 061.8
  ~ gum (1) n 061.8
  ~ mash (1) n 092.9
  ~ mast (2) n 070.7
  ~ mast[N-i] (1) n 088.7
  ~ tree (5) n 061.8
  ~ trees (4) n 061.8
  ~ wood (1) n 008.6
Beech (7) 030.7
  ~ Creek (2) AL TN 030.7
  ~ Lake (1) TN 030.7
  ~ Log Branch (1) TN 030.7
  ~ River (2) TN 030.7
  ~ Spring Creek (1) AR 030.7
Beecher Road (1) 107.8
beeches (3) n 061.8
beechnut (7) n/adj 054.8
  ~ oak (1) n 061.8
  ~ stuff (1) n 088.7
  ~ tree (1) n 061.8
beechnuts (8) n 054.9
beef (190) n/adj 121.2
  ~ calf (1) n 033.8
  ~ cattle (8) n 033.6
  ~ chitlins (1) n 037.3
  ~ clubs (1) n 088.7
  ~ cow (2) n 033.6
  ~ cows (2) n 033.6
  ~ head (1) n 047.1
  ~ herd (1) n 089.9
  ~ hide (2) n 038.7
  ~ liver (4) n 047.2
  ~ livers (1) n 037.2
  ~ neck bones (1) n 121.2
  ~ rennet (1) n 047.7
  ~ ribs (4) n 121.2
  ~ roast (8) n 121.2
  ~ roast[N-i] (1) n 121.2
  ~ roastes (1) n 070.6
  ~ sausage (14) n 121.6
  ~ steers (1) n 033.6
  ~ stew (1) n 091.7
  ~ stroganoff (1) n 121.2
  ~ tallow (1) n 024.3
  ~ tip (1) n 121.2
  ~ tongue (2) n 121.2

~ tripe (6) n 037.2
~ tripes (1) n 037.2
~ wieners (2) n 121.6
Beefalo (1) 033.6
beefeaters (1) n 127.8
beefified (1) adj 033.6
beefing (1) v 080.8
Beefmaster cattle (1) n 033.5
beefsteak (12) n/adj 055.3
~ tomato (2) n 055.3
~ tomatoes (1) n 055.3
beefsteaks (2) n 121.1
beehive (10) n 060A.6
Beehive (4) AL 087.1
beehives (3) n 123.9
Beelzebub (14) 090.1
been (1734) v 026.1
beer (325) n/adj 121.9
~ barrel (1) n 019.1
~ bust (7) n 131.6
~ -drinking (1) adj 089.8
~ faucet (1) n 018.7
~ glasses (2) n 089.9
~ hangouts (1) n 081.8
~ hound (1) n 113.6
~ joint (3) n 088.8
~ joint[N-i] (1) n 016.7
~ joints (3) n 088.7
~ keg (3) n 020.2
~ licks (1) n 071.4
~ parties (1) n 130.7
~ seed (3) n 050.8
~ steins (1) n 048.9
~ taverns (1) n 073.7
~ truck (1) n 050.8
beers (1) n 121.9
bees (301) n/v 060A.4
beeses (1) v 026.1
beeshang tree (1) n 061.8
beestings (2) n 060A.7
beeswax (3) n 080.7
beet (33) n/adj 055.2
~ greens (5) n 055A.5
~ leaves (1) n 055A.5
~ pickle (1) n 055.2
~ sugar (1) n 051.3
~ top (2) n 055A.5
~ tops (7) n 055A.5
beetle (3) n/adj 080.8
~ bugs (2) n 060A.4
Beetle (1) 064.4

beetles (7) n 060A.2
beets (84) n 055.2
beeves (10) n 033.6
beeves' foot oil (1) n 088.7
before (783) conj/prep 089.7
(be)fore (114) conj/prep 066.9
beforehand (2) adv 053.6
(be)forehand (1) adv 092.7
beg (109) v 039.6
began (500) v 102.2
~ to (19) v 072.9
(be)gan (3) v 102.2
beganned (2) v 102.2
beggar (10) n/adj 113.7
~ grass (1) n 015.9
~ -lice (4) n 060A.6
~ -lice roots (1) n 061.4
~ man (1) n 113.7
beggarweed (2) n 015.9
beggarweeds (3) n 015.9
begging (2) n/v 075.7
begin (593) v 102.2
~ to (11) v 007.2
~ with (10) v 102.2
(be)gin (6) v 102.2
~ to (1) v 047.6
begin[V-p] (7) v 083.3
begin[V-r] (169) v 102.2
~ to (28) v 102.2
(be)gin[V-r] (4) v 102.2
~ to (2) v 102.2
begin[V-s] (1) v 102.2
begin[V-t] (46) v 102.2
~ to (1) v 102.2
beginned (3) v 102.2
beginneded (1) v 102.2
beginner (4) n 102.2
beginners (9) n 083.7
beginning (69) n/v 102.2
~ to (32) v 007.2
~ [P-0] (1) v 003.2
begins (87) v 102.2
~ to (1) v 003.3
begot (1) v 080.6
begun (320) v 083.3
~ to (3) v 102.2
(be)gun to (1) v 102.2
behalves (1) n 070.8
behave (8) v 013.1
~ there (1) v 037.5

behaved (1) v 065.3
behaves (5) v 065.3
~ like (2) v 065.3
behave(x2) (1) v 037.5
(be)having (1) v 065.8
behavior (2) n 053.6
behind (973) n/adv/prep 010.5
~ of (1) prep 010.5
(be)hind (13) prep 010.5
behinds (1) n 095.9
behold (1) v 070.5
beholden (68) adj 057.5
behold(en) (1) adj 057.5
beholding (10) adj 057.5
beige (19) adj 066.8
beignet (18) n F 045.2
beignets (9) n F 122.5
being (90) v 026.1
Being (1) 069.4
beings (1) n 088.3
Bel (3) 105.6
~ Air (2) 105.6
~ Air Mall (1) 105.3
Belair (1) 106.2
belch (6) v 080.2
belched (4) v 080.2
~ up (1) v 080.2
Belcher (1) LA 087.3
belches (1) v 080.3
Belen (2) MS 087.2
Belfast (1) GA 087.3
Belfountain (1) AL 087.8
Belgian (2) 031.6
~ block (1) n 031.6
~ blocks (1) n 031.6
Belgians (1) 070.6
Belgium (2) 087.7
Belgreen (2) AL 087.1
Belhaven (2) 105.2
~ College (1) 083.6
belief (1) n 025.5
belier (1) n 034.9
believe (561) v 094.1
~ in (14) v 011.7
~ on (1) v 088.6
believed (2) v 012.5
~ in (1) v 012.5
believes (5) v 025.2
~ in (1) v 093.7
believing (1) v 094.1
Belk community (1) TX 087.2
bell (80) n/adj 065.8

behaved — ~ -bottom trousers (1) n 027.4
~ cow (8) n 033.6
~ fountain (1) n 015.9
~ frog (1) n 060.3
~ mare (1) n 034.2
~ pepper (16) n 055.2
~ peppers (13) n 055.5
~ tomato (1) n 055.3
~ tomatoes (5) n 055.3
~ top (1) n 027.4
Bell (20) TX 087.1
~ Buckle (2) TN 087.2
~ building (3) n 108.5
~ Chapel neighborhood (1) TN 087.3
~ City (1) LA 087.1
~ Creek (1) GA 030.7
~ Island (1) MS 080.9
~ Lake Bottoms (1) AR 092.8
~ Mountain (1) AR 031.1
~ Road (1) 106.1
~ Springs (1) AL 087.5
~ View (1) 106.2
Bellachitto Creek (1) LA 030.7
belladonna (1) n 096.7
Bellaire (2) TX 087.2
Bellamy Gap (1) TN 031.3
belle (3) n 081.6
Belle (35) 106.8
~ Chasse (1) 106.8
~ Cour (1) 105.5
~ d'Eau (1) LA 087.1
~ Isle (1) LA 087.5
~ Isle Bayou (1) LA 030.3
~ Meade (14) 106.1
~ Meade Mansion (2) 106.4
~ Meade Plaza (1) 105.6
~ Meade shopping center (1) n 105.6
~ of Georgia (1) 054.3
~ of Georgia peach (1) n 054.4
Belleair (1) 106.3
belled (1) adj 015.7
Bellefontaine (2) MS 087.1
~ Street (1) 107.9

belles (1) n 125.4
Belles (1) 054.3
Bellevue (2) 105.1
bellied (8) adj 059.9
~ pots (1) n 017.6
bellies (12) n 066.7
belligerent (1) adj 074.8
belling (1) n 082.5
Bellingrath (4) 106.4
~ Garden[N-i] (1) 106.4
~ Gardens (3) 106.4
Bellmead (1) TX 087.2
bellow (120) n/v 036.3
~ out (1) v 036.2
bel(low) (2) v 036.3
bellowed (4) v 036.3
bellowing (40) v/adj 036.3
~ cow (1) n 035.5
~ for (2) v 036.2
bellows (39) n/v 036.3
~ like (1) v 036.2
bellowses (1) n 016.9
bells (3) n 089.2
Bellview (3) LA TN 087.6
~ District (1) GA 087.7
Bellville (1) GA 087.4
bellwether (1) n 096.9
Bellwood (4) LA 087.7
~ Height[N-i] (1) 105.1
~ Lake (2) TX 030.7
belly (703) n/adj 072.4
~ bath (1) n 095.4
~ burst (5) n 095.4
~ burster (1) n 095.4
~ bust (48) n 095.4
~ busted (1) v 095.4
~ buster (461) n 095.4
~ bustering (1) n 095.4
~ busters (3) n 095.4
~ busting (4) n/v 095.4
~ dancing (1) n 092.1
~ -deep (1) adj 074.4
~ dive (21) n 095.4
~ diving (1) n 095.4
~ dock (1) n 095.4
~ flip (1) n 095.4
~ flop (43) n 095.4
~ flopper (4) n 095.4
~ girth (1) n 038.6
~ hit (1) n 095.4
~ land (3) n 095.4
~ landing (9) n 095.4

~ loop (1) n 095.4
~ meat (2) n 046.3
~ part (1) n 046.6
~ plop (1) n 095.4
~ -roll dance (1) n 083.1
~ rubbing (1) n 083.1
~ something (1) n 095.4
~ splash (4) n 095.4
~ splasher (2) n 095.4
~ stroke (1) n 095.4
~ washer (5) n 095.4
~ whop (1) n 095.4
~ whopper (15) n 095.4
~ wool (1) n 035.2
bellyache (8) n/v 080.1
bellyaching (1) v 097.8
bellyband (7) n 038.6
bellyful (3) n 049.1
Belmont (6) 105.5
~ Baptist Church (1) 089.1
~ Heights (3) 105.1
belong (37) v 065.8
~ to (22) v 058.1
~ [P-0] (3) v 040.8
belong[V-p] (6) v 013.6
~ to (5) v 042.7
belong[V-s] (2) v 053.4
~ to (1) v 052.8
belong[V-t] to (1) v 052.5
belonged to (2) v 066.8
belongings (2) n 009.4
belongs (46) v 013.8
~ to (37) v 058.1
below (189) adv 082.7
belt (70) n/adj 022.3
~ dope (2) n 023.7
~ strap (1) n 065.5
Belt (24) 075.8
belted (1) v 065.5
Belters (1) 126.6
belting (3) n 065.5
beltline (1) n 107.2
Belton (6) TX 087.7
~ Creek (1) AL 030.7
belts (11) n 028.5
Belzoni (3) MS 087.5
Bemis (1) TN 087.4
bemoaning (1) v 079.3
ben kins (1) n 059.3
Ben (5) 007A.3

~ Adkins' house (1) n 007A.3
~ Hill (4) 106.2
Bena (1) 087.8
bench (148) n/adj 083.8
~ land (1) n 030.8
~ member (1) n 088.7
~ terrace (1) n 016.6
~ terraces (1) n 016.6
benches (103) n 083.8
bend (28) n/v 096.4
~ down (11) v 096.4
~ like (1) v 058.3
~ over (7) v 096.4
Bend (25) 087.4
bender (2) n 067.8
benders (4) n 072.8
bending (7) v 096.4
~ down (5) v 096.4
bends (1) n 030.6
beneath (1) adv 098.6
benefactor (1) n 066.4
Benevolence (1) GA 087.5
Bengis Creek (1) AL 030.7
Benjamin Franklin Junior High (1) 125.8
Bennetts Mill (1) GA 087.2
bennies (5) n 114.2
Benning (18) 086.4
benny (2) adj 046.1
~ eggs (1) n 046.1
~ hens (1) n 121.5
Benny Craig Park (1) 106.6
Benoit (2) MS 087.2
bent (5) adj 002.7
~ out of (1) adj 075.2
~ over (1) adj 096.4
Bentleys Island (1) FL 087.3
Benton (12) AL AR 087.8
~ County (4) MS TN 087.6
~ County chert (1) n 031.7
~ County Gold (2) 051.3
Bent(on) (2) 086.1
~ sorghum (1) n 087.6
Benzedrine (2) 114.2
Berea (1) TX 087.2
bereaved (1) adj 079.3

bereavement (3) n 079.3
berge (1) n F 014.6
Berkeley (2) CA 087.3
Berkshire (9) 035.5
~ hog (1) n 035.5
~ hogs (1) n 035.5
Berlin (1) 086.1
berm (1) n 090.9
Bermuda (215) 015.9
~ diggers (1) n 021.7
~ grass (68) n 015.9
~ onion (16) n 055.6
~ onions (14) n 055.6
~ pasture (2) n 015.7
~ pastures (1) n 015.7
~ short[N-i] (2) n 123.2
~ shorts (60) n 123.2
~ sod (1) n 015.9
(Ber)muda (36) 015.9
~ grass (32) n 015.9
~ onion (2) n 055.6
~ shorts (1) n 123.2
Bermudan (1) 118.6
Bermudas (24) 123.2
Bern (3) 087.2
Bernard (12) 087.3
~ pine (1) n 061.8
Bernice (1) AR 087.6
Berrien (6) GA 087.9
~ County (4) GA 087.9
berries (57) n 062.5
berry (33) n/adj 062.4
~ acid (1) n 048.5
~ cobbler (1) n 048.3
~ cobblers (1) n 048.3
~ patch (2) n 016.1
~ pie (3) n 048.3
~ tree (1) n 062.5
~ wine (1) n 114.7
Berry (7) 087.2
~ Field (4) 106.6
~ Lane (1) 031.8
Berryville (2) AR GA 087.2
Bertha (1) 125.2
Bertie County (1) NC 087.1
Besa Chitto (1) MS 030.7
Besen (1) n G 010.5
beside (6) adv/prep 088.5
(be)side (1) prep 099.6
besides (1) prep 053.4
besom (1) n 010.5
bessbugs (1) n 060A.7

Bessemer (15) AL 087.8
Bessie Smith (1) 130.8
Bessmay (1) TX 087.1
bessybug (1) n 089.8
best (883) adj 129.4
~ beau (1) n 081.5
~ bedroom (1) n 009.3
~ boyfriend (4) n 081.5
~ buddy (2) n 129.4
~ clothes (2) n 027.7
~ -eating squirrel (1) n 002.8
~ friend (69) n 129.4
~ friends (5) n 129.4
~ girl (13) n 081.6
~ girl friend (5) n 081.6
~ lady (10) n 082.4
~ maid (6) n 082.4
~ man (649) n 082.3
~ -man girl (1) n 082.4
~ men (1) n 082.3
~ mens (1) n 082.3
~ -natured (1) adj 073.2
~ pal (1) n 129.4
~ room (3) n 007.8
~ -up (1) adj 075.7
~ woman (9) n 082.4
Best (1) 050.9
bestering (1) v 095.4
bestest (1) adj 002.6
bet (68) v 072.9
bete (5) n F 059.4
~ puante (3) n F 059.4
~ pue (1) n F 059.4
~ rouge (1) n F 060A.9
betes (1) n F 015.3
Bethany (3) GA MS 086.9
~ Collegiate Institute (1) 055A.9
Bethel (7) GA LA 087.3
~ AME (1) 089.1
~ Church (2) 089.2
Bethesda (5) GA MD 087.3
~ Hospital (1) 070.6
~ Lake (1) AR 087.3
~ Springs (1) AR 087.2
Bethlehem (4) AL GA 087.6
Bethume (1) 080.6
Bethune-Cookman (1) 066.8

betide (1) v 080.7
betrothed (1) adj 082.2
betsey bug (2) n 060A.2
Bettdecke (1) n G 028.7
betted on (1) v 034.2
better (460) adj 079.4
~ -educated (1) adj 083.5
~ -fixed (1) adj 093.8
~ half (77) n 063.2
~ -natured (1) adj 073.2
~ off (1) adj 078.5
~ stand still (1) v 037.5
bet(ter) (4) adj 043.2
Betties (1) 048.3
Betty (15) 048.3
~ lamp (1) n 024.3
between (406) adj/prep 113.7
~ meal (1) n 048.6
~ -meal snack (9) n 048.6
~ -meal snacks (1) n 048.6
~ the North and South (1) 085.8
~ the States (3) 085.8
(be)tween (22) adj/prep 065.8
~ -meal lunch (1) n 048.6
~ -meal snack (1) n 048.6
~ the States (5) 085.8
betwixt (6) prep 080.8
(be)twixt (6) prep 093.5
Beulah (5) LA 087.3
~ settlement (1) LA 082.6
bevel (3) adj 030.2
~ ditches (1) n 030.2
~ siding (2) n 011.2
beveled siding (1) n 011.2
Bevelle (1) AL 087.1
bevels (1) n 062.2
beverage (4) n 065.8
beverages (3) n 121.8
Beverly Acres (1) 106.4
bevy (1) n 055A.8
bewildering (1) adj 065.8
bewitched (1) adj 090.8
Bexar (7) TX 087.5
~ County (1) TX 087.1
~ County Jail (1) 112.8

beyond (9) n/adv 039.5
bezugo (1) n 059.9
bi-tree (1) n 021.3
bias (6) adj/adv 085.2
biased (2) adv 085.2
biasin (1) adv 085.2
biasing (3) v/adj 085.2
biasy (1) adj 085.2
bib (24) n/adj 026.4
~ apron (4) n 026.4
~ aprons (1) n 026.4
~ hats (1) n 099.5
~ overalls (6) n 027.4
Bibb (19) AL GA 087.2
~ County (7) AL GA 087.9
~ lettuce (3) n 055A.6
Bible (32) 070.6
~ bangers (1) n 126.6
~ beater (1) n 067.8
~ Belt (6) 075.8
~ Belters (1) 126.6
~ drills (1) n 130.5
~ reading (1) n 080.8
~ school (3) n 098.6
~ student (2) n 068.7
~ thumpers (1) n 126.6
Bibles (2) 027.7
biblical cord (1) n 065.8
bibs (1) n 018.7
bicentennial (3) n 080.7
biceps (1) n 072.8
bicker (1) v 094.2
bicycle (16) n/adj 070.7
~ policeman (1) n 112.5
~ trail (1) n 031.8
~ tube (1) n 024.4
bicycle[N-i] (2) n 012.9
bicycles (6) n 065.8
bicyc(les) (2) n 039.7
bicycling (2) n 130.2
bid (1) v 101.2
biddable (1) adj 089.9
biddies (74) n 036.7
biddiest (1) adj 088.7
biddy (25) n/adj 036.9
~ breeder (1) n 036.8
~ chickens (1) n 080.7
~ chicks (1) n 036.9
~ coop (6) n 036.8
~ house (2) n 036.8
~ pen (2) n 036.8
~ shelter (1) n 036.8

~ -widdy(x2) (1) interj 038.5
biddy[N-i] (1) n 024.8
biddy(x2) (1) interj 038.5
~ biddies (1) interj 038.5
~ wenny (1) interj 038.5
biddy(x3) (3) interj 038.5
biddy(x4) (5) interj 038.5
~ chick(x4) (1) interj 038.5
biddy(x5) (1) interj 038.5
biddy(x6) (3) interj 038.5
biddy(x7) (1) interj 038.5
Bienvenue (2) 030.7
Bienville (6) 084.3
~ Hotel (1) 084.3
~ Parish (3) LA 087.4
~ Square (1) 106.4
~ Street (1) 107.6
biff (1) n 012.1
bifocals (1) n 052.1
big (1850) adj 065.1
~ as a barrel (1) adj 065.1
~ as a cow (2) adj 065.1
~ -band era (1) n 130.8
~ band music (1) n 130.8
~ bands (3) n 130.8
~ blow (1) n 006.2
~ bone (1) n 037.1
~ boss (2) n 069.6
~ boy (3) n 033.5
~ boys (2) n 129.6
~ brother (9) n 129.5
~ butter bean (1) n 055A.3
~ car (1) n 109.3
~ chief (1) n 068.5
~ chitlins (1) n 037.3
~ corn (1) n 056.2
~ daddies (2) n 128.4
~ daddy (1) n 129.5
~ den (1) n 007.8
~ dog (1) n 093.8
~ drip (1) n 125.6
~ -eyed owl (1) n 059.2
~ flood of rain (1) n 006.1
~ flood rain (1) n 006.1
~ flooded rain (1) n 006.1

~ folks's dance (1) n 083.1
~ freeze (6) n 007.5
~ fresh (1) n 006.1
~ frost (23) n 007.5
~ frostes (2) n 007.5
~ guts (1) n 037.3
~ H (1) n 114.2
~ hard rain (1) n 075.7
~ he rain (1) n 006.1
~ -head (1) n 059.2
~ -head owl (1) n 059.2
~ heavy rain (2) n 006.1
~ heavy rains (1) n 006.1
~ highway (1) n 107.1
~ hominy (18) n 050.6
~ house (23) n 007.8
~ hurricane (1) n 006.2
~ ice (1) n 007.5
~ ice storm (1) n 103.5
~ Indian (1) n 068.5
~ meeting (1) n 089.9
~ -money crop (1) n 041.3
~ mouth (1) n 101.3
~ -name band sounds (1) n 130.8
~ nigger's car (1) n 109.4
~ nose (1) n 126.7
~ -old (220) adj 075.6
~ owl (6) n 059.2
~ pickups (1) n 109.7
~ pie (2) n 048.3
~ pouring rain (2) n 006.1
~ rain (58) n 006.1
~ rains (5) n 006.1
~ ring (1) n 130.7
~ road (7) n 031.6
~ roads (2) n 031.6
~ rock (1) n 123.1
~ room (39) n 007.8
~ school (1) n 083.7
~ shot (5) n 115.3
~ -shot (2) adj 075.8
~ -shot cars (1) n 109.4
~ -shot nigger (1) n 025.9
~ shots (1) n 088.9
~ shower (2) n 006.1
~ shower rain (1) n 006.1

~ sister (4) n 129.5
~ -size (1) adj 064.9
~ sop (1) n 048.5
~ sparkler (1) n 123.1
~ spenders (1) n 129.1
~ spit (1) n 080.3
~ store (1) n 080.7
~ storm (3) n 006.2
~ storms (1) n 006.2
~ striper (1) n 056.9
~ Swede (1) n 128.8
~ swingletree (1) n 021.3
~ time (1) n 082.5
~ time clock (1) n 078.6
~ -time grand affair (1) n 130A.7
~ -timer (1) n 115.3
~ -tooth harrow (1) n 021.7
~ waters (2) n 030.9
~ wheel (2) n 115.3
~ with a baby (1) adj 065.1
~ with child (5) adj 065.1
~ with increase (1) adj 065.1
~ wood (3) n 008.5
Big (237) 030.7
~ Abbie (1) AL 030.7
~ Apple (5) 083.1
~ Armuchee (1) GA 030.7
~ Bahala (1) MS 030.7
~ Bay Ditch (1) AR 030.7
~ Bayou Black (1) LA 030.7
~ Bayou Sorrel Creek (1) LA 030.7
~ Bear Creek (1) AL 030.7
~ Bend (1) 106.4
~ Bertha (1) 125.2
~ Biloxi (1) MS 030.7
~ Bird (2) 088.8
~ Black (2) MS 030.7
~ Black River (6) MS 030.7
~ Boss (1) 069.6
~ Boy (10) 055.3
~ Boy peas (1) n 013.8

~ Boy tomato (1) n 055.3
~ Boy tomatoes (1) n 055.3
~ Boys (3) 055.3
~ Branch (2) AL LA 030.7
~ Brazos River (1) TX 030.7
~ Brother (4) 129.5
~ Brushy (1) AR 030.7
~ Cahaba (1) AL 030.7
~ Canoochee (1) GA 030.7
~ Cat (1) 101.8
~ Cedar (1) GA 030.7
~ Christmas (1) 093.2
~ Clear Creek (1) TN 030.7
~ Colyell (1) LA 030.7
~ Corney (2) AR LA 030.7
~ Corney Bayou (1) LA 030.7
~ Cove (1) 106.1
~ Cow Creek (1) TX 030.7
~ Creek (31) AL AR GA MS TN TX 030.7
~ Creek Gap (1) TN 031.3
~ Creek Lake (1) AL 030.7
~ Creek stream (1) MS 030.7
~ Cypress Creek (1) AL 030.7
~ Dad (2) 064.1
~ Daddy (21) 064.1
~ Dry (1) GA 030.7
~ Elm (2) TX 030.7
~ Fat Mamma (1) 081.6
~ Granddaddy (1) 064.1
~ Granny (1) 064.2
~ Haynes Creek (1) GA 030.7
~ Hill (2) AL 030.8
~ Hook (1) 055A.3
~ House (11) 112.9
~ Iron Ore (1) TX 030.7
~ Island (1) AR 087.3

~ Knob (1) TN 031.1
~ Lake (2) AR TN 030.7
~ Lake Creek (1) AL 030.7
~ Level community (1) MS 105.1
~ Limestone (1) TN 030.7
~ Ma (2) 064.2
~ Mamma (33) 064.2
~ Master (1) 069.6
~ Mountain (1) TN 066.8
~ Nance Creek (1) AL 030.7
~ Nigger's car (1) n 069.3
~ One (1) 064.4
~ Pa (2) 064.1
~ Papa (4) 064.1
~ Pigeon (1) TN 030.7
~ Pine Key (1) FL 087.3
~ Piney (2) AR 030.7
~ Pond (1) AR 087.2
~ Pop (1) 064.1
~ Pottsburg (1) FL 030.7
~ Pottsburg Creek (1) FL 030.7
~ Prairie Creek (1) AL 030.7
~ Red (1) 121.8
~ Reed (1) MS 030.7
~ Ridge (1) TN 030.7
~ Sand (1) MS 030.7
~ Sandy (1) AL 030.7
~ Sandy Creek (2) AL 030.7
~ Sandy River (1) TN 030.7
~ Satilla (1) GA 030.7
~ Scrub (1) FL 087.7
~ Sister (1) 129.5
~ Sisters (1) 129.5
~ Slash (2) AR 029.6
~ South Fork (1) TN 030.7
~ Spring (3) AR TX 030.7
~ Spring Park (1) 106.4
~ Springs (2) GA 087.6
~ Star (1) 105.9

~ Strawberry (1) AR
    030.7
~ Swamp Creek (1) AL
    030.7
~ Sycamore Creek (1)
    TN 030.7
~ Tallabogue (1) MS
    093.7
~ Texas Valley (1) GA
    087.6
~ Thicket (2) TX 029.5
~ Uchee (1) AL 084.8
~ Uchee Creek (1) AL
    030.7
(Big) (2) 030.7
~ Byway (1) MS 030.7
~ Sandy Creek (1) TX
    030.7
bigeye nigger (1) n 069.3
bigged (3) v/adj 065.1
bigger (55) adj 091.7
~ singletree (1) n 021.3
big(ger) (1) adj 043.2
biggest (36) adj 030.6
~ rain (1) n 006.1
biggety (2) adj 092.8
Biggs (1) 107.7
Biggy (1) 064.1
bigheaded (3) adj 074.8
bigmouth (14) n/adj
    059.9
~ bass (10) n 059.9
bigness (1) n 065.1
Bijou (3) 106.7
~ theaters (1) n 084.4
bike (1) interj 037.7
bikes (3) n 075.6
bikini (3) n/adj 123.4
~ shorts (1) n 123.4
bikinis (2) n 123.4
Bilbos (1) 104.3
bilingual (1) adj 080.9
bilious (4) adj 079.9
bill (26) n/adj 094.8
~ folder (1) n 028.2
Bill (426) 067.4
~ Baileys (1) 096.8
billed (6) v/adj 058.3
billet (2) n/adj 008.5
~ wood (1) n 008.5
billets (1) n 008.5
billfold (89) n 028.4
billfolder (3) n 028.2
billfolders (1) n 028.3
billfolds (8) n 028.2

Billie Jo (1) 067.4
billies (6) n 113.2
billion (4) n 001A.2
billions (2) n 093.9
bills (22) n 114.5
Billups (2) MS 087.9
~ Station (1) MS 087.1
billy (274) n 113.2
~ club (50) n/adj 113.2
~ clubs (5) n 113.2
~ goat (125) n 067.4
~ -goat Irish (1) n
    127.9
~ -goat roads (1) n
    031.6
~ -goat weeds (1) n
    061.4
~ goats (9) n 067.4
~ sheep (1) n 034.9
~ stick (15) n 113.2
Billy (693) 067.4
~ Boo (1) 067.4
~ Boy (3) 067.4
~ Carter beer (1) n
    067.4
~ Graham (3) 067.4
~ John (1) 063.9
~ the Kid (6) 067.4
billy(x4) (1) interj
    060A.5
Billy's (3) 067.4
~ Best (1) 050.9
~ sister (1) n 067.4
Billys (2) 067.4
~ Island (1) GA 067.4
~ Lake (1) GA 030.7
Biloxi (64) MS 087.2
~ bacon (3) n 080.6
~ Bay (2) MS 030.3
~ beans (2) n 055A.4
~ Pass (2) MS 030.6
~ River (1) MS 030.7
bimonthly (1) adv 003.8
bin (324) n 014.4
bind (3) v 041.6
binded (1) v 098.7
binder (3) n 041.7
binders (3) n 020.3
binding (2) v 041.6
bing cherries (2) v 062.1
binges (1) n 088.9
Binghamton (2) 105.4
bingo parties (2) n 130.7
binoculars (1) n 033.7
bins (89) n 014.3

biographer (1) n 075.7
biracial (4) adj 069.5
birch (52) n/adj 061.8
~ tree (3) n 061.9
~ trees (2) n 061.9
Birch Creek (2) GA LA
    030.7
birchbark (1) n 061.8
Bircher (1) 129.2
birches (1) n 061.8
birchwood (1) n 061.8
Birchwood Bay (1) AR
    087.9
bird (125) n/adj 065.9
~ beaver (1) n 032.1
~ dog (34) n 033.3
~ -dog boats (1) n
    024.6
~ dogs (21) n 033.1
~ haw (1) n 061.8
~ -hunt (4) v 081.8
~ -hunted (1) v 012.5
~ hunting (2) n 090.9
~ mill (1) n 075.8
~ nestes (4) n 065.9
~ pie (2) n 048.3
~ points (1) n 081.8
~ rights (1) n 084.9
~ shot (2) n 022.4
~ thrashing (2) n 088.8
~ traps (1) n 088.9
~ watchers (1) n 065.9
Bird (9) 088.8
~ Creek (1) TX 030.7
~ Man (1) 088.9
~ Road (1) 107.7
~ tomatoes (1) n 055.3
bird[N-i] (1) n 042.7
bird[N-k]-eye pepper (1)
    n 055A.9
birdhouses (2) n 014.1
birdology (1) n 080.7
bird's-nest fern (1) n
    080.6
birds (113) n 036.6
Birds (1) 055.3
Birdville (1) 106.3
Birmingham (795) AL
    GA 087.2
~ Airport (3) 106.5
~ Green (2) 107.6
~ International Airport
    (1) 106.5
~ Ridge (1) AL 086.2

~ Southern College (1)
    196.4
~ State Choir (1) 087.2
Birming(ham) (1) AL
    087.2
birth (76) n/v/adj 033.9
~ a baby (1) v 065.1
~ a baby calf (2) v
    033.9
~ a calf (8) v 033.9
~ a pig (1) v 033.9
~ certificate (1) n 027.2
~ certif(icate) (1) n
    070.6
~ certificates (1) n
    070.6
~ her calf (1) v 033.9
~ him (1) v 033.9
~ that calf (1) v 033.9
birthday (81) n/adj 093.2
~ cakes (2) n 122.2
~ parties (41) n 130.7
~ party (27) n 130.7
~ ring (1) n 123.1
Birthday Give (1) 093.3
birthdays (3) n 130.7
birthed (3) v 098.7
birthing (6) v/adj 033.9
~ calves (1) v 033.9
~ lady (1) n 065.2
~ that calf (1) v 033.9
birthplace (1) n 106.4
birthright (1) n 080.8
births (1) v 033.9
birthstone (11) n/adj
    123.1
~ ring (5) n 123.1
birthstones (1) n 123.1
Biscayne (22) FL 030.3
~ Bay (2) FL 030.7
~ Boulevard (8) 107.5
~ College (1) 083.6
~ Gardens (2) FL 087.1
~ Gardens Elementary
    (1) 125.7
~ Park (1) 106.4
biscuit (278) n/adj 044.4
~ baker (1) n 017.5
~ board (1) n 010.2
~ bread (30) n 044.4
~ buns (1) n 044.4
~ catcher (1) n 033.3
~ dough (4) n 044.4
~ eater (2) n 033.3
~ eaters (1) n 033.3

~ hoecake (2) n 044.4
~ hoecakes (1) n 044.4
~ maker (1) n 063.2
~ pan (1) n 044.4
~ poultice (1) n 078.2
~ pudding (5) n 048.3
~ roll (1) n 044.4
~ waiter (1) n 017.6
biscuit[N-i] (96) n 044.4
biscuits (577) n 044.4
bis(cuits) (1) n 044.4
bisexual (1) adj 124.2
Bishop College (1) 083.6
bishop's committee (1) n 027.2
Bishop's residence (1) n 106.4
bismarck (5) n 122.6
bisque (1) n 060.8
Bisquick (1) 045.3
Bistineau (2) 030.5
bit (1343) n/v/adj 033.4
~ a bullet (1) v 078.6
~ by (4) v 033.4
~ flies (1) n 060A.7
~ off (2) v 033.4
~ out of (1) v 033.4
~ the dirt (2) v 078.6
~ the dust (6) v 078.6
~ with (1) v 052.6
bitch (104) n 033.6
bitches (13) n 113.3
bitching (2) v/adj 090.9
bite (855) n/v 033.4
~ at (2) v 033.4
~ him (2) v 033.2
~ into (1) v 033.4
~ -size tomato (1) n 055.3
bite[N-i] (1) n 095.9
bite[V-p] (4) v 013.8
bite[V-r] (4) v 033.4
bite[V-t] (4) v 033.4
biters (1) n 060.9
bites (22) n/v 033.4
biting (40) v/adj 033.4
~ dog (4) n 033.4
~ dogs (1) n 045.9
~ fly (1) n 060A.6
~ frost (1) n 007.5
bits (27) n 039.2
bitsy (3) adj 002.6
bitten (464) v 033.4
~ by (4) v 033.4
bittened (1) v 033.4

bitter (32) adj 047.5
~ almonds (1) n 054.9
~ coffee (1) n 032.3
~ haw (1) n 062.5
~ mast (1) n 037.4
~ pecan (5) n 061.9
~ pecan trees (1) n 061.9
Bitter Creek (1) TN 030.7
bitterer (1) adj 039.9
bitterish (1) adj 051.2
bitternut (2) n 061.9
bitters (3) n 078.4
bitterweed (10) n 015.9
bitterweeds (4) n 015.9
bitty (77) adj 064.4
bituminous (2) adj 031.6
~ coal (1) n 088.9
bizarre (2) adj 074.7
blabbermouth (7) n/adj 101.3
~ gabber (1) n 101.3
blabbing (2) v 080.5
black (2703) n/adj 029.8
~ adder (1) n 081.9
~ African (2) n 069.3
~ American (1) n 069.3
~ Americans (3) n 069.2
~ -and-tan hound (1) n 033.3
~ and white (7) n 111.7
~ and white John Dillinger (1) n 092.9
~ -and-white kitty (1) n 059.4
~ -and-white oxfords (1) n 123.8
~ and whites (3) n 111.7
~ angel (1) n 090.1
~ angels (1) n 114.2
~ ant (1) n 060A.2
~ ants (2) n 060A.6
~ antses (1) n 060A.9
~ ape (2) n 069.3
~ apes (2) n 069.3
~ ash (1) n 101.9
~ asphalt (1) n 031.6
~ -ass (1) adj 069.3
~ bakers (1) n 017.6
~ bamboos (1) n 062.5
~ band (1) n 052.6
~ bass (20) n 059.9
~ bastard (3) n 069.3

~ bastards (1) n 069.3
~ bean (1) n 055A.4
~ beans (3) n 055A.4
~ bear (1) n 059.8
~ bears (1) n 089.9
~ beer hangouts (1) n 081.8
~ bitch (2) n 069.3
~ boar (1) n 035.9
~ boarding (1) n 011.2
~ boiling pot (1) n 017.6
~ bottom (1) n 029.4
~ -bottom road (1) n 031.6
~ bottom soil (1) n 029.4
~ bottomland (1) n 029.8
~ box (4) n 079.1
~ boy (8) n 069.3
~ boys (4) n 069.3
~ bread (1) n 044.3
~ bream (1) n 059.9
~ buck niggers (1) n 069.3
~ buckshot (3) n 029.8
~ bugs (2) n 060A.1
~ bumblebee (1) n 060A.7
~ bunch bean (1) n 055A.4
~ Cajuns (2) n 128.3
~ cast-iron pot (1) n 017.6
~ cast pot (1) n 017.6
~ cat (4) n 080.7
~ -cat bone (1) n 081.8
~ cat squirrel (1) n 059.6
~ cement (1) n 031.6
~ cherries (1) n 062.1
~ cherry (2) n 062.1
~ chicks (1) n 088.8
~ children (2) n 069.3
~ clay (9) n 029.8
~ clay land (1) n 029.8
~ coffee (141) n 032.3
~ -collar jobs (1) n 081.9
~ Colombian (2) n 114.1
~ cook pot (1) n 017.6
~ coons (2) n 069.3
~ Creoles (1) n 080.9

~ crow (1) n 069.5
~ cucumber (1) n 062.9
~ cypress (1) n 061.8
~ dark (3) n 096.7
~ day (1) n 005.5
~ dialect (1) n 131.2
~ dinner kettle (1) n 017.6
~ dirt (31) n 029.8
~ dog (2) n 114.1
~ doll (1) n 057.9
~ draft (4) n 078.4
~ drum (1) n 091.8
~ dude (2) n 112.5
~ Dutch (1) n 069.4
~ earth (1) n 029.8
~ -eye peas (6) n 055A.1
~ -eyed (2) adj 055A.1
~ -eyed beans (1) n 055A.4
~ -eyed pea (3) n 055A.3
~ -eyed-pea hoppin Johns (2) n 047.2
~ -eyed peas (84) n 055A.5
~ -eyed table peas (1) n 055A.4
~ family (3) n 069.3
~ fertile soil (1) n 029.3
~ fig (1) n 061.8
~ folk (3) n 069.3
~ folks (19) n 069.3
~ fox squirrel (5) n 059.7
~ fox squirrels (1) n 059.7
~ fraternity (1) n 069.3
~ friends (1) n 069.3
~ frost (7) n 007.5
~ funeral home (1) n 117.4
~ gal (3) n 064.9
~ German bread (1) n 044.4
~ girl (4) n 069.3
~ girls (1) n 069.3
~ gnat (1) n 060A.3
~ gnats (3) n 060A.7
~ gold (1) n 080.9
~ grasshopper (1) n 061.1

~ grasshoppers (1) n 053.8
~ gravel (1) n 029.8
~ ground (1) n 029.8
~ gum (71) n 061.8
~ gum bush (2) n 061.8
~ -gum log (1) n 021.7
~ gum tree (11) n 061.9
~ gum trees (3) n 061.8
~ gumbo (12) n 029.8
~ gumbo land (3) n 029.9
~ gums (5) n 062.2
~ gusty (1) n 007.2
~ guy (1) n 069.3
~ hard-surface roads (1) n 031.7
~ haw (6) n 061.4
~ -haw roots (1) n 061.4
~ haw tree (1) n 055A.9
~ haw trees (1) n 061.9
~ haws (2) n 062.3
~ -headed (1) adj 060A.7
~ -headed bumblebee (1) n 060A.6
~ heel (1) n 069.3
~ hopper (1) n 061.1
~ hound (1) n 033.3
~ hull (3) n 054.8
~ humus soil (1) n 029.8
~ ibis (1) n 081.8
~ iron fryer (1) n 017.5
~ iron pot (1) n 017.6
~ iron pots (4) n 017.6
~ iron skillet (4) n 017.5
~ iron skillets (1) n 017.5
~ jacket (1) n 060A.7
~ Jew (1) n 093.9
~ hip (2) n 090.8
~ joe (5) n 051.2
~ kettle (7) n 017.6
~ kettles (4) n 017.6
~ kids (2) n 064.3
~ labor (1) n 069.3
~ lady (4) n 069.3
~ -like (1) adj 053.4
~ liver (1) n 047.2
~ loam (11) n 029.8

~ loam soil (1) n 029.8
~ locust (10) n 061.9
~ -looking soil (1) n 029.8
~ mamma (1) n 093.5
~ mammies (1) n 069.3
~ mammy (4) n 069.3
~ man (56) n 069.3
~ market (1) n 090.8
~ measles (1) n 079.7
~ meat (2) n 081.8
~ melon (1) n 056.9
~ men (6) n 069.3
~ mens (1) n 016.7
~ MF (1) n 069.3
~ moccasins (2) n 096.8
~ molasses (5) n 051.2
~ moss (3) n 008.6
~ muck soil (1) n 029.8
~ mucky clay (1) n 029.9
~ mud (1) n 029.8
~ mulberries (1) n 062.7
~ mullet (1) n 059.9
~ mushroom (1) n 057.1
~ Negro (1) n 069.3
~ neighborhood (2) n 069.3
~ nigger (12) n 069.3
~ niggers (1) n 069.3
~ night (2) n 096.8
~ oak (28) n 061.8
~ oaks (5) n 061.8
~ oil (4) n 031.6
~ olive trees (1) n 061.8
~ onyx (1) n 123.1
~ overseer (1) n 069.3
~ peach land (1) n 029.8
~ pecks (1) n 069.3
~ people (133) n 069.3
~ peoples (1) n 069.3
~ pepper (65) n 051.7
~ pepper shakers (1) n 051.7
~ peppers (1) n 055A.6
~ perch (2) n 059.9
~ person (12) n 069.3
~ picnics (1) n 081.8
~ pimp (1) n 069.3
~ pine (7) n 061.8

~ pine knots (1) n 008.6
~ polecat (1) n 069.5
~ pot (40) n 017.6
~ pots (17) n 017.6
~ pudding (5) n 047.3
~ race (22) n 069.3
~ racer (7) n 080.6
~ racers (5) n 080.7
~ rascal (2) n 069.3
~ raspberries (4) n 062.5
~ raspberry (1) n 062.5
~ rind (1) n 056.9
~ RJS (1) n 115.6
~ road (1) n 031.6
~ roads (2) n 031.6
~ rock (1) n 130.9
~ root (5) n 061.4
~ roots (1) n 061.4
~ runner (5) n 080.7
~ runners (4) n 089.8
~ sandy land (2) n 029.8
~ schools (1) n 069.3
~ section (1) n 105.4
~ seed (1) n 056.9
~ seed Golden Jubilee (1) n 056.9
~ seed melons (1) n 056.9
~ setter (1) n 080.7
~ sheep (1) n 080.9
~ shell (2) n 054.8
~ shit (1) n 093.6
~ skillet (12) n 017.5
~ skillets (2) n 017.5
~ skunk (1) n 059.4
~ snake (43) n 081.9
~ -snake whip (3) n 019.4
~ snakeroot (6) n 061.4
~ snakeroots (1) n 061.4
~ snakes (28) n 081.8
~ so-and-so (1) n 069.3
~ soil (57) n 029.8
~ son of a bitch (4) n 069.3
~ son (o)f a bitch (2) n 069.3
~ son [P-0] a bitch (1) n 069.3
~ son[N-i] of a bitches (1) n 069.3

~ speckle (1) n 055A.4
~ speech (1) n 131.2
~ spider (2) n 061.3
~ spooks (1) n 069.3
~ squirrel (44) n 059.6
~ squirrels (9) n 059.7
~ straight coffee (1) n 032.3
~ street (1) n 093.9
~ students (1) n 069.3
~ stuff (1) n 008.7
~ sumac (1) n 062.2
~ syrup (1) n 051.2
~ tailors (1) n 069.3
~ tar (6) n 031.6
~ tea (1) n 032.3
~ thing (1) n 069.3
~ things (1) n 008.3
~ -throated (1) adj 059.3
~ tobacco (1) n 057.3
~ tongue (1) n 088.7
~ top (1) n 031.6
~ topsoil (2) n 029.8
~ trash (8) n 069.3
~ truck land (1) n 029.8
~ tubs (1) n 017.6
~ turtles (1) n 060.6
~ walnut (49) n 054.8
~ -walnut (1) adj 054.8
~ -walnut rind (1) n 054.8
~ walnut tree (6) n 054.8
~ walnut trees (2) n 054.8
~ walnut[N-i] (1) n 054.8
~ walnuts (76) n 054.8
~ war-horse (1) n 080.9
~ washpot (6) n 017.6
~ wasp (30) n 060A.6
~ wasp[N-i] (3) n 060A.6
~ water (1) n 093.5
~ widow (7) n 061.3
~ widow spider (8) n 061.3
~ widow spiders (1) n 063.3
~ widows (4) n 063.3
~ wigglers (1) n 060.5
~ woman (12) n 069.3
~ women (2) n 069.3

~ wool (1) n 035.2
~ worm (1) n 060.5
~ worms (1) n 060.5
Black (180) 033.3
~ and Tan (5) 033.3
~ Angle (1) 033.5
~ Angus (14) 033.6
~ Angus bull (1) n 033.5
~ Angus cattle (1) n 036.5
~ Angus cows (1) n 033.6
~ Angus steer (1) n 033.5
~ Bayou (4) LA 030.7
~ Beauties (2) 114.2
~ Beauty (2) 114.2
~ Belt (9) 029.8
~ Belt country (1) n 029.8
~ Belt dairies (1) n 080.6
~ Belt land (1) n 029.8
~ Belt soil (2) n 029.8
~ Bottom (10) 083.1
~ Branch (3) GA TN TX 030.7
~ Cat Thicket (1) TX 080.7
~ Chamber of Commerce (1) 053.4
~ Creek (9) AL GA LA MS TN 030.7
~ Diamond (19) 056.9
~ Diamonds (3) 056.9
~ Dog (1) 033.3
~ Dragon (1) 130.5
~ English (1) 033.6
~ Fork (2) AR TX 030.7
~ Fork Creek (2) TX 030.7
~ Gap (1) TX 031.3
~ Giant (1) 056.9
~ Hawk corn plow (1) n 021.9
~ Hill (1) LA 030.8
~ Holstein (1) 033.6
~ Joe (1) 064.4
~ John (1) 079.8
~ Lake (3) LA 030.7
~ Maria (19) 111.8
~ Mari(a) (1) 111.8
~ Minorcans (1) 093.5

~ Minorcas (2) 080.7
~ Minot (1) 096.7
~ Mollies (3) 114.2
~ Mountain (1) NC 087.8
~ Oak (2) AR 087.5
~ Panthers (1) 066.8
~ Range Mountain (1) NM 031.1
~ River (11) AR LA 030.7
~ Sambo (1) 069.3
~ Sink (1) FL 030.7
~ Snake (2) 056.9
~ Spanish (1) 056.9
~ Swamp (1) AL 119.9
~ Town (1) 105.4
~ Warrior (3) AL 030.7
~ Widow (1) 106.6
(Black) Warrior River (1) AL 030.7
black[N-i] (3) n 069.3
blackball (1) v 091.8
blackberries (576) n 062.6
blackberry (230) n/adj 062.5
~ boil (1) n 077.4
~ brierroot (1) n 093.5
~ bushes (2) n 061.4
~ cobbler (8) n 048.3
~ cobbler pie (1) n 048.3
~ cobblers (1) n 048.3
~ dooby (2) n 093.8
~ dumpling (1) n 048.3
~ jam (3) n 051.6
~ -jam cakes (1) n 051.6
~ jelly (2) n 051.6
~ patch (2) n 016.1
~ pie (6) n 062.4
~ pies (4) n 048.3
~ root (4) n 061.4
~ wine (9) n 114.7
~ winter (1) n 080.8
blackber(ry) (6) n/adj 062.4
~ cobbler (1) n 048.3
~ cobblers (1) n 048.3
~ jelly (1) n 051.6
~ root (1) n 061.4
~ roots (1) n 061.4
blackberry[N-i] (3) n 062.4

blackbird (10) n 059.2
blackbirds (24) n 069.3
blackboard (7) n 075.8
blackbrush (2) n 015.9
blacked out (1) v 034.4
blackest (1) adj 069.3
blackeyes (7) n/adj 055A.3
~ pea (1) n 055A.3
blackface show (1) n 091.9
Blackfeet (1) 080.6
blackfish (17) n 059.9
Blackfish (2) 059.9
~ Bank (1) GA 059.9
~ Bayou (1) AR 030.7
blackfly (1) n 060A.1
Blackfoot (3) 072.6
blackguard talk (1) n 089.9
blackhead (7) n/adj 077.3
~ bumblebee (1) n 060A.4
blackheads (2) n 077.4
blackheart (2) n/adj 062.1
~ cherry (1) n 062.1
blackie (3) n 069.3
blackies (1) n 069.3
blackjack (84) n/adj 113.2
~ country (1) n 029.8
~ land (1) n 029.8
~ molasses (1) n 051.2
~ oak (8) n 061.8
~ oaks (1) n 061.8
~ pine (1) n 061.8
~ tree (2) n 061.8
~ trees (1) n 061.8
blackjacks (9) n 113.2
blackland (95) n/adj 029.9
~ belts (1) n 029.8
~ plow (1) n 021.6
~ prair(ie) (1) n 029.5
~ soil (1) n 029.8
Blackland (2) 107.8
~ Slough (1) LA 030.7
blacklands (2) n 029.4
blackleg (1) v 081.9
Blackley Creek (1) TN 030.7
Blackman Ferry Creek (1) TX 030.7

Blackman's syrup (1) n 051.3
blackout shades (1) n 009.5
blacks (196) n/v 069.3
~ out (1) v 013.9
Blackshear (6) GA 087.4
Blackshirts (1) 129.6
blacksmith (30) n/adj 034.6
~ blowers (1) n 051.4
~ hammers (1) n 020.7
~ shop (14) n 011.8
blacksmithed (1) v 080.7
blacksmithing (3) n/v 090.8
blacksmith's shop (1) n 014.2
blacksmiths (1) n 070.7
Blacksnake Hill (1) MO 087.5
Blackstone laws (1) n 088.7
blackstrap (38) n/adj 051.2
~ molasses (22) n 051.2
Blackton (1) AR 087.4
blacktop (413) n/v/adj 031.6
~ clay (1) n 031.6
~ paving (1) n 031.6
~ road (35) n 031.6
~ roads (35) n 031.6
~ streets (2) n 031.6
blacktopped (24) v/adj 031.6
~ road (2) n 031.6
blacktopping (7) n/v 031.6
blacktops (8) n 031.6
Blackwater (4) FL 030.7
~ Creek (2) AL MS 030.7
~ River (1) FL 030.7
Blackwell (2) OK 087.6
Blackwood Creek (1) AL 030.7
bladder (1) n 037.3
bladders (1) n 081.8
blade (36) n/adj 056.1
~ bone (2) n 072.7
~ fodder pole (1) n 014.7
~ mower (1) n 120.2

~ sharpen(er) (1) n 023.5
bladed (3) adj 080.9
blades (10) n 056.4
Bladon Springs (1) AL 087.5
blah (1) adj 079.4
Blaine (1) GA 087.6
Blairsville (3) GA 087.9
Blakely (10) GA 087.5
blame (22) v/adj 065.7
blame[V-t] (1) v 092.1
blamed (3) adj/adv 092.1
blanc (1) n F 006.8
Blanc (1) 087.4
Blanchard (5) LA 087.6
blanche (1) adj F 037.3
blanching (1) v 046.2
Blanco (4) TX 087.2
   ~ County (1) TX 087.3
Blands Quarter (1) AL 087.5
blank (20) v/adj/adv 032.3
   ~ cartridges (6) n 022.4
   ~ house (1) n 012.1
   ~ out (1) v 079.3
   ~ run (1) n 040.5
   ~ shells (2) n 022.4
   ~ shot (1) n 022.4
Blank (1) 082.6
blanket (96) n/adj 028.7
   ~ road (1) n 031.7
blank(et) (1) n 078.4
blanket[N-i] (1) n 028.6
blankets (49) n 029.1
blanks (4) n 022.4
blaring (2) v 036.2
Blarney (1) 107.7
blase (3) adj 089.9
   ~ -conscious (1) adj 089.9
blast (5) n/v 030.1
   ~ out (1) v 030.1
blasted (1) adv 092.1
blat (1) n 101.3
blaze (10) n/v/adj 057.4
   ~ face (1) n 088.7
   ~ up (1) v 058.5
blazer (4) n 027.1
blazers (1) n 027.1
blazes (1) n 055.2
bleached (2) adj 044.3
   ~ white (1) n 069.4
bleak (1) adj 005.5

bleat (184) v 036.2
bleat[V-p] (3) v 013.6
bleated (2) v 036.2
bleating (90) v/adj 036.2
   ~ for (1) v 036.2
   ~ on (1) v 036.2
   ~ sound (1) n 036.2
bleats (64) v 036.2
bled (3) v 058.8
Bledsoe (1) TN 087.8
bleed (5) n/v 061.4
bleeding (7) v 057.4
   ~ like (1) v 035.5
blemish (1) n 032.3
bless (14) v 089.3
bless[V-p] (1) v 058.6
blessed (8) v/adj 093.2
Blessed (3) 067.1
   ~ Virgin (1) 067.1
   ~ Virgin Mary (2) 067.1
blessing (19) n 049.2
Bleu (1) 030.7
Blevins (3) TX 087.2
blew (640) v 006.3
   ~ away (2) v 006.3
   ~ down (6) v 006.3
   ~ in (1) v 006.3
   ~ it off (1) v 082.1
   ~ off (2) v 006.2
   ~ out (2) v 006.3
   ~ up (9) v 006.3
blewed (5) v 006.3
   ~ up (1) v 006.2
Blieders Creek (2) TX 030.7
blight (9) n/v/adj 055.1
   ~ frost (1) n 007.5
blimeys (1) n 127.8
blimp (1) n 121.8
blind (107) n/adj 009.5
   ~ bridle (2) n 038.6
   ~ cockroach (1) n 060A.1
   ~ Darm (1) n G 080.2
   ~ ditch (4) n 030.2
   ~ fence (4) n 016.2
   ~ fences (1) n 016.2
   ~ gut (1) n 080.1
   ~ man (1) n 099.9
   ~ pole (1) n 053.8
   ~ road (1) n 031.7
   ~ shades (1) n 009.5
   ~ spots (1) n 088.9
   ~ stag (1) n 093.6

~ tiger (16) n 050.8
~ -tiger liquor (1) n 050.9
~ tiger place (1) n 088.7
~ -tigering (1) v 050.8
~ tigers (4) n 050.8
blind[N-i] (6) n 009.5
blinded (1) adj 028.7
blinder (1) n 038.6
blinders (1) n 038.6
blindfold (3) n 098.4
blindfolded (1) adj 129.9
blindman (1) n 052.5
blindman's (12) adj 130.1
   ~ bluff (7) n 130.1
   ~ buff (5) n 098.4
blindmen bluff (1) n 098.4
blinds (416) n 009.5
blink (7) n/v 047.6
blinked (7) v/adj 047.6
blinking (3) v/adj 047.6
   ~ stage (1) n 047.6
blinks (2) v 047.6
blinky (14) adj 047.6
   ~ milk (1) n 047.6
Bliss (7) 055.4
blister (74) n/v/adj 077.7
   ~ bug (2) n 060A.8
   ~ bugs (1) n 077.7
   ~ water (2) n 077.7
   ~ your behind (1) v 065.5
blistered (2) v 065.5
blistering (2) n 065.5
blisters (5) n 077.4
blitzing (1) v 088.9
blizzard (9) n/adj 006.8
   ~ storm (1) n 006.2
blob (1) n 090.8
block (225) n/v/adj 022.1
   ~ and tackle (19) n 104.5
   ~ -and-tackle (1) v 104.5
   ~ fence (5) n 016.6
   ~ -fishing (1) n 080.7
   ~ ice (1) n 080.8
   ~ parties (1) n 130.7
   ~ party (1) n 083.1
   ~ roads (2) n 031.6
   ~ wire (1) n 016.3
block[V-t] (4) v 102.6

blockade whiskey (1) n 050.8
blockade[V-t] (1) v 098.6
blockaded (1) v 102.6
blockbuster (1) n 006.1
blocked (59) v 102.6
   ~ off (3) v 102.6
   ~ up (8) v 102.6
blockers (1) n 110.8
blockheaded (2) adj 074.8
blockheads (1) n 128.8
blockhouse (5) n 098.9
Blockhouse Road (1) 052.2
blockhouses (4) n 118.9
blocking (5) v/adj 015.8
   ~ bait (1) n 093.7
   ~ out (1) v 015.8
blocks (54) n 014.8
Blockton (1) AL 087.7
Blodgett (3) 107.7
   ~ Street (1) 115.8
blond niggers (1) n 069.5
blondies (1) n 128.8
blonds (1) n 095.8
blood (455) n/adj 047.3
   ~ bait (3) n 060.5
   ~ bank (1) n 114.8
   ~ blister (7) n 077.7
   ~ blisters (1) n 077.7
   ~ boil (6) n 077.4
   ~ boils (2) n 077.4
   ~ boudin (5) n 047.3
   ~ cake (1) n 122.8
   ~ cheese (5) n 047.3
   ~ dressing (1) n 047.3
   ~ drippers (1) n 088.8
   ~ kin (13) n 066.6
   ~ meal (1) n 047.3
   ~ pie (8) n 047.3
   ~ pies (14) n 047.3
   ~ poison (5) n 062.6
   ~ poisoning (4) n 078.2
   ~ poison(ing) (1) n 078.2
   ~ pudding (171) n 047.3
   ~ puddings (16) n 047.3
   ~ relation (3) n 066.5
   ~ relative (1) n 066.5
   ~ relatives (1) n 066.5
   ~ ring (1) n 047.3
   ~ sausage (77) n 047.3
   ~ sau(sage) (1) n 047.3

~ sausages (1) n 047.3
~ soup (1) n 047.3
~ stews (1) n 047.3
~ tonic (1) n 061.4
~ vessels (1) n 025.4
~ water (1) n 077.5
~ worm (2) n 060.5
Blood (2) 105.6
~ Alley (1) 105.6
~ River (1) TN 030.7
blooded (11) adj 033.3
~ dog (1) n 033.1
bloodhound (2) n 033.3
bloodhounds (1) n 052.1
bloodied (2) adj 065.9
bloodroot (2) n 061.4
bloodshotten (3) adj 077.7
bloodsucker (1) n 060A.4
bloodweed (2) n 015.9
bloody (12) adj 092.3
~ bucket (1) n 084.4
~ corruption (1) n 077.5
~ hiffle (1) n 060A.5
~ murder (1) n 130.2
~ -shirt Republicans (1) n 129.2
~ water (1) n 077.5
Bloody (3) 030.7
~ Bayou (2) LA 030.7
~ Mary (1) 067.1
bloodybones (1) n 090.2
bloom (16) n/v 101.4
Bloom Hill (1) TX 086.2
bloom[V-t] (1) v 057.8
bloomers (5) n 088.7
Bloomery (8) 053.4
blooming (14) v/adj/adv 082.8
~ time (1) n 081.8
blooms (4) n 055.8
Bloomville (2) TN 075.6
bloomy (2) adj 005.5
~ day (1) n 005.5
~ -looking (1) adj 005.5
blossom (5) n/adj 056.3
Blossom Heights (1) 105.4
blossoms (2) n 101.4
Blossomwood (1) AL 087.2
Blount (12) AL TN 087.1

~ County (5) AL TN 087.3
~ Mansion (2) 106.4
~ Memorial Hospital (1) 108.5
~ National Bank (1) 108.5
Blount's lister (1) n 021.6
Blountstown (1) FL 087.6
Blountsville (3) AL 087.2
blouse (4) n 066.8
blouses (2) n 081.8
blow (649) n/v/adj 006.3
~ away (5) v 006.3
~ back (1) v 123.9
~ beets (1) v 080.3
~ cut (1) n 115.6
~ down (2) v 006.3
~ his groceries (1) v 080.3
~ in (2) v 006.3
~ into (1) v 006.3
~ lunch (3) v 080.3
~ off (5) v 006.3
~ -off (1) adj 096.8
~ on (2) v 006.3
~ out (8) v 006.3
~ outs (1) n 123.9
~ over (2) v 005.7
~ through (1) v 040.6
~ up (17) v 006.3
~ your beets (1) v 080.3
blow[V-p] (2) v 013.6
blow[V-r] (20) v 006.3
~ up (1) v 006.3
blow[V-t] (5) v 006.3
~ down (1) v 006.3
blowed (356) v 006.3
~ away (13) v 006.3
~ down (10) v 006.3
~ in (2) v 006.3
~ off (7) v 006.3
~ out (10) v 006.3
~ over (3) v 006.3
~ up (18) v 006.3
blower (6) n/adj 118.5
~ system (1) n 118.5
blowers (4) n 118.5
blowfish (3) n 059.9
blowflies (2) n 060A.1
blowfly (1) n 060A.2
blowguns (1) n 084.8
blowing (377) v/adj 007.2
~ across (1) v 006.4

~ at (1) v 036.4
~ away (2) v 005.8
~ from (17) v 006.4
~ his nose (1) v 036.4
~ horn (1) n 037.6
~ on (1) v 006.3
~ out of (3) v 006.3
~ over (2) v 005.7
~ rain (3) n 006.1
~ up (13) v 007.2
Blowing (3) 031.5
~ Falls (1) TN 031.5
~ Rock (2) NC 087.5
blown (382) v/adv 006.3
~ away (3) v 006.3
~ down (6) v 006.3
~ off (1) v 006.3
~ out (2) v 006.3
~ over (2) v 006.3
~ up (7) v 006.3
blowned (1) v 006.3
blowout (5) n/adj 083.1
~ Afro (1) n 123.9
blowouts (1) n 098.6
blows (43) n/v 006.3
~ out (1) v 006.3
~ out of (1) v 006.4
~ up (2) v 006.3
blowy (1) adj 006.3
blubbering (1) v 042.5
blucher (3) n/adj 123.8
~ shoe (1) n 123.8
Blucher (2) 106.4
~ Park (1) 106.4
~ Street (1) 107.7
blue (368) n/adj 036.7
~ and gray (1) n 085.8
~ and white (3) n 111.7
~ -and-white car (1) n 111.7
~ and whites (1) n 111.7
~ baby (1) n 080.6
~ bales (1) n 088.7
~ -bellied Yankees (1) n 081.9
~ bellies (1) n 066.7
~ boy (1) n 112.5
~ bream (3) n 059.9
~ buckshot land (1) n 029.8
~ bullets (1) n 093.6
~ cane (3) n 051.3
~ cat (25) n 059.9
~ cat[N-i] (1) n 059.9

~ catfish (5) n 059.9
~ cats (10) n 059.9
~ chambray (1) n 027.4
~ cheese (4) n 048.1
~ -claw crabs (1) n 093.8
~ clay (3) n 029.9
~ crab (1) n 060.2
~ crabs (1) n 060.8
~ day (5) n 005.5
~ denim (5) n 027.4
~ denim pants (1) n 027.4
~ denims (2) n 027.4
~ devils (2) n 114.2
~ dove (1) n 059.3
~ eye (1) n 059.3
~ -eyed (1) adj 053.3
~ -eyed nigger (1) n 069.3
~ films (1) n 114.9
~ flour (1) n 080.7
~ -goose peas (1) n 055A.4
~ granite (1) n 017.6
~ gravel (1) n 031.6
~ gum (2) n 069.3
~ -gum nigger (3) n 069.3
~ -gum niggers (1) n 069.3
~ -gum section (1) n 105.5
~ gums (1) n 069.3
~ heart (1) n 061.8
~ heavens (1) n 114.2
~ heron (1) n 059.2
~ -hill country (1) n 088.8
~ hills (1) n 088.8
~ hole (2) n 030.5
~ holes (2) n 030.4
~ -hull peas (2) n 055A.3
~ jay (3) n 093.6
~ jays (11) n 059.3
~ -jean factory (1) n 027.4
~ -jean material (1) n 027.4
~ jean[N-i] (2) n 027.4
~ jeans (90) n 027.4
~ john (31) n 048.2
~ j(ohn) (1) n 047.6
~ john milk (2) n 047.7

~ jumper (1) n 027.1
~ Kelly (1) n 021.6
~ light (2) n 113.4
~ magnolia (1) n 062.9
~ marlin (2) n 080.6
~ mass (1) n 078.4
~ million (2) n 001A.2
~ mint (1) n 061.4
~ mold (1) n 054.6
~ moon (2) n 089.9
~ movie (1) n 114.9
~ movies (2) n 114.9
~ muck (1) n 090.4
~ mud (1) n 029.8
~ norther (15) n 006.5
~ northers (2) n 007.3
~ overalls (1) n 027.4
~ perch (1) n 059.9
~ racer (7) n 101.9
~ racers (3) n 081.8
~ ribbon (2) n 055A.3
~ -ribbon cane (1) n 051.2
~ -ribbon sugarcane (1) n 051.3
~ rind (1) n 056.9
~ -ring teal (1) n 081.8
~ room (2) n 007A.8
~ runner (2) n 059.9
~ runners (3) n 059.9
~ serge (1) n 027.7
~ -serge suit (1) n 027.7
~ -shell (1) adj 055A.3
~ skies (1) n 005.4
~ sky (4) n 005.4
~ -sky day (3) n 005.4
~ snakes (1) n 080.8
~ soil (1) n 029.8
~ south wind (1) n 006.5
~ -speck hound (1) n 033.3
~ -stem collards (1) n 055A.5
~ string bean (1) n 055A.4
~ tails (1) n 060A.4
~ ticks (1) n 060A.9
~ upper (1) n 019.7
~ whistler (1) n 006.5
~ wigglers (1) n 060.5
~ worms (1) n 060.5
~ yam (1) n 055.5
~ yonder (1) n 052.2

Blue (50) 080.7
~ and Gray Association (1) 080.7
~ and Gray War (1) 085.8
~ and the Gray (1) 085.8
~ Boy (1) 055.3
~ Creek (2) TN 030.7
~ Dash (1) 109.9
~ Dasher (1) 109.9
~ Eye (1) AR 087.4
~ Eye Creek (1) AL 030.7
~ Front (1) LA 087.3
~ Goose (1) TX 087.4
~ -Gray War (1) 085.8
~ Gut (1) AL 030.7
~ Hawks (1) 111.8
~ Hole (1) TN 030.7
~ Lake (1) 055A.4
~ Lake beans (1) n 055A.4
~ Monday (6) 002.1
~ Mountain (5) MS 031.1
~ Pond (1) GA 030.7
~ Ribbons (1) 025.6
~ Ridge (4) GA TN 031.1
~ Ridge Mountains (3) GA 031.1
~ Ridge redbirds (1) n 059.3
~ Sink (1) FL 030.7
~ Spring (2) GA TN 030.7
~ Springs (2) AL TN 030.7
~ Water (1) AL 030.7
blueback (18) adj 080.8
~ speller (15) n 080.8
~ spellers (3) n 080.8
bluebells [J-O] cockle-shells (1) n 130.5
blueberries (194) n 062.5
blueberry (72) n/adj 062.4
~ bread (1) n 044.4
~ bush (1) n 062.4
~ cobbler (5) n 048.3
~ muffins (4) n 044.4
~ tree (1) n 061.9
Blueberry Hill (1) 106.2

bluebill (1) n 059.9
bluebird (8) n/adj 059.5
~ day (1) n 005.4
~ through my window (1) n 130.3
bluebirds (13) n 059.3
bluebonnet (1) n 088.8
bluebonnets (2) n 062.7
bluecoats (1) n 112.5
Bluefield (1) MS 087.9
bluefish (17) n 059.9
bluegill (35) n/adj 059.9
~ bream (2) n 059.9
~ cat (1) n 059.9
bluegills (15) n 059.9
bluegrass (21) n/adj 130.9
~ music (1) n 130.9
~ roots (1) n 061.4
~ tea (1) n 061.4
Bluegrass Branch (1) TN 030.7
bluenette (1) n 070.8
bluenose (2) n/adj 080.9
~ mule (1) n 074.8
blues (30) n/adj 130.9
~ singer (1) n 130.9
Blues (9) 087.7
~ Old Stand (2) AL 087.7
bluestone (1) n 088.9
bluetick (8) n/adj 033.3
~ hound (1) n 033.3
~ hounds (1) n 033.1
blueticks (1) n 033.1
Bluewater (1) AL 030.7
bluff (119) n/adj 031.2
~ blood (1) n 078.9
Bluff (51) AR 087.9
~ City (1) TN 087.1
~ Creek (3) MS TN 030.7
~ Creek Road (1) 030.7
~ Lake (2) MS 030.3
~ Park (1) 106.2
~ Ridge (1) AL 087.4
bluffs (9) n 031.2
Bluffs (1) 080.6
Bluffton (4) GA 087.3
bluing (6) n/adj 080.7
~ tub (1) n 096.7
~ water (1) n 018.2
blunderbuss (4) n 073.3
blundering (3) v/adj 073.3

~ around (1) v 073.3
blunders (1) v 073.3
blunt (4) adj 065.7
~ cut (1) n 123.9
~ cuts (1) n 123.9
~ -nose (1) adj 024.6
blurred (1) adj 005.5
blurry (1) adj 005.5
~ Blue Monday (1) n 005.5
bluster (2) n/v 006.2
~ up (1) v 005.6
blustering (3) v 005.6
blusterous (1) adj 005.5
blustery (24) adj 005.5
~ day (2) n 005.5
~ weather (2) n 005.6
Blutwurst (3) n G 047.3
Blythe Ferry (1) TN 087.7
Blytheville (6) AR 087.9
BM (1) 091.9
boa (2) adj 080.8
~ constrictor (1) n 080.8
~ constrictors (1) n 084.9
boar (1144) n/adj 035.3
~ -bristle brushes (1) n 035.6
~ bristles (1) n 035.6
~ dog (1) n 033.3
~ flank (1) n 046.3
~ hair (1) n 035.6
~ hog (131) n 035.3
~ -hog meat (1) n 035.3
~ hogs (11) n 035.3
~ hunting (1) n 75.9
~ hunts (1) n 035.9
~ pig (16) n 035.3
~ pigs (3) n 035.3
~ sheep (2) n 034.9
~ teeth (2) n 035.7
~ tusks (1) n 035.7
board (525) n/v/adj 016.2
~ -and-batten (20) n 011.2
~ -and-batten roof (1) n 011.4
~ bean (1) n 055A.4
~ -covered house (1) n 007A.7
~ fence (62) n 016.2

~ fences (14) n 016.2
~ froe (1) n 011.8
~ house (5) n 011.2
~ lap fence (1) n 016.2
~ of aldermen (2) n 080.6
~ of education (2) n 083.5
~ roads (1) n 031.6
~ roof (1) n 011.4
~ roofs (1) n 011.4
~ sidewalk (1) n 031.9
~ sidewalks (1) n 031.9
~ siding (1) n 011.2
~ swing (1) n 022.9
~ tanner (1) n 025.4
~ top (1) n 011.4
~ up (1) v 075.6
~ well (1) n 080.7
~ whip (1) n 019.4
Board (2) 030.7
~ Camp (1) GA 030.7
~ Lake (1) LA 030.7
board[V-t] up (1) v 075.6
boarded (3) v/adj 016.2
~ -up fence (1) n 016.2
~ with (2) v 032.4
boarder (3) n 016.7
boarders (1) n 080.6
boarding (5) n/adj 011.2
~ school (2) n 083.6
boardinghouse (25) n/adj 084.3
~ reach (2) n 049.4
boardinghouses (1) n 119.2
boards (106) n 011.2
boardwalk (10) n 031.9
boardwalks (3) n 031.9
boares (1) n 035.3
boaring (3) v 035.5
boarish (1) adj 035.4
boars (123) n 035.3
boat (732) n/adj 024.6
~ blessing (1) n 088.8
~ captain (1) n 068.5
~ corn (1) n 056.2
~ depot (1) n 031.4
~ dock (54) n 031.4
~ docks (8) n 031.4
~ landing (43) n 031.4
~ land(ing) (2) n 031.4
~ landings (1) n 031.4
~ launch (1) n 024.5

~ launches (1) n 024.5
~ launching pad (1) n 031.4
~ lift (1) n 084.8
~ ramp (5) n 031.4
~ ride (4) n 106.6
~ riding (2) n 024.6
~ shoes (1) n 123.8
~ slip (3) n 030.2
~ slips (1) n 106.7
~ stop (1) n 031.4
~ wood (1) n 080.8
Boat (1) 031.4
boater (1) n 012.9
boathouse (3) n 031.4
boating (2) n/v 024.6
boatman (1) n 025.3
boats (288) n 024.7
boatyard (2) n 031.4
Boaz (1) AL 087.2
bob (14) n/v/adj 123.9
~ cut (1) n 115.6
~ for apples (1) v 093.5
~ truck (2) n 109.5
Bob White (1) AL 030.9
bobbed (2) adj 123.9
bobber (1) n 071.7
bobbies (1) n 127.8
bobbing (1) v 022.8
bobby (3) adj 110.4
~ pin (1) n 110.4
~ socks (1) n 002.6
~ stick (1) n 113.2
bobcat (24) n 090.8
bobcats (12) n 059.5
bobo (2) n S 078.9
Bobo (2) MS 030.7
~ Town (1) 088.8
bobolinks (1) n 084.8
bobos (1) n S 073.4
bobs (3) n 123.9
bobtail (8) n/v/adj 080.6
~ bull (1) n 033.5
~ cat (1) n 059.5
~ cats (1) n 059.5
~ dog (1) n 033.1
~ truck (1) n 080.5
bobwhite (4) n 088.8
bobwhites (1) n 080.8
Boca (3) 087.4
~ Chica (1) FL 087.4
~ Grande (1) FL 087.8
~ Raton (1) FL 070.6

Boc(a) Grande Pass (1) FL 087.7
Boche (4) 088.8
bock beer (1) n 121A.9
Bodcau (1) LA 030.7
Bodcaw (1) AR 087.4
bodice (1) n 092.8
bodied (3) adj 073.1
bodies (5) n 052.7
Bodka (1) AL 030.7
bodock (32) n/adj 061.4
~ blocks (1) n 031.6
~ fence (1) n 016.4
~ post (1) n 016.5
~ post[N-i] (1) n 016.5
~ postes (1) n 016.5
~ tree (1) n 061.8
~ trees (2) n 061.9
~ worms (1) n 060.5
bodocks (1) n 061.8
body (29) n/adj 072.4
~ beautiful (1) n 028.1
~ coat (1) n 027.1
~ fluid (1) n 077.7
~ lice (1) n 080.7
~ part (1) n 015.1
~ servant (3) n 088.8
~ towel (3) n 018.6
body's (1) adj 092.8
boeuf (5) n F 033.5
Boeuf (7) 030.7
~ River (4) LA 030.7
bog (67) n/v/adj 029.6
~ disc (3) n 021.7
~ down (2) v 029.6
~ harrow (1) n 021.7
~ swamp (1) n 029.5
~ trotters (1) n 127.9
~ up (4) v 075.8
bog[V-t] (1) v 031.6
Bogalusa (18) LA 087.4
~ Creek (2) LA 030.7
Bogalus(a) (1) LA 087.6
bogeyitis (1) n 090.2
bogeyman (3) n 090.1
bogged (6) v 070.6
~ down (1) v 070.6
~ up (5) v 029.6
boggiest (1) adj 029.6
bogging down (1) v 029.5
boggum by (1) n 022.5
boggy (52) adj 029.6
~ land (8) n 029.6
~ place (1) n 029.6
~ places (2) n 029.6

~ -type land (1) n 029.6
Boggy (10) 030.3
~ Bayou (6) AR LA MS 030.7
~ Bay(ou) (1) LA 030.7
~ Branch (1) GA 030.7
~ Gut Creek (1) GA 030.7
bogholes (1) n 029.6
bogs (5) n 029.6
bogue (3) n 030.6
Bogue (27) 030.7
~ Chitto (12) AL LA MS 030.7
~ Chitto Creek (3) MS 030.7
~ Chitto River (4) LA MS 030.7
~ Chitto Swamp (1) MS 029.5
~ Creek (1) MS 030.7
~ Falaya (2) LA 030.7
~ Falaya River (1) LA 030.7
~ Fellah (1) MS 030.7
~ Homa Creek (1) MS 030.7
Bogueloosa (2) AL 030.7
bogus (1) adj 088.7
Bogy settlement (1) AR 087.8
bohea (2) adj 061.4
~ root (1) n 061.4
~ vine (1) n 061.4
Bohemian (3) 047.3
Bohemians (8) 129.3
bohunk (1) n 130.5
Bohunk (4) 127.6
Bohunks (1) 127.6
boil (1283) n/v/adj 077.4
~ brains (1) n 047.1
~ chicken (1) n 121.5
~ coffee (1) n 048.8
~ corn (31) n 056.2
~ down (1) v 046.1
~ egg (25) n 046.1
~ egg[N-i] (3) n 046.1
~ eggs (24) n 046.1
~ ham (1) n 121.3
~ meat (4) n 046.3
~ pot (2) n 017.6
boil[V-r] (5) v 046.1
boil[V-t] (5) v 046.1

boiled (778) v/adj 046.1
~ cabbage (1) n 046.1
~ coffee (2) n 048.8
~ corn (38) n 056.2
~ corn on the cob (1) n 056.2
~ custard (3) n 048.5
~ egg (95) n 046.1
~ eggs (277) n 046.1
~ food (1) n 048.4
~ greens (1) n 055A.5
~ ham (3) n 046.6
~ in (1) v 053.1
~ intestines (1) n 037.3
~ meat (2) n 046.1
~ okra (3) n 055.8
~ on the cob (1) v 056.2
~ peanuts (1) n 054.7
~ peas (1) n 055A.3
~ rice (1) n 050.7
~ roasting ears (2) n 056.2
~ shrimp (2) n 060.9
~ up (1) v 075.2
boiler (50) n/adj 017.6
~ pan (1) n 017.6
~ shelter (1) n 011.8
~ station (1) n 070.9
boilermaker (1) n 080.6
boilers (6) n 017.6
boiling (177) v/adj/adv 046.1
~ bacon (6) n 046.3
~ coffee (1) n 048.8
~ coffeepot (1) n 048.8
~ corn (4) n 056.2
~ egg (1) n 046.1
~ hot (1) n 046.1
~ meat (38) n 046.3
~ meats (2) n 046.3
~ pork (2) n 046.3
~ pot (16) n 017.6
~ potatoes (1) n 055.4
~ spring (1) n 030.6
~ springs (1) n 030.6
~ things (1) n 080.7
~ up (1) v 030.6
~ water (14) n 046.1
~ white meat (1) n 046.3
Boiling Springs (1) FL 030.7
boilings (1) n 081.9
boils (89) n/v 077.4

bois (14) n/adj F 019.8
~ connu (1) n F 061.7
~ d'arc (6) n F 061.8
~ d'arc trees (1) n 061.9
(bois) connu (1) n F 061.9
Boise (1) ID 087.3
Bois(e) (1) ID 087.6
boisterous (7) adj 074.8
bojacks (1) n 075.7
bok(x3) (1) interj 038.5
Bolatush(a) (1) MS 030.7
bold (5) adj 074.8
~ fence (1) n 016.4
Bold (2) 081.8
~ New City (1) FL 081.8
~ Springs (1) TN 087.2
bole (1) n 061.4
Boleno Creek (1) TX 030.7
boleros (1) n 083.1
Boley Swamp (1) MS 030.7
bolichi (1) n S 047.6
bolillo (2) n S 069.1
Bolivar (11) TN TX 087.1
~ County (3) MS 087.5
boll (55) n/adj 090.8
~ weevil (30) n 084.9
~ -weevil corraller (1) n 025.2
~ weevil monument (1) n 106.4
~ weevil sweep (1) n 021.6
~ weevil[N-i] (1) n 093.5
~ weevils (18) n 060A.4
~ worm (1) n 090.9
Boll Street (1) 105.4
bolled up (1) v 028.9
Bolling (1) AL 087.3
bollos (2) n S 044.8
bolls (1) n 015.8
Bolls Creek (1) MS 030.8
bolo (2) n 104.3
~ knife (1) n 104.3
~ sandwich (1) 121.7
bologna (13) n/adj 046.8
~ sausage (2) n 121.6
bolognas (3) n 121.6
bolster (549) n/adj 028.9

~ bed (1) n 028.9
~ beds (1) n 028.9
~ case (1) n 028.9
~ cover (1) n 028.9
~ pillow (9) n 028.9
~ pillows (4) n 028.9
~ top (1) n 028.9
bolst(er) (1) n 028.9
bols(ter) (1) n 028.9
bol(ster) case (1) n 028.9
bolsters (74) n 028.9
bolt (14) n/adj 026.2
~ ax (1) n 080.6
bolted (2) v 084.8
~ up (1) v 075.8
Bolton (3) GA MS 087.3
bolts (8) n 084.9
Bomar brain (1) n 125.5
bomb (15) n/adj 114.1
~ chuckers (1) n 129.3
bombardment (1) n 130.4
bombed out (1) adj 075.5
bombs (3) n 066.9
bombshell (1) n 103.3
bon (4) adj F 051.1
~ rien (1) adj F 069.9
Bon (5) 087.3
~ Aqua (1) TN 087.3
~ Aqua Junction (1) TN 092.7
~ Secour (2) AL 087.3
~ Secour River (1) AL 030.7
Bonaventure (1) FL 087.4
bond (1) n 058.5
Bond (4) MS TX 086.7
bondage (1) n 032.8
bonded (2) adj 089.9
~ house (1) n 089.9
~ whiskey (1) n 050.8
bonds (1) n 065.8
bone (823) n/adj 037.1
~ -chilling (1) adj 007.4
~ china (3) n 017.1
~ -china egg (1) n 017.1
~ doctor (1) n 039.6
~ feather (1) n 077.6
~ felon (2) n 078.2
~ knives (1) n 017.8
~ orchard (2) n 078.8
~ part (1) n 072.7
~ sucker (1) n 060A.4
~ thumb (1) n 077.7
~ tired (3) adj 075.5

~ wagon (1) n 111.5
~ weary (1) adj 075.5
Bone (7) 069.7
bone[N-i] (1) n 069.4
bonehead (1) n 069.3
boneheaded (1) adj 074.8
boneless (6) adj 054.4
~ cat (1) n 059.9
~ ham (1) n 121.3
~ rump (1) n 121.2
~ steak (1) n 121.1
boner (1) n 092.3
bones (43) n 114.5
Bones (5) 069.7
boneset (2) n/adj 061.4
~ tea (1) n 061.4
boneyard (5) n 078.8
Bonfouca (2) LA 086.2
~ Road (1) 031.8
bong toter (1) n 101.3
bongers (1) n 072.8
bonies (2) n 059.6
boning knife (2) n 017.8
Bonita (3) TX 030.7
~ Creek (1) TX 030.7
~ Springs (1) FL 073.9
bonjour (1) interj F 002.2
bonked (1) v 092.9
Bonne Annee (1) F 093.3
bonnet (10) n/adj 088.7
~ boxes (1) n 009.7
Bonnet (2) 030.7
~ Carre (1) LA 030.7
~ Carre Spillway (1) LA 030.7
bonnets (2) n 088.7
Bonneville Salt Flats (1) NV 087.6
Bonney (1) 068.2
Bonnie and Clyde grave site (1) n 064.2
bonny (2) n 088.8
Bono (1) AR 087.2
bonsoir (1) interj F 003.1
bonus (116) n/adj 095.7
~ gift (1) n 095.7
bony shad (1) n 059.9
boo (108) n/adj/interj 096.5
~ -boo (2) n 078.9
~ -boo gift (1) n 092.7
~ -hoo owl (1) n 059.2
boo(x3) (1) interj 059.1
booby owl (1) n 059.2
boodles (1) n 081.8

boodoodles (1) n 055A.9
boogaloo (2) n 083.1
Boogaloo French (1) 080.6
booger (54) n/adj 069.6
~ bear (9) n 125.2
~ bears (1) n 090.1
~ house (1) n 090.3
~ place (2) n 090.3
Booger Bottom (1) 106.3
boogerman (304) n 090.1
boogerman's out tonight (1) n 090.1
boogermans (1) n 090.1
boogermen (2) n 090.2
boogers (33) n 090.2
Boogertown (1) 106.3
boogery (1) adj 080.4
boogey (4) n/adj 090.1
~ bear (2) n 090.2
~ bears (1) n 084.8
boogeyman (92) n 090.2
boogey(man) (1) n 090.1
boogie (4) n 130.9
~ -woogie (3) n 130.8
boogies (2) n 069.3
boogiest-looking (1) adj 005.8
boohooing (1) v 080.8
booing (1) v 081.4
book (99) n/adj 100.8
~ desk (1) n 083.8
~ freak (1) n 125.5
~ house (2) n 084.1
~ learning (9) n 083.5
~ place (1) n 084.1
~ room (1) n 007A.4
~ satchel (1) n 019.4
~ word (1) n 017.2
Book (1) 013.9
book[N-i] (3) n 016.9
bookcase (1) n 009.4
booked up (1) v 075.7
Booker T Drive (1) 107.7
booking (1) v 095.8
bookish (2) adj 125.5
bookkeeper (15) n 068.8
bookkeeping (1) n 103.1
booklet (1) n 012.2
bookmobile (2) n 084.1
books (28) n 131.2
bookses (1) n 016.9
bookshop (1) n 084.1
bookstore (5) n 084.1
bookworm (117) n 125.5

boom (11) n/adj 111.4
~ and bucket (1) n 111.4
~ potatoes (1) n 055.5
~ trucks (1) n 111.4
boomed (1) v 075.6
boomer (24) n 059.7
Boomer (1) 059.6
boomers (10) n 059.7
booming (1) adj 091.6
boon (1) adj 129.4
boondocks (2) n 099.7
Boone (4) NC 087.1
~ County (2) AR 087.5
Boone's Farm (2) 114.7
Boones (1) 055.5
Booneville (4) AR MS 087.7
boonies (2) n 080.6
boor (1) n 074.8
boos (1) interj 096.4
boose (1) adj 051.5
boost (3) n 097.7
booster (2) n 113.5
boosters (1) n 114.4
boot (26) n/adj 095.7
~ bag (1) n 123.7
~ hill (6) n 078.8
~ liquor (1) n 050.9
booth (2) n 095.7
Booth (3) AL 087.3
~ Station (1) AL 087.4
bootheel (1) n 088.8
boothes (1) n 065.9
booths (1) n 012.1
Boothville (5) LA 087.1
bootleg (193) n/adj 050.8
~ barber (1) n 081.8
~ beer (1) n 050.8
~ booze (1) n 050.8
~ lawyer (1) n 067.8
~ liquor (14) n 050.8
~ moonshine (1) n 050.8
~ place (1) n 050.8
~ preacher (2) n 067.8
~ still (1) n 050.8
~ stuff (1) n 050.8
~ whiskey (53) n 050.8
bootlegged (7) n/v/adj 050.8
~ liquor (1) n 050.9
~ whiskey (1) n 050.9
bootlegger (30) n 050.8
bootleggers (15) n 050.8

bootlegging (27) n/v/adj 050.8
~ whiskey (2) n 050.8
bootlegs out (1) v 053.6
bootlicker (2) n 125.6
boots (96) n 123.8
booty (2) n/adj 131.1
~ roast (1) n 104.6
booty[N-i] (1) n 083.1
booze (47) n/adj 050.8
~ head (2) n 113.6
~ parties (1) n 130.7
boozed up (1) v 115.5
boozehound (1) n 113.6
boozer (3) n 113.6
boozers (1) n 113.9
bop (7) n 083.1
bopeep (1) n 123.9
bopperish (1) adj 080.8
Borax (1) 033.7
Bordeaux (5) 106.3
bordello (4) n 113.4
bordellos (1) n 098.7
border (6) n/adj 031.9
~ oak (1) n 061.8
borderline (1) n 073.6
bore (2) n/v 073.4
bored (8) adj 075.4
~ well (6) n 080.8
Boren Slough (1) AR 030.3
bores (2) n 125.5
Borgne (3) 030.7
boring (1) n 090.4
born (283) v 033.9
~ a calf (1) v 033.9
~ -again experience (1) n 093.1
~ at (5) v 053.4
~ for (1) v 080.8
~ in (30) v 011.1
~ on (7) v 042.3
~ out of wedlock (28) v 065.7
~ to (2) v 053.5
~ with (1) v 053.3
~ without [D-0] father (1) v 065.8
~ [P-0] (2) v 026.7
borned (118) v 056.2
~ a cow (1) v 033.9
~ at (14) v 066.9
~ in (12) v 095.8
~ on (2) v 098.6

~ out of wedlock (8) v 065.7
~ [P-0] (1) v 012.9
borrow (836) v/adj 095.1
~ pit (3) n 080.6
~ pits (1) n 080.8
bor(row) (72) v/adj 095.1
~ ditch (1) n 030.2
~ ditches (1) n 030.2
~ pit (3) n 030.4
~ pits (3) n 080.8
bor(row)[V-t] (2) v 095.1
borrowed (65) v/adj 095.1
borrowing (12) v/adj 095.1
~ pit (1) n 088.7
Bosco bunny (1) n 069.3
bosom (11) n/adj 072.4
~ buddy (1) n 129.4
~ friend (2) n 080.7
~ friends (1) n 080.6
Bosque River (1) TX 030.7
Bosqueville (1) TX 087.1
boss (510) n/adj 069.6
~ man (109) n 069.6
~ men (1) n 069.6
~ mens (1) n 068.5
~ tie (1) n 123.5
~ woman (1) n 063.2
Boss (46) 069.6
~ John (1) 069.6
~ Man (3) 069.6
~ Talbott (1) 056.9
boss(x2) (2) interj 037.5
bossed (1) v 069.6
bosses (6) n 069.6
Bossier (4) LA 087.3
~ City (2) LA 087.3
~ Parish (1) LA 087.2
bossing (1) v 053.7
boss's (7) adj 069.6
~ flunky (1) n 125.6
~ house (1) n 069.6
~ pet (2) n 125.6
~ son-in-law (1) n 115.4
~ work (1) n 069.6
bossy (36) adj/interj 037.6
bossy(x2) (3) interj 037.5

Boston (51) MA TX 087.3
~ blackberry (1) n 062.5
~ brown bread (2) n 044.4
~ butt (3) n 121.2
~ butts (1) n 121.2
~ Celtics (1) 086.9
~ fern (1) n 080.9
~ Mountains (2) AR 031.1
~ potato (1) n 055.5
~ rocker (1) n 008.8
~ roll (2) n 121.2
~ roll roast (1) n 121.2
Bostonberries (2) n 062.5
Bostwick (1) FL 087.4
botah (1) n 055.5
Botan plum (1) n 061.8
botanical (5) adj 106.4
~ garden (1) n 106.4
~ gardens (4) n 106.7
botch (4) v/adj 067.8
~ carpenter (1) n 067.8
botcher (2) n 067.8
botches up (1) v 070.6
both (1087) pron/adj 042.3
bother (96) n/v 057.5
~ with (1) v 057.5
both(er) (1) v 025.3
bother[V-p] (1) v 052.6
bother[V-r] (1) v 039.6
bother[V-t] (2) v 057.5
~ with (1) v 057.5
~ [P-0] (1) v 026.1
botheration (1) n 057.5
bothered (33) v 075.2
~ by (1) v 104.6
~ up with (1) v 053.8
~ with (10) v 032.8
bothering (10) v 053.4
bothersome (1) adj 057.4
bottle (113) n/adj 019.2
~ beer (1) n 121.9
~ cap (6) n 020.4
~ caps (4) n 020.4
~ cleaner (1) n 061.8
~ cork (1) n 020.4
~ doll (1) n 101.5
~ fiends (1) n 090.8
~ lamp (12) n 024.3
~ lamps (4) n 024.3
~ light (8) n 024.3

~ lights (1) n 024.3
~ stopper (10) n 020.4
~ stoppers (2) n 020.4
~ top (7) n 020.4
~ turtle (1) n 060.7
~ wick (1) n 024.3
bottled (1) adj 121.9
bottleneck (2) n 056.6
bottles (14) n 019.2
bottom (517) n/v/adj 029.4
~ country (2) n 029.4
~ dirt (1) n 029.4
~ dollar (1) n 092.8
~ feeders (1) n 059.9
~ fell out (5) v 006.1
~ fell out of (1) v 006.1
~ field (3) n 029.4
~ fields (3) n 029.4
~ ground (1) n 029.4
~ harrow (1) n 021.7
~ has dropped out (1) v 006.1
~ owl (1) n 059.2
~ pasture (1) n 029.4
~ pastureland (1) n 015.7
~ places (2) n 029.4
~ plow (9) n 021.6
~ -plow (1) v 021.6
~ plows (4) n 021.6
~ porch (1) n 010.8
~ rails (1) n 016.4
~ round (1) n 121.1
~ section (1) n 029.4
~ soil (7) n 029.8
~ teeth (1) n 071.8
~ worm (1) n 060.5
Bottom (42) 083.1
~ Creek (1) AL 030.7
bottom[N-i] (1) n 029.4
bottomland (498) n 029.4
Bottomland (1) 029.4
bottomlands (14) n 029.4
bottoms (149) n 029.4
Bottoms (7) 092.8
botulism (1) n 046.9
boucherie (10) n F 046.3
~ campagne (1) n F 046.5
boucheries (1) n F 080.6
bouchon (1) n F 020.4
boudin (77) n F 037.2
boudins (2) n F 047.3

boudoir (5) n 009.3
bouffant (16) n/adj 123.9
~ style (1) n 123.9
bouffants (1) n 123.9
Bougainvillea thorn (1) n 062.3
bougalee (7) n 069.3
Bougalee French (1) 084.8
bougalees (2) n 069.6
bought (864) v/adj 045.1
~ bacon (2) n 046.7
~ biscuit (1) n 045.1
~ biscuit[N-i] (1) n 045.1
~ biscuits (2) n 045.1
~ blanket (1) n 045.1
~ blankets (1) n 029.1
~ bread (123) n 045.1
~ broom (6) n 010.5
~ brooms (5) n 010.5
~ cakes (1) n 045.1
~ candy (1) n 045.1
~ casket (1) n 045.1
~ chair (1) n 045.1
~ chairs (3) n 008.9
~ cheese (1) n 047.1
~ chewing tobacco (1) n 045.1
~ clothes (1) n 045.1
~ coconut (1) n 045.1
~ deal (1) n 045.1
~ dishcloths (1) n 045.1
~ dog irons (1) n 045.1
~ feed (2) n 045.1
~ flour (1) n 045.1
~ food (1) n 045.1
~ furniture (2) n 045.1
~ hammers (1) n 045.1
~ horseshoes (1) n 045.1
~ into (1) v 045.1
~ light bread (5) n 045.1
~ lye (3) n 045.1
~ machinery (1) n 045.1
~ made washcloths (1) n 018.5
~ milk (1) n 045.1
~ mule (1) n 045.1
~ nest egg (2) n 017.1
~ out (3) v 045.1
~ outfit (1) n 045.1
~ outfits (1) n 045.1

~ patterns (1) n 039.7
~ piece (1) n 045.1
~ ready-made hat (1) n 045.1
~ soap (2) n 045.1
~ starch (2) n 045.1
~ sugar (1) n 045.1
~ suit (2) n 045.1
~ syrup (4) n 045.1
~ tea cakes (1) n 045.1
~ the farm (3) v 078.6
~ toothbrush (1) n 045.1
~ towels (1) n 045.1
~ toy (2) n 101.5
~ toys (3) n 045.1
~ up (4) v 045.1
~ vinegar (1) n 045.1
~ washrag (1) n 045.1
~ whetstone (1) n 045.1
~ whiskey (1) n 045.1
boughten (17) v/adj 045.1
~ bread (4) n 045.1
~ stuff (1) n 045.1
~ syrup (1) n 045.1
Boughton (2) AR 087.7
bougre (8) n/adj F 081.5
~ barrow (1) n 035.9
bouilli (2) n F 037.2
bouillon (1) n 048.4
boulder (2) n 028.8
Boulder (3) 030.7
~ Creek (2) MS 030.7
~ Mill Creek (1) AL 030.7
boulevard (66) n 031.9
Boulevard (64) 107.7
boulevards (12) n 107.7
bounce (4) v/adj 022.6
~ board (1) n 022.6
bouncer board (1) n 022.6
bounces (1) v 090.4
bouncing (20) v/adj 022.7
~ board (14) n 022.6
~ swing (1) n 022.9
bound (8) n/v/adj 073.3
boundary (5) n 107.3
bounden (1) adj 057.5
bounds (2) n 065.6
Bountiful (1) 055A.4
bouquet (53) n 101.4
bouquets (7) n 101.4
Bourbe (1) 030.7

bourbon (3) n/adj 050.8
 ~ whiskey (1) n 050.8
Bourbon (3) 031.6
 ~ Street (2) 107.6
bourgeois (2) n/adj 126.6
bourre (1) n F 093.5
bousillage (1) n F 088.8
boutique (1) n F 010.1
Bovina (1) MS 087.4
bovine (2) n 033.6
bovines (1) n 036.5
bow (14) n/v/adj 024.6
 ~ basket (1) n 020.1
 ~ down (1) v 096.5
 ~ vine (1) n 084.8
Bowdon (2) GA 087.4
bowed (5) v 096.5
 ~ down (3) v 096.5
 ~ up (2) v 073.1
bowels (11) n 037.3
Bowersville (1) GA 087.4
bowery (3) n 114.8
Bowery (2) 114.8
bowie (24) adj 104.3
 ~ knife (19) n 104.3
 ~ knives (4) n 104.3
 ~ -type knife (1) n 104.3
Bowie (6) TX 087.3
 ~ County (2) AR TX 087.3
 ~ River (1) MS 030.7
bowl (42) n/adj 017.9
 ~ bath (1) n 018.3
 ~ cut (1) n 123.9
 ~ ivy (1) n 062.3
Bowl (8) 105.7
bowl[V-r] (1) v 130.4
bowlegs (1) n 072.6
Bowlegs (1) FL 087.4
bowlful (1) n 052.5
bowling (22) n/adj 130.4
 ~ green (1) n 085.1
 ~ shoes (1) n 123.8
Bowling Green (5) FL KY 087.6
bowls (6) n 017.3
Bowman (2) AR 087.3
 ~ Hills (1) 087.4
bows (4) n 084.9
bowtie (2) n/adj 088.9
 ~ quilt (1) n 029.1
box (441) n/v/adj 014.5
 ~ boat (1) n 024.6
 ~ cooter (4) n 060.7

 ~ cooters (1) n 060.7
 ~ elder (5) n 061.8
 ~ elder tree (1) n 061.9
 ~ elders (2) n 061.8
 ~ face (1) n 080.8
 ~ heater (1) n 084.9
 ~ house (17) n 007A.1
 ~ -hull terrapin (1) n 060.7
 ~ -hull turtle (1) n 060.7
 ~ moss (1) n 061.9
 ~ plait (1) n 019.4
 ~ seat (1) n 012.2
 ~ -shell (1) adj 060.7
 ~ -shell cooter (1) n 060.7
 ~ -shell terrapin (2) n 060.7
 ~ -shell terrapins (1) n 060.7
 ~ -shell turtle (2) n 060.7
 ~ -shell turtles (1) n 060.7
 ~ snake (1) n 081.8
 ~ stall (1) n 015.2
 ~ style (1) n 115.5
 ~ supper (1) n 104.6
 ~ terrapin (4) n 060.7
 ~ terrapins (1) n 060.7
 ~ three-room house (1) n 007A.2
 ~ toes (1) n 123.8
 ~ turtle (20) n 060.7
 ~ tur(tle) (1) n 060.7
 ~ turtles (8) n 060.7
 ~ -type house (1) n 007A.4
Box (20) 065.8
box[N-i] (3) n 079.1
boxcar (4) n 007A.2
boxcars (1) n 049.3
boxed (10) v/adj 011.2
 ~ building (1) n 011.2
 ~ house (6) n 011.2
 ~ in (1) v 007A.5
 ~ room (1) n 007A.4
 ~ up (1) v 032.4
boxer (4) n/adj 072.2
 ~ shorts (3) n 123.4
boxers (1) n 123.2
boxes (51) n 014.4
boxful (2) n 091.6
boxing (30) n/v/adj 021.2

 ~ plank (2) n 011.2
 ~ planks (1) n 011.2
boxings (1) n 021.8
boxroom (2) n 010.3
Boxtown (2) 105.4
boxwood (1) n 061.8
boxy (1) adj 075.7
boy (826) n/adj 069.3
 ~ bone (1) n 037.1
 ~ calf (2) n 033.8
 ~ child (1) n 068.7
 ~ cow (4) n 033.5
 ~ cows (1) n 033.5
 ~ dog (1) n 033.3
 ~ -girl parties (2) n 130.7
 ~ greasy look (1) n 115.7
 ~ hog (4) n 035.3
 ~ hogs (1) n 035.3
 ~ horse (5) n 034.1
 ~ horses (1) n 034.1
 ~ look (1) n 115.7
 ~ -next-door's father (1) n 053.3
 ~ of honor (1) n 082.3
 ~ pig (1) n 035.3
 ~ sheep (2) n 034.9
Boy (51) 064.4
 ~ Dixie (7) 021.6
 ~ Dixie turn plow (1) n 021.6
 ~ Dixies (1) 021.6
 ~ Friday (1) 081.5
 ~ Scout (1) 097.8
 ~ Scouts (2) 089.2
 ~ Scouts of America (1) 070.8
boy[N-i] (8) n 081.5
Boyce (3) LA 087.5
Boyds Creek (1) TN 030.7
boyed (1) v 053.1
boyfriend (638) n 081.5
boyfriends (19) n 081.5
boyhood (2) adj 025.3
 ~ days (1) n 025.3
 ~ time (1) n 095.8
boyish (5) adj 124.3
 ~ bobs (1) n 123.9
Boyle (2) MS 087.2
 ~ Park (1) 106.4
Boyleston (1) AL 087.2
boy's (4) adj 069.3
 ~ overalls (1) n 027.4

 ~ picture (1) n 053.4
boys (622) n 081.5
Boys (7) 130.8
boys' (37) adj 007A.6
 ~ bedroom (8) n 009.3
 ~ gym (2) n 126.2
 ~ room (22) n 126.3
 ~ rooms (1) n 007A.8
Boys' High (1) 125.9
boysenberries (44) n 062.5
boysenberry (26) n 062.6
bozo (1) n 125.1
bozy (1) adj 076.6
brac (4) n 084.8
brace (21) n/adj 033.7
 ~ face (1) n 125.2
 ~ of horses (1) n 033.7
 ~ of mules (1) n 033.7
 ~ post (1) n 016.5
 ~ postes (1) n 016.5
 ~ yoke (1) n 038.6
bracelet (836) n 028.3
bracelets (73) n 028.3
braces (18) n 028.6
Bracey Creek (1) MS 030.7
bracing (4) n/adj 022.2
 ~ halter (1) n 038.6
bracken bread (1) n 044.6
Brackenridge (8) 106.4
 ~ Park (7) 106.4
 ~ Zoo (1) 106.4
bracket (1) n 020.9
brackish (20) adj 029.5
 ~ water (11) n 030.3
bradder (1) n 096.9
Braden (1) TN 066.8
Bradenton (1) FL 087.2
Bradford (3) AL 086.3
 ~ Bay (1) FL 030.7
Bradley (7) AR 055.3
 ~ County (3) TN 087.2
 ~ Slough (1) LA 030.7
Brady (1) TX 087.1
brag (4) v/adj 053.6
 ~ on (2) v 032.9
 ~ patch (1) n 016.1
Bragg (1) 087.5
braggadocious (2) adj 125.6
braggart (2) n 124.7
bragged on (1) v 090.6
bragging (6) v 025.3
 ~ on (4) v 026.7

brags (1) n 084.9
Brahma (2) 099.8
~ chickens (1) n 099.8
Brahman (20) 033.7
~ bull (3) n 033.5
~ bulls (3) n 033.5
~ calf (1) n 033.8
~ cattle (3) n 081.9
Brahmans (3) 033.5
braid (4) n/v 123.9
braided (10) v/adj 123.9
~ hair (1) n 081.9
~ look (1) n 123.9
braiding (2) n 123.9
braids (18) n 123.9
brain (21) n/adj 125.5
~ head (1) n 125.5
~ -scanning (1) n 070.6
~ tumor (1) n 070.6
~ whiz (1) n 125.5
brain[N-i] (1) n 047.2
brained (2) adj 073.4
Brainerd (5) TN 087.2
~ Road (2) 107.6
brainiac (1) n 125.5
brains (51) n 047.1
brainy (1) adj 125.5
braise (1) n F 089.8
brake (16) n/adj 022.1
~ land (1) n 029.6
brakeman (1) n 115.6
brakes (9) n 030.3
brambleberries (1)   n
062.5
bramblebushes (1)   n
062.3
brambles (1) n 062.3
bran (20) n/adj 019.7
~ bread (3) n 044.4
~ flour (1) n 044.4
~ muffins (1) n 044.4
~ sack (2) n 019.6
brancard (5) n F 020.9
brancards (1) n F 020.8
branch   (588)   n/v/adj
030.6
~ beans (2) n 055A.4
~ bed (1) n 030.5
~ berries (1) n 062.5
~ bottom (6) n 029.4
~ bottoms (2) n 029.4
~ creek (1) n 030.6
~ frog (1) n 060.3
~ head (1) n 029.6
~ heads (2) n 030.6

~ off (2) n/v 031.7
~ -off road (1) n 031.8
~ road (11) n 031.7
~ roads (2) n 031.7
~ run (1) n 030.6
~ side (1) n 029.4
~ spring (2) n 030.6
~ woodcocks   (1)   n
059.4
Branch (155) 087.2
branches (123) n/v 030.6
~ out (1) v 088.3
brand (119) n/adj 080.7
~ -new (117) adj 027.7
~ XXX (1) n 050.8
Brandemere (2) 107.8
~ North (1) 107.8
~ South (1) 107.8
branding (5) adj 081.8
~ day (1) n 081.8
~ iron (3) n 088.8
~ irons (1) n 081.8
Brandon   (5)   FL   MS
087.2
brands (1) n 033.3
brandy (17) n/adj 050.8
~ whiskey (1) n 050.8
brang (8) v 027.5
Brangus (1) 033.6
Brannon (1) 106.5
Brantley (4) AL 087.6
braque (1) adj F 073.4
brash (1) adj 074.8
Brasleton (1) GA 086.3
Brasque (1) 107.8
brass (18) n/adj 009.6
~ beds (1) n 009.6
~ bucket (1) n 017.2
~ eggs (1) n 017.1
~ head (1) n 102.9
~ hoops (1) n 020.3
~ kettle (2) n 017.6
~ kettles (1) n 017.6
~ knobs (2) n 030.8
~ knuckles (1) n 113.2
~ lamp (2) n 024.3
~ pots (1) n 017.6
~ spoon (1) n 012.5
~ wheel (1) n 066.8
brasse de bois (1) n F
019.8
Braswell Branch (1) MS
030.7
brat (17) n 064.4
brats (21) n 068.7

bratty (1) adj 074.9
bratwurst (2) n 121.6
Braunfels (11) 052.6
braunschweiger   (1)   n
047.2
brave (6) adj 074.6
Braves (1) 087.6
bravest (1) adj 052.6
Bravo (1) 030.7
brawlers (1) n 127.9
brawls (1) v 053.7
brawn (2) adj 073.1
brawny (6) adj 073.1
Braxton (2) MS 087.8
bray (58) n/v 036.4
brayed (2) v 036.4
braying   (23)   n/v/adj
036.4
~ noise (1) n 036.4
brays (26) v 036.4
Brays   Bayou   (4)   TX
030.7
Brazell Hill (1) GA 087.3
braziers (1) n 070.6
Brazil (123) 054.8
~ nut (36) n 054.9
~ nuts (75) n 054.9
~ tree (1) n 061.9
~ walnut (1) n 054.8
(Bra)zil (3) 054.8
~ nut (1) n 054.8
~ nuts (2) n 054.8
Brazilian (5) 054.7
~ nut (1) n 054.9
~ nuts (2) n 054.7
~ pepper (1) n 061.8
Brazils (1) 054.8
Brazoria (3) TX 087.3
~ County (1) TX 086.6
Brazos (16) TX 087.5
~ Bottom (1) TX 029.4
~ County (1) TX 087.6
~ River (9) TX 030.7
breach (4) n 082.1
~ of   promise   (3)   n
082.1
~ -of-promise suits (1)
n 082.1
bread (5569) n/adj 044.3
~ -and-butter   knives
(1) n 088.8
~ -and-milk   poultice
(1) n 088.8
~ box (1) n 044.3
~ cabinet (1) n 084.9

~ cake (1) n 044.4
~ -cooking day (1) n
010.6
~ destroy(er)   (1)   n
033.3
~ doughnuts   (1)   n
122.4
~ eater (1) n 033.3
~ eaters (1) n 096.7
~ fish (1) n 059.9
~ griddle (1) n 017.5
~ hoe (2) n 017.5
~ knife (6) n 104.3
~ maker (1) n 088.8
~ man (2) n 044.3
~ oven (2) n 017.5
~ pan (2) n 044.3
~ pans (5) n 017.5
~ powder (1) n 045.5
~ pudding (4) n 050.3
~ sacks (1) n 019.5
~ soda (1) n 045.5
~ toters (2) n 063.1
~ tray (1) n 044.6
~ truck (2) n 109.6
~ wagons (1) n 044.3
Bread (3) 105.6
breadbasket (2) n 071.7
breadfruit   tree   (1)   n
061.9
bread's (1) adj 044.3
breads (21) n 122.4
breadsticks (3) n 044.4
break   (1055)   n/v/adj
048.9
~ a calf (1) v 033.9
~ away (6) v 005.7
~ ball (1) n 130.4
~ beam (1) n 020.8
~ beans (1) n 055A.4
~ blocks (1) n 038.8
~ down (4) v 048.9
~ -even operation (1) n
096.9
~ him down (1) v
065.5
~ in (1) v 048.9
~ -in (1) n 100.2
~ into (1) v 053.4
~ it off (1) v 082.1
~ of dawn (2) n 003.2
~ of day (18) n 003.2
~ of sun (1) n 003.2
~ off (32) v 005.7
~ out (15) v 048.8

~ out of (1) v 052.1
~ peach (1) n 054.4
~ plow (3) n 021.6
~ plows (1) n 021.6
~ pole (2) n 038.8
~ the broomstick (1) v 082.3
~ the engagement (2) v 082.1
~ the neck (1) v 082.2
~ them up (1) v 082.1
~ through (2) v 005.7
~ up (34) v 048.9
~ up with him (1) v 082.1
Break (1) 030.8
break[V-p] off (1) v 005.7
break[V-r] (6) v 048.9
~ up (1) v 048.9
break[V-t] (1) v 057.9
breakdown (14) n/adj 083.1
~ dances (1) n 083.1
~ tunes (1) n 088.7
breakdowns (4) n 083.1
breaker (24) n/adj 110.8
~ plow (2) n 021.6
brea(ker) (1) n 030.3
breakers (45) n 110.8
Breakers (2) 084.3
~ Hotel (1) 084.3
breakfast (312) n/adj 048.6
~ area (2) n 007A.7
~ bacon (117) n 046.7
~ bac(on) (1) n 046.7
~ buns (1) n 044.4
~ cantaloupe (1) n 056.7
~ chop (1) n 121.3
~ dishes (1) n 018.1
~ eating (1) n 046.8
~ food (1) n 048.4
~ foods (1) n 048.4
~ glasses (1) n 048.9
~ ham (1) n 046.3
~ link (1) n 121.6
~ links (1) n 121.6
~ meat (1) n 046.7
~ melon (7) n 056.7
~ melons (1) n 056.7
~ middling (1) n 046.7
~ nook (8) n 007A.6
~ pastries (1) n 122.2

~ roll (4) n 122.2
~ rolls (3) n 122.2
~ room (52) n 007A.2
~ -room nook (1) n 007A.6
~ sausage (3) n 121.6
~ strips (1) n 046.7
~ time (1) n 037.4
~ watermelon (1) n 056.9
breakf(ast)-room nook (1) n 007A.6
break(fast) (1) n 081.3
breakfast[N-i] (2) n 039.6
breakfastes (1) n 016.5
breakfront (2) n 017.1
breaking (191) v/adj 005.6
~ away (4) v 005.7
~ day (1) n 003.2
~ down (3) v 007.3
~ into spring (1) v 005.6
~ off (28) v 005.7
~ -open peach (1) n 054.4
~ out (2) v 092.9
~ peace (1) v 082.5
~ plow (30) n 021.6
~ plows (7) n 021.6
~ spring day (1) n 005.6
~ through (1) v 005.7
~ up (22) v 005.7
~ weather (1) n 005.7
breaks (30) n/v 048.9
~ in (1) v 048.9
~ off (1) v 048.9
~ out (1) v 051.1
~ the engagement (2) v 082.1
~ up (3) v 048.9
~ up with him (1) v 082.1
breakwater (1) n 106.6
bream (355) n/adj 080.8
~ bed (1) n 059.9
~ fish (4) n 059.9
breams (22) n 059.9
breast (206) n/adj 072.4
~ apron (1) n 072.4
~ chain (12) n 021.2
~ chains (6) n 038.7
~ halves (1) n 121.5

~ -high (1) adj 072.4
~ of lamb (2) n 121.4
~ of the lamb (1) n 121.4
~ part (2) n 037.1
~ pieces (1) n 091.8
~ pin (1) n 028.3
~ quarters (1) n 121.5
~ strap (1) n 020.8
~ tree (2) n 020.8
~ yoke (20) n 021.2
~ yokes (2) n 021.3
breast[N-i] (1) n 072.3
breastbone (42) n 037.1
breasted (7) v/adj 090.8
breasts (1) n 037.1
breaststroke (1) n 038.8
breath (8) n 101.3
breathe (4) v 057.7
breathing (2) v/adj 078.6
~ tube (1) n 071.7
breathless (1) adj 075.4
brechas (1) n S 031.7
bred (13) v/adj 076.9
~ boar (1) n 076.9
~ dogs (1) n 033.3
~ gilt (1) n 035.5
~ sow (1) n 035.5
~ up (1) v 033.3
breds (1) n 034.6
Bree Road (1) 107.8
breech (3) n/v/adj 065.8
~ -loader (1) n 022.4
~ -loading (1) adj 022.4
breeches (306) n/adj 027.4
~ leg (6) n 027.4
~ legs (1) n 027.4
~ quilt (1) n 029.1
breeches' pocket (1) n 027.4
breeching (6) n/adj 038.6
~ gear (1) n 038.6
breechings (1) n 020.8
breechloader (1) n 088.8
breechloaders (3) n 084.8
breed (380) n/v/adj 035.3
~ hog (1) n 035.3
~ horse (1) n 034.1
~ in (1) v 092.8
~ out (1) v 092.8
~ sow (1) n 035.5
~ stock (1) n 035.3
breeded (1) n 069.5

breeder (10) n/adj 033.5
~ house (3) n 036.8
~ pen (1) n 036.8
breeders (1) n 080.6
breeding (27) adj 015.2
~ barns (1) n 015.2
~ bull (1) n 033.5
~ bulls (1) n 092.8
~ cattle (1) n 033.5
~ hen (1) n 036.7
~ hog (5) n 035.3
~ horse (2) n 034.1
~ house (2) n 036.8
~ male (1) n 033.5
~ mare (1) n 034.2
~ pen (1) n 015.4
~ sow (1) n 035.5
~ sows (1) n 035.5
~ stock (4) n 035.3
~ -stock horse (1) n 034.1
breeds (31) n 069.5
breeze (22) n/v/adj 006.5
~ through (1) n 080.6
breezes (1) n 030.9
breezeway (82) n/adj 010.8
~ -type deal (1) n 009.9
breezeways (1) n 009.9
breezier (1) adj 007.3
breezing (4) v 007.2
~ up (2) v 007.2
breezy (5) adj 007.2
Bremen (3) GA 087.1
Brenham (4) TX 086.4
Brent (5) AL 087.4
Brentwood (6) TN 105.4
Brer (2) 064.4
~ Rabbit (1) 070.9
Breslau (1) 087.9
bretelles (2) n F 028.5
Brethren Church (1) 089.2
Brevard County (1) FL 087.1
brew (390) n/v 050.8
brewed (5) v 048.8
brewery (1) n 075.8
brewing (8) v 048.8
brews (2) n 050.8
Brewster Road (1) 031.6
Brewton (5) AL 086.5
Briar (7) 030.7
~ Branch (1) GA 030.7

~ Creek (3) GA TX 030.7
~ Hill (2) AL 087.5
Briarcliff (1) 107.7
Briarfield (1) 107.7
Briarwood (2) 105.1
bribe her (1) v 081.4
bribery (1) n 115.3
bric-a-brac (4) n 084.8
brick (220) n/adj 011.2
~ apartments (1) n 119.2
~ area (1) n 008.2
~ barrow (1) n 023.3
~ buildings (2) n 052.1
~ chimley (10) n 008.1
~ chimleys (2) n 008.1
~ chimney (7) n 008.1
~ chimneys (1) n 008.1
~ courthouse (1) n 105.7
~ drive (1) n 031.8
~ facing (1) n 008.2
~ fence (12) n 016.6
~ fences (2) n 016.6
~ flooring (1) n 008.2
~ flue (6) n 008.1
~ foundation (1) n 013.8
~ hearth (3) n 008.2
~ hill (1) n 030.8
~ home (2) n 032.2
~ homes (1) n 014.1
~ house (9) n 014.1
~ houses (17) n 014.1
~ mill (2) n 053.2
~ outhouse (1) n 125.4
~ paper (1) n 011.2
~ patio (1) n 010.8
~ pillars (1) n 007A.7
~ platform (1) n 008.2
~ pressers (1) n 113.7
~ road (3) n 031.6
~ roads (10) n 031.6
~ roofing (1) n 011.4
~ shit house (5) n 012.1
~ siding (10) n 011.2
~ stove flue (1) n 023.2
~ streets (4) n 031.6
~ veneer (4) n 011.2
~ walk (2) n 031.9
~ wall (22) n 016.6
~ walls (4) n 016.6
brick[N-i] (5) n 089.8

brickbat (4) n 032.1
brickbats (2) n 088.8
bricked (1) n 037.1
Brickell (3) 105.2
~ Avenue (2) 106.2
bricklayer (4) n 120.5
brickle (1) n 046.8
brickly (2) adj 047.4
bricks (25) n 031.6
brickyard (2) n 080.7
Brickyard (2) AL 087.8
bridal (7) adj 062.9
~ leaf (1) n 062.9
~ maid (1) n 082.4
~ party (1) n 082.5
~ showers (1) n 130.7
~ wreath (3) n 061.8
bride (16) n 082.4
~ to be (1) n 081.6
bride[N-k] daddy (1) n 082.3
bridegroom (11) n 082.4
bridegrooms (1) n 082.3
bridemaid (40) n 082.4
bridemaids (1) n 082.4
bride's bouquet (1) n 089.9
brides (4) adj 082.4
~ maiden (1) n 082.4
~ matron (3) n 082.4
bridesmaid (342) n 082.4
bridesmaid[N-i] (3) n 082.4
bridesmaids (58) n 082.4
bridesmaids' luncheon (1) n 082.4
bridge (67) n/v/adj 107.8
~ nails (1) n 099.5
~ over (1) v 075.7
~ parties (1) n 130.7
~ tender (1) n 080.6
~ tenders (1) n 080.9
Bridge (45) 107.5
~ Creek (4) AL GA 030.7
~ Creek Church (1) 089.2
~ of Lions (1) 090.9
Bridgeport (4) AL TN 087.3
bridges (12) n 106.4
Bridges (4) 030.7
bridle (340) n/v/adj 038.6
~ bit (1) n 039.2

~ house (1) n 014.4
~ line (2) n 039.2
~ lines (3) n 039.2
~ rein (34) n 039.2
~ reins (87) n 039.2
~ rope (1) n 039.2
~ strap (2) n 039.2
~ straps (1) n 039.2
~ strop (1) n 039.2
~ up (1) v 038.6
brid(le) (1) v 038.6
bri(dle) (1) n 070.6
bridles (14) n 039.2
briefs (1) n 123.4
brier (26) n/adj 070.6
~ blade (1) n 099.9
~ bushes (1) n 015.9
~ corn (1) n 056.2
~ grass (1) n 015.9
~ patch (11) n 016.1
~ -patch (1) adj 065.7
~ -patch babies (1) n 065.7
~ -patch baby (1) n 065.7
~ -patch whiskey (1) n 050.8
~ patches (2) n 016.1
Brier (2) 106.1
~ Grove (1) 106.1
~ Hill (1) AL 030.8
brierberries (7) n 062.4
brierberry (7) n 062.4
brierroot (2) n 061.4
brierroots (3) n 061.4
briers (12) n 062.3
brigade (1) n 108.9
brigadier general (2) n 068.3
Briggsville (1) AR 087.2
bright (119) adj 005.4
~ day (27) n 005.4
~ -eyed (1) adj 076.7
~ girl (1) n 069.3
~ -looking day (1) n 005.4
~ man (2) n 069.5
~ niggers (1) n 069.5
~ people (1) n 069.5
~ -skinned (1) adj 069.5
~ sunshine day (1) n 005.4
Bright[N-k] disease (1) n 080.9

brighten (1) v 090.8
brightening (6) v 005.7
~ off (1) v 005.7
~ up (4) v 005.7
brighter (5) adj 064.7
Brighton (1) TN 087.2
Bright's disease (1) n 078.7
brights (1) n 069.5
Briley Parkway (3) 107.7
brilliant (2) adj 005.4
~ day (1) n 005.4
Brillo sponge (1) n 018.3
Brill's fever (1) n 079.8
brim (1) adj 074.2
brimstone (3) n 070.9
Brimstone (2) TN 087.2
brindle dog (1) n 033.3
brindled-colored (1) adj 080.8
Brindley Creek (1) AL 030.7
brine (3) n 046.6
bring (1503) v 027.5
~ a baby (1) v 033.9
~ a calf (61) v 033.9
~ a child (1) v 065.1
~ a little calf (1) v 033.9
~ back (4) v 027.5
~ birth (1) v 065.1
~ colts (1) v 033.9
~ down (1) v 104.6
~ forth pig (1) v 033.9
~ her calf (2) v 033.9
~ in (15) v 027.5
~ it up (1) v 080.2
~ lambs (1) v 033.9
~ me a calf (1) v 033.9
~ out (1) v 027.5
~ pigs (3) v 033.9
~ the calf (2) v 033.9
~ through (1) v 024.8
~ up (4) v 027.4
~ [D-0] calf (5) v 033.9
bring[V-p] (3) v 027.5
~ out (1) v 013.6
bring[V-r] (10) v 027.5
bringed (1) v 027.5
bringing (32) v 027.5
~ a calf (1) v 033.9
~ in (1) v 025.8
~ up (2) v 065.4
brings (30) v 027.5

~ a calf (2) v 033.9
~ back (1) v 027.5
~ in (2) v 099.5
Brinley (1) 021.6
Brinson (1) GA 087.2
brioche (1) n F 044.3
briquette (1) n F 031.9
Brisbane Park (1) 106.5
brisk (58) adj 007.6
~ morning (2) n 007.4
~ weather (1) n 007.4
brisket (13) n/adj 121.2
~ meat (1) n 121.2
~ stew (2) n 121.2
brisky (3) adj 007.4
bristle (152) n/v/adj
035.6
~ brushes (1) n 035.6
~ hair (1) n 035.6
~ part (1) n 035.6
~ up (5) v 035.6
bristle[N-i] (59) n 035.6
bristled (5) v/adj 035.6
~ up (3) v 035.6
bristles (637) n/v 035.6
~ up (1) v 035.6
brist(les) (1) n 035.6
bristling (2) v 035.6
~ up (1) v 035.6
bristly (2) adj 035.6
Bristol (18) FL GA TN
VA 087.6
Bristow (2) AL 086.4
~ Cove (1) AL 087.2
British (11) 127.8
~ bulldog (1) n 130.2
~ bulldogs (1) n 130.2
~ Columbia (1) 082.6
~ Honduras (1) 060.7
Britishers (1) 069.4
Britoners (1) 127.8
Britons (2) 127.8
Brits (1) 127.8
Brittens Creek (1) GA
030.7
brittle (1) n 054.7
Britton (1) TX 087.4
Britts Landing (1) TN
031.4
Briver (1) LA 087.7
Brizina potatoes (1) n
055.5
bro (1) n 069.3
broached (1) adj 046.2
broad (21) n/adj 125.4

~ oak (1) n 061.8
~ -shouldered (1) adj
072.4
~ -stripe skunk (1) n
089.8
~ wire (1) n 016.3
Broad (32) 107.6
~ Lake (1) MS 030.7
~ River (2) GA 030.7
~ Street (11) 105.3
broadax (13) n 080.7
broadaxes (2) n 080.9
broadcast (6) v/adj 085.2
~ station (1) n 070.8
broadcasting (2) v 088.8
broadcloth (3) n/adj
019.6
~ suit (2) n 027.7
broadleaf weeds (1) n
015.9
broadloom (1) adj 096.7
Broadmoor (3) LA 087.2
~ Park (1) 085.1
broadside (1) adv 021.5
Broadview Square (1)
105.4
Broadway (16) 107.6
~ music (1) n 130.9
~ Shopping Center (1)
106.6
broasted (1) adj 121.5
broccoli (25) n 066.8
Brockton (3) 087.5
Brockwell (1) AR 087.9
brogan (7) n/adj 119.8
~ shoe (1) n 080.9
~ shoes (2) n 093.5
brogans (9) n 097.9
brogue (10) n 131.4
brogues (2) n 123.8
broil (9) v/adj 046.2
~ egg (1) n 046.2
~ eggs (1) n 046.2
broil[V-t] (1) v 046.1
broiled (6) v/adj 046.2
~ egg (2) n 046.1
~ eggs (1) n 046.2
broiler (43) n/adj 036.7
~ house (1) n 036.8
~ houses (2) n 036.8
~ oven (1) n 116.4
~ ovens (1) n 116.4
broilers (20) n 121.5
broiling (2) n/adj 121.5
~ day (1) n 005.4

broke (1515) v/adj 048.9
~ a foot (1) v 065.1
~ away (3) v 048.9
~ class (1) v 083.4
~ classes (1) v 083.4
~ down (19) v 048.9
~ her engagement (5) v
082.1
~ her foot (1) v 065.1
~ her leg (20) v 065.1
~ her neck (1) v 082.2
~ her promise (1) v
082.1
~ her throat (1) v
082.2
~ his heart (5) v 082.1
~ his neck (6) v 071.7
~ in (2) v 089.8
~ into (2) v 048.9
~ it (2) v 082.1
~ it off (26) v 082.1
~ it up (4) v 082.1
~ nose (1) n 035.5
~ off (32) v 005.6
~ off his engagement
(1) v 082.1
~ off the engagement
(5) v 082.1
~ off th(e) engagement
(2) v 082.1
~ off with him (9) v
082.1
~ out (24) v 048.9
~ the engagement (54)
v 082.1
~ the (e)ngagement (1)
v 082.1
~ th(e) engagement
(10) v 082.1
~ the gate (1) v 082.1
~ the leg (1) v 065.1
~ the promise (2) v
082.1
~ their engagement (3)
v 082.1
~ their friendship up
(1) v 082.1
~ their leg[N-i] (2) v
065.1
~ their neck[N-i] (1) v
082.2
~ through (2) v 048.9
~ up (117) v 082.1
~ up the marriage (1) v
082.1

~ up the wedding (1) v
082.1
~ up with him (34) v
082.1
broked (3) v 048.9
~ up (1) v 048.9
broken (559) v/adj 048.9
~ down (2) v 075.5
~ engagement (1) n
082.1
~ English (1) n 048.9
~ -hearted (1) adj
048.9
~ her leg (2) v 065.1
~ into (1) v 048.9
~ off (7) v 082.1
~ up (29) v 079.3
~ up with him (5) v
082.1
~ white lines (1) adj
107.3
Broken (4) 087.5
~ Arrow (1) AL 087.5
~ Ax Ranch (1) 080.7
~ Pot (2) 048.9
broker (3) n 048.9
brokers (1) n 115.5
bronc (2) adj 034.2
~ mare (1) n 034.2
~ mares (1) n 034.2
bronchial (3) adj 066.8
~ condition (1) n 066.8
~ tubes (2) n 076.5
bronchitis (5) n 079.7
broncs (1) n 034.2
brong (1) v 027.5
brooch (3) n 028.4
brooches (2) n 080.9
brood (37) n/adj 055A.8
~ cows (3) n 033.6
~ hen (3) n 036.7
~ house (2) n 036.8
~ houses (4) n 036.8
~ male (1) n 035.3
~ patch (1) n 080.6
~ sow (4) n 035.5
~ sow[N-i] (1) n 035.5
~ sows (7) n 035.5
brooder (92) n/adj 036.8
~ coop (1) n 036.8
~ cow (1) n 033.6
~ hen (6) n 036.7
~ house (17) n 036.8
~ houses (4) n 036.8
~ pen (1) n 015.4

~ sow (1) n 035.5
~ sows (1) n 035.5
brooders (11) n 036.8
brooding (12) v/adj 057.4
~ hen (8) n 036.7
~ hens (1) n 036.7
~ house (1) n 036.8
~ houses (1) n 036.8
broodish (1) adj 036.7
broody (12) adj 036.7
~ hen (7) n 036.7
~ house (2) n 036.8
brook (135) n/adj 030.6
~ frogs (1) n 060.3
~ land (1) n 029.6
Brook (16) 106.1
~ Spring (1) GA 030.7
Brookfield (1) GA 087.4
Brookhaven (18) MS
105.2
~ school district (1) n
025.8
Brookies (1) 084.9
brooklets (1) n 030.6
Brookley Field (1) 106.5
Brooklyn (7) FL MS
087.3
Brooklynese (3) 131.2
brooks (11) n 030.6
Brooks (9) GA TX 087.4
~ County (1) GA 087.5
~ Lake (1) GA 030.7
~ Memorial Art Gallery
(1) 106.7
Brookston (1) IN 087.6
Brooksville (3) FL GA
MS 086.3
Brookwood (5) AL 105.1
~ Mall (1) 105.3
~ Park (1) 105.3
~ Village (1) 085.1
broom (1108) n/adj 010.5
~ brush (1) n 022.2
~ closet (10) n 010.5
~ grass (1) n 010.5
~ handle (4) n 010.5
~ handles (3) n 010.5
~ marks (1) n 010.5
~ over (1) n 130.2
~ peddler (1) n 088.9
~ rake (3) n 120.7
~ sage (36) n 010.5
~ -sage broom (2) n
010.5

~ -sage patch (2) n
016.1
~ skirts (1) n 070.6
~ sweeper (2) n 010.5
~ sweepers (1) n 010.5
broom[N-i] (1) n 053.7
broomcorn (22) n 010.5
brooms (123) n 010.5
broomstick (31) n 010.5
broomstraw (32) n/adj
010.5
~ brooms (2) n 010.5
broth (10) n 048.5
brothel (10) n 113.4
brothels (2) n 113.4
brother (238) n/adj 092.3
~ -in-law (9) n 012.2
~ -in-law[N-k] house
(1) n 043.9
~ -in-law's (1) n 053.6
broth(er) (3) n 065.9
~ -in-law (2) n 086.7
Brother (8) 064.4
~ Bryan (1) 106.4
~ Bryan's statue (1) n
106.9
brother[N-i] (2) n
055A.7
brother's (9) adj 007A.3
~ bedroom (1) n
007A.3
~ room (3) n 007A.4
~ wife (2) n 063.2
brothers (67) n 068.2
Brothers (6) 129.5
~ War (1) 085.8
brougham (3) n 109.4
brought (1482) v/adj
027.5
~ a baby colt (2) v
027.5
~ a calf (1) v 033.9
~ back (8) v 027.5
~ calves (1) v 033.9
~ from (1) v 027.5
~ -home bread (1) n
045.1
~ in (37) v 027.5
~ into (1) v 027.5
~ on (2) v 027.5
~ out (5) v 027.5
~ out of (1) v 027.5
~ over (2) v 027.5
~ pigs (1) v 027.5
~ that calf (1) v 033.9

~ up (95) v 065.4
~ up in (2) v 065.4
broughted (1) v 027.5
Broughton Street (5)
105.2
Broussard (1) LA 087.7
brow (9) n 071.3
Broward (3) FL 087.2
~ Boulevard (1) 107.6
~ River (1) FL 030.7
brown (221) adj 059.7
~ adder (1) n 081.9
~ -and-serve rolls (2) n
044.4
~ baby (1) n 069.5
~ bag (2) n 019.5
~ bags (3) n 019.5
~ bass (1) n 059.9
~ beans (1) n 055A.3
~ Betty (4) n 048.3
~ biscuits (1) n 044.4
~ bottles (1) n 019.2
~ bread (28) n 044.4
~ bunch beans (1) n
055A.4
~ cat (1) n 059.9
~ George (1) n 044.4
~ gravy (11) n 048.5
~ hornet (1) n 060A.5
~ house (2) n 012.1
~ loam (2) n 029.9
~ moccasin (1) n 081.8
~ mullet (1) n 059.9
~ owl (1) n 059.2
~ owls (3) n 059.1
~ paper bag (6) n
019.5
~ paper bags (1) n
019.5
~ paper sack (6) n
019.5
~ potatoes (1) n 055.4
~ rice (3) n 050.7
~ sack (2) n 019.5
~ shack (1) n 012.1
~ shoat gravy (1) n
048.5
~ shrimp (1) n 060.9
~ skin (1) n 069.5
~ -skin nigger (1) n
069.5
~ -skin people (1) n
069.3
~ soil (1) n 029.8
~ spider (1) n 017.5

~ squirrel (17) n 059.7
~ squirrels (11) n 059.7
~ sugar (5) n 051.3
~ thrashers (3) n 059.3
~ trout (4) n 059.9
~ wiggler (1) n 060.5
~ worm (1) n 060.5
~ worms (2) n 060.5
Brown (34) 068.5
~ Bend (1) TN 087.3
~ Creek (1) GA 030.7
~ Mule tobacco (1) n
080.9
~ Park (1) 106.4
~ Spurlock (1) 106.6
Brownfield (1) TX 087.2
brownie (3) n 122.2
Brownie points (3) n
125.6
brownies (9) n 122.2
brownish (3) adj 059.7
brownnose (15) n/v 125.6
brownnoser (21) n 125.6
brownnosers (1) n 125.5
brownnosing (14) v 125.6
browns (2) n 128.7
Brown's (2) 082.7
Browns (46) 082.7
~ Creek (2) MS TN
030.7
Browns' (61) 082.7
~ house (9) n 082.7
~ place (6) n 082.7
~ Surf (3) FL 087.3
Browns[N-k] place (1) n
082.7
Brownsville (24) TN TX
087.1
Brownville (2) AL 087.3
Brownwood (1) TX 087.2
browse around (1) v
015.7
Broxton (1) GA 087.3
brozine (1) n 088.9
Bruce (6) MS 086.2
~ Gap (2) TN 031.3
~ harp (1) n 020.6
~ Reds (1) 055.4
Bruceton (1) TN 087.2
Bruin (1) 030.7
bruise (2) n/adj 077.7
~ blood (1) n 077.7
~ place (1) n 078.1
bruising (1) n 081.3

Brule Sacramento (2) LA 086.1
brumalias (1) n 059.9
Brumby rocker (3) n 008.8
Brummel (2) 028.1
Brummy stew (1) n 065.9
brunch (8) n 048.6
brunches (1) n 130.7
Brundidge (9) AL 087.7
~ Heights (1) 105.4
~ Road (2) 031.7
~ Street (2) 105.5
brunet (1) n 089.6
brung (42) v 027.5
Bruni (1) TX 087.6
Brunson Street (1) 107.6
Brunswick (70) GA 087.7
~ stew (20) n 065.9
brunt (1) n 075.6
brush (1555) n/v/adj 022.2
~ arbor (4) n 091.8
~ arbors (2) n 088.8
~ back (1) v 123.9
~ broom (25) n 010.5
~ brooms (13) n 010.5
~ buddy (1) n 065.7
~ cutter (1) n 022.2
~ deer (1) n 022.2
~ fence (1) n 016.6
~ goats (1) n 015.5
~ heaps (1) n 022.2
~ him off (1) v 022.2
~ -off (5) n 082.1
~ out (1) v 010.4
~ pile (2) n 022.2
~ piles (1) n 022.2
~ up (1) v 022.2
Brush (4) 030.7
~ Creek (3) AL GA 030.7
~ Sicilians (1) 013.9
brush[N-i] (1) n 022.2
brush[V-r] (1) v 022.2
brushed (28) v 022.2
~ him off (1) v 082.1
~ off (1) v 022.2
brusher (1) n 022.2
brushes (36) n/v 022.2
brushing (45) n/v 022.2
~ up (2) v 010.4
brushy (4) adj 022.2
~ swamp (1) n 029.6
Brushy (14) 030.3

~ Bayou (2) LA 030.3
~ Branch (1) MS 030.7
~ Creek (8) AL GA LA MS TX 030.7
~ Knob (2) AR 022.2
Brussels (4) 087.9
~ sprouts (3) n 055A.1
brutality (1) n 112.4
brute (7) n 124.3
brutish (1) adj 088.8
Bryan (11) GA TX 087.4
~ Neely log cabin (1) n 106.4
~ Tower (1) 108.5
~ University (1) 065.9
Bryan's (1) 106.9
Bryant Creek (1) LA 030.7
Bubba (4) 064.4
bubble (3) v/adj 130.8
~ gum (1) n 130.8
~ -gum music (1) n 130.8
bubbles (2) n 123.9
bubbly (1) n 121.9
bucero (1) n S 033.3
Buchanan (3) GA TN 087.1
~ community (1) TX 087.3
buche (1) n S 008.5
buchta (1) n 092.7
buck (228) n/v/adj 034.9
~ ague (2) n 077.8
~ agues (2) n 076.1
~ beer (1) n 050.8
~ bench (1) n 022.1
~ brush (3) n 010.5
~ dance (5) n 083.1
~ danced (1) v 083.1
~ dancing (10) n 083.1
~ deer (1) n 034.9
~ dough (1) n 029.8
~ -dough land (1) n 029.9
~ fever (6) n 080.6
~ flies (1) n 060A.6
~ fly (2) n 060A.7
~ goat (1) n 034.9
~ head (2) n 050.8
~ horse (1) n 022.1
~ -jump (1) v 034.4
~ naked (1) adj 089.8
~ nigger (3) n 069.3
~ niggers (2) n 069.3

~ nut (1) n 045.2
~ privates (1) n 080.6
~ privy (1) n 012.1
~ rabbit (1) n 034.9
~ rake (2) n 092.7
~ rakes (1) n 014.9
~ sheep (7) n 034.9
~ vine (2) n 061.4
~ yam (1) n 055.5
~ yams (1) n 055.5
Buck (13) 064.4
~ Branch (2) AL LA 030.7
~ Creek (5) AL GA TN 030.7
buck(x7) (1) interj 038.5
buck[V-r] (1) v 034.4
buckaroo (1) n 080.6
Buckatunna (1) MS 030.7
buckberries (1) n 062.4
buckberry bushes (1) n 062.4
buckboard (4) n 081.8
buckboards (1) n 021.3
buckbush (3) n/adj 062.2
~ broom (1) n 062.3
buckbushes (1) n 062.2
bucked (8) v 034.4
~ off (2) v 034.4
bucket (3535) n/v/adj 017.2
~ can (1) n 017.4
~ lid (1) n 017.2
~ lids (1) n 017.2
~ -like (1) n 017.2
~ -raining (1) v 006.1
~ seats (5) n 109.1
~ truck (2) n 111.4
~ -type thing (1) n 095.8
~ water (1) n 048.9
buck(et) (7) n/adj 023.1
~ box (1) n 023.1
Bucket (2) 019.2
bucketful (3) n 023.1
buckets (613) n 017.2
buckeye (10) n/adj 062.7
~ ball (1) n 061.9
~ bush (1) n 061.4
Buckeyes (1) 069.4
Buckhead (19) GA 087.6
~ area (1) n 105.4
Buckhorn (10) AL 087.3
~ Bayou (1) LA 030.7

~ Bend area (1) LA 087.4
~ Creek (1) FL 030.7
~ Landing (1) LA 087.3
~ River (1) FL 030.7
bucking (4) v/adj 022.1
~ horse (1) n 022.1
~ horses (1) n 034.2
Buckingham (1) 106.4
buckle (2) n/adj 038.6
~ string (1) n 038.7
Buckle (2) 087.2
Buckley Woods Branch (1) GA 030.7
buckra (6) n/adj 069.4
~ folks (1) n 069.8
buckras (1) n 069.8
buck's name (1) n 034.9
bucks (26) n 034.9
Bucks Wharf (2) FL 031.4
bucksaw (21) n/adj 081.8
~ rack (2) n 022.1
bucksaws (1) n 080.8
buckshot (116) n/adj 022.4
~ country (1) n 029.8
~ farm (1) n 029.8
~ ground (1) n 029.9
~ land (26) n 029.9
~ plantations (1) n 029.8
~ red worms (1) n 060.5
buckshots (1) n 022.4
buckshotty (6) adj 029.8
~ land (2) n 029.8
~ soil (1) n 029.8
buckskin (3) n/adj 027.3
~ pants (1) n 027.4
buckthorn trees (1) n 061.8
Bucktown (3) 105.1
buckwheat (27) n/adj 044.3
~ bread (2) n 045.3
~ -cake bread (1) n 044.4
~ cakes (14) n 045.3
~ niggers (1) n 069.5
~ pancakes (2) n 045.3
Buckwheat (1) 069.3
bud (13) n/adj 055.7
~ vase (9) n 017.7

Bud (9) 064.4
~ Dickson Creek (1) GA 030.7
budded peach (1) n 054.4
buddies (21) n 129.6
budding willow (1) n 061.9
buddy (72) n/v 129.4
~ up to (1) v 129.8
Buddy (5) 064.4
buddy[N-i] (1) n 053.4
budge for (1) v 093.6
buds (3) n 070.7
Budweiser (1) 020.2
Buena (8) TX 087.9
~ Vista (5) GA MS 087.4
~ Vista area (2) n 105A.4
buenas (1) adj S 002.6
Buenos Aires (1) 087.6
buenos (5) adj S 002.4
buff (5) n 098.4
buffalo (101) n/adj 059.9
~ chips (1) n 080.9
~ cow (1) n 033.6
~ fat (1) n 024.4
~ fish (12) n 092.7
~ gnats (2) n 060A.6
~ grass (1) n 015.9
~ hamburger (1) n 093.7
~ wallows (1) n 029.7
Buffalo (28) NY 086.1
~ Bayou (7) TX 030.3
~ Creek (2) GA TN 030.7
~ Ditch (1) AR 031.4
~ Island (1) TN 087.7
~ River (6) AR MS TN 030.7
~ Road (1) 031.6
~ Speedway (1) 107.8
buffaloes (9) n 059.9
buffel grass (1) n 015.9
buffer (3) n 107.3
buffet (11) n/adj 009.2
~ drawer (1) n 008.9
Buford (6) GA 087.2
bug (979) n/v/adj 060A.2
~ around (1) v 080.7
~ -eyed (1) adj 050.8
~ flies (1) n 060A.9
~ fuck (1) n 092.4
~ jumping (1) n 083.1

~ light (1) n 060A.3
~ off (1) v 082.1
~ out (1) v 027.8
~ -proof safe (1) n 015.5
~ shit (1) n 060A.5
bugaboos (1) n 069.4
bugged (1) v 093.8
bugger (1) n 064.4
buggies (48) n 064.5
bugging (1) v 081.8
buggy (753) n/adj 064.5
~ axle (2) n 021.8
~ carriage (1) n 064.5
~ harness (3) n 038.6
~ hickories (1) n 019.4
~ horse (6) n 034.2
~ horses (2) n 034.2
~ house (11) n 011.7
~ houses (1) n 011.7
~ line (1) n 039.1
~ lines (5) n 039.1
~ mare (1) n 034.2
~ pole (1) n 020.8
~ quirt (2) n 019.4
~ reins (1) n 039.1
~ ride (2) n 064.5
~ road (1) n 031.8
~ rug (1) n 093.5
~ shaft (5) n 020.9
~ shaft[N-i] (3) n 020.9
~ shafts (16) n 020.9
~ shears (1) n 020.9
~ shed (6) n 014.2
~ shelter (1) n 011.7
~ shelters (1) n 014.3
~ staves (1) n 020.9
~ strap (1) n 022.3
~ switch (7) n 019.4
~ switches (1) n 019.4
~ tire (1) n 021.1
~ tongue (2) n 020.8
~ tree (1) n 021.2
~ wheel (1) n 065.9
~ whip (136) n 019.4
~ -whip crackers (1) n 019.4
~ whips (12) n 019.4
Buggy (1) 023.3
buggy[N-i] (1) n 023.3
bugle (1) n 088.9
bugs (735) n/v 059.5
Buick (3) 088.9
~ car (2) n 074.4

build (68) n/v 065.3
~ up (4) v 007.2
build[V-p] (1) v 013.6
build[V-r] (6) v 042.7
~ up (1) v 098.6
build[V-t] (2) v 016.6
~ out of (1) v 016.6
builded (2) v 070.8
builder (1) n 067.7
building (259) n/v/adj 007.2
~ engineer (2) n 119.5
~ horse (1) n 022.1
~ inspectors (1) n 115.6
~ man (1) n 119.5
~ manager (2) n 119.5
~ manag(er) (1) n 119.5
~ site (1) n 108.7
~ supervisor (1) n 119.5
~ up (22) v 007.2
buildings (56) n 108.5
builds (3) v 013.7
built (165) v/adj 065.8
~ around (1) v 090.4
~ by (1) v 052.5
~ for (1) v 012.5
~ from (1) v 025.3
~ -in bump (1) n 110.8
~ -in closet (4) n 010.1
~ -in closets (4) n 009.6
~ -in clothes closet (1) n 009.6
~ -in cupboard (1) n 010.1
~ -in dresser (1) n 009.2
~ -in gutters (1) n 011.5
~ -in lockers (1) n 009.6
~ -in pantry (1) n 010.1
~ -in storage area (1) n 010.1
~ in (1) v 013.7
~ like (4) v 065.3
~ of (1) v 025.6
~ off from (1) v 074.4
~ on (6) v 053.4
~ -on (1) adj 017.5
~ onto (1) v 027.2
~ out (2) v 025.9

~ out of (4) v 016.7
~ to (1) v 015.1
~ up (1) v 096.7
~ -up (2) adj 073.1
~ -up land (1) n 029.4
~ -up soil (1) n 029.3
~ with (2) v 042.5
builted (1) v 098.6
bulb (1109) n/adj 019.9
~ socket (1) n 019.9
bulbs (71) n 019.9
bulge (666) n/v/adj 027.8
~ out (156) v 027.8
~ pockets (1) n 073.5
~ up (1) v 027.8
Bulge (7) 027.8
bulged (34) v 027.8
~ out (23) v 027.8
bulges (6) v 027.8
~ out (1) v 027.8
bulging (70) v/adj 027.8
~ out (15) v 027.8
~ up (1) v 027.8
bulgy (27) adj 027.8
bulk (617) n/v/adj 051.5
~ bacon (1) n 046.5
~ barn (1) n 089.9
~ containers (2) n 051.5
~ crackers (2) n 051.5
~ feed (1) n 051.5
~ flour (1) n 051.5
~ form (4) n 051.5
~ lard (1) n 051.5
~ lot (1) n 051.5
~ meat (3) n 046.3
~ out (5) v 027.8
~ quantities (1) n 051.5
~ rate (2) n 051.5
~ rates (1) n 051.5
~ salt (1) n 051.5
~ sausage (2) n 051.5
~ stuff (1) n 051.5
~ sugar (11) n 051.5
~ up (1) v 027.8
~ weight (1) n 051.5
bulkhead (3) n/adj 050.8
~ clouds (1) n 005.3
bulks (23) n 051.5
bulky (35) adj 027.8
~ butter bean (1) n 055A.3
bull (1448) n/adj 033.5
~ bay (3) n 061.9
~ bream (1) n 059.9

~ calf (90) n 033.8
~ calves (5) n 033.8
~ cat (1) n 059.9
~ corn (2) n 092.3
~ cow (11) n 033.8
~ cows (2) n 033.8
~ crap (1) n 033.5
~ dagger (16) n 124.4
~ daggers (2) n 124.4
~ dyke (4) n 124.4
~ dyker (4) n 124.4
~ -faced (2) adj 057.3
~ -faced bumblebee (1) n 060A.8
~ -faced tobacco (1) n 057.3
~ fence (1) n 016.4
~ finger (1) n 072.5
~ fish (1) n 059.9
~ fries (1) n 081.8
~ gang (1) n 080.7
~ gangs (1) n 093.7
~ grass (7) n 018.9
~ harps (1) n 020.5
~ -hook squash (1) n 056.6
~ in the ring (4) n 130.5
~ light (1) n 024.3
~ maple (1) n 061.5
~ minnow (2) n 061.2
~ minnows (1) n 059.9
~ nettle (11) n 062.3
~ nettles (8) n 015.9
~ nuts (1) n 037.2
~ rake (8) n 014.9
~ session (1) n 129.7
~ sheep (1) n 034.9
~ skate (2) n 033.5
~ snake (4) n 093.7
~ steer (1) n 033.5
~ stuff (1) n 080.7
~ swing (1) n 090.9
~ tongue (33) n 021.6
~ tongue plow (12) n 021.6
~ tongue plows (4) n 021.6
~ tongue scooter (2) n 021.6
~ tongue stock (1) n 021.6
~ tongues (2) n 021.6
~ train (1) n 033.7
~ wagon (1) n 070.9

~ yard (2) n 015.6
~ yearling (10) n 033.8
~ yearling calf (1) n 033.8
~ yearlings (2) n 033.8
Bull (12) 030.7
~ Branch (1) AL 030.7
~ Creek (2) GA 030.7
~ Durham (1) 033.5
~ Mountain (2) AL MS 087.5
~ of the Wood (1) 057.3
~ Run (1) LA 087.3
~ Shoals (1) AR 030.7
~ Street (1) 107.6
bullace (1) n 062.4
bullaces (7) n 062.3
Bullard Township (1) AR 087.2
Bullards Creek (1) GA 030.7
bullbat (6) n 059.2
bullbats (2) n 059.1
bullberries (1) n 062.5
bulldog (27) n/adj 033.1
~ soda (1) n 088.8
bulldogs (7) n 033.1
bulldoze (3) v/adj 120.4
~ work (1) n 084.8
(bull)doze (2) v 088.7
bulldozed (4) v 033.5
bulldozer (10) n 041.4
(bull)dozer (5) n/adj 080.8
~ work (1) n 102.8
bulldozers (6) n 080.8
(bull)dozers (1) n 075.6
bulldozing (1) v 066.8
bullet (226) n/adj 022.4
~ hole (5) n 078.1
~ shell (1) n 022.4
~ shot (1) n 078.1
~ tomatoes (1) n 055.3
~ wound (35) n 078.1
~ wounds (1) n 078.1
bullets (149) n 022.4
Bullets (1) 086.9
bullfight (1) n 033.5
bullfrog (515) n/adj 060.2
~ hop (1) n 095.5
~ legs (1) n 013.7
~ meat (1) n 060.2
bullfrog[N-i] (1) n 060.2

bullfrogs (379) n 060.2
bullhead (4) n/adj 074.8
~ cats (1) n 059.9
bullheaded (152) adj 074.8
bullheads (2) n 080.8
bullies (3) n 129.8
bullikin (1) n 033.8
bulling (3) v/adj 033.8
~ ring (1) n 081.8
bullish (1) adj 074.9
Bulloch (1) GA 087.2
Bullochville (1) GA 087.8
bullock (2) n 033.5
Bullock (4) AL 086.4
~ County (1) AL 086.5
bullpen (8) n 098.6
bullring (1) n 088.8
Bullrun Creek (1) TN 030.7
bull's butt (1) n 125.1
bulls (66) n 033.5
bullshit (13) n/adj 092.1
~ requirement (1) n 092.1
bullshits (1) v 090.8
bullshitter (1) n 100.1
bullshitting (1) v 092.2
bullweed (1) n 015.9
bullwhip (4) n 019.4
bullwhips (2) n 019.4
bully (14) n/adj 075.2
~ bestering (1) v 095.4
~ bull (1) n 033.8
~ frog (1) n 060.2
~ kind[N-i] (1) n 099.7
~ stick (1) n 113.2
bulrush (2) n 029.7
bulrushes (1) n 080.6
Bultry Creek (1) AL 030.7
bum (116) n/v/adj 069.7
~ -around shoes (1) n 123.8
~ bread (2) n 045.1
~ bum bum (2) n 130.2
~ roller (1) n 130.6
~ with (1) v 129.6
bumbershoot (16) n 028.6
bumbershoots (1) n 028.7
bumble-fisted (1) adj 073.3
bumblebee (135) n 060A.5

bumblebee[N-k] nest (2) n 060A.5
bumblebees (144) n 060A.6
bumblefooted (1) adj 073.3
bumbler (2) n 073.4
bumbling (2) v/adj 073.3
~ around (1) v 024.9
bumfuddled (2) adj 088.9
~ up (1) adj 081.8
bumfuzzled (2) adj 080.6
bummer (2) n 080.6
bummy (1) adj 080.7
bump (65) n/v/adj 077.4
~ board (1) n 022.6
~ into (11) v 032.6
~ the bump (1) n 130.8
bumped (15) v 032.6
~ him (3) v 082.1
~ into (9) v 032.6
~ off (1) v 078.6
bumper (39) n/adj 041.5
~ cars (1) n 130.5
~ corn crop (1) n 041.3
~ crop (32) n 041.3
bumpers (2) n 110.8
bumping (2) v 097.4
bumpkin (36) n/adj 069.9
bumpkinish (1) adj 080.8
bumpkins (3) n 069.9
bumps (45) n 110.8
~ -a-Daisy (1) n 130.6
bumptious (2) adj 074.8
bumpy (1) adj 039.7
bums (43) n/v 069.7
bun (34) n 044.4
~ in the oven (6) n 065.1
~ warmer (1) n 116.4
Buna (1) TX 087.3
bunch (1064) n/v/adj 055A.8
~ bean (37) n 055A.4
~ bean[N-i] (1) n 055A.4
~ beans (79) n 055A.4
~ butter bean (4) n 055A.3
~ butter beans (8) n 055A.3
~ green snap bean (1) n 055A.4
~ lettuce (1) n 055A.6
~ onion (1) n 055.7

~ onions (3) n 055.7
~ peanut (1) n 054.7
~ Porto Rico (1) n 055.5
~ potato (2) n 055.4
~ purple-hull (1) n 055A.2
~ snap bean (2) n 055A.4
~ snap beans (2) n 055A.4
~ string bean (2) n 055A.4
~ sweet potato (1) n 055.5
~ tomato (1) n 055.3
~ type (2) n 055A.4
~ up (1) v 077.6
~ yam (7) n 055.5
~ yams (1) n 055.5
Bunch Creek (1) AL 030.7
bunch[N-i] (1) n 055A.6
Bunche (1) 081.8
bunched (3) v 015.8
~ up (1) v 041.6
bunches (42) n 041.6
bunching (5) v/adj 015.9
~ teams (1) n 081.8
bunchy (2) adj 027.8
Bundicks Creek (1) LA 030.7
bundle (415) n/v 041.6
bund(le) (1) n 041.6
bun(dle) (1) n 070.7
bundle[N-i] (7) n 041.6
bundled (4) v 041.6
~ in (1) v 042.1
bundles (346) n 041.7
bundling (4) n/v/adj 081.8
~ board (1) n 028.8
~ boards (1) n 104.6
bung (19) n/adj 020.4
~ disc (1) n 021.7
~ stopper (1) n 020.4
bungalow (31) n/adj 118.8
~ house (3) n 014.1
~ -style (1) n 118.9
~ -style house (1) n 007A.8
Bungalow Town (1) 105.8
bungalows (4) n 118.8
bunghole (8) n 018.7

bungholes (1) n 018.7
bungler (1) n 073.4
bungs (1) n 018.7
bunion (1) n 077.4
bunk (25) n/v/adj 029.2
~ bed (1) n 029.2
~ beds (1) n 007A.6
~ buddy (1) n 129.4
~ meeting (1) n 080.7
~ room (1) n 080.8
Bunker (2) FL 087.5
~ Hill (1) 105.2
bunkers (3) n 080.8
bunkhouse (1) n 113.8
Bunkie (5) LA 087.3
bunking (4) adj 130.7
~ parties (3) n 130.7
~ party (1) n 083.1
bunks (2) n 081.9
bunnies (8) n 061.1
bunny (23) n/adj 069.3
~ hop (2) n 083.1
~ hug (2) n 083.1
~ rabbit (1) n 083.1
Bunny Creek (1) AL 030.7
buns (79) n 044.4
Bunsen burner (1) n 116.4
bunting-and-batten (2) n 011.2
bunuelo (1) n S 122.1
bunuelos (1) n S 045.2
buoy (1) n 096.8
Buras (2) LA 087.8
Burbank (4) 055.4
Burbanks (1) 055.4
burden (18) n 057.5
bureau (189) n/adj 009.2
~ drawer (1) n 009.2
~ drawers (3) n 009.2
bur(eau) drawers (1) n 009.2
Bureau (3) 009.2
bureaucracy (1) n 115.4
bureaucrat (3) n 115.4
bureaus (35) n 009.2
Buren (14) 013.8
burger (1) n 047.2
Burgess (2) MS 087.2
~ Plantation (1) AL 087.1
burglar (1) n 065.9
burglars (1) n 065.8
Burgoyne (1) 106.1

Burgundy (4) 114.7
buriage (1) n 079.2
burial (86) n/adj 079.2
~ box (1) n 079.1
~ case (1) n 079.1
~ ceremony (6) n 079.2
~ ground (18) n 078.8
~ grounds (4) n 078.8
~ lots (1) n 078.8
~ place (4) n 078.8
~ plot (5) n 078.8
~ service (5) n 079.2
~ services (1) n 079.2
~ spot (1) n 078.8
burials (1) n 079.2
buried (14) v 079.2
~ at (1) v 078.9
~ in (2) v 052.5
buritis (1) n 079.6
Burke County (1) GA 087.1
Burkeville (3) TX 087.2
Burkville (1) AL 087.3
burlap (420) n/adj 019.7
~ bag (90) n 019.7
~ bags (33) n 019.7
~ cloth (1) n 019.7
~ sack (68) n 019.7
~ sacks (28) n 019.7
~ stuff (1) n 019.7
~ thing (1) n 019.7
~ tow sack (1) n 019.7
burlaps (3) n 019.7
burled walnut (1) n 054.8
Burlen (1) WI 087.5
Burleson County (1) TX 087.2
Burley (1) 057.2
Burlington (1) IA 087.3
Burlison (1) TN 087.3
burly (2) n/adj 099.5
~ sacks (1) n 019.6
burn (79) n/v/adj 070.6
~ down (1) v 101.2
~ -down baseball (1) n 130.4
~ off (2) v 041.4
~ out (1) v 091.6
~ up (4) v 039.8
~ your fanny (1) v 065.5
burn[V-t] (3) v 098.8
~ out (1) v 075.5
burned (21) v 075.2
~ down (2) v 082.7

~ out (2) v 075.5
~ up (4) v 057.9
Burned Grass (1) 131.3
burner (19) n/adj 019.9
burners (4) n 070.6
Burnet (2) TX 086.6
burning (58) v/adj 057.4
~ ant (1) n 060A.5
~ bush (1) n 062.2
~ in hell (1) v 078.6
~ out (1) v 102.8
Burning Springs (1) TN 031.5
burnout (2) n 008.7
burns (7) v 048.7
Burns Park (3) 106.4
burnside (2) n 071.4
Burnside Lake (1) MS 030.7
burnsides (3) n 088.7
Burnsville (1) AL 086.5
burnt (52) v/adj 065.8
~ down (8) v 052.5
~ out (8) v 075.5
~ squash (1) n 056.6
~ up (5) v 070.2
~ yam (1) n 055.5
Burnt (3) 087.7
~ Fort (1) GA 087.7
~ Mill Creek (2) AL GA 030.7
burp (9) v 036.3
~ it up (1) v 080.2
burped (2) v 080.3
burr (52) n/adj 123.8
~ cut (2) n 123.9
~ cuts (1) n 123.9
~ grass (1) n 015.9
~ haircut (1) n 122.8
~ haircuts (1) n 115.6
~ head (13) n 069.3
~ heads (7) n 069.3
~ squirrel (1) n 059.6
Burr Creek (1) AL 030.7
burrheaded (2) adj 069.3
~ colored people (1) n 069.3
Burris (1) GA 087.6
burro (12) n 033.7
burros (2) n 033.7
burrow owl (1) n 059.2
burrowing owls (1) n 088.8
burrows (2) n 041.2
burrs (11) n 123.9

Bursely (2) 030.7
~ Bayou (1) LA 030.7
~ Creek (1) LA 030.7
bursitis (52) n 079.6
burst (636) v/adj 018.8
~ appendix (1) n 080.1
~ open (3) v 018.8
~ out (1) v 018.8
burst[V-p] (3) v 018.8
bursted (197) v/adj 018.8
~ (ap)pendix (1) n 080.1
~ into (1) v 018.8
~ open (2) v 018.8
burster (1) n 095.4
burstes (5) v 018.8
bursting (7) v 018.8
bursts (1) v 018.8
Burt (2) 106.4
~ Baker Planetarium (1) 106.4
~ Reynolds (1) 073.6
Burton Woods (1) 087.3
Burwell (1) GA 087.1
bury (5) v 095.2
burying (57) n/adj 079.2
~ clothes (1) n 079.3
~ ground (28) n 078.8
~ place (3) n 078.8
~ plot (2) n 078.8
~ tortoise (1) n 060.7
~ yard (2) n 078.8
bus (250) n/v/adj 109.9
~ depot (6) n 084.7
~ depots (1) n 084.7
~ line (2) n 085.3
~ service (5) n 109.9
~ station (68) n 084.7
~ stations (1) n 084.7
~ stop (5) n 084.7
~ system (1) n 109.9
~ terminal (6) n 084.7
~ transportation (1) n 109.9
Busch (2) 106.4
~ Garden (1) 106.4
~ Gardens (1) 106.4
bused (1) v 088.7
buses (84) n 109.6
bush (182) n/adj 062.7
~ -and-bog disc (2) n 021.6
~ -and-bog harrow (1) n 021.7

~ -and-bog harrows (1) n 021.7
~ arbor (1) n 080.7
~ arbors (1) n 084.8
~ ax (1) n 104.3
~ baby (1) n 065.7
~ bean (9) n 055A.4
~ beans (21) n 055A.4
~ blade (1) n 099.9
~ butter bean (1) n 055A.3
~ butter beans (2) n 055A.3
~ child (7) n 065.7
~ colt (1) n 065.7
~ goats (1) n 035.2
~ harbor (2) n 089.8
~ harbor church (1) n 089.9
~ hog (9) n 041.4
~ -hog (4) v 041.4
~ -hog mowers (1) n 120.1
~ -hog team (1) n 080.8
~ -hogged (4) v 041.4
~ -hogging (4) v 041.4
~ hogs (2) n 035.9
~ hook (1) n 023.5
~ huckleberries (1) n 062.5
~ ivy (2) n 062.3
~ limas (1) n 055A.3
~ nettle (2) n 015.9
~ snap bean (1) n 055A.4
~ type (1) n 055A.3
Bush (4) LA 087.3
~ Hills (3) 030.8
bush[N-i] (1) n 012.1
Bushaw Creek (1) AL 030.7
bushberries (2) n 062.5
bushed (51) v 075.5
~ out (3) v 075.5
bushel (485) n/adj 019.8
~ basket (5) n 041.8
~ baskets (2) n 020.1
~ crates (1) n 041.8
~ measures (1) n 019.8
~ quantities (1) n 041.8
~ sack (1) n 019.8
bushel[N-i] (181) n 041.8
bush(el)[N-i] (1) n 041.8
bushelful (1) n 041.8

bushels (636) n 041.8
bushes (61) n 093.9
bushing (2) v 041.4
bushinged up (1) v 021.8
bushings (1) n 021.8
bushwhack (1) n 123.9
bushwhacker (2) n 080.7
bushwhackers (3) n 055A.8
bushy (6) adj 055A.4
~ cut (1) n 092.7
~ -tail gray squirrel (1) n 059.6
~ -tail squirrel (1) n 059.6
~ -tailed (1) adj 076.7
busier (5) adj 066.1
busiest (1) adj 026.3
business (270) n/adj 066.8
~ administration (1) n 065.8
~ area (3) n 105.2
~ boys (1) n 092.8
~ building (1) n 108.5
~ college (9) n 083.6
~ course (1) n 065.8
~ district (18) n 105.2
~ education (1) n 083.5
~ purposes (1) n 103.6
~ school (2) n 065.8
~ section (5) n 025.6
Business (6) 083.6
businesses (4) n 065.8
businessman (3) n 065.9
businessmen (2) n 075.7
busing (3) n/adj 080.6
~ days (1) n 080.6
buss (1) n 081.7
bussed (1) v 081.7
bussing (22) v 081.7
bust (405) n/v/adj 018.8
~ head (2) n 050.9
~ hell (1) v 065.5
~ off (1) v 018.8
~ open (11) v 018.8
~ out (3) v 018.8
~ skull (4) n 050.8
~ up (4) v 018.8
bust[V-p] (6) v 018.8
bust[V-r] (29) v 018.8
~ open (1) v 018.8
~ out (1) v 048.9
bust[V-t] (15) v 018.8
~ open (1) v 048.9

Bustamante (1) TX 087.2
busted (367) v/adj 018.8
~ appendix (1) n 080.1
~ down (1) v 088.8
~ egg (1) n 046.2
~ in (1) v 018.8
~ off (1) v 018.8
~ open (3) v 018.8
~ out (3) v 018.8
~ up (13) v 082.1
~ up with him (1) v 082.1
busten (1) v 018.8
buster (500) n/adj 095.4
~ plow (1) n 021.6
~ plows (1) n 021.6
Buster Brown (2) 123.9
bustering (1) n 095.4
busters (5) n 095.4
bustes (17) v 018.8
~ open (2) v 018.8
~ out (1) v 018.8
~ up (1) v 018.8
busthead (2) n 050.9
busting (19) n/v 018.8
~ loose (1) n 083.1
~ -open peaches (1) n 054.4
bustles (1) n 080.1
busts (2) n/v 018.8
busy (24) adj 074.1
~ bee (1) n 101.3
~ mouth (1) n 101.3
busybodies (2) n 101.3
busybody (4) n 101.3
but (610) conj 060A.5
butane (7) n/adj 070.7
~ stove (1) n 080.6
butch (33) n/adj 124.3
~ cut (1) n 123.9
~ cuts (1) n 123.9
butcher (1141) n/v/adj 046.8
~ -birds (2) n 046.8
~ business (1) n 046.8
~ day (1) n 046.8
~ knife (235) n 104.3
~ -knife bean (1) n 055A.4
~ knife[N-i] (3) n 017.8
~ knives (71) n 017.8
~ man (7) n 046.8
~ paper (1) n 046.8
~ pen (1) n 046.8

~ pens (1) n 046.8
~ shop (12) n 046.8
~ shops (5) n 046.8
~ stone (1) n 023.4
~ wagon (1) n 046.8
Butcher (1) 056.2
butcher[V-r] (1) v 046.8
butcher[V-t] (1) v 046.8
butchered (25) v 046.8
~ on (1) v 092.7
butcherer (1) n 067.8
butchering (25) n/v/adj 046.8
~ house (1) n 080.7
~ knife (2) n 017.8
~ shed (1) n 011.7
~ time (2) n 046.8
butcher's (3) adj 046.8
~ knife (1) n 017.9
~ place (1) n 046.8
butchers (23) n 046.8
butches (3) n 124.4
butler (1) n 089.8
Butler (21) AL GA TN 087.1
~ County (4) AL 087.2
~ Creek (3) AL AR TN 030.7
~ Street (1) 107.6
butler's (16) adj 010.1
~ closet (2) n 007A.2
~ pantry (13) n 010.1
butt (68) n/adj 057.3
~ cut (1) n 008.5
~ end (1) n 046.4
~ ends (1) n 121.2
~ head (1) n 024.6
~ -head boat (1) n 024.6
~ -headed (6) n 074.8
~ -headed boat (1) n 024.6
~ kisser (2) n 125.6
~ kissing (1) n 101.9
~ licker (2) n 125.6
~ logs (1) n 093.7
~ naked (1) adv 130.7
~ portion (1) n 121.2
~ stick (1) n 008.5
butt[N-i] (1) n 040.3
Buttahatchee (3) AL MS 030.7
butte (2) n F 030.8
~ a patates (1) n F 015.6

butted (1) v 080.9
butter (1117) n/adj 051.6
~ bean (173) n 055A.3
~ -bean hulls (1) n 055A.3
~ -bean patch (1) n 055A.3
~ -bean patches (1) n 016.1
~ bean[N-i] (8) n 055A.3
~ beans (751) n 055A.3
~ bowl (1) n 093.9
~ box (1) n 009.8
~ bread (2) n 044.3
~ cat (1) n 059.9
~ house (1) n 011.7
~ knife (9) n 104.3
~ loaf (1) n 044.8
~ mold (4) n 092.9
~ oil (1) n 024.1
~ paddle (1) n 065.5
~ pea (17) n 055A.3
~ -pea beans (1) n 055A.3
~ peas (28) n 055A.3
~ rolls (1) n 044.4
~ sauce (2) n 048.5
~ something (1) n 055A.3
~ spreader (1) n 017.8
~ squash (3) n 056.6
~ teeth (1) n 071.8
but(ter) (1) n 073.3
But(ter) and Egg Road (1) 107.6
buttercup (1) n 056.6
buttercups (1) n 088.7
buttered peas (1) n 055A.3
butterfingers (3) n 073.3
butterfish (3) n 059.9
butterflies (13) n 060A.4
butterfly (38) n/adj 060A.1
~ -like thing (1) n 060A.1
~ root (8) n 061.4
~ roots (1) n 061.4
~ shrimp (1) n 060.9
~ weed (1) n 084.9
Butterfly Gap (1) TN 031.3
buttermilk (214) n/adj 047.6

~ biscuit (1) n 044.4
~ biscuit[N-i] (1) n 044.4
~ biscuits (5) n 044.4
~ bread (1) n 044.6
~ cheese (1) n 048.1
~ custard (1) n 080.6
~ doughnut (1) n 122.8
~ pie (2) n 048.3
~ pine (1) n 061.8
~ rolls (1) n 044.4
Buttermilk (10) 087.9
~ Bluff (1) GA 087.9
~ Bottom (6) 092.7
~ Bottoms (1) 106.3
~ Drop (1) 080.7
~ Spring (1) AR 030.7
butternut (37) n/adj 056.6
~ squash (17) n 056.6
butter(nut) squash (1) n 056.6
butternuts (10) n 054.9
buttes (1) n 030.8
butting (3) v/adj 101.3
~ in (1) v 101.3
~ saw (1) n 080.8
buttocks (8) n 072.8
button (35) n/v/adj 027.2
~ on (1) v 027.2
~ onion (1) n 055.7
~ onions (2) n 055.7
~ root (1) n 061.4
~ shoe (1) n 080.9
~ shoes (4) n 088.9
~ tomatoes (1) n 055.3
~ -top shoes (1) n 088.9
~ up (1) v 027.2
~ willow (3) n 061.7
Button Branch (1) GA 030.7
button[N-i] (2) n 027.2
button[V-r] (1) v 052.1
buttonball (2) n 061.7
buttonbush (1) n 061.7
buttons (71) n/v 027.2
~ up (1) v 027.2
buttonwood (5) n 061.7
buttonwoods (1) n 061.7
Buttram Gulf (1) AL 087.6
buttress (1) n 031.2
butts (14) n 117.7
Butts (5) 087.5

~ County (4) GA 087.1
buxom (3) adj 073.1
buy (180) v 045.1
~ a baby (1) v 065.1
~ from (1) v 039.7
Buy-Rite (2) 116.1
buyed (1) v 045.1
buying (41) n/v 094.2
buys (9) v 053.8
buzz (5) n/adj 123.9
~ saw (3) n 120.9
buzzard (17) n/adj 059.4
~ egg (1) n 065.8
~ wing (1) n 021.6
~ wing sweep (2) n 021.9
Buzzard Gulch (1) AL 087.5
buzzard's roost (1) n 114.8
buzzards (12) n 059.2
buzzing (1) v 024.9
B.V.D.s (1) 090.9
by (1221) adj/adv/prep 082.7
~ and by (137) adv 076.2
~ -blow (1) n 065.5
bye (362) interj 002.4
~ -bye (17) interj 002.4
bygone (1) adj 025.6
Byhalia (1) MS 087.4
byname (1) n 064.4
bypass (25) n/v/adj 107.1
~ road (2) n 031.7
~ roads (1) n 031.7
Bypass (4) 107.7
bypasses (1) n 107.5
bypath (1) n 031.7
Byram (1) MS 087.6
Byrd Creek (1) TN 030.7
byroad (24) n 031.7
byroads (7) n 031.7
Byron (1) GA 087.8
bys (1) n 109.6
byway (18) n 031.8
Byway (1) 030.7
byways (1) n 031.7
byword (3) n 092.9

C

C (11) 108.5
~ and W (1) 130.8
~ line (1) n 080.6
~ -O (1) 021.6
ca (5) pron/prefix F 065.1
~ -nipping (1) v 070.9
cab (18) n/adj 109.9
Cab (2) 109.9
caballos (1) n S 022.1
cabana (1) n 010.8
cabbage (726) n/adj 055A.1
~ collard (1) n 055A.5
~ collards (1) n 055A.5
~ farm (1) n 055A.1
~ field (1) n 016.1
~ greens (2) n 055A.5
~ loaf (1) n 044.4
~ palm (2) n 061.9
~ palmetto (1) n 081.8
~ patch (8) n 016.1
~ peas (1) n 055A.3
~ sack (1) n 019.7
~ slaw (2) n 055A.1
~ squash (1) n 056.6
~ tree (1) n 061.9
~ trees (3) n 061.9
~ worms (1) n 060.5
Cabbage Town (6) 105.4
cabbage[N-i] (210) n 055A.1
cabbagehead (3) n 055A.6
cabbagehead[N-i] (3) n 055A.6
cabbageheads (14) n 055A.6
cabbages (139) n 055A.1
cabbages' head[N-i] (1) n 055A.6
cabin (54) n/adj 014.1
~ cruiser (4) n 024.6
~ cruisers (3) n 024.6
~ melon (1) n 056.9
Cabin (3) 030.7

~ Teele (1) LA 087.5
cabinet (126) n/adj 010.1
~ mantels (1) n 008.4
~ shelf (1) n 008.8
~ -type doors (1) n 010.1
cabin(et) (1) n 010.1
cabinets (34) n 010.1
cabins (12) n 014.1
cable (24) n/adj 104.5
~ car (9) n 085.3
~ cars (12) n 085.3
~ end (1) n 070.9
cables (1) n 085.3
caboodle (17) n 082.8
cabood(le) (1) n 082.8
Cabool (1) MO 087.1
caboose (4) n 009.7
cabriolet (1) n 109.4
cabrito (4) n/adj S 047.3
~ blood (1) n 047.3
~ con sangre (1) n S 047.4
cabritos (1) n S 047.3
cabron (1) n S 069.1
cabs (15) n 109.8
cacaho (1) n 061.2
Cache (1) AR 030.7
cachicky(x3) (1) interj 038.5
cack (1) n 080.8
cackle (2) n 036.6
cackling (3) v 036.7
cactus (4) n/adj 062.8
~ root (1) n 061.4
cactuses (1) n 052.1
Caddies (1) 109.4
Caddo (15) LA 087.2
~ Gap (1) AR 031.3
~ Indians (1) 080.7
~ Lake (3) LA 030.7
~ Parish (1) LA 087.2
~ River (1) AR 030.7
Caddos (1) 070.8
caddy (1) n 092.7
Caddy (3) 109.4
Cades Cove (3) TN 087.4
cadet (3) n 068.7
cadets (2) n 123.8
Cadillac (14) 109.4
Cadillacs (2) 109.4
Cadron (1) 030.7
Caesar (1) MS 087.8
cafe (19) n F/S 070.7
~ au lait (9) n F 032.4

~ negro (1) n S 032.3
~ noir (2) n F 032.3
~ solo (1) n S 032.3
cafes (3) n 065.8
cafeter(ia) religion (1) n 088.7
caffeine (3) n 048.9
(caf)feine (1) n 048.8
caflooey (1) adj 088.7
cage (14) n 036.9
~ a bird (1) n 083.1
cages (3) n 036.8
cagou (1) adj F 072.9
Cahaba (10) AL 030.7
~ River (4) AL 030.7
cahoots (2) n 080.6
caille (3) n F 048.1
~ goutte (2) n F 048.1
caillou (1) n F 084.9
cailloux (1) n F 084.9
Cain (9) 098.9
~ Creek (1) TN 030.7
Cairo (13) GA IL MS TN 087.3
Cajan (4) F 069.4
cajon (1) n S 079.1
Cajun (92) 069.5
~ coons (1) n 128.3
~ folks (1) n 069.3
~ French (2) n 084.9
~ gumbo (1) n 060.7
~ houses (1) n 007A.2
~ people (2) n 069.5
~ stuff (1) n 069.7
Cajun[N-i] (1) 069.8
Cajuns (97) 128.3
cake (390) n/adj 045.2
~ bread (1) n 044.4
~ doughnut (12) n 122.4
~ doughnuts (5) n 122.4
~ dressing (1) n 048.5
~ eater (1) n 067.8
~ filling (1) n 048.5
~ in the oven (1) n 065.1
~ knife (1) n 104.3
~ -like doughnut (1) n 045.2
~ -making (1) n 047.5
~ muffin (2) n 044.4
~ muffins (1) n 044.4
Cake (1) 030.7
cake[N-i] (1) n 045.3

cakes (325) n 122.3
Cakes (1) 064.4
cakewalk (4) n/adj 083.1
~ dance (1) n 083.1
cakier (1) adj 045.2
cala (1) n 045.2
calabaza (1) n S 056.7
Calaboga Sound (1) SC 030.8
calaboose (13) n 112.8
caladiums (1) n 062.7
calamine (7) n/adj 084.9
~ lotion (1) n 102.7
calamitously (1) adv 001A.4
calamondin tree (1) n 061.9
calamus (5) n/adj 061.4
~ root (1) n 061.4
Calcasieu (16) LA 030.7
~ River (7) LA 030.7
calculate (2) v 094.1
calculating (1) v 094.1
Caldwell (6) AR LA TX 087.4
~ Parish (2) LA 087.3
Cale (1) AR 087.1
Calebee Creek (1) AL 030.7
Caledonia (2) AR 087.3
calendar tree (1) n 061.8
Calera (3) AL 087.4
calf (1960) n/adj 033.8
~ beef liver (1) n 033.8
~ fries (1) n 081.8
~ hide (1) n 051.4
~ liver (3) n 047.2
~ livers (1) n 121.2
~ lot (4) n 033.8
~ pasture (3) n 015.7
~ pen (6) n 015.1
~ shed (2) n 011.7
~ slobber (2) n 048.5
~ stalls (1) n 015.1
calf(x2) (61) interj 037.6
calf(x3) (27) interj 037.6
calf(x4) (2) interj 037.6
Calf Creek (1) AR 030.7
calf[N-i] (5) n 033.8
calfes (1) n 033.8
calf's (2) adj 093.6
~ -foot jelly (1) n 093.6
~ liver (1) n 047.2
calfs (3) n 033.8

calfy (33) interj 037.6

calfy(x2) (20) interj 037.6

calfy(x3) (4) interj 037.6

Calhoun (30) AL AR GA LA MS 087.8

~ City (3) MS 087.8

~ County (8) AL FL GA MS TX 087.9

~ Sweet (2) 056.9

~ Sweets (1) 056.9

cali (1) n 114.1

caliber (5) n 113.1

~ thirty-eight (1) n 113.1

caliche (28) n/adj 031.6

~ dirt (1) n 029.8

~ pit (1) n 031.6

~ road (2) n 031.6

~ roads (6) n 031.6

calico (9) n/adj 055A.3

~ bush (1) n 062.7

~ butter beans (1) n 055A.3

~ dresses (1) n 084.8

Calico (3) 055A.3

~ Rock (2) AR 087.5

California (125) 086.3

~ beer (1) n 050.8

~ black-eyed (1) adj 055A.3

~ curls (1) n 123.9

~ fir (1) n 061.9

~ line (1) n 012.9

~ peach (1) n 054.3

~ seed beer (1) n 050.9

~ spruce (1) n 061.9

~ style (1) n 011.2

~ tomato (1) n 055.3

~ walnuts (1) n 054.8

~ whites (1) n 055.4

~ worms (1) n 060.5

Californi(a) (2) 070.7

calk (2) v 088.8

calking mallet (1) n 088.8

call (492) n/v/adj 100.3

~ back (2) v 092.7

~ boy (1) n 080.6

~ girl (20) n 113.3

~ girls (3) n 113.3

~ it a day (1) v 082.1

~ Monroe (1) v 080.3

call[V-p] (2) v 053.5

call[V-r] (4) v 025.6

call[V-t] (18) v 088.2

~ down (1) v 052.6

Callaghan Ranch (1) 053.2

Callahan (2) FL 087.4

Callaway (4) GA 080.6

~ Garden[N-i] (1) GA 080.6

~ Gardens (3) GA 050.5

called (157) v/adj 057.4

~ at (1) v 032.8

~ by (1) v 075.7

~ it off (4) v 082.1

~ off the wedding (1) v 082.1

~ to meet his reward (1) v 078.5

calling (37) v/adj 025.4

~ figures (1) v 083.1

~ on (1) v 053.8

~ on her (1) v 081.4

~ Ralph (2) v 080.3

calliope (1) n 022.7

Callio(pe) (1) 106.3

calliopes (1) n 088.7

callous (2) n 077.4

calls (61) v 053.5

calm (859) n/v/adj/adv 075.3

~ day (1) n 005.4

~ days (1) n 007.3

~ down (224) v 075.3

~ spell (1) n 007.3

calm[V-r] down (5) v 075.3

calm[V-t] (13) v 007.3

~ down (12) v 075.3

calmed (13) v 075.3

~ down (7) v 007.3

~ off (1) v 005.7

calmer (4) adj 007.3

calming (146) v 007.3

~ down (119) v 007.3

calms (1) v 075.3

calomel (20) n/adj 078.4

~ oil (1) n 088.7

~ root (2) n 061.4

calom(el) (1) n 078.4

Caloosahatchee River (1) FL 030.7

calories (1) n 048.4

Calotabs (1) 078.4

Calsa Bayou (1) LA 030.7

Calvary (2) GA 087.5

~ Episcopal (1) 106.7

calvary (4) n/adj 065.9

~ knife (1) n 104.3

calve (137) v 033.9

calve[V-t] (1) v 033.9

calved (3) v 033.9

Calvert (1) TX 087.7

calves (220) n/v 033.8

Calvin (1) 106.5

calving (19) n/v 033.9

Calvinism (1) 080.6

Calvinist (1) 089.2

calvo (1) n S 123.9

calypso (2) adj 123.3

~ pants (1) n 123.3

~ stuff (1) n 123.2

cam (1) v 102.4

Camargo (2) 087.9

cambric (2) n/adj 081.9

~ sacks (1) n 019.6

Camden (16) AL AR TX 087.3

~ County (2) GA 087.5

came (1078) v 102.4

~ across (3) v 102.4

~ along (9) v 102.4

~ (a)long (1) v 080.6

~ around (1) v 078.5

~ back (47) v 102.4

~ back from (1) v 102.4

~ by (7) v 102.4

~ down (24) v 102.4

~ down with (13) v 076.3

~ for to (1) v 080.5

~ fresh (2) v 033.9

~ from (29) v 102.4

~ in (55) v 102.4

~ in at (1) v 075.6

~ into (3) v 080.7

~ off (2) v 102.4

~ on (12) v 102.4

~ out (10) v 102.4

~ out of (4) v 075.6

~ over (21) v 102.4

~ through (3) v 102.4

~ to (13) v 102.4

~ up (40) v 003.3

~ with (1) v 032.4

~ [P-0] (1) v 012.9

camel (3) adj 061.4

~ flies (2) n 060A.1

~ roots (1) n 061.4

Camel cigarettes (1) n 057.3

camelback (3) n/adj 118.9

~ house (1) n 118.9

camellia (5) n/adj 062.7

~ tree (1) n 061.8

camellias (13) n 062.7

Camelot (2) 107.9

Camels (1) 057.3

cameo (3) n/adj 028.4

~ ring (1) n 123.1

camera (4) n 066.9

Cameron (17) LA TX 087.4

~ Hill (1) TN 030.8

~ Parish (1) LA 087.6

Camilla (8) GA 086.4

~ Heights (1) GA 087.7

Camille (6) 006.4

Camino (1) 109.7

camisole-top dresses (1) n 080.6

Cammack Village (1) 106.2

camp (44) n/v/adj 090.3

~ bread (2) n 044.4

~ cooks (1) n 088.7

~ fryer (1) n 116.4

~ house (4) n 088.8

~ houses (1) n 014.1

~ light (1) n 024.3

~ meeting (8) n 091.8

~ meetings (4) n 081.9

~ pot (1) n 017.5

~ shorts (1) n 123.3

~ stew (4) n 047.1

Camp (31) 114.8

~ Berry (1) AR 087.2

~ Claiborne (1) LA 087.3

~ County (1) TX 087.2

~ Creek (1) GA 030.7

~ Douglas (1) LA 080.7

~ Fire Girls' corn bread (1) n 044.7

~ Gordon (1) GA 086.5

~ Grant (1) IL 087.2

~ Hill (2) AL 087.3

~ Livingston (1) LA 087.3

~ Maxwell (1) AL 087.3

~ Pike (2) AR 087.2
~ Polk (1) LA 087.4
~ Shelby (1) MS 087.4
~ Stewart (1) GA 087.3
~ Wallace (1) TX 087.2
~ Walton (1) FL 087.3
~ Wisdom Road (1) 105.9
campagne (1) n F 046.5
campaign (3) n/adj 049.5
~ sofa (1) n 009.1
Campbell (10) MO TN 087.2
~ County (4) TN 087.1
Campbellite (4) 089.2
~ church (1) n 089.9
~ Church of Christ (1) 089.1
Campbellites (6) 089.1
Campbells Hill (2) 105.5
Campbellton (1) 107.8
camper (10) n/adj 109.6
~ top (1) n 109.6
~ truck (1) n 109.6
~ van (1) n 109.6
campers (2) n 109.7
Campground (3) TN 087.4
campgrounds (2) n 080.8
Campho-Phenique (2) 078.3
camphor (24) n/adj 078.4
~ berries (1) n 062.5
~ eggs (1) n 017.1
~ gum (2) n 061.4
~ roots (1) n 061.4
~ tree (8) n 061.9
~ trees (4) n 061.9
camping (5) v/adj 070.7
~ on her doorstep (2) v 075.8
~ out (1) v 070.7
~ planters (1) n 021.9
camps (8) n 090.3
Camps (1) AL 007A.3
Campti (1) LA 087.8
Campton (1) FL 087.1
campus (5) n 085.1
can (3505) n/v/adj 057.6
~ cutter (1) n 023.4
~ goods (2) n 066.8
~ ham (1) n 121.3
~ house (4) n 010.1
~ opener (3) n 023.4
~ room (2) n 010.1

~ see (3) n 003.2
~ shrimp (1) n 060.9
(ca)n (3) v 049.6
Can (1) 069.2
can[N-i] (2) n 019.2
can[V-r] (1) v 052.6
Canaan (4) AR LA TX 087.6
Canada (31) 087.5
Canadian (18) 128.9
~ bacon (15) n 046.7
~ night crawlers (1) n 060.5
Canadians (7) 128.9
canal (365) n/adj 030.4
~ branch (1) n 030.7
~ ditch (1) n 030.2
~ -like (1) adj 030.2
~ -type thing (1) n 030.2
Canal (38) 030.2
~ Boulevard (1) 107.5
~ Street (14) 031.8
canals (66) n 030.2
Canals (1) 030.2
canaries (2) n 099.8
canary (1) n 096.7
Canaveral (2) 087.7
cancer (66) n/adj 078.2
~ stick (10) n 117.7
~ sticks (29) n 117.7
~ twigs (1) n 117.7
~ weed (1) n 117.7
~ weeds (2) n 117.7
candelabra (1) n 088.7
candied (17) adj 045.2
~ cherries (1) n 062.1
~ sweet potato (1) n 055.5
~ sweet potatoes (1) n 055.5
~ yam (2) n 055.5
~ yams (11) n 055.5
candies (1) n 124.1
Candies (1) 123.8
candle (399) n/adj 024.3
~ bat (3) n 060A.1
~ bug (13) n 060A.1
~ bugs (15) n 060A.1
~ flappers (1) n 060A.1
~ flies (140) n 060A.1
~ fly (208) n 060A.1
~ -fly-like thing (1) n 060A.1
~ miller (1) n 060A.1

~ moth (1) n 060A.1
~ runners (1) n 080.6
cand(le) bugs (1) n 060A.1
candlelight (5) n/adj 060A.3
~ bug (1) n 060A.1
Candlelight Square (1) 105.5
candlelights (1) n 060A.1
Candler (8) GA 087.8
~ building (1) n 106.4
~ Field (2) 089.7
~ Park (2) 106.7
candles (11) n 065.9
candlestick holder (1) n 024.3
candlesticks (2) n 024.3
candy (60) n/adj 019.5
~ breaking (2) n 080.7
~ bucket (1) n 017.4
~ curls (1) n 080.7
~ drawing (1) n 096.8
~ drawings (1) n 083.1
~ kitchen (1) n 009.9
~ makings (1) n 083.1
~ pulling (6) n 083.1
~ pullings (7) n 083.1
~ pulls (1) n 097.6
~ yam (2) n 055.5
~ yams (3) n 055.5
cane (340) n/adj 051.2
~ -back chairs (1) n 008.8
~ baskets (1) n 020.1
~ beer (4) n 050.8
~ -bottom (2) adj 008.8
~ -bottom chair (11) n 008.9
~ -bottom chairs (16) n 008.8
~ -bottom rockers (1) n 008.8
~ -bottom rocking chairs (1) n 008.9
~ bottoms (1) n 008.8
~ buck (3) n 050.8
~ butter (2) n 051.3
~ chairs (1) n 008.8
~ crop (1) n 041.3
~ crops (1) n 041.3
~ cutter (1) n 088.7
~ cutters (1) n 080.8
~ demijohns (1) n 080.7

~ field (1) n 016.1
~ fodder (1) n 014.7
~ grass (1) n 015.9
~ grinding (1) n 081.9
~ juice (3) n 051.2
~ knife (2) n 104.3
~ maple (1) n 061.5
~ mill (6) n 084.8
~ -mill thing (1) n 051.3
~ molasses (5) n 051.2
~ patch (17) n 016.1
~ patches (1) n 016.1
~ plumbings (1) n 084.8
~ post (1) n 016.5
~ press (1) n 081.9
~ rockers (2) n 008.8
~ shoes (1) n 051.3
~ skimming (2) n 080.8
~ -skimming whiskey (1) n 050.8
~ skimmings (6) n 050.8
~ -skimmings liquor (1) n 050.8
~ snake (2) n 092.9
~ snakes (1) n 089.8
~ stack (1) n 014.6
~ sugar (1) n 051.3
~ syrup (62) n 051.3
Cane (35) LA 030.7
~ Bayou (2) LA 030.7
~ Branch (1) AR 030.7
~ Creek (14) AL GA MS TN 030.7
~ Creek Falls (1) TN 031.5
~ Lake Outlet (1) MS 030.7
~ River (5) LA 030.7
cane[N-i] (1) n 052.1
canebrake (2) n 088.9
caned (1) v 088.7
Canehill (1) AR 087.7
~ area (1) n 087.4
canes (4) n 015.8
Caney (14) TX 087.2
~ Creek (10) AR MS TN TX 030.7
~ Fork River (2) TN 030.7
~ Island Ditch (1) AR 030.2
~ Lake (1) LA 030.7

Cane(y) Fork River (1) TN 030.7
canine (3) n/adj 125.2
~ teeth (1) n 071.8
canister (4) n/adj 116.7
~ deal (1) n 080.8
canisters (1) n 019.2
canker (7) n/v 077.4
cankered (8) adj 046.9
canky (2) adj 046.9
Canman (1) 024.6
cannabis (2) n/adj 114.1
~ root (1) n 061.4
canned (14) v/adj 054.6
~ apples (1) n 054.6
~ biscuit[N-i] (1) n 044.4
~ biscuits (1) n 044.4
~ ham (1) n 121.3
~ him (1) v 082.1
~ huckleberries (1) n 062.4
~ mushroom (1) n 056.8
~ on (1) v 098.6
~ shrimp (1) n 060.9
~ spinach (1) n 075.7
~ yams (1) n 055.5
canner (1) n 119.7
canners (2) n 055A.4
Cannes (1) 030.3
cannibalism (1) n 104.7
canning (13) v/adj 010.1
~ house (1) n 010.1
~ kitchen (1) n 010.1
~ peach (2) n 054.3
~ peaches (1) n 054.4
~ plants (1) n 080.7
~ room (1) n 010.1
~ shed (1) n 014.2
~ tomatoes (2) n 055.3
cannon (1) n 113.9
Cannon (7) LA TN 087.2
~ Bluff (3) GA 087.1
~ County (1) TN 087.3
~ County grammar (1) n 131.2
cannonball (2) n/adj 095.4
~ bed (1) n 080.8
Cannonball (15) 056.9
cannonballs (1) n 081.9
cannons (1) n 052.1
cannot (92) v 057.7
canoe (188) n/adj 024.6

~ boat (1) n 024.6
~ boats (1) n 024.6
~ type (1) n 024.6
~ -type boat (1) n 024.6
Canoe Creek (1) AL 030.7
canoeing (2) v 024.6
canoes (76) n 024.6
Canoochee (4) GA 030.7
~ River (1) GA 030.7
canoodling (2) v 081.7
canopy (6) n 028.7
canover (1) n 095.5
cans (227) n 019.2
can't (2727) n/v 057.7
~ see (5) n 003.4
Can't (2) 057.7
~ Get Away Club (1) 115.8
cant (2) adj 093.5
~ hook (1) n 093.5
~ -hook handle (1) n 084.9
cantaloupe (546) n/adj 056.7
~ melon (1) n 056.7
~ melons (1) n 056.7
~ patch (4) n 056.7
cantaloupe[N-i] (2) n 056.7
cantaloupes (335) n 056.7
cantankerous (10) adj 074.8
canter (1) v 034.3
Canton (24) GA MS OH 086.5
Can(ton) (1) MS 087.5
Cantonment (2) FL 087.8
Cantrell (3) 107.7
~ Road (1) 107.6
cants (1) n 080.7
Canuck (2) 128.9
Canucks (7) 128.9
canvas (14) n/adj 014.7
~ bag (2) n 019.7
~ bags (2) n 019.7
~ curtains (1) n 009.5
~ sack (1) n 019.7
canyon (46) n/adj 030.4
~ -like (1) adj 030.4
~ wall (1) n 031.2
Canyon (5) 087.5
canyons (6) n 030.4
Canyons (2) 030.4

caouaine (4) n F 060.6
cap (119) n/v/adj 041.6
~ -and-ball pistols (1) n 022.4
~ bread (2) n 044.3
~ bundle (1) n 041.7
~ bundles (4) n 041.7
~ house (1) n 118.9
~ loaf (1) n 044.4
~ off (1) v 014.7
~ plank (1) n 016.2
Cap (64) 068.5
capable (4) adj 074.1
capacity (1) n 084.9
cape (3) n 027.1
Cape (25) 087.7
~ Canaveral (2) FL 087.7
~ Cod (5) MA 087.4
~ Cods (1) 118.9
~ Coral (1) FL 105.7
~ Girardeau (2) MO 087.8
~ Hatteras (2) NC 087.8
~ jasmine (8) n 062.9
~ jasmine bush (1) n 062.6
~ jasmines (1) n 061.9
~ Kennedy (1) FL 087.7
caper up (1) v 075.8
capes (1) n 027.1
capital (38) n/adj 085.5
~ center (1) n 085.5
Capital (2) 107.7
~ Avenue (1) 107.7
capitalistic (1) adj 053.7
capitals (1) n 085.5
capitan (1) n S 112.5
capitol (9) n/adj 106.4
~ building (1) n 106.8
Capitol (18) 107.6
~ City (1) 105.5
~ Heights (6) AL 087.3
~ Homes (1) 105.5
~ of the Confederacy (1) 106.6
~ Street (2) 107.5
Caplis (2) LA 087.6
capon (5) n 036.9
caponize (1) v 036.1
caponized (2) v 036.1
capons (1) n 121.5
capped (5) v/adj 041.7

~ sheaves (1) n 041.7
cappella (1) adj 089.5
capping (3) v 041.7
Capps (1) AL 087.5
caps (28) n 041.7
capsize (1) v 101.2
capsule (3) n 078.5
capsules (6) n 070.6
captain (915) n 068.5
Captain (195) 068.5
~ Kangaroo (3) 068.5
~ Shreve (4) 068.5
~ Sigsbee (1) 068.5
~ so-and-so (1) n 068.5
captained (1) v 068.6
captain's (7) adj 068.5
~ chair (1) n 008.8
~ chairs (1) n 008.8
~ deck (2) n 068.5
~ name (1) n 068.5
~ watch (1) n 068.5
captains (18) n 068.5
Captiva (1) 106.4
Captive County (1) 088.9
capture (5) v 130.4
~ the flag (4) n 130.4
~ the fly (1) n 098.4
captured from (1) v 089.9
Capuchin (1) TN 087.7
capush (1) n 082.8
car (1994) n/adj 023.6
~ axle (1) n 021.8
~ body shop (1) n 012.2
~ city (1) n 131.2
~ club (1) n 023.6
~ dealer (1) n 023.6
~ driveway (1) n 031.8
~ games (1) n 130.5
~ house (11) n 011.7
~ inspector (1) n 023.6
~ knockers (1) n 080.6
~ line (1) n 107.3
~ lot (1) n 023.6
~ pocket (2) n 110.2
~ porch (3) n 010.8
~ road (1) n 031.6
~ seat (1) n 064.5
~ seats (1) n 064.5
~ shed (17) n 011.7
~ storage (1) n 108.4
~ tire (1) n 023.6
~ tires (1) n 023.6
~ trouble (1) n 023.6
~ trucks (2) n 109.7

~ wreck (5) n 023.6
car[N-i] (2) n 005.1
caramel (5) n/adj 066.8
~ puffes (1) n 122.7
~ puffs (1) n 122.7
~ sauce (1) n 048.5
Carancahua (1) 115.6
caraway-seed bread (1) n 044.4
Caraway (1) AR 087.7
carbide (11) n/adj 045.4
~ lamp (1) n 024.3
~ lamps (1) n 024.3
~ light (4) n 024.3
~ lights (4) n 088.8
carbolated Vaseline (1) n 078.3
carbolic acid (4) n 084.8
carbon (14) n/adj 008.7
~ copy (3) n 065.3
~ -dough pie (1) n 048.3
~ light (1) n 024.2
~ oil (2) n 024.2
~ rock (1) n 023.4
Carbon Hill (2) AL 087.3
carbonated (4) adj 121.8
~ beverage (1) n 121.8
~ drink (1) n 121.8
~ drinks (1) n 121.8
~ Vaseline (1) n 078.3
Carbondale (1) IL 087.7
carbonique (1) adj F 060A.3
carbons (1) n 061.3
Carborundum (7) 023.4
~ file (2) n 023.4
~ stone (4) n 023.4
carboxes (1) n 023.6
carbuncle (148) n 077.4
carbuncles (18) n 077.4
carcass (1) n 037.2
carcel (1) n S 112.8
card (17) n/v/adj 022.2
~ class (1) n 083.7
~ games (1) n 088.8
~ parties (1) n 130.7
~ shark (1) n 073.4
cardboard boxes (1) n 020.2
carded (2) v 088.8
~ to (1) v 035.1
cardiac (2) adj 111.5
~ care unit (1) n 111.5
cardinal (2) n 090.8

Cardinal[N-i] (1) 087.2
cardinals (3) n 059.1
carding (1) v 029.1
cards (9) n 023.6
care (1446) n/v/adj 013.1
~ about (11) v 013.1
~ (a)bout (6) v 013.1
~ for (563) v 049.6
~ f(or) (1) v 049.6
~ to (18) v 013.1
~ [P-0] (2) v 015.2
care[V-p] about (2) v 013.6
cared (17) v 013.1
~ for (10) v 065.4
career-wise (1) adv 080.6
carefree (4) adj 074.6
careful (145) adj 074.6
carefully (3) adv 005.8
careless (844) adj 074.6
~ man (1) n 124.7
~ weed (10) n 015.9
~ weeds (15) n 015.9
~ woman (1) n 124.8
care(less) (1) adj 074.6
Careless Love (1) 074.6
carelessness (6) n 074.6
cares (2) v 073.2
caressing (1) v 081.7
caretaker (10) n 119.5
caretakers (2) n 119.5
Carey (1) AL 087.9
Cargile Spring (1) AL 030.7
Cargle Creek (1) AL 030.7
cargo truck (1) n 109.6
carhop (1) n 023.6
Caribbean (6) 077.8
~ pine trees (1) n 061.8
Caribou (1) 105.7
caring (1) adj 073.2
Carl (4) 052.5
~ Johnson Park (1) 106.7
~ T. Jones Airport (1) 106.5
Carla (1) 006.3
Carlisle (1) AR 087.4
carload (4) n 023.6
carloads (1) n 023.6
Carls Creek (1) AL 030.7
Carlsbad (3) 087.8
~ Cave (1) NM 087.8

~ Caverns (2) NM 030.5
Carlyss (1) LA 087.3
carman (2) n 023.6
Carmel (1) 089.1
Carmelite (1) 089.2
Carmen (2) 006.4
~ storm (1) n 006.3
carnation bees (2) n 060A.5
carnations (1) n 062.7
carnels (1) n 093.9
Carnesville (1) GA 087.7
carnival (6) n 081.9
Carnival (2) 131.7
~ Parade (1) 131.3
carnivals (1) n 088.8
carnivorous (2) adj 065.8
Carol (7) 105.4
~ City (4) 105.4
~ Villa (2) 007A.6
Carolina (1731) 086.2
~ coast (1) n 086.2
~ Cracker (1) 069.8
~ Hoosier (2) 069.9
~ Southern rock (1) n 097.9
~ tobacco (1) n 086.4
Carolin(a) (15) 086.2
Car(olina) (1) 086.2
Carolina[N-i] (2) 086.2
Carolina's granddaddy (1) n 052.5
Carolinas (27) 086.3
Caroline (5) 106.5
Carolinians (1) 062.8
carols (1) n 130.8
Carondelet (5) 107.6
~ Canal Company (1) 065.9
~ Street (2) 107.9
carotte (1) n F 057.3
carousing (1) v 057.4
carp (96) n/adj 059.9
~ fish (4) n 059.9
carp[N-i] (1) n 059.9
Carpathian (2) 054.8
~ walnut (1) n 054.8
~ walnuts (1) n 054.8
carpenter (164) n/adj 067.8
~ bee (1) n 060A.5
~ burro (1) n 022.1
~ dog (1) n 033.3
~ horse (3) n 022.1

~ horses (6) n 022.1
~ shop (1) n 011.7
~ trestle (1) n 022.1
carpen(ter) (1) n 067.8
carp(enter) (1) n 067.7
carpentered (3) v 088.7
carpentering (7) n/v 096.7
carpentero (1) n S 059.3
carpenter's (6) adj 022.1
~ benches (1) n 022.1
~ horse (3) n 022.1
~ horses (1) n 022.1
~ trestle (1) n 022.1
carpenters (12) n 059.3
carpentry work (3) n 065.8
carpet (23) n/adj 096.7
~ cleaner (2) n 116.7
~ preacher (1) n 089.9
~ rakes (1) n 120.6
~ sweeper (12) n 116.7
~ sweepers (3) n 116.7
carpetbag attitude (1) n 053.3
carpetbagger (2) n 115.5
carpetbaggers (7) n 080.7
carpets (2) n 009.3
carport (73) n 007A.3
carports (2) n 011.9
carps (6) n 059.9
Carr Creek (2) AL TN 030.7
Carrabelle (1) FL 030.7
Carraway (1) FL 087.4
Carre (8) 030.7
carriage (623) n/adj 064.5
~ buggy (1) n 064.5
~ house (7) n 015.2
~ vine (1) n 062.3
car(riage) (3) n 064.5
Carriage Hills (2) AL 030.8
carriages (22) n 064.5
carried (292) v 098.1
~ away (3) v 079.3
~ in (1) v 098.1
~ on (4) v 079.3
~ over (1) v 050.1
~ -over food (1) n 050.1
~ through (1) v 042.1
~ to (3) v 098.9
carrier (22) n 088.8
car(rier) (1) n 023.3

Carriere (3) MS 087.1
carriers (3) n 014.6
carries (17) v 080.7
~ on like (1) v 065.3
carrion crow (1) n 069.3
Carrol City (1) FL 087.2
Carroll (27) GA LA TN TX 087.2
~ County (14) AR GA MS TN 087.8
~ Drive (1) MS 107.6
Carrollton (23) AL AR GA LA MS 087.9
~ Avenue (2) 107.7
Carrollwood (1) 106.1
carrot (18) n/adj 055.2
~ green (1) n 055A.5
~ tobacco (2) n 057.3
carrot[N-i] (1) n 055.2
carrots (102) n 055.8
carrousel (12) n 022.7
carry (429) v 098.1
~ back (2) v 097.5
~ on (8) v 079.3
~ -on bag (1) n 123.7
~ out (1) v 019.8
~ over (1) v 041.8
~ up (1) v 081.9
car(ry) (68) v 097.5
ca(rry) (1) v 097.4
carry[V-p] (1) v 053.4
carry[V-r] (1) v 097.5
carryall (3) n 028.2
carrying (104) v/adj 021.4
~ a baby (3) v 065.1
~ a child (6) v 065.1
~ a heavy load (1) v 065.1
~ a load (1) v 065.1
~ bags (1) n 028.2
~ on (26) v 079.3
~ pail (1) n 017.3
cars (425) n 023.6
cart (66) n/adj 064.5
~ roads (1) n 031.7
CARTA (1) 109.9
Cartecay River (2) TN 030.7
Carter (14) TN 087.1
~ bread (1) n 054.7
~ Hill Road (1) 107.6
Carter's hometown (1) n 070.4

Cartersville (10) GA 087.2
Carthage (4) MO MS TX 087.5
cartilage (2) n 022.4
carting (16) v 021.4
carton (6) n 019.2
cartons (2) n 019.5
cartouche (2) n F 022.4
cartridge (555) n/adj 022.4
~ clip (2) n 022.4
~ pen (1) n 022.4
cartridge[N-i] (1) n 022.4
cartridges (319) n 022.4
carts (13) n 080.7
cartucho (1) n S 022.4
cartwheel (9) n 095.5
cartwheels (6) n 095.5
Caruthersville (3) MO 087.8
carved (2) v/adj 072.5
carver (1) n 017.8
Carver (4) GA 087.2
~ City (1) 106.2
~ Crest (1) 105.4
Carvers Gap (1) TN 031.3
carving (21) n/v/adj 072.5
~ knife (15) n 104.3
~ knives (4) n 104.3
Carwell Creek (1) LA 030.7
Cary Creek (1) AR 030.7
Caryville (1) TN 086.2
casa (1) n S 014.1
Casa (1) AR 087.7
casaba (6) n/adj 056.7
~ melon (3) n 056.7
Casanova (5) 125.3
cascade (7) n/adj 031.5
~ falls (1) n 031.5
Cascade (7) 107.9
~ Heights (2) 106.2
cascading (2) v 080.3
Cascare (1) LA 030.7
Cascilla (1) MS 087.5
case (75) n/adj 028.8
~ dime (1) n 114.5
~ knife (25) n 017.8
~ knives (9) n 017.8
~ quarter (1) n 114.5
cases (8) n 037.3
Caseytown (1) AR 087.5

cash (64) n/adj 114.5
~ cold dollars (1) n 001A.2
~ crop (4) n 041.3
~ money (3) n 080.6
Cash (2) AR 087.7
~ Lake Canal (1) LA 030.7
cashed (11) v 078.6
~ his chips (1) v 078.6
~ his chips in (3) v 078.6
~ in (2) v 078.6
~ in his chips (4) v 078.6
cashew (19) n/adj 054.7
~ nut (4) n 054.8
~ nuts (7) n 054.8
cashews (28) n 054.8
cashiers (1) n 070.9
Cashmere Gardens (1) 105.4
casing (17) n/adj 037.3
~ factory (1) n 081.9
~ plant (1) n 081.9
casings (22) n 037.3
casino (2) n S 070.6
Casino (2) 105.6
~ Club (1) 105.6
casitas (1) n S 012.1
cask (3) n 020.2
casket (613) n/adj 079.1
~ box (2) n 079.1
~ maker (1) n 079.1
cask(et) (4) n 079.1
caskets (48) n 079.1
caso (1) n S 048.1
Cason (1) TX 087.3
casoo(x3) (1) interj 037.6
Casotte (1) 030.3
casperate (1) v 036.1
casperated (1) v 036.1
Caspiana (1) LA 087.8
Cass (4) 107.8
~ County (1) TX 086.6
~ Creek (1) TN 106.4
~ Street (1) 107.7
casse-cou (1) n F 093.6
casserole (2) n 046.1
Cassville (1) GA 087.3
cast (102) n/v/adj 032.1
~ at (1) v 032.1
~ him off (1) v 082.1
~ iron (30) n 017.5

~ -iron black skillet (1) n 017.5
~ -iron cookstove (2) n 080.6
~ -iron eyes (1) n 010.9
~ -iron fences (2) n 016.4
~ -iron frying pan (1) n 017.5
~ -iron kettle (2) n 017.6
~ -iron lid (1) n 044.7
~ -iron pan (1) n 044.7
~ -iron pot (11) n 017.6
~ -iron pots (4) n 017.6
~ -iron rack (1) n 008.3
~ -iron skillet (14) n 017.5
~ -iron skillets (5) n 017.5
~ -iron stove (3) n 084.9
~ -iron washpot (1) n 017.6
~ -iron washpots (1) n 017.6
~ net (2) n 081.8
~ off (2) v 024.5
~ -off furniture (1) n 010.2
~ plow (1) n 021.6
~ plows (1) n 021.6
castana (1) n S 009.2
caste[N-i] (1) n 069.5
castel(lated) (1) adj 021.7
casteraise (1) v 036.1
casterize (11) v 036.1
casterize[V-t] (1) v 036.1
casterized (3) v 036.1
castile (1) n 080.7
Castillo de San Marcos (1) 080.9
casting (2) v/adj 034.8
~ rod (1) n 068.9
castle (3) n/adj 012.1
~ -type buildings (1) n 075.9
Castle (3) 106.1
~ Hills (1) 106.1
~ walk (1) n 083.1
castoff (2) n 033.3
castoffs (4) n 123.5
castor (16) adj 061.7

~ bean tree (1) n 061.7
~ oil (15) n 024.1
cast(or) oil (4) n 024.1
castracized (1) v 036.1
castrate (443) v 036.1
~ on (2) v 036.1
castr(ate) (1) v 036.1
castrate[V-r] (3) v 036.1
castrated (203) v/adj 036.1
~ boar (2) n 035.4
~ bull (3) n 033.5
~ bulls (1) n 036.1
~ hog (5) n 035.4
~ male hog (1) n 035.4
~ pig (3) n 035.4
castrater (2) n 096.8
castrating (18) v/adj 036.1
~ day (1) n 081.9
castration (6) n 036.1
Castro Convertible (1) 009.1
Castroville (5) TX 087.6
casual (13) n/adj 123.8
~ shoe (1) n 123.8
~ shoes (10) n 123.8
casuals (2) n 123.8
Casualty (2) 108.5
cat (569) n/v/adj 059.9
~ and mouse (1) n 130.3
~ ball (2) n 130.4
~ boil (1) n 077.4
~ boils (2) n 077.4
~ bread (1) n 044.7
~ chimleys (1) n 008.1
~ eye (2) n 130.6
~ eyes (1) n 130.6
~ hook (1) n 088.7
~ hunting (1) n 059.6
~ licker (1) n 126.5
~ lickers (1) n 080.8
~ -looking owl (1) n 059.2
~ on (1) v 080.9
~ owl (3) n 059.1
~ owls (1) n 059.2
~ squirrel (153) n 059.6
~ squirrels (44) n 059.6
~ whiskey (2) n 050.8
Cat (10) 101.8
~ Creek (4) GA 030.7
~ Island (3) LA MS 087.9

cat[N-i] (2) n 059.9
Catahoula (45) LA 030.7
~ cur (9) n 033.3
~ cur dogs (1) n 033.3
~ curs (1) n 033.3
~ dog (2) n 033.3
~ dogs (3) n 033.3
~ hog dog (2) n 033.3
~ hounds (2) n 033.3
~ leopards (1) n 033.3
~ Parish (5) LA 087.8
~ River (1) LA 030.7
Catahoulas (1) 033.3
catalog paper (1) n 019.5
catalpa (15) n/adj 062.9
~ tree (1) n 062.8
~ trees (4) n 061.8
~ worm (4) n 060.5
~ worms (3) n 060.5
(ca)talpa (4) adj 062.9
~ tree (2) n 062.9
~ worms (2) n 060.5
(cat)alpa (3) n/adj 061.9
~ trees (1) n 061.9
catamaran (1) n 024.6
catamount (3) n 059.5
catamounts (2) n 059.5
cataplasme (1) n F 061.2
cataract (6) n 031.5
catarrh (2) n 076.3
catawampus (58) adj/adv 085.2
catawampused (3) v/adj 085.2
catawba (99) n/adj 056.7
~ flies (1) n 060A.3
~ tree (13) n 062.9
~ trees (10) n 061.8
~ worm (15) n 060.5
~ worms (40) n 060.5
(ca)tawba worms (2) n 060.5
catawbas (2) n 060.5
catbird (3) n 059.4
catbirds (1) n 088.9
catch (1606) n/v/adj 098.5
~ -as-come (1) adj 080.6
~ dog (3) n 033.3
~ him (90) v 033.2
~ -him(x3) (1) v 033.2
~ it (4) v 033.2
~ lot (1) n 015.6
~ on (8) v 098.5

~ onto (1) v 053.4
~ out (1) v 038.6
~ pen (6) n 015.6
~ -rope (1) n 097.9
~ the bacon (1) n 130.2
~ the flag (1) n 130.2
~ them (5) v 033.2
~ up (14) v 098.5
catch[V-p] (2) v 098.5
catch[V-r] (14) v 098.5
catch[V-t] (4) v 098.5
catchall (18) n/adj 010.3
~ place (1) n 010.3
~ room (5) n 010.3
~ rooms (1) n 010.3
catched (25) v 098.5
catcher (13) n 098.5
catchers (5) n 069.8
catches (35) v 098.5
~ on (1) v 013.8
~ up (1) v 098.5
catching (94) v/adj 098.5
~ up (1) v 024.7
catechism (5) n 083.7
categories (1) n 025.2
category (1) n 082.8
cater (502) v/adv 085.2
~ angling (1) v 085.2
~ bias (5) adj/adv 085.2
~ -biasing (3) v 085.2
~ -cornered (483) adj/adv 085.2
~ crooked (1) adv 085.2
~ cross (1) v 085.2
~ cut (1) v 085.2
~ -mac-biased (1) adv 085.2
~ ranging (1) v 085.2
~ to (1) v 069.3
~ way (1) n 085.2
catercorner (196) adj/adv 085.2
catercorn(er) (6) adv 085.2
catercorners (1) adv 085.2
catergodlin (1) adv 085.2
catering (2) v 085.2
caterpillar (9) n/adj 060.5
~ bugs (1) n 060A.1
~ nest (1) n 061.3
~ worms (2) n 060.5
Caterpillar (4) 041.5
~ tractor (2) n 021.6

caterpillars (2) n 060A.1
Caterpillars (2) 084.8
catfaces (1) n 077.8
catfish (626) n/adj 059.9
~ bait (1) n 059.9
~ Charley (1) n 080.6
~ dinner (1) n 059.9
~ man (1) n 080.9
~ pond (1) n 059.9
~ steak (1) n 088.9
~ stew (2) n 080.9
~ swamp (1) n 029.6
Catfish (6) 030.7
~ Bend (1) LA 030.7
~ Creek (2) GA TN 030.7
~ Point (1) MS 030.7
~ Town (2) 080.8
catfishes (6) n 059.9
catfishing (1) n 059.9
catharized (1) v 036.1
cathartic (2) adj 066.8
~ pill (1) n 066.8
~ pills (1) n 089.9
Cathay corn (1) n 051.1
cathead (4) n/adj 044.4
~ biscuits (2) n 044.4
catheads (1) n 044.4
cathedral (3) n/adj 089.1
~ window (1) n 029.1
Cathedral (4) 106.6
~ of the Immaculate Conception (1) 106.6
~ Towers (1) 119.2
Catherine (7) 030.7
Catherines (1) 030.7
Catholic (108) 126.5
~ cemetery (1) n 078.8
~ church (20) n 089.2
~ High (1) 070.7
~ lovers (1) n 129.1
~ Maritime Club (1) 113.9
~ orphanage (1) n 066.3
~ school (2) n 126.5
Catholics (31) 126.5
cathouse (16) n 113.4
cathouses (2) n 113.4
catnip (16) n/adj 061.4
~ tea (7) n 061.4
catnips (1) n 061.4
Cato (1) NY 087.8

Catoma Creek (3) AL 030.7

Catoosa (3) GA 087.2
~ seat (1) n 085.5
~ Springs (1) GA 030.7

cat's (3) adj 130.6
~ eye (2) n 130.6
~ vine (1) n 062.3

cats (121) n 059.9
~ and dogs (2) n 006.1

Cats (1) 080.7

catsup (1) n 069.2

Cattail Branch (1) GA 030.7

cattail chimley (2) n 008.1

cattails (1) n 061.5

catting (1) v 081.7

cattle (742) n/adj 036.5
~ barn (15) n 014.2
~ barns (5) n 015.1
~ bugs (1) n 060A.6
~ business (4) n 036.5
~ chutes (1) n 031.8
~ corral (1) n 015.6
~ country (2) n 099.8
~ crossing (3) n 031.8
~ crossings (1) n 031.8
~ deal (1) n 088.8
~ dogs (1) n 033.3
~ drive (1) n 031.8
~ drives (1) n 080.8
~ egret (1) n 090.9
~ farm (4) n 036.5
~ farms (1) n 036.5
~ feed (2) n 036.5
~ fence (2) n 016.3
~ fencing (1) n 016.3
~ gap (7) n 036.5
~ gaps (3) n 031.3
~ gate (1) n 031.8
~ guard (5) n 015.3
~ horse (1) n 034.2
~ horses (1) n 034.2
~ hustling (1) n 088.7
~ inspector (1) n 036.5
~ lane (1) n 031.8
~ lot (2) n 015.6
~ pass (2) n 031.8
~ path (3) n 031.8
~ pen (5) n 015.3
~ people (1) n 013.8
~ prods (1) n 113.3
~ -raised (1) v 098.7
~ raising (1) n 036.5

~ ranch (3) n 033.6
~ range (1) n 015.7
~ ranges (1) n 081.8
~ road (1) n 031.8
~ sales (1) n 036.5
~ shed (8) n 015.1
~ sheds (1) n 015.1
~ shelter (3) n 015.1
~ thing (1) n 031.8
~ ticks (1) n 060A.8
~ town (1) n 036.5
~ trail (4) n 031.8
~ trailer (1) n 084.8
~ underpass (1) n 031.8
~ wire (3) n 016.3

cattleman (1) n 036.5

cattlemen people (1) n 084.9

Cattlemen's Association (1) 080.6

cattles (10) n 036.5

catty (1) adj 075.1

catwalk (6) n/v 010.8

catwalking (1) v 088.9

Caucasian (203) 069.4
~ American (1) 069.2
~ group (1) n 069.4
~ race (3) n 069.4

Caucasians (21) 069.4

Caucasoid (1) 069.4

caucus (1) n 081.8

caught (2039) v 098.5
~ at (1) v 098.5
~ in (2) v 098.5
~ on (7) v 098.5
~ out (1) v 098.5
~ up (21) v 098.5
~ up with (2) v 098.5

cauldron (9) n 017.6

cauldrons (1) n 017.6

cauliflower (23) n 055.7

cauliflowers (2) n 055.7

cause (15) n/v 073.6

Cause (1) 085.8

cause[V-r] (3) v 088.6

caused (8) v 040.6
~ from (1) v 040.6

causes (2) v 048.9

causeway (24) n 107.5

Causeway (6) 107.5
~ Bridge (1) 107.5

causeways (4) n 107.5

causing (1) v 053.6

cauterize (1) v 078.2

cauterized (2) v 078.2

caution strip (1) n 107.3

cautious (4) adj 073.5
~ area (1) n 108.7

cavalla (1) n 088.8

cavallas (1) n 059.9

cavalry (2) n/adj 065.8
~ leader (1) n 070.7

Cavalry (1) 001A.3

Cavanaugh (2) 107.6
~ Levee (1) 031.4

cavani haircut (1) n 115.7

cave (6) n/adj 030.4
~ -in (2) n 030.4
~ spring (1) n 015.5

Cave (10) 087.8
~ City (6) AR 087.2
~ Spring (2) AL GA 087.8

caved in (1) v 025.4

cavern (1) n 030.4

caverners (1) n 077.7

Caverns (2) 030.5

caves (2) n 030.4

caviar (1) n 046.3

caving (2) v 024.9
~ in (1) v 024.9

cavity (3) n 071.8

cavorting around (1) v 083.1

caw (1) n 038.9

CAW fish (1) n 060.8

cawfish (1) n 060.8

Cayce (1) KY 087.8

cayenna (1) n 089.9

cayenne pepper (3) n 055.7

cayennes (1) n 055A.9

cayuco (1) n S 024.6

cazo (1) n S 017.6

CB radios (1) n 080.6

CBD (2) 105.2

CBS (3) 118.9
~ house (1) n 118.9

CC (4) adj 013.8
~ camps (1) n 013.8
~ rider (2) n 067.8
~ roads (1) n 031.7

cease (11) v 007.3
~ down (1) v 007.3

cease[V-t] (1) v 007.3

ceased (26) v 007.3

ceaseded (12) v 007.3
~ down (4) v 007.3

ceaseding down (1) v 007.3

ceases (3) v 007.3

ceasing (50) v 007.3
~ down (1) v 007.3

Cebu Island (1) LA 070.7

Cecil (3) AR 087.8
~ Field (2) 106.5

cedar (454) n/adj 061.8
~ bark (1) n 057.3
~ brake (1) n 084.8
~ brush (1) n 061.8
~ bucket (51) n 017.2
~ buckets (39) n 017.2
~ cabinet (1) n 009.7
~ chest (52) n 009.7
~ chest[N-i] (1) n 009.2
~ chestes (4) n 009.2
~ chests (2) n 081.9
~ chifforobe (2) n 009.7
~ choppers (1) n 069.9
~ churn (1) n 099.5
~ closet (7) n 009.7
~ faucet (1) n 018.7
~ fence (3) n 016.4
~ glade (1) n 080.8
~ groves (1) n 061.6
~ kindlings (1) n 008.6
~ limb (1) n 061.8
~ -lined closet (1) n 009.6
~ logs (3) n 007A.2
~ pail (7) n 017.2
~ pencils (1) n 025.6
~ pines (1) n 061.8
~ post (7) n 016.5
~ -post fence (1) n 016.4
~ post[N-i] (13) n 016.5
~ postes (1) n 016.5
~ rail (1) n 016.4
~ rails (1) n 016.4
~ shake (1) n 011.2
~ shavings (2) n 088.8
~ shingles (1) n 008.6
~ splinters (1) n 008.6
~ swamp (1) n 029.6
~ thicket (2) n 015.1
~ tree (28) n 061.8
~ tree[N-i] (1) n 061.8
~ trees (35) n 061.8
~ wardrobe (2) n 009.7
~ water bucket (9) n 017.2

~ water buckets (5) n 017.2
~ waxwing (1) n 084.8
~ well buckets (1) n 017.2
Cedar (33) 107.7
 ~ Bayou (1) LA 030.7
 ~ Bluff (1) MS 087.6
 ~ Creek (8) AL GA LA TX 030.7
 ~ Creek Swamp (1) AL 029.6
 ~ Ford (1) AL 030.7
 ~ Grove (6) TN 087.2
 ~ Hill (1) TX 087.3
 ~ Key (2) FL 087.1
 ~ Keys (2) FL 087.1
 ~ Lake Bridge (1) 030.7
 ~ Lawn (1) 106.1
 ~ Mill (1) TX 087.7
 ~ Point (1) MS 087.7
 ~ Springs (1) AL 087.2
 ~ Street (1) 061.8
 ~ Valley (1) AR 087.3
Ced(ar) Grove (1) FL 087.5
cedarized (1) v 123.7
cedarrobe (18) n 009.7
(cedar)robe (1) n 009.7
cedarrobe[N-i] (1) n 009.7
cedarrobes (5) n 081.9
cedars (24) n 061.8
Cedars (1) 106.2
Cedartown (5) GA 086.3
Ceia (2) 105.4
ceiling (35) n/adj 011.4
 ~ fan (3) n 118.5
 ~ heat (1) n 118.5
 ~ height (1) n 007.9
 ~ vents (1) n 118.5
ceiling[N-i] (1) n 001.6
ceilings (22) n 007.9
celebrate (3) v 082.5
celebrates (2) v 025.9
celebrating (18) v 082.5
celebration (12) n/adj 082.5
 ~ outfit (1) n 089.9
Celebration (2) 106.4
 ~ Grounds (1) 106.4
celery (43) n 055A.6
Celia (1) 112.1
cell (8) n/adj 112.8

cellar (148) n/adj 015.5
 ~ flies (1) n 060A.1
 ~ fly (1) n 060A.1
 ~ house (2) n 007A.1
cellars (35) n 015.6
cellophane (9) n/adj 066.8
 ~ bag (4) n 123.7
 ~ bags (2) n 123.7
 ~ paper (1) n 019.5
cells (1) n 077.5
celluloid (4) n/adj 070.6
 ~ collar (1) n 065.9
 ~ egg (1) n 017.1
Celtics (1) 086.9
celts (1) n 081.8
cement (414) n/v/adj 031.6
 ~ back porch (1) n 031.6
 ~ -block fence (1) n 016.3
 ~ blocks (3) n 031.6
 ~ border (1) n 065.8
 ~ brick (1) n 031.6
 ~ bridge (2) n 031.6
 ~ bridges (1) n 031.6
 ~ container (1) n 017.7
 ~ culvert (1) n 030.2
 ~ doorstep (1) n 023.4
 ~ eggs (2) n 017.1
 ~ farm-to-market roads (1) n 031.7
 ~ feedlots (1) n 015.4
 ~ fence (3) n 016.6
 ~ finisher (1) n 120.5
 ~ floor (2) n 031.6
 ~ highway (1) n 031.6
 ~ lime (1) n 031.6
 ~ pavement (2) n 031.6
 ~ paving (1) n 031.6
 ~ plant (1) n 031.6
 ~ porch (1) n 024.7
 ~ road (25) n 031.6
 ~ roads (11) n 031.6
 ~ slab (2) n 031.6
 ~ stone (1) n 023.5
 ~ -surface road (1) n 031.6
 ~ trough (1) n 035.8
 ~ trowels (1) n 088.7
 ~ walk (2) n 031.9
 ~ wall (1) n 016.6
 ~ water trough (1) n 035.8

cemented (10) v/adj 031.6
 ~ roads (1) n 031.6
cements (1) v 031.6
cemeteries (38) n 078.8
cemetery (955) n/adj 078.8
 ~ lot (1) n 078.8
 ~ lots (1) n 078.8
 ~ plot (2) n 078.8
cemeter(y) (28) n 078.8
Cemetery (14) 078.8
Cemeter(y) (2) 078.8
cen(dre) (1) n F 008.7
cenelle (1) n F 062.4
ceniza (2) n S 008.7
census (1) n 088.6
cen(sus) (1) n 070.7
cent (41) n/adj 026.6
cent[N-i] (115) n 016.7
centaur (1) n 124.7
Centennial (11) 055.5
 ~ Park (8) 106.4
center (101) n/adj 085.1
 ~ base (1) n 098.4
 ~ breast piece (1) n 091.9
 ~ cut (3) n 121.3
 ~ -cut pork chops (2) n 121.3
 ~ cuts (1) n 121.3
 ~ furrow (2) n 041.2
 ~ fur(row) (1) n 041.2
 ~ -furrowing (1) v 092.7
 ~ line (16) n 107.3
 ~ section (1) n 106.2
 ~ strip (1) n 107.3
 ~ stripe (5) n 107.3
 ~ table (2) n 065.8
 ~ way (1) n 031.9
cent(er) (2) n 054.5
Center (35) 107.6
 ~ City (1) 105.1
 ~ Hill (3) GA MS 087.6
 ~ Point (4) 105.1
 ~ Street (1) 107.6
centered (1) adj 074.8
centers (25) n 116.2
Centerville (5) LA MS TN TX 087.4
centipede (4) n 066.9
central (132) adj 118.5
 ~ air (21) n 118.5

~ air and heat (6) n 118.5
~ air-condition (1) n 118.5
~ air conditioning (5) n 118.5
~ air system (1) n 118.5
~ air [J-0] heating (1) n 118.5
~ business district (5) n 105.2
~ ducts (1) n 118.5
~ fire station (1) n 112.6
~ furnaces (1) n 118.4
~ gas heat (1) n 118.5
~ gas heating (1) n 118.4
~ hall (1) n 007A.4
~ hallway (1) n 007A.3
~ heat (25) n 118.5
~ heat and air (3) n 118.5
~ -heated (1) adj 096.7
~ heating (21) n 118.5
~ heating air (1) n 118.5
~ heating and air (4) n 118.5
~ heating and cooling (1) n 118.5
~ heating system (2) n 118.5
~ lockup (4) n 112.8
~ part (1) n 105.1
~ police station (1) n 112.7
~ stove (1) n 093.9
~ system (1) n 118.5
~ unit (2) n 118.5
Central (45) TN 087.4
~ Atlanta (1) 105.2
~ Avenue (6) 107.6
~ Baptist (1) 089.1
~ City (2) 106.3
~ City district (1) n 105.2
~ City Park (1) 106.8
~ community (1) AL 087.1
~ Expressway (2) 107.5
~ Florida (1) 086.4
~ Gardens (1) 106.2
~ Georgia (1) 086.3

~ Georgia Railroad (2) 090.8
~ High (1) 125.9
~ Park (2) 106.4
~ Standard (1) 004.2
~ Station (1) 084.7
~ Texas (1) 093.9
Centralia (1) MS 087.7
Centre (4) AL 087.2
Centreville (7) AL MS 087.8
cents (713) n 026.6
Century (2) FL 087.5
~ Plaza (1) 105.4
ceramic (2) adj 017.1
ceramic[N-i] (1) n 013.8
ceramics (1) n 017.1
cercle (1) n F 020.3
cerc(le) (1) n F 021.1
cereal (7) n 050.7
cereals (2) n 070.6
ceremony (18) n 079.2
certain (49) adj/adv 091.1
certainly (185) adv 091.1
certificate (4) n 065.8
certifi(cate) (1) n 065.8
certif(icate) (1) n 070.6
certificates (1) n 070.6
cervelat (1) n 121.6
cesion (1) n S 088.8
cesspool (4) n/adj 088.7
~ toilets (1) n 012.1
c'est (2) pron F 008.3
cette (2) pron F 065.1
cha (5) n/interj 083.1
~ -cha (2) n 083.1
chab (1) n 059.3
Chablis (2) 114.7
Chacahoula (4) LA 087.2
~ River (1) LA 030.7
Chack (4) 059.3
Chacon Creek (2) TX 030.7
chaetodon (1) n 059.9
chaff (11) n 042.1
chaffing (1) v 042.1
chain (338) n/adj 028.4
~ block (1) n 104.5
~ dogs (1) n 097.9
~ drive (2) n 011.3
~ fence (4) n 016.3
~ fences (4) n 126.1
~ food store (1) n 116.1

~ food stores (1) n 116.1
~ gang (1) n 090.8
~ groceries (1) n 116.1
~ grocery (1) n 116.1
~ grocery store (1) n 116.1
~ hoist (9) n 104.5
~ link (43) n 126.1
~ link fence (51) n 126.1
~ link fences (5) n 016.3
~ link fencing (2) n 016.3
~ -link sausage (1) n 121.6
~ -link saw (1) n 120.9
~ link wire (2) n 016.3
~ link wire fence (1) n 126.1
~ -linked (1) adj 016.3
~ links (2) n 016.3
~ of bead[N-i] (1) n 028.4
~ of beads (3) n 028.4
~ purse (1) n 028.2
~ saw (99) n 120.9
~ saws (1) n 120.9
~ store (8) n 116.1
~ stores (6) n 116.1
~ swing (1) n 022.9
~ tongs (1) n 091.8
chain[V-t] together (1) v 082.2
chained (2) v 041.4
chains (35) n 028.4
chair (1055) n/adj 008.8
~ back (1) n 008.8
~ factory (1) n 008.8
~ lift (1) n 008.8
~ makers (2) n 008.8
~ -type desk (1) n 002.6
chair[N-i] (2) n 008.8
chairman (7) n 068.6
chairs (537) n 008.8
chaise (6) n/adj 008.9
~ longue (1) n F 008.9
~ lounge (5) n 009.1
chal-bal(x2) (1) interj 037.5
chaleco (3) n S 027.3
chalk (21) n/adj 017.1
~ egg (3) n 017.1

~ eggs (7) n 017.1
~ gully (1) n 088.7
Chalk (3) 087.3
~ Bay (1) LA 087.3
~ Bluff (2) TX 030.8
chalked (1) v 032.1
chalkies (1) n 130.6
chalking (1) v 029.2
chalky (1) adj 029.8
challenge (1) v 129.8
Chalmette (3) LA 087.5
chalupas (2) n S 131.9
Cham-Chack (4) 059.3
chamber (20) n/adj 009.3
~ mugs (1) n 012.1
~ music (1) n 130.8
~ pot (2) n 012.1
~ pots (2) n 012.1
Chamber of Commerce (2) 053.4
chambers (3) n 012.1
Chambers (9) AL 087.4
~ Branch (2) TN 030.7
~ County (1) AL 087.1
~ Creek (2) TN TX 030.7
Chamblee (4) GA 087.4
Chambless Water Mill (1) AL 030.7
chambray (2) n 028.9
chambre (3) n F 009.3
~ (de) debarras (1) n F 010.3
~ en avant (1) n F 007.8
chameleon (1) n 090.8
chamomile tea (1) n 061.4
chamorra (1) n S 072.8
champ (1) n F 088.7
champagne (8) n/adj 114.7
~ glass (1) n 048.9
~ glasses (3) n 048.9
Champagnolle (3) AR 087.1
~ Creek (1) AR 030.7
Champaign (2) IL 087.9
champignon (6) n F 057.1
champignons (1) n F 056.8
Champion Creek (1) AL 030.7
chance (963) n/v/adj 019.8

~ length (1) n 126.1
~ lengths (1) n 126.1
Chance (1) 099.2
chance[N-i] (2) n 099.2
chanced (3) v 032.6
~ into (1) v 032.6
~ upon (2) v 032.6
Chancellor (1) AL 087.8
chancery clerk (1) n 068.5
chances (32) n 099.2
chancy (1) adj 074.6
chandelier (6) n 019.9
chandeliers (1) n 088.7
change (290) n/v/adj 005.6
~ bag (1) n 028.2
~ for the worse (1) n 078.5
~ from (1) v 131.7
~ pocketbook (2) n 028.2
~ pouch (1) n 028.2
~ purse (134) n 028.2
~ purses (4) n 028.2
~ up (1) v 005.6
~ with (1) v 032.4
change[V-p] (1) v 005.7
change[V-r] (3) v 070.1
change[V-s] (2) v 005.6
change[V-t] (17) v 089.7
~ from (1) v 005.7
~ to (1) v 005.7
changeable (18) adj 005.6
~ weather (2) n 005.7
changed (66) v/adj 036.1
~ her mind (8) v 082.1
~ up (1) v 032.8
changes (11) n/v 005.6
changing (296) v/adj 005.6
~ (a)round (1) v 090.7
~ to (2) v 005.7
~ up (3) v 005.7
~ weather (4) n 005.6
chankies (1) n 060A.1
channel (126) n/v/adj 030.2
~ bass (3) n 059.9
~ cat (39) n 059.9
~ catfish (1) n 081.8
~ cats (6) n 059.9
~ mullets (1) n 059.9
~ out (1) v 030.1
chan(nel) cat (1) n 059.9
Channel (16) 030.2

~ Branch (1) GA 030.7
~ Eleven (1) 001.6
channelization (1) n 080.6
channels (13) n 011.5
chanteys (1) n 130.9
Chantilly (1) 086.3
chap (5) n 064.3
chaparral (1) n 062.2
Chaparral (1) 107.7
Chapel (29) 087.2
~ Church (2) 089.2
~ Hill (6) NC TX 087.8
~ Isle Levee (1) LA 087.7
chaperon (3) n 082.5
chaperoned dances (1) n 083.1
chaperons (1) n 095.8
Chaplin Lake (1) LA 030.7
Chapman (3) AL 087.8
~ Highway (1) 107.6
Chappepeela (1) LA 030.7
chaps (26) n 064.3
char (2) n/adj 023.6
~ keg (1) n 020.2
character (12) n 070.7
characteristics (4) n 065.3
charades (2) n 130.9
charcoal (20) n/adj 008.7
~ bucket (1) n 023.1
~ burners (2) n 070.6
~ burning (1) n 070.9
~ furnace (1) n 081.8
~ irons (1) n 010.6
~ schooners (1) n 088.9
~ stove (1) n 008.3
~ wagons (1) n 091.9
chard (8) n 055A.6
Charenton (1) LA 087.2
charge (18) n/v 075.9
charges (2) n 099.5
chariot (2) n 023.6
charismatics (1) n 126.6
charity (4) n/adj 123.5
~ hospitals (1) n 084.5
charivari (17) n/adj F 082.5
~ wedding (1) n 082.5
Charles (72) 063.5
~ Atlas (1) 073.1
Charleston (701) MS SC WV 087.2

~ dance (1) n 087.2
~ Gray (20) 056.9
~ Grays (3) 056.9
~ Green (1) 056.9
~ High School (1) 087.1
~ Red (1) 056.9
charley (6) adj 078.4
~ horse (4) n 078.4
~ horses (2) n 079.6
Charley (9) 112.5
~ balls (1) n 061.8
~ Creek (1) FL 030.7
~ Lake (1) LA 087.3
Charleys (2) 126.5
Charlie Brown Airport (1) 106.7
Charlotte (23) FL NC TX 087.3
~ Harbor Bay (1) FL 087.9
charlotte russe (1) n 093.6
Charlottesville (2) NC VA 087.5
Charlton (4) GA 087.2
~ Park (1) 087.2
charm (6) n/adj 028.4
~ bracelet (3) n 028.3
~ bracelets (1) n 028.3
charming (3) adj 073.2
Charmingdale (1) 106.1
Charolais (13) 033.6
charpentier (1) n F 067.9
charred (1) v 050.9
charrue (5) n F 021.6
~ double (1) n F 021.6
~ doub(le) (1) n F 021.6
~ simple (1) n F 021.6
~ simp(le) (1) n F 021.6
chart (11) n/adj 083.7
~ class (4) n 083.7
charter (2) adj 024.8
~ boats (1) n 024.6
~ member (1) n 089.2
chase (17) n/v 130.2
~ the red ball (1) n 130.4
~ -women parties (1) n 130.7
Chase (1) AL 087.8
chaser (1) n 090.3
chasing (3) v/adj 081.4

~ her (2) v 081.4
chasm (2) n 031.3
Chasse (1) 106.8
chassis (4) n/adj 065.8
~ grease (1) n 023.7
Chastain Park (2) 106.6
chaste woman (1) n 065.2
chastise (8) v 065.5
chastising (3) n/v 065.5
Chataignier (5) LA 087.1
Chatawa (1) MS 087.8
Chateaubriand (2) 121.2
chateaux (1) n F 088.7
Chatham (8) GA MS 087.2
~ County (2) GA 087.5
Chatsworth (2) GA 087.2
Chattahoochee (58) AL FL GA 030.7
~ County (2) GA 087.3
~ River (25) AL GA 030.7
~ Valley (1) AL 087.9
Chattahooch(ee) (1) AL 030.7
Chattanooga (736) TN 087.4
~ breaking plow (1) n 021.6
~ Choochoo (2) 106.9
~ Creek (1) TN 030.7
Chattanoo(ga) (1) TN 087.4
Chattanoogan (2) 080.6
Chattooga (3) GA 030.7
~ County (1) GA 030.7
~ River (1) GA 030.7
chaud (1) adj F 093.5
chaudiere (1) n F 017.6
chaudin (3) n F 037.3
chauffeur (2) n 088.8
chauffeured (1) v 080.6
chauffeuring (1) v 088.7
chautauqua (2) n 070.6
Chautauqua Beach (1) FL 086.8
chautauquas (1) n 088.8
chauve(-souris) (1) n F 059.1
Chauvin (1) LA 028.8
chaw (9) n/v 050.2
chaw(x3) (1) interj 037.5
chawed (3) v 050.2
chawer (1) n 069.9
chawers (1) n 069.8

chawing (2) v 050.2
chayote (1) n S 015.9
Cheaha (3) AL 030.7
~ Creek (1) AL 030.7
~ Park (1) AL 087.7
cheap (95) adj/adv 114.7
~ booze (1) n 050.8
~ clothing (1) n 123.5
~ hotel (11) n 113.8
~ hotels (7) n 113.8
~ motel (1) n 113.8
~ rooming house (1) n 113.8
~ screw (1) n 073.5
~ soil (1) n 029.8
~ theater (1) n 114.9
~ thrills (1) n 114.9
~ whiskey (8) n 050.8
~ wine (4) n 114.7
cheaper (45) n/adj/adv 094.5
cheapest (1) adj 013.9
cheapo (1) n 073.5
cheapskate (11) n 073.5
cheat (6) n/v 073.5
cheated (2) v 082.1
cheater (2) n 073.5
Cheatham (9) TN 087.2
~ County (3) TN 087.2
~ Hill (2) GA 030.8
~ Lake (1) TN 030.7
~ River (1) TN 030.7
cheating (2) v 124.8
cheats (1) v 073.5
check (26) n/v 025.4
check(x4) (1) interj 038.5
check[V-r] it in (1) v 078.6
checked (8) v/adj 085.2
~ homespun (1) n 084.9
~ out (4) v 078.6
checkedy (2) adj 065.8
~ -looking bird (1) n 059.3
checker bird (1) n 059.3
checkered (2) adj 065.5
checkers (8) n 080.8
checkerwood (1) n 059.3
checking (2) v 078.6
~ out (1) v 078.6
checkline (4) n 039.1
checklines (27) n 039.1
checkpoints (1) n 090.4
checkrein (2) n 039.2

checkreins (3) n 039.1
checks (5) n 052.1
Cheddar (7) 047.1
~ cheese (4) n 048.1
chee(x2) (1) interj 038.5
chee(x4) chick (1) interj 038.5
cheek (2) n 071.3
cheekbone (1) n 130.2
cheeks (1) n 028.1
Cheer (2) 093.2
cheerful (20) adj 073.2
cheering (1) v 082.5
cheerleader (4) n/adj 088.7
~ shoes (1) n 123.8
cheerleaders (1) n 068.5
cheerleading (1) v 101.7
cheers (1) n 093.2
cheese (1328) n/v/adj 048.1
~ bread (2) n 044.7
~ cake (1) n 122.1
~ eater (6) n 125.6
~ grits (2) n 050.6
~ knife (2) n 104.3
~ -like (1) adj 047.5
~ shop (1) n 116.3
~ spread (1) n 047.2
~ up (1) v 047.6
cheeseburger (1) n 121.7
cheesecake (1) n 125.4
cheesecloth (2) n 048.2
cheesehead (2) n 047.1
cheeses (3) n 048.1
cheesy (3) adj 073.5
chef (2) n/adj 017.7
~ cooks (1) n 080.6
chegro (1) n 069.3
chegroes (2) n 060A.9
Chehaw (2) AL 087.3
Chelsea (5) 107.6
chemical (4) n/adj 081.8
~ foam (1) n 081.8
~ truck (2) n 111.4
chemicals (6) n 017.1
chemin travers (1) n F 031.7
cheminee (2) n F 008.1
chemise (2) n 026.3
chemistry (2) n 083.4
Chene (6) 030.7
chene gris (1) n F 061.8
chenets (2) n F 008.3
Cheney (1) 088.9

Cheneyhatchee (1) AL 030.7
Cheneyville (4) LA 087.3
chenier (4) n F 061.6
Cheniere (16) LA 087.3
~ au Tigre (6) LA 087.3
~ le Croix (1) LA 087.7
chenille (3) n/adj F 028.7
~ spread (1) n 028.7
Cheraw (1) SC 087.1
Cherokee (37) AL AR GA NC TN 030.7
~ Boulevard (1) 107.8
~ County (3) AL GA 087.4
~ County seat (1) n 085.5
~ Heights (1) 106.1
~ Indian (2) 126.5
~ Indians (2) 080.7
~ Lake (2) TN 030.7
~ rose (1) n 062.7
~ Village (1) AR 087.5
Cherokees (2) 092.8
cheroot (5) n 057.3
cheroots (1) n 117.7
cherries (114) n/adj 062.1
~ jubilee flambeau (1) n 080.6
~ trees (1) n 062.1
cherry (1208) n/adj 062.1
~ -bark oak (1) n 061.8
~ -bark red oak (1) n 061.9
~ -blossom tree (1) n 062.1
~ bounce (1) n 062.1
~ bushes (1) n 062.1
~ cobbler (3) n 048.3
~ cobblers (2) n 048.3
~ core (1) n 054.1
~ Danish (1) n 122.2
~ -filled (1) adj 122.6
~ filling (1) n 122.6
~ hedge (2) n 062.1
~ kernel (1) n 054.1
~ laurel (11) n 062.8
~ laurels (1) n 062.8
~ pepper (1) n 055.2
~ picker (4) n 111.4
~ pickers (4) n 062.1
~ pie (6) n 062.1
~ pit (3) n 054.1

~ pits (1) n 054.1
~ red (1) adj 062.1
~ roots (1) n 061.4
~ seed (18) n 054.1
~ seeds (1) n 054.1
~ tomato (32) n 055.3
~ tomatoes (164) n 055.3
~ (to)matoes (2) n 055.3
~ top (1) n 111.7
~ tree (541) n 062.1
~ trees (61) n 062.1
~ turnover (1) n 122.7
~ -type tomatoes (1) n 055.3
~ wine (2) n 114.7
~ wood (2) n 061.8
cher(ry) (8) adj 111.4
~ picker (1) n 111.4
~ pie (1) n 062.1
~ seed (1) n 054.1
~ tree (4) n 062.1
~ trees (1) n 062.1
Cherry (10) 030.7
~ Creek (1) GA 030.7
~ Creek Road (1) 106.6
~ Hill (1) AR 087.7
~ Ridge (1) LA 062.1
~ Street (4) 105.4
Cher(ry) Ridge (1) LA 062.1
cherry[N-i] (1) n 025.8
cherrystone (7) n 054.1
cherrystones (1) n 090.8
chert (29) n/adj 029.9
~ bottomland (1) n 029.8
~ road (4) n 031.6
~ roads (3) n 031.6
cherty lands (1) n 029.8
Chesapeake Bay (1) VA 030.3
Cheshire (1) 087.2
chess (4) adj 048.3
~ pie (1) n 048.3
~ pies (3) n 048.3
chest (1583) n/adj 072.4
~ bone (1) n 072.4
~ cold (1) n 072.4
~ colds (1) n 076.3
~ cough (1) n 076.5
~ in drawer[N-i] (1) n 009.2
~ of (1) n 009.2

~ of drawer[N-i] (56) n 009.2
~ of draw(er)[N-i] (12) n 009.2
~ of drawers (461) n 009.2
~ on chest (2) n 009.2
~ [P-0] drawer[N-i] (1) n 009.2
~ [P-0] drawers (4) n 009.2
chest[N-i] (8) n 009.2
~ of drawers (5) n 009.2
Chestatee (1) GA 030.7
chester (13) n/adj 009.2
~ drawers (1) n 009.2
Chester (6) MS TN 087.7
~ Creek (1) AR 030.7
~ white (1) n 080.6
chesterfield (7) n 009.1
Chesterfield (1) TN 087.1
chesterfields (1) n 009.1
chestes (13) n 009.2
~ of drawers (1) n 009.2
chestnut (136) n/adj 061.9
~ blight (2) n 081.8
~ burr (1) n 054.8
~ nut (1) n 054.8
~ oak (10) n 062.9
~ orchard (2) n 053.2
~ postes (1) n 016.5
~ rail fence (1) n 016.4
~ rails (2) n 016.4
~ tree (7) n 061.8
~ trees (21) n 061.9
~ wood (2) n 061.8
Chestnut (2) AL 030.7
~ Street (1) 107.5
chestnuts (103) n 054.7
chests (6) n 009.2
~ of drawers (1) n 009.2
cheval (2) n F 034.1
Cheval (1) 030.7
Chevrolet (3) 023.6
Chevrolets (1) 066.9
chew (878) n/v 050.2
~ on (9) v 050.2
~ up (2) v 050.2
Chewacla (1) AL 084.8
Chewalla Bottom (1) MS 087.4

chewed (65) v 050.2
  ~ up (4) v 050.2
chewened (1) v 050.2
chewer (4) n 069.4
chewers (1) n 069.8
chewing (64) v/adj 050.2
  ~ gum (7) n 071.9
  ~ tobacco (10) n 057.3
  ~ wax (1) n 061.5
chews (10) v 050.2
Cheyenne (3) WY 087.8
  ~ Boulevard (1) 107.7
chi(x4) (1) interj 038.5
chic (13) adj 123.6
Chica (1) 087.4
Chicago (824) IL 087.2
  ~ blues (1) n 130.9
  ~ Fire (1) 087.2
  ~ Mill (2) 087.2
  ~ Park (1) 106.3
Chicag(o) (1) IL 087.2
Chi(cago) (1) IL 087.2
(Chi)cago (3) IL 087.2
Chicagoese (1) 080.7
Chicano (26) 128.6
  ~ town (1) n 105.4
Chicanos (23) 128.7
chicharrones (4) n/adj S 046.8
  ~ peppers (1) n 055A.7
chiche (1) n F 073.5
chick (75) n/adj/interj 038.5
  ~ -a-chick chicks (1) interj 038.5
  ~ bone (1) n 072.7
  ~ chickoo chick (1) interj 038.5
  ~ chickoo(x2) (1) interj 038.5
  ~ -chickoo(x2) (1) interj 038.5
  ~ chicky (6) interj 038.5
  ~ chicky chick(x2) (1) interj 038.5
  ~ chicky chick(x3) chicky (1) interj 038.5
  ~ coop (1) n 036.8
  ~ gehee chicky (1) interj 038.5
chick(x2) (84) interj 038.5

~ check(x4) (1) interj 038.5
~ chicka (1) interj 038.5
~ chicken (1) interj 038.5
~ chickies(x2) chick(x3) (1) interj 038.5
~ chicko (1) interj 038.5
~ chickoo (3) interj 038.5
~ chickoo(x3) (1) interj 038.5
~ chicks (1) interj 038.5
~ chicky (10) interj 038.5
~ chicky(x2) (2) interj 038.5
~ chicky(x2) chick (1) interj 038.5
~ chicky(x2) chick chicky (1) interj 038.5
chick(x3) (176) interj 038.5
~ chicko (1) interj 038.5
~ chickoo (3) interj 038.5
~ chickoo(x2) (1) interj 038.5
~ chicko(x2) (1) interj 038.5
~ chicky (16) interj 038.5
~ chicky(x3) (2) interj 038.5
chick(x4) (127) interj 038.5
~ chickoo(x4) (1) interj 038.5
~ chicky (16) interj 038.5
~ chicky(x2) (2) interj 038.5
~ chicky chick (1) interj 038.5
~ whoo chicky(x2) (1) interj 038.5
chick(x5) (66) interj 038.5

~ buck(x3) chick(x2) interj (1) 038.5
~ chickoo (1) interj 038.5
~ chicky (6) interj 038.5
~ twoo chick(x6) (1) interj 038.5
chick(x6) (33) interj 038.5
~ chickeroo (1) interj 038.5
~ chicky (3) interj 038.5
~ chicky chick(x5) chicky (1) interj 038.5
chick(x7) (11) interj 038.5
chick(x8) (1) interj 038.5
chick(x9) (2) interj 038.5
chick(x11) (1) interj 038.5
chick(x13) (1) interj 038.5
Chick (13) 012.1
~ Sale (7) 012.1
~ Sales (6) 012.1
chicka(x2) (2) interj 038.5
~ chick (1) interj 038.5
~ chicky(x2) (1) interj 038.5
chicka(x4) chick (1) interj 038.5
chickabies(x2) (1) interj 038.5
chickadee (1) n 038.5
chickadees (1) n 059.3
Chickamauga (12) GA TN 087.5
~ Battlefield (1) 106.8
~ Creek (4) TN 030.7
~ Lake (1) TN 030.7
Chickasaw (30) AL MS 087.3
~ Basin (1) TN 030.7
~ Bayou (1) MS 030.7
~ Bluffs (1) TN 080.6
~ Bogue (1) AL 030.7
~ County (2) MS 087.6
~ Female College (1) 083.6
~ Garden (3) 105.3
~ Gardens (5) 106.1

Chickasawhatchee (1) GA 030.7
Chickasawhay (4) MS 030.7
~ River (2) MS 030.7
chicken (1653) n/v/adj 121.5
~ apartments (1) n 036.8
~ barn (5) n 036.8
~ bone (2) n 037.1
~ box (1) n 036.8
~ breast (2) n 121.5
~ brooder (2) n 036.8
~ bucket (1) n 017.4
~ cage (2) n 036.8
~ change (2) n 028.2
~ chicken macranny crow (1) n 080.8
~ coop (340) n 036.8
~ -coop houses (1) n 118.6
~ -coop wire (2) n 036.8
~ coops (36) n 036.8
~ crates (1) n 036.8
~ crib (2) n 036.8
~ dressing (11) n 044.8
~ dumplings (4) n 044.4
~ eater (2) n 059.5
~ eaters (1) n 059.5
~ -eating animal (1) n 059.5
~ -eating animals (1) n 059.5
~ -eating hog (2) n 058.5
~ entrails (2) n 037.2
~ family (1) n 036.6
~ feed (4) n 036.6
~ -feed sack (1) n 019.7
~ -feed sacks (1) n 019.6
~ fence (9) n 016.3
~ fertilizer (1) n 069.7
~ fever (1) n 080.6
~ fight (1) n 090.8
~ fighting (1) n 130.6
~ fillet (1) n 037.2
~ -foot bean (1) n 055A.4
~ frizz (1) n 090.0
~ frog (1) n 060.2

~ giblets (1) n 037.2
~ gizzard (2) n 037.2
~ -gizzard plant (1) n 080.6
~ goozle (1) n 071.7
~ gravy (1) n 048.5
~ gumbo (3) n 055.8
~ guts (1) n 037.2
~ hash (1) n 037.2
~ hawk (12) n 059.5
~ hawks (11) n 059.5
~ healer (1) n 067.8
~ heart (1) n 037.2
~ house (424) n 036.8
~ -house coop (1) n 036.8
~ houses (53) n 036.8
~ hovers (1) n 036.8
~ hut (1) n 036.8
~ innards (1) n 052.5
~ killer (1) n 059.5
~ killers (1) n 059.5
~ leg (1) n 121.5
~ lice (1) n 060A.9
~ liver (3) n 037.2
~ livers (2) n 037.2
~ lot (7) n 036.8
~ mite (1) n 060A.9
~ nest (1) n 036.8
~ netting (1) n 016.3
~ out (2) v 080.8
~ owl (10) n 059.2
~ owls (2) n 059.2
~ pasture (1) n 036.8
~ pea (1) n 036.8
~ pen (49) n 036.8
~ pens (5) n 036.8
~ pies (1) n 044.4
~ pilaf (1) n 089.8
~ plants (1) n 081.9
~ pops (1) n 079.7
~ pox (16) n 079.7
~ -rice stew (1) n 050.7
~ room (1) n 036.8
~ roost (21) n 036.8
~ roost[N-i] (1) n 036.8
~ run (2) n 036.8
~ salad (1) n 057.7
~ shack (2) n 036.8
~ shed (4) n 036.8
~ shelter (3) n 036.8
~ snake (67) n 081.8
~ snakes (41) n 080.8
~ soup (1) n 060.6

~ stealer (1) n 059.5
~ stealers (1) n 059.5
~ stock (1) n 037.2
~ suckers (1) n 059.5
~ thief (3) n 059.5
~ thieves (1) n 059.5
~ trash (1) n 037.2
~ tree (2) n 061.8
~ trough (1) n 035.8
~ trough[N-i] (1) n 035.8
~ turtle (1) n 060.6
~ wing (1) n 121.5
~ wire (97) n 016.3
~ -wire (6) adj 016.3
~ -wire fence (11) n 016.3
~ -wire fences (3) n 016.3
~ yard (94) n 036.8
~ -yard fence (1) n 016.3
~ yards (6) n 036.8
chicken(x2) (6) interj 038.5
chicken(x3) (1) interj 038.5
chicken(x4) (1) interj 038.5
Chicken (9) 113.4
~ Farm (1) 113.4
~ Gardens (1) 106.2
~ House (1) 113.4
~ Shacks (1) 113.4
chicken[N-i] (10) n 055A.7
chickened out (1) v 082.1
chickenhearted (2) adj 073.2
chickens (397) n 036.6
chickens(x2) (1) interj 038.5
chickety-wee (1) interj 059.4
chickies (1) interj 038.5
chickies(x2) (1) interj 038.5
chicklets (1) n 047.1
chickoo (14) interj 038.5
~ chickoos (1) interj 038.5
~ chick(x6) (1) interj 038.5
~ chicky (1) interj 038.5

~ chicky(x2) (1) interj 038.5
chickoo(x2) (5) interj 038.5
chickoo(x3) (5) interj 038.5
~ chick(x4) (1) interj 038.5
chickoo(x4) (1) interj 038.5
chicko(x2) (3) interj 038.5
chicko(x3) CLICK(x3) (1) interj 038.5
chicks (18) n 038.5
chickweed (2) n 015.9
chicky (123) adj/interj 038.5
~ baby (1) interj 038.5
~ bugs (1) n 060A.1
~ chick (3) interj 038.5
~ chick chicky (1) interj 038.5
~ chick(x2) (5) interj 038.5
~ chick(x3) (2) interj 038.5
~ chick(x4) (1) interj 038.5
~ chick(x5) buck(x3) chick(x2) (1) interj 038.5
~ -chick(x2) (1) interj 038.5
~ chick(x2) chickoo (1) interj 038.5
~ chick(x2) chicky(x2) (1) interj 038.5
~ chick(x2) chicky (2) interj 038.5
~ chick(x3) chicky (2) interj 038.5
~ chick(x4) chicky (2) interj 038.5
~ chick(x5) chicky (2) interj 038.5
~ GRUNT(C) chicka(x2) (1) interj 038.5
chicky(x2) (66) interj 038.5
~ chick (8) interj 038.5
~ chick chicky (1) interj 038.5

~ chick(x2) (1) interj 038.5
~ chick(x2) chicky (1) interj 038.5
~ chick(x4) (1) interj 038.5
chicky(x3) (72) interj 038.5
~ chick (2) interj 038.5
~ chick tick chicky(x2) chick(x2) (1) interj 038.5
~ chick(x3) (1) interj 038.5
chicky(x4) (22) interj 038.5
chicky(x5) (6) interj 038.5
chicky(x6) (3) interj 038.5
chicle (2) n 061.8
Chico (3) 080.8
~ tomato (1) n 055.3
chicory (3) n 070.6
Chicot (11) AR 087.6
~ City (1) AR 086.4
~ County (3) AR 087.5
~ Lake (1) AR 030.7
Chicota (2) TX 087.2
~ Bottom (1) TX 029.4
chiddy (1) interj 038.5
chief (26) n/adj 111.6
~ fire station (1) n 112.6
~ justice (1) n 068.6
~ of police (2) n 115.5
~ [P-0] police (2) n 032.9
Chief (4) 068.5
chief[N-k] (8) adj 111.6
~ car (4) n 111.6
Chiefland (2) FL 087.8
chief's car (41) n 111.6
chiefs (1) n 111.6
chien (2) n F 033.1
~ (de) terre (1) n F 060A.6
chiffonette (1) n 009.7
chiffonier (43) n 009.7
chiffoniers (8) n 009.2
chiffonrobe (1) n 009.7
chifforobe (529) n/adj 009.7
~ scarf (1) n 009.2
chiffo(robe) (1) n 009.2

chifforobe[N-i] (1) n 009.2
chifforobes (68) n 009.7
chigger (151) n/adj 060A.9
~ bite (1) n 060A.9
~ bites (2) n 060A.9
~ bug (3) n 060A.9
~ bugs (2) n 060A.9
~ fleas (1) n 060A.9
~ weed (2) n 015.9
Chigger (1) 064.4
chigger[N-i] (1) n 060A.9
chiggers (390) n 060A.9
chignon (2) n/adj 080.7
~ style (1) n 115.7
Chihuahua (38) 033.3
Chihuahuas (11) 033.3
chikees (1) n 080.8
child (644) n 068.7
~ of the woods (1) n 065.7
~ out of wedlock (4) n 065.7
Child (12) 064.4
child[N-i] (2) n 016.8
childbed fever (1) n 080.6
childbirth (1) n 033.9
childer (1) n 064.3
Childersburg (3) AL 087.2
childhood (4) n 064.4
childish (4) adj 075.1
children (2052) n 064.3
Children (3) 064.3
~ of Mary (1) 067.1
children[N-k] (5) adj 043.9
~ clothes (1) n 043.9
~ disease (1) n 079.7
~ dresses (1) n 064.3
~ play-pretty (1) n 101.5
~ room (1) n 007A.6
children's (9) adj 064.3
~ camp (1) n 064.3
~ children (1) n 025.7
~ clothes (1) n 012.2
~ home (1) n 066.3
~ room (4) n 007A.4
childrens (63) n 064.3
Childress (2) 107.9
~ plow (1) n 021.6
child's (6) adj 053.4
~ father (5) n 053.4

childs (3) n 088.9
Chilhowee (3) 106.4
~ Park (2) 106.5
Chilhow(ee) Mountain (1) TN 031.1
Chilhowees (1) TN 031.1
chili (15) n/adj 081.9
~ beans (2) n 055A.5
~ bowl (1) n 123.9
~ dog (3) n 121.6
~ peppers (1) n 055.5
~ sauce (1) n 053.5
~ sausage (2) n 121.6
chil(i) pepper (1) n 051.7
chilis (2) n 055A.9
chill (29) n/v/adj 076.3
~ box (1) n 015.5
~ out (1) v 096.7
~ tonic (15) n 078.4
Chill (1) 078.4
chill[V-t] (1) v 076.3
Chillatery (1) MS 087.4
chilled (2) v 070.8
Chilled (1) 021.6
Chillicothe (2) MO OH TX 087.3
chillier (3) adj 007.4
chilling (4) n/adj 091.7
~ fever (1) n 078.4
chillish (1) adj 007.4
chills (12) n/adj 079.4
~ tonic (1) n 078.4
chilly (682) adj 007.4
~ cool (1) n 121.9
~ day (3) n 007.4
~ morning (3) n 007.4
~ night (1) n 007.4
~ weather (1) n 007.4
Chilsey Creek (1) MS 030.7
Chiltipin Creek (2) TX 030.7
Chilton (12) AL 087.5
~ County (4) AL 087.8
chimenea (2) n S 008.1
chimley (657) n/adj 008.1
~ backlogs (1) n 008.5
~ board (1) n 008.1
~ clean (1) n 008.1
~ connection (1) n 008.1
~ corner (2) n 008.1
~ -cornered lawyers (1) n 067.8
~ daubing (1) n 083.1

~ fence (1) n 016.6
~ hawk (1) n 089.8
~ -like (1) adj 023.2
~ mud (1) n 008.1
~ pipe (2) n 023.2
~ pot (1) n 008.1
~ rock (1) n 008.1
~ sticks (1) n 008.1
~ swallows (1) n 008.1
~ sweep (5) n 059.2
~ sweeper (2) n 008.1
~ sweepers (3) n 081.9
~ sweeps (8) n 008.1
~ swift (1) n 008.1
~ wood (1) n 008.5
chimley[N-i] (2) n 008.1
chimleys (97) n 008.1
chimney (746) n/adj 008.1
~ breast (1) n 008.4
~ corner (1) n 008.2
~ flue (3) n 023.2
~ funnel (1) n 008.1
~ pipe (2) n 023.2
~ shelf (2) n 008.4
~ smut (1) n 008.7
~ sweep (4) n 059.2
~ sweep bird (1) n 081.8
~ sweeper (1) n 060A.8
~ sweepers (4) n 008.1
~ sweeps (6) n 008.1
~ swifts (1) n 096.7
Chimney (4) 088.7
~ Creek (1) GA 088.7
~ Park (2) 008.1
~ Top Mountain (1) TN 031.1
chimneypiece (2) n 008.4
chimneys (49) n 008.1
chin (43) n/adj 071.7
~ hopper (1) n 071.6
~ whiskers (9) n 071.4
china (1251) n/adj 017.1
~ bowl (2) n 017.1
~ cabinet (25) n 010.1
~ cabinets (1) n 017.1
~ closet (19) n 010.1
~ cup (1) n 017.1
~ cups (1) n 017.1
~ dish (1) n 017.1
~ dishes (11) n 017.1
~ doll (4) n 017.1
~ dolls (1) n 090.8
~ egg (380) n 017.1

~ eggs (60) n 017.1
~ jugs (1) n 017.2
~ magnolia (1) n 062.9
~ nest egg (4) n 017.1
~ nest eggs (3) n 017.1
~ nesting egg (1) n 017.1
~ painting (1) n 017.1
~ pitcher (1) n 017.1
~ plate (1) n 017.1
~ plates (1) n 017.1
~ press (1) n 009.6
~ shop (1) n 073.3
~ store (1) n 017.1
~ stuff (3) n 017.1
~ tea set (1) n 017.1
~ thing (1) n 017.1
~ tree (4) n 061.8
~ trees (6) n 061.8
~ vases (1) n 017.1
chin(a) (1) n 017.1
China (76) 017.1
~ chestnut (1) n 054.8
~ Grove (4) AL 087.3
~ hogs (1) n 017.1
~ Spring (1) TX 087.2
chinaball (14) n/adj 061.8
~ tree (5) n 061.8
~ trees (5) n 061.8
chinaballs (1) n 061.8
chinaberries (20) n 061.9
chinaberry (73) n/adj 062.4
~ balls (1) n 080.7
~ beads (1) n 028.4
~ tree (20) n 061.8
~ trees (18) n 061.9
chinaber(ry) (1) n 017.1
Chinaman (19) 126.4
Chinaman's (3) 095.9
~ chance (1) n 095.9
~ store (1) n 080.8
Chinamans (1) MS 084.9
Chinamen (3) 017.1
Chinamens (2) 126.4
Chinas (1) 035.5
Chinatown (3) 105.4
chinaware (58) n 017.1
chinch (16) n/adj 060A.8
~ bats (1) n 080.6
~ bug (3) n 060A.8
~ bugs (4) n 060A.9
~ harbors (1) n 088.9
chinches (15) n 059.5
chinchy (8) adj 073.4

~ bugs (1) n 060A.9
Chinee (2) 066.8
~ people (1) n 126.4
Chinese (76) 126.4
~ -American (1) 069.2
~ boy (1) n 126.4
~ buggy (1) n 023.3
~ cabbage (7) n 055A.1
~ chase (1) n 130.2
~ checkers (2) n 130.6
~ cherry (1) n 061.8
~ chestnut (2) n 061.8
~ chestnuts (5) n 054.8
~ cling (1) n 054.3
~ egg (1) n 017.1
~ eggs (1) n 017.1
~ elm (3) n 061.9
~ elms (1) n 061.8
~ girl (1) n 053.6
~ jump rope (1) n 130.6
~ laundry (2) n 010.6
~ matting (1) n 080.6
~ plum trees (1) n 061.9
~ red light (1) n 130.5
~ tallow (7) n 061.8
~ tallows (1) n 061.8
Ching (4) 126.5
~ -Ching Chinaman (2) 126.5
chink (5) n/adj 123.6
~ chimney (1) n 008.1
Chink (21) 126.4
chinkers (1) n 060A.9
chinking (1) n 065.8
Chinkos (1) 069.8
Chinks (53) 126.4
Chinky (2) 119.6
~ -Chinky-Chinamen (1) 119.6
chinny (2) interj 038.3
chinois (1) n F 017.1
chinooks (1) n 080.7
chinquapin (42) n/adj 054.7
~ nuts (1) n 054.8
~ oak (2) n 061.8
~ tree (1) n 061.8
~ trees (4) n 054.8
chinquapins (57) n 054.8
chintzy (5) adj 073.5
chip (71) n/v/adj 008.6
~ kindling (1) n 008.6
~ marbles (1) n 080.7

~ off (1) v 008.6
Chipley (4) FL 087.6
chiplings (1) n 008.6
chipmonkey (1) n 059.8
chipmunk (349) n 059.8
chipmunks (101) n 059.8
Chipola River (1) FL 030.9
Chippendale (1) 096.7
chipper (20) adj 074.1
Chippewa (1) 107.7
chippy (5) n/adj 074.1
chips (70) n 008.6
chipules (1) n S 060A.3
chiquito (1) n S 064.4
chiropractor (1) n 012.5
chirping frog (1) n 060.2
Chisca Hotel (1) 084.3
chisel (6) n/adj 020.7
~ harrow (1) n 021.7
~ plow (2) n 021.6
~ plows (1) n 021.6
chiseler (6) n 073.5
chisels (2) n 080.7
Chisholm (13) AL 105.1
~ Road (1) 107.6
~ Trail (2) TX 031.8
chitlin (46) n/adj 037.3
~ addict (1) n 037.3
~ bread (1) n 044.5
~ eating (1) n 037.3
~ man (1) n 037.3
~ supper (3) n 037.3
~ suppers (4) n 037.3
~ time (1) n 037.3
chitlin[N-i] (13) n 037.3
chitlins (782) n 037.3
chitterling (17) n/adj 037.3
~ supper (2) n 037.3
chitterling[N-i] (3) n 037.3
chitterlings (167) n 037.3
Chitto (21) 030.7
chitty(x2) kitty gitty (1) interj 038.5
chitty(x5) (1) interj 038.5
chiva (1) n S 075.8
chivalrous (2) adj 082.5
chivalry (5) n 082.5
chive (1) n 055.7
chives (8) n 055.7
Chiwapa (2) 030.7
~ Channel (1) MS 030.7

~ Creek (1) MS 030.7
cho(x4) (1) interj 038.3
Choccolocco Valley (1) AL 087.4
Choccoloc(co) (5) AL 030.7
~ Creek (4) AL 030.7
chock-full (3) adj 075.7
chocolate (69) n/adj 070.6
~ bar (1) n 066.8
~ cake (4) n 065.8
~ cakes (2) n 044.4
~ -chip cookies (1) n 045.2
~ -coated doughnuts (1) n 122.4
~ Coke (1) n 121.8
~ -covered (5) adj 045.2
~ -covered doughnut (1) n 122.4
~ -covered doughnuts (4) n 122.5
~ doughnut (5) n 122.4
~ doughnuts (3) n 122.4
~ drops (2) n 069.3
~ eclairs (2) n 122.3
~ -frosted (2) adj 122.4
~ glaze (1) n 122.3
~ icing (1) n 122.4
~ layer cake (1) n 122.1
~ motherfucker (1) n 069.3
~ pies (1) n 048.3
~ sauce (5) n 048.5
~ sauces (1) n 048.5
~ syrup (4) n 048.5
~ tops (1) n 045.2
Chocolate Bayou (3) TX 030.7
chocolates (1) n 069.5
Choctafaula (1) AL 030.7
Choctaw (26) MS 092.8
~ Bayou (4) LA 030.7
~ County (1) MS 086.3
~ Indian (1) 069.3
~ Indians (2) 088.7
Choctawhatchee (9) AL FL 030.7
~ Bay (1) FL 030.7
~ River (5) AL FL 030.7

Choctaws (1) 080.8
choice (5) n/adj 121.1
~ top prime hog (1) n 035.5
choicy (2) adj 088.7
choir (11) n/adj 089.5
~ parties (1) n 130.7
~ song (1) n 089.5
Choir (3) 087.2
~ Creek (1) MS 030.7
choirmaster (1) n 080.6
choirs (3) n 089.5
choke (3) v/adj 044.4
~ biscuits (1) n 044.4
~ chain (1) n 028.4
choke[V-r] (1) v 020.4
chokeberries (3) n 062.4
chokeberry (2) n 062.5
choked (5) v 085.8
~ on (1) v 057.2
~ up (3) v 076.4
Chokee District (1) GA 087.1
choker (17) n/adj 028.4
~ collar (1) n 028.4
chokers (3) n 055.5
choking (4) n/adj 076.5
~ asthma (1) n 079.7
~ quinsy (2) n 079.7
cholah (2) n 044.4
cholera (13) n/adj 079.6
~ epidemic (1) n 078.7
~ infantum (1) n 080.6
cholesterol count (1) n 077.9
chomp (5) n/v 050.2
~ away (1) v 050.2
~ down (1) v 050.2
~ on (1) v 050.2
chomping (3) v 050.2
choo (3) interj 037.5
~ -cow(x2) (1) interj 037.5
~ -pig(x2) (1) interj 038.3
choo(x2) (3) interj 038.3
Choochoo (2) 106.9
chooey(x3) (1) interj 038.3
chook(x3) (1) interj 038.3
choop(x3) (1) interj 038.3
choose (5) v 049.6
~ to (2) v 049.6

choosy (2) adj 081.8
chop (391) n/v/adj 015.8
~ ax (3) n 080.6
~ bag (1) n 019.7
~ block (20) n 022.1
~ for (1) v 075.7
~ liver (4) n 047.2
~ meat (1) n 047.4
~ on (1) v 098.6
~ out (7) v 015.8
~ steak (2) n 121.1
~ steaks (1) n 121.1
~ through (2) v 015.8
chop[V-r] (5) v 015.8
chopa (2) n 061.2
chopas (1) n 061.2
chopped (47) v/adj 015.8
~ down (1) v 088.7
~ out (6) v 015.8
~ steak (1) n 121.1
chopper (20) n 111.9
choppers (13) n 111.9
chopping (298) v/adj 041.4
~ ax (2) n 020.7
~ block (22) n 022.1
~ knife (1) n 017.8
~ knives (1) n 017.8
~ on (1) v 015.8
~ out (6) v 093.9
~ up (1) v 015.8
chops (227) n/v 121.4
choral (3) n/adj 115.8
~ music (1) n 130.9
~ works (1) n 130.9
chore (41) n/adj 037.4
~ time (36) n 037.4
chore[N-i] (1) n 037.4
chores (126) n/adj 010.4
~ time (1) n 037.4
chorice (1) n 037.3
choristers (1) n 088.9
chorizo (2) n S 046.8
chosen people (1) n 126.7
chouette (5) n F 059.1
choupique (8) n 059.9
Choupique (1) MS 030.7
choux (3) n F 080.7
chow (16) n/v/adj 048.4
~ down (1) v 048.3
~ time (2) n 049.2
Chow (2) 033.3
Chowchow (1) 083.1
chowder (1) n 047.1
chowhound (1) n 048.4

Christ (125) 089.3
~ Church (1) 106.5
~ Episcopal Church (1) 089.2
~ killer (1) n 126.9
Christ[N-k] (3) 093.2
~ birthday (1) n 093.2
~ sake (2) n 092.2
christen (19) v 024.5
Christenberry Heights (1) 105.6
christened (3) v 024.5
christening (3) v 023.5
Christes' (3) 093.2
~ birthday (1) n 093.2
~ mother (1) n 016.5
~ picture (1) n 043.9
Christi (33) 030.3
christian (2) v 024.5
Christian (38) 089.2
~ church (9) n 089.2
~ freak (1) n 126.5
~ man (1) n 091.8
~ Methodist (1) 089.1
~ Methodist Episcopal (1) 089.1
~ music (1) n 130.8
~ people (1) n 052.6
~ Science (4) 078.3
~ Scientist (2) 089.1
Christianity (1) 070.7
christianize (2) v 088.7
Christians (5) 073.2
Christmas (1586) 093.2
~ Aid (1) 093.2
~ baskets (1) n 020.1
~ bush (1) n 062.2
~ cake (1) n 044.4
~ carols (1) n 130.8
~ Cheer (2) 093.2
~ Creek (1) GA 030.7
~ Day (10) 093.2
~ dinner (1) n 093.2
~ Eve (10) 093.2
~ Eve Day (1) 093.2
~ Eve Gift (24) 093.2
~ Eve Night (1) 093.2
~ Eve party (1) n 093.2
~ gift (4) n 093.2
~ Gift (351) 093.2
~ gift[N-i] (1) n 093.2
~ gifts (1) n 093.2
~ Gifts (1) 093.2
~ Give (48) 093.2
~ Gives (3) 093.2

~ Greeting (7) 093.2
~ Greetings (11) 093.2
~ Kiss (1) 093.2
~ money (1) n 093.2
~ paper (1) n 019.5
~ parties (4) n 130.7
~ party (3) n 130.7
~ present (3) n 093.2
~ Present (2) 093.2
~ presents (3) n 093.2
~ shopping (1) n 094.2
~ stick (1) n 008.5
~ story (1) n 082.8
~ toy (1) n 101.5
~ toys (1) n 101.5
~ Treat (1) 093.2
~ tree (3) n 093.2
~ -tree forts (1) n 130.3
~ trees (5) n 093.2
~ turkey (1) n 125.5
~ whiskey (1) n 050.8
~ -wrapped (3) v 094.3
Chri(stmas) (1) 093.2
Christmasberry (1) 062.4
Christmastime (24) 093.2
Christmastimes (1) 093.2
Christopher Columbus (3) 087.7
Christ's (2) 066.9
~ commandments (1) n 066.9
~ sake (1) n 092.1
chronic (1) adj 078.2
chronological (1) adj 065.8
chrysanthemum (1) n 070.6
Chrysler roadster (1) n 023.6
chu(x2) (1) interj 038.3
chu(x3) (1) interj 038.3
chub (2) n 061.2
Chubbehatchee (1) AL 030.7
chubby (8) adj 073.2
chubs (2) n 061.2
chuc (1) n 069.3
Chucalissa (2) 106.4
~ Village (1) 106.6
chuck (62) n/v/adj 121.1
~ -a-luck (1) v 080.3
~ beef (1) n 121.2
~ roast (22) n 121.2
~ steak (8) n 121.1

~ steaks (1) n 121.1
~ up (1) v 080.3
~ wagon (3) n 080.8
chucked (3) v 032.1
chuckers (1) n 129.3
chuckhole (3) n 030.3
chuckholes (2) n 031.6
chucking (1) v 032.1
chuckmunk (1) n 059.8
chuckwood (1) n 059.3
chuckwoods (1) n 059.3
chucs (1) n 080.8
chufa (16) n/adj 054.7
~ bellies (1) n 069.7
~ patch (3) n 016.1
Chufa Gray (1) 056.9
chufas (31) n 054.7
chufases (5) n 016.7
chugging (1) v 097.4
chuh(x3) (1) interj 037.5
chukkas (1) n 122.8
Chula (1) GA 087.2
Chulafinnee (1) AL 087.3
chum (8) n 129.4
chums (1) n 088.9
Chumuckla (1) FL 087.6
chunk (195) n/v/adj 008.5
~ after (1) v 032.1
~ at (5) v 032.1
~ floater (7) n 006.1
~ floaters (1) n 006.1
~ meat (6) n 046.4
~ mover (1) n 006.1
~ movers (1) n 006.1
~ out (1) v 032.1
chunk[V-r] (3) v 032.1
chunked (114) v 032.1
~ at (11) v 032.1
~ in (1) v 032.1
chunker (1) n 006.1
chunking (27) v 032.1
~ at (2) v 032.1
chunks (19) n/v 046.4
~ at (1) v 032.1
chunky (5) adj 073.1
chupa hueso (1) n S 060A.4
Chuquatonchee (1) MS 030.7
church (1766) n/adj 089.2
~ bells (1) n 089.2
~ benches (2) n 083.8
~ books (1) n 099.5
~ building (1) n 089.2

~ buildings (1) n 089.2
~ burying ground (1) n 078.8
~ camp (1) n 089.2
~ cemeteries (1) n 078.8
~ cemetery (13) n 078.8
~ ceremony (1) n 079.2
~ choir (1) n 089.2
~ circle (1) n 089.2
~ clothes (2) n 027.7
~ clubs (1) n 089.2
~ day (3) n 002.1
~ door (1) n 032.5
~ doors (1) n 089.2
~ dues (1) n 094.8
~ funeral (1) n 079.2
~ graveyard (4) n 078.8
~ ground (1) n 078.9
~ groups (2) n 089.2
~ house (10) n 089.2
~ houses (3) n 014.1
~ job (1) n 089.2
~ lot (1) n 089.2
~ members (1) n 089.2
~ mouse[N-i] (1) n 104.6
~ music (4) n 089.5
~ parties (6) n 089.2
~ party (2) n 130.7
~ picnics (1) n 089.2
~ plot (1) n 078.8
~ rallies (1) n 089.2
~ records (1) n 130.8
~ revivals (1) n 088.7
~ school (1) n 089.2
~ services (1) n 089.2
~ singing (1) n 130.8
~ social (1) n 089.2
~ suit (1) n 027.7
~ wedding (1) n 089.2
~ work (3) n 089.2
Church (220) 107.8
~ of Christ (69) 089.2
~ of Christ people (1) n 075.7
~ of England (1) 089.2
~ of God (44) 089.3
~ of God in Christ (1) 089.2
~ of Gods (1) 089.3
~ Point (1) LA 087.1
~ Street (12) 089.2
~ Street Viaduct (1) 107.8

churches (68) n 089.2
churchgoer (2) n 089.2
churchgoers (1) n 089.2
churchgoing (2) adj 080.6
~ people (1) n 080.6
~ person (1) n 089.2
churchy (1) adj 075.7
churchyard (26) n/adj 089.2
~ cemeteries (1) n 078.8
~ cemetery (1) n 078.8
Churchyard (1) 089.2
churchyards (1) n 078.8
churn (47) n/adj 080.8
~ bellies (1) n 065.1
~ dasher (3) n 080.7
~ jar (1) n 015.5
churning (2) v 075.9
churns (9) n 080.7
chute (12) n 008.1
Chute (2) 030.7
chutes (3) n 033.5
cibleme (2) n F 056.6
Cibolo (4) TX 030.7
~ Creek (2) TX 030.7
cicada (1) n 081.9
cider (16) n/adj 050.8
~ barrels (1) n 019.1
~ mill (2) n 096.8
~ press (1) n 081.8
~ time (1) n 026.1
cig (2) n 117.7
cigaboos (1) n 117.7
cigar (247) n/adj 057.3
~ box (3) n 057.3
~ cigarettes (1) n 057.3
~ factory (2) n 057.3
~ lighter (1) n 057.3
~ maker (1) n 057.3
~ minnows (1) n 061.2
~ store (1) n 057.3
cigar[N-i] (2) n 057.3
cigarette (204) n/adj 057.3
~ ashes (1) n 057.3
~ butts (1) n 057.3
~ factory (1) n 057.3
~ papers (1) n 057.3
~ -smoke (1) v 057.3
~ smoking (1) n 057.3
~ stand (1) n 057.3
cigarette[N-i] (4) n 057.3
cigarettes (683) n 057.3
cigars (593) n 057.3

cigs (5) n 117.7
ciment (1) n F 031.8
cimetiere (1) n F 078.8
cinchona (1) n 078.4
Cincinnati (641) OH 087.9
~ bacon (1) n 046.7
~ Reds (6) 087.9
Cincinna(ti) (2) OH 087.9
cinder (3) adj 016.7
~ blocks (1) n 016.7
~ days (1) n 090.8
~ trains (1) n 089.9
Cinderella (3) 130.6
~ quilts (1) n 029.1
cinders (11) n 008.7
cinema (12) n 084.4
Cinema (2) 114.9
cinnamon (101) n/adj 122.3
~ bar (1) n 045.2
~ bread (8) n 044.3
~ bun (3) n 045.2
~ buns (6) n 122.8
~ cake (1) n 044.4
~ cookies (1) n 044.4
~ Danish (1) n 122.2
~ doughnuts (1) n 122.4
~ loaves (1) n 044.3
~ roll (27) n 122.5
~ rolls (29) n 122.2
~ stick (2) n 122.7
~ sweet rolls (1) n 122.2
~ toast (1) n 045.3
~ twist (6) n 122.7
~ twist doughnuts (1) n 045.2
~ twists (2) n 122.7
~ -type roll (1) n 122.2
cinnam(on) buns (1) n 122.6
cinnamons (1) n 017.1
cinq (1) n F 001.3
cipher (1) v 100.5
circle (19) n/adj 085.1
~ dance (1) n 083.1
~ porch (1) n 010.8
~ rake (1) n 014.8
~ rod (1) n 080.9
~ saw (2) n 120.9
~ saws (1) n 020.7
Circle (12) 105.4

~ Drive (1) 011.3
circle[V-p] (1) v 087.3
circles (10) n 107.5
circuit (30) n/adj 067.8
~ clerk (1) n 068.6
~ judge (6) n 068.6
~ judges (1) n 068.6
~ preacher (1) n 067.8
~ rider (11) n 067.8
~ rider preacher (1) n 067.8
~ riders (4) n 070.7
~ -riding preacher (1) n 080.6
~ -type preacher (1) n 088.7
circular (2) adj 065.8
~ mule baler (1) n 084.8
circulars (1) n 065.8
circulate (1) v 070.6
circulating heater (2) n 118.5
circulation (2) n 097.4
circulator (5) n 118.4
circumcise (4) v 036.1
circumstances (1) n 094.7
cirrhosis (4) n 078.7
cirrus (2) n/adj 005.3
~ clouds (1) n 005.3
cistern (64) n/adj 080.9
~ gutter (1) n 011.5
~ gutters (1) n 011.5
~ house (1) n 015.5
~ room (1) n 007A.5
~ trough (1) n 011.5
~ troughs (2) n 011.5
cisterns (11) n 011.5
cities (5) n 039.7
citified (3) adj 069.8
citizen (33) n/adj 069.2
Citizen[N-i] [J-O] Southern National Bank (1) 108.5
citizens (5) n 069.2
citizenship (1) n 069.2
Citra (1) FL 087.4
citron (23) n/adj 056.7
~ melon (1) n 056.9
~ melons (1) n 056.7
~ preserves (1) n 051.6
Citronelle (3) AL 087.2
citrons (3) n 056.7
citrus (12) n/adj 055.1
~ field (1) n 053.2

~ garden (1) n 080.8
~ grove (2) n 061.6
~ groves (1) n 061.6
~ grower (1) n 080.6
~ trees (1) n 061.8
Citrus Belt (1) 080.7
city (222) n/adj 085.5
~ block (1) n 091.1
~ bomb shelter (1) n 089.8
~ boy (3) n 081.5
~ boys (1) n 069.9
~ bus (6) n 109.9
~ bus lines (1) n 109.9
~ bus system (1) n 109.9
~ buses (2) n 109.9
~ cemetery (2) n 078.8
~ center (1) n 106.4
~ cesspool (1) n 080.6
~ cogger (1) n 080.6
~ commissioners (1) n 080.6
~ commons (1) n 085.1
~ council (1) n 068.6
~ councilman (1) n 115.4
~ cowboy (1) n 099.5
~ cracker (1) n 080.6
~ dock (1) n 031.4
~ dude (26) n 069.8
~ dudes (3) n 069.6
~ employee (1) n 115.4
~ fish (1) n 037.3
~ flunky (1) n 115.4
~ folks (1) n 089.8
~ fountain (1) n 080.6
~ gal (1) n 064.9
~ gardens (1) n 050.5
~ girl (2) n 064.9
~ government (2) n 085.6
~ guy (2) n 069.4
~ hall (24) n 112.7
~ hall annex (1) n 106.9
~ ham (1) n 121.3
~ hoodlum (1) n 069.9
~ jail (19) n 112.8
~ kitty (3) n 112.5
~ library (1) n 084.1
~ limits (1) n 053.5
~ lot (2) n 015.6
~ manager (1) n 115.3
~ marshall (1) n 084.8

~ ordinance (1) n 075.9
~ palms (1) n 107.8
~ park (4) n 085.1
~ parks (1) n 085.1
~ payroll (1) n 115.4
~ people (1) n 081.8
~ person (1) n 069.9
~ police (1) n 112.5
~ property (1) n 031.9
~ right-of-way (1) n 031.9
~ road (1) n 031.7
~ school (1) n 045.8
~ sheik (1) n 069.9
~ shorts (1) n 123.3
~ slicker (13) n 069.9
~ slickers (5) n 069.9
~ square (2) n 085.1
~ street (2) n 031.7
~ streets (2) n 031.7
~ trucks (1) n 109.7
~ water (2) n 048.9
~ workers (1) n 115.4
cit(y) hall (1) n 070.9
City (438) 082.6
~ Auditorium (2) 106.4
~ Girl (1) 099.8
~ Hall (1) 082.6
~ Hospital (1) 084.5
~ Line buses (1) n 109.9
~ National (1) 105A.8
~ of Roses (1) 087.2
~ Park (23) 085.1
~ Park Lake (1) LA 088.7
~ [J-O] County building (1) n 108.5
civet (60) n/adj 059.4
~ cat (57) n 059.4
civ(et) cat (1) n 059.4
civets (1) n 059.4
Civic Center (8) 106.4
civic-type things (1) n 070.4
civil (3) adj 085.8
~ lawyer (1) n 053.3
Civil (906) 085.8
~ Right[N-i] (1) 085.8
~ Rights (2) 090.9
~ War (873) 085.8
~ War between the States (2) 085.8
~ War camp (1) n 085.8

~ War days (3) n 085.8
~ War Hospital (1) 106.7
~ War prison camp (1) n 085.8
~ War rifle (1) n 085.8
~ War times (1) n 085.8
~ War tokens (1) n 085.8
~ War veteran (3) n 085.8
~ War's (1) 085.8
civilize (1) adj 073.6
civilized (2) adj 080.7
CJ Throbber (1) 124.5
clabber (767) n/v/adj 047.6
~ biscuits (3) n 044.4
~ board (1) n 011.2
~ buttermilk (1) n 047.6
~ cheese (46) n 048.1
~ clouds (1) n 005.3
~ cottage cheese (1) n 048.1
~ milk (93) n 047.6
~ pie (2) n 047.6
~ pudding (1) n 047.6
~ puddings (1) n 047.6
~ stage (1) n 047.6
~ up (4) v 047.6
clabbered (168) v/adj 047.6
~ buttermilk (1) n 047.6
~ cheese (6) n 048.1
~ cream (1) n 048.1
~ milk (68) n 047.6
~ -milk cheese (1) n 048.1
clabbering (3) v 047.6
~ up (1) v 005.6
clabbers (30) n/v/adj 047.6
~ milk (1) n 047.6
clacker (1) n 019.4
clacking (1) v 057.4
Claiborne (14) AL LA TN 087.3
~ Elementary (1) 083.2
~ Parish (2) LA 102.9
claim (5) n/v 084.8
claimed (5) v 103.4
claims (4) n/v 035.6

~ to (2) v 067.8
Clair (4) 087.4
Claire (1) 087.3
Clairmont Avenue (1) 093.5
clam (32) n/v/adj 060.1
~ digger (1) n 122.8
~ diggers (6) n 123.3
~ up (2) v 096.3
clamber up (1) v 005.6
clammed (6) v 096.3
clammy (2) adj 023.8
~ dirt (1) n 029.8
clamp (6) n/v 036.1
clamped on (1) v 082.2
clamping down (1) v 091.6
clamps (3) n 110.4
clams (16) n 060.8
clamshells (2) n 031.6
clan (11) n 066.5
clannish (2) adj 129.6
Clanton (7) AL 087.3
clap (5) n/v 092.9
~ him over (1) v 081.3
clapboard (81) n/adj 011.2
~ fence (1) n 016.2
~ house (4) n 011.2
~ houses (3) n 011.2
~ roof (2) n 011.4
clapboarding (4) n 011.2
clapboards (55) n 011.2
clapped (1) adj 011.2
clapper rail (1) n 091.7
Clara (2) 087.4
Clarendon (3) AR TX 087.1
claret (1) n 114.7
Claridge Hotel (1) 084.3
clarify (1) v 088.7
clarinet (1) n 065.9
Clark (9) 087.4
~ County (2) AR 087.4
~ Range (1) TN 087.4
~ River (1) GA 030.7
~ Tower (3) 108.5
~ Towers (2) 105.2
Clarke (10) AL MS 087.3
~ County (4) AL GA MS 087.2
Clarkesville (8) GA 087.3
Clark's Funeral Home (1) 079.2
Clarks Mill (1) 030.9

Clarksdale (13) AR MS 087.8
Clarkston (1) GA 087.7
Clarksville (18) AR TN TX 087.5
clasp (1) n 028.2
class (246) n/adj 083.7
~ clown (1) n 125.6
~ parties (2) n 130.7
~ ring (12) n 123.1
~ rings (2) n 123.1
Class (1) 080.9
classed (2) v 069.5
~ as (1) v 069.5
classer (2) n 070.8
classers (1) n 088.9
classes (39) n 083.4
classic (2) n/adj 130.8
~ music (1) n 130.8
classical (48) n/adj 130A.8
~ music (19) n 130.8
classicals (1) n 130.9
classified (2) adj 039.6
classify (1) v 013.7
classmate (1) n 129.6
classmates (3) n 129.6
classroom (2) n/adj 083.9
~ teachers (1) n 067.6
classy (2) adj 123.6
Claus (11) 012.8
Clauson (1) AL 087.9
claw (35) n/adj 120.6
~ hammer (22) n 020.7
~ hammers (6) n 020.7
~ thing (1) n 020.8
clawdaddy (1) n 060.8
clawed (1) v 013.8
clawfish (1) n 060.8
claws (7) n 120.6
Claxton (4) GA 087.3
clay (636) n/adj 029.8
~ bank soil (1) n 029.8
~ banks (1) n 052.1
~ base (1) n 029.8
~ -base road (1) n 031.6
~ bottom (1) n 029.4
~ buckshot (1) n 029.9
~ cats (1) n 008.9
~ chimley (1) n 008.1
~ chimleys (1) n 008.1
~ cups (1) n 081.9
~ dauber (1) n 060A.6
~ dirt (12) n 029.8

~ egg (1) n 017.1
~ fields (1) n 029.8
~ foundation (3) n 029.8
~ ground (2) n 055.5
~ hard dirt (1) n 029.8
~ hill (1) n 030.8
~ hills (6) n 029.8
~ hole (1) n 029.8
~ land (29) n 029.8
~ -like (1) adj 029.8
~ -like soil (1) n 029.8
~ loam (11) n 029.8
~ marble (1) n 090.4
~ marbles (1) n 093.7
~ mud (4) n 029.8
~ pea (1) n 055A.1
~ peas (2) n 055A.2
~ pipe (5) n 023.2
~ pit (1) n 029.8
~ pitchers (1) n 052.1
~ pot (3) n 017.7
~ pots (1) n 017.7
~ ridges (1) n 030.8
~ road (15) n 031.6
~ roads (10) n 031.6
~ root (1) n 061.4
~ sand (2) n 029.8
~ soil (47) n 029.8
~ stone peach (1) n 054.4
~ -type soil (2) n 029.8
Clay (16) AL AR FL GA 087.6
~ County (7) FL GA 087.4
~ Station (1) TX 087.3
~ Street (2) 107.7
clayey (1) adj 029.8
Clayton (13) AL AR GA 087.7
~ County (4) GA 087.3
clean (687) v/adj/adv 041.4
~ -cut (1) v 041.4
~ day (1) n 010.4
~ off (2) v 041.4
~ out (9) v 041.4
~ rags (1) n 018.4
~ sand yard (1) n 010.5
~ up (179) v 010.4
~ up with (1) v 080.5
~ -up woman (1) n 119.5
clean[V-p] (9) v 010.4

~ up (5) v 010.4
clean[V-r] (9) v 041.4
~ up (1) v 041.4
clean[V-s] (2) v 041.4
clean[V-t] up (1) v 041.4
cleaned (161) v 010.4
~ off (3) v 041.4
~ out (5) v 041.4
~ up (67) v 041.4
cleaner (171) n/adj 010.6
~ bag (3) n 116.8
cleaners (39) n/adj 010.6
~ bag (3) n 123.7
~ bags (1) n 123.7
cleaning (281) n/v/adj 010.4
~ around (1) v 010.4
~ bag (1) n 123.7
~ bags (1) n 123.7
~ day (1) n 010.4
~ off (1) v 041.4
~ out (2) v 041.4
~ up (118) v 010.4
clean(ing) (1) n 010.4
cleans (95) v 010.4
~ up (35) v 010.4
cleanup (1) n 010.4
clear (1184) v/adj 005.4
~ away (3) v 005.7
~ blister (4) n 077.7
~ blue sky (1) n 001A.4
~ bulbs (1) n 019.9
~ corn (1) n 056.2
~ cut (1) n 054.4
~ day (159) n 005.4
~ fluid (1) n 077.7
~ land (2) n 029.8
~ liquid (4) n 077.7
~ morning (1) n 007.4
~ off (62) v 005.7
~ out (2) v 041.4
~ peach (2) n 054.4
~ peaches (1) n 054.4
~ peanut (1) n 054.7
~ seed (239) n 054.4
~ seed peach (34) n 054.4
~ seed peaches (6) n 054.4
~ seeded (1) adj 054.4
~ seeded peach (2) n 054.4
~ seeded peaches (1) n 054.4

~ seeds (3) n 054.4
~ sing peaches (1) n 054.4
~ sky (2) n 005.4
~ stone (46) n 054.4
~ stone peach (3) n 054.4
~ stone peaches (2) n 054.4
~ stuff (1) n 077.7
~ sunset (1) n 003.4
~ up (145) v 005.7
~ water (6) n 048.9
~ -water shrimp (1) n 060.9
~ weather (4) n 005.4
~ wool (1) n 035.2
Clear (23) 030.7
~ Bayou (1) LA 030.7
~ Creek (15) AL AR GA MS TN TX 087.4
~ Creek Lake (1) GA 030.7
~ Fork (1) TN 080.6
~ Lake (2) LA 030.7
~ Point (1) AL 087.7
~ Spring (1) MS 088.8
clear[V-p] up (1) v 005.7
clear[V-r] (3) v 041.4
~ up (1) v 041.4
clear[V-t] up (1) v 005.7
cleared (581) v/adj 041.4
~ away (3) v 005.7
~ land (7) n 041.4
~ off (17) v 005.7
~ out (7) v 041.4
~ up (62) v 005.7
~ with (1) v 032.4
clearing (461) n/v/adj 005.7
~ away (2) v 005.7
~ off (46) v 005.7
~ out (3) v 005.7
~ skies (1) n 006.7
~ up (189) v 005.7
clears (13) v/adj 054.4
~ off (3) v 005.7
~ peach (1) n 054.4
~ up (6) v 005.7
Clearwater (14) FL 087.3
~ Airport (1) 106.6
~ Beach (1) FL 087.5
Cleary (2) MS 086.6
cleats (2) n 123.8

cleaver (12) n 104.3
cleavers (2) n 104.3
Cleburne (4) AL TX 087.9
~ County (2) AL 087.2
cleft (1) n 031.2
Clements Road (1) 107.6
clerical (1) adj 068.8
clerk (23) n 068.6
clerks (1) n 053.2
Cleveland (60) AL AR FL GA MS OH TN TX 087.9
~ Avenue (4) 107.6
~ big boll (1) n 090.8
~ Road (1) 107.8
~ Street (1) 107.6
clever (6) adj 073.2
clevis (7) n 021.3
Clewiston (3) FL 087.8
CLICK (11) interj 038.1
CLICK(x2) (23) interj 038.1
CLICK(x3) (22) interj 037.8
CLICK(x4) (6) interj 038.1
CLICK(x5) (1) interj 038.1
CLICK(x25) (1) interj 038.3
click to (1) v 038.1
cliff (688) n 031.2
Cliff (10) 031.2
cliff[N-i] (9) n 031.2
cliffs (314) n 031.2
cliffside (2) n 031.2
Clifton (3) AL TN TX 087.3
clim (48) v 096.3
~ up (4) v 096.3
climate (2) n/adj 070.1
~ -control unit (1) n 118.5
Climax (2) GA 087.1
climb (718) n/v 096.3
~ like (1) v 052.1
~ on up (1) v 096.3
~ out (1) v 096.3
~ over (2) v 096.3
~ up (24) v 096.3
climb[V-p] (1) v 096.3
climb[V-r] (61) v 096.3
~ up (2) v 096.3
climb[V-t] (38) v 096.3

climbed (980) v 096.3
~ up (16) v 096.3
climber (3) n/adj 055A.3
~ fence (1) n 016.3
climbers (1) n 096.3
climbing (33) n/v/adj 096.3
~ tomato (1) n 089.9
climbs (17) v 096.3
climmed (3) v 096.3
clinch peach (1) n 054.3
Clinch (15) GA TN 030.7
~ County (3) GA 087.3
~ Mountain (1) TN 031.1
~ River (6) TN 030.7
~ Street (1) 107.6
clincher (1) n 112.8
Clines Prairie (1) TX 087.2
cling (333) n/v/adj 054.3
~ free (4) n 054.4
~ peach (92) n 054.3
~ peaches (29) n 054.3
~ pit peaches (1) n 054.3
~ seed (26) n 054.3
~ seed peach (1) n 054.3
~ seeded peach (1) n 054.3
~ sing peaches (1) n 054.3
~ to (1) v 054.3
~ -type peach (1) n 054.3
clinged (1) v 054.3
clinger (2) n 054.3
clinging (7) v/adj 054.3
~ peach (1) n 054.3
~ stone (1) n 054.3
~ to (1) v 054.3
~ type (1) n 054.3
Clingmans Dome (1) TN 031.1
clings (7) n/v 054.3
~ to (1) v 054.3
clingstone (156) n/adj 054.3
~ peach (9) n 054.3
~ peaches (2) n 054.3
clingstones (3) n 054.3
clinic (7) n 084.5
clinics (2) n 084.5
clink (6) n 112.8

clinker (6) n 112.8
~ -built (1) adj 011.2
clinkers (4) n/v 008.7
~ up (1) v 081.8
Clinton (20) AR LA MS SC 087.8
~ Drive (1) 107.4
~ Parish (1) LA 087.4
Clintonville (4) AL 087.7
Clio (1) AL 087.3
clip (183) n/v 110.4
~ -ons (1) n 110.4
clipped (3) v/adj 036.1
clipper (16) n 120.8
Clipper (1) 024.6
clippers (116) n 120.8
clipping (1) v 036.1
clips (25) n 110.4
clique (7) n 129.6
cliques (2) n 129.6
cliquish (1) adj 105.4
cloak (4) n 027.1
cloakroom (1) n 009.6
cloaks (1) n 027.1
clobber (2) n/v 047.6
clobblers (1) n 123.8
clock (25) n/adj 004.3
~ shelf (1) n 008.4
~ tinker (1) n 088.9
clocks (2) n 012.2
clockwise (1) adv 085.2
clod (22) n/adj 124.7
~ buster (3) n 021.7
~ busters (1) n 021.7
~ crusher (1) n 006.1
~ flesh (1) n 078.2
~ harrow (1) n 021.7
~ masher (2) n 021.7
clodhopper (6) n 069.9
clodhoppers (5) n 123.7
clods (9) n 123.8
clogging (2) n 083.1
cloggy (1) adj 029.6
clogs (9) n 123.8
clomb (5) v 096.3
cloo(x3) (1) interj 038.5
cloom (1) v 096.3
clos (1) n F 016.5
close (915) v/adj 083.2
~ bag (1) n 019.6
~ body coat (1) n 027.1
~ brother (1) n 129.4
~ -built (1) adj 073.1

~ -casket funeral (1) n 079.2
~ friend (9) n 129.4
~ friends (2) n 129.6
~ -in porch (1) n 010.8
~ -minded (5) adj 074.8
~ off (2) v 052.5
~ pen (2) n 015.4
~ -toed shoes (1) n 123.8
~ -up pen (1) n 015.6
~ up (1) v 024.7
~ wire (1) n 016.3
close[B-w] (1) adv 039.6
close[V-p] (6) v 083.2
close[V-r] (3) v 083.2
close[V-t] (3) v 102.6
closed (47) v/adj 102.6
~ in (1) v 123.8
~ -in back porch (1) n 010.9
~ -in front porch (1) n 007A.5
~ -in porch (1) n 010.9
~ -in shoe (1) n 123.8
~ out (1) v 083.2
~ over (1) v 102.6
~ shoe (1) n 123.8
closefisted (3) adj 073.5
closer (19) adj/adv 011.3
closers (1) n 009.5
closes (44) v 083.2
closest (14) adj 064.6
closet (1256) n/adj 009.6
~ -like (1) adj 009.6
~ queen (3) n 124.2
~ space (2) n 009.6
closet[N-i] (1) n 009.6
closets (281) n 009.6
closewad (1) n 073.5
closing (8) v/adj 011.1
~ time (1) n 083.2
~ up (1) v 016.1
cloth (691) n/adj 018.4
~ bag (49) n 019.6
~ bags (37) n 019.6
~ curtain (1) n 009.5
~ poke (2) n 019.6
~ pouches (1) n 028.2
~ sack (64) n 019.6
~ sack[N-i] (1) n 019.6
~ sacks (47) n 019.6
~ sample (1) n 026.2
~ top (1) n 096.7

~ torch (1) n 024.3
cloth[N-i] (1) n 019.6
clothes (1609) n/adj 025.1
  ~ bag (35) n 123.7
  ~ bags (6) n 123.7
  ~ basket (224) n 020.1
  ~ bas(ket) (1) n 020.1
  ~ baskets (6) n 020.1
  ~ bin (5) n 020.1
  ~ boilers (1) n 020.1
  ~ box (2) n 020.1
  ~ brush (8) n 022.2
  ~ bucket (1) n 020.1
  ~ cabinet (2) n 009.7
  ~ case (1) n 123.7
  ~ chest (9) n 009.7
  ~ cleaners (1) n 010.6
  ~ closet (135) n 009.6
  ~ closets (17) n 009.6
  ~ container (1) n 123.7
  ~ cupboard (1) n 009.6
  ~ drawer (1) n 009.2
  ~ hamper (79) n 020.1
  ~ hanger (5) n 009.7
  ~ hangers (1) n 009.7
  ~ locker (1) n 009.6
  ~ moth (4) n 060A.2
  ~ moths (2) n 060A.2
  ~ pot (2) n 017.6
  ~ pots (1) n 017.6
  ~ rack (14) n 009.7
  ~ racks (1) n 009.6
  ~ rod (2) n 009.6
  ~ room (2) n 009.6
  ~ sacks (1) n 020.1
  ~ shelf (10) n 009.2
  ~ shelves (4) n 009.6
  ~ wardrobe (1) n 009.6
  ~ washing (1) n 010.6
clothesline (2) n 020.1
clothespin (3) n 026.5
clothespins (6) n 026.5
clothespress (28) n 009.7
clothespresser (1) n 009.7
clothespresses (3) n 009.7
clothing (26) n/adj 025.1
  ~ bag (3) n 123.7
  ~ bags (2) n 123.7
  ~ room (1) n 009.6
cloths (19) n 018.5
clotted cream (1) n 048.5
cloud (124) n/v/adj 005.3
  ~ buster (4) n 006.1
  ~ busters (1) n 006.1

~ cover (1) n 005.3
~ covering (1) n 005.3
~ up (9) v 005.6
Cloud Creek (1) TN 030.5
cloud[N-i] (13) n 005.3
cloudburst (177) n 006.1
cloudburst[N-i] (1) n 006.1
cloudburster (1) n 006.1
cloudbust (2) n 006.1
clouded (10) v 057.9
  ~ up (9) v 005.6
cloudier (1) adj 005.6
clouding (55) v 005.6
  ~ over (1) v 005.6
  ~ up (54) v 005.6
cloudless (8) adj 005.4
  ~ day (5) n 005.4
clouds (800) n/v 005.3
cloudy (476) adj 005.5
  ~ day (190) n 005.5
  ~ days (2) n 005.5
  ~ -looking (1) adj 005.6
  ~ -looking day (1) n 005.5
  ~ norther (1) n 006.4
  ~ sky (1) n 005.5
  ~ weather (5) n 005.5
cloudying (2) v 005.5
  ~ up (1) v 005.6
clout (24) n 115.3
Cloutierville (1) LA 087.8
cloven hoof (1) n 034.7
clover (18) n/adj 041.4
  ~ hay (2) n 014.7
  ~ hulls (1) n 042.1
  ~ land (1) n 029.5
  ~ pomace (1) n 042.2
  ~ sack (1) n 019.6
Cloverdale (8) AL 105.2
  ~ Road (1) 031.6
cloverleaf (4) n 107.4
clovers (3) n 015.9
cloves (1) n 082.8
clown (5) n 125.6
Clown City (1) 105.2
clownish (1) adj 080.6
club (164) n/adj 121.7
  ~ bush (1) n 061.9
  ~ cab (1) n 109.1
  ~ chair (3) n 008.8
  ~ coupe (3) n 109.1
  ~ coupes (1) n 109.1

~ due[N-i] (2) n 094.8
~ dues (11) n 094.8
~ fees (1) n 094.8
~ money (1) n 094.8
~ parties (1) n 130.7
~ ring (1) n 123.1
~ sandwich (6) n 121.7
~ sandwiches (1) n 121.7
~ steak (6) n 121.1
~ steaks (2) n 121.1
Club (17) 104.6
clubber (1) n 053.4
clubbing (1) n 065.5
clubfoot (1) n 072.6
clubs (30) n 113.2
clubwoman (1) n 080.7
cluck (31) n/v 038.1
  ~ at (1) v 038.1
  ~ like (1) v 038.5
  ~ to (12) v 038.1
  ~ t(o) (1) v 038.1
clucker (2) n 036.7
clucking (10) n/v/adj 036.7
  ~ hen (2) n 036.7
  ~ noise (1) n 038.5
  ~ noises (1) n 038.5
  ~ sounds (1) n 038.1
cluck(x2) (1) interj 038.5
cluck(x4) (1) interj 038.5
clueca (2) n S 036.7
clum (144) v 096.3
  ~ out (1) v 096.3
  ~ up (9) v 096.3
clummed (4) v 096.3
  ~ up (1) v 096.3
clump (6) n 061.6
clumps (2) n 014.8
clumpy (1) adj 029.9
clumsy (497) adj 073.3
  ~ foot (1) n 073.3
Clumsy Claude (1) 073.3
clunch down (1) v 096.4
clung to (1) v 054.3
clunker (2) n 123.1
cluster (10) n/adj 061.6
  ~ curls (1) n 123.9
  ~ maple (1) n 061.6
  ~ onions (1) n 055.7
clust(er) of beads (1) n 028.4
clusters (2) n 123.1
clutch (23) n/adj 110.6
  ~ bag (2) n 028.2

~ purse (1) n 028.2
~ seed peach (1) n 054.3
Clyde Fant Parkway (2) 106.4
Clyo (1) GA 087.2
CME Methodist (1) 089.1
CNA building (1) n 108.5
CNB building (1) n 108.5
co (101) interj/prefix 037.8
  ~ -ah (1) interj 037.5
  ~ -ak (1) interj 037.5
  ~ -ank (1) interj 037.5
  ~ -ank co-ant (1) interj 037.5
  ~ -ank(x2) (1) interj 037.5
  ~ -antsy (1) interj 037.5
  ~ -antsy(x2) (1) interj 037.5
  ~ -atch(x3) (1) interj 037.5
  ~ -ay (1) interj 037.5
  ~ -ay(x2) (1) interj 037.5
  ~ -ay(x3) (2) interj 037.5
  ~ -Betty(x2) (1) interj 037.5
  ~ -dan(x2) (1) interj 038.4
  ~ -ed (7) n 068.7
  ~ -ed fraternity (1) n 080.6
  ~ -eds (3) n 068.7
  ~ -eh (2) interj 037.5
  ~ -eh(x2) (1) interj 037.5
  ~ -ench (2) interj 037.5
  ~ -ench(x2) (4) interj 037.5
  ~ -et(x3) (1) interj 037.5
  ~ -inch (5) interj 037.5
  ~ -inch coey (1) interj 037.5
  ~ -inch(x2) (4) interj 037.5
  ~ -ip(x2) (1) interj 037.5
  ~ -it (2) interj 037.5
  ~ -it(x2) (2) interj 037.5

˜ -it(x3) (1) interj 037.5

˜ -it(x4) (1) interj 037.5

˜ -op (5) n 119.3

˜ -ops (2) n 116.2

˜ -pig(x2) (2) interj 038.3

˜ -sheep(x2) (1) interj 038.4

˜ -sheepy(x2) (1) interj 038.4

˜ -sheepy(x3) (1) interj 038.4

˜ sook (1) interj 037.5

˜ sook co (1) interj 037.5

˜ sooky (1) interj 037.6

˜ -up (3) interj 037.5

˜ -up(x2) (1) interj 037.8

˜ -up(x3) (1) interj 037.5

˜ -workers (1) n 052.6

co(x2) (6) interj 037.8

co(x3) (6) interj 037.8

Co-op (1) 081.8

coach (13) n 109.2

coaches (1) n 095.7

coachwhip (28) n/adj 084.8

˜ look (1) n 075.8

coachwhips (6) n 080.8

Coahoma (3) MS 087.5

˜ County (1) MS 087.4

Coahulla Creek (1) GA 030.7

coal (1357) n/adj 024.2

˜ -and-wood stove (1) n 088.7

˜ basket (3) n 023.1

˜ bin (45) n 023.1

˜ bins (1) n 023.1

˜ -black nigger wench (1) n 069.3

˜ box (15) n 023.1

˜ bucket (240) n 023.1

˜ -buck(et) box (1) n 023.1

˜ buckets (18) n 023.1

˜ burner (1) n 118.4

˜ -burning chimley (1) n 008.1

˜ -burning stove (1) n 008.3

˜ camps (1) n 013.9

˜ chute (2) n 023.1

˜ chutes (1) n 080.7

˜ container (1) n 023.1

˜ dust (1) n 023.1

˜ furnace (3) n 118.4

˜ furnaces (1) n 118.5

˜ grates (1) n 008.3

˜ hamper (2) n 023.1

˜ hauler (1) n 023.1

˜ heater (2) n 118.4

˜ heaters (1) n 118.4

˜ hod (18) n 023.1

˜ hods (2) n 023.1

˜ hopper (1) n 023.1

˜ house (16) n 011.7

˜ houses (1) n 011.7

˜ iron (3) n 010.6

˜ kiln (1) n 089.8

˜ kilns (2) n 023.2

˜ oil (584) n 024.2

˜ -oil bottle (2) n 024.3

˜ -oil burner (1) n 024.2

˜ -oil can (1) n 024.2

˜ -oil cat (2) n 024.2

˜ -oil cob (1) n 008.6

˜ -oil icebox (1) n 024.2

˜ -oil irons (1) n 024.2

˜ -oil johnny (1) n 050.9

˜ -oil jug (1) n 024.2

˜ -oil lamp (33) n 024.2

˜ -oil lamps (24) n 024.2

˜ -oil lantern (3) n 024.3

˜ -oil lanterns (1) n 024.2

˜ -oil light (2) n 024.3

˜ -oil lights (1) n 024.2

˜ -oil stove (5) n 118.4

˜ -oil torch (1) n 024.3

˜ pail (5) n 023.1

˜ pan (1) n 023.1

˜ pot (2) n 023.1

˜ rack (1) n 023.1

˜ room (2) n 014.2

˜ sack (1) n 019.7

˜ schooner (1) n 084.9

˜ scoop (1) n 023.1

˜ scoops (1) n 023.1

˜ scooter (1) n 023.1

˜ scuttle (170) n 023.1

˜ scut(tle) (1) n 023.1

˜ scuttles (9) n 023.1

˜ shed (2) n 011.7

˜ sheds (2) n 011.7

˜ shovel (1) n 023.1

˜ shuttle (17) n 023.1

˜ soot (1) n 008.7

˜ -stoked furnace (1) n 118.4

˜ stove (13) n 008.7

˜ stoves (3) n 118.4

˜ tar (7) n 031.6

˜ thing (1) n 023.1

˜ truck (1) n 109.7

˜ tub (1) n 023.1

˜ vase (1) n 023.1

˜ yard (1) n 080.7

Coal Hill (2) TN 030.8

coal[N-i] (2) n 052.1

coalosene (1) n 024.2

coals (18) n 023.1

coarse (17) adj 076.4

˜ -grain sand (1) n 029.8

˜ greens (1) n 055A.5

˜ grits (3) n 050.6

˜ hominy (1) n 050.6

˜ soil (1) n 029.8

coarser (2) adj 050.6

coast (21) n 029.5

˜ -guard protection (1) n 024.9

˜ -guard station (1) n 070.6

Coast (43) 030.9

coast[N-i] (2) n 016.7

coastal (7) adj 015.9

˜ Bermuda grass (1) n 014.9

˜ canal (1) n 030.2

˜ plain (2) n 029.4

˜ prairie (2) n 029.5

Coastal (2) 078.8

˜ (E)lectric (1) 065.9

coaster (10) n/adj 083.1

˜ wagon (1) n 084.8

Coaster (1) 106.3

coastline (3) n 086.5

coastlining people (1) n 069.5

coastwise (1) adv 080.6

coat (1062) n/adj 027.1

˜ bags (1) n 123.7

˜ hanger (1) n 027.1

˜ pocket (2) n 027.1

˜ -style shirt (1) n 089.8

˜ suit (1) n 027.7

Coat (1) 030.7

coat[N-i] (11) n 043.6

coated (5) v/adj 122.3

˜ with (2) v 007.6

coating (5) n 054.8

coatracks (2) n 009.7

coats (253) n 027.1

cob (296) n/adj 020.4

˜ corns (1) n 056.2

˜ pipes (1) n 088.7

˜ stopper (1) n 020.4

Cob (4) 056.3

cobalt blue (1) adj 080.7

Cobb (7) GA 087.3

˜ County (2) GA 087.8

˜ Memorial Hospital (1) 084.5

cobble (5) n/adj 031.6

˜ set (2) n 020.9

cobbled (1) v 095.8

cobbler (748) n/adj 048.3

˜ pie (60) n 048.3

˜ pies (17) n 048.3

co(bbler) (1) n 048.3

cobblers (73) n 048.3

cobbles up (1) v 067.8

cobblestone (18) n/adj 031.8

˜ fence (1) n 016.6

˜ street (1) n 031.7

˜ wall (1) n 016.7

cobblestones (6) n 031.6

Cobbs Creek (1) GA 030.8

Cobbtown (2) GA 086.5

cobia (1) n 089.8

Cobman Creek (1) AL 030.6

cobra (6) n 080.7

cobras (1) n 080.9

cobs (9) n 056.4

cobweb (219) n 061.3

cobweb[N-i] (1) n 061.3

cobwebs (209) n 061.3

Coca (22) 121.8

˜ -Cola (22) 121.8

˜ -Cola bottles (1) n 017.7

˜ -Cola people (1) n 058.6

~ -Cola route (1) n
   066.8
~ -Colas (1) 080.8
Co(ca) (34) 121.8
   ~ -Cola (30) 121.8
   ~ -Cola bottle (2) n
     024.3
   ~ -Cola Company (1)
     108.5
   ~ -Colas (4) 066.8
cocaine (87) n 114.2
cochere (5) n F 081.8
cocheres (1) n F 098.6
cochon (6) n F 035.5
   ~ de lait (1) n F 035.5
   ~ -de-lait festivals (1) n
     035.5
   ~ garde (1) n F 035.3
cochons (2) n F 015.4
Cochran (4) GA 087.6
cock (15) n/adj 039.7
   ~ fence (1) n 126.1
   ~ fish (1) n 059.9
   ~ hound (1) n 124.5
   ~ loft (2) n 009.8
   ~ robin (1) n 098.8
Cocke (1) TN 087.2
cocker (2) adj 033.3
   ~ spaniel (1) n 033.3
   ~ Spanish (1) n 070.6
cockeyed (4) adj/adv
   085.2
   ~ -looking (1) adj
     115.9
cocking (2) v 014.8
cocklebur (16) n/adj
   015.9
   ~ weeds (1) n 015.9
Cocklebur (1) AR 030.7
cockleburras (1) n 015.9
cockleburs (99) n 015.9
cockleshells (1) n 130.5
Cockney (3) 127.8
cockpit (1) n 080.9
cockroach (4) n 060A.1
cockroaches (2) n 060A.2
cocks (3) n 014.8
cocksman (5) n 124.7
cocksucker (4) n 092.6
cocksuckers (1) n 039.7
cocksure (3) adj 074.8
cocktail (55) n/adj 130.7
   ~ fork (1) n 017.8
   ~ glass (1) n 048.9
   ~ glasses (1) n 048.9

~ onion (1) n 055.7
~ parties (3) n 130.7
~ party (1) n 130.7
~ ring (2) n 123.1
~ rings (1) n 123.1
~ tomato (2) n 055.3
~ tomatoes (7) n 055.3
cocktails (1) n 024.3
cocky (3) adj 125.6
coco (24) n/adj 015.9
   ~ grass (17) n 015.9
cocoa (2) n/adj 078.4
   ~ quinine (1) n 078.4
Cocoa (2) FL 087.6
   ~ Beach (1) FL 087.1
cocodrie (2) n F 030.7
Cocodrie (3) LA 030.7
   ~ Bayou (1) LA 030.7
coconut (23) n/adj 122.3
   ~ cake (2) n 045.2
   ~ cakes (1) n 044.4
   ~ doughnuts (1) n
     122.4
   ~ macaroon (1) n 122.2
   ~ macaroons (1) n
     122.8
   ~ palm (1) n 081.8
   ~ palm trees (1) n
     061.8
   ~ tree (2) n 061.8
   ~ trees (7) n 061.8
Coconut Grove (15) FL
   087.3
coconuts (2) n 054.5
cocoon (1) n 066.8
cocozelle (1) n 056.6
cod (4) n/adj 059.9
   ~ -liver oil (2) n 078.3
Cod (5) 087.4
coda (1) n 041.2
coddle (3) v 046.2
coddled (11) v/adj 046.2
   ~ egg (1) n 046.2
   ~ eggs (3) n 046.2
coddling (1) v 046.2
code (1) n 085.7
Code (3) 088.7
   ~ A Three One (1)
     088.7
codeine (4) n 114.2
Coden (2) AL 086.5
codfish (3) n 059.9
codger (5) n 074.1
Cods (1) 118.9
coey (12) interj 037.5

~ co (1) interj 037.5
~ -cow(x2) (2) interj
   037.6
coey(x2) (5) interj 037.5
coey(x3) (8) interj 037.5
   ~ hee hoo (1) interj
     037.5
coey(x4) (2) interj 037.5
Coffadeliah (1) MS 087.4
coffee (1839) n/adj 048.8
   ~ au lait (1) n F 032.4
   ~ bean (1) n 055A.6
   ~ black (2) n 032.3
   ~ boiler (1) n 048.8
   ~ bread (2) n 044.4
   ~ break (2) n 048.6
   ~ cake (100) n 122.1
   ~ cakes (13) n 044.4
   ~ -colored (1) adj
     048.8
   ~ cream (1) n 048.8
   ~ cup (3) n 048.8
   ~ doughnuts (1) n
     122.7
   ~ grinder (3) n 081.9
   ~ grinders (1) n 088.8
   ~ grounds (3) n 048.8
   ~ maker (1) n 048.8
   ~ milk (2) n 032.4
   ~ mill (12) n 048.8
   ~ mills (1) n 048.8
   ~ percolator (2) n
     048.8
   ~ plain (2) n 032.3
   ~ ring (2) n 122.1
   ~ rings (1) n 122.1
   ~ roll (1) n 122.2
   ~ rolls (7) n 088.7
   ~ sack (1) n 019.7
   ~ sacks (1) n 019.7
   ~ shop (2) n 048.8
   ~ spoon (2) n 017.8
   ~ straight (2) n 032.3
   ~ table (19) n 048.8
   ~ tables (3) n 008.9
   ~ time (2) n 048.8
   ~ toper (1) n 080.7
   ~ worm (1) n 060.5
cof(fee) (1) n 048.8
Coffee (16) AL GA 048.8
   ~ Bayou (1) LA 030.7
   ~ County (7) AL GA
     TN 087.4
   ~ Crossing (1) LA
     087.9

~ Stretch (1) LA 087.9
coffeehouse (2) n 080.6
coffeepot (41) n/adj 017.6
   ~ preacher (1) n 067.8
coffeepots (4) n 048.8
coffees (2) n 048.8
Coffeeville (3) MS 087.4
coffeeweed (12) n 015.9
coffeeweeds (8) n 015.9
coffin (583) n/adj 079.1
   ~ bone (1) n 084.8
   ~ box (4) n 079.1
   ~ car (1) n 117.5
   ~ nail (1) n 117.7
   ~ nails (7) n 057.3
   ~ tacks (2) n 117.7
cof(fin) (1) n 079.1
coffin[N-i] (1) n 016.8
coffins (73) n 079.1
cogger (1) n 080.6
cohabitating (1) v 081.7
cohorts (2) n 129.6
cohosh (1) n 061.4
Cohutta (1) GA 087.2
coiffures (1) n 123.9
coil (3) n/v 050.8
   ~ up (1) v 070.8
coiled up (1) v 070.7
coin (209) n/adj 114.5
   ~ bag (3) n 028.2
   ~ case (2) n 028.2
   ~ laundries (2) n 116.5
   ~ laundry (9) n 116.5
   ~ of the realm (1) n
     114.5
   ~ -op (1) n 116.5
   ~ -operated launderette
     (1) n 116.5
   ~ -operated Laun-
     dromat (1) n
     116.5
   ~ -operated laundry (4)
     n 116.5
   ~ -operated self-service
     laundry (1) n 116.5
   ~ pouch (2) n 028.2
   ~ purse (169) n 028.2
   ~ purses (6) n 028.2
coincidence (1) n 065.8
coins (14) n 114.5
coke (31) n/adj 114.2
   ~ freak (1) n 114.3
   ~ heads (1) n 114.3
   ~ -sniffing set (1) n
     114.3

Coke (112) 121.7
~ fiend (1) n 088.7
~ machine (1) n 121.8
~ syrup (1) n 121.8
Cokes (14) 065.8
Cokle Spur (1) 080.6
cola (11) n/adj 121.8
~ drink (1) n 121.8
Cola (53) 095.7
colander (1) n 048.2
Colas (6) 080.8
Colbert (6) GA 087.1
~ County (4) AL 087.1
colchas (1) n S 029.2
cold (1629) n/adj 076.3
~ biscuit (1) n 044.4
~ -blooded (1) adj 033.3
~ cash money (1) n 090.8
~ chisels (1) n 020.8
~ day (5) n 007.4
~ days (1) n 091.7
~ drink (12) n 121.8
~ drinks (10) n 121.8
~ flesh (1) n 078.2
~ foot (1) n 082.1
~ -footed (1) adj 072.6
~ front (4) n 112.3
~ fronts (1) n 006.4
~ -greased (1) v 023.7
~ hard cash (1) n 114.5
~ hours (1) n 080.6
~ house (1) n 015.5
~ lunch (1) n 050.1
~ -meat fork (1) n 017.9
~ mix (1) n 031.6
~ morning (2) n 007.4
~ -natured land (2) n 075.8
~ night (3) n 007.4
~ nights (1) n 090.4
~ -packing (1) v 080.8
~ sandwich (1) n 050.3
~ shoulder (4) n 082.1
~ -shoulder treatment (1) n 129.8
~ snacks (1) n 050.1
~ snap (7) n 007.5
~ soap (1) n 096.7
~ spell (22) n 007.5
~ tune (1) n 130.8
~ -water corn bread (2) n 044.6

~ -water spring (1) n 030.7
~ wave (1) n 005.6
~ waves (1) n 007.5
~ weather (20) n 007.4
~ well (1) n 015.5
~ winters (1) n 091.7
Cold (6) 030.7
~ Creek (3) TN 030.7
~ Spring (2) GA 087.7
~ Springs (1) TN 030.7
colder (9) adj 007.4
coldest (1) adj 053.6
coldovers (1) n 050.1
colds (6) n 076.3
Coldwater (15) AL MS 087.1
~ Bottom (1) MS 029.4
~ Creek (4) AL FL GA MS 030.7
~ River (5) MS 030.7
Cole (2) 131.4
~ planter (1) n 075.9
Coleman (11) AL GA 087.5
~ Creek (1) AR 030.7
~ lantern (2) n 024.2
~ lanterns (1) n 024.3
~ yams (1) n 055.5
Colemans Store (1) 087.3
Coles Creek (5) MS 030.7
Coleto (4) TX 030.7
~ Creek (3) TX 030.7
Colet(o) (4) TX 030.7
~ Creek (1) TX 030.7
Coletoville (3) TX 087.2
~ area (1) TX 087.2
Coley's ass (1) n 091.8
Colfax (3) LA 087.7
colic (61) n 080.1
~ -catching den (1) n 093.7
coliseum (8) n 106.4
Coliseum (7) 106.3
~ Park (1) 105.4
colitis (3) n 079.6
collaborated (1) v 052.5
collapse (1) v 025.3
collar (63) n/adj 038.6
~ box (3) n 081.8
~ pad (1) n 038.6
collarbone (2) n 072.4
collard (179) n/adj 055A.5
~ cabbage (1) n 055A.1

~ green (5) n 114.5
~ green[N-i] (5) n 055A.5
~ greens (115) n 055A.5
~ leaf (1) n 061.4
~ leaves (2) n 055A.5
~ patch (2) n 016.1
~ plant (1) n 096.7
~ sallet (1) n 055A.5
~ stems (1) n 055A.5
collard[N-i] (5) n 055A.5
collards (250) n/adj 055A.5
~ greens (1) n 055A.5
collars (10) n 038.6
collateral (1) n 114.5
collation (1) n 082.4
collect (4) n/v 101.4
~ all (1) n 010.3
collect[V-r] (1) v 074.4
collected (2) v/adj 075.3
collection (3) n 001A.3
collector (19) n/adj 115.2
~ street (1) n 107.7
collect(or) (1) n 116.8
collector's bag (1) n 116.8
collectors (12) n 115.2
college (1200) n/adj 083.6
~ -age students (1) n 068.7
~ -bound students (1) n 068.7
~ boys (2) n 068.7
~ cheese (1) n 048.1
~ co-ed (1) n 068.7
~ courses (1) n 083.6
~ degree (2) n 083.5
~ -educated (3) adj 083.6
~ education (8) n 083.6
~ girls (1) n 083.6
~ graduate (6) n 083.6
~ graduates (5) n 083.6
~ Joe (1) n 068.7
~ kid (1) n 068.7
~ kids (2) n 083.6
~ library (1) n 084.1
~ life (1) n 083.6
~ man (1) n 083.6
~ pupil (1) n 068.7
~ student (36) n 068.7
~ students (1) n 068.7
~ teacher (2) n 083.6

~ work (3) n 083.6
College (52) 083.6
~ Grove (1) TN 087.3
~ Hill (5) MS 083.6
~ Hills (1) 105.8
~ Homes (1) 105.5
~ Park (8) AL GA 087.6
~ Station (2) AR 087.4
~ Street (1) 107.6
colleges (16) n 083.6
collegian (2) n 068.7
collegiate (1) n 068.7
Collegiate (1) 055A.9
collie (11) n/adj 033.2
~ dog (4) n 033.3
Collier (6) 107.7
~ Drive (1) 107.7
~ Heights (4) 105.4
~ Road (1) 107.7
collies (1) n 033.2
Collindale Canal (1) LA 030.7
Collins (8) GA MS 087.5
~ Avenue (1) 107.6
~ Bridge (1) 107.5
~ Highway (1) 107.6
Collinwood (1) TN 087.3
collision (1) n 065.9
colloquial (6) adj 065.8
~ expression (1) n 131.3
colloquialism (4) n 065.8
colloquialisms (4) n 131.2
colloquially (1) adv 065.8
colmillos (1) n S 035.7
Colombian (20) 114.1
~ Gold (5) 119.6
~ Red (2) 119.6
~ smoke (1) n 114.1
Colomokee (2) GA 088.7
colonel (590) n 068.4
Colonel (261) 068.4
~ Cullman's dream (1) n 068.4
~ Sanders (214) 068.4
~ Sand(ers) (1) 068.4
~ Sanders' chicken shop (1) n 068.4
~ somebody (1) n 068.4
colonel's car (1) n 023.3
colonels (12) n 068.4
Colonels (1) 068.4
Colonial (22) 107.6

~ Drive (1) 107.6
~ home (1) n 007A.2
~ homes (1) n 118.9
~ houses (1) n 118.9
~ Manor (1) 106.1
~ Penn(sylvania) (1) 087.5
~ style (3) n 118.8
~ -type houses (1) n 014.1
colony (3) n 069.3
Colony (5) 080.8
~ Park (1) 106.1
~ Square (1) 106.4
color (76) n/adj 069.3
~ -blind (1) adj 025.2
~ crayon (1) n 081.8
~ difference (1) n 025.4
~ doctor (1) n 069.3
~ folk (1) n 069.3
~ folks (3) n 069.3
~ man (1) n 069.3
~ people (5) n 069.3
~ peoples (1) n 069.3
~ sample (1) n 028.2
~ town (1) n 105.1
~ woman (1) n 069.3
~ women (1) n 069.3
Colorado (58) 086.5
~ County (1) TX 087.3
~ grass (1) n 015.9
~ Kool-Aid (1) 121.9
~ potatoes (1) n 055.5
~ Rattlesnake (1) 056.9
~ River (5) TX 086.9
~ Springs (2) CO 087.8
colored (1000) n/adj 069.3
~ areas (1) n 106.6
~ baby (1) n 069.3
~ Baptist church (1) n 069.3
~ beans (2) n 055A.4
~ boy (18) n 069.3
~ boys (12) n 069.3
~ butter bean (1) n 055A.3
~ butter beans (3) n 055A.3
~ children (1) n 069.3
~ church (5) n 069.3
~ churches (1) n 089.2
~ college (1) n 069.3
~ community (1) n 042.5

~ custodian (1) n 069.3
~ customers (1) n 069.3
~ darky (1) n 069.3
~ doctor (3) n 069.3
~ dude (1) n 069.3
~ ex-principal (1) n 069.3
~ expression (1) n 007.3
~ families (2) n 069.3
~ family (2) n 069.3
~ fellow (22) n 069.3
~ fellow's hair (1) n 069.3
~ fellows (2) n 069.3
~ folk (7) n 069.3
~ -folk ways (1) n 065.3
~ folks (65) n 069.3
~ -folks' molasses (1) n 051.2
~ friends (2) n 069.3
~ gal (1) n 069.3
~ gentleman (1) n 069.3
~ girl (13) n 069.3
~ girls (1) n 064.9
~ grammar school (2) n 069.3
~ grocery stores (1) n 105.6
~ guy (3) n 069.3
~ help (6) n 069.3
~ high school (1) n 083.8
~ houses (3) n 014.1
~ kids (1) n 069.3
~ lady (13) n 069.3
~ maid (1) n 069.3
~ mammy (1) n 069.3
~ man (75) n 069.3
~ mans (1) n 041.9
~ men (5) n 069.3
~ nigger (1) n 069.3
~ parade (1) n 069.3
~ part (1) n 105.5
~ people (289) n 069.3
~ peoples (5) n 069.3
~ person (40) n 069.3
~ picture (1) n 069.3
~ pine (1) n 061.9
~ preacher (1) n 069.3
~ race (11) n 069.3
~ school (2) n 069.3
~ section (5) n 069.3

~ servant (1) n 069.3
~ -spotted limas (1) n 055A.3
~ stevedores (1) n 069.3
~ store (1) n 069.3
~ student (1) n 069.3
~ teacher (1) n 069.3
~ teachers (2) n 067.6
~ town (4) n 106.3
~ trade (1) n 069.3
~ trash (1) n 069.3
~ woman (32) n 069.3
~ women (7) n 065.2
Colored Only station (1) n 069.3
coloreds (25) n 069.3
colorful (2) adj 052.7
coloring (1) v 084.8
colorless (1) adj 072.9
colors (10) n 123.6
Colquitt (13) GA 087.6
~ County (1) GA 087.7
colt (157) n/adj 034.2
~ horse (2) n 034.2
Colt (6) AR 087.1
~ forty-five (3) n 113.1
colt(x2) (1) interj 037.8
colter (1) n 021.6
colters (1) n 021.6
coltish (1) adj 073.3
colts (26) n 034.1
Columbia (70) AL AR FL GA LA MO MS SC TN 087.6
~ County (4) AR FL GA 087.7
~ Mutual Tower (1) 108.5
~ River (1) AL 030.7
~ weed (1) n 114.1
Columbi(a) (6) FL SC TN 087.7
Columbiana (1) AL 087.3
Columbias (1) 054.8
Columbus (639) AL GA MS NC OH 087.7
~ Bayou (1) FL 030.7
~ Iron Works (1) 087.7
~ Road (1) 087.7
~ Street (1) 087.7
Colum(bus) (2) AL MS 087.7
column (17) n/adj 110.7

~ -mounted shift (1) n 110.7
~ shift (3) n 110.7
Column (2) 129.6
~ of Hell (1) 129.6
~ [P-0] Fire (1) 129.6
columns (11) n 066.9
Colyell (3) 030.7
Com-Pak (1) 116.2
Comal (3) TX 030.7
~ County (1) TX 087.2
~ Creek (1) TX 088.7
Comanche (8) TX 107.7
~ County (1) TX 087.1
~ Crossing (1) TX 087.1
~ Park (1) 106.5
Comanches (1) 080.8
comas (1) n 088.7
comb (69) n/v/adj 011.5
comb[V-t] (1) v 026.1
combat boots (3) n 129.9
combeille (1) n F 081.9
combination (11) n/adj 033.3
~ dog (2) n 033.3
~ pills (1) n 078.5
~ salad (1) n 055A.5
~ sandwich (2) n 121.7
~ stock (1) n 021.6
combine (45) n/v 041.7
combined (12) v 042.1
combiner (3) n 042.1
combines (6) n 042.1
combing (3) v 022.2
combining (1) v 042.1
combs (2) n 104.6
come (3580) n/v/interj 102.4
~ across (4) v 102.4
~ after (2) v 095.8
~ along (5) n/v 081.9
~ along with (1) v 032.4
~ and get (1) v 033.2
~ and get it (2) v 049.2
~ around (5) v 038.2
~ (a)round (1) v 040.9
~ -as-you-are party (1) n 130.7
~ -baa(x2) (1) interj 038.4
~ back (681) v 093.1
~ back from (1) v 047.8

~ back here (12) v 033.2
~ back here now (1) v 033.2
~ back in the pen (1) v 033.9
~ -Bessie(x3) (1) interj 037.8
~ by (37) v 102.4
~ by chance (2) n 065.7
~ -Daisy(x2) (1) interj 037.4
~ down (14) v 102.4
~ down with (5) v 076.1
~ fresh (24) v 033.9
~ from (107) v 102.4
~ here (94) v 037.8
~ -here(x2) (3) interj 038.5
~ in (172) v 033.9
~ in foal (1) v 033.9
~ in fresh (8) v 033.9
~ in here (1) v 037.8
~ in the pen (8) v 033.9
~ in with a calf (1) v 033.9
~ in with her calf (1) v 033.9
~ into (1) v 095.9
~ into the pen (1) v 033.9
~ off (6) v 102.4
~ on (254) v 038.1
~ -on (2) n 094.5
~ on and eat (1) v 049.2
~ on back (2) v 038.2
~ -on-calf(x2) (1) interj 037.6
~ on calfy (1) interj 037.6
~ -on-calfy(x2) (2) interj 037.6
~ on here (8) v 037.5
~ -on-here(x2) (1) interj 037.6
~ on in (13) v 102.4
~ (o)n in (1) v 077.8
~ -on-John(x2) (1) interj 037.5
~ on now (1) v 037.8
~ on over (3) v 102.4

~ -on-pig(x2) (1) interj 038.3
~ on up (3) v 037.6
~ on [J-0] get it (1) v 038.5
~ -on(x2) (12) interj 038.1
~ -on(x3) (8) interj 037.5
~ -ons (1) n 093.6
~ out (45) v 102.4
~ out from (1) v 101.9
~ out of (4) v 069.9
~ out with (1) v 052.6
~ out [P-0] (1) v 030.6
~ over (22) v 093.1
~ over there (1) v 037.7
~ through (8) v 102.4
~ to (20) v 038.4
~ to barn here (1) interj 037.5
~ to Mamma (1) v 037.6
~ to me (1) v 033.2
~ to pail (1) v 033.9
~ to the pail (1) v 033.9
~ to the pen (4) v 033.9
~ to town (2) v 080.6
~ up (212) v 003.3
~ -up crop (1) n 041.5
~ up here (6) v 038.1
~ up now (1) v 038.1
~ up there (2) v 038.1
~ up with (1) v 102.4
~ -up(x2) (7) interj 038.1
~ with (7) v 102.4
~ [P-0] the pail (1) v 033.9
COME room (1) n 007A.7
come(x2) (1) interj 033.2
come(x4) (1) interj 037.5
come[V-p] (66) v 102.4
~ back (1) v 025.6
~ by (1) v 013.6
~ in (1) v 013.6
~ on (1) v 089.7
~ out (3) v 013.8
~ out from (1) v 042.5
~ over (1) v 043.5
~ through (1) v 052.8

~ to (3) v 102.4
~ under (2) v 053.4
~ up (9) v 102.4
come[V-r] (880) v 102.4
~ across (2) v 053.2
~ (a)cross (1) v 001A.4
~ along (16) v 102.4
~ around (1) v 102.4
~ (a)round (2) v 102.4
~ at (2) v 075.5
~ back (46) v 102.4
~ back to (1) v 102.4
~ by (4) v 013.8
~ down (17) v 102.4
~ down with (3) v 076.3
~ for (1) v 102.4
~ fresh (1) v 033.9
~ from (35) v 102.4
~ (fro)m (1) v 096.8
~ in (55) v 102.4
~ in contact with (1) v 032.6
~ into (1) v 102.4
~ off (3) v 102.4
~ off of (1) v 034.4
~ offen (4) v 034.4
~ on (15) v 102.4
~ on back (1) v 097.1
~ on in (1) v 102.4
~ on out (1) v 102.4
~ out (23) v 102.4
~ out of (5) v 102.4
~ over (12) v 102.4
~ through (4) v 102.4
~ to (30) v 102.4
~ up (73) v 003.3
~ [P-0] (4) v 102.4
come[V-s] on (1) v 092.5
comed (2) v 102.4
~ up (1) v 102.4
comedor (1) n S 007A.5
comedown (1) n 089.9
comely (1) adj 125.4
Comer (2) AL 087.7
~ building (1) n 108.5
comes (192) v 102.4
~ (a)cross (1) v 097.8
~ around (1) v 052.8
~ back (6) v 102.4
~ by (1) v 065.3
~ down (7) v 082.6
~ down in buckets (1) v 006.1

~ from (8) v 102.4
~ in (19) v 033.9
~ in fresh (1) v 033.9
~ off (4) v 102.4
~ off of (1) v 052.6
~ out (8) v 102.4
~ out from (1) v 095.2
~ out of (2) v 006.4
~ out [P-0] (1) v 053.2
~ over (1) v 102.4
~ through (1) v 102.4
~ to (5) v 102.4
~ under (1) v 052.5
~ up (17) v 005.6
~ up with (1) v 053.4
Comet (3) 070.7
comeuppance (2) n 088.7
comfort (142) n/v/adj 029.1
~ quilt (1) n 029.1
~ station (3) n 107.2
Comfort (13) 088.9
comfortable (8) adj 070.9
~ day (1) n 005.4
comforter (90) n 029.1
comforters (8) n 029.1
comforts (40) n 029.1
comfy (1) adj 091.7
comical (5) adj 073.3
comics (1) n 099.2
coming (564) v 102.4
~ along (6) n/v 033.9
~ (a)long (6) v 065.6
~ apart (1) v 102.4
~ at (1) v 032.5
~ back (50) v 093.1
~ back up (1) v 095.8
~ by (2) v 032.5
~ down (3) v 007.3
~ down on (1) v 080.6
~ down with (6) v 076.3
~ for (1) v 099.1
~ fresh (2) v 033.9
~ from (37) v 102.4
~ -home party (1) n 130.7
~ in (23) v 094.7
~ in fresh (3) v 033.9
~ into (1) v 102.2
~ off (2) v 096.7
~ on (9) v 080.6
~ out (11) v 092.7
~ out of (8) v 006.1

~ -out party (1) n 130.7
~ out [P-0] (4) v 006.4
~ over (9) v 042.4
~ through (4) n/v 130.5
~ to (18) v 043.5
~ to calf (1) v 033.9
~ to the pail (2) v 033.9
~ to the pen (2) v 033.9
~ toward (7) v 032.5
~ towards (5) v 032.5
~ up (104) v 065.6
~ with (11) v 032.4
Coming 'Round the Mountain (1) 031.1
comings (1) n 025.2
cominos (2) n S 080.8
Comitas (1) TX 087.1
Comite (5) LA 030.7
~ River (3) LA 030.7
command (2) n/adj 033.2
~ cars (1) n 023.6
commander (4) n 068.5
commanders (1) n 130.5
commandments (2) n 065.8
comme ca (1) adj F 065.1
commence (42) v 083.3
~ to (6) v 096.2
commence[V-p] (1) v 102.2
commence[V-r] (45) v 102.2
~ to (13) v 102.2
commence[V-t] (1) v 102.2
commenced (45) v 102.2
~ to (4) v 102.2
commences (7) v 083.3
commencing (1) v 102.2
comment (1) adv F 092.6
Commerce (19) GA MS TX 087.3
~ Square (1) 108.9
~ Street (5) 105.2
commercial (18) adj 045.1
~ bread (4) n 045.1
~ crab fisherman (1) n 084.9
~ crop (1) n 041.3
~ dairy (1) n 015.5
~ fertilizer (1) n 029.3

~ light bread (1) n 045.1
~ peanuts (1) n 054.7
~ side (1) n 105.4
~ traveler (1) n 080.7
~ -type dairy (1) n 015.5
~ worms (1) n 060.5
Commercial (3) 107.7
~ Avenue (2) 107.7
~ Boulevard (1) 107.6
commercially (1) adv 102.8
Commie (2) 127.5
~ hippie bomb throwers (1) n 129.3
Commies (3) 127.5
commissaries (1) n 064.5
commissary (12) n/adj 080.6
~ store (1) n 090.8
commission (1) n 032.3
commissioner (3) n 057.4
commissioners (7) n 080.6
committed (4) v 044.2
~ suicide (1) v 082.2
committee (5) n 027.2
commode (35) n 118.3
commodes (2) n 012.1
commodities (1) n 048.4
(com)modities (1) n 093.2
Commodores (1) 055A.4
common (1072) adj 073.6
~ law (1) n 065.7
~ -looking (5) adj 073.6
~ man (25) n 073.6
~ men (1) n 073.6
~ -old (6) adj 033.3
~ property (1) n 073.8
~ rain (1) n 006.6
~ road (1) n 031.7
~ school (4) n 073.6
~ -school education (1) n 083.5
~ sense (13) n 073.6
~ snapper (1) n 060.6
~ touch (1) n 073.6
~ -type person (2) n 073.6
com(mon) (1) adj 073.6
Common (1) 107.6
commoner (2) n 069.7
commonly (3) adv 073.6

commons (2) n 085.1
Commonwealth (3) 083.6
commotion (3) n 012.3
commune (3) n/adj 119.3
~ farm (1) n 088.8
communicant (1) n 089.2
communicating (1) v 013.5
communication (3) n 039.8
Communism (1) 073.6
Communist (5) 127.5
communistic (1) adj 127.5
Communists (5) 127.5
communities (4) n 088.3
community (93) n/adj 119.3
~ barbecue (1) n 093.6
~ cemetery (1) n 078.8
~ church (1) n 089.2
~ college (1) n 083.6
~ dance (1) n 083.1
~ dirt road (1) n 031.7
~ gardens (1) n 050.5
~ handbooks (1) n 025.7
~ house (1) n 014.1
~ road (10) n 031.7
~ roads (3) n 031.7
~ social (1) n 083.1
~ store (1) n 081.8
~ telephone line (1) n 081.9
~ trails (1) n 031.7
~ -wise (1) adv 080.6
commuter trains (1) n 109.9
commutes (1) v 102.4
como (1) adv S 052.4
Como (2) MS 088.7
~ Park (1) 085.1
comoda (1) n S 009.2
compact (19) n/v/adj 109.1
~ car (7) n 109.1
~ cars (2) n 109.2
~ garbage disposal (1) n 117.1
~ pickups (1) n 109.7
compactor (91) n 117.1
compact(or) (2) n 117.1
compac(tor) (2) n 117.1
compactors (13) n 117.1
compacts (2) n 109.1
companies (9) n 015.5

companion (4) n 063.1
company (97) n/adj 007A.8
~ bedroom (3) n 007A.4
~ bread (1) n 045.1
~ commander (1) n 068.3
~ dishes (2) n 017.1
~ food (1) n 075.8
~ parlor (1) n 007.8
~ room (16) n 007.8
~ rooms (1) n 007.8
Company (12) 069.2
~ Row (1) 104.5
company's room (1) n 007A.2
comparable (1) adj 065.8
compared to (2) v 073.6
comparison (3) n 040.7
compartment (148) n 110.2
compart(ment) (1) n 110.2
compartments (2) n 065.8
compass (2) n 081.8
compatible (4) adj 073.2
Compere (1) F 064.1
compete with (1) v 052.5
competent (2) adj 125.4
competition (2) n 039.6
complacent (1) adj 073.2
complain (3) v 057.7
complaints (3) n 092.5
complected (2) adj 080.7
complete (3) v/adj 073.4
completed (1) v 042.5
completely (16) adv 028.9
complex (38) n 119.2
complexes (8) n 119.2
complexion (2) n 095.9
complicated (2) adj 042.5
compliment (3) n 066.8
composed of (1) v 053.4
composer (1) n 117.3
composing room (1) n 099.9
composition (3) n/adj 066.9
~ material (1) n 009.5
~ roof (1) n 011.4
compost (7) n/adj 015.3
~ heap (1) n 029.3
~ pile (1) n 052.8

composted rice hulls (1) n 050.7
composure (1) n 075.3
compound (2) n/adj 080.9
~ lard (1) n 023.7
comprehend (1) v 057.7
compress (1) n 088.7
compressor (9) n 117.1
compressors (11) n 117.1
Compton Township (1) AR 087.5
compulsory (1) adj 040.7
computer (2) n 125.5
con (5) v/adj/prep S 073.5
~ man (1) n 073.5
~ men (2) n 113.6
Conant (1) 107.7
Conasauga (4) GA 030.7
~ Creek (1) TN 030.7
~ River (1) GA 030.7
conbrick (1) n 031.6
concave (1) adj 011.6
conceited (7) adj 074.8
conceived (1) v 065.1
concentration camp (1) n 089.9
concentric circles (1) n 065.8
Concepcion (3) 106.4
~ Park (1) 106.4
concept (1) n 024.7
Conception (1) 106.6
concern (10) n 088.8
concerned (55) v/adj 074.2
concert (2) adj 084.4
~ hall (1) n 084.4
~ music (1) n 130.9
concertin(a) (1) n 130.9
concertizing (1) v 088.8
concerts (1) n 102.1
Concession (1) 088.7
conch (7) n/adj 080.9
~ shell (1) n 060.8
~ shells (1) n 060.1
Conch (7) 080.6
~ accent (1) n 104.7
~ flitters (1) n 044.8
~ houses (1) n 088.7
conchs (4) n 060.1
Conchs (5) 069.7
concocted (1) v 065.9

Concord (4) AR FL GA 087.6
~ Spring (1) AR 030.7
Concordia (2) LA 087.4
Concordi(a) (2) LA 087.4
concrete (617) n/adj 031.7
~ baths (1) n 015.4
~ benches (1) n 031.6
~ block (2) n 031.6
~ blocks (3) n 031.6
~ bridge (1) n 031.6
~ cellar (1) n 031.6
~ dividers (1) n 107.4
~ doorsteps (1) n 010.7
~ driveway (1) n 031.8
~ fence (5) n 016.6
~ floor (5) n 031.6
~ floors (2) n 031.6
~ highway (1) n 031.6
~ highways (2) n 031.6
~ house (1) n 010.3
~ men (1) n 031.6
~ outfit (1) n 031.4
~ pave (1) n 031.6
~ pavement (1) n 031.6
~ porch (1) n 007A.2
~ post[N-i] (1) n 016.5
~ road (35) n 031.6
~ roads (25) n 031.6
~ sidewalk (1) n 031.9
~ slab (2) n 010.8
~ slab road (1) n 031.6
~ stack (1) n 008.1
~ stone (1) n 032.1
~ street (1) n 031.6
~ streets (1) n 031.8
~ tanks (1) n 031.6
~ vault (4) n 079.1
~ walk (1) n 031.9
~ walks (1) n 031.9
~ walkway (2) n 031.6
~ wall (4) n 016.6
~ walls (1) n 016.6
concrete[V-r] (1) v 031.6
concreted (8) v/adj 031.6
~ floor (1) n 031.6
~ up (1) v 031.6
concretement (1) n 031.7
concussion (1) n 065.8
condemned (3) adj 108.7
~ area (1) n 108.7
condensed (1) v 125.7
condiments (3) n 051.7

condition (24) n/adj 118.5
conditioned (2) adj 065.9
conditioner (12) n 118.5
conditioners (7) n 118.5
conditioning (29) n 118.5
conditions (3) n 088.7
condo (11) n 119.3
condominia (1) n 119.3
condominium (82) n 119.3
condomini(um) (1) n 119.3
(condo)minium (2) n 082.9
condominiums (59) n 119.3
condos (4) n 119.3
Condos for Christ (1) 119.3
conduct[V-p] (1) v 053.4
conducted (2) v 079.3
conductor (3) n 081.8
cone (3) n 019.3
Cone Avenue (2) 107.6
Conecuh (12) AL 030.7
~ County (1) AL 087.5
~ River (8) AL 030.7
Coney Island (1) 066.9
confection (2) n/adj 065.8
~ sugar (1) n 065.8
confectionaries (1) n 088.8
confectionary (2) n/adj 116.2
~ sugar (1) n 088.7
Confederacy (11) 085.8
Confederama (1) 106.8
Confederate (104) 085.8
~ Army (5) 085.8
~ bill (1) n 001.8
~ cemetery (1) n 078.8
~ dish (1) n 080.6
~ doctor (1) n 085.8
~ general (1) n 068.3
~ Park (3) 106.4
~ rose (1) n 061.9
~ soldier (1) n 085.8
~ veteran (1) n 085.8
~ War (70) 085.8
(Con)federate (3) 085.8
~ War (2) 085.8
Confederates (5) 085.8
confess up (1) v 080.7

confidant (1) n 129.5
confidence (6) n 066.8
confident (1) adj 085.6
confidente (1) n S 009.2
confine[V-t] (3) v 065.1
confined (11) v/adj 065.1
confinement (1) n 065.1
confirmation name (1) n 012.2
confirmed (1) v 089.2
Conflict (2) 085.8
~ between the North and the South (1) 085.8
confliction (1) n 080.6
confluence (1) n 030.6
confused (3) v/adj 090.4
confusing (1) adj 091.7
confusion (2) n 129.7
Cong (1) 126.4
congealed (1) adj 047.6
congenial (29) adj 073.2
congested urban areas (1) n 106.3
congestion (2) n 079.6
congestive chill (1) n 079.6
conglomerate (1) n 070.9
conglomeration (3) n 088.7
Congo (21) 056.9
~ cookie (1) n 069.3
~ Gray (1) 056.9
Congoes (6) 056.9
Congolean (1) 056.9
congregating (1) v 119.8
congregation (4) n 082.8
Congregational Methodist (1) 089.2
Congregationalist (1) 089.1
Congress (6) 085.6
~ Square building (1) n 108.6
conical (1) adj 065.8
conjunction (2) n 107.4
conjured (1) v 080.7
conjuring bags (1) n 080.6
conked (10) v/adj 123.9
~ out (8) v 078.6
~ over (1) v 078.6
connect (2) v 057.6
connected (2) v 043.9
connecter (1) n 031.8

Connecticut (11) 086.1
~ Cornfield (1) 056.5
connection (5) n 115.3
connection[N-i] (1) n 115.3
connections (24) n 115.3
Connector (1) 107.5
Connerly (2) 030.7
~ Bayou (1) AR 030.7
~ Bay(ou) (1) AR 030.7
conniption (1) n 089.8
conniptions (1) n 089.8
connotate (1) v 096.8
connotates (1) v 065.8
connotation (1) n 080.6
connu (3) adj F 061.8
~ tree (1) n 061.9
Conroe (1) TX 087.5
conscience (1) n 012.2
conscientious (2) adj 073.8
conscious (2) adj 074.1
consciously (1) adv 081.1
conscripted (1) v 080.7
consecrated (1) adj 070.6
consent (1) n 039.8
conservation (1) n 093.5
conservative (6) n 085.7
conservatives (2) n 129.2
conservator (1) n 066.4
conservatory (1) n 089.5
conserve (1) v 058.1
conserves (2) n 051.6
conserving (1) v 066.8
consider (3) v 058.7
considerable (3) adj 005.8
considerate (1) adj 073.2
consideration (1) n 114.5
considered (3) v 053.5
considering (2) v 079.4
consistency (2) n 070.6
consistes (1) v 052.5
consolation prize (1) n 080.6
console (7) n 110.2
(con)solidate (1) v 070.7
consolidated (2) v/adj 057.8
~ schools (1) n 088.7
consorting (1) n 081.4
constable (4) n 068.6
~ on patrol (1) n 112.5
constantly (1) adv 093.9
constitution (2) n 072.9

constrictor (1) n 080.8
constrictors (2) n 091.9
construction (8) n/adj 108.7
~ site (2) n 108.7
consumption (8) n 088.9
contact (4) n/v 102.4
contacted (1) v 076.3
contacts (4) n 115.3
container (22) n/adj 017.4
~ bed (1) n 080.9
containers (9) n 117.3
contaminated (1) adj 046.9
Conte (1) 070.6
contemporaries (2) n 129.6
contemporary (7) n/adj 130.8
~ classic (1) n 130.8
~ clothing (1) n 123.6
~ rock (1) n 130.8
Contender (2) 055.5
~ bunch green snap bean (1) n 055A.4
Contenders (1) 055A.4
contented (1) adj 073.2
contentious (3) adj 074.8
contest (2) n 131.1
contestes (1) n 016.7
continental (2) n 088.8
Continental (4) 109.4
~ Divide (1) 081.8
continual rain (1) n 006.6
continue (2) v 070.3
continuous (1) adj 066.8
contour (3) n/adj 030.2
~ farming (1) n 080.6
~ plowing (1) n 021.6
contoured (1) v 070.9
Contraband Bayou (1) LA 030.7
contract (2) n/adj 032.4
~ work (1) n 102.8
contracted (8) v 076.1
contractions (1) n 074.4
contractor (1) n 117.1
contracts (1) n 085.6
contraption (2) n 104.6
contrarious (1) adj 074.8
contrary (43) adj 074.8
contrar(y) (1) adj 074.8
contra(ry) (1) adj 074.8
contribution (1) n 094.8

contributors (1) n 030.6
control (14) n/v/adj 025.4
controlled (2) v/adj 113.6
~ alcoholic (1) n 113.6
controlling (2) v/adj 025.2
~ factor (1) n 025.2
controls (2) n/v 110.8
convalescent (3) adj 072.9
convalescing (1) v 072.9
convene (1) v 083.4
convenience (53) n/adj 116.3
~ centers (1) n 116.2
~ store (32) n 116.2
~ stores (15) n 116.2
convenient (6) adj 116.2
~ corner store (1) n 116.2
~ food market (1) n 116.2
~ food store (1) n 116.2
convenientest (1) adj 064.7
Convention (6) 106.4
~ Center (3) 106.4
~ Hall (1) 106.6
conventional shift (1) n 110.7
conventions (1) n 083.1
conversation (5) n 065.9
conversing (2) v 013.5
convert (1) v 089.2
converted (19) v 089.2
~ to (1) v 089.2
convertible (50) n/adj 109.3
~ sofa (1) n 009.1
Convertible (1) 009.1
convertibles (9) n 109.1
converts (1) v 089.2
conveyor belt (1) n 022.3
convict (2) adj 044.5
~ bread (1) n 044.5
~ town (1) n 080.6
convicts (1) n 074.4
convincer (1) n 022.3
convulsion (1) n 079.9
convulsions (1) n 070.9
Conway (11) AR 087.6
~ River (1) FL 030.7
Conyers (6) GA 087.2
coo (50) interj 037.5

~ -sheep(x2) (10) interj 038.4
~ -sheep(x3) (5) interj 038.4
~ -sheepy(x2) (6) interj 038.4
~ -sheepy(x3) (4) interj 038.4
~ -sheepy(x4) (1) interj 038.4
coo(x2) (4) interj 038.4
cooey (5) interj 037.5
~ coey(x3) hee hoo (1) interj 037.5
cooey(x2) (1) interj 038.3
cooey(x3) (2) interj 037.5
cooey(x4) (1) interj 037.5
cooing (1) v 057.4
cook (167) n/v/adj 048.8
~ apron (2) n 026.4
~ bread (1) n 044.7
~ case (1) n 048.1
~ cheese (3) n 048.1
~ food (1) n 010.1
~ grease (1) n 023.7
~ in (2) v 017.6
~ kitchen (1) n 009.9
~ meat (1) n 080.8
~ off (1) v 095.8
~ on (1) v 074.4
~ out (2) v 102.9
~ over (1) v 097.7
~ pot (9) n 017.6
~ shack (1) n 009.9
~ shed (1) n 009.9
~ spoon (1) n 017.8
~ table (6) n 009.8
~ up (2) v 048.4
~ with (5) v 032.4
~ wood (2) n 008.9
Cook (10) 086.2
~ Branch (1) AL 030.7
~ Convention Center (1) 106.4
~ County (6) GA IL 087.9
cook[V-r] (4) v 053.4
~ for (1) v 053.4
~ to (1) v 012.9
cook[V-t] (1) v 057.9
cookbook (1) n 053.3
Cooke County (1) TX 087.5
cooked (91) v/adj 078.6
~ at (2) v 012.5

~ cane juice (1) n 051.3
~ cream (1) n 090.8
~ down (1) v 099.7
~ eggs (1) n 046.2
~ ham (1) n 121.3
~ in (2) v 026.1
~ kraut (1) n 055A.2
~ on (3) v 025.8
~ out (2) v 092.7
~ over (7) v 050.1
~ -over (1) adj 050.1
~ -over food (3) n 050.1
~ over[N-i] (1) n 050.1
~ salami (1) n 099.9
~ turnips (1) n 055A.5
~ up (2) v 055.9
cooker (11) n 017.7
cookers (2) n 081.9
Cookeville (3) TN 087.3
cookhouse (13) n 009.9
cookhouses (1) n 009.9
cookie (3) n 045.2
cookies (81) n 122.2
cooking (111) n/v/adj 010.4
~ apron (1) n 026.4
~ bar (1) n 008.3
~ deal (1) n 053.5
~ grease (1) n 023.7
~ hen (1) n 121.5
~ house (1) n 009.9
~ kettle (1) n 017.6
~ knife (1) n 104.3
~ knives (1) n 104.3
~ meat (4) n 046.3
~ oil (17) n 024.1
~ pot (5) n 017.6
~ pots (3) n 017.6
~ rod (1) n 008.2
~ room (1) n 009.9
~ soda (2) n 045.5
~ stove (1) n 008.5
~ syrup (1) n 051.3
~ tomatoes (1) n 055.3
~ utensils (1) n 017.5
~ vessels (2) n 088.7
~ with (1) v 032.4
~ wood (1) n 092.9
cookingest (1) adj 080.9
Cookman (1) 066.8
cookout (2) n 084.8
cookouts (2) n 130.8
cookroom (24) n 009.9

cookrooms (2) n 007A.1
cook's house (2) n 007A.9
Cook's fence (1) n 126.1
cooks (13) n/v 010.4
~ on (1) v 038.8
cookstove (36) n 008.5
cookstoves (3) n 088.9
Cooktown (2) LA 087.5
~ Road (1) 031.6
cookware (1) n 017.1
cool (603) n/v/adj 007.4
~ afternoon (1) n 005.4
~ day (2) n 007.4
~ down (16) v 075.4
~ drink (3) n 121.8
~ evening (1) n 005.4
~ fronts (1) n 006.4
~ -headed (1) adj 073.3
~ morning (4) n 007.4
~ night (1) n 007.4
~ off (16) v 075.3
~ snap (1) n 007.5
~ spell (5) n 007.4
~ studs (1) n 123.6
~ weather (2) n 007.4
cool[V-p] (1) v 013.6
cool[V-r] (1) v 049.3
cooled (3) v 082.1
~ him down (1) v 082.1
~ off (1) v 090.4
Cooleewahee (1) GA 030.7
cooler (58) n/adj 015.5
~ kit (1) n 018.7
coolers (9) n 015.5
coolie (1) n 126.5
cooling (15) n/adj 079.1
~ board (10) n 079.1
~ house (2) n 015.5
~ off (1) n 006.6
~ room (1) n 015.5
coolish (2) adj 007.4
coolly (1) adv 007.4
coolrator (1) n 066.9
cools (1) n 075.3
coolsome (1) adj 007.4
coon (78) n/adj 069.3
~ car (1) n 109.4
~ dog (11) n 033.1
~ dogs (12) n 033.3
~ -grease oil light (1) n 024.1
~ hounds (3) n 033.3

~ -hunted (1) v 088.8
~ hunting (2) n 033.1
~ neck (2) n 069.8
~ short (1) n 123.3
~ -tail rattler (1) n 080.9
Coon (6) 063.9
~ biscuit (1) n 044.4
~ Bottom (1) 029.4
~ Creek (1) TN 030.7
~ Shine Baby (1) 070.6
coonass (76) n/adj 069.9
~ ice cream (1) n 050.7
coonass[N-i] (1) n 084.8
coonasses (25) n 080.8
coonies (25) n 069.9
coon's age (4) n 090.6
coons (37) n 069.3
Coons (1) 063.9
coony (11) n 088.7
coonyass (2) n/adj 069.8
~ people (1) n 069.1
coop (861) n 036.8
Coop (1) 036.8
coop(x2) (4) interj 037.5
coop(x3) cup coop(x4) (1) interj 037.8
coop(x4) (2) interj 037.8
cooped up (3) v 036.8
cooper (408) n/adj 067.7
~ shop (1) n 067.7
Cooper (687) 067.7
~ Creek (3) TN 030.7
~ girl (1) n 067.7
~ Green Park (1) 106.6
~ River (1) GA 067.7
~ Road (8) 067.7
~ Street (1) 067.7
~ Tire (1) 067.7
cooperage (5) n/adj 067.7
~ business (1) n 065.8
~ company (2) n 067.7
cooperate (1) v 065.8
cooperative (7) adj 073.2
cooperat(ive) (1) adj 025.5
Cooper's (3) 067.7
~ Tire Shop (1) 067.7
coopers (9) n 067.7
Coopers (5) 067.7
Coopersmith (1) 067.7
Cooperstown (22) NY 067.7
Coopersville (1) TN 067.7
coops (124) n 036.8

Coops Creek (2) TN 030.7
coordinated (1) adj 073.3
coordinates (1) n 027.7
Coors distributing beer trucks (1) n 075.6
Coosa (28) AL GA 030.7
~ County (6) AL 087.7
~ River (14) AL GA 030.7
~ River Church (1) 087.3
(Coo)sada Ferry Road (1) 107.6
Coosawattee (1) GA 030.7
coot (1) n 080.7
Coot (2) 064.4
cootchie (1) n 083.1
cootchies (1) n 045.2
cooter (104) n/adj 060.7
~ cages (1) n 123.9
~ hole (1) n 080.8
~ hull (3) n 076.9
~ turtle (1) n 060.6
Cooter (2) MO 060.6
cooters (52) n 060.7
Cooters Point (3) LA 087.2
cootie(x2) (1) interj 038.3
cop (72) n/adj 112.5
~ car (9) n 111.7
~ cars (2) n 111.7
~ -out (2) n 115.6
~ shop (1) n 112.7
Copano (1) TX 087.8
Copenhagen (1) 086.9
Copiah (3) MS 087.9
~ County (2) MS 087.5
copied off of (1) v 075.6
copies (1) n 012.2
coping (4) n/adj 016.6
~ saw (1) n 020.8
~ saws (1) n 080.7
copped (8) v 100.2
~ out (1) v 083.4
copper (26) n/adj 112.5
~ band (1) n 089.8
~ -belly (4) n 093.9
~ -belly moccasin (1) n 081.9
~ bottom (1) n 080.8
~ cents (1) n 026.6
~ cork (1) n 020.4

~ kettle (3) n 017.6
~ pan (1) n 052.6
~ shell (1) n 022.4
~ skin (1) n 055.5
~ still (2) n 050.8
~ vaults (1) n 080.7
~ -wire (1) adj 016.3
copperhead (40) n/adj 101.7
  ~ adders (1) n 089.9
  ~ bream (1) n 059.9
  ~ moccasin (4) n 089.8
  ~ rattler (1) n 084.8
  ~ snakes (2) n 084.8
copperheads (30) n 080.7
Copperhill (2) TN 087.6
coppermouth (1) n 090.8
coppers (5) n 092.7
coppersmith (1) n 067.7
copping out (1) v 083.4
cops (73) n 112.5
  ~ and robbers (11) n 130.2
copse (1) n 061.6
copter (1) n 111.9
copters (1) n 111.9
copy (5) n 026.2
copying (1) v 065.3
coque (1) n F 054.8
coqueluche (1) n F 079.7
Coquille Bay (1) LA 030.7
coquina (9) n/adj 080.8
  ~ fences (2) n 016.6
  ~ rock (3) n 088.7
  ~ shell (1) n 031.6
corail (1) n F 015.3
coral (39) n/adj 084.9
  ~ fence (1) n 016.6
  ~ rock (2) n 029.8
  ~ snake (18) n 088.7
  ~ snakes (14) n 092.8
Coral (17) 105.7
  ~ Gables (15) FL 105.8
  ~ Way (1) 107.6
corcho (1) n S 020.4
Corcoran (1) AL 075.8
cord (63) n/adj 019.8
  ~ rack (1) n 022.1
  ~ stack (1) n 019.8
  ~ wood (1) n 008.6
Cord (2) AR 086.5
cord[N-i] (1) n 001A.2
corded (9) v/adj 009.3
  ~ bed (1) n 009.3

~ beds (1) n 084.8
~ bedstead (2) n 009.2
~ bedsteads (1) n 009.4
~ stuff (1) n 019.7
Cordele (15) GA 087.6
cordial (4) n/adj 073.2
cording (2) v 021.4
Cordova (1) AL 087.6
cords (11) n 027.4
corduroy (13) n/adj 031.6
  ~ land (1) n 029.8
  ~ pants (2) n 027.4
  ~ road (1) n 031.7
  ~ roads (3) n 031.7
  ~ suit (1) n 027.7
cordwood (9) n 008.5
core (967) n/v/adj 054.5
  ~ corruption (1) n 077.5
  ~ out (1) v 054.5
  ~ part (1) n 054.5
core(x2) (1) interj 037.5
cored stuff (1) n 077.5
cores (4) n 054.5
Corey (1) LA 087.4
Corf Avenue (1) 107.7
coring knives (1) n 104.4
Corinth (8) AR LA MS 087.4
  ~ Baptist (1) 089.1
cork (925) n/adj 020.4
  ~ concern (1) n 020.4
  ~ cork (1) n 020.4
  ~ leg (2) n 020.4
  ~ line (1) n 020.4
  ~ lining (1) n 020.4
  ~ shoe (1) n 123.8
  ~ stopper (84) n 020.4
  ~ stop(per) (1) n 020.4
  ~ stoppers (26) n 020.4
  ~ stopple (2) n 020.4
  ~ top (1) n 020.4
  ~ tree (1) n 061.9
Cork (3) 020.4
corked up (1) v 095.8
corker (1) n 080.9
corkers (3) n 059.9
corking (1) v 020.4
corks (45) n 020.4
corkscrew (11) n 020.4
corkscrews (2) n 020.4
corkwood (1) n 020.4
Cormo(rant) (1) 030.4
corn (4926) n/adj 056.2
  ~ bags (1) n 019.7

~ balls (1) n 044.6
~ barn (7) n 014.3
~ batter (1) n 044.5
~ beards (1) n 056.4
~ beef (2) n 121.2
~ -beef stew (1) n 084.9
~ beer (5) n 050.8
~ belt (1) n 081.8
~ bin (34) n 014.3
~ bins (9) n 014.3
~ bloom (1) n 056.3
~ box (1) n 001.4
~ bread (1245) n 044.5
~ -bread battercakes (3) n 044.6
~ -bread buns (1) n 044.6
~ -bread cake (1) n 044.7
~ -bread cakes (1) n 044.6
~ -bread dodgers (2) n 044.7
~ -bread dressing (5) n 044.6
~ -bread dumpling (3) n 044.7
~ -bread dumplings (10) n 044.7
~ -bread flapjacks (1) n 044.6
~ -bread flitter (1) n 044.7
~ -bread fritters (2) n 045.3
~ -bread griddle (1) n 017.5
~ -bread hoecake (1) n 044.6
~ -bread hotcakes (1) n 045.3
~ -bread mix (1) n 044.5
~ -bread muffin (3) n 044.6
~ -bread muffins (32) n 044.7
~ -bread mush (4) n 050.3
~ -bread pancakes (4) n 045.3
~ -bread patties (11) n 044.6

~ -bread patty (1) n 044.7
~ -bread pone (3) n 044.5
~ -bread pudding (3) n 050.3
~ -bread skillet (1) n 017.5
~ -bread skillets (1) n 017.5
~ -bread slapjack (1) n 044.6
~ -bread-stick pan (1) n 044.6
~ -bread sticks (16) n 044.7
~ breads (3) n 044.5
~ broom (2) n 010.5
~ brooms (2) n 010.5
~ buck (5) n 050.9
~ buns (1) n 044.8
~ cake (20) n 044.6
~ cakes (37) n 044.6
~ cover (1) n 080.7
~ crop (18) n 041.3
~ crops (2) n 041.3
~ cups (1) n 044.6
~ dodger (243) n 044.6
~ dodger bread (2) n 044.6
~ -dodger style (1) n 044.6
~ dodgers (121) n 044.6
~ dog (21) n 044.6
~ dogs (11) n 121.6
~ dumpling (6) n 044.6
~ dumplings (41) n 044.7
~ -fed hogs (1) n 035.5
~ -fed rabbit (1) n 121.6
~ flitter (4) n 045.3
~ flitters (6) n 045.3
~ fodder (2) n 014.7
~ fritter (1) n 044.7
~ fritters (41) n 044.6
~ gin (1) n 050.8
~ gran(ary) (1) n 014.4
~ griddles (1) n 017.5
~ grinder (1) n 019.8
~ grit (1) n 050.6
~ grits (4) n 050.6
~ gruel (1) n 050.3
~ hair (2) n 056.4

~ hash (1) n 047.4
~ hoecake (1) n 044.7
~ hoecakes (2) n 044.7
~ hominy (3) n 050.6
~ husk (5) n 056.1
~ -husk doll (1) n 101.5
~ huskes (1) n 044.6
~ husks (3) n 010.5
~ in the cob (2) n 056.2
~ in the ear (1) n 056.2
~ juice (1) n 050.8
~ knife (1) n 104.3
~ light bread (13) n 044.7
~ lightning (1) n 050.8
~ liquor (51) n 050.8
~ loaf (4) n 044.5
~ manger (1) n 014.3
~ mash (2) n 050.8
~ mill (6) n 080.7
~ muffin (12) n 044.6
~ muffins (106) n 044.6
~ mush (38) n 050.3
~ off the cob (4) n 056.2
~ oil (4) n 024.1
~ on the cob (239) n 056.2
~ on the cobs (1) n 056.2
~ on [D-0] cob (5) n 056.2
~ pancakes (1) n 045.3
~ patch (41) n 016.1
~ patches (2) n 016.1
~ patties (7) n 044.6
~ pile (1) n 041.7
~ piles (1) n 041.7
~ planter (2) n 021.6
~ planters (2) n 021.6
~ pokes (1) n 044.8
~ pone (179) n 044.7
~ pone bread (1) n 044.6
~ pones (38) n 044.6
~ pudding (9) n 050.3
~ puppies (1) n 044.6
~ roll (2) n 044.6
~ rolls (1) n 080.7
~ room (3) n 014.3
~ shed (15) n 014.3
~ sheller (9) n 014.3
~ shelters (1) n 014.3

~ shock (1) n 041.7
~ shocks (1) n 041.7
~ shorts (1) n 084.8
~ shuck (8) n 056.1
~ -shuck mop (1) n 018.9
~ shucking (4) n 056.1
~ shuckings (7) n 084.9
~ shucks (21) n 056.1
~ silk (68) n 056.4
~ silking (1) n 056.4
~ silks (20) n 056.4
~ snake (3) n 084.8
~ snakes (1) n 080.8
~ soup (1) n 050.3
~ squeezings (11) n 050.8
~ stall (1) n 014.3
~ stick (9) n 044.6
~ -stick pan (1) n 044.6
~ -stick pans (1) n 044.6
~ -stick type (1) n 044.6
~ stick[N-i] (1) n 044.6
~ sticks (140) n 044.7
~ sweet bread (1) n 044.6
~ syrup (22) n 051.3
~ tarpaulin (1) n 014.7
~ tassel (7) n 056.3
~ tassels (2) n 056.3
~ tortillas (3) n 044.6
~ weevils (1) n 088.8
~ whiskey (63) n 050.8
~ wienie (1) n 044.6
~ worms (1) n 060.5
~ [P-0] [D-0] cob (1) n 056.2
Corn (2) 044.7
~ Dodger meal (1) n 044.7
~ Silk (1) 056.4
cornballs (1) n 069.9
corncob (27) n/adj 020.5
~ mop (1) n 061.4
~ pipe (4) n 057.3
~ pipes (1) n 057.3
~ stoppers (1) n 020.4
corn(cob) stopper (1) n 020.4
corncobs (10) n 020.4
corncrib (339) n 014.3
corncribs (30) n 014.3

Cornelia (6) GA 087.4
corner (135) n/adj 011.6
~ board (1) n 011.2
~ cabinet (4) n 010.1
~ cupboard (3) n 010.1
~ drugstores (1) n 116.1
~ fence (1) n 016.4
~ groceries (1) n 116.2
~ grocery (3) n 116.2
~ grocery store (5) n 116.2
~ lot (1) n 016.1
~ market (2) n 116.2
~ neighborhood store (1) n 116.2
~ post (12) n 016.5
~ post[N-i] (1) n 016.5
~ postes (2) n 016.5
~ store (14) n 116.2
Corner (8) 086.9
cornered (488) adj/adv 085.2
corners (12) n 085.2
cornerstone (1) n 070.9
Cornersville (1) TN 070.7
cornerwise (2) adv 085.2
cornery (1) n 014.3
Corney (6) 030.7
~ Bottom (1) LA 029.4
cornfield (112) n/adj 016.1
~ bean (16) n 055A.4
~ beans (20) n 055A.3
~ niggers (1) n 069.3
~ peas (4) n 090.9
Cornfield (1) 056.5
cornfields (3) n 016.1
cornflakes (1) n 045.5
cornflower (2) n 056.3
cornhouse (18) n 014.3
cornhouses (1) n 014.3
cornice (2) n/adj 011.5
~ board (1) n 009.5
corniche (1) n F 008.4
Corning (1) AR 086.4
Cornish (15) 121.5
~ game hen (2) n 121.5
~ hen (5) n 121.5
~ hens (8) n 121.5
cornmeal (203) n/adj 044.5
~ balls (3) n 044.6
~ bread (7) n 044.5
~ cake (1) n 044.6

~ cakes (1) n 045.3
~ dodger (1) n 045.2
~ dumpling (3) n 044.6
~ dumpling[N-i] (1) n 044.8
~ dumplings (24) n 044.7
~ flitters (1) n 044.7
~ fritters (2) n 044.8
~ gravy (2) n 050.3
~ grits (1) n 050.6
~ gruel (2) n 050.3
~ mill (1) n 019.8
~ mix (1) n 044.7
~ muffin (1) n 044.6
~ muffins (15) n 044.8
~ mush (86) n 050.3
~ patties (2) n 044.6
~ pudding (3) n 047.4
~ solution (1) n 044.7
~ soup (3) n 050.3
~ sticks (1) n 044.6
cornmealy (1) adj 088.8
cornrow (12) n 123.9
cornrows (18) n 115.7
corns (3) n 077.7
cornsack (25) n 019.7
cornsacks (11) n 019.7
cornstalk (1) n 056.5
cornstalks (4) n 123.9
cornstarch (1) n 066.9
Cornwell (1) FL 087.9
corny (10) adj 121.6
~ dog (3) n 044.6
~ dogs (4) n 044.6
~ man (1) n 069.9
coroner (1) n 001A.1
corporal (2) n 068.3
corporals (1) n 068.4
Corporation (2) 030.9
corporations (1) n 013.8
corps (2) n 081.9
Corps (2) 068.9
~ of Engineers (1) 088.7
corpse (4) n 066.9
Corpus (42) TX 087.5
~ Bay (1) TX 030.7
~ Christi (26) TX 087.9
~ Christi Bay (1) TX 030.3
~ Christi Beach (2) 106.8
corral (107) n/adj 015.6
~ pen (1) n 015.3

corraller (1) n 025.2
corrals (15) n 015.2
correct (13) adj 025.6
correction (1) n 112.8
correctly (3) adv 100.3
correspond (1) v 066.8
corresponded (1) v 081.4
correspondence (1) n 066.8
corresponder (2) n 081.5
corridor (1) n 007A.5
Corrine (1) 107.7
corroded (1) v 047.5
corrupt (2) v/adj 080.1
corrupted (4) v 077.5
corruption (255) n 077.5
corrup(tion) (1) n 077.5
(cor)ruption (3) n 077.5
(cor)rup(tion) (1) n 077.5
corruptions (1) n 077.5
corset cover (1) n 093.7
Corsicana (6) TX 087.3
Cortez Street (1) 031.8
cortinas (1) n S 009.5
Coryell (1) TX 087.4
Cosby (8) TN 030.7
cosmetics (1) n 028.1
cosmopolitan city (1) n 131.1
cosmos (1) n 041.5
Cossack (1) 127.5
cost (285) n/v 094.6
cost[N-i] (2) n 094.6
cost[V-p] (643) v 094.6
~ to (1) v 094.6
costes (19) v 094.6
costing (4) v 094.6
costly (8) adj 094.6
costs (23) v 094.6
costume (11) n/adj 123.1
~ jewelry (4) n 123.1
~ party (3) n 130.7
~ ring (2) n 123.1
~ rings (1) n 123.1
costumes (2) n 066.8
cot (25) n 029.2
Cotaco Creek (1) AL 030.7
cotch (2) v 098.5
cotched (2) v 098.5
cote (3) n F 020.4
~ de mais (1) n F 020.4
coteau (1) n F 030.8

Coteau (1) 087.4
cotense (2) n S 019.6
cotillion (3) n 083.1
cotillions (1) n 083.1
cotonnier (1) n F 061.7
cots (2) n 064.5
cottage (585) n/adj 048.1
~ cheese (550) n 048.1
~ -fashion (1) adv 011.2
~ house (3) n 014.1
~ type (1) n 007A.1
~ -type house (1) n 118.9
cot(tage) (1) adj 048.1
Cottage Hill (3) 105.5
cottages (3) n 118.9
cotton (1180) n/adj 015.8
~ allotments (1) n 016.1
~ areas (1) n 084.9
~ bag (2) n 019.6
~ bag[N-i] (1) n 019.6
~ bagging (1) n 019.6
~ baggings (1) n 019.6
~ bags (8) n 019.6
~ bales (1) n 041.7
~ -ball tree (1) n 061.8
~ barns (1) n 014.2
~ basket (6) n 020.1
~ baskets (6) n 020.1
~ bin (1) n 014.5
~ broker (1) n 080.8
~ business (1) n 070.9
~ chopper (2) n 015.8
~ choppers (2) n 015.8
~ chopping (5) n 015.8
~ -chopping time (1) n 015.8
~ classer (2) n 070.8
~ cloth (2) n 019.6
~ -cloth sack (1) n 019.6
~ country (1) n 091.9
~ cribs (1) n 014.3
~ crop (18) n 041.3
~ crops (3) n 041.3
~ dishcloth (1) n 018.3
~ farm (1) n 015.8
~ farmer (2) n 015.8
~ farmers (1) n 025.7
~ farms (1) n 052.1
~ field (83) n 016.1
~ fields (13) n 016.1
~ gin (15) n 080.7

~ ginner (1) n 080.6
~ gins (1) n 025.2
~ house (30) n 014.3
~ houses (9) n 011.9
~ lane[N-i] (1) n 080.8
~ leaf (1) n 070.7
~ lint (1) n 070.8
~ -lisle stockings (1) n 088.8
~ mesh (1) n 019.7
~ mill (4) n 084.9
~ -mill people (2) n 080.6
~ -mill school (1) n 075.8
~ -mill village (1) n 080.8
~ mop (1) n 010.5
~ oak (1) n 061.9
~ oil (2) n 024.1
~ patch (89) n 016.1
~ -patch (1) adj 056.9
~ -patch watermelon (1) n 056.9
~ patches (6) n 016.1
~ pen (2) n 011.8
~ pens (1) n 014.4
~ pick sacks (1) n 019.7
~ picker (4) n 080.6
~ pickeries (1) n 092.8
~ pickers (4) n 081.9
~ picking (1) n 080.6
~ -picking (1) adj 075.2
~ -picking baskets (1) n 020.1
~ -picking hands (1) n 015.8
~ -picking nigger (1) n 069.3
~ -picking sack (3) n 019.6
~ -picking sacks (1) n 019.7
~ -picking thing (2) n 080.7
~ -picking time (2) n 015.8
~ pile (1) n 007A.2
~ pillow (1) n 028.8
~ planter (3) n 088.7
~ planters (4) n 021.6
~ plow (1) n 021.6
~ presses (1) n 092.8
~ rack (1) n 022.1

~ raiser (1) n 015.9
~ -raising days (1) n 080.6
~ room (1) n 014.5
~ sack (44) n 019.6
~ -sack ducking (1) n 019.6
~ sacks (22) n 019.7
~ scales (1) n 080.6
~ scraper (3) n 021.6
~ shed (1) n 010.3
~ squares (2) n 081.8
~ -storage houses (1) n 014.1
~ tick (1) n 029.1
~ tree (3) n 061.9
~ trees (1) n 061.8
~ trousers (1) n 027.4
~ wagon (1) n 080.6
~ wagons (1) n 080.8
~ warehouse (1) n 088.7
~ wharf (1) n 030.4
cot(ton) (4) n/adj 015.8
~ house (1) n 014.2
~ patch (1) n 016.1
Cotton (16) GA 087.5
~ Belt (1) 087.5
~ Bowl (1) 105.7
~ Creek (4) AL MS TX 030.7
~ Hill (3) GA 087.1
~ Lake (1) TN 030.7
~ Methodist (1) 089.1
Cottondale (1) FL 087.6
cottonfish (1) n 059.9
cottonmouth (46) n/adj 101.8
~ moccasin (18) n 084.8
~ moccasins (5) n 080.6
~ water moccasin (1) n 081.8
cottonmouths (6) n 080.9
Cottonport (1) LA 087.7
cottonseed (29) n/adj 069.9
~ bin (3) n 014.4
~ bins (1) n 014.2
~ house (7) n 014.4
~ hulls (2) n 080.9
~ meal (5) n 080.6
~ oil (1) n 024.1

~ -oil executive (1) n 080.6
cottonseed[N-i] (2) n 052.1
cottonseeds (1) n 014.4
cottontails (1) n 121.7
cottonwood (106) n/adj 061.8
~ tree (7) n 061.8
~ trees (8) n 061.8
Cottonwood (3) AL 087.4
~ Creek (1) TX 030.7
~ Point (1) AR 087.3
cottonwoods (8) n 061.8
cou (1) n F 093.6
couch (613) n/adj 009.1
~ fever (1) n 009.1
couch[N-i] (1) n 009.1
couches (53) n 009.1
cougar (3) n 093.5
cougars (1) n 059.5
cough (828) n/v/adj 076.5
~ drop (1) n 076.5
~ drops (1) n 076.5
~ medicine (4) n 076.5
~ syrup (3) n 061.4
~ syrups (1) n 051.3
~ up (2) v 076.5
coughed (9) v 076.5
coughing (84) v 076.5
coughs (8) n/v 076.5
coughy (1) adj 076.5
could (1001) v 058.6
~ might (1) v 058.7
couldn't (523) v 065.8
could've (13) v 058.6
coulee (19) n 030.6
Coulee (5) 030.7
~ Creek (1) LA 030.7
~ Croche (1) LA 030.7
~ Mine (2) LA 030.7
coulees (2) n 030.5
council (11) n/adj 085.5
~ meeting (2) n 070.8
councilman (6) n 069.1
councilmen (3) n 080.6
councilmens (1) n 081.8
counselor (2) n 066.4
count (23) n/v 057.6
Count (4) 064.4
~ Basie (1) 130.8
~ No-(Ac)count (1) 080.6
counted (4) v 042.5

counter (6) n/adj 019.2
~ spread (1) n 028.7
~ -top grill (1) n 116.4
counterclockwise (1) adv 085.2
counterpane (253) n 028.7
(counter)pane (1) n 028.7
counterpanes (64) n 028.7
counterpiece (2) n 028.7
counties (11) n 013.8
counting (3) v 098.4
countinghouse (1) n 092.7
countra (2) n 095.7
countries (6) n 042.3
countrified (13) adj 069.9
~ -looking (1) adj 069.9
country (1212) n/adj 130.8
~ accent (1) n 131.8
~ and western (9) n 130.8
~ (a)nd western (1) n 130.8
~ bacon (3) n 121.3
~ bastard (1) n 069.9
~ booger (1) n 069.9
~ boy (122) n 069.9
~ boy's overalls (1) n 027.4
~ boy's piston (1) n 099.6
~ boys (2) n 069.9
~ bum (1) n 069.9
~ bumpkin (29) n 069.9
~ -bumpkin type (1) n 125.1
~ bumpkins (2) n 069.9
~ bums (1) n 065.4
~ butter (1) n 080.6
~ Cadillac (1) n 023.3
~ cemetery (1) n 078.8
~ children (1) n 069.9
~ childrens (1) n 092.7
~ church (3) n 089.2
~ clod (1) n 069.9
~ club (3) n 088.8
~ -club area (1) n 106.1
~ clubs (1) n 113.9
~ codger (1) n 069.9
~ colored (1) n 069.3
~ come to town (2) n 069.9

~ cooking (1) n 081.8
~ coon (1) n 069.9
~ country (1) n 096.7
~ cousins (2) n 066.5
~ cracker (37) n 069.9
~ crackers (6) n 069.9
~ -cured (1) adj 046.3
~ -cured ham (2) n 046.5
~ -cured side bacon (1) n 046.5
~ dance (5) n 083.1
~ dances (3) n 083.1
~ dancing (1) n 083.1
~ dinner (1) n 013.9
~ dirt road (2) n 031.7
~ doctor (1) n 069.9
~ dude (10) n 069.9
~ dudes (2) n 069.9
~ eating (1) n 012.2
~ farmer (2) n 069.9
~ -farmhouse porch (1) n 010.8
~ fellow (11) n 069.9
~ fence (2) n 016.4
~ flat talk (1) n 084.8
~ fool (1) n 069.9
~ -fresh vegetables (1) n 050.4
~ -fried ham (1) n 121.3
~ gal (4) n 069.9
~ gentleman (1) n 069.9
~ girl (12) n 069.9
~ girls (1) n 069.9
~ grave (1) n 078.8
~ graveyard (3) n 078.8
~ -grown food (1) n 048.4
~ guy (13) n 069.9
~ ham (22) n 121.3
~ hams (1) n 121.3
~ heathen (1) n 069.9
~ hens (1) n 121.5
~ hick (83) n 069.9
~ hicks (15) n 069.9
~ highway (1) n 031.7
~ home (2) n 007A.6
~ homemade corn bread (1) n 044.5
~ homes (1) n 053.4
~ honky (1) n 069.9
~ hoodlum (3) n 069.9
~ hoosier (55) n 069.9

~ hoosiers (11) n 069.9
~ house (2) n 014.1
~ hunk (2) n 069.9
~ hunks (1) n 069.9
~ idiots (1) n 069.9
~ Ike (1) n 069.9
~ Ikes (1) n 069.9
~ jake (12) n 069.9
~ jakes (6) n 069.9
~ jinx (1) n 069.9
~ kettles (1) n 017.6
~ kid (1) n 069.9
~ lane (3) n 031.8
~ lard (1) n 019.3
~ lawyer (1) n 081.8
~ man (26) n 069.9
~ meat (1) n 046.5
~ men (1) n 069.9
~ molasses (1) n 051.2
~ motherfucker (1) n 069.9
~ music (26) n 130.9
~ Nick (1) n 069.9
~ nigger (2) n 069.3
~ Paddy (1) n 069.9
~ party (1) n 083.1
~ peck (1) n 069.9
~ people (66) n 069.9
~ peoples (1) n 069.9
~ person (10) n 069.9
~ pork (1) n 046.5
~ pork sausage (1) n 121A.5
~ preacher (3) n 096.9
~ rats (1) n 069.9
~ red-necks (1) n 069.9
~ rib eye (1) n 121.1
~ road (116) n 031.7
~ roads (30) n 031.7
~ rock (8) n 130.8
~ route (1) n 031.7
~ rubes (1) n 069.9
~ sager (2) n 069.7
~ sausage (3) n 121.6
~ school (2) n 088.8
~ -school education (1) n 083.5
~ schoolteacher (1) n 012.9
~ side road (1) n 031.8
~ side roads (1) n 031.7
~ singing (1) n 130.8
~ slick (2) n 069.9

~ smoked ham (1) n 121.6
~ soul (1) n 130.8
~ Southern (1) n 081.8
~ store (2) n 094.1
~ stores (1) n 116.2
~ style (2) n 121.5
~ -style cut (1) n 091.8
~ -style light bread (1) n 044.3
~ -style sausage (1) n 121.6
~ sucker (1) n 092.8
~ syrup (1) n 051.3
~ toilet (2) n 012.1
~ tramp (1) n 069.9
~ trash (3) n 069.7
~ -type talk (1) n 131.2
~ wolf (1) n 069.9
~ women (1) n 069.9
~ [J-0] western (5) n 130.8
~ [J-0] western music (1) n 130.8
Country (11) 106.1
~ Club (1) 106.1
~ Club Estates (1) 106.2
~ Estates (1) 075.8
~ Gentleman (1) 056.2
~ Music Hall of Fame (1) 106.4
countryfolk (9) n 069.9
countryfolks (37) n 069.9
countryman (41) n 069.9
countrymans (1) n 069.7
countrywoman (1) n 081.9
counts (1) v 013.7
county (851) n/adj 085.5
~ agent (1) n 085.5
~ assessor (1) n 085.5
~ chair (1) n 085.5
~ city (2) n 085.5
~ co-op board (1) n 085.5
~ commissioner (2) n 057.4
~ coroner (1) n 001A.1
~ court (2) n 085.5
~ courthouse (4) n 014.1
~ courthouse square (1) n 085.1
~ election (1) n 077.4

~ farm (1) n 080.6
~ farm road (1) n 031.7
~ government (1) n 013.9
~ grade (1) n 031.7
~ home (1) n 032.2
~ hospital (1) n 084.5
~ jail (17) n 112.8
~ judge (28) n 068.6
~ library (2) n 084.1
~ library board (1) n 084.1
~ line (1) n 085.5
~ -maintained road (1) n 031.7
~ -maintained roads (1) n 031.6
~ Mountie (3) n 112.5
~ Mounties (1) n 112.5
~ museum (1) n 106.4
~ nursing home (1) n 084.6
~ police (1) n 112.5
~ road (29) n 031.7
~ roads (17) n 031.7
~ seat (641) n 085.5
~ seat town (1) n 085.5
~ seats (8) n 085.5
~ site (9) n 085.5
~ square (3) n 085.1
~ town (2) n 085.5
~ water (1) n 048.9
~ workhouse (1) n 112.8
County (897) 085.5
~ Armaugh (1) 087.7
~ Cowboys (1) 119.8
~ Line Cemetery (1) 078.8
~ of Knox (1) 085.5
~ Seat (1) 085.5
Count(y) (1) 087.7
Coun(ty) (1) 087.4
coup d(e) main (1) n F 088.7
coupe (105) n/adj F 109.1
~ blanche (1) n F 037.3
~ convertible (1) n 109.1
Coupe (3) 109.7
~ de Ville (1) 109.2
~ Ridge (1) LA 087.3
Coupee (3) 087.5

coupes (12) n 109.1
couple (130) n 033.7
~ doub(le) long (1) adj 073.3
~ of (1) n 033.7
~ of mules (4) n 033.7
~ of ox[N-i] (1) n 033.7
~ of oxteam[N-i] (1) n 033.7
coupl(e) (2) n 003.8
couple[N-i] (1) n 052.7
coupled (1) v 082.2
couples (2) n 001.5
coupling (33) n/adj 018.7
~ pole (28) n 080.7
~ poles (1) n 021.8
~ tongue (3) n 020.8
coupon (1) n 081.9
coupons (3) n 070.9
cour (2) n F 015.6
Cour (1) 105.5
cour bois (1) n F 016.2
courage (1) n 012.2
course (86) n/adv 091.2
courses (4) n 083.6
coursing (1) v 088.8
court (86) n/v/adj 081.4
~ ball (1) n 130.4
~ -bouillon (1) n F 048.4
~ building (1) n 112.7
~ her (4) v 081.4
~ lawn (2) n 085.1
~ park (1) n 085.1
~ square (42) n 085.1
~ them (1) v 081.4
~ trials (1) n 065.8
Court (6) 106.8
~ Square Fountain (1) 106.7
~ Street (2) 107.6
court[V-r] (1) v 081.4
Courtableau (1) 030.3
courted (26) v 081.4
~ each other (1) v 081.4
~ her (1) v 081.4
~ him (1) v 081.4
~ in (1) v 081.4
courteous (4) adj 073.2
courter (1) n 081.5
courtesy (5) n/adj 095.7
~ bus (1) n 109.8
~ car (1) n 023.6

~ gift (2) n 095.7
courthouse (277) n/adj 085.1
~ area (1) n 085.1
~ greens (1) n 085.1
~ grounds (6) n 085.1
~ lawn (24) n 085.1
~ lawns (1) n 085.1
~ lot (1) n 085.1
~ property (1) n 085.1
~ square (88) n 085.1
~ square park (1) n 085.1
~ steps (1) n 010.7
~ yard (14) n 085.1
Courthouse (1) 085.1
courthouses (2) n 014.1
courtiers (1) n 123.6
courting (708) v/adj 081.4
~ a girl (2) v 081.4
~ age (1) n 081.4
~ along (1) v 081.4
~ couple (1) n 081.4
~ days (2) n 081.4
~ heavy (6) v 081.4
~ her (143) v 081.4
~ her mighty close (1) v 081.4
~ her pretty (1) v 081.4
~ on her (2) v 081.4
~ place (2) n 081.4
~ pretty close (1) v 081.4
~ pretty heavy (7) v 081.4
~ right along (1) v 081.4
~ steadily (1) v 081.4
~ that lady (1) v 081.4
~ thing (1) n 081.4
~ this girl (1) v 081.4
~ under the hay (1) v 081.4
Courtland (3) AL MS 105.7
Courtney Campbell Causeway (1) 107.6
(Courtney) Campbell Causeway (1) 107.5
courts (7) n/v 081.4
Courts (1) 105.5
courtship (10) n/adj 081.4
~ days (1) n 081.4

Courtview Towers (1) 108.6

courtyard (44) n/adj 085.1

~ square (2) n 085.1

Coushatta (4) LA 087.8

cousin (52) n 066.2

cous(in) (1) n 066.5

cou(sin) (1) n 075.7

Cousin (4) 064.4

~ John (1) 068.2

cousin[N-i] (3) n 066.5

cousin[N-k] wife (1) n 063.2

cousin's (2) adj 053.4

~ brother (1) n 053.4

~ husband's father (1) n 096.7

cousins (57) n 066.6

cous(ins) (1) n 066.5

couteau de poche (1) n F 104.4

couth (1) adj 096.9

couturier (1) n 123.6

couve (1) v F 036.7

couveuse (1) n F 036.7

couvre-pied (2) n F 028.7

cove (12) n 030.3

Cove (38) 087.2

~ Boulevard (2) 105A.7

~ Creek (6) AR TN 030.7

~ Mountain (1) TN 031.1

~ section (1) n 105.1

Covemont (1) 106.1

Coventry Road (2) 093.7

cover (105) n/v/adj 028.7

~ crop (9) n 041.5

~ crops (4) n 041.3

~ porch (1) n 010.8

~ stone (1) n 031.6

~ up (1) v 080.8

coverages (1) n 107.2

coverall (3) n/adj 025.4

~ aprons (1) n 026.4

~ suit (1) n 027.4

coverall[N-i] (5) n 027.4

coveralls (109) n 027.4

covered (57) v/adj 070.8

~ boards (1) n 011.2

~ bridge (1) n 080.7

~ bridges (2) n 088.9

~ dish (2) n 048.4

~ -dish dinner (1) n 048.3

~ -dish party (1) n 130.7

~ ditches (1) n 030.2

~ hall (1) n 009.9

~ haystack (2) n 014.7

~ patio (2) n 007A.3

~ pie (1) n 047.6

~ platform (1) n 014.7

~ porch (1) n 010.8

~ shelter (1) n 015.1

~ stairway (1) n 009.6

~ up (4) v 070.7

~ wagon (6) n 080.8

~ wagons (1) n 080.8

~ walkway (4) n 007A.6

coverhaul[N-i] (1) n 027.4

coverhauls (6) n 027.4

covering (19) n/v 011.2

coverings (1) n 039.8

coverlet (91) n 028.7

coverlets (22) n 028.7

coverlid (1) n 028.7

covers (9) n/v 028.7

coves (1) n 031.3

covey (3) n 055A.8

coveys (1) n 088.7

Covington (29) AL GA KY LA TN 087.9

~ County (1) AL 087.8

~ Highway (1) 105.9

cow (2234) n/adj 033.5

~ ants (1) n 060A.8

~ bag (1) n 091.8

~ barn (113) n 015.1

~ barns (9) n 015.1

~ beef (1) n 121.2

~ bees (1) n 060A.7

~ bird (1) n 059.3

~ brain (1) n 121.2

~ break (1) n 015.6

~ bug (1) n 060A.5

~ business (1) n 033.6

~ calf (1) n̄ 033.8

~ chitlins (1) n 037.3

~ college (2) n 091.9

~ corn (1) n 056.2

~ country (1) n 084.9

~ dog (4) n 033.1

~ dogs (1) n 033.3

~ drive (1) n 033.6

~ farm (1) n 015.5

~ farmer (1) n 089.9

~ farms (1) n 015.5

~ feed (1) n 036.5

~ -feed sack (1) n 019.6

~ fence (1) n 015.1

~ -fertilized (1) adj 029.3

~ fields (1) n 016.1

~ flies (1) n 060A.2

~ fly (1) n 060A.4

~ frog (1) n 060.4

~ gap (3) n 015.3

~ gut (1) n 037.2

~ hairs (1) n 071.4

~ head (1) n 033.6

~ heel (1) n 081.8

~ horn (3) n 037.5

~ horn okra (1) n 055.8

~ horns (1) n 056.7

~ horse (1) n 034.2

~ horses (1) n 034.2

~ house (2) n 014.2

~ intestines (1) n 037.2

~ jumped over the fence (1) n 130.6

~ kicker (1) n 069.9

~ killer (2) n 060A.6

~ lane (1) n 031.8

~ lice (1) n 075.6

~ lick (1) n 051.2

~ liver (1) n 047.2

~ lot (135) n 015.3

~ lots (3) n 015.6

~ manure (2) n 029.3

~ maw (1) n 037.2

~ milk (2) n 048.2

~ oak (1) n 061.8

~ oaks (1) n 061.8

~ pass (2) n 031.8

~ pasture (16) n 015.7

~ -pasture road (1) n 031.8

~ path (30) n 031.8

~ paths (1) n 031.8

~ paunch (1) n 037.2

~ pen (271) n 015.6

~ -pen (2) v 015.3

~ -pen gate (1) n 015.3

~ -penned (1) v 015.3

~ -penning (1) v 015.3

~ pens (20) n 015.1

~ pies (1) n 056.8

~ piss (1) n 33.6

~ pumpkin (1) n 056.5

~ pumpkins (1) n 056.5

~ shed (95) n 015.1

~ -shed barn (1) n 015.1

~ sheds (17) n 015.1

~ shelter (7) n 015.1

~ shit (2) n 096.7

~ stable (2) n 015.3

~ stables (2) n 015.1

~ stall (28) n 015.1

~ stalls (17) n 015.3

~ tea (1) n 080.9

~ ticks (1) n 060A.9

~ tongue (2) n 121.2

~ town (1) n 074.4

~ towns (1) n 090.8

~ trail (19) n 031.8

~ trails (2) n 031.6

~ train (1) n 033.7

~ tripe (1) n 037.2

~ trough (1) n 035.8

~ troughs (1) n 035.8

~ turds (1) n 080.9

~ vine (3) n 062.3

~ whip (8) n 019.4

~ whips (2) n 019.4

~ wire (1) n 016.3

~ yard (2) n 015.6

Cow (12) 030.7

~ Creek (3) GA TX 030.7

~ High Creek (1) TX 030.7

~ Island (2) LA 086.2

~ Suck Bayou (1) LA 030.3

COW (1) interj 037.5

c(ow) fence (1) n.015.1

cow[N-i] (13) n 036.5

coward (9) n 074.3

cowardly (2) adj 074.3

Cowarts Creek (1) AL 030.7

cowbell (2) n 037.5

cowbellions (1) n 082.5

cowberry (1) n 062.5

cowbird (2) n 080.7

cowboy (27) n/adj 033.6

~ boots (6) n 123.8

~ bread (1) n 044.6

~ dances (1) n 083.1

~ -like (1) adj 124.3

~ piss (1) n 088.8

~ stew (3) n 047.2

˜ style (1) n 032.3
˜ yell (1) n 037.5
cowboy[N-i] and Indians (1) n 098.6
cowboying (1) v 084.8
cowboys (23) n 080.8
  ˜ and Indians (16) n 098.6
  ˜ [J-0] Indians (1) n 130.6
Cowboys (1) 119.8
cowcatchers (3) n 060A.4
cowee (1) interj 037.8
Coweta (6) GA 087.2
  ˜ County (1) GA 087.1
Cowhead Creek (2) AL 030.7
cowhide (18) n/adj 051.4
  ˜ chairs (1) n 008.9
cowhides (1) n 065.8
cowish (1) adj 033.6
cowitch (36) n/adj 062.3
  ˜ berry (1) n 035.6
  ˜ vine (19) n 062.3
cowlick (1) n 062.3
cowman (1) n 090.9
cowpea (3) n 055A.4
cowpeas (7) n 033.6
cowpoke (1) n 069.9
cow's (4) adj 033.6
  ˜ brother (1) n 033.6
  ˜ milk (1) n 033.5
  ˜ stomach (1) n 033.6
cows (903) n 033.6
cows' (3) adj 033.8
  ˜ calves (1) n 033.8
  ˜ horns (1) n 104.6
  ˜ path (1) n 031.8
Cox (6) 068.5
  ˜ Creek (1) AL 030.7
  ˜ fence (3) n 126.1
Coxes Creek (1) AL 030.7
Coxey's Army (1) 082.8
Cox's fence (1) n 126.1
coy (2) interj 037.5
coy(x2) (2) interj 037.5
coy(x3) (2) interj 037.5
coyote (23) n/adj 059.5
  ˜ wolves (1) n 059.5
coyote[N-i] (1) n 059.5
coyotes (19) n 059.6
cozy (2) adj 007.4
crab (82) n/adj 060.1
  ˜ apple (9) n 061.8

˜ -apple switch (1) n 104.3
˜ apple trees (2) n 061.9
˜ apples (3) n 062.4
˜ business (1) n 060.7
˜ fish (4) n 060.8
˜ fisherman (1) n 084.9
˜ meat (1) n 059.9
˜ roll (1) n 080.8
Crab Orchard (2) KY 053.2
crab[N-i] (2) n 060.8
crabbing (5) n 060.7
crabbish (2) adj 075.1
crabby (7) adj 074.8
crabeater (1) n 089.8
crabgrass (254) n/adj 015.9
  ˜ hay (1) n 041.4
crabs (56) n 060.8
crack (39) n/v/adj 030.5
  ˜ corn (3) n 084.8
  ˜ egg (1) n 046.2
  ˜ licker (1) n 125.6
  ˜ linings (1) n 011.2
  ˜ of dawn (9) n 003.2
  ˜ of day (3) n 003.2
  ˜ of daylight (1) n 003.2
  ˜ shot (1) n 093.8
  ˜ -the-whip (3) n 130.2
  ˜ -wheat bread (1) n 044.3
  ˜ your lunch (1) v 080.2
crack[N-i] (1) n 053.5
crackbrain (1) n 073.4
cracked (13) v/adj 074.7
  ˜ open (1) v 052.6
  ˜ stone (1) n 031.6
  ˜ up (1) v 074.7
  ˜ up to (1) v 025.8
  ˜ wheat (4) n 044.4
  ˜ -wheat bread (1) n 044.3
cracker (230) n/adj 069.8
  ˜ barrel (7) n 019.1
  ˜ barrels (1) n 019.1
  ˜ box (4) n 118.9
  ˜ -box houses (1) n 118.9
  ˜ boxes (1) n 118.7
  ˜ honky (1) n 069.4
  ˜ neck (2) n 069.4

˜ stand (1) n 019.2
˜ talk (1) n 069.9
Cracker (108) 069.9
  ˜ Barrel (1) 019.1
  ˜ State (2) 067.2
crackerjack (3) n 069.7
crackerjacks (1) n 069.7
crackers (81) n 069.7
Crackers (59) 069.7
  ˜ Neck (2) TN 069.9
cracking (7) v/adv 081.8
  ˜ up (2) v 080.7
crackling (212) n/adj 084.8
  ˜ bread (157) n 044.6
  ˜ corn bread (23) n 044.6
cracklings (98) n 037.4
cracks (6) n 129.7
Craddock Creek (2) TX 030.7
cradle (67) n/v 041.6
cradled (2) v 041.6
cradles (6) n 041.7
cradling (1) v 042.1
craft (3) adj 019.5
  ˜ bag (1) n 019.5
  ˜ paper (1) n 019.5
  ˜ sack (1) n 019.5
crag (2) n 031.1
Craig (6) 115.9
  ˜ Airfield (1) 106.5
  ˜ Field (3) 106.5
Craighead (3) AR 087.1
cram (1) adv 027.8
cramp (34) n/adj 080.1
  ˜ colic (28) n 080.1
cramps (5) n 078.4
Cramton Bowl (1) 106.6
cranberries (19) n 062.5
cranberry (14) n/adj 062.7
  ˜ bread (2) n 044.4
  ˜ sauce (1) n 048.5
crane (9) n 008.3
Crane Street (1) 107.7
cranes (4) n 066.9
Cranes Mill (1) TX 087.1
Cranesville (1) TN 087.4
crank (6) n/v/adj 073.4
  ˜ stone (1) n 023.5
cranked out (1) v 078.6
cranky (28) adj 074.9
crap (42) n/adj/interj 010.2

˜ house (5) n 012.1
˜ mills (1) n 099.8
˜ operators (1) n 099.8
˜ -shooter's squat (1) n 096.4
crapaud (2) n F 060.3
crape (42) adj 062.7
  ˜ myrtle (34) n 062.7
  ˜ myrtle tree (2) n 061.9
  ˜ myrtle trees (2) n 061.8
  ˜ myrtles (4) n 061.8
crapper (12) n 012.1
crappie (150) n/adj 059.9
  ˜ fish (1) n 059.9
crap(pie) (1) n 059.9
crappie[N-i] (2) n 059.9
crappies (39) n 059.9
crappy land (1) n 029.8
craps (3) n 084.8
crash (8) n/adj 019.6
  ˜ cotton (1) n 070.5
  ˜ houses (1) n 113.8
  ˜ -in (1) n 111.8
  ˜ material (1) n 070.9
  ˜ truck (1) n 111.5
crate (9) n 036.8
crater face (2) n 129.8
crates (9) n 036.8
cravat (1) n 027.3
cravate (1) n F 070.9
craw (6) n/adj 071.7
  ˜ mollies (1) n 060.8
crawdab (3) n 060.8
crawdabs (6) n 060.8
crawdad (102) n/adj 060.8
  ˜ holes (1) n 060.8
  ˜ land (3) n 029.9
  ˜ tails (1) n 060.8
crawdaddies (3) n 060.8
crawdaddy (2) n 060.8
crawdads (84) n 060.8
crawfish (798) n/adj 060.8
  ˜ bisque (1) n 060.8
  ˜ bowl (1) n 060.8
  ˜ clay (1) n 029.9
  ˜ country (1) n 029.8
  ˜ dirt (1) n 029.8
  ˜ farming (1) n 060.8
  ˜ ground (2) n 029.6
  ˜ gumbo (1) n 060.8
  ˜ land (16) n 029.8

~ mud (1) n 029.9
~ nets (1) n 060.8
~ pie (1) n 060.8
~ pond (1) n 060.8
~ soil (3) n 029.9
~ tail (1) n 042.7
~ tails (1) n 060.8
craw(fish) (1) n 060.8
Crawfish (1) TX 030.7
crawfished (1) v 060.8
crawfishes (13) n 060.8
crawfishing (4) v 060.8
crawfishy (31) adj 029.9
~ area (1) n 029.6
~ land (15) n 029.9
~ stuff (1) n 029.8
Crawford (9) AR MS TX 087.4
~ County (1) GA 087.3
~ Long (1) 105.9
~ Park (1) 106.4
Crawfordville (1) GA 087.3
crawl (425) v/adj 096.2
~ in (1) v 096.2
~ off (2) v 096.2
~ on (1) v 096.2
~ out of (1) v 096.2
~ over (2) v 096.2
~ space (2) n 009.8
~ through (2) v 096.2
~ under (1) v 096.2
~ up (4) v 096.2
crawl[V-p] (14) v 096.2
~ around (1) v 013.6
crawl[V-r] (5) v 096.2
crawl[V-t] (2) v 080.7
~ under (1) v 080.7
crawled (36) v 096.2
~ out (1) v 096.2
~ over (2) v 096.2
~ under (1) v 096.2
~ up (4) v 096.2
crawler (40) n/adj 060.5
~ worms (1) n 060.5
crawl(er) (1) n 060.6
crawler[N-i] (1) n 060.5
crawlers (54) n 060.5
crawling (36) v 096.2
~ on (1) v 096.2
crawls (336) v 096.2
~ around (1) v 096.2
crawly (4) adj 090.8
~ bottom (2) n 060.8
~ way (1) n 085.2

crawpa (1) n 060.8
cray (1) n 060.8
craydad (1) n 060.8
crayfish (145) n 060.8
(cray)fish (1) n 060.8
crayon (2) n 070.9
crazed (1) adj 124.5
crazier (1) adj 103.1
crazy (334) adj 074.7
~ about her (5) adj 081.4
~ bone (5) n 072.7
~ -driver Cuban (1) n 128.5
~ houses (1) n 012.1
~ -like (2) adj 074.7
~ over her (1) adj 081.4
~ quilt (7) n 029.1
~ quilts (1) n 029.1
creak (1) n 060.3
creaking (2) v/adj 070.7
~ joints (1) n 079.6
cream (464) n/adj 048.5
~ cheese (84) n 048.1
~ churn (1) n 088.7
~ color (2) n 056.9
~ corn (1) n 056.2
~ cottage cheese (1) n 048.1
~ doughnut (2) n 122.6
~ doughnuts (1) n 122.6
~ -fill (2) adj 122.6
~ -fill doughnut (3) n 122.6
~ -filled (10) adj 122.6
~ -filled doughnut (3) n 122.6
~ -filled doughnuts (1) n 122.5
~ fills (1) n 122.4
~ gravy (1) n 048.5
~ horns (2) n 122.7
~ in the coffee (1) n 069.5
~ meat (1) n 056.9
~ melon (1) n 056.7
~ melons (1) n 056.7
~ milkshake (1) n 048.5
~ nut (3) n 054.9
~ nuts (3) n 054.9
~ -of-mushroom soup (1) n 056.8

~ of wheat (6) n 050.3
~ peas (2) n 055A.4
~ pitcher (1) n 017.1
~ potatoes (1) n 055.4
~ puff (5) n 080.6
~ puffs (5) n 122.6
~ roll (1) n 122.7
~ sauce (9) n 048.5
~ separator (2) n 080.6
~ -style corn (3) n 056.2
~ watermelons (1) n 056.9
creamed (6) adj 032.4
~ corn (1) n 056.2
~ onions (1) n 055.6
~ potatoes (2) n 055.4
creameries (5) n 015.5
creamery (15) n 015.5
creamy (3) adj 002.6
crease (2) n/v 027.2
~ up (1) v 055.9
Creaseback (3) 055A.4
Creasebacks (1) 055A.3
created (1) v 002.5
creation (1) n 089.7
creator (1) n 089.3
Creator (1) 078.6
creature (3) n 059.5
creatures (2) n 059.5
credit (10) n 066.8
cred(it) (1) n 066.8
credits (1) n 065.9
creed (1) n 089.8
creek (1103) n/adj 030.6
~ bank (3) n 030.6
~ banks (1) n 082.7
~ bed (11) n 031.3
~ bottom (25) n 029.4
~ -bottom land (5) n 029.4
~ -bottom lands (1) n 029.4
~ bottoms (20) n 029.4
~ branch (1) n 030.7
~ gravel (1) n 031.5
~ ivy (1) n 062.8
~ land (2) n 029.4
~ laurel (1) n 062.7
~ maple (1) n 061.9
~ minnows (2) n 059.9
~ rock (1) n 016.7
~ run (1) n 030.7
~ sand (1) n 029.8
~ suckers (1) n 059.9

~ swamp (2) n 029.6
~ swamp hills (1) n 030.8
~ swamps (1) n 029.6
~ -water breeches (1) n 027.4
Creek (1396) 030.3
~ Circle (1) 105.4
~ Indians (2) 080.6
creeks (197) n 030.6
Creeks (2) 030.7
creep (22) n/v/adj 096.2
~ feed (1) n 037.4
~ feeding (1) v 037.4
~ up (1) v 096.2
~ up on (1) v 125.3
creeped down (1) v 096.4
creeper (7) n 017.5
creepers (1) n 060.5
creeping (5) v 096.2
~ around (1) v 096.4
creeps (12) n/v 096.2
creepy (4) adj 074.3
~ houses (1) n 090.3
cremation (3) n 078.9
crematorium (1) n 117.6
crematory (2) n 117.6
creme patissiere (1) n F 048.5
Crenshaw (8) AL 056.7
~ County (2) AL 087.4
~ melon (2) n 056.7
creole (25) n/adj 055.4
~ bread (1) n 044.4
~ cottage (1) n 118.9
~ food (1) n 048.4
~ horses (1) n 034.2
~ mule (1) n 033.7
~ mushmelon (2) n 056.7
~ nigger (1) n 095.8
~ onion (2) n 055.6
~ onions (1) n 055.7
~ pony (1) n 034.2
~ tomato (1) n 055.3
~ tomatoes (6) n 055.3
~ yam (1) n 055.5
cre(ole) (2) n/adj 019.7
~ sauce (1) n 070.6
Creole (74) 128.3
~ French (1) 080.8
~ lady (1) n 025.6
~ man (1) n 069.5
~ people (5) n 069.5
Creoles (23) 128.3

~ ass (1) n 069.9
creolized (1) v 080.8
creosote (12) n/adj 031.6
~ oil (1) n 031.6
~ plant (1) n 080.8
~ post[N-i] (1) n 016.5
~ postes (1) n 016.5
~ posts (1) n 016.5
~ -treated posts (1) n 016.5
~ wood-block roads (1) n 031.6
creosoted (2) adj 016.5
~ post[N-i] (1) n 016.5
~ wood blocks (1) n 031.6
creosoting (1) v 070.6
crepe (5) n F 045.3
~ suzette (1) n F 122.1
crepes (2) n F 045.3
crescent (5) adj 012.1
~ house (1) n 012.1
~ rolls (4) n 044.4
Crescent (43) 105.8
~ Beach (1) 105.8
~ City (2) FL 087.5
~ River (1) GA 030.7
crescents (1) n 044.4
cress (2) n 055A.5
cresses (5) n 055A.5
crest (8) n 031.2
Crest (3) 105.4
Crestline (2) 087.2
Crestview (3) FL 087.4
Crestwood (1) MO 086.6
cretonne (1) n F 009.6
crevasse (2) n F 030.4
crevice (9) n 011.6
crevices (1) n 030.5
crew (63) n/adj 082.9
~ boats (2) n 024.6
~ cut (36) n 115.6
~ cuts (9) n 123.9
crews (1) n 098.8
crib (539) n/adj 014.3
~ house (1) n 014.3
~ houses (1) n 014.3
~ shed (2) n 011.8
cribbed (1) v 100.2
cribful (2) n 041.3
cribs (66) n 014.3
Crichton (7) AL 105.1
~ Towers (1) 108.5
cricket (34) n 060.2
Cricket (2) 064.4

~ Averys (1) 021.6
crickets (47) n 061.1
Cricks Creek (1) AR 030.7
cried (5) v 036.2
cries (8) v 036.2
crime (5) n/adj 040.6
~ rate (1) n 095.8
criminal sheriff (1) n 092.7
crimp (3) v 022.4
~ up (1) v 055.9
crimper (1) n 080.8
crimson clover (1) n 041.6
Crimson (3) 056.9
~ Sweet (1) 056.9
~ Sweets (1) 056.9
~ Tide (1) 114.7
crinch owl (2) n 059.1
crinchy (1) adj 059.1
crinkle (1) v 055.9
crinkled (2) v 055.9
~ up (1) v 055.9
crinkles (1) n 114.5
crinkly (1) adj 055.9
cripple (8) n/adj 047.4
~ foot (1) n 072.6
cripple[V-r] up (1) v 098.6
cripple[V-t] (1) v 052.5
crippled (3) v 088.6
~ up (1) v 075.6
Crisco (1) 026.1
crisis (1) n 007.1
crisp (28) adj 007.4
~ day (1) n 007.4
Crisp (3) GA 087.3
~ County (1) GA 087.4
crisped up (1) v 077.8
crispy (6) adj 007.4
~ doughnut (1) n 122.4
~ showers (1) n 006.6
~ weather (1) n 007.4
crisscross (9) adj/adv 016.4
Crisscross (1) 056.9
crisscrossed (2) v 016.4
critical (1) adj 080.9
critter (12) n 059.5
critters (26) n 059.5
croak (6) v 078.6
croak[V-r] (1) v 078.6
croaked (58) v 078.6
~ out (1) v 078.6

~ over (1) v 078.6
croaker (25) n/adj 059.9
~ fish (3) n 059.9
croakers (30) n 059.9
croaking (3) v/adj 078.6
~ frog (2) n 060.2
croaks (1) v 078.6
croaky (1) adj 076.4
Croche (1) 030.7
crochet (4) n/v F 029.2
crocheted (5) v/adj 028.7
~ on (1) v 012.5
crocheting (2) n 094.1
crock (36) n/adj 017.7
~ bowl (1) n 017.7
~ churn (1) n 080.7
~ pot (12) n 116.4
~ pots (2) n 116.4
crockerware (2) n/adj 017.1
~ pots (1) n 017.7
crockery (6) n/adj 017.1
~ ware (1) n 017.1
Crockett (4) TX 087.6
Crocketts (2) 106.1
~ Ridge (1) 106.1
crocks (12) n 015.5
crocodile (1) n 080.8
crocs (1) n 035.7
crocus (339) n/adj 019.7
~ bag (20) n 019.7
~ bags (3) n 019.7
~ grass (1) n 015.9
~ sack (233) n 019.7
~ sacks (70) n 019.7
croc(us) (2) adj 019.7
~ sack (1) n 019.7
~ sacks (1) n 019.7
cro(cus) (2) adj 019.7
~ sack (1) n 019.7
~ sacks (1) n 019.7
croker (211) n/adj 019.7
~ bag (31) n 019.7
~ bags (14) n 019.7
~ sack (124) n 019.7
~ sacks (34) n 019.7
crokers (1) n 019.7
Cronanville (1) TN 087.4
cronies (1) n 129.6
crony (1) n 129.4
cronyism (2) n 115.3
crooch (1) n 033.3
crook (17) n/adj 115.4
~ -necked (1) adj 056.6

~ -necked squash (2) n 056.6
~ -shank (1) adj 056.6
Crook (2) 064.4
crook[V-p] in (1) v 025.9
crooked (61) adj 085.2
~ bone (1) n 037.1
~ fence (4) n 016.4
~ lawyer (1) n 067.8
~ -neck (14) adj 056.6
~ -neck cushaw (1) n 056.6
~ -neck cymling (1) n 056.6
~ -neck squash (12) n 056.6
~ -rail fence (5) n 016.4
~ rail fences (1) n 016.4
~ something (1) n 037.1
Crooked (11) 030.7
~ Bayou (1) AR 030.7
~ Creek (5) AL FL GA TN 030.7
~ Dick (1) AL 030.7
~ Fork (1) TN 030.7
~ River (2) GA 030.7
~ Run (1) LA 087.3
crookedest (1) adj 052.5
crookneck (53) n/adj 056.6
~ squash (16) n 056.6
~ yellow (1) n 052.1
crooknecks (1) n 056.6
crooks (2) n 129.2
croop down (1) v 096.4
crop (1219) n/v/adj 041.3
~ duster (3) n 096.7
~ dusters (1) n 080.7
~ grass (2) n 015.9
~ growing (1) n 041.3
~ -making time (1) n 041.3
~ money (1) n 041.3
~ reporter (1) n 041.3
~ season (1) n 041.3
~ time (5) n 041.3
~ up (1) v 041.3
~ year (2) n 041.3
Crop (1) 056.2
crop[N-i] (2) n 041.3
cropland (4) n 029.8
cropped (2) v 088.9

~ down (1) v 088.9
cropper (1) n 088.7
croppers (3) n 080.6
cropping (8) n/v 041.4
crops (196) n 041.3
croquet (10) n 081.9
croquette (2) n 045.2
croquettes (2) n 044.6
croquignole (15) n F 123.9
Crosland (1) GA 087.8
cross (78) n/v/adj 075.1
~ -back (3) n 126.5
~ -backs (2) n 126.5
~ bone (1) n 037.1
~ corner (1) adv 085.2
~ -cut (1) v 021.6
~ -eyed peas (1) n 090.9
~ -eyed snap (1) n 083.1
~ fence (5) n 016.3
~ fencing (1) n 025.7
~ H (1) n 080.8
~ hall (1) n 080.6
~ hog (1) n 080.7
~ horse (1) n 022.1
~ lines (1) n 039.1
~ log (1) n 022.1
~ member (1) n 021.3
~ over (1) v 057.7
~ race (1) n 069.5
~ reference (1) n 053.4
~ spelling (1) n 080.6
~ street (1) n 031.7
~ streets (1) n 031.7
~ tops (1) n 114.2
~ vine (2) n 062.3
~ vines (1) n 057.3
~ wire (1) n 016.3
~ -wood fence (1) n 016.4
~ -wood fences (1) n 016.4
Cross (16) 030.7
~ Bayou (1) LA 030.7
~ City (1) FL 087.1
~ Creek (1) FL 030.7
~ Lake (7) AR 030.7
~ Mountain (1) TN 031.1
cross[V-r] to the other side (1) v 078.5
crossbar (5) n 021.8
crossbred (2) adj 033.3

~ cattle (1) n 033.3
crossbreed (28) n/adj 069.5
~ dog (1) n 033.3
crossbreeded (2) adj 081.9
~ dog (1) n 033.3
crossbreeds (1) n 069.5
crossbuck (1) n 022.1
crossbucks (1) n 022.1
crosscountry road (1) n 031.7
crosscut (37) adj/adv 085.2
~ bun (1) n 045.2
~ saw (32) n 081.9
~ saws (1) n 080.7
crossed (8) v/adj 069.5
~ between (1) v 069.5
~ fences (1) n 016.4
~ -up dog (1) n 033.3
crosses (3) n 052.5
Crossett (3) AR 087.3
~ Camp (2) AR 102.9
crosshaul (1) n 093.6
crossing (32) n/v 031.8
Crossing (5) 087.9
crossings (2) n 107.8
crosspiece (2) n 021.2
crossrail fence (2) n 016.4
crossroad (25) n 031.8
crossroad[N-i] (1) n 031.6
crossroads (9) n 031.6
Crossroads (8) 086.6
~ community (1) GA 087.2
crosstie (1) n 053.5
crosstied fence (1) n 016.4
crossties (6) n 016.4
crosstown (4) n/adj 105.3
~ expressway (2) n 107.5
Crosstown (3) 105A.6
crosstree (5) n 021.2
Crossville (5) TN 087.6
crosswalk (1) n 031.9
crossway (3) adv 085.2
crossways (34) adv 085.2
crosswise (9) adv 085.2
crotch scratcher (1) n 124.9
crotchety (2) adj 074.8
crouch (87) v/adj 096.4

~ down (28) v 096.4
~ peach (1) n 054.3
crouch[V-r] down (1) v 096.4
crouched (14) v 096.4
~ down (1) v 096.4
crouches (5) v 096.4
~ down (1) v 096.4
crouching (19) v/adj 096.4
~ down (2) v 096.4
~ position (1) n 096.4
croup (35) n/v 079.6
~ up (1) v 079.8
croupy (4) adj 079.7
crow (16) n 069.6
Crow (5) 030.7
~ Creek (2) AL GA 030.7
crowbar (4) n 020.7
crowd (282) n 082.8
crowded (2) adj 013.8
crowder (40) n/adj 055A.3
~ pea (6) n 055A.3
~ peas (25) n 055A.4
Crowder (2) MS 087.9
crowders (14) n 055A.1
crowds (6) n 082.8
crowfoot (12) n/adj 015.9
~ grass (7) n 015.9
crowing (1) v 057.4
Crowley (12) AR LA TX 087.2
Crowleys Ridge (6) AR 031.1
crown (5) n/adj 011.6
~ roast (2) n 121A.1
crow's (4) adj 098.4
~ eye (1) n 098.4
~ -foot (2) n 029.1
~ nest (1) n 019.8
crows (10) n 059.3
Crows (1) 069.4
crud (4) n/interj 125.5
~ of [D-0] earth (1) n 069.7
crudded milk (1) n 047.6
cruddy (2) adj 005.5
~ day (1) n 005.5
crude (11) adj 073.6
~ oil (4) n 024.2
cruder (1) adj 051.2
cruds (1) n 047.6
cruel (3) adj 025.9

Cruel (1) TX 087.1
cruet (3) n 019.2
cruise (2) n 088.7
cruiser (14) n 111.7
cruisers (13) n 024.6
cruising for (1) v 081.3
cruller (16) n 045.2
crul(ler) (2) n 122.7
crullers (27) n 045.2
crumb (2) adj 122.3
~ cake (1) n 122.3
~ crushers (1) n 064.4
crumbles (2) n/v 048.6
~ up (1) v 055.9
crumblified (1) adj 029.8
crumbs (1) n 080.9
Crumley Chapel (1) AL 086.2
crummy (4) adj 084.8
~ cheap hotel (1) n 113.8
~ day (1) n 005.5
~ -looking (1) adj 080.7
Crump Boulevard (2) 107.8
crumped up (2) v 055.9
crumple (1) v 096.4
Crumrod (1) AR 087.6
crunch (3) n 088.7
crunched (2) v 096.4
~ down (1) v 096.4
crunching (2) v 096.4
~ down (1) v 096.4
crunchy (1) adj 007.6
crupper (1) n 038.7
crush (11) n/v/adj 031.6
~ bottles (1) n 031.6
~ on her (2) n 081.4
~ rock (3) n 031.6
~ stone (1) n 031.6
crushed (11) v/adj 031.6
~ rock (7) n 031.6
~ shells (1) n 031.6
~ -stone road (1) n 031.6
~ up (1) v 096.4
crusher (3) n 080.9
crushers (1) n 064.4
crust (12) n 046.6
crusted (3) v 007.5
~ over (2) v 007.6
crustes (6) n 016.7
crusting over (1) v 007.6
crusty (3) adj 055.9

crutches (2) n 123.8
crutchous (1) adj 075.1
cry (33) n/v 036.2
~ like (1) v 036.2
cry[V-p] (1) v 036.2
crybaby (2) n 061.8
crying (32) v/adj 079.3
~ about (1) v 036.3
~ for (2) v 071.6
~ f(or) (1) v 036.2
~ noise (1) n 036.2
~ off (3) v 024.9
crypt (17) n 117.6
crystal (9) n/adj/adv 048.9
~ clear (1) adj 050.8
~ meth (1) n 115.5
Crystal (7) 087.7
~ City (1) TX 087.7
~ Hill (2) GA 087.1
~ Hill Spring (1) GA 030.7
~ River (1) FL 030.7
~ Spring (1) AR 030.7
~ Springs (1) AR 087.7
crystallize (2) v 070.6
Cs (2) 114.2
cuarteron (2) n S 069.5
Cuates (1) 030.7
cub (1) n 080.6
Cuba (18) AL LA NM TX 070.9
~ Landing (2) TN 031.4
Cubahatchee Creek (1) AL 030.7
Cuban (52) 066.8
~ bananas (1) n 096.7
~ bread (3) n 044.3
~ coffee (4) n 048.8
~ doctors (1) n 128.5
~ fellow (1) n 128.5
~ groceries (1) n 116.2
~ motherfucker (1) n 128.5
~ public market (1) n 105.4
~ Queen (5) 056.9
~ sandwich (9) n 121.7
~ -sandwich place (1) n 121.7
~ sandwiches (6) n 121.7
~ section (1) n 105.4
Cubana (1) 128.5

Cubanos (2) 128.5
Cubans (24) 128.5
Cubas (1) 055.5
cube (11) n/adj 121.1
~ mushmelon (1) n 056.7
~ steak (8) n 131.8
cubes (1) n 007.7
cuckoo (8) n/adj 074.7
~ owl (2) n 059.2
cucumber (93) n/adj 062.9
~ bush (1) n 062.9
~ fields (1) n 016.1
~ patch (2) n 016.1
~ pickle (1) n 080.8
~ pickles (1) n 089.9
~ plant (1) n 062.9
~ squash (1) n 056.6
~ tree (15) n 062.9
~ trees (6) n 062.9
cucumbers (74) n 062.9
cud (5) n 033.6
cuddle up (1) v 096.4
cuddling (1) v 081.7
cudgel (1) n 032.1
cue (5) n/adj 056.7
~ melon (2) n 056.7
~ pumpkin (1) n 056.5
Cuero (3) TX 087.4
cues (1) n 056.7
cuey (1) interj 037.5
cuey(x2) (1) interj 037.5
cuff (1) n 021.8
cuffs (2) n 081.8
cuisine (1) n F 009.8
cul-de-sac (1) n 107.7
cull tomatoes (1) n 055.3
Culleoka (2) TN 094.9
Cullman (10) AL 087.9
~ County (1) AL 087.2
Cullman's (1) 068.4
Culloden (1) GA 087.3
culls (1) n 055.3
culottes (10) n 123.3
Culpepper (1) VA 087.8
culti-mulcher (1) n 021.7
Culti-Packer (1) 021.7
Cul(ti) (3) 021.7
~ -Packer (2) 021.7
~ -Packers (1) 021.8
cultivatable (1) adj 093.7
cultivate (8) v 021.6
cultivated (2) v/adj 029.3

cultivating (9) v/adj 041.4
~ harrow (1) n 021.7
~ land (1) n 029.8
~ tool (1) n 120.6
cultivation (2) n 013.1
cultivator (117) n/adj 021.7
~ harrow (1) n 021.7
~ plow (2) n 021.6
cultivators (42) n 021.6
cults (1) n 129.6
Cultural Center (1) 106.8
cultural journalism (1) n 080.6
culture (4) n 105.9
Culture (1) 106.6
Culver Creek (1) MS 030.7
culvert (7) n 031.8
culverts (6) n 015.5
Cumberland (49) TN 086.7
~ Avenue (1) 107.6
~ chain (1) n 031.1
~ City (1) TN 087.3
~ clouds (1) n 005.3
~ County (1) TN 086.6
~ Drive (1) 107.7
~ (E)states (1) 106.2
~ Gap (13) TN 031.3
~ Mall (1) 106.5
~ Mountain (3) TN 031.1
~ Mountains (3) TN 031.1
~ Plateau (1) TN 031.1
~ Presbyterian (1) 065.8
~ Presbyterians (1) 089.1
~ River (14) TN 030.7
~ section (1) n 107.7
Cumberlands (1) TN 031.1
cumbersome (1) adj 073.3
cumbia (1) n S 083.1
cumbias (1) n S 083.1
cumerating (1) v 082.5
cummerbund (1) n 027.3
Cumming (1) GA 087.4
Cummings (2) 106.6
cumpfolos (1) n 044.5
cumulus clouds (2) n 005.3

cunt (2) adj 039.7
~ lappers (1) n 039.7
~ lickers (1) n 039.6
cunted (1) adj 006.1
cup (201) n/adj/interj 048.8
~ berry (1) n 062.5
~ coal (1) interj 037.8
~ grease (2) n 023.7
~ towel (53) n 018.4
~ towels (13) n 018.4
Cup (2) 026.6
cup(x2) (2) interj 037.8
cup[N-i] (1) n 016.7
cupboard (87) n 010.1
cupboards (7) n 010.1
cupcake (3) n 122.2
cupcakes (13) n 122.5
cupid (1) adj 072.9
cupola (5) n/adj 007A.4
~ porch (1) n 010.8
cuppen land (1) n 015.3
cups (38) n 019.2
cur (296) n/adj/interj 033.3
~ -cow(x2) (1) interj 037.5
~ dog (106) n 033.3
~ dogs (25) n 033.3
~ -looking dog (1) n 033.3
curandero (2) n S 075.6
curb (35) n/adj 031.9
~ base (1) n 031.9
~ market (7) n 065.8
~ parking (3) n 108.1
~ well (1) n 080.8
Curbie (2) 117.3
curbing (8) n 031.9
curbs (2) n 110.8
curbside parking (1) n 108.1
curbstones (1) n 110.9
curd (38) n/adj 047.6
~ cheese (2) n 048.1
curd[N-i] (2) n 047.7
curding (1) v 047.6
curdle (16) v/adj 047.6
~ milk (5) n 047.6
curdle[V-t] (1) v 047.5
curdled (53) v/adj 047.6
~ cheese (1) n 048.1
~ milk (16) n 047.6
curdles (8) v 047.6
curds (21) n 047.6

cure (38) n/v/adj 070.7
~ hams (1) n 121.3
~ meat (2) n 046.5
~ out (3) v 066.8
~ -out deal (1) n 092.9
~ up (1) v 093.5
cure[V-p] (1) v 025.6
cure[V-t] [P-0] (1) v 045.8
cured (105) v/adj 046.5
~ bacon (8) n 046.7
~ breakfast bacon (1) n 046.7
~ ham (17) n 121.3
~ ham meat (1) n 046.5
~ hams (2) n 121.3
~ hog meat (1) n 046.5
~ meat (20) n 046.5
~ meats (1) n 046.3
~ onion (1) n 055.6
~ out (3) v 092.7
~ pork (2) n 046.5
~ sausage (1) n 121.6
~ side (1) n 046.5
~ up (1) v 078.2
cures (1) v 039.9
curfew (1) n 080.6
curing (12) v/adj 014.5
~ out (1) v 055.6
~ racks (1) n 014.7
~ room (1) n 099.8
~ sheds (1) n 014.5
curiosity (12) n 065.9
curious (43) adj 074.7
curiouser (1) adj 066.1
curl (5) n/v/adj 123.9
~ doughnut (1) n 122.7
~ up (1) v 013.1
curled (3) v 123.9
curlers (2) n 122.7
curlies (1) n 123.9
curling (3) adj 084.8
~ iron (1) n 084.8
~ irons (2) n 080.9
curls (7) n/v 123.9
~ up (2) v 055.9
curly (12) adj 123.9
~ Afro (1) n 123.9
~ (A)fro (2) n 123.9
~ edge (1) n 055A.6
~ -headed (1) adj 040.5
~ look (1) n 115.8
~ maple (1) n 061.9
~ top (2) n 123.9

Currahee Mountain (1) GA 031.1
currant (3) adj 062.4
~ bush (2) n 062.4
~ bushes (1) n 062.5
currants (2) n 062.4
currency (2) n 114.5
current (3) n 065.8
curried (1) v 038.6
curry (4) v 038.6
cur(ry) (4) v 038.6
Curry (1) AL 087.8
currycomb (4) n 080.9
Curryville (1) GA 087.2
curs (18) n 033.3
curse (31) n/v/adj 092.1
~ like (1) v 092.1
~ word (4) n 065.7
~ words (7) n 092.1
cursed (3) v/adj 075.7
curser (1) n 091.6
curses (1) n 092.2
cursing (11) n/v 092.1
cursingest (1) adj 064.7
curtain (85) n/adj 009.5
~ blinds (1) n 009.5
~ stretchers (1) n 080.6
Curtain (2) 127.5
curtain[N-i] (1) n 009.5
curtains (292) n 009.5
Curtis (2) 107.9
~ Lane (1) 107.9
~ Quarter (1) 105.4
curve (4) n/v/adj 107.4
~ around (1) v 013.1
~ spoons (1) n 017.8
curved (3) v/adj 096.7
~ around (1) v 096.7
cush (196) n/adj 050.3
~ bread (1) n 044.6
~ -cush (48) n 050.3
cushaw (93) n/adj 056.6
~ nuts (1) n 054.8
~ pumpkin (2) n 056.5
cush(aw) melons (1) n 056.7
cushaws (31) n 056.6
cushes (1) n 035.7
cushion (5) n 028.8
cushions (2) n 027.2
cuspidors (1) n 070.7
cusps (1) n 070.7
cuss (4) n 088.7
Cusseta (5) AL GA 087.4
custard (33) n/adj 048.5

~ sauce (3) n 048.5
custards (5) n 048.3
custodian (25) n 119.5
custodians (3) n 119.5
custom (2) adj 111.6
~ car (1) n 111.6
~ work (1) n 090.9
customary (1) adj 025.7
customer (7) n 095.7
customers (5) n 069.3
customhouse (1) n 014.1
customs (2) n 069.4
cut (1004) n/v/adj 101.4
~ a class (4) v 083.4
~ a rug (1) n 083.1
~ across (20) v 085.2
~ back (1) v 103.5
~ bait (12) n 060.5
~ beans (1) n 055A.4
~ boar (1) n 035.4
~ class (44) v 083.4
~ classes (14) v 083.4
~ corn (1) n 056.2
~ down (2) v 041.4
~ flowers (1) n 101.4
~ glass (1) n 012.2
~ -glass vases (1) n 017.7
~ green beans (1) n 055A.4
~ her throat (1) v 082.2
~ him off (6) v 082.1
~ him out (1) v 082.1
~ his class (1) v 083.4
~ his classes (1) v 083.4
~ hog (3) n 035.4
~ it (1) v 037.7
~ it out (1) v 033.2
~ -leaf maples (1) n 061.8
~ log (1) n 008.5
~ off (6) v 032.6
~ off from him (1) v 082.1
~ out (10) v 041.4
~ out of (1) v 065.3
~ pea (1) n 129.4
~ pennies (1) n 092.8
~ -pipe clay (1) n 029.9
~ price (2) n 094.5
~ -rate prices (1) n 094.5
~ school (5) v 083.4

~ -short bean (1) n 055A.4
~ -short beans (1) n 055A.4
~ shorts (3) n 055A.8
~ the class (5) v 083.4
~ through (2) v 085.2
~ up (5) v 073.1
~ -up chickens (1) n 121.5
~ wood (1) n 008.6
~ you out (1) v 082.1
Cut (2) 030.3
cut[V-p] (2) v 052.7
cut[V-s] (1) v 026.1
cutaway (17) n/adj 021.6
~ coats (1) n 027.1
~ harrow (10) n 021.7
~ harrows (1) n 021.7
cutdown (2) n 129.6
cute (65) adj 080.7
~ ass (1) n 124.7
~ chick (1) n 125.4
cuter (2) adj 066.1
cutest (1) adj 053.4
Cuthbert (13) GA 087.7
cutie (3) n 125.3
Cutlass (1) 109.2
Cutler (1) 106.1
cutlery (3) n 017.8
cutlet (1) n 121.2
cutlets (1) n 121.4
cutoff (22) n/adj 031.7
~ fence (1) n 016.3
~ pants (2) n 123.3
~ road (3) n 031.7
~ roads (2) n 031.7
~ saw (1) n 081.8
~ shorts (1) n 123.4
cutoffs (15) n 123.2
cutout sandals (1) n 123.8
cutouts (1) n 123.8
cutover (3) n/adj 041.5
~ land (1) n 041.4
cuts (41) n/v 030.4
~ classes (1) v 083.4
~ off (1) v 018.9
~ through (1) v 085.2
~ up (1) v 053.2
cutter (30) n/adj 046.8
~ plow (1) n 021.6
cutters (12) n 120.8
cutthroats (1) n 114.8
cutting (355) n/v/adj 036.1

~ across (3) v 085.2
~ (a)cross (1) v 085.2
~ class (7) v 083.4
~ classes (3) v 083.4
~ disc (1) n 021.7
~ down (3) v 080.6
~ harrow (7) n 021.7
~ har(row) (3) n 021.7
~ horses (1) n 034.2
~ knife (1) n 017.8
~ knives (1) n 104.3
~ off (1) v 030.2
~ on (2) v 024.9
~ out (1) v 015.8
~ over (1) v 041.4
~ pens (1) n 015.3
~ plow (3) n 021.6
~ room (2) n 014.3
~ scrape (1) n 081.8
~ the fool (1) v 082.5
~ through (3) v 085.2
~ up (6) v 080.9
cuttings (13) n 041.5
cutup (1) n 073.4
cutworm (2) n 060.5
cutworms (4) n 060.5
cycle (2) n 001.4
cycles (2) n 111.7
cyclone (55) n/adj 112.2
~ cellar (1) n 015.5
Cyclone (55) 016.3
~ fence (28) n 016.3
~ fences (3) n 016.3
~ fencing (3) n 016.3
~ wire (1) n 016.3
~ wood fence (1) n 016.2
cyclones (26) n 112.2
Cyclorama (6) 093.5
cylinder (4) n/adj 022.4
cylindrical (1) adj 066.8
cymling (13) n/adj 056.6
~ gourd (1) n 056.6
cymlings (12) n 017.1
Cynthiana (1) KY 087.1
cypress (252) n/adj 062.7
~ barn (1) n 014.2
~ batten (1) n 011.2
~ blinds (1) n 009.5
~ board (1) n 016.2
~ -board roof (1) n 011.4
~ boards (2) n 016.4
~ boat (3) n 024.6
~ boats (2) n 024.6

~ bores (1) n 060A.6
~ boxing (1) n 011.2
~ brakes (1) n 029.6
~ bucket (1) n 017.2
~ chip (1) n 008.6
~ chips (1) n 061.8
~ fence (4) n 016.4
~ fish (1) n 075.8
~ gutters (1) n 011.5
~ house (1) n 014.1
~ kindling (1) n 008.6
~ knee (2) n 081.9
~ knees (2) n 088.7
~ log (2) n 008.5
~ logs (2) n 008.5
~ lumber (2) n 061.8
~ pieu (1) n 016.2
~ planks (1) n 014.3
~ pond (1) n 061.8
~ shingle (1) n 011.4
~ shingles (2) n 008.6
~ skiff (1) n 024.6
~ slabs (1) n 016.7
~ swamp (4) n 029.6
~ swamps (4) n 029.6
~ timber (3) n 061.8
~ top (1) n 011.4
~ tree (6) n 061.8
~ -tree land (1) n 029.6
~ trees (24) n 061.9
~ trout (2) n 059.9
~ wood (4) n 061.8
Cypress (25) LA TX 107.7
~ Creek (11) AL AR FL GA TN 030.7
~ Creek Bottom (1) AR 029.4
~ Creek drainage ditch (1) n 030.2
~ Gardens (1) FL 087.9
~ Lake (1) 105.7
~ Point (1) FL 087.3
~ Pond (1) GA 030.7
~ Street (1) 115.9
cypress[N-i] (2) n 061.8
cypresses (1) n 061.8
cypriere (1) n F 061.6
cyst (11) n 078.2
Czech (15) 127.6
~ section (1) n 127.6
Czechoslovakia (2) 127.6
Czechoslovakian (3) 127.6
Czechs (36) 127.6

D

D (11) 010.4
  ~ and C (1) 010.4
  ~ Daddy (1) 064.1
  ~ -line skiff (1) n 024.6
dab (4) n/adv 019.9
dabber (1) n 060A.1
Dach (1) n G 011.4
dachshund (4) n 033.3
dachshunds (1) n 033.4
Dacron (1) 070.7
Dacula (1) GA 087.4
dad (201) n/adj/interj 063.4
  ~ -blasted (1) adj 092.1
  ~ -gone (5) adj 092.1
  ~ -gum (9) adj 092.1
  ~ -in-law (1) n 063.4
Dad (326) 063.1
Dada (5) 064.1
daddies (4) n 063.4
Daddies (1) 063.5
daddle-do (1) n 067.8
daddy (710) n/adj 063.4
  ~ barlows (1) n 104.3
  ~ cow (2) n 033.5
  ~ horse (1) n 034.1
  ~ -in-law (7) n 063.4
  ~ longlegs (1) n 061.3
  ~ pig (1) n 035.3
  ~ rabbit (1) n 034.9
  ~ truck (1) n 111.2
dad(dy)-in-law's uncle (1) n 053.4
Daddy (758) 063.5
  ~ Man (1) 063.5
  ~ Pa (1) 064.1
Daddy[N-k] (2) 063.5
  ~ name (1) n 063.5
  ~ room (1) n 007A.3
daddyless (2) adj 065.7
  ~ child (1) n 065.7
daddy's (44) adj 063.4
  ~ brother (2) n 063.4
  ~ daddy (3) n 064.1

  ~ disposition (1) n 065.3
  ~ eyes (1) n 065.3
  ~ family (1) n 026.1
  ~ farm (1) n 063.4
  ~ father (1) n 064.1
  ~ father's time (1) n 064.1
  ~ folks (1) n 013.8
  ~ footsteps (2) n 065.3
  ~ habits (2) n 065.3
  ~ house (1) n 063.4
  ~ idea (1) n 092.4
  ~ job (1) n 063.4
  ~ land (2) n 063.4
  ~ life (1) n 063.4
  ~ name (1) n 063.4
  ~ people (3) n 066.5
  ~ place (1) n 063.4
  ~ renter's house (1) n 095.8
  ~ room (2) n 007A.5
  ~ side (5) n 063.4
  ~ sister (1) n 063.4
  ~ uncle (2) n 063.4
Daddy's (33) 063.5
  ~ bedroom (3) n 007A.4
  ~ father (2) n 063.5
  ~ kind (1) n 065.3
  ~ mammy (1) n 063.6
  ~ name (1) n 063.5
  ~ parents (1) n 063.8
  ~ people (4) n 063.5
  ~ picture (1) n 065.3
  ~ room (5) n 063.5
  ~ side (5) n 063.5
  ~ sister (1) n 067.9
  ~ uncle (1) n 068.2
Daddys Creek (1) TN 030.7
Dade (13) FL 087.4
  ~ City (3) FL 087.2
  ~ County (4) FL 087.2
  ~ County Jail (1) 112.8
Dadeville (1) AL 087.4
dad's (5) adj 063.5
  ~ father (1) n 063.5
  ~ side (2) n 063.4
Dad's (4) 063.5
  ~ chair (1) n 063.5
  ~ folks (1) n 066.5
  ~ room (1) n 007A.8
dag (1) interj 092.2
dagger (32) n 104.3

Dagger (3) 030.7
  ~ Branch (1) AL 030.7
daggers (8) n 124.4
dago (54) n/adj 127.3
  ~ bunch (1) n 099.6
  ~ children (1) n 088.9
  ~ peddlers (1) n 099.7
  ~ shop (1) n 088.8
Dago (1) 064.4
dagos (31) n 127.3
Dagwood (13) 121.7
  ~ sandwich (2) n 121.7
dahlia (1) n 084.8
Dahlonega (8) GA 087.7
daily (8) adj/adv 065.8
dairied (3) v 015.5
dairies (88) n/v 015.5
Dairies (1) 015.5
dairy (1052) n/adj 015.5
  ~ animals (1) n 015.5
  ~ barn (49) n 015.5
  ~ barns (16) n 015.5
  ~ box (1) n 015.5
  ~ building (1) n 015.1
  ~ business (13) n 015.5
  ~ calves (1) n 033.8
  ~ case (1) n 015.5
  ~ cattle (9) n 015.5
  ~ company (2) n 015.5
  ~ cow (12) n 033.6
  ~ cows (10) n 015.5
  ~ cream (1) n 032.4
  ~ farm (159) n 015.5
  ~ farmer (2) n 015.5
  ~ farmers (2) n 015.5
  ~ farming (1) n 015.5
  ~ farms (14) n 015.5
  ~ feed (2) n 015.5
  ~ goats (1) n 015.5
  ~ herd (1) n 015.5
  ~ house (8) n 015.5
  ~ industry (1) n 015.5
  ~ lot (1) n 015.5
  ~ milk (1) n 015.5
  ~ milk products (1) n 015.5
  ~ operation (1) n 015.5
  ~ operations (1) n 015.5
  ~ people (3) n 015.5
  ~ place (1) n 015.5
  ~ plant (1) n 015.5
  ~ products (14) n 015.5
  ~ room (4) n 015.5
  ~ shed (2) n 015.3

  ~ spreads (1) n 015.5
  ~ stores (1) n 015.5
  ~ tours (1) n 015.5
dair(y) (2) n/adj 015.5
  ~ farm (1) n 015.5
dai(ry) (4) n/adj 015.5
  ~ cattle (1) n 015.5
  ~ cows (1) n 055A.8
Dairy (4) 015.5
  ~ Bar (1) 015.5
  ~ Queen (2) 015.5
dairying (12) n/v/adj 015.5
  ~ barns (1) n 015.5
Dairymaid (1) 015.5
dairyman (7) n 015.5
dairymen (1) n 081.9
daisies (6) n 025.9
Daisy (4) TN 087.2
  ~ Lake (1) AR 030.7
daisy churn (1) n 080.7
Dakota (15) 086.1
dale (3) n 030.8
Dale (6) 087.2
  ~ County (2) AL 087.2
  ~ Mabry (3) 107.6
Daleville (2) AL MS 087.3
Dalkeith (2) FL 087.2
Dallas (204) AL AR GA TX 087.4
  ~ Airport (3) 106.8
  ~ Branch (1) GA 030.7
  ~ Chamber of Commerce (1) 053.4
  ~ County (3) AL 087.1
  ~ -Fort Worth (2) 106.8
  ~ -Fort Worth Airport (1) 106.6
  ~ Freeway (1) 107.1
  ~ Highway (1) 106.3
  ~ North Toll Road (1) 107.5
  ~ Road (1) 013.8
dalle (1) n F 011.5
Dalraida (1) 106.2
Dalrymple (1) 031.6
Dalton (21) GA 087.7
dam (23) n/v/adj 030.6
  ~ buster (1) n 006.1
  ~ party (1) n 130.7
  ~ up (1) v 030.5
Dam (13) 086.4
damage (8) n/v/adj 012.6

~ deposit (1) n 081.8
damage[V-p] (1) v 013.6
damaged (2) v 013.9
Damascus (12) AL GA
  TN VA 087.2
  ~ Freewill Baptist (1)
    089.1
dame (4) n/adj 125.4
  ~ school (1) n 083.7
dames (1) n 067.6
damn (591) n/v/adj/
  adv/ interj 092.1
  ~ -fool (3) adj 092.1
  ~ -it list (1) n 093.7
  ~ Yank (1) n 075.7
  ~ Yankee (10) n 066.7
  ~ Yankees (8) n 066.7
damn[V-t] (13) v 092.1
damnation (4) adj/interj
  092.3
damned (33) v/adj/adv
  092.2
damnedest (2) adj 092.1
damp (31) adj 007.4
  ~ day (7) n 005.5
  ~ land (3) n 029.6
  ~ place (1) n 029.6
  ~ spells (1) n 006.6
  ~ weather (1) n 097.9
damper (11) n 023.2
dampers (2) n 023.2
dampness (2) n 006.7
dams (6) n 031.5
damselflies (1) n 060A.4
damson (2) adj 061.8
  ~ plum (1) n 061.8
  ~ tree (1) n 061.8
Dan May Creek (1) FL
  030.7
dance (939) n/v/adj
  083.1
  ~ band (1) n 083.1
  ~ clubs (1) n 083.1
  ~ floor (3) n 083.1
  ~ hall (18) n 083.1
  ~ halls (2) n 083.1
  ~ music (3) n 130.8
  ~ parties (5) n 130.7
  ~ party (3) n 083.1
Dance (1) 083.1
dance[N-i] (2) n 083.1
dance[V-r] (1) v 083.1
danced (12) v 083.1
  ~ across (1) v 092.8
dancer (2) n 083.1

dances (230) n 083.1
dancing (345) n/v/adj
  083.1
  ~ game (1) n 081.8
  ~ hall (2) n 083.1
  ~ -like (1) adj 083.1
  ~ music (1) n 130.8
  ~ party (2) n 083.1
  ~ pumps (1) n 122.9
Dancing (3) 080.6
dandelion (11) n/adj
  055A.5
  ~ digger (1) n 120.5
  ~ greens (5) n 055A.5
dandelions (3) n 055A.5
dander (1) n 079.5
dandified (1) adj 028.5
Dandridge (3) TN 087.7
  ~ soil (1) n 029.9
dandruff (1) n 071.4
dandy (12) n/adj 028.1
Danes (1) 128.8
dang (37) n/v/adj/adv/
  interj 092.1
danger (3) n 101.6
dangerous (29) adj 066.9
dangest (1) adj 092.1
Dania (1) FL 087.8
Daniel (2) 107.9
  ~ Place (1) 107.9
  ~ Street (1) 107.6
Danielsville (1) GA 087.1
Danish (79) 122.2
  ~ bun (1) n 122.2
  ~ go-(a)rounds (1) n
    122.2
  ~ pastries (2) n 122.2
  ~ pastry (11) n 122.2
  ~ ring (1) n 122.1
  ~ roll (4) n 122.2
  ~ rolls (8) n 122.2
  ~ -type thing (1) n
    122.1
Danishes (3) 122.2
Danneel (1) 065.8
Dannelly (5) 016.1
  ~ Field (4) 106.5
Danny Duz Its (1) 018.3
Danvers (2) 055.6
Danville (3) AR IL 087.4
dap (1) adj 125.3
Daphne (4) AL 087.7
Daphus Hotel (1) 106.8
dapper (2) adj 125.3
DAR (2) 084.9

~ type (1) n 084.8
D'Arbonne (9) AR LA
  030.7
  ~ Bayou (1) LA 030.7
d'arc (7) adj F 061.9
Darden (1) MS 087.8
dare (188) n/v/adj 058.2
  ~ base (3) n 098.4
  ~ to (6) v 058.2
dare[V-p] (1) v 058.2
dared (6) v 058.2
daredevil (1) n 130.6
daren't (16) v 058.2
dares (2) v 058.2
daresay (4) v 013.1
daresome (2) adj 088.9
Darien (7) GA 087.6
dark (326) n/adj 003.5
  ~ boudin (1) n 047.3
  ~ bread (4) n 044.4
  ~ cloudy (1) adj 005.5
  ~ coffee (1) n 032.3
  ~ day (13) n 005.5
  ~ folks (1) n 069.3
  ~ land (2) n 029.8
  ~ -looking (2) adj
    042.5
  ~ meat (1) n 088.8
  ~ person (1) n 069.3
  ~ place (1) n 010.3
  ~ -skinned man (1) n
    069.5
  ~ soil (4) n 029.8
Dark (5) 086.9
  ~ Corner (1) AR 086.9
  ~ Hollow (1) AR 087.5
  ~ Hollows (1) 105.2
  ~ Town (2) 105.4
darkening up (1) v 005.6
darker (10) adj 051.2
  ~ -skinneded blacks (1)
    n 063.8
darkies (61) n 069.3
darkish (1) adj 026.1
darkness (1) n 003.4
Darkness (1) 090.1
darkroom (1) n 007A.7
darky (49) n 069.3
darling (9) n 063.1
Darling (24) 064.4
Darlingtons (1) 056.9
Darm (1) n G 080.2
darn (176) n/v/adj/adv/
  interj 092.1
  ~ -fool (1) adj 073.4

darn[V-t] (7) v 092.2
darned (14) v/adj 092.1
darnedest (1) adj 092.2
darning (16) adj 017.1
  ~ egg (9) n 017.1
  ~ eggs (6) n 017.1
  ~ needle (1) n 060A.4
dart (4) n/v/adj 130.6
  ~ game (1) n 130.6
  ~ school (1) v 083.4
Dart (1) 109.8
darter (1) n 061.2
darts (6) n 130.6
darty (2) adj 097.8
Darvon (1) 115.8
das (2) adj G 035.5
DAs (1) 123.9
dash (48) n/v/adj 110.1
  ~ box (1) n 110.2
  ~ churn (1) n 081.8
  ~ pocket (2) n 092.7
  ~ rain (1) n 006.1
Dash (1) 109.9
dashboard (128) n 110.1
dasher (11) n/adj 008.9
  ~ churn (1) n 088.7
Dasher (1) 109.9
Dashers (2) 013.8
dasn't (33) v 058.1
date (60) n/v/adj 081.6
  ~ bread (1) n 044.4
  ~ her (3) v 081.4
  ~ -nut bread (4) n
    044.4
  ~ palm (1) n 061.9
  ~ tree (1) n 061.9
  ~ trees (1) n 061.8
dated (2) v 081.4
dates (6) n 081.4
dating (208) n/v 081.4
  ~ a girl (1) v 081.4
  ~ her (26) v 081.4
  ~ her steadily (1) v
    081.4
  ~ pretty heavy (1) v
    081.4
  ~ seriously (1) v 081.4
  ~ steadily (2) v 081.4
  ~ steady (2) v 081.4
Datsun truck (1) n 109.6
daub (10) n/v/adj 080.9
  ~ chimney (2) n 008.1
daubed (1) v 008.3
dauber (421) n/adj
  060A.6

dauber[N-i] (4) n 060A.6
dauber[N-k] (5) adj 060A.6
dauber's (1) adj 060A.6
daubers (223) n 060A.6
daubing (3) n/v 083.1
daubs (1) n 060A.6
daughter (872) n 064.8
~ -in-law (17) n 064.8
~ -in-laws (1) n 064.8
daught(er)-in-law (2) n 064.8
Daughter of the American Revolution (1) 064.8
daughter[N-i] (1) n 064.8
daughter[N-k] room (1) n 043.9
daughter's (19) adj 064.8
~ bedroom (1) n 064.8
~ boyfriend (1) n 064.8
~ father (1) n 064.8
~ house (1) n 064.8
~ name (1) n 064.8
~ wedding (1) n 064.8
daughters (310) n 064.8
Daughters (7) 084.5
~ of America (1) 064.8
~ of the Confederacy (3) 064.8
~ of the Republic of Texas (2) 088.7
Dauphin (12) 087.5
~ Island (6) AL 087.5
~ Island Parkway (1) 107.6
~ Street (5) 105.3
Daus (3) TN 087.2
Dauterive (2) 030.7
davender (2) n 009.1
davenette (45) n 009.1
davenettes (10) n 009.1
davenport (152) n/adj 009.1
~ bed (1) n 009.1
Davenport (1) 009.1
davenports (14) n 009.1
David (3) 030.7
~ Blevins Branch (1) TN 030.7
~ -Lipscomb (1) 106.6
Davidson (9) TN 087.1
~ County (1) TN 105.1
~ Creek (1) TX 030.7
Davies' Arithmetic (1) 099.6

Davis (41) 107.6
~ Avenue (7) 105.4
~ Avenue community (1) n 105.1
~ Aviation Air College (1) 083.6
~ Boulevard (2) 107.6
~ Causeway (1) 107.6
~ Creek (1) AR 030.7
~ Crossing (2) AL 087.1
~ Crossroads (1) AL 087.4
~ Falls (1) AL 030.7
~ Island (7) 106.1
~ Park (1) 106.9
~ Street (2) 107.6
~ weed (1) n 015.9
Daviston (1) AL 087.4
Davy Crocketts Tavern (1) 106.4
dawn (152) n/adj 003.2
~ time (1) n 003.2
Dawn (1) 056.2
Dawson (6) GA 087.5
Dawsonville (1) GA 087.4
day (2658) n/adj 003.2
~ bust (1) n 003.2
~ clothes (1) n 080.9
~ lilies (1) n 062.8
~ scholars (2) n 080.6
~ students (1) n 068.7
Day (198) 002.2
day[N-i] (16) n 103.4
daybed (21) n/adj 009.1
~ sofas (1) n 088.9
daybeds (3) n 009.1
daybreak (80) n 003.2
Daybright (1) MS 087.3
daydream (1) n 097.2
daylight (200) n 003.2
daylights (2) n 074.2
dayroom (1) n 007A.2
day's (6) adj 089.8
~ travel (1) n 090.4
~ work (4) n 057.8
days (920) n 076.2
Days (2) 126.7
daytime (6) n 040.9
Dayton (14) OH TN TX 087.1
~ Mountain (1) TN 031.1
Daytona (24) FL 087.6
~ Beach (13) FL 087.9

dayworking (1) v 080.6
DC (606) 087.1
de (42) prep/prefix F/S 051.3
~ -nut (3) v 036.1
d(e) (3) prep F 088.7
De (66) 070.6
~ Armanville (1) AL 087.5
~ Foor Ferry Road (1) 107.8
~ Funiak Springs (3) FL 087.4
~ Funiak (Springs) (1) FL 087.2
~ Kalb (9) GA MS TX 086.3
~ Kalb Avenue (1) 107.6
~ Kalb County (5) GA TN 087.5
~ Land (4) FL 087.8
~ Lay (1) MS 087.7
~ Lisle (1) MS 087.5
~ Queen (6) AR 087.3
~ Ridder (12) LA 086.7
~ Soto (8) FL GA LA MS 087.3
~ Soto County (2) MS 082.6
~ Soto Landing (1) AR 070.7
~ Soto Park (1) 106.6
~ Witt (2) AR 087.5
(De) (3) 087.1
~ Kalb County (2) GA 087.1
~ Soto (1) GA 087.1
deacon (4) n 067.8
deacons (1) n 070.8
deacons' (2) adj 009.1
~ benches (1) n 009.1
~ chair (1) n 009.1
dead (662) adj/adv 057.9
~ and gone (1) adj 057.9
~ as a doornail (3) adj 078.5
~ as [D-0] doornail (1) adj 057.9
~ (Ber)muda grass (1) n 041.5
~ brush (1) n 008.6
~ duck (1) n 078.6
~ end (6) n 031.7

~ -end road (2) n 031.7
~ -ends (1) v 107.7
~ flesh (11) n 078.2
~ grass (21) n 041.5
~ hay (1) n 041.5
~ house (1) n 117.6
~ land (1) n 029.5
~ man (2) n 130.6
~ -man filler (1) n 117.4
~ -man[N-k] flesh (2) n 060.6
~ nigger (1) n 080.8
~ people (2) n 090.3
~ rise (1) n 024.6
~ sage grass (1) n 041.5
~ set (5) adj 074.8
~ set in his ways (1) adj 074.8
~ skin (6) n 078.2
~ stream (1) n 030.6
~ things (1) n 090.2
~ tired (2) adj 075.5
~ to the world (1) adj 075.4
~ trash (1) n 041.5
~ wagon (2) n 117.5
~ white cells (1) n 077.5
Dead (5) 087.7
~ Lake (1) AL 087.7
~ Man Lane (1) 031.7
~ River (2) FL 030.7
deadbeat (9) n 069.7
deadbeater (1) n 073.5
deadbeats (5) n 069.7
deaden (1) v 041.4
deadening (4) n/v/adj 029.8
~ plow (1) n 021.6
deader (2) adj 078.6
deadhead (3) n 115.4
deadline (2) n 098.4
deadly (2) adj 062.6
deadwood (2) n 008.6
deaf (968) adj 077.2
~ -and-dumb (1) adj 077.2
~ ear (1) n 077.2
~ owl (2) n 059.1
Deaf Smith (3) TX 087.4
deafen (1) v 070.2
deafer (1) adj 077.2
deafs (1) n 077.2

deafy (1) adj 077.2
deal (111) n/v 037.2
~ with (3) v 032.4
dealed (1) v 065.8
dealer (47) n 114.4
dealers (6) n 114.4
dealies (1) n 080.6
dealing (5) n/v 094.2
~ with (2) v 013.8
dealings (1) n 039.7
deals (2) n 085.3
dealt with (1) v 012.5
dean (1) n 043.7
Dean Street (1) 107.9
Deans Landing (1) AR 087.7
dear (51) n/adj/interj 081.6
~ friend (2) n 129.4
~ friends (1) n 129.4
Dear (31) 064.4
~ John (3) 082.1
~ John letter (5) n 082.1
~ -John-letter-type thing (1) n 082.1
dearest (1) n 081.6
deary (1) interj 092.2
death (149) n/adj 078.5
~ angel (1) n 090.8
~ house (1) n 113.4
~ owl (4) n 059.1
~ owls (1) n 059.1
~ shower (2) n 006.1
~ wagon (2) n 117.5
~ widow (1) n 063.3
death[N-i] (1) n 090.9
deathly (3) adj/adv 074.3
deaths (1) n 078.5
d'eau (1) adj F 080.7
d'Eau (1) 087.1
Deb club (1) n 052.6
deball (2) v 036.1
deballed (1) v 036.1
debarras (1) n F 010.3
debarrasser (1) v F 010.2
debeaking (1) v 066.8
debilitated (1) v 072.9
debris (3) n 065.8
debt (33) n 057.5
debts (1) n 094.7
Debussy (1) 130.8
debutante (2) n/adj 130.7
~ ball (1) n 083.1
debutantes (1) n 125.4

decanter (2) n 020.4
Decatur (65) AL GA MS 087.6
~ County (6) GA TN 087.6
~ -De Kalb area (1) n 106.2
~ Street (3) 107.6
~ Theatre (1) 084.4
(De)catur (3) AL 087.4
~ Street (2) 105.3
(De)cat(ur) (1) GA 087.4
Decaturville (2) TN 088.7
decay (1) n 046.9
decayed (3) v 046.9
decease (5) v 078.5
decease[V-r] (2) v 078.5
decease[V-t] (2) v 078.5
deceased (73) v 078.5
(de)ceased (4) v 078.5
deceaseded (1) v 078.5
(de)ceaseded (2) v 078.5
deceasing (2) v 007.3
Deceiper Creek (1) AR 030.7
deceiver (1) n 090.1
deceivers (1) n 045.3
deceiving him (1) v 082.1
December (987) 001A.9
Decemb(er) (2) 001A.7
decent (4) adj/adv 073.2
~ -dressed (1) adj 073.6
~ -looking (1) adj 057.3
Decherd (1) TN 087.4
decide (5) v 057.7
decided (10) v 053.4
~ on (1) v 024.7
~ to break up (1) v 082.1
decidedly (1) adv 052.8
deck (69) n/v/adj 010.9
~ out (2) v 028.1
~ shoes (5) n 081.8
decked (6) v 028.1
~ out (5) v 028.1
~ up (1) v 028.1
deckhand (1) n 080.9
deckhead (1) n 023.2
decking (5) n 011.4
decks (9) n 010.8
declare (67) v 092.2
(de)clare (1) v 064.4
decline (2) n/v 082.1

declined (5) v 082.1
decompose (1) v 102.2
decomposer (1) n 117.1
decorated (2) v 075.8
decorative (2) adj 065.8
~ fences (1) n 016.2
decorator (1) n 053.8
(de)coy (1) n 084.8
decrease (2) n/v 007.3
decreased (1) v 090.4
decreases (1) v 007.3
decreasing (25) v/adj 007.3
~ moon (1) n 080.9
decrepit (2) adj 072.9
Deduce (1) 030.3
Dee (3) 012.8
deed (3) n 102.2
deed[V-t] (1) v 057.8
deep (238) adj 007.9
~ apple pie (17) n 048.3
~ chest colds (1) n 076.3
~ dish (8) n 048.3
~ -dish (1) adj 048.3
~ -dish apple pie (28) n 048.3
~ -dish apple something (1) n 048.3
~ -dish cobbler (2) n 048.3
~ -dish peach pie (1) n 048.3
~ -dish pie (34) n 048.3
~ -dish pies (4) n 048.3
~ -down potato pie (1) n 080.8
~ -fat fryers (1) n 017.4
~ fry (1) n 116.4
~ fryer (3) n 017.5
~ mourning (2) n 079.3
~ -pan apple (1) n 048.3
~ -pan apple pie (2) n 048.3
~ -pan pie (1) n 048.3
~ pie (1) n 048.3
~ sand (4) n 029.8
~ sandy loam soil (1) n 029.8
~ soil (2) n 029.8
~ soils (1) n 029.8
~ waders (1) n 027.4

~ well (9) n 015.5
~ -well pump (1) n 081.9
~ -well water (1) n 025.4
~ wells (3) n 015.5
Deep (11) 030.7
~ Branch (2) FL MS 030.7
~ Creek (4) AL FL GA LA 030.7
~ East Dallas (1) 105.1
~ River (1) LA 030.7
~ South (2) 086.6
deeper (6) adj/adv 013.1
Deepfreeze (8) 007.7
Deepfreeze[N-i] (2) 016.7
Deepstep (2) GA 087.1
deepwater (2) adj 030.3
~ channel (1) n 030.3
~ well (1) n 018.7
deer (74) n/adj 059.5
~ Chihuahua (1) n 033.1
~ dog (3) n 033.1
~ dogs (11) n 033.1
~ head (1) n 027.2
~ -head flies (1) n 060A.6
~ -head turtle (1) n 060.7
~ hide (1) n 065.9
~ hound (1) n 033.1
~ hounds (1) n 033.1
~ hunt (2) n 059.4
~ -hunt (5) v 080.7
~ -hunted (1) v 095.8
~ hunting (3) n 065.8
~ lease (1) n 080.6
~ -lick place (1) n 029.9
~ -meat sausage (1) n 121.6
~ sausage (2) n 121.6
~ tick (2) n 060A.9
Deer (19) 030.7
~ Creek (5) AL GA MS 030.7
~ Island (2) MS 087.2
~ Lake (1) FL 030.7
~ Park (2) MS TX 087.5
~ Park Plantation (2) MS 070.6
Deere (1) 068.2

Deerfield (1) FL 070.6
deerflies (4) n 060A.7
deerfly (4) n 060A.8
Deerford (2) LA 087.4
deerhorn (1) n 037.5
deers (9) n 041.9
Deerwood (3) 105.1
Defeated Creek (1) TN 030.7
defend (1) v 013.3
defendant (1) n 070.7
defender (1) n 021.7
definite (2) adj 091.1
definitely (18) adv 091.1
deflower (1) v 036.1
deflowered (1) v 036.1
defrost (1) v 018.8
defunked (1) v 084.8
degenerate (1) adj 075.8
degenerates (1) n 113.7
degree (11) n 085.7
~ -wise (1) adv 080.6
Degree (1) 001A.1
degrees (7) n 001.3
dehorn (2) v 084.9
dehorned (2) v 081.8
dehorners (1) n 084.8
dehydrated (2) v 055.9
dehydrates (1) v 055.9
Deity (1) 089.3
dejoint (1) v 072.3
del (3) prep S 030.7
Del Rio (3) TX 087.8
delaisse (1) n F 063.3
Delano Park (1) 105.6
Delaroche Creek (1) GA 030.7
Delaware (3) 086.7
Delawares (1) 070.8
delayed (1) v 057.9
Delco (6) 081.9
~ light plant (1) n 081.9
~ lights (2) n 019.9
~ plant (2) n 081.8
~ system (1) n 063.4
Delegal Creek (1) GA 088.7
delft (8) n/adj 017.1
~ blue (1) adj 017.1
~ dishes (1) n 017.1
~ egg (1) n 017.1
~ eggs (2) n 017.1
Delhi (2) LA 087.4
deli (25) n 116.3

deliberately (12) adv 103.6
delicacy (1) n 070.7
delicate (3) adj 066.8
delicatessen (118) n/adj 116.3
~ section (1) n 116.3
~ style (1) n 116.3
~ type (1) n 116.3
delicatessens (5) n 116.3
delicious (14) adj 051.2
Delicious (1) 055.6
delight (3) n 104.6
Delight (1) AR 070.6
delighted (21) adj 090.6
delightful (2) adj 073.2
delinquent child (1) n 065.7
delinquents (1) n 064.3
delinting plant (1) n 088.8
delis (3) n 116.3
deliver (28) v 033.9
~ a calf (2) v 033.9
~ her calf (1) v 033.9
delivered (4) v 027.5
~ a calf (1) v 033.9
delivering (20) v 021.4
delivers (4) v 021.4
delivery (36) n/adj 109.6
~ boy (1) n 080.9
~ truck (25) n 109.6
~ trucks (2) n 109.6
~ van (3) n 109.6
~ wood (1) n 021.4
dell (10) n/adj 130.3
~ peppers (1) n 055A.4
Dell (2) 106.9
Delmar (1) AR 086.4
Delmonico (9) 121.1
~ steaks (1) n 121.1
~ strip (1) n 121.1
Delray (3) GA 087.4
~ Beach (2) FL 087.3
delta (105) n/adj 029.4
~ bottomland (1) n 029.4
~ country (2) n 030.9
~ farmer (1) n 080.7
~ folks (1) n 069.9
~ land (9) n 029.4
~ lowlands (1) n 029.4
~ people (2) n 025.8
~ red (1) n 069.4
~ section (1) n 029.4

~ soil (2) n 030.9
Delta (17) MS 087.3
~ Bridge (1) LA 087.4
~ Cotton (1) 088.8
~ Drive (1) 105.6
~ Queen (1) 024.5
~ Towers (2) 106.9
deltas (2) n 071.2
deluder (1) n 090.1
deluge (23) n 006.1
delve into (1) v 013.1
Dement Creek (1) AL 030.7
Demeter (1) LA 087.7
demi-black hip (1) adj 028.2
demigodger (1) n 129.1
demijohn (8) n 066.9
(demi)john (1) n 068.2
demijohns (5) n 017.2
Deming (1) NM 087.1
demised (3) v 078.5
demitasse (2) adj 048.8
~ coffee (1) n 048.8
~ spoon (1) n 017.9
Demo (1) 129.1
Democrat (42) 129.1
Democratic (10) 129.1
Democratics (1) 129.1
Democrats (46) 129.1
(de)moiselle (1) n F 060A.4
demolition (2) adj 108.7
~ area (1) n 108.7
~ site (1) n 108.7
demon (17) n 090.1
demons (5) n 090.2
demonstration (2) n 070.6
Demonstration (1) 032.2
demonstrations (1) n 102.7
Demopolis (10) AL 087.4
Demorest (3) GA 087.5
Demos (1) 129.1
Dempsey (3) 117.3
~ Vanderbilt (1) 077.8
Dempsey (7) 117.3
~ Dumpster (4) 117.3
~ Dumpsters (3) 117.3
Dempster (35) 117.3
~ dump (1) n 117.3
~ Dumpster (25) 117.3
~ Dumpsters (6) 117.3
Dempsty Dumpster (1) 117.3

Demsty Dumpster (1) 117.3
demusked (1) v 059.4
den (446) n/v/adj 007A.3
~ area (2) n 007.8
~ furniture (1) n 009.4
~ up (1) v 053.6
Den (3) 087.7
denatured (1) v 036.1
dence (1) n 030.2
dengue (2) n/adj 078.5
~ fever (1) n 079.7
Denham (4) LA 087.2
~ Springs (2) LA 087.7
denied him (3) v 082.1
denim (21) n/adj 027.4
~ jacket (1) n 027.4
~ overalls (1) n 027.4
~ shirts (1) n 027.4
denims (5) n 027.4
Denison (3) TX 087.1
Dennis (2) FL 030.7
~ Creek (1) AL 030.7
denomination (1) n 095.8
(de)nomination (2) n 089.1
denominations (1) n 025.2
dens (15) n 007A.2
dense (2) adj 005.5
~ weather (1) n 006.7
Dent (3) 056.2
dental floss (1) n 075.9
dentist (5) n 088.7
Denton (8) TX 087.1
~ County (1) TX 087.3
denude (1) v 036.1
denutting (1) v 036.1
Denver (22) AR CO 087.9
~ crossing (1) n 085.2
~ Harbor (1) 105.4
~ Heights (1) 105.2
~ lights (1) n 089.8
~ Side (1) 106.2
~ system (3) n 089.8
Denver's (1) 130.8
deny (1) v 065.3
depart from this life (1) v 078.5
departed (11) v 078.5
~ this life (2) v 078.5
department (58) n/adj 001A.9
~ store (1) n 108.1

~ truck (1) n 109.7
(de)partment (2) n 065.8
Department (3) 083.5
departments (1) n 039.6
depend (3) v 057.7
~ on (2) v 057.7
~ upon (1) v 053.2
(de)pend (1) v 070.9
dependable (1) adj 064.7
dependencies (1) n 011.7
dependent (2) adj 057.5
depends (14) v 055.2
~ on (7) v 088.2
~ upon (3) v 096.8
depense (1) n F 010.1
depicting (1) v 070.6
deplore (1) v 131.2
deposit (3) n 081.8
Deposit (3) 087.8
(De)posit (1) 087.5
(de)posits (1) n 029.8
depot (662) n/adj 084.7
~ station (3) n 084.7
~ yard (1) n 084.7
Depot (4) 030.7
~ Creek (1) FL 030.7
depots (5) n 084.7
depressed (2) adj 074.2
depressing (2) adj 005.5
~ day (1) n 005.5
depression (2) n 002.6
Depression (5) 075.6
~ baby (1) n 075.6
(De)pression (1) 065.8
depressions (1) n 112.1
deputies (2) n 112.5
deputy (7) n/adj 070.8
~ sheriff (3) n 070.8
deranged (2) adj 073.4
derby (1) n 081.9
Derby (3) 086.5
derelict (41) n/adj 113.7
~ house (1) n 113.8
~ street (1) n 114.8
derelicts (6) n 113.7
dermatitis (1) n 081.8
Dermott (1) AR 087.7
derogatory (1) adj 077.8
derrick (4) n 104.5
derricks (2) n 104.5
derringer (7) n 027.3
dervish (3) n 112.2
des (3) pron F 030.3
Des (10) 087.2
~ Arc (6) AR 087.2

~ Arc Bayou (2) AR
030.3
~ Moines (2) IO 087.3
descendant (1) n 069.2
descendants (3) n 066.5
descended (1) v 078.5
descent (3) n 084.8
describe (2) v 013.1
desert (4) n/adj 029.8
~ boots (2) n 123.8
deserted (7) v/adj 063.3
~ her (2) v 082.1
~ him (1) v 082.1
~ house (2) n 090.3
~ the school (1) v
083.4
deserts (1) n 078.6
deserve (1) v 053.8
deserved (3) v 078.6
desex (1) v 036.1
desexed (1) v 036.1
Desha (7) AR 087.7
~ County (2) AR 087.2
design (3) n/v 102.7
designate (1) v 006.1
designed (4) v 052.5
~ for (1) v 052.5
~ on (1) v 096.7
designer (3) adj 123.6
~ clothes (2) n 123.6
~ fashions (1) n 123.6
desire (3) n 052.8
Desire (2) 106.3
~ project (1) n 106.7
desisting (1) v 007.3
desk (879) n/adj 083.8
~ chair (1) n 083.8
~ deal (1) n 083.8
~ jobs (1) n 083.8
~ lamp (2) n 019.9
~ seats (2) n 083.8
desk[N-i] (562) n 083.8
deskes (97) n 083.8
desks (163) n 083.8
deskunk (4) v 059.4
deskunked (2) v 059.4
despair (1) v 079.5
despensa (1) n S 010.1
desperadoes (2) n 080.7
despise (1) v 077.8
despised (4) v 091.6
despondent (1) adj 075.6
dessert (5) n/adj 048.5
~ set (1) n 070.6
~ topping (1) n 048.5

dessertspoon (5) n 017.8
Destin (3) FL 087.2
destitute (2) adj 113.6
~ alcoholic (1) n 113.6
destroy (2) v 088.4
destroy[V-t] (1) v 096.7
destroyed (2) v 102.6
destroy(er) (1) n 033.3
destructive (1) adj 091.7
det (2) adj 006.1
~ shower (1) n 006.1
~ showers (1) n 006.1
detached kitchen (2) n
009.9
detachment (1) n 065.8
detail (2) n F 081.9
details (1) n 070.4
detective (2) n 112.5
detectives (2) n 112.5
detention (2) n 014.1
deteriorate (1) v 055.9
deteriorated (3) v 046.9
deteriorates (3) v 078.3
deteriorating (1) v 065.8
determinator (1) n 070.6
determine (5) v 074.8
determined (13) v/adj
074.8
determited (1) v 088.9
detour (8) n/adj 031.7
~ road (1) n 031.7
detoxification center (1) n
112.8
Detroit (49) MI 087.4
~ Purple Gang (1)
097.8
deuce (17) n/adj 109.4
~ and a quarter (12) n
080.8
~ and a quarters (1) n
109.4
~ wagon (1) n 109.4
Deutsch (1) n G 127.2
deux (1) n F 001.1
dev off (1) v 095.3
devant (1) prep F 072.7
devastating (1) adj 065.8
deveined (1) v 060.8
develop (1) v 058.5
developed (10) v 073.1
developing (1) v 007.2
development (2) n 025.8
Development (1) 080.6
developments (2) n 106.3
Devers (1) TX 087.4

deviate (1) n 113.7
devices (2) n 052.1
devil (1042) n/adj 090.1
~ aspirin (1) n 080.7
~ bread (1) n 057.1
~ doctors (1) n 060A.4
~ egg (1) n 046.1
~ fly (1) n 060A.4
~ hawk (2) n 060A.4
~ head (1) n 056.8
~ in the ditch (1) n
130.2
~ -may-care (1) adj
090.1
~ (o)possum (1) n
080.8
Devil (2) 088.7
DEVIL (1) 090.1
devil[N-k] (22) adj 099.5
~ child (1) n 099.5
~ food (1) n 056.8
~ food cake (1) n
045.2
~ food cakes (1) n
122.1
~ horse (11) n 060A.4
~ horses (3) n 060A.4
~ mushroom (1) n
057.1
~ snuff (2) n 057.1
~ stools (1) n 057.1
deviled (10) adj 046.1
~ eggs (5) n 046.2
~ ham (2) n 090.1
devilish (8) adj 090.1
Deville (1) LA 086.2
devilment (14) n 090.1
devilments (1) n 088.8
devil's (47) adj 010.3
~ den (1) n 010.3
~ dive (1) n 095.4
~ flames (1) n 090.1
~ food (1) n 122.8
~ horse (16) n 060A.4
~ imps (1) n 090.2
~ lane (1) n 016.5
~ little horse (1) n
060A.4
~ lye (1) n 090.1
~ pincushion (1) n
057.1
~ shoestrings (1) n
061.4
~ snuff (4) n 057.1
~ -snuffbox (2) n 057.1

~ -snuff(box) (1) n 057.1
~ something (1) n 057.1
~ -walking-stick (2) n 060A.4
~ work (2) n 090.1
devils (29) n 090.1
Devils (5) 087.7
~ Den (1) AR 087.7
~ Lake (2) LA TX 030.7
~ Pocket (1) TX 088.9
~ River (1) TX 090.1
Devine (1) TX 087.7
Devon (2) GA 087.2
(de)vote (1) v 070.7
devoted (3) v/adj 066.8
~ friend (1) n 129.4
~ to one another (1) v 081.4
devout (1) adj 126.5
dew (78) n/adj 094.7
~ cracks (1) n 089.9
~ melon (12) n 056.7
~ melons (2) n 056.7
~ poison (1) n 088.8
~ poisoning (1) n 094.7
~ shower (1) n 006.6
~ turtles (1) n 060.7
~ web (3) n 061.3
Dew (2) 056.9
dewberries (283) n 062.5
dewberry (107) n/adj 062.5
~ jelly (1) n 062.4
~ pies (1) n 048.3
~ sling (1) n 048.3
~ vines (1) n 062.3
dewber(ry) (4) n/adj 062.4
~ cobbler (2) n 048.3
dewclaws (3) n 096.4
dewdrop (1) n 061.9
dewlap (1) n 084.9
dewy (1) adj 006.6
Dexamyl (1) 114.2
Dexedrine (1) 114.2
Dexter (3) 107.6
~ Avenue (2) 107.7
DFW (2) 106.5
~ Airport (1) 106.5
D'Hanis (1) TX 087.9
d'herbe (2) adj F 055A.4
diaberry (1) n 080.4

diabetes (8) n 065.8
diabetic (1) adj 070.7
diable (2) n F 090.2
diab(le) (1) n F 090.1
diabolo (1) n S 090.1
Diabolo (2) 030.7
diagnose (1) v 070.7
diagnostic (1) adj 085.2
diagonal (66) adj/adv 108.3
~ parking (7) n 108.3
diagonally (54) adv 085.2
diagram (2) n/v 025.1
dial (1) n 110.2
dialect (6) n 131.6
dialects (2) n 131.3
dialog (1) n 131.4
Dials Knob (1) GA 030.8
diamond (32) n/adj 123.1
~ belly (1) n 060.7
~ ring (9) n 123.1
~ rings (3) n 123.1
Diamond (19) 056.8
diamondback (28) n/adj 088.7
~ rattler (4) n 090.8
~ rattlers (2) n 088.8
~ rattlesnake (2) n 081.8
~ rattlesnakes (1) n 088.8
~ turtle (4) n 060.6
diamondbacked rattler (1) n 080.8
diamondbacks (1) n 060.7
Diamondbacks (1) 056.8
diamonds (4) n 123.1
Diamonds (4) 056.9
Dian Lake (1) AR 087.9
diangling (1) v 085.2
diaper (32) n/adj 026.5
~ pin (26) n 026.5
~ pins (4) n 026.5
diarrhea (3) n 090.8
diarrhea's mammy (1) n 081.8
dias (5) n S 002.4
Diaz (1) 068.3
D'Iberville (3) MS 087.7
dice (3) n/adj 130.9
~ mobile (1) n 109.4
diced ham (1) n 121.3
dick (7) n/adj 059.4
~ licker (1) n 039.7
~ teaser (1) n 124.9

Dick (1) 030.7
Dickard Bay(ou) (1) LA 030.3
dickens (22) n 064.4
dicks (1) n 112.5
Dick's hatband (1) n 042.8
Dickson (6) TN 087.4
dictionary (5) n 084.1
did (2515) v 102.8
~ away (1) v 102.8
~ away with (7) v 102.8
~ him wrong (2) v 082.1
~ without (2) v 032.3
d(id) (14) v 076.1
(di)d (44) v 043.8
diddies (1) n 036.9
diddle(x2) (1) interj 038.5
Diddleham Street (1) 107.6
diddling around (1) v 081.4
diddy diddies (1) n 036.9
didies (1) n 099.9
didn't (2731) v 102.8
~ do right (1) v 082.1
~ go to class (1) v 083.4
~ make it (6) v 078.5
~ treat him right (1) v 082.1
~ want him (9) v 082.1
~ want to (1) v 085.4
~ want to marry him (3) v 082.1
(di)dn't (4) v 052.4
Dido (1) LA 087.5
didy pin (1) n 026.5
die (101) n/v 078.5
~ away (1) v 079.3
~ down (10) v 007.3
~ from (2) v 078.7
~ -up (1) n 080.6
~ with (8) v 078.7
die[V-p] (2) v 081.8
die[V-r] (17) v 078.5
~ of (1) v 078.7
~ with (1) v 078.7
die[V-s] (1) v 024.9
die[V-t] down (1) v 099.6
died (1885) v/adj 078.5

~ by (2) v 078.5
~ dead (1) v 078.6
~ down (11) v 007.3
~ flesh (1) n 078.2
~ from (100) v 078.7
~ of (194) v 078.7
~ off (6) v 078.5
~ out (11) v 078.5
~ with (206) v 078.7
Diego (11) 082.6
dies (14) v 095.8
~ down (2) v 007.3
~ of (1) v 078.7
diesel (6) n/adj 109.6
~ engines (1) n 111.1
~ oil (1) n 024.1
~ truck (1) n 109.6
~ trucks (1) n 109.7
diesels (1) n 032.4
diet (5) n/adj 114.7
~ bread (2) n 044.4
difference (118) n 070.8
different (171) adj 074.7
differently (2) adv 013.7
difficult (7) adj 075.1
dig (59) v 030.2
~ in (12) v 043.4
~ on (2) v 092.9
~ under (1) v 096.7
~ with (1) v 120.7
digest (5) v 070.8
digged (1) v 030.1
digger (76) n 120.6
digger's (1) adj 007.4
diggers (24) n 030.2
digging (10) v/adj 057.4
~ time (1) n 080.9
digital (2) adj 004.3
~ watch (1) n 004.3
~ watches (1) n 004.3
dignity (1) n 032.3
digs (4) v 042.7
~ up (1) v 089.9
dike (11) n/v 030.2
~ up (7) v 028.1
diked (8) v 028.2
~ out (5) v 028.1
~ up (3) v 028.1
dikes (2) n 030.2
diking (3) v 028.1
~ up (2) v 028.1
dilatory (1) adj 074.6
dilemma (1) n 131.2
dill (2) n/adj 055.9
~ bread (1) n 044.4

Dillard (1) GA 087.7
diller (1) n 007.5
Dillinger (2) 092.9
Dillon (1) MS 087.2
dillweed (1) n 089.9
dillydally (1) v 094.5
dimanche (1) n F 002.1
dimbo (1) n 069.3
dime (22) n/adj 114.6
~ a dozen (1) n 033.3
~ bag (4) n 114.1
~ bags (1) n 114.1
~ store (2) n 088.9
Dime Box (2) TX 087.5
dime[N-i] (1) n 001.5
dimensions (1) n 052.5
dimes (2) n 114.1
diminishing (11) v 007.3
dimity (1) n 089.9
Dimsty Dumpster (1)
  117.3
dimwit (2) n 073.4
dine (3) v 048.7
~ with (2) v 048.7
dinero (3) n S 114.5
dinette (9) n/adj 007A.6
~ area (1) n 007A.4
~ suite (1) n 007A.6
ding (3) n/adj 083.1
dingbats (1) n 080.7
dingbusted (1) adj 092.1
dinged (1) v 080.9
dinghies (2) n 024.6
dinghy (8) n 024.6
dingy-looking (1) adj
  005.5
dining (754) n/v/adj
  007A.2
~ area (23) n 007A.8
~ chair (2) n 008.9
~ chairs (1) n 008.8
~ den (1) n 007A.5
~ hall (1) n 065.9
~ her (1) v 081.4
~ nook (1) n 007A.5
~ room (697) n 007A.3
~ -room (1) adj 007A.6
~ -room chair (1) n
  008.8
~ -room chairs (3) n
  008.8
~ -room closet (1) n
  009.6
~ -room furniture (1) n
  009.4

~ room-kitchen (1) n
  009.9
~ -room outfit (1) n
  080.6
~ -room suite (3) n
  009.4
~ rooms (4) n 007A.4
~ table (2) n 007A.6
din(ing) room (8) n
  007A.5
dink (2) adj 067.8
dinks (1) n 126.5
dinky (2) adj 097.9
dinner (336) n/adj 002.3
~ -and-dance parties
  (1) n 083.1
~ bell (2) n 084.8
~ bucket (1) n 017.3
~ chop (1) n 121.3
~ dance (1) n 083.1
~ dances (1) n 083.1
~ fork (3) n 017.9
~ hour (1) n 080.7
~ kettle (10) n 017.6
~ kettles (1) n 017.6
~ knife (2) n 017.8
~ music (1) n 130.8
~ parties (1) n 130.7
~ party (3) n 130.7
~ pot (16) n 017.6
~ pots (4) n 017.6
~ ring (22) n 123.1
~ rings (3) n 123.1
~ rolls (4) n 044.4
~ room (1) n 007A.4
~ spoon (1) n 017.9
~ table (1) n 073.7
~ wine (1) n 114.7
~ wines (1) n 114.7
Dinner Key (5) 106A.2
dinner[N-i] (1) n 080.2
dinners (6) n 130.7
dinnertime (14) n/adj
  037.4
~ stories (1) n 080.6
dinnerware (2) n/adj
  017.1
~ dishes (1) n 017.1
dinosaurs (1) n 080.2
Diom Motel (1) 084.3
dip (91) n/v/adj 048.5
~ bucket (1) n 019.2
~ net (2) n 084.8
~ out (1) v 040.7
~ piles (1) n 014.8

~ sauce (1) n 048.5
dip[V-r] (2) v 080.8
diphtheria (620) n 079.7
diphtheri(a) (219) n
  079.7
diphther(ia) (7) n 079.7
diphthe(ria) (1) n 079.7
(diph)theria (2) n 079.7
(diph)theri(a) (3) n
  079.7
diploma (5) n 070.6
diplomas (2) n 070.7
dipped (7) v/adj 122.4
Dipped (1) 122.4
dipper (66) n/adj 026.6
~ drag (1) n 081.8
~ gourds (2) n 088.7
~ land (1) n 029.8
dippers (13) n 048.8
dipping (14) v/adj 057.3
~ days (1) n 088.8
~ out (1) v 051.5
~ vat (2) n 080.8
~ vats (2) n 060A.8
dips (9) n/v 048.5
~ with (1) v 048.4
Dipster Dumpster (1)
  117.3
Dipsty Dumpster (3)
  117.3
Dipsy (5) 117.3
~ Dumpster (3) 117.3
~ Dumpsters (1) 117.3
~ Dumpsy (1) 117.3
direct (7) v/adj/adv 065.9
direction (20) n 006.4
directions (3) n 001.2
(di)rections (1) n 070.8
directly (72) adv 070.3
director (52) n 117.4
director[N-i] (1) n 082.7
director's chair (1) n
  008.8
directors (1) n 080.8
directs (1) v 052.5
dirge (2) n 079.2
dirk (1) n 104.3
dirks (1) n 104.3
dirt (1812) n/v/adj/adv
  031.7
~ -and-jam fireplace (1)
  n 008.2
~ -and-stick chimleys
  (1) n 008.1

~ -and-stick chimney
  (1) n 008.1
~ bag (1) n 116.8
~ bank (1) n 031.4
~ basement (1) n 031.6
~ bikes (1) n 075.6
~ box (1) n 079.1
~ catcher (1) n 116.8
~ cellars (1) n 015.5
~ cheap (1) adj 031.6
~ chimley (12) n 008.1
~ chimleys (3) n 008.1
~ chimney (2) n 008.1
~ chimneys (2) n 008.1
~ -clod battles (1) n
  130.5
~ country road (1) n
  031.7
~ dauber (373) n
  060A.6
~ dauber[N-i] (4) n
  060A.6
~ -dauber[N-k] (1) adj
  060A.6
~ dauber[N-k] den (1)
  n 060A.6
~ dauber[N-k] nest (2)
  n 060A.6
~ dauber's nest (1) n
  060A.6
~ daubers (193) n
  060A.6
~ dodger (1) n 060A.6
~ farmer (2) n 031.6
~ floor (1) n 031.6
~ flooring (1) n 031.6
~ floors (1) n 031.6
~ frog (1) n 060.4
~ garden (1) n 050.5
~ gobblers (1) n
  060A.6
~ house (1) n 031.6
~ kiln (1) n 015.5
~ -land farmers (1) n
  069.7
~ machines (1) n 089.8
~ -moving equipment
  (1) n 031.7
~ pen (1) n 015.4
~ poor (3) n 053.1
~ pot (1) n 114.1
~ rake (7) n 120.7
~ road (380) n 031.7
~ -road sport (1) n
  028.1

~ roads (235) n 031.6
~ sidewalk (2) n 031.9
~ street (3) n 031.6
~ streets (4) n 031.6
~ trails (1) n 031.6
~ turtle (1) n 060.7
~ up (1) v 021.6
~ wagon (1) n 089.8
~ wagon road (1) n 031.7
~ wasp (4) n 060A.6
~ worm (1) n 060.5
dirtier (1) adj 066.1
dirtiest (2) adj 092.1
dirting (1) v 015.8
dirty (143) adj 114.9
~ clothes (4) n 025.1
~ -clothes bag (3) n 116.6
~ -clothes basket (19) n 116.6
~ -clothes baskets (2) n 020.1
~ -clothes box (3) n 116.6
~ -clothes bucket (1) n 116.6
~ -clothes cabinet (1) n 116.6
~ -clothes closet (1) n 080.7
~ -clothes corner (1) n 010.6
~ -clothes hamper (26) n 116.6
~ -clothes pail (2) n 116.6
~ devil (1) n 114.5
~ dozen (1) n 129.7
~ dozens (1) n 129.7
~ houses (1) n 114.9
~ man (1) n 124.7
~ money (1) n 114.5
~ mother (1) n 080.7
~ movie (5) n 114.9
~ -movie theater (1) n 114.9
~ movies (3) n 114.9
~ rice (4) n 090.8
~ woman (1) n 124.8
Dirty Half Dozen (1) 129.6
disability (1) n 115.4
disabled (2) adj 072.9
disagreeable (8) adj 075.1

disappeared (2) v 083.4
disappearing (2) adj 010.7
~ stair (1) n 010.7
~ staircase (1) n 009.8
disappoint (1) v 081.2
disappointed (135) v 081.1
~ him (5) v 082.1
disaster (3) n/adj 065.9
~ area (2) n 108.7
disband (1) v 043.5
disbands (1) v 083.2
disc (357) n/adj 021.7
~ -and-bog harrow (1) n 021.7
~ breaker (1) n 021.7
~ cultivator (1) n 021.9
~ harrow (74) n 021.7
~ har(row) (8) n 021.7
~ -harrowed (1) v 021.7
~ harrower (1) n 021.7
~ -harrowing (1) v 021.7
~ harrows (18) n 021.7
~ machine (1) n 021.7
~ plow (27) n 021.6
~ plows (3) n 021.6
~ tiller (1) n 021.7
~ tractor (1) n 021.7
~ turner (1) n 021.6
disc[N-i] (20) n 016.7
discard (1) v 010.2
discarded (7) v/adj 065.9
~ him (1) v 082.1
discards (3) n/v 010.2
disces (13) n 021.7
discharge (5) n/v 077.5
discharged (1) v 101.2
disciplinarian (1) n 066.8
discipline (4) n/adj 070.6
disciplines (1) n 025.2
disco (28) n/adj 130.8
~ dances (1) n 083.1
~ dancing (3) n 083.1
~ music (3) n 130.8
~ shoes (1) n 123.8
discolating (1) v 084.8
discontented (1) adj 074.2
discontinued (1) v 095.2
discos (1) n 081.8
discotheque (3) n 083.1
discotheques (1) n 080.9
discount (88) n/adj 094.5
~ base (1) n 094.5

~ price (2) n 094.5
discouraged (3) v 073.7
discourages (1) v 053.4
discovered (1) v 057.8
discriminate [P-0] (1) v 039.6
discs (14) n 021.7
discus (1) n 021.7
discuss (2) v 043.3
discussed (1) v 053.6
discussing (4) v 013.5
disease (22) n/adj 071.9
~ questions (1) n 079.6
diseases (1) n 053.6
disencouraged (1) v 088.9
disgusted (5) adj 074.2
disgusting (2) adj 073.8
dish (462) n/v/adj 017.7
~ cabinet (1) n 010.1
~ cabinets (2) n 010.1
~ -cleaning towels (1) n 018.4
~ closet (1) n 010.1
~ cupboard (1) n 010.1
~ in (1) v 049.2
~ pie (1) n 048.3
~ safe (3) n 010.1
~ towel (299) n 018.4
~ tow(el) (2) n 018.4
~ towels (34) n 018.4
~ -wash cloth (1) n 018.3
~ washing (5) n 010.2
~ wiper (1) n 018.4
dishcloth (323) n/adj 018.3
~ gourds (1) n 056.6
dishcloths (29) n 018.3
dished out (1) v 049.4
dishes (497) n/adj 018.1
~ cloth (1) n 018.3
dishing up (1) v 049.4
dishmop (2) n 018.3
dishpan (26) n/adj 018.1
~ hands (1) n 072.5
dishpans (3) n 020.1
dishrag (596) n/adj 018.3
~ gourd (1) n 056.6
~ gourds (1) n 056.6
dishrags (27) n 018.3
dishwash (1) v 018.1
dishwasher (9) n 018.1
dishwashers (1) n 018.1
dishwashing cloth (1) n 018.3

dishwater (4) n 048.8
disinfect (1) n 078.3
disjoint (1) v 072.3
disk (44) v 021.7
disk[V-r] (1) v 021.7
disked (2) v 021.7
diskes (3) v 021.7
~ up (2) v 021.7
disking (7) v/adj 021.7
~ machine (1) n 120.4
~ procedure (1) n 021.7
dismal (10) adj 005.5
~ day (2) n 005.5
dismiss (13) v 083.2
dismiss[V-p] (3) v 083.2
dismiss[V-r] (2) v 083.2
dismiss[V-t] (4) v 083.2
dismissed (17) v 083.2
dismisses (23) v 083.2
dismounted (1) v 034.4
Disney (1) 106.4
Disneyland (1) 065.9
dispatcher (2) n 025.4
dispensers (1) n 117.3
disperse (1) v 005.7
display (5) n/adj 019.2
~ concern (1) n 084.9
~ stand (1) n 019.2
displays (1) n 065.8
disposable (3) adj 116.8
~ bag (1) n 116.8
~ trash bag (1) n 116.8
~ vacuum-cleaner bag (1) n 116.8
disposal (26) n/adj 117.1
disposals (3) n 117.1
dispose of (2) v 099.4
disposed (2) v/adj 065.3
disposer (4) n 117.1
(di)sposer (1) n 117.1
disposition (47) n 073.2
(dis)position (2) n 065.3
dispositioned (3) adj 073.2
(di)spute (3) n/v 066.9
disrecollect (1) v 100.4
disremember (28) v 100.4
dis(remember) (1) v 100.4
disrespective (1) adj 096.8
dissatisfied (2) adj 101.6
dissipate (1) v 007.3
distance (261) n/adj 040.1
dis(tance) (1) n 039.5

distance[N-i] (1) n 053.5
distances (1) n 039.5
distant (13) adj 040.1
distill (2) v 081.8
(di)still (3) v 088.8
distilled into (1) v 048.8
distillery (2) n 050.8
(di)stillery (1) n 075.6
Distillery Branch (1) AR
    030.7
distinction (3) n 040.7
distress sale (1) n 094.5
distributing (1) 075.6
distributor (5) n 021.6
(di)stributor (2) n 065.9
(di)stributors (1) n 021.6
district (63) n/adj 070.7
    ~ attorney (1) n 068.6
    ~ (at)torney (1) n
        070.8
    ~ courthouse (1) n
        065.8
    ~ judge (5) n 068.6
District (48) 087.5
    ~ of Columbia (6)
        087.1
    ~ of Columbi(a) (1)
        087.1
    ~ of Columbus (1)
        087.1
    ~ [P-0] Columbia (1)
        087.1
districts (5) n 065.8
disturbance (2) n 082.5
disturbed (10) adj 075.2
    ~ weather (1) n 005.5
disunabled (1) adj 088.7
ditch (1057) n/v/adj
    030.1
    ~ bank (5) n 030.2
    ~ banks (1) n 030.2
    ~ channel (1) n 030.5
    ~ digger (1) n 030.2
    ~ him (2) v 082.1
    ~ line (2) n 031.9
    ~ off (1) v 030.2
Ditch (11) 030.7
    ~ Eighty-One (1) AR
        030.7
    ~ Eighty-Two (1) AR
        030.3
    ~ Forty-Three (1) AR
        030.7
ditchdigger (1) n 030.2
ditchdiggers (1) n 030.2

ditched (20) v/adj 030.1
    ~ him (8) v 082.1
    ~ off (2) v 030.1
ditcher (2) n 030.2
ditches (307) n 030.2
ditching (33) v/adj 030.1
    ~ him (1) v 082.1
    ~ machine (2) n 030.2
    ~ machines (1) n 030.2
dittany tea (1) n 061.4
ditty (2) adj 080.6
    ~ bags (1) n 080.6
    ~ box (1) n 080.6
div (79) v 095.3
    ~ in (13) v 095.3
    ~ off (7) v 095.3
    ~ over (2) v 095.3
divan (146) n/adj 009.1
    ~ chair (1) n 008.8
(di)van (1) n 009.1
divan[N-i] (1) n 009.1
divans (12) n 009.1
divd in (1) v 095.3
dive (624) n/v/adj 095.3
    ~ board (2) n 022.6
    ~ in (26) v 095.3
    ~ off (18) v 095.3
    ~ off in (1) v 034.4
    ~ on (1) v 095.3
dive[V-r] (48) v 095.3
    ~ off (3) v 095.3
dive[V-t] (14) v 095.3
    ~ off (1) v 095.3
dived (751) v 095.3
    ~ in (48) v 095.3
    ~ off (24) v 095.3
    ~ off of (1) v 095.3
diven (22) v 095.3
    ~ in (1) v 095.3
diver (1) n 025.7
diverger ditch (1) n 030.2
diversion (2) adj 030.2
    ~ ditch (1) n 030.2
dives (33) n/v 095.3
    ~ off of (1) v 095.3
divide (12) n/v 031.3
    ~ up (1) v 065.1
Divide (1) 081.8
divided (6) v/adj 105.7
    ~ at (3) v 105.7
    ~ esplanade (1) n 107.3
    ~ lane (1) n 107.3
    ~ skirts (1) n 080.7
Divided (1) 085.8
divider (23) n/adj 107.3

~ drainage (1) n 011.6
~ line (2) n 107.3
~ lines (1) n 107.3
~ strip (1) n 107.3
(di)vider strip (1) n 031.9
dividers (6) n 107.3
dividing (17) adj 107.3
    ~ line (11) n 107.3
    ~ lines (5) n 107.3
    ~ ridge (1) n 030.9
divine (1) adj 089.6
diving (103) n/v/adj
    095.3
    ~ board (20) n 095.3
    ~ boards (4) n 022.6
    ~ in (2) v 095.3
di(ving) board (1) n
    075.9
division (5) n/adj 001A.3
    ~ line (2) n 107.3
    ~ town (1) n 080.6
Division (1) 080.7
divisions (1) n 065.8
Divisions (1) 084.9
divorce (2) adj 130.7
    ~ party (1) n 130.7
    ~ widow (1) n 063.3
divorced (11) v/adj 063.3
divorceded (1) v 070.6
divorcee (37) n 063.3
divvy up (1) v 089.9
dix (1) n F 001.5
Dixie (69) FL TX 021.6
    ~ Avenue (1) 107.7
    ~ Baptist (2) 089.1
    ~ Blue Steel (1) 022.3
    ~ Boy (1) 021.6
    ~ Gem (1) 056.9
    ~ Highway (4) 031.6
    ~ Home[N-i] (1) 106.3
    ~ Lee peas (1) n
        055A.4
    ~ plow (2) n 021.6
    ~ plows (1) n 021.6
    ~ Queen (20) 056.9
    ~ Queen watermelon
        (2) n 056.9
    ~ Queens (1) 056.9
    ~ Rattlesnake (1) 056.9
    ~ runner (1) n 054.7
    ~ sweep (1) n 021.6
    ~ Sweet (1) 056.9
    ~ Sweets (1) 056.9
    ~ Yarn Mills (1) 013.8
Dixieland jazz (1) n 130.8

Dixies (2) 021.7
Dixon (3) MS 087.6
    ~ -Mason line (1) n
        080.8
dizzy (5) adj 076.6
    ~ day (1) n 005.5
    ~ spell (1) n 076.1
diz(zy) (1) adj 076.6
D'Lo (1) MS 086.8
do (5936) n/v/interj
    102.8
    ~ a hook (1) v 083.4
    ~ away (1) v 024.7
    ~ -away bed (1) n
        029.2
    ~ away with (2) v
        099.4
    ~ (a)way with (1) v
        099.4
    ~ -do-do (1) interj
        092.8
    ~ drop in (1) n 080.6
    ~ for (4) v 044.2
    ~ -for (9) n 009.1
    ~ -fors (2) n 009.1
    ~ -it-yourself lawn
        mower (1) n 120.1
    ~ -nothing (2) n 069.7
    ~ -right boy (1) n
        112.5
    ~ -right boys (1) n
        112.5
    ~ to (2) v 052.7
    ~ up (13) v 102.8
    ~ with (29) v 088.4
    ~ without (28) v 032.3
    ~ (wi)thout (2) v 032.3
d(o) (17) v 057.5
Do-Right (1) 112.5
do[V-p] (267) v 012.8
    ~ for (1) v 102.9
do[V-r] (5) v 102.8
do[V-s] (2) v 092.6
do[V-t] (3) v 058.3
do[+V] (1) v 026.1
DOA (1) 081.9
Doakes Creek (1) TN
    030.7
Doberman (1) 033.3
Doc (5) 064.5
docile (4) adj 073.3
dock (490) n/v/adj 031.4
    ~ weeds (1) n 015.9
Dock (1) 031.4
dockboard (1) n 031.4

docked (4) v 031.3
docks (60) n/v 031.4
Docks (4) 031.4
docs (1) n 084.6
doctor (396) n/v/adj 068.7
~ book (1) n 088.8
~ on (1) v 099.9
~ snake (3) n 060A.4
~ woman (1) n 065.2
doc(tor) (1) n 060A.4
Doctor (9) 068.5
~ Pepper (2) 121.8
doctoral (1) adj 065.8
doctored (8) v 080.7
doctoring (7) v 084.9
~ on (2) v 101.7
doctor's (2) adj 053.4
~ degree (1) n 053.4
~ office (1) n 084.2
doctors (151) n 025.5
Doctors' Hospital (1) 108.2
Doddsville (2) MS 094.9
dodge (37) v/adj 130.4
~ ball (34) n 130.4
~ down (1) v 096.4
Dodge (7) GA TX 087.2
~ City (2) 106.3
~ County (2) GA 087.2
dodger (276) n/adj 044.5
~ balls (1) n 044.8
~ corn bread (2) n 044.6
Dodger (2) 044.7
dodgers (150) n 044.6
dodging (5) v/adj 096.4
~ ball (1) n 080.6
~ bread (1) n 044.6
~ cars (1) n 106.6
dodo (13) n/adj F 073.4
~ bird (1) n 125.2
dodos (1) n F 083.1
doe (35) n 035.1
Doe Creek (1) TN 030.7
doer (1) n 074.2
Doerun (1) GA 087.6
does (1312) n/v 012.8
(doe)s (1) v 049.5
doesn't (757) v 013.1
dog (2563) n/adj 033.1
~ and the rabbit (1) n 098.4
~ bees (1) n 060A.7
~ bite (17) n 033.4

~ -blay (1) adj 044.3
~ bread (8) n 044.6
~ breeze (1) n 099.9
~ -caught (1) v 033.4
~ -chained (1) v 021.5
~ chains (1) n 084.8
~ day (2) n 091.9
~ days (7) n 033.1
~ days weather (1) n 080.6
~ do (1) n 129.8
~ do-do (1) n 033.2
~ dog (2) n 033.3
~ eater (1) n 080.6
~ eye (1) n 033.1
~ fennel (5) n 061.4
~ finger (1) n 091.8
~ firedogs (1) n 008.3
~ flies (3) n 088.7
~ fly (1) n 060A.6
~ food (7) n 048.4
~ gnats (1) n 060A.8
~ horns (1) n 008.3
~ iron (34) n 008.3
~ iron[N-i] (6) n 008.3
~ irons (313) n 008.3
~ links (1) n 084.8
~ luck (1) n 081.8
~ mush (1) n 050.3
~ owl (1) n 059.2
~ -paddle (2) v 095.6
~ pen (1) n 118.7
~ pound (1) n 070.6
~ run (5) n 080.8
~ -run house (1) n 118.7
~ sticks (1) n 008.3
~ strangler (1) n 006.1
~ tags (1) n 092.8
~ teeth (1) n 071.8
~ thumb (1) n 061.4
~ tick (2) n 060A.8
~ ticks (1) n 060A.4
~ tired (6) adj 075.4
~ tracks (1) n 106.3
~ tree (1) n 061.9
~ urns (1) n 008.3
~ windows (1) n 080.6
~ yard (1) n 095.8
Dog (17) 109.3
~ Creek (1) AR 030.7
~ Face (1) 125.1
~ Keys (1) MS 087.8
~ Road (1) 031.7

~ Tail Creek (1) TN 030.7
dog(x2) (1) interj 033.2
dog[N-i] (4) n 008.3
dog[V-t] (18) v 092.7
dogbit (271) v 033.4
~ by (2) v 033.4
~ in (1) v 033.4
dogbite (1) v 033.4
dogbite[V-t] (1) v 033.4
dogbitten (38) v 033.5
dogcatcher (2) n 088.8
dogcatchers (1) n 070.6
dogfights (1) n 033.1
dogfire (1) n 008.3
dogged (21) v 033.1
dogging (2) v 081.4
doggone (81) v/adj/adv/ interj 092.4
doggonedest (1) adj 092.1
doggy (3) n/adv 074.9
Doggy (1) 033.1
doghouse (10) n/adj 009.8
~ windows (1) n 097.8
doghouses (3) n 009.8
dogie (7) n 033.8
dogies (1) n 033.8
dogman (1) n 084.9
dogmatic (5) adj 074.8
dog's back (1) n 015.9
dogs (664) n 033.1
dogtrot (68) n/adj 118.7
~ cabin (1) n 080.6
~ house (6) n 118.7
~ houses (4) n 088.8
dogtrots (1) n 007A.5
dogwood (213) n/adj 061.8
~ brush broom (1) n 010.5
~ brush brooms (1) n 080.7
~ bush (1) n 061.8
~ bushes (3) n 062.2
~ sprouts (3) n 010.5
~ tree (17) n 061.9
~ trees (18) n 061.8
Dogwood (2) 075.7
~ Acres (1) AL 075.7
~ Lake (1) MS 030.7
dogwoods (26) n 061.8
doilies (1) n 080.6
doing (551) v 102.8
~ around (1) v 095.9

~ without (1) v 032.3
doings (3) n 080.8
Doles (1) GA 087.4
doll (102) n/v/adj 101.5
~ baby (1) n 064.4
~ up (42) v 028.1
Doll (3) 064.4
dollar (38) n/adj 095.9
~ bill (1) n 080.7
~ hoarder (1) n 073.5
~ quilt (1) n 029.1
~ vine (1) n 061.4
~ wine (1) n 114.7
dol(lar) (1) n 051.8
dollar[N-i] (23) n 057.4
dollar's (1) adj 051.5
dollars (260) n 114.5
Dollarway (1) 031.6
dolled up (19) v 028.1
dollhouse (1) n 118.9
dolling up (7) v 028.1
dolls (30) n 101.5
dolly (4) n 023.3
Dolores Creek (2) TX 030.7
dolphin (8) n 059.9
dolphins (3) n 059.9
Dom Perrito (1) 075.6
Domas (1) 107.8
Dome (3) 031.1
~ Stadium (1) 106.8
domestic (13) n/adj 019.6
~ animals (3) n 036.5
~ bags (1) n 019.6
~ cloth (1) n 095.9
~ fowls (1) n 036.6
~ wood (1) n 092.7
~ work (2) n 065.8
dominant animal (1) n 039.4
Domineck owl (1) n 059.2
Dominecker (2) 059.3
~ peckerwood (1) n 059.3
Domineckers (1) 036.7
domineering (2) adj 074.8
~ woman (1) n 124.3
Dominique (5) 036.7
~ chicken (2) n 121.5
Domi(nique) (1) 036.9
Dominiques (1) 036.6
domino (6) v/adj 065.1
~ halls (1) n 084.9
dominoed (1) v 078.6

dominoes (6) n 130.7
Don (9) 124.5
~ Juan (8) 124.5
dona (1) n S 069.6
Donahue (1) TX 030.7
Donaldson (2) AR 087.4
Donaldsons Point (1) TN 087.4
Donaldsonville (4) LA 087.2
~ Graveyard (1) 078.8
Donaldson(ville) (1) LA 087.2
Donaldsville (1) LA 086.2
Donalsonville (5) GA 087.4
donate (2) v 070.6
donated (1) v 053.4
donates (1) v 075.6
donation (2) n 095.7
donations (2) n 123.5
done (2325) v/adj 102.8
~ and (5) v 057.8
~ away (5) v 102.8
~ (a)way (1) v 102.8
~ away with (21) v 032.4
~ (a)way with (3) v 099.4
~ bar (1) n 099.5
~ by (1) v 036.1
~ food (2) n 048.4
~ for (1) v 045.9
~ in (6) v 075.5
~ out (1) v 075.5
~ over (3) v 102.8
~ up (7) v 094.3
~ with (2) v 012.9
~ without (1) v 032.3
done[+A] (53) v 057.9
done[+B] (3) v 057.9
done[+N] (1) v 057.9
done[+V] (1398) v 057.8
Donegans Slough (1) AL 030.7
donkey (57) n/adj 033.7
donkeys (28) n 033.7
Donna (1) TX 087.5
don't (5383) v 058.2
~ -care person (1) n 074.6
~ do that (1) v 033.2
~ move (1) v 037.5
(do)n't (5) v 092.2

don't[V-p] (1267) v 013.1
~ like him (1) v 082.1
~ want him (1) v 082.1
~ want to marry him (1) v 082.1
don't[V-r] (1) v 013.3
don'ter (1) n 119.7
dooby (4) n 048.3
dood (3) v 102.9
doodads (3) n 081.9
doodle (5) n/adj 060A.3
~ buggy (1) n 081.9
~ doodles (1) n 060A.7
doodlebug (7) n/adj 080.7
~ cars (1) n 081.9
~ legs (1) n 060A.8
~ train (1) n 088.7
doodlebugs (4) n 080.7
doodled (2) v 080.7
doodles (2) n 060A.7
doofus (2) n 073.4
doolack (1) n 026.5
Dooley (15) 055.5
~ gravy (1) n 048.5
~ potato (1) n 055.5
~ yam (2) n 055.5
~ yams (7) n 055.5
Dooleys (3) 055.5
doolies (1) n 062.6
Doolittle Road (1) 107.6
doolunkum (1) n 048.3
Dooly (6) GA 087.3
~ County (3) GA 087.1
~ District (1) GA 087.1
doom (1) n 129.4
doomajiggers (1) n 096.9
door (1934) n/adj 010.5
~ bolt (3) n 030.8
~ facing (2) n 011.1
~ garden (1) n 050.5
~ porch (1) n 010.8
~ stoop (1) n 010.9
doorknob (186) n 030.8
(door)knob (2) n 030.8
doorknobs (21) n 030.8
doornail (5) n 078.5
doorprop (1) n 011.1
door's (1) adj 053.3
doors (108) n 011.1
doorstep (24) n 010.7
doorsteps (68) n 010.7
doorstop (1) n 011.1
doos (14) v 074.1

doozer (1) n 006.1
dope (122) n/adj 114.2
~ addict (17) n 114.3
~ addicts (5) n 114.3
~ charges (1) n 099.5
~ dealer (1) n 114.4
~ dealers (1) n 114.4
~ fiend (9) n 114.3
~ fiends (1) n 114.3
~ freak (1) n 114.3
~ grease (1) n 023.7
~ parties (1) n 130.7
~ peddler (7) n 114.4
~ pusher (3) n 114.4
~ seller (1) n 114.4
~ thing (1) n 099.5
doped (1) v 023.7
dopehead (6) n 114.3
dopeheads (3) n 081.8
doper (4) n 114.3
dopes (1) n 090.8
dopey (2) adj 114.3
doping (3) v 057.4
Dora (1) 073.4
Dorado (23) 087.5
(Do)rado (1) 087.2
Doran Cove (1) AL 087.3
Dora's batch (1) n 055A.8
Doraville (2) GA 086.2
Dorcas (1) 063.5
Dorcheat (2) LA 030.3
~ Bayou (1) LA 030.3
Dorchester (1) TX 087.8
dork (1) n 125.2
dormer (6) n/adj 007A.5
~ room (2) n 009.8
~ window (1) n 009.8
~ windows (1) n 007A.7
dormers (1) n 084.8
dormitories (2) n 053.5
dormitory (5) n 065.8
dorms (3) n 108.7
Dorsey (3) MS 105.1
Dort (2) 023.6
dos (1) n 083.1
dose (7) n/v 070.7
~ out (1) v 075.8
doses (1) n 016.7
Dossville (1) MS 087.3
doted (1) adj 099.5
Dothan (47) AL 087.4
~ Road (1) 107.7
dots (1) n 107.3

double (480) n/adj/adv 001A.5
~ -A harrow (1) n 021.7
~ -A harrows (1) n 021.7
~ armful (1) n 019.8
~ -B ax (1) n 088.8
~ -barrel shotgun (1) n 096.8
~ bath (1) n 007A.8
~ bed (4) n 065.9
~ -bed couch (1) n 009.1
~ beds (1) n 009.3
~ bit (3) n 021.6
~ -bit (1) adj 081.8
~ -bit axes (1) n 080.6
~ -blade ax (1) n 080.7
~ -blade plow (1) n 021.6
~ -bladed plow (1) n 021.6
~ block (1) n 080.7
~ -breaking (1) v 033.7
~ -breasted (1) adj 090.8
~ buggy (3) n 019.4
~ bugs (1) n 060A.4
~ buster (2) n 093.8
~ -car garage (2) n 007A.8
~ carport (2) n 007A.7
~ chair (1) n 009.1
~ chimley (7) n 008.1
~ chimney (5) n 008.1
~ closet (1) n 009.6
~ -cooked (1) adj 050.1
~ cottage (3) n 118.9
~ cousin (1) n 088.7
~ crop (3) n 041.5
~ -cropping (1) v 041.5
~ cultivator (1) n 021.6
~ -cunted (1) adj 006.1
~ -cut (1) v 041.5
~ cutting harrow (1) n 021.7
~ -dare (4) v 058.2
~ desk[N-i] (1) n 083.8
~ -dipping (1) v 081.8
~ disc (2) n 021.6
~ -dog dare (4) v 058.2
~ -dog dared (1) v 058.2
~ dresser (2) n 009.2

~ -end sack (1) n 019.6
~ -ended pirogue (1) n 024.6
~ -ender (4) n 024.6
~ -enders (1) n 024.6
~ ~ fact (1) n 080.7
~ fireplace (7) n 007A.1
~ -fireplace chimley (1) n 008.1
~ fireplaces (1) n 008.2
~ first cousin (2) n 099.7
~ first cousins (1) n 088.9
~ fist[N-i] (6) n 072.2
~ fistes (1) n 072.2
~ floor (2) n 010.8
~ flue (1) n 023.2
~ foot (4) n 021.6
~ -footed plow (1) n 021.6
~ -freeze (1) v 007.6
~ funeral (1) n 079.2
~ gallery (1) n 010.8
~ harness (2) n 021.3
~ harrow (2) n 021.7
~ hay (1) n 041.5
~ -headed rising (1) n 077.4
~ hill plow (1) n 021.6
~ hole (1) n 012.1
~ -horse plow (2) n 021.6
~ -horse wagon (1) n 021.3
~ house (6) n 118.9
~ hull (1) n 024.6
~ image (1) n 131.4
~ -joint (2) adj 088.7
~ -jointed (2) adj 074.1
~ kin (1) n 066.6
~ laning (1) n 058.1
~ line (2) n 107.3
~ lines (1) n 107.3
~ log house (4) n 007A.1
~ mind (1) n 053.7
~ -mule plows (1) n 021.6
~ mules (1) n 033.7
~ -named (1) adj 064.4
~ parlor (1) n 007.8
~ pen (3) n 007A.3
~ -pen (1) adj 010.9

~ -pen barn (1) n 118.7
~ -pen house (3) n 118.9
~ -pen houses (1) n 014.1
~ -pen log house (2) n 007A.2
~ -penned house (1) n 014.1
~ pillow (1) n 028.9
~ planting (1) n 041.5
~ plow (18) n 021.6
~ plow stock (1) n 021.6
~ plow stocks (1) n 021.6
~ plows (3) n 021.6
~ pneumonia (1) n 078.6
~ pole (2) n 020.9
~ porch (2) n 010.8
~ -S hill (1) n 030.8
~ sack (1) n 019.7
~ scrape (1) n 021.6
~ sets (1) n 021.7
~ shaft (1) n 020.9
~ sheds (1) n 014.4
~ shovel (62) n 021.6
~ -shovel (1) v 021.6
~ -shovel blade (1) n 021.6
~ shovel plow (4) n 021.6
~ shovels (12) n 021.6
~ shuffle (1) n 083.1
~ singletree (40) n 021.3
~ singletrees (3) n 021.3
~ sliding door (1) n 011.1
~ somersault (1) n 095.5
~ somerset (3) n 095.5
~ somersets (1) n 095.5
~ spruce (1) n 061.9
~ stables (1) n 015.2
~ stack chimley (1) n 008.1
~ stock (6) n 033.7
~ -strain (2) v 048.2
~ strainer (1) n 048.2
~ strap (1) n 022.3
~ string (3) n 033.7
~ swing (1) n 022.9

~ swingletree (9) n 021.3
~ swings (1) n 022.9
~ tandem (1) n 033.7
~ team (44) n 033.7
~ team of horses (2) n 033.7
~ team of mules (1) n 033.7
~ -teamed (1) v 093.9
~ -tenant house (2) n 118.9
~ tenants (1) n 119.1
~ tenements (1) n 118.7
~ -tongue (1) n 021.3
~ -top persimmon tree (1) n 075.9
~ trace (2) n 021.3
~ U (1) n 092.7
~ ugly (1) adj 125.1
~ wagon (2) n 020.8
~ wedding ring (2) n 088.8
~ -wedding-ring ceremony (1) n 082.3
~ -whip (1) v 019.4
~ X (1) n 114.9
~ yellow lines (1) n 107.3
~ yoke (1) n 033.7
~ yoke of oxen (2) n 033.7
~ yokes (1) n 033.7
doub(le) (1) adj F 073.3
Double (8) 030.7
~ Bayou (1) FL 030.7
~ Branch (3) AL FL TX 030.7
~ Bridges Creek (1) AL 030.7
~ OMs (1) 119.7
~ Pond Branch (1) FL 030.7
~ Springs (3) AL MS 087.3
doubled (4) v 001A.5
doubleheader (1) n 012.1
doubles (2) n 118.6
doubletree (502) n 021.3
doubletrees (28) n 021.3
doubling tree (1) n 021.3
doubt (14) n/v 025.4
doubtful (1) adj 088.3
doubts (1) n 012.2

dough (87) n/adj 114.5
~ bait (2) n 060.5
~ board (1) n 080.9
~ bread (2) n 044.8
~ doughnut (1) n 122.4
~ stage (3) n 080.7
~ tray (1) n 017.8
~ trays (1) n 088.7
doughball (3) n 061.2
doughballs (1) n 044.6
doughboy (3) n/adj 045.3
~ bread (1) n 044.4
doughboys (4) n 044.6
Dougherty (5) GA 087.6
doughnut (667) n/adj 045.2
~ centers (1) n 045.2
~ cutter (1) n 045.2
~ hole (4) n 045.2
~ holes (9) n 045.2
~ kettle (1) n 017.6
~ parlor (1) n 045.2
~ shop (1) n 045.2
~ twist (7) n 122.7
~ twists (1) n 122.7
doughnuts (575) n 045.2
doughs (1) n 044.7
doughty bread (1) n 044.6
Douglas (22) AZ GA 030.7
~ County (2) GA 087.6
~ Lake (3) TN 030.7
~ Road (5) 031.7
Douglass (4) 083.2
Douglasville (2) GA 087.4
douze (1) n F 001.6
dove (448) n/v/adj 095.3
~ hunting (1) n 093.6
~ hunts (1) n 089.8
~ in (31) v 095.3
~ in the window (1) n 029.1
~ off (9) v 095.3
~ -shoot (1) v 012.8
Dove Creek (1) GA 030.3
dove[N-i] (2) n 036.6
doved (2) v 095.3
doven (1) v 095.3
Dover (2) NJ TN 088.9
Dover's powder (1) n 078.4
doves (15) n 059.3
dovetail (2) n/v 097.8
Dow (5) 021.6

~ -Law (2) 021.6
~ -Law cotton plows (1) n 021.9
~ -Law planter (1) n 021.6
~ -Law planters (1) n 021.9
Dowd Creek (1) MS 030.7
dowdy-looking (1) adj 067.6
dowel (1) n 120.5
Dowling (1) 105.4
down (7529) adj/adv 082.6
~ -and-out (7) adj 113.7
~ -and-out hotel (1) n 113.8
~ -and-outer (1) n 113.7
~ bed (5) n 029.2
~ comfort (2) n 029.1
~ comforter (1) n 029.1
~ gutters (1) n 011.5
~ in the mouth (1) adj 072.9
~ in the valley (1) n 130.6
~ in the weathers (1) adj 072.9
~ on your case (1) adv 129.6
~ -South brogue (1) n 104.8
~ time (1) n 090.8
~ -to-earth (3) adj 073.6
Down (9) 082.6
~ Eastern (1) 082.6
~ -Home Baptist[N-i] (1) 089.1
~ the Bay (6) 105.1
~ the Hill (1) 105.1
down[N-i] (2) n 123.5
downed (1) v 065.2
downer (3) n 114.2
downers (39) n 114.2
downest (1) adj 064.7
downfall (3) n 006.1
downflow (1) n 006.1
downhearted (1) adj 074.2
downhill (4) adv 030.8
downies (1) n 029.1

downing pour (1) n 006.1
downpour (411) n/adj 006.1
~ rain (2) n 006.1
~ shower (1) n 006.1
downpours (4) n 006.1
downright (10) adv 005.9
downs (137) n 083.1
Downs (2) 087.3
~ community (1) GA 087.3
downside (1) prep 075.9
downspout (25) n 011.5
downspouts (12) n 011.5
downstair[N-i] (1) n 010.8
downstairs (37) n/adj 007A.3
~ bath (1) n 118.3
~ front porch (1) n 010.8
~ porch (1) n 010.8
downtown (313) n/adj 105.2
~ airport (2) n 106.5
~ area (12) n 105.3
~ are(a) (1) n 105.3
~ areas (1) n 105.2
~ Atlanta (3) n 106.4
~ Dallas (4) n 105.2
~ Houston (1) n 105.3
~ Huntsville (1) n 105.2
~ Jackson (1) n 105.2
~ Memphis (1) n 105.3
~ Miami (2) n 105.3
~ Mobile (1) n 105.6
~ River Walk (1) n 106.7
~ school (1) n 080.8
~ section (4) n 105.2
~ store (1) n 105.3
Downtown Connector (1) 107.5
downward (1) adv 040.4
downwash (1) n 006.1
downy (4) n/adj 059.3
~ woodpecker (3) n 059.3
dowry (1) n 063.3
Doza (1) 030.7
doze (1) v 076.6
dozed (1) v 041.4
dozen (31) n 129.7
Dozen (1) 129.6

dozen[N-i] (10) n 129.7
dozens (28) n 129.7
doz(ens) (1) n 129.7
dozing (2) v/adj 076.6
~ off (1) v 076.6
drab (3) adj 073.6
~ day (2) adj 005.5
drabby (1) adj 005.5
Draculas (1) 065.8
draft (31) n/adj 023.2
~ animals (1) n 033.7
~ beer (5) n 121.9
~ horses (3) n 034.2
~ pipe (1) n 008.1
drafted (3) v 012.2
~ in (1) v 057.9
~ up (1) v 075.7
drafting (1) v 021.4
drafts (1) n 020.9
drag (751) n/v/adj 021.5
~ along (1) v 021.5
~ around (1) v 021.5
~ harrow (34) n 021.7
~ har(row) (5) n 021.7
~ harrows (8) n 021.7
~ lights (1) n 096.5
~ out (1) v 041.4
~ -out (2) adj 021.5
~ -outs (2) n 080.6
~ queen (5) n 124.2
~ race (2) n 021.5
~ sackers (1) n 021.5
~ saw (1) n 021.5
~ scrapers (1) n 021.6
~ seine (1) n 080.7
~ set (1) n 124.2
~ -tooth harrows (1) n 021.7
~ -type tooth harrow (1) n 021.7
~ up (1) v 021.5
Drag (2) 030.7
~ Nasty (1) GA 030.7
drag[V-p] (1) v 021.5
drag[V-r] (15) v 021.5
drag[V-t] (8) v 021.5
dragged (419) v/adj 021.5
~ land (1) n 041.4
~ out (3) v 021.5
dragger (1) n 069.3
dragging (76) v 021.5
~ along (1) v 021.5
draggy (1) adj 076.6
dragline (10) n 021.5
draglines (1) n 021.5

dragnet (1) n 021.5
dragnets (1) n 060A.4
dragon (11) n/adj 090.1
~ berry (1) n 062.2
~ bugs (1) n 060A.4
Dragon (2) 090.1
dragonflies (69) n 060A.4
dragonfly (280) n 060A.4
dragon(fly) (1) n 060A.4
drags (9) n/v 123.6
drain (779) n/v/adj 011.5
~ board (6) n 018.2
~ canal (1) n 030.2
~ ditch (15) n 030.2
~ ditches (13) n 030.2
~ down (1) v 030.1
~ drip board (1) n 018.4
~ gutter (2) n 011.5
~ lines (1) n 011.5
~ off (25) v 030.1
~ out (12) v 030.1
~ rack (1) n 030.1
~ spout (3) n 011.5
~ tile (2) n 030.1
~ troughs (1) n 011.5
drain[V-p] out (1) v 013.6
drain[V-r] (2) v 030.1
drain[V-s] (1) v 030.1
drain[V-t] (2) v 030.1
drainage (175) n/adj 030.2
~ ~ area (1) n 030.1
~ areas (1) n 030.2
~ canal (5) n 030.2
~ canals (1) n 030.2
~ ditch (75) n 030.2
~ ditches (13) n 030.2
~ ditching (1) n 030.2
~ furrow (1) n 030.2
~ pipes (2) n 011.5
~ pit (1) n 030.2
~ purposes (1) n 030.1
~ structure (1) n 030.2
~ system (1) n 030.1
Drainage (1) 030.1
drainages (2) n 011.5
drained (69) v 030.1
~ off (6) v 030.1
~ out (2) v 030.1
drainer (10) n 030.1
drainers (2) n 011.5
draining (269) v/adj 030.1

~ off (1) v 030.1
~ out (1) v 030.1
~ pan (2) n 030.1
~ rack (1) n 018.2
drainpipe (23) n 011.5
drainpipes (8) n 011.5
drains (55) n/v 011.5
~ off (6) v 030.1
~ out (2) v 030.1
drake (3) n 036.8
drakes (2) n 055A.8
dram (1) n 050.8
dramas (1) n 126.3
drame (1) v 097.2
drank (884) v 049.1
~ out of (1) v 049.1
~ up (1) v 049.1
dranked (38) v 049.1
drankeded (1) v 049.1
dranken (11) v 049.1
drape (4) n 009.5
draped (1) adj 009.5
draperies (31) n 009.5
drapery (9) n 009.5
drapes (112) n 009.5
draps on down (1) v 117.8
drat (4) v/interj 092.3
drats (2) n/interj 092.3
Draughons Business College (1) 083.6
draw (374) n/v/adj 104.4
~ back (2) v 104.4
~ back up (1) v 027.9
~ bed (1) n 055.4
~ bit (1) n 039.2
~ bucket (3) n 017.3
~ chain (2) n 038.6
~ curtains (2) n 009.5
~ day (1) n 080.6
~ draperies (1) n 009.5
~ drapes (4) n 009.5
~ horse (3) n 039.4
~ horses (1) n 022.1
~ like (1) v 012.7
~ lines (1) n 038.9
~ up (173) v 027.9
~ with (1) v 040.6
draw[V-r] (5) v 104.4
drawbridge (3) n 080.7
drawed (399) v 104.4
~ back (1) v 104.4
~ off (1) v 021.5
~ out (4) v 104.4
~ out of (2) v 104.4

~ over (1) v 104.4
~ up (218) v 027.9
~ -up (2) adj 027.9
drawer (21) n 009.2
draw(er) (2) n 009.2
drawer[N-i] (58) n 009.2
draw(er)[N-i] (13) n 009.2
drawers (539) n/adj 027.4
drawing (46) n/v/adj 021.4
~ knife (8) n 020.8
~ knives (2) n 017.8
~ room (5) n 007.8
~ rooms (1) n 007.8
~ up (1) v 027.9
drawings (1) n 083.1
drawknife (14) n 017.8
drawknives (2) n 017.8
drawl (2) n 080.6
drawl[V-r] (1) v 104.4
drawls (1) n 131.4
drawn (74) v/adj 104.4
~ by (1) v 025.5
~ sauce (1) n 048.5
~ up (28) v 027.9
drawned up (1) v 027.9
draws (25) n/v 104.4
~ from (1) v 103.4
~ up (12) v 027.9
drawy (1) adj 088.8
dray (17) n/adj 084.9
~ harrow (1) n 021.7
~ line (1) n 102.3
~ wagon (1) n 021.4
~ wagons (1) n 021.1
drayman (2) n 080.8
draymen (1) n 080.6
drays (2) n 080.6
Drayton (1) GA 087.3
drazzle (1) n 006.5
dread (4) v 091.6
~ to (1) v 091.6
dread[V-r] (1) v 091.6
dreaded (35) v 091.6
~ to (4) v 091.6
dreadful (1) adj 005.5
dreadfully (2) adv 091.7
dreads (3) v 091.6
dream (599) n/v 097.2
~ of (1) v 097.2
dream[V-r] (41) v 097.2
~ about (2) v 097.2
~ of (1) v 097.2
dream[V-t] (32) v 097.2

~ of (1) v 097.2
dreamboat (1) n 109.4
dreamed (811) v 097.2
~ about (12) v 097.2
~ (a)bout (1) v 097.2
~ of (9) v 097.2
dreaming (47) v 097.2
Dreamland Drive (1) 106.1
dreams (26) n/v 097.2
dreamt (329) v 097.2
~ about (3) v 097.2
~ (a)bout (1) v 097.2
~ of (3) v 097.2
dreamy (1) adj 005.5
dreary (164) adj 005.5
~ day (79) n 005.5
~ -looking day (3) n 005.5
~ -old (1) adj 005.5
~ -type (1) adj 005.5
dredge (26) n/v/adj 030.1
~ boat (2) n 024.6
~ boats (1) n 024.6
~ ditch (5) n 030.2
~ ditches (5) n 030.2
~ horses (1) n 034.5
dredge[V-r] (1) v 030.1
dredged (11) v/adj 030.2
~ ditch (2) n 030.2
~ out (1) v 030.1
dredger (1) n 099.7
dredgers (1) n 080.7
dredges (1) n 030.2
dredging (11) v 030.2
~ out (1) v 030.1
dregs (1) n 114.8
drench (3) n/v 018.2
drenched (1) v 077.3
drencher (1) n 006.1
drenching (5) v/adj 080.8
~ rain (1) n 006.1
Dresden (4) TN 017.1
~ china (1) n 017.1
dress (665) n/v/adj 028.1
~ bag (2) n 019.5
~ bedspread (1) n 028.7
~ boots (3) n 123.8
~ clothes (2) n 123.6
~ coat (4) n 027.1
~ in (1) v 074.3
~ like (1) v 123.6
~ lumber (1) n 070.7
~ out (2) v 080.6

~ pair of pants (1) n 027.4
~ pants (6) n 027.4
~ pantses (1) n 027.4
~ pattern (1) n 084.9
~ shirt (1) n 027.6
~ shoe (2) n 123.8
~ shoes (35) n 123.8
~ suit (5) n 027.7
~ suits (2) n 027.7
~ (su)spenders (1) n 028.5
~ up (309) v 028.1
~ -up (1) n 028.1
~ -up clothes (1) n 027.7
~ -up shoes (1) n 123.8
dress[V-p] (2) v 073.7
dress[V-t] (3) v 028.1
dressed (143) adj/v 028.1
~ for (1) v 027.1
~ in (4) v 079.3
~ lady (1) n 113.3
~ oak (1) n 061.8
~ off (1) v 084.9
~ up (84) v 028.1
~ -up (1) adj 028.1
~ -up shoes (1) n 123.8
~ [P-0] (1) v 079.3
dresser (638) n/adj 009.2
~ drawer (11) n 009.2
~ draw(er) (2) n 009.2
~ drawers (12) n 009.2
~ robe (1) n 009.2
~ scarves (1) n 009.2
dresserette (1) n 009.2
dressers (113) n 009.2
dresses (15) n/v 026.3
~ up (1) v 028.1
dressier (3) adj 080.7
dressing (209) n/v/adj 048.5
~ bread (1) n 044.6
~ closet (1) n 007A.8
~ down (2) n 065.5
~ pen (1) n 015.4
~ room (20) n 118.3
~ table (15) n 009.2
~ tables (2) n 009.2
~ up (38) v 028.1
dress(ing) (1) n 044.8
dressings (5) n 044.6
dressmaker (1) n 039.6
dressy (6) adj 028.1
~ shoe (2) n 123.8

~ shoes (2) n 123.8
~ stuff (1) ñ 028.1
drew (531) v 021.5
~ back (1) v 104.4
~ out (2) v 104.4
~ to (1) v 032.5
~ up (85) v 027.9
Drew (5) AR MS 088.8
~ County (1) AR 087.3
drewing (1) v 021.5
dribble (1) n 030.6
dribbling rain (1) n 006.6
driblets (2) n 037.2
dried (606) v/adj 055.9
~ apple (30) n 054.6
~ -apple cake (1) n 048.3
~ -apple pies (1) n 054.6
~ -apple snip (1) n 054.6
~ apple[N-i] (4) n 054.6
~ apples (308) n 054.6
~ -apricot pie (1) n 054.6
~ apricots (1) n 054.6
~ -back turtle (1) n 060.7
~ beans (10) n 055A.2
~ chips (1) n 008.6
~ creek (1) n 090.8
~ fruit (111) n 054.6
~ fruits (7) n 054.6
~ grass (1) n 041.5
~ Johnson grass (1) n 041.5
~ lima beans (1) n 055A.3
~ meat (3) n 046.3
~ onions (1) n 055.6
~ out (8) v 055.9
~ over (1) v 090.4
~ peach (3) n 054.6
~ -peach pie (1) n 054.6
~ peaches (54) n 054.6
~ pear (1) n 054.6
~ peas (1) n 055A.4
~ pieces (1) n 054.6
~ pies (1) n 054.6
~ prunes (1) n 054.6
~ salt pork (1) n 046.5
~ up (25) v 055.9
~ -up hay (1) n 041.5

drier (1) n 092.7
dries (6) v 018.4
~ up (2) v 055.9
drift (5) n/v/adj 031.5
~ in (1) v 053.4
~ track (1) n 114.8
drifter (6) n 066.7
drifters (1) n 069.7
driftes in (1) v 098.7
drifting (1) adj 006.9
driftwood (4) n 075.6
drifty music (1) n 130.8
drill (15) n/v/adj 088.8
~ press (1) n 075.8
~ team (1) n 033.7
~ worm (1) n 060.5
drilled (1) v 098.6
drillers (1) n 081.8
drilling (11) n/v/adj 019.7
~ rigs (1) n 098.7
~ room (1) n 007.8
drills (3) n 041.2
drink (1211) n/v/adj 049.1
~ box (1) n 084.9
~ from (1) v 049.1
~ glass (1) n 048.9
~ houses (1) n 113.8
~ of (1) v 049.6
~ out of (2) v 049.1
~ up (1) v 076.9
~ with (1) v 049.1
drink[V-p] (1) v 049.1
drink[V-r] (68) v 049.1
drink[V-t] (44) v 049.1
drinkable (1) adj 049.1
drinked (85) v 049.1
~ up (1) v 049.1
drinkeded (1) v 049.1
drinken (17) v 049.1
drinker (12) n 113.6
drinkers (1) n 109.4
drinking (121) n/v/adj 049.1
~ bucket (1) n 017.2
~ cup (3) n 049.1
~ fountain (21) n 108.8
~ fountains (2) n 108.8
~ glass (4) n 048.9
~ gourd (1) n 026.6
~ man (1) n 049.1
~ parties (1) n 130.7
~ party (1) n 130.7
~ places (1) n 002.8

~ purposes (1) n 103.6
~ trough[N-i] (1) n 035.8
~ water (3) n 048.9
~ woman (1) n 080.7
Drinking Methodist (1) 126.7
drinks (72) n/v 048.9
Drinkyville (1) 105.6
drip (50) n/v/adj 048.8
~ cheese (1) n 048.1
~ clabber (2) n 048.1
~ coffee (9) n 048.8
~ control (1) n 081.9
~ -dry (1) v 018.4
~ -dry pants (1) n 027.4
~ lye soap (1) n 080.6
~ noodle (1) n 080.6
~ pan (1) n 081.8
~ pot (2) n 048.8
~ process (1) n 048.8
drip[V-r] (1) v 048.8
dripolate (1) v 048.8
dripolator (9) n/adj 048.8
~ pot (1) n 048.8
dripolators (1) n 048.8
dripped (3) v 048.8
~ out of (1) v 051.2
dripper (2) n/adj 048.8
drippers (1) n 088.8
dripping (7) v 006.6
Dripping (2) 030.7
~ Rocks (1) GA 030.7
~ Springs (1) TX 086.3
drippings (5) n 046.5
drips through (2) v 048.8
drit drats (1) n 060.3
driv (34) v 011.3
~ across (1) v 011.3
~ through (1) v 011.3
drive (1165) n/v/adj 011.3
~ along (1) v 011.3
~ and park (1) n 108.4
~ around (1) v 011.3
~ down (1) v 011.3
~ in (3) v 011.3
~ -in (21) n/adj 031.8
~ -in market (2) n 116.2
~ -in movie (2) n 084.4
~ -in store (1) n 116.2
~ -in stores (1) n 116.2

~ -in theater (7) n 084.4
~ -ins (3) n 116.2
~ on (1) v 011.3
~ on out (1) v 011.3
~ out (1) v 011.3
~ outs (1) n 031.8
~ rein (1) n 039.2
~ through (1) v 091.8
~ up (4) v 011.3
Drive (70) 107.8
drive[V-p] (2) v 011.3
drive[V-r] (5) v 011.3
drive[V-t] (3) v 011.3
drived (8) v 011.3
driven (387) v/adj 011.3
~ in (7) v 011.3
~ off (1) v 011.3
~ through (1) v 011.3
driver (15) n/adj 011.3
driver's license (1) n 011.3
drivers (3) n 039.4
drives (35) n/v 011.3
driveway (426) n 031.8
driveways (8) n 031.8
driving (135) n/v/adj 011.3
~ along (4) v 011.3
~ at (1) v 053.7
~ for (1) v 053.4
~ horse (1) n 039.4
~ in (3) v 025.5
~ license (1) n 040.6
~ lines (6) n 039.2
~ rein (1) n 039.1
~ reins (1) n 039.1
~ well (1) n 093.6
~ whip (1) n 019.4
drizzle (356) n/v/adj 006.6
~ -drazzle (1) n 006.6
~ rain (3) n 006.6
drizzle[V-r] (1) v 006.6
drizzled (3) v/adj 006.6
~ rain (1) n 006.6
drizzles (4) n 006.6
drizzlies (1) n 091.8
drizzling (98) v/adj 006.6
~ rain (9) n 006.6
drizzly (10) adj 006.6
~ day (4) n 005.5
~ weather (2) n 006.6
drone (2) n 091.8
droop (3) v 027.9

drooped up (1) adj 072.9
droopy (11) adj 072.9
~ -drawers day (1) n 005.5
drop (299) n/v/adj 033.9
~ a baby (1) v 033.9
~ a calf (117) v 033.9
~ a child (1) v 065.1
~ a foal (1) v 033.9
~ around (1) v 093.1
~ biscuit (1) n 044.4
~ biscuits (2) n 044.4
~ boxes (1) n 093.7
~ by (1) v 080.9
~ cake (1) n 044.4
~ cliff (1) n 031.2
~ door (1) n 088.7
~ doors (1) n 014.3
~ edge (1) n 011.2
~ her (1) v 082.1
~ her calf (2) v 033.9
~ him (2) v 082.1
~ it (6) v 033.9
~ lines (1) n 019.9
~ my handkerchief (1) n 130.3
~ off (1) v 070.7
~ -off (14) n 031.5
~ -offs (1) n 031.2
~ out of (1) v 025.5
~ over (1) n 011.2
~ pipe (1) n 030.1
~ pit (1) n 084.8
~ roof (2) n 011.4
~ shed (2) n 015.1
~ side (2) n 011.2
~ side lumber (1) n 011.2
~ siding (35) n 011.2
~ siding board (1) n 011.2
~ that calf (2) v 033.9
~ the calf (5) v 033.9
~ the handkerchief (37) n 130.3
~ the thimble (1) n 083.8
~ them (1) v 033.9
~ tongue (1) n 020.8
Drop (1) 080.7
drop[V-r] (7) v 078.5
~ dead (5) v 078.5
~ my handkerchief (1) n 130.3
~ the calf (1) v 033.9

drop[V-t] (1) v 057.8
dropout (5) n 083.4
dropped (74) v/adj 033.9
~ a calf (5) v 033.9
~ cookies (1) n 045.2
~ dead (3) v 078.6
~ egg (3) n 046.2
~ eggs (1) n 046.2
~ her (3) v 082.1
~ her calf (1) v 033.9
~ him (35) v 082.1
~ his lunch (1) v 080.3
~ off (3) v 078.6
~ out (5) v 083.4
~ out of school (2) v 058.7
~ siding (1) n 011.2
dropper (1) n 021.7
droppers (4) n 081.9
dropping (32) v/adj 033.9
~ a calf (3) v 033.9
~ a handkerchief (1) n 098.4
~ calves (1) v 033.9
~ off (2) v 041.4
~ on (1) v 006.1
~ out (2) v 078.6
~ rain (1) n 006.6
~ the handkerchief (7) n 080.9
droppings (1) n 091.9
drops (8) n/v 006.6
~ him (1) v 082.1
dropsies (1) n 088.7
dropsy (3) n/adj 088.6
~ vine (1) n 062.3
dross (1) n 008.6
drought (827) n/v/adj 007.1
~ out (2) v 007.1
~ weather (1) n 007.1
drought[N-i] (1) n 007.1
droughts (9) n 007.1
droughty (2) adj 007.1
drove (979) n/v 011.3
~ down (4) v 011.3
~ in (18) v 011.3
~ off (3) v 011.3
~ on (1) v 011.3
~ over (2) v 011.3
~ through (1) v 011.3
~ to (3) v 075.6
~ up (10) v 011.3
droven (9) v 011.3
~ in (2) v 011.3

droves (10) n 055A.8
drown (544) v 096.1
~ out (3) v 096.1
drown[V-p] out (2) v 013.6
drown[V-r] (117) v 096.1
drown[V-t] (81) v 096.1
drownded (361) v 096.1
~ out (3) v 096.1
drownden (1) v 096.1
drownder (4) n 006.1
drownding (13) v 096.1
drowndings (1) n 096.1
drowned (689) v 096.1
~ off (1) v 096.1
~ out (1) v 096.1
drowner (1) n 006.1
drowning (45) v 096.1
~ out (1) v 096.1
drowns (4) v 096.1
drowsy (126) adj 076.6
drubbed (1) v 065.5
drubbing (1) n/v 065.5
drudge boat (1) n 030.2
drudgery (2) n 065.8
drug (857) n/v/adj 021.5
~ addict (36) n 114.3
~ addiction (1) n 114.3
~ addicts (2) n 114.3
~ along (1) v 021.5
~ around (2) v 021.5
~ culture (1) n 105.9
~ dealers (2) n 114.4
~ down (2) v 021.5
~ in (2) v 021.5
~ off (2) v 021.5
~ out (6) v 021.5
~ out of (1) v 021.5
~ pusher (6) n 114.4
~ pushers (1) n 114.4
~ seller (1) n 114.4
~ up (2) v 021.5
~ vendor (1) n 114.4
drugged (21) v 021.5
druggie (2) n 114.3
druggies (1) n 114.3
drugs (16) n 114.1
drugstore (11) n/adj 116.2
~ cowboy (4) n 069.9
~ quarterback (1) n 067.8
~ -type operation (1) n 116.2
drugstores (3) n 116.1

droves (10) n 055A.8
Druid Hills (4) 106.1
drum (63) n/adj 019.1
~ table (2) n 008.9
Drum (2) 087.9
drumfish (3) n 059.9
drummed (1) v 097.2
drummer (5) n 080.8
drummers (5) n 080.8
drummers' room (2) n 007A.5
drums (17) n 019.2
drumstick (10) n 037.1
drumsticks (1) n 091.8
drunk (539) n/v/adj 049.1
~ Catholic (1) n 126.6
~ tank (40) n 112.8
~ throw-up (1) n 080.3
~ up (1) v 049.1
drunkard (22) n 113.6
drunkard's Pat (1) n 089.8
drunkards (11) n 113.6
drunked (1) v 049.1
drunken (16) n/v/adj 049.1
~ bum (1) n 113.7
~ sprawl (2) n 049.1
drunks (29) n 113.6
drupe (1) n 054.4
druv (5) v 011.3
dry (1094) n/v/adj 007.1
~ apple (2) n 054.6
~ ap(ple) (1) n 054.6
~ apple[N-i] (2) n 054.6
~ apples (4) n 054.6
~ bean (1) n 055A.3
~ beans (5) n 055A.4
~ bed (2) n 030.4
~ bottom (1) n 029.4
~ branch (2) n 030.6
~ branches (1) n 030.5
~ butter beans (1) n 055A.3
~ cattle (2) n 033.6
~ cedar (1) n 008.6
~ chips (1) n 008.6
~ -clean laundry (1) n 010.6
~ cleaner (3) n 010.6
~ cleaners (5) n 010.6
~ -cleaning bag (1) n 123.7
~ cloth (61) n 018.4

~ cloths (2) n 018.4
~ corn (2) n 056.2
~ cough (1) n 076.5
~ cows (3) n 033.6
~ creek (3) n 030.4
~ creek bed (1) n 030.6
~ creeks (1) n 030.5
~ cypress (1) n 008.6
~ day (1) n 007.1
~ days (1) n 007.1
~ dishrag (2) n 018.4
~ ditch (1) n 030.4
~ dock (2) n 031.4
~ -done (1) adj 002.6
~ drizzle (2) n 006.6
~ drought (7) n 007.1
~ frogs (1) n 060.4
~ fruit (5) n 054.6
~ good (1) n 070.7
~ -good store (2) n 081.9
~ goods (2) n 088.9
~ -goods store (2) n 084.8
~ graft (1) n 007.1
~ grass (4) n 041.5
~ hardwood (1) n 008.6
~ heaves (3) n 080.3
~ house (1) n 011.7
~ iron (1) n 010.6
~ kiln (1) n 080.8
~ kindling (7) n 008.6
~ land (1) n 060.4
~ -land (4) n/adj 060.7
~ -land cooters (1) n 060.7
~ -land farming (1) n 080.9
~ -land fellow (1) n 060.7
~ -land fish (6) n 056.8
~ -land frog (6) n 060.4
~ -land terrapin (29) n 060.7
~ -land terrapins (1) n 060.7
~ -land toad-frog (1) n 060.4
~ -land turtle (20) n 060.7
~ -land turtles (8) n 060.7
~ -lander (1) n 060.7

~ lima beans (1) n 055A.3
~ line (1) n 040.5
~ look (1) n 123.9
~ meat (2) n 046.5
~ murrain (1) n 015.6
~ off (1) v 012.8
~ out (3) v 055.9
~ peach (1) n 054.6
~ peach[N-i] (1) n 054.6
~ peaches (2) n 054.6
~ peas (3) n 055A.3
~ pen (1) n 015.4
~ period (4) n 007.1
~ pork (2) n 046.5
~ postes (1) n 016.5
~ preserve[N-i] (1) n 054.6
~ rag (37) n 018.4
~ roads (1) n 031.6
~ rot (2) n 050.8
~ salt (9) n 046.3
~ salt bacon (1) n 046.5
~ salt meat (7) n 046.3
~ salt pork (1) n 046.3
~ season (13) n 007.1
~ seasons (2) n 007.1
~ sink (2) n 009.2
~ sitting (1) n 088.9
~ slab (1) n 015.4
~ soil (2) n 029.8
~ spell (475) n 007.1
~ spells (3) n 007.1
~ squash (1) n 056.6
~ sticks (1) n 008.6
~ stone (1) n 023.4
~ streak (2) n 007.1
~ summer (2) n 007.1
~ swamp (1) n 029.6
~ time (3) n 007.1
~ toilet (2) n 012.1
~ toilets (2) n 012.1
~ towel (14) n 018.4
~ towels (1) n 018.4
~ turtle (1) n 060.7
~ up (8) v 055.9
~ wall (1) n 080.6
~ walls (1) n 016.6
~ weather (61) n 007.1
~ -weather branch (1) n 030.6
~ -weather branches (1) n 030.6

~ wind (1) n 006.5
~ wines (2) n 114.7
~ wood (4) n 008.6
~ year (2) n 007.1
~ years (1) n 088.8
~ yeast (2) n 045.5
Dry (11) 030.7
~ Bayou (2) LA 030.7
~ Branch (2) GA LA 030.7
~ Creek (3) AL TX 030.7
~ Hollow (1) AL 087.4
Dryades (2) 107.7
dryer (18) n/adj 018.4
~ cloth (1) n 018.4
drying (377) n/v/adj 018.4
~ cloth (182) n 018.4
~ cloths (7) n 018.4
~ dish towel (1) n 018.4
~ dishcloth (1) n 018.4
~ dishrag (1) n 018.4
~ down (1) v 007.3
~ out (1) v 112.8
~ -out tank (1) n 112.8
~ rag (101) n 018.4
~ rags (1) n 018.4
~ room (1) n 112.8
~ tank (1) n 112.8
~ towel (59) n 018.4
~ towels (2) n 018.4
~ up (1) v 033.9
dryness (1) n 007.1
DSAs (1) 083.1
DTs (2) 112.8
du (2) prep F 016.5
dual (1) adj 103.6
Dubach (1) LA 087.3
dubious (21) adj 074.2
Dublin (14) AL GA 087.2
~ Road (1) 053.4
dubs (1) n 081.9
Dubuque (1) IA 087.3
duck (77) n/v/adj 036.6
~ -blood pudding (1) n 047.3
~ down (4) v 096.4
~ duck goose (5) n 130.3
~ fit (1) n 075.1
~ -hunt (2) v 081.9
~ hunting (2) n/v 012.5
~ lagoon (1) n 106.4

~ supper (1) n 080.9
Duck (16) TN 030.7
~ Heads (3) 027.4
~ Hill (1) MS 030.8
~ Port (1) LA 087.1
~ River (9) TN 030.7
~ River Ridge (1) TN 030.8
duck[N-i] (1) n 059.5
duck[N-k] nest (1) n 080.8
ducked (3) v 096.4
~ him (1) v 082.1
~ school (1) v 083.4
ducker (1) n 130.3
Ducker Station (1) GA 075.7
duckies (1) n 114.5
ducking (18) n/v/adj 101.9
~ breeches (1) n 027.4
~ cloth (1) n 014.6
~ down (1) v 096.4
~ overalls (1) n 027.4
~ pants (1) n 027.4
~ suit (1) n 027.4
duckling (2) n 036.8
duck's ass (1) n 123.9
ducks (69) n 036.6
ducktail (5) n/adj 115.6
~ haircuts (1) n 115.6
ducktails (2) n 123.9
Ducktown (4) GA TN 087.3
duct (2) n 118.5
ducts (11) n 118.5
ductwork (4) n 118.5
dud (2) n 073.4
dude (112) n/v/adj 028.1
~ stuff (1) n 088.7
~ up (2) v 028.1
Dude (1) 114.4
duded up (7) v 028.1
dudes (17) n 069.8
duding (4) v 028.1
~ up (2) v 028.1
dudish (2) adj 028.1
Dudley (2) 086.1
~ Lake District (1) AR 086.1
~ Lake Township (1) AR 086.1
Dudlow Joe (1) 080.6
duds (12) n 025.1

due (753) adj/adv/prep 094.7
~ bill (4) n 094.7
~ bills (1) n 094.7
~ credit (1) n 094.2
~ date (1) n 094.7
~ to (15) prep 088.6
~ to deliver (1) adv 033.9
due[N-i] (10) n 094.8
Dueling Oaks (1) 106.4
dueling pistol (1) n 113.1
dues (705) n/adj 094.8
~ book (1) n 094.8
duff (3) n/adj 048.3
~ can (1) n 099.5
duffdies (1) n 099.5
duffdy (1) n 099.5
Duffee (1) MS 087.2
duffel bags (1) n 088.7
dug (61) v/adj 030.2
~ cellars (1) n 084.9
~ deep well (1) n 015.5
~ ponds (1) n 030.5
~ up (4) v 102.6
~ well (27) n 080.9
~ wells (8) n 015.5
Dugdemona (1) LA 030.7
duggers (1) n 060A.6
dugout (14) n/adj 015.5
~ boats (1) n 024.6
dugouts (12) n 024.6
dugs (1) n 129.2
duked (1) v 046.4
duke's mixture (12) n 033.3
Dulce (1) 030.7
dulce de frijole (1) n S 096.7
dull (15) adj 005.5
~ day (7) n 005.5
~ weather (2) n 005.5
dullard (1) n 069.7
dullheaded (1) adj 074.8
Duluth (6) GA MN 086.3
Dumaine (1) 089.8
Dumas (8) AR 087.6
Dumasites (1) 080.6
dumb (96) adj 073.3
~ ass (7) n 073.4
~ -ass (1) adj 128.7
~ bunnies (1) n 069.7
~ bunny (2) n 073.4
~ -dumb (1) n 073.4
Dumbarton (1) 107.7

dumbbell (8) n 073.4
dumber (2) adj 026.3
dumbest (1) adj 064.7
dumbhead (2) n 073.4
dumbheaded (1) adj 074.9
Dumbo (1) 073.4
dummies (1) n 099.7
Dummkopf (1) n G 067.8
dummox (1) n 073.4
dummy (60) n/adj 073.4
~ egg (4) n 017.1
~ eggs (3) n 017.1
~ line (3) n 085.3
~ lines (1) n 085.3
dump (43) n/v/adj 010.3
~ boys (1) n 099.7
~ can (1) n 117.3
~ hole (1) n 012.1
~ house (1) n 012.1
~ rake (3) n 088.7
~ reaper (1) n 041.6
~ truck (9) n 109.7
~ trucks (4) n 109.6
dumped (12) v 082.1
~ her (1) v 082.1
~ him (10) v 082.1
~ on him (1) v 082.1
dumping (3) v/adj 019.6
~ sack (2) n 019.7
dumpling (63) n/adj 044.4
~ dunker (1) n 071.7
~ guzzard (1) n 071.7
~ knocker (1) n 071.7
~ pie (1) n 048.3
~ snatcher (1) n 071.7
Dumpling (1) 064.4
dumpling[N-i] (2) n 044.8
dumplings (221) n 044.7
dumps (1) n 072.9
dumpster (25) n 117.3
Dumpster (40) 117.3
dumpsters (14) n 117.3
Dumpsters (10) 117.3
Dumpsy (1) 117.3
dumpy (1) adj 073.1
dun (3) v/adj 057.7
~ time (1) n 094.7
Dunbar (3) TN 087.2
~ Creek (1) MS 030.7
Duncan (4) MS 087.5
~ Pfyfe sofa (1) n 009.1

Duncanville (2) AL TX 087.2
dunce (6) n 073.4
Dundee (1) MS 087.3
dune (4) n/adj 030.8
~ buggies (1) n 023.6
~ ridge (1) n 080.7
dunes (6) n 029.6
dung (1) adj 061.9
dungaree (1) v 027.4
dungarees (21) n 027.4
dunga(rees) (1) n 027.4
dungeon (2) n 009.8
dunghill (2) n 081.8
dunk (3) v 050.3
~ down (1) v 096.4
dunker (2) n 045.2
dunkers (1) n 045.2
dunking doughnut (1) n 122.5
dunks (2) n 069.9
Dunlap (5) TN 087.1
~ Springs (1) TN 087.3
Dunlay (1) TX 087.5
Dunmoreland (1) 107.7
Dunn Lake (1) AL 030.7
Dunnellon (2) FL 087.9
duns (1) n 094.7
dupey (1) adj 073.3
Duplessis (1) LA 087.4
duplex (53) n/adj 007A.1
~ apartment (1) n 119.4
~ apartments (1) n 119.2
~ home (1) n 007A.1
~ houses (1) n 118.9
~ stove (1) n 008.4
duplexes (10) n 119.2
Dupre Street (1) 075.7
Dupree (1) AL 087.4
Duquesne (1) 030.7
Durand (1) GA 087.6
Durant (3) MS OK 087.7
Durham (11) NC 087.4
~ bulls (1) n 033.5
Durhamville (1) TN 087.8
during (53) prep 065.8
Durkee (2) 105.6
~ Field (1) 105.6
~ Field Ball Park (1) 106.4
Duroc (15) 035.5
~ Jersey (5) 035.5

~ Jersey hogs (1) n 035.5
~ Jerseys (1) 035.5
Durocs (3) 035.5
durstn't (1) v 058.2
dusk (64) n/adj 003.4
~ dark (7) n 002.3
dusky (6) adj 003.4
~ dark (4) n 003.4
Duson (3) LA 087.3
dust (107) n/v/adj 010.4
~ around (1) v 010.4
~ bag (22) n 116.8
~ bowl (2) n 007.1
~ catcher (1) n 116.8
~ catchers (1) n 010.9
~ collect(or) (1) n 116.8
~ dark (1) n 096.7
~ machines (1) n 091.8
~ mop (11) n 010.5
~ mops (1) n 010.5
~ pouch (1) n 089.8
~ rag (1) n 010.5
~ road (1) n 031.6
~ roads (1) n 031.7
~ ruffle (2) n 028.7
~ settler (2) n 006.8
~ storm (5) n 112.2
~ web (1) n 061.3
~ webs (1) n 061.3
dustcloth (1) n 010.4
dustcoats (1) n 026.4
dusted (5) v 010.4
~ out (1) v 030.5
duster (11) n 026.4
dusters (5) n 080.6
dusting (12) v/adj 010.4
~ brush (1) n 010.5
~ rag (1) n 010.4
dustpan (1) n 010.5
dusts (1) v 010.4
dusty (5) adj 002.5
~ dark (1) n 002.5
Dutch (189) 127.1
~ apple (2) n 048.3
~ apple pie (1) n 048.3
~ boy (4) n 123.9
~ -boy cut (1) n 123.9
~ cheese (2) n 048.1
~ Creek (1) AR 030.7
~ daggers (1) n 104.3
~ elm disease (1) n 061.8
~ Germans (1) 127.2

~ girls (1) n 029.1
~ Island (1) 106.1
~ onion (1) n 055.7
~ oven (118) n 017.5
~ -oven bread (1) n 044.4
~ -oven pie (1) n 048.3
~ ovens (17) n 017.5
~ people (2) n 127.2
~ pie (1) n 048.3
~ ruffle (1) n 028.7
~ soup (1) n 050.4
~ style (1) n 029.1
Dutchman (9) 069.2
Dutchmans Bend (1) LA 087.1
Dutchmen (2) 127.1
Dutchmens (3) 016.8
Dutchy (1) 069.8
duties (3) n 094.8
duty (4) n/adj 094.7
Duval (9) FL 086.8
~ Branch (1) FL 030.7
~ County (2) FL 087.2
~ Street (1) 069.4
Duvalls Bluff (1) 031.2
DW Ten (1) 001.5
dwarf (8) adj 055A.5
~ beans (2) n 055A.4
~ corn (1) n 056.2
~ tomatoes (4) n 055.3
~ trees (1) n 061.8
dwarfs (1) n 070.6
dweller (1) n 069.9
dwelling (18) n/adj 014.1
~ home (1) n 080.6
~ house (12) n 014.1
~ houses (1) n 014.1
dwellings (3) n 014.1
DWI (2) 113.6
dwindle down (1) v 070.6
dwindle[V-t] down (1) v 057.8
dwindled away (1) v 055.9
dwindling (2) v 007.3
~ out (1) v 007.3
DWIs (1) 113.6
Dyas Creek (1) AL 030.7
dye (1) n 054.7
Dye community (2) LA 087.1
dyed (3) adj 035.2
~ -in-the-wool (1) adj 035.2

~ -in-the-wool Southerner (1) n 080.7
Dyer (4) AR TN 087.1
~ County (1) TN 087.3
Dyers Creek (1) TN 030.7
Dyersburg (9) TN 087.1
dying (189) v 007.3
~ away (4) v 007.3
~ down (141) v 007.3
~ like (1) v 078.6
~ off (1) v 007.3
~ out (10) v 007.3
dyke (26) n 124.3
Dyke (1) 091.9
dyker (4) n 124.4
dykes (3) n 124.4
Dykes Creek (1) GA 030.7
dykish (1) adj 124.3
dynamite (7) n/adj 066.8
~ shed (1) n 011.7
~ threads (1) n 123.6
Dynamite Hill (1) 105.5
dynamites (1) n 016.7
dynamo (1) n 088.7
dysentery (3) n 079.9
dyspepsi(a) (3) n 080.2
dystrophy (1) n 088.8

E

E (25) 107.7
~ -Eighty (1) 069.3
~ -Z Stop (1) 116.2
~ -Z Stores (1) 116.2
each (82) pron 042.9
eager beaver (1) n 125.6
eagle (10) n 059.4
Eagle (5) 087.2
~ Ford (1) TX 087.2
~ Lake (2) LA TX 030.7
~ Pass (1) TX 087.8
~ Scout (1) 088.7
eagles (1) n 080.7
Eagleton (3) AR 087.5
~ Village (1) 106.2
Eagleville (1) TN 087.6
ear (2167) n/adj 071.5
~ corn (28) n 056.2
~ infection (1) n 071.5
~ music (1) n 089.5
~ problems (1) n 071.5
~ -to-ear (1) adv 056.2
ear[N-i] (7) n 071.5
earache (1) n 071.5
earbobs (2) n 028.3
eared (4) adj 071.5
earful (1) n 071.5
earlier (8) adj/adv 003.6
earlobe (15) n 071.5
Earls Farm (1) 080.6
early (78) adj/adv 003.6
~ bean (1) n 055A.4
~ corn (12) n 056.2
~ onion (1) n 055.7
~ peach (2) n 054.3
~ peas (1) n 084.8
~ roasting ears (1) n 056.2
~ tender corn (1) n 056.2
Early (26) FL GA 087.7
~ American (5) 069.2
~ Attic (1) 010.2
~ Birds (1) 055.3
~ Bliss (1) 055.4
~ County (4) GA 087.7
~ Dixie (1) 056.9
~ Flat Dutch (1) 055A.1
~ Jersey Wakefield (1) 055A.1
~ June (1) 054.3
~ June peach (1) n 001A.7
~ June peas (1) n 055A.2
~ Richmond (1) 062.1
~ Rose (3) 055.4
(Early) Bird tomatoes (1) n 055.3
earmark (2) n/v 089.9
earmarked (1) v 071.5
earned (1) v 065.9
earphones (1) n 071.5
earrings (3) n 028.3
ears (820) n 071.5
Ears (1) 125.1
earth (26) n/adj 060.5
~ medicine (1) n 061.4
~ place (2) n 008.2
Earth (9) 123.8
~ shoe (3) n 123.8
~ shoes (6) n 123.8
earthen (8) adj 066.8
~ crocks (1) n 066.8
~ jars (1) n 080.6
~ jugs (3) n 019.2
~ plates (1) n 017.1
~ reservoir (1) n 090.8
~ tank (1) n 030.3
earthenware (4) n/adj 017.1
~ jugs (1) n 017.2
earthly (2) adj 092.4
earthquake (3) n 065.8
earthworm (149) n 060.5
earth(worm) (1) n 060.5
earthworm[N-i] (1) n 060.5
earthworms (295) n 060.5
earthy (1) adj 092.9
earwig (2) n 060A.1
ease (9) n 074.2
eased around (1) v 090.4
easement (6) n 108.6
easier (8) adv 007.3
easiest (1) adv 042.1
easily (12) adv 040.2
easing (13) v 007.3

~ off (2) v 007.3
~ up (7) v 007.3
east (366) n/adj 006.4
~ bedroom (2) n 007A.5
~ forty (1) n 001A.1
~ house (1) n 007A.1
~ -northeast (2) adj 006.5
~ porch (3) n 010.8
~ room (1) n 007A.6
~ west (3) adj 006.5
~ -west freeway (1) n 107.2
~ wind (25) n 006.5
~ winds (1) n 006.5
East (243) 105.2
~ Atlanta (4) 105.3
~ Avenue (1) 105A.7
~ Baton Rouge (8) LA 087.7
~ Baton Rouge Parish (3) LA 087.7
~ Bay Street (1) 107.6
~ Birmingham (3) 106.2
~ Broadway (1) 105A.8
~ Carroll (3) LA 087.3
~ Carroll Parish (1) LA 087.7
~ Central (1) 106.3
~ Chattanooga (3) 105.1
~ Coast (5) 006.5
~ Coast States (1) 086.9
~ Coast West Coast (1) 114.2
~ Dallas (9) 105.1
~ Dougherty (1) GA 069.8
~ Ellijay (1) GA 087.1
~ End (8) 006.4
~ End Park (1) 106.7
~ Fayetteville (2) AR 087.8
~ Feliciana (1) LA 087.1
~ Feliciana Parish (1) LA 087.5
~ Flagler Street (1) 107.6
~ Florence (1) 105.1
~ Fork (2) LA TN 030.7

~ Forsyth Street (1) 107.6
~ Fort Myers (1) 105.1
~ Hanna (1) 106.5
~ Harlem (1) NY 087.4
~ Hillsborough County (1) FL 087.4
~ Houston (1) 105.5
~ Indi(a) (1) 055.5
~ Jackson (2) 105.1
~ Jacksonville (4) 105.5
~ Kentucky (1) 086.5
~ Knoxville (2) 105.1
~ Lake (1) 106.3
~ Lake Club (1) 106.7
~ Lake Meadow (1) 105.5
~ Lake Park (2) 106.7
~ Lane Street (1) 107.6
~ Liberty (1) TX 087.7
~ Main Road (1) 031.6
~ Main Street (1) 105.4
~ Memphis (4) 106.2
~ Middle (1) LA 030.7
~ Montgomery (1) 105.1
~ Myrtle Avenue (1) 107.6
~ Nashville (8) 105.1
~ Navidad (1) TX 030.7
~ Ninth Street (1) 114.8
~ Paces Ferry (1) 106.1
~ Paces Ferry Road (1) 107.8
~ Panama City (1) 105.3
~ Parkway (1) 107.6
~ Pearl (1) LA 030.7
~ Point (4) GA 087.6
~ Ponce de Leon (1) 093.6
~ Prong (2) MS 030.7
~ Rice (1) 050.7
~ Ridge (1) 106.2
~ River (1) MS 030.7
~ Saint Louis (1) MO 087.1
~ Sandy (2) TX 030.7
~ section (1) n 105.4
~ Side (39) 105.1
~ Springfield (1) 105.2

~ Tallahatchie (2) MS
006.5
~ Tennessee (12) 086.6
~ Tennessee Pack-
inghouse (1)
086.6
~ Texas (7) 086.8
~ Texas Baptist (1)
089.1
~ Texas nigger (1) n
069.5
~ Texas piney woods
(1) n 088.7
~ Tex(as) Freeway (1)
107.1
~ Thomas Park (1)
106.7
~ Tupelo (1) 010.5
Eastbrook (1) 106.2
easter (2) n 006.5
Easter (11) 065.1
~ duties (1) n 065.1
~ egg[N-i] (1) n 046.1
~ eggs (3) n 017.1
~ Festival (1) 080.8
~ Place (1) AR 087.3
~ Sunday (2) 002.1
~ Week Festival (1)
080.6
easterly (8) adj 006.4
~ wind (1) n 006.5
eastern (11) adj 088.9
~ diamondback (1) n
093.7
~ gale (1) n 006.5
~ north winds (1) n
006.5
~ part (3) n 105.1
~ section (1) n 105.4
~ shore (1) n 086.1
~ wind (1) n 006.5
Eastern (20) 086.9
~ Boulevard (1) 107.7
~ music (1) n 130.9
~ Oklahoma (1) 086.8
~ Seaboard (3) 086.9
~ Shores (1) 106.1
~ Star (1) 051.8
~ States (6) 086.9
~ Virginia (1) 086.2
easternly (1) adj 006.5
Eastgate (2) 105.2
~ Park (1) 085.1
Eastman (5) GA 087.4
Eastmanite (1) 081.8

eastnorth (2) adj 006.5
~ wind (1) n 006.5
Eastover (2) 106.1
eastsouth (2) adj 006.5
~ wind (1) n 006.5
eastward (1) adv 006.5
Eastwood (3) 105.7
~ Mall (1) 105.4
~ Village (1) 105.4
easy (202) adj 073.2
~ chair (11) n 008.8
~ chairs (4) n 008.8
~ fuck (1) n 124.9
~ lady (1) n 124.6
~ lay (3) n 124.6
~ listening (3) n 130.8
~ -listening (1) adj
130.8
~ -listening music (1) n
130.8
~ -listening rock (1) n
130.8
~ mark (1) n 073.6
~ over (2) adj 046.2
~ pay (1) n 115.4
~ -rolling (1) adj 073.2
~ -tempered (1) adj
073.2
Easy (2) 116.2
~ Foods (1) 116.2
~ Shops (1) 116.2
easygoing (98) adj 073.2
eat (1613) v 048.7
~ a root (2) n 048.7
~ around (1) v 048.7
~ at (3) v 048.7
~ in (2) v 048.7
~ like (1) v 058.3
~ of (1) v 049.6
~ off (1) v 048.7
~ off of (4) v 034.4
~ on (3) v 048.7
~ out of (1) v 048.7
~ up (7) v 048.7
~ with (13) v 048.7
eat[N-i] (1) n 081.8
eat[V-p] (7) v 034.4
~ with (1) v 048.7
eat[V-r] (227) v 048.7
~ like (1) v 048.7
~ out (1) v 048.7
~ up (4) v 048.7
eat[V-s] up (1) v 096.8
eat[V-t] (306) v 048.7
~ down (2) v 048.7

~ off (2) v 048.7
~ out (1) v 048.7
~ up (17) v 048.7
~ up with (2) v 048.7
eatable (11) adj 047.5
eated (3) v 048.7
eaten (632) v 048.7
~ up (1) v 050.1
~ up with (1) v 048.7
eater (23) n 048.4
Eater (3) 031.7
eaters (21) n 033.3
Eaters (1) 120.8
eating (195) n/v/adj
048.7
~ area (1) n 007A.2
~ bread (1) n 044.4
~ cheese (2) v 125.6
~ corn (2) n 056.2
~ fish (1) n 084.9
~ joint (1) n 072.3
~ money (1) n 080.7
~ nook (1) n 088.7
~ on (1) v 024.9
~ onion (1) n 055.6
~ onions (1) n 055.7
~ peach (2) n 054.4
~ peaches (2) n 054.4
~ place (2) n 051.8
~ places (1) n 053.8
~ potatoes (1) n 055.4
~ pumpkinseed[N-i]
(1) v 065.1
~ room (3) n 007A.4
~ shebang (1) n 093.5
~ squirrel (1) n 059.6
~ table (2) n 093.5
~ time (3) n 037.4
~ troughs (1) n 035.8
~ type (1) n 054.3
~ watermelon[N-i] (1)
v 065.1
Eatonton (2) GA 087.3
eats (94) n/v 048.4
~ like (2) v 048.4
~ up (1) v 013.8
Eau (3) 087.3
~ Claire (1) WI 087.3
eave (66) n/adj 011.6
~ comb (1) n 011.5
~ trough (2) n 011.5
~ troughs (2) n 011.5
eave[N-i] (2) n 011.5
eaves (99) n/adj 011.5
~ trough (4) n 011.5

~ troughs (3) n 011.5
~ valley (1) n 011.6
Ebbetts Theater (1) 084.4
Ebenezer (9) AL GA
087.3
~ Baptist Church (1)
089.1
~ community (1) AL
087.4
~ Creek (1) GA 030.7
Eber (2) n G 035.3
ebony (7) n/adj 061.9
~ dirt (1) n 029.4
~ wood (2) n 008.5
Ebro (1) FL 087.2
eccentric (19) adj 074.7
(ec)centric (1) adj 074.7
(e)chalote (2) n F 055.7
Echeconnee Creek (1) GA
030.7
(E)checonnee (1) GA
030.7
echelon (1) n 075.8
Echols (1) GA 087.7
eclair (8) n 122.5
eclairs (10) n 122.5
Eclectic (2) AL 087.5
(e)clipse (1) v 070.8
Econfina (3) 030.7
~ Creek (1) FL 030.7
~ River (2) FL 030.7
economical (1) adj 091.7
economy (4) adj 109.1
~ car (2) n 109.1
~ cars (2) n 109.2
(e)conomy cars (1) n
109.2
Ecore (1) 087.8
Ector (2) 107.8
~ Place (1) 107.8
~ Road (1) 107.8
eczema (1) n 088.9
Ed Waters College (1)
106.4
eddy (3) n/adj 030.3
~ water (1) n 030.3
Eden (5) MS 087.3
~ Gardens (1) 105.5
~ Station (1) MS 087.1
edge (27) n/adj 031.2
~ cutter (1) n 120.8
edged in (1) v 099.8
Edgefield (1) SC 087.8
Edgehill (3) 105.1
~ Village (1) 106.3

Edgemont (1) 106.2
edger (19) n/adj 120.8
~ trimmer (1) n 120.4
edges (8) n 031.2
Edgewater (2) 107.7
~ Garden (1) 050.5
(Edge)water (1) 048.9
edgeways (1) adv 090.9
Edgewood (11) TX 093.9
~ area (1) n 105.7
~ Avenue (5) 107.5
~ Drive (1) 107.8
edgy (13) adj 075.1
edible (5) adj 065.9
Edina Creek (1) AR 030.7
Edinburg (6) MS TX 087.6
~ Lake (1) TX 030.7
Edinburgh (1) AR 086.6
Edison (6) GA 087.7
~ Mall (1) 105.3
~ Park (1) 106.4
edition (1) n 081.2
editor (3) n 075.6
editorials (2) n 065.9
Edna (3) TX 087.5
educate (9) v 083.5
educated (76) v/adj 083.5
~ for (1) v 083.5
~ up on (1) v 096.9
educating (2) v 083.5
education (1100) n 083.5
~ -minded (1) adj 083.5
Education Department (1) 083.5
educational (7) adj 083.5
~ fraternity (1) n 083.5
educationese (1) n 131.2
educations (3) n 083.5
educator (2) n 083.5
educators (2) n 083.5
Edward Street (1) 107.7
Edwards (3) MS 087.1
~ Airport (1) 106.5
~ Creek (1) FL 030.7
Edwin Warner Park (1) 106.4
Edwina Creek (1) TN 030.7
ee (3) interj 037.8
~ -oo(x2) (1) interj 037.5
eeby iby over (1) n 130.5

eeh(x2) (1) interj 037.5
eel (24) n/adj 081.9
~ fish (3) n 059.9
~ scrape (1) n 021.6
Eelbeck (1) GA 087.3
eels (12) n 059.9
eelworm (2) n 060.5
eelworms (7) n 060.5
e'er (13) pron 040.5
eerie (6) adj 074.2
effect (1) n 029.3
effects (1) n 009.4
effeminate (31) adj 124.1
~ guy (1) n 124.1
~ type (1) n 124.1
effervescent (1) adj 074.1
effete (2) adj 124.1
efficiency (5) n/adj 119.2
~ apartment (3) n 119.2
~ apartments (1) n 119.2
efficient (1) adj 053.5
Effie (1) LA 070.8
Effingham (3) GA 087.1
~ County (1) GA 087.8
effort (1) n 070.9
(ef)fusions (1) n 007.4
egg (1818) n/v/adj 017.1
~ -and-onion (1) n 055.3
~ balls (1) n 045.2
~ basket (2) n 020.1
~ batter (2) n 051.8
~ bread (96) n 044.6
~ -bread muffin (1) n 044.8
~ cartons (1) n 130.6
~ casserole (1) n 046.1
~ change (1) n 088.9
~ concern (1) n 017.1
~ corn bread (4) n 044.5
~ custard (5) n 048.5
~ cymling (2) n 017.1
~ cymlings (2) n 017.1
~ farm (1) n 046.1
~ gourd (6) n 046.1
~ gourds (9) n 017.1
~ house (1) n 011.9
~ -like squash (1) n 056.6
~ money (2) n 091.9
~ muffins (1) n 044.8
~ nest (1) n 017.1

~ pie (4) n 048.3
~ pies (1) n 048.3
~ poacher (4) n 046.1
~ rolls (2) n 044.4
~ sallet (2) n 046.1
~ sauce (1) n 048.5
~ stew (1) n 046.1
~ suckers (2) n 059.5
~ tomato (1) n 055.3
~ white (9) n 045.6
~ whites (2) n 045.6
~ yellow (2) n 045.6
~ yolk (3) n 045.6
~ yolks (1) n 045.6
Egg (2) 107.6
egg[N-i] (22) n 046.1
eggbeater (5) n 111.9
egghead (8) n 125.5
eggheaded (1) adj 125.5
eggheads (2) n 125.5
eggnog (8) n 048.5
eggplant (41) n 055.8
eggplants (8) n 055.8
eggs (1353) n 046.1
eggshell (2) n 048.8
eggshells (2) n 046.1
Eglin (1) FL 087.6
egomaniac (1) n 125.6
egotistical (1) adj 074.8
egress (2) n/adj 107.4
~ roads (1) n 031.7
egret (1) n 090.9
egrets (4) n 088.7
Egypt (2) 080.7
~ Ridge (1) MS 087.1
Egyptian (1) 095.8
eh-ooh (1) interj 038.5
Ehuaverdi Creek (1) TX 030.7
eiderdown (2) n 029.2
eiderdowns (1) n 029.1
eight (2466) n/adj 001.4
~ -barrel (1) adj 019.6
~ -by-eight (2) adj 001.4
~ -by-eight-by-eight (1) adj 001.4
~ -by-ten (2) adj 001.4
~ -day clock (2) n 125.1
~ -feet (2) adj 007.9
~ -fifteen (3) n 004.5
~ -foot (22) adj 007.9
~ -forty-five (2) n 004.5
~ -gallon (1) adj 020.2

~ -handed reel (1) n 083.1
~ hooter (1) n 059.2
~ -hour shift (1) n 001.4
~ -hundred-acre (1) adj 001A.2
~ -inch (3) adj 001.4
~ -nineteen (1) n 001.4
~ -nut tree (1) n 061.9
~ -oh-five (1) n 001.3
~ -oh-one (1) n 001.1
~ -oh-three (1) n 001.4
~ -plait whip (1) n 019.4
~ -point buck (2) n 080.9
~ -pound (7) adj 017.2
~ -room home (1) n 051.8
~ -row equipment (1) n 099.7
~ -row planter (1) n 001.4
~ -thirty (48) n 004.4
~ -thirty-five (1) n 004.4
~ -wheel (1) adj 001.4
~ -year (1) adj 001.4
~ -year-old (2) adj 005.1
Eight (24) 001.4
~ Mile (1) AL 105.2
~ Row (1) 056.2
~ Street (7) 001A.3
~ Twenty-Six (1) 107.6
~ Ward (1) 001A.3
eighteen (239) n 001.9
~ -and-eighty (1) n 001.9
~ -and-fifty (1) n 001.9
~ -and-fifty-eight (1) n 001.9
~ -and-fifty-five (1) n 001.3
~ -and-forty-five (1) n 001.8
~ -and-forty-one (1) n 001.9
~ -and-forty-six (1) n 001.3
~ -and-forty-two (1) n 001A.1
~ -and-nine (1) n 001.9

~ -and-nineties (1) n 001.9

~ -and-ninety (1) n 001.7

~ -and-ninety-eight (3) n 001.4

~ -and-ninety-nine (4) n 001.9

~ -and-ninety-three (1) n 001A.6

~ -and-ninety-two (1) n 001.9

~ -and-seventy-two (2) n 001.4

~ -and-sixty (1) n 001.9

~ -and-sixty-seven (1) n 001.4

~ -and-twenty-eight (1) n 001.9

~ -and-twenty-three (1) n 001.9

~ -eighty-eight (1) n 001.9

~ -eighty-nine (1) n 001.5

~ -fifty-four (2) n 001.2

~ -fifty-something (1) n 001.9

~ -fifty-two (1) n/adj 025.1

~ -forty-eight (1) n 001A.1

~ -forty-five (2) n 001.3

~ -forty-seven (1) n 001.4

~ -forty-six (1) n 001.3

~ -hundred-and-eighteen (1) n 001.9

~ -hundred-and-fifty-three (1) n 001.2

~ -hundred-and-ninety-three (1) n 001.2

~ -nine (1) n 001.5

~ -nineteen (3) n 001.7

~ -ninety (1) n 001.9

~ -ninety-five (1) 001.9

~ -ninety-four (1) n 001.2

~ -ninety-one (4) n 001.1

~ -ninety-six (2) n 001.9

~ -ninety-some-odd (1) n 001.9

~ -ninety-three (2) n 001.2

~ -ninety-two (1) n 001.9

~ -seventy (2) n 001A.2

~ -seventy-six (1) n 001A.6

~ -seventy-two (1) n 001A.2

~ -sixty-five (1) n 001.3

~ -thirty-nine (1) n 001A.1

~ -thirty-three (1) n 001A.1

~ -to-forty-five draft (1) n 001A.1

~ -twelve (3) n 001.6

~ -twenty (2) n 001.8

~ -twenty-four (1) n 001.2

~ -twenty-nine (1) n 001.5

~ -twenty-seven (1) n 001.8

~ -twenty-two (1) n 001.8

~ wheeler (1) n 109.6

Eighteen (8) 001A.2

~ -Hundreds (2) 001A.2

~ -Tens (1) 001.9

~ -Thirties (1) 001.9

~ -Twenties (1) 001.9

eighteenth (1) n 001A.6

Eighteenth (3) 107.6

~ Avenue East (1) 001.2

eighth (857) n/adj 001A.3

~ -grade education (4) n 001A.3

Eighth (7) 001A.3

~ Air Force (1) 001A.3

~ Avenue (1) 105.4

~ District (1) 001A.3

~ Street (1) 001A.3

eighths (1) n 001A.4

Eightmile Creek (1) AL 030.7

eights (2) n 001A.3

eighty (193) n/adj 001A.1

~ -eight (8) n 001.4

~ -five (20) n/adj 078.5

~ -four (21) n/adj 001.2

~ -nine (12) n/adj 001.5

~ -one (14) n/adj 001.9

~ -seven (21) n/adj 001.4

~ -six (12) n/adj 001.3

~ -something (4) n/adj 103.2

~ -three (8) n/adj 001.2

~ -two (12) n/adj 001.1

Eighty (28) 031.5

~ -Eight Street (1) 107.8

~ -Five South (1) 107.1

~ -Four (2) 031.6

~ -Nines (1) 001.5

~ -Seven Highway (1) 031.6

~ -Two (3) 031.6

Eisen (1) n G 008.3

Eisenhower (9) 068.3

~ jacket (1) n 027.1

either (1170) pron 071.2

eje (1) n S 021.8

el (3) adj S 112.5

El (57) 085.3

~ Camino (1) 109.7

~ Dog (2) 109.4

~ Dorado (23) AR 087.5

~ (Do)rado (1) AR 087.2

~ Paso (26) TX 087.3

elaborate (1) adj 025.7

Elaine (2) AR 087.5

elastic (12) n/adj 110.3

~ band (5) n 110.3

~ rubber (1) n 110.3

elastics (1) n 028.5

Elba (7) AL GA 087.9

Elbert County (2) GA 087.8

Elberta (111) 054.4

~ free (1) n 054.4

~ peach (18) n 054.4

~ peach trees (1) n 054.4

~ peaches (16) n 054.4

~ trees (1) n 061.8

Elbert(a) (1) 054.4

Elbertas (33) 054.4

Elberton (1) GA 087.1

elbow (66) n/adj 072.3

~ fence (1) n 016.4

~ grease (2) n 023.7

~ pipe (1) n 023.2

~ stovepipes (1) n 023.2

elbows (5) n 072.6

Elbridge (1) TN 087.4

elder (25) n/adj 064.7

~ bushes (1) n 061.8

~ leaf (1) n 061.8

elderberries (19) n 062.5

elderberry (15) n/adj 061.4

~ bush (1) n 062.2

~ strawberries (1) n 062.4

~ tree (1) n 061.9

elderly (2) adj 080.7

elders (5) n 061.5

eldest (19) n/adj 064.7

elected (6) v 024.8

election (2) n 077.4

(e)lection (1) n 075.6

electric (318) adj 118.4

~ air-conditioner (1) n 118.5

~ air conditioning (1) n 118.5

~ boats (1) n 024.6

~ broiler (1) n 116.4

~ brooder (1) n 036.8

~ broom (1) n 116.7

~ bulb (9) n 019.9

~ bulbs (1) n 019.9

~ car (3) n 085.3

~ cars (3) n 085.3

~ clipper (1) n 120.8

~ clippers (8) n 120.8

~ cloud (2) n 005.3

~ fans (1) n 118.5

~ fence (26) n 016.3

~ fences (6) n 016.3

~ fencing (1) n 016.7

~ fryer (1) n 116.4

~ frying pan (14) n 116.4

~ frypan (9) n 116.4

~ furnace (1) n 118.4

~ grass clippers (1) n 120.8

~ grill (1) n 116.4

~ grills (1) n 116.4

~ handsaw (1) n 120.9

~ heat (7) n 118.4

~ heater (5) n 118.4
~ heaters (8) n 118.4
~ heating (1) n 118.4
~ hedge clippers (5) n 120.8
~ hedge cutter (1) n 120.8
~ hedge shears (2) n 120.8
~ hedge trimmer (1) n 120.8
~ hedger (1) n 120.8
~ icebox (1) n 039.6
~ lawn mower (2) n 120.2
~ lawn mowers (1) n 120.2
~ light (2) n 065.8
~ -light bugs (1) n 060A.1
~ light bulb (5) n 019.9
~ light bulbs (1) n 019.9
~ light globe (1) n 019.9
~ lights (5) n 019.9
~ motor (1) n 027.2
~ mower (3) n 120.2
~ mowers (2) n 120.2
~ oven (1) n 116.4
~ oven cooker (1) n 116.4
~ pan (1) n 116.4
~ power (1) n 118.5
~ push mower (1) n 120.2
~ ranges (1) n 118.4
~ rock (1) n 023.4
~ sausage mill (1) n 046.8
~ saw (14) n 120.9
~ sharpeners (1) n 023.4
~ shears (3) n 120.8
~ skillet (33) n 116.4
~ skillets (6) n 116.4
~ spreads (1) n 028.7
~ storm (42) n 006.2
~ storms (3) n 006.2
~ stove (15) n 118.4
~ stoves (1) n 118.4
~ sweeper (3) n 116.7
~ switch (1) n 010.5
~ toaster (2) n 116.4
~ train (1) n 085.3

~ trains (1) n 085.3
~ trucks (1) n 111.4
~ warmers (1) n 116.4
~ wire (5) n 016.3
~ -wire fence (1) n 016.3
~ wires (2) n 016.3
(e)lectric (290) adj 065.8
~ baker (1) n 116.4
~ bath heater (1) n 090.8
~ blanket (6) n 029.1
~ blankets (1) n 029.1
~ blowers (1) n 065.8
~ box (1) n 088.9
~ broiler (1) n 116.4
~ broom (2) n 010.5
~ bulb (10) n 019.9
~ bulbs (2) n 019.9
~ buses (1) n 085.3
~ car (7) n 085.3
~ cars (2) n 085.3
~ chair (2) n 070.9
~ clipper (1) n 120.8
~ clippers (1) n 120.8
~ cloud (3) n 006.2
~ coach (1) n 085.3
~ engine (1) n 070.6
~ fan (1) n 118.5
~ fence (27) n 016.3
~ fences (14) n 016.3
~ fish (1) n 098.8
~ fryer (1) n 116.4
~ frying pan (8) n 017.5
~ frying pans (1) n 116.4
~ frypan (1) n 116.4
~ globe (2) n 019.9
~ guitars (1) n 065.9
~ hammers (1) n 020.7
~ heat (4) n 118.5
~ heater (1) n 118.4
~ heaters (1) n 118.4
~ heating (1) n 118.4
~ hedge trimmers (1) n 120.8
~ irons (1) n 065.8
~ lawn mower (1) n 120.3
~ light (9) n 070.6
~ light bulb (3) n 019.9
~ lights (14) n 019.9
~ logs (1) n 008.5
~ mower (4) n 120.2

~ mow(er) (2) n 120.2
~ oven (3) n 116.4
~ percolator (3) n 048.8
~ plate (1) n 116.4
~ pole (1) n 075.9
~ range (1) n 116.4
~ saw (7) n 120.9
~ saws (2) n 120.9
~ sharpeners (1) n 023.4
~ shears (1) n 120.8
~ skillet (16) n 017.5
~ skillets (6) n 116.4
~ space heater (1) n 118.4
~ storm (51) n 006.2
~ storms (2) n 006.2
~ stove (5) n 118.4
~ stoves (1) n 065.8
~ streetcars (1) n 085.3
~ sweeper (4) n 116.7
~ trains (1) n 066.9
~ trimmer (1) n 120.8
~ trolleys (1) n 085.3
~ trucks (1) n 089.8
~ wire (10) n 016.3
~ -wire fence (2) n 016.3
(E)lectric (1) 065.9
electrical (120) adj 118.4
~ cloud (1) n 006.2
~ fence (1) n 016.3
~ fences (1) n 016.3
~ furnaces (1) n 118.4
~ plant (1) n 053.4
~ saw (3) n 120.9
~ shears (1) n 120.8
~ storm (99) n 006.2
~ storms (3) n 006.2
~ wire fence (1) n 016.3
(e)lectrical (90) adj 006.2
~ saws (1) n 120.9
~ storm (81) n 006.2
~ storms (2) n 006.2
~ wire (1) n 016.3
electrician (1) n 067.8
(e)lectrician (4) n 065.8
(e)lectricians (1) n 063.4
electricity (6) n/adj 118.5
~ clippers (1) n 120.8
~ fence (1) n 016.3
electrici(ty) (1) n 070.8
electric(ity) (1) n 053.5

(e)lectricity (21) n 065.8
~ -driven (1) adj 011.3
~ heat (1) n 118.5
~ storm (5) n 006.2
(e)lectrici(ty) (1) n 066.8
(e)lectric(ity) (2) n 039.8
electrification (1) n 080.7
electrified (1) adj 016.3
(e)lectrocute (2) v 065.9
(e)lectrocuted (3) v 085.8
(e)lectrowave oven (1) n 116.4
element (6) n 073.6
elementary (209) adj 125.7
~ education (1) n 083.5
~ grades (1) n 083.7
~ school (107) n 083.7
~ schools (2) n 125.7
~ schoolteacher (1) n 067.6
~ students (1) n 125.7
Elementary (6) 125.7
elephant (21) n/adj 129.2
~ ear (1) n 062.8
~ ears (2) n 062.7
~ giraffe (1) n 130.3
~ tush (1) n 035.7
~ tusk[N-i] (1) n 035.7
elephants (10) n 129.2
elevate (1) v 104.5
elevated highway (1) n 107.5
elevation (2) n 030.9
elevator (27) n/adj 014.4
~ grain company (1) n 014.4
~ truck (1) n 111.4
elevators (10) n 014.4
eleven (871) n/adj 001.6
~ -fifty-five (1) n 001.6
~ -foot (1) adj 007.9
~ -forty-five (2) n 004.5
~ -forty-one (1) n 001.6
~ -hundred (1) adj 001.6
~ -ten (1) n 001.5
~ -thirty (10) n 004.4
~ twenty-nine (1) n 096.8
(e)leven (729) n/adj 001.6
~ -fifteen (1) n 004.5
~ -fifty (1) n 001.6

~ -fifty-eight (1) n 001.6

~ -forty-five (4) n 004.5

~ -hundred (1) adj 001.6

~ -o'clock (1) adj 001.6

~ -oh-five (1) n 001.6

~ -seventeen (1) n 001.6

~ -thirty (36) n 004.4

(el)even (2) n 004.5

Eleven (38) 001.6

~ Street (1) 001A.3

(E)leven (5) 116.2

Elevenmile Creek (1) FL 030.7

Elevens (5) 116.2

eleventh (31) n/adj 001A.3

(e)leventh (30) n/adj 001A.3

Eleventh Street (1) 105A.8

(E)leventh Street (1) 001.1

Elgin (8) AR TN TX 087.3

~ Crossroads (1) AL 087.1

eligible (1) adj 070.6

Elijah (1) 007.1

(e)liminated (1) v 065.9

Elite (1) 055A.5

elixir (1) n 061.4

(E)lizabeth Mountain (1) 031.1

Elizabethan (1) 096.8

Elizabethton (2) TN 087.8

(E)lizabethton (3) TN 087.5

Elk (7) 129.2

~ River (4) AL TN 030.7

~ Valley (2) TN 011.6

Elkhorn (2) TN 087.1

Elkins (4) AR 087.7

~ Creek (1) GA 030.7

~ Lake (1) TX 030.7

Elkmont (1) AL 087.3

Elks (1) 013.8

Elkton (1) TN 087.8

ell (59) n/adj 011.7

~ house (8) n 014.1

~ joint (1) n 011.6

~ porch (7) n 007A.6

~ room (3) n 007A.4

~ rooms (1) n 011.6

Ella (2) 067.3

Ellaville (3) GA 087.3

elle (1) pron F 065.1

elled off (1) v 096.7

Ellen (5) 067.3

Ellendale (1) LA 087.4

Ellenwood (1) GA 087.6

Ellerslie (1) GA 087.7

Ellijay (4) GA 087.2

~ River (1) GA 030.7

Ellis (5) 106.2

~ Acres (1) 106.2

~ County (2) TX 087.4

~ Creek (1) GA 030.7

Ellisville (3) AL MS 087.7

Elly (4) 067.3

elm (208) n/adj 061.9

~ bark (2) n 061.8

~ stick (1) n 066.9

~ tree (14) n 061.8

~ trees (16) n 061.8

~ wood (1) n 061.9

Elm (8) 107.7

~ Grove (1) LA 086.3

Elmo (2) 087.3

Elmore (9) AL 087.5

~ County (4) AL 087.5

elms (26) n 061.9

Eloise (1) 006.2

elope (2) v 082.2

(e)lope (1) v 082.1

eloped (3) v 082.2

Elrod (1) AL 087.8

Els (1) 085.3

else (255) adj/adv 095.7

else's (1) adj 042.9

Elsie (1) MS 087.9

Elvis Presley's house (1) n 106.4

elwise (1) n 059.9

Elwood wire (1) n 016.3

Elyton (4) 106.9

~ section (1) n 087.4

~ Village (2) 106.3

EMA ambulance (1) n 111.5

emaciated (3) adj 072.9

Emancipation Park (1) 085.2

(E)mancipation Day (1) 085.8

Emanuel (3) GA 087.2

~ County (2) GA 087.2

emasculate (1) v 036.1

emasculated (1) v 036.1

emasculation (1) n 036.1

emasculator (1) n 036.1

(e)masculator (1) n 036.1

embalm (3) v 053.4

embalmer (15) n 117.4

embalming fluid (1) n 114.7

embankment (3) n 031.2

embarrass (2) v 129.7

embarrassed (1) v 075.2

Embayment (1) 030.9

embers (7) n 008.7

embetee (1) v F 065.1

embrace (1) v 081.7

embroider (2) v 070.7

embroidered (1) v 028.7

embroidery (3) n/v 081.8

emerald board (1) n 023.4

Emerald Mound (1) MS 030.8

emergency (39) n/adj 111.5

~ ambulance (1) n 111.5

~ car (3) n 111.5

~ medical something (1) n 111.5

~ squad (2) n 111.5

~ stop (1) n 107.2

~ stores (1) n 116.2

~ truck (7) n 111.5

~ trucks (2) n 111.5

~ unit (3) n 111.5

~ vans (1) n 111.5

~ vehicle (10) n 111.5

~ vehicles (2) n 111.5

emergen(cy) (2) n/adj 070.6

~ call (1) n 111.5

(e)mergency (7) adj 111.5

~ ambulance (1) n 111.5

~ squad (1) n 111.5

~ truck (4) n 111.5

~ vehicles (1) n 111.5

Emergency (3) 080.6

~ Medical Technician (1) 080.6

~ Medical Technicians (2) 111.5

emeries (2) n 023.5

Emerson Lake (1) TX 030.7

emery (137) n/adj 023.4

~ cloth (1) n 023.4

~ file (1) n 023.4

~ grindstone (1) n 023.5

~ rock (37) n 023.4

~ rocks (2) n 023.5

~ sharpener (1) n 023.4

~ sickle (1) n 023.4

~ stone (19) n 023.5

~ stones (1) n 023.4

~ wheel (52) n 023.5

~ wheels (5) n 023.5

emigre (1) n F 066.7

EMO (1) 111.5

Emoroid (1) 125.5

Emory (7) 105.9

~ College (1) 083.6

~ University (1) 024.7

emotional (2) adj 075.2

emphasis (1) n 040.6

emphysema (4) n 066.8

Empire (5) AL GA 087.7

~ building (1) n 108.5

Empires (1) 108.5

emplatre (1) n F 073.3

employed (1) v 012.5

employee (2) n 115.4

employ(ee) (1) n 065.9

employees (1) n 053.6

employer (24) n 069.6

employment (1) n 065.9

emporium (1) n 116.3

empties (1) v 013.7

empty (19) v/adj 022.4

~ house (1) n 090.3

~ lot (10) n 108.7

~ lots (2) n 108.7

emp(ty) (1) v 098.6

emptying (1) v 096.4

EMS truck (1) n 111.5

EMT (1) 111.5

EMTs (1) 111.5

emulate (1) v 065.3

emulates (1) v 065.3

en (6) prep F 007.8

~ avant (1) adj F 007.8

~ famille (3) adj F 065.1

enamel (9) n/adj 070.7

~ bucket (1) n 017.3
~ buckets (2) n 017.3
~ milk pails (1) n 017.3
(e)namel (3) n/adj 017.4
~ stuff (1) n 075.8
enamelware (1) n 017.6
encampments (1) n 131.3
enceinte (2) adj F 065.1
enchiladas (2) n 070.6
Encinal (2) TX 087.3
enclose porch (3) n 010.8
enclosed (6) adj 007A.6
~ back porch (1) n 010.8
~ porch (1) n 007A.6
~ rear porch (1) n 007A.4
~ truck (1) n 109.6
enclosure (1) n 015.4
Encore Febre (1) AR 087.2
encouragement (1) n 085.6
(en)cyclopedia (1) n 066.8
end (111) n/v/adj 046.6
~ bacon (1) n 046.6
~ chimley (1) n 008.1
~ cuts (2) n 121.3
~ gate (1) n 084.9
~ room (1) n 007A.3
~ table (5) n 009.2
~ tables (4) n 008.9
End (47) 107.6
ended (11) v/adj 083.2
ender (4) n 024.6
enders (1) n 024.5
endeuille (1) n F 079.3
endive (4) n 055A.5
endorse (3) v 100.7
ends (49) n/v 083.2
~ and odds (1) n 080.7
~ over (1) v 083.2
~ up with (1) v 053.4
endure (1) v 070.6
enemies (1) n 040.6
enemy (4) n 051.8
energetic (41) adj 074.1
energy (13) n 074.1
Energy (1) MS 087.2
enfilade (1) n F 031.9
enforce (1) v 085.7
enforcement (14) n/adj 066.8
engage (2) v 081.4

~ in (1) v 053.4
engage[V-t] (3) v 081.4
~ to her (1) v 081.4
~ to marry (1) v 081.4
engaged (21) v 081.4
engagement (111) n/adj 123.1
~ parties (1) n 130.7
~ party (1) n 130.7
~ ring (15) n 123.1
~ rings (4) n 123.1
(e)ngagement (2) n/adj 123.1
~ rings (1) n 123.1
engagements (1) n 081.4
engine (67) n/adj 111.1
~ oil (1) n 024.1
~ truck (1) n 111.2
engineer (14) n 115.2
engineers (7) n 112.4
Engineers (1) 088.7
enginehouse (3) n 112.6
engines (19) n 066.8
England (628) 066.8
~ Acres (1) 106.2
Eng(land) (1) 086.9
Englanders (1) 127.8
Englands (1) 086.9
English (281) 127.8
~ -American people (1) n 069.4
~ bone china (1) n 017.1
~ book (2) n 051.8
~ Creek (2) GA 030.7
~ cut (3) n 121.2
~ -cut roast (2) n 121.2
~ Mountain (1) TN 030.8
~ muffins (3) n 044.4
~ mulberry (1) n 061.8
~ net (1) n 089.8
~ nuts (1) n 054.8
~ pea (7) n 055A.2
~ peaches (1) n 054.3
~ peas (79) n 055A.2
~ people (1) n 069.4
~ red worm (1) n 060.5
~ spar(row) (1) n 059.2
~ States (1) 086.9
~ sucker (1) n 097.8
~ teacher (5) n 131.2
~ walnut (35) n 054.8

~ walnut trees (2) n 054.8
~ walnuts (66) n 054.8
~ women (1) n 052.1
~ worm (1) n 060.5
~ worms (1) n 060.5
Englishman (4) 069.6
Englishmans (2) 041.9
Englishmen (5) 127.8
Englishwoman (3) 051.8
Enid (4) MS OK 088.8
~ Dam (1) MS 087.7
enjoy (6) v 012.8
enjoyed (16) v 091.6
enjoying (2) v 074.1
enjoyment (3) n 025.8
enjoys (3) v 025.6
enlist in (1) v 024.8
Ennes (1) TX 086.4
Enoka Plantation (1) LA 087.4
Enon (2) AL 086.4
enormous (1) adj 103.3
enough (236) adv 043.3
(e)nough (133) adv 035.9
enraged (1) adj 075.2
enrich bread (1) n 044.3
enriches (1) v 029.3
ensilage (2) n 014.4
Ensley (7) AL 087.2
enter (3) v/adj 107.4
~ point (1) n 107.4
entered apprentice (1) n 067.8
entering ramp (1) n 107.4
Enterprise (16) AL MS 087.3
entertainer (2) n 069.1
entertaining (1) v 082.5
entertainment (3) n/adj 066.8
~ place (1) n 051.8
entertains to (1) v 098.6
enthused (1) adj 088.7
entice (1) v 096.7
entire (23) adj 082.8
entirely (4) adv 028.9
entitled (1) v 024.8
entrail (9) n 037.2
entrail[N-i] (5) n 037.3
entrails (226) n 037.2
entrance (81) n/adj 107.4
~ hall (12) n 007A.4
~ patio (1) n 010.8
~ porch (1) n 010.8

~ porch way (1) n 010.8
~ ramp (18) n 107.4
~ ramps (1) n 107.4
~ road (2) n 031.8
entranceway (2) n 007A.6
entries (1) n 107.4
entry (14) n/adj 007A.5
~ hall (1) n 007A.6
~ ramp (2) n 107.4
enty (1) interj 012.6
enunciations (1) n 069.3
envelope (22) n 110.3
envelopes (1) n 100.7
environmentalists (1) n 099.5
Eola (1) 106.6
epi de mais (2) n F 024.2
epidemic (5) n 070.7
epiglottis (1) n 090.2
epilepsy (1) n 065.8
epileptic (3) n/adj 079.6
~ fits (1) n 065.8
Episcopal (19) 089.2
~ cathedral (1) n 089.1
~ church (6) n 089.1
(E)piscopal (8) 089.2
~ church (2) n 089.2
Episcopalian (14) 089.1
~ heathen (1) n 089.7
(E)piscopalian (2) 089.3
Episcopalians (5) 089.2
(E)piscopalians (1) 089.1
epsom salt (1) n 078.2
equal (5) v/adj 070.9
equalized day (1) n 003.4
equalizer (1) n 113.1
equally (1) adv 033.6
equestrian statue (1) n 084.9
equine (1) n 104.6
equinox (2) n/adj 112.9
~ storm (1) n 006.2
Equinox (1) 083.1
equipment (10) n/adj 066.9
~ room (1) n 011.7
~ shed (2) n 011.7
~ sheds (1) n 011.7
Equitable (3) 108.5
~ building (2) n 108.5
ER (1) 104.7
era (2) n 025.6
Era (2) 087.3
ERA (1) 024.7

eradicate (1) v 099.4
eradicated (1) v 099.5
eradication program (1) n
080.8
erase (1) v 070.7
(e)rase (2) v 075.6
Erath (1) TX 087.1
eretz Mechuleh (1) n G
096.7
Eridu (1) FL 086.2
Erin (2) TN 087.2
Ermine River (1) FL
030.7
Ernest Tutt Record Shop
(1) 106.4
erode (1) v 030.4
eroded (6) v/adj 030.5
 ~ land (1) n 030.4
 ~ lands (1) n 030.5
eroding (1) v 080.7
erosion (23) n/adj 030.5
 ~ ditch (1) n 030.5
erp(x2) piggo (1) interj
038.3
errand (1) n 053.5
errands (6) n 094.2
error (2) n 070.7
Erskine College (1) 083.6
erudite (1) adj 125.5
Erwin (2) TN 087.4
Escambia (11) AL FL
075.6
 ~ County (1) AL 087.6
 ~ Creek (1) AL 030.7
 ~ River (1) FL 030.7
Escambi(a) (2) AL 030.7
 ~ River (1) FL 030.7
(E)scambia (2) FL 087.2
 ~ River (1) FL 030.7
(E)scambi(a) (2) AL
087.3
 ~ River (1) AL 030.7
escape (17) n/v/adj 075.6
(e)scape (1) n 010.7
(e)scape[V-r] school (1)
v 083.4
escape[V-t] (1) v 053.4
escaped (1) v 070.3
escapes (2) v 070.6
(e)scapes (1) n 070.6
escaping (4) v 065.8
escarpment (3) n 031.2
Escatawpa (3) MS 087.6
 ~ community (1) MS
087.5

 ~ River (1) MS 030.7
(es)condileto (1) v S
096.4
escort (121) n/v/adj
097.5
 ~ services (1) n 113.5
(e)scort (6) v 097.5
(es)cort (1) v 097.5
escorting (4) v 081.4
(e)scuadria (1) n S 083.1
Eskimo (2) 011.1
 ~ spitz (1) n 033.3
Eskridge (1) KS 087.2
esophagus (12) n 071.7
(e)sophagus (3) n 071.7
Espada (2) 106.5
espadrilles (1) n 123.8
especially (5) adv 065.8
(e)specially (4) adv 070.7
Esperson (2) 106.4
 ~ building (1) n 106.4
 ~ buildings (1) n 108.5
esplanade (6) n 085.1
Esplanade (4) 107.7
 ~ Avenue (1) 106.3
 ~ Ridge (1) LA 084.8
esplanades (2) n 107.3
espoused (1) v 081.6
espresso (1) n 048.8
Essex (2) MS 082.6
est (2) v F 093.5
establish[V-r] (2) v 065.8
establish[V-t] (1) v 065.8
established (1) v 065.8
establishment (1) n 070.8
establishments (1) n 066.8
estancia (1) n S 007A.2
estate (9) n/adj 090.7
 ~ wagons (1) n 109.5
Estates (13) 087.5
(E)states (2) 106.2
Estill (1) MS 087.4
estimable (1) adj 065.8
estimate (1) v 057.7
estimation (4) n 080.7
estrange (1) v 063.3
estranged (4) v 063.3
estuaries (2) n 029.7
estuary (4) n 030.3
et (179) v/conj F 048.7
 ~ off (1) v 048.7
 ~ out (1) v 048.7
 ~ up (6) v 048.7
etagere (1) n 095.9
etalon (3) n F 034.1

eten (3) v 048.7
eternal rest (1) n 078.5
Eternity Square (1) 105.5
Ethel (1) MS 087.3
Ethiopia (1) 069.3
Ethiopian (2) 069.3
 ~ race (1) n 069.3
Ethiopians (2) 069.3
ethnic (1) n 069.5
etiquette (2) n 065.9
Etonia (2) FL 030.7
etouffee (2) n F 060.9
Etowah (15) AL GA TN
087.1
 ~ County (1) AL 087.2
 ~ River (4) GA 030.7
etranger (1) n F 066.7
eucalyptus (4) n/adj
061.8
 ~ trees (1) n 061.9
Eucheeanna (1) FL 087.6
Euclids (1) 089.8
Eudora (5) AR MS 087.6
Eufaufee (1) AL 030.7
Eufaula (21) AL 087.4
 ~ Lake (1) AL 030.7
Eugene (1) OR 087.1
Eula (2) 106.5
 ~ Park (1) 106.5
eulogy (4) n 079.2
Eunice (4) LA 087.6
eunuchs (1) n 033.5
Eurasian (2) 069.5
Eureka (6) AR MS TN
087.5
 ~ Springs (3) AR MS
087.5
Europe (9) 087.9
European (2) 065.9
 ~ country (1) n 065.9
 ~ theater (1) n 084.4
Eustis (3) FL 087.1
Eutaw (2) AL 087.4
Euvida Road (1) 107A.6
Evangeline (4) LA 086.5
 ~ Parish (1) LA 087.2
evangelist (14) n 067.8
Evans (5) 087.6
 ~ County (1) GA 087.6
 ~ Creek (2) MS 030.7
 ~ Drive (1) 107.6
Evanston (1) WY 087.2
Evansville (3) GA IN MS
087.5

(e)vaporate away (1) v
055.9
evaporated peaches (2) n
054.6
evaporator (2) n 017.7
(e)vaporator (4) n/adj
090.8
 ~ pan (1) n 017.6
eve (2) n 002.5
Eve (49) 070.1
Evelyn (1) 107.7
even (126) adj/adv 070.1
 ~ -dispositioned (1) adj
073.2
 ~ -keeled (1) adj 073.2
 ~ -tempered (23) adj
073.2
 ~ up (1) adj 004.9
ev(en) (1) adv 048.9
evener (6) n 021.3
even(er) (1) n 021.3
evening (1409) n/adj
002.5
 ~ bag (1) n 028.2
 ~ chores (1) n 037.4
 ~ courses (1) n 002.5
 ~ dress (1) n 123.6
 ~ food (1) n 002.5
 ~ gray (1) n 104.6
 ~ meal (3) n 002.5
 ~ paper (1) n 002.5
 ~ parade (1) n 002.5
 ~ part (1) n 002.5
 ~ purse (1) n 028.2
 ~ red (1) n 104.5
 ~ shoes (1) n 123.8
 ~ snack (1) n 048.6
 ~ sun (1) n 002.5
 ~ time (3) n 002.5
 ~ work (1) n 037.4
even(ing) (2) n 002.5
Evening (8) 002.1
 ~ Shade (7) AR 086.2
evenings (13) n 002.3
eveningtide (3) n 002.5
Evenridge (1) 105.4
Evensong (1) 089.9
event (3) n 065.8
eventually (10) adv 076.2
event(ually) (1) adv
076.2
(e)ventually (3) adv
075.7
ever (702) adv 025.5
ev(er) (3) adv 053.8

Everett (4) 106.7
~ Hill (1) 106.7
~ Lake (1) TN 030.7
~ Springs (1) GA 087.3
~ Square (1) 085.1
Everglades (24) FL 029.6
(Ever)glades (1) FL 029.6
evergreen (23) n/adj 061.9
~ bushes (1) n 052.1
~ multiplying shallots (1) n 055.7
~ oaks (1) n 061.9
~ onion (7) n 055.7
~ onions (1) n 055.7
~ tree (1) n 061.8
Evergreen (6) AL LA 087.4
evergreens (3) n 061.8
everhow (9) adv 042.7
everlasting (14) n/adj 057.3
~ spring (1) n 030.6
~ stream (1) n 030.6
~ tea (3) n 061.4
everwhat (5) pron 042.7
everwhich (5) pron 042.7
everwho (3) pron 042.8
every (204) adj 070.8
~ cotton-picking thing (1) n 080.7
~ damn thing (4) n 092.1
~ which way (1) adv 081.8
ever(y) (25) adj 075.6
ev(ery) (1) adj 002.2
everybody (161) pron 082.8
everyday (22) adj 073.6
~ dog (1) n 033.3
~ pants (2) n 027.4
~ school (1) n 083.6
~ shoes (2) n 123.8
everyone (18) pron 070.1
everyplace (1) adv 040.2
everything (151) pron 066.8
everywhat (1) pron 088.8
everywhere (48) adv 040.2
everywheres (8) adv 040.2
evidence (1) n 066.8
evidently (2) adv 065.8
evil (10) adj 090.1

~ one (1) n 090.1
~ spirit (2) n 090.1
~ spirits (4) n 090.2
~ weed (2) n 117.7
evils (1) n 113.3
evolution (1) n 053.4
ewe (642) n/adj 035.1
~ lamb (1) n 035.1
~ sheep (1) n 035.1
EWE (4) 035.1
ewe[N-i] (1) n 035.1
ewes (37) n 035.1
Ewing (1) 080.8
ex (2) prefix 069.3
~ -principal (1) n 069.3
~ -slaves (1) n 069.3
exactly (31) adv 065.8
(e)xactly (6) adv 065.8
exaggerating (1) v 080.7
Exall Lake (1) TX 030.7
exalt (1) v 067.8
exalted (1) n 067.7
example (13) n 026.2
exams (2) n 057.7
exasperated (3) adj 075.4
excavated (1) v 102.6
Excel (3) AL 087.4
excel at (1) v 068.9
excellent (1) adj 051.8
Excelsior Band (1) 131.8
except (8) prep 065.8
(e)xcept (3) prep 025.3
(ex)cept (1) prep 053.2
excepting (1) prep 032.9
(e)xcepting (3) prep 096.7
(ex)cepting (3) prep 066.8
exceptional child (1) n 080.9
excercise (1) n 070.8
excess baggage (1) n 115.3
exchange (3) adj 028.2
~ purse (1) n 028.2
~ store (1) n 116.1
Exchange (54) 108.5
~ Bank (2) 108.5
~ building (1) n 108.5
~ National Bank (1) 108.5
~ Street (1) 106.3
exchangeable (1) adj 005.6
exchanging (1) v 115.3

excitable (2) adj 075.1
excite (1) v 080.5
excited (7) v/adj 090.6
exciting (2) adj 090.5
exclusive (1) adj 123.6
(e)xcursion boats (1) n 024.6
excusado (1) n S 012.1
excuse (6) n/v 099.4
(e)xcuse (6) v 052.4
excused (1) v 083.2
excusing (1) prep 052.6
(e)xcusing (3) prep 092.7
executive (1) n 080.6
exercise (4) n/v/adj 022.6
~ bars (1) n 022.6
exhaust (2) v 075.4
exhausted (237) v 075.5
(e)xhausted (3) v 075.4
exhibition (1) n 024.7
exhibitionist (4) n 124.7
exhilarating (1) adj 007.4
exhorter (3) n 067.8
exiled from (2) v 013.9
exiles (2) n 070.7
exist (1) v 095.2
existence (3) n 053.4
(e)xistence (1) n 055.1
exit (123) n/v/adj 107.4
~ feeder (1) n 107.4
~ ramp (31) n 107.4
~ ramps (2) n 107.4
~ road (1) n 031.7
~ roads (1) n 107.4
~ route (1) n 107.4
exit[N-i] (1) n 107.4
exits (12) n 107.4
expand (2) v 018.9
expansion (1) adj 081.9
expect (38) v 101.2
~ to (10) v 101.2
(e)xpect (44) v 075.7
~ to (1) v 101.2
expectant mother (1) n 065.1
expected (16) v 065.1
~ to (2) v 058.1
(e)xpected mother (1) n 065.1
expecting (252) v/adj 065.1
~ a baby (7) v 065.1
~ a calf (4) v 033.9
~ her baby (1) v 065.1
~ mother (1) n 065.1

~ nurse (1) n 065.2
~ the stork (1) v 065.1
~ to (2) v 025.6
~ to mother (1) v 065.1
~ [D-0] baby (1) v 065.1
(e)xpecting (11) v 065.1
~ a baby (1) v 065.1
(e)xpects to (1) v 094.4
expedition (1) n 080.7
expell (1) v 080.2
expelled (1) v 080.2
expense (1) n 090.7
expensive (59) adj 123.6
~ cars (1) n 109.4
~ clothes (2) n 123.6
experience (4) n 093.1
experiences (1) n 013.7
(e)xperiment station (1) n 065.9
experimental (1) adj 066.8
experimentation (1) n 080.6
expert (2) n/adj 070.6
expertise (1) n 070.6
experts (1) n 065.9
expire (1) v 078.5
expired (66) v 078.5
~ in (1) v 078.5
(e)xpired (2) v 078.5
explain (8) v 057.6
~ to (1) v 053.4
expletives (2) n 065.8
explode (1) v 050.8
exploded (2) v 018.8
exploiter (1) n 073.5
(e)xplosive (1) adj 050.8
explosives plant (1) n 051.8
expose logs (1) n 008.5
exposure (1) n 065.9
(e)xposure (1) n 065.8
express (7) n/v/adj 107.2
~ bus service (1) n 109.9
~ turnpike (1) n 107.2
expressing (1) v 021.4
expression (14) n 070.7
(e)xpression (1) n 093.5
expressions (3) n 032.7
expressway (46) n 107.1
(e)xpressway (1) n 031.5
Expressway (7) 107.5
(E)xpressway (1) 031.7

expressways (12) n 107.5
extended dry spell (1) n 007.1
extension (4) n/adj 107.8
~ style (1) n 115.8
~ truck (1) n 111.3
Extension (1) 031.6
extensive (2) adj 090.7
extensively (1) adv 012.5
extent (1) n 025.6
exterminate (4) v 099.4
(e)xterminators (1) n 070.6
extinct (3) adj 066.8
extra (69) adj/adv 065.9
~ bed (1) n 029.2
~ bedroom (2) n 009.3
~ box (1) n 079.1
~ -heavy sand (1) n 029.9
~ -high (1) adj 065.9
~ house (2) n 010.3
~ pockets (1) n 084.8
~ room (3) n 007A.3
Extra Years of Zest (1) 088.8
extras (1) n 070.7
extravagant (1) adj 028.1
(e)xtravagant (1) adj 065.8
extremely (9) adv 090.4
(e)xtremely (1) adv 090.4
extremes (1) n 104.7
Exxon building (1) n 108.5
ey (1) interj 092.7
eye (265) n/adj 071.4
~ -catcher (2) n 051.8
~ hoe (2) n 051.8
~ loss (1) n 094.5
~ of the round (5) n 121.2
~ -opener (1) n 050.8
~ round (2) n 121.2
~ round roast (1) n 121.2
~ -see dog (1) n 033.3
~ stone (1) n 023.4
Eye (2) 087.4
eyeballed (1) v 088.9
eyebrow (1) n 071.3
eyebrows (3) n 071.3
eyed (118) v/adj 053.3
eyeglasses (1) n 027.6
eyeing (1) v 096.7

eyelashes (1) n 075.6
eyes (78) n 071.5
Eyes (1) 070.8
eyeteeth (9) n 071.8
Eyetie (1) 127.3
eyetooth (12) n 071.8
Ezekiel (1) 052.5

F

F (10) 073.4
~ -Twenty tractor (1) n 080.6
fabric (4) n/adj 026.2
~ sample (1) n 026.2
~ scrap (1) n 026.2
face (239) n/adj 031.2
~ basin (1) n 018.9
~ board (1) n 110.1
~ bowl (3) n 118.3
~ cord (1) n 019.8
~ hair (3) n 071.4
~ rag (25) n 018.5
~ rags (2) n 018.5
~ towel (49) n 018.6
~ tow(el) (1) n 018.5
~ towels (6) n 018.5
Face (2) 064.4
face[N-i] (7) n 040.4
facecloth (57) n 018.5
faced (13) v/adj 057.3
facedown (5) adv 040.4
faces (2) n/v 006.4
facial towel (1) n 018.5
facilities (9) n 012.1
facility (1) n 012.9
facing (4) n/v 008.2
Fackler (2) AL 087.5
fact (14) n 075.6
factor (1) n 025.2
factories (9) n 092.9
factory (40) n/adj 035.3
~ bread (3) n 045.1
~ -built (1) adj 045.1
~ -made (4) adj 045.1
~ -made bread (4) n 045.1
~ -made casings (1) n 046.8
~ -made whip (1) n 045.1
~ town (1) n 080.7
~ work (1) n 040.7
Factory (1) AL 030.7
facts (4) n 075.7

faddish (1) adj 123.6
fade (2) v 027.9
faded (1) adj 090.4
fading (2) v 007.3
fads (1) n 123.6
fag (65) n/v 124.2
~ out (1) v 075.5
Fagan (2) 030.7
~ Creek (1) AL 030.7
~ Ranch (1) TX 087.7
fagged (29) v 075.4
~ out (25) v 075.5
faggish (1) adj 124.2
faggot (19) n 124.2
faggots (3) n 117.7
faggy (2) adj 124.1
fags (20) n 117.7
fail (1) v 057.4
fail[V-r] on him (1) v 082.1
failing (1) n 104.5
fails to (1) v 053.8
faint (4) v/adj 080.4
fainted (5) v 076.1
~ away (1) v 079.3
~ out (1) v 070.2
faintest (1) adj 092.4
fainting couch (3) n 009.1
faints (1) v 034.4
faiou(let) (1) n F 055A.3
fair (323) n/v/adj 005.7
~ day (73) n 005.4
~ days (1) n 005.4
~ -haired boy (1) n 115.3
~ off (60) v 005.7
~ -size (1) adj 090.4
~ sky (1) n 005.4
~ soil (2) n 029.8
~ up (31) v 005.7
~ weather (8) n 005.7
Fair (15) 054.4
~ Beauties (1) 054.4
~ Beauty (1) 054.4
~ Park (8) 106.4
~ Park Boulevard (1) 031.7
Fairburn (4) GA 087.3
~ Road (1) 105A.1
faire (1) v F 052.8
faired (14) v 005.7
~ off (11) v 005.7
~ up (2) v 005.7
Fairfax (1) AL 087.6

Fairfield (10) AL FL 106.3
fairground (5) n 093.7
fairgrounds (5) n 106.4
Fairhope (3) AL 086.5
fairies (3) n 124.2
fairing (75) v 005.7
~ clear (1) v 005.7
~ off (44) v 005.7
~ up (22) v 005.7
Fairlawn (1) 105.4
fairly (58) adv 079.4
Fairport (2) NY 087.4
fairs (2) n/v 070.8
~ off (1) v 005.7
Fairs Mill (3) AR 087.3
Fairsey Road (1) 107.6
Fairview (5) AL IN TN 087.1
~ Heights (1) 106.2
~ Street (1) 107.7
fairy (27) n/adj 124.2
~ caps (1) n 056.8
~ circles (1) n 057.1
~ ring (1) n 056.8
~ rings (1) n 057.1
~ seats (1) n 057.1
~ stools (2) n 057.1
~ tale (1) n 039.6
fais (9) n F 083.1
~ -dodo (8) n F 083.1
~ -dodos (1) n F 083.1
faisande (1) adj F 046.9
faisander (1) v F 080.8
faith (5) n 080.6
faithful (1) adj 079.4
fake (5) adj 067.8
~ china egg (1) n 017.1
~ egg (3) n 017.1
faked (4) v 100.1
~ knowing (1) v 100.1
~ like (1) v 100.1
fakes (1) n 017.1
Falaya (3) 030.7
falcon (1) n 059.3
Falcon (2) TX 087.3
Falfurrias (3) TX 087.5
fall (285) n/v/adj 031.5
~ cleaning (1) n 010.4
~ down (7) v 034.4
~ garden (1) n 050.5
~ in (1) v 030.6
~ into (1) v 034.4
~ -like (1) adj 007.4
~ off (55) v 034.4

~ off of (8) v 034.4
~ offen (1) v 034.5
~ on (3) v 027.2
~ on off (1) v 034.5
~ onions (1) n 055.6
~ out (26) v 034.5
~ out of (4) v 034.5
~ out [P-0] (4) v 034.5
~ over (4) v 034.4
~ potatoes (2) n 055.4
~ term (1) n 083.5
~ time (1) n 002.8
Fall (6) 030.7
~ Creek (4) AR GA TN 030.7
~ Creek Falls (1) TN 031.5
~ River (1) TN 030.7
Fall[N-i] (5) 031.5
fall[V-r] (10) v 070.2
~ off (1) v 034.4
fall[V-t] (6) v 034.4
~ down (1) v 070.2
~ down from (1) v 034.5
~ off (1) v 034.5
~ out (2) v 034.5
falled off (1) v 034.4
fallen (280) v 034.4
~ down (5) v 070.2
~ -down section (1) n 108.7
~ from (1) v 034.5
~ in love (5) v 081.4
~ off (96) v 034.5
~ off of (9) v 034.4
~ offen the log (1) v 083.2
~ out (11) v 034.5
~ out of (81) v 034.5
~ out [P-0] (5) v 034.5
falling (61) n/v/adj 007.3
~ back (1) v 057.4
~ down (10) v 070.2
~ for her (1) v 081.4
~ in love (3) v 081.4
~ off (6) v 034.4
~ off of (1) v 034.5
~ out (3) v 034.5
~ out with him (1) n 082.1
~ tide (1) n 093.9
~ water (1) n 031.5
~ weather (7) n 005.6

Falling Creek (2) GA 030.7
fallish (1) adj 007.4
falloff (2) n 123.9
fallout (2) n 083.4
fallow (3) adj 029.5
falls (81) n/v 031.5
~ in (1) v 010.5
~ off (1) v 034.5
Falls (63) 031.5
~ building (1) n 108.5
~ County (1) TX 087.3
false (31) adj 017.1
~ bottom (1) n 080.6
~ egg (21) n 017.1
~ eggs (3) n 017.1
~ faces (1) n 052.1
~ flesh (1) n 078.2
~ prophet (1) n 090.1
~ teeth (2) n 071.6
False River (3) LA 030.7
fame (3) n 113.4
Fame (4) 106.4
fames (1) n 106.5
familiar (15) adj 065.8
(fa)miliar (1) adj 025.3
families (36) n 066.5
famille (3) n F 065.1
family (870) n/adj 066.5
~ bedroom (5) n 007.8
~ burial ground (4) n 078.8
~ burial place (1) n 078.8
~ burying ground (5) n 078.8
~ burying plots (1) n 078.8
~ butcher (1) n 046.8
~ car (12) n 023.6
~ cars (1) n 109.3
~ cemeteries (1) n 078.8
~ cemetery (31) n 078.8
~ cemeter(y) (1) n 078.8
~ chores (1) n 010.6
~ cow (1) n 033.6
~ cows (1) n 080.7
~ custard (1) n 048.3
~ dance (1) n 083.1
~ dining room (1) n 007A.5
~ farm (1) n 088.7

~ Florida room (1) n 118.1
~ folks (1) n 066.5
~ garden (4) n 050.5
~ graveyard (19) n 078.8
~ graveyards (4) n 078.8
~ grocery store (1) n 116.2
~ heirlooms (1) n 010.2
~ house (3) n 007.8
~ lot (2) n 078.8
~ lots (1) n 078.8
~ name (3) n 064.4
~ pallet (1) n 029.2
~ parlor (1) n 007.8
~ peanut patch (1) n 016.1
~ pie (17) n 048.3
~ pies (3) n 048.3
~ plot (27) n 078.8
~ pudding (1) n 048.3
~ records (2) n 039.8
~ resemblance (1) n 065.3
~ room (131) n 007.8
~ rooms (1) n 007.8
~ sitting room (1) n 007.8
~ sports car (1) n 109.2
~ style (1) n 049.4
~ trait (1) n 065.3
~ tree (1) n 012.2
~ -type car (1) n 109.3
~ vans (1) n 109.6
~ wagon (1) n 090.8
~ wash (1) n 010.6
~ washing (1) n 010.6
~ way (29) n 065.1
~ yard (1) n 078.9
fam(ily) (1) n 070.6
Family (4) 093.8
~ Pantry (1) 116.3
family[N-i] (2) n 016.7
family's (2) adj 066.5
~ cemetery (1) n 078.9
~ pie (1) n 048.3
famine (2) n 007.1
Famine (2) 055.4
famous (4) adj 053.5
fan (34) n/v/adj 118.5
~ blower (1) n 118.5
~ rake (1) n 120.7
~ -shaped (1) adj 120.7

~ -thrash (1) v 042.1
~ your fanny (1) v 065.5
fanatic (4) n 075.2
fanatics (1) n 126.6
fancied up (1) adj 088.7
fancier (3) adj 026.3
fancy (50) v/adj 123.6
~ -built (1) adj 007A.7
~ duds (2) n 123.6
~ groceries (1) n 088.8
~ house (2) n 113.4
~ Toms (1) n 123.6
~ up (2) v 028.1
~ work (2) n 080.8
fandangle thing (1) n 080.9
fangs (10) n 035.7
fanner (1) n 084.9
fanners (1) n 091.9
fannies (2) n 083.8
Fannin (7) GA TX 087.2
~ County (1) GA 087.2
fanning (1) v 057.4
fanny (13) n 072.8
Fanny Gresham Branch (1) GA 030.7
fanny[N-i] (1) n 040.3
fans (13) n 118.5
Fant (2) 106.4
fantail squirrel (1) n 059.7
Fantastic (1) 114.3
fantasy (1) n 088.7
far (1865) adj/adv 070.4
~ bedroom (3) n 070.4
~ -out (6) adj/adv 129.3
~ side (1) n 039.4
Far (3) 070.4
~ East (1) 070.4
~ North Dallas (2) 105.2
farer (1) adv 039.5
farest (8) adj/adv 043.3
farewell (5) adj/interj 002.4
~ parties (1) n 130.7
farfetched (1) adj 066.6
Fargo (4) GA 087.8
faring (2) v 057.4
Farley (1) AL 087.4
farm (504) n/v/adj 016.1
~ -and-market roads (1) n 031.6

~ animals (12) n 036.5
~ bell (1) n 084.9
~ boy (4) n 069.9
~ -bureau man (1) n 084.9
~ children (1) n 064.3
~ cooler (1) n 015.5
~ country (1) n 065.8
~ ditches (2) n 030.2
~ gal (1) n 064.9
~ girl (1) n 064.9
~ guy (1) n 069.9
~ home (1) n 007A.1
~ in (1) v 095.8
~ -junk antique store (1) n 092.7
~ lot (1) n 015.6
~ pool (2) n 015.6
~ road (33) n 031.8
~ roads (12) n 031.8
~ sacks (1) n 019.7
~ to market (3) n 031.7
~ -to-market (6) adj 031.7
~ -to-market road (20) n 031.7
~ -t(o)-market road (1) n 031.7
~ -to-market roads (30) n 031.7
~ to markets (1) n 031.7
~ tractor (1) n 021.9
~ wagon (1) n 053.4
~ wagons (1) n 090.9
~ with (2) v 021.6
~ work (2) n 102.8
~ -worked (1) v 095.8
Farm (7) 114.7
~ Bureau (3) 009.2
farm[V-p] (1) v 040.8
farm[V-r] (1) v 052.6
farm[V-s] (1) v 039.7
farmed (22) v 070.6
farmer (80) n/adj 065.8
~ in the dell (9) n 130.3
~ preachers (1) n 067.8
farm(er) (2) n 069.9
Farmer (2) 027.4
~ Brown (1) 027.4
~ Field (1) 106.5
farmer's (4) adj 081.9
~ friend (1) n 081.9
~ truck (1) n 109.7

~ wife (2) n 063.2
farmers (60) n/adj 048.1
  ~ cheese (1) n 048.1
  ~ market (1) n 116.2
Farmers (3) 088.8
  ~ Alliance (1) 088.8
  ~ Branch (1) TX 030.7
  ~ Home Administration (1) 088.8
farmers' pants (1) n 027.4
Farmerville (1) LA 087.4
farmhouse (15) n/adj 014.1
farmhouses (3) n 014.1
farming (77) n/v/adj 075.7
  ~ land (1) n 029.5
  ~ operation (1) n 081.8
  ~ section (1) n 102.4
  ~ sense (1) n 012.5
Farmington (2) AR 106.2
farmland (3) n 029.9
farms (41) n/v 055A.8
farmwife (2) n 063.2
farmwives (1) n 063.2
farmyard (6) n 015.6
Farnsworth building (1) n 108.5
Farragut Hotel (1) 108.5
Farrah Fawcett (1) 123.9
farrow (7) n/v 033.9
far(row) (1) v 024.7
farrowing (16) v/adj 035.5
  ~ house (6) n 015.4
  ~ houses (4) n 015.4
  ~ pen (1) n 015.4
  ~ pens (2) n 015.4
  ~ shed (1) n 015.4
  ~ sheds (1) n 014.2
far's (1) adv 043.3
fart (6) n/v/adj 064.4
  ~ bag (1) n 080.8
  ~ blossom (1) n 099.4
  ~ fruit (1) n 055.5
farther (93) adv 039.5
fartherest (43) adv 043.3
farthest (77) adv 043.3
farts around (1) v 088.8
farty (1) adj 097.8
fascinated (3) v/adj 081.4
fascinating (1) adj 091.6
fascinator (1) n 027.1
Fascism (1) 070.7

fashion (24) n/adj 123.6
  ~ parade (1) n 028.1
  ~ ring (1) n 123.1
fashionable (9) adj 123.6
  ~ clothes (2) n 123.6
  ~ dresser (1) n 028.1
  ~ things (1) n 123.6
fashioned (5) adj 088.7
fashions (1) n 123.6
fasola (2) n 089.5
fast (68) adj/adv 074.1
  ~ buck (1) n 114.5
  ~ dance (2) n 083.1
  ~ dancing (1) v 083.1
  ~ -food (1) adj 048.4
  ~ -food store (2) n 116.2
  ~ -like (1) adv 001A.4
  ~ music (3) n 130.8
fastback (1) n 109.5
fasten (4) v 011.1
fasten[V-t] (1) v 102.8
fastened (1) v 057.9
fasteners (1) n 110.4
fastens in (1) v 038.6
faster (7) adv 038.1
fastest (2) adj/adv 039.4
  ~ horse (1) n 039.4
fastly (1) adv 005.8
fat (455) n/adj 046.3
  ~ bacon (11) n 046.3
  ~ belly (3) n 046.3
  ~ cats (1) n 115.4
  ~ chips (1) n 008.6
  ~ city (1) n 112.8
  ~ kindling (5) n 008.6
  ~ kindling wood (1) n 008.6
  ~ -lean pork (1) n 046.3
  ~ lighter (3) n 008.6
  ~ lighter splinter (1) n 008.6
  ~ lighter wood (1) n 008.6
  ~ lighterd (49) n 008.6
  ~ lighterd limbs (1) n 008.6
  ~ lighterd log (2) n 008.6
  ~ lighterd pine (2) n 008.6
  ~ lighterd pinewood (1) n 008.6

  ~ lighterd post (1) n 016.5
  ~ lighterd rails (1) n 016.4
  ~ lighterd splinters (11) n 008.6
  ~ lighterd stump (1) n 008.6
  ~ lighterd tree (1) n 008.6
  ~ lighterd wood (1) n 008.6
  ~ lighters (1) n 008.6
  ~ lightwood (11) n 008.6
  ~ light(wood) (1) n 008.6
  ~ lightwood splinters (1) n 008.6
  ~ log (1) n 008.5
  ~ meat (70) n 046.3
  ~ pig (1) n 112.5
  ~ pine (57) n 008.6
  ~ pine splinters (1) n 008.6
  ~ pinewood (2) n 008.6
  ~ pork (7) n 046.3
  ~ pork meat (1) n 046.3
  ~ salt pork (5) n 046.3
  ~ side (1) n 046.3
  ~ splinter (2) n 008.6
  ~ splinters (10) n 008.6
  ~ tree (1) n 008.6
  ~ white meat (1) n 046.3
  ~ women (1) n 125.2
Fat (4) 080.6
  ~ City (3) 080.6
fatal (1) adj 078.5
fatalities (1) n 078.6
fatally (1) adv 078.5
fatback (435) n/adj 046.3
  ~ meat (5) n 046.3
fathead (1) n 073.4
father (2169) n 063.4
  ~ -in-law (1) n 063.4
fath(er) (1) n 063.4
Father (107) 063.5
  ~ Time (1) 088.3
  ~ worshipers (1) n 126.5
Father[N-i] (1) 089.8
father[N-k] (7) adj 065.3
  ~ double (1) n 065.3

  ~ house (1) n 043.9
  ~ mother (1) n 043.9
  ~ people (2) n 042.9
  ~ ways (2) n 065.3
Father[N-k] (1) 007A.3
fatherless (52) adj 066.3
  ~ baby (1) n 066.3
  ~ child (21) n 066.3
  ~ children (1) n 066.3
  ~ mother (1) n 066.3
father(less) (1) adj 066.3
father's (58) adj 063.4
  ~ characteristics (2) n 065.3
  ~ child (1) n 065.3
  ~ death (1) n 063.4
  ~ father (1) n 063.4
  ~ features (4) n 065.3
  ~ folks (2) n 066.5
  ~ footstep[N-i] (1) n 065.3
  ~ habits (3) n 065.3
  ~ image (1) n 065.3
  ~ images (1) n 065.3
  ~ mother (1) n 063.4
  ~ name (2) n 032.5
  ~ parents (3) n 063.8
  ~ people (9) n 066.5
  ~ Purple Heart (1) n 063.7
  ~ side (4) n 063.4
  ~ sister (1) n 063.4
  ~ temperament (1) n 065.3
  ~ way (1) n 065.3
  ~ ways (7) n 065.3
Father's (22) 007A.2
  ~ death (1) n 063.4
  ~ father (1) n 063.4
  ~ folks (1) n 066.5
  ~ mother (1) n 063.6
  ~ name (1) n 063.4
  ~ parents (2) n 063.8
  ~ people (3) n 063.5
  ~ ranch (1) n 063.4
  ~ side (7) n 063.4
fathers (1) n 053.3
fathom (1) n 099.5
fatigue (3) v/adj F 075.4
fatigue[V-t] (2) v 075.5
  ~ out (1) v 075.5
fatigued (23) v/adj 075.4
fatigues (2) n 027.4
fatras (1) n F 010.2
fats (3) n/v 130.8

Fatso (1) 063.9
fatten (6) v 058.5
fattening (24) v/adj 065.9
　~ coop (1) n 036.8
　~ hog (3) n 035.4
　~ hogs (3) n 035.5
　~ pen (9) n 015.4
　~ pens (3) n 015.4
　~ time (1) n 081.9
fatter (2) adj 125.5
Fatti (1) G 064.1
fatty (3) n/adj 125.1
　~ bread (1) n 044.5
　~ wood (1) n 008.6
Fatty (1) 063.9
fatwood (40) n/adj 008.6
　~ pine (1) n 008.6
　~ tinder (1) n 008.6
Faubourg Marigny (1)
　080.6
Faubus (1) 053.4
faucet (1166) n/adj 018.7
　~ thing (1) n 018.7
　~ water (1) n 018.7
faucets (66) n 018.7
Faulk (1) 107.7
Faulkner (4) MS 087.5
　~ County (2) AR 087.1
fault (3) n 070.2
Fauna (1) TX 087.6
Fauntleroy (1) 088.7
fava (1) n 055A.3
favor (50) n/v 065.3
favor[V-p] (9) v 065.3
favored (32) v 065.3
favoring (2) v 065.3
favorite (20) n/adj 070.9
Favorite (5) 056.9
favorites (2) n 125.6
favoritism (1) n 115.4
favors (272) n/v 065.3
fay (1) n 069.5
Fayette (25) AL GA MS
　TX 087.2
　~ County (8) AL GA
　　MS 087.2
Fayetteville (32) AL AR
　GA NC TN TX 087.5
fazed (1) v 075.5
Fe (3) 087.2
fear (6) n/v/adj 074.3
feared (1) v 074.3
fearful (3) adj 074.3
fearing (1) adj 089.3
feast (1) n 056.8

feather (55) n/adj 021.1
　~ bed (14) n 080.7
　~ bedder (2) n 115.4
　~ beds (14) n 080.7
　~ brooms (1) n 010.5
　~ duster (3) n 010.5
　~ mattress (1) n 028.7
　~ pillow (7) n 028.8
　~ pillows (6) n 028.8
　~ tick (1) n 088.7
　~ -tick pillows (1) n
　　028.8
　~ ticking (1) n 080.8
featherbedding (1) v
　115.4
feathercut (2) n 123.9
feathercuts (1) n 123.9
feathered (6) n/adj 123.9
　~ animals (2) n 036.6
　~ back (1) n 123.9
　~ fowl (1) n 036.6
　~ friends (1) n 036.6
featheredge (2) n/adj
　096.8
　~ siding (1) n 011.2
feathers (12) n 040.5
feature (1) v 057.7
feature[N-i] (2) n 065.3
feature[V-p] (4) v 065.3
featured (3) v 065.3
　~ like (1) v 065.3
features (16) n/v 065.3
Febre (1) 087.2
February (911) 001A.6
Februar(y) (68) 001A.6
Fe(bruary) (1) 001A.6
feces (1) n 088.8
fed (22) v/adj 036.5
　~ up (1) v 052.7
federal (105) adj 085.6
　~ agen(cy) (1) n 085.6
　~ buildings (1) n 108.5
　~ court (1) n 085.6
　~ government (78) n
　　085.6
　~ government's (1) adj
　　085.6
　~ grants (1) n 085.6
　~ green (1) n 114.5
　~ highway (1) n 107.1
　~ highways (1) n 031.7
　~ hospital (1) n 084.5
　~ housing (1) n 106.3
　~ judge (2) n 068.6
　~ judiciary (1) n 085.6

　~ man (1) n 085.6
　~ pen (1) n 026.5
　~ people (1) n 085.6
　~ prison (2) n 112.8
　~ program (1) n 092.1
　~ programs (1) n 085.6
　~ road (1) n 031.6
Federal (8) 108.5
　~ Road (1) 088.8
　~ War (5) 085.8
Federals (2) 085.9
feds (1) n 085.6
fee (6) n 094.8
feeble (18) adj 072.9
feeblemind (1) adj 074.7
feed (735) n/v/adj 037.4
　~ bag (10) n 019.6
　~ barn (2) n 014.2
　~ basket (4) n 017.4
　~ bin (3) n 035.8
　~ bins (3) n 014.4
　~ box (2) n 010.1
　~ boxes (1) n 035.8
　~ bucket (10) n 017.4
　~ cattle (2) n 036.5
　~ corn (2) n 056.2
　~ cow[N-i] (1) n 033.6
　~ house (13) n 014.4
　~ houses (2) n 015.4
　~ mill (2) n 081.9
　~ mills (1) n 084.8
　~ on (1) v 040.8
　~ out (1) v 084.8
　~ pen (2) n 036.9
　~ room (8) n 014.3
　~ rooms (2) n 014.3
　~ roots (1) n 061.4
　~ sack (34) n 019.7
　~ sacks (31) n 019.7
　~ shed (2) n 014.3
　~ store (1) n 014.4
　~ time (48) n 037.4
　~ tower (1) n 014.4
　~ trough (27) n 035.8
　~ trough[N-i] (2) n
　　035.8
　~ troughs (10) n 035.8
　~ up (37) v 036.5
feed[V-p] (1) v 053.4
feeder (73) n/adj 035.8
　~ bus (1) n 109.8
　~ -class pig (1) n 035.5
　~ cows (1) n 055A.7
　~ pan (1) n 035.8
　~ parlors (1) n 015.4

　~ pen (1) n 015.4
　~ pig (2) n 035.5
　~ pigs (4) n 035.5
　~ road (3) n 031.7
　~ roads (2) n 031.7
　~ shed (1) n 015.2
　~ streams (1) n 030.6
　~ streets (2) n 107.3
feeders (50) n 060A.4
feeding (549) n/v/adj
　037.4
　~ barn (1) n 015.1
　~ coop (1) n 036.9
　~ hours (1) n 037.4
　~ lot (1) n 015.6
　~ pen (5) n 015.6
　~ place (2) n 015.6
　~ stall (1) n 015.3
　~ the fish (2) v 080.3
　~ time (489) n 037.4
　~ times (1) n 037.4
　~ trough (7) n 035.8
　~ troughs (2) n 035.8
　~ up (1) v 037.4
　~ -up time (2) n 037.4
fee(ding) time (1) n
　037.4
feedlot (20) n 015.6
feedlots (5) n 015.4
feeds (3) v 030.6
feel (127) v 079.4
　~ like (11) v 074.1
　~ of (1) v 051.1
　~`[P-0] (1) v 053.6
feel[V-p] (3) v 072.9
feel[V-r] (1) v 070.9
feel[V-t] like (1) v 058.9
feeled (1) v 072.9
feelers (1) n 126.5
feeling (224) n/v 057.4
　~ his oats (1) v 081.4
　~ like (4) v 025.4
feelings (11) n 012.2
feels (6) n/v 072.9
feely (2) adj 080.8
　~ -feely (1) adj 080.8
fees (11) n 094.8
feet (2087) n/adj 072.6
　~ place (1) n 039.3
　~ -wise (1) adv 081.9
feeting (1) n 075.6
feets (45) n 072.6
feist (427) n/adj 033.3
　~ dog (42) n 033.3
　~ dogs (12) n 033.3

feist[N-i] (6) n 033.3
feister (1) n 033.3
feistes (14) n 033.3
feisting around (1) v 084.8
feists (5) n 033.3
feisty (95) adj 033.3
~ breeches (1) n 088.7
Felcianas (1) LA 087.5
Feld (1) n G 016.1
Feliciana (3) 087.1
Felicity (1) 115.6
Feliz (5) S 093.3
~ Ano Nuevo (1) S 093.3
~ Navidad (4) S 093.2
fell (1198) v 034.4
~ apart (1) v 070.2
~ back (3) v 040.3
~ down (52) v 034.4
~ from (11) v 034.4
~ in (9) v 070.2
~ in love (1) v 034.4
~ off (492) v 034.4
~ off in (1) v 034.5
~ off of (54) v 034.4
~ offen (7) v 034.4
~ on (9) v 070.2
~ out (49) v 034.5
~ out for (1) v 075.2
~ out of (115) v 034.5
~ out with him (1) v 082.1
~ out [P-0] (31) v 034.5
~ over (3) v 034.4
~ through (1) v 034.4
~ with (1) v 032.4
Fellah (1) 030.7
fellen (7) v 034.5
~ off (5) v 034.5
~ offen (1) v 034.5
~ out [P-0] (1) v 034.5
fellies (50) n 021.1
fellow (366) n/adj 081.5
~ horse (1) n 034.1
fellow[N-i] (1) n 055A.7
fellow[N-k] bullet (1) n 043.9
fellow's (3) adj 070.2
~ house (1) n 053.4
~ language (1) n 104.8
fellows (48) n 060A.8
fellowship (1) v 053.7
Fellowship (2) MS 087.2

Fellsmere (1) FL 087.2
felly (147) n/adj 021.1
~ band (1) n 021.1
felon (2) n 078.2
felt (28) v/adj 079.4
~ like (9) v 076.1
~ of (1) v 051.1
~ pen (1) n 026.5
~ siding (1) n 011.2
felted (1) v 019.5
female (78) n/adj 034.2
~ calf (6) n 033.8
~ cow (2) n 033.6
~ gilts (1) n 035.5
~ girl (1) n 064.9
~ hog (3) n 035.5
~ homosexual (1) n 124.4
~ horse (9) n 034.2
~ impersonator (1) n 124.1
~ jackass (1) n 033.8
~ parking (1) n 108.3
~ queer (1) n 124.4
~ sheep (10) n 035.1
~ sheeps (1) n 035.1
~ sow (1) n 035.5
~ teacher (2) n 067.6
fe(male) (1) n 035.5
Female (1) 083.6
females (4) n 035.1
feminine (11) adj 124.1
~ man (1) n 124.1
feminist (2) n 124.1
femme (4) n F 065.1
~ -la (2) n F 065.1
fence (2863) n/v/adj 126.1
~ corners (1) n 016.4
~ jamb (2) n 016.4
~ law (7) n 080.6
~ off (1) v 016.2
~ paling (1) n 016.2
~ pole (1) n 016.5
~ poles (1) n 016.5
~ post (32) n 016.5
~ post[N-i] (24) n 016.5
~ postes (1) n 016.5
~ posts (3) n 016.5
~ rail (5) n 016.4
~ rails (4) n 016.4
~ road (1) n 031.8
~ wire (11) n 016.3
~ worm (3) n 016.4

fence[N-i] (6) n 016.2
fenced (26) v/adj 016.2
~ against (1) v 080.6
~ in (11) v 016.2
~ -in (1) adj 015.4
~ off (1) v 015.6
~ up (2) v 016.2
~ with (2) v 016.6
fencerow (2) n 016.2
fencerows (1) n 016.6
fences (777) n 016.3
fencing (53) n/v/adj 016.2
~ -plank fence (2) n 016.2
~ wire (1) n 016.3
fend (2) v 044.2
fender (3) n 122.7
Fenimore (1) 067.7
fennel (5) n 061.6
Fenton (1) MS 087.5
Fentress (4) TN 086.7
~ County (1) TN 086.8
ferdootin (1) n 065.5
Ferguson (2) MS 087.6
ferme (1) v F 011.1
ferment (2) v 047.6
fermented (2) v 047.5
fern (7) n/adj 062.8
~ stands (1) n 019.2
Fernandina (7) FL 087.7
~ Beach (2) FL 087.4
~ (Beach) (1) FL 087.3
Fernando (2) 106.4
fernery (1) n 080.6
ferns (1) n 017.7
ferocious (1) adj 065.8
Ferriday (4) LA 087.3
ferries (1) n 109.9
Ferris (11) TX 087.2
~ wheel (10) n 080.8
ferry (13) n/adj 024.6
~ boat (1) n 098.5
~ landing (1) n 031.4
Ferry (20) 087.9
ferryboat (6) n 024.6
ferryboats (1) n 024.6
fertile (570) adj 029.3
~ bottomland (1) n 029.4
~ land (19) n 029.3
~ soil (15) n 029.3
fertiler (1) adj 066.1
fertility (4) n 029.3

fertilize (166) n/v/adj 029.3
~ sack (6) n 019.7
~ sacks (5) n 019.7
~ soil (1) n 029.3
fertilize[V-t] (7) v 029.3
fertilized (28) v/adj 029.3
~ soil (1) n 029.3
fertilizer (145) n/adj 029.3
~ bags (4) n 019.6
~ sack (1) n 019.6
~ sacks (1) n 019.7
~ shed (1) n 011.9
~ soil (1) n 029.8
~ spur (1) n 120.5
fertilizers (1) n 029.3
fertilizing (8) n/v 029.3
fescue (8) n/adj 014.9
~ grass (1) n 015.9
fester (17) n/v 077.5
festered (7) v 077.5
festering (1) n 077.5
festers (3) n/v 077.5
festival (10) n 106.7
Festival (4) 080.8
festivals (1) n 035.5
festoony (1) adj 088.7
Festus (1) MO 087.2
fetch (129) v 098.2
~ him (1) v 033.2
~ it (6) v 033.2
fetch[V-r] (1) v 098.3
fetched (14) v 027.5
~ up (1) v 065.3
fetcher (4) n 071.7
fetchers (1) n 071.7
fetching (2) v 021.4
fetlock (1) n 034.7
fetlocks (1) n 034.7
fettle (1) n 073.1
feud (1) n 129.7
feuding with (1) v 025.9
feuds (1) n 013.8
feve plate (1) n F 055A.5
fever (201) n/adj 076.2
~ breaker (1) n 090.8
~ grass (11) n 061.4
~ -grass medicine (1) n 061.4
~ medicine (1) n 078.4
~ powders (1) n 078.4
~ tick (2) n 084.8
~ ticks (3) n 080.6
~ tonic (1) n 078.4

fe(ver) (1) n 079.8
feverweed (2) n 078.4
fevi (2) adj F 055.8
few (621) adj 070.3
FFA (1) 082.9
FHA (1) 012.9
fi-f(ille) (1) n F 088.8
fiance (91) n 081.5
fianc(e) (1) n 081.5
fiancee (42) n 081.6
fianc(ee) (1) n 081.6
fibber (2) n 101.3
fibbers (1) n 101.3
fiber (7) n/adj 054.8
~ butter (1) n 048.1
~ glass (3) n 024.6
~ -glass boats (1) n 024.6
~ wood (1) n 062.2
fiction (2) n/adj 052.8
~ books (1) n 052.8
fiddle (22) n/v/adj 020.6
~ downs (1) n 083.1
~ -fooled with (1) v 081.8
~ music (1) n 089.5
~ string (1) n 104.5
~ worm (2) n 060.5
~ worms (2) n 060.5
Fiddle Route Road (1) 031.7
fiddledeedee (2) interj 092.1
fiddler (5) n/adj 060.5
~ worms (1) n 060.5
Fiddler Knob (1) AL 030.9
fiddlers (6) n 080.6
fiddlers' conventions (1) n 083.1
fiddlesticks (2) n/interj 130.7
fiddling (4) v/adj 080.6
~ around (1) v 080.6
~ for (2) v 080.6
~ worms (1) n 060.5
fidgets (1) n 074.1
fidgety (15) adj 074.1
fido (1) n 033.3
Fido (2) 033.2
field (1476) n/adj 016.1
~ artillery (1) n 016.1
~ beans (2) n 055A.4
~ calf (1) n 033.8
~ colt (1) n 065.7

~ corn (80) n 056.2
~ corn on the cob (1) n 056.2
~ cresses (1) n 055A.5
~ crops (1) n 016.1
~ days (1) n 088.9
~ dodger (1) n 035.9
~ fence (4) n 016.3
~ -fence wire (1) n 016.3
~ fences (1) n 016.2
~ fencing (4) n 016.2
~ goal (3) n 098.4
~ grass (11) n 015.9
~ grasses (1) n 015.9
~ -grown (1) adj 050.4
~ hockey (3) n 130.5
~ house (1) n 126.2
~ mice (4) n 059.7
~ Negroes (2) n 069.3
~ notes (1) n 075.7
~ of diamonds (1) n 029.1
~ onions (1) n 055.6
~ party (1) n 130.7
~ pea (3) n 055.6
~ peas (39) n 055A.2
~ pine (1) n 061.4
~ poppy (1) n 062.3
~ pumpkins (1) n 056.5
~ rake (1) n 120.7
~ rally (1) n 060.6
~ rat (1) n 059.3
~ rats (1) n 059.5
~ road (22) n 031.8
~ road[N-i] (1) n 031.8
~ roads (5) n 031.7
~ rock (4) n 016.1
~ -rock fence (1) n 016.6
~ servant (1) n 088.9
~ spider webs (1) n 061.3
~ squirrel (1) n 059.6
~ time (1) n 077.9
~ -trial dog (1) n 033.4
~ trips (1) n 016.1
~ worm (1) n 060.5
Field (48) 016.1
~ House (1) 106.4
~ Street (1) 107.6
field[N-i] (2) n 016.1
fields (224) n 016.1
Fields (1) 105.5

fieldstone (7) n/adj 007A.3
~ wall (2) n 016.6
fieldstones (1) n 016.6
fieldwork (3) n 016.1
fieldworker (1) n 067.8
fiend (15) n 114.3
fiends (2) n 090.8
fierce (2) adj 006.3
fiery (6) adj 075.1
fiesta (1) n 131.1
fife (1) n 020.5
fifollets (1) n F 090.4
fifteen (577) n/adj 001.7
~ after (11) n 004.5
~ before (1) n 004.5
~ -feet (1) adj 026.6
~ -foot (1) adj 007.9
~ -gallon (1) adj 009.7
~ minutes (2) n 070.3
~ minutes after (1) n 004.5
~ minutes before (1) n 070.1
~ minutes (be)fore (1) n 004.5
~ minutes of (3) n 004.5
~ minutes of being (1) n 004.5
~ minutes past (1) n 004.5
~ minutes till (39) n 004.5
~ minutes to (36) n 004.5
~ minutes until (4) n 004.5
~ minutes [P-0] (1) n 004.5
~ of (1) n 004.5
~ past (1) n 004.5
~ till (75) n 004.5
~ to (14) n 004.5
~ until (1) n 004.5
Fifteen (2) 031.6
fifteenth (4) n/adj 001A.3
Fifteenth (5) 008.9
~ Street (4) 106.3
fifth (987) n/adj 001A.3
~ wheel (5) n 020.8
Fifth (21) 001A.3
~ Avenue (1) 082.6
~ Avenue hotels (1) n 113.8

~ Street (9) 107.7
~ Ward (7) 105.1
fifths (1) n 001A.4
fifties (1) n 001A.1
Fifties (1) 130.8
fiftieth (1) n 001A.3
fifty (537) n/adj 001.9
~ -cent (3) adj 026.6
~ -eight (23) n/adj 001.4
~ -fifty (1) n 001A.1
~ -five (27) n/adj 001.3
~ -four (20) n 001.2
~ -gallon (4) adj 019.1
~ -nine (24) n 001.5
~ -one (16) n/adj 001.1
~ -pound (29) adj 019.6
~ -seven (23) n/adj 001.4
~ -seven varieties (5) n 033.3
~ -seven variety (3) n 033.3
~ -six (17) n/adj 001.3
~ -some (1) n 084.8
~ -some-odd (2) adj 080.7
~ -something (1) n 103.2
~ -third (1) n 001A.3
~ -three (15) n/adj 001.2
~ -two (15) n/adj 001.1
fift(y) (2) n 001.2
~ -four (1) n 001.2
~ -seven varieties (1) n 033.3
fif(ty) (1) adj 016.7
Fifty (69) 107.1
~ -Five (1) 107.1
~ High One (1) 031.6
~ -Nine (1) 031.6
~ -Ninth Street (1) 001A.3
~ -One (2) 031.6
~ -One Government Street (1) 112.6
~ -One Highway (1) 031.6
~ -One North (1) 107.1
~ -Seven Heinz (1) 033.3
~ -Seventh Avenue (1) 107.8

~ -Six (1) 107.7
~ -Six Street (1) 105.6
fig (62) n/adj 061.8
~ bush (1) n 012.2
~ leaf (1) n 061.4
~ (me)theglin (1) n 050.9
~ nuts (1) n 054.7
~ pie (1) n 048.3
~ preserves (2) n 051.6
~ tomato (1) n 055.3
~ tomatoes (2) n 055.3
~ tree (14) n 061.9
~ trees (28) n 061.9
fight (823) n/v/adj 104.2
~ back (1) v 104.2
~ off (1) v 104.2
~ -or-flight words (1) n 104.8
~ over (2) v 104.2
~ your mammy (1) n 114.7
Fight between the Rebels and the Yankees (1) 085.8
fight[V-r] (4) v 104.2
fight[V-t] (9) v 104.2
fighted (4) v 104.2
fighten (1) v 104.2
fighter (18) n 104.2
fighters (13) n 112.4
fighting (155) v/adj 104.2
~ back (1) v 099.5
~ bull (1) n 033.5
~ cocks (1) n 080.7
~ over (1) v 052.7
~ words (1) n 042.6
fightingest (1) adj 104.2
fights (27) n/v 104.2
fighty (1) adj 075.1
figmentation (1) n 079.7
figs (16) n 055.1
figue (1) n F 055.3
figure (31) n/v 070.6
~ eight (2) n 122.7
~ out (1) v 078.7
figured (22) v 094.1
~ out (2) v 012.5
figurehead (2) n 115.4
figures (3) n 083.2
figurine (1) n 045.2
figuring (11) v 065.8
~ on (7) v 101.2
~ to (1) v 101.2
filbert (2) n 054.9

filberts (4) n 054.8
filched (4) v 100.2
file (213) n/adj 023.4
~ clerk (1) n 068.8
~ gumbo (4) n 055.7
filed (1) v 023.4
filer (2) n 023.4
files (11) n 023.4
filet mignon (23) n 121.1
filing (2) n/adj 010.9
Filipino (1) 069.3
Filipinos (2) 126.3
fill (31) n/v/adj 007.9
~ doughnut (2) n 122.6
~ doughnuts (6) n 122.6
~ in (1) v 030.1
~ -in preacher (1) n 067.8
~ mattress (1) n 029.2
~ -out (1) n 067.8
f(ille) (1) n F 088.8
filled (58) n/v/adj 122.6
~ doughnut (5) n 045.2
~ doughnuts (2) n 122.5
~ in (1) v 057.8
~ -in (1) adj 029.8
~ out (1) v 057.8
~ up (5) v 057.8
filler (6) n 048.5
fillet (14) n/adj 121.1
~ knife (1) n 104.3
~ knives (1) n 104.3
~ steak (1) n 121.1
~ steaks (1) n 121.1
filleted (1) v 065.9
fillets (2) n 121.1
fillies (1) n 034.2
filling (29) n/v/adj 048.5
~ out (1) v 088.3
~ station (8) n 107.2
~ stations (1) n 107.2
fillings (1) n 044.6
fills (3) n/v 020.9
filly (68) n 034.2
film (9) n/adj 114.9
~ bag (1) n 123.7
~ flick (1) n 114.9
films (10) n 114.9
filter (8) n/v 116.8
filtering (1) v 048.2
filth (7) n 015.8
filthier (1) adj 066.1
filthy (6) adj 023.8

~ lucre (3) n 114.5
fin (8) n/v 114.5
finagler (2) n 073.5
final (6) adj 027.2
~ resting place (2) n 078.8
~ reward (1) n 078.5
~ rites (1) n 079.2
finally (9) adv 078.5
finance (5) n/v 095.1
financial (10) adj 105.2
~ center (2) n 105.2
~ district (7) n 105.2
Financial (1) 108.5
financially (1) adv 053.4
financier (1) n 081.5
Fincastle (1) TN 087.5
find (253) v 033.9
~ a baby (2) v 065.1
~ a baby calf (1) v 033.9
~ a calf (84) v 033.9
~ calf[N-i] (1) v 033.9
~ calves (1) v 033.9
~ her a calf (1) v 033.9
~ her calf (1) v 033.9
~ out (11) v 057.6
~ pigs (3) v 033.9
find[V-t] out (1) v 057.9
finding (4) v 033.9
~ a calf (1) v 033.9
~ pigs (1) v 035.5
findings (1) n 080.6
finds (2) v 052.6
~ pigs (1) v 035.5
fine (521) adj 079.4
~ babe (1) n 125.4
~ broad (1) n 125.4
~ chick (1) n 125.4
~ china (1) n 017.1
~ clothes (2) n 123.6
~ day (27) n 005.4
~ grits (3) n 050.6
~ -looking (1) adj 055A.2
~ -looking guy (1) n 125.3
~ -mesh wire (1) n 016.3
~ mist (13) n 006.6
~ morning (1) n 007.4
~ piece of ass (1) n 125.4
~ rain (1) n 006.6
~ rock (1) n 031.6

~ rocks (1) n 031.6
~ -tooth harrow (2) n 021.7
~ wood (1) n 008.6
Fine (1) 106.8
finery (1) n 028.1
fines (1) n 002.6
finest (3) adj 081.8
finger (57) n/adj 065.8
~ joints (1) n 072.3
~ pea (1) n 081.8
~ ring (1) n 123.1
~ roll (1) n 122.2
~ trip (1) n 057.8
~ waves (2) n 123.9
finger[N-i] (1) n 072.3
fingered (1) adj 073.3
fingerlings (1) n 088.8
fingernails (3) n 072.5
fingers (57) n 072.3
fingertip towels (1) n 018.6
fingy (1) adj 089.8
finicky (5) adj 074.8
finish (23) v/adj 083.2
~ carpenter (1) n 067.8
~ up on (1) v 012.5
~ with (1) v 089.7
finish[V-r] (3) v 039.6
~ in (1) v 096.8
finish[V-t] (4) v 057.4
finished (32) v 075.5
~ out (1) v 075.7
finisher (1) n 120.5
finishes (2) v 083.2
finishing (3) v/adj 053.1
~ school (1) n 083.6
fink (4) n 101.3
Finley (1) TN 087.6
Finney (1) 021.7
fir (5) n/adj 061.8
~ tree (1) n 061.9
~ wood (1) n 061.8
fire (1027) n/v/adj 070.6
~ ant (5) n 060A.5
~ ants (15) n 060A.8
~ antses (1) n 060A.8
~ backs (1) n 008.5
~ basket (2) n 008.3
~ blight (2) n 080.7
~ -blight (1) v 080.7
~ boats (1) n 111.1
~ bricks (1) n 008.2
~ bush (1) n 062.2
~ car (9) n 111.6

~ chief (6) n 111.6
~ chief[N-k] (1) adj 111.6
~ -chief[N-k] car (3) n 111.6
~ -chief's car (30) n 111.6
~ chiefs (1) n 111.6
~ clay (1) n 016.3
~ coals (2) n 008.7
~ department (20) n 112.6
~ (de)partment (2) n 065.8
~ -department ambulance (1) n 111.5
~ -department ambulances (1) n 111.6
~ -department car (2) n 111.6
~ -department garage (1) n 112.6
~ -department house (1) n 112.6
~ depot (1) n 112.6
~ door (1) n 008.2
~ -eaters (2) n 112.4
~ engine (51) n 111.1
~ engine trucks (1) n 092.8
~ engines (13) n 111.1
~ escape (9) n 010.7
~ (e)scape (1) n 010.7
~ -escape ladders (1) n 108.6
~ exit (1) n 108.2
~ faucets (1) n 108.2
~ fighter (14) n 112.4
~ fighters (12) n 112.4
~ fighting (1) n 104.2
~ -fish (1) n 098.8
~ fliers (1) n 060A.3
~ freak (1) n 112.4
~ front (1) n 008.2
~ gem (1) n 008.2
~ grate (1) n 008.3
~ grates (1) n 008.3
~ hazard (1) n 024.3
~ hazards (1) n 032.7
~ headquarters (1) n 112.6
~ hearth (20) n 008.2
~ hook (1) n 008.3

~ hose (2) n 111.3
~ hot-pepper ropes (1) n 130.6
~ hydrant (71) n 108.2
~ hydrants (31) n 108.2
~ in the mountain (1) n 062.7
~ iron (9) n 008.3
~ irons (63) n 008.3
~ jack (1) n 024.3
~ jenny (1) n 091.8
~ kindling (1) n 008.6
~ length (1) n 008.5
~ log (11) n 008.5
~ logs (9) n 008.5
~ mantel (2) n 008.4
~ -marshal's car (1) n 111.6
~ pepper (1) n 051.8
~ poker (2) n 008.2
~ pokers (1) n 008.3
~ poppers (1) n 091.8
~ pots (1) n 024.3
~ pumper (3) n 111.2
~ rack (2) n 008.3
~ restes (1) n 008.3
~ screen (3) n 008.3
~ shelf (2) n 008.4
~ shovel (1) n 084.9
~ stairs (1) n 010.7
~ starter (1) n 008.6
~ station (87) n 112.6
~ stations (3) n 112.6
~ steamers (1) n 108.2
~ stick (2) n 008.3
~ sticks (1) n 008.5
~ tong (2) n 008.3
~ tongs (5) n 008.4
~ tree (1) n 062.2
~ truck (91) n 111.1
~ trucks (35) n 111.1
~ vessels (1) n 080.7
~ wagon (12) n 111.4
~ wagons (1) n 084.8
Fire (6) LA 030.7
~ Island (1) LA 087.2
firearms (2) n 008.3
fireball (2) adj 055A.2
~ beans (1) n 055A.2
~ party (1) n 024.3
fireballs (1) n 024.3
firebirds (1) n 060A.3
fireboard (80) n 008.4
fireboards (6) n 008.4
fireboats (1) n 111.2

firebox (4) n 008.6
firebug (9) n 060A.3
firebugs (11) n 060A.3
firecracker (1) n 075.2
fired (13) v 099.4
~ for (1) v 053.4
~ up (5) v 075.2
firedog (15) n/adj 008.3
~ things (1) n 008.3
firedog[N-i] (8) n 008.3
firedogs (260) n 008.3
fireflies (73) n 060A.3
firefly (122) n 060A.3
firehall (14) n 112.6
firehorses (2) n 008.3
firehouse (63) n 112.6
Firehouse Number Eight (1) 112.6
firehouses (1) n 112.6
fireless cooker (1) n 118.5
fireman (83) n 112.4
fireman's car (1) n 111.6
firemans (4) n 112.4
firemen (41) n 112.4
firemen's home (1) n 112.6
Firemen's Ball (1) 131.2
fireplace (292) n/adj 008.2
~ baker (1) n 017.5
~ dogs (1) n 008.3
~ grate (1) n 008.3
~ heat (1) n 075.6
~ irons (2) n 008.3
~ mantel (1) n 008.4
~ room (21) n 007.8
~ shelf (3) n 008.4
~ wood (7) n 008.5
fireplaces (43) n 118.4
fireplug (40) n 108.2
fireplugs (7) n 108.2
fireroom (14) n 007.8
fires (12) n 070.6
Firestone peach (1) n 054.3
firewater (4) n 050.8
firewood (83) n/adj 008.6
~ blocks (1) n 008.3
~ dogs (1) n 008.3
firing (3) v 080.9
firm (4) n/adj 074.8
firmer (1) adj 066.1
firs (1) n 061.9
first (2341) n/adj 001A.3
~ aid (2) n/adj 111.5

~ -aid truck (1) n 111.5
~ -aid vehicle (1) n 111.5
~ base (5) n 001A.3
~ book (1) n 083.7
~ class (19) n/adj 083.7
~ -class letter (1) n 083.7
~ -class overhauls (1) n 001A.3
~ cousin (12) n 001A.3
~ cousins (8) n 025.5
~ dark (3) n 002.5
~ floor (5) n 007A.4
~ grade (627) n 083.7
~ -grade level (1) n 083.7
~ -grade school (1) n 083.7
~ -grade teacher (1) n 001A.3
~ grader (5) n 068.7
~ graders (2) n 083.7
~ grades (3) n 083.7
~ light (1) n 003.2
~ love (1) n 081.6
~ man (1) n 082.3
~ mate (1) n 001A.3
~ primary (1) n 083.7
~ primer (1) n 083.7
~ quarter (1) n 046.4
~ -rate (1) adj 079.4
~ reader (34) n 083.7
~ room (1) n 007A.3
~ school (1) n 083.7
~ speller (1) n 083.7
~ water (1) n 075.7
~ year (3) n 083.7
First (103) 107.6
~ African Baptist Church (1) 089.1
~ Avenue (4) 114.8
~ Baptist (11) 089.1
~ Baptist Church (18) 089.1
~ Christian (1) 089.1
~ Christian Church (2) 001A.3
~ Christians (1) 089.1
~ Creek (5) AL MS TN 030.7
~ Federal Bank (1) 108.5

~ Financial Tower (1) 108.5
~ International building (1) n 108.7
~ Methodist (1) 001A.3
~ Methodist Church (3) 089.2
~ National (5) 108.5
~ National Bank (12) 108.5
~ National Bank building n 108.5
~ Slough (1) AR 030.3
~ Southern Methodist Church (1) 089.2
~ State Bank (1) 108.5
~ Street (3) 107.7
~ War (1) 085.8
~ Ward (2) 106.3
~ World War (9) 001A.3
~ World's War (1) 092.8
firstborn (3) n 001A.3
firsthand (1) adv 001A.3
Fischer (1) TX 087.9
fish (390) n/v/adj 059.9
~ bait (27) n 061.2
~ -bait worm (1) n 060.5
~ -bait worms (1) n 060.5
~ balls (1) n 096.8
~ boat (3) n 024.6
~ -boat trio (1) n 129.6
~ boats (1) n 024.6
~ bread (1) n 044.8
~ corn bread (1) n 044.6
~ die-up (1) n 080.6
~ dish (1) n 093.6
~ dock (1) n 031.4
~ doughs (1) n 044.7
~ eater (2) n 126.5
~ eaters (6) n 126.6
~ eel (1) n 068.9
~ eels (2) n 059.9
~ fry (2) n 083.1
~ gar (2) n 059.9
~ grease (3) n 023.7
~ -grease biscuits (1) n 044.6
~ hawks (1) n 060A.4
~ lake (3) n 030.6
~ market (2) n 105.5

~ meal (1) n 080.7
~ mulligan (1) n 088.8
~ oil (1) n 093.6
~ roe (1) n 080.6
~ room (2) n 007A.7
~ sandwich (1) n 070.6
~ sticks (1) n 044.7
~ time (1) n 060.2
~ trail (2) n 031.7
~ trap (1) n 088.8
~ traps (1) n 080.6
~ trees (1) n 051.8
~ with (2) v 040.9
~ [P-0] (1) v 084.8
Fish (5) 059.9
~ Creek (2) TX 030.7
~ River (2) AL 030.7
fish[V-r] for (1) v 001.5
fished (9) v 070.7
~ with (1) v 032.4
Fisher Project (1) 106.3
fisheries (2) n 080.6
fisherman (6) n 060.1
fisherman's (8) adj 031.4
~ landing (1) n 031.4
~ luck (7) n 040.5
fishermens (3) n 016.7
fishery (1) n 082.7
fishes (15) n/v 059.9
~ with (1) v 053.4
fishhook (1) n 055A.3
fishing (293) n/v/adj 020.4
~ bait (1) n 065.8
~ baits (1) n 060.5
~ boat (105) n 024.6
~ boats (29) n 024.6
~ buddy (1) n 091.9
~ docks (1) n 031.4
~ floats (1) n 053.1
~ for (1) v 053.4
~ hole (1) n 030.4
~ license (1) n 039.9
~ rigs (1) n 024.6
~ with (2) v 032.4
~ worm (9) n 060.5
~ worms (37) n 060.5
fishnet sack (1) n 019.7
fishpond (3) n 030.6
fishponds (1) n 030.6
fishworm (11) n 060.5
fishworms (17) n 060.5
Fisk (2) 106.5
~ Road (1) 107.6
fist (849) n 072.2

~ -and-skull chimleys (1) n 008.1
~ and skulls (1) n 008.1
fist[N-i] (646) n 072.2
fisted (6) adj 073.3
fistes (70) n 072.2
fistfight (14) n/v 104.2
fistfighting (1) v 104.2
fistfights (2) n 104.2
fisticuffs (1) n 104.2
fisting (1) n 065.5
fists (129) n 072.2
fistular (2) n 078.2
fisty (1) adj 081.8
fit (346) n/v/adj 027.6
~ behind (1) v 053.7
~ in (2) v 027.6
~ sheet (1) n 028.7
fit[V-p] (3) v 027.6
fit[V-r] (436) v 027.6
~ in (1) v 027.6
~ into (1) v 027.6
~ on (2) v 027.6
fit[V-t] (8) v 027.6
fits (24) n/v 027.6
~ in (1) v 053.2
~ on (1) v 053.5
fitted (147) v/adj 027.6
~ in (2) v 027.6
~ sheet (1) n 027.6
~ sheets (1) n 027.6
~ with (1) v 027.6
fitten (2) adj 075.7
fitting (19) v/adj 095.8
Fitzgerald (5) GA 107.7
Fitzger(ald) (1) GA 087.3
five (3102) n/adj 001.3
~ -acre (1) adj 015.7
~ -and-dime store (1) n 080.6
~ -and-ten (1) n 116.2
~ bar (1) n 021.7
~ -bushel (2) adj 041.8
~ -cent piece (1) n 114.1
~ cents (2) n 114.1
~ -eight (1) n 001.3
~ -fifteen (1) n 004.5
~ -finger bread (1) n 044.7
~ -foot plow (1) n 021.6
~ -foot-two (1) n 007.9

~ -footed plow (1) n 021.6
~ -forty-five (3) n 004.5
~ -gaited horse (1) n 084.8
~ -gaited saddle horse (1) n 096.7
~ -gallon (20) adj 019.2
~ -hole (1) adj 001.3
~ -holer (1) n 012.1
~ hundred (1) n 088.8
~ -leaf (2) adj 062.3
~ -leaf poison vine (3) n 062.3
~ -man committee (1) n 001.3
~ -minute bell (1) n 001.3
~ -mule team (1) n 033.7
~ on the floor (2) n 110.7
~ -pound (44) adj 045.4
~ -room house (3) n 007A.1
~ -seed (1) adj 055A.3
~ -speed (5) n 110.7
~ -star general (4) n 068.3
~ -teeth har(row) (1) n 021.7
~ -ten (1) n 026.6
~ -ten-five (1) n 001.5
~ -thirty (31) n 004.4
Five (84) 107.5
~ Point[N-i] (1) 105.2
~ Points (13) 105.2
~ Runs Creek (1) AL 030.7
Fivemile Creek (1) MS 030.7
fives (1) n 113.1
fix (99) n/v 048.8
~ for (1) v 053.4
~ to (1) v 101.2
~ up (10) v 028.1
fix[V-r] (1) v 025.9
fix[V-s] to (1) v 101.2
fixed (72) v/adj 036.1
~ for (2) v 099.1
~ like (1) v 013.8
~ me up good (1) v 065.1
~ to (2) v 101.2

~ up (10) v 028.1
fixers (1) n 080.7
fixes (2) v 028.1
fixing (495) v 101.2
~ for (1) v 101.2
~ to (370) v 101.2
~ t(o) (2) v 101.2
~ to be confined (1) v 065.1
~ to marry her (1) v 081.4
~ up (10) v 028.1
~ [P-0] (21) v 007.3
fixings (6) n/v 101.2
fixture (2) n 019.9
fixtures (3) n 009.4
fixy (4) adj 099.6
fizz[V-p] (1) v 053.4
fizzing (1) v 088.7
flabbergasted (1) adj 075.5
flabby (2) adj 046.8
flag (13) n/adj 080.6
~ station (1) n 084.7
~ stop (1) n 084.7
Flag (1) 087.4
Flagg Lake (1) AR 030.8
Flagler (11) 105.2
~ College (1) 083.6
~ Hospital (1) 084.5
~ Street (1) 107.7
~ System (1) 095.8
flagman (1) n 080.6
Flagon (2) 030.4
~ Bayou (1) LA 030.3
~ Creek (1) LA 030.7
Flagpole (1) MS 087.2
Flags (4) 106.4
flagstone walks (1) n 016.6
flagstones (1) n 008.2
flagweeds (2) n 015.9
flail (5) n/v 042.1
flailing (1) v 042.1
flake (1) n 073.4
flaked (4) v 078.6
~ off (1) v 078.6
~ out (3) v 078.6
flakes (1) n 050.6
flaky (2) adj 074.7
flam (1) adv 028.9
flambeau (193) n/adj 024.3
~ deal (1) n 024.3
~ light (1) n 024.3

~ lights (1) n 024.3
~ pots (1) n 024.3
Flambeau (1) 024.3
flambeaux (21) n 024.3
flamdozier (2) n 024.3
flame (2) n 024.3
flames (3) n 018.9
flamethrower (1) n 024.3
flaming (3) v/adj 114.9
~ flickers (1) n 114.9
~ out (1) v 078.2
~ sumac (1) n 062.2
Flamingo (3) FL 087.8
~ Park (1) 106.7
flamme (1) n F 024.3
flammed (1) v 042.1
flange (2) n 017.6
flank (19) n/adj 121.3
~ steak (8) n 121.1
~ steaks (2) n 121.1
~ strop (1) n 038.8
flannel (4) n/adj 035.2
~ cakes (1) n 045.3
~ trousers (1) n 027.4
flap (4) n/adj 099.6
~ cakes (1) n 045.3
~ flitters (1) n 045.3
~ -head cat (1) n 059.9
flapcakes (1) n 045.3
flapjack (33) n/adj 045.3
~ molasses (1) n 051.2
flapjack[N-i] (2) n 045.3
flapjacket (1) n 045.3
flapjackety (1) adj 045.3
flapjacks (256) n 045.3
flapjackses (1) n 013.8
flapper (2) n 081.5
flappers (1) n 060A.1
flare (11) n 024.3
~ -like (1) adj 024.3
flares (6) n/v 024.3
~ up (2) v 075.2
flaring (2) v 017.8
flash (33) v/adj 080.1
~ flood (24) n 006.1
~ -flood-like (1) adj 006.1
~ floods (3) n 006.1
~ lightning (1) n 006.2
~ shower (2) n 006.1
Flash (1) 080.6
flasher (2) n 124.7
flashing (2) n/v 011.6
flashy (7) adj 123.6
~ cars (1) n 109.4

~ clothes (2) n 123.6
~ dresser (1) n 028.1
flat (346) n/adj/adv 119.4
~ apartment (1) n 119.4
~ bean (2) n 042.8
~ beans (1) n 055A.4
~ bed (1) n 029.2
~ -bedded boat (1) n 024.6
~ boards (1) n 011.2
~ body (1) n 109.7
~ bottom (11) n 024.6
~ -bottom (2) adj 024.6
~ -bottom aluminum boat (3) n 024.6
~ -bottom aluminum boats (1) n 024.6
~ -bottom bateau (1) n 024.6
~ -bottom boat (38) n 024.6
~ -bottom boats (10) n 024.6
~ -bottom fishing boat (1) n 024.6
~ -bottom homemade boat (1) n 024.6
~ -bottom plow (3) n 021.6
~ -bottom plows (1) n 021.6
~ -bottom rock (1) n 016.7
~ -bottom rowboats (1) n 024.6
~ -bottom turners (1) n 021.6
~ -bottom turning plow (1) n 021.6
~ -bottom wood chair (1) n 008.8
~ bow (1) n 024.6
~ bread (2) n 044.8
~ -break (9) v 081.9
~ -break plows (1) n 021.6
~ -breaking (6) v 021.6
~ cake (4) n 044.4
~ cakes (1) n 044.4
~ country (4) n 029.5
~ dive (3) n 095.4
~ Dutch onion (1) n 055.7
~ fence (1) n 016.2

~ field (1) n 029.5
~ -footed (1) adv 080.9
~ frog (1) n 099.7
~ grain (1) n 050.7
~ harrow (1) n 021.7
~ johnboat (1) n 024.6
~ -like (1) adj 090.4
~ lowland (2) n 029.4
~ marshy place (1) n 029.7
~ milkweed (1) n 015.9
~ muckland (1) n 029.9
~ ponds (1) n 029.6
~ porch (2) n 010.8
~ rake (2) n 120.7
~ red land (1) n 029.8
~ riverboats (1) n 024.6
~ rock (1) n 023.5
~ roof (2) n 011.4
~ -roofed (1) adj 011.4
~ sandal (1) n 123.8
~ shoes (1) n 123.8
~ silver (2) n 017.8
~ skillet (1) n 017.5
~ squash (7) n 056.6
~ stream (1) n 030.6
~ swamp (1) n 029.6
~ tails (1) n 059.9
~ talk (1) n 093.5
~ tank (1) n 018.7
~ tire (3) n 089.7
~ truck (1) n 109.7
~ turtle (1) n 060.6
~ walking shoes (1) n 123.8
~ -weed (1) v 015.8
~ white (1) adj 056.6
Flat (35) 086.2
~ Creek (13) AL AR GA TN 030.7
~ Dutch (1) 055A.1
~ Lake (1) AR 087.7
~ Rock (1) AL 087.6
flatbed (18) n/adj 109.7
~ truck (3) n 109.7
~ trucks (2) n 109.7
flatbeds (2) n 109.7
flatboat (23) n 024.6
flatboats (6) n 024.6
flatcars (1) n 023.6
flateau (1) n 031.1
flatfeet (4) n 112.5
flatfoot (13) n 112.5
flatfoots (2) n 112.5
flatform (3) n 010.9

flathead (2) n 060.5
flatheads (3) n 060.5
flatiron (7) n 010.6
Flatiron building (1) n 106.4
flatirons (8) n 081.8
flatjacks (1) n 045.3
flatland (52) n/adj 029.4
~ foreigner (1) n 066.7
flatlanders (1) n 088.8
flatlands (12) n 029.4
Flatoni(a) (1) TX 087.7
flats (53) n 123.8
Flats (3) 087.6
flatter (4) adj 045.3
~ cakes (1) n 045.3
flattop (18) n 123.8
flattops (9) n 118.9
flatty (1) adj 090.4
flatware (6) n 017.8
flatways (1) adv 090.9
flatwood (2) adj 035.9
~ hog (1) n 035.9
~ land (1) n 029.9
Flatwood (1) 105.4
flatwoods (5) n/adj 029.9
~ land (1) n 029.4
~ mud turtle (1) n 060.6
flatworm (1) n 060.5
flatworms (1) n 060.5
flavor (4) n 053.7
flavored up (1) v 080.7
flavoring (1) n 042.7
flax (1) n 081.8
flaxseed (1) n 053.5
flea (15) n/adj 060A.8
~ hoppers (1) n 061.1
~ market (2) n 114.6
~ merkle (1) n 088.7
~ raisers (1) n 033.3
fleabag (16) n/adj 113.8
~ hotel (3) n 113.8
~ joint (1) n 113.8
fleabags (5) n 113.8
fleas (24) n 059.5
fleche (2) n F 020.8
~ du wagon (1) n F 020.8
flee (1) v 062.3
fleece (11) n 035.2
Fleenora Park (1) 085.2
fleet (3) n/adj 089.9
~ side (1) n 109.7
Fleetwood (2) AL 075.8

Fleming Street (1) 032.9
Flemington (3) FL 087.3
Flemming Prairie (5) TX 029.5
flesh (677) n/adj 078.2
~ wound (12) n 078.1
f(lesh) (1) n 078.2
fleshened up (1) v 099.9
fleshpots (1) n 084.9
fleshy (3) adj 073.1
Fletcher (2) 084.8
fleur de sirop (1) n F 061.4
flew (16) v 080.7
~ on around (1) v 102.3
~ the coop (1) v 083.4
flexible (1) adj 024.4
flibbertigibbet (1) n 074.1
flick (19) n/adj 114.9
~ houses (1) n 114.9
flicked (1) v 100.2
flicker (14) n 059.3
flickers (3) n 059.3
flicking (1) v 057.4
flicks (16) n 114.9
fliers (2) n 130.4
flies (227) n 060A.6
flight (15) n/adj 123.7
~ bag (5) n 123.7
flights (2) n 016.7
flighty (2) adj 074.1
flimsy (1) adj 073.3
flinch drains (1) n 030.1
fling (5) v/adj 032.2
~ ding (1) n 083.1
~ horses (1) n 022.7
flinging off (1) v 075.9
Flinn Street (1) 107.7
flint (20) n/adj 023.4
~ -ridge farm (1) n 029.7
~ rock (6) n 023.5
~ rocks (3) n 017.1
~ stone (5) n 023.5
~ stones (1) n 023.4
Flint (36) GA MI 087.2
~ Creek (1) GA 030.7
~ River (29) GA 030.7
flinty (1) adj 029.8
flip (153) n/v/adj 095.5
~ -flop (6) n 095.5
~ -flops (15) n 095.5
~ ons (1) n 123.8
~ over (1) v 095.5

~ plows (1) n 021.6
~ -top lids (1) n 020.4
flip[V-r] (2) v 100.2
~ the bucket (1) v 078.6
flipjack grits (1) n 050.6
flipjacks (3) n 045.3
flipped (1) v 075.5
flips (24) n 123.9
flirt (2) n/v 028.1
flirting (9) v 081.4
~ with her (4) v 081.4
flirty (3) adj 073.8
flitch (2) n 046.6
flitter (22) n/adj 045.3
~ cake (1) n 045.3
~ cakes (3) n 045.3
~ trees (1) n 045.3
flitters (105) n 045.3
flitty (1) adj 074.1
flivver (1) n 023.6
flivvers (1) n 109.3
float (19) n/v/adj 024.5
~ chunker (1) n 006.1
floated off (1) v 081.8
floater (11) n 006.1
floaters (3) n 006.1
floating (5) v/adj 115.4
~ bridge (1) n 081.8
~ dock (1) n 031.4
~ down (2) v 024.9
floats (3) n 115.8
flock (97) n 036.6
flocked in (1) v 055A.8
flocking (3) v 102.4
~ to (2) v 025.6
flocks (11) n 036.6
flog (1) v 065.5
flogging (4) n 065.5
flood (208) n/adj 006.1
~ -like (1) adj 006.1
~ of rain (1) n 006.1
~ pasture (1) n 029.7
~ rain (14) n 006.1
~ rains (1) n 006.1
~ washer (1) n 006.1
flooded (9) v/adj 006.1
~ land (1) n 029.6
~ out (2) v 070.6
~ rain (1) n 006.1
floodgates (1) n 031.5
flooding (4) v/adj 006.2
~ rain (1) n 006.1
floodland (6) n 029.4
floodplain (7) n 029.4

floodplains (2) n 029.4
floods (9) n 006.6
floodwater (1) n 081.9
floodwaters (1) n 048.9
floor (317) n/adj 070.6
~ coverings (1) n 039.8
~ dance (1) n 083.1
~ fan (1) n 118.5
~ furnace (15) n 118.5
~ furnaces (6) n 118.5
~ heat (1) n 118.4
~ heater (2) n 118.4
~ heaters (3) n 118.5
~ lady (1) n 080.6
~ lamp (2) n 007A.7
~ manager (1) n 089.9
~ pack (1) n 029.2
~ pallet (1) n 029.2
~ pallets (1) n 029.2
~ pipe (1) n 023.2
~ plan (1) n 014.1
~ rag (1) n 088.9
~ shift (10) n 110.7
~ stick (1) n 110.7
~ sweeper (2) n 010.5
~ sweepers (1) n 116.7
~ vents (2) n 118.5
floor[N-i] (1) n 005.3
floored (6) v/adj 096.7
~ pen (4) n 015.4
~ pens (1) n 015.4
flooring (4) n 008.2
floors (38) n 065.9
floozies (1) n 113.3
floozy (2) n 113.3
flop (59) n/v/adj 096.5
~ around (1) v 074.4
~ cake (1) n 044.4
~ -eared (2) adj 071.5
~ -flip (1) n 095.5
Flop Ears (1) 125.1
flopdown (1) n 006.1
flophouse (47) n 113.8
flophouses (14) n 113.8
flopped cake (1) n 091.8
flopper (5) n 009.2
flopping (3) v/adj 057.4
~ stage (1) n 075.5
flops (1) n 069.7
Floradale (2) 105.6
Florahome (1) FL 087.4
floral bloom (1) n 080.8
Florala (1) AL 087.3
Flora(la) (1) AL 087.8

Florence (35) AL MS SC TN 086.2
~ Avenue (1) 107.7
~ Boulevard (1) 107.6
Floresville (2) TX 087.6
Florida (1195) 086.4
~ area (1) n 086.3
~ Avenue (2) 106.7
~ Calico (1) 055A.3
~ City (2) FL 087.3
~ Coast (1) 086.4
~ Cracker (13) 069.9
~ Crackers (4) 069.9
~ day (1) n 005.4
~ East Coast (1) 095.9
~ Favorite (4) 056.9
~ Giant (1) 056.9
~ Grays (1) 056.9
~ lobster (2) n 060.8
~ Mountains (1) NM 031.1
~ National Bank (1) 108.5
~ oranges (1) n 055.1
~ palm (1) n 061.8
~ peach (1) n 054.3
~ Power and Light man (1) n 115.1
~ Rattlesnake (1) 056.9
~ room (49) n 118.1
~ rooms (6) n 118.1
~ scrubs (1) n 080.6
~ Southern rock (1) n 097.8
~ Speckled (2) 055A.3
~ Specks (1) 055A.3
~ Sweet (1) 056.9
~ tomatoes (1) n 055.3
~ Turnpike (2) 107.1
~ water (1) n 088.8
~ worm (1) n 060.5
~ worms (2) n 060.5
~ yam (2) n 055.5
Flori(da) (2) 086.4
Flor(ida) (1) 086.4
Florid(a) Avenue (1) 107.5
Floridian (4) 086.4
Floridians (2) 069.5
Florien (2) LA 087.9
~ City (1) LA 087.4
florist truck (1) n 109.4
florist's truck (1) n 109.6
florunners (1) n 054.7
floss (1) n 075.9

flounder (60) n 059.9
floundered (1) v 081.9
floundering (2) v/adj 093.8
~ expedition (1) n 080.7
flounders (27) n 059.9
flour (477) n/adj 066.8
~ bag (5) n 019.6
~ bags (8) n 019.6
~ barrel (34) n 010.1
~ barrels (10) n 019.1
~ bin (4) n 019.2
~ bins (1) n 019.1
~ biscuit (1) n 044.4
~ bread (28) n 044.3
~ cake (1) n 045.3
~ can (2) n 019.1
~ chest (1) n 010.1
~ chestes (1) n 010.1
~ cupboard (1) n 010.1
~ dough (1) n 044.4
~ doughnuts (1) n 045.2
~ dumpling[N-i] (1) n 044.4
~ dumplings (2) n 044.8
~ flitter (1) n 045.3
~ fritters (1) n 045.3
~ gravy (1) n 048.4
~ hoecake (4) n 044.4
~ house (1) n 014.4
~ light bread (1) n 044.3
~ mill (2) n 019.8
~ muffin[N-i] (1) n 044.4
~ muffins (4) n 044.4
~ pokes (2) n 019.6
~ sack (117) n 019.6
~ -sack cloth (1) n 019.6
~ -sack gowns (1) n 019.6
~ sacks (59) n 019.6
~ tortillas (1) n 044.4
flow (3) n/v 031.4
flower (306) n/adj 101.4
~ (ar)rangements (1) n 101.4
~ arranging (1) n 101.4
~ basket (3) n 017.7
~ bed (8) n 050.5

~ -bed shovel (1) n 120.5
~ beds (3) n 101.4
~ bins (1) n 017.7
~ bottle (1) n 017.7
~ bowl (7) n 017.7
~ box (4) n 017.7
~ boxes (1) n 017.7
~ bucket (3) n 017.7
~ can (1) n 017.7
~ child (2) n 129.3
~ -child mentality (1) n 129.3
~ children (9) n 129.3
~ container (1) n 017.7
~ -covered (1) adj 101.4
~ decanter (1) n 017.7
~ dirt (1) n 029.8
~ dish (1) n 017.7
~ fork (1) n 120.6
~ garden (22) n 050.5
~ -garden quilt (1) n 029.1
~ gardens (4) n 101.4
~ girl (19) n 082.4
~ girls (4) n 082.4
~ house (1) n 017.7
~ jar (5) n 017.7
~ maid (1) n 082.4
~ nursery (1) n 101.4
~ pail (1) n 017.7
~ patches (1) n 016.1
~ people (1) n 124.2
~ pit (3) n 081.8
~ planters (1) n 017.7
~ plow (1) n 021.6
~ room (1) n 118.1
~ route (1) n 101.4
~ scoop (1) n 120.5
~ shop (1) n 101.4
~ spots (1) n 081.8
~ squash (1) n 056.6
~ stand (1) n 017.7
~ time (1) n 101.4
~ tray (1) n 017.7
~ tree (4) n 061.8
~ trucks (1) n 109.6
~ urn (1) n 017.7
~ vase (38) n 017.7
~ vases (9) n 017.7
~ yard (2) n 015.6
flow(er) (1) n 101.4
Flower (2) 129.3
~ Power Age (1) 129.3

flower[N-i] (15) n 101.4
Flowerie (1) MS 087.4
flowering (6) adj 061.8
~ dogwoods (1) n 061.8
~ laurel (1) n 062.7
~ peach (1) n 062.9
~ quince (1) n 062.7
~ tool (1) n 120.5
~ trees (1) n 061.9
flowerpot (266) n 017.7
flowerpots (56) n 017.7
flowers (963) n/adj 101.4
~ vase (1) n 017.7
flowery (1) adj 019.6
Flowery Branch (2) GA 087.7
flowing (5) adj 030.5
~ stream (1) n 030.6
~ streams (1) n 030.6
~ well (3) n 030.6
flows (2) v 080.9
Floyd (9) GA LA 087.1
~ County (3) GA 087.1
~ Creek (1) GA 030.7
flu (31) n/adj 076.3
~ epidemic (2) n 080.8
~ weather (1) n 006.6
~ years (1) n 080.6
fluctuation (1) n 070.8
flue (464) n/adj 023.2
~ connection (1) n 023.2
~ -cured tobacco (1) n 081.8
~ deal (1) n 023.2
~ -like (1) adj 023.2
~ line (1) n 023.2
~ pipe (4) n 023.2
fluently (1) adv 090.4
flues (17) n 023.2
fluff (1) n 055.5
fluffed (2) v/adj 123.9
~ him off (1) v 082.1
fluffles (1) n 075.8
fluid (52) n/adj 077.7
~ drive (2) n 059.4
fluked out (1) v 075.8
flume (1) n 023.2
flumes (2) n 011.5
flung (9) v 032.2
flunk (1) n 069.5
flunked (2) v 083.4
~ out (1) v 078.6
flunkies (2) n 115.4

flunky (16) n 115.4
fluorescent light (1) n 019.9
flurry (1) n 007.5
flush (9) n/v/adj 030.3
~ cloud (1) n 006.1
~ rains (1) n 006.1
flushed him (1) v 082.1
flusher (2) n 012.1
flustered (1) adj 075.2
flustrated (7) adj 073.3
flute (5) n 020.5
fluttering (1) v 057.4
flux (3) n 080.3
fly (325) n/v/adj 060A.8
~ ants (1) n 060A.7
~ around (1) v 073.7
~ bream (1) n 061.2
~ bugs (1) n 060A.1
~ -by-night (1) adj 124.1
~ -by-night carpenter (1) n 067.8
~ fire (1) n 060A.3
~ in (2) v 095.9
~ jenny (1) n 022.7
~ -like thing (1) n 060A.1
~ line (1) n 084.8
~ net (1) n 096.7
~ paddle (1) n 080.8
~ up (2) v 075.2
Fly (1) 106.3
fly[N-i] (2) n 070.7
fly[V-p] (2) v 075.1
~ off (1) v 075.1
Flyer (1) 093.8
flyers (1) n 060A.6
flying (675) v/adj 059.7
~ ants (3) n 060A.2
~ (ap)prentices (1) n 060A.4
~ (a)round (1) v 026.1
~ clouds (1) n 005.3
~ Dutchman (5) n 022.7
~ fish (1) n 059.9
~ gnat (1) n 060A.8
~ grasshopper (1) n 061.1
~ horse (3) n 022.7
~ -horse thing (1) n 022.7
~ horses (4) n 022.7
~ jennies (39) n 022.7

~ jenny (342) n 022.7
~ jib (1) n 084.9
~ mare (1) n 022.7
~ mares (1) n 022.7
~ outrig(ger) affair (1) n 089.8
~ roaches (1) n 060A.2
~ saucers (1) n 056.6
~ sausage (1) n 045.2
~ squirrel (176) n 059.7
~ squirrels (68) n 059.7
~ termites (1) n 060A.1
~ turtle (1) n 060.6
~ wheel (1) n 022.7
fly(ing) mare (1) n 022.7
Flying Fortress (1) 089.9
flyswatter (1) n 098.3
flytraps (1) n 080.7
Flyway (1) 030.7
foal (26) n/v 033.9
~ with pig (1) v 033.9
foaled (4) v 033.9
foaling (2) v 033.9
foals (1) v 033.9
foam (8) n/v/adj 081.8
~ up (1) v 090.4
Foard County (1) TX 087.8
fob (4) n 004.3
fodder (151) n/adj 051.4
~ beans (1) n 055A.4
~ bones (1) n 091.8
~ field (2) n 016.1
~ loft (5) n 014.5
~ pullings (1) n 104.6
~ shower (3) n 006.1
~ showers (1) n 006.1
~ stack (6) n 014.6
~ stacks (5) n 014.6
~ time (2) n 037.4
foddering (1) n 014.6
fog (841) n/v/adj 006.7
~ bank (1) n 006.8
~ lamps (1) n 006.7
~ lights (2) n 006.7
~ rain (2) n 006.7
~ up (1) v 006.7
fogged (6) v 006.7
~ in (3) v 006.7
~ up (1) v 006.7
foggier (12) adj 006.7
foggiest (11) adj 006.7
~ day (1) n 006.7
fogging (3) v 006.7
~ up (1) v 006.7

foggy (776) adj 006.7
~ day (135) n 006.7
~ -like (1) adj 007.4
~ -looking (1) adj 006.7
~ mist (1) n 006.7
~ morning (12) n 006.7
~ mornings (1) n 006.7
~ night (1) n 006.7
~ nights (1) n 006.7
~ rain (3) n 006.7
~ weather (2) n 006.7
fog(gy) (1) adj 006.7
fogs (7) n/v 006.7
fogy (9) n/adj 069.9
foie (1) n F 047.2
foil (2) n 020.4
foin (1) n F 014.8
fold (9) n/v 033.9
~ -over bag (1) n 123.7
~ up (3) v 080.7
foldaway bed (1) n 009.1
folder (1) n 028.2
folding (8) adj 009.1
~ bed (3) n 009.1
~ cot (1) n 008.9
~ cots (1) n 029.2
~ couch (1) n 009.1
~ money (1) n 114.5
~ seats (1) n 083.8
Foley (9) AL FL 087.7
foliage (1) n 077.8
folk (51) n/adj 066.5
~ dance (2) n 083.1
~ dances (1) n 083.1
~ music (7) n 130.8
~ -rock (2) n 130.8
~ songs (1) n 089.5
folk[N-i] (9) n 013.8
folk[N-i][N-k] talk (1) n 093.5
folks (563) n 066.5
folks' (7) adj 044.6
~ house (1) n 014.1
folkses (7) n 016.8
folks's (6) adj 043.6
~ car (1) n 043.6
Folkston (6) GA 086.7
Follette (4) 087.4
follow (16) v 058.3
~ in (1) v 065.3
~ -the-leader (5) n 130.2
fol(low) (2) v 096.7
followed (8) v 066.8

~ in (1) v 065.3
follower (1) n 039.4
following (24) v/adj 066.8
~ in (1) v 065.3
~ through (1) v 066.8
follows (4) v 065.3
folly (1) n 083.3
Folsom Lake (1) TN 030.3
fond (5) adj 081.4
~ of her (3) adj 081.4
fondu pot (1) n 116.4
Font (1) 106.1
Fontaine House (1) 106.7
Fontainebleau Park (1) 106.4
food (971) n/adj 048.4
~ broker (2) n 088.7
~ cellar (1) n 010.1
~ center (1) n 048.4
~ chains (1) n 116.1
~ chopper (1) n 048.4
~ closet (3) n 010.1
~ closets (1) n 009.7
~ company (1) n 048.4
~ crop (2) n 048.4
~ house (1) n 010.1
~ locker (1) n 010.1
~ market (5) n 094.3
~ poisoning (4) n 048.4
~ safe (1) n 010.1
~ shop (2) n 116.2
~ stamps (3) n 048.4
~ storage (1) n 048.4
~ store (16) n 116.2
~ -store chains (1) n 116.1
~ stores (7) n 116.1
~ value (2) n 048.4
Food (4) 116.3
~ Mart (1) 116.3
Foodliner (1) 116.1
foods (24) n 048.4
Foods (1) 116.2
foodstuff (4) n 048.4
foodstuffs (1) n 048.4
fool (644) n/v/adj 073.4
~ around (5) v 084.9
~ -like (1) adj 073.4
~ man (1) n 073.4
~ way (1) n 073.4
~ with (54) v 073.4
FOOL (1) 073.4
fool[V-r] (2) v 096.7

~ around (1) v 096.7
~ with (1) v 040.6
fool[V-t] (1) v 073.4
fooled (10) v 073.4
~ around (2) v 073.4
~ her (1) v 082.1
~ him (1) v 082.1
~ with (4) v 073.4
foolers (1) n 017.1
foolhardy (2) adj 074.6
fooling (19) v 081.7
~ around (7) v 081.7
~ around with her (1) v 081.4
~ with (9) v 081.7
foolish (135) adj 073.4
foolisher (2) adj 066.1
foolishness (11) n 073.4
fools (43) n 073.5
Fools' (2) 001A.6
Foor (1) 107.8
foot (1282) n/adj 072.6
~ adz (5) n 020.7
~ ditches (1) n 030.5
~ feed (2) n 110.6
~ -long (2) n 121.7
~ -long beans (1) n 055A.4
~ -long hot dog (1) n 121.6
~ -long red worms (1) n 060.5
~ -long sandwich (2) n 121.7
~ -long worms (1) n 060.5
~ patrolmen (1) n 112.5
~ ped(al) (1) n 092.8
~ pedals (1) n 072.6
~ peddlers (1) n 127.7
~ piece (1) n 021.8
~ pone (1) n 044.7
~ roll (1) n 028.9
~ shaking (1) n 083.1
~ speed (1) n 110.6
~ track (1) n 072.6
~ tub (23) n 118.9
~ tubs (1) n 020.1
~ washing (2) n 072.6
~ -washing Baptist (3) n 126.6
~ -washing days (1) n 088.7
~ worm (1) n 060A.9

foot[N-i] (513) n 072.6
footback (2) adv 072.6
football (99) n/adj 130.4
~ dances (1) n 083.1
~ fields (1) n 096.7
~ games (3) n 130.4
~ party (1) n 088.6
~ practice (1) n 126.2
~ shoes (2) n 123.8
~ team (1) n 055A.8
footboard (1) n 072.7
Foote (2) 072.6
~ Home[N-i] (1) 106.3
footed (10) adj 072.6
~ glasses (1) n 048.9
foothill (1) n 030.8
foothills (6) n 030.8
foothold (1) n 082.1
footing (1) n 070.2
footlocker (3) n 009.7
footlog (11) n/adj 022.5
~ preacher (1) n 067.8
footlogs (2) n 022.6
footloose (2) adj 088.7
footpads (1) n 080.8
footpath (5) n 031.8
footpaths (1) n 031.8
footrace (2) n 072.6
footraces (2) n 072.6
foots (55) n/adj 072.6
~ pedal (1) n 023.5
footses (1) n 072.6
footstep[N-i] (2) n 072.6
footsteps (6) n 010.7
fop (1) n 028.1
fopped (1) v 080.8
for (3080) prep 032.7
~ purpose (4) prep 103.6
~ sure (129) adv 041.1
~ to (54) prep 080.5
f(or) (3) prep 049.6
forage (4) n 041.5
Foran Gap (1) AR 087.3
forbid (1) v 032.8
Forbus (1) TN 087.5
force (15) n/v 065.8
Force (3) 106.5
forced (10) adj 118.4
~ air (6) n 118.4
~ -air furnace (1) n 118.4
~ -air heating (1) n 118.5

~ -entry tools (1) n 111.3
forceful (1) adj 124.3
forces (1) n 089.2
forcible entry (1) n 088.7
ford (3) n 031.3
Ford (48) 088.8
~ automobile (1) n 023.6
~ car (2) n 023.6
~ coupe (1) n 109.1
~ Creek (1) LA 030.7
~ touring car (2) n 023.6
forded (1) v 095.6
Fordhook (14) 055A.3
~ bean (1) n 055A.3
~ beans (1) n 055A.3
~ lima (2) n 055A.3
~ lima bean (1) n 055A.3
~ limas (1) n 055A.3
Fordhooks (4) 055A.3
Fordhurst (1) 055A.3
Fordoche (1) LA 087.4
fords (2) n 030.3
Fords (4) 109.2
~ Lake (1) MS 087.2
Fordson (1) 021.9
fore shoulder (1) n 046.4
forearm (4) n 075.8
forefeet (4) n 072.6
forefoot (1) n 070.8
foreground (1) n 029.5
forehead (1043) n 071.3
fore(head) (1) n 071.3
foreign (37) n/adj 066.7
~ car (3) n 109.1
~ cars (1) n 109.1
foreigner (506) n 066.7
foreign(er) (2) n 066.7
foreigners (39) n 066.7
foreland (1) n 029.5
foreleg (4) n 072.7
forelegs (1) n 046.4
foreman (16) n 069.6
Foreman (1) AR 087.5
foremost (14) adv 040.4
forenoon (4) n 002.3
foreparents (1) n 064.1
forepart (3) n 002.5
forequarter (1) n 046.4
foreroofer (2) n 008.6
foreroom (1) n 007A.4
fores (1) n 071.3

foresail (1) n 084.8
forest (39) n/adj 061.6
~ land (1) n 029.9
~ maple (1) n 061.8
~ pine (2) n 061.8
Forest (35) MS 087.6
~ Avenue (1) 107.7
~ Chapel (2) 055.1
~ Grove (2) FL 061.6
~ Hills (1) 105.1
~ Home (1) AL 087.6
~ Park (5) GA 087.5
~ River (1) GA 030.7
Forestburg (1) TX 087.4
Forestdale (1) MS 087.5
forestick (13) n 008.5
foresticks (3) n 008.5
forestry people (1) n 061.7
forests (1) n 039.7
forever (1) adv 103.4
forge (2) n 075.8
Forge (3) 087.2
forget (99) v 100.4
~ about (1) v 100.4
~ him (1) v 082.1
(for)get (1) v 100.4
forget[V-r] (1) v 100.4
forget[V-t] (4) v 057.8
forgetful (8) adj 074.6
forgets (7) v 100.4
forgetter (1) n 104.6
forgetting (1) adj 074.6
forgive (3) v 099.2
forgive[V-t] (1) v 098.6
forgot (198) v 100.4
~ about (4) v 100.4
forgotten (59) v 100.4
~ about (2) v 100.4
forjo (1) n 015.9
fork (828) n/v/adj 017.8
~ -and-knife setting (1) n 017.8
~ around (1) v 080.6
~ -leaf (1) n 061.8
Fork (42) 030.7
~ Creek (1) TN 030.7
forked (10) adj 037.1
~ bone (2) n 037.1
~ -leaf yam (1) n 055.5
~ lightning (1) n 006.2
~ -tail cat (1) n 059.9
~ -tail lightning (1) n 006.2
Forked (9) 030.7

~ Deer (1) TN 030.7
~ Deer River (6) TN 030.7
~ Island (1) LA 086.3
~ Lake (1) AR 030.7
forks (259) n 017.8
Forks (2) 106.8
~ of Cypress (1) 106.8
form (8) n 051.5
formal (21) n/adj 083.1
~ dance (3) n 130.7
~ dining room (1) n 007A.2
~ dress shoes (1) n 123.8
~ education (1) n 083.5
~ living room (1) n 007.8
~ round dancing (1) n 083.1
~ schooling (1) n 083.5
~ shoes (1) n 123.8
~ teas (1) n 088.8
formaldehyde (1) n 114.8
formals (3) n 083.1
formed (4) v 052.6
~ on (1) v 053.5
former (1) adj 032.4
fornent (3) adv/prep 085.1
fornicator (1) n 119.4
Forrest (8) MS 087.8
~ City (6) AR 087.5
Forsyth (18) GA 087.3
~ County (3) GA 087.8
~ Park (2) 106.4
~ Street (2) 107.6
fort (4) n 106.4
Fort (252) 087.1
~ Adams (1) MS 087.1
~ Bayou (2) MS 087.5
~ Benning (18) GA 086.4
~ Bragg (1) NC 087.5
~ Brown (2) TX 082.6
~ Caroline (3) 106.5
~ Caroline Road (2) 105.1
~ Deposit (3) AL 087.8
~ (De)posit (1) AL 087.5
~ Drum (2) FL 087.9
~ Gaines (10) GA 087.4

~ George Inlet (1) FL 030.3
~ George Island (1) FL 087.9
~ Gibson (3) MS OK 087.2
~ Gordon (1) GA 087.6
~ Green (1) FL 087.1
~ Griffin (1) TX 082.6
~ Henry (2) TN 087.2
~ Hood (1) TX 087.4
~ Humbug (1) 106.4
~ Jefferson (1) FL 087.6
~ King George Road (1) 065.8
~ Knox (2) KY 087.5
~ Lauderdale (13) FL 087.2
~ Lauderdale International (1) 106.5
~ Lauderdale News building (1) n 106.4
~ Lauderdale Yankee Stadium (1) 106.4
~ Lavaca (1) TX 087.5
~ Loudoun (2) TN 087.4
~ Loudoun Dam (1) TN 030.7
~ Loudoun Embayment (1) TN 030.9
~ Loudoun Lake (2) TN 030.7
~ Massachusetts (1) MS 086.8
~ McPherson (1) GA 087.6
~ Meade (7) FL 087.1
~ Morgan (5) AL 087.7
~ Myers (13) FL 087.9
~ Myers Airport (1) 106.5
~ Myers Beach (1) 106.4
~ Myers proper (1) n 105.1
~ Nashborough (2) 106.5
~ Nashville (1) 106.4
~ Negley (1) 106.4
~ Ogden (2) FL 087.2

~ Oglethorpe (1) GA 087.6
~ Parker (1) TX 087.5
~ Payne (2) AL 087.2
~ Pierce (7) FL 087.2
~ Polk (1) LA 087.2
~ Providence (1) TX 087.3
~ Pulaski (2) 106.5
~ Rucker (6) AL 087.3
~ Rucker Boulevard (1) 107.6
~ Sam Houston (2) 106.4
~ Screvin (1) GA 087.4
~ Sheridan (1) IL 087.5
~ Smith (27) AR 087.5
~ Stewart (2) GA 087.2
~ Stockton (1) TX 087.3
~ Sumter (1) SC 087.1
~ Valley (13) GA 080.8
~ Vinton (1) FL 087.7
~ Walton (11) FL 087.2
~ Walton Beach (8) FL 087.5
~ Wayne County (1) GA 082.6
~ Worth (33) TX 087.4
~ Worth-Dallas Airport (1) 106.5
forth (16) adv 053.7
forties (8) n 001A.1
Forties (17) 001A.1
fortieth (1) adj 001A.1
Fortieth (3) 107.7
Fortification (1) 080.8
fortnight (177) n 003.8
fortnights (1) n 003.8
Fortress (1) 089.9
forts (2) n 106.4
fortunate (10) adj 025.5
fortune bone (1) n 037.1
forty (1864) n/adj 001A.1
~ -acre (4) adj 001A.1
~ -disc tandem (1) n 021.7
~ -eight (53) n/adj 001.4
~ -eight-pound (4) adj 001.4
~ -five (344) n/adj 004.5
~ -five after (4) n 004.5

~ -five Colt (1) n 113.1
~ -five minutes after (5) n 004.5
~ -five minutes past (2) n 004.5
~ -five past (1) n 004.5
~ -five-pound (1) adj 045.4
~ -fives (1) n 113.1
~ -four (45) n/adj 001A.1
~ -four Chattanooga breaking plow (1) n 021.6
~ -hour week (1) n 001A.1
~ -nine (31) n/adj 001.5
~ -odd (2) adj 088.1
~ -one (37) n 001A.1
~ -page (1) adj 001A.1
~ -pound (1) adj 019.2
~ -seven (38) n/adj 001A.1
~ -seven-foot (1) adj 001A.1
~ -six (34) n/adj 001.3
~ -some (2) n/adj 001A.1
~ -some-odd (2) adj 001.9
~ -something (1) adj 001A.1
~ -thirty (1) n 004.4
~ -three (29) n/adj 001A.1
~ -two (35) n/adj 001A.1
fort(y) (3) n 001.4
~ -eight (1) n 001.4
~ -six (1) adj 005.1
Forty (33) 001A.1
~ -Eight Highway (1) 107.1
~ -Fifth Street (1) 001A.1
~ -Five (2) 114.8
~ -Five Highway (1) 031.6
~ -Four (1) 078.4
~ -Nine (1) 107.1
~ -One (3) 031.6
~ Quarters (1) 105.5
~ -Three Canal (1) 030.2

fortyish (1) adj 001A.1
forward (594) n/adj/adv 040.4
~ gears (1) n 110.7
~ horse (1) n 039.4
~ -looking (1) adj 040.4
~ roll (3) n 095.5
~ shifts (1) n 040.4
~ with calf (1) adj 033.9
for(ward) (1) adv 040.4
forwards (261) adv 040.4
foster (124) adj 129.5
~ baby (1) n 065.7
~ child (10) n 066.3
~ children (2) n 064.3
~ daughter (1) n 066.3
~ father (3) n 066.4
~ home (3) n 066.4
~ -mother (9) n 129.5
~ parent (38) n 066.4
~ parents (54) n 066.4
Foster Creek (1) TX 030.7
fostered (1) v 065.4
fotch (4) v 098.3
~ a calf (1) v 033.9
Fouborge (1) LA 087.3
fought (926) v 104.2
~ against (2) v 104.2
~ in (2) v 085.8
~ on (1) v 053.6
~ over (1) v 104.2
~ with (1) v 104.2
foughten (2) v 104.2
foul (16) v/adj 005.5
~ day (2) n 005.5
~ play (1) n 081.7
~ weather (4) n 005.6
fouled up (1) v 096.7
fouls up (1) v 075.7
found (35) v 033.9
~ a calf (5) v 033.9
~ her a calf (1) v 033.9
~ her calf (2) v 033.9
~ her kitten (1) v 033.9
~ out (1) v 057.9
~ that calf (1) v 033.9
~ the baby (2) v 033.9
~ the calf (1) v 033.9
foundation (10) n/adj 070.7
~ bread (1) n 044.3
founded (3) v 053.5

foundered (2) v 093.5
foundering (2) v 088.8
Founders (3) 080.7
~ Day (1) 080.7
~ Park (2) 085.1
Foundry Bottom (1) TN 030.7
fount (1) n 089.9
fountain (259) n/adj 108.8
~ pen (78) n 026.5
~ pens (6) n 026.5
fount(ain) (4) n 108.8
~ pen (1) n/adj 026.5
Fountain (8) 106.1
~ Brook (1) 106.1
~ City (3) 105.2
~ City Park (1) 106.7
Fountainebleau (1) MS 087.7
fountains (13) n 108.8
four (2792) n/adj 001.2
~ -and-twelve (2) adj 001.2
~ bar (1) n 021.7
~ -barbwire fence (1) n 016.3
~ -bedroom (1) adj 119.1
~ bits (5) n 075.6
~ -bottom stuff (1) n 092.7
~ -bushel (1) adj 041.8
~ -by-four (4) n/adj 109.7
~ -by-four wire (1) n 016.3
~ -by-fours (2) n 001.2
~ -bys (1) n 109.6
~ -door (44) n/adj 109.3
~ -door car (14) n 109.3
~ -door cars (2) n 109.3
~ -door coupe (1) n 109.1
~ -door hardtop (1) n 109.3
~ -door sedan (25) n 109.3
~ -door sedans (1) n 109.3
~ doors (9) n 109.3

~ -eighty-two (1) n 001.2
~ -eleven (2) n 001.6
~ -(e)leven (1) n 001.6
~ -eye (1) adj 096.7
~ -eyed stove (1) n 080.9
~ -eyes (1) n 001.2
~ -fifteen (2) n 004.5
~ -fifty-nine (1) n 001.5
~ -flusher (1) n 073.5
~ -foot (3) adj 021.6
~ -foot plow (1) n 021.6
~ -forty (3) n 001A.1
~ -forty-five (12) n 004.5
~ -forty relay (1) n 130.2
~ -forty-three (1) n 004.5
~ -furrow (2) n/v 089.9
~ -fur(row) (1) v 084.8
~ hitch (1) n 033.7
~ -hole (1) n 001.2
~ -holer (1) n 012.1
~ -horse team (3) n 033.7
~ -hour (1) adj 001.2
~ hundred and ten re-break (1) n 050.8
~ in the floor (13) n 110.7
~ -inch (1) adj 088.7
~ -lane (11) n/adj 001.2
~ -lane highway (3) n 107.1
~ -lane highways (2) n 107.6
~ -lane job (1) n 080.9
~ -lanes (1) n 107.5
~ -laning (1) v 096.9
~ -lead team (1) n 039.4
~ -leaf poison vine (1) n 062.3
~ -leaf tea (1) n 061.4
~ -legged stools (1) n 008.8
~ -legged straight chair (1) n 008.8
~ -mule hook (1) n 020.8

~ -mule team (6) n 033.7
~ -mule teams (2) n 033.7
~ -mule wagon (1) n 033.7
~ -note music (1) n 096.9
~ -oh-five (1) n 001.2
~ -oh-two (1) n 001.2
~ on the floor (26) n 110.7
~ -passenger (1) adj 109.3
~ plait (1) n 019.4
~ plex (1) n 119.2
~ -ply (1) n 001.2
~ -post beds (1) n 016.5
~ -poster (1) n 088.7
~ -pound (2) adj 042.5
~ -room (2) adj 007A.4
~ -room house (13) n 001.2
~ -room houses (1) n 014.1
~ -room shotgun house (1) n 007A.2
~ seater (1) n 109.3
~ -seven-three (1) n 001.2
~ -speed (13) n/adj 110.7
~ square (2) n 130.3
~ -star general (3) n 068.3
~ -strand (1) adj 016.3
~ -strand barbwire (1) n 016.3
~ -strand barbwire fence (1) n 016.3
~ -ten (1) adj 113.1
~ -thirty (43) n 004.4
~ -thirty-two (1) n 004.4
~ up (2) n 039.4
~ -up team (2) n 033.7
~ -up teams (1) n 033.7
~ -way highway (1) n 031.6
~ -ways drive road (1) n 031.6
~ -ways road (1) n 031.6

~ -wheel drive (3) n 110.7
~ -wheel-drive country (1) n 080.9
~ -wheel wagon (1) n 023.3
~ -wire (2) adj 001.2
~ -wire fence (3) n 016.3
~ -wire law (1) n 080.6
~ -year (1) adj 080.8
~ -year college (2) n 001.2
~ -year degree (1) n 001.2
~ -year-old (1) n 034.1
~ -year stint (1) n 080.6
Four (35) 001.2
~ -F (1) 088.7
~ -Forty-One (3) 107.1
~ -H (2) 001.2
~ Points (1) TN 087.6
four[N-i] (3) n 072.8
Fourche (5) 030.7
~ Bottom (1) AR 030.7
~ Creek (4) AR 030.7
Fourmile (2) 030.7
~ Branch (1) AL 030.7
~ Creek (1) MS 030.7
fours (28) n 072.8
foursies (1) n 130.7
foursquare (3) n 130.4
fourteen (1214) n/adj 001.7
~ -by-fourteen (1) adj 001.7
~ -by-sixteen (1) adj 001.7
~ castel(lated) (1) n 021.6
~ -foot (6) adj 001.7
~ -inch (2) adj 001.7
~ -ninety-two (1) n 001.7
~ -tooth harrow (1) n 021.7
Fourteen (3) 001.7
~ Street (1) 107.6
Fourteenmile Creek (4) MS 030.7
fourteens (1) n 115.6
Fourteens (1) 001.7
fourteenth (6) n/adj 001A.3

Fourteenth (5) 107A.8
~ Street (4) 107.6
fourth (1003) n/adj 001A.3
~ -class (1) adj 001A.3
~ -grade education (3) n 001A.3
~ renters (1) n 080.6
Fourth (46) 001A.3
~ Alley (1) 108.6
~ Arkansas (1) 001A.3
~ Avenue (1) 001A.3
~ District (1) 001A.3
~ of July (20) 001A.3
~ of July parties (2) n 130.7
~ of July picnic (1) n 001A.3
~ Street (4) 107.7
~ Ward (7) 105.1
~ [P-0] July (1) 001A.3
fourthing (1) v 098.6
fourths (8) n 001A.3
fout (20) v 104.2
~ out (1) v 104.2
fowl (189) n/adj 036.6
~ family (2) n 036.6
~ house (7) n 036.8
~ houses (1) n 036.8
~ yard (2) n 036.8
Fowler (1) 107.6
fowls (128) n 036.6
fox (815) n/adj 059.5
~ and goose (1) n 088.9
~ and hounds (2) n 130.1
~ and the geese (1) n 130.2
~ and the hounds (1) n 130.2
~ and the rabbit (1) n 098.4
~ dog (1) n 033.3
~ dogs (5) n 033.1
~ feist (1) n 033.3
~ feistes (1) n 033.3
~ fire (3) n 060A.3
~ grapes (1) n 062.4
~ hound (1) n 033.1
~ hunt (1) n 098.4
~ -hunt (3) v 081.9
~ hunting (2) n 088.8
~ in a wall (1) n 088.8

~ race (1) n 080.9
~ snake (1) n 084.8
~ squirrel (399) n 059.7
~ squir(rel) (1) n 059.7
~ squirrel[N-i] (3) n 059.7
~ squirrels (101) n 059.7
~ terrier (5) n 033.1
~ ter(rier) (1) n 033.1
~ -terrier feist (1) n 033.3
~ terriers (1) n 033.3
~ -trot (28) n 083.1
~ -trots (1) n 083.1
~ -trotting (2) n/v 083.1
~ -trotting horses (1) n 034.2
Fox (9) AL 087.3
~ Den (2) 106.1
~ River (1) AL 030.7
~ Street (1) 107.7
~ Theatre (3) 106.4
fox[N-i] (16) n 059.5
Foxborough (1) 105.7
Foxcroft (1) 105.1
foxed up (1) v 028.1
foxes (67) n 059.5
foxhound (1) n 033.1
foxhounds (3) n 033.1
foxtail (1) n 015.9
foxy (13) adj 125.4
~ chick (1) n 125.4
~ lady (1) n 125.4
~ little lady (1) n 125.4
foyer (29) n/adj 118.8
~ area (1) n 007A.5
foyers (1) n 010.8
fracas (2) n 065.9
fractious (38) adj 075.1
~ -tempered (1) adj 075.1
fraidycat (17) n 074.3
frail (19) v/adj 042.3
~ pole (2) n 042.1
frailed (3) v 042.1
frailing (4) n/v 065.5
frame (151) n/v/adj 011.2
~ box houses (1) n 118.9
~ building (1) n 014.1
~ dwelling (1) n 014.1
~ home (1) n 014.1

~ house (44) n 014.1
~ houses (7) n 014.1
~ table (1) n 022.1
~ up (1) v 082.5
framed house (1) n 014.1
framer (1) n 008.4
frames (22) n 022.1
Frameville (1) TX 087.1
framing (7) n/adj 011.2
~ square (2) n 080.7
~ table (1) n 022.1
framis fish (1) n 099.6
France (488) 087.9
Francis (14) FL 087.8
Francisco (23) 030.8
Francisville (9) 087.3
Francis(ville) (1) 087.2
frank (9) n/adj 121.6
Frank McCall Funeral Home (1) 079.2
Frankenstein (1) 125.1
Frankford (2) 105.4
Frankfort (6) KY 087.4
Frankfurt (1) 087.8
frankfurter (10) n 121.6
frankfurt(er) (1) n 121.6
(frank)furter (1) n 121.7
frankfurters (11) n 121.6
Franklin (52) AL AR FL GA LA MS NC TN 087.6
~ Bridge (1) 107.6
~ County (5) AL GA MS 087.3
~ Creek (2) AR MS 030.7
~ Drive (1) 106.2
~ heater (2) n 095.9
~ Hotel (1) 084.3
~ Parish (3) LA 087.1
~ Road (3) 105.5
~ stoves (2) n 118.4
~ Street (3) 105.2
Franklinton (4) LA 086.6
Franklinville (1) GA 087.6
frankly (1) adv 090.4
franks (10) n 121.6
frat (1) n 088.7
fraternity (9) n/adj 069.3
~ brother (1) n 129.4
~ house (1) n 014.1
~ initiation (1) n 129.8
~ initiations (1) n 129.8
~ parties (1) n 130.7

Frayser (5) TN 106.2
Fraziers (1) GA 087.2
frazzle (11) n 075.5
frazzled (2) v/adj 075.5
~ out (1) v 075.5
freak (39) n/v/adj 114.3
~ out (2) v 114.3
~ shower (1) n 006.1
freak[V-r] (1) v 053.6
freaked out (1) v 114.3
freaking out (1) v 091.9
freakish (1) adj 091.8
freaks (15) n 129.3
freaky (3) adj 074.7
~ people (1) n 129.3
~ women (1) n 124.3
Frederic Fruit (1) 124.2
Frederica Road (1) 087.7
Fredericksburg (10) TX 087.3
Fredonia (1) TN 087.3
Fredric (1) 033.3
free (137) n/v/adj 054.4
~ base (1) n 098.4
~ burial ground (1) n 078.8
~ child's tray (1) n 080.8
~ cling (2) n 054.4
~ gratis (1) adj 095.7
~ hotel (1) n 112.8
~ jack (6) n 069.5
~ jacks (6) n 069.5
~ -lance preacher (1) n 067.8
~ land (1) n 080.6
~ man of color (1) n 069.3
~ milker (1) n 037.7
~ people of color (1) n 069.3
~ prize (1) n 095.7
~ range (22) n 015.7
~ rider (2) n 115.4
~ run (1) n 050.9
~ -running branch (1) n 030.6
~ school (2) n 083.7
~ seed (7) n 054.4
~ stand (1) n 041.5
~ stock law (2) n 016.2
~ tray (1) n 080.7
Free (3) 088.9
~ State of Winston (2) AL 088.9

freebies (2) n 092.7
freed (3) v 069.2
freedom (3) n/adj 123.9
~ (A)fro (1) n 123.9
Freedom (3) 087.2
~ Hills (1) AL 087.2
~ Shrine (1) 106.4
~ War (1) 085.8
freehearted (1) adj 074.6
Freeland (2) LA 087.2
freeloader (13) n 115.4
freeloaders (1) n 092.7
freeloading (1) v 115.4
Freeport (6) FL TX 087.6
freer (2) adj 102.3
Freerun (1) MS 087.1
freestone (372) n/adj 054.4
~ Elberta (1) n 054.4
~ Indian peach (1) n 054.4
~ peach (27) n 054.4
~ peaches (4) n 054.4
~ water (2) n 080.7
Freestone County (1) TX 086.2
freestones (8) n 054.4
freeway (35) n 107.2
Freeway (15) 107.1
freeways (6) n 031.6
freewheeling (1) adj 096.7
Freewill (10) 089.1
~ Baptist (8) 089.1
~ Baptist Church (1) 089.1
freeze (1231) n/v/adj 007.5
~ frog (1) n 007.5
~ out (3) v 007.7
~ over (113) v 007.6
~ storm (1) n 112.3
~ tag (5) n 130.2
~ time (1) n 007.5
~ up (28) v 007.7
Freeze Out (1) TX 087.5
freeze[V-p] (3) v 007.6
~ up (1) v 007.7
freeze[V-r] (2) v 007.6
freeze[V-t] (1) v 007.7
freezed (8) v 007.7
~ over (1) v 007.6
~ up (2) v 018.9
freezeproof (1) adj 015.6
freezer (10) n/adj 080.8
~ beans (1) n 055A.4

~ burn (1) n 046.9
~ corn (1) n 056.2
~ locker (2) n 015.5
~ melon (1) n 056.8
~ room (1) n 007A.7
freezers (2) n 007.6
freezes (47) n/v 007.7
~ over (8) v 007.6
freezing (76) n/v/adj 091.7
~ day (1) n 007.5
~ over (1) v 007.6
~ owl (1) n 059.1
~ rain (7) n 112.3
~ storm (1) n 112.3
~ weather (6) n 007.5
freight (16) n/adj 024.7
~ boats (1) n 024.6
~ car (1) n 023.6
~ depot (2) n 031.4
~ depots (1) n 084.7
~ hauler (1) n 021.4
~ hauling (1) v 021.4
~ house (1) n 084.7
~ train (1) n 088.3
freighting (1) n 033.7
French (588) 128.2
~ Avenue (1) 107.7
~ bean (1) n 055A.4
~ braid (1) n 123.9
~ braids (2) n 080.8
~ bread (59) n 044.4
~ Broad (10) TN 030.7
~ Broad River (2) TN 030.7
~ bun (1) n 123.9
~ Cajun stuff (1) n 069.7
~ Camp (5) MS 094.9
~ Canadians (2) 128.9
~ chair (1) n 008.9
~ china (1) n 017.1
~ coffee (2) n 032.4
~ Concession (1) 088.7
~ cooking (1) n 093.5
~ country (1) n 080.9
~ Creole (1) 069.7
~ Cs (1) 128.9
~ curl (1) n 122.7
~ -cut (1) adj 122.5
~ doors (1) n 080.6
~ doughnut (2) n 045.2
~ doughnuts (2) n 045.2
~ drip (1) n 048.8

~ drip coffee (1) n 048.8
~ duck (1) n 044.7
~ fort (1) n 105.5
~ general (1) n 052.6
~ girls (1) n 064.9
~ harp (326) n 020.5
~ harps (21) n 020.5
~ horn (1) n 020.5
~ Huguenots (1) 088.8
~ loafs (1) n 044.3
~ Market (7) 106.4
~ Market doughnut (1) n 045.2
~ Market doughnuts (1) n 045.2
~ minnows (1) n 061.2
~ mulberries (1) n 062.6
~ mulberry roots (1) n 061.4
~ music (1) n 089.5
~ oven (1) n 017.5
~ owl (1) n 059.2
~ pastries (1) n 122.6
~ pastry (1) n 045.2
~ people (6) n 069.5
~ Quarter (23) 087.7
~ Quarters (1) 082.6
~ roll (2) n 115.6
~ rolls (1) n 044.4
~ skillet (1) n 017.5
~ sofas (1) n 009.1
~ -speaking niggers (1) n 097.8
~ style (3) n 055A.4
~ toast (6) n 045.2
~ Town (5) 105.1
~ twist (7) n 115.7
~ walnut (2) n 054.8
~ whore (2) n 128.2
~ word (1) n 087.9
Frenchies (5) 128.2
frenching (1) v 081.7
Frenchman (7) 128.2
Frenchmans (5) 016.7
~ Creek (1) LA 030.7
Frenchmen (11) 128.2
Frenchmens (10) 128.2
Frenchy (8) 128.2
frenzy (1) n 079.3
frequency oscillator (1) n 088.7
frequent (1) adj 001A.4
frequently (4) adv 071.1

Freret (1) 119.7
fresh (245) n/adj/adv 033.9
~ beans (1) n 055A.4
~ cold (5) n 076.3
~ corn (14) n 056.2
~ corn on the cob (1) n 056.2
~ cow (1) n 033.8
~ eating onions (1) n 055.7
~ ground (1) n 041.4
~ ham (2) n 121.3
~ -killed cowhide (1) n 084.8
~ land (2) n 041.4
~ marsh (1) n 029.6
~ onions (10) n 055.7
~ seed (1) n 054.4
~ shallots (1) n 055.7
~ spring onions (1) n 055.7
~ vegetables (1) n 050.4
Fresh Water Bayou (1) LA 030.3
freshen (118) v/adj 033.9
~ time (1) n 033.9
freshened (4) v 033.9
~ up (1) v 007.2
freshening (9) v 007.2
~ up (2) v 007.2
freshens (1) v 033.9
fresher cooker (1) n 066.8
freshes (3) n 006.1
freshet (4) n 030.5
freshets (2) n 006.2
freshly (1) adv 041.4
freshman (3) n 068.7
freshmen (1) n 129.8
freshwater (21) adj 030.6
~ bayou (1) n 030.6
~ boats (1) n 024.6
~ bream (1) n 059.9
~ breams (1) n 059.9
~ cat (1) n 084.9
~ catfish (2) n 059.9
~ city (1) n 089.9
~ cooters (1) n 060.7
~ creeks (1) n 030.6
~ drum (1) n 059.9
~ eel (1) n 059.9
~ fish (1) n 059.9
~ fishing boats (1) n 024.6

~ flowing streams (1) n 030.6
~ mullet (1) n 059.9
~ shrimp (2) n 060.9
~ streams (1) n 030.6
~ trout (1) n 091.9
~ turtle (1) n 060.6
fresno (2) n/adj 080.6
~ slip (1) n 084.8
fret (31) v 079.5
~ about (1) v 079.5
~ over (2) v 079.5
fretful (7) adj 075.1
fretted (5) v 075.2
Freyburg (1) TX 087.3
frez (1) v 007.7
Friar (2) 030.7
~ Branch (1) TN 030.7
~ Road (1) 107.8
Friars (4) 030.7
~ Creek (1) TN 030.7
~ Point (3) MS 087.2
fricassee (2) n 088.9
friction (1) n 053.7
Friday (1037) 002.1
~ afternoon (3) n 002.3
~ evening (12) n 002.6
~ evenings (1) n 002.1
~ fish eaters (1) n 126.5
~ morning (5) n 002.1
~ night (17) n 002.1
~ night week (1) n 003.7
~ week (5) n 003.7
Fridays (3) 002.1
fried (164) v/adj 046.2
~ and over (1) v 046.2
~ apple pie (2) n 048.3
~ bacon (1) n 046.5
~ battercakes (1) n 045.3
~ beignet (1) n 045.2
~ biscuits (2) n 044.4
~ bread (10) n 044.7
~ breeches (1) n 080.8
~ chicken (4) n 121.5
~ corn (4) n 056.2
~ corn batter (1) n 044.5
~ corn bread (18) n 044.7
~ corn cakes (2) n 044.9
~ cornmeal (1) n 044.7

~ dough (3) n 045.3
~ egg (1) n 046.1
~ eggs (9) n 046.1
~ flapjacks (1) n 045.3
~ fritter (1) n 045.2
~ green tomatoes (2) n 055.3
~ grits (3) n 050.6
~ ham (1) n 046.5
~ hobbies (1) n 045.3
~ hoecake (1) n 044.6
~ hominy (1) n 050.6
~ in (1) v 050.3
~ Irish potatoes (1) n 055.4
~ liver (4) n 047.2
~ meat (6) n 046.5
~ mush (9) n 050.3
~ okra (7) n 055.8
~ onions (1) n 055.6
~ out (1) v 075.4
~ oysters (3) n 060.1
~ pancakes (2) n 045.3
~ peach pies (1) n 048.3
~ pie (3) n 048.3
~ pies (8) n 048.3
~ plantains (1) n 099.7
~ pork rinds (1) n 046.6
~ rabbit (1) n 121.4
~ roasting ear (1) n 056.2
~ shrimp (3) n 060.9
~ souse (3) n 047.4
~ squirrel (1) n 059.6
~ sunny-side up (1) v 046.1
~ syrup (1) n 051.3
~ veal (1) n 121.2
Fried (5) 086.5
friedcake (1) n 044.7
friedcakes (2) n 044.6
friend (902) n/adj 081.5
~ boy (3) n 081.5
~ girl (1) n 081.6
~ lady (1) n 053.4
friend[N-i] (4) n 129.6
friend[N-k] house (1) n 043.4
friendly (114) adj 073.2
~ -natured (1) adj 073.2
friend's (2) adj 052.5

~ grandmothers (1) n 052.5
~ house (1) n 082.7
friends (131) n 129.6
friendship (11) n/adj 129.4
~ quilt (1) n 081.9
~ quilts (1) n 088.9
~ ring (5) n 123.1
Friendship (8) AR GA MS TN 087.3
~ Missionary Baptist Church (1) 089.1
~ Park (2) 106.4
fries (5) n 081.8
frig (1) v 053.6
frigate bird (1) n 091.8
fright (4) n 125.1
frighten (10) v 074.3
frighten[V-r] (1) v 074.3
frighten[V-t] (2) v 074.3
frightened (72) v 074.3
frightening (1) adj 074.3
frightful (2) adj 074.3
frightfulest (1) adj 066.1
frigid (2) adj 007.4
~ women (1) n 124.4
Frigidaire (12) 015.5
~ watermelon (1) n 056.9
~ watermelons (1) n 056.9
Frigidaires (6) 084.9
Frigidairy (1) 015.5
frijole (3) n/adj S 055A.3
~ beans (1) n 055A.3
~ pinto beans (1) n 055A.4
frijol(e) beans (1) n 055A.4
frijoles (1) n S 128.7
frijolillo (1) n S 062.7
frilled up (1) v 028.1
fringe (8) n/adj 027.2
~ tick (1) n 060A.8
~ tree (1) n 061.8
fringed (1) adj 009.5
Frisco (4) LA 087.6
~ Bridge (1) 106.7
~ City (1) AL 087.1
frisking around (1) v 101.9
frisky (29) adj 074.1
~ morning (1) n 007.4
fritada (1) n S 047.4

fritons (1) n F 046.4
Fritos (1) 044.7
fritter (23) n/adj 044.6
~ cake (1) n 045.3
~ cakes (1) n 045.3
fritters (127) n 044.8
Fritz (2) 127.1
frivolous (1) adj 064.3
friz (8) v 007.6
~ over (2) v 007.6
~ up (1) v 007.7
frizen (1) v 007.7
frizz (1) n 090.9
frizzed out (1) v 075.6
frizzies (1) n 123.9
frizzle (1) n 007.6
frizzled up (1) v 055.9
frizzlings (1) n 021.2
frizzy (2) adj 074.7
fro (1) adv 075.7
frock (1) n 026.4
froe (48) n/adj 020.7
~ ax (1) n 020.7
~ knife (1) n 017.8
froes (1) n 080.7
frog (1312) n/adj 060.2
~ beds (2) n 057.1
~ bench (3) n 057.1
~ bread (1) n 057.1
~ breath (1) n 057.1
~ croaker (1) n 006.1
~ drownder (2) n 006.1
~ drowner (1) n 006.1
~ frog (1) n 060.3
~ fucker (1) n 039.8
~ gigging (7) n 090.8
~ hats (1) n 057.1
~ house (4) n 088.7
~ houses (8) n 057.1
~ -hunted (1) v 060.2
~ hunting (2) n 060.2
~ in the meadow (1) n 098.4
~ leg (1) n 072.6
~ legs (8) n 060.2
~ level (1) n 029.6
~ loaves (1) n 044.8
~ nest (1) n 057.1
~ noodles (1) n 057.1
~ owl (1) n 059.1
~ pond (4) n 029.6
~ -pond mud (1) n 029.9
~ pond[N-i] (1) n 029.6

~ sack (1) n 019.7
~ strangle (1) n 006.1
~ strangler (18) n 006.1
~ stranglers (1) n 006.1
~ stuff (1) n 057.1
~ tail (1) n 096.8
~ -tail coats (2) n 027.1
~ toadstool (1) n 057.1
~ umbrellas (3) n 028.6
Frog (3) 030.7
~ Bayou (1) AR 030.7
~ Mountain (2) GA TN 066.9
frog[N-i] (3) n 060.2
frogfish (1) n 059.9
frogging (3) n 060.3
froggy (1) adj 076.4
Frogmore (1) LA 087.7
frog's (2) adj 057.1
~ feet (1) n 057.1
~ umbrella (1) n 057.1
frogs (931) n 060.2
frogstool (48) n 057.1
frogstools (60) n 057.1
Frogtown (2) 105.4
frolic (21) n/v 083.2
~ around (1) v 083.1
frolicking (3) n 083.1
frolics (10) n 083.1
from (1569) prep 078.7
~ his stomach (1) adv 080.4
(fro)m (1) prep 096.8
fromage (2) n F 047.1
front (1239) n/adj 040.4
~ -and-side porch (1) n 010.8
~ axle (1) n 021.8
~ bedroom (52) n 007A.1
~ bedrooms (2) n 007.8
~ burning bar (1) n 008.2
~ door (33) n 011.1
~ doors (1) n 007A.5
~ doorstep (1) n 010.7
~ doorsteps (1) n 010.7
~ drive (1) n 031.8
~ -end loader (1) n 080.9
~ entrance (1) n 007A.3
~ feet (3) n 072.6
~ foot[N-i] (1) n 072.6
~ gallery (21) n 010.8

~ hall (6) n 007A.3
~ hallway (1) n 007A.3
~ hoof (1) n 034.7
~ hounds (1) n 080.7
~ legs (1) n 121.3
~ living room (1) n 007A.3
~ log (4) n 008.5
~ lot (1) n 015.6
~ of town (1) n 091.9
~ panel (1) n 110.1
~ parlor (2) n 007.8
~ plows (1) n 021.6
~ porch (591) n 010.8
~ -porch steps (1) n 010.8
~ porches (10) n 007A.5
~ quarter (1) n 046.4
~ rake (1) n 024.6
~ ridge (2) n 030.8
~ road (1) n 031.6
~ room (302) n 007A.5
~ rooms (19) n 007.8
~ screen porch (1) n 010.8
~ seat (1) n 049.3
~ shed (1) n 010.8
~ shoulder (1) n 046.5
~ side (1) n 040.4
~ stairs (1) n 010.7
~ stairway (1) n 010.7
~ step (1) n 010.7
~ step[N-i] (1) n 010.7
~ steps (17) n 010.7
~ stick (4) n 008.5
~ sticks (3) n 008.5
~ stomp (1) n 011.7
~ stoop (7) n 007A.5
~ team (1) n 039.4
~ teeth (2) n 071.8
~ tooth (8) n 071.8
~ veranda (3) n 010.8
~ walk (1) n 007A.9
~ wood (1) n 008.5
~ yard (5) n 015.6
~ yards (1) n 010.4
Front (4) 107.5
~ Street (1) 087.5
frontage (2) adj 107.6
~ road (1) n 107.6
~ roads (1) n 107.5
frontier-style (2) adj 070.9
Frontier (1) 107.7

fronts (2) n 006.4
frontward (10) adv 040.4
frontwards (38) adv 040.4
frontways (1) adv 040.4
frost (1043) n/v/adj 007.5
~ cold (1) n 007.5
~ freeze (1) n 007.5
Frost (31) 007.5
frost[N-i] (2) n 007.5
frost[V-p] (2) v 007.5
frostbit (8) v/adj 007.7
frostbite (1) n 007.5
frostbitten (3) v 033.4
frosted (15) v/adj 007.4
~ Coke (1) n 008.8
~ doughnut (2) n 122.4
~ doughnuts (3) n 122.4
~ -looking (1) adj 007.5
~ over (1) v 007.7
frostes (8) n 007.5
frosting (64) n 122.3
Frostproof (1) FL 087.8
frosts (3) n/v 007.3
frosty (18) adj 007.5
~ day (1) n 007.5
~ morning (3) n 007.4
~ night (1) n 007.5
froug (1) n 083.1
frowned on (1) v 090.4
froze (1266) v/adj 007.7
~ corn (1) n 007.7
~ down (2) v 007.6
~ him out (1) v 082.1
~ like (1) v 007.7
~ over (343) v 007.7
~ up (54) v 007.7
~ with (1) v 007.6
frozed (14) v 007.6
~ off (1) v 007.7
~ over (6) v 007.7
frozen (533) v/adj 007.7
~ corn (1) n 056.2
~ dew (1) n 007.5
~ food (1) n 007.7
~ ice (1) n 007.6
~ over (47) v 007.7
~ shrimp (1) n 060.9
~ shrimp[N-i] (1) n 060.9
~ up (5) v 007.6
frozened up (1) v 007.7
frugal (8) adj 073.5

fruit (221) n/adj 054.3
~ basket (1) n 080.7
~ basket turnover (2) n 081.8
~ bowl (1) n 048.3
~ buzzard (1) n 119.7
~ cellar (2) n 010.1
~ cellars (1) n 010.1
~ closet (1) n 010.1
~ cobbler (1) n 048.3
~ cobblers (1) n 048.3
~ Danish (1) n 122.2
~ dumplings (1) n 048.3
~ -filled (1) adj 122.6
~ fritters (1) n 045.3
~ house (3) n 010.1
~ jar (9) n 017.7
~ -jar filler (1) n 019.3
~ knife (1) n 017.8
~ of the vine (2) n 114.7
~ orchard (6) n 053.2
~ orchards (1) n 061.8
~ pie (7) n 048.3
~ pies (2) n 048.3
~ room (1) n 010.3
~ salad (2) n 114.2
~ sauce (1) n 048.5
~ seller (1) n 080.7
~ shelf (1) n 010.1
~ syrup (1) n 051.6
~ tarts (1) n 122.2
~ tree (1) n 061.9
~ trees (11) n 061.9
Fruit (4) 087.4
~ Cove (3) FL 087.4
fruitcake (18) n 048.3
fruitcakes (2) n 044.5
fruits (9) n 054.6
fruity (1) adj 074.7
frump (1) n 125.2
frustration (1) n 066.8
fruz (1) v 007.7
fry (40) n/v/adj 046.2
~ bread (2) n 044.5
fryer (92) n/adj 121.5
~ chicken (1) n 121.5
fry(er) (1) n 017.5
fryers (44) n 121.5
frying (605) n/v/adj 121.5
~ bacon (1) n 046.7
~ chicken (7) n 121.5
~ chickens (1) n 121.5

~ corn (1) n 056.2
~ hen (2) n 121.5
~ pan (547) n 017.5
~ pan skillet (1) n 017.5
~ pans (31) n 017.5
~ skillet (3) n 017.5
frypan (55) n 017.5
frypans (4) n 017.5
Fuchsschwanz (1) n G 015.9
fuck (31) n/v/adj/interj 092.1
~ around (1) v 093.7
~ film (1) n 114.9
~ off (2) v 045.8
~ over (1) v 093.9
~ with (1) v 096.8
fucked (8) v 090.8
~ around (1) v 090.8
~ up (7) v 102.6
fucker (2) n 039.8
fuckers (1) n 081.8
fucking (16) v/adj 092.1
~ around (1) v 093.6
~ off (1) v 089.8
fudge (1) n 122.2
fudging (1) v 048.6
fuel (21) n/adj 066.8
~ gauge (3) n 110.2
~ house (1) n 011.7
~ lights (1) n 024.3
~ oil (10) n 024.2
~ -oil burner (1) n 084.9
~ -oil heater (2) n 118.4
fuffed up (1) v 075.2
fulcrum (1) n 022.2
fulfill (1) v 097.8
fulfilled (1) v 081.1
Fulford (3) FL 087.4
~ School (1) 125.8
full (167) adj/adv 027.8
~ attic (1) n 009.8
~ bath (1) n 118.3
~ -blood (2) adj 069.9
~ -blooded (2) adj 081.9
~ -blown (1) adv 006.3
~ -bred (1) adj 035.5
~ -dress suit (1) n 027.7
~ -grown (2) adj 064.7
~ moon (3) n 080.9

~ mourning (1) n 079.3
~ -room house (1) n 007A.3
~ -size (1) adj 109.3
~ team (1) n 033.7
~ -term (1) adj 065.1
~ tester (1) n 099.7
~ -time (2) adj 052.7
Fuller (3) 106.4
~ Park (1) 106.6
fulling (1) v 065.9
fullness (1) n 040.4
fully (1) adv 033.2
Fulton (28) AR GA KY TN TX 087.2
~ Bag (1) 087.1
~ Beach (1) TX 087.6
~ County (4) GA 087.2
~ County Jail (1) 112.8
~ County seat (1) n 085.5
~ National Bank (1) 108.5
fumble (4) n/adj 130.4
~ -fingered (1) adj 073.3
~ -fisted (2) adj 073.3
fumbler (3) n 073.4
fumblified (1) adj 073.3
fumbling (1) v 073.3
fumbly (1) adj 073.3
fume hood (1) n 023.2
fun (39) n/adj 070.8
~ house (1) n 113.4
~ job (1) n 080.6
~ room (1) n 118.2
fundamentalist (2) n 080.6
funds (3) n 114.5
funeral (1050) n/adj 079.2
~ arrangements (1) n 079.2
~ attendant (1) n 117.4
~ business (1) n 079.2
~ car (9) n 117.5
~ cars (3) n 117.5
~ ceremony (1) n 079.2
~ clothes (2) n 079.3
~ coach (1) n 117.5
~ director (45) n 117.4
~ directors (1) n 080.8
~ dirge (2) n 079.2
~ home (83) n 079.2

~ -home director (3) n 117.4
~ -home limousine (1) n 117.5
~ -home man (1) n 079.2
~ homes (9) n 079.2
~ man (1) n 079.2
~ parlor (2) n 117.6
~ parlors (2) n 079.2
~ procession (4) n 079.2
~ rites (2) n 079.2
~ service (36) n 079.2
~ services (3) n 079.2
~ thing (1) n 079.2
~ time (1) n 079.2
~ yard (1) n 078.8
funer(al) (2) n 079.2
fun(eral) (2) n/adj 079.2
~ director (1) n 117.4
Funeral (2) 079.2
funeralize (2) v 079.3
funeralizing (1) v 079.2
funerals (29) n 079.2
fungicides (1) n 027.2
fungus (4) n 057.1
~ -looking (1) adj 002.6
funguses (1) n 057.1
Funiak (4) 087.4
funk (2) n/adj 130.9
~ wood (1) n 047.5
funked out (1) v 047.5
funky (95) adj 047.5
~ chicken (5) n 083.1
~ drunk (2) n 099.8
~ films (1) n 114.9
~ -like (1) adj 047.5
~ -looking (1) adj 047.5
~ -smelling (1) adj 047.5
~ -wearing clothes (1) n 123.6
funkying out (1) v 080.7
funnel (879) n/adj 019.3
~ cloud (2) n 112.2
~ clouds (4) n 112.2
~ -like (1) adj 019.3
~ -like thing (1) n 112.2
fun(nel) (1) n 019.3
funnels (17) n 019.3
funnies (2) n 124.2

funniest (1) adj 013.8

funning around (1) v 129.7

funny (264) adj 074.7
~ -acting (1) adj 074.7
~ bone (7) n 072.8
~ -looking (4) adj 080.8
~ weather (1) n 005.6

funs (1) n 130.6

Funston (1) GA 086.3

fur (28) n/adj 035.2
~ coats (2) n 027.1
~ hides (1) n 074.1
~ house (1) n 010.3

Fur Bayou (1) LA 030.7

furious (15) adj 075.2

furlough (2) n 032.2

furlows (1) n 041.2

Furman (1) 115.9

furnace (75) n/adj 118.4
~ heater (1) n 008.5
~ room (2) n 007A.6
~ top (1) n 008.1
~ -type heater (1) n 118.4

Furnace (2) 030.7
~ Creek (1) TN 030.7

furnaces (18) n 118.4

furnish (10) n/v 009.4

furnish[V-r] (1) v 080.9

furnished (10) v 009.4

furnishing (6) n/v/adj 009.4

furnishings (14) n 009.4

furniture (1054) n/adj 009.4
~ business (4) n 009.4
~ company (1) n 009.4
~ dealer (1) n 009.4
~ factories (1) n 009.4
~ factory (2) n 009.4
~ -finishing department (1) n 009.4
~ man (1) n 009.4
~ place (2) n 009.4
~ salesman (1) n 009.4
~ set (1) n 009.4
~ store (79) n 009.4
~ stores (4) n 009.4

furnit(ure) (4) n 009.4

furni(ture) store (1) n 009.4

furnitures (5) n 009.4

furrow (443) n/v/adj 041.2
~ horse (5) n 039.4
~ mule (2) n 039.4

fur(row) (107) n/v/adj 041.2
~ horse (1) n 039.4
~ opener (1) n 021.6

furrow[N-i] (11) n 041.2

fur(row)[N-i] (4) n 041.2

furrowing (3) v/adj 092.7
~ plow (2) n 021.6

furrows (352) n 041.2

furs (1) n 070.6

further (378) n/adv 043.3

furth(er) (1) adv 039.7

fur(ther) (1) n/adv 043.3

furtherer (1) adv 070.4

furtherest (42) adv 043.3

furthest (57) adv 043.3

fuse (2) n 075.3

fusee (1) n 024.3

fusion (1) n 075.1

fuss (31) n/v/adj 104.2
~ at (2) v 075.6
~ box (1) n 033.3
~ maker (2) n 033.3
~ over (1) v 104.2

fussed (1) v 104.2

fusses (1) v 080.9

fussing (9) v 104.2
~ at (1) v 025.8
~ over (1) v 028.1

fussy (3) adj 074.8

futile (1) adj 090.4

future (7) n/adj 081.6
~ bride (1) n 081.6
~ home (1) n 078.5
~ husband (1) n 081.5
~ wife (2) n 081.6

futures (1) v 065.3

fuzz (61) n 112.5

fuzzies (1) n 123.8

fuzzmobile (1) n 111.7

fuzzy (3) adj 090.7
~ -looking (1) adj 090.7

G

g-string (1) n 104.6
G (4) 104.7
ga-zip (1) interj 088.7
gabber (2) n 101.3
Gabbettville (1) GA 087.4
gabbing (1) v 101.3
gabby (1) adj 101.3
gable (35) n/adj 011.6
~ roof (2) n 011.6
~ things (1) n 011.6
Gable (1) 090.1
gabled (2) v/adj 011.6
~ roof (1) n 011.4
gables (10) n 011.6
Gables (15) 105.8
gabling (3) n 011.6
Gabriel (2) 030.7
gad (1) interj 092.3
gadabout (1) n 067.8
gadget (1) n 101.5
gadgets (3) n 088.7
Gadsden (20) AL TN 087.3
gaffs (2) n 081.9
gafftopsail (1) n 084.6
gag (7) n/v 080.2
~ of maggot[N-i] (1) n 125.2
gaga (1) n 073.3
gagged (1) v 080.2
gagging (2) v 080.2
gain (1) v 013.1
gained (1) v 057.8
Gaines (13) 030.7
~ Creek (1) AL 030.7
~ Road (1) 031.7
Gainesboro (4) TN 087.2
Gainesville (47) AL FL GA MS TN TX 087.2
~ Road (1) 031.6
gaining (3) v 007.2
gains (1) v 094.5
gait (1) n 005.9
gaited (4) adj 100.9
gaiters (4) n 027.1

Gaitherville (1) TN 087.8
gal (82) n/adj 064.9
~ friends (2) n 061.6
~ -struck (1) adj 098.8
gala (1) n 082.5
Galbraith (1) LA 087.5
gale (14) n 112.2
galeria (2) n S 010.9
galerie (10) n F 010.8
Galerie (1) n G 010.8
gales (1) n 112.1
galette (8) n F 044.4
Galilee (3) 066.8
galing (1) v 081.4
gall (3) n/adj 080.6
Gallatin (2) TN 087.1
~ Street (1) 107.6
gallberries (11) n 061.8
gallberry (17) n/adj 062.2
~ bushes (7) n 062.4
~ honey (2) n 090.8
~ yard broom (1) n 010.5
gallber(ry) (1) n 062.4
gallbladder (1) n 070.6
galled (2) adj 096.8
galleries (43) n 010.8
gallery (300) n 010.8
Gallery (2) 106.7
galley (5) n 009.9
galleys (1) n 009.9
Galliano (1) LA 087.3
Gallican Bottoms (1) MS 035.9
gallicized (1) v 088.8
gallineros (1) n S 036.8
galling (1) n 096.9
gallinipper (9) n 060A.8
gallinippers (9) n 060A.8
Gallinule area (1) n 106.3
Gallion (1) AL 087.4
gallo (1) n S 082.5
gallon (108) n/adj 019.2
~ bucket (15) n 019.2
~ buckets (15) n 019.2
~ can (4) n 019.2
~ cans (5) n 019.2
~ glass jugs (1) n 019.2
~ jug (4) n 017.2
~ jugs (1) n 019.2
~ molasses can (1) n 019.2
~ pail (1) n 017.3
~ syrup bucket (1) n 017.2

~ syrup can (1) n 051.3
~ tins (1) n 019.2
gallon[N-i] (34) n 045.4
gallons (14) n 001.3
gallop (3) v 034.3
galloping (5) adj 093.7
~ consumption (2) n 093.7
~ fence (1) n 016.4
~ TB (2) n 081.8
gallows (8) n 085.8
gallus (19) n/adj 028.5
~ strap (1) n 028.5
~ strop (1) n 039.2
gallus[N-i] (10) n 028.5
galluses (491) n 028.5
gallus(es) (1) n 028.5
gallu(ses) (1) n 028.5
galope (1) n 059.9
galore (1) adv 059.8
galoshes (3) n 084.8
Galphin's Cow Pen (1) 084.8
gal's (5) adj 064.9
gals (10) n 064.9
galvanize (30) n/adj 017.3
~ banding (1) n 020.3
~ bucket (8) n 017.3
~ buckets (1) n 017.4
~ fence (1) n 016.3
~ fencing (1) n 126.1
~ pail (1) n 017.3
~ tin (3) n 017.3
~ tub (1) n 018.9
galvanized (49) n/adj 017.3
~ aluminum (1) n 017.3
~ bucket (7) n 017.3
~ buckets (9) n 017.3
~ fence (1) n 126.1
~ flues (1) n 008.1
~ iron buckets (2) n 017.3
~ metal (1) n 017.3
~ pail (2) n 017.3
~ pails (1) n 017.3
~ roofing (1) n 011.4
~ steel (1) n 017.3
~ steel fence (1) n 126.1
~ tank (1) n 011.4
~ tin (1) n 026.6

~ tin bucket (1) n 017.3
~ tub (1) n 020.1
~ tubs (1) n 084.8
Galveston (60) TX 087.4
~ Bay (6) TX 030.3
~ Freeway (1) 107.1
gamble (5) v/adj 066.9
~ stick (1) n 081.8
gambling (9) n/v/adj 130.9
~ game (1) n 065.9
~ pole (3) n 096.7
~ stick (3) n 080.6
gambrel (2) v/adj 084.9
~ stick (1) n 096.8
gambreling (4) v/adj 046.4
~ stick (3) n 081.9
game (116) n/adj 036.6
~ chicken (1) n 036.9
~ chickens (5) n 080.6
~ fish (4) n 059.9
~ hen (1) n 121.5
~ hens (2) n 121.5
~ laws (1) n 039.9
~ room (10) n 118.2
~ wardens (1) n 066.8
games (23) n 101.5
gamut (1) n 082.8
gander (6) n 036.6
Gandy Street (1) 084.9
gang (268) n/v/adj 082.8
~ around (1) v 049.2
~ bang (1) n 082.5
~ fight (1) n 129.8
~ harrow (2) n 021.7
~ in (1) v 084.9
~ plow (6) n 021.6
~ plows (2) n 021.6
~ up around (1) v 082.8
Gang (1) 097.8
gangling (27) adj 073.3
gangly (41) adj 073.3
gang(ly) (1) adj 073.3
gangplank (2) n 022.6
gangrene (14) n 078.2
(gan)grene (1) n 078.2
gangs (10) n 129.6
gangster (5) n/adj 123.6
~ ride (2) n 109.4
~ suit (1) n 123.6
gangway (1) n 009.8
ganja (1) n 114.1

Gantt (4) AL 087.5
gap (216) n 031.3
~ through (1) n 031.8
Gap (48) 031.3
gappy (1) adj 076.6
gaps (20) n 031.3
gar (57) n/adj 080.6
~ hole (1) n 080.8
garage (302) n/adj 007A.3
~ apartment (3) n 088.7
~ closet (1) n 010.3
~ roof (1) n 011.4
~ sale (1) n 010.3
~ sales (1) n 096.8
Garage (1) 108.4
garages (19) n 011.8
garb (1) n 015.6
garbage (573) n/adj 010.2
~ bag (7) n 116.8
~ bags (2) n 019.5
~ barrel (1) n 017.4
~ baskets (1) n 020.1
~ bin (18) n 117.3
~ bins (1) n 117.3
~ box (1) n 117.3
~ bucket (6) n 017.4
~ can (218) n 017.4
~ cans (10) n 017.4
~ collection (1) n 115.2
~ collector (10) n 115.2
~ collectors (12) n 115.2
~ compactor (7) n 117.1
~ compac(tor) (1) n 117.1
~ compressor (2) n 117.1
~ compressors (5) n 117.1
~ container (3) n 117.2
~ department (1) n 115.2
~ disposal (18) n 117.1
~ disposal bin (1) n 117.3
~ -disposal people (2) n 115.2
~ disposals (3) n 117.1
~ disposer (4) n 117.1
~ (di)sposer (1) n 117.1
~ dump (3) n 117.3

~ dumpster (1) n 117.3
~ house (1) n 010.3
~ man (107) n 115.2
~ men (14) n 115.2
~ pail (29) n 017.4
~ pickers (1) n 088.9
~ pickups (1) n 115.2
~ presser (1) n 117.1
~ smashers (1) n 117.1
~ train (1) n 117.3
~ trash can (1) n 117.2
~ truck (1) n 109.7
~ trucks (3) n 115.2
garbologist (1) n 115.2
Garcitas Creek (2) TX 030.7
garcon haircut (1) n F 123.9
garde (3) n/adj F 035.3
~ -manger (2) n F 010.1
garden (2610) n/adj 050.5
~ apartment (2) n 119.4
~ apartments (1) n 119.2
~ area (2) n 050.5
~ bean[N-i] (1) n 055A.3
~ bed (1) n 050.5
~ bushes (1) n 050.5
~ club (9) n 050.5
~ clubs (1) n 050.5
~ corn (7) n 056.2
~ cultivator (1) n 120.4
~ dust (1) n 080.6
~ farm (1) n 050.5
~ farmer (1) n 050.5
~ faucet (1) n 018.7
~ fence (37) n 016.2
~ -fence wire (1) n 016.3
~ fences (3) n 016.2
~ fencing (1) n 016.3
~ foods (1) n 050.4
~ fork (5) n 120.6
~ -fresh (1) adj 050.4
~ frog (1) n 060.4
~ frogs (1) n 060.3
~ -grown (1) adj 050.4
~ hand tool (1) n 120.5
~ house (9) n 012.1
~ lot (1) n 016.1
~ melons (1) n 056.7
~ netting (1) n 016.3

~ onion (1) n 055.7
~ onions (5) n 055.7
~ patch (16) n 016.1
~ peas (8) n 050.5
~ picks (1) n 120.5
~ pipe (1) n 018.7
~ place (1) n 050.5
~ plot (4) n 050.5
~ plow (14) n 021.6
~ plows (1) n 021.6
~ produce (1) n 050.5
~ rake (24) n 120.7
~ rakes (2) n 120.7
~ room (1) n 118.1
~ sass (2) n 050.4
~ scissors (1) n 120.8
~ shears (1) n 120.8
~ shingle (1) n 016.2
~ shovel (3) n 120.5
~ size (1) n 050.5
~ snake (5) n 081.9
~ snakes (10) n 080.6
~ soil (1) n 029.4
~ spot (15) n 050.5
~ spots (1) n 016.1
~ squash (3) n 056.6
~ stuff (10) n 050.4
~ tiller (4) n 021.7
~ toads (1) n 060.4
~ tool (1) n 120.5
~ -tool house (1) n 011.7
~ tools (3) n 050.5
~ trowel (1) n 120.5
~ truck (4) n 050.4
~ type (1) n 119.2
~ vegetable[N-i] (2) n 050.4
~ vegetables (12) n 050.4
~ wire (20) n 016.3
~ work (2) n 050.5
gard(en) (1) n 050.5
Garden (33) 050.5
~ City (2) AL GA 087.1
~ District (11) 106.1
~ Hills (3) 105.1
garden[N-i] (1) n 050.5
Garden[N-i] (2) 106.4
Gardendale (1) 106.3
gardener (2) n 050.5
gardeners (2) n 050.5
gardenia (11) n/adj 062.7
~ tree (1) n 062.8

gardenias (5) n 062.7
gardening (3) n/adj 120.5
~ shovel (1) n 120.5
gardens (107) n 050.5
Gardens (25) 050.5
Gardner (1) FL 087.2
garfish (38) n/adj 059.9
~ catcher (1) n 059.9
garganta (1) n S 071.7
gargerate (1) v 081.8
gargle (1) n 071.7
Garland (13) AL AR TN TX 087.3
~ City (1) AR 087.7
~ County (3) AR 087.4
~ Mountain (1) GA 031.1
garlic (37) n/adj 055.6
~ bread (7) n 044.3
~ salt (1) n 051.7
garlics (2) n 055.6
garment (37) n/adj 027.7
~ bag (29) n 123.7
~ bags (5) n 123.7
garments (3) n 009.7
garner (10) n 014.4
Garner Creek (2) TN 030.7
garners (3) n 014.4
garret (24) n/adj 009.8
~ loft (4) n 009.8
Garrett Coliseum (1) 106.8
Garretts Bluff (1) TX 031.2
Garrison (5) TN TX 087.4
~ Baptist Church (1) 089.1
Garris(on) Gray (1) 056.9
Garrisonian (2) 056.9
Garrisons (1) 056.9
gars (27) n 059.9
garter (34) n/adj 028.5
~ snake (25) n 101.8
~ snakes (7) n 080.7
garters (6) n 028.5
Gary (12) IN 082.2
~ Cooper (7) 067.7
Garyville (1) LA 087.1
gas (295) n/adj 118.5
~ air conditioning (1) n 118.5
~ bomb (1) n 024.3

~ bombs (1) n 113.2
~ burner (2) n 023.6
~ burners (1) n 109.4
~ circulator (1) n 118.5
~ companies (1) n 075.7
~ drinkers (1) n 109.4
~ -driven lawn mowers (1) n 120.2
~ -fired central-heating furnaces (1) n 118.4
~ -fired floor furnaces (1) n 118.4
~ floor furnace (1) n 118.4
~ furnace (5) n 118.4
~ furnaces (2) n 118.4
~ gauge (2) n 110.1
~ guzzler (8) n 109.4
~ guzzlers (7) n 109.4
~ heat (5) n 118.5
~ heater (11) n 118.4
~ heaters (11) n 118.4
~ heating (4) n 118.4
~ hog (8) n 109.4
~ hogs (5) n 109.4
~ iron (1) n 010.6
~ jobs (1) n 111.1
~ lamp (2) n 024.3
~ lamps (1) n 024.3
~ lanterns (1) n 024.3
~ log (3) n 008.5
~ logs (14) n 008.5
~ mower (2) n 120.2
~ pedal (50) n 110.6
~ pipe (1) n 023.1
~ power (1) n 120.2
~ -power mower (1) n 120.2
~ -powered (1) adj 120.2
~ saw (1) n 120.9
~ starters (1) n 008.6
~ station (2) n 107.2
~ stove (22) n 118.4
~ stoves (5) n 118.4
~ throttle (1) n 110.6
~ wall heaters (1) n 008.4
Gas (6) 106.5
~ Light building (1) n 108.5
~ Light Tower (1) 108.5
~ Tower (1) 108.5

gasboat (1) n 024.6
Gascon (1) 128.2
gash (5) n 078.1
gasket (2) n 020.4
gaslights (1) n 024.2
gasoline (20) n/adj 120.9
~ -driven plow (1) n 120.4
~ feed (1) n 110.6
~ gauge (1) n 110.9
~ guzzlers (1) n 109.4
~ lamp (1) n 024.3
~ lawn mow(er) (1) n 120.2
~ mower (1) n 120.2
~ plow (1) n 120.4
~ stove (1) n 080.8
~ trucks (1) n 111.4
gaspergou (23) n 059.9
gasper(gou) (1) n 059.9
(gasper)gou (3) n 059.9
gaspergous (3) n 059.9
gaspers (1) n 117.8
gassed saw (1) n 120.9
Gassville (1) AR 082.6
Gaston (4) 106.1
~ Estates (1) 106.1
~ Point (3) 105.3
Gastonian (1) 056.9
gate (27) n/adj 016.5
~ fences (1) n 016.4
~ pole (1) n 042.7
Gate (4) AR 087.3
gatepost (3) n 016.5
gatepost[N-i] (1) n 016.5
gates (7) n 013.9
gateway (1) n 080.8
gather (154) v 070.6
~ around (1) v 049.2
~ (a)round (2) v 049.2
~ up (3) v 082.9
gathered (14) v 101.4
~ up (1) v 101.4
gathering (40) n/v/adj 101.4
~ in (1) v 005.6
~ time (2) n 005.6
~ up (1) v 005.6
gathers (1) v 042.1
Gatlinburg (40) TN 087.5
gator (3) n/adj 130.5
~ bait (1) n 069.3
Gator Bowl (1) 106.4
Gatorade (2) 121.8
gattling stick (1) n 099.7

gaucho pants (1) n 123.3
gauchos (7) n 123.3
gaudy (6) adj 109.4
~ car (1) n 109.4
gauge (16) n/adj 110.5
gauges (2) n 110.2
gaunt (6) adj 072.9
Gautier (2) MS 086.8
gave (778) v 102.1
~ birth (2) v 033.9
~ her the air (1) v 082.1
~ him back his ring (1) v 082.1
~ him the air (5) v 082.1
~ him the boot (1) v 082.1
~ him the brush-off (3) v 082.1
~ him the door (1) v 082.1
~ him the gate (3) v 082.1
~ him the go-by (1) v 082.1
~ him the mitten (1) v 082.1
~ him the no sign (1) v 082.1
~ him the runaround (1) v 082.1
~ him the shaft (4) v 082.1
~ him the slip (1) v 082.1
~ him up (1) v 082.1
~ his ring back (2) v 082.1
~ it up (2) v 078.6
~ out (10) v 075.4
~ to (1) v 102.1
~ up (10) v 102.1
~ up the ghost (7) v 078.6
gaved (1) v 102.1
gaven (2) v 102.1
gawking (2) v 057.4
gawky (70) adj 073.3
gay (94) n/adj 074.8
~ places (1) n 081.8
~ side (1) n 124.1
Gay (7) 105.3
~ Street (4) 105.3

~ Street Bridge (1) 114.8
~ Street Cinema (1) 114.9
~ Street Viaduct (1) 107.8
Gaylor (1) 087.4
gays (3) n 124.2
gazebo (4) n 081.8
GB (1) 082.1
GD (1) 092.1
gear (141) n/v/adj 038.6
~ change (1) n 110.7
~ house (12) n 011.7
~ houses (1) n 014.4
~ room (10) n 038.6
~ stick (4) n 110.7
~ up (13) v 038.6
geared up (2) v 012.9
gearing (5) n/v 038.6
~ up (1) v 038.6
gears (45) n 038.7
gearshift (72) n/adj 110.7
~ lever (2) n 110.7
gee (831) v/adj/interj 037.7
~ harrows (1) n 021.7
~ haw (11) interj 037.7
~ horse (6) n 037.7
~ land (2) n 039.3
~ ox (1) n 039.4
~ right (1) interj 037.7
~ side (5) n 039.4
~ up (3) v 038.1
~ whillikins (1) interj 092.2
~ whiz (68) n/interj 021.7
~ whiz harrow (3) n 021.7
~ whiz harrows (1) n 021.7
~ whiz Joe harrow (1) n 021.7
~ whiz plow (1) n 021.6
~ -whiz (1) v 096.7
~ whizzes (5) n 021.7
gee(x2) (1) interj 037.7
gee(x3) (1) interj 037.7
gee(x4) (1) interj 037.7
Geechee (5) 069.4
Geech(ee) (2) 080.9
~ nigger (1) n 069.5
Geechees (8) 069.2

gees (1) n 037.7
geese (76) n 036.6
geeses (4) n 036.6
geezer (1) n 074.1
geezers (1) n 080.6
gelatin (1) n 047.1
gelawin (1) n 061.4
geld (15) v 036.1
gelded (7) v 036.1
gelding (79) n/adj 034.1
~ horse (1) n 034.2
geldings (3) n 034.1
gem (2) n 125.4
Gem (53) 110.4
~ clip (39) n 110.4
~ clips (10) n 110.4
gems (1) n 123.1
gendarmes (1) n F 093.5
genealogy (1) n 066.6
general (757) n/adj 068.3
~ boss (1) n 069.6
~ hospital (2) n 084.5
~ manager (2) n 068.3
~ merchandise (1) n 081.8
~ -merchandise store (1) n 068.3
~ practitioner (1) n 069.7
~ rain (3) n 006.1
~ science (1) n 068.3
~ store (9) n 068.3
gene(ral) (1) n 068.3
gen(eral) (2) n 068.3
General (219) 068.3
~ Clarke (2) 068.3
~ Dwight D. Eisenhower (1) 068.3
~ Eisenhower (7) 068.3
~ Forrest (1) 068.3
~ Grant (4) 068.3
~ Houston (1) 068.3
~ Jackson (3) 068.3
~ Lee (115) 068.3
~ Lee's (1) 068.3
~ MacArthur (8) 068.3
~ Maddox (1) 068.3
~ Motors (1) 068.3
~ of the Army (1) 068.3
~ Patton (32) 068.3
~ Pershing (1) 068.3
~ Robert E. Lee (12) 068.3

~ Robert Lee (1) 068.3
~ Sam Houston (1) 068.3
~ Sam Houston's monument (1) n 068.3
~ Sherman (2) 068.3
~ so-and-so (1) n 068.3
~ Stonewall Jackson (1) 068.3
~ Westmoreland (1) 068.3
~ William Westmoreland (1) 068.3
generally (19) adv 070.8
general(ly) (1) adv 103.4
generals (16) n 068.3
Generals (1) 068.3
generation (10) n/adj 066.5
~ gap (1) n 069.5
(gene)ration (1) n 073.8
generation[N-i] (1) n 012.9
generations (4) n 001.2
generator deal (1) n 075.7
generators (1) n 111.5
generous (2) adj 091.8
Genesis (2) 065.9
genetic (1) adj 065.8
Geneva (10) AL AR 087.8
~ County (3) AL 087.2
genial (1) adj 073.2
genius (6) n 125.5
genteel (3) adj 051.4
Gentile (7) 069.4
~ American (1) 069.2
Gentiles (2) 069.4
gentility (1) n 069.4
Gentilly Ridge (1) LA 084.9
gentle (77) adj 073.2
~ rain (10) n 006.6
gentleman (43) n/adj 065.8
~ cow (10) n 033.5
~ farmer (1) n 080.8
~ friend (1) n 081.5
~ horse (1) n 034.1
~ pig (1) n 035.3
Gentleman (2) 056.2
gentleman's (3) adj 029.2
~ bow (1) n 029.2

~ chair (1) n 008.8
~ chifforobe (1) n 009.2
gentlemen (10) n 065.8
~ of color (1) n 069.3
gentlemens (3) n 073.7
gentles (1) v 075.3
gentlest (1) adj 073.2
Gentry (3) AR 087.4
~ Creek (2) TN 030.7
gentry (1) adj 080.6
gent's bowtie (1) n 088.9
genuflect (3) v 096.5
genuflected (1) v 096.5
genuine (816) adj 051.4
genuinely (1) adv 051.4
geographical-wise (1) adv 080.8
geography (3) n/adj 070.7
~ student (1) n 068.7
geologist (1) n 053.4
George (30) MS 087.4
~ Dempster (1) 117.3
~ Wallace Drive (1) 107.6
~ Ward Park (1) 106.4
~ Washington (3) 087.1
~ Washington celebration (1) n 084.8
~ Washington's time (1) n 087.1
~ Washingtons (2) 114.5
Georgetown (17) GA 086.7
Georgia (1640) 086.3
~ Baptist (1) 105.9
~ Baptist Assembly (1) 089.1
~ Baptist Hospital (1) 089.1
~ bedstead (1) n 080.8
~ Belle (5) 086.3
~ Belle peach (2) n 054.3
~ Belles (1) 054.3
~ -born (1) adj 063.1
~ boys (1) n 061.1
~ Boys (1) 054.4
~ buggies (4) n 023.3
~ buggy (45) n 023.3
~ Buggy (1) 023.3

~ buggy[N-i] (1) n 023.3
~ cane syrup (2) n 051.3
~ cat (1) n 059.9
~ clay (2) n 029.8
~ coastline (1) n 086.3
~ collards (1) n 055A.5
~ Cracker (65) 069.9
~ Crackers (40) 069.9
~ dimes (1) n 013.8
~ gal (1) n 088.9
~ goobers (2) n 054.7
~ grasshopper (1) n 061.1
~ Gray (1) 068.9
~ hills (1) n 030.8
~ Hoosier (2) 069.9
~ hopper (1) n 061.1
~ ice cream (1) n 050.6
~ Infirmary (1) 010.5
~ Lifesavers (1) 054.7
~ man (1) n 043.6
~ marble business (1) n 080.6
~ melon (1) n 056.9
~ melons (1) n 056.9
~ peach (14) n 054.3
~ peaches (4) n 054.4
~ people (2) n 086.3
~ plow (1) n 021.6
~ plow stock (1) n 021.6
~ potato (1) n 055.5
~ Power (1) 086.3
~ Prolific (1) 056.2
~ Railroad (4) 084.7
~ ratchet (1) n 021.6
~ Rattlesnake (21) 074.9
~ Rattlesnake[N-i] (1) 056.9
~ Rattlesnakes (3) 056.9
~ red-neck (1) n 069.4
~ Red (2) 055.5
~ Reds (3) 055.5
~ shale (1) n 031.6
~ soil (1) n 029.8
~ Southern rock (1) n 097.8
~ State (1) 086.3
~ State complex (1) n 106.4
~ stock (50) n 021.6

~ Stock College (1) 083.6
~ stock plow (1) n 021.6
~ -stock sorghum (1) n 051.3
~ stocks (4) n 021.6
~ stumpers (1) n 061.1
~ Sweet (2) 056.9
~ syrup (1) n 051.3
~ Tech (12) 086.3
~ thumper (5) n 060A.4
~ thumpers (3) n 061.1
~ truck (1) n 023.3
~ wagon (1) n 023.3
~ watermelon (1) n 056.9
~ white trash (1) n 069.8
~ wigglers (2) n 060.5
Georgiamens (1) 069.5
Georgian (4) 086.3
Georgiana (1) AL 087.8
Georgians (4) 080.8
Georgia's (1) 086.3
Geraldine (2) AL 087.4
geraniums (1) n 017.7
Geritol (1) 114.8
germ (6) n/adj 054.2
~ cold (1) n 076.3
German (54) 127.1
~ ancestry (1) n 053.3
~ bread (2) n 044.4
~ brown (1) n 058.9
~ cabbage (1) n 055A.1
~ carp (1) n 059.9
~ dances (1) n 083.1
~ Jews (2) 127.1
~ Luger (1) 113.1
~ people (2) n 127.1
~ police (9) n 033.1
~ police dog (2) n 033.3
~ police dogs (1) n 033.3
~ sausage (2) n 121.6
~ sausages (1) n 121.6
~ sea captain (1) n 068.5
~ settlement (2) n 069.6
~ shepherd (2) n 033.3
~ shepherd dog (1) n 033.1

~ shepherds (1) n 033.3
~ (to)mato (1) n 055.3
German's (1) 088.9
Germans (26) 083.1
Germantown (12) LA TN 087.1
~ Road (1) 031.6
Germany (23) 086.3
~ Street (1) 105.5
Geronimo (1) 075.9
Gertie (1) 125.2
Gertrudis (5) 033.7
(Ger)trudis (1) 033.6
gestation (1) n 065.2
gesture (2) n 095.7
get (5493) v 098.3
~ a calf (1) v 033.9
~ about (3) v 075.6
~ after (1) v 081.3
~ after him (1) v 033.2
~ along (10) v 038.1
~ along there (1) v 038.1
~ along with (39) v 073.2
~ (a)long with (2) v 074.8
~ around (16) v 074.1
~ around to (2) v 058.7
~ at (3) v 057.7
~ away (8) v 038.3
~ away from (1) v 052.2
~ away from there (1) v 038.3
~ away with (1) v 053.5
~ back (14) v 038.3
~ back at (1) v 101.2
~ back here (1) v 038.2
~ back in there (1) v 038.2
~ back out (1) v 039.9
~ back up (1) v 076.7
~ behind (1) v 010.5
~ by (3) v 057.7
~ -by (1) n 067.8
~ down (29) v 033.2
~ -down films (1) n 114.9
~ down on your case (1) v 129.6
~ -down party (1) n 130.7

~ down with (1) v 099.5
~ -drunk-and-chase-women parties (1) n 130.7
~ going (4) v 038.1
~ gone (2) v 032.1
~ him (229) v 033.2
~ -him(x2) (6) interj 033.2
~ him off (1) v 033.2
~ him there (1) v 033.2
~ in (35) v 075.6
~ in there (2) v 038.2
~ in with (1) v 089.7
~ into (5) v 053.6
~ it (11) v 033.2
~ my breeches tanned (1) v 065.5
~ off (594) v 085.4
~ off at (26) v 085.4
~ off of (7) v 034.4
~ off on (1) v 088.8
~ off with (1) v 053.4
~ on (25) v 038.1
~ on back there (1) v 037.5
~ on him (3) v 033.2
~ on my case (2) v 024.8
~ on out (1) v 038.1
~ on out of here (1) v 038.3
~ on up (1) v 038.1
~ on up here now (1) v 038.1
~ on up there (1) v 038.1
~ on your case (1) v 024.8
~ onto (2) v 107.4
~ our breeches tore up (1) v 065.5
~ our butts tore up (1) v 065.5
~ out (74) v 083.2
~ out from here (1) v 038.3
~ out of (14) v 076.7
~ out of here (2) v 038.3
~ out [P-0] (1) v 038.3
~ -out (3) n 075.2
~ over (10) v 070.4

~ over there (2) v 037.7
~ overs (2) n 115.4
~ that dog (1) v 033.2
~ that leg back (1) v 037.5
~ the knot tied (2) v 082.2
~ the rod (1) v 065.5
~ them (16) v 033.2
~ these bits (1) v 038.6
~ through (14) v 070.6
~ to (71) v 057.7
~ -together (16) n 083.1
~ -together parties (1) n 130.7
~ -together party (1) n 130.7
~ -togethers (3) n 130.7
~ up (848) v 038.1
~ (u)p (2) v 038.1
~ -up(x2) (17) interj 038.1
~ -up(x3) (4) interj 038.1
~ -up-and-get-it (1) n 069.7
~ -up-and-go (3) n 074.1
~ -up-and-going (1) n 080.6
~ up here (8) v 038.1
~ up off (1) v 073.5
~ -up piece (1) n 096.7
~ up there (14) v 038.1
~ with (1) v 032.4
~ your food (1) v 038.5
~ your jacket (1) v 065.5
Get (1) 115.8
get[V-p] (39) v 025.6
~ around (2) v 074.1
~ into (2) v 099.7
~ off (1) v 013.6
~ on (1) v 013.8
~ out (1) v 083.2
~ over (1) v 025.3
~ up (2) v 003.2
get[V-r] (6) v 076.3
~ up (1) v 095.8
get[V-s] (3) v 098.6
~ after (1) v 098.6
get[V-t] (1) v 057.8

Gethsemane (2) AR 087.7
gets (220) v 076.3
~ about (3) v 074.1
~ after (2) v 025.6
~ along (3) v 013.7
~ along with (1) v 013.8
~ around (12) v 074.1
~ away with (1) v 095.9
~ back (2) v 075.7
~ down (1) v 104.5
~ in (2) v 025.9
~ off (3) v 085.4
~ off of (1) v 034.4
~ on (2) v 028.1
~ out (34) v 083.2
~ over (1) v 083.2
~ to (8) v 024.9
~ up (6) v 097.3
getter (6) n 060A.7
getting (883) v 101.2
~ a baby (1) v 065.1
~ along (45) v 079.4
~ (a)long (33) v 079.4
~ around (4) v 074.1
~ at (3) v 024.7
~ away (1) v 013.8
~ back (1) v 088.7
~ by (1) v 079.4
~ -by-easy guy (1) n 125.6
~ close (1) v 081.4
~ down (6) v 081.7
~ down to gritty (1) v 081.4
~ engaged (1) v 081.4
~ for (2) v 012.9
~ in (4) v 024.7
~ in love (3) v 081.4
~ interested in her (1) v 081.4
~ into (1) v 039.8
~ off (2) v 115.5
~ -off place (1) n 085.4
~ offen (1) v 034.4
~ on (7) v 070.1
~ on his case (1) v 080.7
~ on your case (1) v 129.6
~ out (4) v 083.2
~ out of (2) v 083.2
~ out [P-0] (1) v 012.9
~ over (1) v 125.6

~ pretty serious (1) v 081.4
~ pretty thick (1) v 081.4
~ real serious (1) v 081.4
~ serious (8) v 081.4
~ serious about her (2) v 081.4
~ steady (1) v 081.4
~ struck on her (1) v 081.4
~ the neck broke (1) v 082.2
~ thick (2) v 081.4
~ thick with her (1) v 081.4
~ through (1) v 066.9
~ to (2) v 070.1
~ too thick (1) v 081.4
~ up (40) v 007.2
~ with (1) v 089.4
Gettysburg (1) PA 087.4
Getwell (1) 107.7
gewgaws (2) n 010.2
Geyer Springs (1) 105.1
geyser (3) n 031.5
ghetto (20) n/adj 114.8
~ section (1) n 105.6
~ test (1) n 091.8
ghettos (4) n 114.8
ghost (271) n/adj 090.2
~ chaser (1) n 090.3
~ house (33) n 090.3
~ houses (4) n 014.1
~ people (2) n 090.2
~ stories (4) n 090.2
~ tale (1) n 090.2
~ tales (1) n 090.2
~ town (1) n 090.2
Ghost (11) 089.1
~ Hill (1) 090.2
ghost[N-i] (450) n 090.2
ghostes (39) n 090.2
ghostly troll (1) n 090.2
ghosts (101) n 090.2
ghosty (6) adj 090.3
~ home (1) n 090.3
~ house (2) n 090.3
ghoul (1) n 090.2
ghouls (4) n 090.2
GI (3) 123.9
~ Bill (1) 065.8
~ Joe (1) 123.9
giant (23) n/adj 073.1

~ oaks (1) n 061.8
~ pig farmer (1) n 069.9
~ red worms (1) n 060.5
~ snake (1) n 080.7
~ step (2) n 130.2
~ steps (2) n 130.2
~ stride (1) n 022.7
Giant (6) 116.3
giants (2) n 073.1
gibbers (1) n 060A.9
Gibbs Street (1) 107.8
gibelotte (1) n F 056.5
giblet (23) n/adj 037.2
~ corn (1) n 050.6
~ gravy (5) n 037.2
~ stew (1) n 037.2
giblet[N-i] (2) n 037.2
giblets (78) n 037.2
Gibsland (2) LA 087.3
Gibson (18) LA TN 087.2
~ County (4) MS TN 087.3
~ Street (1) 107.7
Gid (1) AR 087.3
giddap (8) interj 038.1
giddap(x3) (1) interj 038.1
Giddens Chapel (1) AL 087.7
Giddings (2) TX 087.5
giddy (2) adj 074.1
~ wasp (1) n 060A.6
giddyup (201) interj 038.1
~ there (3) interj 038.1
giddyup(x2) (2) interj 038.1
Gideon (1) LA 086.2
Giebel (1) n G 011.6
Gifford (1) FL 087.8
gift (146) n/adj 095.7
~ shop (1) n 084.6
~ wrap (10) v 094.3
~ wrapped (10) v 094.3
~ -wrapped (1) adj 094.3
Gift (439) 093.2
gift[N-i] (1) n 093.2
gifted (1) adj 064.7
gifts (3) n 027.5
Gifts (2) 093.2
gig (21) n/v 060.2
gigged (1) v 060.2
gigging (13) n/v 060.2

~ on (1) v 052.7
gigoless (1) n 124.6
gigolo (5) n 124.5
gigolos (1) n 128.2
gigs (4) n 069.3
Gilbert (1) AR 087.2
Gilchrist (1) 107.9
Giles County (2) TN 087.1
gill (4) n/adj 089.8
~ net (2) n 089.8
~ well water (1) n 088.7
gill[N-i] (1) n 072.9
Gillette Street (1) 107.7
gillnetting (1) n 097.8
gills (2) n 072.9
Gilmer (4) GA TX 087.2
~ County (1) GA 087.2
gilt (263) n/adj 035.5
~ hog (2) n 035.5
~ pig (2) n 035.5
~ shoat (1) n 035.5
gilt[N-i] (1) n 035.5
gilts (45) n 035.5
Gim (1) 088.7
gimlet (2) n 071.8
~ -ended (1) adj 079.1
gimmick (1) n 095.7
gin (69) n/v/adj 015.8
~ head (1) n 113.6
~ job (1) n 075.7
~ pole (2) n 014.6
~ wood (1) n 092.8
Gin Creek (1) AL 030.7
Ginans Branch (1) TN 030.7
ginger (21) n/adj 066.8
~ ale (4) n 121.8
~ breakfast cake (1) n 122.2
~ cake (3) n 069.5
~ -cake color (3) n 069.5
~ -cake nigger (1) n 069.5
~ cakes (4) n 045.3
~ mill (1) n 080.7
~ plants (1) n 061.4
~ tea (2) n 061.4
Ginger Cake Creek (1) GA 030.7
gingerbread (22) n/adj 044.4
~ cake (1) n 121.2

~ roof (1) n 088.9
gingerbready (1) adj 075.8
gingerman (1) adj 051.4
gingerroot (2) n 061.5
gingersnaps (3) n 069.3
gingham (5) n 019.6
ginghams (1) n 080.8
ginhouse (7) n/adj 011.7
~ shelter (1) n 011.8
ginkgo (1) n 061.8
ginned (7) v/adj 101.7
~ cotton (1) n 088.7
~ out (1) v 015.9
ginner (1) n 080.6
ginning (5) n/v/adj 032.8
~ wheel (1) n 022.7
gins (5) n 001.2
ginseng (38) n/adj 061.4
~ root (3) n 061.4
~ roots (1) n 061.4
giraffe (1) n 130.3
Girard (1) AL 087.2
Girardeau (2) 087.8
girdle (2) n 028.6
girdled (1) adj 098.6
girdlers (1) n 028.5
girl (1895) n/adj 064.9
~ calf (1) n 033.8
~ child (1) n 064.9
~ days (1) n 088.9
~ friend (655) n 081.6
~ friends (8) n 081.6
~ goblin (1) n 125.2
~ hog (2) n 035.5
~ horse (2) n 034.2
~ marm (1) n 067.6
~ of honor (1) n 082.4
~ talk (1) n 095.8
~ -watch (1) v 080.7
~ wed man (1) n 082.4
girl(x2) (1) interj 037.5
Girl (9) 063.2
~ Friday (3) 068.8
~ Scouts (1) 064.9
girl[N-i] (12) n 064.9
girl[N-i][N-k] houses (1) n 130.7
girl[N-k] daddy (1) n 043.9
girlie (2) adj 114.9
~ houses (1) n 114.9
~ show (1) n 114.9
girlified (1) adj 124.1
girlish (4) adj 074.1

girl's (6) adj 064.9
~ daddy (1) n 064.9
~ house (1) n 081.6
~ land (1) n 080.9
~ place (1) n 053.5
girls (650) n 064.9
girls' (38) adj 007A.6
~ bedroom (3) n 064.9
~ club (1) n 064.9
~ gym (2) n 126.2
~ mouth[N-i] (1) n 052.1
~ room (15) n 126.3
~ school (6) n 064.9
~ seminary (1) n 064.9
~ sparking room (1) n 007A.2
Girls' (2) 044.7
~ High (1) 064.9
girth (5) n/adj 080.7
~ strap (1) n 088.7
GIs (2) 123.9
gist (2) n 070.8
gitty (1) interj 038.5
give (1979) v 102.1
~ (a)way (1) v 102.1
~ away (1) v 045.8
~ birth (46) v 033.9
~ him the air (2) v 082.1
~ him the ax (1) v 082.1
~ him the gate (2) v 082.1
~ in (1) v 058.5
~ it up (1) v 078.6
~ milk (1) v 033.9
~ off (1) v 102.1
~ on (1) v 102.1
~ on out (1) v 075.4
~ out (13) v 075.4
~ out of (1) v 080.7
~ over there (1) v 037.5
~ them the mischief (2) v 065.5
~ to (1) v 013.5
~ up (5) v 102.1
~ up the ghost (2) v 078.5
Give (58) 093.3
give[V-p] (5) v 053.6
~ to (1) v 095.8
give[V-r] (443) v 102.1
~ away (4) v 102.1

~ for (2) v 102.1
~ him her sack (1) v 082.1
~ him the brush-off (1) v 082.1
~ him the GB (1) v 082.1
~ him the heigh-ho (1) v 082.1
~ it up (1) v 078.6
~ out (22) v 102.1
~ over (1) v 075.8
~ up (9) v 102.1
give[V-t] (350) v 102.1
~ away (1) v 102.1
~ by (2) v 052.5
~ out (226) v 075.5
~ to (5) v 102.1
~ up (5) v 102.1
giveaway (4) n/adj 094.5
~ price (1) n 094.5
~ program (1) n 080.6
giveaways (3) n 123.5
gived (3) v 102.1
given (525) v/adj 102.1
~ away (1) v 102.1
~ him the air (1) v 082.1
~ him the gate (1) v 082.1
~ name (9) n 064.4
~ names (3) n 064.4
~ out (28) v 075.5
~ to (2) v 102.1
~ up (3) v 102.1
gives (25) v 102.1
~ away (1) v 102.1
~ out (3) v 102.1
~ up the ghost (1) v 078.6
Gives (3) 093.2
givey morning (1) n 007.4
giving (37) v 102.1
~ away (1) v 007.3
gizlet (1) n 037.3
gizmo (1) n 099.7
gizzard (126) n/adj 037.2
gizzards (15) n 037.2
glad (959) adj 081.2
~ rags (1) n 028.1
glade (9) n/adj 029.5
~ land (1) n 029.9
Glade Creek (1) GA 030.7
glades (2) n 029.6

Glades (3) FL 087.5
Gladewater (1) TX 087.8
gladiolas (1) n 070.6
glads (1) n 091.8
glady (2) adj 029.8
~ land (1) n 029.8
Gladys (2) GA 087.6
glain (1) v F 016.5
glamor boy (1) n 125.3
gland (1) n 077.6
glands (1) n 081.9
Glascock (1) GA 087.1
Glasgow (1) 087.7
glass (1205) n/adj 048.9
~ beads (1) n 028.4
~ bottle (1) n 048.9
~ bottle tops (1) n 020.4
~ bowl (1) n 019.2
~ container (1) n 019.2
~ cork (2) n 020.4
~ corks (1) n 020.4
~ darning egg (1) n 017.1
~ dipper (1) n 048.9
~ dippers (1) n 013.9
~ door (1) n 048.9
~ doors (3) n 048.9
~ egg (75) n 017.1
~ egg[N-i] (1) n 017.1
~ eggs (35) n 017.1
~ elevator (1) n 048.9
~ eye (3) n 033.3
~ -eyed (1) adj 033.3
~ -eyed curs (1) n 033.3
~ eyes (1) n 025.6
~ house (1) n 118.1
~ jalousies (1) n 009.5
~ jar (9) n 019.2
~ jars (4) n 081.7
~ jug (5) n 018.7
~ jugs (6) n 048.9
~ -like (1) adj 017.1
~ -like eggs (1) n 017.1
~ marbles (1) n 130.6
~ nest eggs (1) n 017.1
~ outfit (1) n 076.9
~ panes (1) n 048.9
~ pots (1) n 048.9
~ rags (1) n 018.5
~ roof (1) n 011.4
~ snakes (1) n 080.8
~ stopper (18) n 020.4
~ stoppers (2) n 020.4

~ top (1) n 020.4
~ tops (1) n 020.4
~ tubes (1) n 024.4
~ turkey eggs (1) n 017.1
~ window (2) n 065.9
~ windows (7) n 007A.4
Glass (1) MS 030.7
glass[N-i] (2) n 048.9
glassed (6) adj 017.1
~ egg (1) n 017.1
~ -in porch (4) n 118.1
~ -in porches (1) n 010.9
glasses (83) n 048.9
glassful (6) n 048.9
glassware (2) n 048.9
glasswork (1) n 048.9
glaze (120) n/adj 048.5
~ doughnut (16) n 122.4
~ doughnuts (14) n 122.4
glazed (34) adj 122.4
~ buckets (1) n 017.3
~ doughnut (7) n 122.4
~ doughnuts (7) n 122.4
~ granite (1) n 075.8
~ ham (1) n 121.3
glazing (5) n/v 122.3
gleaning (2) v 041.5
gleanings (1) n 014.7
glee club (1) n 088.7
glen (3) n 030.9
Glen (5) 087.7
~ Allan (3) MS 087.7
Glendale (1) TN 087.4
Glenmary (3) TN 087.4
Glenmor(a) (2) LA 087.3
Glenmore (2) GA LA 087.2
Glenn (2) GA 087.3
~ Miller (1) 130.8
Glennville (3) GA 087.2
Glenobey (1) TN 087.4
Glenview (1) 106.5
Glenwood (5) AL 087.9
~ area (1) n 105A.4
~ section (1) n 105.1
glib (11) adj 074.1
glide (2) n 083.1
glimmery (1) n 006.7
Glimp (1) TN 087.2

glimpsed (2) v 032.6
glisten (1) v 077.3
glitter (2) adj 130.8
~ rock (1) n 130.8
~ stuff (1) n 123.6
glittering glass (1) n 123.1
globe (41) n/adj 019.9
~ light (1) n 019.9
Globe watermelon (1) n 056.9
globes (8) n 019.9
glommed (2) v 100.2
~ on (1) v 100.2
~ onto (1) v 100.2
glooey (1) n 045.6
gloom (2) n/adj 005.5
~ day (1) n 005.5
gloomy (155) adj 005.5
~ day (69) n 005.5
~ -looking (1) adj 005.5
~ -looking day (1) n 005.5
Gloria Street (1) 107.9
glories (13) n 015.9
Gloriosa (li)ly (1) n 061.9
glorious (3) adj 089.6
glory (19) n/adj/interj 092.6
~ hole (2) n 007A.2
~ hound (1) n 125.6
~ rollers (1) n 126.6
glossing (1) n 122.3
Gloster (2) LA MS 087.3
Gloucester (2) VA 087.2
~ Street (1) 065.9
glove (153) n/adj 053.4
~ box (7) n 110.2
~ compartment (138) n 110.2
~ compart(ment) (1) n 110.2
~ department (4) n 076.9
~ pocket (1) n 110.2
gloves (6) n 027.4
glow (4) v/adj 077.3
~ bug (1) n 060A.3
glowworm (7) n 060A.3
glucken (1) n 050.9
glucky (1) adj 088.9
glucose (1) n 070.8
glue (2) n 114.2
gluey (1) adj 025.9

glut (4) n 016.4
gluts (3) n 020.7
glycerin (1) n 025.9
Glynlea Park (1) 106.2
Glynn (12) GA 087.8
~ County (2) GA 087.2
GN (1) 090.8
gnarled (1) adj 079.6
gnat (18) n 060A.2
gnats (46) n 060A.7
gnaw (2) v 050.2
go (3807) n/v 038.1
~ across (1) v 028.9
~ (a)cross (3) v 028.9
~ after (1) v 025.8
~ after him (2) v 033.2
~ (a)head (1) v 038.1
~ along (3) v 097.5
~ along with (4) v 013.3
~ and (102) v 081.3
~ and fetch it (1) v 071.7
~ and get him (2) v 033.2
~ and get it (1) v 033.2
~ around (1) v 052.3
~ -around (1) n 022.7
~ (a)round (6) v 040.8
~ -(a)round (2) n 080.8
~ -(a)rounds (1) n 122.2
~ at him (1) v 033.2
~ (a)way (1) v 033.2
~ back (43) v 083.3
~ bite him (1) v 033.2
~ by (3) v 065.5
~ -by (1) n 082.1
~ -cart (22) n 064.5
~ -carts (5) n 064.5
~ catch him (2) v 033.2
~ -devil (20) n 021.7
~ -devils (4) n 021.9
~ down (20) v 003.4
~ dry (1) v 033.9
~ -easy (1) n 028.1
~ faster (1) v 038.1
~ fetch it (5) n 071.7
~ fetcher (4) n 071.7
~ fetchers (1) n 071.7
~ find him (1) v 033.2
~ for (1) v 053.4
~ -for (1) n 080.6
~ from (1) v 035.5

~ get him (44) v 033.2
~ get it (2) n/v 071.7
~ get them (4) v 033.2
~ -getter (3) n 074.1
~ -go boots (1) n 123.8
~ in (33) v 096.8
~ in at (1) v 052.6
~ in the house (1) v 065.1
~ into (3) v 079.3
~ -it(x3) (1) interj 037.5
~ off (4) v 074.3
~ on (19) v 038.1
~ (o)n (1) v 075.3
~ on out (1) v 043.5
~ on to (1) v 049.4
~ on up (1) v 066.8
~ out (41) v 083.2
~ out there (1) v 033.2
~ out with (1) v 069.6
~ over (13) v 082.7
~ section (1) n 071.7
~ sit (1) v 033.2
~ steady (1) v 081.4
~ through (20) v 032.1
~ through with (1) v 053.4
~ to (370) v 098.3
~ to it (1) v 038.1
~ together (5) v 081.4
~ up (11) v 082.6
~ with (42) v 081.4
~ with him (1) v 081.4
~ without (1) v 032.3
~ [P-0] (5) v 052.5
g(o) (1) v 080.8
Go (7) 023.9
~ -Jo (1) 023.9
go(x2) (1) interj 038.3
go[V-p] (62) v 013.8
~ across (1) v 028.9
~ along (1) v 088.4
~ (a)round (1) v 013.6
~ back (1) v 013.8
~ down (3) v 053.7
~ from (1) v 013.8
~ in (2) v 083.3
~ like (1) v 098.9
~ on (3) v 025.9
~ out (1) v 013.8
~ through (2) v 053.4
~ to (7) v 024.9
~ to see her (1) v 081.4
~ with (2) v 088.4

go[V-r] (3) v 024.9
~ to (2) v 024.9
go[V-s] (24) v 025.4
~ to (1) v 033.9
~ t(o) (1) v 100.1
~ [P-0] (21) v 024.7
goad (3) n 019.4
goal (253) n/adj 098.4
~ line (37) n 098.4
goalpost (45) n 098.4
goalpost[N-i] (4) n 098.4
goalposts (2) n 098.4
goals (9) n 098.4
goat (177) n/adj 034.9
~ barn (1) n 014.2
~ country (1) n 099.9
~ grass (1) n 015.9
~ head (1) n 015.9
~ -headed (2) adj 074.8
~ hoof (1) n 124.7
~ house (1) n 014.2
~ lips (1) n 084.8
~ lot (1) n 015.6
~ meat (1) n 053.2
~ milk (1) n 048.2
~ roper (2) n 069.6
~ ropers (1) n 069.9
~ shed (1) n 015.2
Goat Hill (1) 106.7
goat(x3) (1) interj 038.4
goat[N-i] (1) n 016.7
goatee (21) n/adj 071.4
~ beard (1) n 071.4
goat's milk (1) n 048.2
goats (41) n 033.6
goatweed tea (1) n 061.3
goaty(x2) (1) interj 038.4
goaty(x3) (2) interj 038.7
gob (1) n 055A.8
gobble (1) v 049.7
gobbler (3) n 080.6
gobbler's (1) adj 080.9
gobblers (3) n 048.9
gobbles (1) v 060.4
Gober (1) GA 087.6
goblet (37) n 048.9
goblets (15) n 048.9
goblin (8) n 090.2
goblins (42) n 090.2
gobs (2) n 090.7
god (39) n 089.3
God (1361) 089.3
~ Almighty (37) 089.3
~ Almighty[N-k] sake
(1) n 092.2

~ -awful (1) adj 047.7
~ called her (1) v 078.5
~ -called man (1) n
089.3
~ -dang (2) adj 092.1
~ dog (5) interj 092.6
~ -fearing (1) adj 089.3
~ -knows-when (1) adv
089.3
~ -made (1) adj 030.6
~ -sent (1) adj 099.6
~ squad (2) n 126.6
~ the Father (1) 089.3
~ Unlimited (1) 089.3
God[N-k] (7) 089.3
~ children (2) n 089.3
~ sake (3) n 089.3
~ sakes (2) n 089.3
Godbold (1) TX 087.6
goddamn (32) adj 097.8
goddamn[V-t] (3) v
092.2
goddaughter (1) n 089.3
godfather (29) n 066.4
godfathers (1) n 129.5
godforsaken (1) adj 089.3
godlin (1) adv 085.2
godmother (28) n 066.4
godmothers (3) n 129.5
godparent (4) n 129.5
godparents (18) n 129.5
god(parents) (1) n 089.3
God's (18) 089.3
~ Day (2) 089.3
~ earth (2) n 089.3
~ house (1) n 089.3
~ sake (1) n 092.9
~ son (1) n 089.3
~ time (1) n 089.3
~ truth (3) n 089.3
~ will (2) n 089.3
~ word (1) n 089.4
~ work (1) n 053.6
gods (10) n 059.3
Gods (1) 089.3
godsent preachers (1) n
067.8
goed (2) v 098.7
goes (209) v 053.2
~ across (1) v 028.9
~ along (1) v 088.4
~ and (3) v 013.6
~ away (1) v 007.3
~ back (2) v 026.1
~ by (1) v 025.4

~ down (9) v 003.4
~ from (1) v 052.8
~ in (7) v 052.7
~ into (1) v 099.5
~ off (3) v 052.6
~ off of (1) v 031.7
~ on (5) v 060.4
~ on down (1) v 007.3
~ out (10) v 083.2
~ out for (1) v 013.7
~ out from (1) v 052.5
~ over (3) v 052.5
~ steady (2) v 081.4
~ through (1) v 013.8
~ to (34) v 053.2
~ under (1) v 053.4
~ up (3) v 052.7
~ with (5) v 025.6
~ with her (1) v 081.4
~ without (1) v 013.7
goge (1) n 010.8
goggle (35) adj 059.9
~ -eye (14) n 059.9
~ -eye catfish (1) n
059.9
~ -eye fish (1) n 059.9
~ -eye perch (8) n
059.9
~ -eye perches (1) n
059.9
~ -eyed (1) adj 081.4
~ -eyed perch (3) n
059.9
~ -eyes (5) n 084.9
~ pipe (1) n 071.7
going (4552) v 024.7
~ a-courting (2) v
081.4
~ about (1) v 010.4
~ across (1) v 082.7
~ after her (1) v 081.4
~ all the way (1) v
081.7
~ along (1) v 026.1
~ (a)long (1) v 092.5
~ (a)round (1) v 024.8
~ away (2) v 007.3
~ -away parties (2) n
130.7
~ -away party (2) n
130.7
~ back (11) v 023.9
~ down (24) v 007.3
~ for (3) v 024.7
~ in (45) v 025.5

~ in and out the
windows (1) n 130.3
~ into (1) v 056.9
~ like (1) v 105.7
~ off (3) v 024.7
~ on (45) v 070.1
~ on up (1) v 053.6
~ out (27) v 024.7
~ out a lot (1) v 081.4
~ out courting (1) v
081.4
~ out of (2) v 062.4
~ out together (1) v
081.4
~ out with (2) v 081.4
~ out with her (3) v
081.4
~ over (9) v 042.4
~ regular (3) v 081.4
~ steady (170) v 081.4
~ steady together (1) v
081.4
~ steady with (1) v
081.4
~ steady with her (3) v
081.4
~ through (7) v 085.2
~ to (1714) v 024.7
~ t(o) (1) v 024.7
~ to bed (1) v 065.1
~ to bribe her (1) v
081.4
~ to Europe (1) v
080.3
~ to marry her (1) v
081.4
~ to see her (2) v 081.4
~ to see them (1) v
081.4
~ to the pen (1) v
033.9
~ -to-town (1) adj
075.6
~ to up (1) v 080.2
~ together (40) v 081.4
~ up (9) v 022.8
~ up Swift Creek (1) v
078.6
~ with (37) v 081.4
~ with a girl (1) v
081.4
~ with each other (1) v
081.4
~ with her (35) v 081.4
~ with him (4) v 081.4

~ with one another (1) v 081.4
~ with that girl (2) v 081.4
~ with this boy (1) v 081.4
~ with this girl (1) v 081.4
~ word (1) n 075.9
~ [P-0] (1205) v 024.7
(go)ing [P-0] (1) v 057.8
goings (2) n 025.2
~ on (1) n 080.8
goiter (1) n 077.4
gold (29) n/adj 114.1
~ beads (1) n 028.4
~ bug (1) n 060A.3
~ rings (2) n 123.1
~ squash (2) n 056.6
~ watch (5) n 004.3
~ wedding band (1) n 123.1
Gold (25) 119.8
~ Creek (1) GA 030.7
~ Ridge (1) GA 087.6
~ Rush potato (1) n 055.5
~ Rushes (1) 055.5
~ Seal (1) 114.7
goldbrick (4) n 115.4
goldbricker (2) n 115.4
goldbricking (3) v 115.4
Golddust (1) TN 087.3
golden (9) adj 090.4
~ corn (1) n 056.2
~ dewdrop (1) n 061.9
~ rain (1) n 061.9
~ retriever (1) n 081.9
~ shiner (1) n 061.2
~ something (1) n 056.9
Golden (20) 056.2
~ Bantam (2) 056.2
~ Beach (3) 106.2
~ Dawn (1) 056.2
~ Dent (1) 056.2
~ Giant (1) 056.2
~ Honey (1) 056.9
~ Honeymoon mushmelon (1) n 056.7
~ Jubilee (1) 056.9
~ Meadow (4) 029.5
~ Pa liquor (1) n 050.9
~ Strand (1) 105.7

~ Triangle Airport (1) 106.5
goldenrod (1) n 062.2
goldenseal (2) n 061.4
goldfish (13) n 061.2
Goldilocks (1) 064.4
Goldman (1) LA 087.7
Golds (1) 088.9
golf (19) n/adj 123.3
~ ball (1) n 080.7
~ balls (4) n 017.1
~ club (1) n 070.8
~ course (1) n 106.8
~ shoes (3) n 123.8
~ shorts (1) n 123.3
~ widows (1) n 063.3
Golf Creek (1) AL 030.7
Goliad (7) TX 087.5
gollies (5) interj 092.7
golly (85) adj/interj 092.3
~ whoppers (1) n 059.3
gombo 'zhe'be (1) n F 091.9
Gonalda Branch (1) TX 030.7
gondola (1) n 121.7
gondoleon cars (1) n 080.8
gone (1371) v/adj 055.1
~ above (1) v 078.6
~ and (3) v 081.3
~ away (1) v 096.9
~ back (2) v 070.4
~ back down (1) v 055.1
~ back in (1) v 057.8
~ back to (1) v 024.9
~ by (5) v 055.1
~ bye-bye (1) v 078.6
~ courting (2) v 081.4
~ down (11) v 055.1
~ dry (1) v 033.8
~ from (3) v 032.2
~ gosling (1) n 078.6
~ home (1) v 057.8
~ in (4) v 055.1
~ on (14) v 078.5
~ on to his reward (1) v 078.5
~ out (5) v 025.4
~ out of (1) v 055.1
~ over (1) v 057.8
~ sweet on her (1) v 081.4
~ through (3) v 055.1

~ to (13) v 007.2
~ to Heaven (1) v 078.5
~ to hell (4) v 078.6
~ to his reward (2) v 078.5
~ to meet his Maker (1) v 078.6
~ to rest (2) v 078.5
~ to see his Maker (1) v 078.6
~ to sleep (2) v 078.5
~ to the great beyond (1) v 078.6
~ up (6) v 055.1
~ west (1) v 078.6
Gone with the Wind (1) 055.1
gong (1) n 126.5
Gong (1) 088.7
gonorrhea (2) n 091.9
Gonzales (8) LA TX 087.2
~ Creek (1) TX 030.7
goo (11) n/adj/interj 038.4
~ fish (3) n 059.9
goober (84) n/adj 054.7
~ butter (2) n 054.7
~ nuts (1) n 054.7
~ pea (3) n 054.7
~ peas (34) n 054.7
Goober (6) 054.7
~ Creek (2) MS 030.7
goobers (487) n 054.7
Goobers (1) 021.5
good (6661) adj 071.4
~ and (31) adj 002.6
~ bedroom (1) n 007A.3
~ black dirt (1) n 029.8
~ blackland (1) n 029.8
~ buddy (5) n 129.4
~ -bye (286) interj 002.4
~ clothes (2) n 123.6
~ -conditioned (1) adj 073.2
~ day (17) n/interj 002.4
~ days (1) n 005.4
~ -dispositioned (1) adj 073.2
~ -eating beans (1) n 002.7

~ -eating farm (1) n 096.6
~ -eating squirrel (1) n 002.7
~ fertile land (3) n 029.3
~ for ducks (1) adj 006.1
~ -for-nothing (34) n/adj 069.7
~ -for-nothings (2) n 069.7
~ friend (18) n 129.4
~ friend[N-i] (1) n 129.4
~ friends (1) n 042.4
~ frost (1) n 007.5
~ god (2) n 059.3
~ gods (4) n 059.3
~ ground (3) n 029.3
~ -hearted (5) adj 073.2
~ -humored (7) adj 099.3
~ land (14) n 029.3
~ level ground (1) n 029.8
~ living room (2) n 007.8
~ loam (1) n 029.8
~ loam soil (1) n 029.8
~ -looker (3) n 125.4
~ -looking (49) adj 125.3
~ -looking bitch (1) n 125.4
~ -looking broad (1) n 125.4
~ -looking chick (1) n 125.4
~ -looking clothes (1) n 123.6
~ -looking dude (4) n 125.3
~ -looking girl (1) n 125.4
~ -looking man (1) n 125.3
~ -looking outfit (1) n 012.2
~ -looking woman (1) n 125.4
~ -nature (4) adj 073.2
~ -natured (218) adj 073.2

~ -night kiss (1) n 081.7
~ -old (183) adj 073.2
~ playroom (1) n 007A.6
~ -pulling mule (1) n 002.7
~ rain (22) n 006.1
~ rains (1) n 006.8
~ sandy land (1) n 029.8
~ sandy loam (1) n 029.8
~ shower (10) n 006.6
~ -size (16) adj 090.4
~ -sized (5) adj 090.4
~ soaking rain (1) n 006.6
~ soil (21) n 029.8
~ solid rain (1) n 006.1
~ spell of weather (1) n 005.4
~ steady rain (2) n 006.6
~ stuff (2) n 114.1
~ -tasting (1) adj 091.7
~ -tempered (6) adj 073.2
~ -time girl (1) n 113.3
~ wear (1) n 027.7
~ weather (9) n 005.4
~ -will gesture (1) n 095.7
~ [J-0] (1) adj 002.6
Good (16) 013.9
~ Book (1) 013.9
~ Bread Alley (2) 105.6
~ Christmas (5) 093.2
~ Friday (2) 002.1
~ Holiday (1) 093.2
~ Hope (1) AL 087.3
~ Humor man (2) n 099.3
~ Wishes (1) 093.2
~ Year (1) 093.3
good[N-i] (1) n 009.4
Goodbee (1) LA 087.6
gooder (1) adj 079.4
goodest (3) adj 005.8
Goodhope (1) AL 075.6
goodies (5) n 054.8
Goodlett (1) 106.4
goodness (234) n/interj 092.3
goodness' (18) adj 092.2

~ sake (10) n 092.2
~ sakes (8) n 092.2
goods (22) n/adj 010.1
~ box (1) n 010.1
Goodwater (3) AL 087.6
Goodwill (1) LA 087.3
Goodwood (1) 084.9
goody (24) n/adj/interj 054.8
~ -goody (2) adj 125.6
Goodys Creek (1) TX 030.7
gooey (5) adj 029.9
~ land (1) n 029.6
goof (9) n 073.4
~ -off (3) n 115.4
~ -up (1) n 073.4
goofball (3) n 074.7
goofed (5) v 083.4
~ off (3) v 083.4
goofing off (3) v 083.4
goofus glass (1) n 084.8
goofy (48) adj 074.7
google (9) n/adj 071.7
~ bone (1) n 071.7
~ pipe (1) n 071.7
~ vein (1) n 071.7
googly bane (1) n 071.7
gooier (1) adj 002.6
gook (8) n 126.4
gooks (9) n 126.4
goombas (1) n 127.3
goomies (1) n 125.2
goon (2) n 125.1
gooney (1) adj 073.4
goop (2) n/interj 038.3
goos (2) n 059.9
goose (45) n/adj 073.4
~ down (2) n 029.1
~ -drowning (1) n 006.1
~ egg (1) n 046.1
~ grass (1) n 015.9
~ liver (7) n 047.2
~ -liver cheese (1) n 047.2
~ -liver sausage (1) n 047.2
~ nest (1) n 065.1
~ nestes (1) n 016.8
~ picking (3) n 081.8
~ pickings (1) n 015.9
~ pipe (1) n 071.7
~ plucking (1) n 081.8
~ quills (1) n 026.5

Goose (6) 055A.4
~ Branch (1) AL 030.7
~ Hill (2) 105.4
~ Point (1) GA 087.2
goose[N-i] (1) n 016.7
gooseberries (40) n 062.6
gooseberry (18) n 062.5
gooseber(ry) (1) n 062.4
gooseneck (14) n/adj 071.7
~ hoe (4) n 080.6
~ squash (2) n 056.6
~ trailer (1) n 088.8
goosenecks (1) n 112.5
gooses (3) n 041.9
goosey (6) adj 080.8
~ goosey gander (3) n 080.8
gooshy (1) adj 088.7
gooze pipe (2) n 071.7
goozle (501) n/adj 071.7
~ bane (2) n 071.7
~ bone (2) n 071.7
~ part (1) n 071.7
~ pipe (28) n 071.7
~ thing (1) n 071.7
~ vein (2) n 071.7
goozled (1) v 057.2
goozler (3) n 071.7
goozles (1) n 071.7
goozling (2) adj 071.7
~ pipe (1) n 071.7
~ voice (1) n 071.7
GOP (6) 129.2
GOPer (1) n 129.2
gope(x2) (1) interj 037.8
gopher (250) n/adj 059.8
~ hole (5) n 081.8
~ hook (2) n 060.7
~ hooks (1) n 081.8
~ hunting (1) n 060.7
~ kind (1) n 056.6
~ mound (1) n 030.8
~ pilaf (1) n 060.7
~ races (1) n 060.7
~ rat (7) n 059.8
~ rats (1) n 060.7
~ snake (1) n 080.8
~ snakes (1) n 092.8
~ turtle (3) n 060.7
~ turtles (2) n 060.7
Gopher Hill (1) AL 060.7
gopher[N-i] (2) n 060.7
gopherberry (1) n 062.5
gopher's (1) adj 096.7

gophers (68) n 059.9
GOPs (1) 129.2
Gorda (2) 082.6
Gordo (2) AL 087.1
Gordon (12) GA 087.2
~ County (1) GA 087.5
~ Creek (2) MS 030.7
~ Road (2) 105.6
~ Street (1) 107.7
Gordons Creek (1) MS 030.7
Gordonville (1) TX 087.8
Gore (1) GA 087.7
gored (1) adj 091.8
Gorgas (2) 106.5
~ Home (1) 106.5
~ Park (1) 106.5
gorge (64) n 030.4
Gorge (1) 030.7
gorged (1) v 027.8
gorgeous (10) adj 089.6
~ day (3) n 005.4
gorges (3) n 030.4
gorilla (5) n/adj 130.1
~ ball (1) n 130.5
~ cookies (1) n 125.2
gory day (1) n 005.5
gosh (182) interj 092.2
Goshen (8) AL AR 087.3
gosling (4) n/adj 036.7
~ drownder (1) n 006.1
goslings (1) n 036.6
gospel (41) n/adj 130.8
~ message (2) n 089.4
~ music (2) n 089.5
~ quartets (1) n 130.9
~ songs (3) n 089.5
gossip (152) n/v/adj 101.3
~ (a)bout (1) v 101.3
~ box (1) n 101.3
~ lady (1) n 101.3
~ on (1) v 101.3
~ people (1) n 101.3
gossiped (a)bout (1) v 080.5
gossiper (30) n 101.3
gossipers (4) n 101.3
gossiping (38) n/v/adj 057.4
~ room (1) n 007.8
gossips (4) n/v 101.3
gossipy (2) adj 101.3
got (4453) v 012.2

~ a pumpkinseed (1) v 065.1

~ a smash on (1) v 081.4

~ acquainted to (1) v 032.8

~ after (2) v 052.8

~ around to (1) v 099.6

~ away (3) v 057.8

~ away from (1) v 013.7

~ back (5) v 057.8

~ behind (2) v 010.5

~ by (1) v 098.6

~ caught for somebody (1) v 065.1

~ down (18) v 096.4

~ down with (2) v 076.1

~ her bellyful (1) v 065.1

~ her leg broke (1) v 065.1

~ herself in trouble (2) v 065.1

~ him hooked (1) v 081.4

~ his just deserts (1) v 078.6

~ in (11) v 021.4

~ into (3) v 080.8

~ into trouble (1) v 082.2

~ it bad (1) v 081.4

~ my butt tore (1) v 065.5

~ my butt whipped (1) v 065.5

~ off (18) v 085.4

~ off of (5) v 034.4

~ off with (1) v 097.8

~ offen (1) v 034.4

~ on (5) v 095.8

~ on his breeches (1) v 065.5

~ onto (5) v 070.2

~ out (11) v 083.2

~ out of (10) v 075.8

~ out of notion (1) v 082.1

~ out [P-0] (3) v 012.9

~ over (4) v 025.4

~ rid of him (1) v 082.1

~ rocks (1) n 109.4

~ smeared (1) v 078.6

~ something in her (1) v 052.5

~ the ax (1) v 082.1

~ the hots (1) v 081.4

~ the knot tied (3) v 082.2

~ the leg broke (1) v 065.1

~ the letter (1) v 082.2

~ the shaft (1) v 082.1

~ their leg[N-i] broke (1) v 065.1

~ through (4) v 070.6

~ tired and quit (1) v 082.1

~ to (339) v 057.8

~ t(o) (1) v 024.9

`~ turn[V-t] down (1) v 082.1

~ up (55) v 097.3

~ up to (3) v 042.5

~ wasted (1) v 078.6

~ what he deserved (1) v 078.6

~ you (1) v 098.4

~ [P-0] (7) v 012.2

Got (1) 109.4

gotch-eared (1) adj 089.8

gots (5) v 052.7

gotten (45) v 034.4

~ away (1) v 057.8

~ into (1) v 053.6

~ to (1) v 012.5

~ up (2) v 003.3

~ what he deserved (1) v 078.6

Gough (3) GA 087.1

~ Church (1) 089.2

goujon (1) n F 059.9

Goula (2) 087.5

Gou(la) (1) 087.3

goulash (6) n 050.3

Goulds (3) FL 087.3

gourd (138) n/adj 017.1

~ dipper (8) n 080.8

~ dippers (2) n 056.6

~ eggs (3) n 017.1

~ -headed owl (1) n 059.2

~ leaves (1) n 061.4

~ -like (1) adj 056.5

~ melon (1) n 056.7

~ -neck squash (1) n 056.6

~ squash (1) n 056.6

Gourd (1) 117.8

gourdful (1) n 048.9

gourds (96) n 017.1

gourdy (1) adj 002.8

gourmet (6) adj 091.7

~ cooks (1) n 091.7

~ food store (1) n 116.3

~ section (1) n 116.3

~ shop (1) n 116.3

~ shops (2) n 116.3

gout (12) n 079.6

goutte (2) n F 048.1

gov (1) n 069.6

governed (1) v 085.6

governess (2) n 080.6

government (1074) n/adj 085.6

~ agencies (1) n 085.6

~ (a)partment building (1) n 119.2

~ apartments (1) n 119.2

~ apparel (1) n 085.6

~ boat (1) n 085.6

~ bodies (1) n 085.6

~ bookstore (1) n 085.6

~ bream (1) n 059.9

~ building (1) n 085.6

~ cane (1) n 051.9

~ checks (1) n 085.6

~ contracts (1) n 085.6

~ drainage ditches (1) n 030.2

~ help (1) n 085.6

~ houses (1) n 085.6

~ housing (1) n 085.6

~ -inspected (3) adj 085.6

~ inspection (1) n 085.6

~ inspector (1) n 085.6

~ job (2) n 085.6

~ land (8) n 085.6

~ man (1) n 085.6

~ map (1) n 085.6

~ money (1) n 085.6

~ name (1) n 085.6

~ -own houses (1) n 085.6

~ papers (3) n 085.6

~ people (1) n 085.6

~ program (1) n 085.6

~ project (3) n 085.6

~ railroad (1) n 084.7

~ service (1) n 085.6

~ supervision (1) n 085.6

~ thing (1) n 085.6

~ warehouse (1) n 085.6

~ water (1) n 030.6

~ whiskey (2) n 050.8

~ work (3) n 085.6

Government (12) 107.6

~ Cut (1) FL 030.2

~ Street (8) 085.6

government's (1) adj 085.6

governments (4) n 085.6

governor (13) n 115.5

Governor (3) 085.6

~ Hogg (1) 054.3

~ Street (1) 106.1

governor's split (1) n 080.6

Governor's (3) 106.5

~ Palace (2) 106.5

~ Square Mall (1) 105.3

governors (3) n 085.6

Governors Drive (1) 107.6

gowan (1) n 015.9

gowns (3) n 070.6

goy (1) n 088.9

GP killing (1) n 119.7

GQ (1) 123.6

grab (13) n/v/adj 049.4

~ -alls (1) n 116.2

~ fishing (1) n 093.8

~ him (1) v 033.2

Graball (1) AL 087.6

grabbed (5) v 070.9

~ up (1) v 075.8

grabber (1) n 073.5

grabbing (1) v 077.9

grabhook (1) n 093.6

grabs (2) v 075.8

grace (10) n/v 092.7

Grace Business College (2) 083.6

grace[V-r] (1) v 049.7

graceful (1) adj 074.1

gracefully (1) adv 074.1

Graceland (1) 086.8

gracious (82) adj/interj 092.2

grac(ious) (2) interj 092.2
grackles (1) n 059.3
grade (1356) n/adj 065.8
~ kid (1) n 068.7
~ school (95) n 083.7
~ -school friends (1) n 129.6
~ -school student (1) n 068.7
~ schools (3) n 125.7
Grade-A dairies (1) n 084.8
grade[N-i] (4) n 083.7
graded (20) v/adj 031.6
~ road (5) n 031.7
~ roads (7) n 031.6
grader (14) n 120.6
graders (5) n 001A.3
grades (39) n 031.6
grading (8) v 080.9
gradual (1) adv 005.8
gradually (2) adv 075.8
graduate (18) n/v/adj 068.7
~ student (2) n 068.7
graduate[V-r] (2) v 098.6
~ for (1) v 075.6
graduated (4) v 070.7
graduates (8) n 070.7
graduating (3) v 066.8
graduation (4) n/adj 130.7
~ parties (2) n 130.7
~ ring (1) n 123.1
Grady (10) AL GA 087.3
~ County (1) GA 087.4
~ Creek (1) AL 030.7
~ Homes (1) 105.3
~ Hospital (1) 084.5
Grafonola (1) 080.9
Grafonolas (1) 080.7
graft (6) n/v/adj 115.4
~ wood (1) n 092.7
grafted (2) v/adj 080.9
grafter (2) n 115.5
grafting (1) n 065.9
grafts (1) n 070.6
graham (18) n/adj 044.3
~ bread (9) n 044.4
~ flour (5) n 044.4
~ -flour (1) adj 044.4
Graham (5) 107.8
~ Avenue (1) 107.8
~ Park (1) 105.2

grain (192) n/adj 014.4
~ alcohol (1) n 050.8
~ bin (51) n 014.4
~ bins (20) n 014.4
~ box (1) n 014.4
~ boxes (1) n 014.4
~ cradle (2) n 041.6
~ crib (1) n 014.4
~ cribs (1) n 014.4
~ elevator (13) n 014.4
~ elevators (7) n 014.4
~ house (15) n 014.4
~ houses (1) n 014.4
~ -make[V-p] (1) v 052.9
~ mill (1) n 014.4
~ pen (1) n 014.4
~ room (3) n 014.4
~ sack (2) n 019.7
~ sacks (2) n 019.6
~ shed (7) n 014.4
~ sheds (1) n 014.4
~ silo (1) n 014.4
~ sorghum (1) n 051.2
~ storage (4) n 014.4
~ storage bin (1) n 014.4
~ sugar (1) n 051.5
~ trees (1) n 061.8
grainage (1) n 014.4
grains (2) n 014.4
grainy (1) adj 090.4
gram (1) n 099.6
Gram (3) 064.2
grama grass (1) n 015.9
Grambling (1) 083.6
grammar (127) n/adj 083.7
~ school (107) n 083.7
~ -school student (1) n 068.7
~ schools (6) n 083.7
Gramophone (4) 081.8
Gramp (4) 064.1
Gramps (16) 064.1
grampus (1) n 060.8
Grampy (2) 064.2
Gran (9) 064.1
~ -Gran (1) 064.2
Granada (1) TX 087.2
granaries (21) n 014.4
granary (295) n/adj 014.4
~ house (2) n 014.4
~ houses (1) n 014.4
granar(y) (1) n 014.4

gran(ary) (4) n 014.4
Granary (1) 014.4
grand (41) n/adj 081.8
~ affair (1) n 130A.7
~ babies (1) n 026.3
~ boy (3) n 064.3
~ boys (1) n 064.3
~ girl (2) n 053.8
~ kids (13) n 064.3
~ marshall (1) n 093.6
~ people (1) n 063.8
~ young ones (5) n 064.3
Grand (65) 064.1
~ Avenue (1) 031.7
~ Bank (1) 088.8
~ Bay (3) AL 087.8
~ Bayou (8) LA 030.7
~ Boy (1) 011.1
~ Cane (1) LA 087.1
~ Cane Creek (1) LA 030.7
~ Canyon (4) 030.5
~ Canyons (1) 081.8
~ Cheniere (4) LA 087.2
~ Coteau (1) LA 087.4
~ Divisions (1) 084.9
~ Ecore (1) LA 087.8
~ -Grand (1) 064.2
~ Island (2) LA 087.5
~ Isle (8) LA 087.7
~ Isle ham (2) n 080.7
~ Lake (4) LA 030.7
~ Mar(ais) Lake (1) AR 030.7
~ Old Party (4) 129.2
~ Old Party people (1) n 129.2
~ Ole Opry (5) 106.4
~ Ole Opry House (2) 106.4
~ Prairie (3) AR TX 087.6
~ River (1) LA 030.7
grandbabies (1) n 064.3
grandbaby (4) n 064.3
Grandbury (1) TX 086.1
grandchild (3) n 064.3
grandchildren (49) n 064.3
grandchildrens (2) n 016.7
grandchilds (1) n 064.3
Grandda (1) 064.1

granddad (11) n 064.1
Granddad (68) 064.1
granddaddies (5) n 064.1
granddaddy (59) n/adj 064.1
~ graybeard (2) n 061.9
~ graybeards (1) n 062.2
~ house (1) n 014.1
~ spider (1) n 061.3
Granddaddy (313) 064.1
granddaddy's (6) adj 062.3
~ beard (1) n 062.3
~ farm (1) n 064.1
~ land (1) n 064.1
Granddaddy's (9) 064.1
~ farm (1) n 064.1
~ father (1) n 064.1
~ place (1) n 064.1
~ uncle (1) n 068.2
Granddad's side (2) n 064.1
granddads (1) n 064.1
granddaughter (45) n 064.8
granddaughters (11) n 064.8
grande (1) adj S 064.1
Grande (31) 030.3
grandest (1) adj 093.8
grandfather (873) n 064.1
grandfath(er) (1) n 064.1
grandfa(ther) (2) n 064.1
Grandfather (25) 064.1
grandfather's (21) adj 064.1
~ business (1) n 064.1
~ father (1) n 064.1
~ home (1) n 064.1
~ house (2) n 064.1
~ land (1) n 064.1
~ lineage (1) n 064.1
~ name (3) n 064.1
~ people (2) n 066.5
~ sister's chair (1) n 008.8
grandfathers (14) n 064.1
grandiflora (1) n 062.9
grandma (25) n/adj 065.2
~ dust (1) n 080.8
Grandma (485) 064.2
~ Moses (1) 064.2
grandma[N-k] (1) adj 064.2

grandmamma (5) n 064.2
Grandmamma (63) 064.2
grandmamma[N-k] room (1) n 043.8
Grandmamma's (1) 064.2
Grandmammy (2) 064.2
grandma's (4) adj 064.2
~ daddy (1) n 064.2
~ picture[N-i] (1) n 012.2
~ side (1) n 066.5
Grandma's (11) 064.2
~ house (2) n 064.2
grandmas (1) n 064.2
Grandmom (7) 064.2
grandmother (950) n 064.2
grandmoth(er) (3) n 064.2
Grandmother (42) 064.2
grandmother[N-i] (1) n 064.2
grandmother[N-k] (2) adj 043.9
~ time (1) n 064.2
grandmother's (18) adj 064.2
~ fan (1) n 089.9
~ house (2) n 054.2
~ people (1) n 064.2
~ picture (1) n 064.2
~ room (1) n 007A.2
grandmothers (20) n 064.2
grandpa (21) n 064.1
~ clock (1) n 092.7
~ turtles (1) n 060.6
Grandpa (502) 064.1
(Grand)pa (1) 063.5
Grandpap (8) 064.1
Grandpapa (19) 064.1
Grandpapa's (1) 064.1
grandpappy (1) n 064.1
Grandpappy (7) 064.1
grandparent (4) n 064.1
grandparents (135) n 063.8
grandparents' (3) adj 063.8
~ home (1) n 063.8
Grandpa's (8) 064.1
~ chair (1) n 008.8
~ grave (1) n 064.1
~ people (1) n 066.5
~ place (1) n 070.4

~ rocking chair (1) n 008.9
grandpas (1) n 064.1
Grandpop (2) 064.1
Grandpops (1) 064.1
grands (7) n 064.3
Grands (1) 088.9
grandson (7) n 064.2
grandson's house (2) n 014.1
grandsons (2) n 001.2
Grandview Avenue (1) 107.7
Grandy (3) 064.1
Granex (1) 055.6
Grange (26) 070.4
~ Hall (1) TX 087.8
Granger (2) TX 087.2
granite (22) n/adj 031.6
~ bucket (4) n 017.3
~ buckets (2) n 017.3
~ business (1) n 080.6
~ dogs (1) n 008.3
~ -(e)namel type (1) n 002.6
~ pans (2) n 084.9
~ pots (1) n 017.6
~ tubs (1) n 010.6
Granite Mountain (5) TX 105.4
graniteware pots (1) n 017.6
grannied (1) v 065.2
grannies (32) n 065.2
granny (231) n/v/adj 065.2
~ boy (1) n 065.2
~ doctor (3) n 065.2
~ graybeard (1) n 061.9
~ graybeards (1) n 062.3
~ lady (5) n 065.2
~ mother (1) n 065.2
~ nurse (1) n 065.2
~ prints (1) n 084.9
~ rag (1) n 088.7
~ rockers (1) n 008.8
~ sacks (1) n 019.6
~ woman (79) n 065.2
~ women (12) n 065.2
Granny (166) 064.2
~ Branch (1) FL 030.7
~ Ridge (1) TN 080.8
Granny's (2) 008.8

~ prayer chair (1) n 008.8
~ room (1) n 064.2
Grano (1) 055.7
granola bread (1) n 044.3
grant (1) n 100.5
Grant (26) AL AR LA 068.3
~ curs (1) n 033.3
~ Parish (2) LA 087.3
~ Park (10) 106.4
granted (5) v 024.7
grants (2) n 085.6
Grantsboro (1) TN 087.6
Grantsville Hollow Road (1) 107.7
Grantville (1) GA 087.1
granulated (5) adj 066.8
~ coffee (1) n 048.8
~ sugar (2) n 065.8
grape (43) n/adj 121.8
~ arbor (2) n 061.6
~ arbors (1) n 062.4
~ Coke (1) n 121.8
~ drink (2) n 121.8
~ jack (1) n 050.8
~ jelly (8) n 051.6
~ juice (3) n 114.7
~ tomato (1) n 055.3
~ tomatoes (1) n 055.3
~ vineyard (1) n 099.7
~ whiskey (1) n 050.8
~ wine (5) n 050.9
grape[N-i] (1) n 061.8
grapefruit (63) n/adj 055.1
~ knife (2) n 104.3
~ spoon (2) n 017.8
~ tree (5) n 061.8
~ trees (4) n 061.8
~ wars (1) n 130.5
grapefruits (8) n 055.1
Grapeland Road (1) 031.6
grapes (33) n 061.8
grapevine (6) n/adj 057.3
~ swing (4) n 022.9
grapevines (6) n 057.3
graph (1) n 097.9
Graphophone (1) 088.7
graqueno (1) n S 061.8
gras (1) adj F 047.2
Gras (13) 083.2
grasp (1) v 057.5
grasping (1) v 073.5
grass (1303) n/adj 019.7

~ bag (3) n 019.7
~ bags (1) n 019.7
~ broom (1) n 120.7
~ bug (1) n 060A.9
~ bugs (1) n 060A.9
~ burr (3) n 015.9
~ burrs (2) n 015.9
~ cap (1) n 014.6
~ chimley (1) n 008.1
~ clover (1) n 041.5
~ colt (3) n 065.7
~ cot (1) n 031.9
~ cutter (2) n 120.2
~ cutters (1) n 120.8
~ eaters (1) n 061.1
~ field (1) n 029.5
~ frogs (4) n 060.3
~ grinder (1) n 120.4
~ gumbo (1) n 055A.5
~ -gut pony (1) n 080.8
~ hay (5) n 014.7
~ median (2) n 107.3
~ pasture (1) n 029.5
~ patch (1) n 015.6
~ plat (1) n 031.9
~ prairie (1) n 029.5
~ rake (11) n 120.7
~ rakes (3) n 120.7
~ roots (1) n 061.4
~ -roots kind (1) n 088.7
~ sack (60) n 019.7
~ sacks (28) n 019.7
~ shrimp (1) n 060.9
~ shrimps (1) n 060.9
~ snake (6) n 080.8
~ snakes (12) n 081.8
~ strip (16) n 031.9
~ strips (1) n 031.9
~ sweeper (1) n 120.7
~ ticks (1) n 060A.5
~ widow (257) n 063.3
~ widower (4) n 063.3
~ widows (10) n 063.3
~ yard (1) n 076.7
~ young one (1) n 065.7
Grass (1) 131.3
Grassack (1) n G 019.7
grassed (3) v 015.9
~ out (2) v 015.9
~ over (1) v 030.5
grasses (10) n 015.9
grasshopper (473) n/adj 061.1

~ stock (2) n 021.6
(grass)hopper (1) n 061.1
grasshopper[N-i] (1) n 061.1
grasshoppering around (1) v 061.1
grasshoppers (423) n 061.1
grassiest (1) adj 015.9
grassland (19) n 029.5
grasslands (1) n 029.5
grassnut (2) n 054.7
grassnuts (4) n 054.7
grassplot (4) n 031.9
grassy (9) adj 029.5
~ bottom (1) n 029.5
~ lot (1) n 015.6
~ lowlands (1) n 029.5
~ strip (1) n 031.9
Grassy (4) 031.3
~ Cove (1) TN 031.3
~ Knob (1) GA 030.8
~ Lake (2) AR LA 030.7
grate (71) n 008.3
grated (2) v/adj 044.9
~ bread (1) n 044.9
grateful (23) adj 093.4
grates (27) n 008.3
gratis (2) adj 095.7
gratitude (1) n 081.2
graton (1) n F 037.3
gratuity (3) n 095.7
grave (41) n/adj 078.8
~ lots (1) n 078.8
~ rites (1) n 079.2
~ robbers (1) n 090.2
~ site (2) n 078.8
grave[N-i] (1) n 095.2
gravedigger (1) n 117.4
gravediggers (1) n 117.5
gravel (807) n/adj 031.6
~ bar (1) n 080.8
~ beds (1) n 029.9
~ cement (1) n 031.6
~ driveways (1) n 031.8
~ field (1) n 029.8
~ highway (1) n 031.6
~ land (3) n 029.8
~ pike roads (1) n 089.8
~ pit (1) n 031.6
~ pits (1) n 031.6
~ rake (1) n 120.7
~ ridges (1) n 030.8

~ road (131) n 031.6
~ roads (110) n 031.6
~ rock (1) n 031.6
~ -rock road (1) n 031.6
~ soil (2) n 029.8
~ street (1) n 031.7
~ streets (4) n 031.6
~ surface (1) n 031.6
~ tops (1) n 031.6
~ trail (1) n 031.6
~ truck (1) n 031.6
~ way (1) n 031.7
Gravel (2) 125.2
~ Gertie (1) 125.2
~ Ridge (1) AR 087.4
graveled (16) v/adj 031.6
~ road (2) n 031.6
~ roads (2) n 031.6
~ up (1) v 088.7
graveling (1) v 031.6
gravelly (11) adj 029.8
~ land (3) n 029.9
~ lands (1) n 029.4
gravels (15) n 029.8
Gravely tractor (1) n 021.6
graves (3) n 079.1
Graves Creek (1) AR 030.7
graveside (22) n/adj 078.8
~ burial (1) n 079.2
~ ceremony (3) n 079.2
~ rites (1) n 079.2
~ service (8) n 079.2
~ services (3) n 079.2
graveyard (596) n/adj 078.8
~ fences (1) n 016.6
~ hill (1) n 078.8
~ horse (1) n 061.1
~ plots (1) n 078.8
~ services (1) n 079.2
~ shift (2) n 078.8
~ stores (1) n 116.2
Graveyard (3) 030.7
~ Branch (1) AL 030.7
graveyards (28) n 078.8
gravies (2) n 048.5
graviest (2) adj 005.8
gravity (3) n/adj 030.1
~ drain (1) n 030.1
~ -fed (1) adj 118.5

~ -forced heat (1) n 118.5
gravy (236) n/adj 048.5
~ tomatoes (1) n 055.3
~ -train job (1) n 115.4
gray (660) adj 008.7
~ boys (1) n 112.5
~ cat squirrel (1) n 059.6
~ day (2) n 005.5
~ deep sand (1) n 029.8
~ digger (1) n 059.7
~ dirt (2) n 029.8
~ fox (2) n 059.5
~ fox squirrel (1) n 059.6
~ foxes (1) n 059.5
~ frog (2) n 060.2
~ frogs (1) n 060.3
~ grasshopper (1) n 061.1
~ -green (1) adj 075.7
~ hill (1) n 030.8
~ land (10) n 029.8
~ land soil (1) n 029.9
~ loam (1) n 029.8
~ -looking (1) adj 008.7
~ mare (1) n 080.9
~ melon (4) n 056.9
~ mule (1) n 050.9
~ owl (2) n 059.2
~ pot (1) n 017.7
~ sand (1) n 029.8
~ soil (9) n 029.8
~ squirrel (321) n 059.6
~ squirrels (109) n 059.6
~ -throated (1) adj 059.3
~ time (1) n 003.4
~ type (1) n 029.8
~ watermelon (2) n 056.9
Gray (56) 107.6
~ Coat Branch (1) GA 030.7
~ Irish (1) 056.9
~ Stone (2) 056.9
~ Strand (1) 056.9
~ Street (1) 115.7
graybeard (3) n 061.9
graybeards (2) n 062.2
grayfish (1) n 059.9

grayhound (1) n 033.1
grayish (10) adj 059.6
Graymont (2) 087.4
grays (3) n 056.9
Grays (11) 030.7
~ Bayou (1) TX 030.7
~ Branch (1) TN 030.7
~ Creek (1) GA 030.7
~ Mountain (1) TN 031.1
~ Station (2) TN 087.3
Grayson (2) LA TX 087.4
Graysville (2) AL TN 087.1
graze (10) n/v/adj 096.8
~ land (3) n 015.7
~ on (1) v 098.8
grazer patch (1) n 029.5
grazing (35) v/adj 029.5
~ area (2) n 015.6
~ boundary (1) n 015.7
~ field (3) n 029.5
~ field soil (1) n 029.5
~ land (15) n 029.5
~ pasture (4) n 015.7
~ place (1) n 015.7
~ spot (1) n 029.5
grease (1366) n/v/adj 023.7
~ bucket (1) n 017.4
~ buckets (1) n 017.2
~ gravy (2) n 048.5
~ gun (9) n 023.7
~ hog (2) n 035.4
~ job (13) n 023.7
~ lamp (14) n 024.3
~ lamps (10) n 024.3
~ light (6) n 024.3
~ lightning (1) n 050.8
~ -pig contest (1) n 131.1
~ pot (1) n 024.3
~ rack (3) n 023.7
~ rag (2) n 024.3
~ trap (1) n 023.7
~ wheel (1) n 023.5
grease[V-r] (30) v 023.7
grease[V-t] (10) v 023.7
greaseball (1) n 128.7
greased (531) v/adj 023.7
~ lightning (2) n 059.8
~ up (29) v 023.7
greaser (9) n 125.1
greasers (28) n 128.7

greases (1) v 023.7
greasier (2) adj 023.8
greasies (2) n 023.8
greasiest (3) adj 023.8
greasing (32) v 023.7
~ up (1) v 023.7
greasings (1) n 023.7
greasy (928) adj 023.8
  ~ bean (1) n 055A.4
  ~ beans (1) n 055A.4
  ~ bellies (1) n 128.7
  ~ -food restaurants (1) n 080.6
Greasy (3) 031.7
  ~ Cove Road (1) 031.7
  ~ Creek (1) TN 030.7
great (367) adj 089.6
  ~ -aunt (10) n 067.9
  ~ -aunts (1) n 067.9
  ~ beams (1) n 014.5
  ~ day (1) interj 092.2
  ~ -grandchild (1) n 064.3
  ~ -grandchildren (4) n 064.3
  ~ -granddaddy (1) n 064.1
  ~ -granddaddy's farm (1) n 064.1
  ~ -granddaughter (1) n 064.8
  ~ -grandfather (27) n 064.1
  ~ -grandfather's (1) adj 064.1
  ~ -grandfathers (2) n 064.1
  ~ -grandma[N-k] time (1) n 064.2
  ~ -grandmother (17) n 064.2
  ~ -grandparents (5) n 063.8
  ~ -grandparents' (1) adj 063.8
  ~ -grands (4) n 064.3
  ~ -granny (1) n 064.2
  ~ -great-aunt (1) n 067.9
  ~ -great-grandaddy (1) n 064.1
  ~ -great-grandfather (1) n 064.1

~ -great-grandmother (2) n 064.2
~ -great-grandpa (1) n 064.1
~ -great-great-grandpa (1) n 064.1
~ hall (1) n 007A.5
~ horn owl (1) n 059.2
~ horned owl (7) n 059.2
~ horned owls (2) n 059.2
~ house (1) n 012.1
~ looker (1) n 125.4
~ -old (4) adj 008.1
~ reward in the sky (1) n 078.6
~ room (4) n 007.8
~ rooms (1) n 007.8
~ squirrel (1) n 059.7
~ -uncle (6) n 068.2
~ -uncle's children (1) n 068.2
~ -uncles (3) n 068.2
Great (32) 088.7
~ Depression (1) 088.7
~ Fire of Atlanta (1) 131.1
~ -Granddaddy (10) 064.1
~ -Grandma (3) 064.2
~ -Grandma's (1) 064.2
~ -Grandpa (1) 064.1
~ Northern (6) 055A.3
~ Northern bean (1) n 055A.3
~ Northern beans (5) n 055A.3
~ Northerns (1) 055A.3
~ War (1) 085.8
greater (2) adj 066.1
greatest (1) adj 053.5
Grecians (1) 128.4
Greece (2) 087.9
greedy (5) adj 073.5
~ gut (2) n 073.5
Greek (10) 128.4
Greekos (1) 128.4
Greeks (15) 128.4
green (1198) n/adj 056.8
~ -apple quickstep (1) n 091.8
~ around the gills (1) adj 072.9

~ -back speller (1) n 080.6
~ bean (49) n 055A.4
~ bean[N-i] (2) n 055A.4
~ beans (331) n 055A.4
~ beer (2) n 050.8
~ bush bean (1) n 055A.4
~ butter bean (2) n 055A.3
~ butter beans (4) n 055A.3
~ cabbage (2) n 055A.1
~ cane (4) n 088.9
~ -cane syrup (1) n 051.3
~ -cedar limbs (1) n 061.4
~ coffee (5) n 048.8
~ corn (19) n 056.2
~ cover (2) n 054.8
~ crop (1) n 042.1
~ elm (1) n 061.8
~ fig (1) n 061.4
~ frog (42) n 060.3
~ frogs (39) n 060.3
~ frying top[N-i] (1) n 061.4
~ garter snake (1) n 061.9
~ grasshoppers (1) n 061.1
~ gumbo (1) n 055A.5
~ ham (1) n 046.3
~ hay (2) n 014.8
~ hoppergrass (1) n 061.1
~ houses (1) n 012.1
~ hull (7) n 054.8
~ kraut (2) n 002.7
~ light (4) n 130.2
~ light bugs (1) n 060A.1
~ lima bean (1) n 055A.3
~ limas (1) n 055A.3
~ lizards (2) n 060.5
~ log (2) n 008.5
~ logs (1) n 008.5
~ -looking (1) adj 090.4
~ meat (2) n 046.3
~ moss (2) n 081.8

~ muscadine (1) n 062.4
~ oak (1) n 061.8
~ oak tree (1) n 061.8
~ oakwood (1) n 008.5
~ oats (1) n 042.1
~ onion (69) n 055.7
~ -onion top (1) n 055.7
~ onions (267) n 055.7
~ part (1) n 055A.5
~ peach (4) n 054.3
~ peaches (2) n 054.3
~ peas (10) n 055A.4
~ pepper (1) n 055.7
~ peppers (4) n 055.8
~ pine (1) n 008.5
~ plastic bag (1) n 123.7
~ room (1) n 007A.5
~ running bean (1) n 055A.4
~ salad (3) n 055A.5
~ sallet (1) n 055A.5
~ sea turtle (1) n 060.6
~ shades (1) n 009.5
~ shell (4) n 054.8
~ shoots (1) n 055.7
~ snake (20) n 088.9
~ snakes (25) n 084.8
~ snap bean (2) n 055A.4
~ snap beans (4) n 055A.4
~ spring frogs (1) n 060.3
~ spring onions (1) n 055.7
~ squash (1) n 056.6
~ squashes (1) n 056.6
~ stick (1) n 008.5
~ string bean (1) n 055A.4
~ stringless (2) n 055A.4
~ stripe (1) n 056.9
~ stuff (7) n 114.5
~ thumb (2) n 095.8
~ time lady (1) n 098.4
~ -tinted frog (1) n 060.3
~ tobacco (1) n 102.7
~ -tomato pickle (1) n 080.8
~ tomatoes (6) n 055.3

~ top (1) n 055.7
~ -top onion (1) n 055.7
~ -top onions (1) n 055.7
~ tops (2) n 055.7
~ tree frog (2) n 060.3
~ tree frogs (2) n 060.3
~ trout (5) n 059.9
~ turtle (4) n 060.6
~ turtles (3) n 060.6
~ -type shades (1) n 009.5
~ vegetable matter (1) n 081.9
~ vegetables (1) n 050.4
~ watermelon (1) n 056.9
~ whiskey (2) n 050.8
~ widow (1) n 063.3
~ window shades (1) n 009.5
~ wood (8) n 008.5
~ worm (1) n 060.5
~ worms (1) n 060.5
Green (52) 114.5
~ Briar Lake (1) TX 030.7
~ Circle (1) 107.7
~ Cove Springs (3) FL 087.2
~ England (1) 056.9
~ Forest (1) AR 087.6
~ Hill (1) 105.4
~ Hills (1) 105.1
~ Island (1) GA 087.3
~ Mountain (2) 055.4
~ Mountain Branch (1) TN 030.7
~ Oak[N-i] (1) 106.2
~ Pod Stringless (1) 055A.4
~ Pond (1) AL 087.2
~ River (1) TN 030.7
~ Stamps (1) 114.5
~ Street (1) 107.7
~ Valley (2) TX 106.1
~ Wonders (1) 055A.4
green[N-i] (28) n 055A.5
greenback (8) n 114.5
Greenback (1) TN 087.5
greenbacks (12) n 114.5
Greenbriar (2) 105.6
Greenbrier (4) AR 030.7

Greene (13) GA TN 087.1
~ County (6) GA MS TN 087.5
~ Mountain (1) TN 031.1
greener (1) adj 002.6
greeneries (1) n 088.9
greenery (1) n 101.4
Greeneville (2) TN 087.2
Greenfield (2) MS TN 087.5
greengrocers (1) n 052.6
greenhead (3) n/adj 059.3
~ fly (1) n 060A.5
greenheads (2) n 060.6
greenhorn (10) n 069.9
greenhouse (16) n 118.1
greenies (2) n 127.9
greenish (3) adj 055.5
Greenland (1) 086.3
Greenleaf Baptist Church (1) 089.1
Green's (1) 105.9
greens (1211) n 055A.5
Greens (4) TX 030.7
~ Chapel (1) AR 087.2
~ Cove (1) AL 087.4
Greensboro (9) AL GA NC 087.6
Greensbor(o) (1) AL 087.3
Greensburg (8) LA PA 087.9
Greenville (64) AL AR FL GA LA MS NC SC TX 087.6
Greenwood (25) AL AR LA MS 087.5
~ Cemetery (1) 078.8
~ Road (1) 107.7
Greer (1) SC 087.2
Greers Ferry (2) AR 030.7
Greeting (12) 093.2
Greetings (15) 093.2
gregarious (1) adj 074.1
Gregg Addition (1) TX 087.3
Gregorian (1) 119.6
Grenada (17) MS 088.7
~ Arden (1) 113.8
~ County (2) MS 085.5
~ Hills (1) TX 030.8
~ Lake (1) MS 087.2

grenade (2) n 072.5
Greneau (1) FL 087.3
grenier (3) n F 014.3
grenouilles (1) n F 060.3
Gresham (1) 030.7
Gretna (10) LA 087.6
~ Green (1) 087.9
grew (724) v 065.6
~ like (2) v 065.6
~ on (2) v 075.8
~ out (1) v 065.6
~ up (240) v 065.6
~ up in (7) v 065.6
~ up with (5) v 065.6
grewed (7) v 065.6
~ up (4) v 065.6
grewen (1) v 065.6
grewing (1) v 065.6
Grey (3) 056.9
Greyhound bus (3) n 109.9
Greynolds Park (2) 106.7
griddle (74) n/adj 017.5
~ bread (3) n 044.7
~ cake (9) n 045.3
~ cakes (39) n 045.3
griddles (2) n 017.5
gridiron (1) n 023.5
gridirons (1) n 008.3
grie (1) n F 036.8
grief (22) n 079.3
~ -stricken (1) adj 079.3
Griesedieck (1) 121.9
grieve (2) v 079.3
~ over (1) v 025.3
grieved (3) v 079.3
grieving (7) n/v 079.3
griffe (3) n F 069.5
griffes (1) n F 088.7
Griffin (32) GA 087.1
~ Road (2) 031.6
Griflet (1) 107.8
Griggs (1) 115.7
Griggses (1) 053.2
grigne (1) n 055A.6
Grigsby (2) LA 087.5
~ Island (1) LA 087.5
grill (11) n 116.4
grillade (1) n F 081.9
grills (1) n 116.6
Grills Creek (1) AR 030.7
grillwork (1) n 070.9
Grimes County (2) TX 087.8

grimy (2) adj 023.8
grin (1) v 036.4
grind (147) v/adj 023.5
~ rock (120) n 023.5
~ rocks (7) n 023.5
~ up (1) v 013.8
~ wheel (3) n 023.5
grind[V-p] (1) v 053.4
grinder (56) n/adj 023.5
~ stone (1) n 023.5
grinders (7) n 121.7
grinding (294) n/v/adj 023.5
~ cane (1) n 051.4
~ machine (1) n 088.9
~ mill (2) n 019.8
~ rock (113) n 023.5
~ rocks (4) n 023.5
~ stone (128) n 023.5
~ stones (5) n 023.5
~ wheel (28) n 023.5
~ wheels (2) n 023.5
grindle (19) n/adj 059.9
~ fish (1) n 059.9
grindles (4) n 059.9
grinds (1) v 013.8
Grindstaff Branch (1) TN 030.7
grindstone (430) n 023.5
grindstones (14) n 023.5
gringa (1) n S 069.4
gringo (10) n S 069.4
gringos (6) n S 069.4
grinner (7) n 059.9
grinners (5) n 059.9
grinnie (1) n 059.9
grinning (2) v/adj 073.7
~ like (1) v 073.7
~ sound (1) n 036.4
gripe about (1) v 058.2
griper (2) n 073.5
griping (4) adj 073.5
grippe (9) n 076.5
gripy (1) adj 074.7
gris (11) n/adj F 090.4
~ -gris (5) n F 090.4
grist (7) n 019.8
gristle (11) n/adj 046.6
~ bone (1) n 071.7
~ growth (1) n 078.2
gristles (2) n 035.6
gristmill (57) n 019.8
gristmills (6) n 080.9
grit (15) n/v/adj 044.6
~ grats (1) n 060.3

~ lovers (1) n 050.6
grit[N-i] (9) n 050.6
grits (964) n/adj 050.6
  ~ -and-cheese casserole (1) n 050.6
  ~ corn bread (1) n 044.7
  ~ -like (1) adj 050.6
  ~ mush (1) n 050.6
  ~ pot (1) n 050.6
gritses (1) n 070.6
gritsmill (6) n 019.8
gritted (4) v/adj 044.9
  ~ bread (1) n 044.6
  ~ -cornmeal bread (1) n 044.6
gritter (4) n 050.6
gritting (1) v 060.3
gritty (8) n/adj 073.5
grivines (1) n 099.5
grizzly day (1) n 006.6
groan (2) n/v 036.3
groaning (2) v 036.2
groans (1) v 036.3
grocer (4) n/adj 116.2
  ~ store (2) n 116.1
groceries (72) n 094.2
grocers (1) n 052.6
grocery (257) n/adj 094.2
  ~ bag (24) n 019.5
  ~ bags (5) n 019.5
  ~ basket (4) n 020.1
  ~ bin (1) n 010.1
  ~ business (4) n 065.8
  ~ buying (2) n 094.2
  ~ day (1) n 010.6
  ~ going (1) n 092.9
  ~ -mix candy (1) n 095.9
  ~ room (4) n 010.1
  ~ sack (7) n 019.5
  ~ shopping (4) n 094.2
  ~ store (147) n 094.2
  ~ stores (24) n 116.1
  ~ truck (1) n 109.6
  ~ wagon (1) n 080.9
groc(ery) (1) adj 116.1
  ~ store (1) n 116.1
grocery[N-i] (5) n 048.4
grog (1) n 121.9
groggers (1) n 113.9
groggy (3) adj 076.6
groin (1) n 066.8
groom (20) n 038.6

groom[N-k] maid (1) n 082.3
groomed (1) v 028.1
grooming (10) v 028.1
groom's (3) adj 082.3
  ~ maid (2) n 082.3
  ~ waiter (1) n 082.3
groomsman (38) n 082.3
groomsmen (13) n 082.3
groomy (1) adj 028.1
groove (17) n/adj 021.8
  ~ lumber (1) n 011.2
grooves (2) n 017.9
groovy (2) adj 125.2
  ~ goomies (1) n 125.2
Gros Pop (1) F 064.1
grosbeak (2) n 059.2
gross (21) n/adj 125.1
Gross (2) G 093.3
  ~ Neu Jahr (1) G 093.3
  ~ Ranch (1) 081.9
grosse (1) adj G 035.5
Grosse (12) 064.2
  ~ Mom (1) 064.2
  ~ Tete (8) LA 030.7
  ~ Tete Bayou (3) LA 030.3
grossesse (1) n F 065.1
grossest-looking (1) adj 059.6
grossness (1) n 080.7
grouch (6) n 075.1
grouchy (19) adj 075.2
ground (899) n/v/adj 060.5
  ~ almonds (1) n 054.9
  ~ beef (29) n 121.2
  ~ cement (1) n 023.4
  ~ cherries (1) n 054.7
  ~ chuck (9) n 121.2
  ~ cisterns (1) n 052.5
  ~ cornmeal (1) n 074.4
  ~ crawler (1) n 088.8
  ~ dogs (1) n 060.5
  ~ floor (2) n 119.4
  ~ fog (1) n 006.7
  ~ frog (2) n 060.4
  ~ frogs (1) n 060.4
  ~ frost (1) n 060.4
  ~ goobers (1) n 054.7
  ~ hominy (2) n 050.6
  ~ hornet (1) n 060A.5
  ~ huggers (1) n 108.5
  ~ itch (35) n 080.6
  ~ ivy (3) n 061.4

  ~ lamb (1) n 121.4
  ~ limestone (1) n 031.6
  ~ lizards (1) n 060.5
  ~ machine (1) n 023.5
  ~ meat (3) n 046.8
  ~ mole (6) n 059.8
  ~ mullet (2) n 059.9
  ~ mullets (1) n 059.9
  ~ oak (1) n 061.9
  ~ owl (2) n 059.2
  ~ pea (10) n 054.7
  ~ peas (93) n 054.7
  ~ pepper (2) n 051.7
  ~ pipe (1) n 011.5
  ~ poles (1) n 016.4
  ~ potato (1) n 055.5
  ~ puppies (4) n 060.5
  ~ rail (2) n 016.4
  ~ rat (1) n 059.8
  ~ rattle (3) n 092.8
  ~ rattler (8) n 080.9
  ~ rattlers (2) n 080.8
  ~ rattlesnake (2) n 093.9
  ~ rattle(snake) (1) n 088.9
  ~ red pepper (1) n 051.7
  ~ rock (2) n 023.5
  ~ -rock road (1) n 031.6
  ~ roomers (1) n 054.7
  ~ round (6) n 121.1
  ~ runners (1) n 054.7
  ~ sausage meat (1) n 121.6
  ~ slide (1) n 021.9
  ~ snake (2) n 088.7
  ~ soaker (1) n 006.6
  ~ squirrel (239) n 059.8
  ~ squirrels (77) n 059.8
  ~ steak (3) n 121.2
  ~ steps (1) n 010.7
  ~ stone (1) n 023.5
  ~ tomatoes (1) n 055.3
  ~ turtle (3) n 060.7
  ~ up (2) v 052.6
  ~ -up corn (1) n 050.6
  ~ -up meat (1) n 121.2
  ~ wasp (2) n 060A.6
  ~ wasp[N-i] (1) n 060A.6
  ~ waspes (1) n 060A.6
  ~ worm (10) n 060.5
  ~ worms (4) n 060.5

Ground (4) 087.5
groundbreaker (2) n 021.7
groundhog (40) n/adj 059.8
  ~ sawmill (1) n 080.9
  ~ thrasher (1) n 041.9
  ~ whiskey (1) n 050.8
groundhogs (12) n 059.8
groundkeepers (1) n 015.6
groundnut (4) n 054.7
groundnuts (4) n 054.7
grounds (23) n/adj 048.8
  ~ keeper (1) n 119.5
Grounds (1) 106.4
group (198) n/v/adj 082.8
  ~ arrangements (1) n 065.9
  ~ off (1) v 075.6
grouper (21) n/adj 059.9
  ~ fish (1) n 059.9
groupers (8) n 059.9
groups (8) n 129.6
grouse (2) n 121.5
Groust (1) 107.6
grove (313) n/adj 061.6
  ~ disc (1) n 021.7
Grove (129) 061.6
  ~ Hill (4) AL 030.8
  ~ Park (2) 106.1
  ~ River (1) GA 030.7
groves (27) n 061.6
Groves Chill Tonic (1) 078.4
grow (830) v 065.6
  ~ back (1) v 065.6
  ~ back up (1) v 065.6
  ~ in (5) v 055A.6
  ~ like (1) v 096.7
  ~ on (4) v 065.6
  ~ over (1) v 065.6
  ~ up (63) v 065.6
  ~ up on (1) v 053.2
gr(ow) up (1) v 065.6
grow[V-p] (10) v 065.6
  ~ in (1) v 013.3
  ~ out (1) v 013.8
  ~ up (2) v 065.6
grow[V-r] (9) v 065.6
  ~ up (4) v 065.6
grow[V-t] (2) v 065.6
growed (543) v/adj 065.6
  ~ down (1) v 065.6
  ~ in (2) v 053.2

~ on up (1) v 065.6
~ out (1) v 065.6
~ up (137) v 064.7
~ -up (5) adj 065.6
~ up at (1) v 065.6
~ up in (1) v 065.6
~ up on (1) v 065.6
groweder-up (1) adj 066.1
growen (1) v 065.6
grower (1) n 080.6
growers (1) n 065.6
growing (187) v/adj 065.5
~ like (1) v 065.6
~ mash (1) n 060.4
~ moon (1) n 080.9
~ on (1) v 027.2
~ pains (1) n 080.1
~ up (51) v 064.7
growling (2) v 036.2
grown (1078) v/adj 065.6
~ in (5) v 053.3
~ like (1) v 065.6
~ up (79) v 065.6
~ -up (95) adj 064.7
~ up with (1) v 065.6
~ -uppest (4) adj 064.7
~ -ups (3) n 065.6
growned (1) v 065.6
growner (2) adj 064.7
grownest (6) adj 064.7
growny (2) adj 064.7
grows (123) v 065.6
~ in (10) v 002.6
~ like (1) v 104.6
~ on (4) v 053.6
~ up (6) v 065.6
growth (64) n/adj 065.6
grub (63) n/v/adj 041.4
~ boat (1) n 024.6
~ bunks (1) n 080.6
~ hoe (1) n 120.4
~ up (1) v 041.4
grubbed (6) v 041.4
~ out (1) v 041.4
~ up (1) v 090.9
grubbers (1) n 060.5
grubbing (16) v/adj 041.4
~ hoe (5) n 120.4
Grube (1) n G 054.6
grubs (6) n 060.5
grubworm (50) n 060.5
grubworms (73) n 060.5
gruel (91) n 050.3
gruff (1) adj 076.4

Gruier Creek (1) TX 030.7
grumble (a)bout (1) v 012.2
grumblement (1) n 092.9
grumbling (1) v 081.9
grumpy (2) adj 075.1
Grundy (1) TN 087.4
grungy (2) adj 088.9
~ -type person (1) n 069.7
grunt (11) n/v/adj 036.3
~ meat (1) n 046.3
~ -nut worms (1) n 060.5
~ worms (1) n 060.5
GRUNT (3) interj 092.4
GRUNT(A) (1262) interj 103.7
GRUNT(A)(x2) (2) interj 103.7
GRUNT(C) chicka(x2) (5) interj 036.4
GRUNT(C)(x2) (2) interj 038.3
GRUNT(C)(x3) (1) interj 036.4
GRUNT(E) (19) interj 012.6
grunters (1) n 059.9
GRUNT(H) (526) interj 091.5
grunting (3) v/adj 057.4
~ at (1) v 097.8
~ stob (1) n 080.8
GRUNT(N) (757) interj 103.8
GRUNT(O) (23) interj 092.2
GRUNT(R) (353) interj 052.4
grunts (5) n 059.9
Gs (1) 013.7
Guadalajara (1) 087.8
Guadalupe (9) TX 030.7
~ Mountains (1) TX 031.1
~ Pass (1) TX 031.3
~ River (4) TX 030.7
guadre (1) n 081.9
Guana River (1) FL 030.7
guano (46) n/adj 081.8
~ distributor (3) n 021.7
~ knockers (1) n 021.7

~ plant (1) n 068.9
~ sack (10) n 019.7
~ sacks (10) n 019.7
~ stripper (1) n 021.8
guarantee (2) v 070.6
guard (10) n/adj 015.3
~ dog (3) n 033.3
guardhouse (1) n 112.8
guardian (809) n/adj 066.4
~ angel (2) n 066.4
guardi(an) (1) n 066.4
guard(ian) (1) n 066.4
Guardian Angels (1) 066.4
guardians (31) n 066.4
guardianship (1) n 066.4
guarding angel (1) n 066.4
guardrail (4) n 107.3
guardrails (1) n 107.3
guards (3) n 091.8
guava (9) adj 051.6
~ butter (1) n 051.6
~ dumplings (1) n 099.5
~ ice cream (1) n 096.8
~ jelly (2) n 051.6
~ pie (1) n 048.3
~ sugar (1) n 096.8
~ trees (2) n 061.8
guavas (3) n 080.8
Gue (1) 038.7
guegue (4) n F 013.8
guegues (2) n F 101.7
guepe (1) n F 060A.6
Guernsey (7) 033.6
Guernseys (2) 033.6
Guerrero (1) 087.8
guerrillas (1) n 070.9
guess (908) n/v 094.1
guessed (2) v 100.1
guesses (1) v 013.8
guessing (3) v 024.9
guesswork (1) n 025.7
guest (66) n/adj 007A.3
~ bedroom (20) n 007A.3
~ dishes (1) n 017.1
~ room (37) n 007.8
~ rooms (3) n 007.8
~ towel (3) n 018.6
~ towels (1) n 018.6
guest[N-i] (8) n 016.5
guestes (1) n 016.7

guesthouse (5) n 126.3
guesthouses (1) n 084.3
guests (1) n 016.8
Guices Creek (3) TN 030.7
guide (11) n/adj 026.1
~ horse (2) n 039.4
guideline (3) n 039.2
guidelines (4) n 107.2
guides (2) n 020.9
Guilford County (1) NC 052.5
guilty (6) adj 081.7
Guin (3) AL 087.3
guinea (84) n/adj 036.6
~ chickens (1) n 036.6
~ fowl (1) n 036.6
~ grass (5) n 015.9
~ hens (2) n 036.6
~ hog (1) n 035.5
~ nest (3) n 104.7
~ pig (2) n 035.5
~ sapsucker (1) n 059.3
~ squash (1) n 056.6
~ wasp (52) n 060A.6
~ wasp[N-i] (3) n 060A.6
~ waspes (3) n 060A.6
~ wop (1) n 127.3
Guinea (10) 082.6
~ -Nest onions (1) n 055.7
~ -Nest watermelons (1) n 056.9
~ watermelon (4) n 056.9
guineas (37) n 036.6
Guion (2) AR 087.1
guitar (29) n/adj 066.8
~ players (1) n 089.8
~ string (1) n 063.9
guitars (11) n 066.8
gulch (23) n 030.4
Gulch (2) 030.4
gulches (1) n 030.4
gulf (210) n/adj 030.9
~ area (2) n 030.9
~ boat (1) n 024.6
~ breeze (1) n 030.9
~ breezes (1) n 030.9
~ fish (1) n 059.9
~ ocean (1) n 030.9
~ runners (1) n 059.9
~ stream (1) n 030.3
~ winds (1) n 112.1

Gulf (254) 030.9
~ Coast (25) 030.9
~ filling station (1) n 030.9
~ Freeway (4) 107.1
~ Hammock (1) FL 030.9
~ Life (1) 108.5
~ Life Tower (1) 108.5
~ man (1) n 030.9
~ of Mexico (167) 030.9
~ of New Mexico (2) 030.9
~ Oil Corporation (2) 030.9
~ Power (1) 030.9
~ Shores (12) AL 087.2
~ States (4) 055.3
~ station (1) n 030.9
~ Stream (1) 080.7
Gulfport (61) MS 087.6
~ Airport (1) 106.5
~ East High School (1) 125.8
gulfs (1) n 062.9
gull (2) n 080.8
Gullah dialect (1) n 069.4
Gullatte (2) AL 087.4
gullet (11) n 071.7
gullible (2) adj 074.6
gullied (3) adj 030.5
~ hills (2) n 030.5
~ lands (1) n 030.5
gullies (148) n 030.5
Gulls (1) 024.6
gully (884) n/adj 030.5
~ buster (3) n 006.1
~ dirt (1) n 073.6
~ land (2) n 029.8
~ thumper (1) n 006.1
~ type (1) n 030.5
~ wash (6) n 030.4
~ -wash (1) v 006.1
~ washer (160) n 006.1
~ washers (18) n 006.1
~ water (1) n 006.1
gul(ly) (4) n 011.5
Gully (3) 030.7
Gulpha Gorge Creek (1) AR 030.7
gum (728) n/adj 071.9
~ ball (3) n 071.9
~ boots (1) n 026.7
~ coat (1) n 027.1

~ disease (1) n 071.9
~ log (1) n 008.5
~ maple (1) n 061.5
~ oak (1) n 061.8
~ root (1) n 061.4
~ tree (14) n 061.9
~ trees (12) n 061.5
Gum (13) 087.2
~ Branch (4) GA MS 087.2
~ Branch community (1) MS 087.4
~ Creek Baptist Church (1) 089.1
~ Flat (1) TN 087.2
~ Pond (1) MS 030.7
~ Ridge (1) LA 087.6
~ Slough Ditch (1) AR 030.7
~ Swamp (2) TN 029.6
gum[N-i] (12) n 071.9
gumbo (230) n/adj 029.8
~ aux herbes (1) n F 091.8
~ clay (4) n 029.8
~ d'herbe (2) n F 055A.4
~ dirt (1) n 029.9
~ farm (1) n 029.8
~ fevi (1) n F 092.9
~ file (6) n F 061.4
~ land (21) n 029.8
~ -limbo (2) n 061.8
~ mud (1) n 029.8
~ roads (1) n 029.9
~ soil (2) n 029.9
~ 'zhe'be (1) n F 091.8
gumbos (5) n 048.4
gummed (3) v/adj 095.9
~ up (2) v 023.8
gumming up (1) v 028.1
gummy (12) adj 023.8
~ land (4) n 029.6
~ stuff (1) n 029.8
gums (641) n 071.9
gun (169) n/adj 113.1
~ barrel (1) n 019.1
~ -barrel fire (1) n 111.6
~ -barrel fires (1) n 084.8
~ -barrel house (2) n 118.6
~ -barrel houses (1) n 080.7

~ barrels (1) n 019.2
~ grease (1) n 023.7
~ oil (1) n 024.1
~ shell (1) n 022.4
~ shells (1) n 022.4
gun[N-i] (2) n 113.1
gunboat (2) n 080.7
gunk (1) n 060A.9
gunny (3) n/adj 019.7
~ -bags (1) n 019.7
gunnysack (113) n/adj 019.7
~ races (1) n 089.7
gunny(sack) (2) n 019.7
gunnysacks (41) n 019.7
gunplay (1) n 025.4
gunpowder whiskey (1) n 050.9
guns (15) n 113.1
gunshot (8) adj 118.6
~ house (2) n 118.6
~ houses (2) n 118.6
~ wound (4) n 078.1
gunsmith (1) n 080.6
gunt (1) n 092.3
Gunter (6) AL 087.1
~ Air Force Base (1) 106.5
~ building (1) n 108.5
~ Field (2) 106.5
~ Hotel (1) 084.3
Guntersville (7) AL 087.9
~ Dam (1) AL 030.3
~ Lake (1) AL 030.7
Gunters(ville) Lake (1) AL 030.3
Gunther Landing (1) AL 087.5
Guntown (1) MS 087.7
gunwales (1) n 024.6
guppies (1) n 061.2
Gurdon (1) AL 087.5
gur(x2) (1) interj 038.3
gushed (1) v 007.2
gusher (1) n 006.1
gushes (2) n/v 080.8
gushing (1) v 057.4
gushy (2) adj 007.2
Guss (2) GA 030.7
~ Creek (1) GA 030.7
gussied (6) v 028.1
~ up (5) v 028.1
Gussy (1) 092.4
gust (1) n 007.1
gusting (14) v 007.2

~ up (2) v 007.2
gusts (1) n 112.1
gusty (13) adj 007.2
gut (51) n/adj 037.3
~ buster (1) n 006.1
~ knife (1) n 104.3
~ part (1) n 037.2
~ rot (3) n 050.9
~ sausage (1) n 037.3
Gut (2) 030.7
gut[N-i] (1) n 037.2
Guthrie Park (1) 085.1
Gutierrez (1) 086.6
guts (161) n 037.2
gutta-percha (1) n 088.7
gutted (3) v/adj 104.3
gutter (372) n/adj 011.5
~ drain (1) n 011.5
~ line (1) n 011.5
~ pipe (2) n 011.5
~ pipes (2) n 011.5
~ rock (1) n 031.6
~ section (2) n 113.9
~ trough (3) n 011.5
gutter[N-i] (4) n 011.5
guttering (26) n 011.5
gutters (476) n 011.5
guttersnipe (1) n 113.7
gutting (3) v 046.4
gutty (1) adj 092.9
guy (82) n/adj 081.5
~ wires (1) n 065.8
Guy (2) 130.8
~ Lombardo (1) 130.8
Guyno Town (1) GA 087.8
guys (22) n 129.6
Guzerat (1) 099.9
guzzard (1) n 071.7
guzzle (6) n/v 071.7
guzzler (9) n 109.4
guzzlers (9) n 109.4
gwine (23) v 024.7
~ down (2) v 065.8
~ on (2) v 024.7
~ out (1) v 025.3
~ to (6) v 024.7
~ up (2) v 070.8
~ [P-0] (5) v 024.7
Gwinnett (5) GA 087.5
~ County (2) GA 087.4
gym (126) n/adj 126.2
~ hockey (1) n 130.6
~ room (1) n 126.2
~ shoes (2) n 123.8

~ shorts (8) n 123.4
gymnasium (75) n 126.2
gymnasiums (1) n 126.2
gymnastics (1) n 126.2
gymnatorium (1) n 126.2
gyms (1) n 126.2
gyp (10) n/v/adj 033.2
   ~ away (1) v 078.6
   ~ dog (1) n 033.3
gypped him (2) v 082.1
gyppy marts (1) n 116.2
gypsum board (1) n 080.6
gypsy (7) n/adj 061.8
   ~ game (1) n 081.8
   ~ kettles (1) n 017.6
   ~ -like (1) adj 128.7
gyro (1) n 111.9

H

H (16) 114.2
~ -type steering (1) n 110.7
ha (7) interj 037.7
Haas's Creek (1) TX 030.7
haberdashery store (1) n 084.8
Habersham (8) GA 086.3
~ County (1) GA 087.2
~ Street (1) 107.7
habit (6) n 039.4
habitat (1) n 070.7
habits (7) n 065.3
habitually (2) adv 053.4
Hablers Bridge (1) AL 086.3
haceros (1) n S 017.5
Hache (1) 087.9
hacienda (1) n S 014.1
hack (30) n/adj 080.7
~ bushes (1) n 062.1
~ cough (2) n 076.5
~ cutter (1) n 023.4
~ line (1) n 080.6
~ whetter (1) n 023.4
hack(x3) (1) interj 038.2
hackberries (9) n 062.5
hackberry (89) n/adj 061.8
~ bush (1) n 062.2
~ root (1) n 061.4
~ tree (5) n 061.8
~ trees (4) n 061.8
hackber(ry) (1) n 062.4
Hackberry (2) LA 087.8
hacked (1) v 104.3
Hackens Ferry (1) LA 087.8
hacker (1) n 088.7
Hackett (1) AR 087.9
hacking (55) n/v/adj 076.5
~ cough (47) n 076.5
~ egg[N-i] (1) n 046.2

hackleberries (1) n 061.8
hackles (1) n 079.5
hackmore tree (1) n 062.2
hacks (8) n 023.9
hacksaw (1) n 020.9
had (1618) v 012.4
~ a calf (1) v 033.9
~ a date (1) v 081.4
~ it (2) v 078.6
~ on (1) v 053.7
~ that calf (1) v 033.9
~ the knot tied (2) v 082.2
~ to (144) v 012.2
~ [P-0] (4) v 003.2
(ha)d (3) v 057.9
haddock (1) n 059.9
Haddock (1) GA 087.3
Haden (1) 061.9
Hades (1) 090.2
Hadley Park (1) 106.4
hadn't (193) v 012.5
hag (6) n 108.9
hagberries (1) n 061.8
hagberry trees (1) n 061.9
haggard (1) adj 072.9
haggers (1) n 094.9
haggis (1) n 037.3
Haggy (2) 090.1
~ Bill (1) 090.1
Hagler (1) AR 087.6
Hahira (5) GA 087.4
~ Highway (1) 107.6
Hahir(a) (1) GA 087.1
hail (39) n/v/adj 112.3
~ cloud (1) n 005.3
~ -fellow-well-met (1) adj 073.2
~ from (6) v 102.4
~ over (1) n 081.8
hailed (1) v 006.2
hailing (2) v 112.3
hailstorm (12) n 112.2
hailstorms (8) n 112.3
Haiman (7) 021.6
~ plow stock (1) n 021.6
~ plows (1) n 021.6
~ stock (4) n 021.6
~ stock plow (1) n 021.6
Haines (2) 115.8
~ Boulevard (1) 115.8
~ Creek (1) FL 030.7
hain't (69) v 025.4

hair (1562) n/adj 071.4
~ comb (2) n 022.2
~ grease (2) n 023.7
~ jump (1) n 039.5
~ oil (2) n 024.1
~ roots (1) n 061.4
~ screw (1) n 081.8
~ tonic (1) n 071.4
~ trim (1) n 071.4
hairbrush (39) n 022.2
hairbrush[N-i] (1) n 022.2
hairbrushes (5) n 022.2
haircut (26) n 071.4
haircuts (5) n 071.4
hairdo (2) n 102.8
hairdos (2) n 043.7
hairdresser (1) n 071.4
haired (10) adj 129.3
hairless peach (1) n 054.3
hairpin (1) n 053.4
hairpins (1) n 071.4
hairs (27) n 035.6
hairstyles (3) n 123.9
hairy (7) adj 090.4
~ -like (2) adj 090.4
~ -looking (1) adj 090.4
~ woodpecker (1) n 059.3
~ worm (2) n 060.5
~ worms (1) n 060.5
Haiti (2) 087.6
Haitian (1) 080.7
Haitians (1) 128.2
Halawakee (1) AL 084.8
hale (8) adj 073.1
Hale (6) AL 087.4
~ cantaloupe (1) n 056.7
~ County (2) AL 087.5
~ peach (1) n 054.3
Haleburg (1) AL 087.8
Hales Point (2) TN 087.8
Haley (2) 030.7
~ Branch (1) AL 030.7
~ Creek (1) AL 030.7
Haleyville (8) AL 087.4
half (1740) n/adj/adv 004.4
~ a bath (7) n 118.3
~ a bathroom (2) n 118.3
~ -a-dollar beans (1) n 055A.3

~ after (39) n/adj 004.4
~ an hour before (1) n 004.4
~ an hour till (1) n 004.4
~ an hour until (1) n 004.4
~ -and-half (21) adj 033.3
~ -and-half feist (1) n 033.3
~ -and-half flour (1) n 090.8
~ -ass (4) adj 088.7
~ -ass carp(enter) (1) n 067.8
~ -ass lawyer (1) n 067.8
~ -ass mechanic (1) n 067.8
~ -ass preacher (2) n 067.8
~ -assed (4) adj 067.8
~ -assed preacher (1) n 067.8
~ barrel (5) n 019.1
~ barrels (3) n 020.2
~ bath (99) n 118.3
~ bathroom (6) n 118.3
~ baths (2) n 118.3
~ black (5) adj 069.5
~ -black child (1) n 069.5
~ -black kid (1) n 069.5
~ -breed (127) n 069.5
~ -breed dog (2) n 033.3
~ -breed dogs (1) n 033.3
~ -breed water spaniel (1) n 033.1
~ -breeds (20) n 069.5
~ brother[N-i] (1) n 055A.7
~ brothers (1) n 025.5
~ -bushel bucket (1) n 017.3
~ -bushel measure (1) n 019.8
~ -bushel measuring baskets (1) n 020.1
~ cans (1) n 051.3

~ -caste[N-i] (1) n 069.5
~ colored (1) adj 069.5
~ dime (2) n 092.7
~ -done food (1) n 093.6
~ door (1) n 010.5
~ froze (1) n 007.5
~ -gallon (1) adj 019.2
~ gone (1) adj 004.4
~ -growed (1) adj 035.5
~ -grown (5) adj 065.6
~ -handed man (1) n 067.8
~ -handed mechanic (1) n 067.8
~ -handed preacher (2) n 067.8
~ Mexican (1) n 069.5
~ -moon (3) n 004.4
~ -moon castle (1) n 012.1
~ -moon gutter (1) n 011.5
~ -moon house (1) n 012.1
~ -moon pies (3) n 084.8
~ Negro (1) n 069.5
~ nigger (11) n 069.5
~ niggers (1) n 069.5
~ nutria (1) n 069.9
~ -open hall (1) n 102.7
~ orphans (1) n 066.3
~ ounce (1) n 114.1
~ past (522) n/adj 004.4
~ -pint jars (1) n 051.3
~ plow (1) n 021.6
~ porch (4) n 007A.1
~ pregnant (1) adj 065.1
~ rubber (1) n 130.4
~ runner (4) n 055A.4
~ -runner bean (1) n 055A.4
~ -runner beans (1) n 055A.4
~ -runner green beans (1) n 055A.4
~ runners (25) n 055A.4
~ section (1) n 080.6
~ shovel (10) n 021.6

~ shovel plow (1) n 021.6
~ shovel plows (1) n 021.6
~ shovels (5) n 021.6
~ side (1) n 063.2
~ sister[N-i] (1) n 055A.7
~ sisters (1) n 025.6
~ -slip (1) n 093.7
~ story (2) n 009.8
~ tester (1) n 099.7
~ ton (2) n 109.7
~ -ton pickup (2) n 109.7
~ -ton pickups (1) n 109.7
~ -ton truck (1) n 109.7
~ tons (1) n 109.7
~ turner (1) n 021.6
~ white (27) adj 069.5
~ -white child (2) n 069.5
~ -white Negro (1) n 069.5
~ -white nigger (2) n 069.5
~ -white squirrel (1) n 059.7
~ -white trash (1) n 069.5
~ -witted (1) adj 069.3
~ -yellow so-and-so (1) n 069.5
Half (4) 129.6
~ Moon (2) MS 030.7
~ Pone Creek (1) TN 030.7
halfway (17) adj/adv 006.5
~ before (1) adj 004.4
~ house (2) n 084.8
~ houses (2) n 113.8
~ past (1) adj 004.4
~ road (1) n 031.8
~ station (1) n 080.8
Halfway (1) GA 087.4
halibut (3) n 059.9
Halifax (3) FL 030.7
~ River (2) FL 030.7
hall (548) n/adj 007A.2
~ and parlor (2) n 118.8

~ -and-parlor house (3) n 118.8
~ closet (2) n 007A.1
~ curtains (1) n 009.5
~ -like (1) adj 009.9
~ rack (1) n 009.3
~ steps (1) n 010.7
~ tree (8) n 008.9
~ trees (1) n 061.8
Hall (43) GA 087.6
~ County (3) GA 086.1
~ of Fame (1) 106.4
~ of Star fames (1) n 106.4
~ Road (1) 105.4
~ Street (1) 105.5
hallah (2) n 044.4
hallelujah shouts (1) n 080.6
Hallettsville (1) TX 087.3
Halley Bayou (1) TX 030.7
Halley's (4) 070.7
~ Comet (3) 070.7
hallowed (1) adj 072.9
Halloween (12) 130.7
~ night (1) n 066.8
~ parties (4) n 130.7
~ party (2) n 130.7
halls (10) n 007A.6
Halls (9) TN 106.2
~ Branch (1) AL 030.7
~ Creek (1) AL 030.7
Hallsville (2) TX 087.5
hallucinogenics (1) n 114.2
hallucinogens (2) n 114.2
hallway (149) n/adj 007A.3
~ room (1) n 007A.2
hallways (2) n 007A.8
Hallwood (1) MS 087.6
halt (9) v 038.2
halter (14) n/v 039.2
~ up (1) v 038.6
halters (1) n 039.3
halts (1) n 107.2
halve (2) v 080.6
halve[V-r] (1) v 080.6
halved (1) v 005.9
halves (21) n/adj 004.4
~ dollars (1) n 016.7
ham (539) n/adj 046.4
~ fat (1) n 046.3
~ gravy (23) n 048.3

~ grease (1) n 023.7
~ hock (35) n 121.3
~ hocks (40) n 121.3
~ meat (6) n 046.3
~ pie (1) n 044.4
~ roast (2) n 121.3
~ shoulder (1) n 046.6
~ skin (1) n 073.4
~ steak (3) n 121.3
~ steaks (2) n 121.3
Ham (1) 069.3
ham[N-i] (2) n 072.7
Hamblen (1) TN 087.5
hambone (9) n 046.3
Hamburg (1) 080.6
hamburger (67) n/adj 121.2
~ bun (1) n 044.4
~ buns (4) n 044.4
~ fries (1) n 130.7
~ joint (1) n 072.3
~ meat (4) n 121.2
~ onion (1) n 055.6
~ patties (1) n 121.2
~ steaks (1) n 121.2
hamburg(er) (1) n 121.2
hamburgers (4) n 121.2
hame (13) n/adj 038.6
~ chain (1) n 038.6
~ string (4) n 038.7
~ strings (1) n 021.3
hames (42) n 080.7
Hamilton (26) AL GA TN 087.1
~ Bank (1) 108.5
~ County (4) FL TN 087.1
~ Creek (1) FL 030.7
~ National Bank (1) 012.6
~ National Bank building (1) n 108.5
~ Park (2) 106.2
Hammar Creek (1) AL 030.7
hammeltree (1) n 021.3
hammer (1296) n/v/adj 020.7
~ -and-saw carpenter (1) n 067.8
~ house (1) n 011.7
~ knocker (3) n 020.7
~ knockers (2) n 059.3
~ mill (4) n 020.7
~ mills (1) n 080.7

Hammer Creek (1) LA 030.7
hammered (13) v/adj 020.7
~ in (1) v 020.7
~ woodpecker (1) n 059.3
hammerer (1) n 020.7
hammerhead (3) n/adj 059.3
~ shark (1) n 092.9
hammerheads (1) n 059.3
hammering (4) v 020.7
hammers (59) n 020.7
hammock (23) n/adj 029.6
~ land (5) n 029.8
~ road (1) n 088.9
Hammock (3) 030.9
hammocks (4) n 029.4
hammocky (3) adj 029.9
Hammond (18) IN LA TX 087.8
~ Creek (1) LA 030.7
~ Highway (1) 107.1
hamper (279) n/adj 020.1
~ bag (1) n 020.1
~ basket (3) n 020.1
~ sack (1) n 019.7
hamperful (1) n 019.8
hampers (11) n 116.6
Hampshire (18) 035.5
~ hogs (1) n 035.5
Hampshires (5) 080.6
Hampton (5) GA VA 087.4
~ Creek (1) TN 030.7
~ House (1) 106.4
Ham's children (1) n 069.3
hams (90) n 121.3
hamster (1) n 070.7
hamsters (1) n 059.8
hamstring (3) n 072.8
Hanceville (1) AL 087.5
Hancock (8) GA MS 087.2
~ County (3) GA MS 087.4
hand (1859) n/v/adj 072.5
~ ax (1) n 020.7
~ basket (1) n 020.1
~ boat (1) n 024.6
~ -carved (1) adj 072.5

~ carving (1) n 072.5
~ clippers (1) n 072.5
~ clips (1) n 120.8
~ cloth (2) n 018.5
~ cradle (1) n 080.7
~ cultivator (1) n 120.5
~ digger (2) n 120.6
~ dish towel (1) n 018.4
~ -ditched canals (1) n 030.2
~ ditches (1) n 030.2
~ -dovetail (1) v 092.8
~ -drawn maps (1) n 104.4
~ -drip (1) v 048.8
~ -dug water wells (1) n 084.8
~ file (2) n 023.4
~ fork (16) n 120.6
~ gear (1) n 110.7
~ gears (1) n 110.7
~ grenade (2) n 072.5
~ -hewed (1) v 002.6
~ -hewn-log rail fence (1) n 016.4
~ -hewn timbers (1) n 072.5
~ hoe (1) n 021.6
~ hoes (1) n 120.4
~ hooks (2) n 072.5
~ lamp (1) n 024.3
~ lawn mower (1) n 120.1
~ -me-down (24) n/adj 123.5
~ -m(e)-down (1) n 123.5
~ -me-down food (1) n 050.1
~ -me-down furniture (1) n 009.4
~ -me-down[N-i] (2) n 123.5
~ -me-downs (128) n 123.5
~ -me-out (1) n 123.5
~ -me-overs (1) n 123.5
~ -milking (1) v 080.7
~ mill (1) n 019.8
~ mower (9) n 120.1
~ mowers (1) n 120.1
~ over (1) n 080.9
~ -painted bream (1) n 059.9

~ -pick (1) v 072.5
~ -picked cotton (1) n 084.8
~ picker (1) n 072.5
~ pickers (1) n 057.7
~ pistol (1) n 113.1
~ plow (11) n 021.6
~ plows (1) n 021.6
~ pocketbook (1) n 028.2
~ poles (1) n 024.6
~ -powered mowers (1) n 120.1
~ pump (3) n 080.9
~ purse (3) n 028.2
~ -push thing (1) n 120.1
~ rag (1) n 018.5
~ rags (1) n 018.3
~ rake (8) n 120.7
~ razors (1) n 072.5
~ -rinse (1) v 018.2
~ rock (1) n 023.4
~ roll (1) n 057.3
~ sack (1) n 028.2
~ satchel (3) n 028.2
~ seeder (1) n 021.6
~ -sewn (1) adj 072.5
~ shears (1) n 120.8
~ -shell (1) v 055A.2
~ shift (2) n 110.7
~ shovel (10) n 120.5
~ spade (3) n 120.5
~ stick (1) n 022.1
~ swing (1) n 022.9
~ tie (1) n 041.6
~ ties (1) n 080.6
~ tool (1) n 120.5
~ tools (4) n 120.5
~ towel (38) n 018.6
~ towels (16) n 018.6
~ trimmers (1) n 120.8
~ trowel (5) n 120.5
~ truck (1) n 023.3
~ -type operation deal (1) n 080.6
~ -wash (1) v 018.1
~ -washing (2) n 010.6
~ -you-down (1) n 123.5
~ -you-downs (1) n 123.5
~ -[M-0]-downs (1) n 123.5
hand[N-i] (96) n 072.5

handbag (119) n 028.2
handbags (10) n 028.2
handball (3) n 130.4
handbook (1) n 028.2
handbooks (1) n 025.7
handcar (1) n 084.8
handcuffs (4) n 113.2
handed (24) v/adj 053.6
~ down (1) v 053.6
~ in his checks (1) v 078.6
hander (2) n 088.8
handers (1) n 080.8
handful (6) n 019.8
handfuls (1) n 098.6
handgun (13) n 113.1
handguns (3) n 113.1
handiron (3) n 010.9
handiron[N-i] (1) n 008.3
handirons (5) n 008.3
handkerchief (54) n 065.9
handkerchiefs (1) n 070.6
handle (105) n/v/adj 017.8
~ with (1) v 075.6
handlebar moustache (1) n 081.8
handled (3) v/adj 070.9
handler (2) n 114.4
handlers (2) n 114.4
handles (19) n 080.6
Handley (1) TX 087.8
handling (1) v 096.7
handmade (4) adj 072.5
~ rig (1) n 072.5
~ -type deal (1) n 002.7
handoff (1) adv 075.6
handout (5) n 095.7
handpress (1) n 014.6
hands (976) n/v 072.5
~ him a lemon (1) v 082.1
handsaw (20) n 120.9
handsaws (2) n 080.6
Handsboro (2) MS 105.5
handsful (1) n 072.5
handsome (73) adj 125.3
~ fellow (1) n 125.3
~ stud (1) n 125.3
handspring (2) n 095.5
handsprings (1) n 095.5
handsticks (1) n 080.7
handstone (1) n 023.4
handwork (1) n 081.8
handwrite (1) n 095.8

handwriting (7) n 100.5
handwriting[N-i] (1) n 025.6
handwritten (1) v 100.5
handy (12) adj 074.1
~ bag (1) n 019.5
~ basket (1) n 020.1
~ shops (1) n 116.2
~ stores (1) n 116.2
Handy (9) 106.4
~ Branch (1) GA 030.7
~ Packs (1) 116.2
~ Park (2) 106.5
~ Road (1) 031.7
handyman (20) n 119.5
hang (164) v/adj 085.9
~ around (4) v 081.6
~ around with (3) v 053.5
~ closet (1) n 009.6
~ dang (1) n 083.1
~ down (1) v 013.1
~ his hat (1) v 081.4
~ in (1) v 088.7
~ into (2) v 080.6
~ my tennis (1) v 078.6
~ out (1) v 080.6
~ out with (1) v 075.9
~ pole (1) n 084.8
~ together (2) v 129.6
~ up (2) v 039.7
~ -up bag (2) n 123.7
~ with (1) v 081.9
hang[V-r] (14) v 085.9
hang[V-t] (18) v 085.9
hanged (379) v 085.9
~ by (2) v 085.9
hanger (13) n/adj 072.8
~ bag (1) n 123.7
hangers (2) n 009.7
hanging (57) n/v/adj 085.9
~ around (1) v 075.6
~ around after her (1) v 081.4
~ bag (9) n 123.7
~ basket (2) n 017.7
~ bee (1) n 056.3
~ his hat there (1) v 081.4
~ off (1) v 081.8
~ on (2) v 079.4
~ out (2) v 053.8
~ -out cliffs (1) n 031.2
~ over (2) v 027.4

~ robe (1) n 009.7
~ rope (1) n 085.9
Hanging Moss (1) 107.8
hangout (2) n 113.9
hangouts (2) n 081.8
hangover (2) n 050.8
hangovers (1) n 010.8
hangs (5) v 053.4
~ down (1) v 053.4
~ onto (1) v 052.8
~ over (2) v 031.2
hank (3) n/v 084.8
hanker (1) n 084.8
hankering (3) n 088.9
hanky (2) adj 065.2
~ -panky (1) n 065.1
~ -pankying (1) v 081.7
Hanna (1) 106.5
hannah (1) n 059.3
Hannah Spring (1) TN 030.7
hanneton (1) n F 060A.7
Hanover (2) GA 087.8
~ County (1) VA 087.4
Hans (1) 127.1
Hanukkah (1) 093.2
Hapeville (3) GA 087.5
haphazard (4) adj 085.2
~ carpenter (1) n 067.8
happen (103) v 070.6
~ -so (1) n 088.7
~ to (8) v 004.2
~ [P-0] (1) v 024.8
happen[V-p] in (1) v 013.7
happen[V-r] (13) v 013.6
~ to (7) v 032.2
happen[V-s] (1) v 052.8
happen[V-t] (5) v 039.9
happened (25) v 058.7
~ to (3) v 043.8
~ up on (3) v 032.6
~ upon (1) v 032.6
~ [P-0] (1) v 032.6
happening (18) n/v 114.4
happens (3) v 097.8
~ about (1) v 097.8
happier (6) adj 066.1
happiness (1) n 082.3
happy (201) adj 081.2
~ -dispositioned (1) adj 073.2
~ dust (1) n 114.2
~ -go-lucky (17) adj 073.2

~ house (1) n 012.1
~ hunting ground (4) n 078.6
~ juice (1) n 050.8
~ pills (1) n 114.2
Happy (889) 093.2
~ and Prosperous New Year (1) 093.3
~ Christmas (79) 093.2
~ Christmas Day (2) 093.2
~ Christmas Give (1) 093.2
~ Days (1) 093.3
~ Greeting (1) 093.2
~ Hanukkah (1) 093.2
~ Hill (1) 105.3
~ Holiday (5) 093.2
~ Holidays (10) 093.2
~ Hollow (3) AL 087.3
~ New Year (677) 093.3
~ New Year's (96) 093.3
~ New Year's Day (2) 093.3
~ New Year's Eve (1) 093.3
~ Noel (1) 093.2
~ Yule (1) 093.2
~ Yuletide (2) 093.2
hara-kiri (1) n 085.9
Harahan Bridge (1) 106.7
Haralson (4) GA 087.2
~ County (1) GA 087.2
harass (2) v 082.5
harassing (2) v 082.5
harassments (1) n 129.7
harbor (53) n/adj 031.4
~ bridge (1) n 115.5
Harbor (8) 087.9
~ View (1) 106.1
harbors (5) n 031.4
Harbour (3) 106.1
~ Island (2) 087.7
hard (977) adj/adv 054.3
~ acid rock (1) n 130.9
~ back (1) n 060.6
~ bake (1) n 044.7
~ balls (1) n 081.8
~ beating rain (1) n 006.1
~ black shell (1) n 054.8
~ blackland (1) n 029.8

~ -boil (8) adj 046.1
~ -boil egg (2) n 046.1
~ -boil eggs (3) n 046.1
~ -boiled (42) adj 046.1
~ -boiled egg (20) n 046.1
~ -boiled eggs (29) n 046.1
~ butter sauce (1) n 048.5
~ -call preacher (1) n 067.8
~ cash (2) n 114.5
~ cider (1) n 050.9
~ clay (3) n 031.6
~ clay land (1) n 029.8
~ cling peaches (1) n 054.3
~ cold (3) adj 091.7
~ -cook eggs (1) n 046.2
~ -cooked (1) adj 046.1
~ core (1) n 054.3
~ -core porn (1) n 114.9
~ dick (2) n 124.5
~ dope (1) n 114.2
~ down (1) n 126.6
~ -down (1) adv 091.6
~ downpour (2) n 006.1
~ drug (1) n 114.2
~ drugs (5) n 114.2
~ dry spell (1) n 007.1
~ egg (1) n 046.1
~ food (1) n 048.4
~ freeze (63) n 007.5
~ freezes (1) n 007.5
~ frost (14) n 007.5
~ frozen (1) adj 007.7
~ gummy land (1) n 029.9
~ hats (1) n 069.7
~ head (2) n 074.8
~ hull (1) n 054.8
~ -hulled (1) adj 054.8
~ -luck folks (1) n 069.7
~ maple (7) n 061.5
~ maple trees (1) n 061.5
~ -nose (1) adj 074.8
~ -nosed (1) adj 074.8
~ nut (1) n 054.8

~ of hearing (92) adj 077.2
~ -packing rain (1) n 006.8
~ pan (1) n 029.8
~ part (1) n 046.6
~ path (1) n 031.6
~ -pave road (1) n 031.6
~ peach (6) n 054.3
~ peaches (1) n 054.3
~ press peach (1) n 054.3
~ rain (74) n 006.1
~ rains (2) n 006.1
~ rake (1) n 120.7
~ red clay (1) n 029.8
~ red sand (1) n 029.9
~ road (10) n 031.6
~ roads (6) n 031.6
~ rock (15) n 130.8
~ roll (1) n 044.4
~ rolls (1) n 044.4
~ salami (1) n 099.9
~ sauce (3) n 048.5
~ shell (7) n 054.8
~ -shell (24) n/adj 074.9
~ -shell cooter (3) n 060.6
~ -shell pallets (1) n 029.2
~ -shell preacher (2) n 080.6
~ -shell snappers (1) n 060.6
~ -shell terrapins (2) n 060.7
~ -shell ticks (1) n 060A.4
~ -shell turtle (32) n 060.7
~ -shell turtles (5) n 060.7
~ -shelled (1) adj 054.8
~ -shelled turtle (1) n 060.6
~ -shells (3) n 060.7
~ shower (17) n 006.1
~ showering rain (1) n 006.1
~ showers (2) n 006.6
~ soil (1) n 029.8
~ -sole shoes (1) n 123.8

~ soles (1) n 123.8
~ -stand area (2) n 015.6
~ stone (1) n 054.3
~ stuff (3) n 114.2
~ suctions (1) n 080.9
~ surface (6) n 031.6
~ -surface road (9) n 031.6
~ -surface roads (2) n 031.6
~ thundercloud rain (1) n 006.1
~ -time (1) adj 067.8
~ -tooth harrow (1) n 021.7
~ twist (1) n 088.9
~ up (11) adj 080.7
~ winter (1) n 007.5
~ [P-0] hearing (2) adj 077.2
Hard (21) 030.7
~ Labor (1) FL 030.7
~ -Shell (10) 089.2
~ -Shell Baptist (7) 089.1
~ -Shell Baptist church (1) n 089.1
~ -Shell church (1) n 089.1
~ -Shell Methodist (1) 089.1
~ -Shell Primitive Baptist[N-i] (1) 104.7
hardback turtle (1) n 060.6
hardbacks (2) n 060.9
hardcase (2) n 077.7
hardcore Nashville country (1) n 130.8
Hardee (2) FL 087.5
Hardeman (4) TN 087.2
~ County (1) TN 087.5
hardening of the arteries (1) n 076.1
hardens (1) v 090.4
harder (129) adj 007.2
~ freeze (2) n 007.5
~ marshes (1) n 029.7
hardest (2) adj 012.2
hardhead (14) n/adj 074.8
~ cat (1) n 084.5
~ catfish (1) n 059.9
~ lettuce (1) n 055A.6

hardheaded (195) adj 074.8
hardheadedest (1) adj 074.8
hardheads (3) n 055A.7
hardhearted (1) adj 074.8
hardie (1) n 088.7
Hardin (2) TN 087.7
~ Creek (1) TN 030.7
Harding (3) 106.4
~ Park (1) 106.4
~ Place (2) 105.5
hardly (427) adv 095.8
hardl(y) (1) adv 040.6
hardnose (1) adj 074.8
hardpan (3) n 029.8
hardtack (2) n 044.4
hardtacks (1) n 092.9
hardtails (1) n 059.9
hardtop (34) n/adj 031.6
~ mud turtle (1) n 060.7
~ road (3) n 031.6
~ roads (1) n 031.6
hardtopped (2) adj 031.6
~ road (1) n 031.6
~ roads (1) n 031.6
hardtops (1) n 031.6
hardware (6) n/adj 070.7
~ dealer (1) n 065.8
hardwood (11) n/adj 061.8
~ ash (1) n 061.8
~ ashes (1) n 061.9
~ trees (1) n 061.8
hardworking (1) adj 025.5
hardy (10) adj 073.1
Hardy (9) AR 087.9
~ Station (1) MS 087.4
Hardys Creek (1) TN 087.1
harebrained (1) adj 075.1
harelip meat dish (1) n 081.8
harem (1) n 055A.8
hark (1) n 076.5
hark(x4) (1) interj 037.5
Harlandale (1) 105.1
Harlans Midnight Sun (1) 099.6
Harlem (11) GA NY 087.4
~ Square (1) 106.4
Harlen (1) AR 087.2

Harlequin Park (1) 106.4
Harleton (1) TX 086.3
Harlingen (3) TX 086.4
harlot (2) n 113.3
harlots (1) n 113.3
harm (17) n/v 045.8
harmless (2) adj 025.6
Harmon (3) 030.7
~ Branch (1) TN 030.7
~ Creek (1) TX 030.7
~ Knobs (1) TN 030.8
harmonica (499) n/adj 020.5
~ harp (1) n 020.5
harmonic(a) (1) n 020.5
harmoni(ca) (1) n 020.5
(har)monica (2) n 020.5
harmonicas (22) n 020.5
(har)monicas (1) n 020.5
harmonious (2) adj 073.2
harmonizing (1) v 057.4
Harmons Creek (1) TX 030.7
harmony (2) n 020.5
Harmony (3) LA TX 087.4
~ Hills (1) 106.2
harness (788) n/v/adj 038.6
~ -broke (1) v 048.9
~ chain (1) n 038.6
~ house (1) n 015.3
~ leather (1) n 038.6
~ piece (1) n 038.6
~ reins (2) n 039.1
~ room (4) n 011.7
~ rooms (1) n 038.6
~ up (19) v 038.6
harn(ess) (1) n 038.6
harness[N-i] (2) n 038.6
harnessed (9) v 038.6
~ up (4) v 038.6
harnesses (37) n 038.6
harnessing (5) v 038.6
~ up (2) v 038.6
harp (1723) n 020.5
Harp (1) 089.5
Harper (2) 030.7
~ Creek (1) TN 030.7
~ Field (1) 106.5
Harpers Ferry (1) WV 086.5
Harpeth River (4) TN 030.7
harpoon (1) n 020.5

harps (79) n 020.5
harpsichord (2) n 020.5
Harriman (2) TN 087.4
Harrington (1) GA 087.8
Harris (19) TX 087.1
~ Bayou (1) MS 030.7
~ City (2) GA 087.9
~ County (2) GA TX 087.2
~ County Courthouse (1) 085.1
~ Creek (1) TN 030.7
Harrisburg (2) AL GA 087.2
Harrison (23) AR MS TN TX 087.3
~ Avenue (2) 105.7
~ County (5) MS TX 087.6
~ Park (1) 106.4
Harrisonburg (2) LA 087.6
Harrisons Creek (1) FL 030.7
Harris's place (1) n 030.5
Harrisville (2) MS TX 087.7
harrow (893) n/v/adj 021.7
~ disc (1) n 021.7
~ off (1) v 021.7
~ plow (2) n 021.7
~ teeth (1) n 021.7
~ with (1) v 021.7
har(row) (134) n/v 021.7
~ -disking (1) v 021.7
~ tooth (1) n 021.7
Harrow (1) 021.7
harrow[N-i] (1) n 021.7
harrowed (14) v 021.7
~ down (1) v 021.7
harrower (3) n 021.7
harrowing (15) v 021.7
~ off (1) v 021.7
harrows (160) n/v 021.7
Harry (5) 068.3
harsh (3) adj 076.4
Hart (5) GA 087.2
~ Bridge (1) 107.7
~ County (3) GA 087.3
Hartford (5) AL CT 087.5
Hartley (2) AR 087.7
~ (E)states (1) 105.5
Hartsfield (11) GA 106.5

~ Airport (5) 106.5
~ International (2) 106.5
~ International Airport (1) 106.5
Hartwell (3) GA 087.5
Harvard Business School (1) 070.7
harvest (30) n/v/adj 041.3
~ festival (1) n 083.1
harvest[V-t] (1) v 057.8
harvested (5) v 042.1
harvester (1) n 089.8
harvesting (1) v 014.6
Harvey community (1) LA 087.2
has (763) v 012.2
~ -been (1) adj 080.9
~ quit him (1) v 082.1
~ to (22) v 058.1
(ha)s (2) v 053.2
hasenpfeffer (2) n 080.6
hash (160) n 050.1
hashish (12) n 114.1
haslet (120) n/adj 037.2
~ stew (6) n 037.2
haslets (34) n 037.2
hasn't (191) v 012.5
hassle (11) n 074.1
hassling (3) n/v 129.7
hassocks (1) n 009.3
haste (2) n 092.7
Hastings (4) FL GA 087.5
~ Prolific (2) 056.2
hasty pudding (1) n 048.3
hat (30) n/adj 033.8
~ racks (1) n 080.8
Hat Creek (1) GA 030.7
hat[N-i] (1) n 077.8
hatband (1) n 042.8
hatch (13) n/v 110.5
~ off (1) v 026.8
~ one (1) v 065.1
~ out (1) v 036.7
~ outs (1) n 060A.8
Hatch Bottom (1) TX 087.5
hatchback (8) n 109.5
hatchbacks (1) n 109.2
Hatchechubbee (1) GA 030.7
hatched (5) v 001A.4
~ off (2) v 036.8

Hatchee Creek (1) AL 030.7
Hatcher (2) 031.1
~ Mountain (1) TN 031.1
~ Station (1) GA 087.6
hatchery (6) n/adj 036.9
~ hen (1) n 036.7
hatches (1) v 098.9
hatchet (19) n 020.7
hatchets (5) n 020.7
Hatchie (12) 030.7
~ River (11) TN 030.7
hatching (9) v/adj 036.7
~ day (1) n 033.9
~ egg (1) n 017.1
~ hen (2) n 036.7
~ jacket (1) n 065.1
hate (14) n/v 033.3
~ to (5) v 057.5
~ [P-0] (1) v 012.9
Hate (1) 085.8
hate[V-p] (1) v 091.6
hate[V-r] to (1) v 091.6
hated (33) v 091.6
~ to (6) v 091.6
hateful (7) adj 075.1
~ peach (1) n 054.3
hatefulest (1) adj 064.7
hates (15) v 091.6
~ to (3) v 091.6
Hatfield (1) AR 087.6
Hathawa Creek (1) LA 030.7
Hathaway Bridge (1) 105.5
hatpin (1) n 026.5
hats (7) n 027.1
hatted (1) v 093.8
Hatteras (2) 087.8
Hattiesburg (43) MS 087.6
Hatton (2) AL 087.2
haul (371) n/v/adj 021.4
~ across (1) v 021.4
~ away (1) v 021.4
~ in (2) v 021.4
~ off (8) v 021.4
~ out (2) v 021.4
~ road (1) n 031.6
~ trucks (1) n 109.7
~ up (3) v 021.4
~ with (1) v 021.4
Haul (1) 109.6
haul[V-r] (9) v 021.4

~ off (1) v 021.4
haul[V-t] (2) v 021.4
hauled (132) v 021.4
~ in (5) v 021.4
~ off (5) v 021.4
~ to (2) v 021.4
hauler (5) n 109.8
hauling (677) n/v/adj 021.4
~ in (1) v 024.9
~ off (3) v 021.4
~ out (1) v 021.4
~ spear (1) n 021.6
~ up (1) v 021.4
Haulover (2) 106.6
~ Beach (1) 106.6
~ Pier (1) 106.6
hauls (13) n/v 021.4
Hauls (1) 027.4
haunch (11) n/v 072.8
~ down (1) v 096.4
haunch[V-t] down (1) v 096.4
haunchers (1) n 072.8
haunches (300) n 072.8
haunt (87) n/v/adj 090.2
~ house (3) n 090.3
~ tales (1) n 080.7
haunt[N-i] (2) n 090.2
haunt[V-p] (2) v 013.6
haunted (969) v/adj 090.3
~ hollow (2) n 040.8
~ homestead (1) n 090.3
~ house (380) n 090.3
~ houses (28) n 090.3
~ owl (1) n 059.1
~ place (2) n 090.3
~ places (2) n 090.3
Haunted House (1) 080.6
hauntified (1) adj 090.3
haunting house (1) n 090.3
haunts (268) n 090.2
haunty (3) adj 074.7
~ house (2) n 090.3
Haus (1) n G 012.1
Hauschen (1) n G 012.1
Hausley (1) LA 087.3
Haute (1) 087.4
Havana (10) FL 087.3
have (6814) v 012.2
~ a (1) v 033.9
~ a action (1) v 080.1
~ a baby (102) v 065.1

~ a baby calf (3) v 033.9
~ a baby cow (1) v 033.9
~ a calf (310) v 033.9
~ a child (3) v 065.1
~ a cow (1) v 033.9
~ a kid (3) v 065.1
~ a litter (1) v 033.9
~ a little baby (3) v 065.1
~ a little calf (2) v 033.9
~ a little one (1) v 033.9
~ another baby (1) v 065.1
~ babies (1) v 033.9
~ birth (1) v 033.9
~ calves (3) v 033.9
~ her baby (1) v 033.9
~ her calf (1) v 033.9
~ it pretty bad (1) v 081.4
~ on (1) v 052.5
~ one (3) v 033.9
~ pigs (1) v 033.9
~ relations with her (1) v 081.4
~ some calves (2) v 033.9
~ the calf (6) v 033.9
~ to (252) v 070.2
~ [D-0] calf (2) v 033.9
~ [P-0] (4) v 025.8
(ha)ve (7) v 058.3
Have (1) 086.2
have[V-p] (93) v 053.6
~ to (2) v 025.7
have[V-r] (5) v 070.2
~ to (1) v 070.1
have[V-s] (3) v 012.2
have[V-t] (2) v 095.7
Haven (12) 082.6
haven't (897) v 012.5
have(n't) (1) v 090.6
(ha)ven't (5) v 040.6
(have)n't (1) v 100.4
haven't[V-p] (16) v 012.5
haves (6) n/v 025.7
Haviland (2) 017.1
~ china (1) n 017.1
having (88) v 057.4
~ a baby (1) v 033.9

~ a baby soon (1) v 065.1
~ a calf (3) v 033.9
~ a foal (1) v 033.9
~ dates (1) v 081.4
~ intercourse with (1) v 081.4
~ to (23) v 091.6
haw (749) n/adj/interj 037.7
~ apples (1) n 054.6
~ berry (1) n 061.9
~ bush (3) n 062.2
~ horse (5) n 039.4
~ land (1) n 039.3
~ left (1) interj 037.7
~ ox (1) n 039.4
~ side (4) n 039.4
~ there (1) interj 038.2
~ tree (2) n 062.3
haw(x4) (1) interj 037.7
Hawaii (16) 086.1
Hawai(i) (1) 086.4
Hawaiian (2) 065.8
~ girls (1) n 052.1
hawk (305) n/adj 059.5
~ bird (1) n 059.2
~ -neck turtle (1) n 060.6
~ owl (2) n 059.1
Hawk (2) 021.9
hawkbill (2) n 104.3
hawkeye (1) n 059.2
Hawkins (5) TN 087.4
~ County (2) TN 025.6
~ Field (1) 106.6
~ Spring (1) AL 030.7
Hawkinsville (4) GA 087.4
hawks (138) n 059.5
Hawks (1) 111.8
haws (24) n 062.4
hawthorn (4) n/adj 061.8
~ berry (1) n 062.4
Hawthorne (6) FL LA 087.5
~ community (1) FL 087.3
hay (784) n/adj 070.7
~ bale (1) n 014.8
~ baler (11) n 014.9
~ balers (5) n 014.8
~ bales (3) n 014.8
~ baling (1) n 014.8
~ barn (63) n 014.2

~ barns (12) n 014.2
~ barrack (6) n 014.7
~ barracks (2) n 014.7
~ bin (2) n 014.5
~ bottom (1) n 029.4
~ carrier (1) n 014.2
~ carriers (1) n 014.6
~ cart (1) n 014.8
~ chimley (1) n 008.1
~ cover (1) n 014.7
~ crib (1) n 014.4
~ crop (4) n 041.3
~ crops (1) n 041.3
~ cutter (1) n 014.9
~ deck (1) n 014.5
~ farm (1) n 029.5
~ fever (4) n 079.8
~ fodder (1) n 014.4
~ frame (7) n 014.8
~ frames (2) n 014.6
~ grass (3) n 015.9
~ hook (1) n 080.7
~ hooks (1) n 014.6
~ house (15) n 014.3
~ houses (1) n 014.5
~ knife (1) n 104.3
~ land (2) n 029.5
~ -making time (1) n 014.5
~ manger (1) n 014.7
~ mattress (1) n 080.9
~ meadow (18) n 029.5
~ meadows (6) n 029.5
~ mound (2) n 014.6
~ mower (1) n 014.9
~ outfit (1) n 080.6
~ pasture (1) n 029.5
~ patch (1) n 016.1
~ patches (1) n 016.1
~ pen (1) n 014.5
~ pile (10) n 014.6
~ piles (6) n 014.8
~ press (5) n 088.8
~ rake (12) n 014.8
~ rakes (3) n 120.7
~ rider (1) n 014.5
~ rolls (1) n 014.6
~ room (2) n 014.5
~ row (1) n 014.8
~ rows (3) n 014.8
~ sack (1) n 019.7
~ shed (38) n 014.5
~ sheds (3) n 014.7
~ shelter (3) n 014.7
~ shelters (1) n 014.7

~ shock (1) n 014.8
~ shocking (1) n 014.8
~ stackers (1) n 014.6
~ stick (2) n 014.6
~ time (2) n 080.8
~ wagon (3) n 014.9
~ wagons (1) n 014.9
~ windrow (1) n 014.8
haycap (2) n 014.7
haycock (4) n 014.6
haycocks (7) n 014.8
haydoodle (1) n 014.8
Hayes (2) 030.7
~ Branch (1) FL 030.7
hayfield (36) n 029.5
hayfields (2) n 029.5
hayfork (9) n 014.6
hayforks (3) n 017.8
haying (2) n/adj 014.6
~ time (1) n 014.8
haylift (1) n 014.6
hayloft (222) n 014.5
haylofts (5) n 014.5
haymow (19) n 014.6
haymows (2) n 014.6
Haynes (2) 030.7
Haynesville (1) LA 087.6
Hayneville (2) AL 087.1
hayrack (60) n 014.7
hayracks (15) n 014.5
hayrick (23) n 014.6
hayricks (6) n 014.8
hayride (3) n 082.5
hayrides (3) n 130.7
hayriding (1) v 084.8
hays (1) n 014.8
hayseed (24) n 069.9
hayseeded (1) adj 069.9
hayseeds (1) n 069.9
hayshaker (2) n 069.9
hayshock (16) n 014.8
hayshocks (11) n 014.8
Haysop (1) AL 087.8
haystack (466) n 014.6
haystacker (1) n 014.6
haystacks (114) n 014.6
haywire (4) n/adv 014.9
Haywood (6) AR TN 087.2
~ Circle (1) 107.8
~ County (2) TN 085.5
hazard (1) n 024.3
hazards (1) n 032.7
haze (14) n 006.6
hazed (1) v 129.8

hazel (3) n/adj 062.7
~ bushes (1) n 062.7
~ splitters (1) n 035.4
Hazel Grove (2) TN
087.2
hazelnut (16) n/adj 054.8
~ tree (1) n 061.8
~ trees (1) n 054.7
hazelnuts (51) n 054.8
hazels (1) n 054.8
hazing (5) v 129.8
Hazlehurst (6) GA MS
087.8
hazy (43) adj 005.5
~ cloud (1) n 005.3
~ clouds (1) n 005.5
~ cloudy (1) adj 005.5
~ day (10) n 005.5
he (6304) pron/v/adj/
interj 042.5
~ -all (1) pron 043.8
~ calf (2) n 033.8
~ cow (6) n 033.5
~ cows (1) n 033.5
~ goat (1) n 067.4
~ grapevines (1) n
084.8
~ hog (5) n 035.3
~ horse (9) n 034.1
~ horses (1) n 034.1
~ -huckleberry (1) n
088.7
~ -ing and she-ing (1) v
081.4
~ males (2) n 034.9
~ -man (2) n 073.1
~ mule (1) n 034.1
~ -ok(x2) (1) interj
037.5
~ -ooh (1) interj 038.3
~ rain (1) n 006.1
~ she (4) n 124.1
~ sheep (1) n 034.9
~ shes (2) n 113.5
He (3) 013.1
he[M-k] (2) pron 065.3
head (424) n/v/adj 047.2
~ block (1) n 024.7
~ bolster (1) n 028.9
~ bookkeeper (1) n
053.3
~ cold (1) n 076.3
~ count (2) n 055A.7
~ fornicator (1) n
119.5

~ honcho (1) n 068.5
~ -in (1) adj 108.3
~ -in parking (3) n
108.3
~ joints (1) n 072.3
~ knockers (1) n 112.5
~ lettuce (20) n 055A.6
~ lice (1) n 075.6
~ marble shooter (1) n
130.6
~ meat (4) n 047.1
~ mule (1) n 039.4
~ nigger (1) n 068.5
~ nurse (2) n 084.6
~ of the herd (1) n
033.5
~ of the house (1) n
063.1
~ -on (2) adj/adv 108.3
~ -on parking (4) n
108.3
~ out (1) v 084.9
~ over (1) n 088.8
~ ox (1) n 039.4
~ pig (1) n 035.3
~ pillow (1) n 028.8
~ rag (1) n 080.9
~ resident (1) n 119.5
~ sausage (2) n 047.4
~ -set (3) adj 074.8
~ shop (1) n 055A.7
~ shops (1) n 114.9
~ souse (7) n 047.1
~ starts (1) n 083.7
~ teacher (1) n 067.6
~ to head (1) adj 108.3
~ troubles (1) n 093.9
~ truck (1) n 111.2
~ up (8) v 055A.7
~ whipper (1) n 113.2
~ wool (1) n 035.2
Head (5) 106.1
head[N-i] (190) n 055A.6
head[V-p] (1) v 098.8
headache (5) n/adj 076.1
~ juice (1) n 114.7
~ stick (1) n 113.2
headaches (1) n 052.1
headboard (2) n 028.8
headcheese (115) n 047.1
headed (40) v/adj 055A.6
~ for (1) v 041.1
~ up (3) v 055A.6
headers (1) n 052.1
headfirst (3) adv 040.4

headgear (1) n 038.6
headhog cheese (1) n
047.1
heading (5) v/adj 006.5
~ back (1) v 006.5
~ lettuce (1) n 055A.6
~ up (1) v 055A.7
headland (2) n 031.7
Headland (3) AL 087.9
headlight (5) n 024.3
headlong (6) adj 074.8
headlonging (1) adj 073.3
headman (3) n 113.5
headmarks (1) n 080.7
headmaster (2) n 067.6
headmistress (1) n 067.6
headquarters (23) n 112.7
headrest (1) n 028.9
heads (706) n/v 055A.6
~ up (2) v 055A.6
Heads (3) 027.4
headshrinkers (1) n 065.9
headstand (1) n 095.5
headstrong (21) adj 074.8
heal (4) v 042.5
healer (1) n 067.8
healing (3) v/adj 057.4
~ oil (1) n 078.3
health (30) n/adj 070.6
~ bread (1) n 044.3
~ club (1) n 113.9
~ -food store (1) n
116.3
~ studio (2) n 113.4
healthier (3) adj 066.1
healthiest (1) adj 002.6
healthy (89) adj 074.1
~ -looking (4) adj
073.1
heap (161) n/v/adj 041.7
~ row (4) n 014.8
~ up (1) v 052.1
heaping (2) v/adj 014.8
~ piles (1) n 014.8
heaps (16) n 014.8
hear (1029) v 012.4
~ about (5) v 012.3
~ (a)bout (1) v 012.3
~ from (5) v 012.3
~ of (19) v 012.3
~ talk (1) v 012.3
~ talk about (1) v
012.4
~ talk of (4) v 012.4
~ tell (10) v 012.3

~ tell of (19) v 012.4
~ to (1) v 032.8
~ [P-0] (1) v 012.3
hear[V-r] (3) v 012.3
~ about (1) v 012.3
~ from (1) v 012.3
hear[V-t] (8) v 012.3
~ talk of (1) v 012.4
~ tell of (1) v 012.4
heard (2641) v 012.3
~ about (43) v 012.4
~ from (3) v 012.3
~ of (690) v 012.4
~ talk (1) v 012.4
~ talk about (2) v
012.4
~ talk of (26) v 012.4
~ tell (27) v 012.4
~ tell from (1) v 025.9
~ tell of (75) v 012.4
~ tell [P-0] (1) v 012.4
Heard (4) GA 087.1
~ County (3) GA 087.4
heared (332) v 012.3
~ about (2) v 012.3
~ of (39) v 012.4
~ talk (3) v 012.4
~ talk about (1) v
012.4
~ talk of (9) v 012.4
~ tell (7) v 012.4
~ tell of (19) v 012.4
hearing (121) n/v/adj
012.3
~ aid (1) n 012.3
hearn (9) v 012.3
~ talk of (2) v 012.4
Hearn (1) AR 087.1
Hearne (2) TX 107.7
hears (4) v 012.3
~ from (1) v 025.6
hearsay (2) n 039.8
hearse (148) n 117.5
hearses (2) n 023.8
heart (251) n/adj 054.1
~ attack (6) n 078.7
~ attacks (1) n 042.7
~ cypress (1) n 061.8
~ cypress boards (1) n
088.9
~ leaves (1) n 061.4
~ lumber (3) n 008.6
~ pills (1) n 102.7
~ pine (6) n 016.7

~ pine timber (1) n
  088.9
~ poplar logs (1) n
  061.9
~ post (1) n 016.5
~ timber (1) n 061.8
~ trouble (3) n 080.6
~ troubles (1) n 078.7
Heart (3) 056.9
heartbroken (1) adj 079.3
hearted (7) adj 048.9
hearth (1048) n/adj 008.2
~ broom (3) n 008.2
~ rock (6) n 008.2
~ wood (1) n 008.5
hearths (6) n 008.2
hearthstone (3) n 008.2
heartichokes (1) n 099.5
hearts (11) n 008.6
~ of palm (1) n 089.9
heartthrob (1) n 081.6
heartworms (2) n 096.8
hearty (4) adj 103.3
heat (142) n/v/adj 113.1
~ blister (1) n 077.7
~ gauge (1) n 110.1
~ lightning (2) n 006.2
~ plate (1) n 116.4
~ pump (3) n 118.5
~ roller (2) n 118.4
~ storm (1) n 006.2
~ tea (1) n 080.9
~ up (1) v 050.1
~ wave (2) n 007.1
~ with (2) v 032.4
heat[V-t] (1) v 070.8
heated (28) v/adj 050.1
~ by (1) v 008.4
~ over (9) v 050.1
~ up (3) v 050.1
heater (107) n/adj 118.4
~ flue (1) n 023.2
~ pipe (1) n 023.2
~ pipes (1) n 023.2
~ room (3) n 007A.3
~ stove (1) n 008.5
~ wood (2) n 092.9
heaters (71) n 118.4
heath (2) n 054.3
heathen (5) n 069.7
heathens (4) n 081.8
heating (57) n/v/adj
  118.5
~ closet (1) n 080.7
~ deal (1) n 080.8

~ element (1) n 040.6
~ pads (1) n 116.4
~ pump (1) n 118.5
~ stove (4) n 007A.8
~ system (1) n 118.5
~ tapes (1) n 084.9
~ unit (1) n 118.4
~ up (2) v 024.9
~ wood (1) n 008.6
heats (1) n 113.1
heave (39) v 080.3
~ to (1) v 104.5
~ up (3) v 080.3
heaved (17) v 080.3
heaven (12) n/adj 066.8
~ bush (2) n 062.2
Heaven (11) 089.3
heaven[N-k] (7) adj
  092.2
~ sake (4) n 092.2
~ sakes (3) n 092.2
heavenly (4) adj 005.4
~ day (1) n 005.4
Heavenly Father (8) 089.3
heaven's (4) adj 092.3
~ sake (3) n 092.3
~ sakes (1) n 092.2
heavens (38) n/interj
  092.2
heaves (4) n 080.3
heavier (9) adj 007.2
heaving (10) v 080.3
~ up (3) v 080.3
heavy (342) adj 073.1
~ as [D-0] cow (1) adj
  065.1
~ beer (1) n 121.9
~ black gumbo land (1)
  n 029.8
~ blow (1) n 006.1
~ bread (1) n 044.8
~ -built (2) adj 073.1
~ clay (1) n 029.8
~ clay hill land (1) n
  029.8
~ cold (1) n 007.5
~ courting (1) n 081.4
~ dating (1) n 081.4
~ dew (6) n 006.7
~ dirt (1) n 029.9
~ downpour (2) n
  006.1
~ drinker (2) n 113.6
~ ducking (1) n 019.7

~ -duty broom (1) n
  120.5
~ floods (1) n 006.1
~ fog (8) n 006.7
~ freeze (2) n 007.5
~ frost (62) n 007.5
~ frosts (1) n 007.5
~ goods (1) n 027.4
~ ice (1) n 007.6
~ land (2) n 029.8
~ loam (1) n 029.8
~ loam soil (1) n 029.8
~ mist (1) n 006.6
~ on her (2) adj 081.4
~ pour (1) n 006.1
~ pourdown (1) n
  006.1
~ rain (69) n 006.1
~ rain shower (1) n
  006.1
~ rainfall (1) n 006.1
~ rains (5) n 006.1
~ rainstorm (1) n 006.1
~ rake (3) n 120.7
~ sack (1) n 019.7
~ shower (14) n 006.1
~ shower rain (1) n
  006.1
~ showers (1) n 006.1
~ shuck (1) n 056.1
~ soil (2) n 029.8
~ springer (1) n 033.9
~ storm (2) n 006.2
~ syrup (1) n 051.3
~ -thigh brigade (1) n
  108.9
~ weather (1) n 006.2
~ with calf (1) adj
  033.9
~ with child (3) adj
  065.1
~ wood (3) n 008.5
heavyset (5) adj 073.1
heavysot (1) adj 073.1
heavyweight (2) n 073.1
Hebbronville (3) TX
087.8
Hebe (5) 126.8
Heber (2) AR 087.6
~ Springs (1) AR 087.4
Hebes (3) 126.7
Hebrew (1) 069.4
Hebrews (1) 126.7
Hebron (4) 089.1

~ Baptist Church (1)
  089.1
~ Cemetery (1) 078.8
heck (121) n/adj/interj
092.3
~ of a fix (1) n 065.1
Heckscher Drive (1) 107.6
Hector (1) 080.7
he'd (141) pron 101.2
hedge (138) n/adj 031.9
~ apple (2) n 061.8
~ cherry (1) n 062.5
~ clipper (5) n 120.8
~ clippers (43) n 120.8
~ cutter (7) n 120.8
~ cutters (6) n 120.8
~ shear (1) n 120.8
~ shears (9) n 120.8
~ snips (1) n 120.8
~ trees (1) n 061.8
~ trimmer (23) n 120.8
~ trimmers (17) n
  120.8
hedgehog (1) n 060.7
hedger (7) n 120.8
hedgerow (4) n/adj 016.2
~ fencing (1) n 016.6
hedgers (2) n 120.8
hedges (2) n 016.2
hedging (2) adj 120.8
~ clippers (1) n 120.8
~ limb (1) n 065.5
Hedwig (1) 105.2
hee (28) interj 038.3
~ -ah (1) interj 037.5
~ -haw (3) n 036.4
~ -haws (1) v 036.4
~ hoo (2) interj 038.3
~ ooh hee (1) interj
  038.3
~ -ooh(x2) (1) interj
  038.3
hee(x2) (4) interj 036.4
hee(x4) (1) interj 036.4
heebie (2) adj 083.2
~ -jeebie dance (1) n
  083.2
~ -jeebies (1) n 074.3
heed (3) n 025.8
heel (51) n/v/adj 072.8
~ pin (1) n 021.6
~ string (1) n 081.9
heel[N-i] (2) n 095.5
heeled (2) v/adj 124.6
~ up (1) v 078.6

heeler (2) n 115.4
heels (100) n 072.8
heemajeema (1) n 124.2
Heflin (1) AL 087.8
heft (2) v 104.5
hefty (20) adj 073.1
Heidenheimer (1)   TX
    087.2
heifer (430) n/adj 033.8
    ~ calf (51) n 033.8
    ~ calf[N-i] (1) n 033.8
    ~ calves (3) n 033.8
    ~ cow (4) n 033.6
    ~ cows (1) n 033.6
    ~ horse (1) n 039.4
Heifer Ford (1) TN 030.7
heifer(x2) (2) interj 037.5
heifer's name (1) n 034.2
heifers (34) n 033.8
heigh-ho (1) n 082.1
height (14) n 065.8
Height (1) 105.2
Height[N-i] (2) 105.1
heights (1) n 065.8
Heights (73) 106.1
Heil (1) 127.1
hein (2) interj F 012.6
heinous (1) adj 065.8
Heinrich (1) 025.2
Heinz (67) 033.3
    ~ Fifty-Seven   (45)
        033.3
    ~ Fifty-Seven curs (1)
        n 033.3
    ~ Fifty-Seven   varieties
        (3) n 033.3
    ~ Fifty-Seven   variety
        (1) n 033.3
    ~ Fifty-Seven vari-
        ety[N-i] (2) n
        033.3
    ~ Forty-Seven varieties
        (1) n 033.3
    ~ Seven   dog   (1)   n
        033.3
    ~ Sixty-Seven (1) 033.3
    ~ variety (2) n 033.3
    ~ Variety   Fifty-Seven
        (1) 033.3
heir (4) n 075.8
heired (1) v 075.7
heirlooms (2) n 010.2
heirs (2) n 066.9
heist (102) v 104.5
    ~ your leg (1) v 037.5

heistes (2) v 104.5
heisting (13) v 104.5
    ~ up (2) v 104.5
held (21) v 006.4
    ~ off (1) v 007.5
    ~ over (1) v 050.1
Helen (11) GA 087.9
Helena   (23)   AR   MS
    088.6
    ~ Run (1) FL 030.7
Helen(a) (1) AR 087.6
Helenwood (1) TN 087.4
Helicon (1) AL 087.7
helicopter   (124)   n/adj
    111.9
    ~ bug (1) n 060A.4
helicop(ter) (2) n 111.9
heli(copter) (1) n 111.9
(heli)copter (2) n 111.9
helicopters (40) n 111.9
he'll (52) pron 100.6
hell   (399)   n/adj/interj
    092.1
    ~ over (1) n 104.7
    ~ raiser (1) n 080.6
    ~ raisers (1) n 082.8
    ~ -raising (1) adj 089.8
    ~ -raising party (1) n
        130.7
    ~ -[J-0]-damnation
        sermon (1) n 089.4
Hell (4) 129.6
    ~ Gate (2) GA 030.7
hellacious (3) adj 084.8
hellbox (1) n 097.8
hellfire (6) n 092.1
    ~ -and-brimstone
        sermon (1) n 089.4
    ~ -and-damnation
        preacher (1) n
        080.6
hellhole (1) n 096.7
hello (189) interj 003.1
hell's bells (1) n 092.8
Helly (1) 067.3
help (1689) n/v/adj 049.4
    ~ from (1) v 096.7
    ~ maids (1) n 065.2
    ~ out (11) v 049.5
    ~ to (3) v 013.1
help[V-p] (4) v 013.6
    ~ out (2) v 025.6
help[V-r] (105) v 049.5
    ~ to (1) v 049.5
    ~ with (1) v 049.5

help[V-t] (139) v 049.5
helped (1328) v 049.5
    ~ along (1) v 049.5
    ~ out (10) v 049.5
    ~ to (2) v 049.5
    ~ up (1) v 049.5
helper (9) n 082.4
helpful (3) adj 073.2
helping   (127)   n/v/adj
    049.5
    ~ hand (1) n 058.6
helpless (5) adj 049.6
helpmate (2) n 063.1
helps (29) v 049.5
    ~ out (3) v 049.5
    ~ to (1) v 003.3
hem (3) n/v 080.8
hematur(ia) (3) n 077.5
HemisFair (5) 106.6
    ~ Plaza (2) 106.6
    ~ Tower (2) 106.4
Hemisphere (1) 106.7
hemlock (2) n 061.8
Hemming Park (1) 106.4
hemorrhaging (1) v 055.9
hemorrhoids (2) n 088.8
hemp (17) n/adj 019.7
    ~ bag (2) n 019.7
    ~ sack (2) n 019.7
Hemphill   (3)   LA   TX
    030.3
    ~ Creek (1) LA 030.7
Hempstead   (6)   AR   TX
    087.8
    ~ County (2) AR 087.5
    ~ Highway (1) 107.4
hen (1237) n/adj 036.7
    ~ caucus (1) n 081.8
    ~ coop (1) n 036.8
    ~ -dung trees (1) n
        061.9
    ~ egg (4) n 066.8
    ~ eggs (1) n 046.1
    ~ house (290) n 036.8
    ~ -house ways (1) n
        074.8
    ~ houses (11) n 036.8
    ~ nestes (1) n 066.8
    ~ owl (2) n 059.2
    ~ owls (1) n 059.2
    ~ setting (1) n 036.7
    ~ sitting (1) n 036.7
    ~ turkey (1) n 080.9
    ~ wood (1) n 059.3
    ~ yard (4) n 036.8

hen[N-k] (14) adj 036.8
    ~ nest (8) n 036.8
    ~ nestes (1) n 016.6
    ~ teeth (5) n 095.2
hence (1) adv 003.7
Henderson   (17)   AL   AR
    TN TX 087.2
    ~ bush   bean   (1)   n
        055A.3
    ~ County   Fair   (1)
        087.5
    ~ Drive (1) 107.7
    ~ High (1) 052.2
    ~ Mountain   (1)   AR
        087.3
    ~ Road (1) 031.6
Hendersonville   (7)   NC
    TN 087.6
Hendrix (2) 107.7
    ~ Avenue (1) 107.7
    ~ Creek (1) LA 030.7
Hendry County (1) FL
    087.6
Henley Street (1) 107.7
Henleyfield (1) MS 087.8
Henly (2) TX 087.4
hennit (2) n/v F 036.4
henny (1) n 033.7
henpeck preacher (1) n
    067.8
Henpeck Lane (1) 031.8
henpeck[V-t] (1) v 080.6
henpecked (1) v 063.1
Henrietta (1) TN 087.1
Henry   (19)   AL GA TN
    087.2
    ~ County (3) AL GA
        087.6
    ~ Grady monument (2)
        n 106.4
    ~ Road (1) 014.1
    ~ Street (1) 107.9
hen's (17) adj 036.8
    ~ nest (2) n 036.8
    ~ teeth (15) n 095.2
hens (92) n 121.5
Henson Mountain (1) AR
    087.4
hep (2) adj 053.5
hepatitis (56) n 079.8
Hephzibah (1) AL 075.7
her (2568) pron/v 042.5
    ~ him (1) n 113.5
    ~ -ing (1) v 081.4

~ leg broke (2) adj 065.1

~ own self (1) pron 044.2

~ to be husband (1) n 081.5

herb (13) n/adj 114.1

~ doctor (2) n 080.8

~ doctors (1) n 061.4

~ garden (2) n 050.5

~ house (1) n 065.8

~ medicine (2) n 061.4

~ tea (1) n 061.4

herb[N-i] (1) n 061.4

herbes (1) n F 091.8

herbicides (2) n 015.8

Herbie (2) 117.3

~ the Curbie (1) 117.3

~ [D-0] Curbie (1) 117.3

herbs (39) n 061.4

herd (47) n/v/adj 036.5

~ bull (3) n 033.5

~ bulls (1) n 033.5

~ sire (1) n 033.5

~ stock (1) n 033.5

herded (1) v 036.6

herder (1) n 084.8

here (2884) n/adv/interj 025.1

~ -boss(x2) (1) interj 037.5

~ -bossy(x2) (1) interj 037.5

~ chick (1) interj 038.5

~ -chick(x2) (4) interj 038.5

~ -cow(x2) (1) interj 038.4

~ -dog(x2) (1) interj 033.2

~ now (2) interj 033.2

~ pig (1) interj 038.3

~ -pig(x2) (1) interj 038.3

~ -pig(x4) (1) interj 038.3

~ -piggy(x2) (1) interj 038.3

~ -sheepy(x3) (1) interj 038.4

~ -sook(x2) (1) interj 037.5

~ -up (1) interj 037.5

~ we come (2) n 098.3

~ you are (1) interj 038.5

here(x2) (7) interj 033.2

here(x3) (3) interj 038.3

here(x4) (1) interj 033.2

Hereford (18) 033.6

~ cattle (2) n 081.9

~ cows (1) n 033.6

Herefords (3) 033.6

here's (176) adv 025.1

Hergett (1) AR 087.1

heritage native (1) n 088.7

Herlong Field (1) 106.5

Herman Park (2) 106.4

Herman's Hermits (1) 130.8

hermaphrodite (3) n 082.8

(her)maphrodite (1) n 069.5

hermit (29) n/adj 069.9

~ crab (1) n 060.8

Hermitage (9) 106.4

~ Drive (1) 107.6

hermits (7) n 069.9

Hermits (1) 130.8

hern (27) pron 043.4

Hernando (6) MS 087.3

~ County (1) FL 087.5

~ De Soto Bridge (1) 106.4

Herndon (2) 106.5

~ Home[N-i] (1) 105.5

hernia (4) n 065.8

herni(a) (2) n 080.1

hero (24) n/adj 121.7

~ sandwich (4) n 121.7

~ sandwiches (2) n 121.7

~ submarine sandwiches (1) n 121.7

heroes (1) n 121.7

heroin (94) n 114.2

heron (3) n 088.9

Heron Bay (1) MS 087.6

herrings (1) n 059.9

hers (557) pron 043.4

herself (102) pron 044.2

hersen (1) pron 043.4

Hershey (6) 065.9

~ bar (3) n 065.9

Hershey's (1) 065.8

he's (964) pron 060A.5

(he')s (1) pron 032.2

hesitated to (1) v 081.3

Hessmer (1) LA 087.3

Hester (2) 030.7

~ Creek (1) MS 030.7

~ melon (1) n 056.9

het (20) v/adj 050.1

~ over (2) v 050.1

~ roof (1) n 011.4

~ up (6) v 050.1

~ water (1) n 070.6

~ with (1) v 098.8

het(x3) (1) interj 037.9

Heustock (1) n G 014.5

hew (2) adj 017.8

~ ax (1) n 017.8

~ knife (1) n 017.8

HEW (1) 012.9

hewed (5) v/adj 002.6

~ -out (1) adj 008.5

Hewes Avenue (1) 107.6

hewing (1) v 057.4

hewn (3) v/adj 016.4

~ out (1) v 065.9

hex (1) n 093.6

hexes (1) n 102.7

hey (93) n/interj 092.5

~ over (1) n 104.7

hey(x2) (5) interj 037.5

hi (84) interj 092.5

Hialeah (7) FL 087.2

~ area (2) FL 088.8

Hiawassee (3) GA 065.8

~ River (1) TN 030.7

Hibernia building (1) n 075.6

hibiscus (6) n/adj 061.9

~ bush (1) n 062.7

Hibiscus Road (1) 107.6

hibou (1) n F 059.2

hick (164) n/adj 069.9

~ music (2) n 130.8

hickey (5) n 077.4

hickies (2) n 028.7

Hickman (4) KY TN 087.4

~ County (1) TN 087.2

hickories (11) n 061.8

hickory (672) n/adj 061.8

~ ashes (3) n 008.7

~ chips (1) n 008.6

~ ham (1) n 121.3

~ handle (1) n 070.8

~ he owl (1) n 059.1

~ log (1) n 008.5

~ logs (1) n 008.5

~ maul (1) n 020.7

~ meat (2) n 056.8

~ nut (75) n 054.8

~ -nut (4) adj 061.9

~ -nut tree (10) n 061.9

~ -nut trees (13) n 061.8

~ nuts (265) n 054.7

~ sapling (1) n 061.8

~ shad (1) n 059.9

~ shirts (1) n 027.3

~ smoke (1) n 061.8

~ -smoked (1) adj 046.5

~ switch (1) n 065.5

~ tree (29) n 061.8

~ trees (26) n 061.8

~ wood (20) n 061.8

hickor(y) (68) n/adj 061.9

~ chickens (1) n 056.8

~ nut (16) n 054.8

~ -nut grove (1) n 061.6

~ -nut tree (4) n 061.8

~ -nut trees (3) n 061.9

~ nuts (41) n 054.7

hick(ory) (4) n/adj 061.8

~ -nut trees (2) n 070.8

~ nuts (2) n 054.7

Hickory (30) NC TN 030.7

~ Branch (2) LA 030.7

~ Cane (4) 056.2

~ Cane corn (2) n 056.2

~ County (1) MO 087.1

~ Flat (6) AL GA MS 087.1

~ Hill (2) LA 087.5

~ Hills (1) 106.1

~ King (3) 056.2

~ Level (1) GA 087.2

Hickor(y) (2) 029.4

~ Bottom (1) LA 029.4

~ Flat (1) GA 086.2

hickory[N-i] (1) n 055A.7

hicks (40) n 069.9

hicky (1) adj 069.9

Hico (1) LA 087.4

hid (12) v 096.4

~ out (1) v 052.6

Hidalgo (4) TX 087.2

~ County (1) TX 087.6
hidden (1) v 096.4
hide (509) n/v 096.4
   ~ -and-go-get-it (1) n
    130.1
   ~ -and-go-seek (124) n
    130.1
   ~ -(a)nd-go-seek (1) n
    130.1
   ~ -and-seek (314) n
    098.4
   ~ and spy (3) n 080.9
   ~ -and-switching (1) n
    098.4
   ~ -[J-0]- go-get-
    them (1) n
    130.1
   ~ -[J-0]-go-seek (6) n
    130.1
Hide (9) 009.1
   ~ -a-Bed (8) 009.1
   ~ -a-Beds (1) 009.1
hide[V-p] (1) v 070.1
hideaway (13) n/adj
  009.1
   ~ bed (8) n 009.1
   ~ closet (1) n 009.6
Hideaway Lake (1) MS
  030.7
hidebound (1) adj 073.5
hided (1) v 034.3
hideous (2) adj 125.1
hides (7) n/v 096.4
hiding (33) v/adj 096.4
   ~ a basketball (1) v
    065.1
   ~ -and-seek (2) n 098.4
   ~ -and-seeking (1) n
    098.4
   ~ hoop (3) n 098.4
   ~ house (1) n 012.1
   ~ in (1) v 096.4
   ~ place (2) n 098.4
   ~ seat (1) n 097.8
   ~ seek (2) n 098.4
   ~ whip (2) n 098.4
hidy (1) n 098.4
hifaluter (1) n 089.8
hiffle (1) n 060A.5
higger (1) n 069.9
high (1271) adj/adv 125.9
   ~ -ass (1) adj 069.6
   ~ -back chair (1) n
    008.8

~ -back rocker (1) n
  008.8
~ -back rocking chairs
  (1) n 008.8
~ -back straight chairs
  (1) n 008.8
~ bench (1) n 089.7
~ blood (11) n 080.6
~ -blowing spell (1) n
  007.2
~ boot (1) n 123.8
~ brown (2) n 069.5
~ browns (1) n 069.5
~ -built houses (1) n
  118.9
~ -button shoes (1) n
  123.8
~ -capacity gin (1) n
  084.9
~ -class (1) adj 123.6
~ -class call girl (1) n
  113.3
~ -class living (1) n
  091.7
~ classers (1) n 088.9
~ -expansion foam (1)
  n 081.9
~ fashion (3) n 123.6
~ five (1) n 088.9
~ frog (1) n 099.7
~ gear (2) n 041.5
~ ground (1) n 029.5
~ -hatted (1) adj 093.8
~ -headed (1) adj 075.1
~ heel (5) n 123.8
~ -heel (1) adj 123.8
~ -heel dress shoes (1)
  n 123.8
~ -heel shoes (10) n
  123.8
~ -heel spike shoes (1)
  n 123.8
~ -heel thing[N-i] (1) n
  123.8
~ heels (40) n 123.8
~ -lace shoes (1) n
  123.8
~ lifts (1) n 104.5
~ -minded (3) adj
  074.8
~ -moving-type wind
  (1) n 006.5
~ noon (2) n 002.3
~ -powered (1) adj
  033.7

~ -powered saw (1) n
  120.9
~ primer (1) n 083.7
~ rent (1) n 069.4
~ rise (1) n 030.8
~ -rise (80) n/adj 108.5
~ -rise apartment (6) n
  108.5
~ -rise apartment build-
  ing (6) n 108.5
~ -rise apartments (8) n
  108.5
~ -rise building (4) n
  108.5
~ -rise buildings (5) n
  108.5
~ -rise community (1)
  n 119.3
~ -rise dormitory (1) n
  108.5
~ -rise dorms (1) n
  119.2
~ -rise housing (1) n
  108.5
~ -rise parking (2) n
  108.4
~ -rises (7) n 108.5
~ school (205) n 125.9
~ -school combination
  (1) n 080.6
~ -school education (2)
  n 083.5
~ -school girls (1) n
  052.6
~ -school graduate (2)
  n 083.5
~ -school kids (1) n
  064.3
~ -school level (1) n
  070.3
~ -school principal (1)
  n 013.8
~ -school scholar (2) n
  068.7
~ -school student (5) n
  068.7
~ -school students (1) n
  068.7
~ -school sweethearts
  (2) n 081.5
~ schools (7) n 125.9
~ service (1) n 031.6
~ sheriff (6) n 070.8
~ shoes (1) n 123.8
~ sky (1) n 005.4

~ -society places (1) n
  106.1
~ -stepping (1) n 083.1
~ -strung (34) adj
  075.1
~ style (1) n 123.6
~ temper (4) n 075.1
~ -temper (8) adj 075.1
~ -tempered (107) adj
  075.1
~ -tension (1) adj 075.1
~ tides (1) n 027.4
~ -tooting (1) adj 088.9
~ top (2) n 009.7
~ -top (1) adj 096.9
~ -top shoe (1) n 084.9
~ -top shoes (4) n
  123.8
~ tops (3) n 123.8
~ -up (1) adj 002.6
~ water (14) n 048.9
~ -water mark (1) n
  084.8
~ waters (6) n 123.3
~ wind (1) n 075.8
~ -wind rain (1) n
  006.1
~ winds (1) n 006.4
~ wiring (1) n 016.3
~ yellow (66) n 069.5
~ -yellow girls (1) n
  069.5
~ yellows (7) n 069.5
~ -yield soil (1) n 029.3
High (40) 125.9
   ~ Brahman (1) 081.9
   ~ Falls (2) GA 031.5
   ~ Five (1) 112.8
   ~ Flyer (1) 093.8
   ~ German (1) 127.1
   ~ Hill (2) TX 030.8
   ~ Knob (1) TN 030.8
   ~ Museum of Art (1)
    106.4
   ~ Pine Creek (1) AL
    030.7
   ~ Plains (1) TX 087.7
   ~ Point (2) GA NC
    086.8
   ~ School (9) 125.8
   ~ Springs (1) FL 087.3
   ~ Street (2) 107.6
high[A-w] (2) adj 083.5
highball (3) n/adj 066.8
   ~ glass (1) n 089.8

~ glasses (1) n 051.9
highballs (1) n 009.2
Highbank Creek (1) AR 030.7
highboy (23) n 009.2
highboys (3) n 009.2
highchous (1) adj 075.1
higher (51) adj/adv 007.2
~ bushes (1) n 082.1
~ education (1) n 083.5
~ -up (1) adj 091.8
highest (4) adj 075.8
highfalutin (6) adj 088.9
highland (58) n/adj 029.4
~ animals (1) n 060.7
~ copper-belly (1) n 081.9
~ frogs (1) n 060.4
~ gophers (1) n 060.7
~ hard maple (1) n 101.7
~ huckleberries (1) n 062.4
~ moccasin (5) n 080.7
~ moccasins (2) n 088.8
~ myrtle (1) n 062.7
~ rice (5) n 050.7
~ terrapin (7) n 060.7
~ terrapins (2) n 060.7
~ turtle (9) n 060.7
~ turtles (4) n 060.7
Highland (32) AR VA 107.7
~ and Virginia (1) 106.2
~ Creek (1) AL 030.7
~ Lakes (1) TX 030.7
~ Park (13) 106.2
~ Pines (1) 105.1
~ section (1) n 087.5
~ Terrace (1) 107.7
highlander (1) n 060.7
Highlander (1) 128.1
highlanders (1) n 127.2
Highlanders (1) 080.7
highlands (1) n 080.9
Highlands (2) FL 087.5
~ County (1) FL 086.5
highly (3) adv 091.6
Highmound (1) AL 087.3
highs (2) n 125.8
Hightower (4) 105A.2
~ Falls (1) GA 031.5
~ Road (1) 107.7

highway (324) n/adj 031.6
~ barn (1) n 014.2
~ bridge (1) n 031.6
~ divider (1) n 107.3
~ hotel (1) n 113.8
~ lanes (1) n 031.8
~ line (1) n 107.3
~ markers (1) n 107.3
~ markings (1) n 107.3
~ patrol (2) n 112.5
~ patrolman (1) n 112.5
~ road (2) n 031.6
~ robbery (1) n 116.3
~ striping (1) n 107.3
Highway (98) 031.6
~ Eighty (1) 107.7
~ Eighty-Four (2) 107.1
~ Eighty-Two (1) 107.1
~ Fifteen (1) 031.6
~ Fifty-Nine (1) 031.6
~ Fifty-One South (1) 031.6
~ Forty-Nine (3) 107.1
~ Nine-Fifteen (1) 107.6
~ Ninety (10) 107.6
~ Ninety-Eight (2) 105A.8
~ One (2) 001.1
~ Seventeen (1) 107.6
~ Seventy (1) 107.1
~ Seventy-Five (1) 084.8
~ Sixteen (1) 031.6
~ Sixty-Five (1) 107.1
~ Sixty-Seven (1) 107.1
~ Ten (2) 031.6
~ Thirty-Five (1) 107.1
~ Thirty-Seven (1) 107.1
~ Twelve (2) 105.5
~ US One (1) 095.9
highways (89) n 031.6
hike (6) n/v/interj 037.7
~ up (2) interj 038.2
hiking (6) v/adj 123.8
~ boots (4) n 123.8
~ shorts (1) n 123.4
hilarious (1) adj 068.8
Hildebrand (4) 107.7
~ Bayou (2) TX 030.7
hill (1091) n/v/adj 030.8

~ countries (1) n 030.8
~ country (10) n 030.8
~ -drop (1) v 092.8
~ droppers (1) n 021.6
~ farm (1) n 030.8
~ farms (1) n 080.8
~ folk (1) n 069.9
~ folks (1) n 069.9
~ gumbo (1) n 029.8
~ hog (1) n 035.9
~ house (1) n 011.6
~ knob (1) n 030.8
~ knobs (1) n 030.8
~ land (31) n 029.8
~ -like (1) adj 030.8
~ -like thing (1) n 030.8
~ maple (1) n 061.9
~ people (11) n 069.9
~ place (1) n 030.8
~ plow (1) n 021.6
~ racket (1) n 080.7
~ rooters (1) n 035.9
~ section (4) n 030.8
~ sweep (6) n 021.6
~ sweeps (1) n 021.6
~ terrapin (1) n 060.7
~ terrapins (2) n 060.7
~ toad (2) n 060.4
~ up (1) v 090.9
Hill (211) 030.8
~ Plantation (1) 030.8
~ Street (1) 105.5
hill[N-i] (2) n 030.8
Hillabee Creek (3) AL 030.7
hillbillies (107) n 069.9
hillbilly (173) n/adj 069.9
~ -ass (1) adj 069.9
~ coffee (1) n 069.9
~ country (1) n 069.9
~ music (3) n 130.9
~ preacher (1) n 067.8
Hillcrest (9) TN TX 087.6
~ Drive (1) 107.9
~ High School (1) 125.9
Hillcroft (1) 107.5
Hilldale (1) 105.2
hilled (6) v 015.6
~ up (1) v 015.6
Hilliard Street (1) 107.6
hillier (1) adj 030.8
hilling (2) v 015.8

hillock (2) n 030.8
hillocks (1) n 030.8
hills (231) n 030.8
Hills (44) 030.8
Hillsboro (9) AR LA TX 105.3
Hillsborough (17) FL 086.6
~ County (3) FL 086.2
~ River (4) FL 030.7
Hillsbor(ough) (1) FL 086.5
Hillsdale Heights (1) 106.1
hillside (68) n/adj 021.6
~ ditches (1) n 030.2
~ knob (1) n 030.8
~ land (3) n 029.5
~ plow (11) n 021.6
~ plows (4) n 021.6
~ soil (1) n 029.8
~ turner (4) n 021.6
~ turning plow (2) n 021.6
hillsides (6) n 030.8
Hilltonia (1) GA 087.2
hilltop (3) n 030.8
Hilltop (1) AR 087.1
Hillview (3) GA 087.7
~ Church (1) 089.2
hilly (70) adj 029.8
~ country (7) n 030.8
~ ground (1) n 030.8
~ land (21) n 029.8
~ lands (1) n 029.8
~ section (1) n 030.8
hilt (1) n 123.6
Hilton (3) 087.2
~ Head (2) SC 087.2
~ Head Beach (1) SC 087.7
him (8311) pron/v 042.5
~ -ing and her-ing (1) v 081.7
(hi)m (4) pron 102.2
Himalaya (7) 062.6
~ berries (2) n 062.4
~ berry (3) n 062.4
~ blackberry[N-i] (1) n 062.2
Himalay(a) berries (2) n 062.5
Himalayan brier (1) n 062.5

Himmel (1) interj G 092.3
himri (1) n 081.8
himself (1073) pron 044.2
(him)self (3) pron 044.2
Hinch Mountain (2) TN 031.1
hind (34) adj 075.7
   ~ end (3) n 075.7
   ~ feet (5) n 072.6
   ~ feets (1) n 072.6
   ~ foot (1) n 072.6
   ~ foots (1) n 072.6
   ~ hoof (1) n 034.7
   ~ leg (3) n 072.8
   ~ legs (11) n 072.8
   ~ part (3) n 072.8
   ~ parts (1) n 072.8
   ~ stick (1) n 008.5
   ~ team (1) n 039.4
   ~ wheel (1) n 010.5
   ~ wheels (1) n 092.8
hindquarter (4) n 072.8
hindquarters (3) n 072.8
Hinds (9) MS 087.2
   ~ County (6) MS 086.7
hindside (1) n 010.5
Hinesville (1) GA 087.4
hinge (5) n 023.7
hinges (5) n 020.3
Hinkle Branch (1) TN 030.7
hinklebonger (1) n 127.1
hinny (2) n 036.4
Hinsonton (1) GA 087.6
hint (1) n 051.8
hip (60) n/adj 072.8
   ~ apron (1) n 026.4
   ~ bone (1) n 072.8
   ~ platter (1) n 130.8
   ~ roof (7) n 080.9
   ~ -roof house (1) n 096.8
   ~ -roof porch (1) n 010.8
   ~ slangs (1) n 084.8
   ~ to-do (2) n 075.7
   ~ -tote (1) v 098.1
   ~ -type roof (1) n 014.2
   ~ -type room (1) n 011.4
hipped out (1) v 007A.2
hippers (1) n 021.7
hippie (94) n/adj 129.3

   ~ area (1) n 099.5
   ~ culture (1) n 129.3
   ~ cut (1) n 123.9
   ~ haircut (1) n 123.9
   ~ movement (1) n 129.3
   ~ radicals (1) n 129.3
   ~ shoes (1) n 123.8
   ~ stuff (1) n 027.4
   ~ style (2) n 123.9
   ~ -type (1) adj 105.8
   ~ -type clothes (1) n 129.3
   ~ -type word (1) n 100.2
hippie[N-i] (1) n 075.6
hippies (76) n 129.3
hipping (1) n 088.7
hips (21) n 072.8
hire (18) v/adj 075.6
   ~ hands (2) n 066.8
hired (17) v/adj 065.8
   ~ labor (1) n 032.4
   ~ out (2) v 070.6
hiring (4) v/adj 114.8
   ~ corner (1) n 114.8
his (3526) pron 043.4
   ~ own self (8) pron 044.2
(hi)s (8) pron 042.4
hisn (75) pron 043.5
hisns (2) pron 043.4
hiss (16) v 033.2
hissed (1) v 033.2
hisself (637) pron 044.2
histoplasmosis (1) n 088.7
historical (1) adj 053.3
historically (1) adv 025.6
history (10) n/adj 069.2
   ~ test (1) n 026.3
History (1) 106.9
hit (582) n/pron/v/adj 042.5
   ~ -and-run (1) n 060A.5
   ~ at (1) v 104.2
   ~ house (1) n 088.9
   ~ out (1) v 042.5
   ~ the buck(et) (1) v 078.6
   ~ the grit (1) v 078.6
   ~ the road (1) v 082.1
hitch (287) n/v/adj 038.6
   ~ lines (1) n 039.2
   ~ onto (1) v 038.6

   ~ post (1) n 020.8
   ~ reins (2) n 039.1
   ~ to (1) v 038.6
   ~ up (64) v 038.6
hitch[V-r] (3) v 038.6
   ~ to (1) v 038.6
   ~ up (1) v 038.6
hitch[V-t] (4) v 082.2
   ~ to (1) v 038.6
hitched (253) v 082.2
   ~ to (2) v 038.6
   ~ up (27) v 038.6
hitches (3) n/v 020.9
hitchhiker (1) n 053.5
hitchhiking (1) n 131.1
hitching (26) v/adj 098.1
   ~ post (3) n 016.5
   ~ post[N-i] (2) n 016.5
   ~ postes (2) n 016.5
   ~ rack (1) n 088.7
   ~ racks (1) n 088.7
   ~ rail (1) n 038.6
   ~ strap (1) n 022.3
   ~ up (4) v 038.6
hit'd (6) pron 072.7
Hitler (2) 015.9
   ~ grass (1) n 015.9
Hitlerites (2) 127.1
Hitlers (1) 127.1
hit'll (23) pron 042.4
hit's (117) pron 042.5
hits (4) n 114.2
hitself (2) pron 044.1
hitter (1) n 090.4
hitting (11) v 057.4
   ~ at (1) v 089.8
   ~ on her (1) v 081.4
hive weed (1) n 089.8
hives (4) n 060A.5
Hiwassee (9) GA TN 030.7
   ~ River (4) TN 030.7
(Hi)wassee River (1) TN 030.7
Hix (1) TX 087.2
Hixson (5) TN 087.1
   ~ Creek (1) TN 030.7
   ~ Pike (1) 106.2
hiyi (1) interj 038.3
HMT (1) 081.8
ho (62) n/interj 038.2
   ~ -cow(x2) (1) interj 037.5
   ~ -eh (1) interj 037.5
   ~ haw (1) interj 038.2

   ~ -ho (1) n 022.5
   ~ hoey (1) interj 038.3
   ~ up (1) interj 038.1
   ~ -wuh (1) interj 037.6
ho(x2) (4) interj 037.7
hoagie (23) n/adj 121.7
   ~ sandwich (2) n 121.7
hoagies (5) n 121.7
hoarder (5) n 073.5
hoarfrost (7) n 112.3
hoarhound tea (1) n 061.4
hoarse (874) adj 076.4
hoarseness (9) n 076.4
hoarser (1) adj 076.4
hoarses (1) adj 076.4
hoarsy (1) adj 076.4
hoary (4) adj 007.5
   ~ frost (3) n 007.5
   ~ snow (1) n 007.5
hob (1) n 008.2
hobbies (2) n 045.3
hobble (1) v 088.7
hobby (2) n 022.5
Hobby (6) 106.5
   ~ Airport (4) 106.5
   ~ Field (1) 106.5
hobbyhorse (5) n/adj 022.6
   ~ ride (1) n 089.9
hobbyhorses (1) n 022.6
hobgoblins (2) n 090.2
hobnail shoes (1) n 088.8
hobnob with (1) v 088.8
hobo (57) n/adj 113.7
   ~ biscuits (1) n 084.9
hoboes (12) n 113.7
Hoboken (2) GA NJ 087.8
hobs (1) n 008.2
hock (68) n/v/adj 046.5
   ~ bones (3) n 046.4
   ~ house (1) n 114.6
   ~ houses (1) n 114.6
   ~ shop (23) n 114.6
hocked (1) v 100.2
hockey (19) n 130.4
hocks (43) n 121.3
hocus (1) n 090.3
Hocus Pocus (1) 106.6
hod (42) n 023.1
(Hod)chodkee Creek (1) GA 030.7
Hodge (2) 107.6
   ~ Avenue (1) 107.6

~ corn (1) n 056.2
Hodges (3) AL 087.3
   ˘ Creek (1) AL 030.7
   ˘ Gardens (1) LA 087.7
Hodgkin's disease (1) n 084.9
hods (4) n 023.1
hoe (277) n/v/adj 021.7
   ˘ bread (1) n 044.6
   ˘ fork (1) n 090.8
   ˘ handle (2) n 066.8
   ˘ hands (3) n 099.8
   ˘ out (4) v 015.8
   ˘ rake (1) n 120.7
   ˘ -type (1) adj 022.3
hoecake (364) n/adj 045.3
   ˘ baker (10) n 017.5
   ˘ bakers (2) n 017.5
   ˘ biscuits (1) n 044.4
   ˘ bread (23) n 044.5
   ˘ breads (1) n 044.6
   ˘ corn bread (5) n 044.5
   ˘ flour bread (1) n 044.6
   ˘ skillet (2) n 017.5
hoecakes (136) n 044.7
hoed (34) v 015.8
   ˘ out (4) v 015.8
hoedown (29) n/adj 083.1
   ˘ dance (1) n 083.1
hoedowns (5) n 083.1
hoeing (126) v 015.9
hoeing[N-i] (1) n 015.9
hoer (1) n 015.8
hoe's width (1) n 015.8
hoes (16) n/v 120.5
hoey (3) interj 037.8
hoey(x2) (1) interj 037.5
Hoffman Road (1) 031.6
hog (2269) n/v/adj/adv 035.5
   ˘ acorn (1) n 054.8
   ˘ -acorn tree (1) n 061.9
   ˘ and hair (1) n 050.8
   ˘ and hominy (1) n 050.8
   ˘ back (1) n 046.3
   ˘ backbone (2) n 046.4
   ˘ balls (1) n 081.8
   ˘ bank (1) n 030.8
   ˘ barb (1) n 016.3

~ barn (4) n 015.4
~ barrel (1) n 017.4
~ beds (1) n 015.4
~ berry (2) n 062.5
~ bladders (1) n 081.8
~ blood (1) n 047.3
~ bone (1) n 121.3
~ booster (1) n 015.4
~ brains (7) n 047.8
~ bristle (3) n 035.6
~ bristles (3) n 035.6
~ bucket (4) n 017.4
~ business (4) n 035.4
~ -calling (1) v 035.5
~ -calling contest (1) n 038.3
~ cheese (8) n 047.1
~ chitlins (11) n 037.3
~ chitterling (1) n 037.3
~ chitterlings (1) n 037.3
~ chow (1) n 047.4
~ claims (1) n 035.5
~ clean (1) adj 041.4
~ corral (1) n 015.4
~ country (1) n 099.9
~ crackling (3) n 047.4
~ cracklings (2) n 047.1
~ -cured stock (1) n 036.5
~ dog (6) n 033.3
~ dogs (5) n 033.3
~ ear (1) n 071.5
~ ears (1) n 046.3
~ entrails (1) n 037.3
~ -eye gravy (1) n 048.5
~ farm (2) n 035.5
~ -farm road (1) n 031.7
~ farming (3) n 015.3
~ -fashion (1) adv 075.9
~ fat (4) n 035.5
~ -fattening pens (1) n 015.4
~ feed (4) n 092.7
~ feeder (4) n 035.8
~ feeders (1) n 035.5
~ -feeding time (1) n 037.4
~ feet (3) n 037.3
~ fence (7) n 016.3
~ fences (1) n 016.4

~ fencing (1) n 016.3
~ goozle (1) n 071.7
~ gravy (2) n 066.8
~ grease (2) n 023.7
~ gut (2) n 037.3
~ guts (13) n 037.3
~ hair (21) n 035.6
~ -hair brush (1) n 022.2
~ hairs (2) n 035.6
~ ham (1) n 046.5
~ hash (2) n 047.1
~ haslet (8) n 035.5
~ haslet stew (1) n 037.2
~ haslets (1) n 037.2
~ haw (1) n 062.5
~ haws (2) n 062.5
~ heaven (1) n 081.8
~ hide (1) n 046.6
~ hocks (1) n 046.3
~ hoof (1) n 034.7
~ -hoof tea (6) n 093.7
~ house (13) n 015.4
~ houses (8) n 015.4
~ intestines (2) n 037.3
~ jaw (9) n 046.3
~ jaws (4) n 047.1
~ jowl (42) n 046.3
~ jowl[N-i] (1) n 046.3
~ jowls (25) n 047.1
~ killing (5) n 035.5
~ -killing knife (1) n 104.3
~ -killing time (4) n 035.6
~ killings (1) n 084.9
~ lard (3) n 019.2
~ law (4) n 036.5
~ -link sausage (1) n 046.8
~ liver (14) n 047.2
~ livers (1) n 047.2
~ lot (82) n 015.4
~ lots (2) n 015.4
~ mark (1) n 088.7
~ maw (5) n 037.2
~ maws (1) n 037.2
~ meat (13) n 035.5
~ meet (1) n 091.8
~ mollies (3) n 059.9
~ molly (1) n 059.9
~ neck bones (1) n 121.3
~ netting (1) n 016.3

~ nuts (2) n 080.8
~ off (2) v 035.5
~ oil (1) n 024.1
~ pail (3) n 017.4
~ palaces (1) n 015.4
~ pan (2) n 035.8
~ parlor (16) n 015.4
~ parlors (4) n 015.4
~ pasture (24) n 015.4
~ -pasture fencing (1) n 016.3
~ pastures (4) n 015.7
~ patch (1) n 015.4
~ path (1) n 031.8
~ paths (1) n 031.8
~ peanut (2) n 054.7
~ pinder (1) n 054.7
~ places (1) n 015.4
~ plum (1) n 062.4
~ potato (2) n 055.4
~ -proof (1) adj 016.3
~ -proof fence (1) n 016.3
~ -proof fences (1) n 016.3
~ -proof wire (3) n 016.3
~ pudding (4) n 035.5
~ pumpkin (2) n 056.5
~ rifle (2) n 035.5
~ rifles (1) n 080.8
~ rinds (1) n 046.6
~ run (1) n 015.4
~ runner (1) n 015.4
~ sausage (2) n 046.8
~ scalder (1) n 081.8
~ seeds (1) n 037.3
~ shed (11) n 015.4
~ sheds (1) n 015.4
~ shelter (6) n 015.4
~ shelters (2) n 015.4
~ shorts (1) n 084.8
~ skin (1) n 046.6
~ slop (5) n 017.4
~ souse (6) n 047.1
~ sucker (1) n 059.9
~ suckers (1) n 059.9
~ tails (2) n 121.3
~ teeth (3) n 035.7
~ tongue (1) n 037.4
~ trail (1) n 031.8
~ trough (77) n 035.8
~ trough[N-i] (9) n 035.8
~ troughs (42) n 035.8

~ tush (1) n 035.7
~ tushes (1) n 035.7
~ -type wire fences (1) n 016.3
~ up (1) v 098.6
~ wallet (1) n 019.7
~ wallow (7) n 015.4
~ whistle (2) n 093.6
~ wire (101) n 016.3
~ -wire (7) adj 016.3
~ -wire fence (18) n 016.3
~ -wire fences (9) n 016.3
~ -wire mesh (1) n 016.3
~ wiring (1) n 016.3
hog(x3) (1) interj 038.3
Hog (10) 080.7
~ Back (1) TN 080.7
~ Bayou (2) MS TX 030.7
~ Branch (1) LA 030.7
~ Creek (3) AR GA TX 030.7
~ Mountain Road (1) 031.8
~ Slough (1) LA 030.7
~ Swamp (1) MS 030.7
hog[N-i] (22) n 035.5
Hogan (2) 107.7
Hogansville (3) GA 087.3
hogfish (4) n 059.9
Hogg (4) 087.3
hogged (4) v 041.4
hogging (5) v 041.4
hoggish (2) adj 035.4
hoggy (3) adj/interj 038.3
~ hog (1) n 035.5
hoggy(x3) (1) interj 038.4
hoghead (388) n/adj 047.1
~ and cheese (1) n 047.1
~ cheese (311) n 047.1
~ chow (1) n 047.1
~ fry (1) n 047.1
~ hash (2) n 047.1
~ liver (1) n 047.1
~ meat (1) n 047.1
~ mush (3) n 047.1
~ sausage (1) n 047.1
~ side (1) n 047.1
~ souse (47) n 047.1

hogheads (9) n/adj 047.1
~ cheese (3) n 047.1
hoghood (1) n 035.5
hoglet (1) n 035.5
hogman (1) n 091.9
hognose (4) n/adj 081.8
~ green snakes (1) n 091.8
~ snakes (1) n 092.9
hognut (1) n 054.8
hognuts (1) n 054.7
hogpen (347) n/adj 015.4
~ tomatoes (1) n 055.3
hog(pen) (1) n 035.5
Hogpen (3) 030.7
~ Branch (1) FL 030.7
~ Slough (1) TN 030.3
hogpens (36) n 015.4
hog's (102) adj 035.5
~ blood (1) n 047.3
~ chitlins (1) n 037.3
~ ear (1) n 071.5
~ entrails (1) n 037.3
~ feet (1) n 121.3
~ foot (1) n 048.7
~ goozle (1) n 071.7
~ hair (1) n 035.6
~ head (9) n 047.1
~ head cheese (61) n 047.1
~ head meat (1) n 047.1
~ head souse (2) n 047.1
~ intestines (1) n 037.3
~ jaw (3) n 046.3
~ jowl (4) n 046.3
~ liver (2) n 047.2
~ tripe (1) n 037.2
hogs (1309) n 035.5
hogs' (3) adj 037.3
~ guts (1) n 037.3
~ houses (2) n 014.1
hogshead (35) n/adj 019.1
~ barrel (2) n 019.1
hogsheads (2) n 019.1
hogweed (3) n 015.9
hogweeds (9) n 015.9
Hohner (1) 020.5
hoist (462) n/v 104.5
~ up (1) v 104.5
hoist[N-i] (1) n 104.5
hoist[V-p] (1) v 104.4
hoist[V-r] (3) v 104.5

hoisted (8) v 104.5
hoisters (1) n 104.5
hoisting (23) v 104.5
hokey (2) adj 044.8
~ -dokey (1) n 044.8
~ -pokey (1) n 130.3
hokies (1) n 069.4
Holbrook Campground (1) GA 087.3
Holcomb (2) MS 087.1
hold (131) n/v 011.8
~ down (2) v 075.3
~ in (1) v 065.9
~ it (4) v 038.2
~ -it roads (1) n 031.7
~ off (1) v 075.3
~ on (19) v 075.3
~ still (4) v 037.5
~ up (1) v 045.9
hold[V-p] (2) v 074.1
~ up (1) v 074.1
holder (7) n 022.1
holders (7) n 008.3
holding (18) v/adj 096.8
~ bench (1) n 088.7
~ company (1) n 052.5
~ pen (2) n 015.3
~ up (1) v 074.9
holdings (1) n 099.4
holds (6) v 041.8
~ onto (1) v 073.5
holdup (1) n 100.2
hole (199) n/v/adj 078.1
~ diggers (1) n 120.5
~ up (2) v 055A.5
Hole (1) 030.7
hole[N-i] (1) n 052.1
holed (1) adj 016.3
holer (40) n 012.1
holers (7) n 012.1
holes (40) n 045.2
holiday (3) n/adj 002.1
~ party (1) n 130.7
Holiday (9) 093.2
~ Inn (2) 084.3
~ Wishes (1) 093.2
Holidays (10) 093.2
Holiness (19) 089.1
~ church (5) n 089.2
~ faith (1) n 032.8
~ people (1) n 089.2
~ preacher (1) n 091.9
holing (2) v 015.6
~ up (1) v 015.5
Holland (5) 087.9

~ Dutch (1) 069.4
Hollandale (4) MS 087.7
Hollander (1) 127.2
Hollanders (1) 127.2
holler (74) v 036.2
~ at (2) v 038.3
~ for Ralph (1) v 080.3
~ for the dinosaurs (1) v 080.3
holler[V-p] (3) v 036.2
hollered (2) v 058.3
hollering (56) v/adj 036.4
~ at (2) v 090.8
~ distance (2) n 080.7
~ for (1) v 036.3
hollers (16) v 036.3
hollies (3) n 062.7
hollin (4) n S 008.7
hollow (114) n/adj 030.4
~ -ground (1) adj 023.4
~ land (1) n 029.4
~ leg (1) n 048.4
~ wash (1) n 030.4
Hollow (22) 030.4
~ Creek (2) TN 030.7
~ Rock (1) TN 087.3
hollows (17) n 030.5
Hollows (1) 105.2
holly (58) n/adj 062.2
~ berries (4) n 062.4
~ bush (2) n 062.2
~ golly (1) n 083.1
~ poultice (2) n 088.7
~ tree (14) n 061.9
~ trees (3) n 061.8
Holly (22) LA 087.2
~ Bluff (1) MS 031.2
~ Creek (1) TN 030.7
~ Grove (1) TN 087.3
~ Heights (1) 106.3
~ Springs (17) GA MS 087.1
hollygoglin (1) adv 085.2
hollyhocks (1) n 101.4
hollywood bush (1) n 062.7
Hollywood (17) AL AR CA FL MS 087.3
~ beds (1) n 095.8
~ Chelsea (1) 106.3
~ Heights (1) 105.4
Holman settlement (1) AR 086.3
Holmes Bayou (1) LA 030.7

Holmesville (1) MS 087.2
holp (115) v 049.5
~ on (2) v 049.5
holped (44) v 049.5
~ [P-0] (1) v 049.5
holping (2) v 049.5
Holstein (18) 033.6
~ cow (1) n 033.6
Holstein[N-i] (1) 033.6
holster (1) n 072.4
Holston (22) TN 030.7
~ Heights (1) 105.5
~ Hills (3) 106.6
~ Mountain (2) TN 031.1
~ River (8) TN 030.7
~ Valley (2) TN 087.2
Holt (2) GA 086.5
Holtamville (1) AL 087.1
holy (15) adj 092.4
~ day (3) n 002.1
~ rollers (1) n 126.5
~ Sabbath Day (1) n 002.1
Holy (51) 090.2
~ Ghost (11) 090.2
~ Joe (1) 126.6
~ Rolies (1) 126.6
~ Roller (11) 126.6
~ Roller preacher (1) n 067.8
~ Rollers (24) 126.6
~ Roly ones (1) n 089.8
~ Spirit (1) 089.3
Homa (1) 030.7
homage (1) n 079.3
hombre (1) n S 069.9
home (3225) n/adj/adv 032.2
~ address (1) n 100.8
~ -baked (1) adj 045.1
~ -baked bread (1) n 044.3
~ base (136) n 098.4
~ beer (2) n 050.8
~ boy (2) n 125.5
~ bread (2) n 045.1
~ breakers (1) n 124.8
~ brew (304) n 050.9
~ brew beer (3) n 050.9
~ -brew joints (1) n 050.8
~ -brew maker (1) n 050.8

~ brew wine (1) n 050.8
~ -brewing (1) v 050.9
~ brews (2) n 050.8
~ burial (2) n 078.8
~ cemetery (1) n 078.8
~ church (1) n 089.2
~ cradle (1) n 074.9
~ cure (1) n 046.3
~ -cured ham (1) n 081.8
~ -cured hog lard (1) n 046.8
~ -cured meat (1) n 046.5
~ -cured shoulder (1) n 072.4
~ -cut (1) adj 122.4
~ dance (1) n 083.1
~ dances (2) n 083.1
~ done (2) adj 051.2
~ feeling (1) n 080.7
~ folks (6) n 066.5
~ free (21) n 098.4
~ free home (1) n 098.4
~ garden (5) n 050.5
~ -garden stuff (1) n 050.4
~ graveyard (1) n 078.8
~ -growed (1) adj 065.6
~ -growed vegetables (2) n 050.4
~ -kill grease (1) n 080.9
~ lot (1) n 015.6
~ mission (1) n 080.7
~ parties (1) n 083.1
~ party (1) n 083.1
~ place (2) n 098.4
~ plate (13) n 098.4
~ -plate tree (1) n 098.4
~ -raise (1) adj 050.4
~ -raise[V-t] (2) v 050.4
~ -raised (2) adj 050.4
~ -raised vegetables (1) n 050.4
~ remedy (2) n 084.9
~ roads (1) n 031.8
~ roll (1) n 044.4
~ run (2) n 098.4
~ seat (1) n 085.5
~ tree (1) n 098.4

~ -use cotton (1) n 093.9
~ vegetables (1) n 050.4
~ wake (1) n 081.8
~ wedding (1) n 088.7
~ well (1) n 015.5
~ wife (1) n 063.2
~ wood (1) n 092.6
Home (30) 032.2
~ Comfort (5) 088.9
~ Comfort range (3) n 096.7
~ Comfort ranges (1) n 008.5
~ Comfort stove (1) n 096.8
~ Demonstration Club (1) 032.2
~ Ec (1) 075.6
~ Ec departments (1) n 039.6
~ Place (1) LA 087.2
home[N-i] (2) n 039.8
Home[N-i] (5) 106.3
homebody (1) n 080.6
homecoming (4) n/adj 090.9
~ day (1) n 081.8
homecomings (1) n 088.9
homegrown (74) adj 050.4
~ cornmeal (1) n 065.6
~ eggs (1) n 050.4
~ mule (1) n 080.9
~ stuff (1) n 050.4
~ vegetables (17) n 050.4
homeless (1) adj 066.3
homelife (1) n 032.2
homely (31) adj 073.6
homemade (306) adj 045.1
~ bacon (1) n 046.7
~ barbecue sauce (1) n 048.5
~ basket (2) n 020.1
~ bedstead (1) n 009.3
~ beer (9) n 050.9
~ benches (3) n 008.8
~ biscuit (1) n 044.4
~ biscuit pudding (1) n 080.9
~ biscuit[N-i] (2) n 044.4

~ biscuits (5) n 044.4
~ boat (3) n 024.6
~ boats (3) n 024.6
~ boots (1) n 034.6
~ bread (69) n 044.3
~ brew (3) n 050.8
~ broom (6) n 010.5
~ brooms (3) n 010.5
~ bull tongue plow (1) n 021.6
~ carpets (1) n 009.3
~ chair (1) n 008.8
~ chairs (9) n 008.8
~ cheese (7) n 048.1
~ chestes (1) n 009.2
~ chimley (1) n 053.4
~ closet (1) n 009.6
~ clothes (1) n 025.1
~ clothespress (1) n 009.7
~ coffin (1) n 079.1
~ cooked corn syrup (1) n 051.2
~ coops (1) n 036.8
~ cypress boats (1) n 024.6
~ desk[N-i] (2) n 083.8
~ doctors (1) n 061.4
~ dolls (2) n 101.5
~ doughnut (2) n 045.2
~ flambeau (1) n 024.3
~ furniture (2) n 009.4
~ grits (1) n 050.6
~ har(row) (1) n 021.7
~ harrows (1) n 021.7
~ jelly (1) n 051.6
~ kraut (2) n 055A.1
~ lamp (9) n 024.3
~ lantern (1) n 024.3
~ light (1) n 024.3
~ light bread (14) n 044.3
~ liquor (6) n 050.8
~ loaf (1) n 045.1
~ loaf bread (4) n 044.3
~ loom (1) n 035.3
~ lunch (1) n 070.7
~ lye (1) n 045.1
~ lye soap (1) n 088.8
~ maple syrup (1) n 051.3
~ merry-go-round (1) n 022.7
~ molasses (1) n 051.2

~ names (1) n 075.8
~ pants (1) n 027.4
~ quilt (2) n 029.1
~ quilts (6) n 029.1
~ rolls (2) n 044.4
~ safe (1) n 010.1
~ sausage (4) n 121.6
~ sausage[N-i] (1) n 051.1
~ scald cat (1) n 050.8
~ scrub brooms (1) n 010.5
~ shades (1) n 009.5
~ shine (2) n 050.8
~ sin (5) n 088.9
~ soap (1) n 125.2
~ spurs (1) n 089.8
~ straw brooms (1) n 010.5
~ -style bread (1) n 044.3
~ sugarcane syrup (1) n 051.3
~ swing (1) n 022.9
~ syrup (3) n 051.3
~ table (1) n 002.7
~ tobacco (1) n 057.3
~ torch (1) n 024.3
~ toy (4) n 101.5
~ toys (3) n 101.5
~ wagon (1) n 101.5
~ wheat (1) n 044.6
~ wheat bread (1) n 044.3
~ whiskey (9) n 050.8
~ wine (5) n 050.8
~ wines (1) n 050.8
~ yeast (2) n 045.5
~ yeast bread (1) n 044.3
homemaker (4) n 032.2
homeplace (13) n 007A.4
Homer (1) GA 087.2
Homerville (7) GA 087.2
homes (63) n 032.2
Homes (7) 105.4
homespun (6) n/adj 070.8
~ blanket (1) n 029.1
~ dresses (1) n 080.8
homestead (11) n 080.6
Homestead (11) FL 087.6
~ tomatoes (1) n 055.3
~ Twenty-Four (1) 055.3
homesteaded (12) v 070.7

homesteading (1) v 080.6
homesteads (2) n 052.1
hometown (1) n 070.4
Homewood (17) AL MS 105.1
~ Beat (1) 080.7
homework (4) n 057.6
homily (44) n/adj 050.6
~ corn (1) n 050.6
~ grits (2) n 050.6
hominies (1) n 050.6
hominy (851) n/adj 050.6
~ corn (3) n 050.6
~ flakes (1) n 050.6
~ grit[N-i] (1) n 050.6
~ grits (73) n 050.6
~ lye (1) n 092.9
~ -making time (1) n 050.6
~ snow (1) n 007.5
hom(iny) (1) n 050.6
Hominy Creek (2) GA 030.7
hominybirds (1) n 066.8
homo (15) n 124.4
Homochitto (8) MS 030.7
~ River (6) MS 030.7
homogenize (7) v 048.2
(ho)mogenize (1) v 070.8
homogenizing (1) v 039.6
Homosassa (2) FL 087.8
~ River (1) FL 030.7
homosexual (59) n/adj 124.2
~ games (1) n 099.8
~ person (1) n 124.2
homosex(ual) (1) n 124.2
homosexuality (1) n 074.7
homosexuals (10) n 124.2
homosexulars (1) n 124.2
Hon (18) 064.4
honcho (3) n 068.5
honchos (1) n 111.5
Hondo (5) TX 087.7
~ Creek (1) TX 030.7
Honduras (3) 086.2
hone (154) n/v 022.3
honed (2) v 023.4
hones (4) n 023.4
honest (21) adj 066.9
~ -to-God (2) adj 075.9
~ -to-goodness (1) adj 046.5
honestly (2) adv 091.6
honey (87) n/v/adj 081.6

~ -and-wheat bread (1) n 044.6
~ around (1) v 081.7
~ breeches (1) n 081.5
~ bumblebees (1) n 060A.5
~ bun (5) n 122.1
~ buns (3) n 122.2
~ -drip (1) adj 045.2
~ -dripper style (1) n 123.9
~ frog (1) n 060.3
~ -glaze doughnuts (1) n 122.4
~ honey bee ball (2) n 130.1
~ loaf (1) n 044.4
~ locust (2) n 061.9
~ man (2) n 089.7
~ maple (1) n 061.5
~ nest (1) n 060A.7
~ peach (1) n 054.3
~ pie (1) n 081.5
~ tree (1) n 061.5
~ wagon (1) n 081.9
~ yam (1) n 055.5
Honey (137) 064.4
~ Ball (2) 056.7
~ Boy (1) 056.9
~ Child (4) 064.4
~ -Dipped (1) 122.4
~ Hill Road (1) 107A.7
~ Island (1) TX 087.5
~ Island Swamp (1) LA 029.6
~ Mamma (1) 064.2
~ Pie (1) 064.4
~ Rocks (1) 056.9
honeybee (71) n/adj 060A.5
~ comb (1) n 060A.5
honeybees (67) n 060A.6
honeybunch (1) n 081.6
Honeybunch (2) 064.4
honeycomb (4) n/adj 123.9
~ country (1) n 029.4
Honeycorn (1) 056.9
honeydew (209) n/adj 056.7
~ melon (80) n 056.7
~ melons (41) n 056.7
~ squash (1) n 056.6
~ syrup (1) n 051.3
honeydews (15) n 056.7

honeymoon (3) n/adj 084.8
~ bugs (1) n 084.8
~ party (1) n 082.5
Honeymoon mushmelon (1) n 056.7
honeymoon[N-i] (1) n 001A.4
honeymoons (1) n 095.8
honeysuckle (31) n/adj 062.7
~ bush (1) n 062.7
~ vine (1) n 015.9
Honeysuckle (3) 106.2
~ Hills (1) 105.5
~ Road (1) 031.8
honeysuckles (4) n 062.7
hongo (2) n S 056.8
honing (11) v/adj 023.5
~ rock (2) n 023.4
~ steel (1) n 023.4
~ stone (4) n 023.4
~ wheel (1) n 023.5
honk (1) v 037.5
honk(x3) (1) interj 038.3
honkies (47) n 069.4
honking (1) v 036.4
honks (1) v 037.5
honky (112) n/adj 069.4
~ -tonk (7) n 088.7
~ -tonk heaven (1) n 113.4
~ -tonk music (1) n 131.8
~ -tonks (4) n 105.4
~ -tonky (1) n 080.6
~ -tonky bread (1) n 044.3
Honolulu (1) HI 070.6
Honolu(lu) (1) HI 087.5
honor (364) n/adj 082.4
~ attendant (1) n 082.4
~ maid (1) n 082.4
~ matron (1) n 082.4
~ student (2) n 068.7
hon(or) (1) n 082.4
Honor (3) 068.6
honorary aunts (1) n 129.5
honored (1) v 092.6
honors (1) v 104.5
hoo (197) adj/interj 038.2
~ -ba (1) interj 037.5
~ -ba(x4) (1) interj 037.5

~ -bonna(x2) hoo (1) interj 038.2
~ chick (1) interj 038.5
~ cow (2) interj 037.5
~ -cow(x2) (4) interj 037.5
~ ha (1) interj 037.5
~ hee here (1) interj 037.6
~ -hoo-hoo-hoo owl (1) n 059.2
~ -hoo-hoo owl (1) n 059.2
~ -hoo hoosiers (1) n 069.9
~ -hoo owl (12) n 059.2
~ -hoo owls (1) n 059.2
~ hooey(x2) (1) interj 038.3
~ -hoop owl (1) n 059.2
~ oh hoo (1) interj 038.3
~ -oh (1) interj 038.3
~ -oke sooey(x2) (1) interj 037.5
~ ooh hoo (1) interj 059.1
~ owl (65) n 059.2
~ owls (10) n 059.2
~ pee (1) interj 038.3
~ pig (1) interj 038.3
~ -piggy(x2) (2) interj 038.3
~ -pig(x2) (8) interj 038.3
~ -pig(x3) (1) interj 038.3
~ sook(x3) soo-pine(x2) (1) interj 037.5
~ soo(x2) (1) interj 037.5
~ sug(x3) (1) interj 037.5
~ way (1) interj 038.3
~ -wee (1) interj 037.5
hoo(x2) (16) interj 038.3
~ hooey (1) interj 038.3
hoo(x3) (5) interj 038.3
hoo(x4) (4) interj 036.4
hoo(x5) (2) interj 037.5
hoo(x6) (1) interj 059.2

hooch (3) n 114.7
hoochie hoo chick (1) interj 038.5
hood (6) n 075.2
Hood (1) 087.4
hooded (2) adj 059.1
~ owl (1) n 059.1
~ windmill grass (1) n 015.9
hooder (1) n 041.7
hooders (1) n 041.7
hoodgy (1) n 069.8
hoodlum (17) n/adj 088.9
~ box (1) n 111.8
~ joint (1) n 113.7
~ territory (1) n 114.8
~ wagon (4) n 111.8
hoodlums (10) n 113.7
hoodoo (14) n/adj 090.8
~ bag (1) n 081.9
~ doctor (1) n 080.8
hoodooed (4) v 081.8
hoodooer (1) n 069.9
hoodoos (3) n 081.8
hoods (1) n 113.7
hooey (17) adj/interj 038.3
~ dog (1) n 033.3
~ hoey(x2) (1) interj 037.5
~ shooey (1) interj 038.4
hooey(x2) (9) interj 038.3
hoof (880) n/adj 034.7
~ hog (1) n 034.7
~ marks (1) n 034.7
~ part (2) n 034.7
~ rattler (1) n 083.1
~ trimmer (1) n 034.7
hoof[N-i] (55) n 034.7
hoofes (1) n 034.7
hoofs (487) n 034.7
hook (133) n/v/adj/interj 055A.3
~ and ladder (37) n 111.3
~ -and-ladder (1) adj 111.3
~ -and-ladder fire truck (1) n 111.3
~ -and-ladder truck (7) n 111.3
~ -and-ladder trucks (2) n 111.3

~ and ladders (4) n 111.3
~ -and-line boat (1) n 024.6
~ nose (1) n 126.7
~ sook(x2) (1) interj 037.5
~ sook(x3) (1) interj 037.5
~ towel (2) n 018.6
~ up (9) v 038.6
Hook (3) 055A.3
~ Them Horns (1) 093.3
hook[V-r] (2) v 100.2
hooked (57) v 082.2
~ for life (1) v 082.2
~ on (2) v 114.3
~ school (1) v 083.4
~ to (3) v 038.6
~ up (17) v 082.2
hookee (1) n 114.3
hooker (46) n/adj 113.3
~ shops (1) n 113.4
Hooker (1) 090.8
hookers (8) n 113.3
hookies (1) n 083.4
hooking (4) v 100.2
~ up (2) v 038.7
hooks (27) n/v 020.9
~ to (1) v 021.2
Hooks Creek (1) MS 030.7
hookworm (4) n/adj 088.9
~ bench (1) n 080.6
hookworms (2) n 060A.2
hooky (680) n 083.4
hoolios (1) n 128.2
hoop (407) n/adj/interj 020.3
~ barrel (1) n 020.3
~ cheese (23) n 048.1
~ -eyedy (1) interj 096.4
~ game (1) n 034.8
~ iron (2) n 020.3
~ owls (1) n 059.2
~ pig (1) interj 038.3
~ snake (4) n 093.6
~ staves (1) n 020.3
Hoop (42) 020.3
hoop(x2) (5) interj 038.3
hoop(x3) (1) interj 037.5
hoop[N-i] (6) n 020.3

hooped (1) v 075.6
hoopee(x2) (1) interj 037.5
hooping (1) v 057.4
hoople owls (1) n 059.2
hooples (1) n 069.9
hoopoly (1) interj 038.3
hoops (581) n 020.3
Hoops (23) 020.3
hoopskirt (7) n 020.3
hoopskirts (12) n 020.3
hoopy (14) adj/interj 038.3
~ -hide (2) n 098.4
~ -hie (9) n 098.4
~ owl (1) n 059.2
hoosa (1) interj 038.3
hoosegow (6) n 112.8
hoosier (184) n/adj 069.9
~ cabinet (1) n 010.1
~ country (1) n 069.9
Hoosier (59) 069.9
~ State (9) 069.9
~ states (1) n 069.9
hoosiers (67) n 069.9
Hoosiers (13) 069.9
hoot (579) n/adj 059.2
~ owl (484) n 059.2
~ owls (89) n 059.2
hootch (1) n 050.8
hootchie (2) adj 083.1
~ -cootchie (1) n 083.1
~ -cootchies (1) n 045.2
hootchy (1) n 069.4
hootenanny (1) n 083.1
hooter (2) n/adj 059.2
~ owl (1) n 059.2
hooting (113) v/adj 057.3
~ owl (95) n 059.2
~ owls (16) n 059.2
hooty (4) adj 059.2
~ owl (3) n 059.2
~ owls (1) n 059.2
Hoover (25) AL 010.5
~ buggies (1) n 081.8
~ cart (3) n 023.2
~ days (1) n 084.8
~ Dyke (1) FL 091.9
~ hogs (1) n 080.9
~ sweeper (1) n 116.7
~ time (3) n 095.2
~ times (1) n 088.7
hooves (231) n 034.7
hooving iron (1) n 116.7
hoowee (1) interj 037.5

hop (39) n/v/adj 083.1
~ along (1) v 061.1
~ around (1) v 052.5
~ cakes (1) n 045.3
~ -in-[D-0]-yard toad (1) n 060.4
~ skip (2) n 039.5
~ yeast (1) n 045.5
hope (95) v/adj/interj 101.2
~ chestes (1) n 009.2
~ hearts (1) n 122.2
~ hoey (1) interj 038.3
~ to (13) v 058.7
hope(x2) (4) interj 038.2
Hope (20) AR 087.5
~ Villa (1) LA 087.3
Hopeful Church (1) FL 087.2
hopeless (2) adj 009.3
~ chest (1) n 009.3
hopely (1) adv 065.8
hopes (2) n/v 025.6
Hopewell (4) LA MS 087.1
~ Plantation (1) LA 065.8
~ settlement (1) FL 087.2
hopgrasser (1) n 061.1
hophead (2) n 114.3
hopheads (2) n 114.3
hoping (5) v 101.2
~ to (1) v 007A.7
Hopkinsville (2) KY 087.8
hopped (4) v 080.9
~ the broomstick (1) v 082.2
~ up (2) v 065.1
hopper (59) n/adj 080.6
~ cricket (1) n 061.1
~ crickets (1) n 061.1
~ frog (1) n 060.2
~ -type deal (1) n 080.7
hopperful (1) n 019.8
hoppergrass (145) n 061.1
hoppergrasses (21) n 061.1
hopperjacks (1) n 061.1
hoppers (11) n 061.1
hoppety-horse (1) n 022.7
hoppin (3) adj 080.7
~ John (1) n 080.7
hopping (5) v/adj 060.4

~ frog (1) n 060.4
~ frogs (1) n 060.4
~ toads (1) n 060.4
hoppinggrass (2) n 061.1
hoppy (4) adj 130.2
~ scotch (1) n 130.2
~ toad (3) n 060.4
hoppyclopter (1) n 111.9
hops (13) n/v 083.1
~ around (1) v 053.2
hopsack (2) n 019.7
hopscotch (71) n 130.2
hoptoads (4) n 060.4
hopvine (1) n 062.3
Horatio (1) AR 087.3
horehound (4) n 061.4
horizontal (7) adj/adv 085.2
~ fence (1) n 016.4
~ park (1) v 108.3
~ parking (1) n 108.3
horn (139) n/adj 022.3
~ back (1) n 060.4
~ bean (1) n 061.8
~ frog (3) n 060.3
~ frogs (2) n 060.4
~ owl (77) n 059.2
~ owls (13) n 059.2
~ snakes (1) n 099.9
~ toad (3) n 060.4
~ toads (4) n 060.4
~ trout (1) n 059.9
hornbeam (1) n 061.8
Hornbeck (2) LA 087.4
horned (66) adj 060.3
~ frog (3) n 060.3
~ frogs (3) n 060.4
~ Herefords (1) n 070.8
~ hoot owl (1) n 059.2
~ owl (41) n 059.2
~ owls (6) n 059.2
~ toads (2) n 060.4
Horner (1) 130.7
Hornersville (1) MO 087.4
hornet (393) n/adj 060A.5
~ bee (1) n 060A.5
hornet[N-i] (3) n 060A.5
hornet[N-k] (17) adj 060A.5
~ nest (14) n 060A.5
~ nestes (3) n 070.6

hornet's nest (23) n 060A.5
hornets (417) n 060A.5
hornetses (2) n 060A.5
hornies (1) n 114.9
horning (3) n 082.5
horns (16) n 035.7
Horns (1) 093.3
Hornsby (1) TN 087.1
Hornville (1) 087.1
horny (38) adj 124.5
~ frog (4) n 060.4
~ frogs (1) n 060.4
~ hide (1) n 059.9
~ man (1) n 124.7
~ owl (3) n 059.2
~ toad (5) n 060.4
~ toads (3) n 060.4
hornyhead (3) n/adj 059.9
~ owl (1) n 059.2
hornyheads (12) n 059.9
horrible (2) adj 070.6
~ day (1) n 005.5
horriblest (1) adj 070.6
horrid (1) adj 125.2
horrified (1) v 081.3
horror house (1) n 090.3
hor(ror) magazines (1) n 081.8
horse (2852) n/adj 034.2
~ accident (1) n 089.8
~ and a half (1) n 080.7
~ -and-buggy days (4) n 034.2
~ -and-buggy doctor (2) n 080.8
~ -and-buggy peddlers (1) n 080.6
~ -and-wagon road (1) n 031.7
~ apple (2) n 084.8
~ -apple tree (1) n 061.7
~ apples (1) n 061.9
~ barn (33) n 015.2
~ barns (2) n 014.2
~ bee (1) n 060A.7
~ benches (1) n 022.1
~ breeches (1) n 021.2
~ buggy (1) n 022.5
~ cart (1) n 034.2
~ carts (2) n 080.9
~ chestnut (1) n 054.8

~ collar (6) n 038.7
~ colt (1) n 034.1
~ corn (5) n 056.2
~ doctor (2) n 060A.4
~ doctors (2) n 060A.4
~ -drawn (3) adj 034.2
~ -drawn baler (1) n 034.2
~ -drawn cars (1) n 085.3
~ -drawn hearse (2) n 080.6
~ -drawn plow (1) n 021.6
~ -drawn rake (1) n 081.9
~ -drawn transfer (1) n 080.8
~ -drawn wagon (2) n 104.4
~ eggs (1) n 044.7
~ farms (2) n 034.2
~ feed (2) n 066.9
~ feet (1) n 034.2
~ food (1) n 055A.5
~ foot (1) n 034.7
~ frame (1) n 022.1
~ gin (2) n 080.7
~ gins (1) n 081.8
~ grasshoppers (1) n 061.1
~ hitches (1) n 016.2
~ hoofs (1) n 034.7
~ killer (1) n 080.8
~ lane (1) n 031.8
~ limb (1) adj 073.3
~ lot (63) n 015.6
~ mane (1) n 061.4
~ master (1) n 069.6
~ medicine (1) n 093.5
~ mule (6) n 033.7
~ mules (1) n 033.7
~ pasture (2) n 015.6
~ path (1) n 031.7
~ pen (3) n 015.2
~ pens (1) n 015.2
~ people (1) n 034.4
~ piss (1) n 050.9
~ pitch (1) n 034.8
~ plate[N-i] (1) n 034.6
~ plow (3) n 021.6
~ presses (1) n 014.6
~ pumpkin (1) n 056.5
~ races (2) n 034.2

~ racing (3) n 034.2
~ rack (1) n 080.6
~ -riding (1) v 034.3
~ sense (6) n 081.8
~ shed (8) n 015.2
~ sheds (1) n 015.2
~ shelter (3) n 015.2
~ shows (1) n 034.2
~ stable (17) n 015.2
~ stables (7) n 015.2
~ stall (11) n 015.2
~ stalls (10) n 015.2
~ stock (5) n 036.5
~ team (1) n 033.7
~ trace (1) n 020.9
~ track (1) n 089.8
~ trader (2) n 034.2
~ trading (2) n 094.2
~ -trading business (1) n 080.6
~ trail (2) n 031.8
~ trailer (1) n 084.8
~ trails (1) n 031.7
~ transportation (1) n 034.2
~ trough (9) n 035.8
~ troughs (1) n 035.8
~ whip (2) n 034.2
Horse (17) 064.4
~ Branch (2) AL LA 030.7
~ Creek (4) AL FL MS TX 030.7
~ Island (1) AR 030.3
~ Maker (1) 064.4
~ Pen (1) AR 030.7
~ Show Celebration (1) 131.1
horse[N-i] (9) n 034.2
horse[N-k] feet (1) n 034.7
horseback (27) n/adj/adv 034.2
~ riding (3) n 130.5
~ -riding shoes (1) n 123.8
~ -rode (1) v 034.1
horsebean (2) n 055A.3
horsebeans (1) n 055A.4
horseberries (1) n 062.5
horseface (1) n 125.2
horseflies (13) n 060A.4
horsefly (36) n 060A.8
horsehair (3) adj 009.1
~ couch (1) n 009.1

~ sofa (1) n 009.1
~ sofas (1) n 009.1
Horsehead Creek (1) FL 030.7
horsehide (1) n 097.9
horselaugh (3) n 036.4
horseless (2) adj 023.6
~ buggies (1) n 023.6
~ buggy (1) n 023.6
horseman (1) n 034.2
horsemeat (1) n 013.9
horsemint (1) n 061.4
horseradish (16) n 055.2
horseradishes (2) n 055.2
horse's (9) adj 034.2
~ ass (1) n 092.2
~ feet (1) n 034.2
~ foot (1) n 034.7
~ hoof (3) n 034.7
~ neck (1) n 071.7
~ rump (1) n 034.2
horses (1581) n 034.2
horses' shoes (1) n 034.6
horseshit (2) n 092.2
horseshoe (279) n/adj 034.8
~ bend (1) n 034.6
~ cooters (1) n 060.6
~ game (51) n 034.8
~ games (4) n 034.8
~ -like (1) adj 034.6
~ nails (4) n 020.2
~ pitching (9) n 034.8
~ playing (1) n 034.8
~ race (1) n 034.8
~ ring (2) n 034.8
~ shape (1) n 034.6
~ spider (1) n 017.5
Horseshoe (12) AR 034.6
~ Bank (1) MS 088.8
~ Beach (1) FL 087.3
~ Bend (4) AR 087.4
~ Bluff (1) AL 034.6
~ Lake (4) LA TN 030.7
horseshoe[N-i] (60) n 034.8
horseshoed (1) v 034.6
horseshoeing (7) v/adj 034.6
~ outfit (1) n 034.6
horseshoer (3) n 034.8
horseshoes (1125) n/adj 034.6
~ game (1) n 034.8

horsetail (1) n 061.4
horsewhip (11) n/v 019.4
horsewhipping (1) n 065.5
horsey (15) n/adj 075.1
~ company (1) n 034.3
horsey(x2) (1) interj 037.8
horsing (2) v 130.5
~ around (1) v 130.5
Horticulturals (1) 052.1
HOs (1) 113.3
hose (13) n/adj 120.1
~ bib (1) n 018.7
~ bibs (1) n 018.7
~ faucet (1) n 018.7
~ pipe (1) n 018.7
~ truck (3) n 111.2
~ trucks (1) n 111.2
Hose Nose (1) 064.4
hosiery mill (1) n 080.7
hospital (1082) n/adj 084.5
~ ambulance (1) n 084.5
~ board (1) n 084.5
~ vessel (1) n 084.5
~ work (1) n 084.5
hospit(al) (4) n 084.5
hosp(ital) (1) n 084.5
hos(pital) (1) n 084.5
Hospital (21) 084.5
hospital[N-i] (1) n 084.5
hospitalization (1) n 084.5
hospitals (44) n 084.5
host (5) n 055A.8
hostess (3) n/adj 026.4
~ chair (1) n 008.8
hostess's apron (1) n 026.4
hostile (4) adj 070.8
hostler (5) n 080.7
hostling for (1) v 081.8
hot (698) adj 124.6
~ ball (1) n 130.4
~ blanket (1) n 096.9
~ box (1) n 130.4
~ breath (1) n 101.3
~ chocolate (1) n 065.9
~ cross bun (3) n 045.2
~ cross buns (1) n 045.2
~ crossed buns (1) n 045.2
~ day (6) n 005.4

~ dog (118) n 121.6
~ -dog (1) interj 092.6
~ -dog bread (1) n 044.4
~ -dog buns (4) n 044.4
~ -dog parties (1) n 130.7
~ dogs (52) n 121.6
~ dry spell (1) n 007.1
~ feet (1) n 083.1
~ -headed (4) adj 075.2
~ iron (1) n 010.6
~ links (5) n 121.6
~ mamma (2) n 124.6
~ mix (4) n 031.6
~ money (1) n 114.5
~ moonshine (1) 050.8
~ mouth (1) n 121.6
~ movies (1) n 114.9
~ name (1) n 064.4
~ oil (1) n 080.6
~ pants (47) n 123.4
~ papa (2) n 124.5
~ pepper (9) n 055.7
~ -pepper sauce (3) n 051.7
~ peppers (11) n 055.7
~ plate (31) n 116.4
~ plates (6) n 116.4
~ potato (1) n 130.5
~ rod (3) n 074.5
~ rods (2) n 023.6
~ -roll corn bread (1) n 044.7
~ sauce (3) n 048.5
~ sausage (16) n 121.6
~ season (1) n 092.7
~ shrinker (1) n 027.9
~ spell (4) n 007.1
~ spider (1) n 017.5
~ spots (1) n 106.4
~ stack (1) n 045.3
~ stuff (4) n 124.6
~ -stuff stove (1) n 080.8
~ -tail bombs (1) n 024.3
~ tamale (1) n 047.2
~ -tamale fillings (1) n 044.6
~ -tamale pies (1) n 044.6
~ tamales (11) n 081.8

~ tea (1) n 012.7
~ -tempered (17) adj 075.1
~ -to-go bitch (1) n 124.6
~ to spot (1) adj 124.5
~ to trot (4) adj 124.6
~ -to-trot (1) adj 124.5
~ toddy (3) n 089.9
~ top (1) n 031.6
~ water (5) n 118.4
~ -water bread (28) n 044.6
~ -water corn bread (22) n 044.7
~ -water corn cakes (1) n 044.7
~ -water heat (1) n 118.5
~ -water heater (1) n 065.8
~ -water-heater closet (1) n 010.1
~ -water kettle (1) n 017.6
~ -water tank (1) n 118.4
~ weather (5) n 007.1
~ wire (4) n 016.3
~ -wire fence (2) n 015.4
Hot (41) 087.8
~ Air (1) MS 087.8
~ Coffee (1) MS 087.8
~ -Shot (1) 080.9
~ Spring (2) AR 087.7
~ Spring County (1) AR 087.6
~ Springs (32) AR 087.2
~ Springs Creek (1) AR 030.7
~ Springs Mountain (1) AR 031.1
~ Springs Municipal Airport (1) 065.8
hotbed (2) n 055.3
hotbox (1) n 096.8
hotcake (22) n 045.3
hotcake[N-i] (1) n 045.3
hotcakes (243) n 045.3
hotcha-cha (1) interj 037.5
hotel (912) n/adj 084.3
~ business (1) n 084.3

~ row (1) n 106.4
~ work (1) n 084.3
Hotel (33) 108.9
~ Albert (1) 084.3
~ Marie (1) 084.3
~ Regal (1) 084.3
hotels (65) n 084.3
hotfooted (1) adv 096.8
hothead (3) n 075.1
hotheaded (29) adj 075.1
hotheads (3) n 075.1
hothouse (10) n/adj 118.1
~ tomatoes (1) n 055.3
hothouses (2) n 050.5
hots (5) n 081.4
hotshot hoosier (1) n 069.9
hotter (1) adj 095.8
Hotwells (2) LA 086.7
Houdier (1) 030.7
Houlka Creek (1) MS 030.7
houma (1) n 005.8
Houma (13) LA 087.7
~ Indians (1) 005.8
hound (193) n/adj 033.3
~ -colored feist (1) n 033.3
~ dog (50) n 033.3
~ dog's back (1) n 104.7
~ dogs (13) n 033.1
~ gourd (1) n 056.6
hounds (57) n 021.4
hour (127) n/adj 065.8
hours (46) n/adj 075.6
house (5415) n/adj 014.1
~ and the lot (1) n 037.1
~ ape (1) n 074.1
~ -back turtle (1) n 088.7
~ bait (1) n 060.5
~ baits (1) n 060.5
~ broom (3) n 010.5
~ cat (2) n 059.4
~ chores (1) n 010.4
~ -confined (1) adj 065.1
~ dance (2) n 083.1
~ dances (1) n 083.1
~ doctor (1) n 060A.4
~ dog (16) n 033.3
~ dogs (4) n 033.3
~ fence (1) n 016.2

~ fixings (5) n 009.4
~ fixtures (1) n 009.4
~ -furnishing goods (1) n 009.4
~ furnishings (1) n 009.4
~ furniture (4) n 009.4
~ garden (1) n 050.5
~ gutter (1) n 011.5
~ hog (1) n 035.5
~ -home supply preacher (1) n 080.6
~ kimono (1) n 026.7
~ kitchen (1) n 009.9
~ lady (2) n 113.5
~ log (1) n 014.1
~ moth (1) n 060A.2
~ number (2) n 014.1
~ of correction (1) n 112.8
~ of detention (2) n 014.1
~ of flowers (1) n 113.4
~ of ill fame (1) n 113.4
~ of ill repute (21) n 113.4
~ of prostitute (1) n 113.4
~ of prostitution (8) n 113.4
~ of prostitutions (1) n 113.4
~ of the evening (1) n 113.4
~ owl (1) n 059.2
~ paint (1) n 014.1
~ parties (6) n 130.7
~ party (5) n 083.1
~ -party crowd (1) n 042.4
~ people (1) n 080.6
~ plans (1) n 014.1
~ plunder (7) n 009.4
~ raisings (1) n 080.9
~ room (1) n 007A.2
~ servant (1) n 088.9
~ shoe (1) n 123.8
~ shoes (10) n 123.8
~ siding (1) n 011.2
~ slipper (1) n 123.8
~ spiders (1) n 090.8
~ steps (1) n 010.7
~ style (1) n 014.1

~ sweeping (1) n 010.4
~ trail (1) n 031.8
~ wood (2) n 008.5
~ wrens (1) n 059.3
~ -yard frogs (1) n 060.4
House (43) 106.4
~ Creek (1) MS 030.7
house[N-i] (6) n 014.1
houseboat (4) n 024.6
houseboats (5) n 024.6
housebreakers (1) n 124.8
housebroken (1) adj 033.1
houseclean (6) v 010.4
housecleaner (1) n 010.4
housecleaning (45) n/v 010.4
housecleans (1) v 010.4
housecoat (24) n 026.4
housecoats (1) n 026.4
housed (3) v 014.1
~ up (2) v 070.6
housedress (1) n 026.4
houseflies (2) n 060A.2
housefly (4) n 060A.2
houseful (46) n 055A.8
household (27) n/adj 014.1
~ belongings (1) n 009.4
~ chores (2) n 010.4
~ duties (1) n 010.4
~ effects (1) n 009.4
~ furnishing (3) n 009.4
~ furnishings (1) n 009.4
~ furniture (3) n 009.4
~ furnitures (1) n 009.4
~ good[N-i] (1) n 009.4
~ goods (6) n 009.4
~ supplies (2) n 009.4
~ things (1) n 009.4
housekeep (3) v 010.4
housekeeper (16) n 119.6
housekeeping (24) n/v/adj 010.4
~ outfit (1) n 080.6
housekept (1) v 095.8
housemaid (2) n 014.1
housemother (4) n 065.2
house's (1) adj 053.4
houses (1313) n 014.1

~ of hope (1) n 113.8
~ of ill fame (1) n 113.4
~ of ill reputation (1) n 090.8
~ of ill repute (1) n 113.4
housetop (13) n 011.4
housewarming (6) n/adj 082.5
~ parties (1) n 130.7
housewife (172) n 063.2
housewives (4) n 065.2
housework (69) n/adj 010.4
~ chores (1) n 010.4
houseworked (1) v 010.4
houseworking (1) v 024.9
housing (25) n/adj 022.4
~ apartments (1) n 119.2
~ complexes (1) n 119.2
~ inspectors (1) n 115.4
~ project (10) n 106.3
~ projects (1) n 106.3
Houston (216) AL GA MS TN TX 087.5
~ Avenue (1) 107.6
~ clay (1) n 029.9
~ College (1) 083.6
~ College for Negroes (1) 065.8
~ County (4) AL TN TX 087.2
~ Creek (1) GA 088.7
~ Intercontinental (1) 106.5
~ Intercontinental Airport (1) 106.5
~ International (1) 106.5
~ Light and Power (1) 108.5
~ Municipal Airport (1) 106.5
~ River (1) LA 030.7
~ Street (6) 107.8
Houstonians (1) 080.6
Houston's (1) 068.3
hove (1) v 078.5
hovel (1) n 099.8
hover (2) n/adj 036.8
~ fly (1) n 060A.2
hovers (1) n 036.8

how (2139) adv/conj 092.7
~ -do-you-do (1) n 089.9
~ many ever (1) adj 052.6
Howard (3) FL 087.6
~ County (1) AR 087.7
~ Creek (1) FL 030.7
how'd (5) adv 098.6
howdy (81) interj 092.5
~ doody (1) interj 092.5
Howell (5) FL 030.7
~ Mill (1) 106.1
~ Mill Road (1) 107.7
~ Mills Creek (1) GA 030.7
Howes Sanford Park (1) 106.3
however (1) conj 026.1
Howie Maui (1) 114.1
howl (3) n 036.2
howled (8) v 006.3
howling (4) v 057.4
how're (35) adv 092.5
how's (78) adv 092.5
how've (13) adv 092.5
Howze Beach (1) LA 087.6
hoy (2) interj 038.3
hoy(x2) (1) interj 038.3
HTB (1) 108.9
huajillo (2) n S 062.2
huaraches (2) n 123.8
hub (87) n 021.8
Hubbard (17) AL 056.6
~ squash (5) n 056.6
~ Street (1) 107.7
Hubbards (1) 084.8
hubby (21) n 063.1
hubs (2) n 021.1
Huck Strip (1) TX 087.5
huckleberries (195) n 062.4
huckleberry (87) n/adj 062.5
~ bush (1) n 062.4
~ bushes (1) n 062.4
~ cobblers (1) n 048.3
~ picking (1) v 062.5
~ pie (1) n 062.5
~ pies (1) n 048.3
~ pudding (1) n 048.3
huckleber(ry) (4) n 062.4

HUD (1) 091.6
huddle (2) n/v 081.7
~ up (1) v 081.7
huddled up (1) v 096.4
Huddleston (1) 107.6
Hudgins (2) TX 087.2
~ Settlement (1) TX 087.2
Hudson (5) 087.3
~ River (3) FL LA NY 030.7
hueso (1) n S 060A.4
hues(o) (1) n S 054.1
Huey (7) 111.9
~ P. Long (2) 070.8
huey(x2) (1) interj 038.3
Huey's grandfather (1) n 025.6
Hueytown (1) AL 087.7
huff (1) v 081.8
Huffman (1) AL 086.9
huffy (5) adj 075.2
hug (7) n/v/adj 083.1
~ dance (1) n 083.1
~ me tight (1) n 081.9
~ the toilet (1) v 080.3
huge (19) adj 099.3
hugged (2) v 081.7
huggers (1) n 108.5
hugging (29) n/v 081.7
~ and mugging (1) v 083.1
~ -the-mug (1) n 083.1
Hughes (11) 068.6
Huguenots (2) 069.5
Huguley (1) AL 087.3
huisache (12) n/adj S 061.8
~ tree (2) n 061.8
~ trees (1) n 061.8
~ wood (1) n 008.6
huisaches (2) n S 061.8
huit (1) n F 001.4
hula (2) n 020.3
~ -hula (1) n 020.3
Hula (56) 020.3
~ -Hoop (34) 020.3
~ -Hoop skirt (1) n 020.3
~ -Hoops (19) 020.3
~ -Hula-Hoops (1) 020.3
hull (624) n/v/adj 054.8
~ beans (3) n 055A.3
~ digger (1) n 006.1

Hull (1) FL 087.6
hull[N-i] (1) n 054.8
hullabaloo time (1) n 080.8
hulled (6) v/adj 054.8
~ eggs (1) n 046.2
hulling (12) n/v/adj 054.8
hulls (30) n/v 055A.2
human (4) n/adj 088.3
~ beings (1) n 088.3
~ skeletons (1) n 070.7
humanist (1) n 088.7
humanitarianism (1) n 088.7
humanity (1) n 066.9
humble (7) adj 073.6
Humble (1) 087.8
humbles (1) v 070.6
humblish (1) adj 074.8
humbly (1) adv 048.7
Humboldt (2) TN 087.5
humbug (4) n 088.7
Humbug (1) 106.4
humbugging (1) v 084.9
humdinger (1) n 092.7
humid (3) adj 005.7
humidity (1) n 006.6
hummed (2) v 032.1
hummer (1) n 080.7
humming (2) v 036.3
hummingbird (5) n 060A.3
hummingbirds (1) n 059.2
hummocks (2) n 061.6
humongous (5) adj 080.9
humor (761) n/adj 077.7
~ bone (1) n 072.7
Humor (2) 099.3
humored (9) v/adj 099.3
humorless (1) adj 075.1
humorous (7) adj 099.3
humors (2) n 077.5
hump (24) n/v 110.8
~ down (1) v 096.4
~ over (2) v 096.4
humpback (2) adj 059.9
~ blue cat (1) n 059.9
~ dirt road (1) n 031.6
humped (4) v 096.4
~ down (1) v 096.4
~ up (2) v 096.4
Humphrey (1) AR 087.3
Humphreys (5) TN 087.2
~ County (4) TN 099.3

humps (11) n 110.8
humpty-nine (1) adj 078.5
humus (14) n/adj 029.8
Hun (2) 127.1
hunch (13) n/v 096.4
~ down (6) v 096.4
hunchback (1) n 109.4
hunched (3) v/adj 096.4
~ down (2) v 096.4
hunching down (1) v 096.4
hunchy (1) n 130.6
hundred (1935) n/adj 001A.2
~ -and-ten proof (1) n 050.8
~ -and-twenty-third (1) n 001A.2
~ -barrel (1) adj 099.6
~ -dollar (1) adj 001A.1
~ -gallon (1) n 019.1
~ -page (1) adj 001A.2
~ -pound (49) adj 019.6
hund(red) (1) adj 001A.2
hun(dred) (1) n 001A.2
(hund)red (1) adj 088.1
Hundred (12) 107.1
~ and Fortieth Street (1) 107.1
~ -and-Sixty-Seven (1) 091.6
~ -and-Sixty-Third Street (1) 001A.3
~ and Twenty-Fifth Street (1) 107.7
~ North Main building (1) n 108.5
hundreds (23) n 001A.2
Hundreds (5) 001A.2
hundredth (1) adj 001.2
hundredweight (1) n 015.8
hung (873) v 085.9
~ around (2) v 088.7
~ by (3) v 085.9
~ herself (1) v 082.2
~ in (2) v 085.9
~ on (4) v 085.9
~ onto (1) v 085.9
~ out (3) v 085.9
~ out at (1) v 052.5
~ out with (1) v 129.6
~ over (1) v 085.9

~ to (1) v 088.9
~ up (13) v 085.9
~ up his spurs (1) v 078.6
~ up on (3) v 085.9
Hungarian (2) 069.4
hunged (1) v 085.9
hungry (49) adj 065.9
~ -looking (1) adj 064.3
Hungry Jacks (1) 045.3
hunk (37) n 125.3
~ -backed (1) adj 088.7
~ of man (1) n 125.3
~ of meat (1) n 125.3
~ of pussy (1) n 125.4
hunker (179) n/v 072.8
~ around (1) v 096.4
~ down (143) v 096.4
~ over (4) v 072.8
hunk(er) down (1) v 072.8
hunker[N-i] (4) n 072.8
hunker[V-t] down (1) v 096.4
hunkered (56) v 096.4
~ down (40) v 072.8
~ over (1) v 072.8
~ up (2) v 096.4
hunkerer (2) n 072.8
hunkering (47) v 096.4
~ down (34) v 072.8
~ up (1) v 072.8
hunkers (206) n/v 072.8
~ down (4) v 096.4
~ over (1) v 096.4
hunkies (3) n 069.4
Hunkies (1) 127.2
hunking down (1) v 096.4
hunks (5) n 072.8
hunky (9) n/adj 127.6
~ buses (1) n 109.8
~ -dory (2) adj 084.8
Huns (3) 127.1
hunt (51) n/v 033.9
~ a calf (1) v 033.9
~ for (2) v 013.8
~ the hay (2) n 130.1
Hunt (4) TX 087.6
~ County (1) TX 086.4
~ House (1) 106.4
hunt[V-t] (1) v 098.6
hunted (13) v 012.5
~ with (2) v 052.6

Hunter Art Gallery (1) 093.7
hunter (2) n 130.1
~ hunter hero (1) n 130.1
Hunter (6) 105.5
~ Road (1) 105.5
~ Street (5) 105.2
hunters (3) n 013.5
Hunters (3) 030.7
~ Creek (2) LA TX 030.7
~ Village (1) 106.1
hunting (153) n/v/adj 057.4
~ bag (1) n 019.5
~ boots (4) n 123.8
~ buggy (2) n 033.7
~ case (1) n 080.7
~ clubs (1) n 013.8
~ coat (1) n 027.1
~ dog (10) n 033.1
~ dogs (5) n 033.1
~ for (3) v 052.5
~ honeybee ball (1) n 130.1
~ knife (15) n 104.3
~ knives (6) n 104.3
~ lamp (1) n 024.3
~ pants (1) n 027.4
~ squirrels (1) n 059.6
~ the bee ball (1) n 130.1
~ time (1) n 080.6
~ watch (1) n 004.3
~ with (2) v 099.6
~ [P-0] (1) v 095.9
Hunting (1) 104.6
Huntingdon (2) TN 088.8
Huntington (1) TX 087.5
hunts (8) n/v 035.9
Huntsville (83) AL AR GA TN TX 087.3
~ -Decatur (1) 106.5
~ Municipal Airport (1) 106.5
Huntsvillians (1) 080.7
hup (1) interj 038.2
Hup automobile (1) n 023.6
Hupmobile (1) 081.8
hurl (2) v 032.1
hurled (7) v 032.1
hurrah (5) n/v/adj 129.7
~ grass (2) n 015.9

hurrahing (6) v 057.4
hurricane (219) n/adj 006.2
~ force (2) n 112.1
~ lamp (4) n 024.3
~ lamps (2) n 024.3
~ season (1) n 112.1
~ shelter (1) n 015.5
~ siding (1) n 011.2
Hurricane (42) FL MS TN 112.1
~ Audrey (4) 006.1
~ Betsy (2) 112.1
~ Camille (1) 080.8
~ Carla (1) 006.3
~ Carmen (1) 006.4
~ Creek (11) AL GA LA MS TN 030.7
~ Eloise (1) 006.2
~ fence (12) n 126.1
~ fences (1) n 016.2
~ fencing (1) n 016.2
~ Gully (1) LA 030.7
~ -wire fences (1) n 016.3
hurricanes (72) n 112.1
hurry (24) n/v 025.4
~ back (15) v 093.1
~ off (1) v 043.5
~ up (1) v 049.2
hur(ry) back (1) v 002.4
hurrying (1) v 097.8
Hurst (4) LA TX 087.6
~ Nation (2) TN 087.7
hurt (436) n/v/adj 074.2
~ his feelings (1) v 082.1
~ place (1) n 078.1
Hurt (2) 108.5
~ building (1) n 108.5
~ Park (1) 106.4
hurt[V-p] (1) v 013.6
hurted (1) v 082.1
hurting (12) v 057.4
~ for (1) v 095.2
hurts (5) v 065.9
Hurtsboro (1) AL 087.9
husband (1238) n 063.1
husband[N-i][N-k] hairdos (2) n 043.7
husband[N-k] (3) adj 063.1
~ daddy (1) n 063.1
~ name (1) n 063.1
~ peoples (1) n 066.5

husbandry (2) n 070.6
husband's (26) adj 063.1
~ cattle (1) n 036.5
~ favorite (1) n 063.1
~ home (1) n 063.1
~ mother (1) n 063.6
~ name (3) n 063.1
~ office (1) n 063.1
~ parents (1) n 063.8
~ people (3) n 063.1
~ ties (1) n 063.1
husbands (9) n 063.1
husbands' wives (1) n 063.1
hush (610) v/adj 066.9
~ -hush (1) adj 088.8
~ -hush word (1) n 090.8
~ mouth (1) n 011.7
~ puppies (509) n 044.8
~ puppy (70) n 044.6
~ -puppy things (1) n 044.6
~ up (2) v 075.3
Hush (7) 123.8
~ Puppies (6) 123.8
~ Puppy (1) 123.8
husk (218) n/v/adj 056.1
~ off (1) v 056.1
~ out (1) v 075.6
~ tomatoes (1) n 055.3
husk[N-i] (6) n 056.1
husked (3) v 070.6
huskes (2) n 050.6
husking (3) v 056.1
husks (16) n 056.1
husky (121) adj 073.1
~ -built (1) adj 073.1
~ -looking (3) adj 073.1
hussified (1) adj 088.7
hussy (6) n 124.8
hustle (18) n/v 113.4
~ up (2) v 096.9
hustle[V-r] (1) v 075.6
hustled (2) v 081.8
~ around (1) v 099.9
hustler (8) n 113.3
hustlers (4) n 114.4
Hustlers (1) 123.8
hustling (5) v 099.5
~ up (1) v 113.5
hut (2) n 008.5
hutch (2) n 036.8

Hutchins River (1) MS 030.7
Hutchinson stopper (1) n 080.6
huts (4) n 015.1
hy spy (11) n 098.4
hya (1) interj 038.1
Hyatt (2) 106.5
~ House Hotel (1) 106.5
hybrid (12) n/adj 033.3
~ corn (2) n 056.2
~ field corn (1) n 056.2
~ tomatoes (1) n 055.3
~ yellow squash (1) n 056.6
Hyde (15) 080.8
~ and Henry (1) 080.8
~ County (1) NC 087.6
~ Park (12) 105.1
~ Park neighborhood (1) n 087.1
hydrangea (10) n 062.7
hydrangeas (1) n 062.2
hydrant (406) n/adj 018.7
~ water (1) n 018.7
hydrants (56) n 018.7
hydraulic lift (1) n 023.3
hydrau(lic) jack (1) n 065.9
hydrogen (2) adj 084.8
~ bomb (1) n 084.8
~ peroxide (1) n 078.3
hydrolift (1) n 111.4
hydrophobia (1) n 070.9
hydrophobi(a) (4) n/adj 070.6
~ cat (1) n 059.4
~ cats (1) n 059.4
hydros (1) n 024.6
hyenas (1) n 059.5
hymn (5) n 089.5
hymns (13) n 089.4
hyper (4) adj 074.1
hyperactive (8) adj 074.1
hypertense (1) adj 074.1
hypocrite (6) n 067.8
hysteria (1) n 079.3
hysteri(a) (1) n 079.3
hysterical (23) adj 079.3
hysterically (1) adv 079.3
hysterics (2) n 079.3

I

I (23227) 042.2
~ and GN (1) 090.8
~ Eighty-Five (4) 107.1
~ Forty (2) 107.1
~ Four (2) 107.5
~ H Ten (1) 107.1
~ Ninety (1) 107.1
~ Ninety-Five (8) 107.1
~ One-Twenty-Four (1) 107.1
~ Seventy-Five (11) 001A.2
~ Sixteen (1) 107.1
~ Sixty-Five (4) 107.1
~ spy (3) n 130.9
~ Ten (13) 107.1
~ Thirty-Five (1) 107.1
~ Twenty (11) 107.1
~ Twenty-Four (4) 107.1
~ Two-Forty (1) 107.1
~ Two-Twenty Overpass (1) 107.7
Iberia (13) LA 087.1
Iberville (12) LA 070.7
ibis (2) n 081.8
iby (1) interj 130.5
IC (2) 066.8
~ Railroad (1) 080.6
ice (304) n/v/adj/adv 007.5
~ bag (1) n 051.9
~ boat (1) n 024.6
~ bucket (1) n 017.2
~ cakes (1) n 122.3
~ cap (1) n 007.5
~ -cold (1) adj 056.9
~ cooler (1) n 015.5
~ cream (12) n 070.8
~ -cream (1) adj 056.9
~ -cream freezer (1) n 081.9
~ -cream land (1) n 029.8

~ -cream melon (2) n 056.9
~ -cream pants (1) n 027.4
~ -cream parties (1) n 130.7
~ -cream party (1) n 130.7
~ -cream salt (1) n 099.8
~ -cream socials (1) n 130.7
~ -cream suppers (2) n 080.6
~ -cream watermelon (1) n 056.9
~ cubes (1) n 007.7
~ -loading refrigerator (1) n 075.8
~ over (5) v 007.6
~ pick (3) n 051.9
~ rind (1) n 056.9
~ route (1) n 051.8
~ skift (1) n 007.6
~ skim (1) n 007.6
~ slick (1) n 112.3
~ storm (61) n 112.3
~ storms (9) n 112.3
~ tea (2) n 121.8
~ -tea glass (1) n 089.8
~ -tea spoon (2) n 017.9
~ teas (1) n 051.9
~ trucks (1) n 080.9
~ wagon (3) n 088.7
~ wagons (2) n 080.6
~ water (6) n 048.9
Ice Gray (1) 056.9
ice[V-t] up (1) v 007.6
iceberg (4) adj 055A.6
~ lettuce (3) n 055A.6
icebox (125) n/adj 088.9
~ biscuit (1) n 044.4
~ burn (1) n 093.9
~ melon (17) n 056.7
~ melons (9) n 056.9
~ pie (1) n 048.3
~ tomatoes (2) n 055.3
~ watermelon (6) n 056.9
~ watermelons (1) n 056.9
iceboxes (18) n 080.6
iced (37) v/adj 007.6
~ cakes (1) n 044.5

~ doughnut (3) n 122.4
~ over (22) v 007.6
~ up (5) v 007.6
iceded (1) v 007.6
icehouse (6) n 088.8
icehouses (1) n 116.2
iceman (6) n 084.8
ices over (1) v 007.6
(Ichaway)nochaway (2) GA 030.7
~ Creek (1) GA 030.7
icicle (11) n/adj 055.2
~ lettuce (1) n 055A.6
~ radish (2) n 055.2
~ radishes (2) n 055.2
icicles (1) n 007.6
(i)cicles (1) n 089.8
icing (162) n/v 048.5
~ over (1) v 007.6
~ up (2) v 007.6
icky (3) adj 023.8
~ day (1) n 005.5
ICOR (1) 059.4
icy (3) adj/adv 007.6
~ cold (1) adj 007.4
I'd (473) pron 053.4
(I')d (4) pron 090.5
Ida (3) 087.9
Idabel (1) OK 087.6
Idaho (82) 055.4
~ baked (1) n 055.4
~ bakers (3) n 055.4
~ potato (13) n 055.4
~ potatoes (23) n 055.4
~ whites (1) n 055.4
Idahoes (6) 055.4
Idalou (1) TX 086.3
idea (445) n 092.4
ide(a) (442) n 092.4
ideal (2) n 129.4
ideas (38) n 092.4
identical (4) adj 065.3
identically (1) adv 101.9
idiot (136) n/adj 073.4
~ lights (2) n 110.2
~ tape (1) n 097.8
~ tools (1) n 115.8
idiotic (2) adj 073.4
idiots (6) n 073.4
idle (1) adj 025.7
idlesome (1) adj 069.7
idol worshipers (1) n 126.5
if (1059) conj 088.2
(i)f (17) conj 088.2

iffen (1) conj 053.5
ignoramus (3) n 069.9
ignorance (2) n 065.6
ignorant (41) adj 073.4
~ juice (1) n 050.8
ignore (2) v 082.1
~ him (1) v 082.1
Ike (4) 064.4
Ikes (3) 127.3
Ila (1) GA 087.4
I'll (701) pron 081.1
ill (199) adj 072.9
~ at ease (8) adj 074.2
~ -bred (2) adj 073.7
~ -disposed (1) adj 075.1
~ -feeling (1) adj 075.2
~ -humored (1) adj 075.2
~ -mannered (3) adj 073.7
~ -natured (2) adj 075.1
~ repute (2) adj 113.4
~ -tempered (14) adj 075.1
~ will (1) n 040.6
illegal (12) adj 065.7
~ child (1) n 065.7
~ liquor (1) n 050.8
illegitimate (375) n/adj 065.7
~ baby (6) n 065.7
~ bastard (1) n 065.7
~ child (103) n 065.7
~ children (1) n 065.7
~ kid (1) n 065.7
~ kids (1) n 065.7
~ son (1) n 065.7
(il)legitimate (32) adj 065.7
~ baby (2) n 065.7
~ child (12) n 065.7
(ille)gitimate (4) adj 065.7
~ child (2) n 065.7
(il)legiti(mate) (1) adj 065.7
illegitimates (2) n 065.7
(il)legitime (1) adj F 065.7
illest (1) adj 002.7
illicit (2) adj 065.7
~ whiskey (1) n 050.8
Illinois (76) 086.4

~ Central (4) 086.9
~ Central Gulf (1) 030.9
~ Central Railroad (1) 084.7
illiterate (5) adj 069.7
illiterates (1) n 069.7
illness (1) n 076.1
illustrative (1) adj 065.8
I'm (2668) pron 042.6
(I')m (2) pron 101.2
image (121) n 065.3
im(age) (1) n 065.3
images (1) n 065.3
imaginary (1) adj 070.7
imagine (90) v 094.1
(i)magine (144) v 094.1
imbecile (6) n 073.4
imitate (1) v 057.7
imitates (3) v 065.3
imitation (5) n/adj 065.8
~ egg (2) n 017.1
~ grass (1) n 031.9
Immaculate (1) 106.6
immature (1) adj 075.1
immediate (13) adj 066.5
~ family (12) n 066.5
immediately (1) adv 070.1
immersion (1) n 065.8
immigrant (12) n 069.3
immigrants (2) n 066.7
Immigration (1) 080.6
immigrator (1) n 066.7
immodest (1) adj 073.8
immoral (1) adj 065.1
imp (3) n 090.1
impairment (1) n 057.5
impassible (3) adj 102.6
impatient (4) adj 075.1
Imperial Beach (1) CA 087.7
impersonator (1) n 124.1
(im)petigo (1) n 077.4
impinge (1) v 053.6
implement shed (3) n 014.8
import (2) adj 116.3
~ store (1) n 116.3
~ stores (1) n 116.3
important (3) adj 088.2
importantest (1) adj 002.6
impose (3) v 057.5
~ on (2) v 057.5
imposed on (1) v 057.5
imposing (10) v 057.5

~ on (3) v 057.5
~ up on (1) v 057.5
imposition (1) n 057.5
impossible (3) adj 070.2
impoverished (1) adj 091.6
impregnate (1) adj 065.1
impregnated (1) adj 065.1
impressed (1) v 095.8
impressionable (1) adj 088.7
improper (1) adj 131.5
improve (1) v 057.7
improved (7) v/adj 015.7
~ (Ber)muda grass (1) n 015.9
~ country roads (1) n 031.7
~ pasture (1) n 015.7
~ pastureland (1) n 029.9
~ pastures (1) n 015.7
~ peanuts (1) n 054.7
Improved (1) 055.5
improving (3) v 005.7
improvised (1) v 070.6
imps (3) n 090.1
in (8082) adv/prep 075.5
~ a delicate state (2) adj 065.1
~ a family way (48) adj 065.1
~ a fix (1) adj 065.1
~ a jam (1) adj 065.1
~ a motherly way (1) adj 065.1
~ a rocking chair (1) adj 065.1
~ a tangle (1) adj 082.2
~ an interesting position (1) adj 065.1
~ -and-out fence (1) n 016.4
~ and out the windows (1) n 130.3
~ back of (21) prep 010.5
~ between (6) prep 064.7
~ -between (1) n 013.1
~ -between-meal snack (1) n 048.6
~ -between snack (3) n 048.6

~ -between snacks (1) n 048.6
~ company with (1) prep 081.4
~ confinement (1) adv 065.1
~ family (2) adj 065.1
~ foal (1) adj 089.7
~ front (1) adv 039.6
~ front of (11) prep 052.9
~ guts (1) n 088.8
~ his belly (2) adv 080.4
~ his stomach (93) adv 080.4
~ -law (2) n 066.5
~ -laws (11) n 066.5
~ lieu of (1) prep 088.5
~ love (53) adj 081.4
~ love with (1) adj 081.4
~ love with her (24) adj 081.4
~ low cotton (1) adj 072.9
~ motherhood (1) adj 065.1
~ my stomach (15) adv 080.4
~ on (1) prep 075.9
~ place (3) prep 088.5
~ place of (21) prep 088.5
~ preference of (1) prep 088.5
~ purpose (1) adv 103.6
~ road (1) n 031.7
~ sheets (1) adv 104.8
~ spite of (4) prep 088.6
~ style (6) adj 123.6
~ that way (1) adj 065.1
~ the belly (1) adv 080.4
~ the family way (50) adj 065.1
~ the floor (5) adj 110.7
~ the gut (1) adv 080.4
~ the motherly way (1) adj 065.1

~ the oven (2) adj 065.1
~ the place of (1) prep 088.5
~ the stomach (80) adv 080.4
~ the stom(ach) (1) adv 080.4
~ the tummy (1) adv 080.4
~ the weathers (1) adj 072.9
~ trouble (20) adj 065.1
~ trouble by herself (1) adj 065.1
~ type (1) adv 081.4
~ waiting (2) adj 065.1
~ ways (1) adv 091.9
~ your belly (1) adv 080.4
~ your stomach (16) adv 080.4
~ [D-0] family way (45) adj 065.1
~ [D-0] family work (1) adj 065.1
~ [D-0] stomach (1) adv 080.4
~ [M-0] stomach (1) adv 080.4
(i)n (28) prep 070.3
~ his stomach (1) adv 080.4
In (2) 114.9
inattentive (1) adj 070.6
inaugural ball (1) n 083.1
inboard (4) n/adj 070.7
~ hydros (1) n 024.6
~ -outboard boat (1) n 024.6
~ outboards (1) n 024.6
inbreed (1) n 033.3
inch (48) n/adj 051.8
~ a night (1) n 015.9
~ -a-night grass (1) n 015.9
inch[N-i] (7) n 001.7
inches (58) n 001.5
inching (1) v 130.5
inchwise (1) adv 088.7
inchworm (3) n 060.5
inchworms (1) n 060.5
incident (2) n 095.8

incinerator (3) n 117.3
(in)cinerator (1) n 117.2
incinerators (1) n 065.8
incisors (1) n 071.8
inclement (9) adj 005.6
~ weather (1) n 005.6
incline (14) n 031.3
Incline Railway (1) 093.6
inclines (1) n 030.8
include (1) v 013.1
income (4) n/adj 051.8
~ tax (1) n 045.9
incompetent (3) adj 073.4
inconvenience (1) n 057.5
inconvenient (1) adj 066.8
incorporated (1) v 012.5
incorrectly (1) adv 053.4
increase (4) n/v 007.2
increased (1) v 007.2
increasing (58) v 007.2
incubator (8) n/adj 036.8
~ chickens (1) n 036.8
incubators (1) n 036.8
indebted (39) v 057.5
~ to (2) v 057.5
(in)debted (1) v 057.5
indeed (54) adv 091.1
(in)deed (1) adv 091.1
indelible pencil (1) n 065.8
Independence (13) AR LA MO TX 087.1
~ County (2) AR 087.5
~ Square (2) 106.4
independent (9) adj 074.8
~ grocer (1) n 116.2
~ groceries (1) n 116.2
~ neighborhood store (1) n 116.2
~ store (1) n 116.2
Independent (3) 108.5
~ Life building (1) n 108.5
~ Square (1) 108.5
index finger (1) n 072.2
Indi(a) (1) 055.6
Indian (187) 126.8
~ agency (1) n 070.6
~ ancestors (1) n 053.5
~ artifacts (1) n 088.9
~ Bayou (4) LA 030.7
~ Bay(ou) (4) LA 030.7
~ Branch (1) MS 030.7
~ bread (2) n 045.3

~ bungalow type (1) n 080.6
~ canoe (1) n 024.6
~ canoes (1) n 024.6
~ corn (2) n 056.2
~ -corn pudding (1) n 050.3
~ country (1) n 088.8
~ Creek (14) FL LA MS TN TX 030.7
~ dumplings (1) n 044.7
~ face (1) n 028.1
~ fighter (1) n 104.2
~ fire (1) n 079.8
~ firebug (1) n 060A.3
~ head (2) n 059.3
~ Head Acres (1) 106.1
~ hen (12) n 059.3
~ hens (5) n 059.3
~ hill (1) n 015.5
~ Hill (1) TX 087.4
~ knoll (1) n 030.8
~ mound (7) n 030.8
~ mounds (7) n 030.8
~ nuts (1) n 054.8
~ paintbrush (1) n 088.8
~ peach (31) n 054.3
~ peaches (11) n 054.3
~ pickles peaches (1) n 054.3
~ Point (1) TX 087.7
~ portage (1) n 081.8
~ pudding (4) n 050.3
~ reservation (2) n 126.8
~ River (3) FL 030.7
~ River City (1) FL 073.8
~ River Harbor (1) FL 087.7
~ rock (1) n 017.9
~ shoes (1) n 123.8
~ Slough (1) LA 030.7
~ Springs (4) FL GA 085.1
~ summer (2) n 091.8
~ Territory (1) 086.8
~ trails (1) n 031.7
~ turnip (1) n 080.8
~ -type (1) adj 024.6
~ -type corn (1) n 056.2
~ War (1) 085.8

Indiana (40) 086.2
~ Hoosier (1) 069.9
~ Hoosiers (2) 069.9
Indianapolis (8) IN 087.2
Indianola (11) GA MS TX 087.9
Indians (61) 069.5
Indies (2) 016.7
indifferent (4) adj 074.7
indigent (1) adj 069.7
indigestion (11) n 080.2
indigo (4) n/adj 088.9
~ snakes (2) n 092.8
Indigo (4) AL 030.7
~ Head (1) AL 087.4
~ Knob (1) AR 030.8
indiscreet (2) adj 124.7
individual (4) adj 074.8
~ little road (1) n 031.8
~ roads (1) n 031.8
individuals (1) n 053.5
indolent (1) adj 069.7
indoor (11) adj 010.7
~ bathroom (1) n 007A.2
~ court (1) n 126.2
~ garden (1) n 050.5
~ parking (1) n 108.4
~ patio (1) n 118.1
~ running water (1) n 088.6
~ toilet (2) n 012.1
~ toilets (2) n 012.1
indoors (1) adv 032.2
industrial (2) adj 107.6
~ road (1) n 107.6
industries (8) n 065.9
industrious (4) adj 074.1
industry (11) n 065.8
inedible (1) adj 057.1
inexperienced (2) adj 067.8
Inez (2) TX 087.3
infant (3) n/adj 051.9
~ childrens (1) n 066.3
Infant Mystics (1) 115.9
infanticipating (1) v 065.1
infantigo (1) n 077.8
infantine paralysis (1) n 070.9
infants (1) n 066.3
infantum (1) n 080.6
infare (10) n/adj 082.5
~ dinner (1) n 082.5
~ dress (1) n 084.8

infares (1) n 082.5
infatuated (1) adj 081.4
infected (15) v/adj 078.2
~ liver (1) n 079.8
~ material (1) n 077.7
(in)fected (1) adj 078.2
infection (35) n 077.5
(in)fection (1) n 078.3
inferior (1) adj 051.6
infern (2) n 090.1
infestation (1) n 091.8
infidel (3) n 067.8
infidels (1) n 069.7
infierno (2) n S 090.1
infirmary (2) n 084.5
Infirmary (2) 010.5
inflamed (2) adj 078.2
~ appendix (1) n 080.1
inflammable (1) adj 075.9
inflammation (14) n 077.5
inflammatory rheumatism (1) n 079.7
inflation (1) n 075.7
influence (42) n 115.3
influenza (6) n 079.7
inform (1) v 080.5
informal (4) adj 083.1
~ dance (1) n 083.1
~ dances (1) n 130.7
information (5) n/adj 104.1
~ center (2) n 107.3
informer (1) n 101.3
informers (1) n 101.3
Ingleside (1) LA 087.2
Inglis (2) FL 087.8
Ingraham Highway (1) 106.1
ingrain (1) n 080.7
Ingram Park (1) 106.4
ingredients (1) n 013.8
ingroup (1) n 129.6
inheritance (1) n 075.8
inherited (3) v 065.4
inherits (1) v 065.3
initials (2) n 013.8
(i)nitials (1) n 070.7
initiate (6) v 024.5
(i)nitiate (3) v 082.5
initiated (3) v 129.8
initiating (1) v 129.8
initiation (8) n 129.8
(i)nitiation (3) n 129.8
initiations (2) n 129.8
injury (2) n 078.1

ink (121) n/adj 026.5
~ pen (105) n 026.5
~ pencil (4) n 026.5
~ pens (3) n 026.5
inland (2) adj 030.8
~ riverways (1) n 030.6
~ town (1) n 084.8
inlet (40) n 030.3
Inlet (4) 030.3
inlets (6) n 030.3
Inman (3) GA 106.7
~ Park (1) 105.7
inn (11) n 084.3
Inn (5) 084.3
innards (40) n 037.2
inner (338) adj 105.1
~ city (10) n 105.1
~ hollow (1) n 030.4
~ hull (2) n 054.8
~ tube (297) n 024.4
~ -tube swings (1) n
022.9
~ tubes (24) n 024.4
~ tubing (2) n 024.4
~ wife (1) n 065.2
innings (1) n 001.5
innocent (1) adj 040.6
inputs (1) n 037.3
inquire (1) v 080.5
insane (6) adj 074.7
~ hospital (1) n 084.5
insect (8) n 065.9
insect[N-i] (2) n 016.7
insecticide (2) n 077.8
(in)secticide (2) n 065.8
insects (17) n 060A.1
insert (1) adj 116.8
inside (72) adj/adv/prep
024.4
~ bark (1) n 061.4
~ commode (1) n 012.1
~ contact (1) n 115.3
~ hull (3) n 054.8
~ of (1) prep 037.2
~ parking (2) n 108.4
~ plumbings (1) n
016.7
~ pocket (1) n 110.2
~ pull (1) n 115.3
~ road (1) n 031.8
~ spider web (1) n
061.3
~ stair[N-i] (1) n 010.7
~ stairs (2) n 010.7
~ stairway (2) n 010.7

~ stairways (1) n 010.7
~ toilet (1) n 012.1
~ toilets (1) n 126.3
~ track (1) n 115.3
insides (12) n 037.2
inspected (4) v/adj 070.6
inspection (2) n 085.6
inspector (5) n 075.7
inspectors (5) n 115.6
inspirational (1) adj 089.6
inspiring (1) adj 089.6
instamatically (1) adv
088.8
instant (23) n/adj 048.8
~ coffee (11) n 048.8
~ grits (1) n 050.6
~ potatoes (1) n 055.4
instantly (1) adv 065.9
instead (634) adv/prep
088.5
~ of (427) prep 088.5
~ [P-0] (2) prep 088.5
(in)stead (49) adv/prep
088.5
~ of (45) prep 088.5
instep (3) n 075.8
instigate (1) v 070.6
Institute (3) 083.6
~ of Texas Culture (1)
106.6
instruct (1) v 080.5
instructions (1) n 070.6
instructor (9) n 067.6
(in)structor (1) n 067.6
instructors (1) n 067.6
instrument (17) n/adj
085.6
~ panel (9) n 110.1
~ panels (1) n 110.1
instrumental (1) adj 130.9
instrumentals (1) n 130.8
instruments (3) n 066.9
insulate (1) v 097.8
insulated (2) adj 065.8
insulation board (1) n
011.2
insultation (1) n 129.7
insulted (1) v 075.2
insulting (4) v 081.8
insurance (36) n/adj
065.8
~ business (3) n 066.8
~ company (1) n 077.8
~ man (1) n 066.9
~ oil (2) n 024.2

~ shoes (1) n 123.8
Insurance (1) 108.5
insured (1) v 065.8
insurrection (1) n 085.8
integrals (1) n 037.3
integrated (5) adj 070.8
~ equine (1) n 104.6
~ family (1) n 069.5
integration business (1) n
080.7
intellect (2) n 125.5
intellects (1) n 125.5
intellectual (7) n/adj
125.5
intellectuals (2) n 125.5
intelligent (4) adj 125.5
~ person (1) n 125.5
Intelligent (2) 125.5
intend (50) v 101.2
~ to (40) v 101.2
intend[V-r] to (1) v
101.2
intend[V-s] to (1) v
101.2
intended (11) v/adj 101.2
~ husband (1) n 081.5
~ to (1) v 101.2
~ wife (1) n 081.6
intending (8) v 101.2
~ to (4) v 101.2
(in)tending to (1) v 101.2
intends to (2) v 101.2
intensity (1) n 007.2
intensive care (1) n 013.1
intent (1) n 084.8
intention (2) n 103.6
intentionally (18) adv
103.6
intentions (2) n 081.4
Interama tract (1) n 105.8
Interbay (3) 105.2
interbreed (1) n 069.5
intercede into (1) v 093.7
interceptor (1) n 111.7
interchange (4) n 107.4
Interchange (1) 107.5
interchanges (2) n 107.4
intercoastal (3) adj 030.2
~ canal (1) n 030.2
~ canal bridge (1) n
030.2
~ things (1) n 029.7
Intercontinental (4) 106.5
~ Airport (1) 106.5
intercourse (1) n 081.4

interest (8) n 070.7
interested (41) v/adj
065.8
~ in (21) v 024.7
~ in her (4) adj 081.4
~ in that woman (1)
adj 081.4
interestes (1) v 025.9
interesting (46) adj 065.8
~ position (1) n 065.1
interim pastor (1) n 067.8
interloop (1) n 107.5
intermarriage (1) n 069.5
intermediate (2) n 031.9
interment (3) n 079.2
intern (3) n/adj 084.6
~ preacher (1) n 067.8
internal organ (1) n 037.2
internals (1) n 037.2
International (39) 106.5
~ Airport (6) 106.5
~ Trade Mart (2) 108.5
interrace[N-i] (1) n 069.5
interracial (3) adj 069.5
interred (1) v 117.7
Interregional (1) 107.1
interrupt (1) v 021.4
intersection (5) n/adj
085.2
~ road (1) n 031.7
intersections (2) n 107.2
interstate (117) n/adj
107.1
~ highway (11) n 107.1
~ highways (2) n 031.6
Interstate (11) 107.1
~ Fifty-Five (1) 107.1
~ Forty (1) 107.1
~ Ninety-Five (1) 107.1
~ Seventy-Five (2)
107.1
~ Ten (2) 107.1
~ Thirty (1) 107.1
~ Twenty (2) 107.1
~ Twenty-Five (1)
107.1
interstates (11) n 031.7
interview (3) n/v 051.8
interviewed (1) v 053.9
interviews (1) n 001.1
intestinal tract (2) n 037.3
intestine (21) n/adj 037.3
~ part (1) n 037.3
intestine[N-i] (2) n 037.3
intestines (163) n 037.3

(in)testines (3) n 037.3
intimate (1) adj 129.4
into (837) adv/prep 032.6
~ love with (1) adj 081.4
~ trouble (3) adv 065.1
(in)to (1) adv 032.6
intown word (1) n 010.3
intoxicated (2) adj 088.8
~ drinks (1) n 050.8
(i)ntoxicated drinks (1) n 050.8
Intracoastal (3) LA 087.3
~ Canal (1) TX 030.2
introduce (2) v 088.8
intrude on (1) v 057.6
intruding on (1) v 057.5
inundated (1) v 065.8
inundating (1) v 068.9
invalid (1) n 070.5
invasion (1) n 025.6
invented (2) v 053.6
Inverness (6) AL AR MS 106.1
investigation (1) n 111.8
investigator (1) n 065.8
invigorating (3) adj 007.4
invitation (3) n/adj 089.9
~ kind (1) n 096.9
invited (1) v 043.7
invites (1) n 080.8
involve[V-t] with (1) v 076.1
involved (9) v 057.5
~ with (2) v 057.5
Inwood Road (1) 107.7
iodide (1) n 078.3
iodine (888) n 078.3
iodines (1) n 078.3
iodized (1) adj 078.3
Iota (2) LA 087.2
Iot(a) (1) LA 087.2
Iowa (21) 086.9
ipilipil trees (1) n 061.8
IQ (2) 084.8
Ira (1) 070.6
irate (1) adj 075.2
Irby Avenue (1) 107.7
Ireland (434) 087.9
Irene Park (1) 106.7
Irish (844) 055.4
~ biddy (1) n 127.9
~ blood (1) n 069.5
~ brawlers (1) n 127.9
~ brogue (2) n 087.9

~ Channel (8) 105.5
~ cobbler (2) n 055.4
~ cobblers (7) n 055.4
~ cops (1) n 112.5
~ Gray (14) 056.9
~ Grays (1) 056.9
~ Hill (1) MS 030.8
~ ignorance (1) n 023.3
~ people (1) n 066.8
~ piece (1) n 088.9
~ potato (178) n 055.4
~ (po)tato (4) n 055.4
~ -potato bags (1) n 019.7
~ -potato leaves (1) n 055.4
~ -potato patch (1) n 055.4
~ -potato poultice (1) n 061.4
~ -potato sack (1) n 019.7
~ potato[N-i] (1) n 055.4
~ potatoes (479) n 055.4
~ (po)tatoes (2) n 055.4
~ schoolmaster (1) n 067.6
~ sofa (1) n 009.1
~ white potato (1) n 055.4
~ white potatoes (1) n 055.4
~ wife (1) n 051.8
Ir(ish) cobbler (1) n 055.5
Irishman (11) 127.9
Irishmans (1) 016.7
Irishmen (13) 127.9
Irishmens (3) 127.9
iron (1014) n/v/adj 010.6
~ band (14) n 021.1
~ bands (5) n 020.3
~ bars (2) n 008.3
~ -beam (1) adj 021.6
~ -beam stocks (1) n 088.8
~ beds (1) n 009.7
~ bedstead (1) n 009.3
~ bedsteads (1) n 009.4
~ black pot (1) n 017.6
~ block (1) n 008.3
~ bucket (1) n 017.3

~ cat (1) n 017.6
~ cookstove (1) n 008.6
~ crock (1) n 017.6
~ day (7) n 010.6
~ dogs (4) n 008.3
~ door (1) n 011.1
~ fence (13) n 016.3
~ firedogs (1) n 008.3
~ foot (1) n 021.6
~ for (1) v 040.8
~ fryer (5) n 017.5
~ fryers (1) n 017.5
~ frying pan (5) n 017.5
~ gray (1) n 034.1
~ griddle (1) n 017.6
~ harrow (1) n 021.7
~ harrows (1) n 021.7
~ heater (1) n 008.5
~ hoop (2) n 020.3
~ hoops (1) n 020.3
~ horses (2) n 008.3
~ horseshoe (1) n 034.6
~ hub (1) n 021.1
~ kettle (41) n 017.6
~ kettles (8) n 017.6
~ lid (1) n 051.8
~ muzzle (1) n 036.2
~ ore (1) n 031.7
~ -ore gravel (1) n 029.8
~ oven (1) n 017.5
~ pan (2) n 017.5
~ pans (1) n 044.6
~ part (2) n 021.1
~ picket fence (2) n 016.2
~ piece (2) n 051.8
~ pin (1) n 002.6
~ pipe (1) n 023.2
~ plow (1) n 021.6
~ poker (1) n 008.3
~ post (1) n 016.5
~ post[N-i] (2) n 016.5
~ pot (93) n 017.6
~ pots (37) n 017.6
~ props (1) n 008.3
~ railing (1) n 008.3
~ rake (6) n 120.7
~ rim (21) n 021.1
~ rims (1) n 020.3
~ rock (1) n 016.6
~ rocks (1) n 016.6
~ rod (2) n 008.2

~ -shod harrows (1) n 021.7
~ shoe (2) n 034.6
~ shoes (5) n 034.6
~ shutters (1) n 088.7
~ skillet (72) n 017.5
~ skillets (18) n 017.5
~ something (1) n 008.3
~ spider (2) n 017.5
~ stob (1) n 088.9
~ stove (1) n 008.4
~ teakettle (6) n 017.6
~ teakettles (3) n 017.6
~ thimble (1) n 021.2
~ thing (3) n 117.3
~ thingamajigs (1) n 008.3
~ things (2) n 020.3
~ tire (12) n 021.1
~ -tired wagon (1) n 021.1
~ tires (7) n 021.1
~ tongs (1) n 008.3
~ -tooth harrow (2) n 021.7
~ -tooth rake (1) n 120.7
~ tooth[N-i] (1) n 032.4
~ tub (1) n 017.6
~ up (1) v 010.6
~ vessel (1) n 017.5
~ washpot (6) n 017.6
~ wedge (4) n 081.9
~ wedges (1) n 066.9
~ wheel (2) n 021.1
~ -wheel wheelbarrow (1) n 023.3
~ wheels (2) n 021.1
Iron (13) 030.7
~ Bridge Creek (1) TN 030.7
~ City (3) AL TN 087.8
~ Curtain (2) 127.5
~ Eyes (1) 070.8
~ Mountain (4) AR TN 031.1
iron[N-i] (9) n 055A.7
iron[V-r] (3) v 010.6
Irondale (5) AL 087.6
ironed (70) v/adj 010.6
~ out (1) v 010.6

~ -[J-0]-pressed   look
    (1) n 115.7
ironer (3) n 010.6
ironhead (1) n 081.8
ironheaded (1) adj 074.8
ironing   (428)   n/v/adj
    010.6
    ~ board (6) n 010.6
    ~ day (6) n 010.6
    ~ fire (1) n 010.6
    ~ rag (1) n 018.5
    ~ room (1) n 007A.1
    ~ time (1) n 010.6
iron(ing) (1) n 010.6
ironings (2) n 010.6
ironize yeast (1) n 045.5
irons (465) n/v 010.6
ironstone (1) n 017.1
ironstones (1) n 008.3
ironware (1) n 017.5
ironweeds (1) n 015.9
ironwood (8) n/adj 061.9
    ~ locust (1) n 061.8
ironwoods (1) n 061.9
ironwork (1) n 070.8
Iroquois Indians (1) 080.7
irrational (2) adj 074.7
irregardless (1) adv 088.7
irresponsible (5) adj 074.6
irrigate (6) v/adj 030.2
    ~ pipes (1) n 070.7
irrigating (2) v 030.1
irrigation   (17)   n/adj
    030.2
    ~ canal (1) n 030.2
    ~ ditch (8) n 030.2
    ~ ditches (4) n 030.2
    ~ pump (1) n 088.8
    ~ well (1) n 080.8
irritable (22) adj 075.1
irritate[V-r] (1) v 075.6
irritated (8) v/adj 075.2
irritates (1) v 090.4
Irvine (1) FL 087.1
Irving (1) 131.1
Irvington (2) AL 087.4
Irwin (5) GA 087.2
    ~ County (2) GA 087.1
Irwinville (2) GA 087.4
I's (97) pron 025.7
is (3640) v 051.2
(i)s (13) v 025.8
Isaac Hayes (1) 123.9
Isabel (4) LA 087.6
Isbell (3) AL 087.2

isinglass (4) n/adj 048.9
    ~ curtains (2) n 023.6
Islamorada (2) FL 087.1
island (9) n/adj 031.9
    ~ hopping (1) n 092.8
Island (126) 066.9
    ~ Airport (1) 106.5
    ~ Forty (1) TN 087.4
    ~ Thirty-Five (1) TN
        087.7
(Isl)and (1) 087.7
islands (8) n 031.9
Islands (3) 087.5
Isle (14) 030.3
    ~ of Orleans (1) 081.9
Islenos (1) 093.7
Isles (2) 077.9
islet (1) n F 081.8
Isney (2) AL 087.5
isn't (227) v 025.7
    ~ here anymore (1) v
        078.5
is(n't) (1) v 012.6
(is)n't (1) v 104.6
Israel (3) 070.7
Israelites (1) 086.7
Issaquena (5) MS 087.5
    ~ County (2) MS 086.3
issue (4) n/v 051.9
istacayota (1) n S 061.4
istle (1) n S 019.7
Istrouma (1) LA 087.4
it (29662) pron 042.1
(i)t (114) pron 102.5
It (3) 013.1
it[M-i] (1) pron 055A.7
Italian (54) 126.6
    ~ bean (1) n 055A.4
    ~ beans (1) n 055A.4
    ~ bee (1) n 060A.8
    ~ bread (6) n 044.4
    ~ community   (1)   n
        070.6
    ~ cypress (1) n 061.9
    ~ fellow (1) n 070.6
    ~ food (1) n 066.8
    ~ groceries (1) n 116.2
    ~ man (1) n 065.8
    ~ motherfucker   (1)   n
        127.3
    ~ pear tomatoes (1) n
        055.3
    ~ people (2) n 075.6
    ~ sausage (3) n 121.6
    ~ spaghetti (1) n 065.8

    ~ squash (2) n 056.6
Italianos (1) 127.3
Italians (38) 127.3
(I)talians (1) 127.3
Italy (15) 087.9
    ~ mans (1) n 070.8
    ~ wop (1) n 127.3
Itasca (1) TX 087.5
Itawamba (1) MS 086.9
itch (94) n/v/adj 065.8
itched (1) v 075.7
itching (4) v/adj 088.7
    ~ foot (1) n 088.7
itchy (1) adj 075.7
it'd (16) pron 005.6
item (3) n 095.2
Ithaca (2) NY 087.4
itinerant (17) n/adj 113.7
    ~ minister (1) n 067.8
    ~ preacher (9) n 067.8
it'll (60) pron 081.1
it's (1428) pron 025.2
(i)t's (14) pron 005.5
(it')s (10) pron 005.4
It's (1) 024.7
its (43) pron 104.8
    ~ own self (4) pron
        042.7
Its (1) 018.3
itself (56) pron 044.1
itty-bitty (1) adj 088.7
Iuka (3) MS 087.4
Ivanhoe (1) 106.6
I've (2121) pron 012.2
(I')ve (2) pron 012.4
Ives (1) 087.5
ivies (1) n 062.7
ivory (77) n/adj 062.8
    ~ -billed (2) adj 059.3
    ~ -billed   woodpecker
        (2) n 059.3
    ~ -billed   woodpeckers
        (1) n 059.3
    ~ -tower   intellectuals
        (1) n 125.5
ivorybill (13) n/adj 059.3
    ~ woodpecker   (5)   n
        059.3
ivy (721) n/adj 062.7
    ~ bush (1) n 062.8
    ~ bushes (1) n 062.7
    ~ vine (3) n 062.3
iv(y) (1) n 062.3
i(vy) (1) n 062.3
IX (1) 080.9

Izard (4) AR 087.9

J

J (4) 074.4
jab (4) v 104.3
jabalina (18) n/adj S 035.9
  ~ hog (1) n 035.9
  ~ hogs (1) n 035.9
jabalinas (11) n S 035.9
jabbed (6) v 104.3
jabbering (1) v 012.9
jabbing (1) v 104.3
jacal (2) n S 088.7
jacaranda (1) n 061.8
Jacinto (10) 087.5
(Ja)cinto (2) 106.4
jack (201) n/v/adj 033.7
  ~ at all trades (4) n 067.8
  ~ black (1) adj 119.6
  ~ carpenter (2) n 067.8
  ~ frame (1) n 022.1
  ~ game (1) n 130.6
  ~ grindles (1) n 059.9
  ~ grinner (1) n 088.7
  ~ horses (2) n 022.1
  ~ -in-the-box (1) n 101.5
  ~ lampings (1) n 024.3
  ~ lanterns (1) n 060A.3
  ~ mule (1) n 033.7
  ~ -o'-lantern (6) n 080.8
  ~ -o'-lanterns (1) n 099.5
  ~ oak (1) n 061.9
  ~ -of-all-trade[N-i] (3) n 080.9
  ~ -of-all-trade[N-i] man (1) n 067.8
  ~ -of-all-trades (36) n 067.8
  ~ -of-trades (1) n 119.5
  ~ pine (1) n 061.9
  ~ plane (1) n 096.7
  ~ rocks (3) n 130.6
  ~ salmon (1) n 059.9
  ~ snipe hunting (1) n 059.4
  ~ toy (1) n 130.6
Jack (40) 017.2
  ~ -and-Jill method (1) n 017.2
  ~ and the Beanstalk (1) 055A.4
  ~ Creek (1) GA 030.7
  ~ Dempsey (1) 058.3
  ~ Frost (31) 007.5
  ~ Hale (1) FL 030.7
  ~ Horner Pie (1) 130.7
  ~ Wheeler Park (1) 106.6
jack[N-i] (1) n 059.9
jack[V-p] up (1) v 098.7
jackal-headed (1) adj 074.8
jackanapes (1) n 067.8
jackass (40) n/adj 033.7
  ~ at all trades (1) n 067.8
  ~ carpenters (1) n 067.8
  ~ preacher (1) n 067.8
Jackass Prairie (1) TX 029.6
jackasses (13) n 129.1
jacked (3) v 104.5
  ~ up (1) v 090.9
jacket (593) n/adj 027.3
  ~ -like (1) adj 027.4
jack(et) (13) n/adj 060A.7
Jacket (2) 030.7
jacket[N-i] (5) n 027.2
jacket[N-k] (2) adj 060A.7
jacket's (2) adj 060A.7
jackets (445) n 060A.7
Jackets (1) 060A.7
jackfish (24) n 059.9
jackhammer (1) n 020.7
jackknife (6) n/adj 081.8
  ~ game (1) n 130.6
jackknives (2) n 017.8
jackleg (827) n/adj 067.8
  ~ at all jobs (1) n 067.8
  ~ at all trades (1) n 067.8
  ~ blacksmith (2) n 067.8
  ~ bootlegger (1) n 067.8
  ~ bricklayer (1) n 067.8
  ~ builder (1) n 067.8
  ~ car repairman (1) n 067.8
  ~ carpenter (104) n 067.8
  ~ carpen(ter) (1) n 067.8
  ~ carpenter work (1) n 067.8
  ~ carpenters (6) n 067.8
  ~ doctor (12) n 067.8
  ~ electrician (1) n 067.8
  ~ farmer (3) n 067.8
  ~ farmers (1) n 067.8
  ~ governors (1) n 067.8
  ~ horse (1) n 067.8
  ~ lawyer (36) n 067.8
  ~ lawyers (13) n 067.8
  ~ man (1) n 067.8
  ~ mechanic (19) n 067.8
  ~ mechanics (2) n 067.8
  ~ of all trades (3) n 067.8
  ~ painter (1) n 067.8
  ~ plow-hand (1) n 067.8
  ~ plumber (5) n 067.8
  ~ politician (1) n 067.8
  ~ preacher (174) n 067.8
  ~ -preacher type (1) n 067.8
  ~ preachers (14) n 067.8
  ~ president (1) n 067.8
  ~ teacher (3) n 067.8
  ~ teachers (1) n 067.8
(jack)leg lawyer (1) n 067.8
jacklegged (16) n/adj 067.8
  ~ carpenter (1) n 067.8
  ~ lawyer (2) n 067.8
  ~ preacher (9) n 067.8
  ~ preachers (1) n 067.8
  ~ teacher (1) n 067.8
jacklegs (11) n 067.8
jackpot years (1) n 081.9
jackrabbit (2) n 077.8
jackrabbits (1) n 121.6
jacks (113) n 022.1
Jacks (4) 030.7
  ~ Branch (1) FL 030.7
  ~ Creek (2) GA 030.7
Jacksboro (3) TN 087.1
  ~ Station (1) TN 087.2
Jackson (265) AL FL GA LA MS TN 087.9
  ~ Barracks (1) 106.4
  ~ Branch (1) GA 030.7
  ~ Chapel (1) TN 087.1
  ~ chest (1) n 009.2
  ~ Choir (1) MS 087.2
  ~ Country Club (1) 106.1
  ~ County (16) AR FL GA MS TN TX 087.5
  ~ Creek (2) MS 030.7
  ~ Height[N-i] (1) 105.2
  ~ Heights (4) 087.1
  ~ Hill (1) MS 030.8
  ~ Lake (1) AL 087.9
  ~ Lake Park area (1) n 085.1
  ~ Municipal Airport (2) 106.5
  ~ Parish (2) LA 087.2
  ~ Point (1) MS 087.6
  ~ River (1) FL 030.7
  ~ Square (4) 106.4
  ~ Street (2) 107.7
  ~ Street First Baptist Church (1) 089.1
  ~ Theater (1) 084.4
  ~ whites (1) n 069.7
  ~ Wonders (1) 055A.4
Jackson's (1) 106.4
Jacksonville (126) AL AR FL GA 087.6
  ~ Airport (1) 106.6
  ~ Beach (4) FL 087.2
  ~ Highway (1) 107.1
  ~ International Airport (2) 106.5
jackstone (1) n 130.6
jackstone[N-i] (1) n 098.4
jackstones (12) n 098.4
Jacob Creek (1) TN 030.7
Jacobi(a) (2) TX 086.3

Jacob's ladder (1) n 130.6
Jacobs Prairie (1) TX 086.2
jade (2) n/adj 076.6
jaded (8) v/adj 076.6
~ out (1) v 075.4
jag (56) n/v 019.8
jagful (1) n 019.8
jagged (1) v 084.9
jaggedy (2) adj 072.9
jaggers (2) n 016.3
Jaguar (1) 109.2
Jahr (1) G 093.3
jai alai (2) n 093.8
jail (189) n 112.8
Jail (3) 112.8
jailhouse (28) n/adj 112.8
~ lawyer (1) n 067.8
jails (2) n 112.8
jake (29) n/adj 050.8
~ leg (13) n 067.8
~ -leg carpenter (1) n 067.8
~ -leg mechanic (1) n 067.8
~ -leg preacher (1) n 067.8
Jake Leg (1) 067.8
jakes (7) n 012.1
Jakes Bayou (1) LA 030.7
jalapeno (5) n/adj 055.8
~ peppers (2) n 051.7
jalapenos (1) n 044.7
jalopies (2) n 023.6
jalopy (3) n 023.6
jalousies (3) n 009.5
jam (170) n/v/adj 051.6
~ session (1) n 083.1
Jamaica (4) 086.8
~ shorts (3) n 123.4
Jamaican (6) 119.7
~ Gold (1) 114.1
jamb (5) n/adj 008.4
~ rocks (1) n 008.3
jambalaya (4) n 080.8
jambalay(a) (1) n 092.9
jambalayas (1) n 090.8
jambe (1) n F 072.7
jamboree (3) n 082.5
jambs (3) n 008.2
James (17) 087.4
~ County (1) TN 087.4
~ Park (1) 085.1

~ River (1) VA 030.7
~ River Valley (1) VA 087.6
~ Robertson Parkway boulevard (1) n 107.6
~ White Court (1) 106.8
Jamestown (4) LA TN 087.9
jammed (2) v 102.6
jamming (1) v 083.1
jams (25) n 051.6
jane (1) n 126.3
Jane (29) 113.3
Janes (2) 067.1
janitor (59) n/adj 119.5
~ service (1) n 119.5
janitors (6) n 119.5
janker (1) n 081.9
January (943) 001A.6
Januar(y) (61) 001A.6
Jap (21) 126.4
~ slaps (1) n 123.8
Japan (16) 087.9
~ plum (1) n 088.8
Japanese (57) 126.4
~ camphor (1) n 061.8
~ cane (1) n 051.3
~ cherry (1) n 062.1
~ elm (1) n 061.8
~ Gardens (1) 106.4
~ girl (1) n 126.5
~ hornets (1) n 060A.5
~ magnolia (3) n 062.9
~ magnolia[N-i] (1) n 062.9
~ magnolias (1) n 013.9
~ maple (1) n 061.9
~ oil (1) n 024.1
~ persimmon tree (1) n 061.9
~ persimmons (1) n 080.9
~ plum (2) n 062.5
~ plum tree (1) n 061.8
~ plum trees (1) n 061.8
~ squash (2) n 056.6
~ tree (1) n 062.9
~ walnut (1) n 054.8
~ worm (1) n 060.5
~ yew (1) n 061.8
Japans (2) 066.8

japonica (3) n 062.8
Japs (46) 126.4
JAPs (1) 126.7
jar (101) n/adj 065.9
~ lamp (1) n 024.3
jardiniere (2) n 017.7
jardinieres (1) n 017.7
jarflies (1) n 088.9
jarfly (3) n 060A.5
jargon (1) n 131.2
jarred (1) v 095.9
jars (47) n 019.2
jasmine (13) n/adj 077.6
~ tree (1) n 062.8
jasmines (1) n 061.9
Jason (1) 112.5
Jasper (15) AL FL GA TN TX 087.7
~ County (2) MS TX 087.1
jasper (1) n 064.4
jaundice (914) n 079.8
jaun(dice) (3) n 079.8
jaundiced (2) adj 079.8
~ eye (1) n 079.8
jaunt (2) n 077.1
jauntitis (1) n 079.8
Java (21) 032.3
~ time (1) n 049.2
jaw (36) n/adj 071.8
~ harp (3) n 020.6
~ meat (1) n 046.3
~ teeth (3) n 071.8
~ tooth (8) n 071.8
jaw[N-i] (1) n 028.9
jawbone (1) n 075.7
jawbones (1) n 066.9
jawbreaker (1) n 065.8
jawed (3) adj 085.2
jaws (10) n/adj 071.7
~ harp (2) n 020.6
jay (5) n/adv/interj 037.7
~ horsing (1) v 085.2
Jay (2) FL 087.5
jaybird (16) n 059.3
Jaybird (1) 096.8
jaybirds (11) n 059.3
Jaycees (2) 065.8
jayhawk[N-i] (1) n 080.8
Jayhawkers (1) 080.8
jays (12) n 059.3
Jays (1) 114.2
jaywalk (36) v 085.2
jaywalked (11) v 085.2
jaywalker (2) n 085.2

jaywalking (74) v 085.2
jaywalks (6) v 085.2
jazz (62) n/adj 130.8
~ dancing (2) n 083.1
~ festival (2) n 130.8
~ music (3) n 089.5
jealous (2) adj 043.1
jean (10) n/adj 027.4
~ breeches (2) n 027.4
~ cloth (2) n 027.4
~ pants (3) n 027.4
jean[N-i] (3) n 027.5
Jeannetta (1) 105.5
jeans (198) n/adj 027.4
~ breeches (1) n 027.4
~ cloth (1) n 027.4
~ clothes (1) n 027.1
jeebie (3) adj 083.1
~ -jeebie (1) adj 065.7
jeebies (2) n 074.4
jeep (13) n/adj 109.2
~ car (1) n 023.6
jeeps (3) n 109.2
jeet (1) n 130.7
jeez (3) interj 092.2
jefe (1) n S 069.6
Jeff (7) AL 087.4
~ Davis (4) GA LA 087.2
~ Davis pie (1) n 096.7
~ Davis time (1) n 088.8
Jefferson (71) AL AR GA LA MS TN TX 087.2
~ City (4) MO 087.1
~ County (11) AL AR GA TX 086.3
~ county seat (1) n 085.5
~ Davis (1) 066.5
~ Davis State Park (1) 104.6
~ Downs (1) 105.9
~ Highway (1) 107.6
~ Paige Road (1) 080.7
~ Parish (5) LA 087.6
~ Street (3) 105.7
~ Street area (1) n 106.3
~ Township (1) AR 087.1
Jeffersonville (1) GA 087.9
Jehosophat (1) 092.2

Jehovah (8) 089.3
~ God (1) 089.3
~ people (2) n 126.6
Jehovah[N-k] (5) 089.1
~ Witness[N-i] (2) 089.1
~ Witnesses (3) 126.7
Jehovah's Witnesses (3) 089.6
Jehovahs (1) 126.6
Jekyll (4) GA 087.4
~ Island (3) GA 086.3
jell (1) v 058.5
Jell-O (3) 051.6
Jellico (2) TN 087.5
~ Creek (1) TN 030.7
jellied (2) adj 051.6
~ doughnuts (1) n 122.6
jellies (82) n 051.6
jelly (1122) n/v/adj 051.6
~ bean (61) n 028.1
~ -bean dude (1) n 051.6
~ -bean pants (1) n 028.1
~ -bean suit (1) n 028.1
~ beans (4) n 028.1
~ buns (2) n 122.7
~ cake (1) n 051.6
~ Danish (1) n 122.2
~ dish (1) n 051.6
~ doughnut (46) n 122.6
~ doughnuts (18) n 122.6
~ -fill (1) adj 122.6
~ -fill doughnut (7) n 122.6
~ -fill doughnuts (3) n 045.2
~ -filled (12) adj 122.6
~ -filled doughnut (7) n 122.6
~ -filled doughnuts (2) n 045.2
~ glass (1) n 048.9
~ grits (2) n 050.3
~ house (1) n 011.9
~ -like (1) adj 051.6
~ puffs (1) n 122.6
~ roll (33) n 045.2
~ rolls (7) n 122.6
~ stick (1) n 122.8
~ up (1) v 089.8

jellyfish (3) n 060.3
Jemison (2) AL 087.4
Jena (4) FL LA 086.1
Jenkins (4) 087.3
~ County (1) GA 087.3
~ Creek (1) TN 030.7
~ peas (1) n 055A.8
Jenkinsburg (1) GA 087.5
jennet (2) n 033.6
jennets (1) n 033.7
Jennie (1) AR 087.7
jennies (57) n 022.7
Jennings (5) FL LA TX 087.4
jenny (388) n/adj 033.7
~ bright (1) n 060.5
~ horses (1) n 022.5
~ stripe (1) n 022.7
~ wood hen (1) n 059.3
Jenny (3) 030.7
~ Branch (1) GA 030.7
jerk (16) n/v/adj 097.6
~ beef (1) n 096.7
~ -leaf tobacco (1) n 088.7
~ line (1) n 039.1
~ water (1) n 067.8
jerked (7) v 104.4
~ up (1) v 065.4
jerker (1) n 080.6
jerkers (1) n 091.8
jerking (1) v 083.1
jerks (1) n 127.1
jerky (3) n/adj 037.3
~ meat (1) n 080.6
Jerries (5) 127.1
Jerry (2) 112.5
~ curl (1) n 123.9
jersey (1) n 027.3
Jersey (67) 033.6
~ City (1) NJ 087.1
~ cow (8) n 033.6
~ cows (3) n 033.6
~ Mill cow (1) n 033.6
~ pigs (1) n 035.5
~ wagon (2) n 088.7
Jers(ey) (1) 037.6
Jersey(x2) (1) 037.5
Jersey(x3) (1) 037.5
Jerseys (7) 033.6
Jerusalem (9) 061.4
~ artichoke (1) n 061.4
~ artichokes (1) n 055.4
~ oak (5) n 089.9

~ -oak weed (1) n 061.4
~ pot (1) n 114.1
Jessieville (1) AR 087.4
jester (1) n 125.6
Jester (1) 080.8
Jesup (6) GA 087.8
Jesus (79) 089.3
~ Christ (27) 089.3
~ Christ Almighty (1) 092.2
~ freaks (3) n 126.6
~ God (2) 089.3
~ people (1) n 129.3
~ sandals (1) n 115.7
jet (5) v/adj/adv 070.9
~ black (1) adj 070.9
~ boat (1) n 024.6
~ out (2) v 011.6
~ thing (1) n 080.9
Jet Drive-In (1) 114.9
Jetaway (1) 106.5
jets (1) n 025.1
jetties (3) n 080.9
jetty (1) n 031.4
Jeune (1) 105.4
jew (4) v 094.6
Jew (55) 073.5
~ baby (3) n 126.8
~ boy (3) n 126.7
~ boys (2) n 126.9
~ peddler (1) n 053.4
~ person (1) n 096.8
~ store (2) n 116.2
~ town (1) n 080.7
Jew[N-k] harp (14) n 020.6
jewbird (1) n 126.7
jeweler (1) n 070.8
Jewel(la) (1) LA 087.8
jewelries (1) n 041.9
jewelry (14) n 028.3
Jewett (1) TX 087.3
jewfish (7) n 093.6
Jewish (52) 126.7
~ cemetery (1) n 106.6
~ children (1) n 126.7
~ community (1) n 105.7
~ country club (1) n 105.7
~ family (1) n 125.7
~ girl (1) n 126.7
~ harp (3) n 020.6

~ merchants (1) n 092.8
~ people (11) n 126.7
~ person (2) n 126.7
~ population (1) n 126.7
~ Sabbath (1) 002.1
~ store (2) n 116.3
~ temple (2) n 126.7
~ -type (2) adj 044.8
~ white bread (1) n 044.4
Jew's (531) 020.6
~ box (1) n 020.6
~ harp (516) n 020.6
~ harps (14) n 020.6
Jews (60) 126.8
jib (3) n 084.9
jibe (2) v 088.8
~ with (1) v 080.6
jiffy (19) n 070.3
Jiffy (3) 116.3
~ Food Store (1) 116.2
~ Store (1) 116.2
jig (12) n/adv 069.3
~ -jag (1) adv 085.2
jigaboo (11) n 069.3
jigaboos (9) n 069.3
jigged (1) v 080.8
jigger (2) n 060A.9
jiggers (15) n 060A.9
jigging (1) v 022.8
jigglers (1) n 060A.9
Jiggs's dog (1) n 033.3
jigs (9) n 069.3
jigsaw (2) n 022.5
jigzag (1) adv 085.2
Jill (1) 017.2
jillion (5) n 001A.3
jillions (1) n 001A.2
jilt (7) v 082.1
~ her (1) v 082.1
~ him (2) v 082.1
jilted (181) v/adj 082.1
~ her (6) v 082.1
~ him (94) v 082.1
~ lover (1) n 082.1
~ you (1) v 082.1
Jim (20) 069.3
~ Crow (3) 069.3
~ Crow things (1) n 088.9
~ Crows (1) 069.3
~ Cummings (1) 106.4

~ Cummings State Park (1) 106.6
~ Hogg (1) TX 087.3
~ Hogg County (2) TX 087.3
~ stink (1) n 060.5
~ Wheelers (1) 060.5
jiminy cricket (1) n 061.1
jimmy jug (1) n 088.8
Jimmy (2) 052.5
~ Carter (1) 052.5
~ clips (1) n 110.4
jimmyjohn (1) n 019.2
Jimson (2) 015.9
~ grass (1) n 015.9
Jimsonweed (10) 015.9
~ roots (1) n 061.4
Jimsonweeds (7) 015.9
jingo (1) n 092.4
jingoes (1) n 092.2
jinks (1) n 092.1
jinx (14) n 090.3
jinxes (2) n 090.3
jitney (13) n/adj 026.7
~ bus (1) n 085.3
jitneys (6) n 109.9
jitterbug (24) n 083.2
jitterbugged (1) v 083.1
jitterbugging (3) v 083.1
jittering (1) v 083.1
jitters (1) n 060A.9
jittery (9) adj 074.3
jive (13) n/v/adj 080.6
~ ass (1) n 069.3
~ -ass nigger (1) n 069.3
~ clothes (1) n 123.6
~ dudes (1) n 081.8
~ law (1) n 112.5
~ term (1) n 046.7
~ turkey (1) n 088.7
~ with (1) v 101.7
jivester (2) n 073.5
jiving (1) v 084.8
Jo (1) 023.9
Joan of Arc (1) 055.5
Joanna Branch (1) MS 030.7
job (146) n/v/adj 075.6
~ development (1) n 032.4
~ down (1) n 021.6
~ -down plow (1) n 021.6
~ market (1) n 088.7

job[V-t] (1) v 065.8
jobbed (3) v 080.6
~ around (1) v 080.6
jobber (1) n 016.5
Job's umbrella (1) n 062.2
jobs (19) n 057.4
jock (4) n/adj 124.5
~ tickler (1) n 124.9
jockstrap (1) n 090.8
joe (10) n/adj 051.2
~ boat (2) n 024.6
~ boats (2) n 024.6
Joe (51) 032.3
~ harrow (20) n 021.7
~ har(row) (2) n 021.7
~ harrows (1) n 021.7
~ Louis (4) 050.8
~ Namath look (1) n 115.8
~ Radford Thomas (1) 106.4
~ -tooth harrow (1) n 021.7
joes (1) n 081.8
Joes Bayou (1) LA 030.3
jog (4) v 022.6
jogged (2) v 102.3
jogging (6) adj 022.6
~ board (2) n 022.6
~ shoes (2) n 123.8
~ shorts (2) n 123.4
joggle (3) n/v/adj 022.6
~ board (1) n 022.6
~ on (1) v 022.6
joggled (2) v 022.7
joggling (39) v/adj 104.2
~ board (37) n 022.6
~ boards (1) n 022.6
john (162) n/adj 012.1
~ room (1) n 126.3
j(ohn) (1) n 047.6
John (993) 068.2
~ Arnold (1) MS 031.1
~ Arnold Mountain (1) MS 031.1
~ B (1) 092.9
~ B. Stetson hat (1) n 066.9
~ Bircher (1) 129.2
~ Brown things (1) n 092.2
~ Clarke Road (1) 031.6

~ D. Rockefeller (1) 068.2
~ Deere (1) 068.2
~ Denver's music (1) n 130.8
~ Dillinger (1) 092.9
~ Doe (2) 032.6
~ F. (1) 068.2
~ F. Kennedy (1) 068.2
~ F. Kennedy assassination site (1) n 106.4
~ Henry (4) 068.2
~ John (2) 064.4
~ Law (1) 112.5
~ Lydgate (1) 068.2
~ Neely Bryan cabin (1) n 106.4
~ Neely Bryan statue (1) n 106.4
~ Pennekamp State Park (1) 106.4
~ Ross Bridge (1) 106.6
~ Ryan (1) 068.2
~ Wesley (2) 068.2
~ Wilkes Booth (1) 068.2
johnboat (43) n/adj 024.6
~ type (1) n 024.6
johnboat[N-i] (1) n 024.6
johnboats (10) n 024.6
johnnies (10) n 012.1
johnny (84) n/adj 012.1
~ bread (2) n 044.4
~ horses (1) n 022.1
~ house (21) n 012.1
~ houses (2) n 012.1
Johnny (47) 068.2
~ Cut Road (1) 031.7
~ Frazier (1) 104.6
~ Law (1) 112.5
~ mowers (1) n 022.5
~ on the Spot (1) 012.1
johnnycake (40) n/adj 044.8
~ bread (1) n 044.6
Johnnycake Alley (1) 044.8
johnnycakes (19) n 044.8
Johnny's room (2) n 010.3
John's (11) 043.4
~ room (1) n 010.3
johns (27) n 126.3
Johns (38) 068.2

~ Branch (1) TN 030.7
~ Creek (3) GA 030.7
Johnson (233) LA TN 087.3
~ Bayou (2) LA TX 030.3
~ Bay(ou) (1) LA 087.3
~ Blevins Branch (1) TN 030.7
~ brace (1) n 021.6
~ City (9) TN TX 087.2
~ Corner (1) GA 087.6
~ County (3) AR TX 087.7
~ Creek (1) AL 030.7
~ Ferry Road (1) 107.9
~ grass (191) n 015.9
~ -grass (1) adj 015.9
~ grass hay (2) n 015.9
~ -grass roots (2) n 061.4
~ Highway (1) 106.3
~ Ridge (1) TN 031.1
~ root (1) n 061.4
~ weed (2) n 015.9
~ wings (2) n 021.7
Johnsonville (1) TN 087.3
Johnston (5) 107.6
~ wing (1) n 021.6
~ wings (1) n 021.6
Johnstons (1) MS 087.3
join (274) v 089.2
~ in (1) v 049.2
~ right hands (1) v 082.2
~ up (1) v 089.2
join[V-p] (1) v 089.2
join[V-r] (121) v 089.2
join[V-t] (6) v 089.2
joined (531) v 089.2
~ in (2) v 089.2
~ together (1) v 082.2
~ up (5) v 089.2
~ up with (1) v 089.2
Joiner (1) AR 087.3
joining (22) v 089.2
joins (16) v 089.2
~ in (2) v 013.9
joint (510) n/adj 072.3
~ ache (1) n 079.6
~ bone (2) n 072.3
~ mark (1) n 077.8
~ piece (1) n 037.1

~ snake (3) n 088.9
joint[N-i] (4) n 072.3
jointed (9) adj 072.3
~ snake (2) n 080.9
jointing (3) v/adj 072.3
~ place (1) n 011.6
jointly (1) adv 072.3
joints (502) n 072.3
joist (3) n 104.5
joist[N-i] (1) n 104.5
joistes (3) n 016.7
jokal (1) adj 073.2
jokative (1) adj 088.6
joke (36) n/v/adj 084.8
~ bait (1) n 093.7
~ fishing bait (1) n 093.8
~ with (1) v 032.4
~ [P-0] (1) v 092.7
joker (2) n 125.6
jokers (2) n 052.1
jokes (6) n 129.7
jokey (2) adj 099.3
joking (22) v 057.4
~ around (1) v 080.9
jokingly (1) adv 059.6
joli (1) adj F 026.3
jolly (52) adj 073.2
jolted (3) v 082.1
~ him (2) v 082.1
Jonah (7) 082.8
Jonathan (1) 068.2
Jones (25) GA MS 087.3
~ Bayou (1) LA 030.7
~ County (2) GA MS 087.4
~ Creek (2) AL AR 030.7
~ crowd (1) n 082.8
~ Hall (1) 106.9
~ melon (1) n 056.9
~ Park (2) 106.4
~ Road (1) 107.7
~ Valley (2) 106.1
Jones[N-i] (2) 066.6
Jonesboro (23) AR GA TN 087.4
Jonesbor(o) (3) AR GA LA 087.3
Joneses (5) 101.6
Joneses' (1) 082.7
Jonestown (1) MS 087.5
Jonesville (5) LA 087.3
jonquil (1) n 070.7
jonquils (1) n 070.6

joogle (1) n 071.7
joogles (1) n 071.7
Jordan (7) 023.5
~ automobile (1) n 023.6
~ Branch (1) GA 030.7
~ City (1) 081.8
~ Creek (1) TX 030.7
~ Schoolhouse (1) 087.8
Jose (3) 128.5
Joseph (5) 087.1
Jo(seph) (1) 087.7
Josephine Street (1) 107.7
Joseph's (2) 108.9
Joshua (2) TX 087.2
~ Creek (1) FL 030.7
Josie (10) AL 087.3
jostler (1) n 110.9
joto (2) adj S 074.8
Jourdan (3) 030.7
~ Eau (2) MS 030.7
~ River (1) MS 030.7
journalism (1) n 080.6
journey (11) n 040.1
joust (1) n 130.5
Jove (1) 092.2
jovial (9) adj 073.2
Jowers Creek (1) TX 030.7
jowl (79) n/v/adj 046.3
~ bones (1) n 013.9
~ him (1) v 033.2
~ meat (4) n 046.3
jowl[N-i] (1) n 046.3
jowls (53) n 047.3
joy (4) adj 113.4
~ house (1) n 113.4
~ juice (1) n 050.9
~ killer (1) n 080.8
~ wagon (1) n 109.3
Joy (10) 054.9
Joyce Boulevard (1) 031.7
joyful (2) adj 073.2
Joyous (2) 093.2
~ Christmas (1) 093.2
~ Noel (1) 093.2
joyride (1) n 064.6
joyriding (1) v 090.4
Joys (1) 054.9
JP (3) 080.9
Js (1) 114.2
Juan (13) 068.2
Juba (5) 060A.4
jubilee (2) n/adj 060A.4

Jubilee (7) 056.9
Judas (3) 090.1
~ tree (2) n 062.7
Jude (1) 084.5
judge (971) n/v 068.6
~ of probate (1) n 068.6
Judge (84) 068.6
~ Hughes (6) 068.6
~ Marshall (25) 068.6
~ Sarah T. Hughes (1) 068.1
~ so-and-so (1) n 068.6
judge[N-i] (1) n 068.6
judged (3) v 068.6
judge's gun (1) n 068.6
judges (19) n 068.6
Judges (1) 068.6
judgeship (1) n 068.6
judging (1) v 068.6
judgment (12) n 066.9
Judgment Day (1) 068.6
Judice (1) LA 087.3
judiciary (1) n 085.6
Judson (2) GA 087.7
~ College (1) 083.6
jug (113) n/v/adj 019.2
~ -a-rum (1) n 060.2
~ -fish (1) v 080.7
~ handle (1) n 071.7
jugged (1) v 104.3
juggling (2) v/adj 022.1
~ board (1) n 022.6
jugheads (1) n 059.9
jugs (70) n 019.2
jugular vein (5) n 065.8
juice (499) n/adj 077.7
~ fruit (1) n 055.1
~ glass (3) n 048.9
~ glasses (4) n 048.9
~ harp (334) n 020.6
~ harps (13) n 020.6
~ oranges (1) n 055.1
~ peach (1) n 054.4
~ plant (1) n 092.8
Juice (1) 050.9
juices (1) n 048.6
juicier (2) adj 026.2
juicing up (1) v 119.6
juicy (8) adj 081.3
~ harp (1) n 020.6
juke (16) v/adj 075.8
~ houses (1) n 083.1
~ jam (1) n 083.1
~ joint (5) n 081.9

~ joints (4) n 084.9
~ organs (1) n 080.9
juked (2) v 104.3
jukes (2) n 113.8
juking (7) v 083.1
jukum (1) n 050.9
julep (1) n 050.8
Julia (1) 067.9
Julian (1) 107.7
Julienton (1) GA 082.6
Juliet Gordon Lowe's home (1) n 106.5
July (1073) 001A.7
~ bugs (1) n 060A.4
~ flies (4) n 060A.1
~ fly (6) n 060A.4
~ freshes (2) n 006.1
jumbo (15) n/adj 055.5
~ bean (1) n 055A.4
~ frog (1) n 060.2
~ land (1) n 029.9
~ potatoes (1) n 055.4
~ shrimp (1) n 060.9
~ shrimp[N-i] (1) n 060.9
~ size (1) n 060.9
~ soil (1) n 029.9
jumbos (1) n 060.5
Jumbos (1) 054.7
jument (1) n F 034.2
ju(ment) (1) n F 034.2
jump (227) n/v/adj 033.2
~ around (1) v 083.1
~ board (44) n 022.6
~ -board (1) v 022.8
~ class (1) v 083.4
~ from (1) v 095.8
~ in (4) v 095.3
~ into (1) v 032.6
~ jacket (1) n 027.4
~ Josie (2) n 098.4
~ Josie parties (1) n 083.1
~ off (1) v 095.3
~ -off (3) n 031.2
~ off into (1) v 053.7
~ on (2) v 097.9
~ on him (2) v 033.2
~ out (2) v 101.2
~ over (1) v 095.3
~ over there (1) v 037.7
~ plank (1) n 022.6
~ rope (64) n 130.6
~ seats (2) n 109.4

~ springboard (1) n 092.8
~ sticks (1) n 130.2
~ suit (12) n 027.4
~ suits (4) n 027.4
~ the broom (7) v 082.2
~ the broomstick (11) v 082.2
~ the gun (1) v 082.2
~ the line (1) v 082.2
~ the log (1) v 082.2
~ the rope (11) n/v 082.2
~ the stick (1) n 089.8
~ up (1) v 084.8
jump[V-p] (1) v 075.2
jump[V-r] (9) v 016.3
~ class (1) v 083.4
~ the broom (4) v 082.2
~ the broomstick (1) v 082.2
jump[V-t] (1) v 130.6
jumped (45) v 095.3
~ him (1) v 082.1
~ in (2) v 095.3
~ Josie (1) v 083.1
~ off (3) v 095.3
~ off of (1) v 034.5
~ on (2) v 081.8
~ over (1) v 095.3
~ over the broomstick (1) v 082.2
~ the broom (9) v 082.2
~ the broomstick (6) v 082.2
~ the broomstick backwards (1) v 082.2
~ the bucket (1) v 082.2
~ the rope (1) v 130.6
~ up (1) v 065.9
~ up and ran (1) v 082.1
jumper (34) n/adj 027.3
~ church (1) n 080.6
~ suit (1) n 027.4
~ suits (1) n 027.4
Jumper Church (1) 080.6
jumpers (14) n 027.4
jumpets (1) n 016.4
jumping (81) v/adj 022.8
~ around (1) v 083.1

~ bean (1) n 128.7
~ board (32) n 022.6
~ boards (3) n 022.6
~ frog (2) n 060.2
~ horse (2) n 022.6
~ jack (3) n 101.5
~ -off place (2) n 080.8
~ plank (2) n 022.6
~ rope (9) n 130.6
~ ropes (1) n 098.4
~ something (1) n 061.1
~ sticks (1) n 130.7
~ the board (1) n 022.6
~ the broom (4) v 082.2
~ the broomstick (3) v 082.2
~ the rope (2) n 130.6
~ the stick (1) v 082.2
Jumping Josie (1) 083.1
jumpy (5) adj 074.3
~ rope (1) n 130.6
jump(y) (1) adj 075.1
jumunder (1) n 066.7
junco (1) n 061.8
juncos (1) n 088.9
junction (7) n/adj 011.6
~ road (1) n 031.7
Junction (15) AR 087.2
~ City (3) AR 087.4
June (1071) 001A.7
~ apples (2) n 001A.7
~ bride (1) n 001A.6
~ bug (26) n 060A.3
~ bugs (21) n 060A.3
~ corn (2) n 056.2
~ peach (2) n 054.4
~ peaches (1) n 054.4
Juneau (1) AK 087.5
Juneberries (1) 062.5
Juneteenth (1) 001A.6
Juney bugs (1) n 060A.3
jungle (24) n/adj 114.8
~ bunnies (5) n 069.3
~ bunny (15) n 069.3
~ gym (1) n 022.7
~ juice (1) n 050.8
junior (158) n/adj 125.8
~ college (23) n 083.6
~ colleges (1) n 083.6
~ commanders (1) n 130.5
~ high (90) n 125.8

~ high school (32) n 125.8
~ highs (2) n 125.8
~ proms (1) n 083.1
~ school (2) n 125.8
Junior (52) 032.7
~ cultivator (1) n 021.6
~ Food Mart (1) 116.2
~ Food Store (2) 116.2
~ Miss Pageant (1) 106.4
Jun(ior) (1) 069.6
juniors (2) n 125.9
juniper (5) n/adj 061.9
~ bushes (1) n 062.9
Juniper (3) FL 030.7
~ Springs (1) AR 087.4
~ Street (1) 105.8
junk (1254) n/adj 010.2
~ chair (1) n 010.2
~ collector (2) n 007A.4
~ compartment (1) n 110.2
~ corner (1) n 010.3
~ drawer (1) n 010.3
~ food (1) n 048.4
~ furniture (2) n 010.2
~ heap (2) n 023.6
~ hole (1) n 010.3
~ house (72) n 010.3
~ houses (2) n 010.3
~ lumber (1) n 010.2
~ pile (9) n 010.2
~ place (2) n 010.3
~ rags (1) n 010.2
~ room (373) n 010.3
~ rooms (6) n 010.3
~ shed (1) n 011.7
~ sheds (1) n 011.7
~ shop (2) n 010.3
~ snakes (1) n 084.9
~ storage area (1) n 010.3
~ stuff (2) n 010.2
~ tires (1) n 010.2
~ whatnot (1) n 010.2
junked (2) v 010.2
~ off (1) v 010.2
junkets (1) n 088.7
junkie (28) n 114.3
junkies (5) n 114.3
junky (3) adj 010.2
~ cars (1) n 109.4
junkyard (7) n 010.2

jurors (3) n 065.8
jury (4) n 065.8
jus (2) n F 054.4
just (3155) adj/adv 070.3
~ away (1) adj 078.5
Just-Us Club (1) 129.6
justice (12) n 068.6
~ of the peace (4) n 080.8
~ of [D-0] peace (1) n 068.8
justify (2) v 057.7
Justina (2) LA 105.1
Justin(a) (1) LA 087.9
jut out (1) v 075.7
jute (45) n/adj 019.7
~ bag (5) n 019.7
~ bagging (1) n 019.7
~ bags (8) n 019.7
~ sack (9) n 019.7
~ sacks (1) n 019.7
~ -type bag (1) n 019.7
jutted up (1) v 009.7
jutting out (1) v 030.3
juveniles (1) n 064.3

K

K (8) 024.2
~ oil (7) n 024.2
~ Street (1) 107.7
kabobs (1) n 121.2
kahoops (1) interj 038.3
Kaiser blade (2) n 093.8
Kalamazoo (2) MI 087.7
~ stoves (1) n 008.4
kalanchoe (1) n 080.7
Kalb (20) 106.2
kale (49) n/adj 055A.5
~ greens (1) n 055A.5
Kaler Park (1) 106.7
Kallison building (1) n
108.5
Kamikazes (1) 126.4
Kamin Eisen (1) n G
008.3
Kangaroo (3) 068.5
Kanis Park (1) 106.4
Kankakee (1) IL 086.3
Kansas (63) 086.7
~ City (28) KS MO
087.1
~ City Southern (2)
092.8
~ City strip (1) n 131.9
~ City strip steak (1) n
121.1
~ Creek (1) TN 030.7
Kan(sas) City (2) MO
087.5
Kanuga Road (1) 107.7
kaolin (1) n 080.7
Kaopectate (1) 092.9
Kaplan (1) LA 087.8
Kapok Tree Inn (1) 106.4
Karankawa (1) 080.7
Karl (1) 067.1
Karo (8) 051.3
~ nut pie (1) n 054.8
~ pie (1) n 084.9
~ syrup (5) n 051.3
Kartoffel (2) n/adj G
080.7

~ Keller (1) n G 080.7
Kase (1) n G 048.1
Kasiquinempas (1) TN
030.7
Kate Ross Barr Park (1)
085.1
Katy (6) TX 087.4
~ Freeway (5) 106.1
katydid (13) n 060A.4
katydids (9) n 060A.5
Katzen (1) n G 082.5
Katzenjammers (1) n G
127.1
Kavanda Drive (1) 107.8
kawhop (1) interj 095.4
kayaks (1) n 024.6
Kayouche Coulee (1) LA
030.7
Kaywood (1) 107.8
kazoo (4) n 020.6
KC strip steak (1) n
121.1
Keds (2) 123.8
kee(x3) (1) interj 038.5
kee(x6) (1) interj 038.5
keebo(x3) (1) interj 037.6
keel over (2) v 095.5
keel[V-r] over (1) v
078.6
keelboat (1) n 024.6
keeled (17) v/adj 073.2
~ over (16) v 078.6
keelihopters (1) n 111.9
keen (4) adj/adv 016.3
keener (1) adj 101.7
keep (701) v 075.3
~ away (4) n 130.4
~ company (1) v 081.4
~ down (1) v 080.5
~ for (1) v 042.5
~ from (5) v 006.5
~ on (5) v 024.7
~ out (2) v 075.3
~ still (1) v 037.5
~ up (5) v 095.7
~ up with (2) v 032.4
~ your tail still (1) v
037.5
k(eep) (1) v 053.2
keep(x2) (1) interj 038.5
keep[V-p] (9) v 057.4
~ on (3) v 053.5
keep[V-t] (1) v 058.6
keeper (3) n 101.3
keepers (1) n 130.5

keeping (36) v/adj 081.4
~ company (9) v 081.4
~ her company (2) v
081.4
~ quality (1) n 092.8
~ room (1) n 010.1
~ up (1) v 025.3
~ up with (1) v 032.4
keeps (22) v 057.4
~ up with (1) v 013.7
keepsake (1) n 010.2
keepsakes (1) n 010.2
keet (1) n 036.6
keg (851) n/adj 020.2
~ beer (1) n 121.9
~ box (1) n 020.2
~ hole (1) n 020.2
~ hoops (1) n 020.3
~ parties (2) n 130.7
~ party (2) n 020.2
keg[N-i] (3) n 020.2
kegs (308) n 020.1
Kehle (1) n G 071.8
Keller (3) TX 087.2
Kellum Creek (1) TN
030.7
Kelly (13) 105.3
~ day (2) n 080.8
~ Field (1) 106.6
~ Gap (2) AR 031.2
~ Ingram Park (1)
106.4
~ plow (1) n 021.6
~ settlement (1) MS
086.3
~ weed (2) n 015.9
Kellys Mill (1) GA 030.9
Kelso (2) AR 086.2
Kembletown (1) LA 087.4
Kemmerer (1) WY 087.2
Kemp Street (1) 107.7
Kemper (5) 087.2
~ City (1) TX 087.2
~ County (3) MS 087.1
Kenans Mill (1) AL 086.6
Kendall (3) FL 087.4
Kennebec (3) 055.4
Kennebecs (6) 055.4
Kennedy (15) AL 105.1
~ Boulevard (1) 105.6
~ Boulevard Bridge (1)
106.4
~ Drive (1) 105.7
~ Hotel (1) 084.3

~ Pasture Company (1)
015.7
~ Plaza (2) 106.4
~ Ranch (1) TX 087.4
Kenner (4) LA 087.8
Kennesaw (3) GA 086.3
Keno (2) 080.9
Kensington Park (1)
106.2
Kent (1) AL 087.7
Kentucky (993) 086.5
~ board fence (1) n
016.4
~ colonel (5) n 068.4
~ Derby (3) 086.5
~ fences (1) n 016.4
~ Fried Chicken (4)
086.5
~ Lake (1) TN 086.5
~ oysters (1) n 037.3
~ rifling (1) n 090.9
~ white wooden fence
(1) n 016.2
~ wife (1) n 086.5
~ Wonder (44) 055A.4
~ Wonder bean (3) n
055A.4
~ Wonder beans (11) n
055A.4
~ Wonder pole beans
(1) n 055A.4
~ Wonder runners (1)
n 055A.4
~ Wonder string beans
(1) n 055A.4
~ Wonders (62) 055A.4
(Ken)tucky (3) 086.5
~ Fried Chicken (1)
086.5
~ Green Pods (1)
055A.4
~ Wonders (1) 055A.4
Kentwood (4) LA MS
087.4
Kenwood (10) GA 087.2
kept (101) v/adj 066.8
~ on (3) v 057.4
~ over (1) v 050.1
~ up (3) v 093.7
~ woman (1) n 113.3
~ women (1) n 113.3
KER (1) 084.9
kernel (306) n/adj 054.2
~ seed (1) n 054.1
kern(el) (3) n 054.2

kernels (10) n 054.2
kerosene (1024) n/adj 024.2
~ barrel (1) n 012.1
~ bomb (1) n 024.3
~ burner (1) n 024.2
~ -burning heater (1) n 008.6
~ -burning refrigerator (1) n 024.2
~ candle (1) n 024.3
~ heater (3) n 118.4
~ heaters (4) n 118.4
~ lamp (56) n 024.3
~ lamps (42) n 024.2
~ lantern (2) n 024.2
~ lanterns (4) n 024.2
~ light (1) n 024.2
~ lights (3) n 024.2
~ oil (69) n 024.2
~ -oil lamp (3) n 024.2
~ -oil lamps (1) n 024.2
~ -oil lights (1) n 024.2
~ oven (1) n 116.4
~ refrigerator (2) n 024.2
~ stove (3) n 024.2
~ stoves (1) n 024.2
~ student lamps (1) n 081.8
~ torch (1) n 024.3
Kerrville (4) TX 087.5
Kessler Park (1) 106.2
kettle (732) n/adj 017.6
~ house (1) n 080.6
~ pots (1) n 017.6
Kettle (2) 017.6
kettles (99) n 017.6
key (3) n 053.4
~ of G (1) n 115.4
Key (45) 087.3
~ Biscayne (3) FL 087.7
~ Largo (2) FL 087.1
~ West (23) FL 086.3
~ Wester (1) 073.6
~ Westers (1) 088.8
keyhole saw (1) n 020.7
keys (3) n 113.2
Keys (14) FL 087.2
khaki (22) n/adj 027.4
~ breeches (1) n 027.4
~ clothes (1) n 027.4
~ pants (13) n 027.4

~ shirt (1) n 027.4
khakis (22) n 027.4
ki-yea (2) interj 037.5
kick (67) n/v/adj 078.6
~ his ass (2) v 065.5
~ hole (1) n 010.3
~ in (1) v 075.8
~ off (1) v 075.8
~ soccer (1) n 130.4
~ the bucket (6) v 078.6
~ the can (32) n 130.4
~ the cans (1) n 130.4
~ the stick (1) n 130.4
~ the tin can (1) n 130.4
~ tin cans (1) v 130.4
~ up (1) v 032.8
kick[V-r] (283) v 078.6
~ out (1) v 078.6
~ the bucket (279) v 078.6
~ the bucket out (1) v 078.6
~ the old bucket (1) v 078.6
~ [D-0] bucket (1) v 078.6
kick[V-t] the bucket (6) v 078.6
Kickapoo (2) 030.7
~ Creek (1) TX 030.7
~ Joy Juice (1) 050.9
Kickapoos (1) 070.8
kickback (1) n 095.7
kickball (29) n 130.4
kicked (229) v 078.6
~ him (14) v 082.1
~ him out (3) v 082.1
~ off (21) v 078.6
~ out (17) v 078.6
~ out the bucket (1) v 078.6
~ over (1) v 078.6
~ the bucket (161) v 078.6
~ the bucket over (1) v 078.6
~ the can (1) v 078.6
~ the light out (1) v 078.6
~ up (2) v 006.3
kicker (23) n/adj 024.6
~ dance (1) n 083.1
~ dancing (1) n 083.1

~ music (3) n 088.8
~ shirt (1) n 088.7
kickers (3) n 088.7
kicking (14) n/v/adj 065.5
~ a can (1) v 130.4
~ fit (1) n 080.8
~ stock (1) n 088.7
~ the bucket (2) v 078.6
~ up (1) v 007.2
kicks (3) n/v 082.1
~ him (1) v 082.1
~ up (1) v 080.7
kid (199) n/v/adj 064.3
~ around (1) v 082.5
~ fight (1) n 129.7
~ friend (1) n 129.4
~ on a corner (1) n 080.7
~ out of marriage (1) n 065.7
~ out of wedlock (1) n 065.7
Kid (9) 064.4
kid[N-i] (3) n 005.2
kid[V-p] (1) v 013.6
kiddie car (1) n 064.5
kidding (21) v 013.3
~ with (1) v 025.3
Kiddles (1) 080.8
kiddlingly (1) adj 080.8
kiddo (1) n 064.4
kiddos (1) n 064.3
kiddy(x2) (1) interj 038.5
kidnapped (1) v 083.4
kidney (33) n/adj 037.2
~ bean (8) n 055A.3
~ beans (11) n 055A.3
~ colic (2) n 080.1
~ stew (1) n 037.2
~ stone (1) n 076.1
~ trouble (1) n 080.9
kidneys (22) n 037.2
kid's (1) adj 064.3
kids (819) n 068.7
kids' (2) adj 081.3
~ butts (1) n 081.3
~ room (1) n 007A.7
kids's (2) adj 043.9
~ lunch[N-i] (1) n 013.6
Kiefers (1) 054.3
kielbasa (1) n 121A.6
Kiest (1) 106.4

kike (11) n 126.8
kikes (11) n 126.8
Kilburn (1) GA 087.9
Kilby (1) 112.8
Kilgore coffee (1) n 032.3
Kilkenny (1) 107.7
kill (127) n/v/adj 104.3
~ floor (1) n 080.9
~ him (2) v 033.2
~ out (1) v 080.8
~ the man with the ball (4) n 130.5
~ [P-0] (1) v 075.6
kill[V-r] (30) v 098.7
kill[V-t] (6) v 013.8
killdeer (5) n 060A.4
Killearn Estates (1) 107.7
killed (143) v/adj 057.9
~ off (1) v 053.5
~ out (2) v 059.4
~ with (1) v 061.9
Killeen (2) TX 087.9
Killen (3) AL 087.2
killer (19) n/adj 055.6
~ ball (1) n 130.5
~ bees (1) n 060A.2
~ -diller (1) n 007.5
~ frost (1) n 007.5
killers (3) n 110.8
Killin (1) AR 087.7
killing (123) n/v/adj 065.5
~ freeze (2) n 007.5
~ frost (86) n 007.5
~ hogs (2) n 098.7
~ out (1) v 099.9
~ time (1) n 028.1
~ up (1) v 053.4
killings (1) n 084.9
killjoy (1) n 075.1
kills (6) v 053.5
kiln (23) n 015.6
~ -dried (1) adj 091.8
Kiln (5) MS 087.2
kilns (3) n 023.2
kilo (2) n 114.7
kilos (1) n 114.5
kilt (32) v/adj 066.9
~ wearers (1) n 128.1
kilted (1) v 065.9
Kilties (1) 128.1
Kimbrough (2) AL 087.4
kimono (4) n 026.4
kin (770) n/adj 066.6
~ line (1) n 066.5

~ networks (1) n 066.5
~ people (59) n 066.5
~ peoples (4) n 066.5
kination (1) n 066.5
Kinchafoonee (5) GA 030.7
~ Creek (3) GA 030.7
Kinchafoo(nee) (1) GA 030.7
Kinch(afoonee) Creek (1) GA 030.7
kind (910) n/adj 073.2
~ of (677) adv 090.4
~ [P-0] (2) adv 090.4
kind[N-i] (85) n 070.1
kinder (1) adj 066.1
Kinder (1) LA 087.2
kindergarten (49) n 083.5
kindergart(en) (1) n 083.7
kindhearted (3) adj 073.2
kindle (9) n/v/adj 008.6
~ with (2) v 008.6
~ wood (3) n 008.6
kindled (1) v 008.6
kindler (1) n 008.6
kindling (846) n/adj 008.6
~ basket (1) n 020.1
~ house (1) n 011.7
~ lighter (1) n 008.6
~ -like (2) adj 008.6
~ pieces (1) n 008.6
~ pine (1) n 008.6
~ room (1) n 011.7
~ shed (1) n 011.7
~ splinters (1) n 008.6
~ wood (66) n 008.6
kindlings (12) n 008.6
kindly (185) adj/adv 090.4
~ of (3) adv 090.4
kindred (2) n 066.5
kindry (2) n 040.7
kinds (49) n 055A.8
kine (1) n 036.5
kinfolk (76) n 066.5
kinfolk[N-i] (4) n 066.5
kinfolks (367) n 066.5
kinfolkses (1) n 066.6
king (110) n/adj 131.4
~ and queen (1) n 130.2
~ -and-queen ball (1) n 083.1

~ bee (1) n 069.6
~ bolt (2) n 081.8
~ fishermens (1) n 084.8
~ king can do (1) n 098.4
~ king can I go? (1) n 088.7
~ mackerel (10) n 088.9
~ of the hill (1) n 130.6
~ of the mountain (3) n 130.5
~ of the woods (1) n 033.5
~ rafter (1) n 011.6
~ rail (1) n 091.7
~ snake (44) n 084.8
~ snakes (29) n 080.7
~ -tail snake (1) n 080.8
~ worms (1) n 060.5
King (24) 107.9
~ Arthur (1) 107.9
~ Cole (1) 131.4
~ Cotton (2) 102.4
~ Nigger (1) 069.3
~ of the Negroes (1) 115.9
~ Ranch (3) TX 087.4
~ William (3) 106.1
kingdom (1) n 092.3
kingfish (11) n 059.9
kingfisher (1) n 059.5
kingpin (1) n 069.6
King's X (1) 098.4
kings (1) n 088.8
Kings (8) 030.7
~ Creek (1) TN 030.7
~ Ferry (1) GA 086.4
~ Fork (1) TN 030.7
~ Lake (1) MS 087.2
~ Pass (1) NC 032.3
~ Point (2) 105A.6
Kingsland (1) GA 087.2
Kingsport (11) TN 087.2
Kingston (11) AR MS NY TN 087.2
~ Mill (1) TN 087.6
~ Pike (3) 107.5
~ Station (2) GA 084.7
Kingsville (3) TX 073.8
kinked (1) adj 123.9
kinks (1) n 022.2

kinky (3) adj 088.7
~ heads (1) n 069.3
kinman (1) n 066.5
kinnery (4) n 066.5
Kinsey (1) AL 087.2
kinsfolk (1) n 066.5
kinsfolks (2) n 066.5
kinsman (3) n 066.5
kinsmen (2) n 066.5
kinspeople (2) n 066.5
kip(x2) chicky(x2) (1) interj 038.5
Kirby Drive (1) 107.7
Kirbyville (1) TX 087.2
Kirkham Branch (1) MS 030.7
Kirkland (1) 087.7
Kirkwood (2) 105.2
~ section (1) n 105.7
Kisatchie (2) LA 030.7
~ Creek (1) LA 030.7
kiss (46) n/v/adj 081.7
~ ass (4) n 125.6
~ -ass (1) v 080.7
~ for final (1) v 081.7
Kiss (1) 093.3
kiss[V-r] (1) v 081.7
kissed (29) v 081.7
~ by (2) v 081.7
kisser (11) n 071.6
kissers (1) n 125.6
Kissimmee (3) FL 087.3
~ River (1) FL 030.7
kissing (410) v/adj 081.7
~ around (1) v 081.7
~ ass (1) v 125.6
~ cousin (1) n 088.9
~ cousins (1) n 091.9
~ kinfolks (1) n 066.5
kissy face (1) n 081.7
kit (17) n 082.9
~ and caboodle (14) n 082.9
~ and caboose (1) n 082.9
Kitalou (1) TX 086.3
kitchen (2582) n/adj 009.9
~ area (8) n 007A.5
~ breakfast-room combination (1) n 007A.2
~ broom (1) n 010.5
~ building (1) n 009.9
~ cabinet (18) n 010.1

~ cabinets (2) n 010.1
~ chair (3) n 008.8
~ chairs (1) n 008.9
~ closet (24) n 010.1
~ closets (2) n 010.1
~ cloth (1) n 018.4
~ cupboard (2) n 010.1
~ curtains (2) n 009.5
~ den (1) n 007A.4
~ door (4) n 009.9
~ dry towel (1) n 018.4
~ faucet (2) n 018.7
~ flue (1) n 023.2
~ fork (1) n 017.8
~ forks (1) n 017.8
~ furniture (1) n 009.4
~ garbage can (1) n 117.2
~ garden (7) n 050.5
~ house (2) n 009.9
~ knife (5) n 104.3
~ knives (4) n 104.3
~ pantry (2) n 010.1
~ part (1) n 009.9
~ porch (6) n 010.8
~ range (1) n 009.8
~ room (1) n 007A.4
~ safe (8) n 010.1
~ safes (1) n 010.1
~ sinks (1) n 009.9
~ stove (3) n 080.6
~ stoves (1) n 009.9
~ supplies (1) n 009.9
~ towel (7) n 018.4
~ -type thing (2) n 007A.3
~ utensils (1) n 070.6
~ wood (1) n 008.6
kitchenette (8) n 007A.2
kitchenettes (1) n 009.9
kitchens (20) n 007A.2
kite (3) n/adj 059.2
~ flying (1) n 130.9
kite[N-i] (1) n 016.7
kites (2) n 098.4
kith (1) n 066.5
kitten (4) n 033.9
~ with fluid drive (1) n 059.4
kitten's nest (1) n 093.8
kittens (2) n 059.4
kitties (2) n 059.4
kittledee (1) n 090.8
kitty (14) n 130.4

~ wants a corner (1) n 098.4
Kitty (2) 109.4
  ~ Cat (1) 109.4
  ~ Mitchell (1) 059.9
kitty(x2) (1) interj 038.5
kitty(x3) (4) interj 038.5
kitty(x4) (2) interj 093.5
kitty(x6) (1) interj 038.5
kiwi fruit (1) n 080.7
KKK (1) 080.9
Klan (8) 068.5
Klans (1) 088.9
Klatsch (1) n G 048.6
Kleckley Sweet (16) 056.9
Kleiderschrank (2) n G 009.7
kleines Haus (1) n G 012.1
kleptomaniacs (1) n 113.7
Klondike (3) MS 105.4
Klondyke (1) 062.4
Klotzville (1) LA 087.5
klutz (10) n 073.4
klutzy (2) adj 073.3
Klux (7) 065.8
knack (1) n 048.6
knacking (1) v 048.6
knapsack (2) n 028.2
knee (101) n/adj 072.6
  ~ baby (1) n 088.7
  ~ bone (5) n 072.6
  ~ breeches (4) n 027.4
  ~ -high (2) adj 104.7
  ~ -high shorts (1) n 123.2
  ~ joint (1) n 072.3
  ~ joints (1) n 072.3
  ~ knockers (11) n 123.2
  ~ -length pants (2) n 123.2
  ~ -length shorts (1) n 123.2
  ~ -length walking shorts (1) n 123.2
  ~ pants (11) n 027.4
  ~ -pants boy (1) n 080.7
  ~ shorts (2) n 123.2
  ~ trousers (1) n 027.4
kneecap (6) n 070.9
kneed (1) adj 073.3
kneehole (1) n 009.4
kneel (170) v 096.5

~ down (53) v 096.5
kneel[V-r] (71) v 096.5
  ~ down (59) v 096.5
kneel[V-t] down (1) v 096.5
kneeled (187) v 096.5
  ~ down (27) v 096.5
  ~ to (4) v 096.5
kneeling (36) v 096.5
  ~ down (3) v 096.5
kneels (23) v 096.5
  ~ down (3) v 096.5
knees (56) n 072.8
knelt (366) v 096.5
  ~ by (1) v 096.5
  ~ down (101) v 096.5
Kneppel (1) n G 008.5
knew (910) v 101.6
  ~ about (1) v 101.6
  ~ of (17) v 101.6
  ~ to (2) v 101.6
knewed (4) v 101.6
Knickerbocker (1) 130.3
knickerbockers (10) n 123.2
knickerbottoms (2) n 123.2
knickers (46) n 123.2
knickknack (13) n/adj 008.8
  ~ snack (1) n 048.6
  ~ stuff (1) n 010.2
knickknacking (1) v 048.6
knickknacks (11) n 048.6
knife (1543) n/v/adj 017.8
  ~ -and-fork clubs (2) n 080.6
  ~ blade (1) n 017.8
  ~ clams (1) n 090.8
  ~ grinder (3) n 023.5
  ~ rock (3) n 023.4
  ~ sharpener (15) n 023.4
  ~ sharpen(er) (2) n 023.4
  ~ stone (1) n 023.4
  ~ wound (5) n 078.1
knife[N-i] (38) n 017.8
knifed (1) v 104.3
knifings (1) n 104.3
Knight (2) 030.7
  ~ Creek (1) TN 030.7
Knights (2) 081.8
  ~ of Pythias (1) 081.8

~ of Revelry (1) 119.6
knit (5) v/adj 019.7
  ~ bag (1) n 019.7
  ~ pants (1) n 027.4
  ~ sack (1) n 019.7
knits (1) n 027.4
knitted (1) adj 088.8
knitting (1) adj 008.9
knives (887) n 017.8
knob (421) n/adj 030.8
  ~ hill (4) n 030.8
  ~ hills (3) n 030.8
Knob (41) 030.8
  ~ Hill (7) TN 030.8
knobby (2) adj 030.8
  ~ land (1) n 030.8
knobs (52) n 030.8
Knobs (1) 030.8
knock (34) n/v/adj 104.2
  ~ -down (4) adj 083.1
  ~ off (1) v 080.7
  ~ -off (1) n 095.7
  ~ skinners (1) n 053.9
  ~ your block off (1) v 065.5
  ~ your head off (1) v 065.5
knock[V-r] (4) v 070.2
knock[V-t] (3) v 053.8
  ~ down (1) v 053.8
  ~ up (2) v 065.1
knockabout clothes (1) n 027.4
knockabouts (1) n 123.8
knockaway (1) n 061.8
knockdown (5) n 022.2
knocked (86) v 053.4
  ~ him cold (1) v 082.1
  ~ him flat (1) v 082.1
  ~ him off (1) v 078.6
  ~ out (10) v 075.5
  ~ up (62) v 065.1
knocker (14) n 069.7
knockers (18) n 127.1
knocking (5) v 057.4
  ~ around (1) v 081.4
  ~ off (1) v 041.4
knockout (5) n 080.6
knocks (2) v 091.4
  ~ out (1) v 091.4
  ~ up (1) v 065.1
knockum (1) n 050.9
knockwurst (7) n 121A.6
knoll (135) n 030.8
Knoll (1) 107.7

knolls (10) n 030.8
Knollwood (1) 107.7
knot (105) n/adj 008.6
Knot (1) 030.7
knothead (3) n 069.8
knotheaded (1) adj 074.8
knot's been tied (1) v 082.2
knots (137) n 031.3
Knots (1) 056.9
knotting up (1) v 005.6
knotty (5) adj 033.3
  ~ dog (1) n 033.3
  ~ haircut (1) n 115.8
  ~ pine (3) n 008.6
know (2242) n/v 101.6
  ~ about (8) v 095.8
  ~ (a)bout (4) v 013.3
  ~ from (2) v 025.8
  ~ -how (2) n 088.9
  ~ -it-all (3) n 074.8
  ~ of (75) v 101.6
know[V-p] (19) v 013.6
  ~ about (1) v 013.6
know[V-r] (6) v 101.6
know[V-t] (2) v 101.6
knowed (379) v 101.6
  ~ about (2) v 101.6
  ~ of (16) v 101.6
  ~ to (3) v 101.6
knowing (21) v 057.4
knowledge (4) n/adj 083.5
  ~ trees (1) n 061.8
knowledgeability (1) n 080.8
Knowles (3) 087.2
  ~ community (2) LA 087.2
  ~ post office (1) n 084.2
Knowlton (3) AR 087.3
  ~ Landing (1) AR 087.4
known (60) v 101.6
  ~ to (1) v 013.8
knows (75) v 013.8
  ~ about (1) v 096.9
  ~ (a)bout (1) v 075.7
  ~ of (9) v 013.8
Knox (8) TN 087.5
  ~ County (1) TN 087.7
  ~ Road (1) 107.6
Knoxville (679) TN 087.4
  ~ College (1) 106.4

knuckle (11) n/adj 072.3
~ purple hull (1) n 088.8
~ sandwich (1) n 065.5
knucklebone (1) n 072.3
knucklebones (1) n 046.4
knucklehead (5) n 073.4
knucklehead[N-i] (1) n 055A.2
knuckles (8) n 072.3
knuckling (1) v 081.4
knucks (3) n 081.8
KNUKS (1) 059.4
Kochkase (1) n G 048.2
kohlrabi (5) n 055A.5
Koinonia (1) GA 087.1
Kojack (1) 037.8
kolaches (1) n 092.7
Kolb Gem (2) 056.8
kong(x2) (1) interj 038.3
kook (3) n 073.4
kooks (2) n 124.2
kooky (2) adj 074.7
kook(y) (1) adj 074.7
Kool-Aid (4) 121.8
koop (1) interj 037.8
koop(x2) (1) interj 037.8
kope (25) interj 037.8
~ coop(x2) (1) interj 037.8
~ -coop(x2) (1) interj 037.8
~ gope(x2) (1) interj 037.8
~ hope(x2) (1) interj 037.8
~ -horsey(x2) (1) interj 037.8
~ -John(x3) (1) interj 037.8
~ kwope(x2) (1) interj 037.8
kope(x2) (11) interj 037.8
kope(x3) (17) interj 037.8
kope(x4) (5) interj 037.8
kope(x5) (1) interj 037.8
Kopfkisse (2) n G 028.8
Korea (5) 087.9
Kore(a) (1) 086.6
Korean (10) 126.6
~ War (3) 065.8
Koreans (8) 126.4

Kornspeicher (1) n G 014.3
Kosciusko (11) MS 087.3
kosher (12) adj 025.3
~ Jews (1) n 126.7
~ market (1) n 116.3
~ sandwich (1) n 121.7
~ sausage (2) n 121.6
~ store (2) n 116.3
Kountze (1) TX 087.4
KPs (1) 081.8
Krapfen (1) n G 045.2
kraut (25) n/adj 055A.1
~ cutters (1) n 092.7
~ eaters (1) n 127.1
~ heads (3) n 127.1
Kraut (10) 127.1
Krauts (35) 127.1
Krebs Lake (1) MS 030.7
Kreme (1) 122.4
Krepletz (1) n G 045.2
Krispy Kreme (1) 122.4
Kroger sack (1) n 019.7
Kroger's (3) 048.4
Krum (1) TX 087.1
KTL (1) 109.8
Ku (7) 069.1
~ Klux (2) 069.1
~ Klux Klan (5) 065.8
Kuche (1) n G 007A.5
kudzu (9) n/adj 096.7
~ hay (1) n 014.7
~ vine (1) n 015.9
Kuhstall (1) n G 015.3
kumquat (6) n/adj 055.2
~ tree (1) n 061.8
~ trees (2) n 061.8
kumquats (7) n 055.1
kup (4) interj 037.8
~ kope kup koop(x2) (1) interj 037.8
kup(x2) (1) interj 037.8
kwa(x2) (1) interj 037.5
kwa(x6) (1) interj 038.5
kwaw pig (1) interj 038.3
kwep(x3) (1) interj 037.5
Kwik-Chek (2) 116.2
kwo (6) interj 037.5
~ -it (1) interj 037.5
~ -it(x2) woo(x2) (1) interj 037.5
~ -it(x3) (2) interj 037.6
kwoo (2) interj 038.3

kwoop(x2) kwoo-pig(x2) (1) interj 038.3
kwope (11) interj 037.8
~ -Bess(x2) (1) interj 037.8
~ kope kwope (1) interj 037.8
kwope(x2) (7) interj 037.8
kwope(x3) (4) interj 037.8
kwoy (2) interj 037.5
kwoy(x2) (2) interj 037.5
kwup (4) interj 037.5
~ kup(x2) (1) interj 037.8
~ wup (1) interj 037.8
kwup(x3) (1) interj 037.8
kwurk kwur(x3) (1) interj 037.5
kwur(x3) (1) interj 037.5
kwy(x2) hoo(x5) (1) interj 037.6
Kyle (1) TX 087.1
kyoodle (14) n 033.3
kyood(le) (1) n 033.3
kyoodles (1) n 033.3

L

L (33) 011.6
~ and A depot (1) n 084.7
~ and B building (1) n 084.9
~ and C Tower (2) 108.5
~ -shape (6) n 118.8
~ -shape house (2) n 007A.5
~ -shape porch (1) n 010.8
~ -shape porches (1) n 010.8
~ -shaped (5) adj 118.8
~ -shaped home (1) n 011.6
~ -shaped house (7) n 118.8
~ -shaped porches (1) n 010.8
la (56) n/adj F/S 031.9
~ la (1) n 126.3
~ -las (1) n F 083.1
La (56) 087.3
~ Fayette (1) GA 087.7
~ Follette (4) TN 087.4
~ Grange (25) AR GA TX 087.2
~ Groust (1) 107.6
~ Lomita (1) TX 086.5
~ Minita (1) TX 030.7
~ Nana Creek (1) TX 030.7
~ Nan(a) Creek (1) LA 030.7
~ Paz (1) 115.6
~ Salle (4) LA TX 086.6
~ Speranda (1) TX 030.7
~ Strip (1) 113.4
~ Vernia (1) TX 087.8
~ Villita (5) 106.4
~ -Z-Boy (1) 008.8

~ -Z-Boy chair (1) n 008.9
~ -Z-Boy recliner (1) n 008.9
~ -Z-Boys (1) 008.9
Labadieville (6) LA 087.7
label (2) v 081.1
Label (1) 114.7
labor (15) n 088.9
Labor (1) 030.7
laboratory (2) n 012.1
labored (2) v 057.8
Labrador (2) 033.3
~ retrievers (1) n 081.9
Lac (1) 109.3
Lacamp (1) LA 087.2
Lacassine Bayou (2) LA 030.7
lace (19) n/v/adj 075.6
~ curtains (6) n 009.5
~ panels (1) n 009.5
~ shoes (1) n 123.8
~ up (1) v 123.8
~ -up shoes (3) n 123.8
~ -ups (2) n 123.8
~ wire (1) n 016.3
laced (3) v/adj 123.8
~ shoes (2) n 123.8
~ up (1) v 048.3
lacerate (1) v 036.1
lacing-up shoes (1) n 123.8
lack (2) v 090.6
lacked (2) v 098.8
lackey (1) n 115.4
lackeys (1) n 115.4
lacking (3) v 095.2
lacks (5) v 070.1
Lacombe (5) LA 087.5
lacquered doors (1) n 009.7
LaCrosse (1) AR 087.5
lacuite (4) n/adj F 051.5
~ cakes (1) n 051.2
lacy bread (3) n 044.7
lad (1) n 064.3
ladder (118) n/adj 010.7
~ -and-hook rig (1) n 111.3
~ -back rockers (1) n 008.8
~ company (1) n 111.3
~ jack (1) n 104.5
~ snake (1) n 080.9
~ steps (1) n 010.7

~ things (1) n 111.3
~ truck (24) n 111.3
~ trucks (2) n 111.3
laddered scaffold (1) n 088.7
ladders (14) n 010.7
ladies (39) n 089.1
~ in red (1) n 113.3
~ -in-waiting (1) n 082.4
~ of color (1) n 069.3
~ of evils (1) n 113.3
~ of the evening (6) n 113.3
~ of the night (4) n 113.3
~ of the nights (1) n 113.3
ladies' (11) adj 124.5
~ man (4) n 124.5
~ room (7) n 126.3
ladle (3) n 017.9
lady (490) n/adj 063.2
~ folks (6) n 091.8
~ friend (7) n 081.6
~ horse (1) n 034.2
~ -in-waiting (1) n 082.4
~ -killer (2) n 124.5
~ lock (1) n 045.2
~ love (1) n 081.6
~ managers (1) n 113.5
~ mule (1) n 034.2
~ of ill fame (1) n 113.3
~ of ill repute (1) n 113.3
~ of leisure (1) n 113.3
~ of the evening (14) n 113.3
~ of the house (2) n 063.2
~ of the night (10) n 113.3
~ pea (5) n 055.8
~ peas (7) n 055A.2
~ slipper (1) n 061.4
~ teacher (8) n 067.6
~ teachers (1) n 067.6
~ turtle (1) n 060.6
Lady (6) 064.4
~ Baltimore cake (1) n 122.8
lady[N-i] (1) n 063.2
lady[N-k] (2) adj 028.2

~ purse (1) n 028.2
~ yard (1) n 043.9
Ladybird (1) 064.4
ladybug (4) n 060A.3
ladybugs (3) n 061.2
ladyfinger (6) n/adj 090.9
~ pea (2) n 055A.3
~ peas (2) n 055A.2
ladyfingers (4) n 122.3
ladyfish (4) n 059.9
lady's (5) adj 008.8
~ chair (1) n 008.8
~ house (2) n 082.7
~ name (1) n 053.5
~ uncle (1) n 063.2
Lafayette (86) AL FL LA MS 087.8
~ County (3) AR FL 087.9
~ Highway (1) 107.7
~ Parish (1) LA 087.1
~ Park (1) 106.4
~ Springs (3) MS 087.4
~ Square (4) 105.1
~ Street (2) 031.7
LaFayette County (1) MS 086.6
Lafferty (1) AR 087.1
Lafitte (9) LA 024.8
~ skiff (2) n 024.6
~ skiffs (1) n 024.6
Lafourche (16) LA 087.5
~ Parish (1) LA 087.5
lag (2) v 080.9
~ for (1) v 080.9
lager (2) n/adj 121.9
~ beer (1) n 121.9
lagged (3) v 130.6
lagging (2) v 080.8
lagniappe (129) n/adj 095.7
~ coupons (1) n 095.7
Lagniappe (3) 095.7
lagniappes (1) n 095.7
lagoon (20) n/adj 029.6
~ bayou (1) n 030.3
Lagoon Park (1) 106.9
lagoons (7) n 029.4
LAGS (1) 030.9
Laguna (3) 106.7
~ Beach (1) 106.7
~ Madre (2) TX 030.3
laid (381) v/adj 097.1
~ around (19) v 097.1
~ aside (1) v 057.8

~ back (2) v 097.1
~ -back style (1) n 130.8
~ by (23) v 015.8
~ corpse (1) v 078.5
~ down (45) v 097.1
~ -down bed (1) n 029.2
~ for (1) v 075.6
~ off (1) v 083.4
~ on (7) v 097.1
~ out (39) v 083.4
~ out from school (1) v 083.4
~ out of (1) v 083.4
~ out of school (12) v 083.4
~ up (3) v 097.1
lain (11) v 097.1
~ down (2) v 097.1
~ out (1) v 096.6
~ over (1) v 096.6
lait (14) n F 032.4
lake (118) n/adj 030.6
~ bottom (1) n 029.4
~ bottoms (2) n 092.9
~ fish (1) n 059.9
~ pond (1) n 030.6
~ water (1) n 048.9
Lake (414) TN 087.5
~ Adair (1) FL 106.4
~ Allatoona (1) GA 106.7
~ Ann (1) TN 030.7
~ Arthur (3) LA 087.2
~ Austin (1) TX 030.7
~ Barre (1) LA 030.7
~ Bird (1) FL 030.7
~ Bistineau (2) MS 030.7
~ Blackshear (1) GA 030.7
~ Bolivar (1) MS 030.7
~ Borgne (3) LA 030.7
~ Bruin (1) LA 030.7
~ Butler (1) FL 087.2
~ Catherine (2) AR LA 030.7
~ Charles (50) LA 086.5
~ Chickamauga (2) TN 030.7
~ City (10) FL TN 087.5

~ Claiborne (1) LA 030.7
~ Cliff Park (1) 106.4
~ Cormo(rant) (1) MS 030.7
~ County (5) FL TN 087.1
~ Crook (1) TX 030.7
~ D'Arbonne (2) LA 030.7
~ Dauterive (2) LA 030.7
~ Denham (1) FL 087.7
~ Douglas Road (2) 106.1
~ Elaine (1) TN 030.7
~ Eola Park (1) 106.6
~ Eufaula (1) GA 030.7
~ Eula (1) FL 106.4
~ Eustis (2) FL 030.7
~ Forest (1) 105.1
~ George (1) FL 087.8
~ Griffin (2) FL 030.7
~ Hamilton (2) AR 087.9
~ Hamilton Division (1) AR 080.7
~ Hancock (1) FL 030.7
~ Harris (2) FL 030.7
~ Houston (1) TX 030.7
~ Ivanhoe (1) FL 106.6
~ Jackson (1) FL 106.1
~ Jordan (2) AL 030.7
~ Kissimmee (1) FL 086.4
~ Lamar Bruce (1) MS 030.7
~ Lanier (2) GA 030.7
~ Lavon (1) TX 030.7
~ Lee (1) MS 030.7
~ Lurleen (1) AL 030.7
~ Martin (2) AL 030.7
~ Mary (5) MS 087.6
~ Maurepas (2) LA 030.7
~ Michigan (2) 086.1
~ Misere (1) LA 030.7
~ Monroe (1) FL 087.2
~ Murvaul (1) TX 030.7

~ Natchez (1) MS 030.7
~ Nellie (2) FL 030.7
~ Okeechobee (7) FL 087.6
~ Oliver (2) GA 030.7
~ Ouachita (1) AR 087.6
~ Paradise (1) AR 030.7
~ Park (1) GA 087.8
~ Placida (1) FL 030.7
~ Pontchartrain (20) LA 087.8
~ Pontchartrain Airport (1) 106.5
~ Providence (7) LA 087.5
~ Ray Hubbard (1) TX 030.7
~ Richland (1) TN 030.7
~ Saint John (2) LA MS 030.7
~ Seminole (3) FL 030.7
~ Shepherd Springs (1) AR 030.7
~ Somerville (2) TX 030.7
~ Street (1) 107.6
~ Sumter (1) FL 030.7
~ Tahoe (1) CA 087.8
~ Tawakoni (1) TX 030.7
~ Texoma (1) AR 086.8
~ Tuscaloosa (1) AL 030.7
~ Tyler (1) TX 030.7
~ Tyler East (1) TX 030.7
~ Vernon (1) LA 030.7
~ Verret (3) LA 030.7
~ Village (6) AR 087.4
~ Vista (3) 106.1
~ Wales (3) FL 087.8
~ Washington (2) MS 030.7
~ Whittington (3) AR MS 030.7
~ Worth (2) FL 087.4
~ Yardley (1) FL 030.7
Lakefront (5) 106.2
~ Airport (1) 106.5

Lakeland (23) FL GA 087.2
~ Drive (1) 107.7
~ Hospital (1) 084.5
lakers (1) n 099.5
lakes (33) n 030.3
Lakes (3) 030.7
Lakeshore (3) MS 087.7
~ High (1) 083.3
Lakeside (5) 105.3
~ Acres (2) 105.5
~ Park (1) 085.1
Lakeview (4) LA 087.6
~ Gardens (1) 106.2
~ Park (1) 106.4
Lakewood (9) AR 087.1
~ Boulevard (1) 105.1
~ Heights (1) 106.3
Lakey (1) TX 087.9
lallygag (2) v 088.7
~ around (1) v 088.7
~ off (1) v 075.6
Lamanto (1) 107.8
Lamar (12) AR MS TX 087.6
~ County (5) GA MS 087.3
Lamartine (1) AR 087.3
lamb (235) n/adj 035.1
~ butt roast (1) n 121.4
~ chop (5) n 121.4
~ chops (75) n 121.4
~ fur (2) n 035.2
~ patties (1) n 121.4
~ pot roast (1) n 121.4
~ ribs (1) n 121.4
~ roast (13) n 121.4
~ shank (1) n 121.4
~ shanks (2) n 121.4
~ shoulder (2) n 121.4
~ stew (3) n 121.4
lamb[N-k] (2) adj 061.4
~ -quarter (1) n 061.4
~ wool (1) n 035.2
lamb(x3) (1) interj 038.4
Lambert (1) MS 087.7
Lambeths Bee Creek (1) GA 030.7
lambrequin (1) n F 081.9
lamb's (4) adj 121.4
~ kidneys (1) n 121.4
~ -quarter (2) n 055A.5
~ tail (1) n 070.3
lambs (7) n 035.1
lame (5) adj 124.6

~ -brained (2) adj 073.4
Lamesa (1) TX 087.3
Lamont (1) FL 087.4
Lamourie (4) LA 087.1
lamp (310) n/adj 024.3
~ bug (4) n 060A.1
~ bugs (1) n 060A.1
~ bulb (6) n 019.9
~ bulbs (1) n 019.9
~ candles (1) n 060A.1
~ chimneys (1) n 008.1
~ fly (2) n 060A.1
~ globe (1) n 019.9
~ jug (1) n 024.3
~ oil (44) n 024.2
~ splinters (1) n 008.6
~ tables (1) n 008.9
Lampasas (1) TX 087.3
lamp(er) eel (1) n 060A.4
lampings (1) n 024.3
lamplight (1) n 024.2
lampreys (1) n 080.6
lamps (130) n 024.3
lampwick (1) n 024.3
Lana Turner[N-k] daughter (1) n 042.4
Lancashire (1) 087.3
Lancaster (2) SC 087.8
lance (3) v/adj 066.8
lanced (2) v 066.9
lancelate (1) v 036.1
lancia (1) n S 020.8
lancias (1) n S 020.9
Lancing (1) TN 087.5
land (1982) n/adj/interj 108.7
~ frog (1) n 060.4
~ frogs (1) n 060.4
~ gopher (1) n 060.7
~ grants (1) n 084.8
~ levelers (1) n 092.9
~ line (1) n 025.5
~ lottery (1) n 084.8
~ off (1) n 021.2
~ -poor (2) adj 053.1
~ port (1) n 080.8
~ sake (8) interj 092.2
~ sakes (18) interj 092.2
~ terrapin (2) n 060.7
~ tortoise (2) n 060.7
~ turtle (29) n 060.7
~ turtles (13) n 060.7
Land (6) 087.8

land[N-k] sakes (2) interj 092.2
land[V-r] (1) v 095.8
landed (4) v/adj 053.7
~ at (1) v 053.7
~ -gentry place (1) n 080.6
lander (1) n 060.7
landfill (2) n 108.7
landholdings (1) n 090.7
landing (148) n/adj 031.4
~ area (1) n 007A.7
~ field (1) n 106.5
~ net (1) n 093.5
~ place (2) n 031.4
~ port (1) n 031.4
land(ing) (2) n 031.4
Landing (23) 031.4
landings (3) n 031.4
landlady (3) n 065.2
landlord (27) n 119.5
landlords (1) n 119.5
landmarks (2) n 106.5
Landrace (1) 035.8
Landracers (1) 035.6
Landry (3) 087.2
land's (2) adj 092.2
~ sake (1) interj 092.2
~ sakes (1) interj 092.2
Land's End (1) VA 087.3
lands (16) n 029.8
landscaped (1) v 041.4
landside (3) n/adj 021.6
~ plow (1) n 021.6
~ plows (1) n 021.6
landslide down (1) v 098.6
lane (507) n/adj 031.7
~ barriers (1) n 107.3
~ cake (1) n 122.8
~ divider (1) n 107.3
~ dividers (2) n 107.3
~ marker (1) n 107.3
~ markers (4) n 107.3
~ road (4) n 031.8
Lane (17) 031.8
~ Meadow (1) 106.2
~ Park (1) 106.4
~ Parkway (1) 107.6
lane[N-i] (3) n 031.7
Laneburg (1) AR 070.9
lanes (39) n 031.8
Lanett (7) AL 087.5
laneway (1) n 031.8
Langdale (2) AL 087.7

Langley community (1) AR 087.4
language (14) n 065.8
L'Anguille River (1) AR 030.7
langusta (1) n 060.8
Langwood Addition (1) 105.4
Lanier (8) 107.8
~ Boulevard (1) 107.8
~ County (4) GA 087.3
~ side (1) n 105.2
laning (2) n/v 058.1
lanky (34) adj 073.3
Lansing (1) MI 087.3
lantana (1) n 062.1
lantern (62) n 024.3
lanterns (25) n 024.3
lap (24) n/adj 011.2
~ baby (1) n 080.6
~ children (1) n 064.3
~ fence (3) n 016.2
~ jack (1) n 021.8
~ joints (1) n 011.2
~ robes (2) n 080.7
~ roll (1) n 080.9
~ secretary (1) n 068.8
~ sheeting (1) n 090.8
~ -side planking (1) n 011.2
~ siding (5) n 011.2
~ wood (1) n 011.2
lap[N-i] (1) n 100.5
lapboard (2) n 011.2
lapboarded (2) v 011.2
lapboards (5) n 011.2
lapdogs (6) n 033.3
lapid (2) adj 002.7
Lapile Creek (1) LA 030.7
Lapine (1) AL 087.7
Laplace (4) LA 087.7
LaPorte (1) TX 087.8
lapped (6) v/adj 011.2
~ over (1) v 011.2
~ -over walls (1) n 011.2
~ siding (1) n 011.2
lappers (1) n 039.7
lapping (5) n/adj 011.2
~ boards (1) n 011.2
~ sides (1) n 011.2
laps (1) v 011.2
lapstrake (3) n/adj 011.2

~ aluminum siding (1) n 011.2
lard (320) n/v/adj 047.8
~ barrel (3) n 019.2
~ barrels (2) n 019.2
~ bucket (21) n 019.2
~ buck(et) (1) n 019.2
~ buckets (13) n 019.2
~ can (55) n 019.2
~ can[N-i] (1) n 019.2
~ cans (34) n 019.2
~ container (1) n 019.2
~ fat (1) n 046.3
~ grease (1) n 023.7
~ hog (1) n 035.5
~ oil (1) n 024.3
~ paddle (1) n 092.7
~ press (1) n 080.8
~ renderings (1) n 081.8
~ squeezer (1) n 081.8
~ stand (29) n 019.2
~ stand[N-i] (1) n 019.2
~ stands (10) n 019.2
~ tin (1) n 019.2
~ tub (3) n 019.2
~ tubs (3) n 019.2
~ up (1) v 049.2
Lard Bucket (1) 019.2
larder (5) n 010.1
larders (1) n 010.1
lards (1) n 019.2
Laredo (12) TX 087.3
large (211) adj 065.1
~ curd (1) n 047.6
~ day (1) n 005.4
~ -leaf magnolia (1) n 062.9
~ rain (1) n 006.1
~ -size (1) adj 051.5
~ -sized (1) adj 073.1
largemouth (9) n/adj 059.9
~ bass (7) n 059.9
larger (22) adj 075.8
~ -size (1) adj 018.6
largest (6) adj 064.7
Largo (2) 087.1
lariat (6) n/adj 080.8
~ rope (4) n 080.8
lark (1) n 012.6
Larkin (2) AR 087.4
larks (4) n 059.2
Larose (1) LA 087.2

larruping (5) n/adj 065.5
~ pole (1) n 065.5
Larry (2) GA 087.9
laryngitis (45) n 076.4
larynx (19) n/adj 071.7
~ goozle (1) n 071.7
las (3) n/adj F/S 012.1
Las (7) 030.7
~ Vegas (6) NV 087.5
lash (5) n/v 019.4
lashes (1) n 029.6
lashing (14) n 065.5
lasso (3) n 130.6
last (613) v/adj 005.1
~ chance (1) n 080.8
~ class (1) n 069.8
~ cooking (1) n 075.6
~ hammer (1) n 020.7
~ rites (6) n 079.2
Last Chance (1) 099.2
last[V-p] (2) v 094.6
lasted (3) v 053.4
lastes (13) v 065.9
lasting fence (1) n 075.8
latch (5) n/adj 030.9
~ pin (2) n 026.5
latched onto (2) v 100.1
latching (1) n 065.5
late (63) adj/adv 070.1
~ cold spell (1) n 007.5
~ corn (2) n 056.2
~ crop (1) n 041.5
~ freeze (3) n 007.5
~ frost (2) n 007.5
~ -hour-type (1) adj
116.2
~ -model (1) adj 123.6
~ -model deal (1) n
081.9
~ potatoes (1) n 055.5
~ roasting ears (1) n
056.2
Late (3) 055A.3
~ Flat Dutch (1)
055A.3
~ Unpleasantness (2)
085.8
lately (11) adv 025.4
later (136) adj 076.2
~ peas (1) n 055A.1
lateral (3) adj 030.2
~ ditches (1) n 030.2
~ road (2) n 107.4
laterals (2) n 030.1
latest (2) adj 080.5

lath (3) n 016.2
lath[N-i] (1) n 016.7
Latham (2) AL 087.5
lathe (4) n 023.4
latheman (1) n 080.6
lather (1) v 053.5
lathing (1) n 011.5
lathings (1) n 081.8
laths (1) n 016.2
Latin (12) 128.7
~ -American (5) 128.7
~ -Americans (3) 069.4
~ area (1) n 105.4
~ dances (1) n 083.1
~ kinds (1) n 128.7
~ -style (1) adj 010.8
Latinos (1) 128.5
Latins (5) 128.5
latitude (1) n 080.7
latrine (17) n 126.3
latrines (3) n 126.3
latter (3) adj 075.9
lattermath (2) n 041.5
lattice (8) n/adj 007A.1
~ fence (5) n 016.2
~ fences (1) n 016.2
latticed (2) v/adj 007A.5
~ in (1) v 007A.5
latticework (2) n 088.7
~ -type (1) adj 065.8
laudanum (6) n 080.6
Lauderdale (31) AL FL
MS TN 087.4
~ -by-the-Sea (1) 105.1
~ County (6) AL MS
TN 087.2
~ Lakes (1) 105.1
Lauder(dale) (4) TN
087.5
~ County (2) TN 087.2
l'auge (1) n F 035.8
laugh (8) n/v 036.4
laugh[V-r] (1) v 070.2
laughed (4) v 057.5
~ at (1) v 053.8
laughing (256) v/adj
057.4
~ at (1) v 099.6
~ noise (1) n 036.4
~ owl (2) n 059.2
~ water (1) n 050.8
laughs (3) n/v 036.4
~ at (1) v 131.2
launch (587) n/v/adj
024.5

~ boat (1) n 024.6
~ out (1) v 024.5
launched (18) v 024.5
launches (8) n/v 024.5
launching (69) n/v/adj
024.5
~ ceremony (1) n 024.5
~ docks (1) n 031.4
~ pad (3) n 031.4
~ pads (1) n 024.5
~ ramps (1) n 024.5
launder (2) v 010.6
laundered (7) v 065.8
launderette (21) n 010.6
launderettes (1) n 116.5
laundering (3) v 010.6
laundress (1) n 010.6
laundries (13) n 010.6
Laundromat (125) 010.6
Laundromats (5) 116.5
laundry (763) n/v/adj
010.6
~ bag (24) n 019.5
~ basket (71) n 020.1
~ baskets (4) n 020.1
~ box (1) n 116.6
~ day (5) n 010.6
~ days (1) n 010.6
~ hamper (6) n 116.6
~ places (1) n 010.6
~ powder (1) n 010.6
~ room (28) n 007A.2
~ shop (1) n 010.6
~ time (1) n 010.6
~ truck (1) n 010.6
~ tub (3) n 017.6
~ -type stove (1) n
008.5
~ -washing business (1)
n 010.6
~ work (6) n 010.6
laun(dry) (1) n 010.6
laundrywoman (1) n
010.6
laurel (321) n/adj 062.7
~ ivy (1) n 062.7
~ leaves (1) n 061.4
~ thicket (1) n 062.7
~ tree (6) n 062.7
~ trees (2) n 062.7
lau(rel) (1) n 062.7
Laurel (40) MS 107.7
~ Bloomery (8) TN
087.3
~ Branch (3) TN 030.7

~ Creek (2) 030.7
~ Grove Cemetery (1)
078.8
~ Hill (5) FL 087.2
Laur(el) (1) MS 087.4
laurels (13) n 062.7
Laurens (3) GA 087.3
~ County (1) GA 087.7
laurier (1) n F 062.8
Lavaca (4) AR 087.9
lavage (2) n F 010.6
lavaliere (15) n 028.4
lavalieres (2) n 028.4
lavatories (7) n 126.4
lavatory (50) n 118.3
lavato(ry) (2) n 118.3
lavender bush (1) n 062.2
lavette (1) n F 018.3
Lavilla (1) 105.4
Lavon (1) 030.8
law (1146) n/adj/interj
092.2
~ -abiding (2) adj
085.7
~ book (1) n 085.7
~ books (1) n 085.7
~ building (1) n 085.7
~ degree (1) n 085.7
~ enforcement (11) n
085.7
~ -enforcement officer
(1) n 112.5
~ offices (1) n 085.7
~ orders (1) n 085.7
~ school (8) n 085.7
~ student (1) n 068.7
Law (21) 088.9
law[N-k] (1) adj 043.9
lawful fence (1) n 016.4
lawless (1) adj 082.8
lawlessness (1) n 085.7
lawman (2) n 112.5
lawn (348) n/adj 085.1
~ darts (1) n 130.6
~ fences (1) n 016.2
~ markers (1) n 110.8
~ mower (208) n 120.1
~ mow(er) (18) n
120.2
~ -mowering (1) v
025.8
~ mowers (14) n 120.1
~ party (1) n 130.7
~ rake (10) n 120.7
~ rakes (2) n 120.7

~ tractor (1) n 120.3
~ -wire fence (1) n 016.3
Lawn (7) 120.2
~ Boy (1) 120.2
lawns (2) n 031.9
Lawrence (15) AL TN 087.3
~ County (5) AL MS TN 087.7
~ County seat (1) n 085.5
~ Drive (1) 107.6
~ Street (1) 082.7
~ Welk (4) 130.8
Lawrenceburg (2) TN 087.6
Lawrenceville (6) AL GA 086.3
law's (2) adj 082.7
laws (49) n 085.7
Lawson (6) AR 107.8
~ chair (1) n 008.9
~ Street (1) 107.7
lawsuit (2) n 085.7
lawsuits (1) n 027.7
lawsy (1) interj 092.2
Lawther Lane (1) 105.3
Lawton Bayou (1) MS 030.7
lawyer (160) n 067.8
lawyer's wife (1) n 004.4
lawyers (44) n 067.7
Lax (2) GA 087.6
lay (949) n/v/adj 096.6
~ across (2) v 096.6
~ around (17) v 096.6
~ back (6) v 096.6
~ by (10) v 015.8
~ -by season (1) n 090.8
~ -by time (3) n 081.9
~ down (423) v 097.1
~ in (2) v 096.6
~ minister (3) n 067.8
~ off (3) v 041.3
~ -off plow (5) n 021.6
~ -off plows (1) n 021.6
~ on (23) v 096.6
~ out (19) v 083.4
~ out of school (2) v 083.4
~ preacher (27) n 067.8
~ reader (1) n 067.8

~ speaker (1) n 067.8
~ to (1) v 095.8
~ up (5) v 097.1
~ up on (1) v 081.8
Lay (1) 087.7
lay[V-p] down (1) v 096.6
Laybefoyer (1) TN 030.7
laydown (1) n 097.1
layer (25) n/adj 036.7
~ cake (2) n 048.3
~ cakes (1) n 044.4
~ cuts (1) n 119.6
~ pies (1) n 048.3
layer[N-i] (1) n 016.9
layered (2) adj 123.9
~ doughnuts (1) n 122.7
layers (4) n 036.7
laying (321) v/adj 007.3
~ around (9) v 096.6
~ by (7) v 015.8
~ -by time (4) n 080.9
~ down (19) v 096.6
~ egg (2) n 017.1
~ for (1) v 088.7
~ hen (54) n 036.7
~ hens (10) n 036.7
~ house (3) n 036.8
~ houses (1) n 036.8
~ mash (5) n 017.1
~ off (6) v 021.6
~ -off plow (5) n 021.6
~ -off stock (1) n 021.9
~ on (8) v 096.6
~ out (11) v 083.4
~ out of (1) v 083.4
~ out of school (3) v 083.4
~ to rest (1) v 079.2
~ up on (1) v 095.9
~ with (1) v 124.8
layman (22) n 067.8
laymans (1) n 067.8
laymens (2) n 067.8
layover (2) n 040.1
lays (23) v 096.6
~ about (1) v 097.1
~ around (4) v 096.6
~ down (3) v 096.6
~ in (1) v 096.6
~ out (1) v 083.4
~ out of school (1) v 083.4

Lazaretto Creek (1) GA 030.7
lazed around (1) v 097.1
Lazer Creek (2) GA 030.7
lazing around (1) v 088.8
lazy (137) adj 069.7
~ boy (1) n 017.7
~ chairs (1) n 008.8
~ -man's chair (1) n 008.8
~ -man's manger (1) n 014.7
~ pie (1) n 048.3
~ Susans (1) n 080.6
Lazy Ike (1) 060.5
lazybones (1) n 069.7
LBJ Freeway (1) 093.7
le (21) adj F 051.3
Le (4) 030.3
~ Bayou (1) LA 030.3
~ Conte pear (1) n 070.6
~ Jeune Road (1) 105.4
~ Moyne Garden (1) 106.3
lea (1) n 029.5
Leachville (1) TN 087.9
lead (374) n/v/adj 039.4
~ bullet (1) n 022.4
~ car (1) n 111.6
~ coffin (1) n 079.1
~ cow (5) n 033.6
~ horse (241) n 039.4
~ horses (7) n 039.4
~ -in road (1) n 031.7
~ line (1) n 039.4
~ lines (1) n 039.1
~ mule (13) n 039.4
~ mules (5) n 039.4
~ ox (2) n 039.4
~ oxen (1) n 039.4
~ pencil (1) n 026.5
~ side (2) n 039.4
~ steers (2) n 039.4
~ swing (1) n 090.9
~ team (18) n 039.4
~ troughs (1) n 011.5
lead[V-p] (4) v 013.6
~ off (1) v 013.6
~ to (3) v 053.2
leader (37) n 039.4
leader[N-i] (1) n 039.4
leaders (6) n 072.3
leadership (1) n 073.1

leading (8) v/adj 039.4
~ maid (1) n 082.4
~ road (1) n 031.7
~ to (2) v 031.8
leads (2) v 053.2
~ to (1) v 031.8
leaf (105) n/adj 056.1
~ broom (1) n 010.5
~ cart (1) n 023.3
~ catchers (1) n 011.5
~ fat (2) n 046.3
~ -head stub (1) n 057.3
~ lard (2) n 046.4
~ lettuce (11) n 055A.6
~ mold (1) n 029.6
~ mover (1) n 006.1
~ rake (38) n 120.7
~ rakes (5) n 120.7
~ ticks (1) n 060A.8
Leaf (9) MS 030.7
~ River (7) MS 030.7
leafy vegetable (1) n 050.4
league (3) n 065.8
League (7) 069.2
~ of Voters (1) 091.6
leak (15) n/v 042.5
leak[V-p] (1) v 024.8
Leake County (2) MS 087.5
Leakesville (1) MS 087.2
leaking (4) v 057.4
lean (276) n/v/adj 046.4
~ -back chairs (1) n 008.8
~ fatback (1) n 046.3
~ -in shed (1) n 011.7
~ meat (16) n 046.7
~ pompano (1) n 059.9
~ salt pork (1) n 046.3
~ streak (1) n 046.3
~ streaked meat (1) n 046.3
~ -to (45) n 015.1
~ -to baths (1) n 012.1
~ -to ell (1) n 011.7
~ -to kitchen (1) n 009.9
~ -to outfit (1) n 080.8
~ -to porch (1) n 010.8
~ -to porches (1) n 010.8
~ -to shed (2) n 011.7
~ -tos (4) n 015.1

Lean (1) 092.9
leaner (1) n 034.8
leaning (1) v 057.4
leap year (1) n 004.7
leaped (2) v 095.3
 ~ off (1) v 095.3
leaper (2) n 060.3
leapfrog (12) n 060.3
leapfrogs (6) n 060.3
leaping frog (1) n 060.2
leaps (2) n 065.6
learn (111) v 101.1
 ~ to (6) v 101.1
learn[V-r] (21) v 101.1
 ~ to (1) v 100.5
learn[V-t] (3) v 101.1
learned (100) v 101.1
 ~ to (2) v 101.1
Learned (1) MS 087.4
learner (1) n 074.6
learning (70) n/v/adj
 083.5
 ~ age (1) n 096.9
learn(ing) (1) n 083.5
learns (2) v 042.5
learnt (127) v 101.1
 ~ to (4) v 070.6
leary (1) adj 074.3
Leary (1) GA 075.7
lease (3) n/v 075.6
leaseded (1) v 075.6
leash (3) n 039.2
least (10) adj 091.6
leather (194) n/adj 022.3
 ~ apron (1) n 026.4
 ~ bank (1) n 028.2
 ~ belt (6) n 022.3
 ~ belts (1) n 051.4
 ~ breeches (3) n
 055A.4
 ~ hide (1) n 022.3
 ~ hone (1) n 022.3
 ~ jacket (1) n 027.1
 ~ lines (1) n 039.1
 ~ pocketbook (2) n
 028.2
 ~ pouch (1) n 028.2
 ~ pouches (1) n 028.2
 ~ razor strap (1) n
 022.3
 ~ reins (2) n 039.2
 ~ shoe (1) n 123.8
 ~ shoes (4) n 123.8
 ~ strap (59) n 022.3
 ~ straps (1) n 022.3

 ~ strips (1) n 022.3
 ~ strop (21) n 022.3
 ~ -vane bat (1) n 089.8
 ~ -winged bat (1) n
 059.4
leatherback (1) n 060.6
leatherleaf (1) n 091.8
leathers (1) n 123.8
Leatherwood (1) TN
 030.7
leathery-type state (1) n
 002.6
leave (105) v/adj 041.2
 ~ (a)bout (1) v 026.7
 ~ out (4) v 083.2
 ~ overs (1) n 050.1
 ~ to (1) v 078.6
leave[V-p] (1) v 013.8
leave[V-s] (1) v 010.4
leaven (5) n/adj 045.5
 ~ bread (3) n 044.3
leavened (6) adj 045.5
 ~ bread (5) n 044.3
leavening (3) n/adj 045.5
 ~ agent (1) n 045.5
Leavenworth (1) KS
 086.8
leaves (45) n/v 062.2
 ~ for (1) v 040.9
 ~ out (1) v 083.2
leaving (14) v 101.2
 ~ out (2) v 075.6
leavings (1) n 050.1
Leawood Heights (1)
 105.1
Lebanese (1) 126.9
Lebanon (10) AL TN
 087.2
 ~ Pike (1) 107.6
leche (1) n F 060.5
lechuza (1) n S 059.1
lechuzas (1) n S 059.1
Lecompte (1) LA 087.1
lecture (2) n 089.4
led him on (1) v 082.1
ledge (52) n 031.2
lee (1) n 035.1
Lee (202) AL FL GA MS
 068.3
 ~ Circle (2) 119.8
 ~ County (14) AL AR
 GA MS TX 086.3
 ~ Creek (2) TN TX
 030.7
 ~ Park (1) 106.4

 ~ -Phillips Drainage
 District (1) 030.1
 ~ Post Office (1) AR
 087.2
 ~ side (1) n 105.2
 ~ Street (1) 107.9
leech (12) n/adj 073.5
 ~ onions (1) n 055.7
 ~ worms (1) n 060.5
leeches (3) n 060.5
Leeds (2) AL 086.3
leek (2) n/adj 055.7
 ~ soup (1) n 055.7
leeks (6) n 055.6
Leeland (2) 107.6
leery (6) adj 074.2
Lee's (1) 068.3
Lees (4) 087.8
 ~ Creek (2) AR LA
 030.7
 ~ Creek Church (1) LA
 087.8
 ~ Crossing (1) GA
 087.6
Leesburg (14) FL GA LA
 TN 087.1
 ~ Creek (1) TN 030.7
Leesville (17) LA TX
 086.6
 ~ Highway (1) 087.4
Leetown (2) MS 087.1
Leflore County (1) MS
 087.5
left (1192) n/v/adj 071.5
 ~ at the church (1) v
 082.1
 ~ behind (1) v 010.5
 ~ from (1) v 075.6
 ~ -hand (2) adj 021.6
 ~ -hand horse (3) n
 039.4
 ~ -hand Johnston wing
 (1) n 021.6
 ~ -hand plow (2) n
 021.9
 ~ -hand plows (1) n
 021.6
 ~ -hand side (7) n
 072.5
 ~ -hand thread (1) n
 075.6
 ~ -hand turning plow
 (2) n 021.6
 ~ -handed (11) adj
 072.5

 ~ -hander (1) n 074.7
 ~ here (1) v 078.6
 ~ him (10) v 082.1
 ~ him flat (1) v 082.1
 ~ him out (1) v 082.1
 ~ horse (4) n 039.4
 ~ lead (1) n 039.4
 ~ -legged (1) adj 073.3
 ~ off (3) v 090.4
 ~ out (6) v 075.6
 ~ out from (1) v 053.4
 ~ over (95) v/adj 050.1
 ~ the scene (1) v 078.6
 ~ to (2) v 042.7
 ~ town (1) v 078.6
 ~ us (10) v 078.5
 ~ wheel (1) n 039.4
 ~ -wing radicals (1) n
 129.3
leftover (64) n/adj 050.1
 ~ chicken (1) n 050.1
 ~ food (8) n 050.1
 ~ foods (2) n 050.1
 ~ rice (1) n 050.1
 ~ roast (1) n 050.1
 ~ soup (1) n 050.1
leftover[N-i] (11) n 050.1
leftovers (428) n 050.1
(left)overs (1) n 050.1
lefty (1) n 072.6
leg (1153) n/adj 072.6
 ~ bone (8) n 072.7
 ~ broke (4) adj 065.1
 ~ condition (1) n 072.6
 ~ of a lamb (1) n
 121.4
 ~ of lamb (43) n 121.4
 ~ of mutton (3) n
 121.4
 ~ of the lamb (1) n
 121.4
 ~ skillet (2) n 017.5
Leg (1) 067.8
leg[N-i] (7) n 072.5
legal (20) adj 070.6
 ~ father (1) n 066.4
 ~ fence (1) n 016.3
 ~ guardian (7) n 066.4
 ~ guard(ian) (1) n
 066.4
 ~ heirs (1) n 066.4
 ~ mother (1) n 066.4
 ~ secretary (1) n 068.8
 ~ stenographer (1) n
 068.8

~ tender (1) n 114.5
~ tutors (1) n 066.4
legalized whiskey (1) n 050.9
legals (1) n 088.8
legged (22) adj 080.8
Legged (2) 036.7
leggies (1) n 055A.4
Legging (1) 036.7
leggings (2) n 027.3
leggy (1) adj 073.3
Leghorn (4) 036.6
Leghorns (3) 080.6
Legion (9) 069.2
~ Field (1) 106.4
Legionnaire (1) 069.2
legislature (1) n 070.6
legitimate (1) adj 065.7
legs (379) n 072.6
legume (4) adj 041.3
~ crop (3) n 041.3
~ crops (1) n 088.7
legumes (2) n 055A.4
Leighton (1) AL 087.4
Leila Street (1) 107.7
leisure (7) n/adj 087.7
~ suit (2) n 027.7
~ suits (2) n 027.7
~ time (1) n 075.6
leisurely (1) adj 065.8
Lejeune Cove (2) LA 087.7
Leland (6) MS 087.8
Lem Turner Road (1) 107.7
lemon (57) n/adj 055.1
~ cakes (1) n 122.8
~ doughnut (1) n 122.4
~ -filled (2) adj 122.6
~ filling (1) n 122.5
~ peach (2) n 054.3
~ pies (1) n 048.3
~ puff (4) n 122.6
~ puffs (1) n 122.5
~ sauce (4) n 048.5
~ tea (1) n 081.8
~ tomatoes (1) n 055.3
~ tree (1) n 061.8
~ trees (3) n 061.9
~ watermelon (1) n 056.9
Lemon (4) 107.7
~ City (2) 105.1
~ Street (1) 107.6
lemonade (2) n 075.8

lemonfish (4) n 089.8
lemons (13) n 055.1
Len Evans Creek (1) GA 030.7
lena (2) n S 008.6
Lena Street (1) 107.7
lend (5) v 114.5
lend[V-t] (1) v 098.7
lending (1) n 070.8
length (25) n/adj 065.8
lengths (10) n/adj 065.8
~ fence (1) n 126.1
lengthways (3) adv 065.9
lenient (2) adj 070.6
Lenny Harris Bluff (1) TN 087.4
leno (2) n S 008.5
Lenoir (4) NC 087.3
~ City (2) TN 087.2
lenos (1) n S 008.5
Lenox (2) 106.1
~ Park (1) 106.1
~ Square (1) 106.4
lens (2) n 066.8
lent (2) v 098.6
Leoma (2) TN 087.1
Leon (16) FL 087.2
~ County (1) FL 087.3
~ Creek (1) TX 030.7
Leonard man (1) n 081.8
leopard (6) n/adj 060.3
~ frog (4) n 060.3
~ frogs (1) n 060.3
Leopard (1) 115.6
leopards (2) n/adj 033.3
~ dogs (1) n 033.3
leopardy-looking (1) adj 033.3
leprosy (1) n 079.7
Leroy (2) AL 087.1
les (5) adj F 009.7
Les (1) 124.4
Lesbian (81) 074.7
Lesbians (5) 124.4
Lesbo (1) 124.4
Lesbos (1) 124.4
Leslie (11) AR GA 087.1
~ Highway (1) 031.7
lespedeza (16) n/adj 014.6
~ hay (2) n 014.7
~ seed (1) n 014.8
(les)pedeza (1) n 015.9
less (44) adj 094.5
lessen (22) conj 088.4

lessening (5) v 007.3
lesser (2) adj 063.2
~ half (1) n 063.2
~ wind (1) n 007.3
Lessley (2) MS 087.1
lesson (10) n 083.5
lessons (7) n 074.4
lest (1) conj 088.4
let (330) v 052.6
~ down (2) v 076.6
~ her rip (1) v 080.3
~ him alone (1) v 033.2
~ him down (5) v 082.1
~ him go (2) v 082.1
~ him out (1) v 082.1
~ it come back (1) v 080.2
~ me down (1) v 082.1
~ off (1) v 085.4
~ on (3) v 100.1
~ on like (3) v 100.1
~ out (52) v 083.2
~ the bluebird out (1) n 130.3
~ up (4) v 007.3
let[V-p] out (2) v 083.2
Letang blackberry (1) n 062.4
let's (168) v 049.2
~ eat (1) v 038.5
~ go (20) v 038.1
lets (120) v 083.3
~ in (1) v 083.3
~ out (113) v 083.2
~ up (2) v 007.3
letter (180) n/adj 100.6
~ carrier (3) n 115.1
letter[N-i] (1) n 089.2
lettering (1) n 102.7
letters (11) n 089.2
letting (56) v 007.3
~ down (2) v 007.3
~ off (2) v 007.3
~ on (1) v 100.1
~ out (2) v 083.2
~ up (45) v 007.3
lettuce (869) n/adj 055A.6
~ head (2) n 055A.6
~ heads (6) n 055A.6
~ patch (1) n 016.1
~ salad (1) n 055A.6
lettuce[N-i] (2) n 055A.6
lettuces (4) n 055A.6

leukemi(a) (1) n 079.7
levee (60) n/adj 029.4
~ plow (1) n 021.6
~ work (1) n 102.8
Levee (4) 031.4
leveed (3) v 029.7
~ in (1) v 029.7
levees (14) n 030.2
level (55) adj 029.6
~ fields (1) n 029.5
~ ground (2) n 029.8
~ -headed (2) adj 073.2
~ land (1) n 029.4
~ -land plow (3) n 021.6
Level (5) 105.1
leveler (1) n 021.2
levelers (1) n 092.9
leveling (2) n 045.5
levels (2) n 108.4
lever (12) n/adj 070.9
~ carts (1) n 085.3
leverage (1) n 115.3
levers (1) n 073.8
Levi[N-k] (1) 027.4
levies (2) n 038.4
Levi's (11) 027.4
Levy (3) FL 087.1
lewd house (1) n 113.4
lewdity houses (1) n 114.9
Lewis Creek (1) AL 030.7
Lewisville (2) AR LA 087.7
Lexington (24) AL KY TN TX WV 086.5
Lexing(ton) (1) TN 087.3
Leyte (1) 070.6
Lez (4) 124.4
Lezzie (5) 124.4
l'herbe a la puce (3) n F 062.3
liable (44) adj 041.1
liar (17) n 101.3
~ -type games (1) n 099.7
liars (1) n 101.3
libber (1) n 124.3
liberal (6) n/adj 129.1
liberals (2) n 129.1
liberated (2) adj 124.8
~ woman (1) n 063.2
libertine (1) n 124.7
Liberty (46) AL GA LA MS TN TX 087.2

~ Baptist Church (2) 089.1
~ Church (2) AL 087.2
~ City (9) FL 106.3
~ City jitney (1) n 109.9
~ County (7) FL GA 087.3
~ Hill (1) MS 087.7
~ Park (1) 105.3
~ Street (1) 107.6
~ Theater (1) 084.4
librarian (5) n 084.1
librarianship (1) n 084.1
libraries (10) n 084.1
library (921) n/adj 084.1
~ board (3) n 084.1
~ books (1) n 084.1
~ building (1) n 084.1
~ club (1) n 084.1
~ resources (1) n 084.1
~ room (1) n 007A.4
~ science (2) n 084.1
~ -service program (1) n 084.1
~ table (7) n 080.9
~ -type study (1) n 084.1
librar(y) (39) n 084.1
libra(ry) (1) n 084.1
Library (1) 080.6
Librar(y) of Congress (1) 084.1
libras (1) n 114.2
lice (20) n/adj 060A.9
license (16) n 066.8
licensing (1) v 065.9
licensor (1) n 067.8
lices (3) n 060A.6
licey (1) adj 088.7
lichen (2) n 061.3
lichens (1) n 057.1
Lichtenstein (1) TX 087.7
lick (36) n/v/adj 065.5
~ -and-stick class (1) n 088.8
~ log (2) n 008.5
Lick (4) 089.1
~ Creek (2) TN TX 030.7
licked (1) v 017.5
licker (5) n 125.6
lickers (2) n 080.8
lickety-split (3) adv 081.9
licking (69) n/v 065.5

licks (4) n 065.5
Lickskillet (1) TN 087.2
licorice (1) n 070.6
lid (50) n 017.4
lids (6) n 114.1
lie (500) n/v 096.6
~ around (1) v 096.6
~ back (1) v 096.6
~ down (419) v 096.6
~ down on (1) v 096.6
~ on (8) v 096.6
~ out (2) v 075.7
lie[V-p] down (1) v 097.1
lie[V-r] (9) v 097.1
~ around (1) v 097.1
~ down (7) v 097.1
lie[V-s] (1) v 097.1
lied (29) v 097.1
~ around (4) v 097.1
~ down (7) v 097.1
~ on (2) v 101.3
Liederhosen (1) n G 123.3
liefer (1) adv 090.5
lies (6) n/v 101.3
~ between (1) v 104.7
~ down (1) v 096.6
lieu (1) n 088.5
lieutenant (18) n/adj 068.4
~ colonel (6) n 068.4
~ general (1) n 068.3
lieutenants (2) n 068.4
life (135) n/adj 114.5
~ belt (1) n 110.3
~ everlasting (9) n 057.3
~ -everlasting tea (1) n 061.4
~ ring (1) n 123.1
~ science (1) n 053.6
~ -support vehicle (1) n 111.5
Life (11) 108.5
~ and Casualty building (1) n 108.5
~ and Casualty Tower (1) 108.5
~ of Georgia building (1) n 108.5
life[N-i] (4) n 013.8
lifeboat (1) n 024.6
lifeboats (1) n 024.6
life's partner (1) n 063.2

Lifesaver game (1) n 130.9
Lifesavers (1) 054.7
lifetime[N-i] (1) n 043.4
lift (159) n/v/adj 104.5
~ backs (1) n 109.3
lifted (19) v 100.2
lifter (7) n 073.1
lifters (4) n 093.6
lifting (6) v/adj 104.5
~ rags (1) n 018.3
~ up (1) v 104.5
lifts (3) n/v 123.8
light (1904) n/v/adj 019.9
~ beer (4) n 121.9
~ bills (1) n 019.9
~ Brahma (1) n 099.8
~ bread (812) n 045.1
~ -bread rolls (1) n 044.4
~ bug (35) n 060A.3
~ bugs (26) n 060A.1
~ bulb (463) n 019.9
~ bulbs (35) n 019.9
~ -burr wool (1) n 035.2
~ -colored (2) adj 069.5
~ -colored Negro (1) n 069.5
~ -complected (2) adj 080.7
~ crop (1) n 050.4
~ dabber (1) n 060A.1
~ day (1) n 005.4
~ drizzle (6) n 006.6
~ fixture (2) n 019.9
~ fixtures (1) n 019.9
~ fly (2) n 060A.1
~ freeze (22) n 007.5
~ freezes (2) n 007.5
~ frost (60) n 007.5
~ frostes (1) n 007.5
~ globe (6) n 019.9
~ globes (2) n 019.9
~ greens (1) n 055A.5
~ insects (1) n 060A.1
~ land (5) n 029.8
~ loaf bread (1) n 044.3
~ material (1) n 008.6
~ millers (1) n 060A.1
~ mist (2) n 006.6
~ nigger (1) n 069.5
~ out (6) v 080.6

~ plants (1) n 080.7
~ pole (3) n 019.9
~ post (2) n 016.5
~ post[N-i] (1) n 019.9
~ rain (48) n 006.6
~ roll[N-i] (1) n 044.4
~ rolls (7) n 044.4
~ sacks (1) n 019.6
~ salt bread (1) n 044.3
~ sandy land (2) n 029.8
~ sandy loam (1) n 029.8
~ shower (31) n 006.6
~ show(er) (1) n 006.6
~ showers (1) n 006.6
~ skin (1) n 069.5
~ -skin darky (1) n 128.3
~ -skinned (1) adj 069.5
~ -skinned Negro (1) n 069.5
~ -skinned Negroes (1) n 069.5
~ -skinneded niggers (1) n 063.9
~ snack (1) n 048.6
~ snow (1) n 007.4
~ soil (1) n 029.8
~ sprinkle (7) n 006.6
~ supper (1) n 048.6
~ tribe (1) n 069.5
~ truck (1) n 111.3
~ water (1) n 084.8
~ wires (1) n 019.9
Light (5) 108.5
~ -Horse Harry (1) 068.3
light[N-i] (10) n 037.2
light[V-p] (1) v 019.9
lighted torch (1) n 024.3
lighten (4) v/adj 060A.3
~ bug (1) n 060A.3
~ down (1) v 007.3
~ up (2) v 005.7
lighten[V-p] (1) v 006.2
lightened up (2) v 005.7
lightening (4) v 007.3
~ up (3) v 007.3
lightens up (1) v 007.3
lighter (102) n/adj 008.6
~ knot (8) n 008.6
~ -knot floater (1) n 006.1

~ -knot floaters (1) n
006.1
~ knots (18) n 008.6
~ load (1) n 080.7
~ pine (4) n 008.6
~ -skinneded (1) adj
063.8
~ stumps (1) n 008.6
~ wood (14) n 008.6
~ -wood torch (1) n
024.3
lighterd (336) n/adj 008.6
~ heart (1) n 008.6
~ knot (22) n 008.6
~ -knot floater (2) n
006.1
~ -knot sweeper (1) n
006.1
~ knots (34) n 008.6
~ logs (1) n 008.6
~ pine (5) n 008.6
~ post (1) n 016.5
~ posts (1) n 016.5
~ rail (1) n 008.6
~ rails (1) n 016.4
~ scaffold (1) n 008.3
~ splinters (10) n 008.6
~ stumps (3) n 008.6
~ torch (1) n 024.3
~ trees (1) n 008.6
~ wood (10) n 008.6
lighters (1) n 008.6
Lightfoot (1) TN 087.8
lightheaded (1) adj 073.3
lighthearted (1) adj 073.2
lighthouse (4) n 014.1
lighthouses (2) n 025.2
lighting (6) adj 060A.3
~ bug (4) n 060A.3
~ wood (2) n 008.6
lightly (1) adv 046.2
lightning (1350) n/adj
006.2
~ bog bug (1) n
060A.3
~ bug (616) n 060A.3
~ -bug bug (1) n
060A.3
~ bugs (277) n 060A.3
~ bulb (1) n 060A.3
~ rod (1) n 015.9
~ rods (1) n 011.5
~ storm (35) n 006.2
~ storms (2) n 006.2
~ wood (1) n 008.6

Lightning (4) 064.4
~ Point (1) MS 087.5
lightnings (1) n 006.2
lightproof (1) adj 075.7
lights (399) n/adj 037.2
~ and liver (3) n 037.2
~ and livers (1) n 037.2
~ and the liver (4) n
037.2
~ building (1) n 108.5
~ [J-0] the liver (1) n
037.2
lightweight (3) n/adj
124.1
~ rake (1) n 120.7
lightwood (130) n/adj
008.6
~ kindling (1) n 008.6
~ splinters (2) n 008.6
light(wood) (2) n 008.6
Lightwood Knot Creek
(1) AL 030.7
lignum vitae (1) n 091.8
likable (19) adj 073.2
like (3408) v/adj/adv/
prep/conj 100.1
~ to (578) v/adv 070.2
~ t(o) (2) adv 070.2
like[V-p] (11) v 013.6
~ to (5) v 013.8
like[V-r] (4) v 013.6
~ to (1) v 053.2
like[V-t] (3) v 013.3
~ to (2) v 052.6
liked (16) v 041.1
~ to (1) v 083.5
likeded (2) v 095.9
~ to (1) v 095.8
likely (62) adj/adv 041.1
liken to (5) prep 096.7
liken[V-t] to (1) v 075.9
likeness (2) n 065.3
likes (70) v 013.8
~ like (1) v 100.1
~ to (25) v 028.1
liking (9) n/v 081.4
~ to (1) v 041.1
lilac bush (1) n 062.7
Lilburn (1) GA 086.4
lilies (2) n 062.8
Lillie (1) LA 082.7
lily (8) n/adj 062.8
~ bugs (1) n 060A.2
~ of the valley (1) n
062.7

(li)ly (1) n 061.9
Lily Flag (1) AL 087.4
lima (481) n/adj 055A.3
~ bean (98) n 055A.3
~ beans (330) n 055A.3
~ butter bean (1) n
055A.3
~ butter beans (3) n
055A.3
lima[N-i] (1) n 055A.3
limas (71) n 055A.3
limb (29) n/adj 072.6
~ lines (1) n 099.7
~ rats (1) n 059.7
limber (16) adj 074.1
~ board (2) n 022.6
~ jack (3) n 022.6
~ -legged (1) adj 073.3
~ twigs (1) n 087.7
limb(er) (1) adj 093.6
limbo (2) n 061.6
limbs (9) n 072.3
lime (41) n/adj 055.1
~ barrel (1) n 019.1
~ base (1) n 029.8
~ egg (1) n 017.1
~ melons (1) n 056.7
~ oak (1) n 061.8
~ quarters (1) n 015.9
~ rock (7) n 031.6
~ -rock roads (2) n
031.6
~ -rock soil (1) n 029.8
~ sack (2) n 019.7
~ sinks (1) n 029.6
~ soil (2) n 029.8
~ tree (1) n 061.8
~ trees (7) n 061.8
Limerick (2) 087.8
limes (5) n 055.1
limestone (24) n/adj
029.8
~ courthouse (1) n
085.1
~ rock (3) n 016.6
~ rocks (1) n 029.8
~ soil (2) n 029.8
~ water (1) n 030.6
Limestone (16) AL TN
087.1
~ County (3) AL 087.1
~ Creek (4) AL TN
030.7
limewood (1) n 008.6
Limey (11) 127.8

Limeys (19) 127.8
limit (39) n 043.3
limited (12) adj 107.5
~ access (2) n 107.5
~ -access highway (2) n
107.5
~ -access highways (2)
n 107.5
~ -access road (2) n
107.5
~ -access roads (1) n
107.5
Limited (1) 109.4
limits (3) n 053.5
limo (3) n 088.9
limon trees (1) n 061.8
Limousin (1) 033.6
limousine (168) n/adj
109.8
~ car (1) n 109.8
~ service (5) n 109.8
limousined (1) v 109.8
limousines (17) n 109.8
limp (2) adj 075.5
~ -wristed (1) adj 124.1
limper light (1) n 060A.3
limy (2) adj 029.8
~ land (1) n 029.8
~ soil (1) n 029.8
Lincoln (24) AL LA MS
087.3
~ Avenue (1) 107.7
~ Continental (1) 109.4
~ County (4) GA MS
087.1
~ Garden (2) 106.2
~ Junior High (1)
125.8
~ Parish (2) LA 087.2
~ Park (3) 105.7
~ Road (1) 106.5
Linc(oln) (1) MS 087.2
Lincoln's War (1) 085.8
Lindale Mill (1) GA
087.8
linden (1) n 061.8
Linden (9) AL FL TX
087.2
~ -Hall (1) 107.7
~ Island (2) AR 087.4
Lindsey Creek (1) GA
030.7
line (339) n/adj 039.1
~ bait (1) n 061.2
~ bone (1) n 046.5

~ fence (2) n 016.3
~ gauge (1) n 097.8
~ horse (1) n 039.4
~ markings (1) n 107.3
~ mule (2) n 039.4
~ mules (1) n 039.4
Line (11) 107.6
~ Avenue (2) 107.6
~ Creek (3) AL 030.7
line[N-i] (4) n 039.1
lineage (2) n 064.1
linear house (1) n 118.6
lined (2) adj 009.6
lineman (2) n 081.8
linen (19) n/adj 026.5
~ closet (9) n 009.6
~ closets (2) n 009.6
~ cloth (1) n 019.7
~ suit (1) n 027.7
liner (1) n 116.8
liners (1) n 117.2
lines (608) n 039.1
Linesville (1) GA 087.6
ling (2) n 059.9
lingerie chest (1) n 009.2
lingo (1) n 080.7
Linguistic Atlas of the Gulf States (1) 030.9
liniment (10) n 078.3
Liniment (2) 025.9
lining (4) n 029.2
linings (2) n 011.2
link (197) n/adj 121.6
~ fence (3) n 126.1
~ form (1) n 121.6
~ meat (1) n 046.8
~ sausage (59) n 121.6
~ sausages (3) n 121.6
~ -wire fence (1) n 016.3
linked (2) adj 016.3
~ wire (1) n 016.3
links (26) n 121.6
Links (1) 129.6
linky (1) adj 073.4
linn (5) adj 061.8
~ tree (2) n 061.8
~ wood (2) n 008.6
~ wood tree (1) n 061.9
Linneville Creek (1) TX 030.7
Linsburg (1) LA 087.8
linseed oil (4) n 024.1
linsey (1) n 028.8

lint (5) n/v/adj 116.8
~ catcher (1) n 116.8
~ cotton (1) n 080.7
~ filter (1) n 116.8
~ your jacket (1) v 065.5
linterna (2) n S 060A.3
linthead (2) n 069.7
lintheads (1) n 069.4
Linwood (1) AL 087.7
lion (3) n 059.4
lions (1) n 031.1
Lions (2) 085.1
lip (6) n/adj 071.6
~ rouge (1) n 028.1
Lipans (1) 080.7
lips (11) n 071.5
Lipscomb (1) 106.6
lipstick (2) n/adj 081.7
~ plant (1) n 080.6
liquid (22) n/adj 077.7
~ embroidery (1) n 081.8
~ kind (1) n 081.3
~ sugar (1) n 122.3
liquidating (1) v 094.5
liquids (1) n 053.2
liquor (231) n/adj 050.8
~ -drinking (1) v 049.1
~ heads (1) n 089.9
~ joint (1) n 050.8
~ still (4) n 050.8
~ stills (1) n 050.8
~ store (1) n 070.7
~ stores (1) n 050.9
liquored up (1) v 050.9
lisle (2) n/adj 092.7
Lisle (1) 087.5
Lisman (1) MS 087.7
list (8) n 021.4
listed (1) v 021.4
listen (64) v 070.5
~ at (35) v 075.6
~ for (8) v 103.8
~ to (9) v 095.8
listened (4) v 032.9
~ at (3) v 032.9
listening (14) v 057.4
~ at (2) v 095.9
lister (2) n 021.6
listing (2) n/v 041.2
listless (2) adj 072.9
lit (16) v 044.2
~ into (1) v 104.7
~ off (1) v 092.9

~ out (7) v 052.6
~ up (1) v 075.2
literary (2) adj 131.3
~ school (1) n 083.7
literature (2) n 065.9
Lithia Springs (1) 106.4
Lithonia (6) GA 087.1
Lithos (2) 127.7
Lithuanian (3) 127.7
Lithuanians (5) 127.7
litter (16) n 055A.8
litters (1) n 080.8
little (2703) n/adj 090.4
~ -bitsy (3) adj 080.7
~ -bitty (55) adj 080.8
~ -bitty-old (10) adj 080.6
~ -bone Duroc (1) n 036.6
~ boss (1) n 069.6
~ -boys' room (3) n 012.1
~ brown house (2) n 012.1
~ brown shack (1) n 012.1
~ buddy (1) n 129.4
~ bull (29) n 033.8
~ bulls (4) n 033.8
~ chitlin (1) n 037.3
~ chitlins (1) n 037.3
~ dry spell (1) n 007.1
~ freeze (1) n 007.5
~ girls (1) n 037.6
~ -girls' room (1) n 126.3
~ gut (1) n 037.3
~ guts (4) n 037.3
~ hog (1) n 038.3
~ hominy (1) n 050.6
~ house (28) n 012.1
~ (in)testines (1) n 037.7
~ male (5) n 033.8
~ name (1) n 064.4
~ necks (1) n 090.8
~ -old (273) adj 080.8
~ -old-bitty (11) adj 080.7
~ ones (4) n 064.3
~ penny store (1) n 116.2
~ road (3) n 031.7
~ roads (2) n 031.7
~ room (4) n 010.3

~ sheep (1) n 038.4
~ shower (2) n 006.6
~ silver (1) n 114.5
~ small shower (1) n 006.6
~ sofa (1) n 009.1
~ sprinkle (4) n 006.6
~ steer (2) n 033.8
~ white house outside (1) n 012.1
~ wishbone (1) n 037.1
~ woman (5) n 063.2
~ wood (6) n 008.6
lit(tle) (2) adj 039.5
Little (270) 030.7
~ Abbie (1) AL 030.7
~ Allen Creek (1) TX 030.7
~ Armuchee (1) GA 030.7
~ Baby (1) 064.4
~ Barren Mill (1) TN 087.2
~ Bay (1) MS 030.7
~ Bay Ditch (1) MS 030.7
~ Bayou (1) LA 030.3
~ Bayou Black (1) LA 087.2
~ Bear Creek (1) AL 030.7
~ Beaverdam Creek (1) GA 030.7
~ Biloxi (1) MS 030.7
~ Black Sambo (1) 069.3
~ Booger (1) 064.4
~ Boss (2) 069.6
~ Boy (1) 055.3
~ Cahaba (1) AL 030.7
~ Canoochee (1) GA 030.7
~ Cedar (1) GA 030.7
~ Cheniere (1) LA 087.4
~ Choctaw (1) LA 030.7
~ Choctaw Bayou (1) LA 030.7
~ Coldwater Creek (1) GA 030.7
~ Corney (2) AR LA 030.7
~ Cove (1) TN 030.3

~ Cow Creek (1) TX 030.7
~ Creek (8) AR GA MS TN TX 030.7
~ Cypress Creek (1) AL 030.7
~ Deep Lake (1) AR 030.7
~ Dry (1) GA 030.7
~ Ebenezer (1) GA 030.7
~ Elm (1) TX 030.7
~ Emory (1) TN 030.7
~ Five Points (1) 105A.2
~ General (1) 116.2
~ Georgia (2) 105.9
~ Granny (1) 064.2
~ Hatchie (1) TN 030.7
~ Havana (7) 105.4
~ Haynes Creek (1) GA 030.7
~ Hooker (1) 090.8
~ Italy (2) 105.4
~ Korea (1) 105.2
~ Lady (1) 064.4
~ Lake Bay(ou) (1) AR 030.7
~ League parks (1) n 106.8
~ Louisiana (1) AR 087.8
~ Mamma (3) 064.2
~ Master (1) 069.6
~ Maumelle (1) AR 030.7
~ Mexico (3) TX 105.4
~ Mineral (1) TX 030.7
~ Mountain (1) TN 031.1
~ Mulberry (1) TN 030.7
~ Pickaninny (1) 116.2
~ Pigeon (2) TN 030.7
~ Pigeon River (1) TN 030.7
~ Pilot Knob (1) TN 030.8
~ Piney (1) AR 030.7
~ Poland (1) 105.4
~ Pottsburg (1) FL 030.7
~ Prairie Creek (1) AL 030.7

~ Rice Creek (1) FL 030.7
~ River (23) AL AR FL GA LA MS TX 030.7
~ Rock (111) AL AR 087.1
~ Rock Airport (1) 106.5
~ Rock paper (1) n 087.3
~ Saint Marys (1) GA 030.7
~ Sally Salter (1) 130.3
~ Sally Saucer (1) 130.3
~ Sally Walker (19) 130.3
~ Sand (1) MS 030.7
~ Sandy (1) AL 030.7
~ Satilla (1) GA 030.7
~ Springs (1) MS 087.3
~ Strawberry (1) AR 030.7
~ Sycamore (4) TN 030.7
~ Sycamore Creek (1) TN 030.7
~ Tallabogue (1) MS 093.8
~ Tallapoosa River (2) GA 030.7
~ Tennessee (2) GA TN 030.7
~ Tennessee River (1) TN 030.7
~ Texas (2) TN 086.8
~ Tobesofkee (1) GA 030.7
~ Town (1) 105.1
~ Uchee (2) AL 030.7
(Little) Cow Creek (1) TX 030.7
Littlefield (1) TX 087.5
Littlejohn Creek (1) FL 030.7
littlemouth (3) adj 059.9
~ bass (2) n 059.9
littler (2) adj 026.3
littlest (3) adj 026.3
live (213) v/adj 074.1
~ around (1) v 052.8
~ at (4) v 075.6
~ bait (2) n 060.5
~ baits (1) n 061.2

~ -box (1) n 096.7
~ devil aspirin (1) n 080.7
~ fish bait (1) n 060.5
~ in (22) v 032.9
~ -in help (1) n 049.5
~ oak (51) n 061.8
~ -oak pond (1) n 029.6
~ oak tree (1) n 061.8
~ oak trees (3) n 061.8
~ oaks (9) n 061.8
~ on (7) v 027.2
~ wire (4) n 074.1
~ wires (1) n 074.1
~ with (4) v 032.4
Live (10) 087.3
~ Oak (6) FL 087.3
~ Oak community (1) LA 087.1
~ Oak Creek (1) TX 030.7
~ Oak Plantation Road (1) 106.1
~ Oak Point (1) FL 087.7
live[V-p] (22) v 053.4
~ across (1) v 053.2
~ in (1) v 013.6
~ over (3) v 052.6
live[V-r] (8) v 082.7
~ down (2) v 082.7
~ to (1) v 053.4
~ with (2) v 053.6
live[V-t] (1) v 039.9
lived (145) v 053.4
~ around (1) v 082.7
~ at (6) v 082.7
~ in (26) v 052.5
~ off of (1) v 034.4
~ on (5) v 053.3
~ out (1) v 039.5
~ to (1) v 065.6
~ up (1) v 082.7
~ with (8) v 052.5
~ [P-0] (2) v 082.6
livelier (1) adj 097.8
lively (112) adj 074.1
liver (921) n/adj 047.2
~ and light[N-i] (4) n 037.2
~ and lights (67) n 037.2
~ (a)nd lights (3) n 037.2

~ and the light[N-i] (2) n 037.2
~ and the lights (14) n 037.2
~ and the lungs (1) n 037.2
~ beef (1) n 121.2
~ bread (1) n 047.4
~ burger (1) n 047.2
~ cheese (55) n 047.2
~ dumplings (2) n 047.2
~ hash (32) n 047.2
~ -heart-and-light stew (1) n 047.2
~ loaf (23) n 047.2
~ loafs (1) n 047.2
~ medicine (1) n 078.2
~ mush (27) n 047.2
~ paste (5) n 047.2
~ pate (1) n 047.2
~ patty (1) n 047.2
~ pea (1) n 047.2
~ pie (1) n 047.2
~ pudding (139) n 047.2
~ puddings (6) n 047.2
~ roll (1) n 047.2
~ sausage (64) n 047.2
~ spots (1) n 077.4
~ spread (2) n 047.2
~ stew (1) n 047.2
~ trouble (1) n 079.9
~ worm (1) n 060.5
~ [J-0] light[N-i] (1) n 037.2
~ [J-0] lights (6) n 037.2
~ [J-0] the lights (1) n 037.2
liv(er) and lights (2) n 037.2
livered (2) adj 073.8
liverelle (2) n 037.2
Liverpool (2) FL 087.7
livers (27) n 037.2
~ and lights (3) n 037.2
liverwurst (84) n 047.2
livery (14) adj 080.9
~ stable (12) n 080.9
~ stables (2) n 015.2
liver(y) (2) adj 014.2
~ barn (1) n 014.2
~ stables (1) n 015.2
lives (89) v 039.1

~ at (1) v 082.7
~ in (20) v 053.4
~ out (1) v 052.8
~ with (1) v 053.4
livestock (151) n/adj 036.5
~ farm (1) n 036.5
~ feed (1) n 036.5
livestocks (1) n 037.4
livid (1) adj 075.2
living (1915) v/adj 007.8
~ area (10) n 007.8
~ at (2) v 053.2
~ children (1) n 064.3
~ daylights (1) n 074.3
~ -dining area (1) n 007A.6
~ doll (1) n 125.3
~ front room (2) n 007.8
~ houses (3) n 014.1
~ image (1) n 065.3
~ in (6) v 053.5
~ off (1) v 115.4
~ on (1) v 013.6
~ quarters (5) n 007A.2
~ room (1642) n 007A.3
~ -room (1) adj 007.8
~ room area (1) n 007A.3
~ -room chair (1) n 008.8
~ -room chairs (1) n 008.8
~ -room couch (1) n 009.1
~ -room dining-room combination (1) n 007A.3
~ -room furniture (15) n 009.4
~ -room parlor (1) n 007.8
~ -room set (2) n 009.4
~ -room suite (17) n 009.4
~ -room suites (3) n 009.4
~ rooms (30) n 007.8
~ things (1) n 052.5
~ with (3) v 082.7
~ [P-0] (1) v 070.9
Livingston (12) AL LA TX 087.6

~ Parish (1) LA 087.5
~ Road (1) 107.6
Livonia (3) LA 087.6
lizard (22) n/adj 060.4
~ lips (1) n 125.2
lizards (18) n 060A.3
Lizzie (6) 124.4
Lizzies (2) 113.3
Llano (1) TX 030.7
llanos (1) n S 029.8
llantas (1) n S 021.1
Llewellin setter (1) n 033.3
L&N station house (1) n 106.9
lo and behold (1) interj 070.5
Loachapoka (4) AL 087.4
load (375) n/v/adj 019.8
~ up (1) v 048.4
load[N-i] (2) n 088.9
loaded (8) v 057.8
~ against (1) v 057.8
~ for bear (1) adj 028.1
~ with (2) v 032.4
loader (5) n 080.6
loaders (2) n 022.4
loading (24) v/adj 021.4
~ chute (1) n 080.7
~ dock (5) n 031.4
~ docks (2) n 031.4
~ places (1) n 031.4
~ port (1) n 031.4
~ ramp (1) n 031.4
loads (5) n 022.4
loaf (501) n/adj 045.1
~ bread (321) n 044.3
~ breads (1) n 045.1
~ cake (2) n 122.7
~ light bread (1) n 044.3
loafed bread (1) n 044.3
loafer (21) n/adj 123.8
~ step-ins (1) n 123.8
loafers (78) n 069.7
loafing (10) n/v/adj 083.4
~ barn (1) n 015.3
~ dog (2) n 033.3
~ shed (3) n 015.1
~ sheds (1) n 015.1
loafs (8) n 044.5
loam (496) n/adj 029.8
~ deposit (1) n 029.8
~ field land (1) n 029.8

~ ground (2) n 029.9
~ land (18) n 029.9
~ sand (1) n 029.8
~ soil (28) n 029.8
loams (1) n 029.9
loamus soil (1) n 029.8
loamy (87) adj 029.8
~ field (1) n 029.9
~ land (10) n 029.8
~ sand (2) n 029.9
~ soil (30) n 029.9
loan (41) n/v/adj 095.1
~ office (1) n 114.6
~ shark (1) n 114.6
~ sharks (1) n 114.6
~ shop (3) n 114.6
~ shops (1) n 114.6
loan[V-r] (3) v 101.7
loan[V-t] (1) v 101.1
loaned (7) v 098.5
~ [P-0] (1) v 095.1
loans (1) n 095.2
loaves (28) n 044.3
lob (1) v 021.8
lobar pneumonia (1) n 078.7
lobby (4) n 010.8
lobbyist (1) n 115.3
Loblockee (1) AL 030.7
loblollies (1) n 061.9
loblolly (19) n/adj 061.9
~ pine (9) n 061.9
lobster (19) n 060.8
lobsters (11) n 060.9
local (21) n/adj 112.5
~ buses (1) n 109.9
~ Methodist preacher (1) n 080.7
~ preacher (6) n 067.8
~ preachers (1) n 067.8
~ shower (1) n 006.6
localisms (1) n 131.2
locate (1) v 088.6
located (2) v 095.8
location (1) n 012.9
Lochinvar (1) 090.3
Lochlin (2) LA 087.4
lock (14) n/v/adj 016.4
~ bowels (4) n 080.1
~ box (1) n 088.7
~ gate (1) n 099.5
Locka (5) 106A.1
Locke Creek (1) 107.7
locked (12) v/adj 080.1
~ bowels (2) n 080.1

~ in (1) v 025.9
~ up (2) v 082.2
locker (34) n/adj 009.6
~ room (1) n 010.3
lockers (8) n 009.6
Lockesburg (3) AR 087.7
locket (30) n 028.4
lockets (7) n 028.4
Lockhart (7) AL MS TX 087.8
~ Stadium (1) 106.4
Lockheed (1) 052.5
locking (1) v 080.7
lockjaw (4) n 079.7
Lockloosa Lake (1) FL 030.7
Lockport (1) LA 087.8
locks (4) n/v 031.4
lockup (9) n/adj 099.6
~ room (2) n 007A.9
Lockwood (1) AL 087.3
loco (2) adj S 073.4
Loc(o) (1) TX 030.7
locomotive (2) n/adj 065.8
~ machinist (1) n 065.8
locomotives (1) n 053.4
locoweed (1) n 114.1
locoweeds (1) n 061.4
locust (42) n/adj 061.8
~ beer (2) n 050.9
~ post[N-i] (1) n 016.5
~ postes (1) n 016.5
~ tree (3) n 061.9
~ trees (6) n 061.8
Locust (5) TX 087.7
~ Grove (2) GA 087.5
~ Mountain (1) TN 080.7
~ Street (1) 107.6
locust[N-i] (5) n 061.1
locustes (3) n 055A.3
locusts (1) n 061.1
lodestone (3) n 023.4
lodge (5) n/v/adj 084.3
~ in (1) v 040.9
Lodge (3) 087.7
~ Corner (2) AR 087.7
Loehmanns Village (3) 106.3
loess (4) n/adj 029.8
~ soil (1) n 029.8
loft (1075) n/adj 014.5
~ part (2) n 014.5
~ room (1) n 009.8

lofted (1) v 014.5
Lofton Creek (1) FL 030.7
lofts (17) n 009.8
lofty (1) n 014.5
log (772) n/v/adj 008.5
~ barn (5) n 014.2
~ barns (1) n 014.2
~ boats (1) n 024.6
~ boom (1) n 081.7
~ building (2) n 008.5
~ cabin (24) n 007A.1
~ cabin house (1) n 014.1
~ cabinets (1) n 066.8
~ cabins (5) n 008.5
~ camp (1) n 008.5
~ cart (2) n 008.5
~ chain (2) n 008.5
~ courthouse (2) n 008.5
~ crib (3) n 014.3
~ cribs (1) n 014.3
~ cushion (1) n 028.9
~ cutter (1) n 008.5
~ dogs (3) n 008.3
~ dray (1) n 084.9
~ fence (21) n 016.4
~ fences (7) n 016.4
~ fire (3) n 008.5
~ fires (1) n 008.5
~ frame (2) n 022.1
~ god (1) n 059.3
~ head (1) n 060.7
~ -head turtle (1) n 060.6
~ heap (2) n 088.7
~ holder (1) n 022.1
~ holders (2) n 008.3
~ horse (1) n 022.1
~ house (113) n 014.1
~ houses (25) n 014.1
~ hut (1) n 008.5
~ huts (1) n 008.5
~ irons (2) n 008.3
~ jailhouse (1) n 008.5
~ kitchen (3) n 009.9
~ landings (1) n 031.4
~ lighter (1) n 008.5
~ -like (1) adj 024.6
~ mover (1) n 006.1
~ pile (1) n 070.9
~ rack (3) n 022.1
~ raisings (1) n 008.5
~ road (2) n 031.6

~ roads (3) n 031.7
~ room (8) n 007A.3
~ rooms (1) n 007A.6
~ saloon (1) n 007A.2
~ scaffold (1) n 022.1
~ schoolhouse (5) n 008.5
~ sheds (1) n 015.2
~ smokehouse (2) n 008.5
~ structure (1) n 008.5
~ team (2) n 093.9
~ tree (1) n 061.8
~ -type (1) adj 008.5
~ wagon (4) n 008.5
~ -wagon team (1) n 033.7
~ wagons (2) n 008.5
~ with (1) v 081.9
~ woods (1) n 008.5
Log (5) 030.7
~ Cabin Syrup (1) 051.3
~ Creek (1) AR 030.7
Logan (4) AR WV 087.3
~ Bayou (1) LA 030.7
~ Gap (1) AL 031.3
loganberries (4) n 062.4
loganberry (4) n 062.5
Logansport (4) LA 030.7
Loganville (1) GA 087.2
loge (1) n 007A.4
logged (7) v 008.5
~ off (1) v 021.4
~ with (1) v 084.8
logger (3) n/adj 080.9
~ back (1) n 060.6
logger[N-k] dream (1) n 090.8
loggerhead (94) n/adj 060.6
~ beer (2) n 050.8
~ cooter (2) n 060.6
~ cooters (1) n 060.6
~ turtle (27) n 060.6
~ turtles (9) n 060.6
Loggerhead Key (1) FL 087.5
loggerheaded (2) adj 060.6
~ turtle (1) n 060.6
~ turtles (1) n 060.6
loggerheads (16) n 060.6
logger's dream (2) n 090.8

loggers (3) n 080.6
logging (27) n/v/adj 021.4
~ dogs (1) n 084.9
~ engines (1) n 013.9
~ grab (1) n 021.4
~ road (2) n 031.7
~ team (1) n 033.7
~ time (1) n 092.9
logjam (1) n 075.6
logjams (1) n 088.8
logroll (1) n 130A.4
logroller (2) n 130.6
logrolling (9) n 091.8
logrollings (12) n 081.9
logs (462) n 008.5
Logtown (3) MS 087.5
loin (53) n/adj 121.2
~ bone (1) n 080.7
~ chops (2) n 121.3
~ cuts (1) n 121.4
~ meat (1) n 048.4
~ part (1) n 121.3
~ roast (1) n 121.3
~ steaks (3) n 121.1
~ tip roast (2) n 121.2
loins (9) n 121.3
loiter (1) v 033.3
loiterer (1) n 113.7
Lollie (1) GA 087.3
lollipop tomatoes (1) n 055.3
Lomax (1) TX 087.9
Lombardo (1) 130.8
Lomita (1) 086.5
London (21) 086.5
~ Bridge (3) 130.3
~ Bridge is breaking down (1) n 089.9
~ Bridge is falling down (6) n 130.3
~ Bridges (3) 130.3
~ broil (5) n 121.2
~ town (1) n 022.8
londri (1) n 046.5
lone (1) adj 064.4
Lone (3) 107.8
~ Star (2) 107.8
~ Star State (1) 086.8
loner (2) n 069.9
loners (1) n 065.7
lonesome day (1) n 005.4
long (1722) adj/adv 040.1
~ arm (1) n 049.4

~ -bladed ax (1) n 080.9
~ boy (1) n 121.7
~ breeches (1) n 027.4
~ bucket (1) n 017.2
~ chair (2) n 009.1
~ -coat Chihuahua (1) n 012.2
~ cotton (3) n 081.9
~ curls (1) n 123.9
~ -distance hauling (1) n 021.4
~ drawers (2) n 080.6
~ drought (4) n 007.1
~ dry period (1) n 007.1
~ dry spell (15) n 007.1
~ eye (1) n 065.9
~ eyes (1) n 055A.5
~ fire (1) n 022.4
~ forage (1) n 014.5
~ giants (1) n 055A.6
~ -grain Honduras (1) n 050.7
~ gravy (1) n 059.9
~ green (3) n 114.5
~ greens (1) n 055A.4
~ hair (19) n 123.9
~ -haired (3) adj 129.3
~ -haired hicks (1) n 129.3
~ -haired hippies (3) n 115.8
~ -haired people (1) n 129.3
~ hairstyles (1) n 115.5
~ -handle drawers (1) n 092.8
~ -handle gourd (1) n 026.7
~ -handle underwear (1) n 088.9
~ -handled underwear (1) n 092.8
~ handles (5) n 080.6
~ head (1) n 074.8
~ house (3) n 007A.1
~ john (15) n 122.5
~ johns (14) n 060.5
~ jumpers (1) n 060.5
~ leg (1) n 072.6
~ -leg stockings (1) n 072.6
~ -legged (3) adj 073.3

~ -legged frogs (1) n 060.2
~ line (1) n 039.1
~ -lived (1) adj 091.7
~ livers (1) n 092.9
~ loaf (1) n 044.3
~ pants (4) n 027.4
~ -pants suit (1) n 027.7
~ quart (1) n 050.8
~ sandwich (1) n 121.7
~ seat (1) n 009.1
~ shag (1) n 115.5
~ shorts (4) n 123.3
~ squashes (1) n 056.6
~ -staple cotton (1) n 015.8
~ -stem clay pipe (1) n 065.9
~ -stem limas (1) n 055A.3
~ -straw pine (1) n 061.8
~ style (1) n 123.9
~ suit (1) n 027.7
~ sweetening (17) n 051.3
~ -tail shinny (1) n 104.6
~ team of oxen (1) n 033.7
~ -teethed (1) adj 035.7
~ thigh (1) n 072.5
~ -tooth rake (1) n 021.7
~ trousers (1) n 095.9
~ underwear (2) n 080.6
~ wood (1) n 008.5
~ worms (1) n 060.5
Long (28) 087.7
~ Beach (3) CA FL 087.7
~ Branch (2) TN 030.7
~ Bull (1) AL 087.6
~ Cane (1) GA 087.4
~ Creek (5) AL MS TN 030.7
~ Guy (1) 055A.4
~ Island (2) LA NY 087.1
~ Island Creek (1) GA 030.7
~ John beans (1) n 055A.3

~ John Silver's (1) 068.2
~ Key (1) FL 087.7
~ Lake (1) MS 030.7
~ Point (1) 107.5
~ Springs (1) LA 087.4
~ Street (1) 107.6
Longacre (1) LA 087.3
longer (26) adj 028.5
~ hair (1) n 123.9
~ -legged (1) adj 080.8
longest (29) adj 040.1
longhair (3) n/adj 129.3
~ music (1) n 130.8
longhairs (3) n 123.9
longhand (1) n 072.2
longheaded (2) adj 074.9
longhorn steer (1) n 048.1
Longhorn (6) 033.5
~ cheese (1) n 048.1
~ steer (1) n 033.5
longitude (1) n 080.7
longleaf (38) n/adj 061.8
~ heart pine (1) n 061.8
~ pine (22) n 061.9
~ pines (4) n 061.8
~ timber (1) n 061.8
~ yellow pine (1) n 061.8
~ yellow pine timber (2) n 061.8
longleafed pine (1) n 061.6
longleaves (1) n 061.9
longlegs (1) n 061.3
longneck (4) n/adj 069.4
~ squash (1) n 056.6
longnecks (3) n 069.8
Longs (1) 055.5
longshoreman (2) n 088.7
Longshot Road (1) 031.7
longtime (1) adj 053.6
longue (1) adj F 008.9
Longview (8) LA MS TX 087.7
Longville (1) LA 087.2
longways (3) adv 016.7
Longwood (4) FL 087.8
Lonoke (3) AR 087.6
~ County (1) AR 087.4
Lonsdale (4) 105.1
~ Project (1) 105.7
look (654) v/interj 102.5

~ -a-here (55) interj 070.5
~ -a-there (16) interj 070.5
~ -a-yonder (3) interj 070.5
~ after (6) v 065.4
~ around (1) v 024.7
~ as if (1) v 088.3
~ at (85) v 070.5
~ back (2) v 057.6
~ for (7) v 081.1
~ forward (5) v 040.4
~ forward to (6) v 040.4
~ in (3) v 098.3
~ like (42) v 065.3
~ on (1) v 070.5
~ out (3) v 070.5
~ out for (5) v 044.2
~ out [P-0] (1) v 025.8
~ over (1) v 070.5
~ through (1) v 080.7
~ to (5) v 088.7
~ [P-0] (1) v 090.8
Look magazine (1) n 075.6
look[V-p] (69) v 072.9
~ like (54) v 065.3
look[V-r] (10) v 098.8
~ like (9) v 065.3
looked (48) v 072.9
~ after (5) v 065.4
~ as if (1) v 088.3
~ at (2) v 090.6
~ down upon (1) v 025.5
~ for (1) v 032.6
~ forward (1) v 040.4
~ like (19) v 065.3
lookeded (1) v 098.8
lookee (14) interj 070.5
looker (7) n 125.4
looking (355) v/adj 057.4
~ after (1) v 024.9
~ at (4) v 025.7
~ at the stars (1) v 078.6
~ for (21) v 025.7
~ for a baby (4) v 065.1
~ for a calf (1) v 033.9
~ for an offspring (1) v 065.1

~ for higher bushes (1) v 082.1
~ forward (6) v 040.4
~ forward to (4) v 040.4
~ glass (10) n 009.2
~ in (1) v 057.4
~ like (5) v 065.3
~ out (1) v 024.8
~ over (1) v 013.5
~ to (4) v 065.1
lookout (4) n/adj 031.2
~ point (1) n 084.9
Lookout (221) 031.1
~ Mountain (21) TN 031.1
looks (350) n/v 065.3
~ after (1) v 053.4
~ as if (1) v 088.3
~ like (259) v 065.3
loom (8) n 029.8
looms (1) n 052.5
loon (2) n 074.9
loony (12) adj 074.8
~ shaft (1) n 020.9
loop (6) n/adj 095.4
~ road (1) n 031.7
~ -the-loop (1) n 080.7
~ -[D-0]-loop (1) n 095.5
Loop (5) 107.1
~ Four-Ten (1) 107.1
~ Twelve (1) 107.1
looped (1) adj 093.8
looping (1) v 034.8
loops (1) n 052.1
Loosahatchie (2) TN 030.7
loose (359) adj 051.5
~ flesh (1) n 078.2
~ girls (1) n 081.9
~ -headed (1) adj 090.9
~ -jointed (1) adj 073.3
~ juice (1) n 121.9
~ -knit (1) adj 091.7
~ -laid fence (1) n 016.6
~ -leaf lettuce (3) n 055A.6
~ lettuce (1) n 055A.6
~ peach (1) n 054.3
~ woman (7) n 073.7
~ womens (1) n 083.8
loosening up (1) v 024.9
looser (1) adj 029.8

loot (4) n 114.5
lope (2) n 102.3
Lopeno (1) TX 087.2
loping (1) v 034.3
loppers (1) n 120.8
lopsided (3) adj 085.2
loquat (3) n 062.8
Loraine Drive (1) 107.7
lord (35) n/adj 063.1
~ and master (1) n 063.1
~ god (28) n 059.3
~ god bird (1) n 059.3
~ gods (3) n 059.3
Lord (563) 089.3
~ Fauntleroy suit (1) n 088.7
~ God (12) 089.3
~ Jesus Christ (2) 089.3
~ taken her (1) v 078.5
Lord[N-k] sake (1) n 092.2
Lord's (37) 089.4
~ business (1) n 089.3
~ Day (28) 002.1
~ help (1) n 032.4
~ sake (1) n 037.9
~ sakes (2) n 092.2
~ side (1) n 089.3
~ will (1) n 058.7
~ work (1) n 089.3
Lordy (27) interj 092.2
Loreauville (2) LA 087.2
Loretto (2) FL 087.5
Lorman (6) MS 087.1
Lorraine (1) LA 087.5
Los (32) 087.3
~ Angeles (24) CA 087.3
~ Ang(eles) (1) CA 087.8
~ Olmos (2) TX 030.7
~ Olmos Creek (1) TX 030.7
~ Saenz (1) TX 087.2
~ Tomates (2) TX 055.3
(Los) Olmos (1) TX 030.7
lose (33) v 096.9
~ his breakfast (1) v 080.2
~ his groceries (1) v 080.3

~ his lunch (1) v 080.3
~ your breakfast (1) v 080.2
~ your lunch (3) v 080.3
lose[V-p] (1) v 075.2
losed on (1) v 094.5
loser (4) n 125.1
loses (3) v 092.8
losing (10) v 094.5
~ on (1) v 094.5
~ their biscuits (1) v 080.3
loss (610) n/adj 094.5
~ leader (1) n 094.5
~ price (1) n 094.5
lossage (2) n 096.8
losses (2) n 094.5
lost (128) v/adj 094.5
~ bread (3) n 044.4
~ child (1) n 066.7
~ her husband (2) v 078.5
~ her notching stick (1) v 065.1
~ him (1) v 078.5
~ his cookies (2) v 080.3
~ his dinner (4) v 080.2
~ his foothold (1) v 082.1
~ his happiness (1) v 082.2
~ his meal (1) v 080.2
~ his supper (1) v 080.2
~ interest (1) v 082.1
~ it all (1) v 080.3
~ john (1) n 044.6
~ my dinner (1) v 080.2
~ my husband (1) v 078.5
~ my wife (1) v 078.5
~ off (1) v 038.8
~ their dinner[N-i] (1) v 080.2
~ their lunch[N-i] (1) v 080.3
~ tribe (1) n 024.8
~ your dear one (1) v 078.5
~ your husband (1) v 078.5

~ your love one (1) v 078.5
~ your lunch (1) v 080.2
~ your stomach (1) v 080.3
Lost (5) 085.8
~ Cause (1) 085.8
~ Creek (2) GA TN 030.7
~ Horse (1) MS 030.7
~ John (1) 083.1
lot (2488) n/adj 015.6
~ fence (5) n 015.6
~ fences (1) n 016.2
~ -like (1) adj 015.3
~ pasture (1) n 015.4
~ pen (1) n 015.4
lotion (2) n 061.4
lots (282) n 025.3
lotted off (1) v 015.3
lottery (2) n 084.8
Lottie's eye (1) n 096.8
Louann (1) AR 087.7
loud (18) adj/adv 074.8
louder (7) adv 047.1
loudmouth (1) n 033.3
Loudon (3) TN 087.2
~ Lake (1) TN 030.7
~ River (1) TN 030.7
Loudoun (6) 030.7
Louis (745) MO 087.1
~ [D-0] Fifteenth chair (1) n 008.9
Lou(is) (1) 087.1
Louise (3) TX 087.3
Louisiana (1084) 086.5
~ Avenue (1) 107.5
~ Baptist (As)sociation (1) 086.5
~ bayou (1) n 030.6
~ Cajun (1) 069.5
~ cane (5) n 086.5
~ Cattlemen's Association (1) 080.6
~ coffee (1) n 032.4
~ coons (1) n 069.9
~ cypress (1) n 061.8
~ Delta (1) 029.5
~ French (1) 080.6
~ green (1) n 055A.3
~ Improved (1) 055.5
~ law (1) n 086.5
~ line (1) n 086.5

~ marsh (2) n 029.7
~ molasses (1) n 051.2
~ people (2) n 086.5
~ pink (6) n 060.5
~ pinks (5) n 060.5
~ pure cane syrup (1) n 051.3
~ red beans (1) n 055A.3
~ red-hot (1) n 051.7
~ Red (1) 080.8
~ style (1) n 055A.3
~ syrup (3) n 051.3
~ waters (1) n 081.8
~ yam (1) n 055.5
~ yams (4) n 055.5
Louisian(a) (6) 086.5
~ Avenue (1) 086.5
Louisiana's (1) 086.5
Louisville (661) AL AR GA KY LA MS TX 087.9
~ Academy (1) 055A.9
~ Park (1) 106.4
~ Slugger (1) 087.9
Louis(ville) (1) KY 087.9
lounge (67) n/adj 009.1
~ chair (4) n 009.1
~ chairs (1) n 008.8
lounger (1) n 008.8
lounges (4) n/v 009.1
~ around (1) v 097.1
lounging (6) adj 008.8
~ chair (4) n 008.8
~ chairs (1) n 009.1
~ couch (1) n 009.1
Loup (2) 029.5
louse (1) n 060A.7
lousy (15) adj/adv 005.5
~ day (4) n 005.5
~ rich (1) adj 075.8
Lousy Level (1) LA 087.4
Loutre (4) AR LA 030.7
~ Creek (2) AR 030.7
L'Outre (2) LA 030.7
louvers (4) n 009.5
lovable (6) adj 066.1
love (328) n/v/adj 081.4
~ apple (2) n 061.4
~ apples (4) n 055.3
~ baby (1) n 065.7
~ bone (4) n 037.1
~ breakers (1) n 124.8
~ bug (3) n 060A.3
~ bugs (5) n 060A.3

~ chairs (2) n 008.8
~ child (13) n 065.7
~ gift (1) n 095.7
~ house (1) n 113.4
~ -it-or-leave-it (1) adj 080.6
~ knots (1) n 123.9
~ lots (1) n 009.1
~ melons (1) n 056.9
~ of his life (1) n 081.6
~ offering (1) n 095.7
~ one (1) n 081.6
~ seat (127) n 009.1
~ seats (25) n 009.1
~ song (1) n 130.8
~ -struck (1) adj 081.4
~ to (4) v 040.7
~ tomatoes (1) n 055.3
Love (12) MS 064.4
~ community (1) MS 088.5
~ Hitlers (1) n 127.1
~ Lane (1) FL 031.8
~ Station (1) MS 088.5
~ Street (2) 114.8
love[V-p] (7) v 089.3
~ her (1) v 081.4
~ to (5) v 125.5
love[V-r] (1) v 091.6
love[V-t] (1) v 053.5
~ by (1) v 053.5
loved (3) v/adj 053.5
~ ones (1) n 066.5
~ to (1) v 080.6
Lovejoy (4) GA 087.2
Lovelady (1) TX 087.2
lovelier (24) adj 066.1
Lovell (2) 106.5
~ Field (1) 106.5
~ Lake (1) TX 030.7
lovely (34) adj 125.4
~ day (7) n 005.4
~ person (1) n 129.4
lover (51) n/adj 081.5
~ boy (1) n 081.5
~ girl (1) n 081.6
lovers (6) n 081.5
lovers' (3) adj 031.8
~ lane (1) n 031.8
~ lanes (1) n 031.8
~ seat (1) n 009.1
loves (17) v 025.6
~ to (5) v 013.8
Lovey (1) 064.4
lovier (4) adj 066.1

loving (215) n/v/adj 081.7
~ one another (1) v 081.4
~ up (2) v 081.7
lovinger (26) adj 066.1
low (403) v/adj 036.3
~ -(ac)count (2) adj 069.7
~ Afro (1) n 123.9
~ bench (1) n 089.7
~ blood (1) n 079.8
~ bottom (4) n 029.4
~ bottoms (1) n 029.4
~ -bush berry (1) n 062.5
~ class (8) n 069.8
~ -class (2) adj 069.7
~ -class hotels (1) n 113.8
~ -class motel (1) n 112.8
~ -class people (3) n 069.7
~ -class person (1) n 069.7
~ -class trash (1) n 069.7
~ -class white man (2) n 069.7
~ -class whites (1) n 069.7
~ cotton (1) n 072.9
~ country (1) n 029.5
~ cut (1) n 123.9
~ -cut shoe (1) n 123.8
~ cuts (1) n 123.9
~ -down (36) adj 073.6
~ -downest (1) adj 064.7
~ English (1) n 123.9
~ first (1) n 083.7
~ flatland (1) n 029.4
~ for (2) v 036.3
~ foundation (1) n 029.4
~ grade (2) n 050.9
~ -grade (3) adj 073.6
~ -grade whiskey (1) n 050.8
~ grades (1) n 069.8
~ ground (6) n 029.4
~ heel (1) n 123.8
~ -heel pumps (1) n 123.8

~ -heel shoes (2) n 123.8
~ heels (9) n 123.8
~ level (1) n 119.2
~ -life (1) n 069.7
~ -lying (3) adj 029.4
~ -lying land (1) n 029.4
~ -lying lands (1) n 029.4
~ middling (1) n 088.8
~ pastureland (1) n 029.4
~ place (15) n 030.4
~ places (1) n 029.4
~ primer (1) n 083.7
~ quarters (3) n 123.8
~ -rated (1) adj 090.4
~ road (1) n 031.3
~ shoes (1) n 123.8
~ spot (1) n 029.4
~ tide (1) n 030.3
~ -water bridges (1) n 081.8
~ -water mark (1) n 084.9
~ wetland (1) n 029.4
~ wind (2) n 007.3
~ wine (6) n 050.8
Low (3) 031.3
~ Gap (2) AR 032.3
~ Germans (1) 127.2
low[V-p] (2) v 036.3
lowboy (4) n 009.2
lowbrow (1) adj 073.6
lowed (2) v 036.3
Lowell (6) 019.7
~ cloth (1) n 019.6
~ sack (1) n 019.7
~ sacks (1) n 019.7
Lowells (2) 019.7
lower (52) adj 007.3
~ bottom (1) n 029.4
~ class (4) n 069.7
~ -class people (3) n 069.7
~ -class white people (1) n 069.7
~ college (1) n 083.6
~ flat (1) n 029.4
~ forty (1) n 016.1
~ gallery (1) n 010.8
~ hall (1) n 007A.2
~ land (4) n 029.4
~ leg (1) n 072.7

~ limb (1) n 072.6
~ limbs (1) n 012.5
~ McKinney (1) 105.4
~ porches (1) n 010.9
~ school (1) n 125.7
~ terrace (1) n 010.9
Lower (9) 016.2
~ Branch Patch (1) 016.2
~ Creek (1) 030.7
~ Garden District (2) 106.6
~ Jackson Road (1) 031.7
~ Josie (1) AL 086.5
~ Little River (1) MS 030.7
~ Mississippi Valley (1) 097.8
~ Peach Tree (1) AL 087.1
Low(er) (2) 114.8
~ Commerce (1) 114.8
~ Wetumpka Road (1) 107.7
lowering (2) v/adj 036.3
~ day (1) n 005.5
Lowe's (1) 106.5
lowest (2) adj 064.7
lowing (149) v/adj 036.3
~ for (3) v 036.2
~ sound (1) n 036.3
lowland (196) n/adj 029.4
~ areas (1) n 029.4
~ bottom (1) n 029.4
~ farm (1) n 030.8
~ field (2) n 016.1
lowlanders (1) n 080.9
lowlands (37) n 029.4
Lowndes (19) AL GA MS 087.7
~ County (9) AL FL GA 087.3
~ Park (1) 106.4
Lowndesboro (3) AL 087.9
Lowry (4) 087.6
~ City (1) MO 086.7
~ Park (3) 106.4
lows (51) v 036.3
~ for (1) v 036.3
Loxahatchee (2) FL 087.8
~ River (1) TN 030.7
Loyd (1) MS 087.8
Loyola (2) 070.6

LPN (1) 084.6
LSD (47) 114.2
LSU (3) 070.9
   ~ Dairy (1) 015.5
   ~ Sugar House (1) 090.9
Lubbock (10) TX 087.1
   ~ County (1) TX 087.9
lube (4) n/v/adj 024.1
   ~ job (1) n 023.7
   ~ oil (1) n 024.1
lubed (1) v 023.7
lubricate (6) v 024.1
lubricated (4) v 023.7
lubricating (2) v/adj 023.8
   ~ oil (1) n 024.1
lubrication (1) n 023.7
Lucedale (4) MS 087.1
Lucie (2) 087.3
luciernagas (1) n S 060A.3
Lucifer (62) 090.1
Lucile (1) GA 087.3
Lucius (1) 090.1
luck (73) n/v/adj 012.9
   ~ upon (1) v 032.6
lucked (2) v 088.6
   ~ up (1) v 088.6
   ~ up on (1) v 053.5
luckiest (1) adj 053.5
lucky (55) adj 073.2
   ~ bone (5) n 037.1
   ~ ladies (1) n 115.7
   ~ piece (1) n 037.1
   ~ shoe (1) n 034.6
   ~ sucker (1) n 115.4
Lucky (2) 107.6
lucrative (1) adj 091.7
lucre (4) n 114.5
Lucy (13) 107.7
   ~ Street (1) 107.7
Ludington (1) LA 087.6
(Lue) Gim Gong oranges (1) n 088.7
Lufkin (1) TX 087.5
lug (60) v 098.1
   ~ with (1) v 098.1
lug[V-t] (1) v 098.1
Luger (3) 113.1
Lugers (1) 113.1
luggage (4) n/adj 123.7
   ~ bag (1) n 123.7
   ~ compartment (2) n 110.5

~ rack (1) n 110.5
lugged (144) v 098.1
luggers (2) n 024.6
Luke (4) 068.2
Lukens (1) FL 087.3
Luke's (1) 106.8
lukewarm Lizzie (1) n 124.4
Lula (1) MS 087.2
Luling (1) TX 087.5
lull (6) n/v 005.7
   ~ down (2) v 007.3
lullabies (1) n 130.8
lulled (1) v 007.3
lulling (3) v 007.3
Lullwater (1) 106.1
Lulu (1) 030.7
lumbago (11) n 079.6
lumber (58) n/adj 010.2
   ~ -board house (1) n 011.2
   ~ business (2) n 080.6
   ~ fence (2) n 016.4
   ~ fences (3) n 016.2
   ~ horses (1) n 022.1
   ~ house (2) n 007A.5
   ~ houses (1) n 014.1
   ~ mill (1) n 080.6
   ~ room (8) n 010.3
   ~ shed (1) n 084.9
Lumber City (2) GA 087.6
lumbered (1) v 080.9
Lumberton (6) MS 087.1
lumberyard (3) n 070.6
Luminol (1) 092.9
lump (13) n/v/adj 030.8
   ~ milk (1) n 047.6
   ~ sum (2) n 051.5
   ~ sums (1) n 051.5
   ~ up (2) v 037.2
Lump (1) 055.3
Lumpkin (7) GA 087.2
   ~ County (2) GA 087.1
lumps (4) n 030.8
lumpy (2) adj 090.4
Luna (1) AR 087.3
Lunar Landing (1) 031.4
lunatic (3) n 073.4
Lunceford (1) AR 087.8
lunch (148) n/adj 048.6
   ~ bags (1) n 019.5
   ~ basket (2) n 020.1
   ~ box (1) n 019.2
   ~ bucket (1) n 096.9

~ meats (1) n 121.6
~ pail (4) n 017.3
~ pails (1) n 019.2
~ sack (1) n 019.5
lunch[N-i] (3) n 080.3
luncheon (5) n/adj 048.6
   ~ meat (1) n 121.3
luncheons (1) n 130.7
lunches (2) n 048.6
lunching (1) v 048.6
lunchtime (2) n 002.3
Lunenberg (1) AR 087.9
Lunen(berg) (1) AR 087.9
lung (2) adj 052.1
   ~ things (1) n 052.1
   ~ trouble (1) n 076.4
lungeroni knife (1) n 090.8
lungs (19) n 037.2
Lunn (4) 044.4
Lunsford (1) AR 087.2
Lupia (1) 087.5
Lupton (2) 087.5
   ~ City (1) TN 087.5
   ~ Drive (1) 107.7
Lurleen (1) 030.7
lush (9) n/adj 113.6
   ~ head (2) n 113.6
lusty (2) adj 124.5
Luther (7) 068.6
Lutheran (18) 089.1
   ~ church (2) n 089.2
   ~ Church (1) 089.2
Lutherans (2) 089.2
Luthersville (1) GA 087.5
Lutherville (1) AR 087.2
Luverne (10) AL 087.3
Luxapallila (3) AL 030.7
Luxomni (1) GA 086.4
Luxor(a) (1) AR 025.8
luxuries (1) n 080.6
luxurious (1) adj 119.2
luxury (19) n/adj 109.4
   ~ car (11) n 109.4
   ~ cars (3) n 109.4
   ~ model (1) n 109.4
lyceum (2) n/adj 088.9
   ~ program (1) n 131.2
Lyceum (1) 084.4
lyceums (1) n 088.8
Lydgate (1) 068.2
lye (168) n/adj 084.8
   ~ corn (11) n 050.6
   ~ homily (6) n 050.6

~ hominy (74) n 050.6
~ hom(iny) (1) n 050.6
~ hopper (2) n 080.9
~ pot (1) n 017.6
~ soap (47) n 080.6
~ water (1) n 008.8
lyed (8) adj 050.6
   ~ corn (5) n 050.6
   ~ hominy (3) n 050.6
lying (43) v/adj 007.3
   ~ about (1) v 012.5
   ~ down (7) v 097.1
   ~ on (2) v 096.6
   ~ out (2) v 083.4
   ~ to (1) v 025.3
lymph (2) n 077.7
lynch (6) v 085.8
lynch[V-t] (1) v 085.9
Lynchburg (3) KY TN 087.2
lynched (6) v 085.9
lynching (6) n/v/adj 085.9
lynchings (1) n 085.9
Lynn (5) 087.5
   ~ Haven (3) FL 087.5
   ~ Mar Estates (1) 106.1
   ~ Mar Hills (1) 106.1
Lynnville (1) TN 087.2
Lynwood (7) 105.1
   ~ Creek (1) TX 030.7
lynx (1) n 059.5
Lyons (4) GA 087.2
   ~ Avenue (1) 105.4
   ~ Park (1) 106.4
Lyric Theater (1) 084.4

M

M (3) 030.6
~ and O Railroad (1) 030.6
~ -Fourteens (1) 001.7
ma (16) n 063.7
Ma (158) 063.7
~ -Mom (2) 064.2
maa (12) n/interj 036.2
maa(x2) (2) interj 036.2
ma'am (608) n 067.6
(m)a'am (1) n 091.4
(ma'a)m (45) n 100.4
Ma'am (2) 067.6
ma'ams (1) n 067.6
Mabelvale (1) AR 087.6
Maben (3) MS 087.3
Mableton (1) GA 087.6
Mabry (3) 107.6
mac (1) infix 085.2
Mac (2) 113.5
macadam (25) n/adj 031.7
~ paving (1) n 031.6
~ road (2) n 031.6
~ roads (1) n 031.6
macadamia (3) n/adj 054.8
~ nuts (2) n 054.8
macadamize (3) v/adj 031.6
~ road (2) n 031.6
(ma)cadamize (1) adj 031.4
macadamized (10) adj 031.6
~ road (1) n 031.6
~ roads (1) n 031.6
macadams (1) n 031.6
macaroni (3) n/adj 044.3
~ line (1) n 080.8
macaroon (1) n 122.2
macaroons (2) n 122.2
MacArthur (11) 068.3
~ Park (3) 106.4

MacArth(ur) Cemeter(y) (1) 078.8
MacArthur's birthplace (1) n 106.4
MacDill (1) FL 087.3
MacDonald (1) 098.4
mace (7) n 113.1
maced (1) v 098.6
Macedonia (3) AL GA LA 087.1
Macedoni(a) Ridge (1) MS 086.8
MacGregor (4) TX 030.7
~ Street area (1) n 105.5
~ Way (1) 106.2
Machado (1) 088.8
machen (1) v G 011.2
machete (31) n/adj 104.3
~ knife (1) n 104.3
~ knives (1) n 104.3
machetes (5) n 104.3
(ma)chetes (1) n 104.3
Machetunim (2) n G 066.5
machine (91) n/adj 023.6
~ house (1) n 011.7
~ oil (5) n 024.1
~ -oil (1) v 024.1
~ operator (1) n 063.4
~ shed (1) n 011.7
(ma)chine oil (1) adj 024.1
Machine (1) 130A.3
machinery (4) n/adj 045.1
~ companies (1) n 108.5
machines (20) n 109.5
machinist (1) n 065.8
machismo (1) n 080.8
macho (6) adj 125.3
machoism (1) n 084.8
mack (1) n 028.1
Mack (5) 111.2
~ chassis (1) n 111.2
~ truck (3) n 109.7
~ trucks (1) n 109.7
mackerel (77) n/adj 059.9
~ fish (3) n 059.9
~ snappers (4) n 126.6
Mackeroy Creek (1) LA 030.7
Mackey Branch (1) TN 030.7

mackinaw (2) n 027.1
Macon (587) AL GA MS NC 087.7
~ Bayou (1) AR 030.7
~ County (3) AL 087.2
~ home (3) n 025.5
~ Ridge (1) LA 030.8
~ Road (3) 031.6
macranny (1) n 080.8
mad (852) adj 075.2
~ dog (8) n 033.1
~ -dog bit (1) v 033.4
~ -dog bitten (1) v 033.4
~ spell (1) n 075.2
Mad (7) 114.7
~ Dog (5) 114.7
~ Dog parties (1) n 130.7
~ Dog Twenty Twenty (1) 114.7
Madagascar (2) 088.8
madam (71) n 113.5
Madam Queen (1) 063.2
madame (1) n 113.5
Madame (1) 067.7
madam's house (1) n 113.4
madams (8) n 113.5
madax (1) n 066.9
madder (4) adj 075.2
Maddox (2) 068.3
~ Park (1) 087.5
made (571) v/adj 048.8
~ a mistake (1) v 082.2
~ as if (2) v 100.1
~ away (1) v 100.2
~ benches (2) n 081.9
~ -down bed (3) n 029.2
~ for (1) v 045.9
~ from (5) v 025.2
~ him sorry (1) v 082.1
~ in (4) v 048.8
~ into (4) v 121.3
~ it (1) v 078.6
~ it legal (1) v 082.2
~ lake (1) n 030.6
~ lakes (1) n 081.8
~ lamps (1) n 024.3
~ land (8) n 081.9
~ like (20) v 100.1
~ love (1) v 081.4
~ of (8) v 074.4
~ off with (1) v 100.2

~ on (2) v 013.8
~ on like (1) v 100.1
~ onto (1) v 027.2
~ out (14) v 100.1
~ out for (1) v 041.1
~ out like (65) v 100.1
~ out of (37) v 019.6
~ over (6) v 036.1
~ soil (2) n 029.4
~ to (2) v 095.8
~ up (6) v 013.6
~ -up mind man (1) n 074.8
~ washcloths (1) n 018.5
~ with (4) v 011.7
mademoiselle (1) n 113.3
madera (1) n S 008.6
mades (1) n 027.7
Madison (46) AL FL GA LA MS TN TX 087.5
~ Avenue (6) 107.6
~ County (9) AR GA TN TX 087.4
Madisonville (8) LA TN TX 087.4
madman (1) n 124.5
madness (2) n 075.2
Madre (3) 030.3
Madrid (4) 087.4
madrigal singers (1) n 130.9
madstone (3) n 061.4
madstones (1) n 088.9
Mafia (3) 127.3
magasin (2) n F 014.3
magazine (3) n/adj 022.4
~ freak (1) n 125.5
Magazine (6) 107.6
~ Point (1) 106.3
~ Street (2) 107.6
magazines (2) n 081.8
Magdalen (8) 067.1
Magee (3) MS 087.7
Magees Creek (1) MS 030.7
Magevney House (1) 106.4
Maggie (1) GA 087.4
Maggie's dog (1) n 033.3
maggot[N-i] (1) n 125.2
maggots (1) n 081.8
magic lantern (1) n 084.4
magistrate (4) n 068.6

Magnesia Springs (1) FL
030.7
magnetic (2) adj 020.7
~ hammer (1) n 020.7
~ marbles (1) n 130.6
magneto (1) n 088.8
magnets (1) n 060A.5
magnificent (1) adj 089.6
magnolia (697) n/adj
062.9
~ bay (2) n 062.9
~ bays (2) n 062.9
~ building (1) n 106.7
~ bush (2) n 062.9
~ bushes (1) n 062.9
~ family (1) n 062.9
~ fig (1) n 062.9
~ leaves (1) n 062.9
~ logs (1) n 062.9
~ tree (59) n 062.9
~ trees (37) n 062.9
magnol(ia) (2) n 062.9
(mag)nolia tree (1) n
062.9
Magnolia (36) AL AR
MS 107.6
~ Avenue (1) 107.6
~ Bay (1) LA 030.3
~ Gardens (1) 105.6
~ grandiflora (1) n
062.9
~ Grove (2) 105.3
~ Park (1) 105.5
~ Petroleum Company
(1) 062.9
~ River (2) FL LA
030.7
~ Springs (2) AL 087.9
~ State (1) 062.9
magnolia[N-i] (1) n
062.9
magnolias (97) n 062.9
magnum (6) n 113.4
magnums (3) n 113.2
maguey (1) n 096.9
Mahan (3) 030.7
~ Creek (2) AL 030.7
mahogany (3) n/adj
061.8
~ wood (1) n 053.5
Mahogany Island (1) FL
087.3
maid (308) n/adj 082.4
~ bride (1) n 082.4
~ lady (1) n 065.2

~ nurse (1) n 084.6
~ of honor (235) n
082.4
~ sister (1) n 075.8
~ work (1) n 075.6
Maid (1) 055.7
maiden (11) n/adj 082.4
~ cane (1) n 015.9
~ canes (1) n 015.9
~ girl (1) n 082.4
~ name (2) n 085.4
~ of honor (1) n 082.4
~ voyage (2) n 024.5
maidish (1) adj 124.1
maids (11) n 082.4
~ of honor (1) n 082.4
mail (42) n/v/adj 027.5
~ boat (1) n 080.7
~ -boat landing (1) n
031.4
~ carrier (12) n 115.1
~ clerk (1) n 115.1
~ office (1) n 084.2
~ person (2) n 115.1
~ route (1) n 074.4
~ truck (3) n 109.6
~ trucks (1) n 109.6
~ woman (5) n 115.1
Mail (1) 087.5
mailbox (4) n 084.2
mailed (1) v 057.9
mailing address (3) n
100.8
mailman (109) n 115.1
mailmen (3) n 115.1
main (117) adj 107.6
~ artery (1) n 107.6
~ axle (1) n 021.8
~ bedroom (1) n
007A.3
~ bone (1) n 037.1
~ boss (1) n 069.6
~ business district (1) n
105.2
~ channel (3) n 032.7
~ city (2) n 085.5
~ dining room (1) n
007A.4
~ drag (4) n 107.6
~ drive (1) n 031.8
~ dwelling (1) n 014.1
~ family room (1) n
007.8
~ girl (2) n 081.6
~ guy (1) n 081.5

~ heater (1) n 118.4
~ highway (10) n 031.6
~ highways (2) n 031.6
~ horse (1) n 039.4
~ house (6) n 014.1
~ man (8) n 081.5
~ nigger (1) n 081.5
~ place (1) n 112.8
~ road (13) n 031.6
~ roads (2) n 107.6
~ room (6) n 007A.4
~ run (1) n 030.4
~ sitting room (1) n
007.8
~ squeeze (2) n 081.6
~ street (8) n 031.6
~ streets (4) n 107.6
~ thing (2) n 081.5
~ thoroughfare (2) n
107.6
~ thoroughfares (1) n
107.6
~ whore (1) n 113.5
Main (53) 107.6
~ Street (42) 107.6
Maine (13) 086.1
mainest (2) adj 026.3
mainline (1) adj 114.3
mainlined (1) v 115.6
mainliners (1) n 114.3
mainly (1) adj 074.4
maintain (1) v 080.7
maintained (3) adj 053.4
maintains (1) v 074.1
maintenance (78) n/adj
065.9
~ engineer (2) n 119.5
~ man (57) n 119.5
~ men (1) n 115.2
~ person (1) n 119.5
~ personnel (1) n 119.5
~ shop (1) n 011.7
~ upkeeper (1) n 119.5
mais (3) n F 020.4
Maishaus (1) n G 014.3
maison (5) n F 007.8
~ bois (1) n F 011.7
Maitland (1) FL 105.1
maitre (1) n F 068.5
maize (15) n 056.2
Majestic (1) 084.4
Majik (4) 116.2
~ Market (2) 116.2
~ Mark(et) (1) 116.2
~ Markets (1) 116.2

major (45) n/adj 068.4
~ arteries (1) n 107.6
~ artery (1) n 107.6
~ general (4) n 068.3
~ thoroughfares (1) n
107.6
Major (5) 069.6
Majorca (1) 070.9
majority part (1) n 095.8
majors (1) n 068.3
Majors Creek (1) AL
030.7
make (964) v 048.8
~ down (3) v 029.2
~ for (1) v 037.1
~ in (1) v 012.8
~ like (6) v 100.1
~ out (4) v 081.7
~ out like (14) v 100.1
~ -out parties (1) n
130.7
~ out [J-0] (1) v 100.1
~ up (23) v 028.1
make[V-p] (32) v 013.6
~ up (1) v 013.6
make[V-r] (1) v 013.6
maker (15) n 033.3
Maker (15) 078.6
makers (4) n 008.8
makes (156) v 013.7
~ out like (1) v 100.1
makeshift (12) n/adj
067.8
~ coal-oil lamp (1) n
024.3
~ lamp (2) n 024.3
~ light (1) n 024.3
~ old lamp (1) n 024.3
makeup (11) n/adj 099.7
~ men (1) n 099.7
making (223) v/adj 081.7
~ dates with her (1) v
081.4
~ down (1) v 029.2
~ eyes at her (1) v
081.4
~ eyes at you (2) v
024.9
~ it legal (1) v 082.2
~ like (1) v 100.1
~ love (2) v 081.4
~ love to her (1) v
081.4
~ out (47) v 081.7
~ out like (2) v 075.9

~ up (19) v 028.1
~ up for (4) v 005.6
makings (1) n 083.1
mal anglais (1) n F 079.7
Malabar (1) FL 087.6
Mal(abar) (1) FL 075.8
malabasters (1) n 069.5
maladjusted (1) adj 125.6
malaria (49) n/adj 079.7
~ fever (4) n 078.4
~ mosquito (1) n 060A.8
~ (mo)squitoes (1) n 060A.8
~ pills (1) n 078.4
malari(a) (3) n/adj 078.4
~ fever (1) n 078.4
malarial (19) n/adj 079.7
~ chills (1) n 078.4
~ fever (4) n 079.8
~ hematur(ia) (1) n 088.7
~ (mo)squito (1) n 060A.8
~ shots (1) n 078.4
Malden (1) MO 087.4
male (659) n/adj 033.5
~ animal (4) n 033.5
~ beast (2) n 033.5
~ bulls (1) n 033.5
~ calf (22) n 033.5
~ chicken (1) n 036.8
~ cow (95) n 033.5
~ cows (7) n 033.5
~ hog (114) n 035.3
~ hogs (7) n 035.3
~ homosexual (2) n 124.2
~ horse (64) n 034.1
~ horses (2) n 034.1
~ jenny (1) n 033.7
~ ox (2) n 033.5
~ parking (1) n 108.1
~ pig (4) n 035.3
~ pigs (2) n 035.3
~ prostitute (1) n 124.2
~ sheep (22) n 034.9
~ shoat (1) n 035.5
~ stock (1) n 033.5
~ yearling (2) n 033.5
males (28) n/adj 034.9
~ cow (1) n 033.5
Malibu Beach (1) CA 087.5
malicious (2) adj 101.4

~ apples (1) n 066.8
malignant child (1) n 065.7
maligned (1) v 075.8
malin (1) n F 073.5
malingerer (1) n 115.4
mall (17) n/adj 085.1
~ area (1) n 105.2
~ boulevard (1) n 031.9
Mall (16) 105.3
~ Boulevard (1) 107.7
mallard (2) adj 081.8
~ ducks (1) n 081.8
~ lake (1) n 087.7
mallards (1) n 059.5
mallet (28) n 020.6
Mallet (4) 030.7
~ Branch (2) MS 030.7
mallets (3) n 120.5
mallized (1) v 088.8
malls (14) n 085.1
malpractice suit (1) n 092.7
malt (7) n/adj 048.5
~ corn (1) n 050.8
~ liquor (3) n 121.9
Malvern (4) AR 087.5
Mam (2) 063.7
mama (1) n S 063.6
Mama Grande (1) S 064.2
Maman (2) F 064.2
mambo (1) n 083.1
Mamie (1) 064.2
mamma (170) n/adj 063.6
~ cow (2) n 033.6
~ dog (1) n 033.3
~ hen (2) n 063.6
~ hog (4) n 035.5
~ pig (2) n 035.5
~ sheep (2) n 035.1
Mamma (953) 063.7
Mam(ma) (5) 063.7
mamma[N-k] house (2) n 025.8
Mamma[N-k] room (1) n 043.9
mamma's (10) adj 124.1
~ boy (4) n 124.1
~ brains (1) n 006.3
~ bread is burning (1) n 130.3
~ mother (1) n 063.6
~ pet (1) n 064.4

~ room (1) n 007A.5
Mamma's (28) 063.7
~ bedroom (3) n 007A.6
~ cooking (1) n 063.7
~ half sister (1) n 063.7
~ house (1) n 053.5
~ people (4) n 066.5
~ place (1) n 063.7
~ room (4) n 007A.7
~ side (1) n 063.7
mammas (7) n 063.7
mammies (6) n 063.6
mammoth (1) n 056.9
Mammoth (3) AR 086.7
~ Spring (1) AR 086.2
mammy (39) n/adj 063.6
~ hog (1) n 035.5
~ sheep (3) n 035.1
Mammy (55) 063.7
mammy-peg (1) n 130.9
mammy's (1) adj 063.7
mamou (5) n/adj 061.4
~ tea (2) n 061.4
Mamou (3) LA 063.7
Mamzer (1) n G 080.8
man (2703) n/adj/interj 081.5
~ about town (1) n 124.7
~ cow (4) n 033.5
~ friend (2) n 081.5
~ groom (1) n 082.3
~ hog (2) n 035.3
~ horse (1) n 034.1
~ in the moon (1) n 092.8
~ -made (3) adj 030.6
~ -made channels (1) n 025.2
~ of color (2) n 069.3
~ -of-war (1) n 060.2
~ -of-war bird (1) n 091.8
~ person (1) n 088.7
~ pig (1) n 035.3
~ -powered lawn mower (1) n 120.1
~ preacher (1) n 081.8
~ tall (1) adj 002.6
Man (45) 064.4
~ above (1) n 089.3
man[N-i] (5) n 063.1
man[N-k] (11) adj 012.9
~ arm (1) n 012.9

~ business (1) n 043.9
~ name (2) n 043.9
~ poetry (1) n 043.9
manage (2) v 044.2
~ to (1) v 101.6
manageable (1) adj 073.2
management (1) n 085.6
managements (1) n 016.8
manager (100) n 119.5
manag(er) (1) n 119.5
managers (1) n 113.4
manana (1) n S 004.1
Manassas School (1) 125.9
Manatee (5) FL 087.6
~ County (4) FL 086.5
Manchester (5) GA TN 087.1
~ Highway (1) 107.5
manchineel (1) n 062.3
mandarin (3) n 055.1
Mandarin (3) FL 087.4
mandarins (2) n 081.8
Mandeville (4) LA 087.2
mandolin (2) n 020.5
mane (6) n 035.6
manes (2) n 035.6
maneuverated (1) v 092.7
mange (2) n 084.9
manger (19) n/adj F 014.5
~ place (1) n 015.3
mangers (2) n 080.8
manglier (1) n F 061.4
mango (11) n/adj 056.7
~ swamps (1) n 029.6
~ tree (2) n 061.8
~ trees (4) n 061.8
mangoes (4) n 061.8
mangrove swamp (1) n 029.7
Mangrove Key (1) FL 087.6
mangroves (2) n 029.7
mangy (2) adj 033.3
manhole (1) n 009.8
manhood (1) n 036.9
maniac (21) n 124.5
Manila (3) AR 087.8
~ rope (1) n 088.9
manipulate (2) v 065.8
manipulator (2) n 070.9
manly (1) adj 074.1
manna (1) n 007.5
manner (3) n 099.3

mannered (10) adj 073.7
mannerisms (7) n 065.3
manners (5) n 065.3
Manning (2) LA TX 087.4
mannish (12) adj 124.3
~ girl (1) n 124.3
manojo (3) n S 001.5
Manolo (1) S 064.4
Manor (2) 106.1
Manors (1) 105.1
man's (39) adj 065.5
~ ass (1) n 065.5
~ coat (1) n 027.2
~ job (1) n 001.1
~ mind (1) n 073.4
~ name (3) n 100.4
~ nose (1) n 101.7
~ robe (4) n 009.7
~ room (1) n 016.7
~ secrets (1) n 082.6
~ son (1) n 053.2
~ son-in-law (1) n 043.3
mans (3) n 041.9
manservant (1) n 091.8
Mansfield (13) AR LA TX 087.8
~ Flower Shop (1) 101.4
~ Road (1) 087.7
mansion (8) n 118.9
Mansion (4) 106.4
mansions (4) n 014.1
Mansura (1) LA 087.8
manta (2) adj 098.8
~ ray (1) n 098.8
~ rays (1) n 059.9
Mantachie (1) MS 087.2
manteca (1) n S 019.2
mantel (759) n/adj 008.4
~ board (54) n 008.4
~ boards (6) n 008.4
~ cloth (1) n 008.4
~ log (1) n 008.4
~ place (2) n 008.4
manteling (1) n 008.4
mantelpiece (296) n 008.4
mantel(piece) (1) n 008.4
mantelpieces (8) n 008.4
mantels (19) n 008.4
mantelshelf (44) n 008.4
manteltree (1) n 008.4
mantis (5) n 060A.4
mantises (1) n 060A.4

mantle (6) n 008.4
mantles (1) n 024.2
manual (21) n/adj 110.7
~ hedge trimmer (1) n 120.8
~ lawn mower (2) n 120.1
~ shift (1) n 110.7
~ transmission (4) n 110.7
~ -transmission car (1) n 110.7
~ -type (1) adj 120.1
manuals (1) n 110.7
Manuel Branch (1) FL 030.7
manufactured (2) adj 045.1
~ bread (1) n 045.1
~ gas (1) n 118.4
manufacturer (1) n 025.9
manufactures (1) n 099.5
manufactury bread (1) n 045.1
manure (13) n/adj 029.3
~ list (1) n 093.7
~ parlor (1) n 012.1
many (680) pron/adj 040.5
man(y) (6) pron/adj 090.7
Many (2) LA 086.4
manzanilla (2) n 061.4
map (8) n/adj 012.5
~ compartment (1) n 110.2
~ pocket (2) n 110.2
maple (988) n/adj 061.5
~ cove (1) n 061.6
~ crop (1) n 061.6
~ farm (1) n 061.6
~ forest (4) n 061.6
~ grove (38) n 061.6
~ orchard (24) n 061.6
~ orch(ard) (1) n 061.6
~ root (2) n 061.5
~ stand (1) n 061.6
~ sugar (1) n 051.3
~ -sugar orchard (1) n 061.6
~ syrup (139) n 051.3
~ syr(up) (1) n 051.3
~ -syrup orchard (1) n 061.6

~ -syrup trees (1) n 061.5
~ tree (140) n 061.5
~ -tree farm (1) n 061.6
~ -tree grove (1) n 061.6
~ trees (61) n 061.5
~ wood lot (1) n 061.6
~ worms (1) n 060.5
map(le) (1) n 061.5
Maple (12) 030.7
~ Creek (1) TX 030.7
~ Grove (7) AR KY TN 061.6
~ Hill (1) 061.6
~ Lake (1) TN 030.7
~ Slough Ditch (1) AR 030.3
~ Street (1) 107.7
maple[N-i] (3) n 061.6
Mapleine syrup (1) n 051.3
maples (57) n 061.5
Maplesville (2) AL 087.5
mapped out (1) v 057.8
maps (3) n 069.2
maque choux (3) n F 080.7
Mar (2) 106.1
Mar(ais) (1) 030.7
Marathon (4) FL 087.3
marauder (1) n 059.5
marble (39) n/adj 130.6
~ belt (1) n 080.7
~ company (1) n 012.9
~ egg (2) n 017.1
~ game (2) n 130.6
~ head (1) n 059.9
~ -head cats (1) n 059.9
~ heads (1) n 059.9
~ mantels (1) n 008.4
~ mill (1) n 084.8
~ names (1) n 052.1
~ quarries (1) n 084.8
~ shooter (2) n 098.4
~ tomatoes (4) n 055.3
~ top (1) n 009.2
~ -top dresser (2) n 009.2
~ -top dressers (1) n 009.2
~ -top furniture (1) n 009.4

~ -top table (3) n 080.7
Marble Falls (4) TX 087.8
marble[N-i] (4) n 130.6
marbles (132) n 130.6
Marbury (1) AL 087.3
Marcel (1) 123.9
Marcels (1) 123.9
march (2) n/v 075.6
March (983) 001A.6
~ -and-May dog (1) n 033.3
~ cotton (1) n 001A.6
~ redhorse (1) n 093.8
~ weather (1) n 007.4
marche (1) n F 052.8
marches (1) n 130.8
marching around the levee (1) n 089.9
Marco (2) 095.8
Marcos (7) 087.3
Marcus (1) 030.7
Mardi (13) 080.6
~ Gras (10) 080.6
~ Gras dance (1) n 083.1
~ Gras parades (1) n 098.9
~ Gras season (1) n 080.8
mare (806) n/adj 034.2
~ barns (1) n 015.2
~ colt (1) n 034.2
~ horse (10) n 034.2
~ mule (7) n 033.7
~ mules (1) n 033.7
mare[N-k] tail (1) n 005.3
Marengo (11) AL 087.1
~ County (6) AL 087.6
mare's tail (2) n 034.2
mares (46) n 034.2
Mares Gap (1) TN 031.3
Margaret (7) 067.1
margarine (8) n 065.8
margin (3) n 031.9
margins (1) n 107.3
Marglobe (1) 055.3
Marguerite (1) 067.2
Maria (23) MS 087.6
Mari(a) (1) 111.8
Marianna (7) AR FL 087.6
Marie (5) 067.1

Marietta (35) FL GA
087.6
~ boy (1) n 001A.3
~ boys (1) n 082.8
~ Highway (1) 031.7
~ Street (5) 107.6
Marigny (2) 088.8
marigolds (2) n 101.4
marijuana (157) n/adj
114.1
~ busts (1) n 114.1
~ cigarette (2) n 057.3
~ cigarettes (1) n 057.3
~ pusher (1) n 114.4
marijuan(a) (1) n 114.1
marina (6) n/adj 031.4
~ park (1) n 085.1
Marina (1) FL 087.6
marinade (1) n 048.5
marinas (4) n 031.4
marine (2) n/adj 070.6
~ tree (1) n 061.8
Marine haircut (1) n
123.6
Maringouin (1) LA 087.5
Marion (26) AL FL TN
087.4
~ Baptist Church (1)
089.2
~ County (5) AL FL
GA TN TX 087.3
~ Junction (1) AL
086.2
Maritime (1) 113.9
mark (54) n/v 036.1
~ -up man (1) n 099.8
Mark (4) 109.8
mark[V-p] (2) v 065.3
~ off (1) v 013.6
mark[V-r] (3) v 104.3
mark[V-t] with (1) v
032.3
marked (15) v 036.1
~ like (1) v 065.3
Marked Tree (1) AR
087.8
marker (4) n 107.3
markers (10) n 107.3
market (134) n/adj 116.2
~ bread (2) n 045.1
~ business (1) n 065.8
~ day (1) n 010.6
~ patches (1) n 016.1
~ people (1) n 046.8
Market (25) 106.6

~ Center (1) 106.6
~ Square Mall (1)
105.3
~ Street (2) 107.6
~ Street Bridge (1)
106.7
Mark(et) (1) 116.2
marketing (2) n/v 094.2
marketman (2) n 046.8
markets (6) n 116.1
Markets (4) 116.2
Markham (3) 107.6
~ Street (1) 107.6
marking (8) n/v 036.1
markings (3) n 107.3
marks (2) n 010.5
Marks (5) MS 087.5
Marksville (5) LA 087.2
marl (7) n/adj 029.8
~ soil (1) n 029.8
marlin (10) n 059.9
Marlin (2) TX 087.5
marlins (1) n 059.9
Marlon melon (1) n 056.7
Marlow (1) AL 087.3
marly rock (1) n 029.7
marm (11) n 067.6
Marmaduke (1) AR 087.3
marmalade (32) n 051.6
marmalades (2) n 051.6
Marmot (1) AR 087.6
Marner (1) 073.5
Maroon (1) 069.5
marrana (1) n S 035.5
marriage (23) n/adj 082.2
~ name (1) n 082.2
~ ring (1) n 123.1
marriages (1) n 082.2
married (1595) v/adj
082.2
~ at (1) v 052.5
~ couple (1) n 082.2
~ couples (1) n 025.2
~ daughters (1) n 082.2
~ from (2) v 025.8
~ life (1) n 082.2
~ name (5) n 082.2
~ off (4) v 082.2
~ students (1) n 082.2
~ to (1) v 053.5
~ woman (2) n 082.2
~ [P-0] (1) v 052.7
marries (5) v 082.2
marrow (6) n/adj 070.6
~ guts (3) n 037.3

Marrowbone Creek (2)
TN 030.7
Marrowfat (1) 055A.3
marry (85) v 082.2
~ over (1) v 024.8
mar(ry) (1) v 082.2
marry[V-r] (1) v 082.2
marry[V-t] (7) v 082.2
marrying (6) v 082.2
~ off (1) v 024.9
marse (10) n 069.6
Marse (5) 069.6
marsh (371) n/adj 029.7
~ area (2) n 029.7
~ buggies (2) n 029.7
~ creeks (1) n 030.6
~ field (1) n 029.4
~ grass (10) n 029.7
~ hen (3) n 080.7
~ horses (1) n 034.2
~ owl (1) n 059.2
~ region (1) n 029.7
~ swamp (1) n 029.7
~ wolves (1) n 033.3
Marsh (Isl)and (1) AL
087.7
marshal (3) n 084.8
Marshall (60) AL AR MS
TX 087.5
~ County (4) AL MS
087.8
~ Street (1) 107.6
Marshallville (1) GA
087.3
marshal's (1) adj 111.6
marshals (1) n 080.8
marshes (99) n 029.7
Marshes of Glynn (6) GA
029.7
marshland (112) n 029.7
marshlands (6) n 029.7
marshmellows (3) n 065.9
marshmelon (1) n 056.7
Marshwater (1) LA 087.5
marshy (79) adj 029.7
~ area (1) n 029.7
~ areas (1) n 029.7
~ ground (2) n 029.7
~ land (31) n 029.7
~ place (6) n 029.7
~ places (4) n 029.7
~ swamp (1) n 029.6
~ swampland (1) n
029.6
mart (1) n 116.2

Mart (12) TX 087.4
MARTA (10) 109.9
~ bus (2) n 109.9
Martha (867) 067.2
~ Washington (5) 067.2
~ Washington's son (1)
n 067.2
~ White (2) 067.2
Marth(a) (1) 067.2
Martha's (2) 067.2
~ Vineyard (1) MA
067.2
Marthas (1) 067.2
Marthaville (4) LA 067.2
~ High School (1)
083.2
Martian Mushroom (1)
106.4
martin (9) n/adj 096.7
~ bird (1) n 059.3
~ box (1) n 081.9
~ gourds (1) n 056.6
~ pole (1) n 080.9
Martin (27) GA TN 086.5
~ Creek (1) TN 030.7
~ Island (1) LA 087.3
~ Luther King (2)
066.9
~ Luther King Drive
(4) 107.7
~ Luther King Nursing
Home (1) 105.8
~ Park (1) 106.4
~ Street (1) 105.3
martins (8) n 059.3
Martinville (10) 087.4
marts (3) n 116.2
Marvell (2) AR 087.4
marvelous (1) adj 089.6
Mary (1098) 067.1
~ Jane (22) 114.1
~ Janes (2) 067.1
~ Karl (1) 067.1
~ Magdalen (8) 067.1
~ Pickford (1) 067.1
~ Todd (1) 067.1
~ Worth lye (1) n
081.8
Mar(y) (3) 067.1
Mary[N-k] house (1) n
070.4
Maryland (727) 086.1
~ Club (1) 086.1
~ State (1) 086.1
~ terrapin (1) n 060.7

Mary's (21) 067.1
Marys (17) 067.1
Marysville (1) CA 087.2
Maryville (10) TN 087.1
~ College (1) 106.4
masa (3) n S 080.9
masculine (22) adj 124.3
~ type (1) n 124.3
~ ways (1) n 124.3
mash (52) n/v/adj 050.8
~ potatoes (2) n 055.4
~ up (1) v 058.5
~ whiskey (1) n 050.8
mashed (4) v/adj 080.8
~ potatoes (3) n 055.4
masher (13) n 021.7
mashers (2) n 117.1
mashes (1) v 117.1
mashings (1) n 051.3
Mashulaville (1)   MS
087.1
mashy (5) adj 029.4
~ land (1) n 029.6
~ place (2) n 029.6
mask (2) n/v 012.2
mask[N-i] (1) n 083.8
Masking (1) 119.6
mason (2) n 060A.6
Mason (8) TX 087.4
~ City (2) FL 087.1
~ jars (1) n 090.8
~ Mill Road (1) 093.7
~ Ridge (1) AR 030.8
Masonic (2) 012.9
~ Lodge (1) 012.9
~ ring (1) n 123.1
masonry   home   (1)   n
007A.6
Masons (2) 089.2
~ Mill (1) GA 087.5
Mason(ville)   (1)   AR
087.2
mass (8) n 082.8
mass[N-i] (1) n 001.2
massa (24) n 069.6
Massa (6) 069.6
Massachusetts (719) 086.9
Massachus(etts) (3) 086.9
(Massa)chusetts (1) 086.9
massage (4) n/adj 117.8
~ parlor (1) n 113.4
~ parlors (2) n 113.4
massas (2) n 069.6
(masse)cuite (1)   n   F
051.2

Massee (1) GA 087.9
masses (1) n 012.2
masseuse (1) n 113.3
massive (1) adj 090.4
mast (15) n 065.8
~ -fed (1) adj 035.5
mast[N-i] (2) n 088.7
master (187) n/adj 069.6
~ bath (1) n 007A.9
~ bathroom   (1)   n
007A.5
~ bedroom   (38)   n
007A.4
~ meatcutter   (1)   n
046.8
~ pig (1) n 035.3
Master (23) 069.6
master's (7) adj 053.5
~ degree (1) n 053.5
~ name (1) n 069.6
~ room (1) n 007A.7
~ son (2) n 069.6
masters (8) n 069.6
masters' (1) adj 075.6
masticate (11) v 050.2
Mastin   Lake   Road   (1)
087.3
mat (5) n 029.2
Matagorda (14) TX 087.4
~ Bay (4) TX 030.3
~ Island (1) TX 087.7
~ Peninsula   (2)   TX
087.4
Matamoros (2) 087.5
Matanzas (3) 030.3
~ Inlet (1) FL 030.3
~ River (2) FL 030.7
match (25) n/v/adj 026.2
~ flooring (1) n 104.6
~ piece (1) n 026.2
~ suit (1) n 027.7
matchbox (5) n/adj 118.9
~ car (1) n 066.9
matched (2) adj 027.7
~ suit (1) n 027.7
~ team (1) n 033.7
matches (7) n 025.7
matching (7) v/adj 026.2
~ funds (1) n 084.9
~ scrap (1) n 026.2
~ suit (1) n 027.7
matchstick   (3)   n/adj
130.6
~ curtains (1) n 009.5
~ shades (1) n 009.5

mate (11) n 063.1
Matecumbe (2) FL 087.1
material (23) n 026.2
~ -wise (1) adv 080.6
maternal (6) adj 064.1
~ grandfather   (3)   n
064.1
~ grandmother   (2)   n
064.2
~ grandparents   (1)   n
063.8
mates (1) n 075.8
mathematics (1) n 066.9
Matheson Hammock (1)
106.9
Mathews Bridge (3) 106.4
Mathis Mill Creek (1) AR
030.7
Mathiston (1) MS 087.4
matinee dance (1) n 083.1
mating hog (1) n 035.3
matriarchal society (1) n
090.8
matriculator (1) n 068.7
matron (135) n 066.4
~ of honor   (113)   n
082.4
~ of hon(or)   (1)   n
082.4
~ [P-0] honor   (1)   n
082.4
matrons (3) n 082.4
~ of honor (1) n 082.4
mats (3) n 029.2
Matt (3) 067.5
matter (98) n/v 077.5
mattered (2) v 078.2
Matthew (793) 067.5
Ma(tthew) (1) 067.5
Matthew's (4) 067.5
Matthews (36) 067.5
matting (1) n 080.6
mattock (6) n 041.5
mattocks (1) n 120.6
mattress (30) n/adj 029.2
~ bed (1) n 029.2
~ cover (1) n 028.6
~ quilt (1) n 029.2
mattress[N-i] (1) n 013.7
mattresses (1) n 029.2
mature (28) v/adj 056.3
~ out (1) v 056.3
~ up (1) v 081.8
mature[V-t] (1) v 057.9
matured (6) v 065.6

matzo balls (2) n 044.7
Maud (2) MS 087.3
~ Sanders   Elementary
(1) 125.7
Maui (2) 114.1
~ Wowie (1) 114.1
maul (36) n/adj 020.7
~ head (1) n 075.7
Maulden Spring (1) GA
030.7
mauls (2) n 080.7
Maumelle Lake (2) AR
030.7
Maurepas (3) 030.7
~ Swamp (1) LA 030.7
Mauriceville (1) TX 087.3
Maury (3) TN 087.5
~ County (1) TN 087.2
mausoleum (94) n 117.6
mausoleums (11) n 117.6
maverick (3) n 033.8
maw (36) n 037.2
maws (3) n 037.3
Maxie (1) LA 087.2
maxis (1) n 123.3
Maxville (1) AR 087.6
Maxwell (8) 081.8
~ Air   Force   Base   (1)
106.5
~ Chapel (1) AL 087.6
~ Creek (1) AL 030.7
~ Field (2) 106.5
~ House (1) n 014.1
may (217) v 058.7
~ can (9) v 058.7
~ would (1) v 058.7
May (983) 001A.7
~ beetles (2) n 060A.1
~ horse (1) n 034.2
~ I? (5) 130.2
~ peach (1) n 054.3
~ peaches (1) n 054.3
~ redhorse (1) n 093.9
~ tree (1) n 062.9
mayapple   (25)   n/adj
061.4
~ root (7) n 061.4
~ roots (1) n 061.4
mayapples (4) n 056.8
Maybanks (1) TX 087.6
maybe (60) adv 058.6
mayb(e) (1) adv 070.1
Maybelle (1) TX 087.1
Mayberries (5) 062.5
Mayberry (4) 062.4

Mayersville (8) MS 087.2
Mayesville (4) AL 087.3
mayflies (1) n 060A.5
mayflower root (1) n 061.4
Mayflower (1) TX 087.3
Mayflowers (1) 060A.4
mayhaw (18) n/adj 062.5
~ jelly (1) n 051.6
~ tree (1) n 061.8
Mayhaw (1) GA 087.5
mayhaws (7) n 062.4
Mayhill (1) TX 087.9
Maynardville (1) TN 087.8
Mayo (1) FL 087.1
mayonnaise (3) n 065.9
mayor (22) n 068.8
may(or) (1) n 115.4
mayors (1) n 080.8
Maypole (5) 130.3
maypop (8) n/adj 084.9
~ berries (1) n 062.5
~ vine (1) n 015.9
maypops (4) n 056.8
Mayport (3) FL 087.1
Maysfield (1) TX 087.4
Maysville (2) 106.3
Mazarn Prairie (1) AR 087.8
mazuma (5) n 114.5
mazurka (2) n 083.1
McAlester (2) OK 086.8
McAllen (6) TX 086.8
McAnally Flats (1) 105.8
McArthur (1) AR 087.1
McCain Boulevard (1) 107.6
(Mc)Cain Boulevard (1) 107.6
McCall (3) LA 087.8
(Mc)Call temper (1) n 075.1
McCall(a) (1) AL 087.3
McCallie Avenue (1) 107.6
McCalls (1) MS 087.4
McCally Park (1) 085.1
McCaslan (3) 055A.4
~ beans (1) n 055A.4
McCaslans (2) 055A.4
McCloud Creek (1) MS 030.7
McComb (11) MS 087.4
~ City (3) MS 087.4

McCondy (1) MS 087.1
McCool (3) MS 087.5
McCorvy Mission (1) AR 086.4
McCoy (13) 106.5
~ Airport (1) 106.5
McCrory Creek (1) TN 030.7
McCullough (3) AL 087.9
~ Avenue (1) 107.9
McDaniel Street (1) 107.8
McDonogh Day (1) 080.6
McDonough (8) GA 087.1
McEwen (1) TN 087.1
McFarlane Park (2) 106.4
McGary Creek (1) TX 030.7
McGee (4) 030.7
~ Creek (1) MS 030.7
~ Tyson (1) 106.5
~ Tyson Airport (2) 106.5
(Mc)Gee Tyson Airport (1) 106.5
McGehee (6) AR 087.8
McGhee (5) MS 087.9
~ Estates (3) 106.1
~ Park (1) 106.4
McGlamery (1) TN 087.4
McGraw Creek (1) TX 030.7
McGregor (3) 107.7
~ Avenue (1) 107.7
~ Boulevard (1) 107.6
~ Isles (1) 106.2
McGuffey (2) 080.7
~ First Reader (1) 080.7
~ Speller (1) 084.8
McGuffey's Reader (1) 099.6
McGuire (1) 056.9
McHenry (1) MS 087.2
McIntosh (4) GA 087.5
~ Road (1) 107.7
McIntyre (1) GA 087.2
McKellar Lake (1) TN 030.7
McKenzie (2) AL TN 087.3
McKey Park (1) 085.1
McKims (1) LA 030.7
McKinney (4) TX 087.8
~ Bayou (1) TX 030.3

McKinnon Town (1) GA 086.6
McLennan (5) TX 087.6
~ County (3) TX 087.6
McManus (1) LA 087.5
McMinn (2) TN 087.3
McMinnville (3) TN 087.4
McNairy (2) TN 087.2
McNair(y) (1) TN 087.5
McNeill (1) MS 087.3
McNeils (1) GA 087.8
McPherson (1) 087.6
McQueeney (1) TX 086.8
McShann Road (1) 093.6
MD Twenty Twenty (1) 114.7
MDA (1) 114.2
me (7399) pron 042.5
m(e) (1) pron 123.5
Me Jane (1) 114.1
me[M-k] (1) pron 047.7
Meacham Field (1) 106.5
Meade (27) 106.1
meadow (405) n/adj 029.5
~ field (1) n 029.5
~ road (1) n 031.8
Meadow (9) 029.5
~ Lane (1) 107.9
~ View (1) 106.1
meadowland (10) n 029.5
meadows (50) n 029.5
Meadows (1) 105.5
meal (179) n/adj 048.4
~ bags (1) n 019.7
~ barrel (4) n 019.1
~ barrels (1) n 019.1
~ batter (1) n 044.8
~ bin (3) n 019.2
~ box (1) n 010.1
~ bread (1) n 044.5
~ chest (6) n 010.1
~ dumplings (4) n 050.3
~ gravy (1) n 044.7
~ gruel (2) n 050.3
~ house (1) n 010.1
~ mush (5) n 050.3
~ pokes (1) n 019.6
~ room (8) n 010.1
~ sack (24) n 019.6
~ sacks (3) n 019.6
~ soup (1) n 044.7
Meal (4) 044.4

~ Paymaster (1) 056.2
meal[N-i] (1) n 016.9
meals (19) n 8.6
mealworm (1) n 060.5
mealworms (1) n 060.5
mealy worms (1) n 060.5
mean (191) v/adj 074.9
~ ass (1) adj 080.8
~ day (1) n 005.5
~ green (1) n 114.5
~ -old (2) adj 033.5
~ to (9) v 101.2
mean[V-p] (7) v 039.8
meandering (1) v 088.7
meaner (4) adj 066.1
meanest (2) adj 102.5
meaning (5) n/v 103.4
~ t(o) (1) v 013.5
meanness (4) n 095.8
means (18) v 053.4
~ to (1) v 101.2
Meansville (2) GA 087.2
meant (5) v 074.7
~ to (1) v 103.6
meanwhile (1) n 004.6
meany (1) n 073.5
Mears Creek (1) AR 030.7
measle (2) n 079.7
measle[N-i] (1) n 079.8
measles (29) n 079.7
measure (57) n/v 007.9
meas(ure) (1) v 070.6
measured (3) v 065.9
~ with (1) v 032.4
measurement (4) n 065.8
measures (4) n 046.6
measuring (8) v/adj 065.9
~ baskets (1) n 020.1
~ container (1) n 007.9
~ spoon (1) n 017.8
meat (1640) n/adj 054.8
~ bench (2) n 065.8
~ box (2) n 046.3
~ butcher (1) n 046.8
~ cleaver (2) n 104.3
~ cow (1) n 080.6
~ curing (1) n 074.4
~ -curing time (1) n 080.6
~ eater (1) n 033.3
~ fork (1) n 017.9
~ grease (1) n 023.7
~ hog (12) n 035.4
~ hogs (4) n 035.5

~ hound (1) n 033.3
~ house (6) n 011.7
~ knife (3) n 104.3
~ knives (1) n 104.3
~ loaf (1) n 121.2
~ market (7) n 046.8
~ -market man (1) n 046.8
~ markets (2) n 116.3
~ -packer (1) n 046.8
~ patties (1) n 046.8
~ pie (1) n 048.4
~ pounder (1) n 088.9
~ skin (7) n 046.6
~ skins (9) n 046.6
~ store (1) n 116.3
~ wagon (4) n 111.5
~ wagons (1) n 117.5
Meat (1) 056.9
meatball (1) n 127.3
meatcutter (24) n 046.8
meated (55) adj 056.9
meatman (13) n 046.8
meats (9) n 046.2
MEBD Club (1) 080.7
mechanic (63) n 067.8
(me)chanic (1) n 067.8
mechanical-minded (1) adj 075.6
mechanics (8) n 067.8
Mechanicsville (8) 105.1
mechon (1) n S 024.3
Mechuleh (1) n G 096.7
Mecklenburg County (1) NC 087.5
med tech (1) n 080.6
medallion (2) n 028.4
Medallion bean (1) n 055A.3
Medart (1) FL 087.2
meddle (2) v 075.6
~ with (1) v 075.6
meddler (3) n 101.3
meddlesome (5) adj 101.3
~ butt (1) n 101.3
meddling (6) v 101.3
~ at (1) v 104.2
media (1) n 070.6
Media (1) 080.6
medial (1) 107.7
median (102) n/adj 031.9
~ strip (11) n 107.3
medians (5) n 031.9
medic truck (1) n 111.5
Medic (2) 111.5

medical (8) adj 111.5
~ center (6) n 106.4
Medical (5) 108.5
~ Arts (1) 108.5
~ College of Georgia (1) 083.6
medicated egg (1) n 017.1
medicinal (2) adj 061.4
~ herbs (1) n 061.4
~ purposes (1) n 053.5
medicine (50) n/adj 065.9
~ closets (1) n 009.6
~ doctor (1) n 099.5
~ shelf (1) n 008.4
medicines (1) n 061.4
medieval (1) adj 115.9
Medina (5) 087.3
~ County (2) TX 087.3
~ Lake (1) TX 030.7
~ River (2) TX 030.7
medinar(y) (1) adj 079.4
medio (1) n S 004.4
Mediterranean (3) 118.9
medium (30) n/adj 079.4
~ heel (1) n 123.8
~ land (1) n 029.9
~ rain (2) n 006.6
~ rock (1) n 130.8
~ shower (1) n 006.6
~ -size car (1) n 109.2
~ strip (2) n 107.3
Medulla (2) FL 087.6
meek (2) adj 073.2
Meek (1) AL 087.8
meet (303) v 091.8
~ his Father (1) v 078.5
~ his Maker (4) v 078.5
~ his reward (1) v 078.5
~ their Maker (1) v 078.5
~ up with (9) v 032.6
meet[V-p] (2) v 013.6
meeting (64) n/v/adj 089.2
~ bug (1) n 061.3
~ suit (1) n 027.7
meetings (8) n 081.9
meets (4) n/v 053.5
Meigs (3) GA 087.5
~ Field (1) 081.8
mejicano (2) n S 069.9
melaleuca (1) n 061.9

Melbourne (9) AR FL 087.7
mellow (11) v/adj 130.8
~ bugs (1) n 060A.3
~ melon (1) n 056.9
~ music (1) n 130.8
~ peach (1) n 054.4
~ -type dirt (1) n 029.8
~ up (1) v 084.8
~ yellow (1) n 069.5
Mellwood (1) AR 087.5
Melly (1) 067.3
Melmac (1) 080.7
melodic (1) adj 130.8
melodicon (1) n 088.9
melon (269) n/adj 056.7
~ bug (1) n 060A.4
~ eaters (1) n 069.3
~ patch (3) n 016.1
melon[N-i] (1) n 097.8
melongena (1) n 081.8
melongen(a) (1) n 081.8
melons (113) n 056.6
Melrose (3) LA TX 087.2
~ Drive (1) 107.7
melt (48) n/v 037.2
~ aways (1) n 122.2
melt[V-p] (1) v 013.6
melted (3) v/adj 047.5
melting (1) v 025.8
Melton Branch (1) TX 030.7
melts (2) n 037.2
Melungeons (2) 069.5
member (15) n 051.8
members (7) n 089.2
membership (3) n/adj 094.8
~ fees (1) n 094.8
memberships (1) n 102.4
membrane croup (1) n 079.7
membranous croup (3) n 079.7
memento (1) n 090.4
Memere (2) F 064.2
memorial (10) n/adj 078.8
~ garden (4) n 078.8
~ park (2) n 078.8
~ parks (2) n 078.8
~ service (1) n 079.2
Memorial (27) 106.1
~ Cemetery (1) 078.8
~ Drive (9) 107.7

~ Forest lots (1) n 078.8
~ Hospital (1) 084.5
~ Park (7) 106.4
memorials (1) n 106.4
memories (1) n 025.6
memorize (3) v 070.9
memorized (1) v 070.7
memory (8) n 075.6
Memphis (840) TN 087.5
~ International (3) 106.5
~ International Airport (3) 106.5
~ Mail (1) 087.5
~ soil (2) n 029.9
~ State (2) 087.5
men (145) n 082.8
Men (2) 126.8
men[N-k] (3) adj 095.8
~ clothes (1) n 095.8
~ garters (1) n 043.9
~ haircuts (1) n 123.9
Mena (13) AR 087.4
~ library (1) n 084.1
~ public school (1) n 083.5
~ Street (1) 087.4
menablers (1) n 044.6
menace (1) n 065.8
menage (1) n F 010.4
menagerie (1) n 055A.8
mend (2) n 088.3
mended (1) v 025.8
Mendenhall (4) MS 087.2
mending (1) v 057.4
Menefee (1) LA 087.5
menfolk (2) n 081.9
menfolks (12) n 080.6
menhaden (6) n 059.9
meningitis (8) n 079.7
Menlo (1) GA 087.7
Mennonites (1) 090.8
men's (16) adj 126.3
~ apparel (1) n 065.8
~ button shoes (1) n 092.8
~ clothes (1) n 025.1
~ pants (2) n 027.4
~ robe (1) n 009.7
~ room (7) n 126.3
~ suits (1) n 027.7
~ trousers (1) n 027.4
Men's Bible Class (1) 080.9

mens (20) n 053.4

mental (2) adj 080.8
~ (a)rithmetic (1) n 080.8
~ hospital (1) n 084.5

mentality (2) n 129.3

mentally (4) adj/adv 074.7

mention (2) v 024.7

mention[V-s] (1) v 013.8

mention[V-t] (1) v 058.3

mentioned (7) v 057.9

Menton (1) 087.9

Mentone (1) AL 087.7

menudo (3) n S 037.3

meow (1) n 036.2

Mephistopheles (4) 090.1

Mer Rouge (1) LA 087.8

mercantile (4) n/adj 080.9
~ business (1) n 065.8
~ store (2) n 065.9

Mercantile Bank building (2) n 108.5

merchandise (3) n/adj 081.8

Merchandise Mart (2) 108.5

merchant (8) n/adj 046.8
~ business (1) n 080.6
~ gift (1) n 095.7

merchants (1) n 092.8

Merchants' National Bank parking lot (1) n 108.5

merciful (1) adj 092.3

Mercurochrome (137) 078.3

(Mer)curochrome (19) 078.3

mercury (1) n 078.3

mercy (129) n/adj/interj 092.2
~ vehicle (1) n 111.5

mere d(e) vache (1) n F 033.6

Mere (2) F 064.2

merge (2) n/v 107.4

meridian (3) n 031.9

Meridian (33) MS 087.3

merienda (4) n S 048.5

meringue (10) n 048.5

Meriwether (5) GA 087.2
~ County (3) GA 087.3

merkle (1) n 088.7

Mermentau (7) LA 087.6

~ River (5) LA 030.7

Merriman's (1) 067.7

Merritts (1) 107.6

merry (471) adj 093.2
~ -go-around (1) n 022.7
~ -go-ride (1) n 022.7
~ -go-round (434) n 022.7
~ -go-rounds (20) n 022.7
~ -[V-0]-round (2) n 022.7

mer(ry) (25) adj 022.7
~ -go-round (22) n 022.7
~ -go-round swing (1) n 022.7
~ -go-rounds (2) n 022.7

me(rry)-go-round (1) n 022.7

Merry (847) 093.2
~ Christmas (826) 093.2
~ Chri(stmas) (1) 093.2
~ Christmas Gift (1) 093.2
~ Land (1) 093.2
~ New Year (3) 093.3
~ New Year's (2) 093.3

Mer(ry) (18) 093.2
~ Christmas (13) 093.2

Merryville (2) LA 087.2

Merthiolate (96) 078.3

(Mer)thiolate (3) 078.3

mesa (2) n 029.4

mesas (1) n 031.2

mescal (1) n 096.9

mescaline (11) n 114.2

mesh (43) n/adj 016.3
~ bag (6) n 019.7
~ bags (4) n 019.7
~ garden wire (1) n 016.3
~ sack (3) n 019.7
~ wire (11) n 016.3

mesquite (53) n/adj 061.7
~ leaves (1) n 061.4
~ limbs (1) n 016.4
~ post (1) n 016.5
~ tree (4) n 061.8
~ trees (9) n 061.8
~ wood (3) n 008.5

~ -wood fences (2) n 016.4

Mesquite (3) 131.2
~ Street (2) 107.7

mesquites (3) n 061.9

mess (123) n/v/adj 055A.8
~ around (1) v 080.9
~ facilities (1) n 088.9
~ hall (1) n 088.9
~ maker (1) n 101.3
~ up (1) v 082.5
~ with (9) v 084.9

message (74) n/adj 089.4
~ parlors (1) n 113.4

messages (1) n 089.4

messed (39) v 082.1
~ him up (1) v 082.1
~ up (36) v 102.6

messes (6) n 055A.5

Messiah (1) 089.3

Messiers Creek (1) GA 030.7

messieurs (1) n F 128.3

messing (15) v 080.3
~ around (3) v 081.7
~ (a)round (3) v 081.8
~ at (1) v 024.9
~ up (1) v 081.7
~ with (4) v 081.7

messy (17) adj 074.6
~ day (1) n 005.5
~ weather (1) n 005.5

met (66) v 032.6
~ his Maker (6) v 078.5
~ their glory (1) v 078.5
~ up (3) v 032.6
~ up with (5) v 032.6
~ with (1) v 032.6

Metairie (12) LA 087.5
~ Ridge (1) LA 084.9

Metair(ie) (1) LA 087.8

metal (168) n/adj 021.1
~ band (15) n 020.3
~ bands (11) n 020.3
~ barn (2) n 014.2
~ boat (3) n 024.6
~ bucket (21) n 017.3
~ buckets (7) n 017.3
~ building (2) n 011.7
~ can (1) n 019.2
~ cans (1) n 026.6
~ cap (1) n 066.9

~ casket (1) n 079.1
~ chunk (1) n 070.7
~ circles (1) n 020.3
~ collar (1) n 014.7
~ container (2) n 017.3
~ fence (5) n 126.1
~ fences (1) n 126.1
~ hammer mill (1) n 088.6
~ hoop (2) n 020.3
~ jalousies (1) n 009.5
~ locker (1) n 010.1
~ pail (6) n 017.3
~ pails (1) n 017.3
~ pipe (2) n 023.2
~ pipes (1) n 042.7
~ post (2) n 016.5
~ pot (1) n 017.6
~ rake (1) n 120.7
~ rim (14) n 021.1
~ rims (2) n 021.1
~ ring (2) n 020.3
~ rings (3) n 020.3
~ rod (1) n 009.7
~ roof (1) n 011.4
~ roofing (3) n 011.4
~ shoe (1) n 034.6
~ shoes (1) n 034.6
~ stand (1) n 008.3
~ strapping (1) n 020.3
~ strip (1) n 021.1
~ strips (3) n 020.3
~ syrup cans (1) n 019.2
~ tap (1) n 020.4
~ things (2) n 020.3
~ tin cans (1) n 019.2
~ tire (5) n 021.1
~ tires (1) n 020.3
~ tub (1) n 017.6
~ weatherboarding (1) n 011.2

metatarsus (1) n 072.1

meter (8) n/adj 110.1
~ parking (1) n 108.1
~ reader (2) n 115.2
~ readers (1) n 115.3

meterman (1) n 115.3

meth (1) n 115.5

metheglin (2) n 049.7

(me)theglin (1) n 050.9

method (3) n 017.2

Methodist (202) 089.1
~ church (37) n 089.2
~ Church (6) 089.2

~ kinfolks (1) n 012.2
~ pallet (2) n 029.2
~ pallets (1) n 029.2
~ preacher (2) n 089.4
Meth(odist) church (1) n 089.2
Methodist[N-i] (4) 089.1
Methodists (1) 089.1
Meto (4) 030.7
Metro (5) 111.7
~ Airport (2) 106.5
~ Plaza (1) 105.6
~ thing (1) n 111.5
metropolis (1) n 085.5
metropolitan (2) adj 077.8
~ area (1) n 077.8
~ government (1) n 085.6
Metropolitan Airport (2) 106.5
Metros (1) 112.5
Metter (3) GA 087.3
mettre (1) v F 025.8
meule de foin (1) n F 014.8
meulon (1) n F 014.7
mew (2) n 036.3
mewing (1) v 036.3
mews (3) v 036.3
Mex (12) 128.7
Mexboro (1) AL 087.2
Mexia (3) AL TX 087.6
Mexican (107) 114.1
~ alfalfa (1) n 014.8
~ -American (15) 128.7
~ -Americans (13) 128.7
~ boll weevil (1) n 080.7
~ bread (3) n 044.6
~ cooking (1) n 052.6
~ corn bread (8) n 044.6
~ cornmeal (1) n 044.7
~ Creek (1) AL 030.7
~ dance (1) n 083.1
~ descent (1) n 070.7
~ element (1) n 069.6
~ food (2) n 048.4
~ garden (1) n 050.5
~ general (1) n 068.3
~ girl (1) n 064.9
~ Gold (1) 114.1
~ grease (1) n 069.9

~ greaser (1) n 080.8
~ hat dance (1) n 083.1
~ hogs (1) n 035.9
~ house (1) n 088.6
~ hydraulic lift (1) n 023.3
~ lion (1) n 084.9
~ locust (1) n 061.2
~ marijuana (1) n 119.8
~ national (1) n 069.2
~ party (1) n 130.7
~ school (1) n 065.8
~ squash (1) n 056.6
~ squirrel (1) n 059.7
~ -style corn bread (1) n 044.8
~ wasp (1) n 060A.6
~ wets (1) n 069.3
~ woman (2) n 052.7
Mexican[N-i] (1) 052.6
Mexicanos (1) 128.7
Mexicans (45) 128.7
Mexico (273) 030.9
~ City (5) 087.5
~ dog (1) n 033.3
~ -grown (1) adj 114.1
Mexis (1) 128.7
Meyerland (1) 105.6
mezquite (1) n S 061.8
mezzanine (1) n 010.8
MF (3) 069.3
~ -er (1) n 069.8
Miami (188) FL OK 087.2
~ Avenue (3) 107.6
~ Beach (16) FL 087.3
~ International (1) 106A.3
~ International Airport (2) 106.5
~ River (4) FL 030.7
~ Shores (2) 106.3
miasma (1) n 081.9
Micanopy (1) FL 087.3
Micco (1) FL 087.4
mice (13) n 059.5
mices (3) n 016.7
Michigan (43) 086.3
mick (8) n 127.9
mickey (2) n 127.9
Mickey Metros (1) 112.5
micks (9) n 127.9
micro (4) n/adj 116.4
~ oven (2) n 116.4

~ ovens (1) n 116.4
microwave (84) n/adj 116.4
~ oven (39) n 116.4
~ ovens (8) n 116.4
microwaves (4) n 116.4
mid (19) adj/prefix 123.3
~ -calf (1) n 123.3
~ lady (3) n 065.2
~ -meal (1) n 048.6
~ -meal lunch (1) n 048.6
~ school (1) n 125.8
~ -thigh shorts (1) n 123.4
~ woman (9) n 065.2
~ women (2) n 065.2
Mid (4) LA 087.1
midafternoon (3) n 002.4
midday (7) n/adj 002.3
~ meal (1) n 002.3
~ snack (1) n 048.6
middies (1) n 092.8
middle (132) n/adj 064.7
~ age (2) n 064.7
~ -age (1) adj 073.1
~ back room (1) n 007A.4
~ bedroom (9) n 007A.4
~ breaker (1) n 021.6
~ brother (1) n 053.2
~ child (2) n 064.7
~ class (4) n 065.8
~ -class neighborhoods (1) n 106.2
~ cutting (1) n 041.5
~ day (1) n 002.3
~ dinner (1) n 080.8
~ finger (1) n 072.5
~ hand (1) n 072.1
~ line (1) n 107.3
~ man (2) n 093.8
~ name (3) n 012.2
~ porch (2) n 007A.4
~ room (11) n 010.3
~ school (23) n 125.8
~ schools (5) n 125.8
~ -size cars (1) n 109.2
~ students (1) n 125.8
~ swing (1) n 090.9
mid(dle) (2) n 004.4
Middle (24) 086.4
~ Atlantic States (1) 086.4

~ City (2) TN 087.5
~ Colyell (1) LA 030.7
~ Creek (5) LA TN TX 030.7
~ Fork (2) AR TN 030.7
~ Georgia (2) 086.3
~ Prong (1) TN 030.7
~ River (1) LA 030.7
~ Shop (1) 106.3
~ Slough (1) AR 030.3
~ Sulphur (1) TX 086.5
~ Tennessee (3) 086.6
~ Tennessee soap trough (1) n 080.8
middlebreaker (1) n 021.9
middlebreakers (1) n 021.6
Middlebrook Pike (1) 106.9
Middleburg (1) TN 087.7
middlebust (3) v 021.6
~ up (1) v 021.6
middlebusted (1) v 021.6
middlebuster (145) n 021.6
middlebusters (24) n 21.6
middles (17) n 041.2
Middlesboro (2) KY 087.3
middlesplitter (3) n 021.6
middleways (2) adv 084.9
middling (446) n/adj 046.4
~ meat (57) n 046.4
~ -meat gravy (1) n 048.5
~ meats (1) n 046.4
~ part (2) n 046.4
~ side (1) n 046.4
middlings (97) n/adj 046.4
~ slab (1) n 046.4
middy (4) n/adj 123.3
~ blouses (2) n 081.8
~ shorts (1) n 123.4
midevening (4) n/adj 002.3
~ snack (2) n 048.6
Midfield (3) AL 087.4
midget (5) n/adj 056.7
~ dog (1) n 073.8
~ snake (1) n 093.5
Midland (2) TX 086.2
Midlothian (1) TX 087.8

midmorning snack (1) n
048.6

midnight (179) n/adj
002.7

~ special (3) n 113.1

Midnight (1) 099.6

midrib (1) n 070.9

midsection (1) n 046.4

midsize (2) n 109.2

midterm exams (1) n
101.2

Midtown (11) 105.1

~ Center (1) 105.3

~ Cinema (1) 114.9

midway (3) n/adj 028.9

~ wife (1) n 065.2

Midway (6) AL GA TX
087.4

midways (1) n 123.3

midwest (1) n 070.7

Midwest (2) 015.5

~ Dairies (1) 015.5

Midwestern topsoil (1) n
029.8

midwife (793) n/adj
065.2

~ woman (1) n 065.2

(mid)wife (4) n 063.2

midwife[N-i] (1) n 065.2

midwifery (1) n 065.2

Midwife's Association (1)
065.2

midwifing (1) n 065.2

midwives (72) n 065.2

Mier (2) 087.7

might (1827) v 058.7

~ can (55) v 058.7

~ can't (1) v 058.8

~ could (248) v 058.7

~ couldn't (2) v 058.7

~ could've (1) v 058.7

~ ought to (4) v 058.8

~ should (3) v 058.8

~ will (2) v 058.7

~ would (45) v 058.7

~ wouldn't (3) v 058.7

mightily (1) adv 081.8

mighty (397) adj/adv
090.6

mignon (23) adj 131.3

migraine (1) n 066.8

migrant (2) adj 108.6

~ work shacks (1) n
108.6

~ workers (1) n 080.8

migrate[V-t] from (1) v
095.7

migrated (3) v 131.3

~ from (1) v 131.3

migrator (1) n 075.6

Miguel (1) 087.4

mike (1) n 080.7

Milam (6) TX 107.8

~ building (1) n 108.5

~ Warehouse (1) 106.4

milan (1) n 084.8

Milan (5) GA TN 087.4

milch (1) n 033.6

Milchschup(pen) (1) n G
015.5

mild (33) adj 007.4

~ day (2) n 005.4

~ days (1) n 005.4

~ -mannered (7) adj
073.2

~ sausage (2) n 121.6

~ -tempered (3) adj
121.6

milder (6) adj 026.3

mildew (3) n/v 047.5

~ on (1) v 093.5

mildewed (2) v 047.5

mile (76) n/adj 088.1

~ jumper (1) n 060.4

~ leaper (1) n 060.3

Mile (8) 030.7

~ Branch (1) GA 030.7

mile[N-i] (305) n 088.1

milepost (1) n 074.8

miles (1337) n 088.1

Miles Landing (2) MS
087.6

mileses (1) n 088.1

Milford (1) GA 087.8

military (7) n/adj 066.8

~ cemetery (1) n 078.8

~ cut (1) n 123.9

~ heels (1) n 123.8

~ road (3) n 031.7

Military Highway (1)
031.6

Militia (1) 087.5

milk (2596) n/v/adj 048.2

~ barn (16) n 015.3

~ bottles (1) n 070.9

~ box (9) n 015.5

~ bread (4) n 044.6

~ break (2) n 015.3

~ bucket (129) n 017.3

~ buckets (30) n 017.3

~ calf (1) n 033.8

~ can (5) n 048.2

~ cans (4) n 017.3

~ cap (1) n 015.3

~ cattle (1) n 015.3

~ check (1) n 081.8

~ cheese (3) n 048.1

~ closet (2) n 015.5

~ coffee (2) n 032.4

~ companies (1) n
015.5

~ cooler (9) n 015.5

~ coolers (2) n 015.5

~ country (1) n 048.2

~ cow (144) n 033.6

~ cows (71) n 033.6

~ crock (1) n 017.3

~ crocks (1) n 080.8

~ cup (1) n 017.3

~ dairies (2) n 015.5

~ dairy (40) n 015.5

~ dai(ry) (1) n 015.5

~ drinker (1) n 048.2

~ farm (4) n 015.5

~ gap (24) n 015.3

~ glass (2) n 048.9

~ gravy (3) n 048.5

~ hole (1) n 015.5

~ house (36) n 015.5

~ houses (6) n 015.5

~ jug (1) n 015.5

~ lot (12) n 015.3

~ pail (130) n 017.3

~ pails (15) n 017.3

~ parlor (2) n 015.3

~ pen (12) n 015.3

~ pens (1) n 015.3

~ pig (1) n 035.5

~ pits (1) n 015.5

~ place (4) n 015.3

~ plant (2) n 015.5

~ punch (1) n 050.8

~ room (5) n 015.3

~ safe (6) n 015.5

~ separators (1) n
090.8

~ shelf (1) n 015.5

~ stall (1) n 015.3

~ stool (1) n 015.3

~ strainer (1) n 048.2

~ -strainer rags (1) n
018.3

~ strainers (2) n 048.2

~ time (5) n 037.4

~ toast (1) n 050.3

~ -toast (1) n 063.1

~ trough (3) n 015.5

~ truck (1) n 109.6

~ trucks (1) n 109.6

~ walk (1) n 080.6

~ well (1) n 015.5

milked (11) v 048.2

milker (1) n 037.7

milking (137) n/v/adj
048.2

~ barn (13) n 015.3

~ barns (2) n 015.3

~ bucket (1) n 017.3

~ buckets (1) n 017.3

~ churn (1) n 019.3

~ corral (1) n 015.3

~ cow (1) n 033.6

~ cows (2) n 033.6

~ gap (1) n 015.3

~ house (3) n 015.3

~ lot (3) n 015.3

~ machine (1) n 039.8

~ machines (1) n 095.9

~ pail (6) n 017.3

~ pails (1) n 017.3

~ parlor (8) n 015.3

~ parlors (2) n 015.3

~ pen (2) n 015.3

~ place (1) n 015.3

~ room (2) n 015.3

~ shed (9) n 015.3

~ sheds (1) n 015.3

~ stall (7) n 015.1

~ stalls (1) n 015.3

~ stool (1) n 049.3

~ time (25) n 037.4

milkman (2) n 048.2

milks (4) n/v 053.5

milkshake (1) n 048.5

milkshed (25) n 015.3

milksheds (3) n 015.3

milkweed (3) n 015.9

milky (3) adj 032.4

mill (206) n/adj 019.8

~ boss (1) n 069.6

~ day (1) n 080.8

~ district (1) n 080.6

~ element (1) n 080.7

~ rock (1) n 023.5

~ town (2) n 080.6

~ village (1) n 080.6

~ work (1) n 031.6

Mill (62) 030.3

~ Bayou (1) TN 030.3

~ Branch (1) MS 030.7

~ Creek (25) AL AR FL GA MS TN TX 030.7
~ Creek School (1) 070.7
Millbrook (1) AL 070.8
milled (2) v 081.8
Milledgeville (13) GA 087.7
miller (47) n/adj 060A.1
~ bug (5) n 060A.1
~ bugs (2) n 060A.1
~ flies (1) n 060A.1
~ fly (5) n 060A.1
~ moths (1) n 060A.1
~ worms (1) n 060.5
Miller (13) AR GA 087.7
~ County (4) AR GA 087.1
~ Count(y) (1) GA 087.7
~ Creek (1) AR 030.7
~ Outdoor Theater (1) 084.4
Millermore (2) 106.4
~ House (1) 106.4
miller's (2) adj 019.8
~ portion (1) n 019.8
~ turn (1) n 019.8
Miller's Garage (1) 108.4
millers (23) n 060A.1
Millers (4) 087.2
~ Chapel (2) AR 087.2
~ Cove (1) TN 030.3
~ Creek (1) TX 030.7
~ Garage (1) 108.4
Millerville (1) LA 087.9
millet (6) n 051.3
millhouse (3) n 011.9
millhouses (2) n 118.9
Millican (1) TX 087.4
Millicent Way (1) 107.7
Millikianates Road (1) 095.9
Millikin Plantation (1) LA 087.3
millinery (1) n 088.7
milling (9) n/v 019.8
Millington (3) TN 087.1
million (733) n/adj 001A.2
~ -dollar (1) adj 001A.2
~ -dollar home (1) n 001A.2

~ -dollar man (1) n 001A.2
~ -dollar smile (1) n 073.9
millionaire (29) n 001A.2
millionaire's play-pretty (2) n 099.8
millionaires (10) n 001A.2
millions (44) n 001A.2
millpond (3) n 030.6
Millpond (1) 030.7
mills (23) n 080.8
Mills (6) GA 087.8
Millsaps (2) 083.6
millstone (1) n 023.5
Millville (2) 105.9
millwright (2) n 080.6
Milneburg (1) LA 087.2
Milner (2) GA 087.6
milo (11) n/adj 041.5
~ corn (1) n 056.2
~ maize (4) n 099.6
Milstead (1) AL 087.1
Milton (7) AL FL MS 087.4
~ Road (1) 107.7
Milwaukee (4) WI 087.3
Mima (15) 064.2
mimeographed (1) v 070.7
Mimi (9) 064.2
mimics (1) v 065.3
mimmytoes (1) n 055.3
mimosa (60) n/adj 061.8
~ tree (10) n 061.9
~ trees (7) n 061.9
mimosas (10) n 061.8
Mims (2) FL 087.6
mincemeat (8) n/adj 047.1
~ pies (1) n 048.3
mind (131) n/v 070.9
~ out (1) v 043.5
mind[N-i] (5) n 075.3
minded (33) v/adj 065.4
Minden (7) LA 087.5
mindful (1) adj 081.9
mindless (4) adj 074.7
mine (441) n/pron 043.4
Mine (4) 030.7
mineral spirits (2) n 118.4
Mineral (2) 030.7
~ Spring Hollow (1) AL 087.7
mines (5) n/pron 043.4

Minette (6) 087.2
mingledy (1) adj 055A.3
Mingo (4) TN 030.7
~ Stream (1) TN 030.7
~ Suck (1) TN 030.7
~ Sucks (1) TN 030.7
~ Swamp (1) TN 029.6
mini (8) prefix 123.9
~ -Afro (1) n 123.9
~ -boot (1) n 123.8
~ -grill (1) n 116.4
~ -kid (1) n 002.6
~ -marts (1) n 116.2
~ -pickups (1) n 109.7
~ -track meets (1) n 130.2
Mini (3) 116.2
~ Market (1) 116.2
~ Markets (2) 116.2
miniature (13) n/adj 065.8
~ dog (1) n 033.3
~ hand shovel (1) n 120.5
~ lobster (1) n 060.8
~ okra (1) n 055.8
~ store (1) n 116.2
~ tomato (1) n 055.3
~ tomatoes (3) n 055.3
miniatures (1) n 055.3
minibus (1) n 109.8
minibuses (3) n 109.6
minie ball (4) n 088.7
minimum (1) n 065.8
mining (2) n 080.6
minishorts (2) n 123.4
minister (18) n 067.8
ministry (1) n 089.5
Minita (1) 030.7
mink (68) n/adj 059.5
~ farming (1) n 066.9
mink[N-i] (1) n 059.5
minks (42) n 059.5
Minneapolis (1) MN 087.5
Minnesota (19) 086.1
minnied (1) v 036.4
minnies (1) n 061.2
minnow (234) n/adj 061.2
~ fish (1) n 061.2
~ fishes (1) n 061.2
~ hatchery (1) n 061.2
~ net (1) n 061.2
~ seine (1) n 061.2

min(now) (1) n 061.2
Minnow Creek (1) AR 030.7
minnow[N-i] (3) n 061.2
minnows (613) n 061.2
minny (1) interj 037.6
Minorca (2) 060.1
Minorcan family (1) n 066.8
Minorcans (2) 128.4
Minorcas (2) 080.7
minors (1) n 068.7
Minot (1) 096.7
minstrel shows (1) n 091.9
mint (7) n 061.4
Mint Spring (1) MS 030.7
Minter City (2) MS 087.5
mintweed (1) n 061.4
minuet (3) n 083.1
minute (780) n/adj 070.5
~ steak (1) n 121.1
~ steaks (1) n 121.1
min(ute) (5) n/adj 045.9
~ savers (1) n 116.2
Minute (6) 116.2
~ Market (3) 116.2
~ Markets (2) 116.2
~ Mart (1) 116.2
minute[N-i] (9) n 070.3
minutes (429) n 070.3
Minutes (1) 070.2
miracle baby (1) n 088.8
Miracle Mile (1) 106.5
mire (3) n 029.6
mirliton (3) n 056.6
mirlitons (1) n 056.5
mirror (51) n 009.2
mir(ror) (2) n 009.2
mirror[N-i] (2) n 027.2
mirrors (6) n 009.2
miry (6) adj 029.7
~ kind (1) n 029.6
misbehaving (1) v 081.7
miscellaneous (1) adj 042.5
mischief (6) n 070.6
mischievous (20) adj 066.8
mischievousness (1) n 075.6
miser (317) n 073.5
miserable (16) adj 005.5
~ day (5) n 005.5

~ -looking weather (1) n 005.6
~ weather (1) n 007.1
Misere (1) 030.7
miseries (3) n 078.5
misering (1) v 073.5
miserly (7) adj 073.5
misers (7) n 073.5
misery (5) n 079.6
misfit (3) n 069.8
misfits (1) n 069.5
misfortune (1) n 080.6
Mishegoss (1) n G 080.9
Mishpokhe (1) n G 066.5
miss (32) n/v 092.8
~ classes (1) v 083.4
~ school (3) v 083.4
Miss (120) 067.6
~ Amy Vanderbilt (1) 125.5
~ Howell's Dancing School (1) 083.1
~ Intelligent (1) 125.5
~ It (1) 125.6
~ so-and-so (1) n 067.7
miss[V-r] (2) v 052.5
~ school (1) v 083.4
miss[V-t] (1) v 083.4
missed (8) v 053.5
~ class (1) v 083.4
~ his class (1) v 083.4
~ the class (1) v 083.4
missing (3) v/adj 055.1
mission (8) n/adj 113.8
~ club (1) n 053.2
Mission (12) TX 087.4
~ Valley (1) TX 087.2
missionary (2) n/adj 067.8
~ meeting (1) n 080.8
Missionary (26) 089.1
~ Baptist (18) 089.1
~ Baptist church (3) n 089.1
~ Baptist preacher (1) n 089.1
~ Ridge (2) 105.2
Missionar(y) (4) 089.1
~ Baptist (2) 089.1
missions (7) n 113.8
Mississippi (1247) 086.7
~ bottom (2) n 086.7
~ bottomlands (1) n 086.7
~ bottoms (1) n 029.4

~ Coliseum (1) 106.4
~ County (4) AR 086.7
~ Cracker (1) 069.7
~ Delta (7) 029.5
~ Delta blues (1) n 130.9
~ Flyway (1) AR 030.7
~ line (2) n 086.7
~ loam (1) n 029.9
~ red-neck (3) n 069.7
~ River (112) AR LA MS TN 030.7
~ River drainage (1) n 030.1
~ River pilot (1) n 084.8
~ River steamboat (1) n 024.6
~ River water (1) n 030.7
~ silt (1) n 029.9
~ Sound (1) LA 030.7
~ State (4) 086.7
~ thin skin (1) n 050.5
~ Valley (5) 086.7
~ water (1) n 030.7
Mississip(pi) (7) 086.7
~ River (2) MS 030.7
(Missis)sippi (1) 086.7
Mississippian (3) 069.8
Mississippians (3) 069.5
Missouri (821) 086.6
~ Kansas Texas (1) 084.8
~ line (1) n 086.6
~ minnow (1) n 061.2
~ minnows (1) n 061.2
~ mule (2) n 033.7
~ Pacific (2) 086.6
~ -Pacific Line Railroad (1) 086.6
~ -Pacific Railroad (1) 086.6
~ River (1) 030.7
~ Wonders (1) 055A.4
Missour(i) (9) 086.6
~ -Pacific Railroad (1) 086.6
missus (20) n 063.2
miss(us) (2) n 063.2
Missus (1) 067.7
missy (2) n 064.9
Missy (5) 067.7
mist (281) n/v/adj 006.6
~ -like (1) adj 006.6

~ onion (1) n 055.7
~ rain (3) n 006.6
mistake (4) n 085.6
mistaken (2) adj 070.6
mistakes (1) n 013.1
misted (2) v 006.6
mister (7) n/adj 063.1
~ rat (1) n 099.4
Mister (267) 069.6
~ -and-Mrs. chest (1) n 009.2
~ Arthritis (1) 079.6
~ Bad Man (1) 090.1
~ Boss (1) 069.6
~ Do-Right (1) 112.5
~ Fantastic (1) 114.2
~ Got Rocks (1) 109.4
~ Intelligent (1) 125.5
~ Natural (1) 114.2
~ Nixon (1) 052.6
~ (O)possum (1) 059.5
~ Policeman (1) 112.5
~ Scrooge (1) 073.5
~ Skunk (2) 059.5
~ so-and-so (8) n 069.6
Mist(er) (6) 069.6
Misters (1) 063.2
misting (80) v/adj 006.6
~ rain (25) n 006.6
mistletoe (6) n 062.2
mistress (28) n 067.6
Mistress (13) 069.7
~ Cooper (1) 067.7
~ Lady (1) 067.7
mistresses (1) n 113.3
mists (1) n 006.6
Mists (1) 119.7
misty (52) n/adj 006.6
~ day (4) n 006.6
~ moisture (1) n 006.6
~ morning (1) n 006.6
~ rain (11) n 006.6
~ rains (1) n 006.6
~ shower (1) n 006.6
~ weather (1) n 006.6
Mitchell (12) GA 087.5
~ County (2) GA 087.4
~ Home (1) 106.4
~ Yellow Meat (1) 056.9
Mitchellville (2) 105.4
mite (11) n F 060A.2
miter (3) adj 022.1
~ box (2) n 022.1
~ saws (1) n 080.7

mites (7) n 060A.9
mitten (1) n 082.1
mix (254) n/v/adj 069.5
~ bag (1) n 075.6
~ -blooded (3) adj 069.5
~ -blooded dog (1) n 033.3
~ bred (1) n 033.3
~ breed (143) n 033.3
~ -breed child (1) n 069.5
~ -breed dog (16) n 033.3
~ -breeded (1) adj 069.5
~ breeds (7) n 069.5
~ child (2) n 069.5
~ children (1) n 069.5
~ colored (1) n 069.5
~ colors (1) n 069.5
~ dirt (2) n 029.8
~ dog (14) n 033.3
~ dogs (3) n 033.3
~ feed (1) n 065.8
~ fertilize (1) n 029.3
~ folks (1) n 069.5
~ hound (1) n 033.3
~ land (3) n 029.8
~ man (1) n 069.5
~ -marriage baby (1) n 069.5
~ people (1) n 069.5
~ race (11) n 069.5
~ sandwiches (1) n 121.7
~ soil (2) n 029.9
~ team (1) n 033.7
~ terrier (1) n 033.3
~ -up (1) n 033.3
~ vegetable[N-i] (2) n 050.4
~ vegetables (1) n 050.4
mix[V-t] with (2) v 029.8
mixblood (10) n 069.5
mixbloods (1) n 128.3
mixed (186) n/v/adj 033.3
~ blood (11) n 069.5
~ -blooded (2) adj 069.5
~ breed (53) n 033.3
~ -breed (1) adj 128.3

~ -breed dog (4) n 033.3
~ -breed people (1) n 069.5
~ breeds (2) n 069.5
~ child (2) n 069.5
~ dog (6) n 033.3
~ dogs (2) n 033.3
~ feed (1) n 014.4
~ greens (1) n 055A.5
~ kid (1) n 069.5
~ land (1) n 029.8
~ marriage (1) n 069.5
~ niggers (1) n 069.5
~ race (6) n 069.5
~ tumor (1) n 069.5
~ up (2) v 058.6
~ -up (4) adj 033.3
~ -up breed (4) n 033.3
~ -up child (2) n 069.5
~ -up cur dog (1) n 033.3
~ -up dog (7) n 033.3
~ -up family (2) n 069.5
~ -up people (1) n 069.5
~ -up race (3) n 069.5
~ vegetables (1) n 050.4
~ with (1) v 076.8
mixer (3) n 048.5
mixers (1) n 130.7
mixing (2) v 057.4
~ up (1) v 098.6
Mixmaster (1) 116.5
mixtry (1) n 090.8
mixture (33) n 033.3
mizzle (1) v 006.6
mizzling (4) v 006.6
MKT Railroad (1) 084.8
mo (1) interj 038.2
moan (7) n/v 036.3
moaning (4) v 036.3
moat (1) n 030.2
mob (30) n/adj 082.8
~ crowd (1) n 082.8
~ squad (1) n 112.5
Mobil Oil (3) 024.1
mobile (5) n/adj 074.1
~ home (2) n 109.5
~ homes (1) n 065.8
Mobile (740) AL 087.3
~ Bay (10) AL 030.3
~ City (1) 105.3

~ Infirmary (1) 108.2
~ Medic (2) 111.5
~ Municipal Airport (1) 106.5
~ nigger (1) n 069.3
~ Port (1) AL 031.4
~ River (2) AL 030.7
~ Street (1) 107.6
(Mo)bile (1) AL 087.3
mobiles (1) n 084.8
Mobilian (4) 080.6
~ turtle (1) n 060.6
moccasin (102) n/adj 123.8
~ snake (2) n 089.8
mocca(sin) (1) adj 080.6
Moccasin (6) TN 030.7
~ Branch (4) AL FL 030.7
~ Gap (1) AR 031.3
moccasins (93) n 123.8
moccasins' heads (1) n 097.4
mocha (1) n 032.4
mock (6) v/adj 065.8
~ orange (1) n 080.6
~ oranges (2) n 099.5
mockies (1) n 126.8
mocking (1) v 129.7
mockingbird (18) n 059.4
Mockingbird (1) 105.3
mockingbirds (18) n 059.2
mod (5) n/adj 123.6
~ cut (1) n 123.9
mode (1) n 123.6
model (14) n/adj 125.4
~ bow (1) n 024.6
~ hulls (1) n 024.6
~ planters (1) n 021.9
~ road (1) n 031.6
Model (53) 109.4
~ -A (6) 109.4
~ -A coupe (1) n 023.6
~ -T (5) 109.3
~ -T car (1) n 023.6
~ -T days (1) n 025.6
~ -T Ford (5) 088.7
~ -T Ford coupe (1) n 023.6
~ -T truck (1) n 088.7
~ -Ts (1) 023.6
Models (3) 109.1
moderate (11) v/adj 005.7

~ rain (3) n 006.6
~ shower (1) n 006.6
~ weather (1) n 007.3
moderated (2) v 007.3
moderately (2) adv 090.4
moder(ately) (1) adv 090.4
moderating (12) v 005.7
~ down (1) v 007.3
moderator (1) n 067.5
modern (39) adj 065.8
~ -day stuff (1) n 130.8
~ jazz (2) n 130.8
Modern (1) 096.8
moderner (1) adj 002.6
modest (1) adj 090.4
Modoc (1) AR 087.1
module (1) n 111.5
Moffat (1) TX 087.9
Mogen David Twenty Twenty (1) 114.7
Mohawk (3) 123.9
Mohican (1) 123.9
Mohicans (1) 081.7
Moines (2) 087.3
Moisant (4) 106.5
~ Airport (2) 106.5
moist (6) adj 029.3
moisture (4) n/adj 088.4
~ land (1) n 029.4
~ places (1) n 029.6
moist(ure) (1) n 029.4
Moko (1) AR 087.7
molar (1) n 071.8
molars (1) n 071.8
molasses (1244) n/adj 051.2
~ ball (1) n 093.6
~ barrel (4) n 019.2
~ barrels (3) n 019.2
~ bread (2) n 044.6
~ bucket (6) n 019.2
~ buckets (2) n 019.2
~ cake (4) n 051.2
~ can (3) n 019.2
~ candy (1) n 051.2
~ container (1) n 019.2
~ gate barrel (1) n 019.2
~ keg (3) n 020.2
~ lick (1) n 051.2
~ mill (4) n 080.9
~ pan (1) n 051.2
~ pitcher (8) n 020.2
~ pitchers (1) n 051.2

~ pudding (2) n 051.2
~ stand (21) n 019.2
~ stands (1) n 019.2
~ syrup (3) n 051.2
~ trees (1) n 051.2
~ works (1) n 051.2
(mo)lasses (42) n/adj 051.2
~ bread (5) n 044.4
~ buckets (1) n 019.2
~ cookies (1) n 051.2
~ pudding (1) n 051.2
~ stand (1) n 019.2
molas(ses) (4) n 051.2
Molasses Creek (1) TX 030.7
mold (23) n 046.9
moldboard (16) n/adj 021.6
~ plow (10) n 021.6
moldboards (1) n 021.6
molded (15) v/adj 046.9
molding (1) v 047.5
molds (3) n/v 046.9
moldy (14) adj 047.5
mole (30) n 059.8
molehill (1) n 030.8
molehills (1) n 030.8
Molena (1) GA 087.9
moles (6) n 059.5
molested (2) v 080.9
Moline (2) 021.7
Molino (1) FL 087.4
mollet (1) adj F 046.1
Mollies (3) 114.2
mollies (4) n 060.8
mollifier (1) n 011.3
molly (2) n 060.8
Molly (15) 067.3
~ blight (1) n 098.4
Molotov (35) 024.3
~ cocktail (32) n 024.3
~ cocktails (1) n 024.3
molting (1) v 057.4
mom (23) n 063.6
~ and pop (1) n 116.2
~ -and-pop store (1) n 116.2
~ and pop's (1) adj 116.2
Mom (176) 063.7
moment (58) n 070.3
moments (2) n 070.3
mommy (1) n 063.7
Mommy (53) 063.7

Mom's (1) 064.2
moms (1) n 063.7
Momus (1) 088.7
Mon Louis Island (2) AL
  087.9
monadnock (1) n 031.1
monastery (1) n 117.6
Moncks Corner (1) SC
  087.2
Moncrief (2) 105.4
  ~ Park (1) 106.4
Monday (1049) 002.1
  ~ evening (2) n 002.3
  ~ morning (15) n 002.1
  ~ night (3) n 002.1
  ~ washing (1) n 010.6
  ~ week (10) n 003.6
Mondays (5) 002.1
monde (1) n F 066.5
Monett (1) MO 074.4
Monette (1) AR 087.7
money (488) n/adj 114.5
  ~ bag (3) n 028.2
  ~ car (1) n 109.4
  ~ clasp (1) n 028.2
  ~ coin (1) n 028.2
  ~ crop (21) n 041.3
  ~ crops (1) n 041.3
  ~ lover (6) n 073.5
  ~ miser (3) n 073.5
  ~ orders (1) n 039.9
  ~ people (1) n 105.7
  ~ pincher (1) n 073.5
  ~ poke (1) n 028.2
  ~ pouch (3) n 028.2
  ~ purse (2) n 028.2
  ~ purses (1) n 028.2
  ~ rent (1) n 075.6
  ~ run (1) v 080.6
  ~ sack (5) n 028.2
  ~ -sent (1) adj 099.6
moneybags (1) n 126.7
moneyed people (2) n
  091.8
moneylenders (1) n 126.7
moneys (1) n 066.7
monger (2) n 033.3
Mongolian dog (1) n
  033.3
Mongolians (2) 069.5
Mongols (1) 069.5
mongoose (1) n 125.2
mongrel (238) n/adj
  033.3
  ~ dog (5) n 033.3

~ hound (1) n 033.3
~ pup (1) n 033.3
mongrels (11) n 033.3
Moniac (1) GA 087.1
Monica (2) 087.2
monitor (1) n 099.6
monk (1) n 125.2
monkey (46) n/adj 069.3
  ~ bars (2) n 022.5
  ~ blood (14) n 078.3
  ~ bread (1) n 044.3
  ~ cactus (1) n 062.3
  ~ face (1) n 125.1
  ~ -face owl (1) n 059.1
  ~ -faced owl (2) n
    059.1
  ~ -faced owls (1) n
    059.1
  ~ grass (1) n 015.9
  ~ junk (1) n 088.7
  ~ owl (1) n 059.2
  ~ ring (1) n 029.3
  ~ suit (2) n 027.7
  ~ swing (1) n 022.9
  ~ wrench (1) n 067.8
monk(ey) (1) n 125.2
Monkey (2) 030.7
  ~ Branch (1) FL 030.7
  ~ Island (1) LA 087.7
monkey's (2) adj 078.3
  ~ blood (1) n 078.3
  ~ face (1) n 101.4
monkeys (1) n 064.4
monkeyshining (1) v
  088.7
monogram (1) n 070.8
mononucleosis (1) n
  065.9
monorail (5) n/adj 085.3
  ~ system (1) n 109.9
Monroe (101) AL AR FL
  GA LA MS TX 087.1
  ~ College (1) 083.6
  ~ County (9) AL AR
    GA LA TN 087.4
  ~ Drive (1) 107.7
  ~ Park (1) 022.8
  ~ Street (7) 107.6
Monroeville (3) AL 087.2
Monrovia School (1)
  080.6
monsoon (2) n/adj 006.1
  ~ rains (1) n 006.1
monsoons (3) n 112.2
monster (9) n 125.2

monsters (3) n 064.3
Montague (1) TX 087.4
Montana (6) 086.8
Montauk (1) NY 087.3
Montclair (1) 107.6
Montdale (1) 106.1
Monte-Sano (3) AL 087.2
Monteagle Mountain (1)
  TN 031.1
Monterey (3) CA LA
  087.5
Monterrey (4) 087.2
Montevallo (16) AL 087.2
  ~ High School (1)
    087.6
  ~ Highway (1) 087.6
Montezuma (3) GA 087.7
Montezuma's revenge (1)
  n 091.8
Montgomery (781) AL
  AR TX 087.3
  ~ County (11) AL AR
    GA TN 087.3
  ~ Crossroads (1) 107.6
  ~ flying field (1) n
    016.1
  ~ Highway (1) 107.5
  ~ Park (1) 106.5
  ~ Ward (4) 087.3
(Mont)gomery (1) AL
  087.3
month (240) n/adj 075.6
  ~ hand (1) n 080.6
month[N-i] (10) n 005.1
monthly (5) adj 094.8
months (173) n/adj 065.9
Monticello (16) AL AR
  FL MS VA 086.5
Montreal (2) 087.7
Montreat (2) NC 086.2
Montrose (9) AR MS TX
  087.2
Montvale (2) 106.4
  ~ Road (1) 107.7
monument (12) n/adj
  117.6
  ~ business (1) n 080.6
monuments (1) n 102.5
moo (339) n/v/adj/interj
  036.3
  ~ ah (1) n 033.5
  ~ cow (1) n 033.6
  ~ -cow(x2) (2) interj
    037.5
  ~ noise (1) n 036.3

moo(x2) (4) interj 036.3
moo[V-p] (2) v 036.3
mooch (3) v 073.5
  ~ on (1) v 073.5
mooched girl friends (1)
  v 081.4
moocher (9) n 101.3
moochers (2) n 115.4
mooching (2) v 081.7
mood (182) n/adj 099.3
  ~ music (1) n 130.8
  ~ rings (1) n 123.1
moody (7) adj 075.1
Moody (7) 087.6
  ~ Field (1) 016.1
  ~ (po)tato (1) n 055.5
  ~ Stretch (1) LA 087.8
mooed (3) v 036.3
Moog synthesizer (1) n
  130.8
mooing (96) v/adj 036.3
  ~ for (1) v 036.2
  ~ sound (1) n 036.3
moola (21) n 114.5
moon (49) n/adj 092.7
  ~ -eyed (2) adj 034.2
  ~ face (1) n 125.1
  ~ grass (1) n 080.7
  ~ house (1) n 012.1
  ~ man (1) n 053.6
  ~ room (1) n 109.1
  ~ signs (1) n 080.9
Moon (9) 056.9
  ~ and Star[N-i] (1)
    056.9
  ~ and Stars (1) 056.9
  ~ and the Stars (1)
    056.9
  ~ Lake (3) MS 030.7
  ~ River (2) GA 030.7
Mooney Lake (1) 106.4
mooning (1) v 129.8
moonlight owl (2) n
  059.1
Moonlight Cemetery (1)
  078.9
moonlighting (1) v 081.7
moonshine (616) n/adj
  050.8
  ~ central (1) n 050.8
  ~ gosh (1) n 050.8
  ~ hills (1) n 050.8
  ~ jug (1) n 017.6
  ~ liquor (11) n 050.8
  ~ stills (2) n 050.8

~ whiskey (29) n 050.8
Moonshine (1) LA 087.2
moonshiner (7) n 050.8
moonshiners (7) n 050.8
moonshining (3) v 050.8
moonshiny (1) adj 084.8
moonstruck (1) adj 081.4
moop (1) interj 037.5
Moore (5) TX 087.8
 ~ County (1) TN 087.3
 ~ Ranch (1) 082.6
 ~ Road (1) 031.6
Moores (5) 087.5
 ~ Bridge (2) AL 087.5
 ~ Mill Road (3) 105.5
Mooresville (1) NC 087.7
Mooretown (1) 105.4
Moorhead (1) MS 087.5
moos (62) v 036.3
moose (1) n 125.2
mop (84) n/v/adj 010.5
 ~ bucket (15) n 017.3
 ~ buckets (1) n 017.4
 ~ pail (6) n 116.9
 ~ rag (1) n 018.3
 ~ up (2) v 010.4
 ~ with (1) v 010.5
mopped (2) v 015.8
mopping (8) v/adj 010.9
 ~ bucket (1) n 116.9
mops (12) n 010.5
moral (2) n/adj 017.9
moral[N-i] (1) n 052.7
morals (3) n 073.6
morass (1) n 029.7
morbid (1) adj 005.5
morcilla (1) n S 047.3
morcil(la) (1) n S 047.3
more (1044) adj/adv
 066.1
Morehouse (2) LA 087.7
 ~ Parish (1) LA 087.4
Moreland (2) GA 087.3
 ~ Avenue (1) 107.6
Morgan (30) AL GA
 087.5
 ~ City (9) LA 087.6
 ~ County (7) AL GA
 TN 086.8
 ~ Creek (1) AL 030.7
 ~ River (1) LA 030.7
 ~ stallion (1) n 034.1
Morgans Bayou (1) LA
 030.7

Morgantown (2) MS WV
 087.5
Morganza (1) LA 087.4
morgue (8) n 079.2
Moriah (1) 075.8
Mori(ah) (1) 088.8
morita tree (1) n 061.8
Mormon (2) 089.1
 ~ church (1) n 089.2
Mormons (3) 089.1
morn (1) n 002.2
morning (1711) n/adj
 002.2
 ~ chores (3) n 010.4
 ~ cleaning (1) n 010.4
 ~ coffee (1) n 048.8
 ~ glories (13) n 015.9
 ~ glory (2) n 015.9
 ~ glory flowers (1) n
 088.8
 ~ -glory vine (2) n
 015.9
 ~ -glory vines (1) n
 062.3
 ~ gray (1) n 104.5
 ~ paper (1) n 002.2
 ~ part (1) n 002.2
 ~ red (1) n 104.6
 ~ snack (1) n 048.6
 ~ sun (1) n 002.2
 ~ time (3) n 002.2
morn(ing) (8) n 002.2
Morning (4) GA 030.7
 ~ Creek (2) GA 030.7
 ~ Star (1) n 002.2
Morn(ing) Creek (1) GA
 030.7
morning[N-i] (2) n 075.7
mornings (20) n 002.2
Morningside (9) 106.2
 ~ area (1) n 105.1
 ~ Park (2) 106.4
moron (5) n 073.4
morphadite (1) n 075.6
morphine (11) n 114.2
morral (1) n S 019.7
Morral (2) TX 030.7
 ~ Creek (1) TX 030.7
morrice out (1) v 021.1
Morrilton (2) AR 029.9
morris chair (3) n 008.7
Morris (6) 107.6
 ~ Avenue (1) 107.6
 ~ Boulevard (1) 107.6

 ~ Hill (2) AL GA
 087.3
Mor(ris) Station (1) GA
 087.3
Morrison (2) 055A.3
 ~ beans (1) n 055A.3
 ~ Campground (1) GA
 087.6
Morristown (3) TN 087.7
 ~ Airport (1) 106.5
Morrow (3) GA 087.8
 ~ Station (1) GA 012.5
Morse (1) LA 086.1
morsel (1) n 012.5
mortal (1) adj 079.7
mortar (1) n 065.9
mortgage (5) n/adj 042.7
 ~ lifter (2) n 056.2
 ~ lifters (1) n 035.5
mortician (63) n 117.4
morticians (5) n 117.4
mortified (1) v 078.2
mortise (2) n 070.7
Morton (2) MS 087.4
 ~ community (1) TN
 087.4
mortuaries (1) n 117.4
mortuary (17) n/adj
 117.6
 ~ college (1) n 083.6
Morvin (1) AL 087.2
Moscow (4) TX 087.9
Moseley Hall (1) FL
 087.2
Mosely Park (1) 106.5
Moses (4) 092.3
 ~ in the cradle (1) n
 080.7
Moses' law (1) n 085.7
mosey around (1) v 093.5
moseys (2) v 080.6
 ~ around (1) v 080.6
 ~ on (1) v 098.7
Moshat (1) AL 087.1
mosque (1) n 117.6
mosquito (724) n/adj
 060A.8
 ~ ball (1) n 104.9
 ~ bar (11) n 060A.8
 ~ -bar net (1) n 060A.8
 ~ -bar netting (1) n
 060A.8
 ~ bars (11) n 081.8
 ~ bites (3) n 060A.8
 ~ bugs (1) n 060A.4

 ~ catcher (1) n 060A.4
 ~ catchers (1) n 060A.4
 ~ cloth (1) n 060A.8
 ~ country (1) n 081.9
 ~ dens (1) n 060A.8
 ~ doctors (1) n 060A.4
 ~ fly (3) n 060A.4
 ~ hatch (1) n 029.6
 ~ hawk (217) n 060A.4
 ~ hawks (72) n 060A.4
 ~ horse (2) n 060A.4
 ~ net (1) n 060A.8
 ~ nets (3) n 060A.8
 ~ netting (3) n 060A.8
 ~ -raising flat (1) n
 093.5
 ~ spray (1) n 060A.8
 ~ tree (1) n 061.8
 ~ veil (2) n 060A.8
mosquit(o) (1) n 060A.8
(mo)squito (93) n/adj
 060A.8
 ~ doctor (1) n 060A.4
 ~ bugs (2) n 060A.8
 ~ flies (1) n 060A.4
 ~ fly (1) n 060A.4
 ~ hawk (47) n 060A.4
 ~ hawks (21) n 060A.4
 ~ juice (1) n 050.8
 ~ net (2) n 060A.8
Mosquito Bay (1) FL
 030.3
mosquito[N-i] (3) n
 060A.8
mosquitoes (656) n
 060A.8
(mo)squitoes (61) n
 060A.8
moss (31) n/adj 056.8
 ~ beds (1) n 080.6
 ~ business (1) n 081.8
 ~ gin (1) n 081.9
 ~ mattress (2) n 028.7
 ~ wood (1) n 061.9
Moss (7) 105.8
 ~ Brothers downtown
 (1) n 105.8
 ~ Point (5) MS 087.7
Mossy Creek (3) GA
 030.7
most (263) adj/adv 064.7
mostest (1) adj 064.7
mostly (33) adv 090.4
mote (1) n 061.6
motel (450) n/adj 084.3

~ room (2) n 084.3
Motel (4) 084.3
~ Row (1) 105.6
motels (34) n 084.3
moth (742) n/adj 060A.2
~ bag (4) n 123.7
~ bags (4) n 123.7
~ bugs (1) n 060A.2
~ -eaten (1) adj 060A.2
~ egg (1) n 017.1
~ family (1) n 060A.1
~ fly (1) n 060A.2
~ hole (1) n 060A.2
~ miller (2) n 060A.2
~ -proof bag (1) n 123.7
~ webs (1) n 061.3
moth[N-i] (61) n 060A.1
mothball (27) n/adj 060A.2
~ bag (3) n 123.7
~ bags (1) n 123.7
mothball[N-i] (1) n 060A.1
mothballs (94) n 060A.2
mother (1757) n/adj 063.6
~ bulb (1) n 019.9
~ cow (1) n 033.6
~ cows (1) n 033.6
~ doctor (1) n 065.2
~ fish (1) n 063.6
~ hen (16) n 036.7
~ horse (2) n 034.2
~ -in-law (8) n 063.6
~ -(i)n-law (1) n 063.6
~ -in-law car (1) n 109.5
~ -in-law seat (2) n 109.1
~ -in-law seats (2) n 109.1
~ -of-pearl (1) n 080.7
~ owl (1) n 063.6
~ sheep (2) n 035.1
~ to be (1) n 065.1
~ turtle (1) n 060.6
~ will (1) n 083.5
~ wit (2) n 070.8
moth(er) (7) n 063.6
~ -in-law (3) n 085.7
~ -in-law seat (1) n 109.2
Mother (337) 063.7
~ Dear (6) 063.7

~ Hubbard (5) 080.8
~ Hubbard squash (1) n 056.6
~ Hubbards (1) 084.8
Moth(er) (3) 063.7
~ Dear (1) 063.7
Mo(ther) (7) 063.7
~ Dear (6) 063.7
(Mother) Hubbard apron (1) n 026.4
mother[N-k] (4) adj 043.9
~ lineage (1) n 043.9
~ room (2) n 007A.4
mother[V-r] (1) v 065.4
mothered (6) v 065.4
motherfuck (1) n 092.9
motherfucker (12) n 039.6
motherfuckers (2) n 093.8
motherfucking (4) adj 093.6
motherhood (1) n 065.1
motherless (62) adj 066.3
~ and fatherless child (1) n 066.3
~ baby (1) n 066.3
~ child (26) n 066.3
~ children (2) n 066.3
~ girl (1) n 066.3
~ [J-0] fatherless child (4) n 066.3
moth(erless) (3) adj 066.3
motherly (2) adj 065.2
mother's (64) adj 063.6
~ brother (2) n 063.6
~ daddy (1) n 063.6
~ daughter (1) n 125.4
~ family (1) n 066.5
~ father (2) n 063.4
~ folks (3) n 066.5
~ husband (1) n 078.5
~ mamma (1) n 063.6
~ mother (2) n 063.6
~ name (4) n 063.6
~ namesake (2) n 032.7
~ parents (1) n 063.8
~ people (9) n 066.5
~ picture (1) n 012.2
~ room (2) n 007A.3
~ side (9) n 063.6
~ sister's husband (1) n 063.1
Mother's (42) 063.7

~ bedroom (3) n 007A.5
~ birth (1) n 063.7
~ daddy (1) n 063.4
~ family (1) n 066.5
~ father (2) n 063.7
~ folks (2) n 066.5
~ house (2) n 063.7
~ mother (2) n 063.6
~ name (1) n 063.6
~ Oats (1) 050.3
~ parents (2) n 063.8
~ people (7) n 066.5
~ Quaker Oats (1) 042.1
~ ring (1) n 123.1
~ room (2) n 007A.5
~ side (8) n 063.7
~ sister (1) n 063.7
mothers (12) n 063.6
mothes (9) n 060A.2
mothproof (12) adj 060A.2
~ bag (5) n 123.7
~ bags (5) n 123.7
mothproofed (1) v 060A.2
moths (742) n 060A.2
mothses (1) n 060A.2
motion (7) n/adj 040.4
~ -picture house (2) n 084.4
~ -picture show (1) n 084.4
~ pictures (1) n 084.4
motley (1) adj 075.6
motor (35) n/adj 023.6
~ buggies (1) n 023.6
~ buggy (1) n 023.6
~ buses (2) n 085.3
~ cop (1) n 112.5
~ court (1) n 084.3
~ -driven (1) adj 120.2
~ inn (1) n 108.4
~ lawn mow(er) (1) n 120.2
~ mower (1) n 120.2
~ oil (4) n 024.1
~ -operated (1) adj 120.9
~ spader (1) n 021.6
~ sweepers (1) n 111.3
~ vehicles (1) n 023.6
~ yacht (1) n 001A.1
motorboat (41) n 024.6

motor(boat) (1) n 024.6
motorboats (21) n 024.6
motorcar (4) n 023.6
motorcycle (13) n/adj 111.8
~ wreck (1) n 066.9
motorcycles (8) n 111.7
motorized (3) adj 120.2
~ outfit (1) n 084.8
~ plow (1) n 120.4
motorman (1) n 081.8
motors (7) n 012.8
Motors (1) 068.3
Motown (1) 105.5
motte (2) n 061.6
motto (1) n 077.7
motts (1) n 059.9
moucheron (1) n F 060A.3
moudage (1) n F 019.9
mought (5) v 058.6
Moulton (5) AL 087.1
Moultrie (18) GA 087.7
~ Creek (1) FL 030.7
~ Road (1) 025.2
mound (122) n/adj 030.8
~ ants (1) n 060A.8
Mound (9) 030.8
~ River (1) LA 030.7
mounds (21) n 014.8
mount (3) n 031.1
Mount (47) 087.5
~ Berry (1) GA 087.5
~ Bethlehem (1) 096.8
~ Carmel Baptist Church (1) 089.1
~ Cheaha (1) AL 031.1
~ Enon (1) 125.7
~ Gaylor (1) AR 087.4
~ Hebron (1) AL 087.2
~ Hope (1) AL 087.5
~ Ida (3) AR 087.9
~ Lebanon (1) LA 087.7
~ Meigs (1) 105.4
~ Moriah (1) AL 075.8
~ Mori(ah) (1) MS 088.8
~ Olive (3) AL AR MS 087.1
~ Olive Church (1) 089.2
~ Parthenon (1) AR 086.1
~ Pinson (1) AL 086.4

~ Pleasant (5) AR GA TN TX 087.4
~ Pleasant Road (1) 031.6
~ Riante (1) AR 031.1
~ Sequoia (1) AR 087.6
~ Tabor (2) FL 087.1
~ Union (1) LA 087.1
~ Vernon (7) AL AR GA 087.2
~ Zion (4) GA TX 087.5
~ Zion Baptist Church (1) 089.1
mountain (1229) n/adj 031.1
~ area (1) n 031.1
~ areas (1) n 031.1
~ ash (2) n 062.8
~ boomer (10) n 069.9
~ boomers (5) n 069.9
~ boy (1) n 069.9
~ cedar (1) n 061.8
~ cliff (1) n 031.2
~ climb (2) n 096.3
~ country (2) n 031.1
~ cut (1) n 031.3
~ dew (18) n 050.9
~ fall (1) n 031.1
~ fever (1) n 080.9
~ flowers (1) n 025.6
~ folk (1) n 069.9
~ folks (2) n 031.1
~ goat (2) n 034.9
~ goats (1) n 069.9
~ hillbillies (1) n 069.9
~ hog (1) n 035.9
~ hogs (1) n 035.9
~ hoosier (22) n 069.9
~ hoosier woman (1) n 069.9
~ hoosiers (16) n 069.9
~ hydrangea (1) n 062.7
~ ivy (1) n 062.7
~ Jack (1) n 069.9
~ juice (1) n 050.8
~ land (1) n 031.1
~ laurel (189) n 062.7
~ lau(rel) (1) n 062.7
~ laurel tree (1) n 062.7
~ laurels (1) n 062.7
~ -like (1) adj 031.1

~ lily (1) n 062.7
~ lion (1) n 066.9
~ lions (1) n 031.1
~ man (2) n 069.9
~ maple (1) n 061.5
~ men (1) n 069.9
~ moccasins (1) n 092.7
~ oak (5) n 061.8
~ owl (1) n 059.2
~ oyster[N-i] (1) n 036.1
~ oysters (10) n 081.8
~ pass (8) n 031.3
~ people (9) n 069.9
~ person (1) n 069.9
~ pinks (1) n 062.7
~ regions (1) n 031.1
~ road (1) n 031.3
~ roads (3) n 031.7
~ rock (1) n 016.6
~ rocks (1) n 031.1
~ rooter (3) n 035.9
~ rooters (1) n 035.9
~ scene (1) n 031.1
~ springs (2) n 030.6
~ squirrel (1) n 059.6
~ stones (1) n 016.7
~ stream (2) n 030.6
~ term (1) n 031.1
~ trout (5) n 059.9
~ wilderness (1) n 031.1
mount(ain) (6) n/adj 031.1
~ laurel (1) n 062.7
~ people (1) n 069.9
Mountain (285) 031.1
~ Brook (13) AL 087.3
~ City (14) GA TN 087.8
~ Crest (1) 106.3
~ Dew (2) 056.9
~ Gray (1) 056.9
~ Home (4) AR 086.6
~ Hoosiers (1) 056.9
~ Sprout (3) 056.9
~ Sprouts (1) 056.9
~ Sweet (3) 056.9
~ View (6) AR 087.4
~ View Inn (1) 031.1
Moun(tain) (2) 087.4
mountain[N-i] (3) n 031.1

Mountainburg (2) AR 087.4
mountaineer (32) n/adj 069.9
~ something (1) n 069.9
mountaineers (20) n 069.9
mountainous (6) adj 031.1
~ area (1) n 031.1
mountains (239) n 031.1
Mountains (34) 087.4
mountainside (2) n 031.2
mountaintops (1) n 031.1
mounted (1) adj 110.7
Mountie (3) 112.5
Mounties (1) 112.5
mourn (12) v 079.3
~ (a)round (1) v 079.3
mourner[N-i] (2) n 016.7
mourners (45) n 079.3
mourners' bench (3) n 079.3
mournful (1) adj 079.3
mourning (823) n/v/adj 079.3
~ about (1) v 079.3
~ bench (1) n 089.9
~ clothes (6) n 079.3
~ dove (2) n 059.6
~ doves (1) n 079.3
~ over (1) v 079.3
mourn(ing) (17) n 079.3
mournings (1) n 079.3
mouse (7) n/adj 059.6
~ owl (1) n 059.1
~ snake (1) n 081.8
~ tight (1) adj 014.4
Mouse (2) 030.7
~ Creek (1) TN 030.7
mouse[N-i] (1) n 104.6
mouser (1) n 084.9
mouse's ear (1) n 104.6
moustache (79) n/adj 071.4
~ cups (1) n 088.8
mousy (1) adj 059.6
mouth (1307) n/adj 071.6
~ harmonica (1) n 020.5
~ harp (85) n 020.5
~ harps (5) n 020.5
~ keeper (1) n 101.3
~ music (2) n 020.5
~ organ (106) n 020.5

~ organs (9) n 020.5
mouth[N-i] (3) n 071.6
mouthed (1) adj 080.8
mouthful (5) n 071.6
mouthing (1) v 129.7
mouthpiece (3) n 071.6
mouths (11) n 071.6
mouton (2) n F 034.9
mouton(x3) (1) interj F 038.4
movable (3) adj 074.1
~ storage closet (1) n 009.7
move (52) v 053.2
~ around (2) v 057.7
~ away (1) v 025.3
~ back (1) v 038.2
~ in (1) v 095.9
~ off (1) v 024.8
~ out (3) v 081.1
~ out of (1) v 069.3
~ over (1) v 037.5
~ that hind leg (1) v 037.5
~ to (1) v 078.6
~ your leg (2) v 037.5
~ your leg back (1) v 037.5
move[V-r] (5) v 082.7
~ from (1) v 082.7
~ out (2) v 013.6
~ up (1) v 013.6
move[V-t] (3) v 098.8
moved (54) v 021.5
~ around (2) v 057.8
~ away (1) v 057.8
~ from (2) v 052.5
~ in (3) v 052.7
~ into (1) v 053.5
~ on (2) v 078.5
~ out (5) v 013.8
~ out of (1) v 034.5
~ out [P-0] (1) v 025.9
~ to (1) v 053.5
movement (3) n 070.6
Movement (1) 088.9
mover (18) n 075.6
Mover of God (1) 126.7
movers (2) n 006.1
moves (2) v 025.9
movie (192) n/adj 084.4
~ actor (1) n 069.1
~ actress (2) n 069.1
~ building (1) n 084.4
~ house (41) n 084.4

~ houses (3) n 084.4
~ picture show (1) n 084.4
~ scores (2) n 130.8
~ show (4) n 084.4
~ shows (1) n 084.4
~ star (38) n 069.1
~ theater (13) n 084.4
~ theaters (1) n 084.4
movies (66) n 084.4
moving (71) n/v/adj 021.4
~ along (1) v 021.4
~ in (1) v 070.3
~ into (1) v 024.8
~ on (1) v 070.1
~ out (2) v 005.7
~ over (1) v 005.7
~ picture (3) n 084.4
~ -picture house (3) n 084.4
~ -picture show (13) n 084.4
~ -picture shows (1) n 084.4
~ pictures (3) n 084.4
~ star (1) n 069.1
~ van (2) n 109.4
~ vans (2) n 109.8
mov(ing)-picture show (1) n 084.4
mow (21) n/v 014.5
mowed (3) v 053.7
~ for (1) v 053.7
mower (419) n 120.1
mow(er) (27) n 120.2
mowering (1) v 025.8
mowers (40) n 120.1
mowing (21) n/v/adj 014.8
~ machine (6) n 021.8
~ machines (2) n 021.7
~ scythe (1) n 080.7
mown (1) adj 041.5
mows (1) n 014.5
Moyne (1) 106.3
Mozart (1) 130.9
Mozart's Requiem (1) 066.8
Mozley (4) 105.6
~ Drive (3) 105.6
~ Park (1) 106.8
mozzarella (1) n 065.8
Mrs. (1030) 067.7
~ Astorbilt (1) 028.1

~ Cooper (598) 067.7
~ Gary Cooper (4) 067.7
~ James Cooper (1) 067.7
~ James Fenimore Cooper (1) 067.7
~ so-and-so (8) n 067.7
~ so-and-so's boarding-house (1) n 067.7
Ms. (3) 067.7
MSCW (2) 083.6
MTA (1) 109.9
much (1442) adj/adv 031.6
muchacho (1) n S 128.8
muching (1) v 025.4
muchly (2) adv 064.7
mucho (3) adv S 124.9
~ mucho macho (1) adj 124.9
muck (43) n/adj 029.8
~ farms (1) n 029.4
~ -like (1) adj 029.8
~ loam (1) n 029.8
~ root (1) n 061.4
~ soil (3) n 029.9
~ -type soil (1) n 029.8
Muckafoonee (1) GA 030.7
Muckalee (6) GA 030.7
~ Creek (4) GA 030.7
Muckaloochee Creek (1) GA 030.7
mucked up (1) v 102.6
muckland (14) n 029.9
mucklands (1) n 029.8
mucks around (1) v 093.8
mucky (30) adj 029.6
~ beer (1) n 121.9
~ land (6) n 029.8
~ place (4) n 029.7
~ soil (4) n 029.8
~ -type black soil (1) n 029.8
mucus (7) n 077.5
mud (311) n/adj 031.6
~ -and-stick chimneys (1) n 008.1
~ black cat (1) n 059.9
~ boat (2) n 081.8
~ -boat run (1) n 081.9
~ boats (1) n 080.7
~ buggy (1) n 090.9
~ cat (22) n 059.9

~ catfish (2) n 059.9
~ cats (10) n 059.9
~ chimley (3) n 008.1
~ chimleys (1) n 008.1
~ chimney (2) n 008.1
~ chimneys (3) n 008.1
~ crawling (1) n 093.9
~ dauber (41) n 060A.6
~ -dauber type (1) n 060A.6
~ daubers (25) n 060A.6
~ daubing (1) n 080.8
~ daubs (1) n 060A.6
~ dirt (1) n 029.8
~ ditches (1) n 030.5
~ duck (1) n 080.7
~ duggers (1) n 060A.6
~ fat (1) adj 080.7
~ fence (1) n 125.2
~ flat (1) n 030.3
~ flats (4) n 029.6
~ horse (1) n 034.2
~ house (1) n 014.1
~ lashes (1) n 029.6
~ mashy place (1) n 029.6
~ mason (1) n 060A.6
~ oven (1) n 008.1
~ pie (1) n 104.6
~ pies (1) n 130.3
~ pond (1) n 029.7
~ pudding (1) n 008.1
~ puddle (2) n 029.6
~ rake (1) n 120.7
~ rat (1) n 069.9
~ road (6) n 031.6
~ roads (6) n 031.6
~ room (2) n 007A.2
~ street (1) n 031.6
~ streets (1) n 031.6
~ terrapin (1) n 060.6
~ things (1) n 052.1
~ trout (1) n 059.9
~ turtle (36) n 060.6
~ turtles (12) n 060.6
~ wasp (4) n 060A.6
~ wasp[N-i] (1) n 060A.6
~ wasps (3) n 060A.6
Mud (8) 030.7
~ Creek (7) AL GA MS TN 030.7
~ River (1) GA 030.7
muddies (1) n 069.8

muddled (1) adj 032.4
muddler (1) n 073.3
muddy (22) adj 029.7
~ butter bean (1) n 055A.3
~ cat (1) n 059.9
~ land (2) n 029.6
~ roads (2) n 031.6
~ swamp (1) n 029.6
Muddy (6) 064.2
~ Creek (3) FL TN 030.7
~ Fork (1) TN 080.6
~ Lake (1) AR 030.7
mudfish (18) n 059.9
mudfoots (1) n 128.3
mudhole (18) n/adj 030.4
~ place (1) n 029.7
mudholes (1) n 031.5
mudminnow (1) n 061.2
mudsuckers (1) n 059.9
Mudville (1) TN 087.5
mudworm (2) n 060.5
mudworms (2) n 060.5
muebles (1) n S 009.4
muenster (1) n 048.1
muffalettas (1) n 121.6
muffin (78) n/adj 044.4
~ bread (11) n 044.8
~ cakes (4) n 044.9
~ pan (5) n 044.7
~ ring (3) n 017.6
~ rings (2) n 044.6
~ tins (1) n 044.6
muffin[N-i] (1) n 044.4
muffins (392) n 044.4
mufflers (1) n 080.8
mug (19) n/v/adj 048.9
~ shot (1) n 093.7
mugging (3) v 081.7
muggles (1) n 114.1
muggy (15) adj 005.5
~ day (4) n 005.5
~ weather (1) n 005.5
mugly (1) adj 125.1
mugs (8) n 012.1
Muhammed (1) 099.8
mukluks (1) n 122.8
mulateral (1) n 069.5
mulato (1) n S 069.5
mulatre (5) n F 069.5
mulatto (249) n/adj 069.5
~ dirt (1) n 029.9
~ folks (1) n 069.5
~ girl (1) n 069.5

~ land (1) n 029.9
~ man (1) n 069.5
~ Negro (1) n 069.5
~ nigger (4) n 069.5
~ niggers (2) n 069.5
~ race (1) n 069.5
~ rice (1) n 069.5
~ woman (1) n 069.5
mu(latto) (1) n 069.5
(mu)latto (1) n 069.5
mulattoes (54) n 069.5
(mu)lattoes (1) n 069.5
mulattress (1) n 069.5
mulberries (56) n 062.4
mulberry (97) n/adj 061.9
~ bush (5) n 081.8
~ tree (16) n 061.9
~ trees (14) n 061.8
mulber(ry) (2) n/adj 062.4
~ trees (1) n 062.5
Mulberry (20) AL AR FL GA LA 030.7
~ and Vance (1) 105.1
~ Creek (1) GA 030.7
~ Fork (1) AL 030.7
~ Inn (1) 012.1
~ Island (1) LA 087.6
~ Lane (1) 031.8
~ River (1) AL 030.7
mulberry[N-i] (1) n 062.4
mulch (12) n/v 041.4
mulcher (1) n 021.7
mulching (3) v/adj 041.5
~ hay (1) n 041.5
~ purpose (1) n 103.6
Muldon (1) MS 087.7
mule (742) n/adj 033.7
~ barn (29) n 015.2
~ barns (1) n 015.2
~ butter (1) n 080.9
~ cane mill (1) n 090.8
~ car (2) n 081.9
~ cars (2) n 085.3
~ collar (1) n 038.6
~ collars (2) n 033.7
~ colt (2) n 034.5
~ corn (2) n 056.2
~ corral (1) n 015.6
~ cotton gin (1) n 070.7
~ cultivator (1) n 021.6
~ days (3) n 092.9
~ disc (6) n 021.7
~ disces (1) n 021.7

~ -drawn harrows (1) n 021.7
~ -drawn rake (2) n 021.7
~ -driven (1) adj 033.7
~ -driving (1) v 033.7
~ farm (1) n 088.7
~ farming (3) n 033.7
~ feed (1) n 033.7
~ -foot hog (1) n 080.9
~ -footed hog (3) n 035.5
~ gear (1) n 038.6
~ gins (1) n 081.9
~ grass (1) n 015.9
~ harrow (1) n 021.7
~ line (1) n 038.1
~ lot (13) n 015.6
~ mill (1) n 090.8
~ mower (3) n 080.6
~ mowers (1) n 014.8
~ pasture (1) n 015.7
~ pen (1) n 015.2
~ plow (2) n 021.6
~ plows (1) n 021.6
~ power (1) n 033.7
~ rake (1) n 081.8
~ rakes (1) n 080.7
~ scraper (2) n 021.9
~ shed (2) n 015.2
~ shoe (2) n 034.6
~ shoes (4) n 034.6
~ stable (4) n 015.2
~ stables (4) n 015.2
~ stall (3) n 015.2
~ stalls (2) n 015.2
~ -tail weed (1) n 015.9
~ team (31) n 033.7
~ -team freighting (1) n 033.7
~ teams (2) n 033.7
~ ties (1) n 038.6
~ times (1) n 088.7
~ train (2) n 033.7
~ trough (1) n 035.8
~ wagon (1) n 033.7
~ whip (1) n 019.4
Mule (2) 033.7
mule[N-i] (26) n 033.7
muleback (2) adj 084.9
~ riding (1) n 034.4
mulehead (3) n 074.8
muleheaded (51) adj 074.8

muleheadedy (1) adj 074.8
mule's (3) adj 033.7
~ gear (1) n 033.7
~ hame (1) n 038.6
~ shoe (1) n 034.6
mules (1028) n 033.7
Muleshoe (2) TX 086.6
muley (1) adj 074.8
muleyheaded (1) adj 074.8
mulish (1) adj 074.8
mull (2) n 050.3
mullein (34) n/adj 061.6
~ beans (1) n 055A.4
~ leaves (1) n 061.4
~ plant (1) n 061.4
~ tea (10) n 061.4
mulleins (3) n/adj 061.4
~ bush (2) n 061.4
muller (1) n 020.4
mullet (116) n/adj 059.9
~ cat (1) n 059.9
~ fish (6) n 059.9
~ gun (1) n 084.8
~ snappers (1) n 069.9
mullets (20) n 059.9
mullican (1) n 088.8
mulligan (1) n 088.8
Mulligan stew (1) n 047.2
mulligatawny soup (1) n 084.8
multi (5) prefix 108.4
~ -level parking lot (1) n 108.4
~ -multi-multi-million aires (1) n 001A.2
~ -unit dwellings (1) n 119.2
~ -units (1) n 119.2
multibag (1) n 019.7
multifamily dwellings (1) n 119.2
multimillion-dollar thing (1) n 001A.2
multimillionaire (1) n 001A.2
multimillionaires (1) n 001A.2
multiplication (1) n 088.2
multiplier (2) n 055.7
multipliers (10) n 055.7
multiplies (1) v 055.7
multiply (8) n/adj 055.7

~ onion (2) n 055.7
~ onions (4) n 055.7
multiplying (60) adj 055.7
~ onion (22) n 055.7
~ onions (29) n 055.7
~ variety (1) n 055.7
multiply(ing) (1) adj 055.7
multiplyingest (1) adj 015.9
multistoried buildings (1) n 108.5
multistory (2) adj 108.5
~ building (1) n 108.5
~ buildings (1) n 108.5
multitude (2) n 129.4
mum (1) n 063.6
Mum (2) 064.2
mumble (25) v/adj 130.6
~ peg (24) n 130.6
mumblety-peg (20) n 130.6
mumbly-peg (5) n 130.6
Mummy (2) 063.7
mumps (18) n 079.8
munch (1) v 014.8
munchies (2) n 048.6
munchy (1) n 048.6
Muncie oven (1) n 116.4
Munford (1) AL 087.1
munguba (1) n 061.8
municipal (4) adj 106.5
~ airport (1) n 106.5
~ judge (2) n 068.6
~ palace (1) n 085.1
Municipal (31) 108.6
~ Airport (13) 106.5
~ Auditorium (4) 106.4
~ Park (4) 106.4
Murchison (1) 087.9
murder (3) n 130.2
~ in the dark (1) n 130.5
Murder Creek (2) FL GA 030.7
murdered (1) v 082.2
mure (1) n F 062.4
Murfreesboro (22) AR TN 087.6
~ Pike (1) 107.9
~ Road (1) 107.9
murky (9) adj 005.5
~ day (1) n 005.5
~ land (1) n 029.3
Murphree (6) 107.7

~ Park (2) 085.1
~ Street (1) 106.2
~ Street Park (1) 106.4
Murphy (9) GA NC 087.1
~ Candler Park (1) 106.8
~ Creek (1) GA 030.7
~ Mountain (1) MS 031.1
~ settlement (1) LA 087.1
murrain (1) n 015.6
Murray (8) GA 087.1
~ County (1) GA 087.1
~ Hill (2) 105.1
Murrayville (2) GA 087.2
Murvaul (1) 030.7
Mus (1) n G 051.6
muscadine (36) n/adj 062.4
~ grapes (1) n 090.9
~ sauce (1) n 048.5
~ vine (2) n 062.4
~ vines (2) n 062.4
~ wine (4) n 114.7
Muscadine (2) AL 030.7
muscadine[N-i] (1) n 097.9
muscadines (21) n 062.5
muscatel (2) n 114.7
muscle (10) n 072.7
~ -bound (1) adj 073.3
~ -built (1) adj 073.1
Muscle (4) 075.6
~ Shoals (3) AL 075.6
~ Shoals City (1) AL 087.9
muscled (4) v/adj 073.1
~ up (3) v 073.1
muscleman (4) n 073.1
muscles (2) n 073.1
Muscogee (14) GA 087.3
~ Airport (1) 084.8
~ County (3) GA 087.3
~ language (1) n 080.7
muscular (49) adj 073.1
~ dystrophy (1) n 088.8
museum (15) n 066.9
Museum (8) 106.7
~ of Fine Art (1) 106.8
~ of Natural History (1) 106.9
museums (3) n 066.8

Musguine onion (1) n 055.6
mush (909) n/adj 050.3
~ bread (1) n 044.9
~ form (1) n 050.3
~ ice (15) n 007.6
~ meal (1) n 050.3
~ -mush (1) n 050.3
~ peas (2) n 099.7
~ -pot bare (1) n 096.8
mushed (1) adj 047.5
musher (1) n 060.6
mushes (1) v 117.1
mushier (1) adj 056.7
mushmelon (372) n 056.7
mushmel(on) (1) n 056.7
mushmelon[N-i] (1) n 056.7
mushmelons (184) n 056.7
mushroom (476) n/adj 056.8
~ gravy (2) n 056.8
~ soup (2) n 056.8
~ toadstool (1) n 056.8
(mu)shroom (1) n 056.8
Mushroom (1) 106.4
mushroom[N-i] (9) n 056.8
(mu)shrooming (1) v 056.8
mushrooms (503) n 056.8
mushroomy-like (1) adj 047.5
mushy (13) adj 050.3
~ ice (1) n 007.6
~ land (2) n 029.6
~ -mushy (1) adj 080.8
~ place (2) n 029.6
~ rot (1) n 092.8
music (1112) n/adj 089.5
~ books (1) n 089.5
~ box (1) n 089.5
~ boxes (1) n 089.5
~ cabinet (1) n 089.5
~ clubs (1) n 089.5
~ conservatory (1) n 089.5
~ hall (2) n 084.4
~ instruments (1) n 070.6
~ lesson (1) n 089.5
~ lessons (3) n 089.5
~ ministry (1) n 089.5
~ room (6) n 007.8

~ root (1) n 055.5
~ roots (5) n 055.5
~ school (3) n 089.5
~ store (1) n 089.5
~ teacher (7) n 089.5
~ teachers (1) n 089.5
mus(ic) (1) n 089.5
Music (4) 131.1
~ Association presentations (1) n 131.1
~ City Hall of Fame (1) 106.4
~ Row (1) 106.4
musica de voca (1) n S 020.5
musical (19) adj 089.5
~ chairs (5) n 130.3
musician (7) n 088.9
musicians (5) n 089.5
musk (11) n/adj 059.4
~ bag (1) n 059.4
~ cat (1) n 059.4
~ rose (1) n 055.4
~ turtle (1) n 060.6
muskie (3) n 059.9
muskies (1) n 059.9
muskmelon (103) n 056.7
muskmelons (40) n 056.7
Muskogee (2) OK 087.7
muskrat (28) n/adj 059.5
~ knife (2) n 104.3
muskrat[N-i] (1) n 075.8
muskrats (7) n 065.8
musky (1) adj 080.9
Muslim (1) 117.6
muslin (2) n/adj 046.8
~ sacks (1) n 019.6
mussed out (1) v 088.8
mussel (26) n/adj 060.1
~ shell (7) n 060.1
~ -shell boats (1) n 024.6
~ shells (7) n 060.1
mussels (10) n 060.1
Mussett (3) 115.9
~ Avenue (1) 107.7
~ River (1) TX 030.7
must (105) v/adj 058.3
~ can (1) v 058.7
~ haves (1) n 088.9
mustafina (1) n 069.5
mustang (8) n/adj 088.9
~ berries (1) n 062.4
~ grapes (1) n 080.7
~ horse (1) n 034.2

~ horses (1) n 034.2
~ mule (1) n 033.7
~ wine (1) n 050.9
mustangs (3) n 065.8
mustard (373) n/adj 055A.5
~ beds (1) n 081.8
~ green (17) n 055A.5
~ green[N-i] (3) n 055A.5
~ greens (123) n 055A.5
~ patch (1) n 055A.5
~ salad (3) n 055A.5
~ sallet (3) n 055A.5
must(ard) (1) n 055A.5
mustards (20) n 055A.5
mustered out (1) v 025.5
mustn't (1) v 058.3
must've (3) v 027.9
musty (6) adj 047.5
mutt (160) n 033.3
Mutti (1) n G 064.2
mutton (53) n/adj 121.4
~ chops (2) n 071.4
~ corn (12) n 056.2
~ grass (1) n 015.9
~ tallow (1) n 024.3
muttonfish (1) n 059.9
muttons (1) n 034.8
mutts (4) n 033.3
Mutual (1) 108.5
MUW (1) 065.8
muzzle (10) n/adj 038.6
~ -loader (3) n 080.8
~ -loaders (2) n 022.4
~ -loading (1) adj 022.4
~ -loading-barrel guns (1) n 061.8
~ -loading shotguns (1) n 022.4
my (5570) pron/adj 043.4
~ god (1) n 059.3
~ own self (12) pron 042.7
m(y) (3) pron 063.2
My Dear (3) 063.7
Myers (18) 106.5
myna birds (1) n 099.8
myriads (1) n 065.8
myrtle (49) n/adj 062.8
~ brush (1) n 010.5
~ bushes (1) n 061.8
~ swamps (1) n 029.6

~ tree (2) n 062.8
Myrtle (13) 107.6
    ~ Avenue (5) 106.3
    ~ Avenue Ball Park (1)
      106.4
    ~ Beach (4) SC 087.3
    ~ Creek (1) FL 030.7
    ~ Lake (1) FL 030.7
myrtles (5) n 061.9
myself (271) pron 044.1
mystery (1) n 052.6
Mystic (2) GA 086.3
Mystics (1) 115.9

N

'n' (42) conj 099.6
N (8) 027.4
~ and W (1) 027.4
'N (4) 105.1
naa (3) interj 036.2
naa(x2) (1) interj 036.2
nab (2) v/adj 092.2
~ Johns (1) n 112.5
nabbed (2) v 100.2
nabbing (1) v 057.4
Naborton (1) LA 087.5
nachos (1) n 131.9
Nacogdoches (15) TX 087.7
~ County (1) TX 087.1
Nacoochee Valley (2) GA 087.7
nag (1) n 125.2
nagging cough (1) n 076.5
nags (1) n 063.2
nail (154) n/v/adj 020.7
~ bar (1) n 080.8
~ barrel (4) n 020.2
~ barrels (3) n 020.2
~ bender (1) n 067.8
~ bucket (1) n 017.2
~ hammer (1) n 020.7
~ keg (76) n 020.2
~ kegs (28) n 020.2
nail[N-i] (5) n 020.2
nailed (6) v 011.3
nailing (3) v/adj 020.7
~ machine (1) n 093.6
nails (63) n 009.7
Nails (2) 030.7
~ Creek (1) TN 030.7
~ Creek Church (1) 089.2
naked (24) adj 032.3
~ coffee (1) n 032.3
~ Coke (1) n 084.8
~ eye (1) n 070.9
~ place (1) n 080.6
naladoc (2) n 061.4

Namath (1) 115.8
name (457) n/v/adj 032.7
~ after (1) v 032.7
~ -calling (1) n 129.7
name[N-i] (6) n 037.8
name[V-r] (6) v 032.7
~ after (1) v 032.7
name[V-t] (24) v 053.1
~ after (2) v 032.7
~ for (12) v 032.7
~ from (1) v 032.7
named (166) v 032.7
~ after (86) v 032.7
~ for (31) v 032.7
~ from (2) v 032.7
~ over (1) v 012.4
names (61) n 075.8
namesake (14) n 032.7
naming (3) v 129.7
nana (1) n S 084.8
Nana (11) 064.2
Nan(a) (1) 030.7
Nanaine (1) F 063.8
Nance (1) 030.7
Nancy (33) 056.9
~ Creek (4) GA 030.7
~ Hall (18) 055.5
~ Halls (5) 055.5
~ yam (1) n 055.5
nandina (9) n 062.2
nandinas (2) n 061.9
Nanna (3) 064.2
Nannie (2) GA 030.7
~ Branch (1) AL 030.7
nannies (4) n 035.4
nanny (42) n/adj 035.1
~ goat (6) n 067.4
~ sheep (1) n 035.1
Nanny (19) 064.2
Nantachie Lake (1) LA 030.7
nap (17) n/adj 096.5
~ towels (1) n 018.4
napkin (6) n 018.5
napkins (1) n 039.8
Naples (4) FL 087.5
Napoleon (2) 107.7
~ bed (1) n 080.7
Napoleonic laws (1) n 088.7
Napoleonville (1) LA 087.2
naps (1) n 096.4
naptha launches (1) n 024.5

narc (2) n 101.3
narcotic (3) n/adj 114.2
~ agents (1) n 114.4
narcotics (2) n/adj 114.2
~ dealer (1) n 114.4
narcs (1) n 112.5
narrator (1) n 065.8
narrow (86) v/adj 065.9
~ bone (1) n 037.1
~ cut (1) n 085.2
~ down (1) v 065.8
~ -gauge railroad (1) n 075.9
~ -minded (5) adj 126.6
~ -stripe skunk (1) n 089.8
nar(row) (7) adj 070.8
~ -minded (1) adj 075.1
Narrowdale (1) 105.1
narrowest (1) adj 066.8
narrowing (2) v 065.8
narrows (4) n 031.3
Narrows (1) 030.7
nary (159) adj 040.6
Nashborough (2) 106.5
Nashville (890) AR GA TN 087.5
~ Airport (1) 106.5
~ country (1) n 130.8
~ Tech (1) 106.4
Nassau (12) FL 086.7
nastied up (2) v 080.8
nastier (3) adj 092.8
nastiest (7) adj 050.8
nastiness (1) n 092.7
nasty (110) adj 023.8
~ -ass (1) adj 069.4
~ day (7) n 005.5
~ film (1) n 114.9
~ -looking (2) adj 023.8
~ -looking day (1) n 005.5
~ -old day (1) n 005.5
~ pictures (1) n 114.9
~ -sounding (1) adj 090.4
~ weather (1) n 005.5
Nasty (1) 030.7
Natchez (84) LA MS 087.7
~ loam (1) n 029.8
~ Trace (11) 087.8

~ Trace Parkway (1) 107.7
~ Trace Trail (1) 106.4
Natchitoches (24) LA 087.3
~ Parish (3) LA 087.4
nation (4) n 069.5
Nation (4) 075.8
national (3) adj 025.7
~ park (1) n 085.1
National (38) 108.5
~ Bank of Commerce (1) 108.5
~ Life Insurance Company building (1) n 108.5
nationality (3) n 066.7
nations (1) n 066.7
Nations (1) 085.8
native (14) n/adj 041.5
~ birds (1) n 080.9
~ -born American (1) n 069.2
~ hog (1) n 035.9
~ hogs (1) n 035.9
~ peach (1) n 054.3
~ pecans (2) n 054.9
~ stone (1) n 016.6
~ tomato (1) n 055.3
natives (5) n 069.3
nativity (1) n 080.8
natty dresser (1) n 028.1
natural (46) n/adj 051.4
~ -born (4) adj 075.8
~ bridge (1) n 031.5
~ crop (1) n 041.5
~ dirt (1) n 031.6
~ foods (1) n 048.4
~ gas (3) n 118.4
~ -gas wall heaters (1) n 008.4
~ man (1) n 125.3
~ rock (1) n 016.6
~ son (1) n 065.7
Natural (5) 106.5
naturalest (1) adj 002.6
naturally (5) adv 070.6
naturals (4) n 123.9
nature (20) n/adj 073.2
~ break (1) n 012.1
natured (237) adj 073.2
~ horse (1) n 034.2
natures (1) n 065.3
naturist (1) n 080.6
naughty (3) adj 073.9

nausea (2) n 080.2
nauseate (1) v 080.2
nauseated (34) adj 080.4
nauseous (1) adj 080.2
Nauvoo (3) AL 087.2
Navajo Trail (1) 107.7
naval (5) adj 106.6
~ air station (1) n 106.6
~ airfield (1) n 081.9
~ base (1) n 105.7
~ station (1) n 070.6
~ -store operator (1) n 080.7
Navarro County (1) TX 087.4
Navasota (3) TX 087.8
navel (9) adj 055.1
~ orange (3) n 055.1
~ oranges (6) n 055.1
Navidad (7) TX 030.7
navies (1) n 055A.3
Navigation (2) 107.4
~ Canal area (1) n 105.7
navigator (1) n 088.8
navy (54) n/adj 055A.4
~ bean (13) n 055A.3
~ beans (27) n 055A.4
~ -blue (1) adj 027.7
~ trash (1) n 069.7
~ -type shoes (1) n 123.8
Navy Yard (1) 070.5
nay (5) interj 037.7
Nayjimo (1) GA 030.7
Naylor (1) GA 087.6
Nazarene (1) 089.1
Nazarenes (1) 089.1
Nazareth (1) KY 086.8
Nazi (8) 127.1
Nazis (14) 127.1
NC and Saint L (1) 087.1
ne plus ultra (1) n 080.7
neap (5) n/adj 020.8
~ tide (1) n 029.7
~ tides (2) n 029.4
near (301) adj/adv 082.6
~ cut (8) n 085.2
~ horse (9) n 039.4
~ lead (2) n 039.4
~ leader (1) n 039.4
~ mule (1) n 039.4
~ shoot (1) n 085.2
~ side (2) n 039.4

Near (3) 105.2
~ North Dallas (2) 105.3
~ North Side (1) 105.1
nearabout (73) adj/adv 070.2
nearby (2) adv 039.5
nearer (3) adj/adv 070.1
nearest (1) adj 100.3
nearing (2) v 070.1
nearly (319) adj/adv 070.2
Nearly-New Shop (1) 010.2
neat (16) adj 026.3
~ clothes (1) n 123.6
~ threads (1) n 123.6
neatening up (1) v 010.4
neater (1) adj 066.2
neating up (1) v 010.4
Nebraska (20) 086.1
necessarily (3) adv 026.1
necessary (10) n/adj 012.1
~ house (2) n 012.1
necessities (1) n 052.1
Nechanitz (1) TX 087.2
Neches (11) 087.6
~ River (9) TX 030.7
neck (1284) n/adj 071.7
~ areas (1) n 071.7
~ bone (3) n 046.3
~ bones (7) n 071.7
~ chain (1) n 028.4
~ hair (1) n 071.4
~ lash (1) n 071.7
~ squash (1) n 056.6
~ yoke (13) n 020.8
Neck (5) 069.7
neck[N-i] (3) n 082.3
necked (4) adj 056.6
necking (163) v 081.7
neckism (1) n 069.8
necklace (456) n 028.4
necklaces (21) n 028.4
neckline (1) n 115.5
neckpiece (1) n 028.4
necks (113) n 071.7
necktie (6) n 088.7
necky (1) adj 069.7
nectar (1) n 050.8
nectarine (3) n 054.3
nectarines (1) n 081.8
Nederland (3) TX 087.3
need (78) n/v 097.5

~ to (9) v 058.3
~ [P-0] (2) v 025.8
need[V-p] (2) v 013.8
needed (13) v 058.3
~ to (3) v 053.5
Needham (1) AL 087.1
needing (2) v 025.1
needle (11) n/adj 088.9
~ darts (1) n 130.6
needlefish (1) n 059.9
needlegrass (1) n 041.7
needlepoint (1) n 081.8
needles (3) n 026.5
Needmore (2) AL 075.7
needn't (2) v 053.7
needs (25) v 013.7
~ out (1) v 085.4
~ to (8) v 058.1
Needville (1) TX 086.5
neeing (2) v 036.4
Neely (4) MS 087.3
ne'er (170) adv 040.5
~ -do-well (3) n 073.6
~ -do-wells (2) n 069.7
Neger (1) n G 069.3
neglectful (2) adj 074.6
neglection (1) n 074.6
neglector (1) n 069.7
Negley (1) 106.4
negligent (1) adj 074.6
negre (1) n F 069.3
Negre (1) F 064.4
Negreet (4) LA 086.3
~ Creek (1) LA 030.7
Negress (1) 069.3
negrette (1) n 069.3
negro (2) n S 069.3
Negro (715) 069.3
~ American (1) 069.2
~ bands (1) n 069.3
~ blood (1) n 095.8
~ boy (2) n 069.3
~ boys (1) n 069.3
~ cemetery (2) n 078.8
~ church (4) n 069.3
~ church association (1) n 069.3
~ College (1) 083.6
~ cook (1) n 069.3
~ crew (1) n 069.3
~ dialect (2) n 089.8
~ doctors (1) n 069.3
~ enunciations (1) n 069.3
~ families (3) n 069.3

~ family (1) n 069.3
~ friends (1) n 069.3
~ girl (3) n 069.3
~ hair (1) n 069.3
~ help (1) n 069.3
~ Hill (1) 069.3
~ hospital (1) n 084.5
~ houses (2) n 014.1
~ joint (2) n 069.3
~ labor (1) n 069.3
~ mammies (1) n 065.2
~ mammy (1) n 069.3
~ man (9) n 069.3
~ midwife (1) n 065.2
~ name (1) n 069.3
~ park (1) n 085.1
~ people (4) n 069.3
~ person (1) n 069.3
~ philosopher (1) n 069.3
~ population (1) n 069.3
~ preacher (1) n 069.3
~ quarters (1) n 069.3
~ race (17) n 069.3
~ section (4) n 105.4
~ sections (1) n 069.3
~ servant (2) n 069.3
~ slaves (1) n 069.3
~ soldiers (1) n 069.3
~ spiritual (1) n 069.3
~ talk (1) n 012.8
~ teachers (2) n 069.3
~ tenants (1) n 069.3
~ thing (1) n 069.3
~ toe (2) n 054.9
~ Town (1) 105.4
~ washwoman (2) n 069.3
~ washwomen (1) n 010.5
~ woman (7) n 069.3
~ woman's name (1) n 069.3
~ women (4) n 069.3
Neg(ro) (1) 069.3
Negro[N-i] (1) 069.3
Negroes (374) 069.3
Neg(roes) (1) 069.3
Negroid (7) 069.3
~ race (1) n 069.3
Negroids (1) 069.3
Negro's (2) 069.3
~ farm (1) n 069.3
~ race (1) n 069.3

Negros (1) 030.7
neigh (164) n/v 036.4
neigh(x2) (1) interj 036.4
neighbor (24) n/adj 065.8
~ lady (1) n 075.7
~ woman (1) n 065.2
neighbor[N-k] (2) adj 043.9
~ house (1) n 043.9
~ yard (1) n 043.3
neighbored with (1) v 080.8
neighborhood (58) n/adj 105.4
~ friends (1) n 129.6
~ grocer (1) n 116.2
~ grocery (8) n 116.2
~ grocery store (1) n 116.2
~ grocery stores (2) n 116.2
~ lane (1) n 031.8
~ nurse (1) n 065.2
~ parties (1) n 130.7
~ road (8) n 031.7
~ roads (3) n 031.7
~ store (6) n 116.2
~ stores (7) n 116.2
~ streets (1) n 107.7
~ youth corps (1) n 065.8
neighbor(hood) road (1) n 031.7
neighborhoods (4) n 106.2
neighborly (1) adj 070.7
neighbor's (2) adj 082.7
~ house (1) n 082.7
neighbors (14) n 089.7
neighed (1) v 036.4
neighing (40) v/adj 036.6
~ sound (2) n 036.4
neighs (57) v 036.4
neither (530) adj/adv 071.2
neith(er) (2) adv 071.2
nei(ther) (2) adv 071.2
Nell (55) 067.3
Nellie (2) 030.7
Nelly (723) 067.3
~ Bell (3) 067.3
~ Gray (2) 067.3
Nellys (2) 067.3
Nelson (2) GA 087.4
~ Creek (1) TX 030.7

nematodes (2) n 054.6
Neon (1) 107.5
Neosho Overpass (1) 031.6
nephew (854) n 066.2
nephew[N-i] (1) n 066.2
nephew's (2) adj 066.2
~ dog (1) n 066.2
~ house (1) n 082.7
nephews (62) n 066.2
nepotism (1) n 115.3
Neptune Beach (1) FL 087.5
nerd (12) n 125.5
nerding out (1) v 125.5
nerve (11) n 092.4
~ -racking (1) adj 065.9
nerves (1) n 079.3
nervine (1) n 061.5
nervous (96) adj 074.2
nervouser (1) adj 066.1
nervy (2) adj 074.6
Neshoba (5) MS 087.4
~ County (2) MS 087.1
nest (544) n/adj 017.1
~ egg (249) n 017.1
~ -egg gourd (4) n 017.1
~ -egg gourds (6) n 017.1
~ -egg onions (1) n 055.7
~ egg[N-i] (1) n 017.1
~ eggs (55) n 017.1
~ hen (1) n 036.7
~ onion (10) n 055.7
~ onions (31) n 055.7
~ tomato (1) n 055.3
Nest (2) 055.6
nest[N-i] (39) n 016.7
Nesta (1) 065.8
nested egg (1) n 017.1
nestes (78) n 016.8
nestful (1) n 046.1
nesting (29) v/adj 036.7
~ boxes (1) n 036.9
~ egg (6) n 017.1
~ hen (14) n 036.7
nests (7) n 016.7
net (99) n/adj 016.3
~ bag (2) n 019.7
~ barbwire (1) n 016.3
~ fence (4) n 016.3
~ fences (1) n 016.3

~ type (1) n 016.3
~ wire (57) n 016.3
~ -wire (5) adj 016.3
~ -wire fence (2) n 016.3
~ -wire fences (4) n 016.3
nets (6) n 060.8
netted fence (1) n 016.3
netting (17) n/adj 016.8
~ fence (2) n 016.3
~ fences (1) n 016.3
~ wire (2) n 016.3
nettle (29) n/v/adj 065.5
~ rash (2) n 062.3
nettles (17) n 062.3
Nettleton (1) MS 087.8
nettly (2) adj 075.1
networks (1) n 066.5
Neu (1) G 093.3
neuf (1) n F 001.5
neuralgia (8) n 079.6
neural(gia) (1) n 079.6
neuritis (9) n 079.6
neurotic (1) adj 074.7
neuter (17) n/v 036.1
neutered (22) v 036.1
neutering (1) v 036.2
neuters (1) n 033.5
neutral (28) adj 031.9
~ ground (20) n 031.9
~ grounds (1) n 031.9
~ strip (6) n 031.9
~ rats (1) n 088.7
Neva (2) TN 087.1
Nevada (13) AR 086.2
~ County (1) AR 087.3
never (1885) adv 103.4
ne(ver) (4) adv 012.5
nevertheless (2) conj 088.8
new (1254) adj/adv 027.7
~ clearing (1) n 041.4
~ corn (1) n 056.2
~ crop (2) n 041.5
~ grapes (1) n 062.4
~ grass (1) n 096.8
~ growth (3) n 041.5
~ house (1) n 007A.7
~ Irish potatoes (2) n 055.4
~ land (11) n 041.4
~ man (1) n 112.4
~ -mown (1) adj 041.5
~ onions (2) n 055.7

~ pasture (1) n 041.4
~ potato (5) n 055.4
~ potato[N-i] (1) n 013.8
~ potatoes (41) n 055.4
~ red potatoes (1) n 055.4
~ rich (1) n 080.6
~ room (1) n 007A.6
~ -style (1) adj 027.7
~ -style house (1) n 091.7
New (3754) 087.4
~ Albany (4) IN MS 087.4
~ Augustine (1) FL 087.5
~ Basin Canal (1) LA 090.8
~ Bern (3) NC 087.2
~ Boston (1) TX 087.3
~ Braunfels (11) TX 087.4
~ Brockton (2) AL 087.5
~ Brunswick (1) NJ 087.7
~ Caledonia (1) MS 087.3
~ Cross (1) 087.9
~ England (156) 086.9
~ Eng(land) (1) 086.9
~ England area (1) n 086.9
~ England State (4) 086.9
~ England State[N-i] (5) 086.9
~ England States (410) 086.9
~ England woodcocks (1) n 059.3
~ Englands (1) 086.9
~ Era (1) LA 087.3
~ Fountain (2) TX 086.6
~ Guinea (3) 086.2
~ Guinea niggers (1) n 091.9
~ Hampshire (11) 086.1
~ Hampshire Reds (1) 036.7
~ Hampshire States (1) 086.9

~ Haven (3) TX 087.8
~ Hebron Baptist (1) 089.1
~ Hope (4) AL GA TN 087.4
~ Hope Baptist Church (1) 089.1
~ Hope Creek (1) AR 030.7
~ Iberia (10) LA 087.4
~ Iberia Parish (1) LA 087.6
~ Inverness (1) GA 087.3
~ Jersey (18) 086.1
~ Knoxville Highway (1) 107.5
~ Leland Road (1) 031.7
~ Madrid (4) MO 087.4
~ Market (1) TN 087.3
~ Mexico (32) 086.4
~ Niles Ferry (1) 107.7
~ Orleanian (1) 096.7
~ Orleanians (2) 101.7
~ Orleans (934) LA 087.8
~ Or(leans) (1) LA 087.8
~ (Or)leans (2) LA 087.8
~ Orleans Airport (2) 106.5
~ Orleans bread (2) n 044.4
~ Orleans East (1) 106.1
~ Orleans International Airport (4) 106.5
~ Orleans molasses (1) n 051.2
~ Philadelphia (1) 106.8
~ Providence (1) AL 087.6
~ River (5) GA TN 030.7
~ Roads (7) LA 087.5
~ Salem (1) AR 086.3
~ Smyrna (2) FL 087.4
~ Smyrna Beach (2) FL 087.1
~ Testament church (1) n 089.2

~ Town (6) TX 093.6
~ Trace (1) 031.7
~ Waverly (1) TX 087.9
~ Year (42) 093.3
~ Year Gift (1) 093.3
~ Year[N-k] Day (1) 093.3
~ Year[N-k] Gift (1) 093.3
~ Year[N-k] Give (2) 093.3
~ Year's (35) 093.3
~ Year's celebration (1) n 093.3
~ Year's Day (17) 093.3
~ Year's Eve (7) 093.3
~ Year's Eve Gift (3) 093.3
~ Year's Eve night (1) n 093.3
~ Year's Eve party (1) n 093.3
~ Year's Gift (58) 093.3
~ Year's Gifts (1) 093.3
~ Year's Give (7) 093.3
~ Year's Greeting (4) 093.3
~ Year's Greetings (2) 093.3
~ Year's Night (1) 093.3
~ Year's parties (1) n 130.7
~ Year's Party Club (1) 115.8
~ Year's spirit (1) n 093.3
~ York (801) NY 086.1
~ York City (37) NY 086.1
~ York Jews (1) 126.7
~ York paper (1) n 086.1
~ York State (179) 086.1
~ York steak (1) n 121.1
~ York strip (7) n 121.1
~ York strip steak (2) n 121.1

~ York stripper (1) n 121.1
~ York Times (1) 086.1
~ York Yankee (1) 086.1
~ Yorker (1) 121.1
~ Yorkers (1) 086.1
~ Zapata (1) TX 087.4
~ Zion Baptist (1) 089.1
~ Zion community (1) MS 087.5
N(ew) (52) 086.9
~ England (2) 086.9
~ Orleans (47) LA 087.7
~ York (1) NY 086.1
~ York City (1) NY 086.1
~ York State (1) 086.1
Newark (1) NJ 087.7
Newbern (2) TN 087.5
Newberry (1) FL 087.2
newborn Democrats (1) n 088.8
Newburg (1) AL 086.2
newcomer (54) n 066.7
newcomers (8) n 066.7
Newellton (1) LA 087.9
newer (3) adj 002.6
newfangle (1) adj 081.9
newground (159) n/adj 041.4
~ harrow (1) n 021.7
~ plow (5) n 021.6
newgrounds (5) n 101.7
Newllano (1) LA 087.6
Newnan (12) GA 087.5
Newport (14) AR TN 087.2
~ Hotel (1) 084.6
~ News (3) VA 087.3
news (64) n/adj 080.5
~ bee (2) n 060A.9
~ bees (1) n 060A.5
~ carrier (2) n 101.3
~ dispatcher (1) n 101.3
~ media (1) n 070.6
~ toter (1) n 101.3
News (4) 106.4
newspaper (18) n 027.7
newspap(er) (1) n 019.5
newspapers (5) n 027.7
newsroom (1) n 099.9

Newton (14) GA MS TX 087.2
~ County (7) AR GA MS TX 087.6
Newtonville (2) AL 087.5
next (499) n/adj/adv 003.6
~ -coming (1) adj 003.7
~ -door child's father (2) n 053.3
~ -door neighbor lady (1) n 088.7
Neyland Stadium (1) 106.5
Nezpique (1) 030.3
Niagara (15) NY 031.5
~ Fall[N-i] (4) NY 031.5
~ Falls (10) NY 031.5
(Ni)agara Falls (1) NY 031.5
nibble (3) n/v 048.6
~ on (2) v 048.6
nibbled (1) v 048.6
nibbling (6) v 048.6
nice (588) adj 073.2
~ broad (1) n 125.4
~ clothes (2) n 123.6
~ clothing (1) n 123.6
~ day (114) n 005.4
~ days (2) n 005.4
~ -looking (19) adj 125.3
~ -looking boy (1) n 125.3
~ -looking fellow (1) n 125.3
~ -looking guy (1) n 125.3
~ -looking lady (2) n 125.4
~ morning (2) n 007.4
~ -old (1) adj 090.7
~ rain (2) n 006.6
~ shower (1) n 006.6
~ -size (1) adj 055A.1
~ spring day (1) n 005.4
~ sunshine day (1) n 005.4
~ weather (10) n 005.4
Nice Christmas (1) 093.2
nicely (5) adv 092.5
nicer (4) adj 026.3
nicest (3) adj 129.4

Niceville (1) FL 087.2
nicey-nice (1) adj 104.7
niche (6) n 031.3
nicho sito (1) n S 012.2
Nicholls (1) GA 087.1
Nicholson Drive (1) 031.6
Nicholsville (1) AL 087.4
nick (3) n 031.3
Nick (14) 069.9
    ~ Springs (2) AR 087.2
Nickajack (1) TN 030.7
nickel (24) n/adj 114.5
    ~ bag (4) n 114.1
    ~ bags (2) n 114.1
    ~ box (1) n 114.1
    ~ boxes (1) n 080.8
    ~ horse (1) n 099.9
    ~ issue (1) n 114.1
nickel[N-i] (1) n 055.7
nickelodeon (1) n 084.4
nickel's worth (1) n 096.8
nickels (1) n 114.1
nicker (184) n/v 036.4
nicker[V-p] (2) v 036.4
nickered (6) v 036.4
nickering (56) n/v 036.4
nickers (60) v 036.4
nickles (1) v 036.4
nickname (343) n 064.4
nicknamed (3) v 064.4
nicknames (41) n 064.4
niece (20) n 066.2
nieces (8) n 066.2
nig (2) n 069.3
nigaroos (1) n 069.3
niggardly (2) adj 073.5
nigger (1007) n/adj 069.3
    ~ area (1) n 105.4
    ~ babies (4) n 069.3
    ~ bastard (1) n 065.7
    ~ blood (1) n 069.5
    ~ boy (13) n 069.3
    ~ boy's (1) adj 069.3
    ~ boys (8) n 069.3
    ~ business (1) n 069.3
    ~ cabin (1) n 099.5
    ~ cake (1) n 084.9
    ~ cakes (1) n 044.4
    ~ car (2) n 109.4
    ~ cemetery (1) n 078.8
    ~ choker (1) n 055.5
    ~ chokers (1) n 055.5
    ~ church (4) n 069.3
    ~ colony (2) n 069.3
    ~ cook (1) n 069.3

    ~ corn (1) n 056.2
    ~ couple (1) n 090.9
    ~ cracker (1) n 069.7
    ~ cut (1) n 091.9
    ~ dance hall (1) n 069.3
    ~ dialect (1) n 069.3
    ~ district (1) n 069.3
    ~ dog (1) n 073.9
    ~ expression (2) n 069.3
    ~ face (1) n 023.7
    ~ family (1) n 069.3
    ~ features (1) n 069.3
    ~ fish (2) n 059.9
    ~ -fish (1) v 088.8
    ~ fishing (5) n 080.8
    ~ French (1) n 097.8
    ~ funeral (1) n 079.2
    ~ gal (1) n 064.9
    ~ girl (2) n 069.3
    ~ graveyard (1) n 069.3
    ~ hair (1) n 069.3
    ~ heel (3) n 054.9
    ~ heels (6) n 054.9
    ~ house (6) n 069.3
    ~ houses (1) n 069.3
    ~ huts (1) n 080.6
    ~ in the woodpile (10) n 069.5
    ~ joint (1) n 069.3
    ~ joints (1) n 080.7
    ~ juke joint (1) n 084.7
    ~ kids (1) n 069.3
    ~ killer (5) n 055.5
    ~ -killer potatoes (1) n 055.5
    ~ killing (1) n 081.8
    ~ knocker (3) n 113.2
    ~ leg (1) n 055.5
    ~ lover (2) n 069.4
    ~ mammies (1) n 069.3
    ~ mammy (1) n 069.3
    ~ man (8) n 069.3
    ~ massa (2) n 069.6
    ~ midwives (1) n 065.2
    ~ minister (1) n 075.7
    ~ nurse (1) n 069.3
    ~ nuts (3) n 054.7
    ~ people (3) n 069.3
    ~ pine (4) n 061.9
    ~ pit (2) n 069.3
    ~ pole (1) n 093.9
    ~ preacher (1) n 069.3
    ~ quarter (2) n 069.3

    ~ quarters (4) n 069.3
    ~ race (3) n 069.3
    ~ rich (2) adj 090.8
    ~ rigging (1) n 024.3
    ~ riot (1) n 069.3
    ~ saying (1) n 075.6
    ~ school (2) n 069.3
    ~ schoolhouse (1) n 069.3
    ~ schools (1) n 069.3
    ~ settlement (2) n 069.3
    ~ shoes (1) n 123.8
    ~ -shooter (7) n 080.8
    ~ -shooters (4) n 022.5
    ~ situation (1) n 069.3
    ~ slave (1) n 069.3
    ~ slaves (1) n 069.3
    ~ stick (1) n 113.2
    ~ stickers (1) n 104.3
    ~ stills (1) n 069.3
    ~ street (1) n 069.3
    ~ tales (1) n 084.8
    ~ talk (3) n 069.3
    ~ token (1) n 115.4
    ~ town (18) n 069.3
    ~ wench (2) n 069.3
    ~ wine (1) n 114.7
    ~ woman (45) n 069.3
    ~ woman's house (1) n 069.3
    ~ women (8) n 069.3
    ~ work (1) n 069.3
    ~ workers (1) n 069.3
    ~ yell (1) n 089.8
nig(ger) killers (1) n 055.5
Nigger (11) 064.4
    ~ Baptist (2) 069.3
    ~ Branch (1) AL 030.7
    ~ in the Cane Patch (1) 051.3
    ~ in the Woodpile (1) 083.1
nigger[N-i] (1) n 069.3
niggeress (1) n 069.3
niggergeese (1) n 099.8
niggerism (1) n 088.9
nigger's (4) adj 069.3
    ~ brother (1) n 069.3
    ~ field (1) n 069.3
Nigger's (1) 069.3
niggers (503) n 069.3
niggers' (2) adj 076.8
    ~ brogue (1) n 076.8

    ~ heads (1) n 131.3
niggertoe (15) n 054.7
Niggertoe Creek (1) AL 030.7
niggertoes (81) n 054.9
niggerwool (1) n 035.2
nigh (31) adj/adv 070.1
    ~ cut (1) n 085.2
    ~ horse (1) n 039.4
nighest (1) adj 002.6
nighing (1) v 036.4
night (1651) n/adj 003.1
    ~ air (1) n 080.9
    ~ bug (1) n 060A.1
    ~ bugs (2) n 060A.1
    ~ chores (2) n 088.7
    ~ court (1) n 112.8
    ~ crawler (36) n 060.5
    ~ crawl(er) (1) n 060.5
    ~ crawler worms (1) n 060.5
    ~ crawler[N-i] (1) n 060.5
    ~ crawlers (50) n 060.5
    ~ creeper (1) n 060.5
    ~ driving (1) n 011.3
    ~ fighter (1) n 069.3
    ~ flies (1) n 060A.4
    ~ fly (2) n 060A.1
    ~ frogs (2) n 060.2
    ~ jasmine (1) n 062.8
    ~ -light (1) n 024.3
    ~ lunch (1) n 080.6
    ~ millers (1) n 060A.1
    ~ -night (2) interj 003.1
    ~ pot (1) n 080.6
    ~ predators (1) n 059.5
    ~ riders (1) n 085.7
    ~ -riding (1) v 080.8
    ~ school (1) n 065.8
    ~ spots (1) n 105A.6
    ~ table (2) n 009.3
    ~ varmints (1) n 059.5
    ~ walker (1) n 060.5
    ~ -watched (1) v 095.9
    ~ -watching (1) v 024.9
    ~ wiggler (1) n 060.5
    ~ woman (1) n 113.3
    ~ work (28) n 037.4
    ~ -work time (1) n 037.4
Night (2) 093.2
Nightbeat (1) 106.4
nightclub (1) n 083.1
nightclubs (1) n 115.6

nightfall (3) n 003.4
nightgown (1) n 093.9
nightgowns (1) n 025.6
nighthawk (2) n 084.8
nighthawking (1) v 119.8
nighthawks (1) n 059.2
nightingale (1) n 059.3
nightmare (16) n 097.2
nightmares (6) n 097.2
nightowl (33) n 059.1
nightowls (6) n 059.1
nights (14) n 001.2
nightshade (2) n 057.1
nightshades (1) n 009.5
nightstand (12) n 080.9
nightstick (54) n 113.2
nightsticks (6) n 113.2
nighttime (27) n 040.9
nigritos (1) n S 069.3
nigs (2) n 069.3
Niles (2) 107.7
nimble (3) adj 074.1
nincompoop (2) n 073.4
nine (1713) n/adj 001.5
~ -drawer dresser (1) n 009.2
~ -feet-high (1) adj 007.9
~ -foot (5) adj 007.9
~ -forty-five (5) n 004.5
~ -gored skirts (1) n 091.8
~ -night show (1) n 099.6
~ patch (1) n 080.7
~ -pound (2) adj 001.5
~ shooters (2) n 001.5
~ -thirty (21) n 004.4
~ -year-old (1) adj 001.5
Nine (19) 107.6
nines (1) n 028.1
Nines (1) 001.5
nineteen (370) n/adj 001.7
~ -and-eight (4) n 001.4
~ -and-eighteen (4) n 001.5
~ -and-fifteen (1) n 001.9
~ -and-fifty (1) n 001.9
~ -and-fifty-three (1) n 001.2
~ -and-five (1) n 001.9

~ -and-forty (1) n 001.9
~ -and-forty-four (2) n 001.9
~ -and-forty-one (1) n 001A.1
~ -and-four (2) n 001.9
~ -and-fourteen (2) n 001.7
~ -and-nine (2) n 001.9
~ -and-nineteen (3) n 001.9
~ -and-one (1) n 001.9
~ -and-seven (2) n 001.9
~ -and-seventeen (3) n 001.9
~ -and-six (1) n 053.4
~ -and-sixteen (3) n 001.9
~ -and-sixty-six (1) n 001.9
~ -and-sixty-two (1) n 001.8
~ -and-ten (2) n 001.9
~ -and-thirteen (2) n 001.7
~ -and-thirty (1) n 001.9
~ -and-thirty-five (1) n 001.9
~ -and-thirty-nine (1) n 001.9
~ -and-thirty-something (1) n 103.2
~ -and-thirty-three (1) n 001A.1
~ -and-three (3) n 001.2
~ -and-twelve (4) n 001.6
~ -and-twenty (4) n 001.9
~ -and-twenty-eight (1) n 001.4
~ -and-twenty-five (1) n 001.9
~ -and-twenty-seven (1) n 001.8
~ -and-twenty-six (3) n 001.3
~ -aught-eight (1) n 001.9
~ -aught-five (1) n 001.3

~ -aught-six (1) n 001.9
~ -aught-three (1) n 001.9
~ -aught-two (2) n 001.9
~ -eight (5) n 001.4
~ -eighteen (3) n 001.9
~ -eleven (9) n 001.6
~ -(e)leven (3) n 001.6
~ -fifty (1) n 001.9
~ -fifty-eight (1) n 001.4
~ -fifty-two (2) n 001.1
~ -five (5) n 001.3
~ -forty (5) n 001A.1
~ -forty-eight (1) n 001A.1
~ -forty-nine (1) n 001.5
~ -forty-one (1) n 001A.1
~ -forty-six (2) n 001.3
~ -four (5) n 001.2
~ -fourteen (14) n 001.7
~ -hundred (5) n 001A.2
~ -hundred-and-eight (1) n 001.4
~ -hundred-and-eleven (1) n 001A.2
~ -hundred-and-five (1) n 001A.2
~ -hundred-and-four (2) n 001A.2
~ -hundred-and-nine (1) n 001.9
~ -hundred-and-one (2) n 001A.2
~ -hundred-and-six (1) n 001.3
~ -hundred-and-ten (2) n 001.5
~ -hundred-and-thirty-three (1) n 001A.2
~ -hundred-and-twelve (3) n 001.9
~ -hundred-and-twenty-six (1) n 001.9
~ -hundred-twelve (1) n 001.6
~ -nine (5) n 001.5

~ -oh-nine (1) n 001.9
~ -oh-one (1) n 001.1
~ -oh-seven (1) n 001.4
~ -one (5) n 001.1
~ -seven (5) n 001.4
~ -seventeen (1) n 001.9
~ -seventy (1) n 001.9
~ -seventy-five (1) n 001A.2
~ -seventy-three (2) n 001A.2
~ -seventy-two (1) n 001A.2
~ -six (5) n 001.3
~ -sixteen (1) n 001.8
~ -sixty-eight (1) n 103.5
~ -sixty-one (1) n 001.1
~ -sixty-seven (1) n 001.4
~ -ten (12) n 001.5
~ -thirteen (8) n 001.7
~ -thirty (4) n 001A.1
~ -thirty-eight (1) n 001A.1
~ -thirty-five (2) n 001A.1
~ -thirty-nine (1) n 001.5
~ -thirty-seven (2) n 001A.1
~ -thirty-six (2) n 001A.1
~ -thirty-two (1) n 001A.1
~ -three (2) n 001.2
~ -twelve (8) n 001.6
~ -twenty (10) n 001.8
~ -twenty-eight (1) n 001.4
~ -twenty-five (4) n 001.8
~ -twenty-four (1) n 001.8
~ -twenty-nine (2) n 001.5
~ -twenty-seven (8) n 001.8
~ -twenty-seven flood (1) n 001.8
~ -twenty-six (1) n 001.3
~ -twenty-six hurricane (1) n 112.1

~ -twenty-six storm (1) n 001.3

~ -twenty-three (1) n 001.8

~ -twenty-two (1) n 001.8

~ -two (4) n 001.1

nine(teen) (1) n 001.5

Nineteen (6) 001.9

~ -and-Twenties (1) 001.9

~ -Hundreds (2) 001A.2

~ -Tens (1) 001.9

~ -Thirties (1) 001A.1

nineteenth (2) n/adj 001.7

Nineteenth (4) 107.6

~ Street (1) 107.6

nineties (1) n 001.9

ninety (155) n/adj 001.5

~ -and-forty (1) n 001.9

~ -day corn (1) n 056.2

~ -eight (7) n/adj 001.4

~ -eight-pound (1) adj 019.1

~ -five (9) n/adj 001.3

~ -four (8) n/adj 001.2

~ -nine (8) n/adj 001.5

~ -ninth (1) n 001A.3

~ -one (5) n/adj 001.1

~ -second (1) n 001A.3

~ -seven (9) n/adj 001.4

~ -six (18) n/adj 001.3

~ -six-pound (1) adj 019.5

~ -some-odd (2) adj 005.1

~ -something (2) adj 007.9

~ -three (10) n/adj 001.5

~ -two (13) n/adj 001.9

~ -two-years-old (1) adj 005.1

Ninety (33) 107.6

~ -Eight (2) 107.6

~ -Five (13) 107.1

~ -Ninth Street (1) 107.2

~ -Six (2) SC 087.2

ninny (4) n 069.3

ninos (1) n S 064.3

ninth (851) n/adj 001A.3

Ninth (20) 107.6

~ District (2) 082.6

~ Street (8) 107.6

~ Ward (4) 001A.3

Niota (1) TN 087.2

nip (3) n/adj 007.4

~ tide (1) n 065.9

Nip (1) 126.4

nipped (1) v 033.4

nipping (3) v/adj 036.4

~ frost (1) n 007.5

nipple (1) n 020.4

nippy (75) adj 007.4

~ morning (1) n 007.4

Nips (1) 126.5

nit (7) n/adj 073.5

~ fly (3) n 060A.4

nits (4) n 069.2

nitty (7) adj 073.5

~ -gritty (5) n 099.8

nitwit (6) n 073.4

nivada (1) n 069.3

Nix building (2) n 108.5

nixed (1) v 100.2

nixie (1) interj 080.6

Nixon (5) 066.6

~ Lake (1) AR 030.7

Nixonites (1) 129.2

Nixons (1) 025.5

no (5383) adj/adv/interj 091.4

~ -account (9) adj 033.3

~ -(ac)count (76) adj 069.7

~ -(ac)counters (1) n 069.7

~ -(ac)counts (1) n 069.7

~ damn body's (1) adj 092.8

~ -fence law (12) n 080.6

~ -for-good (1) adj 010.2

~ goddamn body (1) pron 097.8

~ -good (78) adj 069.7

~ -good-ass (1) adj 128.6

~ -good land (2) n 029.8

~ -good room (1) n 010.3

~ -good stuff (1) n 010.2

~ longer with us (5) adj 078.5

~ more (300) adv 095.2

~ -name cigarette (1) n 114.1

~ -name road (1) n 031.7

~ -name tree (1) n 061.8

~ one (15) pron 057.5

~ -passing line (1) n 107.3

~ place (9) adv 040.2

~ -see-thems (1) n 060A.6

~ -tell motel (1) n 113.8

~ -winner Pedro (1) n 033.3

~ -worm peckerwoods (1) n 069.7

n(o) (1) interj 049.6

No (2) 080.6

~ -Doze (1) 114.2

no(x2) (2) interj 033.2

no(x3) (1) interj 103.8

Noah (7) 070.8

Noah's ark (1) n 010.3

Nobel Hill (1) FL 087.6

Noble Visitors (1) 093.5

nobody (472) pron 080.6

nobod(y) (1) pron 057.5

nobody[M-k] (2) adj 043.9

nobody's (10) adj 092.7

Noccalula Falls (2) AL 106.4

nod (1) v 096.6

nodding (1) v 076.7

noddy (1) adj 076.6

Noel (4) F 093.2

Nogales (2) AZ 086.6

noggin (3) n 070.7

nohow (83) adv 040.7

noir (2) adj F 032.3

Noire (1) 030.7

noise (32) n 036.4

noises (3) n 038.3

noisy (8) adj 033.3

nolessen (1) conj 088.4

Nolichucky (2) TN 030.7

(Noli)chucky (6) TN 087.2

~ Creek (1) TN 030.7

~ River (2) TN 030.7

nominative (1) adj 065.9

non (6) prefix 080.7

~ -fire (1) n 080.7

~ -kosher Jews (1) n 126.7

~ -riding rotary mower (1) n 120.2

~ -tax liquor (1) n 050.8

~ -tax-paid whiskey (1) n 050.8

~ -teased (1) adj 123.9

nonchalant (1) adj 074.6

nonclimber (1) n 016.3

nonconformist (2) n 129.3

Nonconnah Creek (5) TN 030.7

nondairy (1) n 099.5

nondescript (2) adj 033.2

Nondescript Forties Modern (1) 096.8

none (628) pron 040.8

nonny (2) interj 037.5

~ -nonny (1) interj 037.5

nonpoisonous (1) adj 062.6

nonsense (1) n 073.4

nonstandard English (1) n 131.2

noo (1) n 036.2

noodle (3) n/adj 048.5

~ gravy (1) n 048.5

~ shocks (1) n 014.8

noodles (2) n 057.1

nook (14) n 007A.3

noon (35) n/adj 002.2

~ hour (1) n 002.3

noonday (2) n/adj 002.3

~ meal (1) n 075.7

Noonday (4) TX 087.2

~ Creek (1) GA 030.7

noontime (5) n 002.3

noose (1) n 082.3

nope (34) interj 103.8

nor (47) conj 057.7

Norcross (4) GA 086.2

Norfield (1) MS 087.5

Norfolk (14) VA 087.4

~ pine (1) n 061.9

~ Lake (2) AR 030.7

Norma (1) TN 087.6

normal (13) n/adj 073.7
~ college (1) n 083.6
~ school (2) n 080.8
Normal (2) AL 087.3
~ Institute (1) 083.6
normally (2) adv 053.4
normals (3) n 088.6
Norman (5) OK 087.1
~ Bridge Road (2) 107.6
~ horses (2) n 034.1
Norm(an) Park (1) GA 087.6
Normandale (2) AL 105.6
Normandy (2) TN 087.1
Norphlet (2) AR 087.2
Norris (4) TN 087.6
~ Hotel (1) 084.3
~ Lake (1) TN 030.7
Norristown (1) GA 087.4
Norte (1) 030.7
north (513) n/adj 006.4
~ bedroom (2) n 007A.6
~ -northeast (4) adj 006.5
~ porch (2) n 010.8
~ section (1) n 105.5
~ -south (1) adj 006.5
~ wind (26) n 006.5
~ winds (3) n 006.5
North (1193) 107.6
~ Alabama (3) 086.4
~ Alabama girl (1) n 086.4
~ American Baptist Association (1) 069.2
~ and South (19) 085.8
~ and South War (1) 085.8
~ and the South (1) 085.8
~ Atlanta (1) 105.1
~ Avenue (2) 107.8
~ Baton Rouge (1) 087.7
~ Bay Road (1) 106.1
~ Beach (1) 114.8
~ Beach Point (1) 087.8
~ Birmingham (6) 105.1
~ Boulevard (1) 107.5
~ Branch (1) LA 030.7

~ Cadron (1) AR 030.7
~ Candler (1) 093.9
~ Canton (1) GA 087.2
~ Canton Village (1) GA 087.7
~ Cape cruise (1) n 088.7
~ Carolina (859) 086.2
~ Carolin(a) (4) 086.2
~ Car(olina) (1) 086.2
~ Carolina guys (1) n 086.2
~ Carolina people (1) n 013.7
~ Carolina runner peanut (1) n 054.7
~ Carolina runners (2) n 054.7
~ Chattanooga (2) 105.1
~ City (1) FL 086.5
~ Creek (1) FL 030.7
~ Dakota (8) 086.7
~ Dallas (13) 105A.4
~ Dayton (1) 087.2
~ Decatur Road (1) 093.8
~ Florence (1) 105.1
~ Florida (2) 086.4
~ Fork (5) AR TN 030.7
~ Fork Creek (1) TN 030.7
~ Fork Lakes (1) AR 030.7
~ Fort Myers (1) FL 105.2
~ Franklin Street (1) 114.6
~ Fulton (1) 105.1
~ Fulton Park (1) 106.7
~ Georgia (10) 086.3
~ Georgia mountains (1) n 031.1
~ Grove (2) 105.5
~ Gulfport (4) 105.1
~ Helena (1) AR 087.3
~ Highland (2) 107.6
~ Hills (2) 106.2
~ Jackson (6) 107.6
~ Knoxville (1) 106.2
~ Lake (1) TN 030.7
~ Little Rock (6) AR 087.2

~ Main (1) 107.6
~ Market (1) 107.7
~ Memphis (3) 105.1
~ Miami (4) 105.1
~ Miami Beach (5) FL 087.5
~ Miami Beach Boulevard (1) 107A.6
~ Miami Senior High School (1) 125.9
~ Mobile (1) 105.1
~ Montgomery (4) 106.3
~ Nashville (9) 105.1
~ Park (3) 105.2
~ Parkway (1) 107.6
~ part (1) n 105.1
~ Prong (1) LA 030.7
~ Rampart Street (1) 080.6
~ River (3) AL FL TN 030.7
~ Rock (1) 032.1
~ section (1) n 105.1
~ Seventh Street (1) 106.3
~ Shore (1) LA 087.4
~ Shreveport (2) 105.1
~ Side (36) 106.1
~ Side Airport (1) 106.5
~ -South War (1) 085.8
~ Star (1) 106.6
~ State (3) 057.3
~ State Street (1) 107.6
~ Stream (2) TX 030.7
~ Street (3) 107.7
~ Sulphur (1) TX 086.5
~ Tampa (1) 105.1
~ Texas (2) 086.8
~ Three Notch (3) 107.6
~ Three Notch Street (1) 107.6
~ Weathers (1) TX 087.5
~ Wilkesboro (1) NC 086.4
(North) Carolina (1) 087.7
northeast (438) n/adj 006.4
~ storms (1) n 006.5
~ wind (46) n 006.5
~ winds (1) n 006.5

Northeast (43) 105.1
~ Arkansas (1) 086.7
~ Atlanta (1) 106.1
~ Dade County (1) 006.5
~ Elementary (1) 125.7
~ First Street (1) 107.7
~ Houston (1) 106.3
~ Jackson (2) 105.1
~ Preserve (1) 106.8
~ section (4) n 105.1
~ Side (3) 105.5
~ State[N-i] (1) 006.5
~ States (1) 086.9
~ Texas (2) 006.5
northeaster (20) n/adj 006.5
~ storms (1) n 006.2
northeasterly (28) adj 006.5
~ wind (9) n 006.5
northeastern (13) adj 006.5
Northeastern (13) 086.9
~ section (1) n 006.5
~ States (8) 086.9
northeasterner (1) n 006.5
northeasterners (1) n 006.5
northeasternly (1) adj 006.5
northeasters (2) n 006.5
norther (43) n 006.5
northerly (7) n/adj 006.4
northern (8) adj 006.5
~ frame (1) n 091.8
~ part (1) n 106.1
~ turnip (1) n 055A.6
~ wind (2) n 006.5
Northern (48) 055A.3
~ bean (2) n 055A.3
~ beans (3) n 055A.3
~ brogue (1) n 088.7
~ folks (1) n 066.7
~ friends (1) n 091.4
~ Indians (1) 126.4
~ nigger (1) n 069.3
~ people (2) n 129.3
~ pike (2) n 059.9
~ red oak (1) n 061.8
~ rock bass (1) n 059.9
~ States (10) 086.9
~ War (o)f Aggression (1) 085.8
Northerner (7) 066.8

northerners (1) n 128.9
Northerners (4) 066.7
northernly (1) adj 006.5
Northerns (2) 055A.3
northers (11) n 006.5
Northport (2) AL 087.7
Northside (6) 106.5
  ~ Airport (1) 106.5
  ~ Drive (5) 106.1
Northtown (1) 106.2
northward (3) adv 006.5
northwest (424) n/adj
006.5
  ~ -corner room (1) n
006.5
  ~ room (1) n 007A.8
  ~ territories (1) n 006.5
  ~ wind (34) n 006.5
  ~ winds (1) n 006.5
Northwest (33) 105.1
  ~ Atlanta (3) 087.6
  ~ Fourteenth Street (1)
105.3
  ~ Highway (1) 107.5
  ~ Jackson (1) 105.4
  ~ Second (1) 106.3
  ~ Second Avenue (1)
105.5
  ~ section (4) n 105.2
  ~ Side (4) 006.5
northwester (18) n 006.5
northwesterly (32) adj
006.5
  ~ wind (5) n 006.5
northwestern (15) adj
006.5
  ~ wind (1) n 006.5
northwesterner (1) n
006.5
Northwesterner (1) 006.5
northwesters (2) n 006.5
Northwood (1) 105.7
Norton (2) 055.5
  ~ yam (1) n 005.5
  ~ yam potatoes (1) n
005.5
Norwegian (1) 065.9
Norwegians (2) 128.8
Norwood (4) LA 105.6
  ~ Lake (1) AL 030.7
  ~ Park (1) 106.3
Nosa (1) 087.6
nose (64) n/adj 071.5
  ~ pick (1) n 117.8
  ~ smeller (1) n 075.6

Nose (1) 064.4
nose[N-i] (2) n 101.7
nosed (1) adj 074.9
noser (1) n 101.3
nostrils (1) n 065.9
nosy (7) adj 101.3
not (4454) adv 040.5
  ~ going out (1) v 065.1
  ~ in love with him (1)
adj 082.1
  ~ legitimate (1) adj
065.7
  ~ see (1) n 003.2
notary public (2) n 070.6
Notasulga (1) AL 087.4
notch (372) n/v 031.3
  ~ out (1) v 031.3
Notch (10) 030.7
  ~ Creek (1) AL 030.7
notch[V-t] down (1) v
031.3
notched (14) v 031.3
  ~ out (1) v 031.3
  ~ up (1) v 031.3
notchedy (1) adj 075.8
notches (41) n/v 031.3
notching (6) v/adj 031.3
Notchy Creek (1) TN
030.7
note (12) n/adj 025.5
notebook (1) n 040.9
noted (1) adj 063.6
notes (7) n 114.5
nothing (2703) pron/adj
103.1
  ~ necklace (1) n 028.4
nothingness (1) n 103.1
nothings (2) n 069.7
notice (4) n/v 057.8
notice[V-t] (1) v 040.8
noticed (4) v 040.6
notices (1) v 013.9
noticing (2) v 012.9
notion (34) n 093.5
notions bag (1) n 019.5
notre (1) adj F 066.5
Nottely River (1) GA
030.7
nourishing (2) adj 029.3
Nova Scotia (3) 070.7
novels (2) n 052.6
novelty (10) adj 011,2
  ~ boarding (1) n 011.2
  ~ siding (8) n 011.2

  ~ weatherboarding (1)
n 011.2
novel(ty) side (1) n 011.2
November (993) 001A.9
  ~ peaches (1) n 054.3
  ~ the Fifth Street (1)
108.6
Novem(ber) (1) 001A.8
now (920) adv/interj
095.3
now(x2) (1) interj 037.5
nowadays (72) adv 095.2
noway (109) adv 040.7
noways (12) adv 040.7
nowhere (117) pron/adj/
adv 040.7
  ~ road (1) n 031.7
nowheres (18) adv 040.2
Noxubee River (1) MS
030.7
noyau (7) n F 054.1
nozzle (7) n 018.7
nub (2) n/v 075.5
nubbed (1) v 089.9
nubbin (3) n/adj 092.9
  ~ end (1) n 080.6
  ~ head (1) n 074.9
nubbins (6) n 056.3
Nubian goats (1) n 088.9
nuclear (3) adj 070.7
  ~ bomb (1) n 070.7
  ~ peer group (1) n
129.6
  ~ -powered tractor (1)
n 065.9
nudge (1) v 038.1
Nueces (15) TX 030.7
  ~ Bay (1) TX 030.3
  ~ Bay Flats (1) 105.7
  ~ River (6) TX 030.7
Nuevo (2) S 093.3
  ~ Laredo (1) 087.4
nueza (1) n S 071.7
Nugget (1) 055.5
nuisance (25) n 059.5
nuisances (2) n 059.5
nuke them (1) n 130.3
null the tops (1) n 130.6
numb (1) n 073.4
number (72) n/adj 100.8
  ~ eight (1) n 022.4
  ~ eight wood stove (1)
n 080.7
  ~ five (1) n 022.4
  ~ four (1) n 022.4

  ~ line (1) n 107.3
  ~ one (3) n 081.8
  ~ -one (1) adj 025.8
  ~ -one hog (1) n 035.5
  ~ -one hogs (1) n 035.5
  ~ running (1) n 080.6
  ~ ten (1) n 099.7
  ~ -ten Oliver breaking
plow (1) n 021.6
  ~ three (1) n 010.6
  ~ -three tin tubs (1) n
017.6
  ~ -three tub (4) n 080.8
  ~ -three tubs (2) n
081.8
  ~ -three washtub (5) n
017.6
  ~ two (1) n 010.6
  ~ -two washtub (1) n
084.9
Number (10) 112.6
  ~ Five (1) 001.3
  ~ One (2) 031.6
  ~ Twelve (1) 001.6
  ~ Two (1) 069.3
numbers (5) n/adj 052.5
  ~ racket (1) n 080.6
numbskull (5) n 073.4
numbskulls (1) n 069.3
numerous (2) adj 055A.8
Nunnelly (1) TN 087.5
nunnery (1) n 113.4
nuns (1) n 102.3
Nupe (1) 113.5
nups (1) n 093.6
nurse (858) n/v/adj 084.6
  ~ home (1) n 084.6
nurse[N-k] (2) adj 084.6
  ~ aide (1) n 084.6
  ~ aides (1) n 084.6
nurse[V-t] (1) v 075.6
nursed (5) v 065.4
nursemaid (1) n 084.6
nurseries (1) n 084.6
nursery (13) n/adj 125.6
  ~ maple (1) n 061.8
  ~ school (5) n 125.7
nurse's (6) adj 084.6
  ~ aide (3) n 084.6
  ~ course (1) n 084.6
  ~ training (1) n 084.6
nurses (141) n 084.6
nurses' (3) adj 084.6
  ~ aides (1) n 084.6
  ~ home (1) n 084.6

~ school (1) n 084.6
nursing (48) n/v/adj
　084.6
　~ home (25) n 084.6
　~ homes (1) n 084.6
　~ profession (1) n
　　053.4
　~ school (3) n 084.6
　~ service (1) n 084.6
Nursing (2) 084.6
　~ Association (1) 084.6
nut (361) n/adj 073.4
　~ bread (2) n 044.4
　~ grass (36) n 015.9
　~ grasses (1) n 015.9
　~ head (1) n 073.4
　~ house (1) n 032.2
　~ meat (1) n 054.8
　~ part (2) n 054.8
　~ theaters (1) n 114.9
Nut Hill (1) 107.7
Nutbush (1) TN 087.2
nutcake (2) n 122.1
nutcakes (1) n 044.5
nutcracker (2) n 059.7
Nutcracker (1) 066.9
nutmeg (3) n 061.8
nutria (7) n/adj 059.5
　~ rat (1) n 059.5
nutri(a) rat (1) n 059.5
nutrias (3) n 059.5
nuts (460) n 092.3
nutshell (4) n 054.8
nutty (25) adj 074.7
nuzzling (1) v 036.4
nylon (1) adj 123.7
nymph (8) n 124.6
nympho (15) n 124.8
nymphomaniac (32) n
　124.6
nymphomaniacs (1) n
　124.5
nymphos (2) n 124.5
nymphs (1) n 124.6

O

o' (10) prep 012.5
O (10) 021.6
(Oa)cohay Creek (1) MS 030.7
oafish (1) adj 073.3
oak (2032) n/adj 061.9
~ ash (1) n 080.6
~ ashes (7) n 008.7
~ bark (1) n 061.8
~ buckets (2) n 017.2
~ chest (1) n 009.5
~ chunk (1) n 008.5
~ fire (1) n 051.8
~ grove (1) n 061.6
~ kegs (1) n 020.2
~ leaf (3) n 051.8
~ log (11) n 008.5
~ logs (9) n 008.5
~ mite (1) n 060A.9
~ person (1) n 088.7
~ pickets (1) n 016.2
~ pins (1) n 026.5
~ post (1) n 016.5
~ post[N-i] (1) n 016.5
~ rail fence (1) n 016.4
~ scrub (1) n 061.9
~ shingles (1) n 061.8
~ slits (1) n 088.7
~ snake (2) n 088.8
~ snakes (1) n 084.8
~ stick (1) n 008.5
~ stove (1) n 008.4
~ table (1) n 061.8
~ thicket (1) n 029.4
~ timber (2) n 061.8
~ tree (89) n 061.8
~ tree mechanic (1) n 067.8
~ tree[N-i] (1) n 061.9
~ trees (128) n 061.9
~ worms (3) n 060.5
Oak (104) FL 105.1
~ Bowery (1) AL 075.7
~ Cliff (8) TX 086.5
~ Court (2) 105.1

~ Creek Town Park (1) 085.1
~ Forest (1) 105.4
~ Grove (10) AR LA MS TN 061.6
~ Grove community (1) n 105A.4
~ Grove School (1) 061.6
~ Hill Baptist (1) 089.1
~ Hills (2) 106.2
~ Knoll (1) 107.7
~ Lawn (5) 105.5
~ Leaf (1) 093.7
~ Mountain (1) GA 031.1
~ Mountain community (1) GA 087.5
~ Park (1) 106.9
~ Ridge (18) LA MS TN 087.5
~ Ridge Highway (1) 107.7
~ Ridge Museum (1) 106.7
~ Street (2) 061.8
oak[N-i] (3) n 061.9
Oak[N-i] (1) 106.2
Oakdale (5) LA 105.2
oaken (15) adj 017.2
~ bucket (14) n 017.2
~ buckets (1) n 017.2
Oakland (14) CA FL GA MS TX 087.3
~ Cemetery (1) 106.7
~ Heights (1) 105.4
~ Park (1) 106.4
Oaklane Drive (1) 107.9
Oaklawn (2) AR 087.4
Oakleaf (1) 106.3
Oakleigh (1) 106.5
Oakman (1) AL 087.7
Oakmont (1) TN 087.5
oaks (163) n/adj 061.8
~ range (1) n 015.7
Oaks (14) 106.2
Oaktibee (1) MS 030.7
oakwood (51) n/adj 008.6
~ ashes (1) n 008.7
Oakwood (4) 105.6
~ Cemetery (1) 078.8
oaky (3) adj 029.9
Oaky Streak (1) AL 087.4

oar (12) n/v/adj 024.6
~ boat (4) n 024.6
~ boats (2) n 024.6
~ -type paddle (1) n 024.6
oared (1) v 101.7
oaring (1) v 024.6
oars (10) n 024.6
oat (23) adj 014.4
~ bin (4) n 014.4
~ bundle (1) n 041.6
~ cradle (3) n 042.1
~ drill (1) n 093.9
~ field (1) n 016.1
~ granary (1) n 014.4
~ patch (2) n 016.1
~ sack (4) n 019.7
~ sacks (4) n 042.1
~ straw (2) n 096.9
oat[N-i] (3) n 042.1
oatmeal (12) n/adj 050.3
~ bread (3) n 044.4
oats (344) n/adj 042.1
~ patch (1) n 051.8
Oats (2) 050.3
obelisk statue (1) n 093.5
obese (2) adj 073.1
Obey River (1) TN 030.7
Obion (7) TN 087.8
~ River (4) TN 030.7
object (1) adv 085.2
objected to (1) v 095.8
objection (1) n 039.6
objective (1) adj 075.2
obligate (2) v 057.5
obligate[V-t] (2) v 057.5
~ to (1) v 057.5
obligated (275) v 057.5
obligation (13) n 057.5
obligations (2) n 057.5
oblige (164) adj 093.4
(o)blige (4) adj 093.4
obliged (337) adj 093.4
(o)bliged (6) adj 093.4
obliging (2) adj 057.5
oblique (1) adj 085.2
oblong (5) adj/adv 085.2
obnoxious (6) adj 074.9
obscene movies (1) n 114.9
obsequies (1) n 079.2
observations (1) n 053.6
obsessed (3) adj 124.5
obstinate (36) adj 074.8

obstreperous (2) adj 074.8
obvious (1) adj 070.5
Ocala (21) FL 087.2
~ Forest (1) FL 087.4
ocarina (3) n 020.6
ocarin(a) (1) n 020.6
occasion (1) n 039.7
occasional (3) adj 008.8
~ chair (2) n 008.8
~ chairs (1) n 008.8
occasionally (5) adv 081.1
(oc)casionally (1) adv 066.9
occasions (2) n 052.5
Occonechee Trail (1) 107.7
occupation (2) n 065.8
occu(pation) (1) n 040.6
occupations (1) n 040.8
occupied (3) v 080.6
occurrence (1) n 073.6
ocean (22) n/adj 030.6
~ catfish (1) n 059.9
~ meadow (1) n 029.7
~ perch (3) n 059.9
~ traffic (1) n 080.7
~ trout (1) n 059.9
~ turtle (1) n 060.6
~ wave (1) n 083.1
~ well (1) n 022.7
Ocean (13) 030.7
~ Drive (1) 107A.8
~ Front Park (1) 106.8
~ Pond (1) FL 087.5
~ Springs (7) MS 087.5
oceans (1) n 030.6
Ochlockonee (4) FL 030.7
~ River (2) FL 030.7
Ochs (1) n G 033.5
Ocilla (5) GA 087.8
o'clock (226) adv 070.1
(o')clock (5) adv 001.6
Ocmulgee (14) GA 030.7
~ Creek (1) AL 030.7
~ Indians (1) 084.9
~ River (7) GA 030.7
Ocoee (1) TN 030.7
Oconee (7) GA 030.7
~ River (4) GA 030.7
Octagon (5) 070.6
~ soap (4) n 088.8
October (974) 001A.8
~ bean (3) n 055A.3

~ bean[N-i]   (1)   n
  055A.3
  ~ beans (7) n 055A.4
Octo(ber) (1) 001A.8
Octobers (6) 055A.4
octopus (3) n 060.9
octoroon (25) n 069.5
octoroons (9) n 069.5
OD (1) 088.9
OD'd (1) v 078.5
odd (124) adj 074.7
  ~ -acting (1) adj 074.7
oddball (11) n/adj 074.7
oddity (1) n 051.8
odds (12) n 080.7
  ~ and ends (11) n
    010.2
Odenville (1) AL 086.2
Odessa (4) TX 087.8
Odom (1) TX 087.6
odometer (3) n 110.2
O'Donnell (3) TX 087.3
odor (16) n/adj 047.5
  ~ smell (1) n 051.1
oee (1) interj 038.3
oeuf (2) n F 045.6
of (19906) prep 078.7
(o)f (19) prep 069.2
ofay (7) n 069.4
off (4461) adj/adv/prep
  085.4
  ~ -and-on showers (1)
    n 006.1
  ~ balance (1) adj 074.7
  ~ brands (1) n 033.3
  ~ breed (5) n 033.3
  ~ days (1) n 080.6
  ~ drain (1) n 011.5
  ~ from (1) prep 025.8
  ~ horse (39) n 039.4
  ~ in (2) prep 052.6
  ~ into (1) prep 053.7
  ~ kitchens (1) n 009.9
  ~ lead (2) n 039.4
  ~ -lead team (1) n
    039.4
  ~ leader (2) n 039.4
  ~ limits (2) adj 114.8
  ~ mule (7) n 039.4
  ~ of (229) prep 034.4
  ~ on (3) prep 088.8
  ~ ox (2) n 039.4
  ~ ramp (6) n 107.4
  ~ ramps (3) n 107.4
  ~ road (5) n 031.8

~ roads (1) n 107.4
~ side (14) n 039.4
~ -sided (1) adj 021.6
~ steer (1) n 039.4
~ strap (1) n 088.7
~ street (1) n 031.7
~ -street (1) adj 108.3
~ -street parking (2) n
  108.3
~ the cob (3) adj 056.2
~ -the-wall crack (1) n
  096.9
~ wheel (1) n 039.4
~ -wheeler (2) n 039.4
~ -white (1) adj 008.7
~ with (6) prep 053.4
offal (3) n 037.2
offals (4) n 037.2
Offatt Bayou (1) TX
  030.7
offbeat (2) adj 074.7
offen (46) prep 034.4
offended (18) v 075.2
offender (1) n 114.4
offense (3) n 051.8
offer (7) n/v 058.7
offered (5) v 058.6
  ~ to (1) v 058.6
offering (1) n 095.7
Offertory (1) 089.5
offhand (4) adv 039.5
offhanded (2) adv 065.8
office   (1126)   n/adj
  007A.3
  ~ boy (1) n 084.2
  ~ building (8) n 108.5
  ~ buildings (3) n 108.5
  ~ girl (6) n 068.8
  ~ lady (2) n 068.8
  ~ manager (1) n 068.8
  ~ sitting room (1) n
    007A.2
  ~ space (1) n 090.7
  ~ work (1) n 065.8
of(fice) (4) adj 084.1
Office (2) 084.2
officer (16) n 112.5
Officer (5) 112.5
officers (6) n 112.5
offices (14) n 084.2
official (2) n/adj 013.5
officials (2) n 066.8
officiated (1) v 079.2
offs (4) n 031.2
offset (9) n/adj 085.2

~ disc harrow (1) n
  021.7
~ kitchen (2) n 007A.1
offsets (1) v 065.9
offsides (1) n 075.1
offspring (16) n 064.3
offsprings (5) n 064.3
oft (1) adv 071.1
often   (1192)   adj/adv
  071.1
  ~ child (1) n 066.3
oft(en) (1) adv 071.1
oftener (3) adv 071.1
oftentime (3) adv 071.1
oftentimes (8) adv 071.1
ofttime (1) adv 071.1
ofttimes (1) adv 088.8
Ogden (4) UT 087.4
Ogeechee (5) GA 030.7
  ~ River (4) GA 030.7
Ogeech(ee) River (1) GA
  030.7
Ogle Knob (1) TX 030.8
Oglethorpe (10) GA 065.9
  ~ Avenue (3) 107.6
  ~ Mall (1) 106.4
Ogleton Park (1) 085.1
O'Grady's (1) 106.4
ogre (1) n 125.1
oh (1380) interj 091.5
  ~ -a(x2)   (1)   interj
    037.5
  ~ -wee(x2)   (1)   interj
    038.3
Oh (8) 107.6
oh(x2) (2) interj 037.5
Ohio (62) 086.1
  ~ River (2) OH 030.7
oho (1) interj 091.5
Ohoopee (1) GA 030.7
(O)hoopee (3) GA 030.7
  ~ River (2) GA 030.7
OIC (1) 035.5
OICs (1) 080.6
oil (2168) n/v/adj 024.1
  ~ barrel (1) n 019.1
  ~ bean (1) n 024.1
  ~ bomb (1) n 024.3
  ~ boom (1) n 024.1
  ~ -burner stoves (1) n
    080.6
  ~ -burning   (1)   adj
    024.1
  ~ -burning furnaces (2)
    n 118.4

~ business (1) n 024.1
~ can (6) n 020.4
~ changing (1) n 024.1
~ circulator (3) n 118.5
~ companies   (5)   n
  024.1
~ company (6) n 024.1
~ cup (1) n 051.8
~ derrick (1) n 024.1
~ drilling (1) n 024.1
~ drum (1) n 024.1
~ drums (1) n 024.1
~ field (6) n 024.1
~ -field work (1) n
  102.8
~ -field worker (1) n
  024.1
~ -field workers (1) n
  024.1
~ field[N-i] (2) n 016.1
~ fields (12) n 024.1
~ furnace (2) n 118.4
~ gauge (4) n 024.1
~ head (1) n 113.6
~ heat (1) n 118.5
~ heater (3) n 118.4
~ heaters (2) n 118.4
~ industry (1) n 024.1
~ lamp (16) n 024.3
~ lamps (16) n 024.1
~ light (1) n 024.3
~ lights (4) n 024.2
~ mill (6) n 024.1
~ painting (3) n 024.1
~ -producing   (1)   adj
  024.1
~ product (1) n 024.1
~ refinery (1) n 024.1
~ rigs (1) n 024.1
~ road (2) n 031.6
~ roads (1) n 031.6
~ rock (5) n 023.4
~ stove (13) n 024.1
~ tanks (2) n 024.1
~ well (3) n 024.1
~ -well peoples (1) n
  080.9
~ wells (5) n 024.1
~ wick (1) n 024.3
Oil (16) 024.1
~ Trough (1) AR 070.6
oilcan (4) n 024.1
oilcloth (6) n 024.1
oiled (15) v 024.1
oiling (4) n/v 023.7

oils (3) n 127.3
oilstone (15) n 023.4
oilstones (1) n 023.4
oilstove (3) n 024.1
oily (12) adj 024.1
~ -like (1) adj 090.4
~ road (1) n 031.6
~ -type (1) adj 029.8
oink (2) n 112.5
~ -oinks (1) n 112.5
oink(x2) (1) n 037.9
oinks (1) n 112.5
ointment (1) n 078.3
Ojus (1) 105A.5
OK (269) 091.3
~ dinghies (1) n 024.6
(O)K (2) 091.3
ok(x2) (1) interj 037.5
Okahumpka (2) FL 087.1
~ Terrace (1) FL 087.2
Okaloosa (2) FL 087.2
Okatuppa (1) FL 030.7
oke (2) interj 037.5
Okeechobee (14) FL 087.7
~ City (1) FL 087.6
Okeelala (1) MS 030.7
Okefenokee (19) GA 087.7
~ Swamp (10) GA 029.6
Okefenok(ee) Swamp (2) GA 030.7
okeydoke (3) interj 091.1
Okie (1) 084.9
Okies (3) 069.7
Okinawa (1) 065.9
Oklahoma (763) 086.8
~ City (10) OK 087.7
~ drill (1) n 130.5
~ River (1) OK 030.7
~ Silver Mine (2) 056.2
~ State (1) 086.8
Oklahom(a) (3) 086.8
Oklawaha (4) FL 030.7
~ River (2) FL 030.7
Okolona (7) AR MS 087.5
okra (928) n/adj 055.8
~ blooms (1) n 055.8
~ crop (1) n 055.8
~ gumbo (8) n 055.8
~ seed (1) n 055.8
~ seeds (1) n 055.8
~ squash (1) n 056.6

~ stalks (1) n 055.8
okras (8) n 016.7
Oktibbeha (4) MS 087.1
~ County (1) MS 087.1
~ County Lake (1) MS 106.4
Oktoberfest (1) 001A.6
Oktoc (3) MS 087.2
~ Road (1) 087.7
old (4688) adj 047.5
~ -age (1) adj 073.1
~ -age building (1) n 108.5
~ bachelor (1) n 037.3
~ bag (1) n 084.9
~ bags (1) n 126.7
~ battle-ax (3) n 063.2
~ boss (6) n 069.6
~ -country look (1) n 123.9
~ -fashion (12) adj 074.7
~ -fashion tomatoes (1) n 055.3
~ -fashioned (4) adj 073.9
~ -fashioned glasses (1) n 048.9
~ -fogy doings (1) n 080.8
~ -folks' home (1) n 119.2
~ -folks' signs (1) n 006.8
~ -folks's home (2) n 043.9
~ -folks's talk (1) n 016.7
~ ham (1) n 046.2
~ hen (2) n 063.2
~ hen cackle (1) n 083.1
~ highway (2) n 107.1
~ husband (1) n 063.1
~ kitchen (3) n 009.9
~ ladies (1) n 063.2
~ lady (243) n 063.2
~ -lady style (1) n 115.5
~ lady[N-i] (1) n 063.2
~ lady's uncle (1) n 063.2
~ maid (11) n 067.6
~ -maid aunt (2) n 067.9

~ -maid daughter (1) n 064.8
~ -maid schoolteacher (7) n 067.6
~ -maid sisters (1) n 001.1
~ -maid teacher (1) n 067.6
~ -maid uncle (1) n 081.9
~ -maidish (1) adj 124.1
~ maids (2) n 130.3
~ male (2) n 035.3
~ man (274) n 063.5
~ man[N-i] (1) n 063.1
~ -man[N-k]-beard (1) n 089.9
~ man[N-k] business (1) n 043.9
~ marse (2) n 069.6
~ massa (2) n 069.6
~ master (12) n 069.6
~ men (1) n 063.1
~ miss (7) n 063.2
~ missus (1) n 063.2
~ mistress (1) n 069.6
~ parents (1) n 063.8
~ playroom (1) n 007A.6
~ potatoes (1) n 055.4
~ -settlers' cake (1) n 044.7
~ South Side (1) 106.1
~ squaw (1) n 063.2
~ sweetie (1) n 063.2
~ -time (26) adj 009.7
~ -time music (1) n 130.8
~ -timers (4) n 025.3
~ -timers' talk (1) n 048.4
~ -timesy (1) adj 066.8
~ -timey (62) adj 088.7
~ -timey-style couch (1) n 009.1
~ wife (2) n 063.2
~ witch (1) n 130.2
~ wives' tale (3) n 063.2
~ wives' tales (1) n 088.8
~ woman (45) n 063.2
Old (128) 067.3

~ Aunt so-and-so (1) n 067.3
~ Canton (1) 107.7
~ Capitol (1) 084.9
~ Capitol Museum (1) 106.4
~ Christmas Day (1) 080.8
~ Cutler Road (1) 106.1
~ Dallas (1) AR 087.5
~ English (1) 118.7
~ Fields (1) 105.5
~ Golds (1) 088.9
~ Gulf (3) 087.6
~ Haggy (1) 090.1
~ Haggy Bill (1) 090.1
~ Harry (3) 090.1
~ Hickory (3) AL TN 106.1
~ Hickory Lake (2) TN 105.8
~ Huntsvillians (1) 080.7
~ Jack (1) 090.1
~ Johnny Bridge (1) 106.6
~ Kings Road (1) 031.6
~ Knoxville Highway (1) 107.5
~ Leland Road (1) 031.6
~ MacDonald (1) 098.4
~ Man (1) 068.5
~ Master (4) 069.6
~ Mexico (7) 086.4
~ Mill (1) 106.6
~ Miss (3) 069.6
~ Montgomery (1) 105.1
~ Mrs. (1) 067.7
~ Natchez Trace (2) 088.9
~ Natchez Trail (1) 087.5
~ Nick (10) 090.1
~ Niles Ferry (1) 107.6
~ Number Eleven (1) GA 001.6
~ Philadelphi(a) (1) AR 087.3
~ Pitch (1) 090.1
~ River (1) LA 030.7
~ Sally (1) 068.1
~ Scratch (26) 090.1

~ South (2) 052.1
~ Spanish Trail (1) 088.7
~ Sugar (1) 063.2
~ Town (3) AL MS 087.7
~ Town Creek (2) AL MS 030.7
~ Town Plantation (1) 070.3
~ Trace (1) 031.7
~ Uncle (1) 069.3
~ Uncle so-and-so (1) n 068.2
~ War (2) 085.8
~ Woman (1) 063.2
~ Yacona River (1) MS 030.7
~ Year (2) 080.9
olden (11) adj 013.5
Oldenburg (1) TX 086.1
older (259) adj 064.7
~ lady (1) n 065.2
old(er) (4) adj 043.2
olders (1) n 075.6
oldest (227) adj 064.7
olds (1) n 001.5
oldsters (1) n 064.3
Ole (12) 080.9
~ Miss (5) 080.9
oleander (20) n/adj 062.7
~ tree (1) n 080.6
~ trees (1) n 061.8
Oleander (1) 084.3
oleanders (9) n 062.2
Olena (1) AR 087.3
olive (9) n/adj 055.2
~ oil (2) n 024.1
~ tree (1) n 061.9
Olive (8) 107.7
~ Branch (1) MS 087.2
~ Creek (1) AL 030.7
~ Springs (1) TN 075.9
Oliver (19) 021.6
~ A turning plow (1) n 021.6
~ Chilled (1) 021.6
~ Creek (1) AL 030.7
~ Finney (1) 021.6
~ Goober (2) 021.6
~ Goobers (1) 021.6
~ plow (1) n 021.6
~ plows (1) n 021.6
Olivers (3) 021.6
Olivier (1) LA 087.1

Ollie (2) LA 087.4
Olmos (14) 030.7
~ Creek (3) TX 030.7
~ Park (6) 106.1
~ Street (1) 107.7
Oloh (1) MS 087.1
Olustee (3) FL 087.5
~ Creek (1) FL 030.7
(O)lustee Creek (1) FL 030.7
Olympic Peninsula (1) 086.2
Oma (2) G 064.2
Omaha (10) NE 087.2
~ Springs (1) GA 087.8
Omega (2) LA 087.8
omelet (10) n/adj 046.2
~ pan (1) n 017.5
omelets (2) n 046.3
Omelia and Ophelia (1) 089.8
ominous (1) adj 074.3
Omni (5) 106.4
OMs (1) 119.7
(O)musee Creek (2) AL 030.7
on (6634) adj/adv/prep 027.2
~ a cause (1) prep 088.6
~ account (2) prep 088.6
~ account of (133) prep 088.6
~ (ac)count of (11) prep 088.6
~ account [P-0] (1) prep 088.6
~ (ac)count [P-0] (1) prep 088.6
~ apurpose (4) adv 103.6
~ back of (1) prep 010.5
~ his stomach (40) adv 080.4
~ my stomach (1) adv 080.4
~ person (1) adv 103.6
~ purpose (398) adv 103.6
~ ramp (10) n 107.4
~ ramps (2) n 107.4
~ the account of (2) prep 088.6

~ the cob (15) adj 027.2
~ the cobs (1) adj 056.2
~ the count of (4) prep 088.6
~ the gay side (1) adj 124.1
~ the make (1) adj 081.4
~ the nest (1) adj 065.1
~ the stomach (8) adv 080.4
~ their stomach[N-i] (2) adv 080.4
~ top of (16) prep 027.2
~ your case (1) adv 090.9
(o)n (3) adv 075.3
On (3) 130.8
once (1285) n/adv 001A.4
oncle (1) n F 068.2
one (6222) n/pron/adj 001.1
~ -and-a-half stories (1) n 007A.6
~ another (3) pron 042.7
~ -by-four (2) n 001.2
~ -by-fours (1) n 001.1
~ -by-six (2) n 001.1
~ -by-tens (1) n 026.6
~ -by-twelve (3) n 001.6
~ -by-twelves (1) n 001.6
~ -by-wides (1) n 080.6
~ -car garage (1) n 065.8
~ creed (1) n 089.8
~ -door (1) n 109.2
~ eye open (1) adj 046.1
~ -eyed car (1) n 081.9
~ -family (1) adj 118.9
~ -forty-five (2) n 004.5
~ -handed farmer (1) n 080.9
~ -holer (14) n 012.1
~ -holers (2) n 012.1
~ hop (1) n 130.4
~ -horse (3) adj 067.8
~ -horse crop (1) n 041.3

~ -horse cultivator (1) n 023.9
~ -horse farm (2) n 034.2
~ -horse farmer (3) n 084.9
~ -horse hack (1) n 034.2
~ -horse harrow (1) n 021.7
~ -horse harrows (1) n 021.7
~ -horse outfit (1) n 084.9
~ -horse plow (8) n 021.6
~ -horse preacher (1) n 067.8
~ -horse sawmill (1) n 052.7
~ -horse sharecrop (2) n 080.8
~ -horse shay (1) n 084.8
~ -horse single plow (1) n 021.6
~ -horse thing (1) n 034.2
~ -horse town (1) n 106.7
~ -horse wagon (8) n 001.1
~ -horse wagons (2) n 034.2
~ -hundred (1) adj 001A.2
~ in the oven (1) n 065.1
~ -legged bed (1) n 080.8
~ -level (1) adj 119.4
~ -level apartments (1) n 119.4
~ -man boat (1) n 024.6
~ -man operation (1) n 001.1
~ -minded (1) adj 074.8
~ -mule contraption (1) n 021.2
~ -mule crop (1) n 080.6
~ -mule planter (1) n 021.6

~ -night baby (1) n
   065.7
~ -on-one (1) adv 092.7
~ Our Father (1) n
   089.8
~ -plank merry-go-
   rounds (1) n 022.7
~ -room (2) adj 001.1
~ -room cabin (1) n
   010.8
~ -room house (3) n
   007A.2
~ -room houses (1) n
   118.9
~ -room outfit (1) n
   080.6
~ -room school (8) n
   001.1
~ -room schoolhouse
   (5) n 001.1
~ -row cultivator (3) n
   021.6
~ -row planter (4) n
   021.6
~ -row planters (1) n
   096.7
~ -row plow (1) n
   021.6
~ -row stuff (1) n 099.7
~ -seat car (1) n 109.1
~ -seat outfit (1) n
   039.6
~ -seater (1) n 023.6
~ -sided (1) adv 085.2
~ -step (5) n 083.1
~ stock (1) n 021.6
~ -stop plow (1) n
   021.6
~ -story (2) adj 118.9
~ -story (a)partment
   house (1) n 119.4
~ -teacher (1) adj 067.6
~ -teacher school (7) n
   067.6
~ -teacher schools (1) n
   088.7
~ -thirty (9) n 004.4
~ -track mind (7) n
   074.8
~ -upmanship (2) n
   129.9
~ -way (4) adj 074.8
~ -way drive (1) n
   031.8

~ -way street (7) n
   031.7
~ -way streets (12) n
   107.5
(o)ne (15) n 036.7
One (98) 001.1
~ -Forty-Six Street (1)
   107.1
~ -Hundred-and-
   Seventy-Fourth
   Street (1)
   001A.3
~ Hundred building (1)
   n 106.4
~ -Oh-One (1) 074.4
~ -Seventy-Three (1)
   031.6
~ -Sixty-Third Street
   (1) 107.7
one[M-i] (7) pron
   055A.1
one[N-i] (5) n 064.3
one[N-i][N-k] (1) adj
   064.3
Oneida (7) AR TN 087.8
Oneonta (1) AL 087.5
ones (565) n/pron 001.1
(o)nes (2) pron 052.1
ones' (1) pron 064.3
oneself (1) pron 044.2
oneses (4) pron 042.7
onesies (3) n 130.6
onion (692) n/adj 055.6
~ -and-egg bread (1) n
   044.8
~ bag (1) n 019.7
~ -bag sack (1) n 019.7
~ bags (1) n 019.5
~ bread (2) n 044.4
~ bulbs (1) n 055.7
~ buns (1) n 044.4
~ buttons (2) n 055.7
~ dip (1) n 055.6
~ dumplings (1) n
   044.6
~ patch (2) n 016.1
~ plants (2) n 055.7
~ poultice (1) n 061.4
~ rings (3) n 055.6
~ roll (1) n 044.4
~ rolls (3) n 044.4
~ -root tea (1) n 061.4
~ sack (8) n 019.7
~ season (1) n 037.3
~ set (3) n 055.7

~ sets (17) n 055.7
~ slips (1) n 055.6
~ soup (2) n 081.8
~ sprouts (1) n 055.7
~ stalks (1) n 055.7
~ top (1) n 055.7
~ tops (7) n 055.6
on(ion) (1) n 055.7
Onion Creek (3) AR TX
   030.7
onion[N-i] (7) n 055.6
onions (1287) n 055.6
onliest (128) adj 064.7
only (136) adj/adv 070.6
onl(y) (1) adj 025.8
Only (4) TN 087.2
onto (51) adv/prep 027.2
onus child (1) n 065.7
onyx (1) n 123.2
onze (1) n F 001.6
oo (2) interj 038.5
~ -eh (1) interj 038.5
Oochee Creek (1) GA
   030.7
oodles (10) n 084.8
ooey (6) interj 038.3
~ yooey (1) interj 038.3
ooey(x2) (1) interj 038.3
oogy (1) interj 038.3
ooh (35) interj 038.3
~ wee (1) interj 036.2
ooh(x2) (3) interj 038.3
ooh(x3) ow (1) interj
   059.2
oolite limestone (1) n
   031.6
Ooltewah (1) TN 087.4
oompower (1) n 073.1
oop (1) interj 038.3
Oostanaula (3) GA 030.7
~ Creek (1) GA 030.7
Oostanaul(a) River (1)
   GA 030.7
Oostanau(la) (1) GA
   030.7
ooze (1) n 093.5
oozy (1) adj 029.7
Opa (7) G 064.1
~ -Locka (3) FL 087.3
~ -Locka Air Base (1)
   106A.1
~ -Locka Airport (1)
   106.5
OPD (1) 112.5
ope(x2) (1) interj 038.3

Opelika (9) AL FL 087.3
Opelousas (15) LA 087.4
open (420) v/adj 083.3
~ -air coop (1) n 036.8
~ -air safe (1) n 015.5
~ attic (1) n 009.8
~ barn (2) n 014.7
~ barns (1) n 014.7
~ bed (1) n 109.7
~ black pot (1) n 017.6
~ boat (1) n 024.6
~ boats (1) n 024.6
~ country (1) n 029.5
~ ditches (1) n 030.2
~ eggs (1) n 046.2
~ enclosure (1) n 015.4
~ -faced pie (1) n 047.6
~ field (5) n 108.7
~ fireplace (1) n 008.3
~ fireplaces (1) n 065.8
~ free range (1) n
   081.9
~ gilts (1) n 035.5
~ grate (2) n 118.4
~ hall (7) n 010.8
~ -hall breezeway (1) n
   010.8
~ halls (1) n 007A.3
~ hallway (3) n 007A.3
~ hay barn (1) n 014.2
~ heart (1) n 054.4
~ house (1) n 084.8
~ houses (1) n 130.7
~ kettle (1) n 017.6
~ kettle house (1) n
   080.6
~ land (2) n 016.6
~ livestock law (1) n
   080.6
~ load bed (1) n 109.7
~ loft (1) n 014.5
~ lot (4) n 015.6
~ lots (1) n 051.5
~ pasture (3) n 015.7
~ peach (2) n 054.4
~ peaches (1) n 054.4
~ pen (1) n 015.6
~ place (6) n 008.2
~ places (1) n 015.7
~ plow (1) n 021.6
~ porch (13) n 010.8
~ porches (4) n 007A.5
~ range (49) n 015.7
~ range country (1) n
   088.7

~ season (1) n 081.8
~ seed (3) n 054.4
~ shed (2) n 015.1
~ sheds (1) n 015.1
~ shelter (2) n 015.1
~ space (1) n 031.3
~ spaces (1) n 065.9
~ stone (28) n 054.4
~ stone peach (1) n 054.4
~ stones (1) n 054.4
~ store (1) n 054.4
~ -toe (1) adj 123.8
~ -toed (2) adj 123.8
~ -toed pumps (1) n 123.8
~ -toed shoe (1) n 123.8
~ -toed shoes (2) n 123.8
~ toes (1) n 119.8
~ toilet (1) n 012.1
~ toilets (1) n 012.1
~ up (16) v 083.3
~ weave (1) n 019.7
~ well (5) n 015.5
~ woods (1) n 015.6
~ wound (1) n 078.1
o(pen) (1) adj 098.6
Open (2) 029.4
~ Elm Bottom (1) TX 029.4
~ Lake (1) TN 030.7
open[V-p] (2) v 083.2
open[V-r] (1) v 081.3
open[V-t] (2) v 095.8
~ up (1) v 041.4
opened (33) v 094.4
~ into (1) v 052.5
~ up (3) v 083.3
opener (6) n 021.8
opening (9) n/v/adj 051.8
~ plow (1) n 021.6
opens (13) v 083.3
openwork sack (1) n 019.6
opera (42) n/adj 084.4
~ house (28) n 084.4
~ houses (2) n 084.4
operas (4) n 130.8
operate (19) v 036.1
~ on (12) v 036.1
operate[V-t] on (1) v 036.1
operated (23) v/adj 120.9

~ on (13) v 036.1
operating (4) v/adj 110.1
~ buttons (1) n 110.1
~ on (1) v 036.1
operation (16) n/adj 080.1
operations (3) n 015.5
operator (4) n 063.4
operators (1) n 099.8
Ophelia (1) 089.8
opinion (1) n 052.5
opinionated (5) adj 074.8
opinions (2) n 073.1
opium (10) n 114.2
opossum (28) n 059.5
(o)possum (260) n/adj 059.5
~ hide (1) n 059.5
~ -hunt (1) v 080.7
~ hunting (7) n/v 096.7
(O)possum (1) 059.5
(o)possum[N-i] (3) n 059.5
opossums (8) n 059.5
(o)possums (121) n 059.5
Opp (1) AL 087.8
opportunity (1) n 013.8
opposite (8) adj 085.2
opposition (3) n 080.6
Opry (7) 130.8
Opryland (8) 106.4
optimistic (3) adj 070.7
option price (1) n 094.5
or (2628) conj 014.3
(o)r (2) conj 001A.3
Oral Roberts (1) 025.8
orange (632) n/adj 055.1
~ blossoms (1) n 055.1
~ bowl (3) n 055.1
~ bread (1) n 044.4
~ Coke (1) n 121.8
~ color (1) n 055.1
~ -colored (1) adj 055.1
~ crate (1) n 055.1
~ crates (2) n 055.1
~ drink (4) n 055.1
~ flesh (1) n 056.9
~ grove (15) n 061.6
~ groves (8) n 061.6
~ juice (75) n 055.1
~ marmalade (2) n 051.6
~ orchard (1) n 053.2
~ peel (2) n 084.9

~ peeling (3) n 055.1
~ pickers (1) n 080.8
~ pies (1) n 055.1
~ seed (1) n 055.1
~ slice (1) n 055.1
~ snake (1) n 080.7
~ sorghum cane (1) n 055.1
~ square (1) n 055.1
~ squash (1) n 056.6
~ sunshine (1) n 114.2
~ tree (18) n 055.1
~ -tree limb (1) n 055.1
~ trees (21) n 055.1
~ twist (1) n 122.7
~ wars (1) n 130.5
Orange (28) FL TX 087.2
~ Avenue (2) 107.6
~ Beach (1) AL 087.8
~ Bowl (4) 055.1
~ County (1) FL 087.5
~ Hill (1) FL 055.1
~ Mound (6) 105.4
~ Park (1) FL 087.7
~ River (1) FL 030.7
~ Streaker (1) 109.9
~ Street (1) 107.7
~ View (1) FL 087.2
orange[N-i] (5) n 055.1
Orangeburg (3) SC 087.4
~ clay (1) n 029.9
Orangemen (1) 127.8
orangerie (1) n F 053.2
oranges (636) n/adj 055.1
~ trees (1) n 061.8
orchard (1092) n/adj 053.2
~ farm (1) n 053.2
~ harrow (1) n 021.9
orch(ard) (7) n 053.2
Orchard (10) 053.2
~ Beach (1) ME 053.2
~ Knob (4) TN 030.8
orchards (50) n 053.2
orchestra (3) n 130.9
orchid (4) n/adj 070.6
~ trees (2) n 061.9
Orchid Homes (1) 106.2
ordain[V-t] (1) v 057.8
ordained (2) v 067.8
ordeal (1) n 091.6
Ordeman-Shaw complex (1) n 106.4
order (928) n/v 085.7
ord(er) (1) n 085.7

or(der) (1) n 085.7
Order (2) 131.1
~ of De Pineda (1) 131.1
~ of Mists (1) 119.7
ordered (1) v 074.4
orderliness (1) n 085.7
orderly (1) adj 082.8
orders (18) n 085.7
ordinaire (1) adj F 047.2
ordinance (3) n 085.7
ordinary (47) n/adj 073.6
~ ground (1) n 029.8
ordinary's office (1) n 090.8
ore (2) n 029.8
Ore (1) 030.7
Oregon (11) 086.5
Oreo (3) 098.7
Oreos (3) 069.3
orfanato (1) n S 066.3
organ (129) n/adj 130.9
~ loft (1) n 088.8
~ meat (2) n 037.2
~ meats (2) n 037.2
~ music (4) n 089.5
~ room (1) n 007A.3
organic soil (1) n 029.8
organist (1) n 057.9
organization (2) n 065.9
organize (1) v 049.5
organized (2) v/adj 012.2
organs (19) n 037.2
orgies (1) n 130.8
orgy (2) n/adj 083.1
~ seat (1) n 009.1
Orient pear (1) n 070.7
Oriental (4) 069.4
Orientals (4) 126.4
original (7) adj 051.4
originally (2) adv 053.5
origin(ally) (1) adv 065.8
Orion (4) AL 086.8
~ Street (1) 107.7
Orlando (25) FL 087.6
~ Clipper (1) 024.6
Orleanian (1) 096.7
Orleanians (2) 101.7
Orleans (1002) 087.8
~ Parish (2) LA 087.4
~ Street (1) 114.8
Or(leans) (1) 087.8
(Or)leans (2) 087.8
Orme (2) 107.7
~ Circle (1) 107.7

~ Park (1) 106.5
ornament (2) n/adj 066.8
  ~ crab apple (1) n 061.9
ornamental (5) adj 017.1
  ~ eggs (1) n 017.1
  ~ fence (1) n 016.4
  ~ tomatoes (1) n 055.3
  ~ trees (1) n 061.8
  ~ wire (1) n 016.3
ornaments (1) n 028.4
ornate (1) adj 013.8
ornery (42) adj 074.8
orphan (916) n/adj 066.3
  ~ asylum (2) n 066.3
  ~ baby (1) n 066.3
  ~ boy (11) n 066.3
  ~ boys (2) n 066.3
  ~ child (74) n 066.3
  ~ children (11) n 066.3
  ~ childs (1) n 066.3
  ~ girl (2) n 066.3
  ~ home (24) n 066.3
  ~ -home childrens (1) n 066.3
  ~ homes (3) n 066.3
  ~ kid (2) n 066.3
  ~ people (1) n 066.3
Orphan Creek (1) MS 030.7
orphanage (26) n/adj 066.3
  ~ child (2) n 066.3
  ~ children (1) n 066.3
  ~ home (1) n 066.3
orphaned (3) v/adj 066.3
orphans (32) n 066.3
orphans' (21) adj 066.3
  ~ boy (1) n 066.3
  ~ children (1) n 066.3
  ~ girl (1) n 066.3
  ~ home (17) n 066.3
  ~ lady (1) n 065.2
orphlet (1) n 066.3
orris (1) n 088.8
Ortega (5) 105.1
Orthodox (5) 126.7
  ~ Jew (1) 126.7
  ~ Jews (1) 025.2
orts (2) n 037.2
Orvil (2) TX 087.6
Orville Faubus (1) 053.4
Osage (2) 087.7
  ~ orange (1) n 061.9
Osanippi (1) AL 084.8

Osburn Creek (1) MS 030.7
Osceola (7) AR MO 086.7
oscillator (1) n 088.7
oscilloscope (1) n 088.8
Osierfield (2) GA 086.4
Osman (1) 084.9
osnaburg (6) n/adj 019.7
  ~ sack (1) n 019.7
  ~ sacks (1) n 019.6
Oso (2) TX 030.7
Ossabaw Sound (1) GA 030.7
Ossahatchie (1) GA 030.7
ostrich (2) n/adj 052.9
  ~ farm (1) n 088.9
Osyka (2) MS 087.6
other (307) n/adj 069.4
  ~ bedroom (1) n 007A.7
  ~ half (10) n 063.1
  ~ ma (1) n 064.2
  ~ pa (1) n 064.1
  ~ room (5) n 007A.2
  ~ side (2) n 078.5
  ~ -side-of-the-street people (1) n 069.7
  ~ side of the tracks (1) n 114.8
oth(er) (1) adj 057.4
other[N-i] (1) n 052.1
others (45) n 099.1
otherwise (1) adv 040.6
Otoptis (1) MS 030.7
otter (6) n 060.2
Otter (6) FL 030.7
  ~ Creek (4) AR FL 030.7
  ~ Lake Creek (1) FL 030.7
otters (9) n 070.7
ottoman (3) n 008.9
Otwell (2) AR 087.7
  ~ Bayou (1) LA 030.7
Ouachita (43) AR LA 031.3
  ~ basin (1) n 030.5
  ~ Bottoms (1) AR 029.4
  ~ Parish (2) LA 087.2
  ~ River (18) AR LA 030.7
ouch (19) interj 092.1

ought (1344) v 058.1
  ~ to (1013) v 058.3
  ~ to've (2) v 058.3
  ~ [P-0] (4) v 058.3
oughtn't (108) v 058.4
oui (2) n F 128.2
  ~ -oui (1) n F 128.2
ounce (7) n/adj 114.1
ounces (3) n 114.1
our (326) pron 043.4
  ~ own self[M-i] (1) pron 043.3
  ~ own selves (2) pron 044.1
Our (2) 089.8
  ~ Father (1) 089.8
  ~ Father[N-i] (1) 089.8
ourn (27) pron 043.4
ours (684) pron 043.4
ourself[M-i] (16) pron 043.4
ourselves (33) pron 044.2
ousted (1) v 066.9
out (7299) adj/adv/prep 034.5
  ~ barn (1) n 014.2
  ~ bathroom (1) n 012.1
  ~ in the cold (1) adv 082.1
  ~ irons (1) n 008.3
  ~ kitchen (1) n 009.9
  ~ of (833) prep 034.5
  ~ (o)f (1) prep 034.5
  ~ -of-doors toilet (2) n 012.1
  ~ of family (1) adj 065.7
  ~ of his troubles (1) adj 078.5
  ~ of his way (1) adj 078.5
  ~ of it (1) adj 114.3
  ~ of order (1) adj 065.1
  ~ of school (2) adj 083.4
  ~ of sight (1) adj 075.6
  ~ of state (1) adv 066.7
  ~ -of-state person (2) n 066.7
  ~ of stater (1) n 066.7
  ~ of step (1) adv 104.8
  ~ of the saddle (1) adv 082.1

  ~ of the way (1) adv 078.6
  ~ of the wedlock (1) adj 065.7
  ~ of towner (3) n 066.7
  ~ of towners (1) n 066.7
  ~ -of-wed marriage (1) n 065.7
  ~ of wedlock (59) adj 065.7
  ~ -of-wedlock child (1) n 065.7
  ~ -of-wedlock mother (1) n 065.7
  ~ -rebound (1) v 080.6
  ~ road (4) n 031.8
  ~ sheds (1) n 011.7
  ~ toilet (1) n 012.1
  ~ [P-0] (119) prep 048.9
  ~ [P-0] the way (3) adj 078.6
Out (2) 087.5
  ~ Yonder (1) 052.2
outbidded (1) v 097.8
outboard (8) n/adj 024.6
  ~ motorboats (1) n 024.6
  ~ motors (3) n 024.6
outboards (1) n 024.6
outbuilding (20) n 011.7
outbuildings (13) n 011.7
outcast (2) n 065.7
outdo (1) v 058.5
outdone (1) adj 092.3
outdoor (244) n/adj 012.1
  ~ bath (2) n 012.1
  ~ bathroom (6) n 012.1
  ~ bathrooms (1) n 012.1
  ~ blinds (1) n 009.5
  ~ building (1) n 011.7
  ~ buildings (1) n 011.7
  ~ closet (4) n 012.1
  ~ crap shop (1) n 012.1
  ~ facilities (1) n 012.1
  ~ faucet (1) n 018.7
  ~ faucets (1) n 018.7
  ~ house (10) n 012.1
  ~ john (2) n 012.1
  ~ johnny (2) n 012.1
  ~ johns (2) n 012.1
  ~ kitchen (1) n 009.9

~ lavatory (4) n 012.1
~ parlor (1) n 012.1
~ privy (10) n 012.1
~ rest room (3) n 012.1
~ shop house (1) n 011.7
~ sitting room (1) n 010.8
~ spigot (1) n 018.7
~ spiral stairs (1) n 010.7
~ staircase (2) n 010.7
~ stairs (1) n 010.7
~ stairways (1) n 010.7
~ steps (2) n 010.7
~ storage room (1) n 011.7
~ storeroom (1) n 011.7
~ theaters (1) n 084.4
~ toilet (122) n 012.1
~ toil(et) (2) n 012.1
~ toilets (49) n 012.1
Outdoor (1) 084.4
outdoors (9) adj/adv 066.8
~ privy (1) n 012.1
~ toilet (2) n 012.1
~ toilets (1) n 012.1
outdoorsy (2) adj 118.1
outed (1) v 032.2
outen (4) prep 032.8
~ doors (1) adv 032.8
outer (30) n/adj 113.7
~ city (2) n 105.9
~ covering (1) n 054.8
~ house (4) n 012.1
~ houses (1) n 012.1
~ hull (4) n 054.8
~ layer (1) n 054.8
~ pantry (1) n 010.1
~ rim (2) n 021.1
~ rung (1) n 021.1
~ shell (8) n 054.8
~ skin (1) n 054.8
~ toilet (1) n 012.1
~ tube (1) n 024.4
~ wheel (1) n 021.1
outfit (83) n 055A.7
outfits (3) n 009.4
outgoing (6) adj 074.1
outgrew (2) v 065.6
outgrow (5) v 101.8
outgrow[V-r] (1) v 065.6
outgrow[V-t] (2) v 065.8

outgrowed (15) v 065.6
outgrown (7) v 065.6
outhouse (442) n/adj 012.1
~ place (1) n 011.7
~ toilets (1) n 012.1
~ tomatoes (3) n 055.3
outhouses (94) n 012.1
outing (2) n/adj 027.1
~ clothes (1) n 065.8
outlander (3) n 066.7
outlandish (1) adj 081.8
outlaw (10) n/adj 065.7
~ dog (1) n 033.3
~ preacher (1) n 067.8
outlawed (2) v/adj 053.6
~ whiskey (1) n 050.9
outlaws (5) n 080.6
outlet (4) n/adj 015.7
~ faucet (1) n 018.7
Outlet (1) 030.7
outlets (4) n 030.3
outlived (1) v 057.8
outmanned (1) v 065.5
outnig(ger) (1) v 080.9
outrageous (1) adj 075.2
outrageousest (2) adj 064.7
outranked (1) v 129.7
outrig(ger) (1) adj 089.8
outroom (1) n 010.3
outs (8) n/v 123.9
outside (250) n/adj/adv/prep 065.7
~ agitator (1) n 066.7
~ bark (1) n 054.8
~ bath (2) n 012.1
~ bathroom (5) n 012.1
~ bathrooms (1) n 012.1
~ boxing (1) n 011.2
~ bread (1) n 045.1
~ building (1) n 012.1
~ child (12) n 065.7
~ children (3) n 065.7
~ chores (2) n 037.4
~ closets (1) n 012.1
~ commode (1) n 012.1
~ doorsteps (1) n 010.7
~ facilities (1) n 012.1
~ faucet (9) n 018.7
~ fences (1) n 016.3
~ garbage can (1) n 117.2
~ horse (1) n 039.4

~ house (6) n 012.1
~ houses (3) n 012.1
~ hull (4) n 054.8
~ hydrant (1) n 018.7
~ kitchen (5) n 009.9
~ kitchens (1) n 009.9
~ man (1) n 082.3
~ of (1) prep 102.7
~ part (1) n 054.8
~ people (1) n 066.7
~ plumbing (1) n 012.1
~ range (5) n 015.7
~ rest room (1) n 012.1
~ rim (1) n 021.1
~ road (1) n 031.7
~ room (1) n 011.7
~ sealing (1) n 011.2
~ shell (1) n 054.8
~ shorts (1) n 123.2
~ siding (1) n 011.2
~ spicket (3) n 018.7
~ spickets (1) n 018.7
~ stair (4) n 010.7
~ staircase (1) n 010.7
~ stairs (16) n 010.7
~ stairway (12) n 010.7
~ steps (2) n 010.7
~ sweep (1) n 088.8
~ toilet (50) n 012.1
~ toilet facilities (1) n 012.1
~ toilets (13) n 012.1
~ trash can (1) n 117.2
~ two-holer (1) n 012.1
~ walkway (1) n 010.9
~ work (2) n 037.4
outsider (13) n 066.7
outsiders (3) n 066.7
outskirts (2) n 106.2
outspell (1) v 074.4
outspoken (1) adj 080.6
outstandingest (1) adj 064.7
outstingest (1) adj 090.8
outtalk (1) v 039.6
outwards (1) adv 080.8
oval (1) adj 090.4
oven (314) n/adj 017.5
~ bread (3) n 044.6
~ skillet (1) n 017.5
~ toaster (1) n 116.4
ovens (55) n 017.5
over (3678) adj/adv/prep 039.5
~ easy (1) adj 046.2

~ -exaggerating (1) v 080.7
~ hard (1) adj 046.2
~ joist[N-i] (1) n 104.5
~ light (11) adj 046.2
~ lightly (1) adv 046.2
~ medium (1) adj 046.2
~ -rise (1) v 088.7
~ the fence (1) adv 065.7
~ the hill (3) adj 078.6
~ the housetop (1) n 080.9
~ the tracks (2) adv 106.1
~ there (5) interj 039.5
~ well (1) adj 046.2
ov(er) (11) adv/prep 082.7
o(ver) (4) adv 050.1
over[N-i] (5) n 050.1
overall (12) n/adj 027.4
~ gang (1) n 069.9
~ material (1) n 027.4
~ pant[N-i] (1) n 027.4
~ pants (2) n 027.4
~ strap (1) n 027.4
~ unions (1) n 027.4
overall[N-i] (27) n 027.4
overalls (521) n 027.4
overanxious (1) adj 074.2
overbearing (1) adj 073.5
overboard (8) adv 066.8
overbraid (1) n 123.9
overcast (41) adj 005.5
~ day (5) n 005.5
overcloudy (1) adj 005.5
overcoat (117) n/adj 027.1
~ weather (1) n 007.4
overcoating (1) n 027.1
overcoats (8) n 027.1
overcome (3) v 079.3
overcross (1) adj 085.2
overcup (3) n/adj 061.6
~ oak (1) n 061.8
overdone (1) v 076.3
overdrank (1) v 049.1
overdrive (1) n 110.7
overdriven (1) v 124.6
overdue (23) adj 094.7
overed (2) v 079.7
overflooded (1) v 088.7
overflow (23) n/v/adj 006.1

~ land (6) n 029.4
~ lands (1) n 029.4
~ water (1) n 029.5
overflown (1) v 098.6
overgrown (9) v/adj 065.6
overhanded in (1) v 088.7
overhang (2) n 011.5
overhanging eaves (1) n 011.5
overhaul (5) adj 027.4
~ pants (3) n 027.4
~ suit (2) n 027.4
overhaul[N-i] (12) n 027.4
overhauls (112) n 027.4
overhead (17) n/adj 014.5
~ bridge (1) n 107.8
~ bridges (1) n 107.8
~ ramp (1) n 107.8
overheated (2) v 076.3
overhet (3) v 076.4
overlap (3) v/adj 011.2
~ siding (1) n 011.2
overlapping (1) v 011.2
overloaded (1) adj 027.8
overlooks (1) n 107.2
overly (3) adv 124.5
~ sexed (2) adj 124.5
~ -sexed male (1) n 124.6
overnight (7) adj/adv 123.7
~ bag (1) n 123.7
~ bags (1) n 123.7
~ freeze (1) n 007.5
~ log (1) n 008.5
overpass (87) n/adj 107.8
~ bridge (1) n 093.7
Overpass (2) 107.7
overpasses (6) n 107.8
overpath (1) n 107.8
overran (1) v 102.3
overriding (1) v 129.7
overs (28) n 050.1
overseas (6) n/adj 070.9
~ house (1) n 014.1
overseed (2) v 089.9
overseeing (2) v 089.8
overseer (13) n 069.6
overseers (1) n 031.6
oversensitive (2) adj 075.1
oversex (1) adj 124.5
oversexed (12) adj 124.5
overshoes (3) n 080.6

oversize shotgun house (1) n 007A.7
oversized (1) adj 066.8
overstayed (1) v 003.8
overstuff (3) adj 008.8
~ chair (2) n 008.8
~ chairs (1) n 008.8
overstuffed chair (1) n 008.8
overtakes (1) v 076.1
overtalk (1) v 088.8
overtime (3) n/adv 013.1
Overton Park (9) 106.7
Overton's (1) 106.4
overtook (1) v 077.1
Overtown (7) 105.7
overview (1) n 031.2
overweight (2) adj 073.1
overweighted (1) adj 073.1
Ovett (1) MS 087.3
ow (2) interj 092.1
owe (20) v 057.5
owed (6) v 094.7
Owens (2) 087.9
~ Cross Roads (1) AL 087.9
~ Thomas House (1) 106.4
owing (27) v 057.5
~ to (20) v 057.5
~ [P-0] (2) v 098.6
owl (2265) n/adj 059.1
~ family (1) n 059.2
Owl (2) 030.7
~ Creek (1) TN 030.7
~ Hollow Road (1) 031.7
owl[N-i] (1) n 059.2
owlet (4) n 059.1
owlets (2) n 059.1
owls (395) n 059.2
own (175) pron/v/adj 033.9
~ a calf (1) v 033.9
~ up to (1) v 091.8
own[V-p] (23) v 053.2
own[V-r] (5) v 052.7
owned (59) v/adj 098.6
owner (6) n 070.6
owners (2) n 075.7
ownership (1) n 053.9
owns (304) v 053.2
ox (182) n/adj 033.7
~ day[N-i] (1) n 080.7

~ drivers (1) n 039.4
~ shoes (1) n 034.6
~ wagon (12) n 033.7
~ wagons (7) n 081.8
~ whip (1) n 019.4
~ whips (1) n 019.4
~ yokes (4) n 020.8
ox[N-i] (32) n 033.7
oxbows (1) n 088.7
oxcart (12) n 033.7
oxcarts (3) n 081.8
oxen (435) n/adj 033.7
~ cart (1) n 033.7
~ carts (1) n 033.7
~ team (1) n 033.7
~ teams (2) n 033.7
oxen's feet (1) n 034.7
oxens (147) n 016.7
oxes (25) n 033.7
oxford (8) n 123.8
oxf(ord) (1) n 123.8
Oxford (28) AL FL GA MS 087.2
~ County (1) MS 087.6
oxford[N-i] (1) n 033.6
oxfords (31) n 123.8
oxgoad (1) n 019.4
Oxheart (1) 089.8
Oxidine (2) 078.4
Oxmoor section (1) n 105.2
Oxnard (1) CA 087.5
oxtail soup (1) n 080.9
oxtails (1) n 121.3
oxteam (17) n 033.7
oxteam[N-i] (1) n 033.7
oxteams (7) n 033.7
oyster (214) n/adj 060.1
~ bar (1) n 060.1
~ bars (1) n 060.1
~ beds (2) n 060.1
~ boat (2) n 024.6
~ capital (2) n 060.1
~ dressing (1) n 044.6
~ dressings (1) n 060.1
~ factories (3) n 060.1
~ factory (1) n 060.1
~ fisherman (1) n 060.1
~ gumbo (3) n 060.1
~ house (1) n 060.1
~ houses (1) n 060.1
~ king (1) n 053.6
~ knife (1) n 104.3
~ pie (1) n 048.3
~ plant (1) n 060.1

~ plants (1) n 060.1
~ rakes (1) n 011.8
~ roast[N-i] (2) n 060.1
~ season (1) n 060.1
~ shells (1) n 060.1
~ soup (2) n 060.1
~ stew (9) n 060.1
Oyster Bank (1) MS 088.7
oyster[N-i] (8) n 060.1
oysterfish (1) n 098.8
oystering (5) n/v 060.1
oysterize (1) v 080.8
oysterman (1) n 096.7
oysters (784) n 060.1
oysters' fish (1) n 061.2
oystershell (24) n/adj 060.1
~ roads (2) n 031.7
oystershells (17) n 060.1
oystery (1) n 060.1
OZ (1) 114.2
Ozan (1) AR 087.3
Ozark (15) AL AR 087.7
~ Creek (1) AL 030.7
~ Island (1) AR 087.8
~ Mountains (5) AR 031.1
Ozarks (6) AR 031.4
Ozone Falls (1) TN 031.5

P

P (2) 070.8
pa (8) n 063.4
~ -in-law (1) n 063.4
Pa (138) 063.5
Pablo Creek (1) FL 030.7
Pac-A-Sac (5) 116.2
pace (2) v 034.3
Pace (1) FL 087.2
Paces (6) 106.2
~ Ferry (2) 106.2
pachuco (5) n S 069.1
(pa)chuco (1) n S 088.7
pachucos (7) n S 091.8
Pacific (7) 086.6
~ Ocean (1) 030.2
pacifier (2) n 080.8
pacify (1) v 075.3
pacing (3) adj 088.8
~ horse (2) n 088.8
~ horses (1) n 034.2
pack (82) n/v/adj 098.1
~ -a-days (1) n 117.7
~ mules (1) n 033.7
~ peddlers (1) n 093.6
~ -rat stuff (1) n 010.2
~ -rat things (1) n 010.2
~ room (2) n 014.5
package (35) n/adj 051.5
~ store (1) n 116.2
~ sugar (1) n 025.7
~ truck (1) n 109.6
packaged (2) adj 045.1
packages (3) n 019.2
packed (59) v/adj 098.1
~ bowels (1) n 080.1
~ in (1) v 092.7
~ up (1) v 091.9
~ with (1) v 088.7
packer (3) n 046.8
Packer (3) 021.7
packers (1) n 088.7
Packers (1) 021.8
packet (2) n 114.1
packhouse (6) n 011.7

packhouses (1) n 014.2
packing (15) v/adj 098.1
~ boats (1) n 024.6
~ ham (1) n 050.8
~ room (2) n 011.8
~ shed (2) n 081.8
~ sheds (1) n 011.7
packinghouse (5) n/adj 081.8
~ slaughterhouse employee (1) n 046.8
Packinghouse (1) 086.6
packinghouses (1) n 014.1
packs (1) v 029.8
Packs (1) 116.2
packy (2) adj 029.8
pad (33) n 029.2
~ -like (1) adj 029.2
Paddies (1) 069.4
padding (1) n 029.2
paddle (86) n/v/adj 065.5
~ ball (4) n 130.4
~ bill (1) n 059.9
~ boat (31) n 024.6
~ boats (9) n 024.6
~ cat (1) n 081.8
~ -them band (1) n 022.9
paddled (3) v 065.3
paddles (1) n 024.6
paddling (46) n/v/adj 065.5
~ board (1) n 010.6
~ boat (2) n 024.6
~ boats (1) n 024.6
paddlings (1) n 065.5
paddock (4) n 015.6
paddy (114) n/adj 050.7
~ bus (1) n 111.8
~ frog (1) n 060.2
~ wagon (98) n 111.8
~ wagons (12) n 111.8
Paddy (5) 127.9
padlock (1) v 057.6
Padre (1) TX 087.6
pads (4) n 116.4
Paducah (11) KY 087.9
page (4) n/adj 123.9
Page (26) 016.3
~ chain fence (1) n 126.1
~ chain wire (1) n 016.3
~ fence (5) n 016.3
~ wire (8) n 016.3

~ -wire (1) adj 016.3
~ -wire fence (3) n 016.3
~ -wire fences (2) n 016.3
Pageant (1) 106.5
pageboy (14) n/adj 115.5
~ style (1) n 115.6
pageboys (4) n 123.9
pages (4) n 001.5
pagoda rings (1) n 123.1
paid (42) v/adj 094.7
~ flunky (1) n 115.4
~ for (6) v 032.8
~ his debt (1) v 078.6
~ off (1) v 091.6
Paige (1) 080.7
pail (971) n/adj 017.3
~ bucket (5) n 017.3
paila (1) n S 017.6
paillet (1) n F 029.2
pails (112) n 017.3
pain (33) n 125.1
~ (a)mericain (1) n F 044.3
painful (1) adj 090.4
paining (1) v 096.8
pains (6) n 079.6
paint (19) n/v/adj 025.2
~ box (1) n 025.2
~ bucket (1) n 017.3
Paint Rock River (1) AL 030.7
paintbrush (4) n 022.2
paintbrushes (1) n 022.2
painted (6) v/adj 059.9
~ line (1) n 107.3
~ turtle (1) n 060.6
~ up (1) v 025.9
painter (1) n 067.8
painter's overalls (1) n 027.4
painters (1) n 049.1
painting (7) n/v 017.1
~ up (1) v 028.1
paints (1) v 052.6
pair (672) n 033.7
~ of bead[N-i] (2) n 028.4
~ of beads (59) n 028.4
~ of blue jean[N-i] (1) n 033.7
~ of breeches (5) n 027.4

~ of donkeys (1) n 033.7
~ of dress pants (1) n 027.1
~ of horses (18) n 033.7
~ of jeans (2) n 027.4
~ of mule[N-i] (11) n 033.7
~ of mules (199) n 033.7
~ of overalls (2) n 027.4
~ of ox[N-i] (3) n 033.7
~ of oxen (17) n 033.7
~ of oxens (3) n 033.7
~ of pant[N-i] (2) n 027.4
~ of pants (41) n 027.4
~ of pearls (1) n 028.4
~ of slacks (1) n 027.4
~ of trousers (1) n 027.4
~ of Unionalls (1) n 027.4
~ of yearlings (1) n 033.7
~ of young mules (1) n 033.7
~ [P-0] beads (1) n 028.4
~ [P-0] horses (1) n 033.7
~ [P-0] mule[N-i] (1) n 033.7
~ [P-0] mules (7) n 033.7
~ [P-0] overalls (1) n 027.4
~ [P-0] oxen (1) n 033.7
~ [P-0] pants (1) n 027.4
~ [P-0] them mules (1) n 033.7
pair[N-i] (30) n 033.7
~ of mule[N-i] (1) n 033.7
~ of mules (6) n 033.7
~ of oxen (1) n 033.7
~ of oxens (1) n 033.7
~ of pant[N-i] (1) n 027.4
~ of pants (3) n 027.4

paired (1) v 024.7
pairs (19) n 033.8
pajama (1) adj 130.7
pajamas (4) n 070.6
Pak (1) 116.2
pal (36) n 129.4
palace (8) n 070.7
Palace (3) 106.5
palaces (2) n 015.4
Palacios (4) TX 087.8
palate tongue (1) n 088.8
Palatka (9) FL 087.6
palavering (1) v 080.9
pale (261) n/v/adj 072.9
  ~ fence (10) n 016.2
  ~ fences (1) n 016.2
  ~ -looking (1) adj
    072.9
  ~ road (1) n 031.6
  ~ roads (1) n 031.6
  ~ skin (1) n 069.4
paled (4) v/adj 098.7
  ~ in (1) v 016.2
  ~ road (1) n 031.6
  ~ up (1) v 016.2
paleface (6) n 069.4
palefaces (4) n 069.4
palement (3) n/adj 016.2
  ~ fence (1) n 016.2
pales (1) n 016.2
Palestine (10) TX 087.2
  ~ Lake (1) TX 030.7
paling (212) n/adj 016.2
  ~ fence (115) n 016.2
  ~ fences (13) n 016.2
  ~ garden (1) n 016.2
  ~ guards (1) n 016.2
paling[N-i] (1) n 016.2
palings (81) n 016.2
palisade (1) n 031.2
Palisade Drive (1) 106.1
palisades (1) n 016.4
palish (1) adj 072.9
Pall Mall (2) TN 087.6
pallet (813) n/adj 029.2
  ~ parties (1) n 029.2
  ~ party (2) n 029.2
pallets (89) n 029.2
pallid (6) adj 072.9
pallio (1) n 029.2
palm (903) n/adj 072.1
  ~ brush (1) n 022.2
  ~ grove (1) n 061.6
  ~ tree (4) n 061.8
  ~ tree[N-i] (1) n 061.9

  ~ trees (15) n 061.8
Palm (28) 072.1
  ~ Beach (11) FL 087.5
  ~ Beach suits (2) n
    027.7
  ~ Beaches (1) FL 087.5
  ~ River (1) FL 030.7
  ~ Springs (2) FL 087.8
  ~ Sunday (1) 002.1
palma (3) n 061.8
  ~ Christi (1) n 061.8
  ~ Christi leaves (1) n
    061.4
  ~ Christi trees (1) n
    061.8
(palma) Christi leaves (1)
  n 104.8
Palma (3) 105.2
  ~ Ceia (1) 105.2
  ~ Ceia Beach Park (1)
    105.4
Palmas (1) 030.7
palmed (1) v 100.1
Palmer (5) MO MS 072.1
  ~ Creek (1) MS 030.7
  ~ House (1) 014.1
  ~ Lake (1) TX 030.7
Palmersville (1) TN 087.5
palmetto (39) n/adj 061.8
  ~ berries (1) n 062.5
  ~ broom (1) n 010.5
  ~ brooms (2) n 010.5
  ~ camps (1) n 084.8
  ~ fan (2) n 061.8
  ~ fans (3) n 084.8
  ~ land (2) n 029.8
  ~ logs (2) n 008.5
  ~ patch (2) n 016.1
  ~ root (1) n 061.4
  ~ roots (2) n 061.4
  ~ shacks (1) n 118.9
  ~ tree (1) n 061.8
  ~ trees (2) n 061.8
Palmetto (12) FL GA
  087.2
  ~ Branch (1) FL 030.7
  ~ Creek (2) AL 030.7
  ~ Expressway (2) 107.6
  ~ Street (1) 107.6
palmettos (12) n 061.8
palms (9) n 061.8
Palms Center (1) 105.6
Palmyra (3) GA 087.2
  ~ Creek (1) GA 030.7
palo santo (1) n S 061.4

Palo Alto (1) AR 087.6
palomilla steak (1) n S
  047.5
palomino (3) n/adj 034.3
  ~ mare (1) n 080.7
  ~ stud (1) n 034.1
palonnier (1) n F 020.8
Paloopa Swag (1) AR
  029.6
palourde (1) n F 060.2
palpitating (1) v 102.2
pals (10) n 129.6
palsy (1) n 065.8
pampas (1) n 041.6
pamper (1) v 028.1
pan (830) n/adj 020.1
  ~ bread (4) n 044.4
  ~ drippings (1) n 048.5
  ~ -frying size (1) n
    121.5
  ~ gravy (1) n 048.5
  ~ loaf (1) n 122.3
  ~ pie (4) n 048.3
  ~ pies (6) n 048.3
  ~ sausage (14) n 121.6
  ~ trout (1) n 059.9
Pan (3) 069.2
  ~ -American (2) 069.2
Panama (52) FL 087.4
  ~ Canal (3) 030.2
  ~ Canal Zone (1) 086.1
  ~ Canals (1) 030.2
  ~ City (34) FL 087.8
  ~ City Airport (1)
    106.7
  ~ City Beach (3) FL
    087.7
  ~ Red (2) 114.1
Panamagen (1) n G 047.4
Panancy potato (1) n
  055.5
pancake (145) n/adj
  045.3
  ~ bread (2) n 044.4
  ~ dough (1) n 045.3
  ~ -like things (1) n
    045.3
  ~ syrup (2) n 051.3
  ~ turner (1) n 017.5
pancake[N-i] (5) n 045.3
pancakes (652) n 045.3
pancaking (1) v 095.4
pandandy (1) n 048.3
panderer (1) n 113.5
pandowdy (10) n 048.3

(pan)dowdy (1) n 048.3
panel (100) n/adj 109.6
  ~ board (1) n 110.1
  ~ car (1) n 109.6
  ~ fence (9) n 016.2
  ~ fences (1) n 016.2
  ~ fencing (1) n 016.2
  ~ ray (1) n 118.4
  ~ truck (32) n 109.6
  ~ trucks (6) n 109.6
  ~ wagons (1) n 109.6
  ~ wire (1) n 016.3
Panel Bay (1) GA 030.7
paneling (12) n/adj 011.2
  ~ fence (4) n 016.2
panels (5) n 065.9
panes (1) n 048.9
panfish (9) n 059.9
panhandle (1) v 081.8
Panhandle (8) FL TX
  087.6
panhandler (1) n 113.7
panhandling (1) v 113.7
panic (6) v/adj 079.5
  ~ bread (1) n 044.6
Panic (2) 080.8
panicky (1) adj 074.3
Pankey (3) 105.4
panky (1) n 065.2
pankying (1) v 081.7
Panola (9) MS TX 087.2
  ~ County (4) MS 087.1
pans (70) n 017.5
pansies (3) n 028.2
pansy (6) n 124.1
pant[N-i] (17) n/adj
  027.4
  ~ suits (2) n 027.7
pantalon (1) n S 027.4
pantalones (1) n S 027.4
pantaloons (8) n 080.8
panther (9) n/adj 059.5
  ~ piss (1) n 050.8
Panther (5) 030.7
  ~ Creek (3) AR LA
    MS 030.7
  ~ Creek State Park (1)
    106.4
  ~ headquarters (1) n
    066.9
panthers (3) n 059.5
Panthers (1) 066.8
panties (2) n 093.8
pantries (29) n 010.1
pantry (795) n/adj 010.1

~ -like (1) adj 010.1
~ room (6) n 010.1
~ shelf (1) n 010.1
~ thing (1) n 010.1
pantr(y) (1) n 010.1
Pantry (1) 116.3
pants (1084) n/adj 027.4
~ legs (1) n 027.4
~ -style denim (1) n 027.4
~ suit (3) n 027.7
~ suits (1) n 027.7
pantses (6) n 027.4
panty hose (1) n 027.5
Panuco (1) 086.3
Paola (2) FL 087.3
pap (1) n 048.5
Pap (15) 063.5
papa (36) n S 063.4
~ cow (2) n 033.5
~ grande (1) n S 064.1
~ hog (2) n 035.3
~ horse (4) n 034.1
~ pigs (1) n 035.3
~ sute (1) n S 055.3
Papa (609) 063.5
~ Daddy (1) 064.1
~ Johns (1) 068.2
Papalote Creek (1) TX 030.7
Papa's (23) 063.5
~ bedroom (1) n 007A.2
~ brother (2) n 068.2
~ brothers (1) n 063.5
~ cotton (1) n 015.8
~ father (1) n 063.4
~ idea (1) n 092.4
~ people (1) n 066.5
~ room (5) n 063.5
~ shoat[N-i] (1) n 016.8
papas (1) n 043.6
papaw (5) n/adj 054.9
~ tree (1) n 061.9
papaws (2) n 056.8
papaya (3) n 056.7
papayas (2) n 061.8
paper (1449) n/adj 019.5
~ bag (338) n 019.5
~ -bag business (1) n 019.5
~ bags (110) n 019.5
~ clamp (1) n 110.4
~ clip (109) n 110.4

~ clipper (1) n 110.4
~ clips (8) n 110.4
~ company (1) n 019.5
~ cup (3) n 019.5
~ cups (1) n 019.5
~ dolls (2) n 019.5
~ hornet (1) n 060A.5
~ hull (1) n 054.9
~ insert filter (1) n 116.8
~ -mache (1) n 019.5
~ mill (7) n 019.5
~ mills (2) n 019.5
~ money (1) n 040.8
~ moth (1) n 060A.2
~ nestes (1) n 060A.5
~ package (1) n 019.2
~ pep (1) n 019.5
~ plates (2) n 019.5
~ poke (31) n 019.5
~ pokes (7) n 019.5
~ products (1) n 019.5
~ route (1) n 080.9
~ sack (225) n 019.5
~ -sack brown (1) n 069.5
~ sacks (47) n 019.5
~ stack (1) n 019.5
~ stopper (1) n 020.4
~ string (1) n 019.5
~ towel (4) n 018.4
~ tree (2) n 061.8
~ wasp (2) n 060A.6
~ wood (1) n 080.9
~ wood business (1) n 081.8
~ -wood roads (1) n 031.7
pap(er) (1) n 019.5
papered (2) v 011.8
papers (24) n 019.5
papershell (10) n/adj 019.5
~ pecan (3) n 054.9
~ pecans (4) n 054.9
papershells (1) n 054.9
papillon (1) n F 060A.1
Papist (3) 126.5
Papists (1) 126.5
pappy (2) n 065.3
Pappy (34) 064.1
Pappy's (1) 063.4
Paps (1) 064.1
par (6) n 072.9
para (3) adj/prep S 028.6

~ agua (1) n S 028.6
~ un sol (1) n S 028.6
parachute (2) n 028.6
parade (7) n 068.9
Parade (3) 131.3
parades (1) n 098.9
paradise (1) n 088.8
Paradise (3) 030.7
~ Park (2) 106.2
paraffin (6) n/adj 065.8
~ bags (1) n 084.9
~ paper (1) n 019.5
Paragould (6) AR 087.7
parallel (150) adj/adv 108.1
~ park (10) n 108.1
~ -park (3) v 108.1
~ -parks (1) v 108.1
~ parking (59) n 108.1
~ road (1) n 031.7
paralysis (1) n 070.9
paramedic (6) n/adj 111.5
~ truck (2) n 111.5
~ trucks (1) n 111.5
paramedics (10) n 111.5
paramedics' (2) adj 111.5
~ truck (1) n 111.5
~ trucks (1) n 111.5
paramour (1) n 081.6
paranoid (2) adj 074.3
parasite (6) n 115.4
Parasite (1) 106.3
parasitic (1) adj 060.5
parasol (377) n/adj 028.6
~ umbrella (1) n 028.6
Parasol (1) TN 030.7
parasol[N-i] (1) n 028.6
parasols (14) n 028.6
paratrooper knife (1) n 104.3
parboil (3) v 055A.7
parboiled (2) v 046.2
parboiling (1) v 046.1
parc (3) n F 015.4
~ a cochons (2) n F 015.4
~ de betes (1) n F 015.3
parcel (18) n/adj 055A.8
~ post (1) n 084.2
~ shelf (1) n 110.2
parcels (1) n 090.7
parch (28) v 007.2
parch[V-r] (1) v 065.9

parched (12) v/adj 048.8
~ peanuts (1) n 054.7
Parcheesi (1) 130.3
parches (1) v 096.8
parching (8) v 075.8
Parchman (4) MS 087.4
parcipient (1) n 065.9
pardon (177) n/v 052.4
pard(on) (2) n 052.4
paregoric (2) n 081.8
parent (64) n/adj 063.8
~ breed (1) n 063.8
~ high school (1) n 063.8
parent[N-i] (6) n 063.8
par(ent)[N-i] (1) n 063.8
parent[N-k] (2) adj 063.8
~ approval (1) n 063.8
~ name (1) n 025.8
parentless (2) adj 066.3
parents (1156) n 063.8
parents' (20) adj 063.8
~ bedroom (11) n 007A.6
~ home (1) n 063.8
~ room (5) n 063.8
Parham (1) 107.6
parilla (1) n S 008.3
paring (13) n/adj 017.8
~ knife (10) n 017.8
~ knives (2) n 104.3
Paris (24) MS TN TX 087.9
parish (62) n/adj 085.5
~ airport (1) n 077.8
~ capital (1) n 085.5
~ courthouse (1) n 085.1
~ prison (3) n 112.8
~ road (10) n 031.7
~ seat (33) n 085.5
Parish (107) 087.1
~ of Lafourche (1) LA 087.3
parishes (4) n 085.5
Parisian French (1) 080.5
park (304) n/v/adj 085.1
~ and drive (1) n 108.4
~ and ride (1) n 108.4
~ -and-wildlife superin-tendents (1) n 115.3
~ coverages (1) n 107.2
~ observations (1) n 053.6
~ strip (1) n 031.9

Park (437) 085.1
~ Avenue (5) 107.7
~ Boulevard (1) 031.6
~ City (3) 105.2
~ Drive (1) 107.7
~ Hill (1) 105.1
~ National Bank (1) 108.5
~ Road (1) 031.6
~ Row (1) 105.5
~ Street (1) 107.7
~ Street section (1) n 106.1
~ Tower (1) 108.5
Parkay (1) LA 086.4
parked (2) v 058.3
Parker (9) 030.7
~ Bayou (1) MS 030.7
~ berry (1) n 062.5
~ House rolls (3) n 044.4
parkette (1) n 031.9
Parkin (1) AR 087.9
parking (350) n/v/adj 081.7
~ area (4) n 108.4
~ areas (2) n 108.4
~ building (3) n 108.4
~ buildings (2) n 108.4
~ complex (2) n 108.4
~ deck (24) n 108.4
~ decks (2) n 108.4
~ facilities (1) n 108.4
~ garage (37) n 108.4
~ garages (7) n 108.4
~ high-rise (1) n 108.4
~ house (1) n 108.4
~ levels (1) n 108.4
~ lot (51) n 108.4
~ -lot buildings (1) n 108.4
~ lots (18) n 108.4
~ meter (1) n 108.4
~ place (1) n 108.3
~ problem (1) n 108.1
~ ramp (6) n 108.4
~ ramps (1) n 108.4
~ site (1) n 108.4
~ space (4) n 108.3
~ spaces (1) n 108.3
~ spots (1) n 108.1
~ station (1) n 108.4
~ straight (1) v 108.1
~ strip (1) n 031.9
~ ticket (1) n 093.8

Parkinson's disease (1) n 088.8
parks (35) n/v 085.1
parkway (28) n 031.9
Parkway (23) 107.5
~ East (2) 105.2
~ South (1) 105.5
parkways (1) n 107.4
parlor (584) n/adj 007.8
~ chair (1) n 008.9
~ dates (1) n 007.8
~ joke (1) n 084.8
~ luxuries (1) n 080.6
~ parties (1) n 130.7
~ room (1) n 007.8
~ set (1) n 009.1
~ suite (1) n 009.1
~ word (1) n 080.7
parlors (49) n 007.7
Parmisan (1) 047.2
parochial school (2) n 125.7
parole (1) n 053.2
Parrain (1) F 063.8
parrakeet (1) n 126.4
parrakeets (1) n 099.8
Parris Island (1) SC 087.3
parrot (1) n 088.8
parrots (1) n 099.8
parsley (16) n 055A.5
parsnips (6) n 055.8
parsol (1) n S 028.6
parson (2) n 067.8
Parsons (2) TN 087.2
~ Hotel (1) 084.3
part (242) n/adj 054.5
~ Chihuahua (1) n 033.3
~ clay (3) n 029.8
~ dog (1) n 033.3
~ Indian (1) n 069.5
~ nigger (1) n 069.5
~ sand (3) n 029.8
~ -time (4) adj 065.8
~ -time minister (1) n 067.8
~ -time pastor (2) n 067.8
~ -time preacher (17) n 067.8
~ white (1) n 069.5
partake of (1) v 049.6
parted (1) v 013.8
Parthenon (7) 106.4

partial (10) adj 019.8
~ freeze (1) n 007.5
~ showers (1) n 006.6
partially (2) adv 007.5
participate (1) v 053.5
participated (1) v 053.2
particle (2) n/adj 011.1
~ board (1) n 011.2
particular (18) adj 075.1
(par)ticular (1) adj 088.2
particularly (3) adv 070.6
parties (201) n 083.1
partition (4) n 007A.3
(par)tition (5) n/v 014.5
~ off (1) v 066.8
partitioned off (1) v 007A.7
partitions (3) n 007A.1
partly (14) adj/adv 042.5
~ cloudy (6) adj 005.6
~ colored (1) n 069.5
~ fair (2) adj 005.4
~ Negro (1) n 069.5
partner (21) n 050.9
partners (7) n 129.4
partnership (1) n 042.3
partnerships (1) n 016.7
partridge (6) n 036.6
partridges (8) n 059.2
parts (11) n 037.2
party (315) n/v/adj 028.1
~ bags (1) n 089.8
~ boat (1) n 024.6
~ boats (2) n 024.6
~ games (2) n 130.7
~ group (1) n 082.8
~ line (1) n 069.9
~ on (1) v 052.5
~ party (1) n 130.7
~ ring (2) n 123.1
~ tomatoes (1) n 055.3
Party (7) 115.8
partying shoes (1) n 123.8
paruna (1) n 114.7
Pasadena (4) TX 087.2
Pascagoula (23) MS 087.4
~ Swamp (1) MS 030.7
Paso (26) 087.3
Paspalum (1) 062.3
pass (263) n/v 031.3
~ around (1) v 049.4
~ away (9) v 078.5
~ for (1) v 052.8
~ -me-down (1) n 123.5
~ off (3) v 005.7

~ on (3) v 078.5
~ out (6) v 078.5
~ over (2) v 005.7
~ -through (1) n 031.3
~ to (1) v 075.7
Pass (15) 070.7
~ Road (1) 107.6
(Pass) Christian (2) MS 087.6
pass[V-r] (25) v 078.5
~ away (2) v 078.5
~ out (1) v 078.5
pass[V-t] (6) v 078.5
~ and gone (1) v 078.5
~ by (1) v 057.9
passable (1) adj 079.4
passage (4) n/adj 031.3
~ sidewalk (1) n 108.6
passageway (6) n 108.6
passant blanc (1) v F 006.8
passe (1) n 130.5
passed (909) v 078.5
~ along (1) v 123.5
~ and gone (1) v 057.9
~ away (562) v 078.5
~ away with (1) v 078.7
~ down (1) v 123.5
~ him by (1) v 082.1
~ him up (1) v 082.1
~ into the great beyond (1) v 078.5
~ off (1) v 078.6
~ on (139) v 078.5
~ on by (1) v 078.5
~ out (34) v 078.5
~ over (5) v 005.7
~ over the hill (1) v 078.6
passel (432) n/adj 055A.8
~ amount (1) n 055A.8
~ (a)mount (1) n 055A.8
passels (1) n 055A.8
passenger (13) n/adj 109.3
~ car (6) n 111.6
~ cars (2) n 111.6
~ hack (1) n 080.6
passengers (2) n 021.4
passes (12) n/v 031.3
~ away (4) v 078.5
passing (11) v/adj 069.5
~ away (1) v 078.5

~ off (1) v 095.8
~ on off (1) v 007.3
~ rain (1) n 006.1
passion (4) n/adj 027.3
~ mark (1) n 027.3
~ palace (1) n 114.9
passionflowers (1) n 057.1
passovers (1) n 069.5
passway (2) n 085.2
past (626) n/adj 082.7
~ -due (11) adj 094.7
~ queens (1) n 081.8
pasta (2) n 044.4
paste (10) n 051.3
pasteboard (17) adj 019.2
~ box (9) n 019.2
~ boxes (7) n 019.5
~ carton (1) n 019.5
pasteurization (1) n 048.2
pasteurize (14) v 048.2
pasteurized (1) v 048.2
pasteurizer (1) n 017.3
pastime (1) n 029.1
pastor (13) n/v 067.6
pastored (3) v 067.9
pastoring (1) v 095.8
pastors (2) n/v 088.8
pastries (27) n 122.2
pastry (31) n/adj 045.2
~ cake (1) n 122.1
~ cook (1) n 080.6
pasturage (1) n 015.7
pasture (1329) n/adj 015.7
~ area (1) n 015.7
~ fence (10) n 016.4
~ fences (1) n 015.7
~ field (12) n 015.7
~ fields (3) n 015.7
~ gate (1) n 015.7
~ grass (3) n 015.7
~ ground (1) n 029.5
~ lane (1) n 031.8
~ lot (1) n 015.7
~ lots (1) n 015.7
~ road (4) n 031.8
~ -type land (1) n 029.5
past(ure) road (1) n 031.8
Pasture (1) 015.7
pastured (3) v 015.7
pastureland (69) n 015.7
pastures (109) n 015.7
pat (19) n/v 065.5

~ -a-cake (5) n 044.7
~ -a-cakes (5) n 045.3
~ -a-cat (2) n 101.8
Pat (5) 127.9
patassa (2) n 059.9
Patassa (1) 030.7
patates (1) n F 015.6
(Pa)taula Creek (1) GA 030.7
patch (1054) n/v/adj 016.1
~ berries (1) n 062.5
~ farming (1) n 016.1
~ garden (1) n 050.5
~ quilt (4) n 029.1
~ quilts (1) n 029.1
Patch (3) 016.1
patchers (1) n 050.4
patches (102) n 016.1
patching (1) n 016.8
patchwork (11) n/adj 029.1
~ quilt (8) n 029.1
~ quilts (1) n 029.1
pate (13) n F 047.2
~ de foie gras (1) n F 047.2
~ d(e) maison (1) n F 047.2
~ ordinaire (1) n F 047.2
patent (7) n/adj 080.9
~ leather (1) n 123.8
~ -leather pumps (1) n 123.8
~ -leather shoes (1) n 123.8
~ leathers (1) n 123.8
~ medicine (1) n 091.9
~ strap shoes (1) n 123.8
Pater (1) 063.5
paternalistic (1) adj 099.6
path (302) n/adj 031.8
~ -like (2) adj 031.8
~ road (1) n 031.6
path[N-i] (3) n 031.8
pathed (1) adj 031.7
pathetic (2) adj 125.2
paths (39) n 031.8
pathway (12) n 031.8
pathways (1) n 031.8
patience (3) n 075.1
patient (15) n/adj 073.2
patients (1) n 081.8

patio (185) n/adj 010.9
~ boats (1) n 024.6
~ tomatoes (6) n 055.3
patios (7) n 010.8
patissiere (1) adj F 048.5
patois bon charpentier (1) n F 089.9
patootie (2) n 081.6
Patoutville (1) LA 087.5
Patricio (1) 087.3
Patrick's (1) 093.6
patriotic songs (1) n 130.8
patrol (49) n/adj 111.7
~ boat (1) n 084.8
~ car (21) n 111.7
~ cars (9) n 111.7
~ wagon (10) n 111.8
~ wagons (1) n 111.8
(pa)trol cars (1) n 111.7
patrol[N-i] (1) n 112.5
patrolman (3) n 112.5
patrolmen (3) n 112.5
patron (4) n F/S 069.6
patronage (6) n 115.3
patronizing (1) v 099.6
Patsaliga (5) AL 030.7
~ Creek (1) AL 030.7
~ River (2) AL 030.7
patsies (1) n 124.2
patsy (1) n 115.4
patte poule (1) n F 055A.5
pattern (56) n/adj 026.2
~ patch (1) n 026.2
patterned after (1) v 065.3
patterns (1) n 039.7
Patterson (2) GA 087.7
~ Street (1) 107.6
patties (50) n 121.6
patting (1) n 115.3
Patton (34) 030.7
~ Bayou (1) FL 030.7
patty (21) n/adj 121.6
~ bread (1) n 044.7
~ sausage (10) n 121.6
~ sausages (2) n 121.6
~ shell (2) n 080.6
pattypan (11) n/adj 056.6
~ squash (3) n 056.6
pattypans (1) n 056.6
Paul (3) 083.1
~ Jones (1) 083.1
Paulding (1) GA 087.2

paunch (32) n/adj 037.2
~ part (1) n 037.2
Paunch Creek (1) TN 030.7
paunchy (3) adj 073.1
pauper (9) n 069.5
pauper's (4) adj 078.9
~ field (2) n 078.8
~ grave (2) n 078.9
paupers (2) n 069.7
pave (76) v/adj 031.9
~ bridge (1) n 031.6
~ highway (1) n 031.6
~ road (29) n 031.6
~ road[N-i] (1) n 031.6
~ roads (23) n 031.6
~ street (3) n 031.6
~ streets (1) n 031.7
~ walk (1) n 031.9
pave[V-t] (6) v 031.6
paved (196) v/adj 031.6
~ highway (4) n 031.6
~ highways (2) n 031.6
~ road (50) n 031.6
~ roads (51) n 031.6
~ sidewalks (2) n 031.9
~ street (8) n 031.6
~ streets (4) n 031.6
pavement (112) n/adj 031.9
~ road (4) n 031.7
~ roads (2) n 031.6
pavements (5) n 031.6
pavilion (1) n 105.9
pavilions (1) n 080.7
paving (14) n/v 031.6
pawn (3) v/adj 114.6
~ dealer (1) n 114.6
pawnbroker (3) n 114.6
pawnbrokers (1) n 114.6
pawned (1) v 095.8
pawnshop (129) n 114.6
pawnshops (4) n 114.6
paws (1) n 072.5
pay (119) n/v/adj 053.8
~ for (7) v 057.4
~ off (1) v 080.8
~ phone (1) n 012.9
~ -roller (7) n 115.4
~ -rollers (1) n 115.4
payday (2) n 002.1
paying (24) v 057.4
~ attention to her (1) v 081.4

~ for (1) v 025.3
~ up (1) v 012.6
Paymaster (1) 056.2
payment (2) n 065.8
Payne (2) 087.2
payroll (7) n 115.4
pays (6) v 013.8
Paz (1) 115.6
PB (1) 131.2
PCP (5) 117.8
PDQ (1) 119.6
pea (179) n/adj 055A.2
~ beans (2) n 055A.4
~ droppers (1) n 065.7
~ field (1) n 016.1
~ frogs (1) n 060.4
~ gravel (4) n 031.6
~ gumbo (1) n 084.8
~ hay (7) n 014.8
~ hays (1) n 014.8
~ house (2) n 011.7
~ -hulling (1) adj 083.1
~ larks (1) n 059.2
~ liquor (2) n 081.8
~ mite (1) n 060A.8
~ patch (47) n 016.1
~ -patch-farmed (1) v 016.1
~ patches (4) n 016.1
~ -patching (1) n 016.8
~ peeler (1) n 055A.2
~ picker (1) n 111.4
~ pot (1) n 017.6
~ rows (2) n 041.2
~ sack (1) n 019.7
~ sheller (5) n 055A.2
~ shells (1) n 055A.2
~ shelter (1) n 014.2
~ snaps (1) n 055.9
~ trees (1) n 061.8
Pea (13) 030.7
~ Creek (1) GA 030.7
~ Ridge (2) MS TN 087.2
~ River (8) AL 030.7
Peabody (5) 107.6
~ Hotel (1) 084.3
peace (101) n/adj 085.6
~ officers (2) n 112.5
~ turtles (1) n 060.6
Peace River (3) FL 030.7
peaceable (1) adj 093.6
peacebreaker (2) n 101.3
peaceful (2) adj 073.2
peach (1083) n/adj 061.9

~ arbor (1) n 053.2
~ baskets (1) n 020.1
~ brandy (9) n 050.8
~ cobbler (79) n 048.3
~ cobblers (9) n 048.3
~ core (1) n 054.2
~ dumpling (2) n 048.3
~ farm (2) n 053.2
~ farms (1) n 053.2
~ grove (7) n 053.2
~ jelly (3) n 051.6
~ kernel (14) n 054.2
~ kernels (1) n 054.2
~ leather (1) n 054.6
~ leaves (2) n 061.4
~ -limb whippings (1) n 065.5
~ orchard (94) n 053.2
~ orch(ard) (3) n 053.2
~ orchards (3) n 053.2
~ pasture (1) n 053.2
~ patch (2) n 053.2
~ pickle (5) n 054.3
~ pie (13) n 048.3
~ pies (4) n 048.3
~ pit (9) n 054.2
~ pits (1) n 054.2
~ preserves (3) n 051.6
~ puffs (3) n 048.3
~ seed (140) n 054.2
~ -seed almonds (1) n 054.9
~ seeds (2) n 054.2
~ stone (15) n 054.2
~ stones (1) n 054.2
~ tart (1) n 048.3
~ tarts (2) n 048.3
~ tree (29) n 061.8
~ -tree-leaf tea (1) n 061.4
~ -tree leaves (1) n 078.4
~ -tree limb (1) n 065.5
~ -tree poultices (1) n 061.4
~ -tree switch (1) n 104.3
~ tree[N-i] (1) n 061.8
~ trees (63) n 061.9
~ turnovers (1) n 048.3
Peach (9) GA 087.3
~ County (1) GA 087.2
~ Festival (1) 081.8
~ Lake (1) LA 030.7

~ Tree (1) AL MS 087.3
peach[N-i] (2) n 054.6
peaches (298) n 061.8
Peachstone Shoals (1) GA 087.3
Peachtree (34) 107.6
~ Battle (1) 106.2
~ Center (1) 106.4
~ City (1) GA 087.3
~ Creek (9) GA 030.7
~ Plaza (4) 108.5
~ Plaza Hotel (1) 108.5
~ Road (3) 107.6
~ Street (7) 105.2
Peach(tree) Street (1) 082.7
peacock (5) n/adj 093.5
~ gravy (1) n 093.8
~ hen (1) n 080.9
peacocks (2) n 036.6
peafowl (4) n/adj 036.6
~ hens (1) n 036.6
peafowls (4) n 036.9
peak (9) n 031.1
Peak (1) 080.7
peaked (406) adj 072.9
~ -like (1) adj 072.9
~ -looking (2) adj 072.9
peakedy (2) adj 072.9
peakish (6) adj 072.9
peaks (1) n 031.1
peaky (1) adj 072.9
peanut (200) n/adj 054.7
~ bale (1) n 054.7
~ bean (2) n 055A.4
~ beans (1) n 055A.3
~ boiling (2) n 080.9
~ brittle (1) n 054.7
~ butter (10) n 054.7
~ -butter maker (1) n 116.4
~ combine (1) n 096.8
~ country (2) n 054.7
~ crop (3) n 054.7
~ field (5) n 016.1
~ hay (5) n 014.6
~ machines (1) n 054.7
~ mill (1) n 106.4
~ oil (3) n 024.1
~ parching (2) n 082.5
~ patch (9) n 016.1
~ picker (2) n 080.6
~ pickers (2) n 099.8

~ rows (1) n 054.7
~ sacks (1) n 019.7
~ shellings (3) n 090.8
~ stack (4) n 014.6
~ stacks (1) n 081.8
~ thrasher (2) n 080.8
~ -thrashing machines (2) n 042.1
~ vines (1) n 090.8
~ wagon (1) n 111.7
peanut[N-i] (6) n 054.7
peanuts (975) n 054.7
pear (130) n/adj 055.3
~ cobbler (2) n 048.3
~ cobblers (1) n 048.3
~ dumpling (1) n 048.3
~ honey (1) n 051.6
~ orchards (1) n 053.2
~ pies (1) n 048.3
~ preserves (4) n 051.6
~ sallet (1) n 055A.5
~ -shape tomatoes (1) n 055.3
~ -toed (1) adj 073.3
~ tomato (9) n 055.3
~ tomatoes (18) n 055.3
~ tree (21) n 061.8
~ tree[N-i] (1) n 016.8
~ trees (41) n 061.8
Pear (3) 030.7
~ Creek (1) LA 030.7
~ Orchard (2) TX 053.2
pearl (18) n/adj 055.7
~ beads (3) n 028.4
~ necklace (5) n 028.4
~ onions (3) n 055.7
~ pop (1) n 121.9
Pearl (49) MS 086.4
~ River (35) LA MS 030.7
~ River Basin (1) LA 030.7
~ River County (3) MS 087.6
~ River language (1) n 040.5
~ River Swamp (1) LA 029.6
~ Street (3) 107.6
pearl[N-i] (1) n 028.4
Pearline (1) 080.7
Pearlington (3) MS 087.6
pearls (81) n 028.4

pears (27) n 061.8
Pearson (2) FL 087.5
~ Station (1) AL 087.7
Pearsons Spring (1) TN
030.7
peas (699) n/adj 055A.4
~ gumbo (1) n 081.8
peasant (1) n 069.7
Pease (1) 107.6
peat (9) n/adj 029.8
~ moss (2) n 029.9
~ muck (1) n 029.9
~ sack (1) n 019.7
peavine (10) n/adj 014.9
~ hay (6) n 014.7
~ rake (1) n 014.6
Peavine (5) 030.7
~ Creek (4) GA TN
030.7
peavines (2) n 041.5
pebble (9) n 032.1
Pebble (2) AL 087.4
pebbles (9) n 031.6
pebblestone (1) n 031.6
pebbly land (2) n 029.8
pecan (586) n/adj 054.9
~ cake (1) n 122.1
~ crop (1) n 054.9
~ crops (2) n 041.3
~ Danish (1) n 122.2
~ grove (15) n 061.6
~ groves (1) n 061.6
~ hulls (1) n 054.9
~ limbs (1) n 008.6
~ nut (2) n 054.9
~ nuts (4) n 054.9
~ orchard (16) n 053.2
~ orchards (4) n 053.2
~ pie (3) n 054.9
~ roll (1) n 122.2
~ rolls (1) n 122.2
~ time (1) n 099.8
~ tree (70) n 061.8
~ tree[N-i] (1) n 051.8
~ trees (123) n 061.9
~ wood (5) n 008.5
~ worms (1) n 060.5
(pe)can tree (2) n 061.8
Pecan (11) 054.9
~ Creek (2) TX 030.7
~ Grove (1) 061.6
~ Island (6) LA 087.6
~ Valley (1) 106.1
pecan[N-i] (4) n 054.9
pecans (774) n 054.9

(pe)cans (5) n 054.9
peccaries (1) n 035.9
peccary (3) n 035.9
peche (4) n F 054.4
~ a jus (1) n F 054.4
~ au jus (1) n F 054.3
~ au noyau (1) n F
054.3
~ sec (1) n F 054.6
pechers (1) n F 053.2
peck (107) n/v/adj 019.8
~ baskets (1) n 020.1
~ bucket (2) n 017.2
~ measure (1) n 019.8
~ on (1) v 093.9
~ sacks (1) n 019.6
peck[N-i] (1) n 016.7
pecker (15) n/adj 059.3
~ head (2) n 059.3
~ -head (1) adj 059.3
~ heads (1) n 069.9
~ woodpecker (1) n
059.3
~ woodpeckers (1) n
059.3
peckered out (1) v 075.5
peckers (4) n 069.8
peckerwood (710) n/adj
059.3
~ bird (3) n 059.3
~ farmers (1) n 069.7
~ mill (1) n 084.7
~ sawmill (2) n 059.3
~ sawmills (1) n 084.7
~ song (1) n 069.7
Peckerwood Corner (1)
059.3
peckerwooder (1) n 059.3
peckerwood's head (1) n
059.3
peckerwoods (111) n
059.3
pecking (3) v/adj 024.9
~ noises (1) n 052.1
pecks (23) n 019.8
Pecos (1) 056.7
peculiar (116) adj 074.7
~ in their ways (1) adj
074.8
(pe)culiar (1) adj 074.8
pedal (130) n/adj 110.6
~ organ (1) n 092.8
~ pusher (3) n 123.3
~ pusher[N-i] (1) n
123.2

~ pushers (61) n 123.3
ped(al) (1) n 092.8
pedals (2) n 110.6
peddle (2) v 080.6
peddler (18) n 098.9
peddlers (8) n 113.7
peddling (4) v 114.4
Pedenville (1) GA 087.5
pedestrian (1) n 031.9
Pedestrian Mall (1) 106.5
Pedro (6) FL 087.6
pee (18) n/v/adj/interj
038.3
~ go (1) interj 038.3
~ -hee(x2) (1) interj
038.3
~ hoo (1) interj 038.3
~ in (4) v 096.7
~ on (1) v 060.4
~ ooh ee (1) interj
038.3
~ pee (1) n 099.8
~ pots (1) n 012.9
~ -whoo(x3) (1) interj
038.3
Pee Dee (3) AR SC 030.7
pee(x2) (5) interj 038.3
pee(x3) (2) interj 038.3
pee(x4) (1) interj 038.3
pee(x7) (1) interj 038.5
peed (1) v 091.8
peeing on (1) v 091.8
peek (2) adj 096.4
~ -eye (1) n 096.4
~ shows (1) n 114.9
peekaboo (14) n/interj
096.4
peeked up (1) v 003.3
peeking theater (1) n
114.9
peel (22) v 065.9
peel[N-i] (1) n 052.2
peeled (1) v 075.2
peeler (2) n 002.7
peeling (21) n/v/adj
054.5
~ knife (1) n 104.3
peelings (5) n 054.8
peen (9) n/adj 020.7
peep (65) v/adj 096.4
~ -eye (53) n/interj
096.4
~ -eyed (1) v 096.4
~ -eyeing (1) v 096.4
~ frog (2) n 060.3

~ frogs (1) n 060.3
~ owls (1) n 059.1
~ show (1) n 114.9
~ -show place (1) n
114.9
~ shows (1) n 114.9
~ under (1) v 057.7
peeped (1) v 075.5
peeper (1) n 060.3
peepers (7) n 060.3
peeping (4) v 096.4
~ at (1) v 096.4
~ down (1) v 096.4
peer (7) adj 129.6
~ group (6) n 129.6
~ pressure (1) n 063.9
peers (4) n 129.6
peeved (4) v 075.2
peeves (1) n 067.8
peewee tomato[N-i] (1) n
055.3
Peewee (4) 064.4
peewees (1) n 080.7
peg (74) n/v/adj 020.2
~ leg (2) n 027.4
~ -legged (1) adj 091.9
~ out (1) v 078.6
~ pants (1) n 027.4
~ -tooth harrow (3) n
021.7
~ -tooth harrows (1) n
021.7
~ -toothed harrow (1)
n 021.7
~ -top pants (1) n
027.4
Peg (3) 056.2
peg[V-r] (1) v 053.7
pegged (13) v/adj 014.1
~ out (11) v 078.6
peggy-looking fences (1)
n 016.2
pegs (6) n 065.8
Pekingese (1) 033.3
Pelham (2) GA 087.3
~ Range (1) AL 087.3
pelicans (3) n 099.8
pellagra (1) n 088.7
pellagresy (1) n 061.4
pellet (2) n 054.1
pelletize (1) v 090.8
pellets (4) n 022.4
Pellias (1) 107.9
Pellicer Creek (1) FL
030.7

Pellissippi Parkway (1) 107.5
pelted (1) v 032.1
pelvic bones (1) n 070.5
Pembroke (1) GA 087.1
pen (1940) n/v/adj 026.5
~ -like (1) adj 026.5
~ name (1) n 064.4
~ point (1) n 026.5
~ points (1) n 026.5
~ staff (2) n 026.5
~ traps (1) n 052.6
~ -up(x2) (1) interj 037.5
Pen (3) 106.4
Pena (1) TX 087.4
penal farm (1) n 070.7
penalized (1) v 032.3
pencil (141) n/adj 026.5
~ -cob corn (1) n 056.2
Pencil City of the World (1) 131.2
pencils (10) n 070.7
pendaligne (1) n 055.3
pendant (6) n 028.4
pendants (2) n 028.4
pendejo (6) n S 073.4
Pendleton (2) AR LA 087.3
pendulum (1) n 065.8
Peneille (1) LA 030.7
penetrate (2) v 013.1
penetrating (1) v 007.4
Penfield (3) GA 087.2
Penia (1) GA 087.2
peniche (1) n F 024.6
penicillin (2) n 078.4
peninsula (5) n 066.9
Peninsula (3) 087.4
penis (1) n 059.3
penitentiary (12) n/adj 112.9
~ stripe (1) n 056.9
penknife (2) n 104.4
penknives (2) n 088.9
Penne (1) n G 015.3
penned (8) v/adj 015.4
~ up (3) v 015.3
Pennekamp (1) 106.4
Penney's (1) 052.5
pennies (34) n 114.5
penning (3) v 015.6
Pennsylvania (39) AL 086.1
~ Dutch (2) 090.9

Penn(sylvania) (1) 087.5
penny (64) n/adj 026.6
~ grabber (1) n 073.5
~ loafers (5) n 123.8
~ pincher (41) n 073.5
~ pinchers (3) n 126.8
~ -pinching (1) adj 073.5
~ purse (1) n 028.2
penny[N-i] (1) n 026.7
pennyroyal (4) n/adj 061.4
~ tea (2) n 061.4
pennywinkle (2) n 080.6
pennywinkles (2) n 060A.4
Pennzoil (2) 024.1
pens (137) n 026.5
Pensacola (50) FL 087.7
~ Bay (1) FL 030.3
pension (2) n 066.8
Pentecost (4) 089.1
Pentecostal (7) 089.1
~ church (1) n 089.2
~ Holiness (1) 089.1
penthouse (32) n 119.4
penthouses (3) n 119.2
penurious (2) adj 073.5
peon (1) n S 069.3
peony (1) n 062.7
people (2992) n/adj 066.5
~ person (1) n 074.1
people[N-k] (5) adj 043.9
~ baby (1) n 043.9
~ religion (1) n 043.9
~ yard (1) n 012.9
people's (13) adj 066.5
~ horses (1) n 015.2
~ houses (1) n 053.4
~ land (1) n 041.4
~ mind[N-i] (1) n 052.5
~ names (1) n 025.1
peoples (108) n 016.7
Peoples (1) 107.7
pep (22) n/v/adj 074.2
~ assembly (1) n 080.7
~ pills (2) n 114.2
~ rallies (1) n 126.2
Pepere (2) F 064.1
pepid (1) adj 072.9
pepper (1050) n/adj 051.7
~ bellies (5) n 128.7
~ belly (4) n 128.7
~ box (1) n 051.7

~ -box sawmills (1) n 080.6
~ cellars (1) n 051.7
~ gut (1) n 069.9
~ mill (3) n 051.7
~ patch (1) n 016.1
~ -pot sawmill (1) n 080.8
~ relish (1) n 055.8
~ salt (3) n 051.7
~ salts (1) n 051.7
~ sauce (16) n 048.5
~ -sauce bottle (1) n 048.5
~ seed (1) n 051.7
~ shake (2) n 051.7
~ shaker (15) n 051.7
~ shaker[N-i] (1) n 051.7
~ shakers (14) n 051.7
~ tree (1) n 061.9
~ trees (2) n 061.8
Pepper (2) 121.8
peppered with (1) v 088.9
peppergrass (3) n 080.8
peppering down (2) v 006.6
peppers (77) n 051.7
peppies (1) n 127.3
peppy (39) adj 074.1
Pepsi (6) 121.8
~ -Cola (2) 121.8
~ -Colas (1) 089.8
per (4) prep 065.8
~ dime (1) adv 065.8
perambulator (16) n 064.5
perambulators (2) n 064.5
percale (1) n 080.9
percent (16) n 001A.2
percentage (1) n 052.8
perch (415) n/adj 059.9
~ fish (8) n 059.9
~ -fish (1) v 059.9
~ fishing (2) n 059.9
~ pole (1) n 081.9
Perch Creek (1) MS 030.7
perches (26) n 059.9
percolate (41) v 048.8
percolated (11) v/adj 048.8
~ coffee (3) n 048.8
percolates (1) v 048.8
percolating (5) v 048.8

percolator (66) n/adj 048.8
~ coffee (2) n 048.8
percolators (4) n 048.8
Percy (5) MS 088.8
~ Creek (1) MS 030.7
~ Edwin Warner Park (1) 106.4
~ Warner Park (2) 106.4
Perdido (3) FL 030.7
~ River (2) FL 030.7
Pere (1) F 064.1
peregrinations (1) n 088.7
perfect (35) adj 074.8
~ day (5) n 005.4
perfectionist (1) n 028.2
perfectly (21) adv 027.6
perform (1) v 057.7
(per)form (1) v 065.8
performance (1) n 102.7
performer (1) n 069.1
perfume (5) n/adj 065.9
~ cat (1) n 059.4
perhaps (5) adv 091.8
Perimeter (4) 107.5
~ Highway (1) 107.5
period (19) n 070.6
peri(od) (1) n 001A.3
periodically (1) adv 065.8
perish (1) v 066.8
peritonitis (3) n 080.2
periwinkle (2) n 081.8
periwinkles (1) n 060.5
perk (102) v/adj 048.8
~ coffee (5) n 048.8
~ pot (1) n 048.8
~ up (1) v 076.7
perked (15) v/adj 048.8
~ coffee (1) n 048.8
~ up (1) v 080.7
perking (8) v 048.8
Perkins (2) 106.4
~ Long Green (1) 055.8
Perkinston (1) MS 087.2
perkle (1) v 048.8
perks (1) v 048.8
perky (6) adj 074.1
perlite (1) n 080.6
perm (1) n 123.9
permanent (10) n/adj 123.9
~ fence (1) n 016.6
~ process (1) n 123.9
permanents (3) n 123.9

permeable soils (1) n 093.5

permission (3) n 053.2

permit (1) n 070.7

permitted (1) v 025.6

perms (1) n 123.9

pernicious fever (1) n 088.7

peroxide (22) n 078.3

perparing to (1) v 101.2

perpendicular (3) adj 085.2

perpetuated (1) v 070.7

perplexed (1) adj 075.6

Perrine (2) FL 087.2

Perrito (1) 075.6

Perry (33) AL FL GA TN 087.4

~ County (9) AL AR MS TN 087.4

~ Highway (1) 107.1

~ Home[N-i] (1) 105.5

~ plow (1) n 021.6

~ Street (3) 107.6

~ tomatoes (1) n 055.3

Perryville (2) AL TN 087.3

Pershing (2) 107.6

Persian (8) 056.7

~ melon (2) n 056.7

~ melons (5) n 056.7

persimmon (58) n/adj 061.8

~ beer (4) n 050.9

~ bread (1) n 044.4

~ stick (1) n 061.8

~ tree (11) n 061.8

~ trees (13) n 061.9

~ wars (1) n 130.5

(per)simmon (14) n/adj 061.8

~ beer (2) n 050.8

~ tree (4) n 061.8

~ trees (6) n 061.8

Persimmon Creek (3) AL 030.7

persimmons (14) n 061.9

(per)simmons (6) n 061.8

persistent (3) adj 074.8

persnickety (3) adj 080.6

person (526) n 069.3

pers(on) (1) n 069.7

person[N-k] mouth (1) n 095.8

personal (3) adj 005.8

~ friend (1) n 129.4

personality (16) n 073.2

personally (2) adv 013.8

personnel (1) n 119.5

person's (1) adj 046.2

persons (2) n 052.1

perspirate (1) v 077.3

perspirated (2) v 077.3

perspiration (29) n 077.3

perspire (76) v 077.3

perspire[V-r] (2) v 077.3

perspired (170) v 077.3

(per)spired (2) v 077.3

perspires (5) v 077.3

perspiring (20) v 077.3

perstrated (1) v 077.3

persuading (1) v 053.4

pert (64) adj 074.1

pertain (1) v 070.6

pertain[V-r] to (1) v 088.7

pertens up (1) v 060.4

pertly (1) adj 074.1

perturbed (2) adj 075.2

perty (1) adj 074.1

pervert (10) n 124.5

perv(ert) (1) n 124.6

perverts (2) n 124.5

pesky (2) adj 099.4

pesos (1) n 114.5

pest (34) n 033.3

pest[N-i] (11) n 059.5

pestes (3) n 033.3

pesthouse (1) n 082.9

pestle (1) v 042.1

pestles (1) n 080.7

pestling (1) v 050.7

pests (11) n 059.5

pet (202) n/adj 064.4

~ cock (2) n 018.7

~ name (91) n 064.4

~ names (10) n 064.4

~ peeves (1) n 067.7

~ slang (1) n 064.4

~ squirrel (2) n 059.6

~ term (1) n 064.4

pet[N-i] (1) n 053.2

(Pe)taul(a) Creek (1) GA 030.7

Pete (6) 092.1

Pete[N-k] sake (1) n 092.3

Peter (2) 030.7

~ Creek (1) LA 030.7

~ Schuttler (1) 088.8

petered (17) v 075.5

~ out (16) v 075.5

Peterman (1) AL 087.1

Peter's mudhole (2) n 006.1

Peters Branch (1) TN 030.7

Petersburg (17) TN VA 087.4

~ Road (1) 031.7

Peterson Hotel (1) 084.3

Pete's sake (1) n 092.3

petit fours (1) n 122.1

(pe)tit (2) adj F 068.5

~ -maitre (1) n F 068.5

~ noyau (1) n F 054.3

(Pe)tit-Boy (2) 064.5

petition (2) n 053.4

Petrey (1) AL 087.6

petrified (3) adj 096.7

~ liver (1) n 096.7

petroleum (1) n 024.2

Petroleum (2) 062.9

~ Tower (1) 108.5

pets (6) n 036.6

petted (1) v 084.8

petticoat (2) n 088.8

petticoats (3) n 027.1

Pettigrew Creek (1) MS 030.7

petting (24) v 081.7

pew (4) n 083.8

pew(x2) (1) interj 038.3

pews (3) n 083.8

peyote (6) n/adj 114.2

~ buttons (3) n 115.9

~ weed (1) n 114.2

Peyton (1) 107.7

Peytonsville (2) TN 087.6

Pfanne (1) n G 017.5

Pfannkuchen (1) n G 045.3

Pfeiffer Lake (1) AR 030.7

Pferdestall (1) n G 015.2

Pfyfe (1) 009.1

PG (17) 065.2

phaeton (5) n 080.8

phalanges (2) n 072.5

phantoms (2) n 090.2

Pharez (1) 069.3

pharmacist (1) n 088.7

pharmacy (1) n 075.7

Pharr (2) TX 087.5

pheasant (6) n 121.5

pheasants (4) n 088.8

Pheba (1) MS 087.6

Phelps (1) TX 087.3

Phenix (20) AL 087.3

~ City (19) AL 087.5

phenobarbital (2) n 114.2

phenomenon (1) n 070.6

phew (1) interj 092.1

Phi Delta Kappa (1) 052.7

Philadelphia (36) MS PA 087.5

~ cream cheese (2) n 048.1

~ scrapple (3) n 047.4

Philadelphi(a) (3) PA 087.8

philanderer (1) n 124.7

Philip (2) 115.5

Philippine Islands (1) 086.3

Philippines (1) 086.2

Philippinos (1) 069.4

Philip's (1) 106.5

Philips Inlet (2) FL 030.3

Phillips (13) AR 107.5

~ Creek (1) MS 030.7

~ Highway (1) 107.1

~ Highway Plaza (1) 116.1

~ Street (1) 107.6

(Phillips) Bayou (1) AR 087.7

philodendron (2) n 062.8

philosopher (1) n 069.4

Phinizy rooter (1) n 021.6

phlebitis (2) n 070.6

phlegm (1) n 076.5

Phoenix (4) AZ 087.5

phone (7) n/v 100.6

phones (1) n 045.8

phonetic (1) adj 066.8

phonograph (1) n 080.7

phoo (1) interj 092.3

phooey (3) interj 092.3

phosgene (1) n 075.6

phosphate (6) n/adj 080.6

~ district (1) n 080.7

~ land (1) n 029.8

~ mine (1) n 080.6

phosphating (1) v 080.7

photostatic (1) adj 039.6

phrase (1) n 012.3

physical education (1) n 083.5

physically (2) adv 073.1
physician (2) n 084.5
physique (2) n 065.8
PI (1) 101.3
pi(x2) (1) interj 038.3
pi(x5) (1) interj 038.5
pianist (1) n 088.7
piano (35) n/adj 009.4
~ box (1) n 014.4
~ -box buggy (1) n 080.9
~ lessons (2) n 053.4
~ music (2) n 130.8
~ room (1) n 007A.6
~ teacher (1) n 067.6
piazza (92) n 010.8
piazzas (4) n 010.8
pic bois (3) n F 059.3
pica pole (1) n 097.8
picadillo (2) n S 047.3
picayune (1) n 088.7
Picayune (9) MS 087.4
picayunish (2) adj 081.8
piccolo (1) n 020.5
pick (542) n/v/adj 101.4
~ off (1) v 101.4
~ on (3) v 129.8
~ plow (1) n 021.6
~ sack (5) n 019.7
~ -sack material (1) n 018.6
~ sacks (6) n 019.6
~ up (48) v 010.4
~ up sticks (2) n 088.8
pick[V-r] (3) v 013.8
~ up (1) v 052.5
pick[V-t] (2) v 015.8
pickaninnies (2) n 069.3
pickaninny (10) n 069.3
Pickaninny (1) 116.2
picked (64) v/adj 101.4
~ cotton (1) n 075.8
~ out (1) v 001.1
~ up (21) v 100.2
Pickens (11) AL LA MS 087.8
~ County (6) AL GA 086.6
~ Creek (1) GA 030.7
Pickensville (1) AL 087.7
picker (16) n/adj 088.7
pickerel (2) n 059.9
pickeries (1) n 092.8
pickers (16) n 065.9
picket (669) n/adj 016.4

~ boards (1) n 016.2
~ fence (480) n 016.2
~ fence[N-i] (1) n 016.2
~ fences (88) n 016.2
~ fencing (1) n 016.2
~ house (1) n 095.8
~ panel fence (1) n 016.2
~ pegs (1) n 016.2
picket[N-i] (2) n 016.2
pickets (76) n/adj 016.2
~ fence (1) n 016.2
Pickett Street (1) 107.7
Pickford (1) 067.1
picking (274) v/adj 101.5
~ at (3) v 098.7
~ sack (1) n 019.7
~ sacks (2) n 019.7
~ the pin (1) n 096.4
~ up (200) v 010.4
~ up on (2) v 075.9
pickings (2) n 069.7
pickle (37) n/v/adj 019.1
~ barrel (2) n 019.1
~ barrels (1) n 019.1
~ beet (1) n 055.6
~ factory (1) n 106.4
~ feet (1) n 121.3
~ fork (1) n 017.9
~ hog foot (1) n 081.8
~ jam (1) n 052.6
~ meat (3) n 046.3
~ peach (2) n 054.3
~ peaches (2) n 054.3
~ pig[N-i][N-k] feet (3) n 046.4
~ pigs' feet (2) n 121.3
~ pork (2) n 046.3
~ pork meat (1) n 080.7
~ sausages (1) n 121.6
pickled (6) adj 046.6
~ beef (1) n 046.6
~ eggs (1) n 046.2
~ meat (1) n 046.3
~ okra (1) n 055.8
~ peaches (1) n 054.3
~ pigs' feet (1) n 047.3
pickles (3) n 051.7
pickling (10) v/adj 046.5
~ peach (7) n 054.3
~ peaches (1) n 054.3
~ tubs (1) n 089.8
picks (6) n/v 120.5

~ up (1) v 007.2
pickup (150) n/adj 109.7
~ baler (1) n 014.8
~ fryers (1) n 121.5
~ load (2) n 019.8
~ meat (2) n 046.5
~ truck (64) n 109.7
~ trucks (10) n 109.7
pickups (18) n 067.8
picky (2) adj 085.4
picnic (37) n/adj 121.3
~ area (4) n 107.2
~ areas (1) n 107.2
~ basket (2) n 020.1
~ grounds (1) n 107.2
~ ham (10) n 121.3
~ ham[N-i] (1) n 121.3
~ hams (6) n 121.3
~ melons (1) n 056.9
~ shoulders (1) n 121.3
~ swings (1) n 022.9
~ table (1) n 022.1
Picnic (1) FL 087.1
picnicking (1) v 066.8
picnics (8) n 121.3
Picolata (1) FL 087.6
Pictsola (1) 078.3
picture (256) n/v/adj 070.7
~ cinema (1) n 084.4
~ show (145) n 084.4
~ sh(ow) (1) n 084.4
~ shows (12) n 084.4
~ theater (1) n 084.4
~ tube (1) n 048.9
pict(ure) show (1) n 084.4
pic(ture) show (3) n 084.4
picture[N-i] (1) n 012.2
pictures (33) n 065.8
Pid Creek (1) GA 030.7
piddle with (1) v 080.6
piddled (2) v 090.9
~ around (1) v 090.9
~ (a)round (1) v 084.8
piddler (1) n 067.8
piddling (4) v 010.4
~ around (2) v 010.4
pidgin language (1) n 092.8
pie (604) n/adj 048.3
~ closet (1) n 010.1
~ cobbler (2) n 048.3
~ cupboard (1) n 010.1

~ hominy (1) n 044.6
~ melon (17) n 056.5
~ melons (4) n 056.7
~ pumpkin (1) n 056.5
~ pumpkins (2) n 056.5
~ safe (10) n 010.1
~ safes (3) n 010.1
~ shelf (1) n 010.1
~ suppers (1) n 104.6
~ tins (1) n 026.6
Pie (11) 064.4
piece (845) n/v/adj 039.4
~ away (1) v 067.8
~ goods (2) n 080.8
~ of cheese (1) n 125.4
~ quilts (2) n 029.1
~ up (1) v 052.6
piece[N-i] (3) n 016.7
pieced (4) v/adj 029.1
~ oak leaf (1) n 088.8
~ tulip (1) n 080.7
pieces (63) n 054.6
piecing (3) v 029.1
~ up (1) v 011.2
piecrust (13) n 044.4
piecrustes (2) n 016.5
piecrusts (1) n 044.4
pied (10) n/adj F 033.3
~ moccasin (1) n 088.8
pieded (1) adj 055A.3
Piedmont (18) AL 105.1
~ Avenue (1) 107.7
~ Park (9) 106.4
pieing (1) v 099.6
pieplant (4) n 055.6
pier (90) n 031.4
Pier (2) 106.4
Pierce (13) GA 087.1
~ Arrow (1) 109.4
~ County (2) GA 087.1
Pierre (9) 030.7
~ Font Estates (1) 106.1
Pierremont (1) 106.1
piers (11) n 031.4
pies (176) n 122.3
pieu (16) n/adj F 016.2
~ fence (11) n 016.2
~ fences (2) n 016.2
pieux (1) n F 016.7
pig (944) n/adj/interj 035.5
~ barn (3) n 014.2
~ brains (2) n 047.1
~ bristles (1) n 035.6

~ bucket (1) n 017.4
~ can (1) n 017.4
~ car (3) n 111.7
~ country (1) n 080.7
~ dogs (1) n 112.5
~ ears (13) n 121.3
~ farmer (1) n 069.9
~ -foot jelly (1) n 051.6
~ haslet (1) n 037.2
~ head (1) n 074.8
~ hickory nut (1) n 054.8
~ -ho(x2) (1) interj 038.3
~ -hoey(x2) (1) interj 038.3
~ -hog(x3) (1) interj 038.3
~ house (3) n 015.4
~ houses (1) n 015.4
~ in the blanket (1) n 084.8
~ intestines (1) n 037.3
~ iron (2) n 080.6
~ knuckles (3) n 121.3
~ legs (1) n 121.3
~ lot (10) n 015.4
~ maw (1) n 037.3
~ netting (1) n 016.3
~ nuts (1) n 121.3
~ parlor (9) n 015.4
~ parlors (5) n 015.4
~ pasture (1) n 015.4
~ path (2) n 031.8
~ paths (1) n 031.8
~ -piggy(x2) (1) interj 038.3
~ pool (1) n 084.8
~ rocks (1) n 034.8
~ sausage (1) n 121.6
~ shelter (2) n 015.4
~ slops (1) n 017.4
~ stage (1) n 035.5
~ stall (1) n 015.4
~ tail (7) n 121.3
~ -tail sandwiches (1) n 121.3
~ tails (9) n 121.3
~ tongue (2) n 121.3
~ tracks (2) n 073.6
~ trail (8) n 031.8
~ trails (3) n 031.8
~ trash (1) n 073.7
~ trough (11) n 035.8

~ troughs (7) n 035.8
~ wire (1) n 016.3
Pig (2) 064.4
~ Stand (1) 112.5
pig(x2) (63) interj 038.3
~ come-here(x2) (1) interj 038.3
pig(x3) (51) interj 038.3
pig(x4) (21) interj 038.3
pig(x5) (10) interj 038.3
pig(x6) (3) interj 038.3
pig[N-i] (2) n 035.5
pig[N-i][N-k] (30) adj 121.3
~ feet (25) n 121.3
~ feets (3) n 072.6
~ foot[N-i] (1) n 072.6
~ foots (1) n 072.6
pigawee (1) interj 038.3
pigee (1) interj 038.3
pigeon (18) n/adj 101.3
~ gangs (1) n 084.8
~ peas (1) n 055A.3
~ pen (1) n 036.8
Pigeon (22) 030.7
~ Creek (4) AL GA 030.7
~ Forge (3) TN 087.2
~ Key (1) 105A.1
~ River (5) TN 030.7
~ Roost Creek (1) LA 030.7
pigeonhole parking lot (1) n 108.4
pigeonnier (1) n F 014.3
pigeons (7) n 036.6
pigeonwing blinds (1) n 038.6
pigfish (1) n 059.9
piggies (3) n 035.5
piggies(x2) (1) interj 038.3
piggin (5) n 017.2
piggins (2) n 017.2
piggo (7) interj 038.3
piggo(x2) (1) interj 038.3
piggoee (2) interj 038.3
~ oee (1) interj 038.3
piggoo (2) interj 038.3
piggoo(x2) (1) interj 038.3
Piggott (2) AR 087.2
piggy (77) adj/interj 038.3

~ a-piggy (1) interj 038.3
~ perch (1) n 059.9
~ pig(x2) (1) interj 038.3
~ pig(x4) (1) interj 038.3
~ poo (1) interj 038.3
~ wants a signal (1) n 081.8
~ -wiggy-wig(x2) (1) interj 038.3
~ wiggy(x3) (1) interj 038.3
Piggy (2) 064.4
~ Bank (1) 055.4
piggy(x2) (57) interj 038.3
piggy(x3) (73) interj 038.3
~ pee (1) interj 038.3
piggy(x4) (29) interj 038.3
piggy(x5) (7) interj 038.3
piggy(x6) (2) interj 038.3
piggy(x7) (1) interj 038.3
piggy(x8) (1) interj 038.3
pigheaded (20) adj 074.8
piglet (90) n 035.5
piglets (26) n 035.5
pigling (1) n 035.5
pigmy (2) adj 036.8
~ poultry (1) n 036.8
~ rattler (1) n 088.9
pignut (6) n 054.9
pignuts (3) n 054.8
pigoey (1) interj 038.3
pigoo (11) interj 038.3
pigoo(x2) (3) interj 038.3
pigooey (5) interj 038.3
pigooey(x2) (2) interj 038.3
pigoop (1) interj 038.3
pigoy (1) interj 038.3
pigpen (238) n 015.4
Pigpen Branch (1) FL 030.7
pigpens (17) n 015.4
pig's (5) adj 035.5
~ ass (1) n 088.8
~ car (1) n 111.7
~ hair (1) n 035.6
pigs (620) n/interj 035.5
pigs' (27) adj 121.3
~ brains (1) n 121.3

~ bucket (1) n 017.4
~ feet (18) n 121.3
~ -foot jelly (2) n 051.6
~ house (1) n 015.4
~ pen (1) n 015.4
pigs(x2) (1) interj 038.3
pigskin (2) n 035.6
pigsties (2) n 015.4
pigsty (51) n 015.4
pigtail (7) n 121.3
pigtails (11) n 123.9
pigweed (3) n 015.9
pikage (1) n 092.7
pike (42) n/adj 031.6
~ fish (3) n 059.9
~ road (4) n 031.6
~ roads (3) n 031.7
Pike (49) AL GA 087.5
~ County (22) AL AR GA MS 087.2
~ County Museum (1) 106.4
~ Pioneer Museum (1) 106.4
piker (1) n 080.7
pikes (1) n 107.6
Pikes Peak (1) CO 080.7
Pikeville (3) TN 087.9
pilaf (5) n 080.6
pilchards (1) n 061.2
pile (127) n/v/adj 014.6
~ around with (1) v 096.7
~ driver (2) n 020.7
pile[V-t] up (1) v 053.8
pileate (1) n 059.3
pileated (12) n/adj 059.3
~ woodpecker (5) n 059.3
~ woodpeckers (1) n 059.3
piled (4) v 014.8
~ up (1) v 014.6
piles (75) n/v 014.8
pilfered (3) v 100.2
pilfering (5) v 070.8
~ around (1) v 094.2
Pilgrim's Rest (1) 070.6
piling (3) n/v 021.4
pilings (3) n 066.9
pill (13) n/adj 073.4
~ bugs (1) n 060A.2
~ poppers (1) n 114.3
~ pusher (1) n 114.4

pillador (1) n S 090.8

pillaging room (1) n 010.2

pillars (4) n 028.8

pilled (1) v 095.8

pillow (980) n/adj 028.8
~ bolster (1) n 028.9
~ bolst(er) (1) n 028.9
~ cover (1) n 028.8
~ covering (1) n 028.8
~ cushions (1) n 028.8
~ fight (1) n 028.8
~ fights (1) n 028.8
~ rack (1) n 028.8
~ rest (1) n 028.9
~ roll (2) n 028.9
~ sham (24) n 028.8
~ shams (22) n 028.8
~ sheet (1) n 028.8
~ slip (28) n 028.8
~ slips (21) n 028.8

pil(low) (2) n 028.8

pillowcase (66) n 028.8

pillowcases (38) n 028.8

pillowcasing (2) n 028.8

pillowcasings (1) n 028.8

pillows (208) n 028.8

pillroller (2) n 088.7

pillrollers (1) n 067.8

pills (29) n 114.2

Pillsbury crescent rolls (1) n 044.4

pilon (30) n S 095.7

piloncillo (1) n S 051.3

piloncillos (1) n S 095.7

pilot (18) n/adj 093.7
~ license (1) n 053.4

Pilot (11) 086.4
~ Hill (1) AR 086.4
~ Knob (7) AR TX 030.8
~ Point (2) TX 087.3

pilots (6) n 099.6

pimento (4) n/adj 055.2
~ cheese (1) n 066.8
~ peppers (1) n 055.7

(pi)mento cheese (1) n 066.8

pimentos (3) n 055.2

pimp (165) n/v/adj 113.5
~ car (1) n 109.4
~ cars (1) n 109.4
~ clothes (3) n 123.6
~ on (3) v 113.5
~ shirt (1) n 123.6

~ stuff (3) n 123.6
~ town (1) n 114.8

pimped (2) v 113.5
~ on (1) v 113.5
~ up (1) v 109.4

pimping (3) v 101.4

pimple (54) n 077.4

pimples (8) n 077.4

pimpmobile (14) n 109.4

pimpmobiles (2) n 109.4

pimpoter (1) v F 028.1

pimp's car (1) n 109.4

pimps (33) n 113.5

pin (924) n/v/adj 026.5
~ oak (50) n 061.8
~ -oak glades (1) n 029.6
~ oak tree (1) n 061.9
~ oaks (12) n 061.9
~ the donkey tail (1) n 130.2
~ the tail on the donkey (4) n 130.3
~ -ticket machine (1) n 026.5
~ your ears back (1) v 065.5

Pin Hook (1) TX 082.6

pinafore (3) n 026.4

pinafores (1) n 080.8

pinball wizard (1) n 089.8

pinch (12) n/v 066.8
~ off (1) v 101.4

Pinchback Lake (1) MS 030.7

pinched (5) v 100.2

pincher (42) n 073.5

pinchers (6) n 060A.1

pinches (1) v 073.5

pinching (6) v 007.4

pinchpennies (1) n 126.7

pinchpenny (5) n 073.5

pinchy (6) adj 007.4

Pinckneyville (2) GA 086.4
~ District (1) GA 025.8

pincushion (2) n 026.5

pinder (19) n/adj 099.9
~ field (2) n 015.4
~ nut (1) n 054.7
~ nuts (1) n 054.7
~ patch (1) n 054.7

pinders (116) n 054.7

pine (1203) n/adj 061.8
~ beetle (1) n 080.8

~ benches (2) n 083.8
~ box (30) n 079.1
~ boxes (1) n 079.1
~ brush (1) n 022.2
~ brush top (1) n 022.2
~ buckets (1) n 017.2
~ burrs (1) n 061.8
~ chest (1) n 008.8
~ chips (2) n 008.6
~ country (1) n 024.7
~ farms (1) n 061.6
~ fat (1) n 008.6
~ flats (1) n 080.9
~ floors (1) n 010.5
~ grove (1) n 053.2
~ groves (1) n 061.6
~ -gummed (1) v 095.8
~ hearts (1) n 008.6
~ -hill rooter (1) n 030.9
~ -hill rooters (1) n 035.9
~ hills (3) n 030.8
~ kindling (6) n 008.6
~ knot (13) n 008.6
~ -knot fire (1) n 008.6
~ -knot torch (1) n 024.3
~ knots (74) n 008.6
~ light (3) n 024.2
~ lighter (1) n 008.6
~ lighterd (1) n 008.6
~ log (1) n 008.5
~ logs (3) n 008.5
~ lumber (2) n 011.2
~ oil (2) n 078.3
~ poles (1) n 082.8
~ post[N-i] (1) n 016.5
~ rail fence (1) n 016.4
~ railing fence (1) n 016.4
~ resin (4) n 008.6
~ richerd (1) n 008.6
~ -ridge rooter (1) n 035.9
~ rooter (7) n 035.9
~ root(er) (1) n 035.9
~ rooters (7) n 035.9
~ roots (1) n 061.4
~ saplings (2) n 061.8
~ seedlings (1) n 061.8
~ shavings (2) n 008.6
~ shelf (1) n 088.9
~ siding (1) n 011.2
~ splinters (8) n 008.6

~ sticks (1) n 008.6
~ straw (3) n 061.4
~ stump (1) n 061.8
~ stumps (1) n 008.6
~ swamps (1) n 029.6
~ tacky (1) adj 069.9
~ tar (5) n 031.6
~ thicket (4) n 061.6
~ timber (2) n 061.8
~ top (2) n 061.4
~ -top tea (1) n 061.4
~ tops (1) n 010.5
~ torch (6) n 024.3
~ torches (2) n 024.3
~ tree (64) n 061.8
~ -tree post (1) n 016.5
~ tree[N-i] (2) n 061.9
~ trees (145) n 061.8

Pine (64) 087.7
~ Apple (1) AL 087.7
~ Barren (1) AL 030.7
~ Barren Creek (1) AL 030.7
~ Bluff (20) AR 087.4
~ Chapel Church (1) 089.2
~ Creek (2) TN TX 030.7
~ Flat (1) TX 087.8
~ Flat community (1) TX 087.7
~ Grove (2) AR 087.5
~ Grove Church (1) 089.2
~ Harbor (2) GA 087.3
~ Hill (4) AL GA 087.1
~ Island (2) LA 087.7
~ Island Bayou (3) TX 030.7
~ Key (1) FL 087.4
~ Level (1) FL 087.4
~ Log Mountain (2) GA 031.1
~ Mountain (9) GA NC 087.6
~ -O-Lean (1) 092.9
~ Orchard Road (1) 031.6
~ Street (3) 107.7
~ Tree Drive (1) 106.1

pine[N-i] (1) n 061.8

pineapple (3) n/adj 055.2
~ jelly (1) n 051.6
~ tree (1) n 061.9

pineapples (2) n 083.9
Pineda (2) FL 087.4
Pinedale (1) AL 087.2
Pinellas (5) FL 087.5
~ Park (1) 106.2
~ Point (1) 106.1
pinely (3) adv 091.6
Pineola Avenue (1) 061.8
pines (82) n 061.8
Pines (3) 105.1
Pineville (2) LA 087.8
pinewood (31) n/adj
008.6
~ box (1) n 079.1
~ rooters (1) n 035.9
Pinewood (2) TN 087.3
pinewoods (7) n/adj
061.8
~ rooters (1) n 035.9
piney (142) adj 035.9
~ rooter (4) n 035.9
~ rooters (2) n 035.9
~ wood (4) n 069.9
~ -wood cows (1) n
033.6
~ -wood hog (1) n
035.9
~ -wood hogs (1) n
035.9
~ -wood rooter (18) n
035.9
~ -wood-rooter cow (1)
n 033.6
~ -wood rooters (9) n
035.9
~ woods (27) n 008.6
~ -woods cow (2) n
033.6
~ -woods cows (1) n
033.6
~ -woods hog (4) n
035.9
~ -woods hogs (2) n
035.9
~ -woods land (1) n
029.8
~ -woods peckerwood
(1) n 069.9
~ -woods people (1) n
069.9
~ -woods rooter (44) n
035.9
~ -woods rooters (15) n
035.9

~ -woodsiness (1) n
069.9
~ -woodsy (1) adj
069.9
Piney (26) AR 030.7
~ Creek (7) AL AR
MS TN 030.7
~ Grove (3) TN 087.2
~ Grove Church (1)
089.2
~ Point (1) TX 105.2
~ Point Village (1) TX
087.2
~ River (2) TN 030.7
~ Way (1) FL 087.3
~ Wood (1) GA 087.2
~ Woods (2) GA MS
030.7
Pineywoods Branch (1)
AL 030.7
pinfeathers (2) n 026.5
Ping-Pong (2) 130.4
Pinhook Creek (4) AL
030.7
pink (49) n/adj 075.7
~ and blues (1) n 115.8
~ boll worm (1) n
060.5
~ dogwoods (1) n
062.6
~ elder (1) n 062.3
~ -eyed purple hull (1)
n 088.8
~ house (2) n 113.4
~ Irish potato (1) n
055.4
~ lady (1) n 113.3
~ magnolia (1) n 062.9
~ -meat watermelon (1)
n 056.9
~ mulberries (1) n
062.6
~ pampas (1) n 041.6
~ potato (2) n 055.4
~ room (1) n 007A.8
~ salmon (1) n 059.9
~ -skin potatoes (1) n
055.4
~ tips (1) n 055A.4
~ tomatoes (1) n 055.3
~ worm (3) n 060.5
~ worms (3) n 060.5
~ yam (1) n 055.5
Pink Palace (1) 106.4
pinked (1) adj 072.9

pinkeye (6) n/adj 081.9
~ bean (1) n 055A.4
~ purple hull (1) n
055A.8
~ purple-hull pea (1) n
055A.6
pinkie ring (1) n 123.1
pinkish (1) adj 075.8
pinko (1) n 129.1
pinks (8) n 115.7
pinky (1) n 072.9
pinned (2) v 081.4
pinochle (1) n 088.9
pinpoint (2) n/v 026.5
pins (93) n 026.6
Pinson (1) 086.4
pinstriped overalls (1) n
027.4
pint (4) n/adj 051.3
pintail (1) n 081.8
Pintlalla Creek (2) AL
030.7
pinto (117) n/adj 055A.8
~ bean (16) n 055A.3
~ beans (83) n 055A.3
~ box (1) n 079.1
~ (to)matoes (1) n
055.3
pintos (16) n 055A.3
pints (1) n 052.5
piojillo (1) n S 060A.9
pioneer home (1) n 032.2
Pioneer (2) 108.5
~ Bank building (1) n
108.5
~ Museum (1) 106.4
pip (11) n/adj 054.1
~ jennies (2) n 077.4
~ jenny (4) n 077.4
pipe (429) n/v/adj 018.7
~ -cider worms (1) n
060.5
~ clay (2) n 029.9
~ down (2) v 075.3
~ posts (1) n 016.5
~ stack (1) n 023.2
~ tobacco (1) n 057.3
pipe[N-i] (1) n 052.1
piped (4) v 023.2
~ into (1) v 023.2
~ out (1) v 078.6
pipeline (2) adj 008.1
~ canals (1) n 030.2
pipeman (2) n 112.4
piper (1) n 060.3

pipes (95) n 057.3
piping (8) n 023.2
Pippin (1) 106.6
pipping (1) v 080.7
pips (1) n 054.5
piquante (2) adj F 054.9
pique (3) n F 104.3
pirates (1) n 082.8
Pirates House (1) 106.4
pirogue (94) n/adj 024.6
~ boats (1) n 024.6
~ races (1) n 024.6
pirogue[N-i] (1) n 024.6
pirogues (32) n 024.6
piroot (1) v 080.5
PIs (1) 101.3
Pisa (1) 078.3
Pisgah School (1) 087.6
piss (20) n/v/adj/interj
059.4
~ elm (1) n 061.8
~ elms (1) n 061.8
~ -fuck hell (1) interj
092.3
~ house (1) n 126.3
~ in (1) v 017.6
~ on (2) v 096.7
~ pot (1) n 088.8
pissants (1) n 060A.8
pissed (15) v/adj 091.8
~ off (12) adj 075.2
~ on (1) v 075.6
pisses (4) v 092.7
pissing (7) v 081.9
~ fire (1) v 081.9
~ on (6) v 006.1
pissoir (1) n F 012.1
pissy (2) adj 075.1
pistache (5) n F 054.6
pistachio (4) n/adj 054.8
~ nuts (3) n 054.9
pistachios (5) n 054.9
pistol (109) n/adj 113.1
~ ball (1) n 022.4
~ bullet (1) n 022.4
~ cartridges (4) n 022.4
~ -leg pants (1) n 028.1
~ -legged breeches (1)
n 027.4
~ -toter's license (1) n
098.6
Pistol Creek (1) TN 030.7
pistolets (1) n 044.7
pistols (14) n 113.1
piston (1) n 099.6

pit (519) n/adj 054.1
~ stop (1) n 107.2
~ toilet (2) n 012.1
~ toilets (2) n 012.1
pitahaya (1) n S 062.4
pitahayas (1) n S 088.7
pitch (125) n/v/adj 008.7
~ his cookies (1) v 080.3
~ horseshoes (1) v 034.8
~ in (1) v 049.4
~ out (2) v 032.1
~ pine (3) n 008.6
~ pot (1) n 024.3
~ roof (2) n 011.4
~ wood (1) n 008.6
~ your cookies (1) v 080.3
Pitch (1) 090.1
pitched (48) v/adj 032.2
~ his cookies (1) v 080.3
~ in (3) v 070.2
~ off (3) v 034.4
~ roof (1) n 011.4
~ up and (1) v 095.8
pitcher (66) n/adj 017.2
~ -mouth pump (1) n 071.6
~ pump (4) n 088.9
~ pump[N-i] (1) n 080.7
pitchers (9) n 017.2
pitchfork (52) n 120.6
pitchfork[N-i] and nigger babies (1) n 006.1
pitchforks (20) n 021.7
~ and nigger babies (1) n 006.1
pitching (136) n/v 032.1
~ out (1) v 032.1
~ woo (1) v 081.7
pith (3) n 054.1
pitiful (10) adj 072.9
Pitkin (1) TX 087.1
Pitman Creek (1) MS 030.7
pits (31) n 054.1
pitta-pee(x2) (1) interj 038.5
pitted (3) v/adj 062.1
~ peach (1) n 054.3
Pittman (3) GA MS 086.6

~ Park (1) 106.4
Pitts Hollow (1) AR 087.7
Pittsboro (1) MS 087.6
Pittsburg (10) CA GA TN TX 087.3
Pittsburgh (12) PA 105.4
pity (1) v 039.6
pity's sake (1) n 092.2
piup(x6) (1) interj 038.5
pivot fence (1) n 126.1
pixie (7) n/adj 123.9
~ cut (1) n 123.9
~ tomatoes (1) n 055.3
pixies (2) n 123.9
piyoop(x2) (1) interj 038.3
pizza (3) n/adj 070.8
~ lovers (1) n 127.3
pizzaburger (1) n 081.9
pizzles (2) n 037.2
place (475) n/adj 070.6
Place (8) 107.6
place[N-i] (1) n 052.1
placed (2) v 053.4
~ upon (1) v 052.5
Placedo (1) TX 030.7
places (100) n 107.7
Placida (1) 030.7
placing (1) v 040.6
plaftorm concern (1) n 008.4
plague (3) n 070.1
plain (321) adj 032.3
~ coffee (15) n 032.3
~ Jane (3) n 125.2
~ land (1) n 029.5
~ -old (23) adj 029.8
~ talk (1) n 099.8
~ toe (2) n 123.8
~ -toe shoes (1) n 123.8
plainclothes car (1) n 111.7
plains (11) n 029.5
Plains (25) GA LA 087.4
plainspoken (1) adj 073.6
Plainview (3) LA TX 087.4
Plainville (1) GA 087.2
plait (7) n/v/adj 019.4
plaited (9) v/adj 019.4
~ up (1) v 123.9
plaiting (1) v 123.9
plaits (5) n 115.7

plan (70) n/v 101.2
~ on (4) v 101.2
~ to (51) v 101.2
planarian (1) n 060.5
plane (10) n/adj 020.7
~ tree (1) n 061.7
~ trees (2) n 061.7
planed (1) v 084.8
planer mill (1) n 088.9
planes (1) n 052.1
Planetarium (1) 106.4
planing (5) adj 104.3
~ knife (1) n 104.3
~ mill (4) n 080.7
plank (141) n/adj 011.2
~ boat (1) n 024.6
~ closers (1) n 009.5
~ fence (60) n 016.2
~ fences (12) n 016.2
~ fencing (2) n 016.2
~ floor (1) n 039.8
~ flooring (1) n 014.1
~ house (5) n 011.2
~ houses (1) n 014.1
~ mix (1) n 031.6
~ pen (1) n 015.4
~ road (2) n 031.6
~ room (1) n 007A.3
~ steak (1) n 121.1
~ troughs (1) n 035.8
~ walk (7) n 009.9
~ walks (4) n 031.9
~ walkway (1) n 031.9
plank[N-i] (2) n 016.7
planking (1) n 011.2
planks (31) n 011.2
plankton (1) n 015.9
planned (2) v 101.2
~ to (1) v 101.2
planning (148) v 101.2
~ on (33) v 101.2
~ to (51) v 101.2
plans (7) n/v 104.4
~ to (1) v 101.2
plant (91) n/v/adj 065.9
~ bed (2) n 050.5
~ engineer (1) n 119.5
~ in (1) v 092.8
~ mix (2) n 031.6
Plant (7) 087.9
~ City (6) FL 087.9
~ Park (1) 106.4
plantains (2) n 096.9
plantation (72) n/adj 090.7

~ days (1) n 066.8
~ desk (1) n 009.5
~ education (1) n 083.5
~ house (1) n 007A.5
~ houses (2) n 014.1
~ manager (1) n 080.6
~ owner (1) n 069.6
~ road (3) n 031.6
~ roads (1) n 031.6
~ stores (2) n 088.7
~ weeds (1) n 015.9
Plantation (14) 105.1
~ Key (1) FL 087.9
plantations (9) n 065.8
planted (31) v 017.7
~ in (3) v 074.4
~ to (1) v 080.9
planter (59) n 017.7
planter's (2) adj 083.8
~ desk (1) n 083.8
~ pot (1) n 017.7
planters (26) n 017.7
Plantersville (3) AL 087.1
planting (14) n/v/adj 079.2
~ on (1) v 002.1
~ plow (1) n 021.6
~ time (1) n 095.8
plants (31) n/v 080.7
~ in (2) v 025.5
plaque (1) n 001.8
Plaquemine (15) LA 087.5
~ Bayou (2) LA 030.7
Plaquemines (12) LA 086.4
~ Parish (3) LA 087.4
plasma center (1) n 114.8
plaster (3) n 052.1
plastered with (1) v 013.8
plastering (2) v/adj 080.6
~ trowel (1) n 080.6
plastic (216) n/adj 017.1
~ bag (70) n 123.7
~ bags (18) n 019.6
~ barrel (1) n 019.1
~ basket (2) n 020.1
~ bottle cap (1) n 020.4
~ bucket (22) n 116.9
~ buckets (6) n 116.9
~ cleaner bag (1) n 123.7
~ cork (1) n 020.4
~ cover (2) n 014.7

~ drawers (1) n 090.9
~ egg (8) n 017.1
~ eggs (5) n 017.1
~ garbage pail (2) n 116.9
~ garden (1) n 050.5
~ glass (1) n 048.9
~ glasses (1) n 131.5
~ keg (1) n 017.1
~ mop pail (1) n 017.3
~ pail (10) n 116.9
~ pipe (1) n 066.9
~ pumpkins (1) n 056.5
~ restoration surgery (1) n 080.6
~ sack (3) n 019.6
~ sacks (1) n 019.7
~ shutters (1) n 009.5
~ strips (1) n 066.8
~ vessel (1) n 017.3
plat (2) n 107.3
plate (102) n/adj 071.7
~ -bande (1) n F 065.8
~ bones (1) n 037.1
~ meat (1) n 046.3
~ pie (2) n 048.3
~ pies (1) n 048.3
plate[N-i] (3) n 049.5
plateau (15) n 031.2
Plateau (3) 105.1
plateaus (2) n 031.1
plateful (1) n 049.6
plates (24) n 017.8
platform (31) n/adj 010.8
~ heels (1) n 123.8
~ rocker (9) n 008.8
~ shoes (5) n 123.8
(plat)form (2) adj 008.8
~ rocker (1) n 008.8
~ rockers (1) n 008.8
platforms (10) n 123.8
platonic (3) adj 129.4
~ friend (1) n 129.4
~ relationship (1) n 129.4
Platt (2) 107.7
Platte (4) 087.6
~ City (1) MO 087.6
platter (2) n 017.5
platters (1) n 130.8
play (682) n/v/adj 083.1
~ brother (1) n 129.4
~ children (1) n 129.6
~ dad (1) n 129.5
~ daddy (9) n 129.5

~ daughter (1) n 129.5
~ day (1) n 081.8
~ dogs (1) n 033.1
~ down (1) v 090.4
~ father (6) n 129.5
~ for (1) v 080.8
~ group (1) n 129.6
~ hookies (1) v 083.4
~ hooky (38) v 083.4
~ in (1) v 042.3
~ instrument (1) n 101.5
~ like (1) v 100.1
~ mamma (14) n 129.5
~ mother (9) n 129.5
~ mothers (1) n 129.5
~ name (1) n 064.4
~ out (6) v 075.5
~ papa (2) n 129.5
~ parent (1) n 129.5
~ -parties (6) n 130.7
~ partner (1) n 129.4
~ -party (2) n 083.1
~ possum (1) v 080.9
~ -pretties (135) n 101.5
~ -pretty (257) n 101.5
~ school (1) n 083.7
~ sister (3) n 129.4
~ songs (1) n 083.1
~ the dozen[N-i] (1) v 129.7
~ tools (1) n 101.5
~ toy (22) n 101.5
~ toys (20) n 101.5
~ truant (1) v 083.4
~ with (11) v 032.4
play[V-r] hooky (1) v 083.4
play[V-s] (1) v 025.8
playboy (6) n/adj 124.7
~ sports cars (1) n 109.1
played (568) v 052.5
~ (a)round (1) v 083.4
~ down (1) v 080.8
~ hell (1) v 065.1
~ her for a fool (1) v 082.1
~ hide (1) v 083.4
~ hooky (469) v 083.4
~ like (7) v 100.1
~ on (1) v 040.5
~ out (41) v 083.4

~ out of school (2) v 083.4
~ the hooky (2) v 083.4
~ the truant (1) v 083.4
~ truant (1) v 083.4
~ with (3) v 053.5
player (1) n 124.7
players (1) n 089.8
playful (1) adj 074.1
playground (7) n/adj 108.7
~ area (1) n 108.7
~ fence (1) n 126.1
playgrounds (1) n 108.7
playhouse (6) n 084.4
playhouses (2) n 014.1
playing (238) v 022.9
~ around (3) v 081.7
~ hippie (1) v 083.4
~ hooky (120) v 083.4
~ like (1) v 100.1
~ on (11) v 022.8
~ out (4) v 088.7
~ the dozen[N-i] (7) v 129.7
~ the dozens (15) v 129.7
~ the doz(ens) (1) v 129.7
~ up to her (1) v 081.4
~ with (2) v 057.4
~ [D-0] dozens (1) v 129.7
playmate (2) n 129.4
playmate[N-i] (1) n 129.6
playmates (16) n 129.6
playroom (31) n 118.2
playrooms (1) n 007A.5
plays (23) n/v 126.2
~ around (1) v 124.8
~ hooky (9) v 083.4
~ on (1) v 095.8
~ with (3) v 053.4
playsuits (1) n 090.8
plaything (60) n 101.5
playthings (104) n 101.5
plaza (13) n 085.2
Plaza (31) 105.3
~ Park (1) 114.8
~ Tower (1) 108.5
plazas (1) n 107.2
plazuela (1) n S 085.1
plea (1) n 089.8
pleasant (201) adj 005.4

~ day (22) n 005.4
~ -looking (3) adj 073.2
~ morning (1) n 007.4
~ weather (4) n 005.4
Pleasant (28) 087.4
~ Grove (3) FL GA 087.4
~ Hill (5) AL AR MS 087.4
~ Hill area (1) LA 030.8
~ Hill Creek (1) LA 030.7
~ Hill Road (2) 030.8
~ Retreat (1) TX 087.2
~ Ridge (1) MS 087.6
~ Ridge Road (1) 107.7
~ Valley (5) 105.1
~ View (1) TN 087.8
pleasantest (1) adj 073.2
Pleasanton (1) TX 087.8
please (178) adj/v/interj 052.4
~ don't fight in the house (1) n 050.8
~ remits (1) n 131.2
please[V-t] (1) v 091.7
pleased (68) v/adj 081.2
pleaser (1) n 124.5
pleasing (4) adj 073.2
pleasingly (1) adv 073.2
pleasure (24) n/adj 024.6
~ boats (6) n 024.6
~ drink (1) n 002.6
~ horse (1) n 034.2
~ merchant (1) n 113.3
~ pleaser (1) n 124.5
Pleasure (2) 087.1
~ Bluff (1) GA 087.1
~ Island (1) TX 087.1
pleated skirts (1) n 092.9
plebeian existence (1) n 075.7
pleine (1) adj F 065.1
plentiful (6) adj 073.6
plenty (101) n/adv 055A.8
plethor(a) (1) n 055A.8
pleurisy (8) n 080.1
plex (1) n 119.2
pliers (6) n 020.8
plime (1) n 084.8
plinkers (1) n 008.8
plisse (1) adj F 055.9

plop (1) n 095.4
plot (85) n 016.1
plots (4) n 078.8
plow (1634) n/v/adj 021.6
~ cuts (1) n 041.2
~ ditch (1) n 041.2
~ -ears (1) n 021.6
~ furrow (2) n 041.2
~ furrows (2) n 041.2
~ gear (4) n 038.8
~ gears (2) n 038.6
~ -hand (2) n 021.6
~ handle (1) n 021.6
~ -handle share (1) n 021.6
~ handles (1) n 021.6
~ harness (3) n 038.6
~ horse (5) n 034.2
~ mule (1) n 021.6
~ oxen (1) n 021.6
~ stock (17) n 021.6
~ stocks (6) n 021.6
~ team (1) n 033.7
~ tool (2) n 021.6
~ tools (8) n 021.6
~ up (2) v 021.6
~ wings (1) n 021.6
~ with (3) v 021.6
~ [P-0] (1) v 012.9
plowboy (2) n 021.6
plowed (118) v/adj 021.6
~ around (1) v 021.6
~ flesh (31) n 078.2
~ flush (2) n 078.2
~ fresh (14) n 078.2
~ fur(row) (1) n 041.2
~ into (1) v 080.6
~ up (4) v 102.6
~ with (1) v 052.5
~ [P-0] (1) v 084.8
plowing (66) n/v/adj 021.6
~ double (2) v 033.7
~ stock (1) v 036.5
~ time (1) n 021.6
~ with (2) v 021.6
plowline (29) n 039.1
plowline[N-i] (1) n 039.1
plowlines (96) n 039.1
plowpoints (1) n 021.9
plows (224) n/v 021.6
plowshoes (1) n 119.7
pluck (16) n/v 101.4
plucked (3) v 101.4

plucking (4) v 101.4
plucks (1) n 037.2
pluffers (1) n 080.7
plug (17) n/v 108.2
~ knuckling (1) v 081.4
~ up (1) v 020.4
plugged (1) v 101.5
plugging along (1) v 081.9
plugs (7) n 108.2
plum (283) n/adj 054.3
~ berries (1) n 062.4
~ butter (1) n 051.6
~ jam (1) n 051.6
~ jelly (5) n 051.6
~ orchard (3) n 053.2
~ order (1) n 053.5
~ peach (88) n 054.3
~ peaches (14) n 054.3
~ preserves (1) n 051.6
~ pudding (1) n 080.7
~ sauce (1) n 048.5
~ seed (12) n 054.3
~ seed peach (5) n 054.3
~ seed peaches (3) n 054.3
~ seeded (1) n 054.3
~ stone (5) n 054.3
~ stone peach (2) n 054.3
~ stone peaches (1) n 054.3
~ tomato (17) n 055.3
~ tomatoes (30) n 055.3
~ tree (14) n 061.9
~ trees (27) n 061.8
Plum (4) AR 030.3
~ Creek (1) TX 030.7
~ Nelly (2) AR GA 067.3
plumb (418) adv 028.9
plumber (9) n 067.7
plumbers (2) n 039.7
plumbing (6) n/adj 040.7
~ inspectors (1) n 115.6
~ shop (1) n 082.7
plumbings (2) n 084.8
plume bird (1) n 081.9
Plumerville (1) AR 088.7
plumgranite (4) n 056.6
plumgranites (2) n 065.8
plumgrannies (1) n 056.7

Plummers Cove (1) FL 087.5
plummings (2) n 051.3
plump (7) adj 073.2
plums (16) n 061.8
plunder (176) n/adj 010.2
~ box (1) n 010.3
~ house (11) n 011.7
~ houses (1) n 010.3
~ porch (1) n 010.3
~ room (57) n 010.3
~ rooms (3) n 010.3
plunder[V-p] (1) v 010.2
plundering (1) v 010.2
plunders (2) n 009.4
plunge (1) v 095.3
plunged (1) v 095.3
Plunkett Town (1) 105.5
plural (3) n/v 051.2
plus (2) conj 025.8
ply (1) n 001.2
plyboard (1) n 052.6
Plymouth (12) 109.3
~ Rock (7) 082.9
~ Rocks (3) 036.7
plywood mill (1) n 080.6
plywoods (1) n 024.6
PM (4) 002.3
pneumonia (72) n/adj 079.7
~ pain (1) n 066.9
pneumoni(a) (3) n 065.9
pneumon(ia) (1) n 076.3
po (3) n/interj 038.3
~ -pos (2) n 128.5
poach (159) v/adj 046.2
~ egg (21) n 046.2
~ egg[N-i] (2) n 046.2
~ eggs (3) n 046.2
poach[V-r] (1) v 046.2
poach[V-t] (5) v 046.2
poached (647) v/adj 046.2
~ egg (171) n 046.2
~ eggs (163) n 046.2
poacher (9) n 046.2
poacher's rifle (1) n 096.9
poachers (1) n 046.2
poaches (1) v 046.2
poaching (41) v/adj 046.2
~ skillet (1) n 017.5
poc(x2) (1) interj 037.5
Pocahontas (7) AR MS 065.8
poche (1) n F 104.4

pocho (3) n S 080.9
pocket (71) n/adj 028.2
~ haunts (1) n 090.2
~ net (1) n 028.2
~ purse (3) n 028.2
~ stone (1) n 023.4
~ watch (20) n 004.3
~ watches (2) n 004.3
Pocket (1) 088.9
pocket[N-i] (1) n 006.9
pocketbook (378) n 028.2
pocketbooks (29) n 028.3
pocketknife (30) n 017.8
pocketknives (6) n 104.4
pockets (14) n/adj 098.8
~ fence (1) n 016.4
pocosin (2) n 029.6
pocosins (1) n 080.6
Pocus (1) 106.6
pod (10) n/adj 054.8
Pod (8) 055A.4
podding time (1) n 081.8
pods (4) n 062.2
Pods (6) 055A.4
podunk (1) n 069.9
Podunk (17) 069.9
~ High School (1) 091.8
~ Hollow (1) 069.9
~ Junction (1) 069.9
~ town (1) n 093.7
~ U (1) 069.9
poele (3) n F 017.5
poem (3) n 101.1
poet (1) n 040.8
poetry (1) n 043.9
pogies (1) n 084.8
pogrom (1) n 056.8
pogy (8) n/adj 061.2
~ boats (1) n 024.6
~ fish (3) n 059.9
poinciana trees (2) n 061.9
Poinsett (1) AR 087.2
poinsettia (4) n 062.2
poinsettias (2) n 070.6
point (42) n/v 070.6
~ out (1) v 024.7
Point (84) 029.5
~ au Loup (2) LA 029.5
~ Blank (1) TX 082.6
~ Comfort (1) TX 087.8
~ Lafitte (1) LA 087.1

~ Lookout (1) TN 065.9
~ Park (1) 106.6
~ Pleasant (1) LA 072.3
~ Washington (3) FL 087.1
Point[N-i] (1) 105.2
Pointblank (1) TX 082.6
Pointe (4) 087.9
~ (a) la Hache (1) LA 087.9
~ Coupee (1) LA 087.9
~ Coupee Parish (2) LA 087.5
pointed (13) adj 024.6
~ -shingle fences (1) n 016.2
~ star (1) n 029.3
~ toes (1) n 123.8
pointer (2) n 033.3
pointing (33) v 070.8
~ at (1) v 013.6
~ out (1) v 082.6
points (11) n 065.8
Points (15) 105.2
pointy (4) adj 125.5
~ head (1) n 125.5
~ -headed intellectuals (1) n 125.5
~ heads (1) n 059.9
~ toes (1) n 123.8
poise (1) n 104.5
poison (2137) n/v/adj 062.6
~ adder (1) n 093.7
~ ash (4) n 062.3
~ blackberries (1) n 062.6
~ elder (4) n 062.2
~ itch bush (1) n 062.3
~ ivory (62) n 062.3
~ ivy (641) n 062.3
~ iv(y) (1) n 062.3
~ i(vy) (1) n 062.3
~ -ivy bush (1) n 062.3
~ kind (7) n 057.1
~ lily pads (1) n 057.1
~ liquor (1) n 050.9
~ mushroom (7) n 057.1
~ mushrooms (9) n 057.1
~ oak (596) n 062.3
~ -oak vine (8) n 062.3

~ -oak vines (2) n 062.3
~ plants (1) n 062.6
~ side (1) n 062.6
~ snake (3) n 062.6
~ snakes (1) n 062.6
~ stuff (1) n 062.6
~ sumac (41) n 062.2
~ three-leaf (1) n 062.3
~ tree (3) n 062.3
~ type (1) n 062.6
~ vine (37) n 062.3
~ wasp (1) n 062.6
~ whiskey (3) n 062.6
poison[V-r] (1) v 097.7
poison[V-t] (2) v 062.6
poisonberries (8) n 062.6
poisonberry (3) n 062.2
poisoned (10) v/adj 062.6
~ flesh (1) n 078.2
~ ivy (1) n 062.3
~ up (1) v 075.7
poisonest (2) adj 095.9
poisoning (14) n/v/adj 062.6
~ oak (1) n 062.3
~ turnip (1) n 062.6
poison(ing) (1) n 078.2
poisonous (371) adj 062.6
~ berries (2) n 062.6
~ berry (1) n 062.6
~ liquor (1) n 062.6
~ mosquitoes (1) n 060A.8
~ mushroom (3) n 057.1
~ mushrooms (4) n 057.1
~ snake (2) n 062.6
~ snakes (1) n 080.8
~ spiders (1) n 062.6
~ sumac (1) n 062.3
~ trees (1) n 062.6
~ weed (1) n 062.6
poisons (5) n/v 080.8
poisonwood (1) n 062.3
poisony (1) adj 062.6
POJ (3) 051.9
poke (353) n/v/adj 019.5
~ bag (1) n 019.5
~ block (1) n 104.5
~ green[N-i] (1) n 055A.5
~ greens (8) n 055A.5
~ out (8) v 027.8

~ paper (1) n 019.5
~ sacks (1) n 019.7
~ salad (84) n 055A.5
~ -salad berries (1) n 062.6
~ salad greens (3) n 055A.5
~ -salad roots (1) n 061.4
~ sallet (62) n 055A.5
~ -sallet berry (1) n 062.5
~ -sallet bush (1) n 062.2
~ vine (1) n 062.6
~ weed (1) n 062.2
~ wine (1) n 088.9
pokeberries (29) n 062.7
pokeberry (23) n/adj 062.5
~ root (1) n 061.4
~ roots (1) n 061.4
~ tree (1) n 062.2
pokeber(ry) (1) n 061.8
poked (2) v 095.8
poker (15) n 008.2
Poker Keno (2) 080.9
pokeroot (8) n/adj 062.2
~ juice (1) n 061.4
pokeroots (1) n 061.4
pokers (2) n 008.3
pokes (29) n 019.5
pokeweed (1) n 062.2
pokey (9) n 112.9
Polack (36) 127.4
~ jokes (2) n 127.4
Polacks (63) 127.4
Poland (37) 087.9
~ China (29) 035.5
~ China hog (2) n 035.5
~ China hogs (2) n 035.5
~ Chinas (1) 035.5
polar (2) adj 129.9
~ -bear races (1) n 129.9
~ bears (1) n 080.6
polarates (1) v 056.3
pole (385) n/adj 019.4
~ barn (1) n 014.2
~ bean (39) n 055A.4
~ bean[N-i] (2) n 055A.4
~ beans (185) n 055A.4

~ bridge (1) n 006.1
~ butter beans (3) n 055A.3
~ -car (1) n 085.3
~ fence (7) n 016.4
~ fences (4) n 016.2
~ fishing (1) n 091.9
~ -fishing (1) v 090.8
~ jerkers (1) n 091.8
~ Kentucky Wonder (1) n 055A.7
~ kitty (2) n 059.4
~ leaf (1) n 061.8
~ oar (1) n 024.6
~ rack (1) n 022.1
~ roads (2) n 031.6
~ shack (1) n 091.9
~ shed (1) n 015.1
~ snap bean (2) n 055A.4
~ strop (2) n 020.8
~ swing (1) n 022.9
Pole (5) 069.5
pole[N-i] (1) n 016.5
poleax (3) n 088.9
poleaxes (2) n 066.8
polecat (600) n 059.4
Polecat (1) AR 030.3
polecats (80) n 059.5
poles (47) n 016.5
Poles (16) 127.4
Poley (1) 059.4
police (390) n/adj 112.5
~ brutality (1) n 112.5
~ building (1) n 112.7
~ bus (1) n 111.8
~ captain (1) n 068.5
~ car (74) n 111.7
~ cars (30) n 111.7
~ -chief's car (1) n 111.7
~ club (1) n 113.2
~ cruiser (2) n 111.7
~ department (12) n 112.7
~ dogs (2) n 033.2
~ force (5) n 112.5
~ headquarters (11) n 112.7
~ helicopter (2) n 111.9
~ (heli)copter (1) n 111.9
~ helicopters (1) n 111.9
~ house (3) n 112.7

~ jury (4) n 065.8
~ lady (1) n 112.5
~ officer (4) n 112.5
~ officers (1) n 112.5
~ palace (1) n 112.7
~ patrol (1) n 111.8
~ sedan (1) n 111.7
~ service (1) n 111.5
~ special (2) n 113.1
~ station (115) n 112.7
~ stick (1) n 113.2
~ truck (2) n 111.8
~ van (9) n 111.8
~ vehicle (1) n 111.7
~ wagon (6) n 111.8
policeman (74) n 112.4
Policeman (1) 112.5
policemans (2) n 016.9
policemen (26) n 112.5
~ [J-0]   robber[N-i]
   (1) n 130.2
policemens (5) n 053.5
polices (10) n 081.9
policewoman (1) n 063.2
polies (1) n 088.7
polish (4) n/v 080.7
Polish (21) 127.4
~ jokes (1) n 127.4
~ people (3) n 127.4
~ sausage (10) n 121.6
~ sausages (1) n 121.6
~ wedding (1) n 082.5
polish[V-t] (1) v 065.3
polished up (1) v 080.8
polisher (10) n 125.6
polite (10) adj 073.2
politer (2) adj 066.1
politest (1) adj 064.7
political (24) adj 115.4
~ appointee (1) n 115.4
~ authori(ty)   (1)   n
   115.4
~ bums (1) n 115.4
~ favorites (1) n 115.3
~ hack (1) n 115.4
~ influence (11) n 115.3
~ pull (7) n 115.3
~ savvy (1) n 115.3
politician (7) n 115.3
politician[N-i]   (1)   n
   082.8
politicians (1) n 115.4
politicking (2) v 115.3
politics (3) n 115.3

Polk (26) AR FL GA LA
   TN 019.7
~ Colony 106.8
~ County (8) AR FL
   087.3
~ County Memorial Hos-
   pital (1) 084.5
~ side har(row) (1) n
   021.7
polka (9) n 083.3
polkas (6) n 130.9
Polks Tavern (1) 131.1
poll (5) adj 033.3
~ -blood (1) n 033.3
~ Hereford (1) n 033.6
~ parrot (1) n 088.8
~ tax (2) n 070.6
Pollard (3) AL LA 087.7
~ community (1) AR
   087.4
polled Hereford cattle (1)
   n 036.5
pollen (3) n 056.4
pollenates (1) v 070.6
polliwog (4) n 060.3
polliwogs (4) n 060.3
polluted (2) v/adj 062.6
Polly (1) 017.6
polo (2) n 034.8
poltergeist (1) n 090.2
poly (6) n/adj 060A.2
polyester (1) n 066.8
polyethylene (1) n 080.6
Polynes(ian)   restaurant
   (1) n 070.8
pom-pom-pull-away (1) n
   130.5
pomace (4) n 048.4
pomegranate   (9)   n/adj
   054.6
~ trees (1) n 061.9
pomegranates (6) n 056.9
(pome)granates   (1)   n
   055.1
pommel (2) n 039.2
pompadour (9) n 123.9
pompadours (2) n 123.8
pompano (12) n 059.9
Pompano (1) FL 070.7
pompanos (1) n 059.9
pompon-looking (1) adj
   053.6
pompons (1) n 091.9
pompous (1) adj 074.8
Ponce (15) 093:5

~ de Leon (9) 093.5
~ (de) Leon Avenue
   (1) 107.6
~ de Leon Boulevard
   (1) 095.8
~ de Leon Hotel (1)
   084.3
~ de Leon Sears (1)
   108.5
~ de Neon (1) 107.6
Ponchatoula   (2)   LA
   087.3
pond (130) n/adj 030.4
~ catfish (2) n 059.9
~ cats (1) n 059.9
~ cooters (1) n 060.7
~ frog (2) n 060.3
~ frogs (2) n 060.3
~ house (1) n 011.9
~ -like (1) adj 029.6
~ melon (1) n 056.7
~ scoggin (1) n 089.9
~ side (1) n 029.5
~ turtle (1) n 060.6
~ turtles (1) n 060.6
~ wigglers (1) n 060.5
~ worms (4) n 060.5
Pond (12) 030.7
~ Creek (1) TN 030.7
~ Mountain   (1)   TN
   031.1
pond[N-i] (2) n 030.5
ponded up (1) v 007.6
pondering (2) v 013.5
~ about (1) v 013.5
ponderosa (2) adj 061.8
~ pine (1) n 061.9
ponds (36) n 030.6
pondy (4) adj 029.6
~ place (2) n 029.6
~ places (1) n 029.6
pone (465) n/adj 044.6
~ bread (68) n 044.6
~ cake (1) n 044.6
~ corn (1) n 044.5
~ corn   bread   (10)   n
   044.6
~ light   bread   (1)   n
   044.3
Pone (1) 030.7
pone[N-i] (1) n 044.7
poned up (4) v 077.6
pones (119) n 044.7
poney bread (1) n 044.3
Pong (2) 130.4

pongee (1) n 080.9
ponhaws (5) n 047.4
ponies (4) n 034.2
Ponta Creek (1) MS
   030.7
Pontaco(la) (1) MS 087.4
Pontchartrain   (31)   LA
   087.3
~ Beach (3) 106.5
~ Expressway (1) 089.8
~ Park (2) 106.2
Ponte Vedra (1) 106.1
Pontiac (3) MI 087.3
pontoon (3) n/adj 024.6
~ boat (2) n 024.6
Pontotoc (18) MS 087.5
~ County (1) MS 087.1
~ Ridge (1) MS 030.8
~ Road (1) 031.6
~ Street (1) 107.7
pony (18) n/adj 034.2
~ back (1) n 080.6
~ express (1) n 084.2
~ land (1) n 029.6
~ plow (1) n 021.6
~ turner (1) n 021.6
ponytail (18) n 123.9
ponytails (14) n 123.8
poo (3) interj 038.3
~ -sheepy(x3) (1) interj
   038.4
~ wee (1) interj 038.3
poo(x3) (1) interj 038.5
pooch (19) n/v/adj 019.5
~ out (12) v 027.8
~ owl (1) n 059.2
pooched out (4) v 027.8
poocher (1) n 019.5
pooching (2) v 027.8
~ out (1) v 027.8
poodle (13) n/adj 033.3
~ dog (4) n 033.3
~ perms (1) n 123.9
poodles (3) n 033.4
poodoo (1) n 059.2
pooey (2) interj 092.3
poofed (1) adj 075.4
pooh (1) interj 092.3
pook (1) n 008.1
pook(x3) pookaw pook
   (x4) pookaw (1) interj
   038.5
pook(x4) (1) interj 038.5
pookaw (2) interj 038.5
pool (20) n/adj 030.6

~ hall (2) n 013.5
~ -hall game (1) n 131.5
Pool (1) 105.1
Pooler (1) GA 087.1
poolroom (2) n 007A.6
Pools Bluff (2) LA 031.4
poontang (2) n 050.8
poop (2) n 084.8
poop[V-t] (1) v 075.5
pooped (159) v 075.4
~ out (53) v 075.5
pooping (1) v 081.7
poor (1980) adj 053.1
~ black trash (1) n 069.3
~ boy (53) n 121.7
~ -boy (2) adv 088.7
~ -boy cake (1) n 044.4
~ -boy corn bread (1) n 044.6
~ boy sandwich (10) n 121.7
~ boy sandwiches (4) n 121.7
~ -boyed (1) v 053.1
~ boys (6) n 121.7
~ buckra (1) n 069.8
~ -class Cajun (1) n 069.8
~ -class white people (1) n 069.8
~ dirt (3) n 029.8
~ do (4) n 044.7
~ dog (1) n 015.9
~ dunks (2) n 069.7
~ farm (2) n 053.1
~ field (2) n 029.8
~ -folks' bread (1) n 044.6
~ ground (5) n 029.8
~ honky (2) n 069.8
~ hoosiers (3) n 069.8
~ joe (1) n 047.4
~ land (58) n 029.8
~ -land weeds (1) n 015.9
~ loam (2) n 029.8
~ -man[N-k] potato (1) n 059.6
~ -man's bread (1) n 044.8
~ -man's cobbler (1) n 048.3

~ -man's fight (1) n 085.8
~ -man's gravy (1) n 088.8
~ -man's land (1) n 029.8
~ -man's pie (3) n 048.3
~ -man's pudding (2) n 050.3
~ -man's trout (1) n 053.1
~ mouth (1) n 073.5
~ -old (9) adj 053.1
~ peck (5) n 069.8
~ pecker (1) n 069.8
~ peckerwoods (1) n 069.8
~ pecks (1) n 069.8
~ -people's lard (1) n 023.7
~ pine (1) n 080.9
~ puds (1) n 069.8
~ sagers (1) n 069.8
~ sandy land (1) n 029.8
~ sandy soil (3) n 029.8
~ soil (38) n 029.8
~ soul (1) n 044.7
~ spots (1) n 029.8
~ tomato (1) n 055.3
~ trash (33) n 069.7
~ white (19) n 069.7
~ white crackers (2) n 069.4
~ white farmer (1) n 069.4
~ white folk (1) n 069.8
~ white folk[N-i] (1) n 069.8
~ white folks (6) n 060.8
~ white girl (1) n 053.1
~ white man (5) n 069.8
~ white people (23) n 069.7
~ white peoples (1) n 069.8
~ white person (5) n 069.8
~ white pers(on) (1) n 069.7

~ -white section (1) n 106.3
~ white trash (237) n 069.7
~ whites (46) n 069.7
Poor (2) 053.1
~ Boys (1) 053.1
~ Creek (1) AL 030.7
poor[A-w] (1) adj 053.3
poorer (28) adj 053.1
~ ground (1) n 029.8
poorest (6) adj 053.1
poorhouse (3) n 053.1
Poorhouse Branch (2) AL 030.7
poorly (51) adj/adv 072.9
poot roots (1) n 055.5
pop (121) n/v/adj 121.8
~ bug (1) n 061.1
~ country (1) n 130.9
~ fly (2) n 130.4
~ music (2) n 130.8
~ out (1) v 062.2
~ over (1) v 025.8
~ rock (2) n 130.8
~ saw (1) n 120.9
~ the chicken neck (1) n 130.6
~ the rope (2) n 130.2
~ -the-whip (12) n 081.8
~ -top (1) n 121.9
~ whip (1) n 019.4
~ whips (1) n 019.4
Pop (86) 063.4
~ Pop (1) 064.1
~ Tart (1) 122.8
~ Tarts (2) 122.2
popcorn (13) n/adj 056.2
~ patch (2) n 016.1
~ popper (1) n 116.4
~ poppers (1) n 116.4
~ trees (1) n 061.8
Pope lovers (1) n 126.5
Popers (1) 126.5
popeye (2) n/adj 050.8
~ mullet (1) n 084.8
popeyed (2) n/adj 050.8
popgun (4) n/adj 080.7
~ elder (1) n 061.8
~ elm (1) n 062.2
~ wars (1) n 130.5
popguns (2) n 022.5
poplar (170) n/adj 061.8
~ honey (1) n 061.8

~ leaf (1) n 104.6
~ logs (2) n 007A.2
~ root (1) n 061.4
~ tree (6) n 061.9
~ trees (2) n 101.7
Poplar (16) 106.3
~ Avenue (3) 106.1
~ Bluff (1) MO 087.2
~ Grove (1) AR 087.5
~ Pike (1) 107.6
~ Plaza (2) 116.1
~ Springs (1) AL 030.7
~ Street (2) 106.3
poplars (12) n 061.8
Poplarville (2) MS 087.2
Poplins Crossroads (1) TN 087.3
popover (2) n 045.3
popovers (7) n 045.2
popped (6) v 114.4
~ out of (1) v 057.8
popper (1) n 116.4
poppers (4) n 114.2
popping (14) v/adj 130.6
~ a whip (1) n 019.4
~ bugs (1) n 061.1
~ off (1) v 075.8
~ out (1) v 027.8
~ the whip (2) n 130.2
poppy (6) n/adj 062.3
~ nettle (1) n 062.3
~ seed (2) n 057.3
Poppy (7) 063.4
pop's (1) adj 116.2
pops (9) n/v/adj 092.8
~ off (1) v 125.5
~ -type music (1) n 130.8
Pops (1) 063.5
popskull (19) n 050.8
popular (18) n/adj 070.6
~ land (1) n 029.8
~ music (2) n 130.8
~ tunes (1) n 130.8
population (13) n 066.9
populationwise (2) adv 096.7
Populist (2) 088.8
~ days (1) n 088.8
~ Movement (1) 088.9
porcelain (29) n/adj 017.1
~ buckets (1) n 017.3
~ doorknobs (1) n 017.1

~ egg (4) n 017.1
~ eggs (2) n 017.1
~ pot (1) n 070.8
porch (3219) n/adj 010.8
~ area (1) n 007A.1
~ baby (1) n 080.6
~ boxes (1) n 010.8
~ chair (1) n 008.9
~ children (1) n 064.3
~ door (1) n 011.1
~ -like (2) adj 007A.7
~ steps (2) n 010.7
~ swing (2) n 022.9
~ -type thing (2) n 007A.2
~ upstairs (1) n 010.8
porches (91) n 010.8
porcupine (3) n 059.4
pore (2) n 006.1
pores (1) n 077.3
porgies (1) n 059.9
porgy (3) n/adj 059.9
~ boats (1) n 024.6
pork (633) n/adj 046.3
~ bacon (2) n 046.3
~ barrel (1) n 019.2
~ bellies (2) n 046.3
~ belly (2) n 046.2
~ brains (1) n 047.1
~ chop (24) n 121.3
~ chops (117) n 046.3
~ cracklings (1) n 050.7
~ fat (1) n 046.3
~ link (2) n 121.6
~ link sausage (1) n 121.6
~ links (1) n 121.6
~ liver (3) n 047.2
~ loin (12) n 121.3
~ -loin roast (2) n 121.3
~ -loin roasts (1) n 121.3
~ loins (1) n 121.3
~ meat (10) n 046.3
~ neck bones (1) n 121.3
~ patties (1) n 046.8
~ ribs (4) n 121.3
~ rind (6) n 046.6
~ rinds (4) n 046.6
~ roast (27) n 121.3
~ roasts (2) n 121.3
~ round (1) n 121.3
~ sausage (66) n 121.6

~ -sausage patty (1) n 121.6
~ sausages (1) n 046.8
~ shoulder (7) n 121.3
~ -shoulder roast (1) n 121.3
~ shoulders (1) n 046.4
~ side (2) n 046.4
~ sides (1) n 046.4
~ skin (2) n 046.6
~ skins (1) n 046.6
~ steak (5) n 121.3
~ steaks (4) n 121.3
porker (2) n 035.5
porkers (3) n 035.5
porky (1) n 059.9
Porky (2) 064.4
~ Pig (1) 064.4
porn (11) n/adj 114.9
~ flick (1) n 114.9
~ house (3) n 114.9
~ houses (1) n 114.9
~ movie house (1) n 114.9
~ palace (1) n 114.9
~ palaces (1) n 114.9
porno (31) adj 114.9
~ film (1) n 114.9
~ films (3) n 114.9
~ flick (2) n 114.9
~ flicks (1) n 114.9
~ house (6) n 114.9
~ movie houses (1) n 114.9
~ movie theater (2) n 114.9
~ movies (5) n 114.9
~ palace (1) n 114.9
~ place (1) n 114.9
~ shop (4) n 114.9
~ shops (1) n 114.9
~ shows (1) n 114.9
~ theater (2) n 114.9
pornographic (8) adj 114.9
~ bookstore (1) n 114.9
~ film shop (1) n 114.9
~ films (1) n 114.9
~ movie (1) n 114.9
~ movies (1) n 114.9
~ shows (1) n 114.9
~ theater (2) n 114.9
pornography (4) n 114.9
pornos (3) n 114.9
porous (1) adj 029.8

porpoise (6) n/adj 059.9
~ dolphin (1) n 059.9
~ face (1) n 125.2
porpoises (1) n 059.9
porridge (9) n 050.3
port (64) n/adj 031.4
~ horse (1) n 039.4
~ wine (1) n 114.7
Port (50) 087.3
~ Allen (3) LA 087.3
~ Aransas (1) TX 086.5
~ Arthur (12) TX 087.7
~ Barre (2) LA 087.4
~ Caddo (1) TX 087.3
~ Caddo River (1) TX 030.7
~ Gibson (5) MS 087.2
~ Houston (1) TX 087.9
~ Hudson (2) LA 087.3
~ Isabel (3) TX 087.4
~ Lavaca (2) TX 087.8
~ Neches (2) TX 087.6
~ -O-Lets (1) 012.1
~ of Corpus Christi (1) TX 106.6
~ of Savannah (1) GA 031.4
~ Orange (1) FL 087.2
~ Saint Joe (8) FL 087.7
~ Tampa (1) FL 105.1
(Port) Saint Joe (1) FL 087.9
portable (7) adj 009.7
~ closet (1) n 009.7
~ closets (1) n 009.7
~ plow (1) n 120.4
~ plug-in heaters (1) n 118.4
~ saw (1) n 120.9
~ toilets (1) n 012.1
portage (1) n 081.8
Portage (1) LA 030.7
porte (7) n F 007A.7
~ cochere (5) n F 007A.7
~ cocheres (1) n F 098.6
porter (1) n 121.1
Porter (6) 055.3
~ Street (1) 114.8
~ tomato (1) n 055.3

~ tomatoes (1) n 055.3
~ wire (1) n 016.3
Porterdale (1) GA 087.2
porterhouse (34) n/adj 121.1
~ steak (8) n 121.1
porters (1) n 119.5
Porters (5) 055.3
~ Creek (1) MS 030.7
~ Gap (1) TN 030.5
~ River (1) LA 030.7
Porterville (1) TX 087.4
portico (22) n 010.8
porticoes (2) n 010.8
Portier Drive (1) 107.7
portieres (2) n 009.5
portion (6) n 065.9
Portland (7) OR TN TX 087.3
~ Boulevard (1) 107.7
portmanteau (2) n 009.7
Porto (55) 055.5
~ Acorn (1) 055.5
~ Rican (10) 055.5
~ Rican potato (1) n 055.5
~ Rican potatoes (2) n 055.5
~ Rican sweet potato (1) n 055.5
~ Ricans (5) 055.5
~ Rico (25) 055.5
~ Rico potato (3) n 055.5
~ Rico (po)tato (1) n 055.5
~ Rico sweet potatoes (1) n 055.5
~ Rico yams (2) n 055.5
Port(o) Rico sweet potato (1) n 055.5
(Porto) Rico yams (1) n 055.5
Porto Ricos (15) 055.5
portrait (1) n 012.3
ports (4) n 031.4
Portsmouth (1) VA 087.6
Portuguese (2) 065.9
~ man-of-wars (1) n 059.9
pose (2) v S 002.2
poses (1) v 028.1
posies (1) n 130.3
position (6) n 115.3

positive (22) adj 074.7
positively (2) adv 091.1
posse (2) n 082.9
possess (1) v 013.6
possessed (2) v 075.1
possessions (1) n 065.9
possibility (2) n 025.2
possibly (7) adv 041.1
possum (25) n/adj 054.5
~ apple (1) n 054.5
~ dog (6) n 033.1
~ dogs (3) n 033.1
~ grape (3) n 096.7
~ grapes (5) n 062.4
~ haw (1) n 061.4
~ haws (2) n 062.5
~ -hunted (1) v 088.8
~ run (1) n 080.8
~ trot (1) n 080.6
Possum (8) 030.7
~ Creek (3) AL TN 030.7
~ Trot (2) AR 087.5
~ Trot District (1) AR 087.6
~ Walk (2) TX 087.2
Possumneck (2) MS 087.8
post (2072) n/adj 016.5
~ and rail (3) n 016.5
~ -and-railing fence (1) n 016.4
~ -and-wire (1) adj 016.3
~ digger (4) n 016.5
~ fence (2) n 016.5
~ fences (1) n 016.4
~ hammer (1) n 020.7
~ heads (2) n 016.7
~ -hole digger (57) n 016.5
~ -hole diggers (14) n 016.5
~ -hole jobber (1) n 016.5
~ mail (1) n 084.2
~ maul (2) n 020.7
~ oak (80) n 061.9
~ -oak bark (1) n 093.7
~ -oak country (2) n 096.8
~ -oak flats (1) n 029.8
~ -oak land (6) n 029.8
~ -oak mud (1) n 016.5
~ -oak prair(ie) (1) n 029.5

~ oak tree (4) n 061.8
~ oak trees (2) n 061.8
~ oaks (5) n 061.8
~ -oaky dirt (2) n 096.7
~ -oaky-type sand (1) n 029.9
~ office (1004) n 084.2
~ of(fice) (3) n 084.2
~ -office address (1) n 084.2
~ -office box (14) n 084.2
~ -of(fice) box (1) n 084.2
~ office department (1) n 084.2
~ -office gallery (1) n 010.8
~ offices (5) n 084.2
~ over (1) n 080.8
~ roads (1) n 031.6
~ -secondary education (1) n 083.6
~ shift (1) n 110.7
~ split (1) n 016.5
Post (10) 087.3
~ Oak (2) GA 087.2
~ -Oak Belt (1) 091.9
~ Oak Creek (1) TX 030.7
~ Oak Road (1) 107.6
~ -Office Box (1) 084.2
post[N-i] (839) n 016.5
postal (6) adj 084.2
~ office (1) n 084.2
~ people (1) n 084.2
~ service (1) n 084.2
~ truck (1) n 109.7
~ worker (1) n 115.1
~ workers (1) n 115.1
posted (4) v/adj 084.2
~ egg (1) n 046.2
postemergents (1) n 084.9
poster (3) n/adj 009.4
~ bed (1) n 009.4
posterior (1) n 072.8
posters (1) n 028.9
postes (163) n 016.5
posthole (21) n 016.5
postholes (18) n 016.5
postman (95) n 115.1
postmark (1) v 100.7
postmaster (7) n 084.2
postmen (6) n 115.1

postponed it (1) v 082.1
posts (107) n 016.5
postwoman (1) n 115.1
postwomen (1) n 115.1
pot (863) n/adj 017.6
~ cheese (3) n 048.1
~ coffee (1) n 048.8
~ cur (1) n 033.3
~ dealer (1) n 114.4
~ dodger (1) n 044.6
~ dodgers (3) n 044.6
~ flower (1) n 101.4
~ flowers (3) n 017.7
~ guts (1) n 093.6
~ -gutted minnows (1) n 061.2
~ ham (2) n 033.3
~ hound (3) n 033.3
~ hounds (1) n 033.3
~ lifters (1) n 090.9
~ liquor (42) n 084.8
~ -liquor preacher (1) n 067.8
~ -liquor turnip (1) n 055A.5
~ parties (1) n 130.7
~ party (4) n 130.7
~ plant (1) n 017.7
~ plants (1) n 017.7
~ rack (2) n 008.4
~ roast (4) n 121.2
~ soil (1) n 029.8
~ soup (1) n 088.8
~ trammel (1) n 008.2
Pot (2) 048.9
Potacocow(a) (1) MS 030.7
potash (20) n/adj 089.8
~ soap (7) n 080.6
potato (1188) n/adj 055.4
~ -and-onion poultice (1) n 061.4
~ bag (5) n 019.7
~ bags (2) n 019.7
~ bank (27) n 015.5
~ barn (1) n 014.2
~ baskets (1) n 020.1
~ bed (5) n 015.5
~ beer (1) n 050.8
~ bin (4) n 015.5
~ biscuits (1) n 044.4
~ bread (18) n 044.4
~ bug (1) n 060A.2
~ bunk (4) n 015.5
~ burlap (1) n 019.7

~ cellar (4) n 015.5
~ cellars (1) n 015.5
~ chip (1) n 045.3
~ country (1) n 055.4
~ crop (1) n 055.5
~ digger (1) n 080.8
~ draws (1) n 055.4
~ eaters (1) n 127.9
~ farm (1) n 055.4
~ fork (1) n 120.7
~ fritters (1) n 045.3
~ head (2) n 055.4
~ heads (1) n 127.9
~ hill (22) n 015.5
~ hills (1) n 095.8
~ hole (1) n 015.5
~ house (44) n 015.5
~ houses (11) n 015.5
~ kiln (7) n 015.5
~ knife (1) n 088.8
~ lamp (1) n 024.3
~ man (1) n 127.9
~ masher (1) n 070.9
~ mound (1) n 015.5
~ onion (3) n 055.6
~ onions (3) n 055.6
~ oven (1) n 017.5
~ pancake (1) n 045.3
~ pancakes (1) n 045.3
~ patch (39) n 016.1
~ patches (4) n 016.1
~ pie (5) n 055.4
~ pies (3) n 048.3
~ pile (2) n 015.5
~ plow (1) n 021.6
~ pone (4) n 044.7
~ pones (1) n 044.9
~ puddings (1) n 048.3
~ pump (6) n 015.5
~ pumpkin (8) n 056.6
~ pumpkins (1) n 056.6
~ race (1) n 130.2
~ rake (1) n 120.7
~ rick (1) n 015.5
~ room (1) n 015.5
~ sack (21) n 019.7
~ sacks (3) n 019.7
~ salad (3) n 055.4
~ sallet (2) n 055.4
~ shed (1) n 015.5
~ slips (1) n 055.4
~ soup (1) n 081.9
~ squash (3) n 056.6
~ stew (1) n 055.4

~ storage house (1) n 055.4
~ trough (1) n 035.8
~ -vine pea (1) n 055A.6
~ whistle (1) n 099.6
~ yeast (1) n 045.5
po(tato) (1) n 055.5
(po)tato (123) n/adj 055.4
~ bag (2) n 019.7
~ bank (10) n 015.5
~ banks (1) n 015.5
~ bed (2) n 015.5
~ bug (1) n 060A.8
~ bunk (1) n 015.5
~ choker (1) n 006.1
~ cobbler (1) n 048.3
~ creek (1) n 030.6
~ custards (1) n 048.5
~ digger (1) n 088.8
~ -digging time (1) n 080.9
~ hill (5) n 015.5
~ hole (3) n 015.5
~ house (7) n 015.5
~ houses (2) n 015.5
~ kiln (3) n 015.5
~ knob (1) n 030.8
~ melon (2) n 056.7
~ onion (3) n 055.6
~ onions (2) n 055.6
~ oven (1) n 017.5
~ patch (12) n 016.1
~ pie (2) n 055.5
~ pies (1) n 048.3
~ pit (1) n 015.5
~ pone (1) n 044.6
~ pumpkin (1) n 056.5
~ pumpkins (2) n 056.5
~ rolls (1) n 044.4
~ sack (6) n 019.7
~ salad (1) n 055.4
~ skillet (1) n 017.5
~ time (1) n 090.9
~ washer (1) n 006.1
~ yams (1) n 055.5
Potato (6) 030.7
~ Creek (4) GA 030.7
~ Famine (2) 055.4
potato[N-i] (6) n 013.8
potatoes (1889) n/adj 055.4
~ bank (1) n 015.5
(po)tatoes (113) n 055.4

potbellied (15) adj 017.6
~ heater (2) n 008.5
~ stove (8) n 118.4
~ stoves (4) n 008.4
potbelly (3) adj 008.4
~ kettle (1) n 017.6
~ stoves (1) n 118.4
poteau (2) n F 037.5
potent (1) adj 124.6
potful (1) n 017.6
potfuls (3) n 055A.7
pothead (4) n 114.4
potholders (2) n 017.7
pothole (4) n 030.5
potholes (2) n 030.5
pothook (1) n 008.3
potlicker (21) n/adj 033.3
~ hound (6) n 033.3
~ hounds (1) n 033.3
potlickers (4) n 033.3
potluck suppers (1) n 130.8
potpie (8) n 048.3
potpies (1) n 048.3
potpourri (1) n 095.7
pots (234) n 017.6
potted (6) adj 008.8
~ chair (1) n 008.8
~ eggs (1) n 055.3
~ meat (2) n 047.1
~ plant (1) n 017.7
~ plants (1) n 017.7
Potter (3) AR 087.4
~ Junction (1) AR 087.4
potter's (5) adj 078.8
~ field (4) n 078.8
~ grave (1) n 078.9
Potters Chapel School (1) 087.6
pottery (2) n 017.1
potting tool (1) n 120.5
Potts Camp (2) MS 087.2
Pottsburg (3) FL 030.7
potty (3) n/adj 012.1
~ training (1) n 088.8
pouch (21) n 028.2
pouches (3) n 028.2
poulailler (1) n F 036.8
poule (3) n F 080.7
~ d'eau (1) n F 080.7
poules (1) n F 036.8
poulets (1) n F 121.5
poult (1) n 036.7
poultice (15) n 061.5

poult(ice) (1) n 061.9
poultices (4) n 061.4
poultries (1) n 036.6
poultry (145) n/adj 036.6
~ business (2) n 036.6
~ chicken (1) n 121.5
~ company (2) n 036.6
~ farm (1) n 036.6
~ fence (1) n 036.6
~ fences (1) n 016.3
~ house (13) n 036.8
~ houses (1) n 036.8
~ netting (2) n 016.7
~ ranch (1) n 036.6
~ wire (9) n 016.3
~ -wire fence (1) n 016.3
~ yard (2) n 036.8
pound (288) n/adj 045.4
~ bag (1) n 019.6
~ cake (11) n 044.4
~ cake[N-i] (1) n 045.4
~ cakes (3) n 045.4
~ party (2) n 080.7
~ supper (2) n 083.1
~ suppers (3) n 081.8
pound[N-i] (344) n 045.4
pounder (1) n 088.9
pounding (1) v 040.2
pounds (837) n 045.4
pour (31) n/v/prep F 006.1
~ down (5) v 006.1
~ offs (1) n 031.5
~ out (2) v 006.1
pourdown (44) n/adj 006.1
~ rain (6) n 006.1
~ shower (1) n 006.1
pourdowns (2) n 006.1
poured (16) v 006.1
~ down (8) v 006.1
~ on (1) v 053.2
~ out (1) v 075.5
pouring (35) v/adj 006.1
~ consistency (1) n 065.8
~ down (13) v 006.1
~ -down rain (4) n 006.1
~ rain (6) n 006.1
pourover (5) n 031.5
pours (6) v 006.1
~ down (1) v 006.1
pousse-cafe (1) n F 048.8

pouts off (1) v 075.1
poverty (1) n 070.6
powder (95) n/v/adj 022.4
~ doughnut (1) n 122.6
~ doughnuts (1) n 122.4
~ keg (1) n 020.2
~ puff (1) n 061.9
~ room (15) n 118.3
~ rooms (1) n 118.3
~ up (1) v 028.1
powd(er) (1) v 028.1
Powder Springs (2) GA 087.6
powdered (2) adj 122.4
~ sugar (1) n 122.3
Powderly (1) TX 087.3
powders (14) n 045.5
Powell (7) LA TN TX 030.7
~ Creek (1) AL 030.7
~ River (2) TN 030.7
power (122) n/adj 120.2
~ baler (1) n 014.8
~ blade (1) n 120.9
~ brokers (1) n 115.5
~ chain saw (1) n 120.9
~ clippers (2) n 120.8
~ cutters (1) n 120.8
~ -driven (1) adj 120.2
~ flesh (1) n 078.2
~ grass mower (1) n 120.2
~ hedge trimmer (1) n 120.8
~ lawn mower (1) n 120.2
~ mower (36) n 120.2
~ mow(er) (1) n 120.2
~ mowers (1) n 080.8
~ saw (51) n 120.9
~ saws (3) n 120.9
~ take-off unit (1) n 111.2
~ tiller (2) n 120.4
pow(er) mower (1) n 120.2
Power (5) 129.3
powerboat (2) n 024.6
powerboats (2) n 080.8
powered (8) adj 120.2
~ saw (1) n 120.9
powerful (16) adj 073.1
powerhouse (2) n 081.8

powers (2) n 053.2
Powerville (1) GA 087.6
Powhatan (2) LA 087.3
pox (17) n 079.7
poy(x3) (1) interj 037.5
PR (2) 128.6
~ -ing (1) v 088.3
practical (12) adj 053.6
~ nurse (6) n 065.2
~ nurses (2) n 065.2
~ nursing (3) n 084.6
practically (16) adv 070.1
practice (11) n/v/adj
073.6
~ nurse (1) n 084.6
~ togs (1) n 131.3
practicing (1) v 024.9
practitioner (1) n 069.8
pragmatic (1) adj 074.8
pragmatism (1) n 080.6
prairie (173) n/adj 029.5
~ chickens (3) n 080.9
~ country (1) n 029.5
~ dirt (1) n 029.8
~ dog (15) n 059.8
~ dogs (9) n 059.8
~ green (1) n 060.2
~ ground (1) n 029.5
~ gumbo (1) n 029.8
~ hay (3) n 041.7
~ hen (1) n 059.2
~ land (18) n 029.5
~ marsh (1) n 029.7
~ mud (3) n 029.5
~ oysters (1) n 089.8
~ rattlers (1) n 091.9
~ runner (1) n 088.8
~ soil (1) n 029.8
~ stuff (1) n 029.7
~ tremblante (1) n F
029.6
prair(ie) (9) n/adj 029.8
~ land (2) n 029.5
~ meadow (1) n 029.5
~ soil (1) n 029.9
Prairie (38) AL AR TX
087.2
~ Creek (4) AR LA
TX 030.7
~ De Ann (1) AR
070.6
~ Dell (1) TX 087.4
~ Grove (2) AR 087.1
~ Hill (1) TX 087.2
~ Point (1) MS 087.8

~ View (4) AR TX
087.8
Prair(ie) View (1) TX
087.3
prairies (16) n 029.5
praise (2) n/v 089.3
praises (1) n 089.5
praline (3) n 054.9
pralines (6) n 054.9
pram (11) n 066.8
prams (1) n 024.6
prance around (1) v 083.1
prank (1) n 129.8
pranking (4) v 080.8
~ around (1) v 088.7
~ with (2) v 090.9
prankish (1) adj 080.9
pranks (4) n 082.5
Pratt (3) 082.6
~ Avenue (1) 082.6
~ City (1) 106.2
~ City Park (1) 106.4
Prattville (7) AL 087.2
prawn (2) n/adj 060.9
~ fishing (1) n 080.8
pray (13) v 007.1
~ for (1) v 012.7
~ to (6) v 089.3
prayed (7) v 096.5
~ to (1) v 078.5
~ up (1) v 091.9
prayer (9) n/adj 078.3
~ beads (2) n 028.4
~ meeting (1) n 070.8
prayers (2) n 104.1
praying (11) n/v/adj
013.6
~ (a)bout (1) v 013.6
~ mantis (5) n 060A.4
~ mantises (1) n
060A.4
prays (2) v 013.8
pre (3) prefix 066.9
~ -mulch (1) v 066.9
~ -runner (1) n 088.8
~ -sacked (1) adj 051.5
Pre-Civil War homes (1)
n 088.7
preach (24) v 089.4
~ about (4) v 043.8
~ on (3) v 043.8
preach[V-p] (2) v 098.9
preached (5) v 079.3
preacher (393) n/adj
067.8

~ cow (1) n 033.5
pr(eacher) (1) n 067.8
Preacher (3) 069.2
preacher[N-k] (2) adj
095.3
~ seat (1) n 095.4
~ subject (1) n 043.8
preacher's tonic (1) n
022.2
preachers (28) n 067.8
preaches (1) v 089.4
preaching (31) n/v/adj
089.4
~ service (4) n 089.4
precaution (1) n 070.6
precinct (17) n/adj 112.7
~ station (1) n 112.7
precious (2) adj 125.4
precipice (19) n 031.2
precipitation (2) n 066.9
precisely (1) adv 065.3
predator (5) n 059.5
predators (11) n 059.5
predatory (2) adj 059.5
~ animals (1) n 059.5
predestinated (1) adj
081.9
predicted (1) v 101.6
prediction (1) n 006.2
preen (5) v 028.1
preengagement ring (1) n
123.1
preening (1) v 028.1
prefab (1) n 098.7
prefer (25) v 090.5
~ to (1) v 090.5
~ [P-0] (1) v 051.8
preferable (2) adj 066.8
preference (3) n 088.5
preferred (1) v 070.7
prefers (1) v 090.5
pregnancy (2) n 065.1
pregnant (760) adj 065.1
~ animals (1) n 065.1
~ with a baby (1) adj
065.1
~ with a calf (1) adj
033.9
~ woman (4) n 065.1
preg(nant) (1) adj 065.1
preheated (1) v 050.1
prejudice (2) n 026.1
prejudiced against (1) v
052.6

(pre)mature baby (1) n
065.1
prematured (1) adj 065.7
premium (11) n 095.7
premonition (1) n 091.6
prenado (1) adj S 065.1
Prentiss (6) MS 070.6
~ County (2) MS 087.2
prep (2) n/adj 125.8
~ school (1) n 083.6
preparation (4) n/adj
084.9
~ cook (1) n 084.9
~ day (1) n 080.7
~ lady (1) n 084.9
preparations (1) n 101.3
(pre)pare (1) v 073.7
prepared (2) v/adj 041.4
~ chalk (1) n 084.8
preparing (7) v 101.2
~ to (3) v 101.2
preppy (1) n 123.6
presbyterial (1) n 080.6
Presbyterian (50) 066.8
~ church (3) n 089.2
~ circuit rider (1) n
080.6
~ preacher (1) n 089.1
Presbyterians (10) 089.1
presbyteries (1) n 080.6
presbytery (1) n 088.8
preschool (3) n 125.7
Prescott (5) AL AR 087.3
(pre)scription medicine
(1) n 070.8
presence (1) n 053.5
present (35) n/adj 095.7
Present (2) 093.2
presentable (1) adj 085.4
presentations (1) n 131.1
presently (2) adv 070.3
presents (6) n 093.3
preservation (1) n 053.4
preserve (8) n/v/adj
051.6
~ stand (1) n 019.2
Preserve (1) 106.8
preserve[N-i] (4) n 066.8
preserved (10) v 058.3
preserves (151) n 051.6
(pre)serves (1) n 051.6
preserving (5) adj 017.6
~ kettle (1) n 017.6
~ peach (1) n 054.3
~ peaches (1) n 054.3

~ pear (1) n 054.5
~ tomatoes (1) n 055.3
preshrink (2) v 027.9
preshrinked (1) v/adj 027.9
preshrunk (12) v/adj 027.9
president (24) n 065.9
President (6) 032.7
~ George (1) 032.7
~ Nixon (2) 066.6
~ Truman's place (1) n 070.8
presiding judge (1) n 068.6
Presidio (1) TX 087.8
Presley's (1) 106.4
presliced (1) adj 046.7
press (280) n/v/adj 009.6
~ meat (90) n 047.1
~ pan (1) n 047.2
~ peach (65) n 054.3
~ peaches (16) n 054.3
~ seed (3) n 054.3
~ stone (4) n 054.3
~ stone peach (3) n 054.3
Press community (1) TX 087.2
pressed (30) v/adj 010.7
~ into (1) v 054.6
~ meat (15) n 047.1
~ out (1) v 057.8
~ peach (3) n 054.3
presser (7) n 022.2
pressers (1) n 113.7
presses (7) n 054.3
pressing (12) n/v/adj 010.6
~ club (1) n 084.8
~ iron (1) n 010.5
~ peach (1) n 054.3
~ shop (1) n 010.6
~ shops (1) n 010.6
pressure (7) n/adj 096.7
~ cooker (4) n 017.5
prestige (2) n 115.3
Preston (4) GA 105.4
~ Hollow (3) 105.4
presume (12) v 094.2
pretend (5) v 100.1
~ like (1) v 100.1
~ to (1) v 100.1
pretend[V-p] to (1) v 100.1

pretend[V-r] (2) v 100.1
pretended (40) v 100.1
~ like (1) v 100.1
~ to (5) v 100.1
(pre)tended (1) v 100.1
pretending (2) v 100.1
pretends (2) v 100.1
~ like (1) v 100.1
Pretori(a) (1) GA 087.2
prettied up (4) adj 028.1
prettier (426) adj 026.3
pretties (146) n 101.5
prettiest (156) adj 026.3
prettifying (1) v 028.1
pretty (2903) n/v/adj/adv 026.3
~ blue day (1) n 005.4
~ blue sky (1) n 005.4
~ blue-sky day (1) n 005.4
~ boy (4) n 125.3
~ boys (1) n 124.1
~ close (1) adj 081.4
~ clothes (3) n 026.3
~ day (136) n 005.4
~ days (3) n 005.4
~ dude (1) n 125.3
~ girl (5) n 026.3
~ girl's land (1) n 080.9
~ music (1) n 130.8
~ -pretty (2) n 088.7
~ sun day (1) n 005.4
~ sunshine day (3) n 005.4
~ up (5) v 028.1
~ weather (10) n 005.4
~ woman (1) n 125.3
~ women (2) n 026.3
pret(ty) (20) adj/adv 026.3
Pretty (2) 030.7
~ Creek (1) TN 030.7
~ Good Creek (1) MS 030.7
pretty(x4) (1) interj 037.9
pretty[A-w] (1) adj 026.3
pretty[V-s] (1) v 028.1
prettying (6) v 028.1
~ up (5) v 028.1
pretzels (1) n 045.2
prevalent (4) adj 066.8
previous (1) adj 003.6
prey (1) n 059.2
price (82) n/adj 094.5

~ range (1) n 094.6
Price Creek (1) MS 030.7
prices (8) n 103.3
Prichard (8) AL MS 105.1
prick (2) adj 124.8
~ tease (1) n 124.8
~ teaser (1) n 124.8
prickles (1) n 035.6
prickly (7) adj 075.1
~ ash (3) n 061.9
~ ash tree (1) n 061.8
~ pear (2) n 061.4
pride (2) n/v 027.2
Pride (4) LA 087.1
~ of Georgia (2) 056.9
~ of Mobile (1) 131.2
priest (3) n 067.8
priestes (1) n 016.8
priests (1) n 049.5
primarily (1) adv 053.4
primary (117) n/adj 083.7
~ class (3) n 083.7
~ department (2) n 083.7
~ grade (12) n 083.7
~ grades (11) n 083.7
~ roads (2) n 031.7
~ school (19) n 125.7
~ teacher (2) n 067.6
primar(y) (2) n/adj 083.7
prime (8) n/adj 121.1
~ rib (1) n 121.2
~ rib roast (1) n 121.2
~ ribs (1) n 121.2
~ roast (1) n 121.2
primer (168) n/adj 083.7
~ class (3) n 083.7
~ grade (2) n 083.7
~ grades (1) n 083.7
Primer (1) 089.8
primers (3) n 083.7
primitive (2) adj 115.6
Primitive (25) 089.3
~ Baptist (19) 089.1
~ Baptist church (1) n 089.1
~ Baptist churches (1) n 089.1
~ Baptist minister (1) n 089.1
~ Baptist[N-i] (2) 089.1
primp (335) v 028.1
~ up (45) v 028.1

~ with (1) v 032.4
primped (12) v 028.1
~ out (1) v 028.1
~ up (7) v 028.1
primper (1) n 028.1
primping (236) v 028.1
~ up (28) v 028.1
primpish (1) adj 028.1
primps (16) v 028.1
~ up (3) v 028.1
primroses (1) n 065.9
prince (2) v/adj 054.3
~ up (1) v 028.1
Prince (4) 057.3
~ Albert (3) 057.3
~ of Darkness (1) 090.1
princess (3) n/adj 124.2
~ ring (2) n 123.1
Princeton (4) GA KY 107.7
~ University (1) 070.7
princing up (1) v 028.1
principal (12) n 067.8
principles (1) n 068.3
print (5) n/v/adj 034.3
~ sack (1) n 019.6
~ sacks (1) n 019.6
printcloth (1) n 019.6
printed sacks (1) n 019.6
printer's devil (2) n 080.6
printers (1) n 091.5
printing (5) n/v/adj 027.2
~ paper (1) n 091.5
prints (2) n 084.9
Prio (1) 088.9
prison (28) n/adj 112.8
~ camp (1) n 057.4
~ wagon (1) n 091.8
Prison (1) 106.6
prisoner's base (1) n 098.4
priss around (1) v 028.1
prissing (a)round (1) v 100.1
prissy (5) adj 073.7
Prissy (1) 028.1
Pritchard (2) AL 105.1
privacy fence (3) n 016.3
private (133) adj 031.8
~ cars (1) n 111.7
~ cemeteries (1) n 074.4
~ cemetery (8) n 078.8

~ cemeter(y) (1) n 078.8

~ colleges (1) n 083.6

~ drive (12) n 031.8

~ driveway (3) n 031.8

~ driveways (1) n 031.8

~ graveyard (2) n 078.8

~ lane (3) n 031.8

~ office (1) n 012.1

~ -owned stores (1) n 116.2

~ people (1) n 112.5

~ plot (2) n 078.9

~ pupils (1) n 068.7

~ road (78) n 031.8

~ roads (4) n 031.8

~ rooms (1) n 039.6

~ school (2) n 090.4

~ secretary (5) n 068.8

privates (2) n 080.6

privet (6) n/adj 012.1

~ hedge (2) n 061.9

~ house (2) n 012.1

privets (2) n 012.1

privies (79) n 012.1

privilege (1) n 084.8

privileges (1) n 115.3

privy (317) n/adj 012.1

~ house (3) n 012.1

~ tomatoes (1) n 055.3

prix (1) n F 069.7

prize (15) n/v/adj 095.7

~ down (1) v 104.5

~ pole (5) n 022.1

prizefight (2) n/v 104.2

prizefighter (1) n 073.1

prizes (1) n 095.7

prizing up (1) v 104.6

pro (1) n 113.3

probably (101) adv 041.1

probate (9) n/adj 090.9

~ court (1) n 090.9

~ judge (7) n 068.6

problem (17) n 027.5

problems (17) n 012.2

procedure (1) n 021.7

proceeded (1) v 095.8

process (13) n 065.9

processed (2) v 123.9

processer (1) n 015.5

processing (1) n 039.9

procession (4) n 079.2

processors (1) n 015.5

procurer (2) n 113.5

prod (1) n 019.4

prodded flesh (1) n 078.2

prods (1) n 113.2

produce (21) n/v/adj 050.4

~ trucks (1) n 109.7

producer (1) n 046.8

produces (1) v 104.6

producing (1) adj 024.1

product (2) n 050.4

production (2) n 084.8

productive (22) adj 029.3

products (18) n 045.1

profess (3) v 089.2

~ to (1) v 058.3

(pro)fess (2) v 089.2

(pro)fess[V-r] (1) v 075.6

professed (1) v 089.2

(pro)fessed (1) v 089.2

profession (2) n 053.4

professional (4) n/adj 025.4

~ volunteer (1) n 088.7

professions (1) n 089.2

professor (20) n 065.8

(pro)fessor (3) n 067.6

professors (2) n 080.9

(pro)fessors (1) n 067.6

profit (7) n 094.5

program (15) n/adj 089.5

~ dances (1) n 083.1

program[N-i] (1) n 075.9

programs (5) n 070.7

progress (1) n 053.4

progressing (1) v 066.9

progressive (12) adj 130.8

~ country (3) n 130.9

~ dinner party (1) n 130.7

~ dinners (1) n 099.9

~ house party (1) n 095.8

~ jazz (2) n 130.8

~ rock (2) n 130.8

prohibition (2) adj 081.9

~ law (1) n 081.9

~ man (1) n 101.3

project (28) n 119.2

Project (4) 106.3

~ Road (1) 107.7

projected (1) v 101.2

projects (17) n 119.2

proj(ects) (1) n 119.2

Prolific (5) 056.2

~ corn (1) n 056.2

Prolifics (1) 056.2

prom (16) n/adj 083.1

~ parties (1) n 130.7

promenade (1) v 089.8

prominent (2) adj 090.4

promis (1) adj F 081.4

promiscuous (14) adj 124.8

promiscuously (1) adv 096.7

promise (14) n/v/adj 123.1

~ ring (1) n 080.6

promised (1) adj 081.4

promising (1) adj 005.6

promontory (1) n 031.2

promote (1) v 099.4

promptness (1) n 095.7

proms (7) n 083.1

prone (2) adj 073.3

prong (2) adj 126.1

~ fence (1) n 126.1

~ rake (1) n 120.7

Prong (5) 030.7

prongs (5) n 120.6

pronounce (3) v 070.6

pronto (3) adj 044.6

~ puffs (1) n 044.6

~ pups (2) n 121.6

pronunciation (2) n 065.8

proof (15) adj 114.2

~ bags (1) n 123.7

propel (1) adj 120.2

propelled (14) adj 120.2

propelling (1) adj 120.2

proper (12) adj 125.5

properest (1) adj 064.6

properly (1) adv 131.1

property (33) n/adj 070.7

~ road (1) n 031.8

prophet (1) n 090.1

prophets (1) n 052.1

proportion (1) n 039.7

proposal (4) n 082.1

propositions (1) n 091.8

props (2) n 008.3

pros (1) n 113.3

prospect (1) n 026.3

Prospect Heights (1) 106.2

prospective bride (1) n 081.6

prosper (1) v 084.9

prosperous (1) adj 029.3

Prosperous (6) 093.3

Prolifics (1) 056.2

~ New Year (4) 093.3

~ New Year's (1) 093.3

prostitute (63) n/adj 113.3

~ house (1) n 113.4

prostitutes (26) n 113.3

prostitutes' house (1) n 113.4

prostitution (12) n/adj 113.3

~ house (2) n 113.4

~ houses (1) n 113.4

prostitutions (1) n 113.4

prostrate trouble (1) n 066.8

protect (2) v 070.6

(pro)tect (1) v 008.2

protection (7) n/adj 113.8

~ levee (1) n 080.8

protective (2) adj 123.7

~ cover (1) n 054.8

protector (1) n 123.7

protects (2) v 070.6

protein (2) n/adj 065.8

~ foam (1) n 081.9

Protestant (12) 126.6

~ groups (1) n 126.6

Protestants (3) 126.6

protracted (4) adj 090.9

~ meeting (3) n 090.9

~ meetings (1) n 089.8

(pro)tracted meetings (1) n 089.8

protrude (2) v 027.8

proud (993) adj 081.2

~ corruption (1) n 078.2

~ -cut (1) v 036.1

~ flesh (585) n 078.2

~ f(lesh) (1) n 078.2

~ flush (3) n 078.2

~ fresh (36) n 078.2

~ skin (1) n 078.2

proudest (1) adj 090.6

prove (1) v 129.8

Provencal (7) LA 030.7

~ Road (1) 087.6

(Proven)cal Bottom (1) LA 030.7

proverbial (1) adj 073.2

providence (2) n 085.6

Providence (13) AL LA RI TX 087.3

~ Bayou (1) LA 030.3

~ Village (1) 105.1

province (1) n 089.6
provoked (2) v 075.2
provokes (1) v 075.3
prowl (3) adj 111.7
~ car (2) n 111.7
~ cars (1) n 111.7
prowler (2) n 111.7
prowlers (2) n 059.5
PRs (4) 128.6
prune (5) n/adj 055.9
~ -and-raisin wine (1) n
  050.9
~ Danish (1) n 122.2
~ pies (1) n 090.9
pruner (1) n 120.8
pruners (2) n 120.8
prunes (1) n 054.6
pruning (9) adj 120.6
~ fork (1) n 120.6
~ shears (8) n 120.8
Prussia (1) 087.9
Prussians (1) 127.2
Pryor Street (1) 107.6
Ps (1) 080.6
pshaw (17) interj 092.3
psilocybin (2) n 114.2
psilocyb(in) (1) n 114.2
psst (1) interj 033.2
Psyche (1) 123.9
psyched (1) adj 092.2
psychedelic (3) adj 070.7
~ drugs (1) n 114.2
psychedelics (1) n 099.6
psychology (1) n 080.8
PTA work (1) n 012.9
PTO (1) 041.7
ptomaine (4) adj 046.9
~ fever (1) n 046.9
~ poison (2) n 062.6
~ poisoning (1) n 062.6
puante (3) adj F 059.4
public (100) n/adj 031.6
~ alley (1) n 108.6
~ burying ground (1) n
  078.8
~ dance (1) n 083.1
~ dances (3) n 083.1
~ drive (1) n 108.6
~ hauling (1) n 021.4
~ job (2) n 080.8
~ jobs (1) n 076.1
~ library (4) n 084.1
~ nuisance (1) n 113.5
~ park (4) n 085.1

~ parking garages (1) n
  108.4
~ parks (1) n 085.1
~ -relations writer (1) n
  100.5
~ road (28) n 031.7
~ roads (11) n 031.6
~ salt lick (1) n 051.7
~ school (6) n 083.7
~ schools (2) n 083.7
~ schoolteacher (1) n
  067.6
~ square (14) n 085.1
~ store (1) n 116.1
~ work (3) n 065.8
~ -worked (2) v 098.6
~ -working (2) v 024.9
~ -works-minded (1)
  adj 053.5
published (1) v 053.4
puccoon (3) n/adj 061.4
puce (3) n F 062.3
pucker (6) v 027.8
~ out (2) v 027.8
puckered (7) v/adj 055.9
~ out (3) v 075.5
~ up (1) v 055.9
puckering string (1) n
  028.2
puckery (2) adj 055.9
pud (1) n 069.8
pudding (419) n/adj
  047.2
~ pan (1) n 048.3
~ pie (1) n 047.3
~ sauce (2) n 048.5
Pudding (2) 063.2
puddings (30) n 047.3
puddle (3) n 030.5
pudgy (3) adj 073.1
puds (3) n 069.8
pue (1) adj F 059.4
puerco (1) n S 047.3
puerto (1) n S 010.8
Puerto (37) 069.4
~ Rican (6) 069.4
~ Ricans (23) 128.6
~ Rico (8) 086.1
(Puerto) Ricans (1) 128.6
puff (43) n/v/adj 029.1
~ adder (1) n 060A.9
~ cakes (1) n 044.6
~ out (19) v 027.8
~ up (1) v 077.6
puff[V-t] up (1) v 027.8

puffball (1) n 057.1
puffballs (1) n 057.1
puffed (17) v 047.5
~ out (2) v 027.8
~ up (14) v 077.6
puffes (1) n 122.7
puffing adder (1) n 089.8
puffle (1) n 027.8
puffs (23) n/v 054.6
~ out (1) v 027.8
puffy (1) adj 046.7
pug (2) n/adj 033.3
~ dog (1) n 033.3
Pugh River (1) AL 030.7
puke (289) v 080.3
~ like (1) v 080.3
~ like a buzzard (1) v
  080.3
~ my insides out (1) v
  080.3
~ up (4) v 080.3
puke[V-r] my guts up (1)
  v 080.3
puked (60) v 080.3
~ up (6) v 080.3
pukes (3) v 080.3
puking (47) v 080.3
~ up (1) v 080.3
Pulaski (26) AR GA MS
  TN 087.5
~ Heights (6) 105.1
~ Pike (2) 031.6
pull (1585) n/v/adj 097.6
~ across (1) v 097.6
~ away (3) v 097.6
~ back (4) v 097.6
~ bone (28) n 037.1
~ chain (2) n 097.6
~ down (5) v 097.6
~ -down shade (1) n
  009.5
~ -down shades (2) n
  009.5
~ from (1) v 097.6
~ in (2) v 097.6
~ -in parking (1) n
  108.3
~ into (2) v 097.6
~ lawn mower (1) n
  120.2
~ off (12) v 097.6
~ -off places (1) n
  107.2
~ on (8) v 097.6
~ open (1) v 097.6

~ out (15) v 097.6
~ over (1) v 097.6
~ ov(er) (1) v 097.6
~ post (1) n 016.5
~ rake (1) n 120.7
~ shades (1) n 009.5
~ through (32) v 097.6
~ up (14) v 097.6
Pull Tight (1) TN 030.8
pull[V-p] (1) v 120.2
pull[V-r] (17) v 097.6
~ by (1) v 097.6
~ down (3) v 097.6
pull[V-s] (1) v 070.3
pull[V-t] (7) v 097.6
~ by (1) v 097.6
~ down (2) v 097.6
~ off (1) v 097.6
pulled (264) v/adj 097.6
~ by (4) v 097.6
~ down (2) v 097.6
~ off (1) v 097.6
~ out (9) v 097.6
~ toward (1) v 025.8
~ up (8) v 097.6
puller (3) n 115.3
pullers (4) n 020.9
pullet (7) n/adj 036.7
~ bone (3) n 037.1
~ egg (1) n 044.6
pullets (4) n 036.9
pulley (579) n/adj 104.5
~ bats (1) n 059.3
~ bone (556) n 037.1
~ bones (5) n 037.1
pulleys (4) n 104.5
pulling (125) v/adj 097.6
~ bone (4) n 037.1
~ in (1) v 097.6
~ machines (1) n 089.9
~ ox (1) n 039.4
~ rake (1) n 120.7
~ skiff (1) n 024.6
~ up (2) v 097.6
pullings (10) n 083.1
pullout (2) n/adj 097.6
~ job (1) n 097.6
pullover (1) n 027.3
pulls (18) v 097.7
pulmotor (1) n 111.5
pulp (13) n/adj 054.1
~ mill (1) n 021.4
~ mills (1) n 065.9
pulpit (4) n 065.8

pulpwood (15) n/adj 080.6
~ boys (1) n 080.7
~ business (1) n 070.6
~ mill (1) n 084.8
~ roads (1) n 031.7
pulpwooders (1) n 080.6
pulpwooding (1) n 080.7
pulverize (2) v 021.7
pulverizer (3) n 021.7
pulvermulch (1) v 021.7
pumice (3) n 041.5
pummies (1) n 051.2
pummins (4) n 051.3
pump (99) n/v/adj 123.8
~ and ladder (1) n 111.2
~ engine (1) n 111.2
~ engines (1) n 111.2
~ house (19) n 014.7
~ houses (2) n 011.7
~ organ (1) n 089.9
~ organs (1) n 088.7
~ pitchers (1) n 080.9
~ shed (1) n 011.7
~ shoes (1) n 123.8
~ system (1) n 024.9
~ water (1) n 002.7
~ well (2) n 080.6
pump[N-i] (1) n 080.7
pumped (2) v/adj 075.7
~ -in area (1) n 075.7
~ out (1) v 075.4
pumper (33) n/adj 111.2
~ truck (8) n 111.2
~ trucks (1) n 111.2
pumpernickel (22) n/adj 044.4
~ bread (3) n 044.4
~ breads (1) n 044.4
pumpers (11) n 111.2
pumping (5) v/adj 111.2
~ equipment (1) n 111.2
~ system (1) n 111.2
pumpkin (755) n/adj 056.5
~ bread (9) n 044.4
~ bug (1) n 056.5
~ butter (1) n 051.6
~ heads (1) n 073.4
~ in her belly (1) n 065.1
~ melon (1) n 056.7
~ melons (1) n 056.7

~ patch (1) n 056.5
~ pie (17) n 056.5
~ pies (6) n 056.5
~ (po)tato (1) n 056.5
~ potatoes (1) n 015.5
~ squash (2) n 056.6
~ vine (1) n 056.5
~ watermelon (1) n 056.9
~ yam (5) n 055.5
~ yams (1) n 055.5
Pumpkin (7) 064.4
~ Hill Creek (1) FL 030.7
~ Town (1) 093.8
pumpkin[N-i] (2) n 056.5
pumpkins (237) n 056.5
pumpkinseed (39) n/adj 056.5
~ perch (1) n 061.2
pumpkinseed[N-i] (1) n 065.2
pumpkinseeds (2) n 056.5
pumps (40) n 123.8
punch (14) n/v 082.5
~ out (3) v 027.8
punch[V-r] that big time clock (1) v 078.6
punched (2) v 104.3
~ out (1) v 027.8
puncheon (4) n/adj 016.4
~ fence (1) n 016.4
~ lot (1) n 015.6
puncheons (1) n 080.6
punching (5) v/adj 080.7
~ stick (4) n 080.7
~ up (1) v 078.2
puncture (2) n 078.1
pungo (1) n 056.9
punish (29) n/v 065.5
punished (14) v 065.5
punishing (4) v 065.5
punishment (7) n 065.5
punk (24) n/adj 124.2
~ age (1) n 080.6
~ ash (1) n 061.8
~ funk (1) n 130.9
~ rock (1) n 130.9
~ tree (2) n 061.9
~ trees (1) n 061.9
punkah (1) n 088.7
punked out (1) v 075.5
punks (1) n 124.2
punkwood (1) n 061.8
Punta (3) 087.9

~ Gorda (2) FL 087.9
~ Guadalupe Resaca (1) TX 030.7
puny (218) adj 072.9
~ list (1) n 072.9
~ -looking (1) adj 072.9
pup (7) n 033.3
pupil (166) n 068.7
pupils (63) n 068.7
puppies (519) n 044.5
Puppies (6) 123.8
puppy (87) n/adj 033.2
~ dog (5) n 080.6
~ dogs (3) n 070.8
~ love (3) n 081.4
~ lovers (1) n 081.5
~ wolf (1) n 088.8
Puppy (1) 123.8
pups (3) n 121.6
Purdham Hill (1) AR 087.7
pure (172) adj 051.4
~ -bred dog (1) n 033.1
~ cane syrup (1) n 051.4
~ coffee (8) n 032.3
~ music (1) n 130.8
~ -old (6) adj 051.4
~ pine (1) n 008.6
~ -white sand (1) n 029.9
~ white trash (1) n 069.7
Pure Oil (1) 024.1
purebred (1) adj 013.8
purely (26) adv 091.6
purgative (2) n 061.4
purgatory (1) n 090.1
purging medicine (1) n 080.2
purify (4) v 048.2
purloined (1) v 100.2
purple (56) adj 070.9
~ berries (1) n 062.4
~ butter bean (1) n 055A.3
~ butter beans (1) n 055A.3
~ cane (1) n 051.9
~ corn (1) n 056.2
~ hull (14) n 055A.3
~ -hull (2) adj 055A.4
~ -hull crowders (2) n 055A.2

~ -hull pea (1) n 080.7
~ -hull peas (7) n 055A.2
~ -hull speckle pea (1) n 055A.4
~ hulls (2) n 055A.3
~ martin (1) n 081.9
~ martins (1) n 059.2
~ onion (2) n 055.6
~ onions (2) n 055.6
~ passion (1) n 062.4
~ peanuts (1) n 054.7
~ pods (1) n 055A.2
~ stripe (1) n 056.9
~ top (2) n 055A.5
~ -top turnip (1) n 055A.7
~ -top turnips (2) n 055A.5
Purple (2) 097.8
~ Heart (1) 053.7
purplish (1) adj 075.8
purpose (493) n 103.6
purposed (1) v 101.7
purposely (32) adv 103.6
purposes (19) n 103.6
purse (1026) n/adj 028.2
~ chain (1) n 028.2
~ snatching (1) n 080.9
~ -strings (1) n 115.3
purse[N-i] (1) n 028.2
purses (42) n 028.2
purslane (4) n 015.9
pursy (1) adj 073.1
purve (1) n 041.7
Purvis (2) MS 087.6
Puryear (1) KY 087.4
pus (685) n/adj 077.5
~ bag (1) n 077.5
~ -like (1) adj 077.5
push (1355) n/v/adj 097.7
~ and caboodle (1) n 082.9
~ away (1) v 097.7
~ back (4) v 097.7
~ boat (1) n 024.6
~ broom (1) n 010.5
~ buggies (1) n 064.5
~ buggy (2) n 064.5
~ -button (1) n 097.7
~ deal (1) n 021.6
~ down (2) v 097.7
~ lawn mower (6) n 120.1

~ lawn mowers (1) n 120.1
~ mower (56) n 120.1
~ mow(er) (2) n 120.1
~ mowers (3) n 120.1
~ off (1) v 097.7
~ -off (1) n 096.7
~ on (2) v 037.5
~ out (4) v 027.8
~ plow (4) n 021.6
~ plows (1) n 120.4
~ rake (2) n 014.8
~ reel type (1) n 120.1
~ up (2) v 097.7
push[V-r] (2) v 097.7
push[V-t] (3) v 097.7
pushcart (5) n 064.5
pushcarts (1) n 097.7
pushed (80) v 097.7
~ around (3) v 097.7
~ away (1) v 097.7
~ back (1) v 097.7
~ off (1) v 097.7
~ out (4) v 027.8
~ under (1) v 097.7
~ up (3) v 097.7
Pushepatap(a) (1) MS 030.7
pusher (118) n 114.4
pusher[N-i] (1) n 123.2
pushers (70) n 114.4
pushes (10) v 097.7
~ (a)round (1) v 097.7
pushing (81) v/adj 097.7
~ buggy (1) n 064.5
~ down (1) v 097.7
~ job (1) n 097.7
~ mower (1) n 120.1
~ up daisies (3) v 078.6
Pushmataha (1) AL 037.7
puss (1) n 124.1
pussley (18) n 015.9
pussy (10) n/adj 077.5
~ wagon (1) n 109.4
~ willow (1) n 061.8
~ willows (1) n 061.8
pussycat (2) n 059.4
pustule (1) n 088.7
put (2404) v 102.7
~ a switch on you (1) v 065.5
~ a whipping on you (1) v 065.5
~ around (1) v 053.4
~ (a)round (1) v 016.1

~ away (23) v 102.7
~ back (1) v 102.7
~ between (2) v 007A.5
~ down (13) v 102.7
~ -down (4) n 080.6
~ -down connotation (1) n 080.6
~ -down-on-the-floor bed (1) n 029.2
~ -down term (1) n 092.7
~ forth (1) v 102.7
~ her down (2) v 082.1
~ him down (15) v 082.1
~ him in the sack (1) v 082.1
~ him off (1) v 082.1
~ him on the shelf (1) v 082.1
~ him up on the shelf (1) v 082.1
~ in (58) v 102.7
~ in for (1) v 102.7
~ in to (1) v 095.8
~ into (4) v 102.7
~ it on you (1) v 091.8
~ off (4) v 102.7
~ on (194) v 102.7
~ -on (3) n 073.6
~ on top of (1) v 102.7
~ out (16) v 102.7
~ over (4) v 102.7
~ the halter on (1) v 082.2
~ the noose on (1) v 082.2
~ through (1) v 053.7
~ to (1) v 025.8
~ together (1) n 075.8
~ up (37) v 102.7
~ -up (1) adj 102.7
~ up to (1) v 080.6
~ up with (7) v 102.7
~ your foot back (1) v 037.5
~ your leg down (1) v 037.5
~ your little foot (1) n 130.7
Put (1) 017.6
put[V-p] up (1) v 013.6
puta (1) n S 074.8
Putman (2) AL 087.6

Putnam (6) FL GA 087.4
~ County (2) FL GA 087.4
puto (2) n S 074.6
putrid (2) adj 047.5
putrified (1) adj 046.9
puts (42) v 102.7
~ away (1) v 048.4
~ on (4) v 100.1
~ out (2) v 102.7
~ up (3) v 096.7
putter (1) v 080.7
putting (96) v 102.7
~ away (1) v 102.7
~ down (4) v 129.7
~ in (6) v 102.7
~ in the dozen[N-i] (1) v 129.7
~ in the dozens (1) v 129.7
~ on (37) v 028.1
~ out (2) v 081.7
~ them in a dozens (1) v 129.7
puttings upon (1) n 080.6
puzzled (2) v/adj 013.5
~ over (1) v 013.5
PWA (1) 012.1
PWTs (1) 069.7
pygmy (4) n/adj 069.5
~ owl (1) n 059.1
~ rattlers (2) n 092.8
pyoo woo (1) interj 038.3
pyorrhea (4) n 071.9
pyracantha (7) n/adj 061.8
~ bushes (1) n 070.6
pyramid (2) n 117.6
pyramids (1) n 123.9
Pyrenees Mountains (1) 031.1
pyrenes (1) n 020.4
Pythias (1) 081.8
python (1) n 080.7
pythons (2) n 088.7

Q

Q (1) 083.1
Qs (1) 080.6
QT (1) 075.7
Quaalude (2) 114.2
Quaaludes (9) 115.6
quack (24) n/adj 067.8
~ doctor (3) n 067.8
~ doctors (1) n 067.8
quack(x4) (1) interj 038.9
quacker (1) n 069.4
quad (1) n 085.1
quadrangle (1) n 085.1
quadrille (1) n 083.1
quadroon (19) n 069.5
quadroons (10) n 069.5
quahog (1) n 090.8
quail (42) n 088.8
quail[N-i] (1) n 059.3
quails (9) n 059.3
quaint (2) adj 080.8
Quaker (1) 042.1
Quakerish (1) 096.8
Quakers (2) 126.6
qualification (1) n 024.8
qualifications (1) n 039.8
qualified (3) v/adj 053.3
~ for (2) v 053.3
qualities (1) n 051.5
quality (3) n 057.8
quantities (11) n 051.5
quantity (9) n 051.5
quanti(ty) (2) n 051.5
Quantrell (1) 089.2
quarrel (2) v 104.2
quarried (1) v 070.6
quarries (2) n 084.8
quarry (7) n 065.9
quart (16) n/adj 050.8
~ jar (3) n 019.2
quart[N-i] (1) n 016.7
quarter (862) n/adj 004.5
~ after (59) n 004.5
~ bag (1) n 114.1
~ before (4) n 004.5

~ black (1) n 069.5
~ boat (1) n 024.6
~ breed (1) n 069.5
~ breeds (2) n 069.5
~ cuts (1) n 121.3
~ horse (1) n 034.2
~ horses (3) n 034.2
~ hour (1) n 004.5
~ log (1) n 008.5
~ loin (1) n 121.3
~ of (109) n 004.5
~ (o)f (1) n 004.5
~ of an hour to (1) n 004.5
~ ounce (2) n 004.5
~ past (29) n 004.5
~ -sawed oak (1) n 088.9
~ section (1) n 084.8
~ till (324) n 004.5
~ to (243) n 004.5
~ until (4) n 004.5
~ [P-0] (11) n 004.5
quart(er) (4) n 004.5
~ of (2) n 004.5
~ of an hour to (1) n 004.5
~ to (1) n 004.5
Quarter (27) 087.5
~ Creek (1) AL 030.7
quarter[N-i] (1) n 007A.4
quarterage (1) n 081.8
quarterback (1) n 067.8
quartered (4) v 054.6
~ across (1) v 085.2
quarterhouse (1) n 121.1
quarteroons (1) n 069.5
quarters (39) n 010.6
Quarters (5) 082.6
quartets (1) n 130.9
quarts (1) n 001.4
quasi (2) prefix 067.9
~ -hillbilly (1) n 069.9
quatorze (1) n F 001.7
quatre (1) n F 001.2
que (1) pron F 025.8
queasy (4) adj 074.2
Quebec (6) 087.6
queen (28) n/adj 124.2
~ bee (2) n 091.8
~ pig (1) n 035.5
~ potato (1) n 055.4
~ snake (1) n 090.9
Queen (48) 080.8
~ Branch (1) AL 030.7

~ heater (1) n 008.6
~ Mary (1) 067.1
~ of [D-0] South (1) 055.5
queen's kids (1) n 127.8
Queen's lace (1) n 062.7
queens (3) n 124.2
Queens (1) 056.9
Queensboro (3) GA 087.3
~ settlers (1) n 081.8
queer (932) n/adj 074.7
~ -acting (4) adj 074.7
~ -like (2) adj 074.7
~ -looking (1) adj 074.7
~ -thinking (1) adj 074.7
~ -turned (1) adj 074.7
~ women (1) n 124.3
queerer (1) adj 074.7
queerish (2) adj 074.7
queers (18) n 074.7
queery (2) adj 074.7
quelite (1) n S 015.9
queso (1) n S 048.1
question (27) n 092.1
question[N-i] (2) n 104.1
questioning (1) v 053.5
questions (22) n 070.6
Queue (1) 030.7
qui (1) pron F 036 7
quibbling owl (1) n 059.1
quick (218) adj/adv 005.8
~ bread (4) n 044.4
~ breads (3) n 044.4
~ downpour (2) n 006.1
~ flesh (2) n 078.2
~ floods (1) n 006.1
~ grits (1) n 050.6
~ -minded (1) adj 075.1
~ service (1) n 116.2
~ shop (1) n 116.2
~ shower (10) n 006.1
~ storm (1) n 006.1
~ -temper (3) adj 075.1
~ -tempered (51) adj 075.1
Quick (4) 116.2
~ Market (1) 116.2
~ Sacks (1) 116.2
~ Shop (1) 116.2
~ Stop (1) 116.2
quicken (2) v 093.9

quicker (6) adj 065.8
quickie (1) n 116.2
quickies (1) n 080.6
quickly (3) adv 005.8
quicks (1) n 119.7
quicksand (7) n/adj 029.7
~ stuff (1) n 029.8
quickstep (1) n 091.8
quiet (206) n/v/adj 075.3
~ down (22) v 075.3
~ -tempered (1) adj 073.2
quieted (2) v 007.3
~ down (1) v 007.3
quieten down (16) v 075.3
quieten[V-t] down (3) v 007.3
quietening (3) v 007.3
~ down (2) v 007.3
quieter (3) adj 007.3
quieting (15) v 007.3
~ down (12) v 007.3
~ off (1) v 007.3
quiets (1) v 007.3
quietus (1) n 081.8
quiety (1) adj 007.3
Quihi (2) TX 087.3
quill (28) n/adj 056.7
~ melon (18) n 056.7
~ melons (5) n 056.7
quills (1) n 026.5
quilt (694) n/v/adj 029.1
~ box (3) n 009.3
~ boxes (2) n 009.2
~ chest (3) n 009.7
~ frames (1) n 029.1
~ linings (1) n 029.1
~ out (1) v 029.1
~ pack (2) n 009.7
~ pad (1) n 029.1
~ pieces (2) n 029.1
~ scraps (3) n 026.2
~ shelf (1) n 009.2
~ tie (1) n 029.1
~ top (3) n 029.1
~ topping (2) n 029.1
~ tops (3) n 029.1
quilt[N-i] (2) n 029.1
quilt[V-r] (1) v 029.1
quilted (14) v/adj 029.1
~ cover (1) n 028.7
quilting (66) n/v/adj 029.1
~ bee (4) n 029.1

~ bees (5) n 029.1
~ club (1) n 029.1
~ cotton (1) n 029.1
~ frame (2) n 029.1
~ frames (10) n 029.1
~ horse (2) n 022.1
~ parties (7) n 029.1
~ party (10) n 029.1
~ rails (1) n 092.8
quiltings (5) n 083.1
quilts (421) n 029.1
(quim)bombo (2) n S 055.8
quince (8) n/adj 061.8
~ preserves (2) n 051.6
~ tree (1) n 061.8
~ trees (1) n 061.9
quinces (2) n 061.8
Quincy (5) FL 087.4
quinidine (1) n 078.4
quinine (830) n/adj 078.4
~ capsules (2) n 078.4
~ syrup (1) n 078.4
~ tablets (1) n 078.4
~ water (8) n 078.4
quinsy (3) n 079.7
quint (1) n 124.2
quintupled (1) v 088.9
quirt (17) n 019.4
quit (184) v 007.3
~ breathing (1) v 078.6
~ dating him (3) v 082.1
~ going together (1) v 082.1
~ going with him (5) v 082.1
~ her (7) v 082.1
~ him (75) v 082.1
~ out (1) v 095.9
~ out of (1) v 053.8
~ seeing him (1) v 082.1
~ the boy (1) v 082.1
~ you (1) v 082.1
~ [P-0] (1) v 095.8
quite (718) adv 004.6
Quitman (15) AR GA MS 087.6
~ County (6) GA MS 087.9
quits (3) v 007.3
~ dating him (1) v 082.1
~ him (1) v 063.3

quitting (8) v/adj 005.7
~ him (1) v 082.1
~ time (1) n 037.4
~ you (1) v 082.1
Quiver River (1) MS 030.7
quivering (5) v/adj 070.8
~ owl (4) n 059.2
quiz shows (1) n 002.9
quo (1) pron 085.7
Quo Vadis (1) 123.9
quoits (21) n 034.8
Quonset huts (1) n 089.8

R

R (3) 095.8
rab (1) n 126.7
rabbi (1) n 126.7
rabbit (119) n/adj 124.9
~ cage (1) n 088.7
~ dog (6) n 033.3
~ dogs (5) n 033.3
~ ears (1) n 070.7
~ eyes (1) n 062.4
~ fever (1) n 096.8
~ foot (1) n 055A.6
~ hawk (1) n 059.2
~ hound (1) n 033.3
~ -hunt (3) v 080.6
~ hunting (1) n 081.9
~ -hunting (1) v 088.8
~ kin (1) n 066.5
~ mull (1) n 088.9
~ owl (1) n 059.2
~ snake (1) n 080.7
~ tobacco (28) n 057.3
~ -tobacco tea (2) n 061.4
~ wire (1) n 016.7
Rabbit (7) 064.4
~ Branch (2) AL TN 030.7
~ Creek (2) MS 030.7
~ Stole the Pumpkin (1) 056.5
rabbit's foot (1) n 072.6
rabbits (25) n 061.2
Rabelaisian (1) 065.8
rabid (4) adj 070.8
rabies (7) n 065.8
Rabun (6) GA 087.3
~ Gap (2) GA 031.3
~ Gap Junction (1) GA 087.5
~ Moun(tain) (1) GA 087.4
racacha (2) n F 060A.7
raccoon (39) n/adj 059.5
(rac)coon (123) n/adj 059.5

~ hides (1) n 040.1
~ hunt (2) n 059.6
~ -hunt (3) v 081.9
~ -hunted (1) v 081.8
~ hunting (4) n 059.5
~ meat (1) n 048.7
~ trails (1) n 031.8
~ -trapped (1) v 090.9
(rac)coon[N-i] (2) n 059.4
raccoons (20) n 059.5
(rac)coons (101) n 059.5
race (155) n/v/adj 030.5
~ boats (1) n 024.6
~ war (1) n 057.4
raced (1) v 024.6
racehorse (4) n/adj 034.2
~ language (1) n 015.5
racehorses (5) n 034.2
racer (18) n 093.5
racers (12) n 080.7
races (11) n 130.2
rachet stock (1) n 021.6
racially (1) adv 069.5
racing (11) n/v/adj 130.2
~ boats (1) n 024.6
~ cars (2) n 130.2
~ stock (1) n 036.5
racist (2) n 066.8
rack (245) n 022.1
~ -like (1) adj 008.3
~ of lamb (1) n 121.4
racked (3) v 014.6
racket (17) n/adj 088.8
~ ball (2) n 130.4
rackets (1) n 005.4
racking (6) v/adj 075.7
~ (a)cross (1) v 075.7
racks (29) n 022.1
racy car (1) n 109.1
Radagous (1) 089.9
radar (6) n/adj 088.7
~ oven (2) n 116.4
~ ovens (3) n 116.4
Radarange (5) 116.4
Radford (1) 106.5
radiant (8) adj 118.5
~ heat (4) n 118.5
~ heaters (2) n 118.5
radiator (2) n 118.4
radiators (3) n 118.4
radical (1) n 075.1
radicals (2) n 129.3
radio (17) n 065.9
radios (3) n 080.6

radish (414) n/adj 055.2
~ leaves (1) n 055A.5
~ -skin soil (1) n 029.9
~ top (1) n 055A.5
~ tops (3) n 055A.5
radish[N-i] (33) n 055.2
radishes (515) n 055.2
radium ovens (1) n 116.4
radius (1) n 021.1
raft (28) n/adj 024.6
~ eel (1) n 059.9
rafted (1) v 080.6
rafter (6) n 011.4
rafters (13) n 011.6
rafts (3) n 024.6
rag (310) n/adj 018.4
~ ball (1) n 081.8
~ doll (1) n 101.5
~ dolls (4) n 080.6
~ lamp (3) n 024.3
~ mop (1) n 010.5
~ smoke (1) n 024.3
~ stopper (1) n 020.4
~ tag (2) n 130.2
~ torch (1) n 024.3
~ wick (1) n 024.3
Rag Town (1) 105.6
ragamuffin (1) n 084.9
rage (1) n 075.2
ragged (1) adj 084.9
raggedy (3) adj 102.6
ragging (2) v 028.1
raging (3) v 007.2
rags (39) n 010.2
Ragsdale (1) GA 087.4
ragtime (1) n 130.8
ragweed (14) n 015.9
ragweeds (4) n 015.9
raid (1) n 082.8
raiders (2) n 059.5
rail (888) n/adj 016.4
~ benders (1) n 008.3
~ cars (1) n 085.3
~ crossing (1) n 107.8
~ depot (1) n 084.7
~ express (1) n 085.3
~ fence (429) n 016.4
~ fence[N-i] (1) n 016.4
~ fences (202) n 016.4
~ fencing (4) n 016.4
~ junction (1) п 084.7
~ lights (1) n 024.3
~ pen (1) n 015.4
~ pile (1) n 073.3

~ station (15) n 084.7
~ system (1) n 109.9
~ terminal (1) n 084.7
~ timber (1) n 016.4
~ -type fence (1) n 016.4
~ yard (1) n 084.7
~ yard fence (1) n 016.4
rail[N-i] (3) n 039.6
railcars (1) n 085.3
railhead (3) n 084.7
railing (27) n/adj 016.4
~ fence (11) n 016.4
~ fences (4) n 016.4
railing[N-i] (1) n 016.4
railings (6) n 107.3
railroad (599) n/adj 084.7
~ bed (1) n 084.7
~ boss (1) n 068.5
~ bridge (2) n 031.6
~ car (1) n 084.7
~ cars (1) n 023.6
~ clerk (1) n 065.8
~ crossing (16) n 107.8
~ crossties (1) n 084.7
~ dance (1) n 083.1
~ depot (20) n 084.7
~ dock (1) n 031.4
~ drawbridge (1) n 084.7
~ flat (1) n 118.6
~ house (2) n 007A.3
~ houses (1) n 118.9
~ junction (4) n 084.7
~ man (4) n 084.7
~ map (1) n 084.7
~ men (2) n 084.7
~ office (2) n 084.7
~ overpass (3) n 107.8
~ pass (2) n 107.8
~ shed (1) n 084.7
~ -shop team (1) n 084.7
~ station (301) n 084.7
~ -station office (1) n 084.8
~ stations (4) n 084.7
~ stop (1) n 084.7
~ stopping (1) n 107.8
~ terminal (1) n 084.7
~ track (20) n 084.7
~ tracks (5) n 084.7
~ watch (2) n 004.3
~ yard (2) n 084.7

~ yards (1) n 084.7
Railroad (21) 090.8
~ Shop (1) 105.6
railroaded (3) v 084.7
railroading (1) v 095.8
railroads (24) n 084.7
rails (134) n 016.4
railway (74) n/adj 084.7
~ depot (3) n 084.7
~ station (57) n 084.7
~ stations (1) n 084.7
Railway (2) 093.6
rain (957) n/v/adj 006.6
~ barrel (11) n 019.1
~ barrels (5) n 019.1
~ bonnet (1) n 028.6
~ cap (1) n 028.6
~ caps (1) n 028.6
~ cats and dogs (2) v
  006.1
~ check (2) n 051.9
~ crow (3) n 059.3
~ crown (1) n 014.6
~ ditch (1) n 030.5
~ down (1) v 006.1
~ gutter (5) n 011.5
~ gutters (1) n 011.5
~ -out area (1) n 030.5
~ pipes (1) n 011.5
~ plays (1) n 083.1
~ porch (1) n 010.8
~ pour (1) n 006.1
~ shoes (1) n 123.8
~ shower (8) n 006.6
~ showers (1) n 006.6
~ spells (1) n 006.1
~ toad (1) n 060.4
~ trees (2) n 061.9
~ trough (1) n 011.5
~ troughs (2) n 011.5
~ (um)brella (1) n
  028.6
Rain Barrel (1) 019.1
rain[V-p] (3) v 013.6
rain[V-r] (5) v 006.1
~ down bullfrogs (1) v
  006.1
~ down cats and dogs
  (1) v 006.1
~ down frogs (1) v
  006.1
~ like the devil (1) v
  006.1
~ toad-frogs (1) v
  006.1

rain[V-t] (1) v 057.8
rainbirds (1) n 080.7
rainbow (24) n/adj 080.7
~ bass (1) n 059.9
~ frogs (1) n 060.3
~ trout (16) n 059.9
~ -trout farm (1) n
  059.9
~ trouts (1) n 059.9
Rainbow (5) 044.3
~ Avenue (1) 107.6
~ bread (1) n 045.1
~ Drive (1) 107.7
~ River (1) FL 030.7
rainbows (2) n 059.9
raincoat (13) n 027.1
rained (32) v 005.7
~ cats and dogs (1) v
  006.1
~ fish (1) v 006.1
~ on (1) v 089.7
~ pitchforks (1) v
  006.1
~ toad-frogs (1) v
  006.1
rainfall (6) n 006.1
rainfrog (70) n 060.3
rainfrogs (79) n 060.3
raining (167) v 006.8
~ buckets (1) v 006.1
~ bullfrogs (2) v 006.1
~ cats and dogs (18) v
  006.1
~ fish (1) v 006.1
~ in sheets (1) v 006.1
~ like (1) v 006.1
~ nigger babies (1) v
  006.1
~ pitchfork[N-i] and
  nigger babies (1)
  v 006.1
~ pitchforks (1) v
  006.1
~ pitchforks and nigger
  babies (1) v 006.1
~ toad-frogs (4) v
  006.1
rainproof coop (1) n
036.9
rains (32) n/v 006.6
~ cats and dogs (1) v
  006.1
~ out (1) v 006.8
rainspout (4) n 011.5
rainspouts (2) n 011.5

rainsquall (2) n 006.1
rainstorm (48) n 006.1
rainstorms (9) n 006.1
Rainsville (2) AL 087.2
rainwater (7) n 048.9
rainworm (1) n 060.5
rainworms (2) n 060.5
rainy (112) adj 005.5
~ day (56) n 005.5
~ days (7) n 005.5
~ -looking (2) adj
  005.6
~ -looking day (1) n
  005.5
~ season (2) n 006.1
~ spell (3) n 006.1
~ times (1) n 006.1
~ weather (8) n 005.5
raise (288) n/v/adj 065.4
~ a calf (1) v 033.9
~ doughnuts (1) n
  045.2
~ on (1) v 003.3
~ up (6) v 065.4
raise[V-p] (3) v 095.8
raise[V-r] (48) v 065.4
~ up (1) v 065.4
raise[V-t] (38) v 065.4
~ like (1) v 013.9
~ to (2) v 065.4
~ up in (1) v 065.4
~ up to (1) v 093.5
~ [P-0] (1) v 053.4
raised (1107) v/adj 065.4
~ at (6) v 065.4
~ bread (1) n 045.1
~ cottage (1) n 088.9
~ doughnuts (3) n
  045.2
~ for (1) v 013.8
~ from (1) v 065.4
~ gravy (2) n 048.5
~ ham gravy (1) n
  048.5
~ hearth (2) n 008.2
~ in (26) v 065.4
~ like (1) v 065.4
~ on (12) v 065.4
~ to (3) v 065.4
~ up (71) v 065.4
~ up at (1) v 065.4
~ up in (4) v 065.4
~ up on (2) v 065.4
~ up with (5) v 065.4
~ with (5) v 025.7

raiseded (1) v 065.4
raiser (3) n 080.6
raisers (2) n 033.2
raises (17) v 065.4
raiseth (1) v 003.3
raisin (30) adj 122.5
~ bar (1) n 122.5
~ bread (26) n 044.4
~ corn bread (1) n
  044.6
~ muffins (1) n 044.4
Raisin (1) TX 087.2
raising (78) n/v/adj 007.2
~ up (4) v 065.4
raisings (4) n 083.1
raisins (1) n 070.6
rake (402) n/v/adj 120.7
~ -like tool (1) n 120.6
~ -offs (1) n 080.9
~ out (1) v 080.9
~ rake (1) n 120.7
~ type (1) n 021.7
~ up (1) v 081.8
raked (15) v/adj 041.4
~ hay (1) n 014.8
~ -up hay (2) n 014.8
rakes (43) n 120.7
Rakestraw hog (1) n
035.5
raking (4) v 014.8
~ up (1) v 022.2
Raleigh (34) FL MS NC
TN 087.5
~ coupons (1) n 070.8
~ Creek (1) AL 030.7
~ Mall (1) 105.3
~ Springs (1) TN 087.2
~ Springs Mall (1)
  105.8
ralings (2) n 016.4
rallies (3) n 130.2
rally (2) n 080.7
Ralph (10) 080.3
~ Bunche School (1)
  081.8
ram (615) n/v 034.9
~ him (1) v 081.3
~ -jammed (1) adj
  088.7
ramble (2) v 070.6
~ around (1) v 075.9
rambunctious (13) adj
074.9
Ramer (2) AL 087.1
ramess (1) n 035.1

ramming rod (1) n 084.8
ramp (132) n 055.7
rampant (1) adj 065.8
Rampart (7) 065.8
~ Street (1) 107.6
ramps (22) n 055.7
ramrod (3) n 022.4
rams (14) n 034.9
ramshackle (3) adj 096.7
ramshackly (1) adj 099.8
ran (1070) v 102.3
~ across (34) v 032.6
~ (a)cross (2) v 032.6
~ afoul of (1) v 032.6
~ against (3) v 102.3
~ around (1) v 124.6
~ away (13) v 083.4
~ back (1) v 102.3
~ by (1) v 102.3
~ down (1) v 102.3
~ down on (1) v 032.6
~ him off (2) v 082.1
~ in (2) v 102.3
~ into (249) v 032.6
~ (in)to (1) v 032.6
~ like (1) v 092.3
~ off (12) v 102.3
~ off with (1) v 100.2
~ onto (3) v 032.6
~ out (3) v 102.3
~ out of (3) v 102.3
~ out on him (2) v 082.1
~ over (3) v 102.3
~ to (2) v 032.6
~ up (3) v 102.3
~ up on (12) v 032.6
~ upon (3) v 032.6
~ with (2) v 052.5
rance (10) n/adj F 046.9
ranch (55) n/adj 090.7
~ country (1) n 082.7
~ fence (2) n 016.4
~ hand (2) n 069.9
~ hands (1) n 080.6
~ house (4) n 118.8
~ houses (1) n 118.9
~ road (2) n 031.7
~ style (1) n 118.9
~ -style (5) adj 118.9
~ -style house (4) n 118.9
~ -style masonry home (1) n 007A.6
~ type (1) n 118.8

~ -type (1) adj 118.6
~ -type house (2) n 098.6
~ wagons (1) n 109.5
Ranch (13) TX 087.3
rancher (1) n 069.9
ranchers (1) n 069.8
ranches (1) n 053.4
ranching part (1) n 053.4
ranchland (3) n 029.9
Rancho Viejo (2) TX 087.1
rancid (575) adj 047.5
ranc(id) (11) adj 047.5
ran(cid) (1) adj 046.9
rancids (1) v 047.5
rancy (1) v 046.9
Randolph (14) AL GA TN 087.1
~ County (4) AL GA 087.3
~ Road (1) 107.7
randy (2) adj 080.6
rang (22) v 095.8
range (132) n/v/adj 015.7
~ cattle (4) n 036.5
~ child (1) n 065.7
~ cows (1) n 033.6
~ hog (1) n 035.5
~ hogs (3) n 035.9
~ law (1) n 016.4
~ rider (1) n 088.9
~ stove (1) n 070.9
Range (3) 087.4
ranged (1) v 098.6
ranger (1) n 033.5
ranges (7) n 118.4
ranging (1) v 085.2
rangy (1) adj 073.3
rank (255) n/v/adj 047.5
~ stranger (2) n 066.7
~ up (1) v 019.8
ranked (3) v 080.6
ranker (2) adj 047.5
rankid (1) adj 047.5
Rankin (13) TN 087.1
~ County (6) MS 087.3
ranking (9) n/v 129.7
~ on (1) v 129.7
rankish (1) adj 047.5
ranks (2) n 014.8
ranky (7) adj 047.5
ranned (1) v 102.3
rap (5) n/v/adj 096.7
~ partner (1) n 129.6

rape (19) n/v/adj 055A.5
~ sallet (1) n 055A.5
raped (2) v 064.9
Raphael Semmes Home (1) 106.4
rapid (11) n/adj 031.5
~ falls (1) n 031.5
~ transit (5) n 109.9
Rapides (9) LA 087.3
(Ra)pides (2) 087.2
rapidly (2) adv 088.6
rapids (10) n 031.5
rapier (1) n 104.3
rapping (1) n 065.5
raquette (1) n F 070.9
rare (5) adj 095.2
raree (1) n 082.5
rarely (3) adv 065.8
raring (21) adj 070.8
rascal (48) n 073.5
rascals (12) n 069.7
rash (4) n/adj 075.1
rasher (2) n 046.5
rashers (1) n 046.5
rasp (6) n/adj 023.4
~ file (1) n 075.7
raspberries (492) n 062.5
raspberry (240) n/adj 062.5
~ colored folks (1) n 069.3
~ Danish (1) n 122.2
~ Jell-O (1) n 062.5
~ lemon puff (1) n 122.6
~ pancakes (1) n 062.5
~ pie (1) n 062.5
~ puff (1) n 122.6
raspber(ry) (5) n/adj 062.5
~ bushes (1) n 062.5
rasp(berry) (1) n 062.5
raspberry[N-i] (3) n 062.5
raspy (4) adj 076.4
Rastafar(ian) (1) 088.7
Rastus (3) 021.7
~ Row (1) 090.9
rat (132) n/v/adj 059.7
~ cheese (4) n 080.7
~ country (1) n 080.6
~ den (1) n 113.8
~ dog (2) n 033.3
~ fink (2) n 101.3
~ on (1) v 101.3

~ out (1) v 022.2
~ pack (1) n 123.7
~ red (1) n 081.8
~ -roof crib (1) n 014.3
~ shot (1) n 022.4
~ snake (15) n 080.8
~ snakes (13) n 092.9
~ squirrel (1) n 059.6
~ terrier (11) n 033.3
~ ter(rier) (1) n 033.3
~ terriers (1) n 033.3
~ trap (1) n 113.8
rat[N-i] (2) n 059.5
ratbane (1) n 062.2
ratchet (3) n/adj 095.9
~ stock (1) n 021.6
rate (11) n/adj 094.5
~ clerk (1) n 065.8
rated (55) adj 114.9
~ -X theater (1) n 114.9
rates (1) n 051.5
rather (1196) adv 090.5
rath(er) (1) adv 090.5
Rather (1) 090.4
rathole (2) n 113.8
ration (2) n/adj 088.9
~ stamps (1) n 088.9
rations (7) n 048.4
Raton (1) 070.6
ratproofed (1) adj 014.3
rats (85) n 059.5
Rats (1) 069.9
rattail (1) n 033.3
rattan (6) n/adj 088.8
~ dog (1) n 033.3
~ vines (1) n 080.6
rattle (16) n/v 101.5
rattlehead (1) n 033.3
rattler (35) n 101.5
rattlers (25) n 088.8
rattles (2) n 101.5
rattlesnake (94) n/adj 084.8
~ -bit (1) v 033.4
~ color (1) n 056.9
~ meat (1) n 088.9
~ pilot (9) n 080.8
~ pilots (3) n 070.9
~ roundup (1) n 089.9
rattle(snake) (1) n 088.9
Rattlesnake (98) FL 056.9
~ melon (12) n 056.9
~ melons (1) n 056.9
~ Rodeos (1) 080.7

~ stripe (1) n 056.9
~ watermelon (3) n 056.9
~ watermelons (1) n 056.9
Rattle(snake) (1) 056.9
Rattlesnake[N-i] (1) 056.9
rattlesnakes (83) n 080.6
Rattlesnakes (11) 056.9
rattletrap (3) n/adj 088.7
~ Ford (1) n 023.6
~ thing (1) n 080.7
rattletraps (2) n 080.9
rattling (4) v 057.4
~ on (1) v 088.8
raunch (1) v 080.8
raunchy (4) adj 007.4
~ -looking (1) adj 125.2
rave (1) v 066.8
raveling (1) v 080.6
raven (1) n 059.2
Ravenwood (1) MO 087.5
ravine (271) n 030.4
~ -like (1) adj 030.4
Ravine Cheval (1) LA 030.7
ravines (16) n 030.4
raw (23) adj 007.4
~ eggs (1) n 046.1
~ ham (1) n 121.3
~ kraut (1) n 055A.2
~ land (3) n 108.7
~ milk (3) n 048.2
~ sugar (1) n 051.4
rawbony (1) adj 073.3
rawhead and bloodybones (1) n 090.2
rawhide (6) n/adj 051.4
~ chairs (1) n 008.9
~ fight (1) n 104.7
~ whip (2) n 019.4
rawhiding (1) v 115.9
ray (5) n/adj 098.8
Ray (6) 087.7
~ City (3) GA 087.7
~ Creek (1) MS 087.3
Rayburn (2) 107.7
~ Drive (1) 107.7
~ Lake (1) TX 030.7
Raymond (7) LA MS 096.7
Raymondville (4) TX 087.7

Rayne (2) LA 087.5
Rayo(vac) (1) 088.8
rays (2) n 059.9
Rayville (2) LA 087.7
raza (3) n S 080.7
razing (1) v 129.8
razor (347) n/adj 065.8
~ belt (5) n 022.3
~ blades (1) n 023.4
~ clam (1) n 090.8
~ cut (1) n 122.8
~ fish (1) n 059.9
~ hone (25) n 022.3
~ hones (1) n 022.3
~ rock (12) n 023.4
~ rocks (1) n 022.3
~ soup (3) n 065.5
~ stone (4) n 023.4
~ strap (185) n 022.3
~ straps (3) n 022.3
~ strop (85) n 022.3
~ strops (2) n 022.3
raz(or) strap (1) n 022.3
Razor (2) TX 087.3
razorback (95) n/adj 035.9
~ boar (1) n 035.9
~ buffalo (1) n 059.9
~ hog (9) n 035.9
~ hogs (8) n 035.9
~ pig (1) n 035.9
~ rooter (1) n 035.9
Razorback (5) 035.9
razorbacks (51) n 035.9
Razorbacks (9) 035.9
razors (4) n 022.3
razzing (1) v 082.5
RC (3) 121.8
RCA (1) 069.8
RCs (1) 126.5
re (4) prefix 080.7
~ -rectify (1) v 080.7
~ -rinse (1) v 018.2
~ -served (1) v 050.1
~ -snake (1) v 021.5
REA (2) 065.9
reach (50) v 049.4
~ around (1) v 039.6
~ for (4) v 049.4
~ over (2) v 049.4
reach[V-t] (1) v 098.6
reached (3) v 028.9
~ across (1) v 028.9
reaches (2) v 028.9
~ across (1) v 028.9

reaching (2) v 080.7
~ over (1) v 024.9
read (83) v 057.6
read[V-r] (1) v 098.7
reader (67) n 083.7
Reader (2) 099.6
readers (3) n 083.7
Readers (1) 082.6
readily (1) adv 091.7
reading (27) n/v/adj 057.4
~ about (1) v 012.9
~ chair (1) n 008.8
~ ladies (1) n 084.6
~ room (6) n 012.1
~ word (1) n 075.7
reads (3) v 025.7
ready (336) adj 070.2
~ -cooked ham (1) n 121.3
~ for the baby (1) adj 065.1
~ -made (1) adj 045.1
~ -made bread (2) n 045.1
~ -made clothes (1) n 080.6
~ -made coffee (1) n 048.8
~ -made dress (1) n 084.8
~ -made hat (1) n 045.1
~ -made suits (1) n 065.8
~ -mades (1) n 027.7
~ roll (1) n 117.7
~ -roll cigarette (1) n 057.3
~ -roll cigarettes (1) n 057.3
~ rolls (2) n 117.7
~ slice (1) n 046.7
~ Teddy (1) n 124.6
~ -to-wear (1) adj 088.9
read(y) (6) adj 101.2
real (1750) adj/adv 091.7
~ estate (3) n 065.9
~ -estate man (1) n 053.4
reality (1) n 053.8
realize (3) v 013.1
realized (1) v 058.6
realizing (1) v 032.3

realliest (1) adv 100.4
really (1417) adv 091.6
real(ly) (1) adv 091.6
realm (1) n 114.5
reap (6) adj 041.6
~ hook (5) n 041.6
~ hooks (1) n 088.8
reaper (4) n 021.9
reapers (1) n 042.2
reaping (1) v 081.8
rear (29) v/adj 072.8
~ back in (1) v 075.7
~ down (1) v 093.7
~ end (7) n 072.8
~ porch (3) n 010.8
~ up (3) v 065.9
~ wheels (1) n 070.8
reared (250) v 065.4
~ at (1) v 065.4
~ back (3) v 065.9
~ on (2) v 025.6
~ up (7) v 065.4
rearing (5) v 065.4
rearranges (1) v 010.4
rearranging (1) v 010.4
reason (11) n 104.1
reasonable (3) adj 073.2
reasoning powers (1) n 053.4
reasons (2) n 052.7
Reb time (1) n 074.1
rebate (1) n 095.7
rebel (1) n 092.1
Rebel (1) 034.2
rebelled against (1) v 005.8
rebellion (2) n 085.8
Rebellion (10) 085.8
rebellious (1) adj 074.8
Rebels (6) 085.8
reboil (1) v 046.1
reboiled (2) v 050.1
rebound (1) v 080.6
rebreak (2) n 050.8
rebuild (1) v 065.8
rebuilt (1) v 013.6
rec room (1) n 118.2
Rec (1) 106.5
recalcitrant (1) adj 074.8
recall (179) v 100.3
~ of (1) v 025.8
(re)call (1) v 100.4
recalling (1) v 100.3
recaned (1) v 088.7
recede (1) v 007.3

receding (3) v 007.3
receipt (3) n 095.7
receive (1) v 024.8
received (2) v 082.2
receiving (3) adj 007.8
    ~ room (2) n 007.8
    ~ vault (1) n 117.6
recent (1) adj 090.7
recently (9) adv 102.8
reception   (92)   n/adj
    082.5
    ~ are(a) (1) n 007.8
    ~ hall (3) n 007A.3
    ~ party (1) n 130.7
    ~ room (6) n 007.8
(re)ception (2) n 082.5
receptionist (7) n 068.8
receptions (6) n 130.7
recess (3) n/v 083.2
recessed (1) v 083.2
recipe (2) n 091.8
recipes (1) n 091.7
recipients (1) n 069.7
recital (1) n 013.5
recitation (5) adj 083.8
    ~ bench (4) n 083.8
    ~ benches (1) n 096.8
reckless (16) adj 074.6
reckon (696) v 094.1
reck(on) (3) v 094.1
reclaim (1) v 030.1
reclaimed (2) adj 041.4
    ~ clothing (1) n 123.5
recline (1) v 096.7
(re)cline back (1) v 008.9
recliner (15) n 008.8
recliners (1) n 008.8
reclining (7) adj 008.8
    ~ chair (5) n 008.8
    ~ chairs (2) n 008.8
(re)clining chair (1) n
    008.8
recluse (4) n/adj 069.9
    ~ spider (1) n 096.9
recognition (2) n 070.6
recognize (14) v 012.4
recognized (2) v 077.9
recognizing (1) v 070.6
recoil (1) n 102.7
recollect (69) v 100.3
recollection (4) n 100.3
recollections (1) n 081.8
recompense (1) n 095.7
reconciled (1) v 097.9
reconstructed (1) v 053.4

Reconstruction days (1) n
    080.7
recook (1) v 050.1
recooked (9) v/adj 050.1
record (13) n/v/adj 012.2
    ~ parties (1) n 130.7
Record (1) 106.4
recorder (1) n 012.2
recording machine (1) n
    092.1
records (6) n 130.8
recourt (1) v 081.4
recover (3) v 078.5
recovered (2) v 012.5
    ~ from (1) v 012.5
recovering (1) v 072.9
Recovery Room (1) 097.8
recreate (1) v 088.7
recreation   (20)   n/adj
    070.6
    ~ area (1) n 085.1
    ~ areas (1) n 107.2
    ~ center (1) n 106.4
    ~ cent(er) (1) n 126.2
    ~ parks (1) n 085.1
    ~ room (14) n 118.2
rec(reation) area (1) n
    108.7
recreational facilities (1)
    n 106.4
recropping (1) v 041.5
rectangle fence (1) n
    016.4
rectangular (2) adj 090.4
rectify (1) v 080.7
Rector (2) AR 087.2
Rectum of the Mid South
    (1) 131.1
recuperate (1) v 072.9
recuperating (1) v 066.8
recut (7) n/v 041.5
recutting (1) n 041.5
recycled (2) adj 123.5
red (2559) adj 045.7
    ~ alder tags (1) n 061.4
    ~ -and-white car (1) n
      111.6
    ~ ant (2) n 060A.8
    ~ ants (4) n 060A.5
    ~ ash (1) n 008.7
    ~ bait (1) n 061.8
    ~ baits (2) n 060.5
    ~ bamboos (1) n 062.4
    ~ bass (6) n 059.9
    ~ bay trees (1) n 061.8

    ~ bean (7) n 055A.4
    ~ bean[N-i] (2) n
      055A.3
    ~ beans (29) n 055A.3
    ~ bees (1) n 060A.7
    ~ -bellied (1) adj 059.3
    ~ Bermuda (1) n 055.6
    ~ blood pudding (1) n
      047.3
    ~ boudin (9) n 047.3
    ~ bream (1) n 059.9
    ~ -breasted sapsuckers
      (1) n 059.3
    ~ -breasted woodpecker
      (1) n 059.3
    ~ bug (209) n 060A.9
    ~ bugs (315) n 060A.9
    ~ bush (1) n 062.2
    ~ cane (4) n 051.9
    ~ car (12) n 111.6
    ~ cat (1) n 059.9
    ~ cedar (3) n 008.6
    ~ cent (1) n 026.6
    ~ cherry (2) n 061.4
    ~ chiggers (1) n 060A.9
    ~ chipmunk (1) n 059.8
    ~ clay (83) n 029.8
    ~ clay dirt (2) n 029.8
    ~ clay gravel (1) n
      031.6
    ~ -clay hill (1) n 030.8
    ~ -clay hills (3) n 029.8
    ~ clay land (3) n 029.8
    ~ clay-like (1) adj
      029.8
    ~ clay mud (1) n 029.8
    ~ -clay road (1) n
      031.7
    ~ corn (1) n 056.2
    ~ crawfish (1) n 060.8
    ~ devil (3) n 090.1
    ~ devils (4) n 114.2
    ~ dirt (6) n 029.9
    ~ dogwood (1) n 061.9
    ~ earthworm (3) n
      060.5
    ~ earthworms (1) n
      060.5
    ~ elm (1) n 061.8
    ~ elm tree (1) n 061.9
    ~ -eye (10) n/adj 050.8
    ~ -eye gravy (20) n
      048.5
    ~ -eye potato (1) n
      055.4

    ~ -eyed gravy (1) n
      046.5
    ~ -eyed turtles (1) n
      060.6
    ~ eyes (1) n 090.1
    ~ field (1) n 029.8
    ~ -fin minnow (1) n
      061.2
    ~ fire car (1) n 111.6
    ~ fox (9) n 059.7
    ~ fox squirrel (12) n
      059.7
    ~ fox squirrels (4) n
      059.7
    ~ Georgia clay (1) n
      029.8
    ~ girl (1) n 069.4
    ~ goldfish (1) n 061.2
    ~ gravel (2) n 031.6
    ~ gravy (5) n 048.5
    ~ gum (7) n 061.8
    ~ gum tree (1) n 024.6
    ~ gumbo (1) n 029.9
    ~ hard clay (1) n 029.8
    ~ hard-clay land (1) n
      029.8
    ~ haw (8) n 061.9
    ~ haw bush (1) n 062.2
    ~ haw tree (4) n 062.2
    ~ haws (9) n 061.8
    ~ hill (2) n 029.8
    ~ -hill ground (1) n
      029.8
    ~ -hill people (1) n
      069.9
    ~ hills (3) n 029.8
    ~ hornet (1) n 060A.5
    ~ horse trees (1) n
      061.8
    ~ -hot (2) n 121.6
    ~ -hot pepper (1) n
      051.7
    ~ -hot sausage (1) n
      121.6
    ~ -hots (4) n 121.6
    ~ hound (2) n 033.1
    ~ Irish potato (3) n
      055.4
    ~ Irish potatoes (1) n
      055.4
    ~ jacket wasp (1) n
      060A.6
    ~ jackets (1) n 114.2
    ~ kind (1) n 059.7
    ~ lady (1) n 113.3

~ land (25) n 029.8
~ laurel (1) n 062.8
~ -letter ground (1) n 029.8
~ level (1) n 029.8
~ light (13) n 130.2
~ -light district (19) n 113.4
~ -light districts (1) n 113.4
~ light green light (3) n 130.1
~ -light house (3) n 113.4
~ -light houses (1) n 113.4
~ lightning (1) n 050.8
~ lights (1) n 113.3
~ lobster (1) n 060.9
~ -looking (2) adj 095.8
~ man (1) n 090.1
~ maple (5) n 061.8
~ maple tree (1) n 061.8
~ maples (1) n 061.9
~ measles (1) n 079.7
~ meat (11) n 056.9
~ -meat (1) adj 056.9
~ -meat watermelons (2) n 056.9
~ -meated (11) adj 056.9
~ -meated melon (1) n 056.9
~ -meated melons (1) n 056.9
~ -meated watermelon (1) n 056.9
~ melon (1) n 056.9
~ mud (3) n 029.8
~ mulatto (1) n 029.8
~ nation (1) n 005.9
~ navy beans (1) n 055A.4
~ -neck (217) n 069.9
~ -neck cracker (2) n 069.4
~ -neck hippie (1) n 069.7
~ -neck rock (1) n 090.8
~ -neck turtle (1) n 060.6

~ -neck white folk (1) n 069.4
~ -neckism (1) n 069.9
~ -necks (92) n 069.9
~ -necky (1) adj 069.7
~ nigger (1) n 069.5
~ oak (129) n 061.8
~ -oak bark (4) n 061.4
~ -oak ooze (1) n 093.5
~ -oak poultice (1) n 061.4
~ -oak roots (1) n 061.4
~ -oak timber (2) n 061.8
~ oak tree (3) n 061.8
~ oak trees (6) n 061.8
~ oak wood (1) n 008.5
~ oaks (11) n 061.9
~ okra (2) n 055.8
~ onion (13) n 055.6
~ onions (10) n 055.6
~ owl (1) n 059.1
~ part (1) n 045.6
~ pea (1) n 080.8
~ peaches (2) n 054.3
~ peanut (1) n 054.7
~ pecker (1) n 059.3
~ peckers (1) n 069.4
~ peckerwood (2) n 079.4
~ people (1) n 005.8
~ pepper (23) n 051.7
~ -pepper tea (1) n 061.4
~ peppers (4) n 055.7
~ perch (6) n 059.9
~ pill (1) n 114.2
~ pinder (1) n 054.7
~ -pod pepper (1) n 051.7
~ (pome)granates (1) n 055.1
~ Porto Rico potatoes (1) n 055.5
~ potato (14) n 055.5
~ potatoes (30) n 055.4
~ (po)tatoes (1) n 055.4
~ race (1) n 069.3
~ radish (2) n 055.2
~ raspberries (6) n 062.5
~ raspberry (2) n 062.5

~ ribbon cane (1) n 088.9
~ rice (6) n 069.5
~ rock (1) n 031.6
~ roses (1) n 130.2
~ rover (45) n 130.2
~ russets (1) n 055.4
~ sand (4) n 029.8
~ sassafras (1) n 061.4
~ sausage (1) n 047.8
~ seed (1) n 056.7
~ shank (1) n 061.4
~ shrimp (1) n 060.9
~ -skinned (2) adj 055.4
~ snapper (54) n 059.9
~ snappers (13) n 059.9
~ soil (19) n 029.8
~ -soil road (1) n 031.6
~ Spanish (2) n 055.5
~ spider (1) n 061.4
~ squirrel (116) n 059.7
~ squirrels (45) n 059.7
~ sticks (1) n 126.4
~ -striped (1) adj 070.7
~ suckers (1) n 059.9
~ sugar (1) n 051.5
~ sumac (3) n 062.2
~ sunrise (1) n 003.2
~ sweet potato (2) n 055.5
~ sycamore (1) n 061.7
~ -tailed hawk (1) n 059.5
~ tea (1) n 061.4
~ tea weeds (1) n 015.9
~ -time talk (1) n 080.6
~ tomato (1) n 060A.8
~ tomatoes (1) n 055.3
~ (to)matoes (1) n 055.3
~ topsoil (1) n 029.8
~ vein (1) n 071.6
~ war-horse (1) n 080.8
~ wasp (81) n 060A.6
~ wasp[N-i] (5) n 060A.6
~ waspes (5) n 060A.6
~ wasps (1) n 060A.6
~ watermelons (1) n 056.9
~ whiskey (3) n 050.8
~ wiggler (8) n 060.5
~ wiggler worms (1) n 060.5

~ wigglers (32) n 060.5
~ wine (3) n 114.7
~ wines (2) n 114.7
~ wolf (1) n 088.9
~ woodpecker (1) n 059.3
~ worm (80) n 060.5
~ worms (193) n 060.5
~ yam (1) n 055.5
~ yams (3) n 055.5
Red (160) 127.5
~ Acres (1) 106.2
~ Angus (2) 033.6
~ Bank (3) FL TN 075.6
~ Barn (1) 014.2
~ Bay (4) AL 087.3
~ Bayou (1) TX 030.7
~ Bliss (5) 055.4
~ Bliss potatoes (1) n 055.4
~ Bluff Lake (1) TX 030.7
~ Bone (6) 069.9
~ Bone Georgians (1) 069.7
~ Bones (5) 069.7
~ Chute (1) LA 030.7
~ Cob corn (2) n 056.2
~ Creek (3) MS TN 030.7
~ Creek community (1) n 105.1
~ Dagger (2) 114.7
~ Devil lye (1) n 088.7
~ Devon (1) 088.8
~ Duroc (1) 035.5
~ Fox (1) 027.4
~ Goose beans (1) n 055A.4
~ Jersey (1) 035.5
~ Label (1) 114.7
~ Level (1) AL 087.4
~ Lick Baptist Church (1) 089.1
~ Man (3) 126.4
~ Men (4) 126.8
~ Mountain (1) AL 031.1
~ -Neck Club (1) 069.7
~ Oak (1) GA 087.2
~ Oak Creek (2) GA TX 030.7
~ Oaks (1) 106.2
~ Pass (1) LA 030.7

~ Quarters (1) 105.4
~ Ripper (2) 055A.3
~ River (49) AL AR LA MS TN TX 030.7
~ River Bottom (2) LA 029.4
~ River Bottomland (1) 029.4
~ River City (1) TX 087.2
~ River Parish (2) LA 087.1
~ River Valley (1) AR 087.5
~ Road (1) 107.7
~ Rocks (1) 080.7
~ Russians (1) 127.5
~ Sand Creek (1) MS 030.7
~ Seal (1) 039.8
~ Shoot (1) TX 087.1
~ Triumph (3) 055.4
(Red) Devil lye (1) n 090.1
Redan Road (1) 087.3
redback (3) n/adj 083.7
~ primer (1) n 083.7
~ speller (1) n 080.7
redbellies (4) n 059.9
redbelly (8) n/adj 130.5
~ perch (4) n 059.9
redberries (7) n 062.5
redberry (6) n/adj 061.8
~ trees (1) n 061.8
redbird (10) n 031.6
redbirds (20) n 059.3
redbone (9) n/adj 033.3
~ coon dogs (1) n 033.1
~ dog (1) n 033.3
~ hound (2) n 033.1
redbones (1) n 033.3
redbreast (6) n/adj 059.9
~ bream (1) n 059.9
redbud (44) n/adj 029.9
~ land (3) n 029.8
~ tree (4) n 061.8
~ trees (2) n 061.8
redbuds (10) n 061.9
redd (8) v 010.4
~ up (7) v 010.4
redder (1) adj 066.1
Reddick (1) FL 087.4
redding (3) v 010.4

~ up (1) v 010.4
reddish (6) adj 059.7
~ -colored (1) adj 059.7
Reddock (1) 107.7
redds (1) v 010.4
redear sunfish (1) n 059.9
redeye (7) n 059.9
redeyes (6) n 059.9
redfin pike (1) n 059.9
redfins (1) n 061.2
redfish (80) n 059.9
Redfish (2) 030.7
~ Bay (1) LA 030.7
~ Point (1) FL 087.8
redhead (90) n/adj 059.3
~ -and-whitewing peckerwood (1) n 059.3
~ birds (1) n 059.3
~ peckerwood (14) n 059.3
~ peckerwoods (2) n 059.3
~ sapsucker (1) n 059.3
~ sapsuckers (1) n 059.3
~ woodpecker (11) n 059.3
~ woodpeckers (2) n 059.3
redheaded (118) adj 059.3
~ bird (1) n 059.3
~ peckerwood (32) n 059.3
~ peckerwoods (3) n 059.3
~ sapsucker (2) n 059.3
~ sapsuckers (1) n 059.3
~ scorpion (1) n 090.9
~ scorpions (1) n 090.9
~ turtle (1) n 060.6
~ wood hen (1) n 059.3
~ wooden peckers (1) n 059.3
~ woodpecker (46) n 059.3
~ woodpeckers (9) n 059.3
redheads (17) n 059.3
redhearts (1) n 088.8
redhorse (12) n/adj 059.9
~ suckers (1) n 059.9
redhorses (1) n 059.9
redisk (1) v 021.7

Redlands (1) 105.4
redo (2) v 102.8
Redoak (1) LA 087.5
redone (2) v 102.8
redress (1) v 100.7
redrove (1) v 011.3
reds (8) n 131.7
Reds (36) 127.5
redskin (6) n/adj 126.8
~ potatoes (1) n 055.5
redskins (4) n 069.4
Redstone Arsenal (1) 106.4
redtail (4) n/adj 059.9
~ cat squirrel (1) n 059.6
~ minnow (1) n 061.2
~ squirrels (1) n 059.7
redtop (4) n/adj 059.3
~ grass (1) n 014.6
~ hay (1) n 014.7
~ roads (1) n 031.6
reduce (6) adj 094.5
reduced (13) adj 094.5
reducers (1) n 110.8
reducing pills (1) n 114.2
reduction (4) n 094.5
redwood (30) n/adj 061.8
~ fence (8) n 016.4
~ fences (3) n 016.4
~ fencing (1) n 016.4
~ tree (2) n 061.8
Redwood (5) MS 087.2
~ Avenue (1) 105A.7
~ Creek (2) LA MS 030.7
reed (10) adj 029.6
~ brake (2) n 029.6
~ brakes (5) n 029.6
~ chair (1) n 008.8
~ organ (1) n 088.3
~ snake (1) n 081.8
Reed (9) 030.7
~ Creek (2) AR GA 030.7
~ Lake (3) TX 030.7
~ Road (1) 107.7
reeds (2) n 029.7
Reedville (1) AR 087.8
Reedy Creek (4) GA MS TN 030.7
reef (2) n/adj 031.2
~ fish (1) n 059.9
reefer (18) n/adj 119.7
~ parties (1) n 130.7

Reefer Man (1) 114.1
reefers (8) n 114.1
reefs (1) n 092.1
reel (21) n/v/adj 091.7
~ mower (3) n 120.1
~ mowers (1) n 120.1
~ type (2) n 120.1
~ -type lawn mowers (1) n 120.1
~ -type mowers (1) n 120.1
Reelfoot (5) 030.7
~ Creek (1) TN 030.7
~ Ditch (1) TN 030.7
~ Lake (2) TN 030.7
~ Lake-type flatboat (1) n 024.6
reels (2) n 083.1
reentered (1) v 083.3
refer (3) v 024.7
~ back (1) v 024.7
~ to (2) v 013.1
reference (4) n 115.3
referred to (2) v 042.1
referring (2) v 025.8
~ about (1) v 025.8
refers to (1) v 052.5
refined (5) adj 042.1
~ sugar (1) n 051.3
refineries (1) n 066.8
refinery (2) n 024.1
refining (1) n 051.2
reflectors (4) n 107.3
Reform (4) AL MS 087.4
reformed (1) adj 070.7
Reformed (2) 126.7
~ Jews (1) 126.7
refreeze (1) v 007.7
refresher course (1) n 088.7
refreshing (1) adj 007.4
refreshments (2) n 048.6
refried beans (1) n 050.1
refrigeration (2) n 040.7
refrigerator (24) n/adj 015.5
~ cars (1) n 023.6
~ corn (1) n 056.2
~ melon (4) n 056.9
~ melons (1) n 056.9
(re)frigerator (11) n/adj 077.8
~ car (1) n 081.8
~ melons (1) n 056.9
refrigerators (4) n 065.8

(re)frigerators (1) n 070.8

Refuge (1) 087.7

refugee (1) n 066.7

refugees (1) n 077.8

Refugio (5) TX 087.6

refuse (9) n/v/adj 082.1
~ container (1) n 117.3
~ him (1) v 082.1

refuse[V-r] (9) v 082.1
~ him (1) v 082.1
~ to marry him (2) v 082.1

refused (207) v 082.1
~ him (68) v 082.1
~ his proposal (2) v 082.1
~ to accept (1) v 082.1
~ to accept it (1) v 082.1
~ to marry (2) v 082.1
~ to marry him (2) v 082.1

refuses (5) v 082.1

Regal (3) NC 087.7
~ blue marble (1) n 080.7

regardless of (1) prep 088.2

Regency (6) 108.5
~ Hyatt House (1) 108.5
~ Square (1) 116.1

Regen(cy) Hotel (1) 084.3

Regenwurm (1) n G 060.5

region (1) n 029.7

regional (2) adj 131.3
~ dialects (1) n 131.3
~ stores (1) n 105.3

Regional (1) 106.5

regions (1) n 031.1

registered (5) v/adj 092.8
~ nurse (3) n 084.6

registers (2) n 118.6

regret (2) n 032.8

regrowth (2) n 041.5

regular (135) adj/adv 073.6
~ boyfriend (1) n 081.5
~ coffee (1) n 032.4
~ date (1) n 081.5
~ girl (1) n 081.6
~ -old (7) adj 057.3

regularly (3) adv 012.7

regulations (1) n 070.6

Regulators (1) 080.8

regurgitate (62) v 080.2

(re)gurgitate (5) v 080.2

regurgitated (7) v 080.2

regurgitating (2) v 080.3

reharvest (1) v 041.5

rehash (1) v 088.7

rehashed (1) v 050.1

reheat (6) v 050.1

reheat[V-t] (1) v 050.1

reheated (79) v/adj 050.1
~ food (1) n 050.1

reheating (1) v 050.1

Rehobeth (1) TX 087.3

Reid (1) MS 087.6

Reidsville (3) GA 087.2

rein (143) n/v 039.1

rein[N-i] (6) n 039.2

reindeers (2) n 016.7

reinforced sacks (1) n 019.6

Reinhard (1) GA 087.2

reins (983) n 039.2

reject (3) v 082.1
~ him (2) v 082.1

rejected (67) v 082.1
~ him (50) v 082.1

rejecting (2) v 082.1
~ him (1) v 082.1

rejects (5) v 082.1
~ him (4) v 082.1

rejoicing (2) v 082.5
~ in (1) v 039.8

relapse (3) n 076.1

relapsed (1) v 076.3

relate (1) v 066.6

related (184) v/adj 066.6

relation (263) n 066.6

(re)lation (1) n 066.6

relation[N-i] (3) n 066.6

relations (45) n 066.5

(re)lations (1) n 066.5

relationship (3) n 066.5

relative (43) n 066.5

relative[N-i] (5) n 066.5

relatives (552) n 066.5

rela(tives) (1) n 066.5

relatives' (1) adj 066.5

relax (7) v 096.7

relaxation house (1) n 012.1

relaxing (1) v 053.3

relay (5) n/adj 130.2
~ games (1) n 130.2

~ races (2) n 130.2

relays (5) n 130.2

releases (1) v 083.2

relevant (1) adj 066.8

Reliance (1) TN 087.2

relics (9) n 010.2

relief (5) n/adj 094.8
~ office (1) n 012.1

relies on (1) v 090.4

relieved (1) v 100.2

religion (19) n 088.7

(re)ligion (3) n 089.2

religion[N-i] (1) n 016.7

religious (9) adj 130.8
~ commune (1) n 096.8
~ exiles (1) n 070.7
~ music (1) n 130.8
~ records (1) n 130.8
~ world (1) n 089.8

relish (8) n 050.5

remainders (1) n 050.1

remarkable (3) adj/adv 074.1

remarks (3) n 043.8

remarried (9) v 082.2

remarry (2) v 082.2

Rembert (1) AL 087.3

remedies (2) n 075.6

remedy (2) n 084.9

remelt (1) v 097.8

remember (2067) v 100.3
~ of (5) v 032.9
~ to (1) v 100.3

rememb(er) (2) v 100.4

remem(ber) (3) v 100.4

(re)member (218) v/adj 100.4
~ croup (1) n 079.7

(re)memb(er) (1) v 100.4

(re)mem(ber) (1) v 100.3

remember[V-r] (1) v 100.3

remembered (23) v 100.3

remembering (2) v 070.4

remembers (6) v 075.6

(re)members (1) v 100.3

remembrance (2) n 075.7

remind (1) v 090.4

reminds (1) v 065.3

Remington (2) 113.1

remits (1) n 131.2

remitting fever (1) n 080.9

Remlap (1) AL 086.4

remnant (12) n 026.2

remnants (2) n 037.2

remodeled (2) v 081.3

remodify (1) v 012.2

remote-control lawn mowers (1) n 120.2

remove (2) v 104.3

removed (2) v 088.7

removing (1) v 036.1

remuda (2) n 015.7

Remus's (1) 068.2

Renaissance (1) 115.9

renal colic (1) n 080.1

render (2) v 065.8

ren(der) up (1) v 097.8

rendered (2) v/adj 088.7
~ hog fat (1) n 088.7
~ out (1) v 093.5

renderings (1) n 081.8

renegade (1) n 069.9

reneged (2) v 082.1

(re)neged on his class (2) v 083.4

renew (2) v 040.6

renewal (4) n/adj 108.7

renewed (1) v 057.8

rennet (1) n 047.7

Reno (2) NV 087.7

Renoir Street (1) 001.4

renovated (2) adj 108.7
~ bus (1) n 111.8

Rensselaer (1) IN 087.4

rent (16) n/v/adj 091.8
~ from (1) v 053.5
~ house (2) n 080.7
~ houses (1) n 080.6
~ man (2) n 119.5
~ -office man (1) n 119.5

rental (2) adj 108.6
~ apartments (1) n 108.6
~ places (1) n 075.6

rented (4) v 053.4
~ out (1) v 065.8

renter tenant (1) n 080.9

renter's house (1) n 088.8

renters (3) n 080.6

renting (7) v 057.4

rents (3) v 052.5
~ from (1) v 052.5

Renwick (1) 087.1

Reo lamps (1) n 024.3

reopen (5) v 083.3

reopens (1) v 083.3

repair (4) v/adj 023.6

repairing (1) v 067.7
repairman (7) n 119.5
repairmen (1) n 119.5
repale (1) v 098.8
repeat (54) v 050.1
repeating (1) v 001A.5
repetitiously (1) adv 001A.5
replace (1) v 065.9
reply (26) n/v 100.6
report (4) n/v 066.8
~ to (1) v 039.8
reported (1) v 058.1
reporter (1) n 041.3
reptile (1) n 123.8
Repton (1) AL 087.9
republic (1) n 129.2
Republic of Texas (3) 088.7
Republican (48) 129.2
~ and Democrat War (1) 085.8
~ Party (1) 129.2
Republic(an) (2) 129.2
Republicans (42) 129.2
(Re)publicans (1) 085.8
republics (1) n 129.2
reputation (3) n 092.1
repute (26) n 113.4
requiem (1) n 079.2
Requiem (1) 066.8
requirement (1) n 092.1
rerag (1) v 028.1
reroof (2) v 011.4
reroofed (2) v 011.4
reroute (1) v 024.7
rerun (3) n/v 050.1
resaca (5) n S 030.6
Resaca (5) 030.7
~ De Los Cuates (1) TX 030.7
~ del Rancho Viejo (1) TX 030.7
~ la Palma (1) TX 030.7
~ Rivagerra (1) TX 030.7
resacas (1) n S 030.4
resaved (1) v 091.8
rescue (47) n/adj 111.5
~ squad (15) n 111.5
~ squad cars (1) n 111.5
~ squads (1) n 111.5
~ truck (10) n 111.5

~ trucks (4) n 111.5
~ unit (5) n 111.5
~ units (1) n 111.5
~ vehicle (1) n 111.5
~ wagon (3) n 091.9
research (2) n 102.8
Research (1) 084.5
reselect (1) v 070.6
resemblance (2) n 065.3
resemble (18) v 065.3
(res)emble to (1) v 065.3
resemble[V-r] (1) v 065.3
resembled (20) v 065.3
resembles (215) v 065.3
(re)sembles (1) v 065.3
resembling (2) v 065.3
resent (1) v 092.4
resentful (1) adj 058.6
reserboiled (1) v 065.9
reservation (4) n 070.7
reserved (3) adj 066.1
reservoir (15) n 030.3
Reservoir (2) 030.7
reservoirs (2) n 080.7
reshrink (1) v 027.9
residence (3) n 014.1
residences (2) n 014.1
resident (26) n/adj 119.5
~ manager (24) n 119.5
residential (7) adj 031.7
~ -like (1) adj 090.4
~ section (1) n 066.8
~ street (2) n 107.7
~ streets (1) n 107.7
residents (1) n 069.7
residue (2) n 041.5
resifted (1) v 093.5
resigned (4) v 078.6
resin (46) n/adj 065.9
~ berry (1) n 062.5
~ chawer (1) n 069.9
~ chawers (1) n 069.8
~ chewer (2) n 069.9
~ chewers (1) n 069.8
~ lighterd knots (1) n 008.6
~ pine (2) n 008.6
Resinite (1) 069.9
resolve (1) v 013.1
resort hotels (1) n 084.3
resources (2) n 053.4
respect (8) n 094.7
respect[V-p] (1) v 053.5
respectable (1) adj 101.9
respected (2) v 053.4

respond to (1) v 065.8
response (1) n 100.6
responsibilities (1) n 077.1
responsibility (1) n 012.2
responsible (3) adj 053.1
rest (326) n/v/adj 096.6
~ area (57) n 107.2
~ are(a) (2) n 107.2
~ areas (26) n 107.2
~ -broken (3) adj 048.8
~ camps (1) n 107.2
~ chair (1) n 008.8
~ halts (1) n 107.2
~ house (1) n 012.1
~ parks (1) n 107.2
~ period (1) n 107.2
~ places (1) n 107.2
~ room (94) n 126.3
~ rooms (30) n 107.2
~ spots (1) n 107.2
~ station (2) n 107.2
~ stop (23) n 107.2
~ stops (19) n 107.2
Rest (4) 089.2
restaurant (12) n 065.8
Restaurant (1) 001.4
restaurants (5) n 084.8
rested (4) v 075.6
restes (4) v 008.3
~ on (3) v 013.9
resting (8) v/adj 078.5
~ on (1) v 072.8
~ place (5) n 078.8
restless (8) adj 074.2
restoration (3) n/adj 080.6
~ bench (1) n 089.9
restricted (1) adj 114.9
result (1) n 032.8
results (1) n 091.7
resuscitate (1) v 080.2
resuscitating (1) v 111.5
retail (3) n/v 094.5
~ for (1) v 094.6
retainer wall (1) n 016.6
retaining wall (3) n 107.4
retama (6) n 061.8
retarded (3) adj 074.7
~ child (1) n 080.9
retch (6) v 080.2
~ up (1) v 098.7
retches (1) v 080.2
retching (2) v 080.2
reticule (3) n 028.2

retied (1) v 082.2
retire (14) v 096.6
retire[V-t] (1) v 057.8
retired (22) v/adj 075.4
~ from (2) v 090.4
retirement (3) n 065.8
retracted (1) v 095.9
retreads (1) n 123.5
retreat (1) n 007.8
Retreat (1) 087.2
retriever (3) n 099.5
retrievers (1) n 081.9
return (28) n/v/adj 100.6
~ address (15) n 100.8
(re)turn (7) v 049.2
(re)turned (1) v 049.2
returns (2) n/v 100.7
~ to (1) v 081.1
Reuben (1) 121.7
reunion (2) n 066.5
revelant (1) adj 065.8
reveling (1) n 083.1
revelry (2) n 082.5
Revelry (1) 119.6
revenant (1) n F 090.2
revenge (1) n 091.8
revenue (2) adj 081.9
~ men (1) n 081.9
~ people (1) n 080.6
revenuers (3) n 081.9
reverend (3) n 067.8
Reverend (2) 053.1
reverent (1) n 032.3
Reverschon Park (1) 106.7
reverse (5) n/adj 110.7
reversible (3) adj 021.6
~ plows (1) n 021.6
~ turning plow (1) n 021.6
~ vest (1) n 027.3
review (2) n/adj 077.1
~ course (1) n 077.1
revisited (1) v 053.2
revival (11) n/adj 070.6
~ meeting (1) n 080.6
revivals (2) n 080.8
revive (1) v 088.7
revoir (3) n F 002.4
revoke (1) v 053.2
revolution (8) n 085.8
Revolution (14) 085.8
~ War (1) 085.8
revolutionary (1) adj 085.8

Revolutionary (6) 085.8
~ War (5) 085.8
revolver (41) n 113.1
revolvers (3) n 113.1
revolving harrow (1) n 021.7
revorcee (1) n 066.8
reward (10) n 078.5
reward[N-i] (1) n 078.5
rewarm (2) v 050.1
rewarmed (5) v 050.1
rewash (1) v 018.1
rewater (2) v 048.9
reweatherboards (2) v 011.2
reworded (1) v 058.1
reworking (1) v 047.5
Rex (2) 131.1
~ Ball (1) 131.1
~ Motel (1) 084.3
Reynolds (2) GA 087.1
Reynosa (1) 086.5
Reyuda Wonder (1) 056.9
RFD (1) 001.1
Rhea (5) TN 087.2
~ County (2) TN 087.1
rhetoric (1) n 040.9
rheumatic (6) adj 079.6
~ fever (2) n 079.6
~ pains (2) n 079.6
rheumatics (5) n 079.6
rheumatism (588) n 079.6
rheumatis(m) (34) n 079.6
(rheuma)tism (1) n 079.6
rheumatisms (1) n 079.5
rheumatoid (5) adj 079.6
~ arthritis (4) n 079.6
rheumy (1) adj 079.6
Rhine (2) GA 087.1
rhinestones (1) n 123.1
Rhode (21) 086.6
~ Island (10) 086.6
~ Island hen (1) n 036.7
~ Island Red (7) 084.8
~ Island Reds (3) 036.9
Rhodesia (1) 087.6
rhodo-something (1) n 062.8
rhododendron (218) n/ adj 062.8
~ festival (2) n 062.8
rhododen(dron) (3) n 062.8

rhododendrons (20) n 062.8
rhubarb (8) n/adj 055A.6
~ pie (1) n 056.6
rhubarbs (1) n 055.7
rhythm (7) n 130.8
~ and blues (6) n 130.9
Rials Creek (2) MS 030.7
Riante (1) 031.1
rib (73) n/adj 046.4
~ beef (2) n 121.2
~ chops (1) n 121.3
~ eye (25) n 121.1
~ -eye steak (5) n 121.1
~ -eye steaks (1) n 121.1
~ eyes (1) n 121.1
~ meat (1) n 046.4
~ pork (1) n 121.3
~ roast (11) n 121.2
~ steak (4) n 121.1
~ steaks (2) n 121.1
Rib Creek (1) GA 087.5
rib[N-i] (1) n 024.6
Ribault (4) FL 030.7
ribbing (2) n/v 020.3
ribbon (82) n/adj 055A.3
~ cane (53) n 051.3
~ -cane molasses (1) n 051.2
~ -cane syrup (19) n 051.3
~ grass (2) n 029.7
~ snakes (1) n 081.8
Ribbons (1) 025.6
ribs (101) n 046.4
Rica (2) 087.4
Rican (20) 055.5
Ricans (31) 128.5
rice (1110) n/adj 050.7
~ bags (1) n 019.7
~ cooker (1) n 093.6
~ country (3) n 050.7
~ custard (1) n 048.5
~ dressing (2) n 080.7
~ farm (2) n 050.7
~ farming (3) n 050.7
~ farms (2) n 050.7
~ field (5) n 016.1
~ -field area (1) n 050.7
~ fields (7) n 016.1
~ girl (1) n 082.4
~ hulls (1) n 050.7
~ land (3) n 029.4

~ paddy (1) n 050.7
~ pancakes (1) n 045.3
~ patch (2) n 053.2
~ plains (1) n 050.7
~ plantations (1) n 050.7
~ plates (1) n 042.2
~ polish (3) n 080.7
~ pot (1) n 093.7
~ pudding (7) n 050.7
~ puddings (1) n 050.7
~ straw (4) n 041.7
~ throwing (1) n 050.7
Rice (5) 050.7
~ Creek (1) FL 030.7
~ University area (1) n 106.1
ricebird (1) n 084.8
ricebirds (2) n 093.8
rich (1029) n/adj 029.3
~ black dirt (2) n 029.9
~ blackland (2) n 029.8
~ bottom (1) n 029.8
~ dirt (11) n 029.3
~ ground (3) n 029.8
~ kindling (1) n 008.6
~ land (33) n 029.3
~ lighterd (5) n 008.6
~ lighterd pine (1) n 008.6
~ lighterd splinters (2) n 008.6
~ lightning (1) n 008.6
~ loam (4) n 029.3
~ -looking muck (1) n 029.8
~ man (1) n 053.1
~ -man's child (1) n 053.3
~ -man's high (1) n 080.8
~ -man's war (1) n 085.8
~ mucklands (1) n 029.8
~ mud (1) n 029.8
~ -old (3) adj 074.2
~ -pine (51) n 008.6
~ -pine knots (2) n 008.6
~ -pine splinters (1) n 008.6
~ pinewood (1) n 008.6
~ place (1) n 029.3
~ plot (1) n 029.8

~ property (1) n 029.3
~ red land (1) n 029.8
~ red sand (1) n 029.8
~ river-bottom land (1) n 029.4
~ sand (1) n 029.3
~ soil (66) n 029.8
~ soils (1) n 029.3
~ splinters (4) n 008.6
~ stuff (2) n 029.8
~ wood (3) n 008.6
Rich (5) 030.7
~ Bayou (1) AR 030.7
~ Mountain (4) AR 031.1
Richard (2) 090.1
~ Nixon (1) 090.1
~ Street (1) 107.7
Richardson (6) TX 105.3
~ Heights (1) 105.6
~ Landing (1) LA 052.8
Richardsons Landing (2) TN 087.1
Richburg (1) AL 087.4
richen (1) v 029.3
richened (2) v 075.7
~ up (1) v 029.3
richer (14) adj 029.3
richerd (2) n/adj 008.6
~ pine (1) n 008.6
richest (4) adj 029.3
Richland (10) GA 087.4
~ Creek (6) TN 030.7
~ Parish (2) LA 087.4
Richmond (24) AR GA VA 087.9
~ Academy (1) 087.1
~ County (1) GA 087.2
~ Heights (2) 106.2
~ Hill (1) GA 087.6
richness (1) n 029.3
Richton (1) MS 087.5
Richwood (4) GA LA TN 087.1
rick (77) n/v/adj 014.6
~ saw (1) n 120.9
ricked (8) v 014.6
~ out (1) v 014.6
~ up (2) v 019.8
Rickenbacker Causeway (1) 107.5
rickets (1) n 079.4
ricking (1) v 080.7
rickrack (5) n/adj 085.2

~ fence (3) n 016.4
ricks (24) n/v 014.7
Rico (47) GA 087.1
Ricos (15) 055.5
rid (898) v 099.4
~ of (816) v 099.4
~ [P-0] (1) v 099.4
ridded (1) v 041.4
ridden (428) v 034.3
~ in (1) v 034.3
Ridder (12) 053.2
riddle (3) n 030.4
ride (1228) n/v/adj 034.3
~ -and-guide (1) adj 120.3
~ around (2) v 034.3
~ (a)round (1) v 034.3
~ back (1) v 034.3
~ by (1) v 034.3
~ in (5) v 034.3
~ lawn mower (1) n 120.3
~ mower (1) n 120.3
~ off (1) v 034.3
~ on (5) v 034.3
~ up (1) v 089.9
~ with (8) v 097.5
~ [P-0] (1) v 012.9
ride[V-r] (5) v 034.3
ride[V-t] (3) v 034.3
rideau (2) n F 009.5
rider (55) n/adj 016.4
~ lawn mower (1) n 120.3
~ mower (3) n 120.3
riders (12) n 016.4
Riderville (1) AL 087.2
rides (16) n/v 034.3
~ in (1) v 021.9
ridge (92) n/adj 030.8
~ country (3) n 029.8
~ hickory nuts (1) n 061.8
~ land (2) n 029.8
~ roads (1) n 031.7
~ roll (1) n 011.5
~ row (2) n 011.6
~ runner (5) n 069.9
~ -runner hog (1) n 035.9
~ runners (5) n 069.9
Ridge (80) LA 087.1
~ Route (1) 031.6
Ridgecrest (2) NC 087.8
Ridgeland (1) MS 087.5

Ridgely (1) TN 087.5
ridges (16) n 030.8
Ridgeway (1) 106.2
Ridgewood (1) 107.7
ridiculous (2) adj 065.8
riding (355) v/adj 022.8
~ along (1) v 013.5
~ around (1) v 064.6
~ board (2) n 022.5
~ boots (2) n 123.8
~ breeches (2) n 027.4
~ bridle (2) n 039.2
~ car (1) n 023.6
~ child (1) n 074.3
~ crop (2) n 019.4
~ cultivator (4) n 023.9
~ cultivators (2) n 021.7
~ habit (2) n 034.3
~ horse (19) n 022.7
~ -horse barn (1) n 015.2
~ horses (17) n 034.2
~ kind (1) n 120.3
~ lawn mower (29) n 120.3
~ lawn mow(er) (3) n 120.3
~ lawn mowers (3) n 120.3
~ mower (52) n 120.3
~ mow(er) (3) n 120.3
~ mowers (12) n 120.3
~ on (5) v 022.8
~ one-row cultivator (1) n 021.9
~ planter (1) n 021.6
~ planters (1) n 021.6
~ plow (3) n 021.6
~ preacher (1) n 089.9
~ rein (1) n 039.2
~ reins (2) n 039.2
~ rotary mower (1) n 120.3
~ shorts (1) n 123.3
~ skirt (1) n 084.9
~ something (1) n 022.7
~ stable (1) n 015.2
~ stables (1) n 015.2
~ stock (1) n 039.3
~ strap (1) n 019.4
~ sulky plow (1) n 021.6
~ switch (1) n 019.4

~ whip (3) n 019.4
~ your case (1) v 129.7
Ridley (1) GA 087.3
ridley turtle (1) n 060.6
ridleys (1) n 060.6
ridy (51) adj 034.3
~ -horse (43) n 022.5
~ -horses (5) n 022.5
~ -horsey (2) n 022.5
rien (1) n F 069.9
Rienzi (1) MS 087.1
riffle (1) n 031.5
riffraff (2) n 069.7
riffraffs (1) n 033.3
riffs (2) n 014.7
rifle (50) n/adj 022.4
~ balls (1) n 096.9
~ cartridges (2) n 022.4
~ house (1) n 118.6
~ shell (1) n 022.4
~ shells (1) n 022.4
rifles (7) n 113.1
rifling (1) n 090.9
rift (1) n 030.4
rig (12) n/v 035.4
~ up (2) v 038.6
Rigaud (1) 030.3
rigged (3) v 044.2
~ up (2) v 028.1
rigging (2) n 038.7
riggings (2) n 038.6
right (3534) n/adj/adv 071.5
~ -angling (1) v 085.2
~ arm (1) n 129.4
~ -hand (1) adj 021.6
~ -hand animal (1) n 039.4
~ -hand ear (1) n 071.5
~ -hand man (1) n 081.5
~ -hand plow (3) n 021.6
~ -hand side (2) n 039.4
~ -hand turning plow (1) n 021.6
~ -handed (3) adj 072.5
~ horse (3) n 039.4
~ lead (1) n 039.4
~ mule (1) n 039.4
~ -of-way (12) n 031.9
~ on (154) adv 057.4
~ on out (1) adv 057.5

~ smart (806) n/adj 090.7
~ smart-sized (1) adj 090.7
~ smarter (1) adv 090.7
~ wheel (1) n 039.4
~ -wing (1) adj 129.2
r(ight) (3) adv 066.8
Right (2) 112.5
~ -On Store (1) 057.4
Right[N-i] (1) 085.8
righteousness (1) n 057.8
rightly (2) adv 100.3
rights (2) n 084.9
Rights (2) 090.9
righty (4) interj 091.3
Rigolets Road (1) 031.8
rigor (1) n 076.3
rigs (6) n 088.8
riled (27) v 075.2
~ up (21) v 075.2
riles (1) v 075.2
rill (7) n 030.6
rim (721) n/adj 021.1
~ -fire cartridges (1) n 022.4
rime (2) n 046.6
rimming (2) n 021.1
rims (33) n 020.3
rin (1) v 034.3
rind (466) n/adj 046.6
rinds (22) n 046.6
ring (336) n/v/adj 123.1
~ a ring a row (1) n 081.8
~ around (1) n 022.7
~ -around-a-rosy (2) n 130.3
~ around detective (1) n 130.3
~ -around-the-rosary (1) n 088.7
~ -around-the-roses (21) n 130.3
~ -around-the-rosy (27) n 130.3
~ -(a)round-the-rosy (1) n 130.3
~ -around-[D-0]-roses (1) n 130.3
~ -around-[D-O]-rosy (4) n 130.3
~ bearer (5) n 082.3
~ frog (1) n 060.3

~ game (1) n 034.8
~ games (1) n 098.4
~ hoop (1) n 034.8
~ man (1) n 082.3
~ -out stobs (1) n 034.8
~ play (5) n 130.3
~ plays (1) n 022.5
~ the hoop (1) n 034.8
~ -tossing (1) n 034.8
~ up (1) v 089.9
ring[N-i] (1) n 034.8
ringer (2) n 034.8
ringers (5) n 130.6
Ringgold (5) GA LA 087.3
ringing (8) v/adj 057.4
~ shoes (1) n 034.8
~ vine (1) n 062.8
ringneck pheasant (1) n 121.6
ringnecks (1) n 080.7
rings (87) n 039.2
ringtail (3) adj 059.6
~ (rac)coon (2) n 059.5
~ squirrel (1) n 059.6
ringtails (1) n 059.4
ringtoss (18) n/adj 034.8
~ game (2) n 034.8
ringworm (5) n 060.5
ringworms (2) n 060.5
rinky (2) adj 067.8
~ -dink carpenter (1) n 067.8
~ -dink stuff (1) n 130.9
rinse (734) v/adj 018.2
~ cloth (1) n 018.3
~ off (2) v 018.2
~ out (1) v 018.2
~ period (1) n 018.2
~ towel (1) n 018.3
~ tub (1) n 018.2
~ water (12) n 018.2
~ waters (5) n 018.2
rinse[V-p] (15) v 018.2
rinse[V-r] (4) v 018.2
rinse[V-t] (1) v 018.2
rinsed (77) v 018.2
rinser (1) n 018.2
rinses (270) n/v 018.2
rinsing (72) n/v/adj 018.2
~ tub (5) n 020.1
~ water (7) n 018.2

Rio (34) 030.7
~ Bravo del Norte (1) TX 030.7
~ de las Palmas (1) TX 030.7
~ Grande (15) TX 126.1
~ Grande City (4) TX 087.9
~ Grande River (3) TX 030.7
~ Grande Valley (5) TX 087.5
~ Hondo (1) LA 030.7
~ Nosa (1) TX 087.6
riot (2) n/adj 113.2
~ stick (1) n 113.2
rip (18) v/adv 027.8
~ off (3) v 100.2
~ -off (4) n 129.3
~ -off mart (1) n 116.2
~ -roaring (1) adj 080.9
rip[V-r] (1) v 070.2
ripe (17) adj 029.3
~ peach (1) n 054.4
Ripley (13) MS TN 087.3
ripped (43) v 100.2
~ off (20) v 100.2
~ up (1) v 102.6
Ripper (2) 055A.3
Ripple (12) 114.8
rippy marts (1) n 116.2
rips (2) v 080.8
rise (795) n/v/adj 003.3
~ loaves (1) n 044.3
~ up (12) v 003.3
rise[V-p] (9) v 003.3
rise[V-r] (8) v 003.3
rise[V-t] (5) v 003.3
rised (26) v 003.3
~ up (5) v 003.3
risen (421) v/adj 003.3
~ bread (1) n 044.3
~ up (1) v 003.3
riser (1) n 044.3
rises (68) n/v 003.3
~ up (1) v 003.3
rising (614) n/v/adj 077.4
~ bread (4) n 044.6
~ tide (1) n 093.9
~ up (3) v 003.3
ris(ing) (1) n 077.4
Rising Sun (1) MS 087.2
risings (50) n 077.4
risky (3) adj 074.6

rite (1) n 079.2
rites (14) n 079.2
ritual (2) n 070.8
ritzy (9) adj 088.7
~ car (1) n 109.4
~ -like (1) adj 080.7
~ -titzy (2) adj 088.7
riv (2) v 098.9
~ out (1) v 098.9
Rivagerra (1) 030.7
rive (30) v 080.9
~ -board shingles (1) n 011.2
~ out (1) v 066.8
~ up (1) v 016.7
rived (4) v 075.7
~ out (2) v 092.8
~ out of (1) v 098.7
riven (1) v 011.2
river (864) n/adj 030.6
~ basin (1) n 029.4
~ boats (1) n 024.6
~ boomers (1) n 069.9
~ bottom (43) n 029.4
~ -bottom farm (1) n 029.4
~ -bottom land (14) n 029.4
~ -bottom soil (1) n 029.4
~ bottoms (17) n 029.4
~ bread (1) n 044.7
~ chute (1) n 032.7
~ coon (1) n 069.9
~ flat (2) n 029.4
~ freight (1) n 080.6
~ gorge (1) n 030.4
~ land (5) n 029.4
~ landing (1) n 031.4
~ mouth (1) n 071.6
~ narrows (1) n 030.6
~ nigger (1) n 069.9
~ niggers (1) n 093.8
~ perch (1) n 059.9
~ plans (1) n 096.7
~ port (1) n 031.4
~ rat (3) n 069.9
~ rats (9) n 069.9
~ road (1) n 082.7
~ sand (3) n 029.8
~ shrimp (2) n 098.7
~ -slick rocks (1) n 016.8
~ slicks (1) n 016.7
~ swamp (7) n 029.6

~ swamps (2) n 029.6
~ town (1) n 002.6
~ towns (1) n 096.7
~ turtle (1) n 060.6
~ valley (3) n 029.4
~ water (1) n 114.7
riv(er) (1) n 057.8
River (1177) 030.7
~ Bend (2) GA 087.6
~ Grove (2) TN 030.7
~ Junction (1) FL 087.3
~ Oaks (5) 106.1
~ Oaks area (1) n 106.1
~ Oaks Boulevard (2) 107.7
~ Rats (1) 069.9
~ Road (1) 107.6
~ Street (1) 107.7
~ Thames (1) 107.7
~ View (2) AL 087.7
~ View Country Club (1) 106.1
~ Walk (2) 106.4
riverbank (7) n/adj 029.7
~ whore (1) n 113.3
riverbed (18) n 029.4
riverbeds (2) n 029.4
Riverbend (1) 106.1
riverboat (7) n 024.6
riverboats (5) n 024.6
Riverdale (3) GA 087.2
~ Plantation (1) MS 087.1
riverfront (7) n/adj 114.8
~ land (1) n 029.4
~ park (1) n 085.1
Rivergate (1) 105.3
rivermen (1) n 069.9
Rivermont (3) TN 106.1
~ area (1) n 106.1
~ Hotel (1) 106.9
river's (1) adj 030.6
rivers (84) n 030.6
Rivers (2) 106.1
~ Road (1) 106.1
Riverside (19) TX 107.8
~ area (1) n 106.2
~ Avenue (1) 107.7
~ Drive (1) 107.5
~ Park (3) 106.4
~ section (1) n 106.1
~ Terrace (1) 106.2
Riverview (1) 106.2

riverways (1) n 030.6
riveter (1) n 080.9
Rivi(era) (1) 109.4
riving (1) v 066.8
rivulet (20) n 030.6
rivulets (5) n 030.6
riz (106) v 003.3
~ up (5) v 003.3
rized up (1) v 003.3
RJS (2) 114.2
roach (13) n/adj 114.1
~ bug (1) n 060A.1
~ clip (1) n 114.1
~ in their pocket[N-i]
  (1) n 006.9
~ palace (1) n 113.8
roaches (23) n 060A.2
road (2359) n/adj 031.6
~ bikes (1) n 075.6
~ -blocked (1) adj
  102.6
~ breaker (1) n 110.8
~ -building (1) n 031.6
~ camps (1) n 088.7
~ car (1) n 031.6
~ cars (1) n 091.7
~ carts (1) n 080.8
~ ditch (2) n 030.2
~ ditches (1) n 030.2
~ divider (1) n 107.3
~ drag (1) n 080.6
~ field (1) n 031.8
~ foreman (1) n 069.6
~ grader (2) n 080.6
~ graders (1) n 031.5
~ hog (5) n 109.4
~ lines (2) n 107.3
~ markers (2) n 107.3
~ markings (1) n 107.3
~ miles (1) n 080.7
~ oil (1) n 031.6
~ partner (1) n 129.4
~ runner (1) n 088.9
~ scrape (1) n 080.7
~ scraper (1) n 066.8
~ separators (1) n
  107.8
~ slip (1) n 080.6
~ slips (2) n 096.5
~ station (1) n 084.7
~ stop (1) n 107.2
~ system (1) n 091.6
~ tax (2) n 031.6
~ track (1) n 084.7
~ wagons (1) n 081.8

Road (212) 014.1
~ Ninety (1) 031.6
~ Twenty-Five (1)
  107.1
road[N-i] (2) n 031.8
roadhouse (3) n 119.6
roadmaster (1) n 060A.4
roadrunner (6) n 069.9
roadrunners (2) n 084.9
roads (963) n 031.7
Roads (8) 087.5
roadside (20) n/adj 107.2
~ mechanic (1) n 067.8
~ park (15) n 107.2
~ parks (2) n 107.2
~ table (1) n 107.2
roadster (11) n/adj 109.2
~ Ford (1) n 088.7
roadsters (3) n 109.2
roadway (3) n 031.7
roadwork (1) n 001A.3
roam (2) v 028.1
roaming (2) v 097.8
Roan (4) 030.7
~ Creek (2) TN 030.7
~ Mountain (2) TN
  087.2
Roane (1) TN 087.3
Roanoke (5) AL VA
087.2
roar (2) n/v 012.3
roaring (3) v/adj 065.8
Roaring River (2) TN
030.7
roast (249) n/v/adj 121.2
~ beef (16) n 121.2
~ eggs (1) n 046.1
~ ham (1) n 121.3
~ lamb (2) n 121.4
~ lettuce (1) n 055A.6
~ peanuts (1) n 054.7
roast[N-i] (5) n 121.2
roasted (14) adj 056.2
~ bread (1) n 044.8
~ corn (2) n 056.2
~ ears (3) n 056.2
~ egg (1) n 046.1
~ nuts (1) n 054.7
~ peanuts (3) n 054.7
roaster (6) n 121.5
roasters (7) n 080.9
roastes (3) n 016.9
roasting (764) v/adj 121.5
~ chicken (5) n 121.5
~ corn (7) n 056.2

~ ear (133) n 056.2
~ -ear (2) adj 056.2
~ -ear bean (1) n
  055A.4
~ -ear beans (1) n
  055A.3
~ -ear cordial (1) n
  050.9
~ -ear corn (23) n
  056.2
~ -ear field (1) n 016.1
~ -ear patch (7) n
  016.1
~ -ear patches (1) n
  016.1
~ -ear patties (1) n
  044.7
~ -ear pea (1) n 055A.5
~ -ear peas (3) n 056.2
~ -ear shuck (1) n
  056.1
~ -ear stage (6) n 056.2
~ -ear worm (1) n
  060.5
~ ear[N-i] (3) n 056.2
~ ears (552) n 056.2
~ hen (6) n 121.5
~ hens (1) n 121.5
~ oven (1) n 017.6
~ pan (1) n 017.5
~ skillet (1) n 017.5
~ years (1) n 056.2
roast(ing) ears (3) n
056.2
roasts (8) n 121.2
rob (2) v 081.9
robbed (2) v 100.2
robber[N-i] (1) n 130.4
robberies (1) n 025.2
robbers (12) n 130.2
robbery (1) n 116.3
robbing (1) v 100.2
Robbins (3) TN 087.5
robe (11) n 026.4
Robeline (3) LA 087.1
Robert (31) LA 087.7
~ E. Lee (6) 106.4
~ Lee (1) 068.3
~ Road (1) 031.7
Roberts (2) 080.7
~ Street (1) 080.7
Robertsdale (1) AL 087.6
Robertson (4) TN 087.2
~ redback (1) n 080.7
robes (4) n 009.7

Robeson County (1) NC
086.2
robin (6) n/adj 059.5
~ redbreast (1) n 059.2
robinet (1) n 018.7
robins (6) n 059.4
Robins (4) GA 087.5
Robinson (14) TX 087.4
~ Creek (7) AL MS
  TN TX 030.7
~ Park (1) 085.1
~ Pond (1) FL 030.7
~ Road (1) 107.7
~ Springs (1) AL 087.6
~ Street (1) 080.7
Robinsonville (2) MS
087.1
robot (3) n 083.1
robust (64) adj 073.1
robusty (1) adj 073.1
Rochelle (1) LA 070.7
rock (2022) n/v/adj 032.1
~ -and-brick walls (1) n
  007A.4
~ bass (12) n 059.9
~ basses (1) n 099.6
~ battles (1) n 130.5
~ -bench terrace (1) n
  016.6
~ bottom (1) n 031.6
~ candy (3) n 081.8
~ cat (1) n 059.9
~ chimley (8) n 008.1
~ chimleys (6) n 008.1
~ chimney (2) n 008.1
~ chimneys (2) n 008.1
~ chunking (1) n 032.1
~ cliff (10) n 031.2
~ cliffs (1) n 031.2
~ country (2) n 080.8
~ crab (1) n 060.2
~ dancing (2) n 083.1
~ dikes (1) n 098.7
~ elm (1) n 061.8
~ fall (1) n 031.5
~ fence (175) n 016.6
~ fence[N-i] (1) n
  016.6
~ fences (47) n 016.6
~ fencing (1) n 016.6
~ fights (2) n 130.5
~ garden (1) n 050.5
~ gill (1) n 059.9
~ gravel (1) n 029.8

~ -hard Republican (1) n 129.1
~ hearth (2) n 008.2
~ hearths (1) n 008.2
~ hounds (1) n 090.4
~ house (9) n 011.7
~ houses (1) n 014.1
~ ledge (1) n 031.2
~ melons (1) n 056.7
~ mine (1) n 080.8
~ music (13) n 130.9
~ 'n' roll (40) n 130.8
~ -'n'-roll band (1) n 099.6
~ 'n' roll music (1) n 089.5
~ oil (1) n 024.2
~ pavement (1) n 031.6
~ perch (1) n 059.9
~ pile (1) n 016.6
~ piles (2) n 016.8
~ quarry (3) n 032.1
~ rake (1) n 120.7
~ road (16) n 031.6
~ roads (10) n 031.7
~ sharpener (1) n 023.4
~ siding (1) n 011.2
~ squirrel (2) n 059.7
~ stone (2) n 016.6
~ sugar (1) n 051.2
~ terraces (1) n 016.6
~ throwing (1) n 130.5
~ up (1) v 051.9
~ walks (1) n 031.9
~ wall (138) n 016.6
~ wall fence (1) n 016.6
~ walls (20) n 016.6
Rock (175) 083.1
~ Bank (1) MS 088.7
~ Chapel (2) GA 087.4
~ Church (1) GA 087.5
~ City (3) TN 093.6
~ Cornish hen (1) n 121.5
~ Creek (12) AL AR GA TN TX 030.7
~ Hill (4) AL FL GA SC 087.7
~ House (1) 107.7
~ Island (1) IL 086.7
~ Island Depot (1) 084.7
~ Island Station (1) 084.7

~ Lake (1) AR 030.7
~ Mills (1) AL 087.3
rock[N-i] (3) n 021.4
Rockdale (6) GA TX 087.1
rocked (4) v 093.6
~ on (2) v 076.2
~ up (1) v 052.9
Rockefeller (3) 068.2
~ Refuge (1) 087.7
Rockefellers (1) 039.7
rocker (56) n/adj 008.8
~ chair (2) n 008.8
~ chairs (1) n 008.8
rocker[N-i] (1) n 074.6
rockers (28) n 008.8
Rockett (1) TX 087.2
rockfish (6) n 060.1
Rockford (2) AL 087.6
Rockies (1) 080.7
rocking (188) v/adj 008.9
~ bolster (5) n 028.9
~ bolsters (1) n 084.8
~ chair (102) n 008.8
~ chairs (70) n 008.8
~ horse (5) n 022.5
~ horses (1) n 101.5
Rockmart (3) GA 087.4
Rockport (4) TX 087.9
rocks (173) n 031.5
Rocks (10) 030.7
Rockvale (1) TN 087.3
Rockwell (2) TX 016.6
rockwhet (1) n 023.4
Rockwood (3) AL TN 087.2
rocky (50) adj 029.8
~ base (1) n 031.2
~ bottom (1) n 029.4
~ clay dirt (1) n 029.9
~ cliff (1) n 031.2
~ country (1) n 016.6
~ field (1) n 029.8
~ hill (1) n 030.8
~ hills (3) n 030.8
~ horse (8) n 022.5
~ land (6) n 029.9
~ loam (1) n 029.9
~ road (2) n 031.6
~ roads (1) n 031.6
~ side (1) n 031.2
~ soil (6) n 029.8
Rocky (39) AR 087.5
~ Bayou (1) LA 030.7

~ Bayou Creek (1) AR 030.7
~ Branch (3) AL GA TN 030.7
~ Branch Creek (1) TN 030.7
~ Comfort (2) 087.7
~ Creek (2) AL FL 030.7
~ Ford (9) 056.7
~ Ford cantaloupes (1) n 056.7
~ Ford melon (1) n 056.7
~ Fords (1) 056.7
~ Knob (1) GA 030.8
~ Mount (3) NC 087.4
~ Mountain (1) TN 031.1
~ Mountain fever (1) n 080.9
~ Mountains (5) 031.1
~ Ridge (1) 087.6
~ River (2) TN 030.7
~ Way (1) FL 087.7
rococo (1) n 080.7
rod (24) n 110.6
rode (991) v 034.3
~ around (1) v 034.3
~ away (1) v 034.3
~ in (2) v 034.3
~ on (1) v 034.3
~ over (2) v 034.3
~ through (1) v 034.3
~ up (1) v 034.3
~ with (1) v 034.3
rodent (8) n 059.5
rodents (32) n 059.5
rodeo (4) n 080.6
Rodeos (1) 080.7
Rodgers (1) AR 087.2
Rodney (2) MS 087.5
~ Parham (1) 107.6
rods (5) n 113.1
roe (5) n/adj 080.6
Roebuck (2) TX 030.7
Roger Dodger (1) 080.7
Rogers (7) AR TX 104.3
~ Department Stores (1) 108.5
~ knife (1) n 104.3
~ Ridge (1) TN 031.1
Rogersville (2) AL TX 087.3
rogue (6) n 059.5

rogue[N-i] (1) n 069.8
rogued (1) v 100.2
rogues (2) n 113.7
roguing (1) v 088.7
roguish (3) adj 035.9
Rohwer (2) AR 087.1
roke (1) v 098.7
Roland (1) AR 087.3
Rolies (1) 126.6
roll (432) n/v/adj 064.6
~ -around closet (1) n 009.7
~ bop (1) n 083.1
~ bow (1) n 028.9
~ bread (1) n 044.4
~ clipper (1) n 021.6
~ off (3) v 034.5
~ off of (1) v 034.5
~ over (2) v 095.5
~ overs (1) n 088.8
~ pants (1) n 027.4
~ pillow (1) n 028.9
~ roast (1) n 121.2
~ -up pillow (1) n 028.9
Roll (1) 069.4
roll[N-i] (5) n 044.4
roll[V-r] over (1) v 070.2
roll[V-t] off (1) v 034.5
rollaway bed (3) n 009.1
rolled (65) v/adj 123.9
~ off (38) v 034.5
~ off of (5) v 034.5
~ out (3) v 034.5
~ out of (9) v 034.5
~ out [P-0] (1) v 034.5
~ roast (1) n 121.2
~ roofing (2) n 011.4
~ -up paper (1) n 008.6
rollen off (1) v 034.5
roller (34) n/adj 064.6
~ coaster (9) n 083.1
~ curtains (2) n 009.5
~ shade (3) n 009.5
~ shades (4) n 009.5
~ skates (2) n 130.4
~ skating (1) n 098.6
~ towel (1) n 018.6
Roller (13) 106.3
~ Coaster Hill (1) 106.3
rollers (10) n 021.7
Rollers (24) 126.6
rollford bed (1) n 009.1
rollicky (1) adj 007.4

rolling (51) v/adj 057.5
~ around (2) v 064.6
~ chair (6) n 008.8
~ chairs (1) n 064.5
~ clouds (1) n 005.3
~ cutter (1) n 021.7
~ down (1) v 095.8
~ ground (1) n 030.8
~ land (11) n 030.8
~ lands (1) n 029.5
~ like (1) v 095.5
~ pin (1) n 026.5
~ section (1) n 030.8
~ shades (1) n 009.5
~ -type land (1) n 029.5
~ upland (1) n 029.5
Rolling Fork (3) MS 087.1
Rollover Bayou (1) LA 030.3
rolls (446) n 044.4
Rolls (3) 109.4
~ Royce (1) 109.4
~ Royces (1) 077.8
rolltop desk (1) n 009.2
rolly land (1) n 030.8
roly (13) adj 089.8
~ -hole (1) n 089.8
~ -holey (4) n 088.7
~ -oly (1) n 088.7
~ -polies (1) n 088.7
~ -poly (5) n 130.6
~ -poly bugs (1) n 060A.2
Roly (1) 089.8
Roma (6) TX 087.1
Roman (13) 044.4
~ bread (1) n 044.4
~ Catholic (5) 126.5
~ Catholics (4) 126.5
~ Meal (1) 044.4
~ Meal bread (2) n 044.4
romance (2) n 081.4
romancing (2) v 081.4
Romania (1) 087.8
Romans (1) 126.5
Romantic (1) 115.9
Rome (35) AR GA 087.7
Romeo (4) 124.5
romero (2) n S 061.4
rondas (1) n S 080.8
rondo (1) n S 125.3
Rondo (1) AR 087.3

Roney Plaza (1) 077.7
roo(x2) (1) interj 037.5
roof (1152) n/adj 011.4
~ boards (1) n 102.7
~ grass (1) n 011.4
~ gutter (1) n 011.5
~ line (2) n 011.4
~ pipes (1) n 011.5
~ plate (1) n 011.4
~ tinning (1) n 011.4
~ valley (1) n 011.6
~ work (1) n 011.4
roofed (3) v/adj 011.4
roofer (1) n 011.4
roofing (83) n/adj 011.4
~ boards (1) n 011.4
~ metal (1) n 011.4
~ paper (1) n 011.4
~ shingles (1) n 011.4
~ tin (1) n 011.4
~ top (1) n 011.4
roofs (32) n 011.4
rooftop (3) n 011.4
Rook (1) 130.4
rooked (3) v 096.9
rookie (4) n 112.4
rookies (2) n 112.5
Rookies (1) 112.5
room (5253) n/adj 007A.3
~ doom (1) n 129.4
~ mother (1) n 080.7
~ upstairs (1) n 009.8
Room (3) 097.8
room[N-i] (6) n 042.3
roomed (3) v/adj 042.7
roomers (1) n 054.7
roomful (1) n 055A.8
rooming (17) n/adj 119.2
~ house (12) n 014.1
~ houses (4) n 113.8
rooms (286) n 007A.3
Roosevelt (6) 070.6
~ City (1) 106.3
~ Hotel (1) 084.3
~ Park (1) 106.4
~ Spring (1) TX 030.7
roost (63) n/v/adj 036.8
~ in (1) v 012.7
~ pole (2) n 036.8
~ poles (1) n 036.8
Roost (1) 030.7
roost[N-i] (2) n 036.9
roosted (1) v 036.8
rooster (20) n/adj 121.5

~ fighting (1) n 088.9
~ owl (1) n 059.2
rooster[N-i] (1) n 016.7
roostercrat (1) n 098.7
roosters (3) n 036.7
Roosterville (1) GA 087.4
roostes (1) n 016.7
roosting (6) v/adj 036.7
~ hen (1) n 036.7
~ house (1) n 036.8
~ place (1) n 036.8
root (442) n/v/adj 061.4
~ around (1) v 098.6
~ beer (7) n 121.8
~ -beer mugs (1) n 048.9
~ cellar (13) n 015.5
~ cellars (2) n 010.1
~ crops (1) n 041.3
~ cutter (3) n 021.9
~ doctor (1) n 061.4
~ doctors (1) n 061.4
~ for (1) v 039.9
~ herbs (1) n 061.4
~ hog (1) n 035.9
~ -hog-or-die (1) v 061.4
~ medicines (1) n 061.4
~ part (1) n 055A.5
~ perch (1) n 059.9
~ plow (1) n 021.6
~ -plowed (1) v 061.4
~ -plowing (1) v 041.4
~ plows (1) n 021.6
~ rakes (1) n 041.3
~ structure (1) n 061.4
~ system (8) n 061.4
~ the peg (1) n 130.6
~ under (1) v 061.4
~ up (1) v 061.4
root[N-i] (6) n 061.4
rooted (4) v 061.4
rooter (88) n/adj 047.2
~ hog (1) n 035.9
root(er) (1) n 035.9
Rooter (2) 093.9
rooters (44) n 035.9
Rooters (2) 021.7
rooting (3) v 057.4
~ around (1) v 080.7
~ out (1) v 076.9
roots (847) n/adj 061.4
Roots (3) 061.4
rooves (6) n 011.4
ropa vieja (1) n S 047.4

rope (185) n/adj 039.1
~ beads (1) n 028.4
~ lines (2) n 039.1
~ of beads (1) n 028.4
~ swing (15) n 022.9
~ the peg (1) n 034.8
~ the pig (1) n 130.6
roped (2) v 084.8
roper (2) n 069.9
ropero (1) n S 009.7
roperos (1) n S 009.6
ropers (1) n 069.9
rope's end (1) n 099.6
ropes (15) n 039.1
roping (2) v 034.2
Roque (1) 030.7
Rosa (2) 087.7
rosary (4) n 028.4
Roscoe (2) 113.1
~ Boulevard (1) 107.5
rose (720) n/v/adj 003.3
~ apple (1) n 088.8
~ -breasted grosbeak (1) n 059.3
~ business (1) n 088.7
~ -comb lighterd knot (1) n 008.6
~ garden (2) n 050.5
~ on (2) v 003.3
~ tomatoes (1) n 055.3
~ up (6) v 003.3
Rose (10) 030.3
~ Bay (1) FL 030.3
~ Creek (2) FL 030.7
~ Hill (2) GA 030.8
~ Hill Cemetery (1) 078.8
~ Window Mission (1) 106.4
Rosebud (1) TX 087.9
rosebush (1) n 070.7
rosed up (2) v 003.3
Rosedale (15) AL AR GA LA MS TX 087.3
Rosedown (1) LA 087.9
Rosefield (1) LA 087.6
Roseland (2) FL LA 087.9
rosemaries (1) n 061.8
rosemary (5) n/adj 061.4
~ pine (3) n 061.8
~ tea (1) n 080.9
rosen (4) v 003.3
~ up (1) v 003.3
Rosenberg (1) TX 086.4

Rosepine (2) LA 087.1
roses (62) n 062.7
Roses (1) 087.2
rosette (1) n 019.9
rosettes (1) n 080.8
rosewood coffins (1) n 079.1
Rosewood Avenue (1) 107.7
Rosie O'Grady's (1) 106.4
Roslyn Heights (1) 106.1
Ross (7) TX 087.5
~ Avenue (2) 105.2
~ Branch (1) TN 030.7
~ Street (1) 107.6
Rosser (1) TX 087.7
Rossville (1) TN 106.1
Roswell (9) GA 087.7
~ area (1) n 106.1
~ Road (2) 107.7
rosy (35) n/adj 021.6
~ clipper (1) n 021.6
rot (42) n/v 055.9
rot[V-t] (1) v 046.9
rotary (14) n/adj 120.2
~ cutaway (1) n 021.7
~ cutters (1) n 021.6
~ mower (2) n 120.2
~ saw (1) n 120.9
~ tiller (1) n 021.7
~ tillers (1) n 021.7
~ type (1) n 120.2
rotate (1) v 015.7
rotation (2) n/adj 015.7
~ fields (1) n 015.7
rotgut (85) n/adj 050.8
~ whiskey (3) n 050.8
~ wine (1) n 114.7
Rothe Ranch (1) 081.8
roti (1) n F 046.4
rotisserie (2) n/adj 116.4
~ -type things (1) n 116.4
rotisse(rie) (1) n 116.4
rotisseries (1) n 116.4
roto (1) n 120.4
Roto (3) 093.9
~ -Rooter (1) 093.9
~ -Rooters (2) 021.7
rotor cultivators (1) n 021.9
Rotospader (1) 021.6
Rototiller (20) 021.6
rots (1) v 055.9

rotted (13) v 055.9
~ away (1) v 013.8
~ down (2) v 057.8
~ him (1) v 082.1
~ off (1) v 070.2
~ out (1) v 090.4
rotten (52) adj 047.5
~ day (1) n 005.5
~ dirt (1) n 029.8
~ flesh (2) n 078.2
~ milk (1) n 047.6
Rotten Bayou (1) MS 030.7
rottening (2) v 053.6
rottenness (1) n 046.9
Rottenwood Creek (1) GA 030.7
rotting (2) v 075.9
rotty (1) adj 033.3
rotunda (1) n 075.7
rouge (9) n/adj F 028.1
Rouge (752) 087.8
rouged up (1) v 028.1
rough (114) adj/adv 005.5
~ boards (2) n 007A.1
~ carpenter (1) n 067.8
~ day (12) n 005.5
~ -dry (1) v 010.6
~ element (1) n 080.8
~ grass (1) n 015.9
~ -growing boy (1) n 080.7
~ -looking sky (1) n 005.5
~ lumber (1) n 007A.1
~ -old (1) adj 075.7
~ pine (1) n 007A.1
~ roads (1) n 031.6
~ sack (1) n 019.6
~ sacks (1) n 019.7
~ timber (2) n 007A.1
~ toad (1) n 060.4
~ trot (1) n 034.5
~ water (1) n 089.8
~ weather (3) n 006.2
roughage (1) n 014.3
rougher (5) adj 007.2
roughhouse (1) n 130.5
roughneck (6) n 069.9
roughnecks (1) n 080.6
roulette (1) n 130.5
round (704) n/adj 121.1
~ and big (1) adj 065.1

~ -bale presses (1) n 014.6
~ bales (5) n 014.8
~ -bottom boat (2) n 024.6
~ bread (2) n 044.4
~ broom (1) n 010.5
~ dance (36) n 083.1
~ dances (6) n 083.1
~ dancing (19) n 083.1
~ grain (1) n 050.7
~ -heeled (1) adj 124.6
~ melon (1) n 056.9
~ -pole houses (1) n 096.8
~ porch (1) n 010.8
~ porches (2) n 010.8
~ prairie (1) n 029.5
~ roast (7) n 121.2
~ rock (1) n 023.5
~ sausage (1) n 121.6
~ shovel (4) n 021.6
~ shovels (1) n 021.6
~ squash (8) n 056.6
~ steak (41) n 121.1
~ steaks (8) n 121.1
~ -toe shoes (1) n 123.8
~ watermelons (1) n 056.9
~ well (1) n 080.7
~ white squash (1) n 056.6
'Round (1) 031.1
Round (6) 030.7
~ Lick Creek (1) TN 030.7
~ Mountain (2) AR TN 031.1
~ Prairie (2) TX 029.5
~ Top (1) TX 087.8
Roundaway Bayou (1) LA 030.7
rounder (1) adj 002.6
roundhead (1) n 059.2
Roundhill (1) LA 087.2
roundhouse (5) n/adj 080.7
~ board (1) n 022.7
~ foreman (1) n 104.6
rounds (23) n 022.7
Rounds (1) 055.6
roundtop (1) n 007A.2
roundup (3) n 080.9
roundworms (2) n 060.5

rouse (24) v 076.7
~ up (5) v 076.7
roused (5) v 076.7
~ up (4) v 076.7
roust (1) v 076.8
roustabout (3) n 074.1
roustabouts (3) n 080.8
route (23) n/adj 031.7
~ road (1) n 031.7
Route (56) 107.1
~ Eighty (1) 107.1
~ Five (2) 001.3
~ Four (4) 001.2
~ Nine (2) 001.5
~ One (20) 001.1
~ Seven (1) 001.4
~ Six (1) 001.3
~ Three (13) 001.2
~ Two (9) 001.1
routes (5) n 001.3
routine (1) n 065.8
roux (9) n F 092.8
rove (6) v 080.9
~ out (1) v 098.9
rover (47) n 124.8
Rover (2) AR TN 087.6
row (281) n/v/adj 021.7
~ building (1) n 007A.6
~ corn (1) n 056.2
~ crop (2) n 041.3
~ -crop (2) v 041.3
~ -crop farm (1) n 041.3
~ -crop farming (1) n 041.3
~ -cropped (1) v 075.8
~ cropping (1) n 080.8
~ -cropping (4) v 015.7
~ crops (11) n 041.3
~ down (1) v 021.7
~ harrow (1) n 021.7
~ house (29) n 119.1
~ houses (15) n 119.1
~ of beads (2) n 028.4
~ plows (1) n 021.6
~ up (1) v 021.9
Row (9) 080.7
~ Gully Bayou (1) LA 030.7
row[N-i] (4) n 016.7
rowboat (303) n 024.6
rowboats (40) n 024.6
rowdies (1) n 081.8
rowdy (6) adj 074.1
rowed (4) v/adj 014.8

~ with (1) v 024.6
rowing (2) n/adj 041.6
  ~ boats (1) n 024.6
rowlocks (1) n 024.6
row's end (1) n 104.7
rows (141) n 041.2
Roxie (1) MS 087.2
Roxton (1) TX 087.9
Roy (1) 083.1
royal (4) adj 089.8
  ~ palm (3) n 061.8
Royal (11) 105.7
  ~ Family (2) 093.8
  ~ Glades Canal (1) FL 030.2
  ~ Jester (1) 080.8
  ~ Oaks (1) 106.2
  ~ Palm (1) 084.3
  ~ Palm Hotel (1) 106.4
  ~ Palm Park (1) 106.4
  ~ Scot (1) 128.1
  ~ Theater (1) 084.4
royalty (1) n 091.2
Royce (1) 109.5
Royces (1) 077.8
Royston (1) GA 087.3
RPM dial (1) n 110.2
Rs (1) 001.2
rub (86) n/v/adj 070.8
  ~ blocks (1) n 021.2
  ~ board (65) n 010.6
  ~ boards (11) n 010.6
  ~ on (1) v 065.8
  ~ over (1) v 092.7
rubbage (1) n 070.7
rubbed off (1) v 010.4
rubber (193) n/adj 021.1
  ~ ball (1) n 130.4
  ~ band (140) n 110.3
  ~ bands (7) n 110.3
  ~ belts (1) n 022.3
  ~ boats (1) n 024.6
  ~ boots (2) n 123.8
  ~ curtains (1) n 009.5
  ~ foam pillow (1) n 042.9
  ~ gun (1) n 052.5
  ~ rim (1) n 021.1
  ~ stamps (1) n 125.4
  ~ stopper (4) n 020.4
  ~ tire (2) n 021.1
  ~ -tired buggies (1) n 021.1
  ~ tires (6) n 021.1
  ~ tree (1) n 061.9

~ tube (1) n 024.4
~ tubing (1) n 024.4
rubberized suit (1) n 027.7
rubbers (7) n 080.8
rubbing (8) n/v/adj 114.7
  ~ alcohol (2) n 114.7
  ~ board (2) n 010.6
  ~ -board tub (1) n 080.7
rubbish (28) n/adj 010.2
  ~ room (1) n 010.3
rubble (2) n 016.6
rube (8) n 069.9
rubes (2) n 069.9
Rubes Creek (1) GA 030.7
Rubia (1) 061.4
rubies (1) n 123.1
rubstone (1) n 023.4
ruby (1) n 123.1
Ruby (5) 093.7
  ~ Falls (4) 093.7
  ~ Reds (1) 056.9
Rucker (8) 107.6
  ~ Street (1) 107.6
Ruckersville District (2) GA 087.3
ruckus (4) n 083.1
rudder (2) n 095.8
rudders (2) n 011.5
ruddy Indian peaches (1) n 054.3
rude (5) adj 073.3
Rudolphtown (1) TN 087.6
ruffian (1) n 069.9
ruffle (4) n/v 028.7
  ~ up (1) v 077.6
ruffled (1) adj 075.6
ruffles (2) n 026.4
Rufous-Sided Towhees (1) 088.8
rug (11) n/adj 007A.5
  ~ machine (1) n 116.7
  ~ shampooer (1) n 116.7
Rugby Road (1) 087.8
rugged (1) adj 075.7
Rugon (1) LA 087.6
rugs (3) n 040.7
ruin (20) v/adj 046.9
ruin[V-r] (3) v 070.2
ruin[V-t] (6) v 046.9
ruination (1) n 084.8

ruined (129) v/adj 046.9
  ~ by (1) v 070.6
  ~ their life[N-i] (1) v 082.2
ruining (1) v 055.9
ruins (7) n/v 066.8
rule (3) n 068.3
Rule (1) AR 086.5
ruler (1) n 032.1
Ruleville (2) MS 088.8
rum (19) n/adj 050.9
  ~ cake (1) n 122.8
  ~ hound (1) n 088.8
  ~ liquor (1) n 050.8
  ~ still (1) n 050.8
Rum Trail (1) 031.7
rumba (4) n 083.1
rumbas (2) n 083.1
rumble (41) n/adj 090.4
  ~ seat (28) n 109.3
  ~ seats (11) n 109.5
  ~ strips (1) n 110.8
rummage (19) n/adj 010.2
  ~ clothes (1) n 123.5
  ~ room (3) n 010.3
  ~ sale (3) n 123.5
rummy (1) n 113.6
rumored (1) v 013.7
rumors (1) n 025.2
rump (57) n/adj 072.8
  ~ roast (35) n 121.2
rump(x2) (1) interj 093.7
Rumpelkammer (2) n G 010.3
rumps (2) n 121.3
rumpus room (9) n 010.3
rumrunners (2) n 050.8
run (1835) n/v/adj 102.3
  ~ across (27) v 032.6
  ~ around (13) v 102.3
  ~ (a)round (1) v 102.3
  ~ around with (1) v 102.3
  ~ away (15) v 102.3
  ~ away with (1) v 102.3
  ~ by (3) v 102.3
  ~ down (13) v 102.3
  ~ -down (17) adj 075.4
  ~ -down hotel (2) n 113.8
  ~ -down ranch (1) n 029.8
  ~ for (2) v 102.3

~ from (2) v 102.3
~ him away (1) v 033.2
~ him off (1) v 082.1
~ in (7) v 102.3
~ -in (2) n 104.2
~ into (115) v 032.6
~ -mad dog (1) n 033.3
~ off (28) v 102.3
~ off from school (1) v 083.4
~ on (2) v 102.3
~ on out (1) v 102.3
~ out (30) v 102.3
~ out of (4) v 102.3
~ over (14) v 102.3
~ the bases (1) n 130.4
~ through (6) v 102.3
~ to (2) v 053.6
~ together (2) v 102.3
~ trough (1) n 035.8
~ up (12) v 032.6
~ up on (21) v 032.6
~ up to (1) v 053.4
~ up with (2) v 032.6
~ upon (4) v 032.6
~ with (1) v 075.5
Run (5) 087.3
run[V-p] (7) v 102.3
  ~ down (1) v 013.6
run[V-r] (588) v 102.3
  ~ about (1) v 102.3
  ~ across (17) v 032.6
  ~ aground (1) v 102.3
  ~ around (2) v 102.3
  ~ away (10) v 102.3
  ~ away out (1) v 102.3
  ~ away with (1) v 034.2
  ~ back (4) v 102.3
  ~ down (4) v 102.3
  ~ down on (1) v 032.6
  ~ from (3) v 074.4
  ~ in (4) v 052.6
  ~ into (53) v 032.6
  ~ off (16) v 102.3
  ~ off from school (1) v 083.4
  ~ on (1) v 102.3
  ~ onto (1) v 032.6
  ~ out (10) v 102.3
  ~ out of (2) v 102.3
  ~ out on her (1) v 082.1
  ~ outside (1) v 102.3
  ~ over (10) v 102.3

~ through (2) v 102.3
~ under (1) v 102.3
~ up (6) v 065.6
~ up on (9) v 032.6
~ up to (2) v 032.6
~ up with (5) v 032.6
~ upon (1) v 032.6
~ with (3) v 102.3
~ [P-0] (1) v 032.8
run[V-s] (1) v 026.1
runabout (6) n/adj 024.6
~ buggy (1) n 089.8
runabouts (1) n 080.8
runaround (8) n/adj 015.1
~ pen (1) n 015.6
runaway hall (1) n 007A.5
rung (44) n/v 095.8
rungs (1) n 020.3
runned (21) v 102.3
~ around (1) v 118.8
~ away (2) v 083.4
~ out (2) v 102.3
~ over (1) v 102.3
~ up (1) v 102.3
~ up on (1) v 032.6
runnels (1) n 011.5
runner (37) n/adj 055A.4
~ beans (1) n 055A.4
~ fish (1) n 059.9
~ oak (1) n 061.8
~ peanut (1) n 054.7
~ -type peanuts (1) n 054.7
runners (55) n 054.7
running (290) v/adj 102.3
~ after (1) v 052.9
~ after her (1) v 081.4
~ around (1) v 025.5
~ (a)round (2) v 053.5
~ around the mountain (1) n 098.4
~ bean (10) n 055A.4
~ beans (24) n 055A.4
~ board (5) n 109.1
~ boards (3) n 109.5
~ brier (1) n 062.7
~ bush (1) n 062.7
~ butter bean (2) n 055A.3
~ butter beans (4) n 055A.3
~ conch peas (1) n 055A.3

~ creek (1) n 030.6
~ ditch (1) n 030.6
~ dog (1) n 126.4
~ down (1) v 095.9
~ fit (2) n 096.7
~ fits (1) n 081.8
~ frogs (1) n 060.3
~ from (1) v 045.8
~ gear (7) n 080.8
~ gears (1) n 021.8
~ grass (1) n 015.9
~ horse (1) n 034.2
~ in (1) v 102.3
~ into (2) v 032.6
~ lake (1) n 007.6
~ limas (1) n 055A.3
~ off (1) v 052.2
~ okra (1) n 055.8
~ out (3) v 053.7
~ out of (1) v 075.8
~ over (2) v 027.7
~ peanut (2) n 054.7
~ peanuts (1) n 054.7
~ plank (1) n 022.6
~ purple hull (1) n 088.8
~ pus (1) n 077.5
~ room (1) n 015.6
~ shoes (2) n 123.8
~ snap beans (1) n 055A.4
~ sore (2) n 077.4
~ squash (1) n 056.6
~ start (1) n 102.3
~ stream (5) n 030.6
~ streams (1) n 030.6
~ through (1) v 010.3
~ tomato (2) n 055.3
~ tomatoes (2) n 055.3
~ up (1) v 080.8
~ up on (1) v 032.6
~ vine (1) n 062.8
~ water (12) n 030.6
~ waters (1) n 030.6
~ -wire fence (1) n 016.3
runningest (1) adj 088.9
runny (1) adj 091.7
runoff (3) n 030.5
runs (79) v 102.3
~ around (1) v 124.7
~ down (1) v 102.3
~ in (1) v 094.1
~ into (1) v 032.6
~ off (3) v 101.7

~ out (4) v 088.8
~ through (3) v 032.1
~ up on (1) v 102.3
~ with (1) v 084.8
Runs (1) 030.7
runt (20) n 035.5
runts (4) n 035.5
runway (12) n 010.8
runways (1) n 031.4
Runyan (1) AR 030.7
rupture appendix (1) n 080.1
ruptured (10) v/adj 080.1
~ appendix (3) n 080.1
~ (ap)pendix (3) n 080.1
~ gallbladder (1) n 070.6
rural (28) n/adj 065.8
~ areas (1) n 106.3
~ country roads (1) n 031.7
~ dweller (1) n 069.9
~ mail carrier (1) n 065.8
~ people (4) n 069.9
~ road (3) n 031.7
~ roads (4) n 031.7
rurals (2) n 082.7
rush (2) n/v 115.5
~ up (1) v 024.7
Rush (4) 030.7
~ Bayou (1) MS 030.7
~ Creek (2) TX 107.7
rushed (1) v 065.9
rushes (1) n 115.6
Rushes (1) 055.5
rushing (4) v 081.4
~ her (3) v 081.4
Rusk (2) TX 087.1
~ County (1) TX 087.7
Russ (1) n G 008.7
russe (1) adj 093.6
Russell (5) AL 087.8
~ Cave (1) AL 087.3
~ County (1) AL 087.2
Russellville (14) AL AR KY 087.5
russet (7) n/adj 055.4
~ potato (1) n 055.4
~ potatoes (4) n 055.4
russets (6) n 055.4
Russia (437) 087.9
Russian (19) 127.5
~ boar (1) n 035.9

~ boars (2) n 035.9
~ Jew (1) 126.7
~ olive (1) n 061.9
~ roulette (1) n 130.5
~ soccer (1) n 033.3
~ wild boar (2) n 035.9
Russians (19) 087.9
Russki (3) 127.5
Russkies (17) 127.5
rust (5) n/v/adj 013.1
~ color (1) n 059.7
~ out (1) v 080.6
~ through (1) v 052.5
rusted (2) v 103.4
ruster (1) n 019.2
rustes out (1) v 060A.6
rustic (6) n/adj 069.9
rusting on (1) v 023.6
rustling (1) v 080.9
Ruston (21) LA 087.5
rusty (6) adj 046.9
~ coats (1) n 099.7
~ dusty (1) n 049.3
~ lizard (1) n 090.8
rut (17) n/adj 030.5
~ road (1) n 031.6
rutabaga (13) n/adj 055A.6
~ greens (1) n 055A.5
~ salad (1) n 055A.5
~ tops (1) n 055A.5
~ turnip (1) n 055A.5
rutabagas (27) n 065.9
Rutherford (2) 087.2
~ Beach (1) LA 087.2
~ County (1) TN 087.2
ruts (10) n 041.2
rutted (2) adj 031.8
~ yam (1) n 055.5
rutty (1) adj 102.6
Ryals Street (1) 107.6
Ryan (1) AL 087.7
rye (143) n/adj 044.3
~ bin (1) n 014.4
~ bread (84) n 044.4
~ breads (1) n 044.4
~ liquor (1) n 050.9
~ patch (1) n 016.1
~ sack (1) n 019.7
~ whiskey (4) n 050.8
Rye (2) 083.3
~ waltz (1) n 083.1
~ Whiskey (1) 050.8
ryegrass (7) n 014.9
Ryland (1) AL 087.8

Ryman Auditorium (1)
    106.4

S

S house (1) n 012.1
Saba (1) 030.7
sabal palm (2) n 061.9
Sabbath (418) 002.1
~ Day (112) 002.1
~ -school books (1) n 002.1
saber (1) n 104.3
Sabine (34) LA TX 030.7
~ Parish (2) LA 087.2
~ Pass (4) TX 087.1
~ pilots (1) n 053.4
~ River (18) LA TX 030.7
Sabines (1) 069.9
sabot (1) n F 034.7
sac (3) n F 019.7
~ a pique (1) n F 019.7
~ de pique (1) n F 019.7
sacalait (15) n 059.9
sacalaits (5) n 059.9
Sacata Creek (2) TX 030.7
saccharine (1) n 065.8
sachet kitten (2) n 059.4
sack (2314) n/v/adj 019.6
~ coffee (2) n 081.9
~ dresses (1) n 080.7
~ lunch (1) n 019.5
~ out (1) v 096.6
~ race (2) n 101.7
~ races (1) n 130.2
~ swing (2) n 022.9
~ up (1) v 019.6
Sack (1) 068.1
sack[N-i] (3) n 019.6
sackcloth (1) n 019.7
sacked (9) v 082.1
~ him (4) v 082.1
~ up (2) v 019.6
sackers (1) n 021.5
sackful (6) n 019.8
sacking (5) n/v 019.7
sacks (840) n/v 019.5

Sacks (1) 116.2
Saco (3) AL 087.6
~ Road (1) 031.7
Sacramento (7) CA 087.4
sacred (2) adj 130.8
~ music (1) n 130.8
Sacred Harp sings (1) n 089.5
sacrifice (5) n 094.5
sad (4) adj 091.7
~ flesh (1) n 078.2
saddest (1) adj 002.6
saddle (215) n/v/adj 038.6
~ blanket (1) n 029.1
~ board (2) n 011.2
~ -broke (1) v 048.9
~ down (1) v 034.3
~ hoops (1) n 039.3
~ horse (30) n 034.2
~ horse[N-i] (2) n 034.2
~ horses (16) n 034.2
~ house (2) n 011.7
~ mare (3) n 034.2
~ mule (3) n 039.4
~ oxford (1) n 123.8
~ oxfords (7) n 123.8
~ slicker (1) n 081.9
~ stirrup (6) n 039.3
~ stirrups (7) n 039.3
~ stock (1) n 034.2
~ tree (1) n 088.8
~ up (19) v 038.6
~ whip (1) n 019.4
Saddle Dam (1) 085.1
saddleback (2) n/adv 060A.5
saddled (3) v 038.6
~ with (1) v 075.8
saddles (2) n 039.3
saddling (4) v 038.6
sadiron (3) n 010.6
sadirons (7) n 010.6
sadist (1) n 124.7
Saenz (1) 087.2
safe (239) n/adj 009.2
~ area (1) n 098.4
~ closets (1) n 009.7
~ pin (2) n 026.5
safe[N-i] (1) n 010.1
safer (4) adj 070.6
safes (36) n 010.1
safest (1) adj 052.5
safety (414) n/adj 085.7

~ base (1) n 098.4
~ belt (1) n 039.7
~ belts (1) n 052.1
~ building (1) n 112.8
~ bumpers (1) n 110.8
~ bumps (1) n 110.8
~ lines (1) n 107.3
~ pin (365) n 026.5
~ pins (36) n 026.5
~ razor (1) n 081.3
~ razors (2) n 024.9
safet(y) pin (2) n 026.5
saffron (5) n/adj 061.8
~ root (1) n 061.4
sag (8) v/adj 027.8
~ down (1) v 027.8
~ holes (1) n 031.4
sage (91) n/adj 010.5
~ broom (6) n 010.5
~ brooms (6) n 010.5
~ bush (1) n 081.9
~ cloth (1) n 025.6
~ -femme (1) n F 065.2
~ field (5) n 016.1
~ grass (11) n 015.9
~ -grass broom (1) n 010.5
~ -grass brooms (1) n 010.5
~ straw (1) n 010.5
~ tree (1) n 080.8
Sage (2) AR 087.7
~ Park (1) 106.4
Sagebock (1) n G 022.1
sagebrush (4) n 022.2
sagebush (1) n 061.4
sager (8) n 069.6
sagers (5) n 069.6
sagrain (1) n 051.2
said (199) v 070.7
~ about (2) v 039.9
~ no (19) v 082.1
sail (3) n/v 024.5
sailboat (19) n 024.6
sail(boat) (1) n 024.6
sailboats (19) n 081.9
sailfish (9) n 059.9
sailing (9) n/v/adj 057.4
~ lighterd (2) n 008.6
~ schooners (1) n 080.8
~ vessel (1) n 080.6
~ vessels (1) n 024.6
sailor (4) n 124.7
Sailor Brothers (1) 106.4

sailor[N-k] delight (1) n 053.9
sailor's (5) adj 005.8
~ breeches (1) n 005.8
~ choice (1) n 059.9
~ delight (2) n 104.6
~ warning (1) n 104.6
sails (1) n 088.8
Saint (1023) 070.6
~ Aloysius College (1) 070.6
~ Andrew Bay (1) FL 030.7
~ Andrew section (1) n 105.2
~ Andrews (1) AR 030.7
~ Andrews State Park (1) 106.5
~ Augustine (24) FL 087.8
~ Augustine Beach (1) FL 086.7
~ Augustine grass (6) n 015.9
~ Augustine Road (3) 031.7
~ Augustinian (1) 080.7
~ Bernard (6) LA 105.3
~ Bernard dog (1) n 033.1
~ Bernard Parish (3) LA 087.4
~ Bethlehem (1) TN 087.7
~ Catherine Creek (3) MS 030.7
~ Catherines Sound (1) GA 030.7
~ Charles (10) LA 107.6
~ Charles Avenue (3) 107.7
~ Charles corn (1) n 056.2
~ Charles Hotel (2) 075.7
~ Charles Parish (2) LA 087.6
~ Clair (1) AL 087.1
~ Clair County (3) AL AR 087.4
~ Clara (1) 087.5

~ Elmo (2) TN 087.3
~ Francis (5) AR 087.1
~ Francis Bottom (1) AR 030.7
~ Francis County (1) AR 087.2
~ Francis River (5) AR 030.7
~ Francisville (8) LA 087.3
~ Francis(ville) (1) LA 087.2
~ Gabriel (1) LA 087.4
~ George (2) GA 087.2
~ George Street Parade (1) 080.8
~ Helena (2) LA 087.2
~ Ives (1) AL 087.5
~ James (5) LA 087.1
~ James Methodist Church (1) 089.1
~ James Parish (2) LA 087.4
~ James Park (1) 106.4
~ Joe (3) LA 087.4
~ John (3) LA 087.3
~ John Methodist (1) 024.9
~ John Parish (1) LA 087.7
~ John's (4) 068.2
~ Johns (6) FL 086.2
~ Johns County (1) FL 086.4
~ Johns River (19) FL 087.5
~ Joseph (5) FL LA MO 087.1
~ Jo(seph) (1) LA 087.7
~ Joseph's Church (1) 108.9
~ Joseph's Day (1) 093.6
~ Jude Research Hospital (1) 084.6
~ Julian (1) 107.7
~ Landry (2) LA 086.5
~ Landry Parish (1) LA 087.2
~ Louis (719) MO 087.1
~ Lou(is) (1) MO 087.1
~ Louis Blues (6) 087.1

~ Louis Cardinal[N-i] (1) 087.1
~ Louis Fair (1) 087.1
~ Lucie (2) FL 087.3
~ Lucifer (1) 090.1
~ Luke's Church (1) 106.8
~ Martin (4) LA MS 087.2
~ Martinville (10) LA 087.4
~ Mary (5) LA 067.1
~ Mary's (14) 067.1
~ Mary's Cemetery (1) 078.8
~ Mary's Lake (1) MS 030.7
~ Marys (7) GA 067.1
~ Marys Bayou (1) TX 030.7
~ Marys River (4) FL GA 030.7
~ Matthew (5) LA 086.5
~ Matthew's (1) 067.5
~ Nick (1) 090.1
~ Patrick's Day Parade (1) 093.6
~ Paul (3) MN 065.8
~ Pete (4) FL 087.5
~ Petersburg (12) FL 089.3
~ Philip Street (1) 115.5
~ Philip's (1) 106.5
~ Rest Baptist Church (1) 089.2
~ Sebastian River (1) FL 030.7
~ Simons (6) GA 087.7
~ Simons Island (2) GA 087.2
~ Tammany (3) LA 086.5
~ Tammany Parish (3) LA 087.3
~ Thomas (2) 086.7
~ Thomas Park (1) 085.1
~ Vincent Island (1) FL 087.3
(Saint) (2) 087.2
~ Francisville (1) LA 087.2

~ Tammany (1) LA 087.1
Sainte (1) 087.5
saints (1) n 090.2
Saints Rest (1) TX 087.6
sake (39) n 092.2
sakes (41) n 092.2
saki (3) n 050.9
Sal (2) 068.1
sala (3) n S 007A.3
salad (359) n/adj 055A.5
~ bar (1) n 084.8
~ beans (1) n 055A.4
~ fork (8) n 017.8
~ forks (4) n 017.8
~ green (3) n 055A.5
~ green[N-i] (1) n 055A.5
~ greens (14) n 055A.5
~ onion (3) n 055.7
~ onions (6) n 055.7
~ part (1) n 055A.5
~ pear (1) n 054.5
~ tomato (21) n 055.3
~ tomatoes (73) n 055.3
~ turnips (2) n 055A.5
~ -type tomatoes (1) n 055.3
Salado (9) TX 030.7
~ Creek (6) TX 030.7
Sala(do) (2) TX 030.7
saladox (1) n 055A.5
salads (4) n 055A.5
salamander (10) n 059.9
salamanders (1) n 060.2
salami (14) n 037.2
salamis (1) n 121A.5
salary (5) n 063.8
sale (21) n/adj 094.5
~ price (1) n 094.5
Sale (14) 012.1
~ Creek (7) TN 087.2
Salem (21) AL AR GA TN 087.2
~ Church (2) 089.2
~ Churchyard (1) 089.2
~ Graveyard (1) 078.8
~ Springs (1) AR 087.8
Saleries Creek (1) GA 030.7
sales (2) n 036.5
Sales (6) 012.1
salesman (3) n 114.4
salesmen (2) n 052.1

Salim (1) 087.4
Saline (7) LA 030.7
~ Bay(ou) (1) LA 030.3
~ River (4) AR LA 030.7
Salisbury (7) MS NC NY 087.3
~ Creek (1) MS 030.7
~ steak (1) n 121.1
salitre (1) adj S 029.8
saliva glands (1) n 081.9
salivated (1) v 071.8
Salle (4) 086.6
sallet (173) n/adj 055A.5
~ dressing (1) n 055A.5
~ greens (1) n 055A.5
~ onion (3) n 055.7
~ onions (1) n 055.7
~ part (1) n 055A.5
~ patch (1) n 055A.5
~ tomatoes (1) n 055.3
sallets (6) n 055A.5
Sallis (1) MS 087.3
Sallisaw (1) OK 087.1
sallow (4) adj 072.9
~ -looking (2) adj 072.9
Sally (74) 068.1
~ Girl Branch (1) LA 030.7
~ in the saucer (3) n 104.6
~ Lunn (3) 044.4
~ Lunn bread (1) n 044.4
~ Walker (2) 130.3
salmon (17) n/adj 059.9
~ croquettes (1) n 080.8
~ melons (1) n 056.9
salmons (5) n 059.9
Salnienda Fork (1) MS 087.1
salon (4) n F 065.8
saloon (6) n 065.8
Saloon (1) 034.2
saloons (1) n 115.6
salso (1) n S 046.8
salt (1560) n/v/adj 051.7
~ -and-pepper suit (1) n 027.7
~ back (2) n 046.3
~ bacon (30) n 046.3
~ box (1) n 051.7

~ bread (1) n 044.4
~ -cured (2) adj 046.3
~ fish (1) n 051.7
~ flats (4) n 029.7
~ -free bread (1) n 122.4
~ -fried meat (1) n 048.4
~ gourd (1) n 051.7
~ grass (3) n 029.7
~ ham (1) n 046.5
~ hay (3) n 051.7
~ -heavy (1) adj 029.9
~ jowl (6) n 046.3
~ jowls (1) n 046.3
~ land (1) n 029.8
~ lard (1) n 051.7
~ lick (3) n 080.9
~ licks (1) n 096.7
~ marsh (7) n 029.7
~ marshes (7) n 029.7
~ meat (151) n 046.3
~ meats (1) n 046.3
~ mullet (2) n 051.7
~ ponds (1) n 029.7
~ pork (187) n 046.3
~ pot (2) n 017.6
~ -raising (1) adj 044.4
~ -rising (2) adj 044.4
~ -rising bread (18) n 044.4
~ -rising light bread (2) n 044.4
~ sacks (1) n 018.4
~ shoulder (1) n 046.3
~ side (2) n 046.4
~ side meat (2) n 046.3
~ side pork (1) n 046.4
~ sides (1) n 046.3
Salt (12) 030.7
~ Branch (1) AL 030.7
~ Creek (1) FL 030.7
~ Lake (2) TX UT 087.7
~ Lake City (6) UT 087.2
~ Springs (1) LA 087.9
salt(x2) (1) interj 037.5
saltbox (2) n/adj 118.9
~ house (1) n 118.9
saltcellar (2) n 051.7
saltcellars (3) n 051.7
salted (19) v/adj 121.3
~ bacon (1) n 046.5
~ hams (1) n 121.3

~ meat (6) n 046.5
~ nuts (1) n 054.7
~ peanuts (2) n 054.7
~ pork (1) n 046.3
~ side meat (1) n 046.3
Saltillo (3) MS 087.8
saltine (1) n 069.4
salting (2) v/adj 035.6
~ day (1) n 035.6
salts (6) n 051.7
saltshake (2) n 051.7
saltshaker (12) n 051.7
saltshakers (9) n 051.7
saltwater (36) n/adj 048.8
~ bass (1) n 059.9
~ bream (1) n 059.9
~ cat (1) n 084.6
~ catfish (3) n 059.9
~ cedars (1) n 061.8
~ corn bread (2) n 044.7
~ crawfish (1) n 060.8
~ creek (1) n 030.3
~ fish (3) n 059.9
~ flats (1) n 029.7
~ gar (1) n 088.9
~ Geech(ee) (1) n 080.9
~ marsh (3) n 029.7
~ mosquito (1) n 060A.8
~ mullet (1) n 059.9
~ striped bass (1) n 059.9
~ swamp (1) n 029.7
~ trout (2) n 059.9
~ turtles (2) n 060.6
salty (17) adj 029.7
~ ham (1) n 046.3
~ land (1) n 029.9
~ meat (1) n 046.3
~ -natured (1) adj 029.8
~ soil (2) n 029.8
~ trout (1) n 059.9
Salura (1) TX 087.6
saluting (1) v 081.7
Salvador Park (1) 106.4
salvage (5) n/adj 123.5
~ covers (2) n 088.8
~ room (1) n 010.3
~ stuff (1) n 010.2
Salvation Army (2) 113.8
salve (8) n 078.3
salves (1) n 061.4

salvia (1) n S 061.4
Salzburger (2) 065.8
~ antiques (1) n 066.9
Sam (10) 037.8
~ Hollow (1) TN 107.7
~ Houston (1) 054.3
~ Jones harrow (1) n 021.7
~ Rankin Street (1) 107.6
samba (2) n 083.1
sambas (1) n 083.1
Sambo (6) 069.3
Sambos (1) 069.3
same (164) n/adj 026.2
Sampan Sam (1) 126.5
sample (743) n/v 026.2
samp(le) (1) n 026.2
sampled (1) v 026.2
sampler (2) n 026.2
samples (17) n/v 026.2
Samples Fork (1) TN 030.7
sampling (3) n/v 026.2
Sampson (7) 016.5
~ post (1) n 016.5
~ snakeroot (6) n 061.4
Sampsons Branch (1) AL 030.7
Sams Creek (1) TN 030.7
Samson (1) 073.1
San (168) 087.6
~ Angelo (4) TX 087.6
~ Antonio (59) TX 087.6
~ Antoni(o) (1) TX 087.9
~ Anton(io) (8) TX 086.4
~ (An)tonio (3) TX 087.5
~ (An)ton(io) (1) TX 087.5
~ Antonio International Airport (1) 106.5
~ Antonio River (4) TX 030.7
~ Anton(io) River (2) TX 030.7
~ (An)tonio River (3) TX 030.7
~ Antonio Transit System (1) 109.9
~ Augustine (4) TX 087.2

~ Diego (11) CA TX 087.8
~ Fernando Cathedral (2) 106.4
~ Francisco (23) CA 087.8
~ Gabriel River (1) TX 030.7
~ Jacinto (1) TX 087.4
~ Jacinto Battleground (1) 106.4
~ (Ja)cinto Battleground (1) 106.4
~ Jacinto monument (2) n 106.4
~ Jacinto River (5) TX 030.7
~ (Ja)cinto River (1) TX 065.8
~ Jose (2) 106.4
~ Juan (1) 086.8
~ Juan Plantation (1) TX 087.2
~ Juan River (1) TX 030.7
~ Marco (1) 105.2
~ Marco Avenue (1) 095.8
~ Marcos (7) TX 087.3
~ Miguel (1) TX 087.4
~ Patricio (1) TX 087.3
~ Pedro (2) 105.4
~ Pedro Park (2) 106.4
~ Roque Creek (1) TX 030.7
~ Saba (1) TX 030.7
~ Salvador Park (1) 106.4
~ Souci (2) 105.1
~ Ygnacio (3) TX 087.9
sanatorium (1) n 084.5
sanctified (2) adj 067.9
~ fellow (1) n 067.9
Sanctified (7) 089.2
~ church (2) n 089.2
Sanctify (1) 126.6
sanctuary (1) n 098.4
sand (307) n/adj 029.8
~ bass (2) n 059.9
~ bed (1) n 031.7
~ beds (1) n 029.8
~ berry (1) n 062.5
~ bolster (1) n 020.9

~ bream (1) n 059.9
~ clay (4) n 031.6
~ -clay road (1) n 031.6
~ crabs (2) n 060.8
~ dirt (1) n 029.8
~ ditch (1) n 030.2
~ dunes (4) n 029.7
~ field (1) n 029.8
~ flea (3) n 060A.6
~ fleas (2) n 060A.9
~ flies (5) n 084.8
~ fly (5) n 060A.7
~ frog (1) n 060.3
~ glade (1) n 029.6
~ gnat (2) n 060A.7
~ gnats (2) n 060A.4
~ gophers (1) n 060.7
~ -graded roads (1) n 031.6
~ gravel (1) n 031.6
~ -grit wheel (1) n 023.5
~ gullies (1) n 030.5
~ hill (2) n 029.8
~ hills (5) n 029.8
~ jack (2) n 061.8
~ jack acorn tree (1) n 061.8
~ land (5) n 029.8
~ loam (4) n 029.8
~ nigger (1) n 069.3
~ owl (1) n 059.1
~ pail (3) n 116.9
~ pear (1) n 091.8
~ perch (3) n 059.9
~ pine (2) n 061.8
~ ridge (1) n 029.4
~ rim (1) n 029.7
~ road (8) n 031.7
~ roads (7) n 031.6
~ rock (1) n 029.8
~ screen (1) n 016.3
~ sharks (1) n 059.9
~ soak (1) n 029.4
~ -soak land (1) n 029.4
~ soaker (1) n 006.1
~ soil (4) n 029.8
~ ticks (1) n 060A.8
~ trails (1) n 031.6
~ trout (3) n 059.9
~ turtle (1) n 060.7
~ yard (1) n 010.5
Sand (16) 030.7

~ Creek (1) MS 030.7
~ Fly (1) 106.3
~ Grove (1) GA 087.3
~ Hill (1) TX 087.6
~ Mountain (8) AL 087.2
~ Ridge (1) AR 092.7
sandal (9) n 123.8
sandals (98) n/adj 123.8
~ -like (1) adj 123.8
sandbag (2) adj 022.9
~ ditch (1) n 030.2
sandbagging (1) v 096.8
sandbar (2) n 075.9
sandbars (1) n 029.6
sandburs (2) n 062.3
Sanders (220) 068.4
~ Creek (3) TX 030.7
Sand(ers) (1) 068.4
Sanders' (1) 068.4
Sandersville (5) GA MS 087.2
Sandfield (3) 078.8
~ Cemetery (2) 078.8
~ Cemeter(y) (1) 087.5
sandhill (9) n/adj 030.8
~ country (1) n 030.8
~ crane (1) n 081.9
~ cranes (1) n 059.3
~ gopher (1) n 060.7
~ pine (1) n 061.8
~ racers (1) n 089.8
~ red-neck (1) n 069.4
~ tick (1) n 080.7
sandhills (1) n 030.8
Sandhills Mountains (1) TX 031.1
sanding (1) v 010.9
sandlot (6) n/adj 130.4
~ baseball (2) n 130.4
~ football (2) n 130.5
~ stuff (1) n 130.4
sandlots (2) n 080.9
sandman (1) n 090.2
sandpaper (1) n 023.4
sandrock (12) n 010.9
sandrocks (1) n 032.1
sands (2) n 029.4
Sands (1) 105.9
sandsoap land (2) n 029.6
sandspur (5) n/adj 015.9
~ grass (1) n 015.9
~ weeds (1) n 015.9
sandspurs (12) n 015.9
sandstone (2) n/adj 029.9

~ land (1) n 029.8
sandstones (1) n 023.4
sandstorm (2) n 006.3
sandstorms (3) n 104.6
Sandtown (2) MS 087.4
~ Road (1) 087.2
Sandusky (1) OH 087.3
sandwich (97) n/adj 048.6
~ bread (11) n 044.3
~ loaves (1) n 044.3
~ roll (1) n 122.4
~ sack (1) n 019.5
~ shop (1) n 116.3
~ shops (1) n 116.3
sandwiches (24) n 121.6
sandworm (4) n 060A.6
sandy (515) adj 029.8
~ beach (2) n 029.8
~ bottomland (1) n 029.8
~ chocolate loam (1) n 029.8
~ clay (3) n 029.9
~ clay soil (1) n 029.9
~ country (1) n 029.8
~ ground (1) n 029.8
~ hammock (1) n 029.5
~ hills (1) n 029.8
~ lamp (1) n 083.1
~ land (113) n 029.8
~ -land country (1) n 029.8
~ -like (1) adj 029.8
~ -like soil (2) n 029.9
~ loam (130) n 029.8
~ loam land (6) n 029.8
~ loam soil (5) n 029.8
~ -loam-type soil (1) n 029.8
~ loams (1) n 029.9
~ pea (1) n 060A.6
~ peas (1) n 060A.6
~ place (1) n 029.8
~ plain (1) n 029.5
~ poor land (1) n 029.8
~ road (2) n 031.6
~ roads (1) n 031.6
~ soil (112) n 029.8
~ -stone land (1) n 029.8
~ type (1) n 029.8
~ yard (1) n 029.8
~ yards (1) n 015.6

Sandy (37) 030.7
~ Branch Hill (1) GA 030.8
~ Creek (8) AL GA LA MS 030.7
~ Cross (2) GA 087.4
~ Hill (1) AR 087.4
~ Land Ridge (1) AR 092.7
~ Mountain (2) AL 087.9
~ River (1) TN 030.7
~ Springs (10) GA 106.4
~ Springs Park (1) 106.6
Sandy's dog (1) n 033.3
Sanford (7) FL 087.4
Sanforized (1) 103.3
sang (13) n/adj 061.4
~ hoes (1) n 061.4
~ roots (4) n 061.4
Sanger (2) TX 087.1
sanging (1) v 047.5
Sango (1) TN 087.5
sangre (1) n S 047.4
Sanibel (1) 106.4
sanitary (7) adj 085.6
~ collector (1) n 115.2
~ engineers (1) n 115.2
~ inspectors (1) n 115.7
~ men (1) n 115.2
~ toilets (1) n 012.1
~ workers (1) n 115.2
Sanitary Department (1) 115.2
sanitation (10) adj 115.2
~ -department workers (1) n 115.2
~ engineer (3) n 115.2
~ engineers (1) n 115.2
~ worker (2) n 115.2
~ workers (3) n 115.2
sank-in place (1) n 098.6
Sanka (2) 048.8
sanked (1) v 096.1
Sano (3) 087.2
sans (1) prep F 069.7
Sans Souci (1) 106.1
Santa (25) 087.4
~ Clara (1) 087.4
~ Claus (10) 093.2
~ Claus melon (1) n 056.7
~ Fe (3) NM 087.2

~ Gertrudis (4) 033.6
~ Gutierrez (1) TX 086.6
~ Lupia (1) FL 087.5
~ Maria (1) TX 086.2
~ Monica (2) CA TX 087.2
~ Rosa (1) FL 087.7
Sant(a) Gertrudis (1) 033.6
San(ta) (3) 086.4
~ Anna (1) TX 086.4
~ (Ger)trudis (1) 033.6
~ Rosa (1) FL 087.2
Santabarb (2) LA 030.7
Santee (1) SC 030.7
santo (1) adj S 061.6
sap (10) n/adj 113.2
~ pine (1) n 008.6
~ post (1) n 016.5
~ post[N-i] (1) n 016.5
~ tree (1) n 061.5
SAP (2) 059.4
Sapelo (3) GA 087.2
~ River (1) GA 030.7
sapling (5) n/adj 088.7
~ fence (1) n 016.2
saplings (3) n 061.9
sapodilla (3) n/adj 061.9
~ tree (1) n 096.7
sapodillas (1) n 061.8
Sapolio (1) 080.8
sapota (2) n/adj 061.8
~ tree (1) n 061.8
sapped (1) v 057.7
sapphires (1) n 123.1
sappy (1) adj 092.9
sapsuck (3) n 059.3
sapsucker (92) n 059.3
sapsuckers (26) n 059.3
sapsucks (3) n 059.3
Sara (26) 086.3
~ Lee (23) 068.1
~ Lee cakes (1) n 068.1
Sar(a) (1) 069.6
Sarah (698) 068.1
~ Hughes (1) 068.1
Sar(ah) (8) 068.1
Sarah's (1) 068.1
Sarahs (2) 068.1
Saraland (2) AL 105.2
Sarasota (5) FL 086.4
Saratoga (4) MS TX 107.7
sarcastic (1) adj 074.8

sardine (5) n 061.2
sardines (13) n 130.5
Sardis (13) MS TN 087.3
~ community (1) GA 087.1
~ Lake (2) MS 030.7
Sargent (1) TX 087.6
sarrace(nia) (2) n 104.7
sarsaparilla (12) n/adj 062.2
~ roots (4) n 061.4
~ tea (2) n 080.8
~ vine (1) n 061.4
~ vines (1) n 061.4
sash (4) n/adj 009.5
~ curtains (1) n 009.5
sashes (1) n 009.5
sass (8) n 055A.5
sassafras (279) n/adj 061.4
~ bushes (1) n 061.4
~ candy (1) n 061.4
~ leaf (1) n 062.2
~ root (31) n 061.4
~ roots (28) n 061.4
~ sprouts (2) n 061.4
~ tea (67) n 061.4
~ tree (13) n 061.4
~ -tree root (1) n 061.4
~ trees (2) n 061.8
~ worms (1) n 060.5
sassa(fras) tree (1) n 061.8
sas(safras) tea (1) n 061.4
sassed (1) v 091.8
Sasser (1) GA 087.8
Sassers Mill Creek (1) MS 030.7
sassy (8) adj 074.8
sat (631) v 049.3
~ around (6) v 049.3
~ beside (1) v 049.3
~ down (230) v 049.3
~ in (6) v 049.3
~ on (15) v 049.3
~ to (1) v 049.3
~ up (8) v 049.3
Satan (445) 090.1
Sat(an) (1) 090.1
satchel (15) n 028.2
satchels (1) n 028.2
sateen bloomers (1) n 080.9
Satilla (9) GA 030.7

~ Creek (1) GA 030.7
~ River (5) GA 030.7
Satilpa Creek (1) AL 030.7
satinwood (1) n 061.8
satisfactory (1) n 053.4
satisfied (12) adj 070.7
satisfy (1) v 039.8
satsuma (12) n/adj 055.1
~ bushes (1) n 055.1
~ groves (1) n 091.8
~ oranges (1) n 055.1
~ tree (1) n 055.1
~ trees (1) n 061.8
Satsuma (2) 105.2
satsumas (10) n 055.2
Saturday (1186) 002.1
~ afternoon (3) n 002.1
~ afternoons (1) n 002.3
~ dinner (1) n 002.1
~ evening (13) n 002.1
~ Evening Post (1) 002.1
~ evenings (1) n 002.5
~ morn (1) n 002.2
~ morning (9) n 002.2
~ night (32) n 002.1
~ -night frolics (1) n 083.1
~ night special (16) n 113.1
~ night specials (4) n 113.1
~ nights (1) n 002.1
~ week (9) n 003.7
Saturd(ay) evening (1) n 002.5
Saturday[N-i] (1) 002.1
Saturdays (24) 002.1
satyr (2) n 124.7
satyriases (1) n 124.8
satyriasis (1) n 124.5
sauce (502) n/adj 048.5
~ bottle (1) n 051.8
~ piquante (2) n F 048.5
saucepan (8) n 017.5
saucepan[N-i] (1) n 017.5
saucepans (2) n 017.6
saucer (12) n/v/adj 017.2
~ kind (1) n 056.6
~ squash (2) n 056.6
Saucer (1) 130.3
saucered (1) v 084.8

saucering (1) v 032.4
saucers (1) n 056.6
sauces (5) n 048.5
Saucier (1) MS 087.4
saucy (1) adj 048.5
sauerbraten (1) n 121.6
sauerkraut (2) n 055A.1
sauger (2) n/adj 059.9
~ jack (1) n 059.9
saule (1) n F 061.7
Sault Sainte Marie (1) MI 087.5
sausage (1574) n/adj 046.8
~ balls (1) n 046.8
~ cakes (1) n 046.8
~ casing (1) n 037.3
~ casings (2) n 046.8
~ grinder (2) n 046.8
~ grinders (1) n 046.8
~ gumbo (1) n 046.8
~ links (5) n 121.6
~ making (1) n 046.8
~ meat (18) n 046.8
~ mill (14) n 046.8
~ mills (2) n 046.8
~ patties (9) n 121.6
~ roll (1) n 046.8
~ rolls (1) n 121.6
~ sandwich (1) n 046.8
~ stuff (1) n 046.8
~ stuffer (2) n 046.8
sau(sage) (1) n 047.3
sausage[N-i] (2) n 046.8
sausages (34) n 046.8
sauter balai (2) v F 082.2
sauvage (1) n F 069.9
Sauvage (1) 030.4
savage (1) adj 093.5
savane (1) n F 015.9
savanna (2) n 029.7
Savannah (666) GA TN 087.6
~ Bank and Trust (1) 108.5
~ Beach (1) GA 087.6
~ River (13) GA 030.7
~ River Swamp (1) GA 029.6
~ River Valley (1) GA 030.7
~ Sweet (1) 056.9
(Sa)vannah (1) GA 087.6
Savannahian (2) 080.8
Savannahians (1) 080.6

savannas (1) n 029.4
save (24) v 074.4
saved (14) v 057.8
  ˜ by (1) v 053.4
saver (2) n 073.5
Saver (2) 116.2
savers (1) n 116.2
saving (5) v/adj 073.5
savior (1) n 089.3
Savior (4) 089.3
savoy cabbage (1) n 055A.1
savvy (5) n/v 025.4
saw (1742) n/v/adj/interj 037.5
  ˜ a leg (1) interj 037.5
  ˜ after (1) v 090.7
  ˜ bench (15) n 022.1
  ˜ benches (1) n 022.1
  ˜ block (3) n 022.1
  ˜ -boss(x2) (1) interj 037.5
  ˜ brier (1) n 062.3
  ˜ briers (2) n 015.9
  ˜ dogs (3) n 022.1
  ˜ down (1) v 092.7
  ˜ filer (1) n 080.6
  ˜ frame (2) n 022.1
  ˜ frames (1) n 022.1
  ˜ grass (6) n 029.7
  ˜ -grass flats (1) n 029.7
  ˜ jack (6) n 022.1
  ˜ log (1) n 008.5
  ˜ -now(x2) (1) interj 037.5
  ˜ rack (44) n 022.1
  ˜ racks (2) n 022.1
  ˜ rick (1) n 022.1
  ˜ the light (1) v 082.1
  ˜ there (1) interj 037.5
  ˜ to (2) v 102.5
  ˜ tree (1) n 022.1
saw(x2) (17) interj 037.5
saw(x3) (3) interj 037.5
sawback (1) n 022.1
sawbuck (74) n 022.1
sawbucks (3) n 022.1
sawdust (4) n/adj 065.9
  ˜ box (1) n 015.5
  ˜ roads (1) n 031.7
sawed (9) v/adj 102.5
  ˜ into (1) v 075.9
  ˜ -off shotgun (1) n 113.1

  ˜ -off shotguns (1) n 113.1
sawhorse (339) n 022.1
sawhorses (127) n 022.1
sawing (10) v/adj 022.9
  ˜ bar (1) n 022.1
  ˜ log (1) n 022.1
  ˜ rack (2) n 022.1
  ˜ sharpener (1) n 023.4
sawlogs (1) n 093.5
sawmill (40) n/adj 088.9
  ˜ camp (1) n 080.6
  ˜ chicken (1) n 046.3
  ˜ coffee (1) n 032.3
  ˜ license (1) n 082.2
  ˜ man (2) n 080.6
  ˜ mechanic (1) n 067.8
  ˜ mules (1) n 033.7
  ˜ socks (1) n 080.8
Sawmill Creek (1) TN 030.7
sawmill[V-t] (1) v 080.6
sawmilled (3) v 080.9
sawmiller (2) n 080.8
sawmilling (4) n/v 080.6
sawmills (10) n 080.8
saws (18) n 120.9
Sawyahatchee Creek (1) AL 030.7
sawyer (12) n 080.6
Sawyer (5) 105.4
  ˜ City (1) 105.4
  ˜ Creek (3) AL 030.7
sawyers (6) n 060.5
Saxon (16) 099.5
Sax(on) (1) 069.4
Saxons (1) 069.4
saxophone (2) n 066.8
say (1221) v 013.7
  ˜ (a)bout (1) v 013.7
  ˜ no (1) v 082.1
s(ay) (2) v 033.2
say[V-p] (23) v 013.7
say[V-r] (10) v 070.2
say[V-t] (1) v 074.5
saying (48) n/v 057.5
says (93) v 013.7
  ˜ no (1) v 082.1
  ˜ to (1) v 053.3
SB (1) 033.2
scab (28) n 078.2
scabies (1) n 060.8
scads (4) n 055A.8
scaffold (29) n 022.2
scaffolding (5) n 022.1

scaffolds (2) n 022.1
scalawag (5) n/adj 069.7
  ˜ goings on (1) n 080.8
scalawags (2) n 085.8
scald (74) n/v/adj 018.2
  ˜ cat (3) n 050.8
scald[V-p] (1) v 018.2
scalded (16) v/adj 018.1
  ˜ bread (2) n 044.6
  ˜ hoecake (1) n 044.8
  ˜ hot hoecake (1) n 044.8
  ˜ milk (1) n 080.6
  ˜ out (1) v 018.2
scalder (1) n 081.8
scalding (35) v/adj 018.2
  ˜ barrel (10) n 019.1
  ˜ barrels (1) n 019.1
  ˜ box (1) n 098.7
  ˜ bugs (1) n 060A.8
  ˜ pot (2) n 017.6
  ˜ pots (1) n 017.6
  ˜ vat (1) n 035.6
  ˜ water (5) n 070.9
scalds (17) v 018.2
scale (6) n/adj 015.7
  ˜ fish (1) n 059.9
scales (2) n 080.6
scallion (12) n 055.7
scallions (56) n 055.7
scallop (7) n/adj 060.9
  ˜ squash (4) n 056.6
  ˜ squashes (1) n 056.6
scalloped (3) adj 070.7
scallops (8) n 060.1
scalls (1) n 020.9
scalp (2) n 071.3
scalpel (1) n 104.4
scaly (61) adj 060.4
  ˜ back (1) n 060.4
  ˜ bark (29) n 054.8
  ˜ -bark hickory (3) n 061.8
  ˜ -bark hickory nut (3) n 054.8
  ˜ -bark hickory nuts (2) n 054.8
  ˜ -bark maple (1) n 061.8
  ˜ -bark tree (2) n 061.8
  ˜ -bark trees (1) n 061.8
  ˜ barks (17) n 054.8
  ˜ fish (1) n 059.9
  ˜ grass (1) n 015.9

scamp (4) n 080.9
Scandinavian (1) 128.8
Scandinavians (7) 128.8
scanning (2) adj 070.6
Scans (1) 128.8
scantling (2) n 080.7
scanty (2) adj 095.2
scar (19) n/adj 078.2
  ˜ tissue (12) n 078.2
Scarboroughs Landing (1) AR 094.9
scarce (849) adj 095.2
scarcely (6) adv 065.9
scarcer (9) adj 095.2
scarcity (1) n 095.2
scare (49) v/adj 074.3
  ˜ house (1) n 090.3
  ˜ -off boots (1) n 123.8
scare[V-p] (3) v 074.3
scare[V-t] (2) v 074.3
scarecrow (2) n 090.2
scared (881) v/adj 074.3
  ˜ away (1) v 074.3
scaredest (1) adj 074.3
scaredy (46) adj 074.3
  ˜ butts (1) n 074.3
  ˜ -cat (45) n 074.3
scares (12) v 074.3
scarf (3) n 028.8
scarier (1) adj 074.3
scariest (1) adj 074.3
scarifiers (1) n 041.8
scaring (2) v 024.9
scarish (1) adj 074.5
scarlet (18) adj 079.7
  ˜ fever (16) n 079.7
  ˜ maple (1) n 061.5
  ˜ tanagers (1) n 089.8
scarletina (2) n 079.8
scarves (1) n 009.2
scary (174) adj 074.3
  ˜ cat (3) n 074.3
  ˜ house (3) n 090.3
  ˜ -like (1) adj 074.3
  ˜ -looking (1) adj 074.3
scatter pins (1) n 080.9
scatterbrain (3) n 073.4
scatterbrains (2) n 073.4
scattered (6) v/adj 074.9
  ˜ rains (1) n 006.1
  ˜ shower (1) n 006.6
  ˜ thundershowers (1) n 006.2
scattering (1) n 006.6

scatters (1) n 030.9
scavenger (4) n/adj 059.5
~ man (1) n 096.7
~ wagon (1) n 080.9
~ wagons (1) n 089.8
scavengers (6) n 059.5
scene (4) n 031.1
scenic (4) adj 031.6
~ highway (1) n 031.6
~ overlooks (1) n 107.2
~ railway (1) n 084.7
~ road (1) n 107.7
scent (9) n 070.6
Schaeffer Bridge (1) LA 087.2
Schale (1) n G 024.7
Schatz (1) n G 081.5
scheduled (2) v 101.2
~ to (1) v 101.2
schefflera (1) n 080.6
scheffleras (1) n 062.8
schemer (1) n 073.5
Schiffman Branch (1) AL 030.7
Schlappkanne (1) n G 017.4
Schleifstein (1) n G 023.4
Schley (3) GA 087.4
Schlitz (5) 121.9
~ beer (1) n 095.8
Schmear (2) n G 090.8
Schmierkase (1) n G 048.3
Schmuck (1) n G 073.4
Schnitsbrot (2) n G 044.3
Schnitts (2) n G 054.6
schnitzel (1) n 121.4
Schnitzel Grube (1) n G 054.6
scholar (109) n 068.7
scholarly (3) adj 125.6
scholars (14) n 068.7
scholastic age (1) n 083.2
Scholes Field (1) 106.5
school (1480) n/adj 067.6
~ bass (1) n 059.9
~ bathroom (1) n 126.3
~ board (1) n 012.5
~ books (1) n 081.4
~ buddies (1) n 129.6
~ building (2) n 002.6
~ bus (4) n 109.9
~ buses (1) n 065.8
~ cen(sus) (1) n 070.7

~ -closing programs (1) n 083.2
~ dance (2) n 083.1
~ dances (3) n 083.1
~ desk (3) n 083.8
~ desk[N-i] (2) n 083.8
~ desks (1) n 083.8
~ doors (1) n 010.5
~ flops (1) n 069.7
~ hops (1) n 083.1
~ kid (1) n 068.7
~ kids (4) n 068.7
~ ma (1) n 067.6
~ madam (5) n 067.6
~ maid (1) n 067.6
~ maker (1) n 067.6
~ matron (2) n 067.6
~ miss (2) n 067.6
~ nights (1) n 003.1
~ parties (1) n 130.7
~ picnics (1) n 130.7
~ primary (1) n 083.7
~ scholar (2) n 068.7
~ shit (1) n 092.1
~ student (2) n 068.7
~ superintendent (1) n 052.6
~ sweetheart (1) n 081.5
~ system (1) n 103.4
~ term (2) n 083.2
~ time (1) n 083.5
~ wagon (2) n 081.9
~ woman (1) n 067.6
School (26) 065.8
~ Library Media Specialist (1) 080.6
school[N-i] (1) n 091.7
schoolboy (10) n 068.7
schoolchild (11) n 068.7
schoolchildren (7) n 068.7
schooled (1) v 075.6
schoolgirl (8) n 068.7
schoolhouse (33) n 014.1
Schoolhouse (1) 087.8
schooling (67) n 083.6
schoolma'am (24) n 067.6
schoolma'ams (1) n 067.6
schoolmarm (232) n 067.6
(school)marm (1) n 067.6
schoolmarms (10) n 067.6
schoolmaster (7) n 067.6
schoolmates (1) n 129.6
schoolmistress (30) n 067.6

schoolrooms (1) n 001.2
school's (3) adj 083.2
~ out (2) n 075.7
~ -out party (1) n 130.7
schools (70) n 090.7
schoolteacher (342) n 067.6
schoolteach(er) (1) n 067.6
schoolteacher[N-k] name (1) n 067.6
schoolteachers (33) n 067.6
schoolteaching (2) n/v 057.4
schoolwork (1) n 102.8
schooner (5) n 024.6
schooners (7) n 024.6
schottische (6) n 083.1
schottisches (1) n 083.1
Schrank (3) n G 009.7
Schriever (3) LA 087.1
Schubkarren (1) n G 023.3
Schulenburg (4) TX 087.5
Schuttler (1) 088.8
Schwademagen (2) n G 047.1
Schwartz (1) n G 069.5
Schwartze (1) n G 069.5
Schwartzer Mamzer (1) n G 080.8
Schwartzers (2) n G 069.3
Schweinepenne (1) n G 015.4
Schwein (1) n G 035.5
Schwengel (1) n G 021.2
sciatic rheumatism (1) n 079.6
science (7) n 066.9
Science (4) 078.3
scientific (1) adj 052.1
Scientist (2) 089.1
scissor grabs (1) n 090.9
scissorbill gars (1) n 059.9
scissors (9) n 060.8
scitch-him(x2) (1) interj 033.2
Scoco (2) 046.3
Scofield (1) TX 087.4
scoggin (1) n 089.9
scold (3) v 057.6
scolding (7) n 065.5

scones (1) n 044.4
sconions (2) n 125.2
scoop (19) n/v/adj 120.5
~ deal (1) n 023.1
~ stock (1) n 021.6
~ up (2) v 020.3
scooped (1) adj 023.1
scooper (1) n 030.2
scooping (1) v 030.1
scoops (5) n 088.7
scoosh (1) v 055.9
scoot (9) v/adj 096.2
~ along (1) v 058.6
~ down (2) v 096.4
~ mobiles (1) n 084.8
scootched (1) v 096.4
scooted down (1) v 096.4
scooter (49) n/adj 021.6
~ plow (8) n 021.6
~ plows (2) n 021.6
~ pooping (1) v 081.7
~ stock (6) n 021.6
~ stocks (2) n 021.6
scooters (18) n 080.8
scooting plow (1) n 021.6
scoots out (1) v 023.1
scope (3) n 061.6
scorcher (2) n 007.1
scorching (1) adj 007.1
score (2) n/v 065.5
scores (2) n 130.8
scorpion (16) n 060A.7
scorpions (7) n 059.8
Scot (4) 128.1
scotch (2) n/v 130.2
~ out (1) v 075.6
Scotch (24) 128.1
~ burr (1) n 089.9
~ -Irish (13) 128.1
~ people (2) n 128.1
~ tightwad (1) n 128.1
Scotchman (4) 128.1
Scotia (3) 070.7
Scotland (9) 087.8
Scotlandville (1) LA 087.3
Scotland(ville) (3) LA 087.5
Scots (8) 128.1
Scotsman (2) 073.5
Scott (29) AR MS TN 087.2
~ Boulevard (1) 093.6
~ County (8) AR MS TN 087.4

~ Fitzgerald (1) 032.7
~ Mountain (1) AL 031.1
~ River (1) GA 030.7
~ Station (2) AL 087.4
~ Street (1) 107.6
Scottdale (1) TX 087.2
Scotties (2) 128.1
Scottish (7) 128.1
~ Highlanders (1) 080.7
Scotts (2) 087.3
~ Addition (1) TX 087.3
~ Hill (1) TN 087.1
Scottsboro (5) AL 087.3
Scottsville (1) TX 087.6
scoundrel (14) n 069.6
scoundrelly (1) adj 080.6
scoundrels (10) n 059.5
scour (4) v/adj 010.4
~ broom (1) n 010.5
scoured (3) v 070.7
scouring (11) v/adj 010.4
~ mop (3) n 010.5
~ mops (1) n 010.5
~ pad (3) n 018.3
scours (1) v 010.4
scout (10) adj 088.8
~ car (5) n 088.8
~ cars (2) n 111.7
~ knife (2) n 104.3
~ knives (1) n 104.3
Scout (2) 097.8
scouting (2) v 081.8
~ around (1) v 081.7
Scouts (4) 042.3
Scovil (2) 080.8
~ hoe (1) n 080.8
~ hoes (1) n 021.6
scow (7) n 024.6
scrabble (2) n 047.4
scraggly-looking (1) adj 030.9
scramble (32) n/v/adj 046.2
~ eggs (2) n 046.1
scram(ble) (2) v 046.1
scramble[V-r] (1) v 046.1
scrambled (49) v/adj 046.1
~ egg (3) n 046.2
~ eggs (14) n 046.1
scrambles (2) n/v 130.7
scrambling (4) v 046.2

Scranton (3) MS PA 087.3
scrap (111) n/v/adj 026.2
~ bucket (5) n 017.4
~ butter (1) n 047.5
~ can (1) n 017.4
~ fish (1) n 059.9
~ iron (3) n 050.8
~ irons (1) n 010.2
~ land (1) n 029.7
~ lumber (2) n 016.2
~ meat (1) n 046.7
~ meat skin (1) n 046.6
~ pail (1) n 017.4
~ pen (1) n 010.3
~ piece (4) n 026.2
~ plate (1) n 017.4
~ sample (1) n 026.2
~ up (1) v 081.8
~ wood (1) n 008.6
scrap[N-i] (1) n 017.4
scrapbooks (1) n 053.4
scrape (44) n/v 015.8
~ up (1) v 093.6
scraped (1) v 080.7
scraper (19) n 021.7
scrapers (2) n 023.3
scrapes (16) n/v 021.6
scrapified (1) adj 033.4
scraping (21) v/adj 015.8
~ scooter (1) n 021.6
scrapped (1) v 104.2
scrapping (1) v 104.2
scrapple (111) n 047.4
scrap(ple) (1) n 047.4
scraps (27) n 010.2
scratch (16) n/v/adj 114.5
~ feed (1) n 088.8
~ out (1) v 075.8
~ pad (1) n 018.3
~ up (1) v 052.7
Scratch (27) 090.1
scratched (2) v 025.6
scratcher (9) n 120.6
scratchers (4) n 092.8
scratching (2) v 057.4
scratchy (2) adj 076.4
scrawngy (1) adj 072.9
scrawny (3) adj 072.9
screak (2) n/adj 070.7
~ owl (1) n 059.1
screaking (15) v/adj 065.9
~ frog (1) n 060.3

screaks (1) n 070.8
screaky (1) adj 070.6
Scream Machine (1) 130A.3
screaming (6) v/adj 057.4
~ guitars (1) n 088.7
~ owl (2) n 059.1
screech (544) adj 059.1
~ owl (458) n 059.1
~ owls (79) n 059.1
screeched up (1) v 096.4
screeching (12) v/adj 065.9
~ owl (9) n 059.1
~ owls (1) n 059.1
screen (80) n/v/adj 059.1
~ cage (1) n 036.8
~ door (3) n 011.1
~ doors (2) n 011.1
~ house (1) n 014.2
~ in (2) v 010.8
~ -in (1) n 010.9
~ -in back porch (1) n 007A.6
~ -in front porch (2) n 007A.3
~ porch (41) n 010.8
~ porches (5) n 010.8
~ rack (1) n 008.3
~ wire (6) n 016.3
screen[V-t] (1) v 070.7
screened (84) v/adj 007A.5
~ back porch (1) n 010.8
~ box (1) n 015.5
~ cabinet (1) n 015.5
~ in (8) v 010.8
~ -in (2) adj 010.8
~ -in back porch (8) n 007A.t
~ -in front porch (2) n 007A.5
~ -in porch (38) n 007A.6
~ -in porches (3) n 007A.6
~ -in room (2) n 007A.1
~ -in side porch (1) n 010.8
~ out (1) v 009.9
~ porch (12) n 007A.4
screenhouse (1) n 015.5
screens (8) n 065.8

Screven (4) GA 087.7
~ County (3) GA 087.1
Screvin (1) 087.4
screw (26) n/v/adj 112.5
~ caps (1) n 020.4
~ dive (1) n 095.4
~ flies (1) n 060A.2
~ job (1) n 095.4
~ -on (1) adj 020.4
~ -on top (1) n 020.4
~ -on tops (1) n 020.4
~ stopper (1) n 020.4
~ tail (1) n 033.3
~ top (6) n 020.4
~ tops (3) n 020.4
~ -up (1) n 073.4
screw[N-i] (1) n 073.4
screwball (3) adj 073.3
screwdriver (7) n 020.9
screwdrivers (2) n 066.9
screwed (6) v 039.8
~ up (3) v 082.2
~ up his life (1) v 082.2
~ -up (1) adj 093.5
screwing (2) v 057.5
~ around (1) v 081.7
screwman (1) n 092.7
screws (1) n 070.6
screwworm (4) n 060.5
screwworms (3) n 060.5
screwy (2) adj 074.7
scribble (1) v 100.5
scribblings (1) n 046.6
scrim (2) n 019.6
scrimshaw (1) n 096.9
Scrimshaw (1) 056.7
scrinch (33) v/adj 096.4
~ down (2) v 096.4
~ owl (26) n 059.1
~ owls (5) n 059.1
scrinching owl (1) n 059.1
scrip (3) n/adj 095.3
~ dances (1) n 083.1
scriptural (1) adj 089.3
Scripture (1) 089.4
scrooch (136) v/adj 096.4
~ down (18) v 096.4
~ owl (90) n 059.1
~ owls (18) n 059.1
~ up (4) v 096.4
scrooch[V-t] down (1) v 096.4
scrooched (6) v 096.4
~ down (2) v 096.4

~ up (3) v 096.4
scrooches up (1) v 096.4
scrooching (4) v/adj 096.4
    ~ down (1) v 096.4
    ~ outfit (1) n 099.9
    ~ up (1) v 096.4
Scrooge (19) 073.5
scroonch owl (1) n 059.1
scrouch (3) v 049.3
    ~ in (1) v 049.3
scrouched (1) v 096.4
scrouching (1) v 096.4
scrouge (2) v 096.4
    ~ down (1) v 096.4
scrouged down (1) v 096.4
scrounge (2) v 108.9
    ~ around (1) v 099.7
scroungy (2) adj 113.9
    ~ -looking (1) adj 073.9
scrout down (1) v 096.4
scrub (83) n/v/adj 061.9
    ~ broom (7) n 010.5
    ~ brooms (1) n 010.5
    ~ brush (3) n 022.2
    ~ brushes (1) n 022.2
    ~ bucket (4) n 116.9
    ~ bull (1) n 033.5
    ~ cattle (2) n 080.6
    ~ cloth (1) n 018.4
    ~ cows (2) n 033.6
    ~ dogs (1) n 033.3
    ~ heifer (1) n 033.8
    ~ hogs (3) n 035.9
    ~ mop (2) n 010.4
    ~ oak (8) n 061.8
    ~ oak trees (1) n 061.9
    ~ oaks (3) n 061.9
    ~ palmetto (1) n 061.8
    ~ pine (2) n 061.9
    ~ pines (2) n 061.8
    ~ rag (1) n 018.3
    ~ stuff (2) n 088.8
    ~ trees (1) n 093.8
    ~ up (1) v 010.4
    ~ with (2) v 025.7
Scrub (1) 087.7
scrubbed (7) v 010.4
scrubbing (14) v/adj 010.4
    ~ board (1) n 010.6
    ~ boards (2) n 010.6
    ~ brush (2) n 022.2

~ towel (1) n 018.5
scrubbled through (1) v 088.9
scrubboard (12) n 081.8
scrubboards (4) n 010.6
scrubby (1) adj 061.8
scrubland (1) n 029.8
scrubs (5) n 010.5
scrummed up (1) v 096.4
scrunch (11) v/adj 096.4
    ~ down (7) v 096.4
    ~ owl (1) n 059.1
    ~ up (1) v 096.4
scrunched (2) v 096.4
    ~ down (1) v 096.4
scrunching (3) v 096.4
    ~ up (1) v 096.4
scuba (3) adj 095.3
    ~ -dive (1) v 095.3
    ~ diving (2) v 095.3
scud (1) n 007.4
Scudderfield (2) 106.3
scuffle (2) n/v 104.2
scuffled (a)round (1) v 093.6
Scuffletoni(an) (1) 069.5
Scuffletonians (1) 088.7
scuffling (1) v 104.2
scull (1) v 024.7
scum (5) n 069.7
scumgullion (1) n 050.9
scuppernong (15) n/adj 092.8
    ~ arbor (1) n 062.4
    ~ grape (1) n 080.7
    ~ jelly (1) n 051.6
    ~ pie (1) n 048.3
    ~ vines (1) n 062.4
    ~ wine (2) n 114.7
scuppernong[N-i] (1) n 089.8
scuppernongs (19) n 062.4
scurvy (5) n/adj 079.7
    ~ grass (4) n 061.4
scutter (2) n/adj 046.3
    ~ back (1) n 046.3
scuttle (409) n/adj 023.1
    ~ bucket (5) n 023.1
    ~ hole (5) n 009.8
    ~ holes (1) n 009.7
    ~ service (1) n 109.8
scut(tle) (1) n 023.1
scuttles (15) n 023.1
scuttling hole (1) n 009.8

scuzzy (1) adj 125.2
scythe (14) n/adj 042.1
    ~ blade (1) n 023.9
    ~ stone (1) n 023.4
scythes (6) n/adj 023.5
    ~ rock (2) n 023.4
SDI (1) 116.2
SDS (1) 129.3
sea (115) n/adj 030.6
    ~ ash tree (1) n 061.9
    ~ bass (5) n 059.9
    ~ bob (1) n 060.9
    ~ captain (3) n 068.5
    ~ captains (1) n 068.5
    ~ cat (1) n 059.9
    ~ catfish (1) n 059.9
    ~ chanteys (1) n 130.9
    ~ fog (2) n 006.7
    ~ frog (1) n 060.2
    ~ gnat (1) n 060A.6
    ~ grape trees (2) n 061.8
    ~ grapes (1) n 062.4
    ~ grass (4) n 019.4
    ~ -grass-like (1) adj 019.7
    ~ -grass sack (1) n 019.7
    ~ gull (1) n 088.7
    ~ island (1) n 019.6
    ~ marsh (1) n 029.7
    ~ monster (1) n 125.2
    ~ oats (3) n 042.1
    ~ perch (1) n 059.9
    ~ rim (1) n 030.3
    ~ -rim marsh (1) n 029.7
    ~ slope (1) n 029.4
    ~ sponge (1) n 018.3
    ~ spouts (1) n 112.2
    ~ sugar (1) n 080.8
    ~ trout (7) n 059.9
    ~ turtle (32) n 060.6
    ~ turtles (25) n 060.6
    ~ wharf (1) n 031.4
Sea (8) 087.3
    ~ Island (5) GA 087.3
    ~ Island tick (1) n 060A.9
    ~ World (1) 106.4
Seaboard (8) 096.7
    ~ Park (1) 105A.1
    ~ Park Road (1) 107.6
    ~ Railroad (1) 088.8
    ~ station (1) n 084.7

seafood (10) n 048.4
seal (3) n/adj 020.4
    ~ heat (1) n 118.5
Seal (3) 030.7
    ~ Creek (1) GA 030.7
sealed (4) v/adj 011.2
    ~ heat (1) n 118.5
sealer (2) n 020.3
sealing (7) n/adj 011.2
    ~ wax (1) n 020.4
    ~ weatherboarding (1) n 011.2
Sealy (1) TX 086.4
seamen (1) n 066.7
seams (1) n 011.2
seamster (1) n 093.8
seamstress (3) n 070.6
seances (1) n 066.8
seaport (3) n 031.4
search (1) v 080.8
Searcy (23) AR 087.1
    ~ College (1) 083.6
Sears (2) 012.1
    ~ building (1) n 012.1
seas (1) n 013.9
Seas (1) 001.4
seashell (2) n/adj 029.8
    ~ roads (1) n 031.7
seashells (1) n 060.1
seashore (1) n 029.7
season (50) n/v/adj 046.3
    ~ meat (1) n 046.3
    ~ out (1) v 014.8
Season[N-k] Greetings (1) 093.2
season[V-t] (1) v 057.9
seasoned (1) v 032.4
seasoning (22) n/adj 051.7
    ~ bacon (1) n 046.3
    ~ meat (10) n 046.3
    ~ pork (1) n 046.3
Season's Greetings (1) 093.2
seasons (5) n 007.1
Seasons (1) 055.3
seat (1108) n/v/adj 085.5
    ~ belt (1) n 110.3
    ~ boards (1) n 022.9
Seat (1) 085.5
seated (149) v/adj 049.3
    ~ mower (1) n 120.3
seater (9) n 012.1
seats (74) n 083.7
Seats (1) 090.1

Seattle (7) WA 087.7
seawall (1) n 106.7
seaweed-type material (1) n 019.7
Sebastian (4) AR FL 087.9
~ River (1) FL 030.7
Sebring (1) FL 087.5
sec (1) adj F 054.6
secede (3) v 070.6
Secession (3) 085.7
~ War (1) 085.7
secheresse (1) n F 007.1
(se)cheresse (1) n F 007.1
Seconals (1) 115.8
second (1575) n/adj 001A.3
~ base (1) n 001A.3
~ bedroom (3) n 007A.3
~ beer (1) n 050.8
~ bloom (1) n 041.5
~ bottom (1) n 030.8
~ childhood (1) n 074.1
~ -class roads (1) n 031.7
~ cover (1) n 041.5
~ crop (105) n 041.5
~ cut (9) n 041.5
~ -cut hay (1) n 041.5
~ cutting (192) n 041.5
~ dark (1) n 002.6
~ -day dress (2) n 089.8
~ -day's dress (1) n 089.8
~ father (1) n 129.5
~ -floor balcony (1) n 010.8
~ -floor gallery (2) n 007A.9
~ -floor porch (1) n 010.8
~ generation (1) n 041.5
~ -grade molasses (1) n 001A.3
~ growth (47) n 041.5
~ -growth cypress (1) n 093.8
~ -growth hickory (1) n 061.9
~ -growth pine (2) n 041.5
~ harvest (9) n 041.5

~ hull (1) n 054.8
~ joint (2) n 037.1
~ lieutenant (2) n 001A.3
~ mother (3) n 129.5
~ mourning (1) n 079.3
~ mowing (4) n 041.5
~ -oldest (2) adj 064.7
~ -place road (1) n 031.7
~ quarter (1) n 046.4
~ -rate hotel (1) n 113.8
~ serving (1) n 050.1
~ -story porch (4) n 010.8
~ tenor (1) n 001A.3
~ time (8) n 041.5
~ water (2) n 075.7
~ wife (1) n 068.8
~ yield (1) n 041.5
sec(ond) (6) n/adj 070.3
~ cutting (1) n 041.5
Second (47) 107.6
~ Army (1) 001A.3
~ Avenue (5) 001A.3
~ Av(enue) (1) 105.2
~ Christmas Day (1) 093.2
~ Creek (7) AL MS TN 030.7
~ Davidson (1) TX 030.7
~ District (1) 001A.3
~ John (1) 001A.3
~ Ponce de Leon (1) 106.6
~ Revolutionary War (1) 085.8
~ Street (6) 107.7
~ War (2) 085.8
~ War for Independence (1) 085.8
~ Ward (3) 105.4
~ World War (3) 001A.3
~ World's War (2) 001A.3
secondary (20) n/adj 125.8
~ road (8) n 031.7
~ roads (4) n 031.7
~ school (1) n 125.8
~ streets (1) n 107.7

secondhand (60) adj 123.5
~ clothes (22) n 123.5
~ clothing (1) n 123.5
~ food (1) n 050.1
~ garments (1) n 123.5
~ place (1) n 123.5
~ store (2) n 114.6
~ stores (1) n 123.5
secondhanded (7) adj 065.8
~ clothes (1) n 123.5
~ coffee (1) n 050.1
~ food (1) n 050.1
~ store (1) n 080.7
secondhands (4) n 123.5
seconds (17) n 044.4
Secour (3) 087.3
secretarial (10) adj 068.8
~ aide (1) n 068.8
secretaries (25) n 068.8
secretary (862) n/adj 068.8
~ course (1) n 068.8
~ desk (1) n 068.8
~ thing (1) n 068.8
secretar(y) (26) n 068.8
secreta(ry) (1) n 068.8
Secretary (1) 068.8
secretion (1) n 077.5
secrets (1) n 082.6
section (162) n/adj 021.6
~ drag (1) n 021.7
~ foreman (2) n 068.5
~ harrow (33) n 021.7
~ har(row) (11) n 021.7
~ harrower (1) n 021.7
~ harrows (7) n 021.7
sectional (2) n 009.1
sectionals (1) n 009.1
sections (10) n 021.1
security (7) n/adj 119.5
~ guards (1) n 119.5
(se)curity (1) n 115.4
Sedalia (1) MO 087.5
sedan (158) n/adj 109.3
~ car (1) n 109.2
~ delivery (1) n 109.6
~ -type thing (1) n 111.6
sedans (19) n 109.2
sediment (2) n/adj 070.8
~ roads (1) n 031.6
see (2795) n/v/adj 102.5

~ about (9) v 102.5
~ (a)bout (2) v 076.8
~ after (6) v 102.5
~ board (2) n 022.5
~ by (1) v 026.2
~ her (3) v 102.5
~ horse (25) n 022.5
~ horses (2) n 022.5
~ of (1) v 051.1
~ out (2) v 057.7
~ through (1) v 057.7
~ to (3) v 100.9
see[V-p] (4) v 013.6
see[V-r] (4) v 102.5
see[V-t] (6) v 102.5
seed (1918) n/v/adj 054.1
~ about (1) v 102.5
~ after (1) v 080.6
~ bags (1) n 019.7
~ bank (1) n 015.5
~ bed (1) n 080.9
~ beer (1) n 050.9
~ bin (2) n 014.4
~ bins (1) n 014.4
~ change (1) n 036.1
~ corn (2) n 056.2
~ crop (2) n 041.5
~ horse (1) n 034.1
~ house (16) n 014.4
~ -like (1) adj 054.8
~ money (1) n 080.8
~ oats (2) n 042.1
~ oysters (1) n 088.9
~ peaches (1) n 054.3
~ peas (1) n 014.5
~ potatoes (2) n 081.9
~ rice (1) n 050.7
~ sack (2) n 019.7
~ sacks (2) n 019.6
~ tick (12) n 060A.8
~ ticks (18) n 060A.9
~ watermelons (1) n 056.9
Seed (2) 089.1
~ Tick Creek (1) AR 030.7
seed[N-i] (3) n 052.1
seeded (6) adj 054.4
seeder (1) n 021.6
seeders (1) n 080.6
seedless (2) adj 054.4
seedling (6) n/adj 054.3
~ peach (1) n 054.3
~ peaches (2) n 054.3
~ pines (1) n 061.8

~ trees (1) n 061.8
seedlings (1) n 061.8
seeds (61) n 054.1
seeing (72) v 102.5
 ~ a lot of her (1) v 081.4
 ~ each other (5) v 081.4
 ~ her (10) v 081.4
 ~ her regular (1) v 081.4
 ~ that girl (1) v 081.4
seek (453) n 098.4
 ~ -and-hide (4) n 098.4
seeked (1) v 098.8
seeker (2) n 125.6
seekers (1) n 125.5
seeking (1) n 098.4
seem (91) v 013.1
 ~ like (25) v 088.3
 ~ to (54) v 074.5
seem[V-p] (107) v 013.9
 ~ like (91) v 013.6
 ~ to (2) v 013.9
seem[V-r] (17) v 088.3
 ~ like (14) v 088.3
 ~ to (2) v 088.3
seemed (21) v 088.3
 ~ as though (1) v 088.3
 ~ like (16) v 088.3
seems (177) v 088.3
 ~ as (2) v 088.3
 ~ as if (9) v 088.3
 ~ as though (10) v 088.3
 ~ like (99) v 088.3
 ~ to (4) v 088.3
 ~ [J-0] if (1) v 088.3
seen (1912) v 102.5
 ~ after (2) v 102.5
 ~ to (2) v 058.1
seened (1) v 102.5
seep (6) n/adj 029.7
 ~ water (2) n 081.9
seepage (3) n/adj 030.7
 ~ water (1) n 030.3
seeping (1) v 048.8
seepish land (1) n 029.6
seeps (1) n 029.4
seepy place (2) n 029.5
seersucker (1) n 099.6
seersuckers (1) n 027.4
sees (11) v 102.5
 ~ after (1) v 065.4
seesaw (980) n/adj 022.5

~ horse (3) n 022.5
 ~ horsey (1) n 022.5
seesaw[V-s] (1) v 022.8
seesawed (4) v 022.8
seesawing (564) v 022.8
seesaws (24) n 022.5
seesawsied (1) v 022.8
seesawsy (1) n 022.5
seg academy (1) n 088.7
segmented roundworms (1) n 060.5
segregated (2) adj 103.4
 ~ knives (1) n 104.3
segregation (2) n/adj 080.8
 ~ academy (1) n 080.8
Seguin (2) TX 086.8
seine (20) n/v/adj 080.7
 ~ for (1) v 101.7
 ~ net (1) n 060.4
 ~ out (1) v 060.8
seinefish (1) n 059.9
seines (3) n 061.2
seining (4) v 089.9
Seitzes Creek (1) AL 030.7
Selby (1) TN 087.4
seldom (9) adj/adv 070.7
self (96) pron/prefix 074.8
 ~ -assured (1) adj 074.8
 ~ -centered (1) adj 074.8
 ~ -conceited (2) adj 074.8
 ~ -determined (1) adj 074.8
 ~ -done (1) adj 075.6
 ~ -educated (4) adj 083.5
 ~ -education (1) n 083.5
 ~ -feeder (1) n 035.8
 ~ -feeders (1) n 035.8
 ~ -grown (1) adj 050.4
 ~ -made (2) adj 075.7
 ~ -playing piano (1) n 066.9
 ~ -propel (1) adj 120.2
 ~ -propelled (10) adj 120.2
 ~ -propelled lawn mower (1) n 120.2

~ -propelled lawn mowers (1) n 120.2
 ~ -propelled mower (1) n 120.2
 ~ -propelled mow(er) (1) n 120.2
 ~ -propelling (1) adj 120.2
 ~ -rising (3) adj 045.4
 ~ -rising bread (6) n 044.3
 ~ -rising flour (3) n 045.5
 ~ -rising meal (1) n 044.1
 ~ -season (1) adj 045.5
 ~ -service laundry (2) n 116.5
 ~ -sown (1) adj 041.5
 ~ -style (1) n 123.3
 ~ -sufficient (2) adj 074.1
self[M-i] (8) pron 044.1
self[N-i] (1) n 043.6
selfish (15) adj 073.5
selfisher (1) adj 066.1
sell (54) v 025.3
 ~ out (1) v 075.7
 ~ to (1) v 053.2
sell[V-r] (1) v 095.8
seller (3) n 114.4
selling (30) v/adj 057.4
 ~ hogs (1) n 035.5
 ~ size (1) n 035.6
 ~ to (1) v 052.6
sells (11) v 053.4
Selma (40) AL LA MS 087.2
 ~ Road (1) 105.5
Selmer (3) TN 087.1
seltzer water (1) n 045.5
selves (5) pron 044.2
Seman (1) AL 087.9
sembel breed (1) n 035.9
semester (2) n 001A.3
semi (4) n/adj/prefix 109.6
 ~ -brick chimley (1) n 008.1
 ~ trucks (1) n 109.5
semiclassical (3) adj 130.8
 ~ music (1) n 130.9
semiformal (1) n 083.1
semilegal granny (1) n 065.2

semimonthly (1) adv 003.8
seminar (1) n 088.7
seminary (2) n/adj 064.9
 ~ school (1) n 075.6
seminar(y) (1) n 066.9
Seminole (13) FL GA TX 086.4
 ~ County (1) GA 025.8
 ~ Heights (2) 106.3
semiround (1) adj 056.9
semis (2) n 109.6
semitrailer (1) n 109.7
semitrailers (1) n 109.5
Semmes (3) 106.4
Senath (1) MO 087.6
Senatobia (1) MS 087.2
Senatobi(a) (1) MS 087.5
senator (2) n 025.8
send (24) v 052.6
 ~ by (1) v 075.7
 ~ -off (3) n 082.5
 ~ -off party (1) n 082.5
send[V-r] (1) v 098.7
sendero (2) n/adj S 031.8
 ~ road (1) n 031.8
senderos (1) n S 031.8
sends (2) v 025.6
Seneca Chief (1) 056.2
senile (15) adj 074.7
senior (34) adj 064.7
 ~ child (1) n 064.7
 ~ -citizen bus (1) n 109.9
 ~ high (24) n 125.9
 ~ high school (7) n 125.9
 ~ prom (1) n 083.1
Senior (3) 106.4
 ~ Bowl (1) 106.4
seniors (1) n 125.9
Senoi(a) (1) GA 087.3
sense (116) n 026.6
sensible (2) adj 013.5
sensitive (99) adj 075.1
sensuous (1) adj 125.4
sent (18) v 070.7
 ~ by (1) v 075.8
 ~ off (1) v 057.8
 ~ to (1) v 042.1
s(ent) (1) v F 051.1
sentence (1) n 082.2
sentenced (1) v 082.2
sentences (1) n 095.8
sentimental (3) adj 130.8

~ songs (1) n 130.8
Senyah (2) FL 086.1
separate (15) v/adj 013.8
   ~ kitchen (1) n 009.9
separated (10) v/adj
082.1
   ~ from (1) v 052.6
   ~ widow (1) n 063.3
separating (1) v 048.2
separator (7) n/adj 042.1
   ~ house (1) n 011.7
separators (2) n 090.8
sept (1) n F 001.3
September (1004) 001A.8
   ~ storms (2) n 006.1
septic (2) adj 079.7
   ~ sore throat (1) n
079.7
   ~ tanks (1) n 089.9
sepulcher (3) n 078.8
Sequatchie (10) TN 087.1
   ~ County (2) TN 087.2
   ~ Creek (1) TN 030.7
   ~ River (2) TN 030.7
   ~ Valley (2) TN 087.1
Sequoia (2) 055.4
Sequoyah (4) GA 106.1
   ~ Hills (2) 106.1
Sequoy(ah) Hills (1)
106.1
serenade (208) n/v 082.5
serenade[V-r] (1) v 082.5
serenaded (11) v 082.5
serenaders (1) n 082.5
serenades (5) n 082.5
serenading (71) n/v 082.5
Serepta Spring (1) AR
070.8
serge (3) n/adj 027.7
sergeant (10) n 068.3
Sergeant Four-Oh (1)
125.5
sergeants (1) n 068.3
sergical (1) adj 096.7
sericea (3) n/adj 014.7
   ~ hay (1) n 041.5
series (1) n 070.6
serious (36) adj 081.4
   ~ about her (5) adj
081.4
   ~ -minded (1) adj
075.1
seriously (5) adv 075.6
sermon (852) n 089.4
sermonettes (1) n 089.4

sermons (10) n 089.4
serpent (4) n 090.2
Serpent (1) 030.3
serpentine (1) adj 088.7
serum (4) n 075.8
servant (8) n/adj 069.3
servant's house (1) n
011.9
servants' (7) adj 012.1
   ~ bathroom (1) n 012.1
   ~ house (1) n 014.1
   ~ quarters (5) n 080.8
serve (87) v 070.6
   ~ and go (1) n 116.2
   ~ to (1) v 093.7
served (42) v 049.5
serves (1) v 104.5
service (142) n/adj 079.2
   ~ alleys (1) n 108.6
   ~ area (3) n 107.2
   ~ areas (1) n 107.2
   ~ islands (1) n 107.2
   ~ revolver (1) n 113.1
   ~ ring (1) n 123.1
   ~ road (9) n 107.5
   ~ roads (3) n 107.5
   ~ room (5) n 010.3
   ~ station (6) n 107.2
   ~ stations (4) n 107.2
   ~ stop (1) n 107.2
   ~ truck (1) n 109.6
   ~ trucks (1) n 109.7
   ~ worker (1) n 119.5
serviceberries (1) n 062.4
serviceberry (2) n 062.7
serviced (1) v 065.8
serviceman (1) n 119.5
services (16) n 062.4
serving (4) n/v/adj 053.4
   ~ spoon (1) n 017.9
sesame-seed bread (1) n
044.3
session (5) n 129.7
Session (1) 088.7
Sessions (1) 106.4
Sessums (1) MS 087.2
set (994) n/v/adj 049.3
   ~ around (16) v 049.3
   ~ back (5) v 049.3
   ~ by (2) v 049.3
   ~ down (337) v 049.3
   ~ down in (1) v 049.3
   ~ hen (1) n 036.7
   ~ him up (1) v 082.1
   ~ in (8) v 049.3

~ -in (1) n 088.8
~ in her ways (1) adj
074.8
~ in his own way (2)
adj 074.8
~ in his own ways (2)
adj 074.8
~ in his way (2) adj
074.8
~ in his ways (59) adj
074.8
~ in my way (1) adj
074.8
~ in their ways (12) adj
074.8
~ in to (2) v 093.8
~ in your own way (2)
adj 074.8
~ in your own ways (3)
adj 074.8
~ in your way (2) adj
074.8
~ in your ways (62) adj
074.8
~ of beads (3) n 028.4
~ of mules (1) n 033.7
~ of pearls (1) n 028.4
~ off (2) v 009.9
~ on (34) v 049.3
~ onion (1) n 055.7
~ out (14) v 027.8
~ pillows (1) n 028.9
~ rain (1) n 006.6
~ through (1) v 049.3
~ up (33) v 049.3
~ -up (1) n 082.8
~ up with (2) v 079.3
~ -willed (1) adj 074.8
~ with (4) v 074.8
set[N-i] (1) n 028.4
set[V-p] (3) v 003.4
set[V-s] (1) v 095.8
setback (1) n 084.8
sets (55) n/v 055.6
   ~ around (1) v 049.3
   ~ down (3) v 049.3
   ~ up (1) v 031.6
settee (218) n/adj 009.1
   ~ bed (1) n 009.1
   ~ chair (1) n 009.1
settees (43) n 009.1
setter (14) n 036.7
setters (1) n 051.7
setting (817) v/adj 036.7
   ~ back (2) v 049.3

~ block (1) n 009.1
~ chair (2) n 008.8
~ chairs (3) n 008.8
~ down (2) v 049.3
~ duck (2) n 036.7
~ egg (5) n 017.1
~ eggs (5) n 017.1
~ hen (553) n 036.7
~ hens (9) n 036.7
~ in (6) v 049.3
~ on (4) v 036.7
~ room (27) n 007.8
~ up (6) v 079.2
~ up to her (1) v 081.4
~ up with (1) v 082.5
set(ting) (2) adj 036.7
   ~ hen (1) n 036.7
Settingdown Creek (1)
GA 030.7
settings (2) n 036.7
settle (24) v 048.8
   ~ down (15) v 075.3
   ~ up (1) v 094.7
   ~ with (1) v 070.6
settle[V-r] (1) v 053.4
settled (7) v 007.3
   ~ in (1) v 105A.4
settlement (39) n/adj
070.6
   ~ road (10) n 031.7
   ~ roads (4) n 031.7
Settlement (1) 087.2
settler (2) n 006.7
settlers (6) n 013.8
settlers' (1) adj 044.7
settles (2) v 007.3
   ~ down (1) v 007.3
settling (16) v/adj 007.3
   ~ down (10) v 007.3
   ~ time (1) n 075.6
seven (3787) n/adj 001.4
   ~ cents (1) n 114.1
   ~ -day (1) adj 001.4
   ~ -day-a-week job (1) n
001.4
   ~ -fifteen (4) n 004.4
   ~ -fifteen earlier (1) n
004.5
   ~ -fifty (2) n 001.4
   ~ -fifty-one (1) n 001.4
   ~ -foot (3) adj 007.9
   ~ -forty (1) n 004.5
   ~ -forty-five (97) n
004.5

~ -fourteens (1) n 115.6

~ -grade scholar (1) n 068.7

~ -inch Kelly (1) n 021.6

~ -month-old (1) adj 001.4

~ -month school (1) n 001.4

~ -passenger (1) adj 001.4

~ -room brick (1) n 007A.2

~ -room house (1) n 014.1

~ -seventy (2) n 001.4

~ steak (2) n 121.1

~ steaks (1) n 046.3

~ -strand barbwire fence (1) n 016.3

~ -strand fence (1) n 016.3

~ -ten (1) n 001.5

~ -thirty (520) n 004.4

~ -year drought (1) n 007.1

~ -year itch (5) n 062.3

~ -year locust (1) n 061.2

~ -year-old (1) adj 001.4

Seven (131) 033.3

~ -Day Advention (1) 002.2

~ -Day Adventist (2) 089.3

~ -Day Adventist[N-i] (1) 089.1

~ -Days Adventist (1) 126.7

~ -Eleven (32) 116.2

~ -(E)leven (5) 116.2

~ -Eleven store (1) n 116.2

~ -Elevens (5) 116.2

~ Pines (1) MS 087.4

~ Seas Restaurant (1) 001.4

~ Sisters (1) 055.7

~ Street (1) 001A.3

~ -to-Eleven (1) 116.2

~ Top (1) 055A.5

~ Up (4) 121.8

sevenbark (2) n 062.7

sevenbarks (1) n 061.7

seventeen (173) n/adj 001.9

~ -fifty-one (1) n 001.9

~ -forty-one (1) n 001.9

~ -fourteen (1) n 001.7

~ -seventy-seven (1) n 001.4

~ -sixty-eight (1) n 001.4

~ -sixty-nine (1) n 001.9

Seventeen (5) 031.6

~ -Hundreds (1) 001A.2

~ Mile Creek (1) GA 030.7

seventeenth (1) adj 001A.3

seventh (898) n/adj 001A.3

~ day (1) n 002.1

~ -grade education (1) n 001A.3

Seventh (28) 001A.3

~ Avenue (10) 105.4

~ Cavalry (1) 001A.3

~ -Day Adventist (4) 089.2

~ District (2) 001A.3

~ Street (4) 001A.3

~ Ward (1) 105.5

seventies (6) n 001A.1

seventieth (1) adj 001A.2

Seventieth Street (1) 107.7

seventy (1399) n/adj 001A.2

~ -dollar (1) adj 001A.2

~ -eight (32) n/adj 001A.2

~ -fifth (1) adj 001A.3

~ -five (144) n/adj 001A.2

~ -five-dollar (1) adj 001A.8

~ -five-foot (1) adj 001A.2

~ -four (40) n/adj 001A.2

~ -nine (24) n/adj 001A.2

~ -one (38) n/adj 001A.2

~ -seven (45) n/adj 001.4

~ -six (57) n/adj 001A.2

~ -some-odd (1) adj 088.9

~ -three (53) n/adj 001A.2

~ -two (42) n/adj 001A.2

seven(ty) (3) n 001A.2

~ -six (1) n 001A.2

~ -two (1) n 001A.2

Seventy (34) 001A.2

~ -Eight (2) 031.6

~ -Eighth Street (1) 107.7

~ -First Bridge (1) 107.6

~ -Five (21) 107.1

~ -Five (E)xpressway (1) 031.7

~ Highway (1) 001A.2

~ -Nine Highway (1) 013.9

~ -Ninth Street (1) 107.7

~ Street (1) 107.7

several (102) adj 033.4

~ palsy (1) n 065.8

severe (11) adj 091.7

~ drought (2) n 007.1

~ freeze (1) n 007.5

~ frost (1) n 007.5

~ storm (1) n 006.2

severely (1) adv 091.7

severer (1) adj 005.9

Sevier (6) AR TN 087.1

~ County (1) TN 087.3

~ Park (2) 106.6

Sevierville (5) TN 087.3

sew (17) v 027.2

sewage (2) n/adj 030.2

~ pipe (1) n 030.2

Sewanee (3) TN 065.8

sewed (7) v 029.1

~ on (2) v 027.2

~ together (1) v 097.9

Sewell Road (1) 107.8

sewer (3) n/adj 030.2

~ pipe (1) n 030.2

~ system (1) n 030.2

sewers (1) n 030.2

sewing (21) n/v/adj 007A.6

~ area (1) n 007A.6

~ bee (1) n 081.8

~ chair (1) n 008.9

~ lady (1) n 093.6

~ room (9) n 010.3

sewn (1) adj 072.5

sews (1) v 053.2

sex (22) n/adj 124.5

~ -crazed (1) adj 124.5

~ fiend (3) n 124.6

~ maniac (12) n 124.6

~ movies (2) n 114.9

~ theaters (1) n 114.9

sexed (3) adj 124.6

sexious (1) adj 124.6

sexpot (1) n 125.4

sexton (1) n 070.6

sexually overdriven (1) adj 124.6

sexy (5) adj 125.3

Seymour (2) MS 033.3

Seymourville (1) LA 087.1

sh (2) interj 038.5

sh(x2) (1) interj 038.5

sha (1) interj 038.5

shab beans (1) n 055A.4

shabbily (1) adv 080.6

shabby (8) adj 080.7

~ hotel (1) n 113.8

shack (50) n/v/adj 011.7

~ cow shed (1) n 015.1

~ room (1) n 014.3

~ up (2) v 082.2

shack[V-s] (1) v 117.8

shacked up (2) v 092.8

shacker (1) n 063.3

shacking up (3) v 080.9

Shacklesville (1) AL 087.2

shacklety (1) adj 088.7

shackly (1) adj 096.7

shacks (10) n 118.9

Shacks (1) 113.4

Shacktown (1) LA 087.7

shad (37) n/adj 061.2

~ minnows (1) n 061.2

~ roe (1) n 059.9

shade (276) n/adj 009.5

~ blinds (1) n 009.5

~ tree (9) n 067.8

~ -tree (11) adj 067.8

~ -tree mechanic (30) n 067.8
~ -tree (me)chanic (1) n 067.8
~ -tree mechanics (6) n 067.8
~ -tree money (2) n 080.6
~ -tree preacher (4) n 067.8
Shade (7) 086.2
shade[N-i] (5) n 009.5
shaded lane (1) n 031.8
shades (717) n 009.5
Shades (4) 030.7
~ Creek (2) AL 030.7
~ Mountain (2) AL 031.1
shadow (2) n 074.3
Shadow Lane (1) 106.1
Shadowlawn (1) 105.5
shadows (2) n 090.2
shads (9) n 059.9
shady (8) adj 052.7
~ cat (1) n 059.4
~ drive (1) n 031.8
~ lady (1) n 113.3
~ lane (1) n 031.8
~ road (2) n 031.8
Shady (27) TN 087.1
~ Banks (1) 113.4
~ Grove (18) AL AR FL LA MS 061.6
~ Grove Baptist Church (1) 087.7
~ Grove community (1) LA 087.6
~ Side (1) 106.1
~ Valley (3) TN 087.6
shaffs (1) n 041.7
shaft (144) n 020.9
shaft[N-i] (45) n 020.9
shafted (4) v 082.1
~ her (1) v 082.1
~ him (1) v 082.1
shafts (609) n 020.9
shag (38) n/adj 123.9
~ cut (1) n 123.9
~ cuts (2) n 123.9
~ haircuts (1) n 119.6
shaggy (1) adj 080.7
shags (6) n 123.9
shake (20) n/v/adj 070.3
~ a leg (1) n 050.8
~ leg (1) n 083.1

shaked (1) v 042.1
shakedown (4) n 029.2
shakedowns (1) n 083.1
shaker (16) n 075.6
shaker[N-i] (1) n 051.7
Shakers (1) 126.6
shakers (14) n 051.7
shakes (9) n 011.2
Shakespeare (3) 106.4
~ Park (2) 106.4
shakies (1) n 124.2
shaking (4) v 057.4
shaky (11) adj 074.3
shale (4) n 029.8
shall (103) v 081.2
shallot (68) n/adj 055.7
~ onion (5) n 055.7
~ onions (7) n 055.7
shallot[N-i] (3) n 055.7
shallots (203) n 055.8
shallow (10) adj 065.8
~ -draft boats (1) n 024.6
shallower (1) adj 070.6
shallows (2) n/v 030.3
~ back (1) v 080.8
sham (31) n/adj 028.9
~ pillows (1) n 028.8
shame (2) n 092.2
shameless (1) adj 124.8
shamoshack (1) interj 037.5
shampoo (2) n 117.8
shampooer (3) n 116.7
Shamrock (1) LA 087.7
shams (30) n 028.9
Shanghai (4) 011.2
~ house (1) n 007A.3
~ lumber (1) n 011.2
shank (84) n/adj 072.7
~ bone (14) n 072.7
~ cuts (1) n 121.4
~ portion (2) n 072.7
shanks (16) n 072.7
Shannon (2) GA TN 087.1
shan't (1) v 058.5
shanties (7) n 118.9
shanty (7) n/adj 089.8
~ house (3) n 118.6
~ houses (1) n 080.7
shantyboat (2) n 024.6
shantyboats (1) n 127.9
shantytown (1) n 080.7
shape (48) n/v/adj 002.7

~ up (1) v 005.7
shaped (20) adj 054.9
shapes (1) n 095.8
share (16) n/v/adj 024.7
~ dairy (1) n 080.9
~ dairying (1) n 081.9
~ hand (1) n 088.7
~ hands (4) n 072.5
~ plow (1) n 021.6
~ workers (1) n 080.6
sharecrop (16) n/v/adj 069.7
~ renters (1) n 080.7
sharecropped (7) v 041.3
sharecropper (7) n 069.7
sharecropper[N-i] (1) n 081.8
sharecroppers (17) n 069.7
sharecropping (9) n/v 080.6
sharecrops (1) n 041.3
shared (1) v 075.6
shares (6) n 070.7
sharing renters (1) n 080.7
shark (9) n 059.9
sharkites (1) n 084.9
sharks (19) n 059.9
~ and fishes (1) n 130.5
~ and the minnows (1) n 130.1
sharky clay (1) n 029.4
Sharon Church (2) 080.8
sharp (81) adj 007.4
~ chick (1) n 125.4
~ clothes (2) n 123.6
~ -looking (1) adj 125.4
~ -looking clothes (1) n 123.6
~ -nose boat (1) n 024.6
~ show (1) n 125.6
~ suit (1) n 123.6
~ threads (1) n 123.6
Sharp (8) AR 087.1
~ County (3) AR 087.6
~ Mountain (2) GA 030.7
~ Top (1) GA 087.5
sharped up (2) v 028.1
sharpen (10) v/adj 075.6
~ rock (5) n 023.4
~ stone (2) n 023.4

sharpener (36) n 023.5
sharpen(er) (3) n 023.5
sharpeners (2) n 023.4
sharpening (30) adj 023.4
~ rock (7) n 023.4
~ stone (18) n 023.4
~ wheel (4) n 023.5
sharply (1) adv 090.7
sharpshooter (5) n/adj 120.5
~ casket (1) n 079.1
sharpshooters (2) n 079.1
shatter (1) v 048.9
shattered (2) v 048.8
shave (4) n/v 117.8
shaved (3) v/adj 074.4
shavers (2) n 064.4
shavetail (1) n 088.7
shaving (8) v/adj 022.2
~ brush (2) n 022.2
~ mugs (1) n 026.3
~ notion (1) n 091.8
~ strap (1) n 022.3
shaving[N-i] (1) n 008.6
shavings (30) n 008.6
shaw (1) interj 037.5
Shaw (4) MS 087.9
Shawmut (2) AL 087.6
Shawnees (1) 070.7
Shawnette (1) TN 030.7
shay (1) n 084.8
shaying (1) v 036.4
she (2252) pron/v/adj 042.5
~ calf (3) n 033.8
~ -calf(x2) (1) interj 037.6
~ -calf(x3) (1) interj 037.6
~ cow (6) n 033.6
~ dog (2) n 033.3
~ donkeys (1) n 033.7
~ hes (1) n 124.3
~ hog (9) n 035.5
~ horse (4) n 034.2
~ -ing (1) v 081.4
~ lamb (1) n 035.1
~ male (1) n 088.7
~ mule (2) n 033.7
~ pig (1) n 035.5
~ rabbit (1) n 035.1
~ sheep (1) n 035.1
sh(e) (1) pron 076.1
She (1) 064.1
sheaf (73) n 041.6

sheaf[N-i] (2) n 041.6
sheafs (11) n 041.6
shear (13) n/v 035.2
shear[N-i] (1) n 065.9
sheared (6) v 035.2
shearer (1) n 080.7
shearing (4) n/v/adj 089.8
~ outfit (1) n 089.8
~ station (1) n 096.9
shearings (1) n 035.2
shears (49) n 120.6
sheath (5) n 041.6
sheathes (1) n 041.6
sheaths (3) n 041.6
sheave (1) n 041.6
sheaves (63) n 041.6
Sheaves (1) 041.6
shebang (17) n 082.8
she'd (42) pron 104.1
shed (1251) n/v/adj 015.1
~ bedroom (2) n 009.3
~ house (5) n 011.7
~ man (1) n 015.1
~ off (1) v 089.8
~ porch (1) n 010.8
~ roof (2) n 011.7
~ room (49) n 007A.1
~ rooms (13) n 007A.6
~ -type rooms (1) n 007A.2
~ way (1) n 015.1
shed[N-i] (1) n 011.7
shedded (3) v 101.7
shedding (2) n/v 054.8
sheds (145) n 015.1
sheek(x4) (1) interj 037.6
sheenies (2) n 126.9
sheeny (1) n 126.7
sheep (256) n/adj 038.4
~ barn (2) n 014.2
~ board's down (1) n 098.4
~ country (2) n 034.9
~ -dip (1) n 050.8
~ -dip john (1) n 068.2
~ dog (1) n 033.3
~ fertilize (1) n 029.3
~ flies (1) n 060A.5
~ fur (2) n 035.2
~ guts (1) n 037.3
~ horn (1) n 038.4
~ intestines (1) n 037.2
~ -killing dog (2) n 080.8

~ lot (1) n 015.6
~ manure (1) n 061.4
~ meat (1) n 092.7
~ -nose apples (1) n 054.5
~ paths (1) n 031.8
~ pen (2) n 015.2
~ place (1) n 035.2
~ -saffron tea (1) n 061.4
~ shear (1) n 035.2
~ shear[N-i] (1) n 065.9
~ shearing (1) n 084.8
~ shearings (1) n 035.2
~ shed (2) n 015.1
~ shit (1) n 092.9
~ sorrel (2) n 015.9
~ turds (1) n 096.7
~ wool (5) n 035.2
sheep(x2) (14) interj 038.4
sheep(x3) (8) interj 038.4
sheep(x4) (3) interj 038.4
sheep(x7) (1) interj 038.4
sheepdog (1) n 033.3
sheepfold (2) n 034.9
sheepman (1) n 039.6
sheep's (2) adj 015.9
~ -gowan (1) n 015.9
~ tail (1) n 039.5
sheeps (59) n 035.1
sheeps' stuff (3) n 037.3
sheepshead (31) n 059.9
sheepsheads (2) n 088.7
sheepskin coats (1) n 027.1
sheepy (19) interj 038.4
sheepy(x2) (17) interj 038.4
sheepy(x3) (11) interj 038.4
sheepy(x4) (2) interj 038.4
sheer drop (1) n 031.2
sheers (4) n 009.5
sheet (39) n/adj 007.6
~ erosion (2) n 030.5
~ -iron roof (1) n 011.4
~ -iron stove (1) n 008.5
~ lightning (1) n 006.2
~ metal (1) n 026.6
~ music (1) n 089.5

sheet[N-i] (1) n 028.7
sheeted (2) v 080.6
sheeting (7) n 011.4
sheetlap (1) n 011.2
Sheetrock (5) 011.2
Sheetrocked (1) 011.2
sheets (17) n 018.6
Sheffield (6) AL 087.8
~ Road (1) 107.7
sheik (4) n/v 069.9
~ down (1) v 028.1
~ up (2) v 028.1
Shelby (29) AL MS TN 087.2
~ County (12) AL TN TX 087.1
~ Forest (4) 106.4
Shelbyville (10) TN 087.1
shelf (135) n/adj 008.4
~ mantel (1) n 008.4
shelf[N-i] (2) n 009.7
shelfs (1) n 009.7
she'll (16) pron 076.2
shell (1617) n/v/adj 054.8
~ bean (3) n 055A.2
~ beans (15) n 055A.3
~ case (1) n 022.4
~ corn (4) n 002.6
~ dredgers (1) n 080.7
~ dust (1) n 031.6
~ -dust roads (1) n 031.6
~ out (4) v 055A.2
~ pea (1) n 055A.2
~ peanuts (1) n 054.7
~ peas (2) n 055A.2
~ road (20) n 031.6
~ roads (13) n 031.6
~ up (2) v 055A.2
Shell (32) 089.1
~ Creek (4) GA TN 030.7
~ Oil Company (2) 024.1
~ Plaza (1) 108.5
~ Plaza One (1) 108.5
~ Road (1) 115.8
shell[N-i] (1) n 022.4
shell[V-r] (1) v 055A.2
shell[V-t] (1) v 055A.2
shellacker bugs (1) n 060A.1
shellacking (1) n 065.5
shellcracker (11) n 059.9
shellcrackers (20) n 059.9

shelled (37) v/adj 055A.2
~ for (1) v 055A.2
~ out (2) v 055A.2
~ roads (1) n 031.6
sheller (14) n 080.8
Shelley (1) 084.8
shellfish (2) n 060.2
Shellhorn (1) AL 075.6
shellies (5) n 055A.3
shelling (43) n/v/adj 055A.2
~ place (1) n 096.8
shellings (3) n 090.8
Shellman (3) GA 087.2
~ Bluff (1) GA 087.4
shells (138) n 022.4
shelly (27) n/adj 055A.3
~ bean (5) n 055A.3
~ beans (18) n 055A.3
~ Octobers (1) n 055A.3
shelter (114) n/adj 015.2
~ barn (1) n 015.1
~ place (1) n 015.2
shelters (13) n 015.1
Shelton (2) MS 087.9
shelves (23) n 010.1
Shenandoah Valley (1) 087.5
Shephardsville (1) AL 087.6
shepherd (15) n/adj 033.3
~ dog (7) n 033.2
~ dogs (1) n 033.2
~ needle (1) n 060A.4
Shepherd (2) TX 087.6
shepherds (5) n 035.1
Sherard (2) MS 087.4
Sheraton (2) 084.3
~ Hotel (1) 084.3
~ Peabody (1) 108.5
sherbet glass (1) n 048.8
Sheridan (3) TX 087.5
~ Heights (1) 105.5
sheriff (37) n 065.9
sheriff[N-k] office (1) n 112.7
sheriffing (1) n 101.7
sheriff's (4) adj 111.7
~ car (2) n 111.7
~ office (1) n 112.8
~ patrol (1) n 111.7
sheriffs (2) n 066.8
Sherman (13) TX 068.3
~ Avenue (1) 105.8

~ Park (1) 106.4
sherries (1) n 130.8
sherry (2) n/adj 114.7
    ~ glass (1) n 048.9
Sherry Drive (1) 107.6
Sherwood (5) AR LA
    106.2
    ~ Forest (2) 106.1
she's (424) pron 025.6
(she)'s (1) pron 010.4
shes (4) n 113.5
Shetland (4) 034.1
    ~ ponies (2) n 080.6
    ~ pony (1) n 034.3
SHI house (1) n 012.1
shiboop(x4) (1) interj
    033.2
shied (1) v 032.1
shielder (1) n 080.7
Shields Creek (1) MS
    030.7
shift (130) n/v/adj 110.7
    ~ lever (1) n 110.7
shift[V-p] to (1) v 006.5
shifted him (1) v 082.1
shifter (2) n 110.7
shifters (1) n 110.7
shiftgear (4) n/adj 066.9
    ~ car (1) n 110.7
shifting (6) v/adj 007.3
    ~ lever (1) n 110.7
shiftless (15) adj 069.7
shifts (3) n 040.4
Shiloh (17) AL GA LA
    TN TX 087.3
    ~ Baptist Church (1)
        089.1
    ~ Church (1) 089.2
    ~ community (1) LA
        087.5
shim (1) v 075.7
shimmy (2) n 083.1
shin (543) n/adj 072.7
    ~ oak (1) n 061.8
shin[N-i] (2) n 072.7
shinbone (134) n 072.7
shinbones (3) n 072.7
shindig (37) n 083.1
shindig[N-i] (1) n 083.1
shindigs (4) n 083.1
shine (40) n/v/adj 069.3
    ~ bone (3) n 037.3
    ~ through (1) v 013.9
Shine (2) 064.4
shined up (1) v 028.1

shineface (1) n 069.4
shiner (34) n/adj 061.2
    ~ fish (1) n 061.2
    ~ minnows (1) n 061.2
shiners (78) n 061.2
shines (3) n/v 092.8
Shinetown (1) 105A.5
shingle (36) n/adj 011.4
    ~ cuts (1) n 123.9
    ~ -like (1) adj 011.2
    ~ mill (2) n 081.9
    ~ roof (11) n 011.4
    ~ roofing (1) n 011.4
    ~ tick (1) n 088.7
    ~ ticks (1) n 060A.8
    ~ top (1) n 011.4
shingle[N-i] (4) n 014.1
shingled (6) adj 123.9
    ~ roof (2) n 011.4
shingles (161) n 011.4
shingling back (1) v 014.8
shining (10) v 003.3
    ~ like (1) v 125.1
    ~ up (1) v 028.1
    ~ up to her (2) v 081.4
shinnied (2) v 096.3
    ~ up (1) v 096.3
shinny (53) n/v/adj 050.9
    ~ drop (1) n 050.9
    ~ makers (1) n 069.9
    ~ up (1) v 096.3
    ~ whiskey (1) n 050.8
Shinny (2) 030.7
    ~ Creek (1) LA 030.7
    ~ Lake (1) LA 030.7
Shinola (1) 016.3
shins (69) n 072.7
shiny (4) adj 005.4
    ~ stuff (1) n 123.1
ship (26) n/v/adj 109.4
    ~ base (1) n 031.4
    ~ captain (1) n 068.5
    ~ channel (5) n 030.2
    ~ dock (1) n 031.4
    ~ foreman (1) n 068.5
    ~ house (2) n 031.4
    ~ landing (2) n 031.4
Ship (7) 106.4
    ~ Channel (3) 106.4
    ~ Channel area (1) n
        105.7
    ~ Island (2) MS 087.6
    ~ Island Pass (1) MS
        087.4
shiplap (67) n/adj 011.2

~ joint (1) n 011.2
~ siding (3) n 011.2
~ weatherboarding (1)
    n 011.2
shiplapping (1) n 011.2
shiplaps (1) n 011.2
Shipman Creek (1) TN
    030.7
shipped (5) v/adj 055.1
    ~ in (3) v 042.1
    ~ -in (1) adj 055.1
shipping (8) adj 019.7
    ~ bag (1) n 019.7
    ~ dock (1) n 031.4
    ~ lock (1) n 031.4
    ~ melon (1) n 056.9
    ~ port (2) n 031.4
    ~ sack (1) n 019.7
    ~ watermelon (1) n
        056.9
ships (6) n 024.6
ships' captains (1) n
    001.2
shipwrecked (1) adj 090.8
shipyard (6) n/adj 031.4
    ~ community (1) n
        087.5
shipyards (2) n 084.8
Shirley (2) AR 087.6
    ~ Temple (1) 115.6
shirt (52) n/adj 027.4
shirts (17) n 027.3
shirttail (5) n/adj 059.3
    ~ preacher (1) n 067.8
shirttails (1) n 059.3
shirtwaist (2) n 081.8
shit (209) n/v/adj/ interj
    092.1
    ~ ass (2) n 096.7
    ~ -assy (1) adj 069.3
    ~ detail (1) n 081.9
    ~ eater (1) n 033.3
    ~ face (2) n 039.8
    ~ fire (3) interj 092.3
    ~ fly (1) n 060A.7
    ~ head (2) n 039.8
    ~ house (40) n 012.1
    ~ houses (2) n 012.1
    ~ in (2) v 096.8
    ~ kicker (5) n 069.9
    ~ kickers (1) n 123.8
    ~ on (1) v 039.9
    ~ on him (1) v 082.1
    ~ pill (1) n 078.4
    ~ pit (1) n 012.1

~ pot (1) n 088.8
~ sack (1) n 092.1
~ shoes (1) n 123.8
~ stompers (1) n 123.8
~ upon (1) v 092.1
shitlin (1) n 037.3
shitlins (2) n 037.3
shits (1) v 050.3
shitter (1) n 012.1
shitting (3) v/interj 092.3
    ~ -ass (1) adj 082.8
shitty (3) adj 072.9
shiv (1) n 104.3
shivaree (282) n/v/adj
    082.5
    ~ dance (2) n 083.1
shivareed (22) v 082.5
shivareeing (25) n/v 082.5
shivarees (11) n 082.5
shiver (2) adj 059.1
    ~ owl (1) n 059.1
    ~ owls (1) n 059.1
shivered (1) v 082.5
shivering (25) adj 059.1
    ~ owl (24) n 059.1
    ~ owls (1) n 059.1
shivers (1) v 059.1
shoal (2) n 031.4
Shoal (13) 030.7
    ~ Creek (12) AL GA
        TN TX 030.7
    ~ Creek Mountains (1)
        AL 031.1
shoals (7) n 031.6
Shoals (7) 030.7
    ~ Creek (1) AL 030.7
shoat (377) n/adj 035.5
    ~ gravy (1) n 048.5
    ~ hog (1) n 035.5
    ~ pig (5) n 035.5
shoat[N-i] (3) n 035.5
shoats (182) n 035.5
shoats' (1) adj 035.5
shoaty (4) adj 035.5
    ~ pig (2) n 035.5
    ~ pigs (2) n 035.5
shock (408) n/v/adj
    041.6
    ~ buster (1) n 110.9
    ~ piles (2) n 014.6
shock[V-r] (1) v 014.6
shocked (37) v 041.7
    ~ up (1) v 041.6
shockers (1) n 041.7
shocking (41) v/adj 014.7

~ horse (1) n 022.1
shocks (183) n/v 014.8
shod (7) v/adj 034.4
shodded (1) v 034.6
shoe (119) n/v/adj 034.6
  ~ bag (1) n 019.7
  ~ box (1) n 066.8
  ~ -button bradder (1) n 096.9
  ~ factories (1) n 040.8
  ~ factory (1) n 034.6
  ~ head (1) n 098.7
  ~ leather (1) n 044.4
  ~ sack (1) n 019.7
  ~ soles (2) n 080.3
Shoe Peg (1) 056.2
shoe[N-i] (2) n 123.8
shoed (4) v 034.6
shoeing (2) v 034.6
shoelaces (1) n 070.9
shoemaker (11) n/adj 091.7
  ~ bush (1) n 062.2
  ~ root (1) n 062.2
  ~ tree (2) n 062.2
shoemakers (1) n 062.2
shoes (736) n 034.6
shoeshine (2) adj 069.3
  ~ boy (1) n 069.3
  ~ Roy (1) n 083.1
shoestring (1) n 062.2
shoestrings (2) n 019.4
shone like (1) v 104.6
shoo (44) v/interj 038.5
  ~ -ants oil (1) n 024.2
  ~ -(a)round dance (1) n 083.1
shoo(x2) (3) interj 037.5
shoo(x3) (1) interj 038.5
shooey (1) interj 038.4
shooey(x3) (1) interj 038.3
Shoofly (2) 080.7
shook (14) v 096.8
  ~ up (7) v 075.2
shooken up (1) v 079.3
shoot (191) v/interj 092.3
  ~ -'em-up (1) n 091.4
  ~ hooky (1) v 083.4
  ~ off (1) v 075.1
  ~ the buffalo (1) n 088.8
  ~ the chute (2) n 084.9
  ~ the hook (1) v 083.4
  ~ up (2) v 114.2

Shoot (1) 087.1
shoot[V-p] (1) v 013.6
shooter (16) n 130.7
shooter's squat (1) n 096.4
shooters (7) n 093.6
shooting (38) v/adj 057.4
  ~ a hook (1) v 083.4
  ~ at (1) v 042.8
  ~ hooky (3) v 083.4
  ~ match (7) n 082.8
  ~ taw (1) n 080.9
  ~ up (3) v 114.3
shoots (6) n/v 056.3
shop (177) n/v/adj 011.9
  ~ around (1) v 094.2
  ~ foreman (1) n 025.2
  ~ hammer (2) n 020.7
  ~ hammers (2) n 020.7
  ~ house (3) n 011.7
Shop (10) 070.2
  ~ a Minutes (1) 070.2
  ~ and Go (1) 116.2
shopped (2) v 094.2
shopping (824) n/v/adj 094.2
  ~ areas (1) n 105.6
  ~ around (1) v 094.2
  ~ bag (8) n 019.5
  ~ bags (2) n 019.5
  ~ basket (1) n 019.6
  ~ book (1) n 028.2
  ~ center (16) n 105.6
  ~ -center grocery store (1) n 116.1
  ~ centers (22) n 105.3
  ~ day (1) n 094.2
  ~ malls (1) n 105.3
  ~ place (1) n 094.2
  ~ stores (1) n 116.2
  ~ -wise (1) adv 088.9
Shopping (2) 106.6
shops (20) n/v 094.2
Shops (1) 116.2
shore (9) n/v/adj 029.7
  ~ crest (1) n 029.7
Shore (8) 106.1
shoreline (2) n 031.4
shores (1) n 006.4
Shores (15) 106.1
shoring (2) v 080.7
short (442) adj 123.9
  ~ and sassy (1) adj 123.9
  ~ bone (1) n 037.1

  ~ breeches (1) n 027.4
  ~ corn (1) n 056.2
  ~ cotton (4) n 015.8
  ~ crop (1) n 041.3
  ~ drought (2) n 007.1
  ~ dry spell (1) n 007.1
  ~ hair (3) n 123.9
  ~ -haired dog (1) n 071.4
  ~ hall (1) n 007A.3
  ~ handles (1) n 092.8
  ~ -legged niggers (1) n 091.8
  ~ -life people (1) n 042.6
  ~ line (1) n 039.1
  ~ -link sausage (1) n 121.6
  ~ -lived (1) adj 075.7
  ~ loaf (1) n 044.3
  ~ -minded (1) adj 075.1
  ~ name (2) n 064.4
  ~ -needle pine (1) n 061.8
  ~ -order cook (2) n 084.9
  ~ pair of breeches (1) n 123.3
  ~ pants (17) n 123.4
  ~ patience (1) n 075.1
  ~ patient (5) adj 075.1
  ~ porch (2) n 007A.1
  ~ rain (1) n 006.1
  ~ -range cartridge (1) n 022.4
  ~ ribs (4) n 121.2
  ~ road (1) n 031.7
  ~ runs (1) n 055A.4
  ~ sack (1) n 019.7
  ~ shag (2) n 115.5
  ~ -sheeting (1) v 082.5
  ~ -shock (1) v 041.6
  ~ shorts (86) n 123.4
  ~ shower (1) n 006.6
  ~ siding (1) n 011.2
  ~ stack (2) n 045.3
  ~ -straw pine (1) n 061.8
  ~ sweetening (9) n 051.3
  ~ -tempered (20) adj 075.1
  ~ thigh (3) n 072.6
Short (2) 030.7

  ~ Creek (1) AL 030.7
  ~ John (1) 091.8
short[N-i] (2) n 123.2
shortage (1) n 095.2
shortbread (7) n 044.4
shortcake (16) n/adj 044.6
  ~ bread (1) n 044.4
shortcakes (6) n 044.4
shortcut (35) n/adj 085.2
  ~ road (1) n 031.7
shortcuts (1) n 031.9
shortcutting (1) v 085.2
shorted (1) v 088.7
shorten (2) v/adj 046.5
  ~ blade bone (1) n 046.5
shortening (19) n/adj 023.7
  ~ bread (11) n 044.8
  ~ corn bread (1) n 044.6
Shorter College (1) 105.4
shorter (7) adj 052.5
shortest (9) adj 026.3
shorthandess (1) n 068.8
Shorthorn (3) 033.6
Shorthorns (1) 033.6
shortleaf (22) n/adj 061.8
  ~ pine (13) n 061.9
  ~ pines (1) n 061.9
  ~ slash (2) n 061.8
shortleaves (1) n 061.8
shortly (22) adv 076.2
shorts (331) n 019.7
shorty shorts (1) n 123.4
shot (107) n/v/adj 084.8
  ~ a hook (2) v 083.4
  ~ glass (6) n 081.9
  ~ glasses (2) n 048.9
  ~ him down (3) v 082.1
  ~ him out of the saddle (1) v 082.1
  ~ hooky (4) v 083.4
  ~ in (3) v 078.2
  ~ pussy (1) n 083.4
  ~ -scared (1) adj 074.3
  ~ the hook (1) v 083.4
  ~ up (4) v 065.6
Shot (2) 080.9
shotgun (203) n/adj 118.6
  ~ barrel (1) n 019.1
  ~ coffin (1) n 079.1
  ~ doubles (1) n 118.6

~ house (95) n 118.6
~ houses (20) n 118.6
~ kitchen (3) n 007A.6
~ leg (1) n 078.1
~ outfit (1) n 007A.5
~ shack (1) n 118.6
~ shell (4) n 022.4
~ shells (6) n 022.4
~ type (1) n 007A.1
~ wedding (4) n 080.8
~ weddings (2) n 088.7
shotguns (11) n 113.4
shots (13) n 022.4
Shotwell Street (1) 107.7
should (855) v 058.1
shoulder (392) n/adj 072.4
~ bag (7) n 019.5
~ bags (1) n 028.2
~ beef (1) n 121.2
~ blade (4) n 072.4
~ blades (5) n 072.4
~ chops (1) n 121.4
~ cut (1) n 131.9
~ cuts (1) n 121.3
~ ham (2) n 121.3
~ -high (1) adj 072.4
~ hock (1) n 046.3
~ holster (1) n 072.4
~ joint (1) n 072.3
~ joints (2) n 072.3
~ line (1) n 107.3
~ loin (2) n 121.1
~ meat (7) n 046.5
~ of lamb (1) n 121.4
~ roast (12) n 121.2
~ roasts (1) n 121.2
~ steak (1) n 121.1
~ steaks (2) n 121.1
shoul(der) (1) v 098.1
shoulder[N-i] (15) n 072.4
shouldered (3) v 072.4
shoulders (770) n/adj 072.4
~ meat (1) n 046.3
shouldn't (470) v 058.4
should've (20) v 058.3
Shouns (1) TN 070.6
shout (1) interj 092.3
shouting (7) v/adj 088.7
~ Methodist (1) n 089.9
~ revival (1) n 089.9
shouts (1) n 080.6

shove (35) n/v 097.7
shove[V-p] (1) v 024.5
shoved off (1) v 078.6
shovel (265) n/v/adj 021.6
~ -bill cats (1) n 059.9
~ hoe (1) n 065.9
~ -like (1) adj 120.5
~ out (1) v 010.4
~ -out day (1) n 010.4
~ plow (14) n 021.6
~ plow stock (1) n 021.6
~ plows (1) n 021.6
~ stock (5) n 021.6
~ stocks (1) n 021.6
~ sweeps (1) n 021.6
shovelhead (1) n 059.9
shoveling (4) v 093.5
shovels (33) n 021.6
shoving off (1) v 024.5
show (322) n/v/adj 084.5
~ actor (1) n 069.1
~ girl (1) n 069.1
~ music (1) n 130.8
~ off (6) v 028.1
~ -off (11) n 125.6
~ -off things (1) n 092.7
~ out (1) v 100.1
~ tunes (1) n 130.8
~ up (3) v 083.4
~ woman (2) n 069.1
sh(ow) (1) n 084.4
Show (2) 131.1
showboat (3) n 024.6
showdown (1) n 083.1
showed (18) v 082.1
~ him the door (2) v 082.1
~ him the gate (1) v 082.1
~ up (2) v 012.5
shower (641) n/adj 006.6
~ rain (5) n 006.6
~ stick (3) n 028.6
show(er) (2) n 006.1
showered (2) v 006.6
showering (11) v/adj 006.6
~ rain (1) n 006.1
showers (74) n 006.6
showhouse (1) n 084.4
showing (6) v 123.4
~ out (3) v 082.5

~ up (1) v 033.9
shown (1) v 058.4
shows (28) n/v 084.4
shrank (204) v 027.9
~ up (9) v 027.9
shranked (8) v 027.9
~ up (1) v 027.9
shranken (1) v 027.9
shred (4) v 042.1
shredded wheat (1) n 081.8
Shreve (6) 030.7
~ City (1) LA 087.6
Shreveport (160) LA 087.8
~ Regional Airport (1) 106.5
shrewd (3) adj 065.8
shriek owl (1) n 059.1
shrimp (720) n/v/adj 060.9
~ bait (2) n 060.9
~ boat (6) n 060.9
~ boats (19) n 060.9
~ bran (1) n 029.3
~ docks (1) n 031.4
~ family (1) n 060.9
~ festival (2) n 060.9
~ flies (1) n 060A.2
~ fly (1) n 060A.2
~ for (1) v 060.9
~ fork (1) n 060.9
~ gumbo (5) n 060.9
~ industry (1) n 060.9
~ jambalaya (1) n 090.8
~ moth (1) n 060A.1
~ net (1) n 060.9
~ plant (1) n 085.6
~ season (2) n 081.8
~ trawlers (1) n 080.7
~ with (3) v 052.4
shrimp[N-i] (411) n 060.9
shrimped (2) v 060.9
shrimper (1) n 024.6
shrimpers (3) n 060.9
shrimping (6) n/v 060.9
shrimps (116) n 060.9
shrimpses (1) n 060.9
shrine (1) n 106.8
Shrine (3) 066.9
~ ring (1) n 123.1
Shriner (1) 070.7
shrink (804) v 027.9

~ out (1) v 055.9
~ up (58) v 027.9
shrink[V-p] (1) v 027.9
shrink[V-r] (19) v 027.9
shrink[V-t] (14) v 027.9
~ up (1) v 027.9
shrinkable (2) adj 027.9
shrinkage (3) n 027.9
shrinked (101) v 027.9
~ apart (1) v 027.9
~ up (23) v 027.9
shrinkeded (1) v 027.9
shrinken (6) v 027.9
~ up (1) v 027.9
shrinker (4) n 027.9
shrinking (22) v 027.9
~ up (4) v 027.9
shrinkle up (1) v 055.9
shrinks (62) v 027.9
~ up (10) v 055.9
shrivel (321) v/adj 055.9
~ away (1) v 055.9
~ up (106) v 055.9
~ tree (1) n 021.4
shrivel[V-p] up (1) v 055.9
shrivel[V-r] up (1) v 055.9
shrivel[V-t] (7) v 055.9
shriveldy (1) adj 055.9
shriveled (163) v/adj 055.9
~ away (1) v 055.9
~ things (1) n 055.9
~ up (65) v 055.9
~ -up (2) adj 055.9
shriveling (9) v 055.9
~ up (6) v 055.9
shrivels (54) v 055.9
~ up (26) v 055.9
shrively (1) adj 055.9
shroud (1) v 055.9
shrouds (1) n 079.2
Shrove Tuesday (1) 002.1
shrub (10) n/adj 062.2
~ pine (1) n 061.8
shrubbed (2) v 041.4
shrubberies (1) n 070.7
shrubbery (13) n/adj 062.2
~ fence (1) n 016.2
shrubbing (4) v 041.4
~ off (1) v 041.4
shrubs (9) n 065.8
shrugged (1) v 072.4

shrunk (813) v 027.9
~ up (71) v 027.9
shrunked (3) v 027.9
~ up (1) v 027.9
shrunken (37) v 027.9
~ up (1) v 027.9
Shubuta (3) MS 087.6
shuck (714) n/v/adj 056.1
~ baskets (1) n 020.1
~ bed (5) n 028.7
~ bread (1) n 044.7
~ broom (6) n 010.5
~ brooms (1) n 010.5
~ brush (2) n 022.2
~ collars (1) n 080.6
~ factory (1) n 080.8
~ hat (1) n 090.8
~ mattress (2) n 081.9
~ mop (11) n 010.5
~ mops (3) n 010.5
~ out (1) v 056.1
~ pen (1) n 014.3
~ scrub (2) n 010.5
~ tea (3) n 061.4
~ tick (1) n 028.8
~ up (1) v 075.3
~ weed (1) n 015.9
shuck[N-i] (15) n 092.3
shucked (14) v 056.1
shucker's hook (1) n 080.6
shuckers (2) n 041.7
shucking (20) n/v 056.1
shuckings (8) n/interj 084.9
shucks (438) n/interj 056.1
shuckses (1) n 056.1
shucky bean (1) n 055A.3
shuffle (3) n 083.1
shuffleboard (2) n 034.8
shuffled off (2) v 078.6
shuffling (2) adj 058.7
~ mentality (1) n 068.5
shum (1) v 092.1
shun (1) v 080.8
shunkles (1) n 072.7
Shuqualak (3) MS 086.3
Shushan Airport (3) 106.5
shusty (1) n 061.4
shut (1064) v/adj 011.1
~ -door window (1) n 011.1

~ down (12) v 011.1
~ -eye (2) n 011.1
~ -in (1) n 084.9
~ of (184) v 099.4
~ off (2) v 011.1
~ out (1) v 011.1
~ up (41) v 066.9
~ [P-0] (2) v 099.4
Shut-In Mountain (1) LA 031.1
shuts (3) v 011.1
~ off (1) v 011.1
shutter (15) n/adj 011.3
~ window (1) n 096.7
~ windows (1) n 009.5
shutters (95) n 009.5
shutting (2) v 011.1
~ up (1) v 099.9
shuttle (32) n/adj 035.2
~ bus (1) n 090.9
~ buses (2) n 109.8
~ service (1) n 109.8
shy (8) v/adj 074.3
~ away from (1) v 075.6
shylocks (1) n 055.7
Shylocks (1) 126.7
shyster (8) n/adj 067.8
~ lawyer (1) n 067.8
shysters (1) n 069.7
Siard (2) 030.7
Siberia (1) 010.3
Siberi(a) (1) 087.8
Sibley (1) LA 087.5
siblings (4) n 064.3
sic (607) v 033.2
~ him (457) v 033.2
~ -him(x2) (4) interj 033.2
~ -him(x3) (2) interj 033.2
~ it (4) v 033.2
~ it psst (1) v 033.2
~ them (65) v 033.2
~ -them(x2) (2) interj 033.2
sic(x3) (2) interj 033.2
sicced (3) v 033.2
siccing (3) v 033.2
Sicilians (1) 013.9
Sicily (5) 086.2
sick (1589) adj 072.9
~ birds (1) n 081.4
~ box (1) n 104.6

~ -looking (1) adj 125.3
~ nurse (1) n 084.6
~ person's egg (1) n 046.2
~ stomach (14) n 080.4
~ up (1) adj 090.4
sickening (1) adj 090.8
sickety-whick (1) interj 084.9
sickie (1) n 124.2
sickle (16) n/adj 042.1
~ blade (1) n 120.1
~ grinders (1) n 023.5
~ mower (1) n 097.8
~ rock (1) n 023.4
sickles (1) n 120.5
sickly (77) adj 072.9
~ -looking (2) adj 072.9
sickness (8) n 080.6
sicknesswise (1) adv 002.6
side (1454) n/adj 046.4
~ ache (1) n 080.1
~ alley (1) n 108.6
~ back (1) n 046.3
~ bacon (13) n 046.3
~ beef (1) n 046.4
~ blade (1) n 084.8
~ by side (1) adj 108.3
~ -by-side parking (1) n 108.3
~ chair (2) n 008.8
~ chairs (1) n 008.8
~ closet (1) n 010.3
~ curtain (1) n 089.8
~ curtains (1) n 009.5
~ door (4) n 007A.6
~ dressing (3) n 080.6
~ drive (1) n 031.8
~ entrance (1) n 007A.9
~ entry (1) n 108.6
~ gallery (3) n 010.8
~ hall (1) n 007A.4
~ harrow (17) n 021.7
~ har(row) (6) n 021.7
~ -har(row) (3) v 021.7
~ -harrowing (1) v 096.8
~ harrows (9) n 021.7
~ house (3) n 007A.2
~ lane (1) n 031.7
~ meat (260) n 046.4

~ meats (1) n 046.4
~ middling (1) n 046.4
~ panels (1) n 032.4
~ plank (1) n 014.7
~ -plate meat (1) n 046.4
~ pleurisy (2) n 080.1
~ plow (3) n 021.6
~ porch (42) n 010.8
~ porch area (1) n 010.3
~ pork (7) n 046.3
~ rest (are)as (1) n 107.2
~ road (213) n 031.7
~ road strip (1) n 107.3
~ roads (26) n 031.7
~ room (75) n 007A.3
~ rooms (10) n 007A.4
~ screen porch (1) n 010.8
~ shed (5) n 015.1
~ sheds (2) n 011.7
~ shelters (1) n 011.9
~ slab (1) n 046.4
~ storage room (1) n 010.1
~ street (10) n 031.7
~ streets (3) n 031.7
~ sweep (1) n 021.6
~ table (1) n 009.5
~ teeth (1) n 035.7
~ tooth (1) n 025.7
~ -wheel steamer (1) n 080.8
~ wool (1) n 035.2
~ yard (1) n 108.6
Side (189) 106.6
side[N-i] (3) n 042.3
sidearm (4) n 113.1
~ out (1) n 088.8
sidearms (1) n 113.1
sideback (1) n 046.3
sidebar (1) n 021.6
sideboard (33) n/adj 009.2
~ house (1) n 014.1
sideboards (7) n 011.2
sideburn (3) n 071.4
sideburns (22) n 071.4
sidecar (1) n 109.6
sided (4) adj 021.7
Sided (1) 088.8
sidekick (2) n 080.7
sidely (1) adv 021.7

sidepieces (1) n 020.9
sider (1) n 122.8
sides (117) n 046.4
sidesaddle (2) n 039.3
sideswiped (1) v 075.7
sidetrack (2) v/adj 082.1
~ him off (1) v 082.1
~ road (1) n 031.7
sidewalk (723) n/adj
031.9
~ preacher (1) n 067.8
~ tag (1) n 130.2
~ work (1) n 031.9
sidewalks (110) n 031.9
sidewards (2) adv 108.1
sideways (4) adv 040.3
sidewinder (1) n 084.8
sidewise (1) adv 040.3
siding (367) n/adj 011.2
~ boards (1) n 011.2
~ house (1) n 011.2
sidings (4) n 011.2
Sidney (3) AR 086.3
Sierra Madre (1) 031.1
siete medio (1) n S 004.4
sieva bean (1) n 055A.3
sieve (3) n/v 070.7
sieved (1) v 048.2
sifle out (1) v 075.8
sift (1) v 048.2
sifters (1) n 081.8
siftes (1) v 070.9
sigh (2) n 036.4
sight (37) n 025.4
sign (15) n/v 095.1
~ for (1) v 088.4
sign[V-r] (1) v 053.4
signal (2) n/adj 024.2
~ oil (1) n 024.2
Signal Mountain (4) GA
TN 031.1
signed (3) v 100.5
~ up (1) v 081.3
signet (2) n/adj 123.1
~ ring (1) n 123.1
significant (1) adj 091.7
signifying (2) v 129.7
~ a case (1) v 129.7
signs (7) n 090.3
sigodlin (1) adv 085.2
Sigsbee (1) 068.5
silage (16) n/adj 014.4
~ crop (2) n 041.3
~ pit (2) n 014.4
Silas Marner (1) 073.5

silent (2) adj 075.3
silk (565) n/adj 056.4
~ clay loam (1) n 029.9
~ hair (1) n 056.4
~ mill (1) n 081.8
~ oak (1) n 061.8
~ -stocking district (1)
n 080.7
~ stuff (1) n 056.4
~ tassel (2) n 056.4
Silk (1) 056.4
silked out (2) v 056.4
silken (1) v 056.4
silking (6) v 056.4
~ out (1) v 056.4
silks (334) n/v 056.4
~ out (1) v 056.4
silkweed (2) n 078.4
silkworm (1) n 056.4
silkworms (1) n 060.5
silky (2) adj 056.4
sill cock (2) n 018.7
sills (4) n/v 096.7
silly (94) n/adj 074.7
~ -ass (2) adj 104.1
~ -like (1) adj 074.7
~ party (2) n 089.8
silo (229) n/adj 014.4
~ thing (1) n 035.8
silos (55) n 014.4
Silsbee (1) TX 087.3
silt (15) n/adj 029.4
~ loam (1) n 029.8
siltation (1) n 080.8
silty (1) adj 029.7
Siluria (2) AL 087.5
Silur(ia) (1) AL 087.8
silver (57) n/adj 017.9
~ cat (1) n 059.6
~ dime (1) n 026.6
~ dollar (1) n 080.8
~ dollars (2) n 034.8
~ goblet (1) n 048.9
~ harness (1) n 038.6
~ knives (1) n 017.8
~ maple (8) n 061.8
~ maple leaf (1) n
061.5
~ maple tree (1) n
061.8
~ maples (1) n 061.9
~ -mesh-looking (1) adj
126.1
~ oak (1) n 061.8
~ plate (1) n 017.8

~ poplar (1) n 062.8
~ rings (2) n 123.1
~ skins (1) n 055.7
~ spoon (1) n 053.3
~ spoons (1) n 012.2
~ stuff (1) n 017.8
~ teaspoons (1) n 017.8
Silver (21) 087.5
~ Bluff (1) GA 087.5
~ City (1) 119.8
~ Creek (7) GA LA
MS TN 030.7
~ Queen (1) 056.2
~ River (1) FL 030.7
~ Springs (8) FL MD
MS 087.4
silverfish (15) n 061.2
silverfishes (1) n 060A.2
Silverhill (1) AL 087.9
silverleaf (12) adj 061.8
~ maple (11) n 061.8
~ maples (1) n 061.8
silverleaves (1) n 061.8
silvers (1) n 061.2
Silver's (1) 068.2
silverside minnows (1) n
061.2
silversides (1) n 059.9
silversmith (3) n 070.7
Silversmith Creek (1) FL
030.7
silverware (26) n 017.8
Simcoe (1) AL 087.2
similar (18) adj 065.3
simmer down (15) v
075.3
simmering (1) v 048.8
Simmesport (2) LA 087.7
Simms (2) FL 030.7
~ Creek (1) FL 030.7
simon-pure (1) adj 081.9
Simon (5) 065.9
~ Bolivar (2) 065.9
~ says (3) n 080.7
Simons (9) 087.2
simp (2) n 073.4
simple (15) adj 074.7
~ syrup (1) n 051.3
simp(le) (1) adj F 021.6
simpleton (3) n 073.4
simply (3) adv 005.8
Simpson County (3) MS
087.2
Sims Bayou (4) TX 030.7
Simsboro (1) LA 087.6

Simsbor(o) (1) LA 087.5
sin (8) n 052.6
since (1271) adv/conj
103.5
sincere (1) adj 073.2
sing (18) v/adj 057.4
singe (1) v 066.9
singed (1) v 070.8
singer (1) n 130.9
singers (1) n 130.9
singing (321) n/v/adj
057.4
~ choir (1) n 089.5
~ master (1) n 070.8
~ school (1) n 080.7
singings (2) n 083.1
single (130) adj 033.7
~ -axle outfit (1) n
021.8
~ bed (1) n 009.3
~ bit (1) n 021.6
~ -bit ax (1) n 088.8
~ -blade ax (1) n 080.7
~ -bladed plow (1) n
021.6
~ -breasted (1) adj
090.8
~ buggy (1) n 095.9
~ chairs (1) n 008.8
~ chimley (2) n 008.1
~ doubletree (1) n
021.3
~ foot (3) n 021.6
~ -foot (2) n 034.7
~ -footed (1) adj 021.6
~ gee whiz (1) n 021.7
~ harrow (1) n 021.7
~ hole (1) n 012.1
~ house (1) n 007A.6
~ -pen house (1) n
007A.1
~ plow (29) n 021.6
~ plow stock (1) n
021.6
~ plow stocks (1) n
021.6
~ plows (2) n 021.6
~ -point plow (1) n
021.6
~ -row planter (1) n
088.7
~ scooter (1) n 021.6
~ sets (1) n 021.7
~ shaft (1) n 021.6
~ shovel (4) n 021.6

~ shovel plow (1) n 021.6
~ stock (18) n 021.6
~ stock plow (2) n 021.6
~ stock plows (1) n 021.6
~ stocks (5) n 021.6
~ stop (1) n 021.6
~ story (1) n 118.9
~ stripe (1) n 107.3
~ -tackle hoist (1) n 104.5
~ turning plows (1) n 021.6
~ wagon (2) n 020.8
~ woman (2) n 063.3
singles (1) n 080.7
Singleton (1) 105.7
singletree (680) n/adj 021.2
~ ends (1) n 021.2
~ -looking (1) adj 021.2
~ mules (1) n 033.7
~ plow (1) n 021.6
~ two (1) n 021.3
singletrees (86) n 021.2
sings (4) n/v 080.7
~ in (1) v 013.8
singular (2) adj 066.8
sink (29) n 009.8
Sink (2) 030.7
sinkers (3) n 045.2
sinkhole (5) n 029.6
sinkholes (3) n 030.1
sinking (1) v 024.9
Sinking (3) 030.7
~ Creek (3) TN 030.7
~ Springs (1) TN 030.7
sinks (4) n 065.8
sinner (2) n/adj 090.1
~ hogs (1) n 035.9
sins (1) n 073.6
Sinton (3) TX 087.1
sinus (2) n/adj 076.3
~ problems (1) n 012.2
Sioux City (1) IA 087.5
sippers (1) n 080.9
Sipsey (12) AL 030.7
~ Creek (1) AL 030.7
~ Fork (2) AL 030.7
~ River (7) AL 030.7
sir (783) n 069.6
sire (18) n 033.5

siren (11) n 070.9
sirens (2) n 070.6
sirloin (106) n/adj 121.1
~ of lamb (1) n 121.4
~ patties (1) n 121.2
~ steak (19) n 121.1
~ steaks (3) n 121.1
~ strip (1) n 121.1
~ strips (1) n 121.1
~ tip (6) n 121.2
~ -tip roast (3) n 121.2
~ -tip steak (1) n 121.1
~ tips (2) n 121.1
sirloins (3) n 121.1
sirop (3) n F 051.3
~ de batterie (1) n F 051.3
sirree (22) interj 091.4
Sis (5) 064.4
sissies (19) n 124.1
sissified (1) adj 124.1
sissy (117) n/adj 124.1
~ breeches (1) n 083.1
~ cat (1) n 059.4
~ fancy (1) adj 088.8
~ game (1) n 130.3
~ -sounding (1) adj 028.1
Sissy (2) 064.4
sister (155) n/adj 064.9
~ -in-law (2) n 085.7
~ -in-law's (1) adj 082.7
~ school (2) n 067.6
sist(er) (1) n 042.2
Sister (10) 064.4
sister[N-i] (1) n 055A.7
sister[N-k] (3) adj 043.9
~ comb (1) n 043.9
~ room (1) n 043.9
sister's (13) adj 007A.3
~ bedroom (2) n 007A.6
~ book (1) n 052.8
~ house (1) n 082.7
~ land (1) n 043.8
~ room (3) n 007A.2
sisters (69) n 068.2
Sisters (4) 129.5
~ Creek (1) FL 030.7
sit (1061) v/adj 049.3
~ around (16) v 049.3
~ (a)round (1) v 049.3
~ at (2) v 049.3
~ back (5) v 049.3

~ down (626) v 049.2
~ -down mower (1) n 120.3
~ -downs (1) n 080.7
~ him down (1) v 082.1
~ in (12) v 049.3
~ off (1) v 009.9
~ on (71) v 049.2
~ -on dog (1) n 033.3
~ out (8) v 049.3
~ room (1) n 007.8
~ up (17) v 079.3
~ up with (2) v 075.6
~ with (2) v 049.2
sit[V-r] (96) v 049.3
~ around (1) v 049.3
~ down (64) v 049.3
~ in (1) v 049.3
~ on (2) v 049.3
~ up (1) v 049.3
sit[V-t] (86) v 049.3
~ down (61) v 049.3
~ up (2) v 049.3
site (20) n 085.5
sito (1) adj S 012.1
sits (40) v 049.3
~ back (1) v 039.5
~ down (9) v 049.3
~ on (2) v 025.6
~ up (2) v 013.9
sitten (9) v 049.3
~ down (1) v 049.3
sitter (5) n 036.7
sitters (1) n 055A.8
sitting (399) v/adj 049.3
~ area (1) n 007A.7
~ around (2) v 049.3
~ -back fire (1) n 081.9
~ chair (4) n 008.8
~ chairs (1) n 008.8
~ down (6) v 049.3
~ hen (85) n 036.7
~ in (5) v 130.3
~ in a chair (1) n 130.7
~ lawn mower (1) n 120.3
~ on (15) v 059.3
~ room (177) n 007.8
~ rooms (3) n 007.8
~ to (1) v 026.9
~ up to them (1) v 081.4
~ up with (1) v 079.2
situation (4) n 070.8

six (2610) n/adj 001A.3
~ -and-twelve-pitch roof (1) n 088.9
~ bits (4) n 114.5
~ -by (1) n 109.6
~ -by-six (1) n 001.3
~ -by-sixes (1) n 042.8
~ -cent (1) adj 001.3
~ feet under (3) n 078.6
~ -fifteen (2) n 004.5
~ -fifty (1) n 001.3
~ -foot (8) adj 007.9
~ -forty (1) n 001.3
~ -forty-five (15) n 004.5
~ -forty-two (3) n 001.1
~ -four (1) n 001.2
~ -grade education (1) n 001A.3
~ holes across (1) n 093.5
~ -horse farm (1) n 080.8
~ -hour (1) adj 001.3
~ -hundred-room (1) adj 001A.2
~ -inch (2) adj 001.3
~ -months school (1) n 001.3
~ -mule crop (1) n 080.6
~ -mule wagon (1) n 033.7
~ -nineteen (1) n 001.3
~ -plait (1) adj 019.4
~ -room brick house (1) n 007A.2
~ -room house (6) n 001.3
~ -shooter (4) n 113.1
~ -sixty-six (1) n 001.3
~ sticks (1) n 104.6
~ -string fence (1) n 016.3
~ -ten (2) n 001.3
~ -thirty (32) n 004.4
~ up (2) n 033.7
~ -up teams (2) n 033.7
~ -week bean (1) n 055A.4
~ -week pea (2) n 081.9

~ -weeks feeders (1) n 035.5
~ -wire fences (1) n 016.3
Six (40) 001.3
~ District (1) 001A.3
~ District police station (1) n 112.7
~ -Eight-Eight (1) 001.4
~ Flags (4) 106.4
~ Hundred and Sixty-Six (1) 078.4
~ Hundred and Sixty-Six tonic (1) n 078.4
~ Links (1) 129.6
~ Mile (2) AL 087.7
~ Points (1) 105.4
~ -Sixty-Six (2) 078.4
~ Street (5) 001A.3
~ Ward (1) 087.5
Six[N-i] (1) 078.4
sixes (5) n 001.3
Sixes (23) 078.4
Sixmile (5) LA 030.7
~ Creek (3) FL LA 030.7
~ Lake (1) AR 030.7
sixteen (166) n/adj 001.8
~ -fifty (1) n 001.9
~ -foot (3) adj 007.9
~ -foot-square (1) adj 007.9
~ -gauge Remington automatic (1) n 113.1
~ -inch bottom plows (1) n 021.6
~ -ounce (1) adj 048.9
~ -ten (1) n 001.5
Sixteen (3) 001.2
sixth (392) n/adj 001A.3
Sixth (4) 001A.3
~ Street (1) 001A.3
sixty (305) n/adj 001.9
~ -eight (31) n/adj 001.4
~ -fifth (1) n 001A.3
~ -five (43) n/adj 001.3
~ -four (15) n/adj 001.2
~ -gallon (1) adj 016.7
~ -nine (28) n/adj 001A.1
~ -one (11) n/adj 001.1

~ -pound (1) adj 045.4
~ -seven (28) n/adj 001.4
~ -six (20) n/adj 001.3
~ -some-odd (3) adj 001.9
~ -something (1) adj 103.2
~ -something-years-old (1) adj 002.9
~ -three (15) n/adj 001.2
~ -two (15) n/adj 001.1
~ -watt (1) adj 019.9
Sixty (29) 107.1
~ -Five (2) 107.1
~ -One (1) 031.6
~ -Second Street (1) 001A.3
~ -Seven (1) 107.1
~ -Six (2) 078.4
~ -Six chill tonic (1) n 078.4
sizable (2) adj 090.7
size (64) n/adj 035.5
sized (7) adj 090.4
sizes (2) n 095.8
sizzle (1) n 006.6
sizzling (1) n 050.8
skag (10) n 114.1
skags (1) n 125.2
skank (3) n 125.2
skate (5) n/v/adj 130.5
~ bug (1) n 060A.4
skateboards (1) n 130.4
skater bedding (1) n 080.8
skates (3) n 033.7
skating (7) n/v/adj 130.2
~ parties (1) n 130.7
skaw (1) n 050.8
skein (8) n/adj 021.9
skeleton (6) n/adj 090.2
~ hotel (1) n 106.4
skeletons (1) n 070.7
sketch (4) n/v 057.7
sketches (1) n 039.6
sketchy (2) adj 090.4
ski (9) n/adj 024.6
~ boat (2) n 024.6
~ boats (4) n 024.6
~ -lodge house (1) n 118.9
~ nose (1) n 128.4

skid (70) n/v/adj 021.5
~ poles (1) n 021.5
~ row (58) n 114.8
~ -row bum (1) n 113.7
~ -row bums (1) n 113.7
Skidaway (3) 087.2
~ Island (2) GA 087.2
~ Narrows (1) GA 030.7
skidded (6) v 021.5
~ across (1) v 085.2
skidder (2) n 080.8
skidders (1) n 080.6
skidding (7) n/v/adj 021.5
~ dogs (2) n 088.9
skids (3) n 081.9
skidway (1) n 091.8
skidways (1) n 081.8
skies (2) n 005.4
skiff (130) n/adj 024.7
~ boat (6) n 024.6
~ boats (3) n 024.6
~ load[N-i] (2) n 019.8
~ oar (2) n 024.6
skiff[N-i] (2) n 024.6
skiffers (1) n 024.6
skiffs (52) n 024.6
skift (6) n 007.6
skigoglin (2) adv 085.2
skiing (2) adj 024.6
~ boat (1) n 024.6
~ shoes (1) n 123.8
skill (1) n 090.7
skillet (928) n/adj 017.5
~ bread (2) n 044.6
~ cakes (1) n 045.3
~ corn bread (1) n 044.6
~ deal (1) n 116.4
skillet[N-i] (2) n 017.5
skilletes (1) n 017.5
skilletful (1) n 044.6
skillets (116) n 017.5
Skillikalaia Creek (2) MS 030.7
skillpot (2) n 060.6
Skilsaw (2) 080.6
skim (65) n/v/adj 007.6
~ cream milk (1) n 048.5
~ ice (3) n 007.6
~ milk (9) n 048.2
~ off (1) v 065.8

skim[V-r] (1) v 007.6
skimmed (16) v/adj 048.2
~ milk (1) n 047.7
~ off (1) v 081.8
~ over (10) v 007.7
skimmer (1) n 051.3
skimmers (1) n 060A.4
skimming (6) n/v/adj 051.3
~ down (1) v 080.6
skimmings (17) n/adj 050.8
skimping over (1) v 007.6
skimpy (2) adj 095.2
skin (567) n/v/adj 046.6
~ boats (1) n 024.6
~ boil (1) n 077.4
~ fish (2) n 092.7
~ flick (11) n 114.9
~ flicks (13) n 114.9
~ game (1) n 080.6
~ him alive (1) v 065.5
~ my fanny (1) v 080.8
~ pork (1) n 046.6
~ them alive (1) v 065.5
~ up (2) v 096.3
~ you alive (1) v 065.5
Skin Oak (2) 087.3
skinflint (48) n 073.5
skinflints (2) n 073.5
skink (1) n 060A.7
skinks (1) n 060A.8
skinned (21) v/adj 065.9
~ us alive (1) v 065.5
skinneded (3) adj 063.8
skinners (1) n 053.9
skinning (13) n/v/adj 065.5
~ knife (5) n 104.3
~ knives (2) n 104.3
skinnings (2) n 050.6
skinny (17) adj 072.9
~ -dip (1) v 084.9
~ -dipping (2) v 080.6
~ year (1) n 084.8
Skinny Papa (1) 081.6
skins (23) n 046.6
skintight (1) adj 123.6
skip (59) n/v 083.4
~ a class (2) v 083.4
~ across (1) v 085.2
~ class (10) v 083.4
~ classes (3) v 083.4
~ over (1) v 092.7

~ rope (6) v 130.6
~ school (12) v 083.4
~ the rope (2) v 130.6
~ to my Lou (3) n 081.8
skip[V-r] (26) v 083.4
~ class (7) v 083.4
~ classes (3) v 083.4
~ school (13) v 083.4
skip[V-t] school (1) v 083.4
skipjack (1) n 088.9
skipjacks (2) n 059.9
skipped (126) v 083.4
~ a certain class (1) v 083.4
~ class (28) v 083.4
~ classes (6) v 083.4
~ his class (2) v 083.4
~ his classes (2) v 083.4
~ his school (1) v 083.4
~ out (5) v 083.4
~ school (37) v 083.4
skipper (11) n/adj 068.5
~ fly (1) n 088.9
Skipper (1) 069.5
skippers (9) n 088.7
skipping (21) v 083.4
~ class (5) v 083.4
~ classes (1) v 083.4
~ rope (1) v 130.6
~ school (6) v 083.4
~ the rope (1) v 130.6
skips (1) v 083.4
Skipworth (1) MS 087.5
skirt (5) n/adj 088.7
~ -chasing (1) adj 089.9
~ steaks (1) n 121.1
skirts (5) n 070.6
skittish (10) adj 035.9
skrinch (2) adj 059.1
~ owl (1) n 059.1
~ owls (1) n 059.1
skrink owl (1) n 059.1
skull (14) n/adj 074.8
~ bone (1) n 071.3
~ bust (1) n 050.9
~ buster (1) n 050.8
~ orchard (3) n 078.8
skulls (1) n 008.1
Skuna Creek (1) MS 030.7
skunk (728) n/adj 059.4

~ cat (1) n 059.4
~ liquor (1) n 050.8
~ owl (1) n 059.2
Skunk (2) 059.4
skunked (6) v 075.2
skunking (1) n 040.5
skunks (52) n 059.4
sky (26) n/adj 005.4
~ ball (1) n 088.8
~ parlor (2) n 009.8
~ pilot (1) n 067.8
~ scooter (1) n 022.7
Sky Ranch (1) 106.5
Skyland (1) 106.2
skylight (1) n 118.1
skyline (2) n 080.7
skyliner (1) n 108.5
skylines (1) n 089.6
skyscraper (47) n 108.5
skyscrapers (59) n 108.5
Skyview (1) 084.4
skyway (1) n 031.3
Skyway (1) 107.5
slab (179) n/adj 046.6
~ bacon (29) n 046.4
~ fence (1) n 016.2
~ har(row) (1) n 021.7
~ meat (6) n 046.4
~ part (1) n 046.4
slabs (13) n 046.4
slack (15) n/v/adj 074.6
~ barrel (1) n 084.9
~ barrel stave (1) n 019.1
~ lime (1) n 078.4
~ load (1) n 019.8
~ off (1) v 007.3
~ preacher (1) n 067.8
~ -stave barrel (1) n 019.1
~ up (3) v 007.3
slackens (1) v 007.3
slacker (1) n 083.4
slackered (1) v 083.4
slacking (12) v 007.3
~ down (1) v 088.7
~ off (5) v 007.3
~ up (3) v 007.3
slacks (128) n 027.4
slag (26) n/adj 031.6
~ road (3) n 031.8
slaggard (1) n 099.5
slagged road (1) n 031.7
slags (1) n 029.5
slain (2) v 078.5

slam (34) v/adj/adv 028.9
~ word (1) n 088.7
slam[V-r] (1) v 011.1
slammed (2) v 011.1
slammer (20) n 112.9
slang (11) n/adj 131.5
~ expressions (2) n 131.2
~ name (1) n 090.8
~ word (1) n 091.2
~ words (1) n 131.3
slangiest (1) adj 117.8
slangs (4) n 080.6
slangy (1) adj 080.9
slant (22) n/adj 126.4
~ -eye (1) n 126.4
~ -eyed (1) adj 126.4
~ -eyes (15) n 126.4
~ parking (3) n 108.3
slanted (3) adj 108.3
~ parking (1) n 108.3
~ roof (1) n 011.4
slanties (1) n 126.4
slanting (2) v 090.4
slants (2) n 126.4
slantways (1) adv 085.2
slantwise (1) adv 085.2
slap (39) n/v/adj/adv 065.5
~ diving (1) n 095.4
~ out (1) n 098.6
~ -wing plow (1) n 021.6
slap[V-p] (1) v 090.6
slapdab (1) adv 075.8
slaphappy (1) adj 076.6
slapjack (3) n 113.2
slapjacks (8) n 045.3
slapped (1) v 065.5
slapper (3) n 113.2
slappers (1) n 113.2
slapping (4) v 065.5
slaps (1) n 123.8
slapstick (2) n 113.2
slash (21) n/v/adj 061.8
~ land (1) n 029.6
~ pine (8) n 061.8
Slash (2) 029.6
slashed (4) v/adj 104.3
~ at (1) v 104.3
~ ham (1) n 046.7
slashes (2) n 088.7
slashing (2) n/v 065.5
slashways (1) adv 085.2

slat (21) n/adj 016.2
~ boards (1) n 011.2
~ fence (15) n 016.2
~ fencing (1) n 016.2
~ house (1) n 080.7
~ wing (1) n 021.6
slate (10) n/adj 029.9
~ land (2) n 029.8
slates (1) n 066.9
slats (13) n 036.8
slatted fence (1) n 016.2
slaty land (1) n 029.8
slaughter (7) v/adj 130.4
~ ball (1) n 130.4
~ pen (4) n 015.1
~ pole (1) n 081.8
Slaughter (3) 030.7
~ Creek (2) TX 030.7
~ Mountain (1) AR 031.1
slaughtered (1) v 070.7
slaughterer (3) n 046.8
slaughterhouse (6) n/adj 046.8
~ pen (1) n 015.3
slaughterhouses (1) n 014.1
slaughtering knives (1) n 104.4
slave (28) n/adj 070.8
~ cemetery (1) n 078.8
~ days (1) n 069.3
~ driver (4) n 073.5
~ house (2) n 011.7
~ labor (2) n 080.6
~ master (1) n 073.5
~ nigger woman (1) n 069.3
~ owners (2) n 075.7
~ plantation (1) n 093.5
~ quarters (3) n 080.9
~ time (1) n 075.6
~ -time church (1) n 089.2
~ wall (1) n 016.6
slave[N-i] (4) n 070.6
slaved out (1) v 096.7
slaveries (1) n 069.3
slavery (25) n/adj 080.8
~ days (2) n 080.8
~ fight (1) n 085.8
~ graveyard (1) n 078.8
~ maid (1) n 081.8
~ nigger (2) n 081.9

~ time (13) n 080.6
~ times (1) n 069.3
Slavery (1) 085.8
slaves (48) n 070.8
Slaves (1) 085.8
Slavs (2) 127.6
slaw (3) n 055A.1
slayed (1) v 052.6
sleazy (2) adj 113.9
~ hotels (1) n 113.9
~ joints (1) n 113.4
sled (10) n/adj 021.4
~ road (1) n 031.7
sledgehammer (28) n 020.7
sledgehammers (1) n 020.7
sleds (2) n 021.5
sleek (1) adj 123.6
sleekers (1) n 060.6
sleep (81) n/v/adj 065.8
~ hound (2) n 033.3
~ like (1) v 090.8
~ on (2) v 058.7
~ room (2) n 009.3
~ sofas (1) n 080.8
~ with (1) v 093.9
sleep[V-p] (1) v 013.6
sleeper (4) n/adj 009.1
~ -cab trucks (1) n 109.8
~ couch (1) n 009.1
~ trucks (1) n 109.7
sleepers (3) n 080.8
sleeping (143) v/adj 009.1
~ alcove (2) n 007A.8
~ areas (1) n 009.3
~ bag (18) n 029.2
~ bags (7) n 029.2
~ barn (3) n 015.1
~ chamber (1) n 009.3
~ couch (1) n 009.1
~ gallery (1) n 009.3
~ pad (1) n 029.2
~ party (1) n 029.2
~ pill (1) n 114.2
~ porch (58) n 007A.8
~ porches (4) n 010.8
~ quarter[N-i] (1) n 007A.4
~ quarters (1) n 009.3
~ room (27) n 009.3
~ rooms (5) n 009.3
~ set (1) n 080.6
~ with (1) v 093.5

sleeps (5) v 124.8
~ around (3) v 124.8
sleepy (466) adj 076.6
~ ladies (1) n 115.7
~ time (1) n 076.6
~ woman (1) n 114.1
sleepyhead (1) n 076.6
sleepyheaded (3) adj 076.6
sleet (42) n/adj 112.3
~ storm (4) n 112.3
~ storms (1) n 112.3
sleeting (6) v 077.9
sleets (1) v 112.3
sleeve (3) n/adj 028.5
~ holders (1) n 028.5
sleeve[N-i] (1) n 075.1
sleeves (7) n 070.7
sleigh (3) adj 009.1
~ bed (2) n 009.1
~ ride (1) n 080.7
slender (5) adj 073.3
~ grama grass (1) n 015.9
slendered up (1) v 088.9
slept (23) v 097.1
~ at (1) v 032.8
~ away (1) v 078.5
~ in (4) v 083.4
~ on (5) v 098.7
sleven ditch (1) n 030.2
slew (30) n 055A.8
~ -footed (1) adj 081.9
slice (47) v/adj 070.8
~ bacon (32) n 046.7
~ bread (3) n 045.1
~ ham (1) n 046.7
~ lamb (1) n 121.4
~ liver (1) n 047.2
slice[V-t] (1) v 046.7
sliced (49) v/adj 046.7
~ bacon (26) n 046.7
~ bread (6) n 045.1
~ ham (2) n 121.3
~ liver (1) n 047.2
~ meat (2) n 046.7
~ white bread (1) n 044.3
slices (7) n 054.6
slicing knife (1) n 104.3
slick (52) n/v/adj 066.9
~ back (1) adj 123.9
~ down (2) v 028.1
~ dude (1) n 124.7
~ hairs (1) n 127.3

~ -headed scorpion (1) n 090.9
~ -looking (1) adj 090.4
~ off (1) v 089.8
~ pines (1) n 061.8
~ -shaved (1) adj 089.9
~ -tail rat (1) n 059.6
~ up (5) v 028.1
Slick Rock (1) AR 030.7
slick[V-t] down (1) v 028.1
slicked (5) v 080.9
~ off (1) v 080.9
~ up (4) v 028.1
slicker (20) n/adj 073.5
~ coat (1) n 027.1
~ suit (1) n 027.7
slickers (9) n 080.6
slickest (1) adj 030.8
slicking (6) v 028.1
~ down (2) v 028.1
~ up (4) v 028.1
slicks (2) n 069.9
slicksters (1) n 115.3
slickum (1) n 048.3
slicky (1) adj 075.6
slid (7) v 021.5
~ down (1) v 070.2
~ in (1) v 021.5
~ off of (1) v 034.4
~ up (1) v 070.2
slide (23) n/v/adj 031.2
~ off (1) v 034.4
~ out (1) v 024.5
~ plow (1) n 021.6
slided (2) v 080.9
Slidell (16) LA 087.9
sliders (2) n 060.6
slides (8) n/v 123.8
~ down (1) v 024.6
sliding (10) v/adj 080.6
~ board (2) n 022.6
~ boards (1) n 080.7
~ door (1) n 011.1
~ doors (1) n 010.5
~ plank (1) n 022.6
slidy horse (1) n 084.8
slight (6) v/adj 088.7
~ freeze (1) n 007.5
~ him (1) v 082.1
slighted (12) v 082.1
~ him (10) v 082.1
~ you (1) v 082.1
slightest (2) adj 100.4

slightly (2) adv 090.4
slim (9) adj 125.4
~ road (1) n 031.7
slimmed up (1) v 072.9
Slimp Branch (1) TN 030.7
slimy (4) adj 023.8
sling (9) n/v/adj 041.2
~ back (1) n 119.8
~ horses (1) n 022.7
~ pump (1) n 123.8
~ pumps (1) n 123.8
slinged (1) v 032.1
slingers (1) n 080.6
slingshot (7) n/adj 080.8
~ wars (2) n 130.5
slingshots (1) n 084.8
slip (73) n/v/adj 031.4
~ around (1) v 080.9
~ down (1) v 070.2
~ gap (1) n 015.3
~ off (1) v 092.9
~ off of (1) v 034.4
~ -on (1) n 123.8
~ onion (1) n 055.7
~ -ons (6) n 123.8
~ scrape (1) n 021.7
~ seed (1) n 054.4
~ -shuck (1) v 056.3
~ -slung carts (1) n 080.7
~ stones (1) n 023.4
~ teams (1) n 080.6
~ up (1) v 066.9
slip[V-r] (8) v 100.2
~ down (4) v 070.2
slip[V-t] (1) v 100.4
slipover shoes (1) n 123.8
slipped (48) v 070.2
~ around (1) v 083.4
~ away (1) v 078.5
~ down (2) v 070.2
~ off (5) v 034.4
~ on (1) v 052.6
~ out (1) v 070.2
~ up (1) v 070.2
~ up on (2) v 065.1
slipper (6) n/adj 123.8
~ chair (1) n 008.8
~ shoes (1) n 123.8
slippers (27) n 123.8
slippery (7) adj 031.9
~ elm (2) n 061.8
~ -elm bark (1) n 061.4

~ -elm poultices (1) n 065.8
slipping (6) v 080.7
~ around (1) v 081.4
~ up (1) v 102.4
slips (36) n/v 084.8
~ off (1) v 075.7
slit (2) n/adj 031.3
~ mountain (1) n 031.1
slithering (1) v 088.7
slits (3) n 054.6
Sloan's Liniment (1) 025.9
slob (2) n 125.1
slobber (6) n 061.4
slobbering on (1) v 081.7
Slocomb (4) AL 087.1
sloggy (1) adj 029.6
slommack around (1) v 088.8
sloop (2) n/adj 024.6
~ boats (1) n 024.6
sloosh (3) n/v 006.1
~ over (1) v 095.5
slop (890) n/v/adj 017.4
~ around (1) v 017.4
~ barrel (3) n 017.4
~ bucket (601) n 017.4
~ buckets (28) n 017.4
~ can (33) n 017.4
~ cans (2) n 017.4
~ cart (1) n 017.4
~ hog (1) n 035.5
~ jar (31) n 017.4
~ jars (11) n 012.1
~ pail (27) n 017.4
~ pan (1) n 017.4
~ pen (1) n 017.4
~ pots (1) n 017.4
~ trough (5) n 035.8
~ worm (3) n 060.5
~ worms (4) n 060.5
slope (66) n/v/adj 030.8
~ head (1) n 126.4
~ heads (1) n 126.4
~ out (1) v 058.8
slopes (3) n 126.4
sloping (2) adj 030.8
~ land (1) n 030.8
~ lands (1) n 029.4
slopped (5) v 095.8
~ over (1) v 095.8
slopping (10) v/adj 017.4
~ bucket (1) n 017.4
~ trough (1) n 035.8

sloppy (8) adj 074.6
~ carpenter (1) n 067.8
~ day (1) n 005.5
~ joes (1) n 081.8
slops (9) n 017.4
slosh (1) n 029.6
sloshy place (1) n 029.6
slot (1) n 031.3
slothful (1) adj 069.8
slouch (3) n/v 080.9
slouchy (20) adj 073.3
slough (106) n/v/adj 029.6
~ beds (1) n 080.7
~ -like (3) adj 029.6
~ off (2) v 030.1
~ out (1) v 080.9
~ way (1) n 030.3
Slough (13) 030.7
sloughs (35) n 029.6
Slovaks (2) 069.8
Slover Creek (1) AR 030.7
slow (102) v/adj 095.2
~ black music (1) n 130.9
~ bumps (1) n 110.8
~ cookers (1) n 116.4
~ dance (6) n 083.1
~ dancing (6) n 130.8
~ diggers (1) n 096.8
~ down (6) v 082.6
~ drag (1) v 083.1
~ drizzle (6) n 006.6
~ fever (2) n 079.7
~ gin (1) n 084.8
~ mist (1) n 006.6
~ motion (1) n 130.8
~ music (3) n 130.8
~ rain (31) n 006.6
~ rock (1) n 130.8
~ shower (2) n 006.6
slow[V-r] down (1) v 007.3
slower (4) adj 007.3
slowful (1) adj 074.7
slowing (36) v 007.3
~ down (34) v 007.3
~ up (2) v 007.3
slowly (7) adv 050.2
sludge (1) n 023.8
slug (10) n/adj 022.4
~ hammer (2) n 020.7
Slugger (1) 087.9
sluggish (6) adj 073.3

slugs (2) n 022.4
slum (21) n/adj 114.8
~ area (5) n 114.8
~ areas (2) n 114.8
~ hotel (1) n 113.8
~ motel (1) n 113.8
~ people (1) n 069.7
slumber (17) v/adj 130.7
~ chamber (1) n 009.3
~ over (1) v 096.4
~ parties (10) n 130.7
~ party (4) n 130.7
slummy person (1) n 069.8
slump (3) n/v 048.3
~ down (1) v 096.4
slumped (1) v 075.4
slums (26) n 114.8
slung (7) v/adj 032.1
~ out (1) v 080.7
~ out of (1) v 084.9
slur (2) n 069.4
slurp (1) v 070.8
slush (7) n 029.6
slut (46) n 124.8
sluts (1) n 124.6
sly fox (1) n 124.7
smack (32) n/v/adj 114.2
~ tooth (1) n 021.7
smacked (1) v 081.7
smacker (1) n 069.7
smackers (1) n 071.6
smacking (7) v 081.7
Smackover (4) AR 070.7
~ Creek (2) AR TX 030.7
small (386) adj 055.4
~ army (1) n 055A.8
~ bulls (1) n 033.8
~ closets (1) n 009.6
~ curd (1) n 047.6
~ entrails (1) n 037.3
~ flood (1) n 006.1
~ freeze (1) n 007.5
~ gut (1) n 037.3
~ house (1) n 014.1
~ intestine (2) n 037.3
~ intestines (4) n 037.3
~ kindling (1) n 008.6
~ -mesh wire (1) n 016.3
~ oven (2) n 116.4
~ rain (2) n 006.6
~ road (2) n 031.7
~ shower (1) n 006.6

~ spot (1) n 059.9
~ water (2) n 088.7
~ waters (1) n 088.6
~ wood (11) n 008.6
Small World (2) 085.4
smaller (18) adj 057.4
~ bedroom (1) n 007A.7
smallest (1) adj 053.6
smallmouth (9) n/adj 059.9
~ bass (5) n 059.9
smallpox (17) n 079.7
smart (943) adj/adv 100.1
~ -aching (1) adj 090.7
~ -acting (1) adj 088.7
~ aleck (23) n 069.5
~ -aleck niggers (1) n 093.7
~ aleckes (1) n 125.5
~ alecks (4) n 073.4
~ -alecky (1) adj 125.5
~ ass (4) n 125.5
~ asses (1) n 080.9
~ -looking (1) adj 090.7
~ -sized (1) adj 090.7
Smart Street (1) 107.7
smarter (6) adj 002.6
smartest (3) adj 053.4
smarting off (1) v 075.6
smartweed (2) n 015.9
smartweeds (2) n 015.9
smarty (5) n/adj 125.5
~ breeches (1) n 100.1
~ gentleman (1) n 028.1
smash (2) n/adj 130.7
~ bash (1) n 130.7
smasher (3) n 117.1
smashers (1) n 117.1
smear (4) n/v 130.2
~ the queer with the ball (1) n 130.5
smearcase (9) n 048.1
smeared (1) v 078.6
smell (603) n/v/adj 051.1
~ like (5) v 051.1
~ melon (1) n 056.7
~ melons (2) n 056.7
~ of (50) v 051.1
smell[V-p] (30) v 051.1
~ like (2) v 051.1
smell[V-r] (3) v 051.1
smelled (29) v 051.1

~ around (1) v 051.1
~ of (1) v 051.1
~ up (1) v 051.1
smeller (2) n 075.6
smellest (1) adj 092.3
smelling (16) v 051.1
~ around (1) v 081.4
~ like (1) v 128.2
~ of (3) v 051.1
smells (212) v 051.1
~ like (5) v 051.1
smelt (15) v 088.7
~ like (1) v 104.7
smidgen (3) n 092.8
smile (4) n/v 075.6
~ if you love me (1) n 130.3
smiled (1) v 102.9
smirking (2) v 081.7
Smith (83) MS TX 107.7
~ and Wesson (3) 113.1
~ Avenue (1) 105.5
~ Bayou (1) LA 030.7
~ Break (1) LA 030.7
~ County (4) MS TX 087.3
~ Creek (3) AL GA 030.7
~ Ford (1) GA 030.7
~ Fork Creek (3) TN 030.7
~ Lake (3) AL 030.7
~ Lake Road (1) 031.6
~ melon (1) n 056.9
~ Park (2) 106.4
Smithcraft boat (1) n 024.6
Smithfield (6) 087.3
~ area (1) n 105.1
~ Estates (2) 106.1
Smiths (7) 087.8
~ Lake (1) MS 087.8
~ Landing (1) GA 030.7
~ Station (2) AL 087.6
Smithville (8) AR GA MS TN TX 087.2
~ Highway (1) 031.7
smiting (1) v 091.9
smitten (2) adj 081.4
smock (22) n 026.4
smocks (3) n 026.4
smog (7) n 006.7
smoggy (2) adj 006.7

~ day (1) n 005.5
smoke (176) n/v/adj 008.7
~ bacon (20) n 046.5
~ bomb (1) n 024.3
~ eater (1) n 112.4
~ eaters (2) n 112.4
~ ham (2) n 121.3
~ hams (1) n 046.4
~ link sausage (3) n 121.6
~ links (2) n 121.6
~ meat (21) n 046.5
~ on the water (1) n 050.8
~ pipe (8) n 008.1
~ pork (2) n 046.5
~ pot (2) n 024.3
~ pots (2) n 024.3
~ room (2) n 010.1
~ sausage (24) n 121.6
~ shoulders (1) n 046.4
~ webs (1) n 061.3
Smoke Bend (2) LA MS 087.3
smoked (103) v/adj 046.5
~ bacon (14) n 046.5
~ beef (1) n 046.3
~ country ham (1) n 046.5
~ ham (27) n 046.5
~ hams (2) n 121.3
~ house (1) n 084.9
~ -link (1) adj 121.6
~ meat (16) n 046.5
~ middling meat (1) n 046.5
~ pork (4) n 046.5
~ pork sausage (1) n 046.8
~ salt (1) n 046.5
~ salted meat (1) n 046.5
~ sausage (6) n 046.5
~ shoulder (1) n 046.5
~ side (3) n 046.5
~ side meat (2) n 046.7
~ stuff (1) n 046.5
smokehouse (402) n/adj 010.1
~ crib (1) n 011.7
Smokehouse (2) 030.8
~ Hills (1) AR 030.8
~ Slough (1) FL 030.3
smokehouses (32) n 011.7

smoker's cough (1) n 076.5
smokes (20) n/v 117.7
smokestack (202) n/adj 008.1
~ pipe (1) n 008.1
smokestacks (23) n 008.1
smokestacky (1) n 008.1
Smokette (1) 121.6
Smokey (8) 112.5
~ Bear (1) 112.5
~ Bears (1) 112.5
~ the Bear (1) 112.9
smokies (3) n 069.3
Smokies (4) TN 086.5
smoking (16) n/v/adj 057.4
~ jacket (1) n 027.3
smoky (7) adj 006.7
~ breakfast (1) n 046.5
~ day (1) n 005.5
Smoky (12) 031.1
~ Mountain (4) TN 031.1
~ Mountains (8) TN 031.1
smoky soil (1) n 029.8
Smokyville (1) 106.3
smooch (3) n/v 081.7
smooched (2) v 081.7
smooching (250) v 081.7
~ around (1) v 081.7
smooks (1) n 090.2
smooth (21) adj 008.3
~ stone (1) n 054.4
~ -tempered (9) adj 073.2
~ -traveling (1) adj 080.6
~ wire (1) n 016.3
smoother (2) adj 120.5
smoothing (32) v/adj 066.8
~ harrow (1) n 021.7
~ iron (21) n 010.6
~ iron[N-i] (1) n 088.7
~ irons (8) n 010.6
smoted (1) v 104.3
smother (3) n/v 047.2
smothered (4) adj 046.6
~ cabbage (1) n 046.6
~ rabbit (1) n 121.5
~ squash (1) n 046.7
~ string beans (1) n 046.5

smudge (30) n/adj 008.7
~ pot (13) n 024.3
~ pots (14) n 080.7
~ torch (1) n 024.3
smush (2) v 011.3
smut (213) n/v/adj 008.7
~ -burning outfit (1) n 090.4
~ -colored Negro (1) n 096.8
~ mushrooms (1) n 057.1
~ pot (1) n 017.6
~ up (1) v 080.7
smutty (13) adj 008.7
~ buddy (1) n 069.3
Smyrna (7) GA TN 087.6
snack (649) n/v/adj 048.6
~ around (1) v 048.6
~ bar (1) n 107.2
~ family (1) n 048.6
snacked (1) v 048.6
snacker (1) n 071.8
snacking (16) v 048.6
snacks (129) n 048.6
snag (5) n/adj 080.7
~ boat (1) n 024.6
~ har(row) (1) n 021.7
~ lightning (1) n 125.2
~ trees (1) n 096.8
snaggler diagonal (1) adj 085.2
snaggletooth (3) n 071.8
snagline (1) n 097.8
snags (2) n 035.7
snail (7) n/adj 060.6
~ darter (1) n 061.2
snails (7) n 060.6
snake (855) n/v/adj 059.5
~ ass (1) n 092.3
~ bites (1) n 033.4
~ catchers (1) n 090.8
~ doctor (240) n 060A.4
~ doc(tor) (1) n 060A.4
~ doctor flies (1) n 060A.4
~ doctors (118) n 060A.4
~ eater (1) n 101.6
~ feeder (31) n 060A.4
~ feeders (29) n 060A.4
~ fence (4) n 016.4
~ fences (2) n 016.4

~ flies (2) n 060A.4
~ fly (1) n 060A.4
~ -grass (2) n 099.8
~ handlers (1) n 126.6
~ hawk (1) n 060A.4
~ into (1) v 081.8
~ -killing dog (1) n 033.1
~ kit (1) n 088.9
~ line (1) n 084.8
~ lips (1) n 125.2
~ medicine (1) n 060A.4
~ melon (2) n 056.9
~ piss (1) n 050.8
~ -proof boots (1) n 088.8
~ -proof suit (1) n 088.8
~ turtle (1) n 060.6
~ watermelons (1) n 056.9
~ widow (1) n 060A.4
~ widows (1) n 060A.4
~ -[J-0]-rider fence (1) n 016.4
Snake (7) 030.3
~ Bayou (1) TN 030.3
~ Creek (2) TN 030.7
~ Eater Road (1) 031.7
~ River (1) LA 030.7
snake[N-i] (1) n 016.7
snake[N-k] head (1) n 053.7
snake[V-r] (2) v 021.5
snakeberries (4) n 062.6
snakebit (39) v 033.4
~ at (1) v 033.4
snakebite (2) n 033.4
snakebitten (5) v 033.4
snaked (39) v 021.5
snakeheading (1) v 088.7
snakeroot (19) n 061.4
snakeroots (1) n 061.4
snake's belly (1) n 080.7
snakes (249) n/v 059.5
Snakes Creek (1) GA 030.7
Snakeville (1) LA 087.7
snakeworm (1) n 060.5
snaking (36) v 021.5
~ for (1) v 021.5
~ out (2) v 021.5
snap (580) n/v/adj 055A.4

~ bean (65) n 055A.4
~ -bean family (1) n 055A.4
~ bean[N-i] (4) n 055A.4
~ beans (388) n 055A.4
~ block (1) n 104.5
~ bugs (1) n 061.1
~ butter beans (1) n 055A.3
~ green beans (1) n 055A.4
~ holders (1) n 052.6
~ -on pocketbooks (1) n 028.2
~ peas (3) n 055A.4
~ pocketbook (1) n 028.2
~ pole beans (1) n 055A.4
~ runners (1) n 055A.4
~ socials (1) n 130.7
Snap(finger) Creek (1) GA 030.7
snapped (4) v 033.4
snapper (89) n/adj 059.9
~ fish (1) n 059.9
~ turtle (2) n 060.6
~ turtles (1) n 060.6
snapper[N-i] (1) n 059.9
snappers (31) n 059.9
snapping (113) v/adj 055A.2
~ beans (1) n 055A.4
~ jenny (1) n 060.6
~ kind (1) n 060.6
~ terrapin (2) n 060.6
~ turtle (70) n 060.6
~ turtles (27) n 060.6
snappish (1) adj 007.4
snappy (28) adj 007.4
~ -like (1) adj 007.4
~ turtle (1) n 060.6
snaps (7) n 055A.4
snapshots (1) n 099.6
snatch (6) v/adj 100.2
~ team (1) n 033.7
snatch[V-r] (3) v 100.2
snatched (10) v 104.4
snatcher (2) n 065.2
snatching (1) n 080.9
snats (1) n 060A.8
snazzy car (1) n 109.4
Snead (1) AL 087.9
sneak (4) n/v 100.2

sneaker (3) n 123.8
sneakers (30) n 123.8
sneaks around (1) v 053.5
sneaky (2) adj 128.7
sneed (1) n 041.6
Sneed Creek (1) GA 030.7
Sneedville (2) TN 087.2
sneeze (4) n/v 076.5
sneezing (2) n/v 024.9
Snell (2) MS 087.3
~ Island (1) 106.1
snicker (1) v 036.4
snickering (1) v 036.4
snickers (3) v 027.4
Snider (1) 056.9
sniff (26) n/v 051.1
sniffing (4) v/adj 081.4
~ around the bushes (1) v 081.4
sniffles (4) n 076.3
snifter (2) n 048.9
snip (3) n/v 101.4
snipe (6) n/adj 059.5
~ hunt (1) n 129.8
~ hunting (1) n 129.8
~ hunts (1) n 129.8
sniped (2) v 100.2
snipper nose (1) n 120.8
Snipper Creek (1) AL 030.7
snips (4) n 054.6
snit (3) n 054.6
snitch (21) n/v 101.3
~ on (1) v 101.8
snitch[V-r] (4) v 100.2
snitched (59) v 100.2
snitcher (11) n 101.3
snitching (1) v 101.3
snits (12) n 054.6
snivel (1) n 006.6
snob (3) n 125.5
snobbish (1) adj 090.3
snobby (2) adj 074.7
snobs (1) n 091.8
snoofing (1) v 081.7
snook (2) n 080.6
snooked (1) v 100.2
snookers (1) n 059.9
snoop (1) v 101.3
snooper (1) n 101.3
snooping (1) v 025.5
snoot (3) n 047.1
snooter (1) n 090.6
snootiness (1) n 101.8

snooty (1) adj 090.4
snooze (1) n 080.9
snoozing off (1) v 092.9
snoring (1) v 024.9
snorkel (34) n/adj 111.4
~ truck (8) n 111.4
Snorkel (1) 111.4
snorkels (3) n 111.4
snorkling noises (1) n 038.3
snort (23) n/v 036.4
snorting (4) v 036.4
snorts (5) n/v 036.3
snot (2) n/adj 090.8
~ man (1) n 090.9
snotty (1) adj 076.3
snout (8) n 036.4
snouts (1) n 035.9
snow (76) n/v/adj 007.5
~ boots (1) n 123.8
~ bread (1) n 044.8
~ clouds (2) n 005.3
~ fence (2) n 016.2
~ fences (1) n 052.1
~ flurry (1) n 007.5
~ ice (1) n 007.6
~ owl (5) n 059.2
~ weather (1) n 005.5
Snow (3) 087.6
~ Lake (2) AR 087.6
~ White (1) 114.2
snowball (5) n 062.7
snowballs (1) n 069.4
snowbirds (3) n 059.2
Snowden (1) 083.2
snowed (3) v 112.3
~ in (1) v 013.8
snowflake (1) n 007.5
snowflakes (1) n 112.3
snowing (3) v 007.5
snows (1) v 115.3
snowshoes (1) n 115.7
snowstorm (7) n 112.3
snowstorms (1) n 112.3
snowy owl (4) n 059.1
snub nose (1) n 113.1
snuck (3) v 100.2
~ off (2) v 083.4
snudging around (1) v 088.7
snuff (38) n/adj 057.3
~ chewer (1) n 069.9
~ factory (1) n 080.6
~ glass (1) n 048.9
~ glasses (1) n 048.9

snuffbox (4) n 091.8
snuff(box) (1) n 057.1
snuffling (2) n 036.4
snuffy-colored (1) adj 029.8
snug (2) adj 027.6
~ -fitting (1) adj 027.6
so (2098) adv 037.5
~ -and-so (66) n/adj 079.4
~ -and-so's road (1) n 031.8
~ -and-sos (2) n 127.8
~ -called (1) adj 074.7
~ -goody (1) adj 096.7
~ -so (40) adj 079.4
so(x2) (4) interj 037.6
so(x3) (2) interj 037.5
soak (6) n/v/adj 024.5
soaked (4) v 008.6
~ in (2) v 008.6
soaker (2) n 006.6
soaking (9) v/adj 006.8
~ in (1) v 006.8
~ rain (7) n 006.6
soap (90) n/adj 045.1
~ grease (2) n 080.9
~ kettles (1) n 017.6
~ pad (1) n 018.3
~ trough (2) n 035.8
~ wrappers (1) n 081.8
Soap (3) 030.7
~ Creek (1) GA 030.7
~ Hill (1) LA 030.7
~ Sally (1) 090.2
soapbox operas (1) n 088.8
soapers (1) n 114.1
soapstone (7) n/adj 023.5
~ clay (1) n 029.8
~ jug (1) n 017.2
soapsuds (1) n 042.7
soapwood (1) n 008.5
soapy (1) adj 018.3
sob (2) adj/interj 037.5
SOB (6) 065.7
sobbing (2) v/adv 079.3
~ wet (1) adj 018.3
sobby (5) adj 029.8
~ bottomland (1) n 029.4
~ land (2) n 029.4
sobering-up place (1) n 112.8
sobs (3) v 030.2

SOBs (2) 059.5
soccer (13) n/adj 130.5
~ ball (1) n 130.4
sociable (6) adj 073.2
social (22) n/adj 083.1
~ bugs (1) n 060A.3
~ climbers (1) n 096.3
~ crowd (1) n 129.6
~ dancing (1) n 083.1
~ drinker (2) n 113.7
~ party (1) n 130.7
~ rejects (1) n 091.7
~ security (5) n 040.7
~ (se)curity (1) n 115.4
so(cial) security (1) n 039.6
Social (4) 087.3
~ Circle (3) GA 087.3
~ Hill (1) AR 087.5
Socialists (2) 129.1
Socialites (1) 129.2
socials (4) n 080.8
society (7) n/adj 033.3
~ dogs (1) n 033.3
~ gals (1) n 064.9
~ woman (1) n 052.5
sock (21) n/adj 065.5
~ hop (10) n 083.1
~ hops (5) n 083.1
~ in the jaw (1) n 065.5
~ in the nose (1) n 065.5
~ tops (1) n 081.8
socket (4) n/adj 072.3
sockets (1) n 020.7
sockety-peck (2) interj 059.4
socking (1) v 065.5
socks (14) n 027.4
sod (14) n/adj 063.3
~ belt (1) n 031.9
~ ground (1) n 029.8
~ widow (9) n 063.3
~ widows (1) n 063.3
soda (168) n/adj 045.5
~ biscuit (1) n 044.4
~ corn bread (1) n 044.7
~ cracker (3) n 069.4
~ crackers (1) n 069.4
~ jerker (1) n 080.6
~ pop (16) n 080.8
~ pops (1) n 080.6
~ shop (1) n 080.6

~ water (17) n 084.9
~ -water bottle (1) n 080.9
~ waters (1) n 121.8
Sodalities (1) 065.8
sodas (4) n 121.8
sodbuster (3) n 069.9
sodded widow (1) n 063.3
soddy (2) adj 029.8
~ ground (1) n 029.7
Soddy (2) TN 087.9
~ Daisy (1) TN 075.6
Sodomite (1) 069.6
soey(x2) (1) interj 037.5
sofa (782) n/adj 009.1
~ bed (16) n 009.1
~ chair (5) n 009.1
~ lounge (1) n 009.1
~ pillow (2) n 028.8
~ pillows (2) n 028.8
sofas (81) n 009.1
soft (367) adj 046.2
~ -back (1) n 060.6
~ -back turtle (2) n 060.6
~ -backs (1) n 060.6
~ -boil (9) v 046.1
~ -boil egg (2) n 046.1
~ -boil eggs (3) n 046.1
~ -boiled (24) v/adj 046.1
~ -boiled egg (14) n 046.1
~ -boiled eggs (12) n 046.1
~ brick (1) n 080.7
~ cling peaches (1) n 054.4
~ -cooked (1) adj 046.1
~ corn (1) n 056.2
~ dinner music (1) n 130.8
~ dirt (1) n 031.6
~ drink (62) n 121.8
~ drink beverage (1) n 121.8
~ drinks (18) n 121.8
~ ears (1) n 060.6
~ egg (1) n 046.1
~ eggs (1) n 046.1
~ feed (1) n 080.6
~ gravel (1) n 031.6
~ -like (1) adj 002.6
~ maple (3) n 061.6
~ meat (1) n 054.3

~ molasses (1) n 051.3
~ music (2) n 130.8
~ peach (12) n 054.3
~ peaches (2) n 054.4
~ pine (1) n 008.6
~ pop (1) n 121.8
~ rock (4) n 130.9
~ rolls (1) n 044.4
~ scrambled (1) n 046.2
~ shell (1) n 054.8
~ -shell (44) n/adj 060.6
~ -shell cooter (2) n 060.6
~ -shell cooters (2) n 060.6
~ -shell crab (1) n 060.8
~ -shell terrapin (1) n 060.6
~ -shell turtle (75) n 060.6
~ -shell turtles (15) n 060.6
~ -shelled cooter (1) n 060.7
~ -shelled turtle (2) n 060.6
~ -shelled turtles (1) n 060.6
~ -shells (4) n 060.6
~ -skinned (1) adj 075.1
~ -stone rock (1) n 032.1
~ suction (2) n 032.1
~ -water turtle (1) n 060.6
Soft (2) 126.6
~ -Shell (1) 126.6
~ -Shell Baptist (1) 089.8
softball (38) n/adj 130.4
~ team (1) n 130.4
softer (5) adj 070.6
softwood (1) n 061.8
sog (1) interj 037.5
soggy (13) adj 029.6
~ bottom (1) n 029.6
~ land (7) n 029.6
soil (622) n/adj 029.8
~ bank (1) n 084.8
~ cement (1) n 031.6

~ conservation (1) n 093.5
~ testes (1) n 016.8
~ tiller (1) n 120.4
~ tilters (1) n 120.4
soils (5) n 093.5
soiree (3) n 083.1
soke (3) interj 038.3
~ oke (1) interj 037.5
soke(x2) (2) interj 037.5
~ sook(x3) (1) interj 037.5
soke(x3) (1) interj 037.5
sol (2) n S 028.7
solar (2) adj 118.5
~ heat (1) n 118.5
~ room (1) n 118.1
solarium (21) n 118.1
solariums (2) n 118.1
sold (43) v 065.8
~ off (1) v 052.7
~ out (1) v 057.9
soldering iron (1) n 010.6
soldier (5) n/adj 068.5
~ boys (1) n 104.7
Soldier Creek (2) AL 030.7
soldiered (2) v 096.7
soldiering (1) v 082.7
soldiers (6) n 130.2
sole (3) adj 080.7
~ fish (1) n 080.7
~ -frame shoes (1) n 123.8
soles (4) n 080.3
soliciting (1) v 113.5
solicitor (4) n 068.6
solid (37) adj/adv 007.9
~ -black fox squirrel (1) n 059.7
~ cloudy (1) adj 005.5
~ coffee (1) n 032.3
~ doughnut (1) n 045.2
~ fellies (1) n 021.1
~ green (1) adj 056.9
~ -green (1) adj 056.9
~ lines (1) n 107.3
~ melon (1) n 056.9
~ plow (1) n 021.6
~ rain (1) n 006.1
~ wing (1) n 021.6
~ yellow (1) adj 107.3
~ yellow line (1) n 107.3
solitaire (2) n 130.9

Solladies Hill (1) TN 030.8
solo (3) adj/adv S 032.3
~ instrument (1) n 115.8
solution (1) n 044.7
some (2254) adj/pron 088.9
~ -odd (20) adj 001.7
somebody (192) pron 103.2
somebody[M-k] (1) pron 032.2
somebody's (5) adj 053.7
~ mother (1) n 052.8
someday (3) adv 076.2
somehow (3) adv 013.1
someone (62) pron 104.1
someplace (11) adv 040.2
somersault (425) n/v 095.5
(somer)sault (2) n 095.5
somersault[N-i] (1) n 095.5
somersaulted in (1) v 095.3
somersaulting (2) v 095.5
somersaults (57) n 095.5
somerset (195) n 095.5
Somerset (2) KY 086.1
somersets (33) n 095.5
Somerville (4) 105.4
~ Mountain (1) MS 031.1
something (2059) pron/ adj 103.2
~ grain (1) n 050.8
~ harp (1) n 020.6
~ in the water (1) n 065.1
some(thing) (14) pron/ adj 103.2
sometime (38) adv 076.2
sometimes (25) adv 076.2
somewhat (5) adv 090.4
somewhere (38) adv 040.2
somewheres (27) adv 040.2
son (243) n 064.8
~ -in-law (14) n 085.7
~ of (2) n 092.1
~ of a bitch (41) n 092.2
~ (o)f a bitch (3) n 092.2

~ of a bitches (2) n 092.1
~ of a booger (2) n 092.3
~ of a gun (16) n 092.2
~ (o)f a gun (1) n 074.8
~ of [D-0] bitch (2) n 092.4
~ of [D-0] bitches (1) n 092.4
~ of [D-0] gun (2) n 052.5
~ [P-0] a bitch (4) n 092.2
~ [P-0] a gun (2) n 092.2
~ [P-0] [D-0] bitch (14) n 066.9
~ -[P-0]-[D-0]-bitching (1) adj 088.9
Son (9) 064.4
son[N-i] (9) n 055A.6
~ -in-law (1) n 055A.6
~ (o)f a bitches (1) n 099.4
~ of a guns (2) n 092.3
~ of bitches (2) n 069.7
Sondheimer (1) LA 087.4
song (17) n/adj 089.5
~ ballad (1) n 080.6
~ director (1) n 070.6
~ service (1) n 089.5
~ services (1) n 089.5
songbirds (1) n 059.2
songs (15) n 089.5
sonker (1) n 048.3
Sonny (9) 064.4
~ Boy (2) 064.4
Sonora (1) TX 087.8
son's birthday (1) n 098.6
sons (16) n 055A.8
~ of bitches (2) n 074.8
~ [P-0] bitches (1) n 092.8
Sons (1) 084.5
soo (346) interj 038.3
~ -baby(x2) (1) interj 037.6
~ -bossy(x2) (2) interj 037.5
~ -calf(x2) (37) interj 037.6
~ -calf(x3) (13) interj 037.6

~ -calfy(x2) (13) interj 037.6
~ -calfy(x3) (3) interj 037.6
~ -cow(x2) (40) interj 037.5
~ -cow(x3) (8) interj 037.5
~ -cow(x4) (1) interj 037.5
~ -hog(x2) (1) interj 038.3
~ -hog(x3) (1) interj 038.3
~ -pig(x2) (7) interj 038.3
~ -pig(x3) (2) interj 038.3
~ pigee (1) interj 038.3
~ -piggy(x2) (2) interj 038.3
~ -pine(x2) (1) interj 037.5
~ sooey soo (1) interj 037.5
~ there (1) interj 037.5
soo(x2) (27) interj 037.5
soo(x3) (22) interj 038.3
soo(x4) (3) interj 037.5
sooboos (1) n 069.3
soody(x2) (1) interj 038.3
sooey (222) interj 038.3
~ ooey soo(x3) (1) interj 038.3
~ soo (1) interj 037.5
sooey(x2) (38) interj 038.3
sooey(x3) (22) interj 038.3
sooey(x4) (1) interj 038.3
sooey(x5) (2) interj 038.3
sooey(x7) (2) interj 038.3
sook (250) interj 037.5
~ away (1) interj 037.6
~ -baby(x2) (1) interj 037.5
~ -bed(x2) sook(x6) (1) interj 037.5
~ -calf(x2) (20) interj 037.6
~ -calf(x3) (11) interj 037.6
~ -calf(x4) (2) interj 037.6

~ -calfy(x2) (4) interj 037.6
~ -cow(x2) (17) interj 037.5
~ -cow(x4) (1) interj 037.5
~ -cow-there(x2) (1) interj 037.5
~ -heifers (1) interj 037.5
~ -heifer(x2) (2) interj 037.5
~ -him(x3) (1) interj 033.2
~ -Jersey(x2) (1) interj 037.5
~ -Jersey(x3) (1) interj 037.5
~ soo (5) interj 037.6
sook(x2) (43) interj 037.6
~ soo(x3) sook(x2) (1) interj 037.5
sook(x3) (65) interj 037.5
~ ooh sook(x3) (1) interj 037.5
~ soke(x2) so (1) interj 037.5
~ suck (1) interj 037.5
~ swook (1) interj 037.5
sook(x4) (15) interj 037.6
~ sooky (1) interj 037.5
sook(x5) (5) interj 037.5
sook(x6) (5) interj 037.5
sook(x9) (1) interj 037.5
sookaa sook(x3) (1) interj 037.6
sookoo (2) interj 037.5
~ sook(x3) sookoo (1) interj 037.5
sooky (22) interj 037.5
~ kwo aa (1) interj 037.5
~ sook (1) interj 037.6
~ sook(x2) (1) interj 037.5
~ sook(x2) sooky(x2) (1) interj 037.5
sooky(x2) (8) interj 038.3
sooky(x3) (3) interj 037.6
sooky(x4) (3) interj 037.6
soon (230) adv 076.2
~ [P-0] suckle (1) adj 033.9

sooner (69) n/adj/adv 033.3
~ dog (1) n 033.3
~ dogs (1) n 033.3
~ hound (1) n 033.3
sooners (10) n 033.3
soot (1044) n/v/adj 008.7
~ black (1) adj 008.7
~ box (2) n 008.7
~ tag (2) n 061.3
~ tea (1) n 008.7
~ up (1) v 008.7
soothe (1) v 081.2
soothing (1) adj 089.6
sooty (1) adj 008.7
sop (8) n/v 051.3
Sopchoppy (5) FL 087.1
~ River (2) FL 030.7
Sope Creek (1) GA 030.7
sophisticated (2) adj 123.6
sophomores (1) n 125.9
sopped (2) v 051.3
~ up (1) v 080.6
soppers (1) n 045.3
sopping (2) n/v 051.3
Soque River (1) GA 030.7
sore (99) n/adj 075.2
~ eyes (1) n 090.6
~ mouth (1) n 088.7
~ throat (41) n 071.7
sorehead (1) n 075.2
sores (3) n 077.4
sorghum (423) n/adj 051.3
~ barrel (1) n 019.2
~ cakes (1) n 051.2
~ candy (1) n 051.2
~ cane (19) n 051.2
~ field (1) n 016.1
~ grain (1) n 014.4
~ hay (2) n 051.2
~ head (2) n 091.8
~ heads (1) n 089.8
~ maker (1) n 051.2
~ mill (16) n 051.2
~ molasses (64) n 051.2
~ molas(ses) (1) n 051.2
~ (mo)lasses (1) n 051.2
~ molasses syrup (1) n 051.2
~ pan (1) n 075.9

~ patch (2) n 016.1
~ plates (1) n 042.2
~ pomace (1) n 051.2
~ press (2) n 051.2
~ stuff (1) n 051.3
~ syrup (64) n 051.3
~ syrups (2) n 051.3
sorority (3) n/adj 014.1
~ house (1) n 014.1
~ parties (1) n 130.9
sorrel (4) n/adj 034.2
~ horse (1) n 089.8
Sorrel (7) 030.7
Sorrento (3) FL LA 087.5
sorrier (1) adj 073.6
sorries (1) n 084.9
sorriest (12) adj 082.9
sorriness (1) n 069.7
sorrow (5) n 079.3
sorrowing (1) v 079.3
sorrows (1) n 096.1
sorry (181) adj 069.7
~ -ass (1) adj 033.3
~ -looking (1) adj 072.9
~ sack (1) n 090.4
~ soil (1) n 029.8
~ -type folks (1) n 069.7
sor(ry) (1) adj 066.8
sort (282) n 090.4
~ of (272) adv 090.4
~ (o)f (1) adv 090.4
~ [P-0] (2) adv 090.4
sort[N-i] (1) n 080.9
sorts (4) n 055.1
so's (2) conj 025.8
Soso (6) MS 087.4
sot (42) n/v/adj 113.6
~ down (4) v 049.3
~ in her ways (1) adj 074.8
~ in his mind (1) adj 074.8
~ in his ways (4) adj 074.8
~ in the head (1) adj 074.8
~ in your ways (4) adj 074.8
~ out (2) v 070.6
~ up (1) v 049.3
Soto (14) 106.3
sots (1) n 113.7
Souci (3) 105.1

soucoupe (1) n F 066.8
souffle (1) n 081.9
souffled (1) v 055.5
Sougahatchee (2) AL 030.7
~ Creek (1) AL 030.7
Souinlovey (1) MS 030.7
soul (50) n/adj 130.8
~ brother (1) n 069.3
~ food (5) n 089.8
~ music (7) n 130.8
~ rock (1) n 130.9
~ sisters (1) n 096.7
~ -stirring (1) adj 089.6
~ -touching (1) adj 089.6
souls (1) n 090.2
sound (49) n/v 030.9
~ as if (1) v 088.3
~ like (3) v 013.1
Sound (7) 030.7
~ Creek (1) AL 030.7
sound[V-p] like (1) v 088.3
sounded (1) v 090.8
sounding (4) v/adj 080.8
~ board (1) n 080.8
sounds (15) n/v 088.3
~ as if (1) v 088.3
~ like (2) v 088.3
~ [P-0] (2) v 025.8
soup (83) n/adj 055.8
~ bean (1) n 055A.4
~ beans (2) n 055A.3
~ bowl (1) n 123.9
~ bunch (1) n 055.7
~ day (1) n 084.9
~ hound (5) n 033.3
~ kettle (2) n 017.6
~ line (1) n 095.2
~ meat (1) n 121.2
~ spoon (7) n 017.8
~ tomato (1) n 055.3
~ tomatoes (6) n 055.3
soupbone (3) n 046.4
soupbones (2) n 121.2
soupe est chaud (1) n F 093.4
souped-up cats (1) n 059.5
soup's on (8) v 049.2
soupy (1) adj 058.1
sour (247) v/adj 047.6
~ bone (1) n 069.9
~ bread (5) n 044.3

~ buttermilk (4) n 047.6

~ cheese (2) n 048.1

~ clabber (1) n 047.6

~ corn bread (1) n 044.5

~ cream (12) n 048.6

~ -cream cheese (2) n 048.1

~ -cream coffee cake (1) n 122.9

~ gourd (1) n 056.6

~ grapes (1) n 062.5

~ grass (1) n 015.9

~ -like (1) adj 047.6

~ mash (2) n 050.9

~ -mash whiskey (1) n 050.8

~ milk (78) n 047.6

~ -milk biscuits (1) n 044.4

~ -milk cheese (2) n 048.1

~ on (1) v 089.9

~ orange (1) n 055.1

~ stomach (5) n 080.2

~ tomatoes (1) n 055.3

~ vines (1) n 062.3

sourberry (1) n 061.4

source (1) n F 030.6

sourdough (24) n/adj 044.4

~ biscuits (1) n 044.4

~ bread (9) n 044.3

~ light bread (1) n 044.4

soured (61) v/adj 047.6

~ milk (4) n 047.6

souring (3) v 070.7

Sourlake (1) TX 087.5

sourpuss (1) n 074.8

sours (1) v 046.9

soursop (4) n/adj 096.8

~ ice cream (1) n 096.8

~ tree (2) n 061.9

~ trees (1) n 061.8

sourwood (8) n/adj 061.9

~ honey (1) n 061.8

sourwoods (2) n 061.8

souse (715) n/v/adj 047.1

~ meat (279) n 047.1

~ press (1) n 047.1

soused (2) v/adj 113.6

south (653) adj/adv 006.4

~ breeze (1) n 006.5

~ fork (1) n 030.7

~ forty (1) n 001A.1

~ meat (5) n 047.1

~ porch (2) n 010.9

~ side (3) n 006.5

~ -southeast (2) n 006.5

~ -southwest (1) n 006.5

~ wind (30) n 006.4

~ winds (2) n 006.4

South (1137) 105.1

~ Alabama (4) 086.4

~ Alabama University (1) 083.6

~ America (6) 069.2

~ American (1) 069.2

~ Apple Street (1) 001.1

~ Atlanta (1) 105.1

~ Austin (1) 086.2

~ Bayshore (1) 107.6

~ Beach (4) 105.7

~ Bend (1) IN 087.5

~ Boulevard (1) 031.7

~ Branch (1) GA 030.7

~ Carolina (828) 086.3

~ Carolin(a) (10) 086.3

~ Carolina Geechees (1) 084.9

~ Carolina line (1) n 086.3

~ Carolina Mississippians (1) 096.8

~ Carolina types (1) n 086.3

~ Central Bell building (3) n 106.4

~ Chattanooga (1) 105.1

~ Cleveland (1) 082.7

~ corner (1) n 105.4

~ Dakota (6) 086.1

~ Dallas (13) 105.1

~ De Kalb (2) 105.4

~ Dixie Highway (1) 107.6

~ End (2) 105.6

~ Florida (3) 086.4

~ Fork (3) AR TN 030.7

~ Fork Bayou (1) TX 030.7

~ Fork River (1) AR 030.7

~ Georgia (8) 086.3

~ Georgia Cracker (1) 093.5

~ Georgia cure (1) n 080.9

~ Georgia scrape (1) n 021.6

~ Georgia syrup (1) n 051.3

~ Hampton (1) 106.2

~ Haven (1) MS 087.4

~ Holston Lake (1) TN 030.7

~ Holston River (1) TN 030.7

~ Houston (2) 105.6

~ Jackson (5) 107.6

~ Knoxville (1) 105.1

~ Louisiana (2) 086.5

~ MacGregor side (1) n 115.9

~ Memphis (5) 105.1

~ Miami (5) FL 087.1

~ Mississippi (2) 086.7

~ Moore (1) 107.6

~ Nashville (9) 105.1

~ New River Canal (1) FL 030.3

~ Park (3) TX 087.1

~ Park area (2) n 105.5

~ part (2) n 105.1

~ Peachtree (1) 107.9

~ Prong (1) TX 030.7

~ Rampart (1) 105.4

~ River (3) GA 030.7

~ Sawyer Creek (1) AL 030.7

~ Shore (1) LA 087.5

~ Shreveport (2) 105.1

~ Side (43) 105.1

~ Springs (1) TN 087.7

~ State (1) 084.9

~ Sulphur (1) TX 086.5

~ Texas (5) 093.8

~ Three Notch (3) 107.6

~ Three Notch Street (1) 107.6

~ Wall Street (1) 105.2

Southdown (1) LA 087.3

southeast (407) n/adj 006.5

~ wind (52) n 006.5

~ winds (1) n 006.5

Southeast (38) 105.1

~ Alabama (1) 086.4

~ Atlanta (1) 105.1

~ Dallas (2) 105.1

~ Georgia (1) 086.3

~ Jackson (1) 006.5

~ Miami (1) 105.1

~ section (2) n 105.1

~ States (1) 006.5

southeaster (17) n 006.5

southeasterly (28) adj/ adv 006.5

~ breeze (1) n 006.5

~ wind (6) n 006.5

southeastern (18) adj 006.5

~ wind (3) n 006.5

Southeastern (6) 006.5

~ Asian people (1) n 002.6

~ League (1) 006.5

~ States (1) 086.9

southeastwardly (1) adv 006.5

southerly (24) adj 006.5

~ wind (5) n 006.5

southern (13) adj 006.4

~ breeze (1) n 006.5

~ part (1) n 006.5

~ wind (5) n 006.5

Southern (87) 080.6

~ accent (4) n 131.2

~ Army (1) 024.8

~ Baptist (13) 089.1

~ Baptist Convention (1) 089.1

~ Belle (1) 092.9

~ biscuits (1) n 044.4

~ boogie (1) n 130.9

~ brogue (1) n 081.8

~ Bypass (1) 107.7

~ colloquialisms (1) n 084.9

~ cracker (2) n 069.9

~ drawl (1) n 080.6

~ eating (1) n 088.9

~ Frenchmen (1) 069.9

~ -fried chicken (1) n 121.5

~ Georgia hick accent (1) n 131.2

~ greens (1) n 055A.5

~ hicks (1) n 069.9

~ Hills (1) LA 087.7

~ hognose (1) n 093.7
~ magnolia (1) n 062.9
~ Memorial Day (1) 080.6
~ Natural Gas building (3) n 106.4
~ nigger (1) n 069.3
~ Pacific (1) 084.8
~ people (1) n 069.4
~ Pines (1) 087.6
~ Queen (3) 056.9
~ Queen sweet potato (1) n 055.5
~ Railroad (6) 084.7
~ Railway (1) n 084.7
~ rock (1) n 130.9
~ rock 'n' roll (1) n 130.9
~ side (1) n 053.6
~ slang (1) n 080.6
~ speech (1) n 080.6
~ speeches (1) n 131.2
~ spoon bread (1) n 044.6
~ squirrel (1) n 059.7
~ -style porch (1) n 010.8
~ swampy lowlands (1) n 029.6
~ sweet bread (1) n 044.6
~ Texas (1) 082.6
~ University (1) 106.2
~ War (1) 085.8
~ wheat (1) n 044.3
~ whites (1) n 069.4
Southerner (5) 069.2
southerners (1) n 006.4
Southerners (8) 066.9
southernly (4) adj 006.4
Southgate (2) 105.7
~ Plaza (1) 116.1
Southhaven (1) 105.4
Southies (1) 128.3
Southland (3) 108.6
~ Life (1) 108.5
~ Shopping Center (1) 105.2
Southlawn (1) 105.5
southpaw (1) n 080.6
Southport (1) 106.3
Southside (4) 105.1
~ Baptist Church (1) 089.2
~ Expressway (1) 107.1

southward (9) adv 006.4
southwest (466) adj 006.4
~ room (1) n 007A.7
~ wind (67) n 006.4
Southwest (34) 105.2
~ area (1) n 106.2
~ Atlanta (2) 105.1
~ community (1) n 006.5
~ Dallas (1) 105.1
~ Eight Street (1) 105.4
~ First Street (1) 105.3
~ Georgia (1) 006.5
~ Little Rock (1) 105.1
~ Miami (1) 105.1
~ Mississippi (1) 006.5
~ Pass (1) LA 031.3
~ section (2) n 105.1
~ Side (1) 105.4
~ Texas (1) 006.5
southwester (18) n 006.5
southwesterly (30) adj/ adv 006.5
~ wind (13) n 006.5
southwestern (20) adj 006.5
~ wind (7) n 006.5
Southwestern part (1) n 105.1
southwesterner (1) n 006.5
southwesters (1) n 006.5
Southwood (2) 105.7
~ subdivision (1) n 106.2
souvenir (4) n 095.7
Soviet Union (1) 087.9
sow (576) n/adj/interj 035.5
~ bosom (3) n 046.3
~ hog (7) n 035.5
~ pig (12) n 035.5
~ pigs (4) n 035.5
sow[N-i] (1) n 035.5
sowbellies (3) n 046.3
sowbelly (166) n/adj 046.3
~ meat (1) n 046.3
sowed (1) v 081.8
sowee(x2) (1) interj 038.3
SOWEGA (1) 081.8
sowing a watermelon (1) v 065.1
sown (1) v 041.5
sow's belly (1) n 046.3

sows (70) n 035.5
soybean (8) n/adj 055A.2
~ field (1) n 005A.3
~ hay (1) n 014.7
soybeans (70) n 055A.4
SP (2) 070.8
spa (2) n 126.2
space (44) n/adj 009.8
~ cadet (1) n 073.4
~ gas heaters (1) n 118.5
~ heater (8) n 118.4
~ heaters (10) n 118.4
~ launch (1) n 024.5
~ launching (1) n 024.5
Space (2) 106.7
~ Center (1) 106.7
~ Museum (1) 106.4
spaced-out (2) adj 073.4
spaceman (1) n 124.2
spaces (4) n 065.9
spacy (4) adj 074.7
spade (93) n/v/adj 069.3
~ -like tool (1) n 120.6
~ well (1) n 015.5
spaded (11) v 036.1
spader (1) n 021.6
spades (13) n 120.5
spading (5) v/adj 036.1
~ fork (1) n 020.8
~ plow (1) n 021.6
spaghetti (3) n/adj 127.3
~ eaters (1) n 127.3
~ people (1) n 127.3
spaghettis (1) n 041.9
Spain (3) 087.9
spake (1) v 012.3
Spalding (10) GA 087.3
~ County (5) GA 080.6
span (29) n 033.7
~ of mule[N-i] (1) n 033.7
~ of mules (9) n 033.7
~ of oxen (1) n 033.7
Spanian (1) 128.7
Spanians (1) 128.7
Spaniards (4) 128.5
spaniel (3) n 033.3
Spanish (127) 054.7
~ adobe (1) n 118.9
~ -American (3) 069.2
~ -American War (4) 085.8
~ -Americans (1) 128.7
~ bayonet (1) n 062.3

~ bayonets (1) n 062.7
~ dagger (1) n 062.8
~ design (1) n 118.9
~ Fort (1) 106.4
~ girls (1) n 128.7
~ goober (1) n 054.7
~ house (1) n 118.9
~ influenza (1) n 100.9
~ Lake (2) LA 087.2
~ lime trees (1) n 061.9
~ limon trees (1) n 061.8
~ mackerel (12) n 059.9
~ melon (1) n 056.7
~ moss (5) n 080.8
~ mullet net (1) n 089.8
~ music (1) n 130.8
~ needle leaves (1) n 091.8
~ needles (1) n 015.9
~ nuts (2) n 054.7
~ oak (9) n 061.8
~ oaks (1) n 061.8
~ onions (3) n 055.6
~ peanut (7) n 054.7
~ peanuts (10) n 054.7
~ people (2) n 128.5
~ Plaza (1) 106.4
~ potatoes (2) n 055.5
~ rice (3) n 050.7
~ sweet potato (1) n 055.5
~ Town (2) 080.7
~ -type (1) adj 118.9
~ -type-speaking people (1) n 105A.4
~ types (1) n 118.9
~ walnuts (1) n 061.8
~ wasp (2) n 060A.6
~ Wells (1) 087.4
~ yam (1) n 055.5
Spanishy (1) 080.6
spank (186) v 081.3
Spank (1) 083.1
spank[V-t] (1) v 065.5
spanked (19) v 065.5
~ out of (1) v 065.5
spanking (455) n/v 065.5
spankings (3) n 065.5
Spann Quarter (1) AL 087.4
spar (2) v 104.2
spare (12) v/adj 010.3

~ bathroom (1) n 118.3
~ change (1) n 114.5
~ room (6) n 007A.6
~ -time job (1) n 088.6
sparerib (2) n 046.4
spareribs (29) n 121.3
spark (3) v 081.4
~ a girl (1) v 081.4
~ up to (1) v 081.4
sparked (1) v 081.4
sparking (179) v/adj 081.4
~ courting (1) v 081.4
~ heavy (1) v 081.4
~ her (13) v 081.4
~ party (1) v 082.5
~ with her (1) v 081.4
sparkleberries (6) n 062.4
sparkleberry (2) n 080.9
sparkler (2) n 123.1
sparkling (2) v/adj 081.4
~ bug (1) n 060A.3
Sparr (1) FL 087.5
sparrow (6) n/adj 059.3
~ hawks (1) n 059.3
spar(row) (1) n 059.2
sparrows (13) n 059.2
Sparta (6) GA MS TN 087.5
Spartanburg (3) SC 087.1
spastic (2) n/adj 074.7
spats (1) n 088.7
spatter board (1) n 090.9
spatula (6) n 018.3
spawneded out (1) v 098.7
spay (40) v 036.1
spayed (52) v/adj 036.1
~ hog (1) n 036.1
spaying (3) n/v 036.1
speak (53) v 013.6
~ about (6) v 043.8
~ of (6) v 081.8
~ on (4) v 043.8
~ up (3) v 052.4
speaker (6) n 053.1
speakers (1) n 052.1
speaking (18) v/adj 057.4
~ about (1) v 043.8
~ (a)bout (1) v 025.8
~ of (6) v 102.5
~ to (2) v 013.5
~ with (1) v 053.7
speaks (2) v 025.6
spear (5) n/adj 020.8

~ carriers (1) n 069.3
~ dive (1) n 095.3
~ throwers (1) n 069.3
Spearsville (4) LA 087.3
special (57) n/adj 096.9
~ boyfriend (1) n 081.5
~ education (1) n 083.5
~ friend (1) n 070.6
~ gift (1) n 095.7
~ girl (1) n 081.6
~ girl friend (1) n 081.6
~ market (1) n 116.3
~ name (1) n 064.4
~ privileges (1) n 115.3
specialfy (1) v 088.7
specialist (1) n 012.1
Specialist (1) 080.6
specialize (1) v 013.1
specialized (1) adj 090.4
specially (1) adv 040.7
specials (4) n 113.2
specialty (4) adj 116.3
~ food store (1) n 116.3
~ shop (2) n 116.3
~ store (1) n 116.3
species (5) n 065.8
specific (9) adj 070.8
specify (1) v 013.1
specifying (1) v 065.8
speck (5) n/adj 060A.8
~ back (1) n 060A.8
~ -back ticks (1) n 060A.9
~ backs (1) n 060A.9
speckle (76) adj 055A.3
~ bass (1) n 059.9
~ bean (1) n 055A.3
~ butter bean (4) n 055A.3
~ butter beans (3) n 055A.3
~ cat (3) n 080.8
~ crowder (1) n 088.9
~ peas (4) n 099.7
~ peckerwood (1) n 059.3
~ perch (17) n 059.9
~ perches (1) n 059.9
~ runner (1) n 081.9
~ sea trout (1) n 059.9
~ trout (24) n 059.9
~ turtle (1) n 060.6

~ woodpecker (1) n 059.3
Speckle Hamburg (1) 080.6
speckled (38) adj 055A.3
~ beans (1) n 055A.3
~ butter beans (2) n 055A.3
~ cat (2) n 059.9
~ catfish (1) n 081.9
~ limas (1) n 055A.3
~ pea (1) n 055A.5
~ peas (2) n 055A.3
~ perch (1) n 059.9
~ trout (16) n 059.9
~ trouts (2) n 059.9
Speckled (2) 055A.3
speckledy (2) adj 080.8
~ -like (1) adj 065.8
specks (1) n 128.7
Specks (1) 055A.3
specky (1) adj 055A.3
specs (1) n 080.9
specter (1) n 090.2
specters (2) n 090.2
speculators (1) n 053.7
speech (7) n 043.8
speeches (1) n 131.2
speed (172) n/adj 114.2
~ blockers (1) n 110.8
~ breaker (14) n 110.8
~ breakers (40) n 110.8
~ breaks (1) n 110.8
~ bump (8) n 110.8
~ bumps (22) n 110.8
~ controls (1) n 110.8
~ freak (4) n 114.3
~ hump (3) n 110.8
~ humps (2) n 110.8
~ limit (1) n 013.8
~ reducers (1) n 110.8
~ sails (1) n 088.8
~ stoppers (1) n 110.8
~ traps (2) n 110.8
speedboat (3) n 024.6
speedboats (8) n 024.6
speeding up (1) v 007.2
speedometer (9) n 110.1
Speedway (1) 107.8
spell (622) n/v 004.6
~ like (1) v 095.8
spellbinder (1) n 067.8
spelled (2) v 075.6
speller (18) n 080.8
Speller (1) 084.8

spellers (4) n 080.6
spelling (4) n/adj 080.7
~ bees (3) n 080.7
Spellman (1) 032.8
spells (15) n 080.7
spelt (2) v 070.7
Spencer (3) TN 087.1
spend (16) v 082.8
~ -the-night (1) adj 130.7
~ -the-night parties (2) n 130.7
spend[V-s] (1) v 097.9
spenders (1) n 129.1
spending (2) v 040.8
spends (3) v 013.8
spendthrift (10) n 073.5
spent (10) v 098.6
Speranda (1) 030.7
spew (5) v 080.2
~ out (2) v 080.3
spewed (3) v 080.3
~ up (1) v 080.3
spewing (1) v 071.6
spews up with (1) v 007.6
spice (3) adj 047.4
~ boudin (1) n 047.4
~ cake (1) n 044.4
~ sausage (1) n 121.6
spicebush (1) n 061.9
spices (1) n 039.6
spicewood (2) n/adj 061.8
~ tea (1) n 061.4
spick (2) n/adj 075.9
~ -and-span (1) adj 027.7
spicket (403) n 018.7
spickets (22) n 018.7
spicy (1) adj 091.7
spider (827) n/adj 017.5
~ cob (2) n 061.3
~ fingers (1) n 120.7
~ getter (1) n 060A.7
~ house (1) n 061.3
~ legs (1) n 073.3
~ mites (1) n 060A.9
~ nest (6) n 061.3
~ silk (1) n 061.3
~ web (420) n 061.3
~ webs (231) n 061.3
spider[N-i] (1) n 061.3
spider's (9) adj 061.3
~ nest (1) n 061.3
~ web (8) n 061.3

spiders (66) n 061.3
Spiers Turnout (1) GA 086.6
spies (3) n 127.5
spiffy (3) adj 123.6
~ duds (1) n 123.6
~ threads (1) n 123.6
spigot (153) n 018.7
spigots (8) n 018.7
spik (26) n 128.5
spike (23) n/adj 104.4
~ boat (1) n 024.6
~ fence (1) n 016.3
~ harrow (1) n 021.7
~ heels (4) n 123.8
~ jacks (1) n 061.8
~ team (4) n 033.7
~ -tooth (1) adj 021.7
~ -tooth harrow (5) n 021.7
~ -tooth harrows (2) n 021.7
spiked (4) adj 123.8
~ heels (2) n 123.8
~ iron fences (1) n 016.2
~ -tooth harrow (1) n 021.7
spikenard roots (1) n 061.4
spikes (6) n 123.8
Spiko Ricans (1) 128.6
spiks (60) n 127.3
spill (7) v 031.4
~ his cookies (1) v 080.3
~ water (1) n 031.5
~ your guts (1) v 080.3
~ your supper (1) v 080.3
spilled (2) v 080.5
spilling (1) n 088.5
spillover area (1) n 029.6
spillway (18) n 030.3
Spillway (2) 030.7
spilt (1) v 016.4
spin (11) v/adj 130.6
~ the bottle (9) n 130.6
~ wheel (1) n 022.7
spinach (125) n/adj 055A.5
~ greens (2) n 055A.5
spinal meningitis (1) n 079.9
spindle (26) n/adj 021.2

~ -back (1) adj 008.9
~ stairways (1) n 010.7
Spindle Home (1) 106.4
spindles (4) n 021.9
spindly (1) adj 072.9
spinner (1) n 021.1
spinning (40) n/adj 022.7
~ and weaving room (1) n 007A.9
~ board (1) n 022.7
~ jennies (1) n 022.7
~ jenny (9) n 022.7
~ saw (2) n 022.7
~ stone (1) n 023.5
~ the bottle (1) n 083.9
~ the top (1) n 130.9
~ wheel (20) n 023.3
~ wheels (2) n 080.9
spinster (5) n 073.5
spiral (2) adj 010.7
~ staircase (1) n 010.7
spirea (1) n 061.7
spirit (71) n 090.3
Spirit (2) 089.3
~ Lake (1) AR 090.2
spirit[N-i] (1) n 099.3
spirited (2) adj 074.1
spirits (140) n 090.2
spiritual (8) n/adj 115.6
~ hymns (1) n 089.5
~ music (1) n 130.8
~ outfit (1) n 090.2
~ spirit (1) n 090.2
~ transformation (1) n 089.9
spirituals (1) n 130.8
Spiro (1) OK 087.6
spit (79) v/adj 066.9
~ at (1) v 052.6
~ bath (2) n 088.8
~ devils (1) n 061.1
~ feist (1) n 033.3
~ harp (2) n 020.5
~ image (9) n 065.3
~ in (2) v 039.8
~ out (1) v 080.3
~ up (30) v 080.3
spite (4) prep 088.7
spitfire (1) n 075.1
spiting (1) v 104.2
spits (2) n/v 128.7
spitting (70) v/adj 006.6
~ image (66) n 065.3
~ im(age) (1) n 065.3
~ up (2) v 080.2

spittoon (3) n 065.8
spittoons (2) n 017.7
spitz (6) n/adj 033.3
~ feist (2) n 033.3
splash (14) n 095.4
splashdown (1) n 095.4
splashed (1) v 095.4
splasher (2) n 095.4
splatter (1) n 095.4
spleen (4) n 037.4
splews out (1) n 050.8
splice (1) n 026.2
spliced (3) v 082.2
splinter (9) n/adj 008.6
~ box (1) n 008.6
~ light (1) n 024.3
~ lighterd (1) n 008.6
~ wood (2) n 008.6
splinter[N-i] (2) n 016.7
splintered (1) v 066.9
splinters (177) n 008.6
splints (2) n 008.6
split (209) n/v/adj 018.8
~ -bottom chairs (1) n 008.8
~ bottoms (1) n 008.8
~ foyer (1) n 118.8
~ hoof (1) n 034.7
~ house (1) n 096.9
~ -level (22) adj 118.9
~ -level house (4) n 098.8
~ -levels (1) n 118.9
~ log (1) n 008.5
~ -log (1) adj 016.4
~ logs (2) n 016.4
~ -out rails (1) n 016.4
~ pickets (1) n 016.2
~ pine (1) n 061.8
~ rail (27) n 016.4
~ -rail (10) adj 016.4
~ -rail fence (37) n 016.4
~ -rail fences (17) n 016.4
~ railing (1) n 016.4
~ rails (21) n 016.4
~ season (1) n 093.7
~ -shingle roof (1) n 011.4
~ siding (1) n 011.2
~ term (1) n 084.8
~ their blanket (1) v 096.7
~ up (3) v 082.1

splits (8) n/v 080.6
splitted (4) v 095.8
~ up (2) v 025.6
splitters (1) n 035.3
splitting (7) v/adj 055A.2
~ the blanket (1) v 082.1
~ image (1) n 065.3
spliv (1) n 069.3
splo (21) n/adj 050.8
~ drinker (1) n 113.7
~ whiskey (1) n 050.8
splotch (1) n 026.2
Splunge Creek (1) AL 030.7
spocket (1) n 018.7
spoil (137) v/adj 046.9
~ bank (1) n 090.9
~ brat (1) n 046.9
spoil[V-p] (1) v 046.9
spoil[V-r] (2) v 046.9
spoil[V-t] (61) v/adj 047.5
~ -like (1) adj 046.9
spoilage (1) n 066.9
spoiled (707) v/adj 047.5
~ milk (1) n 125.6
spoiling (17) n/v 046.9
spoils (19) v 046.9
spoilsport (1) n 075.2
spoilt (128) v/adj 047.5
~ milk (1) n 047.7
spoke (16) n/v/adj 021.1
~ about (1) v 098.6
~ ax (1) n 020.7
~ fence (1) n 016.4
~ of (3) v 098.6
spoken (3) v 058.3
spokes (84) n 021.1
spokeses (1) n 041.9
sponge (40) n/v/adj 018.3
~ bath (1) n 088.9
~ cake (1) n 122.2
~ cakes (1) n 122.8
~ cloth (1) n 018.3
~ hooks (1) n 088.7
~ off (1) v 073.5
sponger (1) n 073.5
sponges (2) n 018.3
sponging (1) n 057.4
spongy (1) adj 026.1
sponsor (1) n 113.5
spontaneously (1) adv 041.5

spook (38) n/adj 069.3
~ house (11) n 090.3
spooked (8) v/adj 090.3
~ house (1) n 090.3
spookier (1) adj 074.3
spookies (1) n 090.1
spooking (2) v 081.7
~ her (1) v 081.4
spooks (142) n 090.2
spooks' witch (1) n 090.2
spooky (68) adj 074.3
~ house (12) n 090.3
~ -looking (1) adj 090.3
spool (4) n/adj 035.2
~ beds (1) n 009.3
~ wire (1) n 016.3
spoon (887) n/v/adj 017.8
~ biscuits (1) n 044.4
~ bread (103) n 044.7
~ bush (1) n 062.7
~ cat (1) n 084.8
~ harrow (1) n 021.7
~ holder (3) n 017.8
~ rings (1) n 123.1
~ stand (1) n 017.9
~ -type garfish (1) n 059.9
~ with (1) v 081.7
spoon[N-i] (2) n 017.8
spoonbill (5) adj 059.9
~ cat (3) n 059.9
~ catfish (2) n 059.9
spoonbills (1) n 059.9
spoonful (7) n 017.8
spoonfuls (1) n 017.8
spooning (37) v 081.8
~ around (1) v 081.7
spoons (175) n 017.8
sporadic (1) adj 065.8
spores (1) n 057.1
sport (37) n/adj 028.1
~ car (6) n 109.1
~ coat (8) n 027.1
~ fish (1) n 059.9
~ jacket (2) n 027.1
~ model (1) n 109.1
~ -model car (1) n 109.1
~ shirt (1) n 027.4
sporting (3) adj 097.9
~ gentleman (1) n 097.9
~ ladies (1) n 113.3

~ woman (1) n 073.7
sports (74) n/adj 123.8
~ car (46) n 109.1
~ cars (10) n 109.1
~ coat (5) n 027.1
~ coupe (3) n 109.1
~ family car (1) n 109.2
~ jacket (2) n 027.1
~ locker (1) n 009.6
~ model (1) n 109.1
~ parties (1) n 130.7
sporty (4) adj 065.9
~ woman (1) n 080.7
spot (37) n/v/adj 113.4
~ -back tick (1) n 060A.9
~ -fight (2) v 091.8
Spot (2) TN 087.6
spots (17) n 059.9
spottail (2) n 061.2
spottails (3) n 059.9
spotted (11) n/adj 035.6
~ butter beans (1) n 055A.3
~ cat (2) n 059.9
~ catfish (1) n 059.9
~ oak (3) n 061.9
~ oaks (1) n 061.8
~ Poland China (1) n 035.5
spouse (68) n 063.2
spouse's (1) adj 065.9
spout (103) n 011.5
Spout Spring (1) AL 030.7
spouters (1) n 011.5
spouting (1) n 011.5
spouts (7) n 011.5
spraddle legged (1) adv 095.5
Sprague Junction (1) AL 087.8
sprang (1) v 095.3
spraucet (1) n 018.7
sprawl (2) n 049.1
sprawled (1) v 095.8
spray (8) n/v 018.7
~ with (1) v 052.9
sprayer (1) n 012.2
spraying (1) n 058.7
sprays (4) v 013.7
spread (383) n/v/adj 028.7
~ apple pie (1) n 048.3

~ cover (1) n 028.7
~ on (2) v 028.1
~ out (2) v 043.1
~ wide (1) n 044.4
spreaded (3) v 095.8
~ out (2) v 026.1
spreader (4) n 021.3
spreading (19) adj 084.8
~ adder (13) n 084.8
~ adders (5) n 089.9
~ houses (1) n 118.9
spreads (23) n 028.7
sprightly (2) adj 074.1
spring (748) n/v/adj 030.6
~ at (1) v 101.2
~ beans (1) n 055A.4
~ bed (1) n 030.4
~ box (3) n 015.5
~ branch (32) n 030.6
~ branches (7) n 030.6
~ buttons (1) n 055.7
~ chicken (3) n 060.2
~ chickens (1) n 056.8
~ cleaning (5) n 010.4
~ clean(ing) (1) n 010.4
~ creek (1) n 030.6
~ cutting (1) n 041.5
~ day (2) n 005.6
~ fever (1) n 061.4
~ frog (92) n 060.3
~ frogs (65) n 060.3
~ garden (2) n 050.5
~ harrow (1) n 021.7
~ harrows (1) n 021.7
~ industries (1) n 120.2
~ land (2) n 029.6
~ -like (1) adj 005.4
~ line (1) n 084.9
~ lizard (1) n 060.6
~ lizards (3) n 061.2
~ onion (16) n 055.7
~ on(ion) (1) n 055.7
~ onions (94) n 055.7
~ peepers (2) n 060.3
~ piece (1) n 029.4
~ plank (1) n 022.6
~ potatoes (1) n 055.4
~ puppy dog (1) n 060.8
~ roots (1) n 061.4
~ runners (1) n 030.6
~ seat (2) n 020.8
~ seats (1) n 084.8

~ seep (1) n 029.7
~ shed (1) n 015.5
~ shoat (1) n 035.5
~ shower (4) n 006.1
~ shrimping (1) n 089.8
~ sickness (1) n 077.4
~ steel fingers (1) n 120.6
~ stream (1) n 030.6
~ teeth (1) n 021.7
~ thing (1) n 041.3
~ tide (2) n 029.7
~ tides (1) n 029.4
~ toad (1) n 060.4
~ tonic (4) n 078.4
~ tooth (6) n 021.7
~ -tooth (2) adj 021.7
~ -tooth cultivator (3) n 021.9
~ -tooth cultivators (1) n 021.7
~ -tooth deal (1) n 021.7
~ -tooth harrow (31) n 021.7
~ -tooth har(row) (1) n 021.7
~ -tooth harrows (4) n 021.7
~ -type harrow (1) n 021.7
~ wagon (2) n 084.9
~ wagons (1) n 080.6
~ water (9) n 048.9
Spring (101) 107.6
~ Branch (6) AR TX 030.7
~ City (5) TN 087.1
~ Creek (19) AL AR GA LA MS TN TX 030.7
~ Creek Bottom (2) TN 029.4
~ Field (1) 105A.5
~ Garden (1) AL 087.6
~ Hill (14) AL GA TX 087.3
~ Hill College (2) 083.6
~ Hill settlement (1) FL 087.2
~ Lake (3) 105.4
~ Maid onions (1) n 055.7
~ Park (1) 085.1
~ Ridge (1) LA 087.1

~ River (3) AR 030.7
~ Street (2) 107.6
~ Town (1) GA 087.1
~ Valley (1) AL 087.7
spring[N-i] (1) n 039.9
springboard (92) n 022.6
springboarding (1) v 022.8
springboards (2) n 022.6
Springdale (8) AR TN 087.4
~ Plaza (3) 106.2
springed (3) v 031.7
~ off (1) v 031.7
~ up (2) v 007.2
springer (4) n/adj 022.6
~ board (1) n 022.6
springers (2) n 033.9
Springfield (25) FL GA IL MO MS TN 087.1
~ wagon (1) n 081.8
Springflat Branch (1) GA 030.7
springful (2) n 088.7
springhead (2) n/adj 030.6
~ branch (1) n 030.6
springheads (1) n 030.6
Springhill (5) AL 075.9
~ Avenue (2) 107.6
~ community (1) LA 087.3
springhouse (78) n 015.5
springhouses (7) n 015.5
springing (20) v/adj 033.9
~ board (1) n 022.6
~ cow (1) n 033.9
~ like (1) v 033.9
springs (78) n 030.6
Springs (181) 114.7
springtime (3) n 002.7
Springtown (2) AR TX 087.4
Springvale (3) GA 087.1
Springville (2) AL LA 087.5
springy (1) adj 007.4
sprinkle (328) n/v/adj 006.6
~ rain (1) n 006.6
sprinkle[N-i] (1) n 006.6
sprinkled (6) v 006.6
sprinkler (2) n 108.8
sprinkles (10) n/v 006.6

sprinkling (161) v/adj 006.6
~ rain (15) n 006.6
sprints (1) v 010.5
sprite (6) adj 074.1
Sprite (2) 121.8
sprites (1) n 090.2
sprocket (2) n 018.7
sprout (2) n/v 029.9
Sprout (3) 056.9
sprouted wheat (1) n 044.4
sprouting (2) v 024.8
sprouts (11) n/v 055A.1
~ out (1) v 041.5
Sprouts (1) 056.9
spruce (30) n/v/adj 061.8
~ beer (1) n 050.8
~ pine (4) n 061.8
~ pine tree (1) n 061.8
~ pines (1) n 061.8
~ up (8) v 028.1
Spruce Creek (4) FL 030.7
spruced up (4) adj 028.1
sprucing (9) v 081.4
~ up (8) v 028.1
sprucy (4) adj 074.1
sprung (4) v 041.5
~ back out (1) v 041.5
~ in (1) v 095.3
~ off (1) v 098.7
~ up (1) v 065.7
spry (409) adj 074.1
spryer (1) adj 074.1
sprying (1) n 006.6
spud (8) n 055.4
spuds (23) n 055.4
spunk (1) n 074.1
spunky (8) adj 074.1
spur (11) n 031.7
Spur (1) 080.6
Spurlock (1) 106.6
spurned (4) v 082.1
~ him (3) v 082.1
spurs (10) n 019.4
spurts (1) n 001A.4
spy (19) n/v 098.4
squabbling (1) v 057.4
squabby squash (1) n 056.6
squabs (1) n 036.6
squad (66) n/adj 111.7
~ car (31) n 111.7

~ -car men (1) n 112.5
~ cars (12) n 111.7
squadron (1) n 088.8
squads (1) n 111.5
squall (14) n 006.1
squalling (4) v 036.2
squalls (3) n 006.1
squally (1) adj 005.5
square (687) n/adj 085.1
~ acre (1) n 090.8
~ back (2) n 109.5
~ broom (1) n 010.5
~ -built (1) adj 007A.7
~ -built house (1) n 007A.2
~ dance (114) n/v 083.1
~ dance[N-i] (1) n 083.1
~ danced (3) v 083.1
~ dances (52) n 083.1
~ dancing (52) n 083.1
~ doughnut (1) n 045.2
~ feet (1) n 007.9
~ haircut (1) n 115.6
~ heels (1) n 123.8
~ -holed fence (1) n 016.3
~ house (5) n 007A.6
~ loaves (1) n 090.4
~ lot (1) n 085.1
~ mile-wise (1) adv 080.6
~ miles (2) n 088.1
~ nail (1) n 092.8
~ nails (4) n 080.6
~ parking (1) n 108.3
~ -pointed boat (1) n 024.6
~ shoulder (3) n 046.5
~ toes (1) n 123.8
~ wire (1) n 016.3
Square (30) 106.4
squared off (1) v 025.6
squareheads (2) n 128.7
squares (14) n 014.7
squaring (1) n 130.6
squash (1225) n/v/adj 056.6
~ gourd (1) n 056.6
~ out (1) v 060.4
~ pickle (1) n 056.6
squashes (64) n 056.6
squashing (1) v 070.8
squat (364) n/v/adj 096.4

~ behind (2) v 096.4
~ down (162) v 096.4
~ frog (1) n 060.4
~ line (2) n 108.5
~ on (1) v 096.4
squat[V-r] (4) v 096.4
~ down (2) v 096.4
squats (7) v 096.4
~ down (4) v 096.4
~ to (1) v 124.1
squatted (65) v 096.4
~ down (41) v 096.4
squatter (1) n 072.8
squatters (2) n 080.7
squatting (230) v/adj 072.8
~ down (73) v 096.4
~ on (1) v 072.8
~ position (1) n 096.4
squaw (7) n/adj 063.2
~ bread (1) n 044.6
~ vine (1) n 061.4
squawk (1) n 039.9
squaws (2) n 126.8
squeak (6) n/adj 059.1
~ owl (2) n 059.1
~ owls (1) n 059.1
squeaking (3) v 024.8
squeaks (1) v 073.5
squeal (18) n/v 036.2
squealed on (2) v 101.3
squealer (6) n 101.3
squealers (2) n 101.3
squealing (6) v/adj 036.4
~ noise (2) n 036.4
squeals (3) v 036.4
~ on (1) v 101.3
squeaming (1) v 096.7
squeech (6) adj 059.1
~ owl (5) n 059.1
~ owls (1) n 059.1
squeech[V-r] down (1) v 096.4
squeeching owl (2) n 059.1
squeechy eyes (1) n 126.4
squeeze (4) n/v 073.5
squeeze[V-r] (1) v 096.4
squeezer (2) n 081.8
squeezing (1) v 081.7
squeezings (12) n 050.8
squibs (1) n 061.2
squid (2) n 061.2
squiggly (1) adj 016.5
squinch (42) adj 126.4

~ eye (1) n 126.4
~ owl (39) n 059.1
~ owls (2) n 059.1
squinched up (1) adj 055.9
squinches (2) v 059.1
squinchies (1) n 126.4
squinching (3) v/adj 089.8
  ~ around (1) v 089.8
  ~ owl (1) n 059.1
  ~ owls (1) n 059.1
squink owl (1) n 059.1
squinky owl (1) n 059.1
squint (2) adj 126.4
  ~ eyes (1) n 126.4
  ~ owl (1) n 059.1
squire (3) n 080.7
squires (1) n 068.6
squiring (1) v 081.4
squirming with (1) v 055A.8
squirmy (1) adj 081.9
squirrel (2038) n/adj 059.6
  ~ corn (1) n 056.2
  ~ dog (11) n 033.1
  ~ dogs (6) n 059.6
  ~ head (1) n 059.6
  ~ hunt (4) n 059.6
  ~ -hunt (2) v 059.6
  ~ -hunted (1) v 059.6
  ~ hunters (3) n 013.5
  ~ hunting (8) n 059.6
  ~ -hunting (2) v 059.6
  ~ meat (1) n 059.6
  ~ nuts (1) n 054.7
  ~ season (1) n 080.7
  ~ stew (1) n 059.6
  ~ -time season (1) n 093.5
  ~ trap (1) n 059.7
  ~ whiskey (1) n 050.8
squir(rel) (2) n 059.6
squirrel[N-i] (6) n 059.6
squirrel[N-k] nest (1) n 059.6
squirrelbit (1) v 033.5
squirrelfish (1) n 059.9
squirreling (2) v 075.7
  ~ out (1) v 089.9
squirrelly (1) adj 074.7
squirrels (834) n 059.6
squirt (5) n/v/adj 033.3
  ~ -gun wars (1) n 130.5

squirted (1) v 070.8
squirty (1) adj 080.7
squish (1) n 056.6
squished down (1) v 096.5
squush up (1) v 092.9
Ss (3) 078.4
SSS tonic (2) n 078.4
ST (1) 081.8
stab (102) n/v/adj 104.3
  ~ down (1) v 104.3
  ~ wound (4) n 078.1
stab[V-r] (14) v 104.3
stabbed (474) v 104.3
  ~ at (1) v 104.3
  ~ in (2) v 095.8
stabbers (3) n 123.8
stabbing (6) v 104.3
stability (1) n 065.8
stable (400) n/adj 015.2
  ~ boy (1) n 015.2
  ~ business (1) n 015.2
  ~ door (1) n 058.2
  ~ horse (11) n 034.1
  ~ loft (1) n 014.5
  ~ lot (1) n 015.6
  ~ manure (1) n 021.4
stables (173) n 015.2
stabling (1) v 015.2
stabs (4) v 104.3
stack (566) n/v/adj 014.6
  ~ cake (4) n 048.3
  ~ cakes (2) n 048.3
  ~ chimley (25) n 008.1
  ~ chimleys (2) n 008.1
  ~ chimney (12) n 008.1
  ~ chimneys (1) n 008.1
  ~ heel (1) n 123.8
  ~ heels (4) n 123.8
  ~ pie (6) n 048.3
  ~ pies (1) n 048.3
  ~ pipe (1) n 008.1
  ~ pole (2) n 014.6
  ~ poles (1) n 014.6
  ~ rail fence (1) n 016.4
  ~ rail fences (1) n 016.4
  ~ wall (1) n 016.6
stack[V-r] (1) v 080.7
stacked (43) v/adj 014.6
  ~ cake (1) n 045.3
  ~ in (2) v 041.6
  ~ like (2) v 125.4
  ~ out (3) v 014.6
  ~ up (2) v 014.8

~ woman (1) n 125.4
stackers (2) n 014.6
stacking (22) v 041.7
stacks (137) n/v 014.7
stadium (5) n 126.2
Stadium (6) 106.4
stadiums (1) n 106.4
staff (3) n 020.8
staffs (2) n 020.9
stag (67) n/adj 033.5
  ~ film (1) n 114.9
  ~ -film parties (1) n 130.7
  ~ films (2) n 114.9
  ~ horse (1) n 034.1
  ~ male (1) n 035.5
  ~ parties (1) n 130.7
  ~ party (1) n 082.4
  ~ shops (1) n 114.9
stage (28) n/adj 031.4
  ~ flat (1) n 031.4
  ~ planks (2) n 044.4
  ~ rustic (1) n 081.2
  ~ show (1) n 084.4
stagecoach (4) adj 089.9
  ~ horses (1) n 089.9
  ~ inn (2) n 084.8
  ~ road (1) n 031.7
staggering (3) v 070.8
Staggerlee (1) 104.6
staggery (1) adj 073.3
staghorn sumac (1) n 062.2
stagnant (2) adj 029.6
  ~ pond (1) n 029.6
  ~ water (1) n 029.6
stags (5) n 033.5
staid (1) adj 074.8
stain (3) v/adj 026.3
  ~ apron (1) n 026.3
  ~ glass (1) n 009.6
stained water (1) n 047.7
stainless-steel pail (1) n 017.3
stair (22) n 010.7
stair[N-i] (7) n 010.7
staircase (66) n 010.7
staircases (3) n 010.7
staircasing (1) n 010.7
stairs (547) n/adj 010.7
  ~ steps (1) n 007A.6
stairstep (8) n 010.7
stairstep[N-i] (1) n 010.7
stairsteps (112) n 010.7

stairway (334) n/adj 010.7
  ~ steps (1) n 010.7
stairways (25) n 010.7
stairwell (8) n 010.1
stairwells (2) n 010.7
stajoles (1) n S 041.5
stake (42) n/v/adj 016.5
  ~ -and-lighter (1) n 016.4
  ~ -and-rail fence (1) n 016.4
  ~ -and-ride (2) n 016.4
  ~ -and-rider (17) n 016.4
  ~ -and-rider fence (5) n 016.4
  ~ -and-riders (2) n 016.4
  ~ fence (3) n 016.2
  ~ -rail fence (1) n 016.4
  ~ truck (1) n 109.7
  ~ -[J-0]-rider (1) n 016.4
staked out (1) v 016.3
stakes (10) n 016.5
  ~ -and-riders (1) n 016.4
stale (77) adj 046.9
stalk (16) n/v/adj 080.8
  ~ -cutter (3) n 021.8
  ~ heap (1) n 041.7
  ~ stands (1) n 041.7
  ~ tassel (1) n 056.3
stalks (8) n 065.8
stall (237) n/v 015.4
  ~ -feed (1) v 080.9
  ~ -feeding (1) v 015.5
stalled up (1) v 015.1
stalleded up (1) v 098.6
stallion (472) n/adj 034.1
  ~ horse (2) n 034.1
  ~ horses (1) n 034.1
stallions (20) n 034.1
stalls (251) n 015.2
stamp (46) n/v 097.4
stamp[N-i] (1) n 052.1
stamped (28) v 097.4
stamping (16) v 097.4
stamps (6) n 095.7
Stamps (2) LA 087.2
Stan the Man (1) 125.3
stanchion (4) n 015.3
stanchions (12) n 015.3

stand (306) n/v/adj 019.3
~ back (2) v 037.5
~ for (1) v 082.3
~ him up (2) v 082.1
~ in (1) v 013.1
~ irons (1) n 008.3
~ like (1) v 097.8
~ of mules (1) n 033.7
~ off (1) v 014.2
~ out (2) v 027.8
~ still (23) v 037.5
~ table (3) n 008.9
~ there (1) v 038.2
~ to (2) v 093.7
~ under (1) v 081.3
~ up (5) v 098.2
~ -up attic (1) n 009.8
~ up with (1) v 082.4
Stand (3) 087.7
stand[N-i] (1) n 019.2
stand[V-p] (2) v 052.6
standard (40) n/adj 018.7
~ breds (1) n 034.2
~ clutch (1) n 110.7
~ gear (1) n 110.7
~ shift (15) n 110.7
~ shifts (1) n 110.7
~ transmission (5) n 110.7
~ -type construction (1) n 096.7
Standard (10) 107.7
~ Drive (1) 107.7
~ English (5) 131.2
~ Heights (1) 084.7
~ Oil (2) 024.1
standards (4) n 020.8
standby (3) n 081.5
standers (1) n 022.3
standing (24) v/adj 034.1
~ around (1) v 057.4
~ (a)round (3) v 088.5
~ back (1) v 097.8
~ rib roast (2) n 121.2
~ roses (1) n 062.7
~ trunks (1) n 009.7
~ up (1) v 049.2
~ water (1) n 039.7
Standing Rock (1) AL 087.8
standoffish (2) adj 074.7
standpipe (3) n 018.8
stands (37) n/v 019.2
~ out (3) v 091.6
standstill (1) n 088.3

Stanfield Creek (1) MS 030.7
Stanley (3) 030.7
~ Creek (1) TN 030.7
~ Steamer (2) 023.7
Stanley[N-k] store (1) n 025.8
Stanton (2) TN 087.4
~ Road (1) 106.3
staph germ (1) n 077.4
staple (10) n/v/adj 020.4
~ crops (1) n 016.1
staples (4) n 020.2
Staples Street (1) 115.8
Stapleton (1) GA 086.5
Stapletons Mill (1) 029.9
star (84) n/adj 069.1
~ back (1) n 089.8
~ root (6) n 061.4
~ root vine (1) n 061.4
~ -shape squash (1) n 056.6
~ tick (1) n 060A.4
Star (16) 023.5
~ car (1) n 081.2
~ City (1) AR 087.3
~ Island (2) 106.1
~ melon (1) n 056.9
~ Motel (1) 084.3
Star[N-i] (1) 056.9
starboard (1) adj 039.4
starch (8) n/v 065.9
starched (3) v/adj 010.6
~ shirt (1) n 080.8
starching (1) n 010.6
starchy (1) adj 013.9
starfish (1) n 060.1
stargazing (1) v 028.1
staring (1) n 088.5
stark (3) adj/adv/interj 046.9
Starke (3) FL 087.9
Starkville (19) MS 087.9
~ Street (1) 107.6
starling (2) n 093.7
starlings (2) n 059.2
Starlings Park (1) 106.4
Starnes (2) TN 030.7
~ Creek (1) TN 030.7
Starr (3) TX 087.2
~ County (1) TX 087.6
stars (15) n 069.1
stars' homes (1) n 106.4
Stars (2) 056.9
start (723) n/v 083.3

~ back (19) v 102.2
~ in (3) v 102.2
~ in on (1) v 075.9
~ off (4) v 102.2
~ off with (1) v 102.2
~ on (2) v 102.2
~ out (1) v 102.2
~ to (18) v 024.9
~ up (3) v 083.3
~ with (10) v 102.2
start[V-p] (11) v 102.2
start[V-r] (55) v 102.2
~ off (2) v 102.2
~ on (1) v 102.2
~ out (3) v 102.2
~ out with (1) v 053.4
~ to (17) v 102.2
start[V-t] (6) v 102.2
~ out (1) v 102.2
~ to (4) v 007.2
started (765) v 102.2
~ back (1) v 102.2
~ in (2) v 102.2
~ in to (1) v 024.9
~ off (13) v 102.2
~ out (10) v 102.2
~ to (38) v 024.9
~ up (2) v 102.2
~ [P-0] (3) v 102.2
starter (7) n/adj 110.6
~ set (1) n 008.6
starters (1) n 008.6
starting (19) v/adj 102.2
~ in (1) v 102.2
~ out (1) v 102.2
~ to (10) v 007.2
~ wood (1) n 008.6
startled (2) v 084.9
starts (106) v 083.3
~ back (3) v 083.3
~ in (3) v 083.3
~ out to (1) v 024.9
~ to (3) v 095.8
~ up (1) v 083.3
starve (1) v 090.5
starve[V-r] (1) v 070.2
starved (1) v 080.9
starving (1) v 075.7
stash (3) n/v 114.5
stashed out (1) v 050.9
state (79) n/adj 002.6
~ -aid roads (1) n 031.7
~ archives (1) n 106.9
~ bodies (1) n 109.7

~ capital (1) n 085.6
~ college (1) n 083.6
~ government (2) n 085.6
~ grouper (1) n 112.5
~ highway (5) n 031.6
~ highways (1) n 080.8
~ house (1) n 093.7
~ lake road (1) n 031.6
~ land (1) n 053.4
~ law (1) n 085.7
~ legislature (1) n 070.6
~ park (1) n 085.1
~ police (1) n 070.6
~ prison (2) n 112.8
~ rest areas (1) n 107.2
~ road (12) n 031.6
~ roads (7) n 031.7
~ stores (1) n 050.8
~ streets (1) n 031.7
~ teachers college (1) n 083.6
~ trooper (1) n 053.4
~ troopers (2) n 112.5
State (267) 086.1
~ Capitol (3) 106.4
~ Docks (4) 031.4
~ Fair (1) 106.4
~ House (1) 106.4
~ Line (1) MS 087.5
~ of Mississippi (1) 086.7
~ of New York (8) 086.1
~ of Texas (1) 092.8
~ of Washington (1) 087.1
~ Road Eighty-Four (1) 107.7
~ Street (3) 107.6
State[N-i] (15) 086.9
Staten Island (1) NY 087.8
stater (1) n 066.7
Stater (1) 069.2
staterooms (1) n 081.9
states (6) n 069.9
States (794) 085.8
~ Street (1) 107.6
Statesboro (6) GA 087.2
Statesville (3) TN 087.3
statewide stock law (1) n 016.5
static (2) n 092.6

station (1234) n/adj 084.7
~ depot (2) n 064.4
~ house (8) n 112.7
~ wagon (140) n 109.5
~ wagons (9) n 109.5
Station (35) 113.8
stationaried (1) v 022.6
stationed (2) v 053.1
~ in (1) v 084.7
stations (17) n 112.6
statistic (1) n 065.8
statistics (1) n 070.7
Statler House (1) 106.4
statue (12) n 106.4
status (4) n/adj 125.6
~ climber (1) n 125.6
~ quo (1) n 085.7
~ seekers (1) n 125.6
~ symbol (1) n 088.9
staunch (4) adj 065.8
~ in his ways (1) adj
   074.8
Staunton (1) VA 087.2
stave (14) n/adj 020.8
~ factory (1) n 088.7
~ mill (5) n 092.8
staves (54) n 020.9
staveses (1) n 020.3
stay (146) v/adj 033.2
~ at (1) v 052.6
~ away (2) v 098.2
~ away from (1) v
   098.2
~ bolts (1) n 088.7
~ chain (3) n 038.7
~ in (10) v 058.3
~ on (3) v 034.4
~ out (3) v 095.9
~ out of (1) v 057.7
~ still (2) v 037.5
~ up with (1) v 075.6
~ wires (1) n 016.3
~ with (5) v 053.4
stay[V-p] (6) v 040.1
~ (a)round (2) v 026.1
stay[V-r] up in (1) v
   053.6
stay[V-s] (2) v 088.4
~ at (1) v 088.4
~ on (1) v 026.1
stayed (80) v 097.1
~ away (1) v 083.4
~ down (1) v 076.1
~ in (4) v 080.7
~ on (3) v 052.6

~ out (2) v 083.4
~ out of school (4) v
   083.4
~ out with (1) v 092.8
~ with (5) v 032.4
staying (9) n/v 007A.2
~ at (1) v 024.7
~ in (1) v 024.9
~ out of (2) v 084.8
~ with (1) v 032.4
stays (15) n/v 020.3
~ in (3) v 080.6
~ on (1) v 012.9
~ put (1) v 074.8
~ with (1) v 075.6
staysail (1) n 084.9
steadfast (1) adj 074.8
steadily (4) adv 081.4
steady (318) n/adj/adv
081.5
~ beau (3) n 081.5
~ bees (1) n 060A.7
~ boyfriend (6) n 081.5
~ date (5) n 081.5
~ dating (3) n 081.4
~ downpour (2) n
   006.8
~ girl (4) n 081.6
~ girl friend (4) n
   081.6
~ now (1) interj 037.5
~ rain (19) n 006.6
~ rainfall (1) n 006.6
steak (295) n/adj 121.1
~ beater (1) n 099.6
~ houses (1) n 014.1
~ knife (17) n 017.8
~ knife[N-i] (3) n
   017.8
~ knives (63) n 017.8
~ pork (1) n 121.3
~ sauce (1) n 048.5
steaks (67) n/adj 121.1
~ knife (1) n 104.3
steal (21) v 100.2
~ the bacon (1) n 130.1
steal[V-r] (1) v 100.2
stealer (1) n 059.5
stealers (1) n 059.5
stealing (28) v 100.2
~ brick[N-i] (1) n
   053.8
~ chips (2) n 084.9
~ goods (1) n 098.4
~ partners (1) n 080.6

~ stick[N-i] (1) n
   080.8
~ sticks (4) n 098.4
steals (2) v 096.7
steam (27) n/adj 013.8
~ cooker (1) n 116.4
~ dryer (1) n 014.5
~ engine (2) n 066.8
~ grease (1) n 023.7
~ heat (5) n 118.4
~ heater (1) n 118.4
~ iron (1) n 010.6
~ kettle (1) n 017.6
~ launch (1) n 024.5
~ locomotive (1) n
   080.9
~ piano (1) n 088.7
~ shovel (2) n 080.8
~ shovels (1) n 065.8
~ tractor (1) n 042.2
~ train (1) n 080.9
~ tug (1) n 024.6
~ valve (1) n 008.1
steamboat (15) n/adj
024.6
~ bean (1) n 055A.3
~ captain (1) n 068.5
~ channel (1) n 030.2
~ landing (1) n 030.4
steamboats (9) n 024.6
steamed (2) v 048.8
~ up (1) v 075.2
steamer (1) n 080.8
Steamer (2) 023.7
steamers (2) n 024.6
steams (2) n/v 010.5
steeds (1) n 034.1
steel (111) n/adj 021.1
~ -back minnow (1) n
   061.2
~ band (7) n 021.1
~ bands (3) n 020.3
~ barrels (1) n 025.2
~ beam (10) n 021.6
~ -beam Dixie (1) n
   021.6
~ -beam plow (6) n
   021.6
~ -beam turning plow
   (1) n 021.6
~ belt (1) n 020.3
~ bin (1) n 014.4
~ boats (1) n 024.6
~ casket (1) n 079.1
~ container (1) n 017.4

~ cradles (1) n 008.3
~ drags (1) n 021.7
~ fence (4) n 016.3
~ fences (1) n 016.3
~ gaffs (1) n 090.9
~ har(row) (1) n 021.7
~ hoops (1) n 020.3
~ iron (1) n 075.8
~ -mesh fence (1) n
   016.3
~ middlebuster (1) n
   021.6
~ mill (1) n 106.4
~ -netting fence (1) n
   016.3
~ plate (1) n 021.1
~ plow (3) n 021.6
~ plows (1) n 021.6
~ post[N-i] (1) n 016.5
~ pot (1) n 017.6
~ rake (2) n 120.7
~ rim (14) n 021.1
~ rims (1) n 021.1
~ ring (1) n 021.1
~ rings (1) n 021.1
~ round skillet (1) n
   017.5
~ shoe (1) n 034.6
~ shoes (1) n 034.6
~ skillet (1) n 017.5
~ straps (1) n 022.3
~ tire (8) n 021.1
~ tires (1) n 021.1
~ traps (1) n 022.3
~ wing plow (1) n
   021.6
~ wire (3) n 016.3
~ -wire fence (1) n
   016.3
~ -wire fences (1) n
   016.3
Steel (2) 030.7
~ Bridge (1) GA 030.7
Steele Bay(ou) (1) MS
030.7
steelers (1) n 130.6
steelhead (1) n 059.9
steelies (1) n 130.6
steep (27) n/v/adj 048.8
steepest (1) adj 031.1
steeple (1) n 027.2
steeples (3) n 070.6
steer (166) n/adj 033.6
~ calf (4) n 033.8
~ calves (1) n 033.8

~ cow (1) n 033.5
~ shoes (1) n 034.6
~ wagon (1) n 081.9
steer[N-i] (4) n 033.7
steered (1) v 070.7
steering (12) v/adj 110.7
~ column (3) n 110.7
~ -column shift (1) n 110.7
~ wheel (4) n 077.8
~ -wheel column (1) n 110.7
steers (93) n 033.7
stein (1) n 048.9
Steiner building (1) n 108.5
Steinhatchee River (1) FL 030.7
steins (1) n 048.9
stem (9) n/adj 046.6
~ -wind watch (1) n 004.3
stemmed (1) v 092.1
stems (1) n 055A.5
stenographer (61) n 068.8
stenographers (5) n 068.8
step (129) n/v/adj 010.7
~ ants (1) n 060A.8
~ around the mountain (1) n 029.4
~ back (2) v 037.5
~ dad (1) n 129.5
~ daddy (8) n 063.4
~ -down (2) n 085.2
~ downs (1) n 088.8
~ -drop (1) v 021.9
~ in (1) v 129.8
~ -ins (2) n 081.8
~ it back (1) v 037.5
~ kid (1) n 066.3
~ ma (1) n 063.6
~ mammy (1) n 063.6
~ on (3) v 110.6
~ -on cans (1) n 017.4
~ out (1) v 028.1
~ -out (1) n 010.8
~ -out house (1) n 012.1
~ out with him (1) v 081.4
~ over the line (1) v 082.2
~ papa (1) n 063.4
~ roof (1) n 011.4
~ side (1) n 109.7

~ stove (2) n 088.9
~ up (1) v 038.1
~ van (1) n 109.6
Step Daddy (1) 063.5
step[N-i] (8) n 010.7
stepchild (2) n 066.3
stepdaughter (3) n 064.8
stepfather (14) n 066.4
Stephens County (1) GA 087.3
stepladder (5) n 010.7
stepmother (17) n/adj 129.5
~ biscuits (1) n 044.4
stepparent (2) n 129.5
stepparents (3) n 066.4
stepped (5) v 021.4
~ in (1) v 021.4
~ on (2) v 070.2
~ up (1) v 057.8
stepping (3) n/v 083.1
~ on (1) v 002.3
steps (726) n 010.7
stepsister (1) n 042.4
stereo (1) n 065.8
stereoscope (1) n 080.7
Sterick building (1) n 025.2
sterile (8) v/adj 047.5
~ hog (1) n 035.4
sterilize (11) v 048.2
steril(ize) (1) v 036.1
sterilized (3) v 036.1
sterilizing (2) v 018.2
sterling-silver flatware (1) n 017.8
Sterlington (3) LA 094.9
stern (1) n 081.8
sterno (1) n 114.7
Stetson (1) 066.9
stevedore (2) n 066.9
stevedores (2) n 088.7
Stevens (3) TX 030.7
~ Park (1) 106.4
Stevenson (2) AL 087.1
stew (100) n/v/adj 047.2
~ beef (3) n 121.2
~ -boil (1) v 046.1
~ boiler (1) n 017.6
~ meat (10) n 121.2
~ onions (1) n 055.6
~ pan (3) n 017.6
Stewart (13) GA TN 087.1
~ Avenue (2) 107.7

~ County (4) GA TN 087.5
stewed (7) v/adj 048.8
~ coffee (1) n 048.8
~ corn (1) n 056.2
~ fruit (1) n 054.6
~ fruits (1) n 054.6
~ liver (1) n 047.2
~ rabbit (1) n 121.5
stewer (8) n 017.3
stewers (6) n 017.5
stewing (9) adj 121.5
~ chicken (2) n 121.5
~ hen (4) n 121.5
~ hens (2) n 121.5
~ pot (1) n 017.5
stewpot (3) n 017.6
stewpots (1) n 017.6
stews (5) n 121.2
stick (486) n/v/adj 104.3
~ -and-clay chimley (1) n 008.1
~ -and-clay chimney (1) n 008.1
~ -and-daub chimley (2) n 008.1
~ -and-daub fireplace (1) n 088.7
~ and dirt (1) n 008.1
~ -and-dirt chimley (15) n 008.1
~ -and-dirt chimleys (4) n 008.1
~ -and-dirt chimney (1) n 008.1
~ -and-mud chimleys (1) n 008.1
~ -and-mud chimneys (1) n 008.1
~ -and-rag chimney (1) n 008.1
~ bean (6) n 055A.4
~ beans (14) n 055A.4
~ bread (1) n 044.7
~ broom (15) n 010.5
~ candy (2) n 080.6
~ fence (1) n 016.2
~ -handle broom (1) n 010.5
~ harrows (1) n 021.7
~ horse (3) n 101.5
~ horses (2) n 022.5
~ -in-the-mud (1) n 074.8
~ method (1) n 089.9

~ on (1) v 053.5
~ out (40) v 027.8
~ out from (1) v 090.8
~ pan (1) n 044.6
~ pin (1) n 026.5
~ -proof (1) adj 017.7
~ shift (55) n 110.7
~ to (1) v 013.1
~ toter (2) n 088.8
~ types (1) n 060A.8
~ -up onions (1) n 055.7
~ wood (1) n 008.5
stick[N-i] (4) n 052.2
stick[V-p] (1) v 104.3
stickball (6) n 130.4
stick(ball) (2) n 080.6
sticker weeds (1) n 015.9
stickers (5) n 015.9
stickful (1) n 088.9
sticking (10) v/adj 104.3
~ out (7) v 027.8
~ plaster (2) n 081.9
stickler (2) n 058.3
sticks (284) n/v 008.5
~ -and-stones-type stuff (1) n 129.7
~ through (1) v 053.2
~ to (2) v 104.8
sticktight (1) n 060A.9
stickweed (1) n 015.9
stickweeds (2) n 117.7
sticky (15) adj 075.1
~ clay (1) n 029.9
~ ground (2) n 029.4
~ gumbo land (1) n 029.8
~ soil (1) n 029.8
~ soils (1) n 029.8
~ stuff (1) n 029.8
~ wire (1) n 016.3
sties (8) n 015.4
stiff (44) adj 074.8
~ bit (1) n 039.2
~ blackland (1) n 091.7
~ hair (6) n 035.6
~ joints (2) n 079.6
~ land (12) n 029.4
~ -neck (1) adj 127.8
~ -necked (1) adj 074.8
~ rake (1) n 120.7
~ soil (1) n 029.8
~ tongue (1) n 020.8
stiffening (1) n 079.6
stiffer (2) adj 007.2

stifle (1) n 088.7
stigma (1) n 103.3
stile (3) n/adj 080.6
~ fence (1) n 016.4
Stilesboro (1) GA 087.6
stiletto (1) n 104.3
stilettos (1) n 104.3
still (317) n/adj/adv 089.8
~ lake (1) n 007.5
~ resin (1) n 077.9
~ spot (1) n 050.8
~ whiskey (1) n 050.9
stilled (1) v 007.3
Stillmore (1) GA 086.4
stills (10) n 080.8
Stills Crossroads (1) AL 087.2
stilted (1) v 081.8
stilts (3) n 123.8
stimulate (1) v 070.5
stimy (1) n 127.8
sting (28) n/v 130.4
sting[V-p] (2) v 013.6
stingaree (6) n 059.8
stingarees (5) n 062.3
stinge (1) n 073.5
stinger (3) n/adj 073.5
~ Marie (1) n 130.5
stingers (2) n 060A.7
stingiest (1) adj 073.5
stinginess (2) n 128.1
stinging (38) v/adj 057.4
~ ant (3) n 060A.7
~ bee (1) n 060A.5
~ lizard (1) n 060A.6
~ lizards (2) n 060A.9
~ nettle (7) n 062.3
~ nettles (5) n 062.3
~ scorpion (4) n 060A.7
~ scorpions (1) n 060A.5
~ snake (4) n 099.8
~ vine (1) n 062.3
~ weed (1) n 062.3
~ worm (5) n 062.3
~ worms (1) n 060A.4
stingray (3) n 098.8
stings (3) n/v 078.7
stingy (384) n/adj 073.5
~ green (2) n 057.3
~ gut (3) n 073.5
stink (25) v/adj 047.6
~ bait (2) n 061.2

~ base (3) n 053.7
~ bay (1) n 061.9
~ cat (1) n 059.4
~ dog (1) n 125.1
~ house (1) n 012.1
~ Jenny (1) n 060.7
~ Jim (4) n 060.7
~ kitties (1) n 059.4
~ melon (1) n 056.7
~ turtle (1) n 060.7
stinkbug (4) n 060A.2
stinkbugs (3) n 060A.8
stinker (1) n 059.4
stinkers (1) n 064.3
stinking (9) adj 092.4
~ cedar (1) n 061.8
~ Jim (3) n 060.5
~ outfit (1) n 099.9
~ Tom (1) n 060.6
Stinking Creek (2) TN 030.7
stinkingest (3) adj 064.7
stinks (2) v 046.9
~ like (1) v 059.4
stinkweed (1) n 015.9
stinkwood (1) n 062.6
stinky (3) adj 047.5
~ -back (1) n 060.7
stint (1) n 080.6
stipend (1) n 095.7
stir (8) v/adj 076.7
~ (a)round (1) v 076.7
~ mattress (1) n 088.7
stirred up (4) v 075.2
stirring (11) v/adj 007.2
~ up (2) v 007.2
stirrup (214) n/adj 039.3
~ fence (1) n 016.4
~ leather (1) n 039.3
stir(rup) (2) n 039.3
stirrup[N-i] (41) n 039.3
stir(rup)[N-i] (1) n 039.3
stirrups (637) n 039.3
stob (49) n/v 065.9
stob[V-r] (6) v 104.3
stobbed (57) v 104.3
stobbing (3) v/adj 104.3
~ knife (1) n 104.3
stobs (10) n 070.2
stock (872) n/adj 036.5
~ (as)sociation (1) n 065.8
~ barn (13) n 014.2
~ breeder (1) n 033.5
~ bull (4) n 033.5

~ business (1) n 052.6
~ cattle (1) n 036.5
~ cow (17) n 033.5
~ cows (1) n 033.6
~ dog (3) n 033.3
~ farm (3) n 036.5
~ feed (2) n 036.5
~ -feeding time (1) n 037.4
~ fences (1) n 016.3
~ food (1) n 036.5
~ goat (1) n 067.4
~ hog (24) n 035.3
~ hogs (1) n 035.3
~ horse (7) n 034.1
~ horses (1) n 034.1
~ law (46) n 016.4
~ laws (6) n 036.5
~ lot (1) n 015.5
~ male (3) n 033.5
~ market (1) n 036.5
~ pasture (1) n 015.6
~ pen (1) n 015.3
~ plow (1) n 021.6
~ pond (2) n 065.9
~ ponds (1) n 091.9
~ raiser (1) n 036.5
~ -raising (1) v 036.5
~ shelter (1) n 015.1
~ stud (1) n 034.1
Stock (2) 083.6
~ Creek (1) TN 030.7
stockade (10) n/adj 015.6
~ fence (1) n 016.2
~ -type fences (1) n 016.2
Stockbridge (2) GA 087.1
Stockes Creek (1) LA 030.7
stocking (2) v/adj 080.7
stockings (5) n 088.7
stocks (29) n 036.6
Stockton (6) AL GA 087.6
stocky (17) adj 073.1
~ -built (1) n 073.1
stockyard (2) n 015.1
stockyards (3) n 036.5
stogie (5) n 057.3
stogies (2) n 117.7
stoke (1) n 020.8
stoked furnace (1) n 118.4
stoker (2) n 118.4

Stokes Creek (1) LA 030.7
stole (374) v 100.2
~ out (1) v 096.8
Stole (1) 056.5
stole[V-r] (1) v 100.2
stoled (76) v 100.2
stolen (16) v 100.2
stomach (1022) n/v/adj 080.4
~ buster (4) n 095.4
~ colic (1) n 080.1
~ dive (1) n 095.4
~ part (1) n 037.3
~ teeth (2) n 071.8
~ tooth (1) n 071.8
~ trouble (1) n 080.4
~ upset (1) n 080.4
stom(ach) (1) n 080.4
stomach[N-i] (26) n 080.4
stomachache (9) n 072.6
stomacher (2) n 028.7
stomachs (1) n 080.4
stomp (425) v/adj 097.4
~ around (2) v 097.4
~ dance (3) n 097.4
~ down (1) v 097.4
~ -down (1) adv 097.4
~ lot (1) n 015.6
~ on (4) v 097.4
stomp[V-r] (4) v 097.4
stomped (174) v 097.4
~ on (2) v 097.4
stompers (3) n 123.8
stomping (155) v/adj 097.4
~ around (1) v 036.4
~ grounds (1) n 084.8
stomps (3) v 097.4
stone (1069) n/v/adj 032.1
~ barge (1) n 080.7
~ -blind (1) adj 077.2
~ bread (1) n 044.4
~ buildings (1) n 016.6
~ cast (1) n 039.5
~ chimney (2) n 008.1
~ churn (1) n 019.2
~ churns (1) n 015.5
~ coal (5) n 023.1
~ -cold (1) adj 078.6
~ cracker (1) n 069.4
~ -dead (5) adj 057.9
~ -deaf (25) adj 077.2

~ eggs (1) n 017.1
~ fence (78) n 016.6
~ fences (18) n 016.6
~ free (2) n 054.4
~ grinder (2) n 023.5
~ -ground meal (3) n 080.6
~ hearth rock (1) n 008.2
~ house (2) n 014.1
~ houses (1) n 016.6
~ jailhouse (1) n 106.4
~ jar (3) n 017.3
~ jars (3) n 017.3
~ jug (5) n 017.2
~ jugs (6) n 065.9
~ locust (1) n 061.9
~ mantel (1) n 008.4
~ peach (3) n 054.3
~ pecans (1) n 054.9
~ pipes (1) n 088.7
~ plate (1) n 017.1
~ postes (1) n 016.6
~ quarry (1) n 065.8
~ road (1) n 031.6
~ rock (3) n 023.4
~ rocks (1) n 032.1
~ seed peach (1) n 054.3
~ sharpener (1) n 023.5
~ sharpening wheel (1) n 023.5
~ sheeting (1) n 011.2
~ thing (1) n 016.6
~ toter (2) n 059.9
~ trough (1) n 035.8
~ vase (1) n 017.7
~ wall (112) n 016.6
~ walls (12) n 016.6
~ wheel (3) n 023.5
Stone (100) MS 087.5
~ County (1) AR 087.4
~ Creek (1) AL 030.7
~ House (1) 007A.2
~ Mountain (83) GA 080.8
~ Mount(ain) (1) GA 106.4
~ Mountain Freeway (2) 107.5
~ Mountain granite (1) n 081.8
~ Mountain melon (2) n 056.9

~ Mountain watermelon (1) n 056.9
~ Mountains (1) 056.9
~ River (1) AL 030.7
stoneboat (1) n 080.7
stonecutter (2) n 032.1
stoned (1) adj 115.7
stoneless (1) adj 054.3
Stoner Hill (2) 105.4
stone's throw (6) n 039.5
stones (43) n 031.6
Stones River (1) TN 030.7
Stonewall (4) LA 087.7
~ Jackson (2) 056.9
stoneware (1) n 088.7
Stony (2) 030.7
~ Creek (1) TN 030.7
~ Mountain (1) 056.9
stood (27) v 013.5
~ her up (1) v 082.1
~ him up (15) v 082.1
~ up (5) v 077.6
~ up with (1) v 082.3
stook (1) n 041.7
stool (38) n/v/adj 008.8
~ -bottom chair (1) n 008.8
~ chair (2) n 008.8
~ chairs (1) n 008.8
~ pigeon (14) n 101.3
~ pigeons (1) n 101.3
stoolie (2) n 101.3
stools (14) n 009.4
stoop (340) n/v/adj 096.4
~ behind (1) v 096.4
~ down (51) v 096.7
~ method (1) n 089.9
~ over (13) v 096.4
~ place (1) n 007A.1
stoop[V-r] (4) v 096.4
~ down (3) v 096.4
stoop[V-t] down (1) v 096.4
stooped (9) v 096.4
~ down (2) v 096.4
~ over (2) v 096.4
stooping (48) v 096.4
~ down (7) v 096.4
~ over (1) v 096.4
stoops (6) n/v 010.7
~ over (1) v 096.4
stop (176) n/v/adj 038.2
~ areas (1) n 106.2
~ at (1) v 085.4

~ going with him (1) v 082.1
~ it (1) v 033.2
~ off (1) v 085.4
~ out (1) v 083.2
~ out of (1) v 053.4
~ seeing him (1) v 082.1
~ the engagement (1) v 082.1
~ ticking (1) v 078.6
~ to (1) v 025.8
Stop (8) 116.2
~ and Shop (1) 116.2
~ N Go (5) 116.2
stop[V-p] (2) v 013.6
stop[V-r] (2) v 053.5
~ seeing him (1) v 082.1
stop[V-t] (2) v 007.3
stoplight (2) n 130.2
stopover (1) n 107.2
stopped (25) v 007.3
~ dating him (1) v 082.1
~ seeing him (2) v 082.1
~ up (2) v 102.6
stopper (618) n 020.4
stop(per) (3) n 020.4
stoppers (52) n 020.4
stopping (10) v/adj 007.3
~ off (1) v 007.3
~ places (1) n 107.2
stopple (8) n 020.4
stops (24) n 110.8
stopwatch (1) n 004.3
storage (439) n/adj 014.7
~ area (5) n 010.3
~ attic (1) n 009.8
~ bag (20) n 123.7
~ bags (7) n 123.7
~ barn (4) n 014.2
~ bin (8) n 014.4
~ bins (4) n 014.4
~ building (3) n 014.4
~ buildings (1) n 014.2
~ closet (18) n 009.7
~ garage (1) n 108.4
~ house (58) n 011.7
~ houses (1) n 010.3
~ place (7) n 015.5
~ places (2) n 010.3
~ room (237) n 010.3
~ rooms (3) n 007A.6

~ sections (1) n 010.3
~ shed (10) n 011.7
~ shelter (1) n 011.7
~ space (4) n 014.5
~ tanks (1) n 014.4
~ thing (1) n 123.7
~ truck (1) n 109.7
store (812) n/v/adj 094.2
~ away (1) v 048.4
~ bin (1) n 014.3
~ -bought (134) adj 045.1
~ -bought beds (1) n 045.1
~ -bought biscuits (1) n 045.1
~ -bought bread (138) n 045.1
~ -bought broom (3) n 045.1
~ -bought brooms (1) n 045.1
~ -bought cake (1) n 045.1
~ -bought clothes (2) n 090.9
~ -bought coffee (1) n 045.1
~ -bought dress (1) n 045.1
~ -bought food (1) n 045.1
~ -bought hair (1) n 045.1
~ -bought harrows (1) n 021.7
~ -bought jacks (1) n 045.1
~ -bought kind (1) n 045.1
~ -bought loaf bread (1) n 045.1
~ -bought patterns (1) n 039.7
~ -bought products (1) n 045.1
~ -bought stuff (2) n 045.1
~ -bought suit (1) n 045.1
~ -bought tables (1) n 045.1
~ -bought teeth (3) n 071.8

~ -bought tomatoes (1) n 045.1
~ -bought wheat bread (1) n 045.1
~ -boughten (4) adj 045.1
~ -boughten bread (4) n 045.1
~ bread (23) n 045.1
~ business (1) n 084.9
~ closet (2) n 009.6
~ places (1) n 025.6
Store (8) 087.3
store[N-i] (1) n 065.8
stored (1) v 052.5
storehouse (34) n/adj 011.7
~ place (1) n 010.3
storehouses (2) n 014.4
storeman (2) n 046.8
storeroom (200) n/adj 010.3
~ building (1) n 011.7
storerooms (7) n 010.3
stores (97) n 116.2
Stores (2) 116.2
storied (2) v/adj 098.6
~ on (1) v 101.3
stories (15) n 088.9
storing (3) v 057.4
stork (2) n 065.1
storm (769) n/v/adj 006.2
~ Celia (1) n 112.1
~ cellar (6) n 011.7
~ cellars (3) n 015.5
~ cloud (2) n 006.2
~ clouds (3) n 005.3
~ drains (1) n 030.2
~ fence (3) n 016.3
~ fences (3) n 126.1
~ house (8) n 011.7
~ houses (2) n 006.2
~ lamp (1) n 024.3
~ -like (2) adj 006.1
~ parties (1) n 082.5
~ pit (3) n 084.9
~ pits (2) n 015.5
~ rain (1) n 006.1
~ sheet (2) n 011.2
~ -sheeted (2) v 080.6
~ shelter (1) n 014.2
~ shutters (2) n 009.5
Storm (1) 030.7
~ Creek (1) AR 030.7

stormed (1) v 006.1
storming (9) v 005.6
~ up (2) v 005.6
storms (50) n 006.2
stormy (107) adj 005.6
~ day (9) n 005.5
~ -looking (1) adj 005.6
~ shower (1) n 006.6
~ time (1) n 006.2
~ weather (22) n 006.2
story (75) n/adj 092.2
~ -and-a-half (1) n 088.7
~ -and-a-half house (1) n 007A.4
~ -and-a-half type (1) n 004.4
~ -and-a-jump (1) n 080.6
stor(y)-and-a-half (1) n 118.9
storyteller (6) n 101.3
storytellers (1) n 101.3
Storyville (1) 098.8
stout (541) adj 073.1
~ -built (1) adj 073.1
~ -looking (2) adj 073.1
stoutened up (1) v 027.6
stouter (21) adj 073.1
stoutest (5) adj 073.1
Stovall (1) MS 087.9
stove (394) n/v/adj 070.7
~ chimley (1) n 008.1
~ factory (1) n 102.3
~ fingers (1) n 044.6
~ flue (36) n 023.2
~ flues (3) n 023.2
~ in (1) v 080.6
~ joint (1) n 023.2
~ joints (2) n 023.2
~ length (1) n 008.5
~ lengths (1) n 008.5
~ pot (1) n 017.6
~ pots (2) n 017.6
~ rake (1) n 008.8
~ room (25) n 009.9
~ smokestack (1) n 023.2
~ spoon (2) n 017.8
~ stack (2) n 023.2
~ up (4) v 075.5
stove[N-i] (1) n 008.6
stovepipe (518) n 023.2

stovepipes (35) n 023.2
stovepiping (3) n 023.2
stoves (62) n 118.4
stovewood (42) n/adj 008.6
~ box (5) n 023.1
~ house (1) n 011.7
stovewoods (1) n 008.4
stowaway (5) n/adj 010.3
~ closet (1) n 010.1
~ house (3) n 010.3
Stowe Creek (1) AR 030.7
STP (1) 114.2
straddle jack (2) n 021.6
straddled (1) v 080.9
straggler (1) n 041.5
straggling (1) adj 033.3
straggly (1) adj 073.3
straight (611) adj/adv 032.3
~ -back (2) adj 008.8
~ -back chair (5) n 008.8
~ -back chairs (5) n 008.8
~ black (6) adj 032.3
~ black coffee (2) n 032.3
~ blood (1) n 033.3
~ cane-bottom chair (1) n 008.8
~ cane-bottom chairs (1) n 008.8
~ chair (22) n 008.8
~ chairs (36) n 008.8
~ coffee (31) n 032.3
~ comb (2) n 022.2
~ cut (2) n 085.2
~ dancing (1) n 083.1
~ edge (1) n 055A.6
~ fence (3) n 016.4
~ -grain wood (1) n 008.6
~ hair (2) n 071.4
~ house (4) n 118.6
~ in (5) adv 108.3
~ -in parking (4) n 108.3
~ line (1) n 084.8
~ -line (1) adj 016.3
~ look (1) n 123.9
~ neck (3) n 056.6
~ -old (1) adj 032.3
~ -out (2) adj 069.4

~ -out corn bread (1) n 044.5
~ -out farming (2) n 075.6
~ parking (7) n 108.3
~ pin (7) n 026.5
~ pins (2) n 026.5
~ plow (1) n 021.6
~ plows (1) n 021.6
~ porch (2) n 007A.2
~ porches (1) n 010.8
~ potato (1) n 055.4
~ pots (1) n 017.6
~ -rail fence (4) n 016.4
~ razor (4) n 022.3
~ shift (7) n 110.7
~ shoot (1) n 118.6
~ shotgun (1) adj 007A.3
~ shotgun house (2) n 007A.2
~ shovel (5) n 021.6
~ stock (2) n 021.6
~ stocks (1) n 021.6
~ tea (1) n 032.3
~ -through flat (1) n 119.4
~ -through house (1) n 080.8
~ time (1) n 037.4
~ -tooth harrow (1) n 021.7
~ -tooth harrows (2) n 021.7
~ -top plow (1) n 021.6
~ up (2) adv 032.3
~ up and down (1) adj 004.9
~ up [J-0] down (1) adj 004.8
~ -up (2) adj 046.2
~ -up barrel (1) n 019.1
~ wooden box (1) n 079.1
~ yellow squash (1) n 056.6
Straight (2) 031.1
~ Mountain (1) TN 031.1
~ Row Creek (1) MS 030.7
straighten (41) v/adj 010.4

~ comb (2) n 022.2
~ out (1) v 010.4
~ up (28) v 010.4
straighten[V-t] back up
   (1) v 010.4
straightened (4) v 123.9
~ out (1) v 091.6
~ up (2) v 010.4
straightening (52) v/adj
   010.4
~ comb (3) n 022.2
~ combs (1) n 080.9
~ up (38) v 010.4
straightens (8) v 010.4
~ up (5) v 010.4
straightneck (3) adj 056.6
~ squash (2) n 056.6
strain (692) n/v/adj 048.2
~ cloth (1) n 048.2
~ harrow (1) n 021.7
~ out (1) v 048.2
~ up (1) v 048.2
strain[V-p] (1) v 048.2
strain[V-r] (1) v 048.2
strain[V-t] (2) v 048.2
strained (75) v 048.2
~ up (1) v 048.2
strainer (73) n/adj 048.2
~ cloth (1) n 048.2
~ cloths (1) n 048.2
strainers (7) n 048.2
straining (45) v/adj 048.2
~ cloths (1) n 048.2
~ rag (1) n 048.2
~ room (1) n 014.2
strains (7) n/v 048.2
strait (2) n 030.3
straitjackets (1) n 079.2
straitlaced (3) adj 074.8
strand (36) n/adj 028.4
~ of beads (17) n 028.4
~ of pearls (3) n 028.4
Strand (5) 106.4
~ Theater (1) 084.4
strands (5) n 028.4
~ of beads (2) n 028.4
strange (140) adj 074.7
~ -acting (1) adj 074.7
~ -looking (1) adj
   074.7
stranger (678) n 066.7
stran(ger) (1) n 066.7
stranger's (2) adj 066.7
~ name (1) n 066.7
strangers (27) n 066.7

strangle (3) n/v 006.2
strangle[V-t] (1) v 070.2
strangled (4) v 085.8
strangler (40) n/adj 006.1
~ figs (1) n 061.9
stranglers (7) n 006.1
strap (749) n/v/adj 022.3
~ thing (1) n 022.3
~ things (1) n 022.3
strapped (2) v 065.5
strapping (13) n/v/adj
   065.5
straps (44) n 028.5
strata (1) n 073.6
stratheads (1) n 084.8
stratus cloud (1) n 005.3
straw (124) n/adj 041.5
~ -and-dirt (1) adj
   008.1
~ basket (1) n 020.1
~ basket[N-i] (1) n
   020.1
~ bed (2) n 080.7
~ beds (2) n 080.7
~ boss (4) n 069.6
~ broom (49) n 010.5
~ brooms (18) n 010.5
~ field (1) n 029.5
~ -field (1) adj 015.9
~ fields (1) n 016.1
~ mattress (1) n 029.2
~ pillows (1) n 028.8
~ rocking chair (1) n
   008.8
~ shed (1) n 014.7
~ tick (4) n 029.2
~ ticks (2) n 009.4
strawberries (715) n 062.4
strawberry (237) n/adj
   062.4
~ bed (1) n 062.4
~ cobblers (1) n 048.3
~ corn (2) n 062.4
~ Danish (1) n 122.2
~ jam (1) n 062.4
~ jelly (2) n 062.4
~ leaves (1) n 062.4
~ melon (1) n 056.9
~ patch (14) n 062.4
~ patches (2) n 062.4
~ pie (1) n 062.4
~ popcorn (1) n 056.2
~ preserves (1) n 062.4
~ -raising country (2) n
   062.4

~ shortcake (8) n 062.4
~ tree (1) n 062.4
~ wine (1) n 062.4
strawber(ry) (8) n/adj
062.4
~ jam (1) n 062.4
~ patch (1) n 016.1
Strawberrry (10) AR
062.4
~ Hill (1) AR 062.4
~ Belt (1) 062.4
~ River (4) AR 030.7
strawberry[N-i] (4) n
062.4
straws (1) n 084.8
strawstack (2) n 014.8
strawstacks (2) n 014.6
stray (49) n/adj 033.3
~ breed (1) n 033.3
~ colt (2) n 065.7
~ dog (30) n 033.3
~ dogs (3) n 033.3
strays (3) n 033.3
streak (233) n/v/adj
088.7
~ -backed (1) adj 056.9
~ lightning (1) n 006.2
~ meat (1) n 046.3
~ of fat (44) n 046.3
~ of fat streak of lean
   (1) n 046.3
~ of lean (134) n 046.3
~ of lean bacon (3) n
   046.3
~ -of-lean gravy (1) n
   048.5
~ of lean meat (2) n
   046.3
~ of lean streak of fat
   (31) n 046.3
~ of the lean (1) n
   046.3
~ owl (1) n 059.1
~ [P-0] lean (1) n
   046.3
Streak (1) 087.4
streaked (59) adj 046.3
~ bacon (3) n 046.3
~ -head (5) adj 060.6
~ -head turtle (2) n
   060.6
~ -head turtles (1) n
   060.6
~ -headed terrapin (1)
   n 060.7

~ heads (1) n 080.6
~ lean (5) n 046.3
~ meat (24) n 046.3
~ -neck (1) adj 060.6
~ -neck turtle (1) n
   060.6
~ pork (1) n 046.3
~ with lean (1) adj
   046.3
streakedy (5) adj 084.8
~ -head turtle (1) n
   060.7
~ -head turtles (1) n
   060.6
~ -looking (1) adj
   002.6
streaker (2) n/adj 124.7
~ head (1) n 060.7
Streaker (1) 109.9
Streakers (1) 109.9
streaking (2) v/adj 088.8
~ off (1) v 088.8
~ owl (1) n 059.1
streaks (5) n 025.2
~ of lean (1) n 046.3
streaky (3) adj 060.6
~ head (1) n 060.6
~ meat (1) n 046.3
stream (424) n/adj 030.6
~ valleys (1) n 030.6
~ water (1) n 030.6
Stream (6) 030.7
streaming down (1) v
075.6
streamliner (1) n 092.9
streams (81) n 030.7
street (499) n/adj 031.6
~ address (6) n 100.8
~ bum (1) n 113.7
~ bus (2) n 085.3
~ cleaners (2) n 115.3
~ cook (1) n 084.9
~ -corner whore (1) n
   124.6
~ dance (3) n 083.1
~ dances (1) n 083.1
~ dealer (1) n 114.4
~ divider (1) n 107.3
~ dog (1) n 033.3
~ guy (1) n 113.7
~ hockey (1) n 130.4
~ lady (1) n 113.3
~ parking (2) n 108.1
~ people (3) n 113.3
~ person (2) n 113.7

~ pimp (4) n 113.5
~ preachers (1) n 067.8
~ railway (2) n 085.3
~ shoes (1) n 123.8
~ sweepers (1) n 085.3
~ whore (1) n 113.3
~ -wise (1) adj 080.9
~ woman (1) n 113.3
~ women (2) n 113.3
~ worker (1) n 113.3
Street (496) 001A.3
streetcar (228) n/adj 085.3
~ line (3) n 085.3
~ lines (1) n 085.3
~ tracks (1) n 085.3
(street)car (1) n 023.6
streetcars (395) n 085.3
streetlight (1) n 019.9
streetlights (2) n 019.9
streets (123) n 031.6
streetwalker (28) n 113.3
streetwalkers (6) n 113.3
strength (17) n 065.9
strengthening (2) v 007.2
strep throat (44) n 079.7
stretch (24) n/v/adj 130.6
~ bag (1) n 123.7
~ out (7) v 096.6
~ worms (1) n 060.5
Stretch (2) 087.9
stretcher (7) n/adj 111.5
~ rig (1) n 021.3
~ ring (1) n 021.2
stretchers (5) n 021.5
stretches across (1) v 028.9
stretchified (1) adj 076.6
stretching (3) v/adj 057.3
~ time (1) n 075.7
stretchy (1) adj 076.6
streusel (6) n 122.1
streusels (1) n 122.2
strew (1) v 098.6
stribble (1) n 021.7
strick (1) v 098.8
stricken (4) v 006.2
strict (8) adj 074.5
~ low (1) n 088.8
stricter (4) adj 070.7
strictest (1) adj 052.5
strictly (3) adv 085.7
stride (1) n 022.7
stridently (1) adv 090.4
strides (1) n 020.9

striffen (1) n 045.6
strike (12) v 066.8
~ at (1) v 032.1
~ with (2) v 039.7
striker (1) n 067.8
strikes (1) n 101.7
striking (4) v/adj 084.9
~ lightning (1) n 006.2
~ watch (1) n 004.3
string (971) n/v/adj 055A.4
~ bean (75) n 055A.4
~ -bean stuff (1) n 056.4
~ bean[N-i] (2) n 055A.4
~ beans (370) n 055A.4
~ bikini (1) n 092.7
~ music (2) n 083.1
~ neck (2) n 069.4
~ of (2) n 028.4
~ of bead[N-i] (2) n 028.4
~ of beads (327) n 028.4
~ of gold beads (1) n 028.4
~ of oxen (1) n 033.7
~ of pearls (31) n 028.4
~ of them (1) n 028.4
~ puller (1) n 115.3
~ quilts (1) n 029.1
~ [P-0] beads (2) n 028.4
string[N-i] (1) n 016.7
stringer (6) n 080.8
stringers (1) n 081.9
stringier (1) adj 055A.4
stringing (9) n/v/adj 055A.2
~ comb (1) n 080.7
stringless (8) adj 055A.4
~ bean (5) n 055A.4
~ green bean (1) n 055A.4
Stringless (5) 055A.4
~ Green Pod (3) 055A.4
~ Green Pods (1) 055A.4
strings (22) n 019.6
~ of beads (2) n 028.4
stringy (7) adj 073.3
strip (119) n/v/adj 031.9

~ bacon (2) n 046.7
~ boat (1) n 024.6
~ joint (1) n 114.9
~ joints (1) n 113.4
~ meat (1) n 046.7
~ mining (1) n 080.6
~ of fat (1) n 046.3
~ poker (2) n 130.7
~ sirloin steak (1) n 121.1
~ steak (2) n 121.1
~ wire (1) n 016.3
Strip (7) 087.5
stripe (40) n/v/adj 107.3
~ back (1) n 046.3
~ bass (2) n 059.9
~ melon (2) n 056.9
stripe[N-i] (1) n 056.9
striped (107) v/adj 056.9
~ bass (18) n 059.9
~ basses (1) n 059.9
~ beans (1) n 055A.4
~ cane (1) n 080.9
~ garter snake (1) n 081.9
~ gooseneck (1) n 056.9
~ head (1) n 060.6
~ -head terrapin (1) n 060.7
~ -headed (1) adj 060.6
~ heads (1) n 060.6
~ kitty (1) n 059.4
~ ladies (1) n 084.6
~ leg (1) n 060.7
~ like (1) adj 035.9
~ melon (2) n 056.9
~ melons (1) n 056.9
~ moccasin (1) n 088.7
~ -neck (1) adj 056.6
~ -neck turtle (1) n 060.6
~ polecat (1) n 059.4
~ sapsucker (1) n 059.3
~ toads (1) n 060.4
~ trout (1) n 059.9
~ wasp (7) n 060A.6
~ wasp[N-i] (1) n 060A.6
~ watermelon (4) n 056.9
~ watermelons (1) n 056.9
~ white half runners (1) n 055A.4

~ woodpecker (1) n 059.3
Striped (2) 056.9
~ Creaseback (1) 055A.7
stripedy (1) adj 055A.3
striper (1) n 056.9
stripes (15) n 107.3
striping (2) n 065.5
stripped (2) v 041.4
stripper (5) n 124.8
strippers (1) n 088.7
stripping (7) n/v 011.2
strips (25) n 110.8
striptease dance (1) n 083.1
stripy (3) adj 070.8
~ frog (1) n 060.2
~ leg (1) n 060.6
striving (1) v 057.4
stroganoff (1) adj 121.1
stroke (5) n 065.9
strokes (1) n 001A.2
stroll (214) n/v 064.6
~ around (1) v 064.6
~ around with (2) v 064.6
~ with (3) v 064.6
stroller (185) n 064.5
strol(ler) (1) n 064.5
strollers (13) n 064.5
strolling (19) v 064.6
Strolling Jim (1) 099.7
strong (1114) adj 073.1
~ -as-a-horse (1) adj 034.2
~ coffee (6) n 032.3
~ -coffee man (1) n 088.7
~ -like (1) adj 007.3
~ -looking (2) adj 073.1
~ -minded (7) adj 074.8
~ soil (1) n 029.8
~ -tempered (1) adj 075.1
~ -will (1) adj 074.8
~ -willed (7) adj 074.8
Strong (7) AR 087.6
~ River (2) MS 030.7
stronger (127) adj/adv 007.2
strongest (5) adj 073.1

strongheaded (5) adj 074.8
strongly (3) adv 073.1
strooch (1) n 033.3
strop (347) n/v 022.3
stropped (2) v 022.3
stropping (7) v/adj 022.3
strops (15) n 022.3
Stroud (1) AL 087.2
strow (1) v 081.8
strowed (1) v 015.9
struck (19) v/adj 006.2
  ~ at (1) v 032.1
  ~ on her (8) adj 081.4
  ~ on him (1) adj 081.4
  ~ on that girl (2) adj 081.4
  ~ on the girl (1) adj 081.4
  ~ up with (2) v 052.6
structure (3) n 030.2
strudel (15) n 048.3
strudels (3) n 048.3
struggle with (1) v 098.1
struggled with (1) v 098.1
struggling (1) v 057.4
strumpet (1) n 073.6
strung (43) v/adj 075.1
  ~ out (4) adj 114.3
  ~ out on (2) adj 099.5
  ~ out over (1) adj 080.7
  ~ up (1) v 058.3
strut (3) v 027.8
strutted (1) v 027.8
strutting (2) v 057.3
  ~ in (1) v 052.5
strychnine (1) n 078.4
Stuart (6) FL 087.2
  ~ Heights (1) 106.3
Stuarts (1) 054.8
stub (1) n 057.3
stubble (33) n/adj 041.5
  ~ cane (2) n 024.9
  ~ crop (2) n 041.5
  ~ ground (1) n 041.5
  ~ potatoes (1) n 041.5
stubbles (2) n 041.5
stubborn (470) adj 074.8
  ~ -headed (1) adj 074.8
  ~ -minded (1) adj 074.8
stubbornest (2) adj 074.8
Stubbs (2) TX 087.2

~ community (1) TX 087.3
Stubby's store (1) n 082.7
stubs (1) n 041.5
stucco (8) n/adj 007A.9
  ~ fence (1) n 016.6
  ~ flat (1) n 119.4
  ~ house (1) n 014.1
  ~ houses (3) n 014.1
stuccos (1) n 118.8
stuck (81) v/adj 104.3
  ~ him up (1) v 082.2
  ~ in his ways (1) adj 074.8
  ~ in their ways (1) adj 074.8
  ~ in your ways (2) adj 074.8
  ~ on (2) adj 028.1
  ~ on her (8) adj 081.4
  ~ on that gal (1) adj 081.4
  ~ on that girl (1) adj 081.4
  ~ on to her (1) adj 081.4
  ~ out (1) v 027.8
  ~ out from (1) v 053.8
  ~ to (3) v 125.5
  ~ -up (6) adj 080.6
  ~ -ups (1) n 069.7
Stuckey's (1) 107.2
stud (457) n/adj 034.1
  ~ bull (1) n 033.5
  ~ clothes (1) n 123.6
  ~ colt (1) n 034.1
  ~ fee (1) n 034.1
  ~ pony (1) n 034.1
Studebaker (2) 088.8
student (785) n/adj 068.7
  ~ bodies (1) n 068.7
  ~ council (2) n 068.7
  ~ government (1) n 085.6
  ~ pilots (1) n 068.7
students (130) n 068.7
studhorse (132) n 034.1
studhorses (9) n 034.1
studied (7) v 075.7
  ~ about (1) v 075.7
  ~ (a)bout (2) v 013.5
studies (3) n/v 083.5
studio (31) n/adj 007A.3
  ~ apartment (1) n 119.2

~ cot (2) n 009.1
~ couch (18) n 009.1
~ couches (4) n 009.1
~ room (1) n 007A.8
studios (1) n 119.1
studious (8) adj 125.5
studs (21) n 034.1
study (43) n/v 093.7
  ~ about (4) v 057.6
  ~ (a)bout (5) v 013.5
  ~ on (4) v 013.5
  ~ over (2) v 013.5
studying (24) v 088.9
  ~ about (4) v 088.7
  ~ (a)bout (9) v 013.5
  ~ on (1) v 013.5
stuff (319) n/v/adj 010.2
  ~ sausage (3) n 121.6
  ~ shirts (1) n 127.8
stuffed (12) v/adj 027.8
  ~ armchairs (1) n 008.8
  ~ chairs (3) n 008.8
  ~ with (2) v 032.4
stuffer (6) n 046.8
stuffing (12) n/adj 044.6
  ~ box (1) n 089.8
stuffy (1) adj 027.8
stumble (1) v 073.3
stumblebum (2) n 073.4
stumbled (4) v 070.2
  ~ upon (1) v 032.6
stumbles (1) v 073.3
stumbling (7) v/adj 073.3
  ~ blocks (1) n 065.8
stumbly (3) adj 073.3
stump (76) n/adj 050.8
  ~ fit (1) n 050.9
  ~ -hole juice (1) n 050.9
  ~ juice (12) n 050.8
  ~ jumper (3) n 069.9
  ~ jumpers (2) n 069.9
  ~ kickers (1) n 123.8
  ~ leg (1) n 067.8
  ~ liquor (7) n 050.9
  ~ mover (2) n 006.1
  ~ preacher (3) n 067.8
  ~ puller (2) n 021.6
  ~ pullers (2) n 097.6
  ~ pulling (1) v 097.6
  ~ rum (4) n 050.9
  ~ tail (1) n 081.9
  ~ water (6) n 050.8
  ~ whiskey (1) n 050.8
  ~ worm (1) n 060.5

Stump Creek (1) GA 030.3
stumpers (1) n 061.1
stumping (2) v 097.4
stumpknocker (14) n/adj 067.8
  ~ preacher (1) n 067.8
  ~ preachers (1) n 067.8
stumpknockers (7) n 059.9
stumps (19) n 117.7
stung (6) v 039.9
  ~ by (1) v 039.9
  ~ by the trouser worm (1) v 065.1
stunning (1) v 036.2
stunt (2) n 036.1
stunted (2) adj 035.9
stupe (3) n 073.4
stupid (160) adj 073.4
  ~ -ass (3) adj 128.5
sturdier (1) adj 002.6
Sturdivant (1) AL 087.6
sturdy (9) adj 074.1
sturgeon (2) n 059.9
sturgeons (2) n 059.9
Sturgis (1) MS 087.4
Stuttgart (13) AR 087.7
Stuyvesant (1) 086.2
sty (37) n 015.4
style (79) n/v/adj 130.8
  ~ up (1) v 028.1
styling (1) v 088.7
stylish (13) adj 123.6
  ~ clothes (3) n 123.6
suave (3) adj 123.6
sub (10) n/adj 121.7
  ~ rivers (1) n 030.6
  ~ sandwich (3) n 121.7
  ~ sandwiches (1) n 121.7
subcompact (4) n 109.1
subcontracts to (1) v 013.9
subdivided (1) v 025.4
subdivision (2) n 106.2
subdivisions (10) n 105.1
subdued (1) v 053.6
subfloor (2) n 011.8
subgrade (1) n 031.6
subject (12) n 075.1
subjects (1) n 080.9
submarine (69) n/adj 121.7

~ sandwich (22) n 121.7
~ sandwiches (6) n 121.7
submarines (8) n 121.7
subs (5) n 121.7
subscription (2) n/adj 104.5
~ school (1) n 104.5
subsequent (1) adj 100.5
subside (1) v 007.3
subsided (2) v 007.3
subsides (1) v 007.3
subsiding (16) v 007.3
subsoil (4) n/adj 029.8
~ plow (1) n 021.9
subsoiler (6) n 021.6
subsoilers (1) n 021.7
subsoiling (3) v/adj 093.8
~ plows (1) n 021.9
substance (8) n 031.6
substation (1) n 112.8
substations (1) n 112.8
substitute (2) n/adj 067.8
subtract (1) v 076.1
suburb (2) n 105.1
suburban (6) adj 070.8
~ areas (1) n 105.4
~ bus (1) n 109.5
~ neighborhoods (1) n 106.1
~ sedan (1) n 109.5
~ shopping centers (1) n 105.3
suburbs (8) n 105.1
subway (7) n/adj 085.3
~ system (1) n 109.9
subways (3) n 109.9
Sucarnoochee (2) AL MS 030.7
success (2) n 066.8
Success (1) 054.9
successful (1) adj 025.7
succotash (3) n 050.4
succumb (1) v 078.5
succumbed (11) v 078.6
~ to his wounds (1) v 078.5
such (961) pron/adj 103.3
~ and such (49) pron 103.3
suchlike (11) pron 103.3
suck (7) n/v/adj/interj 037.5
~ ass (1) n 125.6

~ bottle (1) n 080.7
~ up (1) v 125.6
Suck (2) 030.3
suck(x3) (1) interj 037.5
sucked under (1) v 096.1
sucker (33) n/adj 059.9
~ list (1) n 080.7
~ rod (1) n 089.8
~ rods (1) n 080.8
suckerfish (4) n 059.9
suckers (54) n 056.3
suckhole (3) n 030.5
suckholes (2) n 030.4
sucking pigs (1) n 035.5
suckle (11) v 033.8
suckling (3) n/adj 035.5
~ calf (1) n 033.8
sucklings (2) n 035.5
sucks (1) v 013.7
Sucks (1) 030.7
suction (4) n/adj 091.7
~ bag (1) n 116.8
suctions (1) n 080.9
suctor (1) n 070.7
sud[N-i] (1) n 121.9
Sudan (1) 041.5
sudden (35) n/adj 005.8
~ downpour (1) n 006.1
~ shower (1) n 006.1
suddenly (16) adv 001A.4
suds (37) n 121.9
sue (2) v 088.2
sued (2) v 092.8
~ by (1) v 092.8
suede (3) adj 123.8
~ shoe (1) n 123.8
~ shoes (2) n 123.8
suet cake (2) n 045.2
Suez Canal (1) 030.2
suffer[V-r] with (1) v 078.7
suffered (3) v 097.1
suffering (2) v 057.4
suffers with (2) v 032.8
sufficient (2) adj 074.1
suffocation (1) n 130.6
sug(x3) (1) interj 037.5
sugan (1) n 029.1
sugar (575) n/adj 051.3
~ ant (1) n 060A.2
~ ants (1) n 060A.9
~ -apple tree (1) n 096.8

~ -apple trees (1) n 061.8
~ babe (1) n 081.6
~ baby (1) n 081.5
~ bags (2) n 019.6
~ barrel (1) n 019.1
~ barrels (1) n 019.1
~ beet tree (1) n 061.5
~ beets (1) n 061.5
~ bin (1) n 096.9
~ boiler (1) n 017.6
~ bone (1) n 071.7
~ bowl (2) n 017.2
~ buns (1) n 122.2
~ camp (1) n 061.5
~ chemistry (1) n 090.9
~ -coated (1) adj 122.4
~ corn (6) n 056.2
~ -covered (1) adj 045.2
~ crowder (1) n 088.9
~ crowder peas (1) n 055A.4
~ cure (1) n 046.7
~ -cure (1) v 046.4
~ -cure ham (1) n 121.3
~ -cured (10) adj 046.3
~ -cured bacon (1) n 046.5
~ -cured ham (3) n 046.5
~ -cured meat (3) n 046.5
~ daddy (3) n 089.7
~ diabetes (4) n 080.9
~ -dipped doughnut (1) n 045.2
~ -dipped doughnuts (1) n 122.4
~ doughnut (2) n 122.5
~ doughnuts (5) n 122.4
~ farm (1) n 061.6
~ foot (1) n 081.6
~ -frosted (1) adj 122.4
~ furnace (1) n 051.5
~ glaze (1) n 122.4
~ -glaze doughnuts (1) n 122.4
~ grove (5) n 061.6
~ gum (1) n 061.8
~ kettle (7) n 017.6
~ kettles (1) n 017.6
~ lump (1) n 081.5

~ mamma (1) n 084.6
~ maple (97) n 061.5
~ -maple grove (2) n 061.6
~ -maple orchard (1) n 061.6
~ maple trees (2) n 061.5
~ maples (17) n 061.5
~ meat (2) n 056.9
~ -meated (1) adj 056.9
~ melon (2) n 056.7
~ mill (2) n 051.2
~ orchard (4) n 061.6
~ peas (2) n 055A.2
~ pie (1) n 064.4
~ potato (1) n 055.4
~ pumpkins (2) n 056.5
~ refinery (1) n 051.2
~ rolls (1) n 122.5
~ sack (15) n 019.6
~ sacks (10) n 019.6
~ shell (4) n 017.8
~ spoon (1) n 017.8
~ squash (1) n 056.6
~ syrup (8) n 048.5
~ tit (1) n 080.7
~ tomatoes (1) n 055.3
~ -top doughnuts (1) n 045.2
~ tree (25) n 061.5
~ -tree grove (1) n 061.6
~ -tree orchard (2) n 061.6
~ trees (8) n 061.5
~ twist (1) n 122.7
~ twisted doughnut (1) n 122.7
~ type (1) n 061.5
~ whiskey (1) n 050.8
~ yams (2) n 055.5
Sugar (53) 064.4
~ Babe (1) 063.2
~ Baby (4) 056.9
~ Bab(y) (1) 056.9
~ Creek (10) AR GA LA TN 030.7
~ Creek Road (1) 031.6
~ Daddy (1) 081.5
~ Dumpling (1) 064.4
~ Foot (2) 063.1
~ Hill (5) 106.3
~ House (1) 090.9
~ Lump (1) 055.3

~ Pie (3) 064.4
~ Pie pumpkins (1) n 056.5
~ Pudding (1) 064.4
~ Town (1) 056.9
~ Valley (1) GA 087.5
Sug(ar) Creek (2) LA 030.7
sugarberries (2) n 062.4
sugarberry (4) n/adj 061.9
~ tree (2) n 061.5
sugarcane (100) n/adj 051.2
~ field (2) n 016.1
~ fields (1) n 016.1
~ molasses (4) n 051.2
~ (mo)lasses (1) n 051.2
~ patch (3) n 016.1
~ syrup (17) n 051.3
~ syrups (1) n 051.3
~ tree (2) n 061.5
sugared (1) adj 122.4
sugarhouse (5) n 011.9
sugaring party (1) n 080.6
Sugarloaf (1) 056.9
Sugartree Creek (1) TN 030.7
sugary coating (1) n 122.4
suggest (1) v 070.9
suggests (1) v 065.8
sugs (1) n 088.9
suh (1) interj 037.5
suicide (4) n/adj 085.9
~ football (1) n 130.5
suie (2) n F 008.7
suit (1266) n/v/adj 027.7
~ bag (16) n 123.7
~ bags (3) n 123.7
~ coat (3) n 027.1
~ up (1) v 038.6
~ vest (1) n 027.3
suit[N-i] (1) n 055A.7
suit[V-p] (1) v 013.8
suitable (2) adj 033.3
suitcase (21) n/adj 027.7
~ college (1) n 083.6
~ teachers (1) n 080.6
suitcases (2) n 098.1
suite (57) n 009.4
Suite (1) 066.9
suiter (2) n 123.7
suites (7) n 009.4

suitor (16) n 081.5
suits (79) n 027.7
sukey (2) adj 070.8
sulfur (13) n/adj 054.4
~ beans (2) n 055A.4
~ mine (1) n 065.9
~ water (3) n 030.7
~ wood (1) n 024.9
sulky (8) n/adj 080.6
~ day (1) n 005.4
~ days (1) n 005.5
~ plow (3) n 021.6
~ rake (1) n 014.9
sullen (1) adj 075.1
Sullivan (4) TN 087.3
~ City (1) TX 087.2
Sullivans Hollow (2) MS 086.2
sully (1) interj 038.3
Sulphur (22) LA TX 087.9
~ Branch (1) TN 030.7
~ Dell Ball Park (1) 106.9
~ Fork (1) TN 030.7
~ River (5) AR LA TX 030.7
~ Spring (1) TN 030.7
~ Springs (6) AR TN TX 106.3
Sulph(ur) Forks (1) TN 030.7
sultan (1) n 056.6
sultry (3) adj 005.5
~ weather (1) n 040.7
Sulze (1) n G 047.1
sum (3) n 001A.4
Sum (1) 116.2
sumac (618) n/adj 062.2
~ berries (3) n 062.2
~ bush (12) n 062.2
~ bushes (4) n 062.2
~ molasses (1) n 051.2
~ plant (1) n 062.2
~ poison ivory (1) n 062.2
~ tree (12) n 062.2
Sumac (2) 030.7
~ Spring (1) GA 030.7
sumacs (10) n 062.2
sumblesault (4) n 095.5
sumblesaults (1) n 095.5
sumbleset (8) n 095.5
sumblesets (1) n 095.5
Sumi Bayou (1) LA 030.7

Sumiton (1) AL 087.7
summer (105) n/adj 056.6
~ breeches (1) n 027.4
~ car (1) n 085.3
~ cold (1) n 076.3
~ crookneck (1) n 056.6
~ crooknecks (1) n 056.6
~ day (1) n 005.4
~ dining room (1) n 080.6
~ evenings (1) n 002.5
~ garden (3) n 050.5
~ gardens (1) n 050.5
~ grapes (1) n 062.4
~ grease (1) n 023.7
~ house (1) n 014.1
~ job (1) n 070.3
~ kitchen (14) n 009.9
~ kitchens (3) n 009.9
~ park (1) n 022.5
~ party (1) n 130.7
~ peaches (1) n 054.3
~ potatoes (2) n 055.4
~ rain (2) n 006.6
~ religion (1) n 090.9
~ sausage (3) n 121.6
~ school (3) n 083.2
~ shower (3) n 006.6
~ showers (1) n 006.6
~ squash (24) n 056.6
~ storm (1) n 006.2
~ suit (1) n 027.7
~ term (1) n 083.6
~ thunderstorm (1) n 006.2
~ trout (1) n 059.9
~ turnips (1) n 055A.8
Summer (3) 107.5
~ Street (1) 107.7
Summerall (1) FL 087.3
Summerdale (1) AL 087.3
Summerfield (1) AL 087.9
Summerhill (3) 106.3
summers (2) n 001A.3
Summers Creek (1) TN 030.7
summertime (5) n 074.4
Summerville (1) GA 087.5
Summit (7) MS TN 087.2
Sumner (6) GA MS TN 087.2
sump (3) adj 030.4

~ hole (1) n 030.4
~ pump (2) n 080.7
Sumrall (4) MS 087.2
sums (1) n 051.5
Sumter (21) AL GA SC 087.2
~ County (7) AL FL GA 087.2
sun (348) n/adj 003.2
~ beans (1) n 055A.4
~ blade (1) n 104.8
~ -blade (1) adj 015.8
~ box (1) n 080.6
~ day (1) n 005.4
~ deck (13) n 010.8
~ decks (4) n 010.8
~ dog (1) n 081.9
~ -dry (1) v 088.9
~ line (1) n 080.6
~ parlor (17) n 118.1
~ parlors (1) n 118.1
~ perch (19) n 059.9
~ perches (3) n 059.9
~ porch (57) n 010.8
~ porches (1) n 010.8
~ -room (68) n 118.1
~ -room porch (1) n 118.1
~ -rooms (2) n 118.1
~ shades (1) n 009.5
Sun (3) 108.5
~ Bank (1) 108.5
sunbath (1) n 007A.3
Sunbeam (5) FL 105.7
~ Street (1) 102.3
sunbonnets (2) n 084.8
sunbreak (2) n 003.2
sunburn (2) n/adj 079.8
~ Americans (1) n 069.2
Sunday (2592) 002.1
~ afternoon (7) n 002.3
~ afternoons (2) n 002.3
~ baby (1) n 065.7
~ best (2) n 027.7
~ brunch (1) n 048.6
~ china (4) n 017.1
~ clothes (30) n 123.6
~ dinner (1) n 002.1
~ dinners (1) n 002.1
~ dishes (10) n 017.1
~ dress (2) n 027.7
~ evening (9) n 002.1

~ -go-to-meeting (2) n 027.7

~ -go-to-meeting clothes (12) n 088.7

~ -go-to-meeting pants (1) n 027.4

~ -go-to-meeting suit (1) n 027.7

~ -go-[P-0]-meeting (1) adj 027.7

~ house (2) n 012.1

~ -meeting clothes (1) n 027.7

~ morning (26) n 002.1

~ morn(ing) (2) n 002.1

~ mornings (1) n 002.1

~ muffin (1) n 044.8

~ night (8) n 002.1

~ -night mullet supper (1) n 083.1

~ -night snack (1) n 048.6

~ outfit (1) n 027.7

~ pants (2) n 027.7

~ riggings (1) n 096.9

~ school (59) n 002.1

~ -school books (1) n 002.1

~ -school class (3) n 002.1

~ -school parties (1) n 130.7

~ -school picnics (1) n 130.7

~ -school teacher (9) n 002.1

~ schools (1) n 002.1

~ set (1) n 017.1

~ shirt (2) n 089.9

~ shoes (1) n 027.7

~ suit (19) n 027.7

~ week (384) n 003.7

Sun(day) (1) 002.1

Sunday[N-i] (1) 003.6

Sundays (41) 002.1

sundown (614) n 003.4

Sundown (1) 003.4

sundry (2) adj 075.6

sunfish (8) n 059.9

sunflower (4) n 056.4

Sunflower (10) LA MS 101.4

~ County (1) MS 087.3

~ River (1) MS 030.7

sunflowers (6) n 101.4

sung (11) v 080.7

sunk (3) v 098.6

Sunk Lake (1) TN 030.7

Sunken Garden (1) 106.7

sunlight (5) n 003.2

sunning (1) n 064.6

sunny (81) adj 005.4

~ day (55) n 005.4

~ -side (1) n 046.2

~ -side up (10) n 046.1

Sunny (2) 077.9

~ Isles Casino (1) 077.9

~ South (1) TX 087.2

Sunnyside (2) 106.2

Sunnyville Road (1) 107.7

sunrise (398) n 003.2

Sunrise (2) 105.1

sunrises (1) n 003.2

sunroof (5) n/adj 118.1

~ top (1) n 109.2

sunset (301) n/adj 003.4

~ trout (1) n 059.9

Sunset (6) LA 087.1

~ Island (1) 106.1

~ Park (1) 105A.7

~ View (1) 106.2

sunsets (2) n 003.4

sunshade (3) n 028.6

sunshades (1) n 028.6

sunshine (21) n/adj 005.4

~ day (11) n 005.4

Sunshine (2) 105.4

~ Additions (1) 105.4

~ Skyway (1) 107.5

sunshining (2) adj 005.4

sunshiny (68) adj 005.4

~ day (55) n 005.4

~ days (2) n 005.4

~ weather (1) n 005.4

sunspots (1) n 077.4

sunstroke (1) n 090.8

suntan (1) n 073.6

sunup (470) n 003.2

sup (1) n 069.6

super (25) n/adj/prefix 119.5

~ black (1) n 097.8

~ fly (1) n 123.6

~ Jew (1) n 126.7

~ jobs (1) n 080.8

~ -macho (1) adj 081.9

~ -sensitive (1) adj 075.1

~ subs (1) n 121.7

~ toggery (1) n 123.6

~ togs (1) n 123.6

Superdome (5) 108.5

supereducated (1) adj 083.5

superfluous (3) adj 070.6

superhighway (6) n 031.6

superhighways (4) n 107.1

superintendent (26) n 119.5

superintendents (1) n 115.3

superior officer (1) n 069.6

Superior (1) WI 087.5

supermarket (80) n/adj 094.2

~ -type store (1) n 116.1

supermarkets (25) n 116.1

supermarts (1) n 116.2

supers (2) n 114.4

superslab (1) n 107.1

superstitious (7) adj 074.3

superstore (2) n 116.1

superstore[N-i] (1) n 080.9

supervision (2) n 085.6

supervisor (11) n 069.6

supervisors (1) n 070.8

supper (97) n/adj 048.6

~ dishes (1) n 018.1

suppers (12) n 066.9

suppertime (16) n 002.5

supple (7) adj 074.1

supplier (5) n 114.4

supplies (4) n 021.4

supply (11) n/adj 067.8

~ pastor (1) n 067.8

~ pastors (1) n 067.8

~ preacher (3) n 067.8

~ room (2) n 011.7

support (6) n/v/adj 022.1

~ shoes (1) n 123.8

supported (1) v 065.4

supporters (6) n 028.5

supporting (1) v 013.8

suppose (133) v 094.1

~ to (4) v 058.4

supposed (395) v 065.8

~ to (383) v 058.1

~ to've (3) v 058.1

~ [P-0] (2) v 052.4

(sup)posed to (2) v 058.1

supposedly (2) adv 066.8

suppository stabbers (1) n 122.8

Supreme Being (1) 069.4

sure (2886) adj/adv 091.2

~ enough (70) adv 091.2

~ (e)nough (124) adv 091.2

Sure Crop (1) 056.2

surely (84) adv 091.1

surel(y) (1) adv 091.2

surf (2) adj 024.6

~ boat (1) n 024.6

~ eaters (1) n 069.4

Surf (3) 087.3

surface (29) n/adj 031.7

~ dog (1) n 033.3

~ rains (1) n 006.6

~ road (3) n 031.6

~ toilets (1) n 012.1

surfaced (3) v/adj 031.5

~ land (1) n 029.6

surfer shoes (1) n 123.8

surfers (1) n 123.3

Surfside (2) 106.1

~ Beach (1) FL 086.4

surgeon (2) n 084.6

surgeons (1) n 025.6

surgery (4) n 080.1

Surinam cherries (2) n 062.1

surlies (1) n 033.5

surly (1) n 033.5

surname (2) n 064.4

surplus (2) adj 010.2

~ junk (1) n 010.2

~ stock (1) n 036.5

surprise (11) n/adj/interj 096.4

~ parties (3) n 130.7

~ party (1) n 130.7

surprise[V-r] (1) v 092.2

surprised (7) v 090.6

surprising shower (1) n 006.1

Surrency (2) GA 087.4

surrey (33) n 066.8

surreys (6) n 081.8

surrogate (4) n/adj 129.5

~ father (2) n 129.5

~ mother (1) n 129.5

surround (1) v 084.8

surrounded by (1) v 106.6

survey (1) n 075.7

surveyor (2) n 066.9

Surveyor Street (1) 106.3
surveys (1) v 068.5
survive (1) v 078.5
survived (1) v 053.5
survivors (1) n 078.5
Susan Drive (1) 107.9
Susans (1) 080.6
Susie Q (1) 083.1
suspect (6) v 013.7
(su)spect (5) v 103.9
suspected (1) v 101.6
suspended porch (1) n 010.8
suspender (9) n/adj 028.5
  ~ -like (1) adj 028.5
  ~ strops (1) n 028.5
(su)spender (2) n 028.5
suspender[N-i] (9) n 028.5
suspenders (824) n 028.5
(su)spenders (92) n 028.5
(sus)penders (2) n 028.5
suspension (1) n 029.8
suspicion (1) v 013.7
suspicioned (5) v 093.6
suspicious (2) adj 074.2
Suss Kartoffel (1) n G 055.5
sut (1) v 049.3
sute (1) adj S 055.3
sute(x3) (1) interj 037.5
Sutton Creek (1) LA 030.7
Suwannee (19) FL GA 087.3
  ~ Coun(ty) (1) FL 087.4
  ~ River (12) FL GA 030.7
suzette (1) adj F 122.1
swag (17) n/v 030.5
  ~ down (1) v 027.8
Swag (1) 029.6
swagging (1) v 033.9
swaggy places (1) n 029.6
swags (2) n 030.5
Swahilis (1) 069.3
Swain Show (1) 088.9
Swainsboro (2) GA 087.4
swale (3) n 031.9
swallow (961) n/v/adj 057.2
  ~ a watermelon seed (1) v 065.1
  ~ fork (6) n 057.2

~ part (1) n 057.2
~ pipe (1) n 071.7
~ with (1) v 053.4
swal(low) (97) v 057.2
swallow[V-r] (4) v 065.1
  ~ a pumpkinseed (2) v 065.1
  ~ a watermelon seed (1) v 065.1
  ~ the whole cabbage (1) v 065.1
swallow[V-t] (1) v 098.6
swallowed (83) v 057.2
  ~ a peach seed (1) v 065.1
  ~ a pumpkinseed (29) v 065.1
  ~ a watermelon (4) v 065.1
  ~ a watermelon seed (11) v 065.1
  ~ the pumpkinseed (1) v 065.1
  ~ the seed (1) v 065.1
  ~ up (1) v 057.2
swallower (3) n 071.7
swallowing (12) v 057.2
swallows (16) n/v 057.2
swam (657) v 095.6
  ~ across (16) v 095.6
  ~ out (2) v 095.6
swammed (9) v 095.5
swamp (768) n/adj 029.6
  ~ angels (1) n 069.9
  ~ area (1) n 029.6
  ~ are(a) (1) n 029.6
  ~ areas (2) n 029.6
  ~ bait (1) n 060.5
  ~ buggy (1) n 109.6
  ~ cabbage (3) n 029.6
  ~ chickens (1) n 080.7
  ~ country (4) n 029.6
  ~ cows (1) n 033.6
  ~ dirt (1) n 029.6
  ~ fever (6) n 081.9
  ~ fields (1) n 029.4
  ~ fish (1) n 059.9
  ~ flies (1) n 060A.4
  ~ frog (1) n 060.3
  ~ grass (3) n 029.6
  ~ ground (1) n 029.6
  ~ hickory nut (1) n 061.8
  ~ hog (1) n 035.9
  ~ hogs (2) n 035.9

~ hook (1) n 088.7
~ hunting (1) n 029.6
~ -like (1) adj 029.6
~ maple (4) n 061.8
~ maples (1) n 061.5
~ marshy land (1) n 029.6
~ nigger (1) n 069.3
~ niggers (1) n 069.3
~ owl (14) n 059.2
~ owls (1) n 059.2
~ people (1) n 128.3
~ pine (1) n 061.8
~ place (1) n 029.6
~ rat (5) n 069.9
~ rats (1) n 069.9
~ root (5) n 061.4
~ -root tea (1) n 061.4
~ squirrel (1) n 059.7
~ stompers (2) n 069.9
~ water (2) n 029.6
~ wiggler (1) n 060.5
~ wigglers (1) n 060.5
~ worm (1) n 060.5
Swamp (32) 119.9
  ~ Church (1) 093.7
  ~ Pool (1) 105.1
swampberries (1) n 062.4
swampberry (1) n 062.4
swamped (1) v 024.7
swampers (1) n 069.9
swamping (3) v/adj 021.4
  ~ land (1) n 029.6
swampland (137) n 029.6
swamplands (3) n 029.6
Swampoodle Creek (1) TX 030.7
swamps (132) n 029.6
swampy (137) adj 029.6
  ~ area (3) n 029.6
  ~ areas (2) n 029.6
  ~ ground (3) n 029.6
  ~ land (48) n 029.6
  ~ -like place (1) n 002.6
  ~ place (6) n 029.6
  ~ places (1) n 029.6
  ~ -type land (1) n 029.6
  ~ water (1) n 029.6
swan (5) adj/interj 095.3
  ~ dive (1) n 095.3
  ~ -neck chair (1) n 008.9
Swan (2) 030.7

~ Creek (1) AL 030.7
swank (1) adj 123.6
swanky (7) adj 123.6
  ~ togs (1) n 123.6
swanny (8) interj 092.3
swap (11) v/adj 065.5
  ~ out (1) v 088.7
  ~ over (1) v 075.6
  ~ shop (1) n 114.6
  ~ shops (1) n 088.7
  ~ up (1) v 093.6
swap[V-r] (1) v 080.6
swapped (9) v 088.8
swapping (5) v 094.2
  ~ slobber (1) v 081.7
swarm (3) n 055A.8
swarming (1) v 059.5
swarthy (3) adj 072.9
Swartz (1) LA 087.7
swat (1) n 075.9
swatch (59) n 026.2
swath (2) n/v 026.2
swayback (2) adj/adv 065.1
  ~ mule (1) n 033.7
swear (10) v 092.1
  ~ to (4) v 089.3
swears (1) v 025.4
sweat (410) n/v/adj 077.3
  ~ bee (25) n 060A.8
  ~ bees (20) n 060A.6
  ~ blossom (1) n 064.4
  ~ fly (1) n 060A.8
  ~ hog (1) n 109.4
  ~ hogs (1) n 128.7
  ~ off (1) v 077.3
sweat[V-p] (3) v 077.3
sweat[V-t] (1) v 077.3
sweated (462) v 077.3
  ~ down (1) v 077.3
  ~ up (1) v 077.3
sweater (44) n 027.1
sweaters (2) n 027.3
sweating (85) v 077.3
  ~ down (1) v 077.3
sweats (23) v 077.3
sweatshirt (1) n 027.3
sweaty (17) adj 077.3
Swede (2) 128.8
Sweden (2) 086.6
Swedes (8) 128.8
Swedish (2) 080.7
  ~ ivy (1) n 080.7
  ~ pastry (1) n 122.2
swee (1) interj 038.3

swee(x2) (1) interj 038.3
sweep (137) n/v/adj 010.4
~ broom (1) n 010.5
~ out (4) v 010.4
~ plow (3) n 021.6
~ rake (1) n 014.8
~ stock (6) n 021.6
~ stocks (1) n 021.6
~ up (7) v 010.4
~ with (2) v 032.4
sweeped with (1) v 098.6
sweeper (43) n/adj 116.7
~ bag (1) n 116.8
sweepers (15) n 116.7
sweeping (33) v/adj 010.4
~ out (1) v 010.4
~ plow (1) n 021.6
~ rake (1) n 120.7
~ up (3) v 010.4
sweeps (60) n/v 010.4
sweet (1801) adj 073.2
~ bacon (1) n 046.3
~ bay (5) n 061.9
~ bay prune (1) n 061.4
~ biscuit (1) n 045.2
~ boudin (1) n 047.3
~ bread (31) n 044.3
~ breads (1) n 044.4
~ buns (1) n 122.2
~ bush (1) n 062.7
~ cake (3) n 044.4
~ cake doughnut (1) n 045.2
~ cakes (1) n 044.4
~ can peaches (1) n 090.8
~ child (1) n 064.4
~ cider (1) n 050.9
~ clabber (1) n 047.7
~ -clabber milk (1) n 048.1
~ corn (272) n 056.2
~ corn bread (2) n 044.6
~ cream (2) n 048.5
~ dirt (1) n 029.9
~ doughnuts (1) n 045.2
~ ear (1) n 056.2
~ feed (2) n 092.8
~ gum (152) n 061.8
~ -gum bark (1) n 061.4

~ gum sapling (1) n 061.8
~ -gum smacker (1) n 069.9
~ -gum stool (1) n 002.6
~ -gum toothbrush (1) n 061.8
~ gum tree (18) n 061.8
~ gum trees (23) n 061.8
~ gums (8) n 061.8
~ guy (1) n 124.1
~ ham (1) n 121.3
~ loaf (1) n 045.2
~ Lucy (2) n 114.7
~ magnolia (1) n 062.9
~ mamma (2) n 081.6
~ man (1) n 124.7
~ maple (2) n 061.5
~ melons (2) n 056.7
~ milk (33) n 048.2
~ mouth (1) n 081.8
~ -mouth (1) v 088.7
~ -mouthed (1) adj 080.8
~ myrtle (1) n 062.8
~ name (1) n 064.4
~ -olive tree (1) n 061.9
~ on her (18) adj 081.4
~ on them (1) adj 081.4
~ onion (4) n 055.6
~ onions (7) n 055.6
~ patootie (1) n 081.6
~ pea (1) n 055A.2
~ peaches (1) n 054.3
~ peas (9) n 055A.3
~ pepper (3) n 055.6
~ peppers (4) n 055.7
~ potato (292) n 055.5
~ -potato (1) adj 055.5
~ po(tato) (1) n 055.5
~ (po)tato (2) n 055.5
~ -potato bed (1) n 015.5
~ -potato bin (1) n 055.5
~ -potato bread (3) n 044.4
~ -potato cobbler pie (1) n 055.5

~ -potato coffee (1) n 048.8
~ -potato crop (1) n 055.5
~ -potato fluff (1) n 055.5
~ -potato house (1) n 015.5
~ -potato patch (9) n 055.5
~ -potato patches (1) n 016.1
~ -potato pie (1) n 055.5
~ -potato pies (1) n 055.5
~ -(po)tato pumpkin (1) n 056.6
~ -potato souffle (1) n 081.9
~ -potato squash (1) n 056.6
~ potato[N-i] (3) n 055.5
~ potatoes (622) n 055.5
~ (po)tatoes (7) n 055.5
~ pumpkin (1) n 056.5
~ pumpkins (1) n 056.5
~ roll (52) n 122.2
~ rolls (37) n 122.2
~ sauce (4) n 048.5
~ shrub (2) n 062.2
~ shrubs (1) n 062.7
~ Spanish onions (1) n 055.6
~ squash (1) n 056.6
~ stone (1) n 023.4
~ talk (2) n 081.4
~ -talk (6) v 081.8
~ -talking (1) v 081.8
~ tender corn (1) n 056.2
~ thing (2) n 124.1
~ tomatoes (1) n 055.3
~ tooth (1) n 025.4
~ water (4) n 051.3
~ -water (1) adj 088.8
~ watermelon (1) n 056.9
~ wine (1) n 114.7
~ wines (1) n 114.7
Sweet (57) 064.4
~ Auburn (1) 107.6

~ Auburn Avenue (1) 107.7
~ Lake (4) LA TX 087.3
~ Lucy (10) 050.9
~ Mamma (1) 063.7
~ Pea (1) 064.4
~ Sweet Sweet (1) 064.4
~ Texas Grano Number Thirty-Two (1) 055.7
~ Valikia (1) 056.9
~ Water (2) AL 087.6
~ Williams (1) 056.9
sweetbread (5) n 037.2
sweetbreads (9) n 037.3
sweeten (2) adj 045.2
~ bread (1) n 045.2
~ cake (1) n 045.2
sweeten[V-t] (1) v 032.4
sweetening (39) n 048.5
Sweetening Town (2) 105.1
sweeter (18) adj 066.1
sweetest (7) adj 025.6
sweetheart (426) n 081.6
Sweetheart (10) 064.4
~ melon (1) n 056.9
sweethearting (1) v 081.7
sweetheart's father (1) n 081.6
sweethearts (31) n 081.5
sweetie (29) n/adj 081.6
~ gum tree (1) n 061.8
~ pie (3) n 081.6
Sweetie (8) 064.4
~ Pie (5) 064.4
sweetmeats (1) n 037.2
sweets (5) n 122.1
Sweets (5) 064.4
sweetshop (2) n 116.2
sweetwater trout (1) n 059.9
Sweetwater (21) TN TX 087.7
~ Branch (3) AL FL GA 030.7
~ breeches (1) n 027.4
~ Creek (5) FL GA TN 030.7
~ Oaks (1) 106.1
Sweetwaters (1) 080.6
swell (507) v/adj 077.6
~ out (3) v 077.6

~ up (112) v 077.6
swell[V-p] (1) v 077.6
swell[V-r] (24) v 077.6
  ~ up (5) v 077.6
swell[V-t] (12) v 077.6
  ~ up (2) v 077.6
swelled (418) v 077.6
  ~ out (2) v 077.6
  ~ up (126) v 077.6
swelleded up (1) v 077.6
swelling (53) n/v 077.6
  ~ up (5) v 077.6
swells (31) v 077.6
  ~ up (12) v 077.6
swelt (2) v 077.6
  ~ up (1) v 077.6
swept (20) v 010.4
swerve (1) v 085.2
swift (8) n/adj 007.2
  ~ piece (1) n 088.8
  ~ water (1) n 031.5
Swift Creek (6) AL FL GA 030.7
swifter (1) adj 066.1
swiftly (2) adv 074.1
Swiftown (1) MS 087.2
swifts (1) n 096.7
swiggling across (1) v 080.7
swill (19) n/adj 017.4
  ~ bucket (9) n 017.4
  ~ pail (3) n 017.4
swiller (1) n 017.4
swillers (1) n 112.5
swim (746) n/v/adj 095.6
  ~ across (3) v 095.6
  ~ along (1) v 095.6
  ~ around (1) v 095.6
  ~ back (1) v 095.6
  ~ hole (3) n 095.6
  ~ holes (2) n 095.6
  ~ in (3) v 095.6
  ~ like (1) v 095.6
  ~ out (1) v 095.6
swim[V-p] (2) v 095.6
swim[V-r] (55) v 095.6
  ~ across (1) v 095.6
  ~ out (2) v 095.6
swim[V-t] (50) v 095.6
swimmed (83) v 095.6
  ~ across (4) v 095.6
  ~ out (2) v 095.6
swimmer (2) n 095.6
swimming (164) n/v/adj 095.6

~ across (1) v 104.5
~ hole (9) n 095.6
~ holes (2) n 095.6
~ out (1) v 095.6
~ parties (2) n 130.7
~ party (1) n 130.7
~ pool (5) n 095.6
~ suit (1) n 095.6
~ turtle (1) n 060.6
swimmingest (1) adj 002.6
swimmy (1) adj 090.9
swims (15) v 095.6
swimsuits (1) n 095.6
swinch owl (1) n 059.2
swindle (2) n/v 073.5
  ~ away (1) v 088.8
swindler (3) n 073.5
swine (24) n 035.3
swines (3) n 035.5
swing (886) n/v/adj 022.9
  ~ around (1) n 083.1
  ~ arounds (1) n 022.7
  ~ bands (1) n 130.9
  ~ billy (1) n 089.8
  ~ blade (2) n 120.1
  ~ boards (1) n 022.9
  ~ couch (1) n 009.1
  ~ dance (1) n 083.1
  ~ dancing (1) n 083.1
  ~ fly (1) n 083.1
  ~ horse (1) n 039.4
  ~ Josie (1) n 083.1
  ~ mules (2) n 039.4
  ~ music (1) n 130.8
  ~ out (2) v 022.9
  ~ seat (2) n 022.9
  ~ set (4) n 022.9
  ~ team (2) n 039.4
  ~ the statue (1) n 130.5
  ~ tire (1) n 022.9
swing[V-t] (1) v 098.7
swinger (14) n 022.9
  ~ -go-round (1) n 022.7
swingers (1) n 022.9
swinging (16) v/adj 083.1
  ~ board (1) n 022.6
  ~ dance (1) n 083.1
  ~ horse (1) n 022.7
  ~ jenny (1) n 022.7
  ~ -ladder (1) adj 111.3
  ~ scythe (1) n 120.6
  ~ scythes (1) n 070.8
  ~ Willy (1) n 120.6
swingle (2) n 021.2

swingles (1) v 021.2
swingletree (72) n 021.2
swingletrees (11) n 021.2
swings (83) n 022.9
swink owl (1) n 059.1
swipe (11) v 100.2
swipe[V-r] (20) v 100.2
swiped (146) v 100.2
swipes (1) v 100.2
swiping (1) v 100.2
swipy stick (1) n 113.2
swirled around (1) v 032.5
swirls (1) n 122.7
Swiss (11) 047.2
  ~ Avenue (1) 105.4
  ~ chard (5) n 055A.5
  ~ cheese (2) n 048.1
  ~ cut (1) n 084.9
  ~ steak (1) n 131.8
switch (75) n/v/adj 065.5
  ~ broom (1) n 010.5
  ~ harp (1) n 020.5
  ~ thing (1) n 019.4
Switch (2) 087.3
switchback (1) n 031.8
switchblade (20) n/adj 104.3
  ~ knife (2) n 104.3
switchblades (2) n 081.9
switched (5) v 065.5
Switched-On Bach (1) 130.8
switcher herder (1) n 084.8
switches (8) n 019.4
switching (36) n 065.5
switchman (2) n 065.9
Switzerland (2) 087.9
swivel (11) n/v/adj 021.5
  ~ chair (3) n 008.8
  ~ chairs (1) n 008.8
  ~ tree (3) n 021.2
  ~ windlass (1) n 017.4
swivels (1) n 021.2
swizzled (1) v 055.9
swole (186) v 077.6
  ~ up (57) v 077.6
swoled (29) v 077.6
  ~ up (17) v 077.6
swoleden (1) v 077.6
swoles (1) v 077.6
swollen (574) v/adj 077.6
  ~ up (30) v 077.6
swollened (1) v 077.6

swoo (4) interj 037.5
  ~ swook (1) interj 037.5
swoo(x2) (2) interj 037.5
swook (2) interj 037.5
sword (9) n 104.3
swordfish (5) n 059.9
swords (3) n 104.3
swore (2) v 081.8
swum (361) v 095.6
  ~ across (12) v 095.6
  ~ out (1) v 095.6
  ~ over (1) v 057.8
swummed (4) v 095.6
swump (1) adj 046.9
swung (5) v 022.9
  ~ in (1) v 012.9
sycamore (752) n/adj 061.7
  ~ tree (125) n 061.7
  ~ trees (35) n 061.7
sycam(ore) tree (1) n 061.7
Sycamore (19) AL IL TN 061.7
  ~ Creek (4) AL TN 030.7
  ~ River (2) TN 030.7
  ~ Street (1) 061.7
sycamores (61) n 061.7
sycophant (1) n 125.6
Sykes Creek (1) AR 030.7
Sylacauga (6) AL 087.3
syllables (1) n 055.4
syllabub (1) n 048.5
Sylvan (2) 106.2
  ~ Hills (1) 106.2
  ~ Park (1) 106.2
Sylvania (3) AL GA 087.3
Sylvester (6) GA 087.2
symbol (1) n 088.9
sympathy (2) n 079.3
symphonic (3) adj 130.9
  ~ music (1) n 130.9
symphony (2) n 130.8
synagogues (1) n 126.7
synthesizer (1) n 130.8
synthesizers (1) n 088.8
synthetic (1) adj 017.1
syphilis (2) n 070.7
Syracuse (2) NY 021.6
Syrian (1) 084.8
Syrians (1) 126.9
syrup (1846) n/adj 048.5

~ barrel (2) n 051.3
~ barrels (3) n 019.1
~ boiler (2) n 017.6
~ bread (3) n 044.4
~ bucket (12) n 019.2
~ buckets (15) n 017.4
~ cake (4) n 045.3
~ cakes (1) n 051.3
~ can (4) n 019.2
~ candy (6) n 081.9
~ cane (5) n 051.3
~ -cane patch (1) n 051.3
~ cans (1) n 019.2
~ eaters (1) n 051.3
~ farm (2) n 061.6
~ funnels (1) n 019.3
~ furnace (1) n 080.6
~ grinding (1) n 081.9
~ house (3) n 010.3
~ jar (1) n 019.2
~ jug (2) n 019.2
~ jugs (1) n 051.3
~ kettle (27) n 017.6
~ kettles (4) n 017.6
~ liquor (1) n 050.8
~ maker (1) n 051.3
~ making (1) n 051.3
~ -making kind (1) n 061.5
~ mill (20) n 051.3
~ -mill furnace (1) n 080.7
~ mills (4) n 051.3
~ pan (3) n 051.3
~ pie (1) n 084.8
~ pitcher (10) n 019.2
~ pitchers (1) n 019.2
~ pullings (2) n 084.8
~ season (1) n 051.3
~ shelter (1) n 088.7
~ soppers (1) n 045.3
~ stand (5) n 019.2
~ sweet water (1) n 051.3
~ tree (2) n 061.5
~ trees (1) n 061.5
~ trough (1) n 035.8
~ troughs (1) n 035.8
~ vats (1) n 051.3
syr(up) (1) n 051.3
Syrup (1) 051.3
syrups (15) n 051.3
syrupy (1) adj 051.2
system (34) n 111.2

System (2) 109.9
systems (1) n 049.2

T

T (164) 070.9
~ and T (1) 070.9
~ bar (1) n 021.2
~ -Bird (2) 114.7
~ -bone (63) n/adj 121.1
~ -bone steak (29) n 121.1
~ -bone steaks (2) n 121.1
~ -bones (7) n 121.1
~ -hall (1) n 080.6
~ -Model (11) 109.1
~ -Model car (3) n 023.6
~ -Model Ford (9) 080.6
~ -Model Fords (1) 080.8
~ -Model truck (2) n 023.6
~ -Model trucks (1) n 109.7
~ -Models (2) 109.1
~ -shape (2) n 118.9
~ -shirt (1) n 102.7
~ -shirts (1) n 013.7
~ strap (1) n 123.8
~ straps (1) n 123.8
~ -top (2) adj 109.4
tab (1) n 125.2
tabby (6) n/adj 092.7
~ cat (3) n 059.9
~ house (1) n 080.8
tabernacle (1) n 084.8
table (155) n/adj 009.8
~ captain (1) n 068.5
~ corn (2) n 056.2
~ gardens (1) n 050.5
~ knives (2) n 104.3
~ onions (1) n 055.7
~ pea (3) n 055A.2
~ pot (1) n 017.6
~ salt (3) n 051.7
~ scraps (1) n 017.4

~ syrup (1) n 051.3
~ tapper (1) n 067.8
~ tennis (2) n 130.4
~ use (1) n 048.4
tablecloth (1) n 040.6
tableland (4) n 031.2
tables (18) n 083.8
tablespoon (14) n 017.8
tablespoonful (2) n 017.8
tablespoons (1) n 017.8
tablet (3) n 025.7
tablets (1) n 078.4
tableware (2) n 017.8
taboo (1) n 130.7
Tabor (2) 087.1
TAC (1) 114.2
tache (2) n F 016.4
tachometer (2) n 110.2
taciturn (1) adj 075.1
tack (20) n/v/adj 038.7
~ comfort (1) n 029.1
~ hammer (4) n 020.7
~ mattress (1) n 080.8
~ quilt (1) n 029.1
~ room (4) n 099.9
~ rooms (1) n 015.5
~ up (1) v 038.6
tacked (8) v 029.1
~ on (1) v 027.2
tackiest (3) adj 131.6
~ -looking (1) adj 052.6
tacking (1) v 093.6
tackle (39) n/v/adj 038.6
~ and smear (1) n 130.5
~ basketball (1) n 130.5
~ football (4) n 130.5
~ room (1) n 011.7
~ the man with the ball (1) n 130.5
tackling (1) n 130.5
tacks (2) n 117.7
tacky (34) n/adj 080.7
~ parties (2) n 130.7
~ party (1) n 130.7
taco (4) adj 128.7
~ bender (1) n 128.7
~ benders (2) n 128.7
~ eater (1) n 128.7
tacos (5) n 044.5
tad (4) n 064.4
tadpole (14) n/adj 060.3
~ frog (1) n 060.3

~ stools (1) n 057.1
tadpoles (13) n 060.3
tadpoly (2) adj 029.6
~ land (1) n 029.6
taffy (4) n/adj 051.3
~ pulling (1) n 104.7
~ pulling parties (1) n 130.7
tag (70) n/v/adj 130.2
~ along (2) v 075.7
~ bicycle (1) n 130.2
~ dance (1) n 083.1
~ football (2) n 130.5
~ games (1) n 130.1
~ out of jail (1) n 130.2
tagging (1) n 081.8
tags (5) n 088.8
Tahoe (2) 043.3
Tahoka (1) TX 087.4
tail (69) n/adj 072.7
~ end (1) n 099.5
~ oiling (1) n 065.5
Tail (1) 030.7
tailed (2) adj 076.7
tailgate (4) n/adj 021.9
~ drawers (1) n 089.8
tailing off (1) v 007.3
tailor (3) n 090.4
~ -made (1) adj 123.6
~ -made suits (1) n 027.7
tailored (1) adj 123.6
tailor's goose (1) n 081.8
tailors (1) n 069.4
tails (21) n 060A.4
Tails Creek (2) GA 030.7
taint (3) v 046.9
taint[V-t] (1) v 046.9
tainted (143) v/adj 046.9
taints (1) v 046.9
tainty (1) adj 046.9
take (2399) v 077.1
~ a limb to (1) v 065.5
~ a piece off your butt (1) v 065.5
~ a walk (1) v 082.1
~ after (16) v 065.3
~ and (63) v 081.3
~ away (2) v 036.1
~ back up (1) v 083.3
~ care (40) v 077.1
~ care of (85) v 077.1
~ care [P-0] (2) v 015.2

~ down with (1) v 076.3
~ him (4) v 033.2
~ in (26) v 083.3
~ it easy (1) v 037.5
~ off (8) v 077.1
~ on (14) v 080.8
~ on a date (1) v 081.4
~ out (15) v 077.1
~ out from (1) v 021.6
~ over (4) v 077.1
~ to (5) v 077.1
~ up (32) v 083.3
~ up for (1) v 077.1
take[V-p] (23) v 077.1
~ after (2) v 065.3
~ and (1) v 081.3
~ care of (4) v 013.1
~ off (1) v 013.8
take[V-r] (10) v 077.1
take[V-s] (1) v 053.8
take[V-t] (2) v 077.1
~ up with (1) v 077.1
taked (5) v 077.1
taken (1225) v 077.1
~ after (9) v 065.3
~ and (2) v 081.3
~ away (1) v 077.1
~ back (1) v 076.1
~ by his Creator (1) v 078.5
~ care (11) v 077.1
~ care of (24) v 077.1
~ down (3) v 077.1
~ from (1) v 077.1
~ her (1) v 077.1
~ in (6) v 077.1
~ like of her (1) v 081.4
~ of (1) v 077.1
~ off (10) v 077.1
~ out (16) v 077.1
~ out of (1) v 077.1
~ over (13) v 077.1
~ to (4) v 088.2
~ up (6) v 077.1
~ with (3) v 076.3
~ [P-0] (1) v 076.1
takened (19) v 100.2
~ away (1) v 096.7
~ off (1) v 077.1
~ on (2) v 119.6
takes (239) v 077.1
~ after (141) v 065.3
~ af(ter) (1) v 065.3

~ back in (1) v 083.3
~ care (3) v 013.1
~ care of (7) v 013.1
~ in (11) v 083.3
~ over (1) v 064.7
~ to (1) v 039.7
~ up (9) v 083.3
taketh (1) v 080.7
taking (181) v 077.1
  ~ after (6) v 065.3
  ~ at (1) v 065.3
  ~ care (3) v 013.1
  ~ care of (12) v 013.1
  ~ her out (3) v 081.4
  ~ in (2) v 083.3
  ~ on (21) v 079.3
  ~ out (1) v 049.4
  ~ out after (1) v 065.3
  ~ over (2) v 077.1
  ~ up (2) v 077.1
  ~ up aft(er) (1) v 065.3
Talbot (3) GA 087.2
  ~ County (2) GA 087.5
Talbott (2) TN 087.1
Talbotton (3) GA 087.1
tale (17) n/adj 101.3
  ~ carrier (1) n 101.3
  ~ -teller (5) n 101.3
  ~ -tolder (2) n 080.5
talebear (1) n 101.3
talebearer (5) n 101.3
talebearers (1) n 101.3
talent (2) n 089.5
tales (13) n 101.3
taletattler (2) n 101.3
taletattlers (1) n 101.3
Taliaferro (2) GA 087.4
  ~ County (1) GA 087.3
Talisheek (1) LA 087.4
talk (238) n/v 089.4
  ~ about (58) v 013.5
  ~ (a)bout (1) v 013.5
  ~ in (1) v 131.2
  ~ like (4) v 100.1
  ~ to (20) v 043.5
  ~ with (4) v 032.4
Talk of the Town (1) 099.7
talk[V-p] (2) v 013.5
  ~ to (1) v 013.5
talk[V-r] (2) v 013.5
  ~ to (1) v 013.5
  ~ with (1) v 013.5

talk[V-s] about (1) v 013.5
talk[V-t] (7) v 052.7
  ~ to (5) v 057.8
  ~ with (1) v 032.4
talked (27) v 013.5
  ~ about (7) v 057.9
  ~ like (2) v 100.1
  ~ out (1) v 057.9
  ~ to (3) v 013.9
  ~ with (3) v 013.5
talker (2) n 091.9
talkie (1) n 113.3
talkies (1) n 084.4
talking (755) n/v 057.4
  ~ about (230) v 013.5
  ~ (a)bout (265) v 013.5
  ~ among (1) v 044.1
  ~ for my mamma (1) v 129.7
  ~ on (1) v 101.3
  ~ over (3) v 013.5
  ~ to (64) v 053.5
  ~ to her (2) v 081.4
  ~ with (6) v 013.5
  ~ [P-0] (4) n/v 102.1
Talking Rock River (1) GA 030.7
talks (3) v 090.6
  ~ with (1) v 032.4
tall (286) adj 043.1
  ~ building (1) n 108.5
  ~ buildings (2) n 108.5
  ~ -old (1) adj 090.9
  ~ -tale teller (2) n 101.3
Tall (2) 106.2
  ~ Timber (1) 106.2
  ~ Timbers (1) 106.1
Talla (2) 030.3
  ~ Bena (1) LA 087.8
Tallabogue (4) MS 030.7
Talladega (31) AL 087.1
  ~ County (2) AL 087.1
  ~ Creek (3) AL 030.7
  ~ National Forest (2) AL 087.7
  ~ Springs (1) AL 087.4
Tallahaga Creek (1) MS 030.7
Tallahala Creek (1) MS 030.7
Tallahassee (44) FL 087.8

~ Municipal Airport (1) 106.5
Tallahatchie (18) MS 086.5
  ~ Bottom (2) MS 087.1
  ~ County (3) MS 086.3
  ~ River (5) MS 030.7
Tallahatta Creek (1) AL 030.7
Tallahoma (3) MS 030.7
  ~ Creek (2) MS 030.7
Tallapoosa (24) AL GA 087.2
  ~ Creek (1) AL 030.7
  ~ River (7) AL GA 030.7
Tallassee (9) AL 087.5
tallboy (2) n 121.9
taller (63) adj 042.6
tallow (34) n/adj 065.9
  ~ candles (1) n 024.2
  ~ face (1) n 069.4
  ~ lamp (1) n 024.3
  ~ tree (3) n 061.8
  ~ trees (3) n 061.9
tallows (2) n 061.8
Tallula (1) MS 086.8
Tallulah (19) LA 087.4
  ~ Falls (10) GA 086.3
  ~ River (1) GA 030.7
tally (2) n/adj 009.7
  ~ ho (1) n 088.8
tam-o'-shanter hat (1) n 081.8
tamale (5) n/adj 044.6
  ~ men (1) n 081.8
  ~ pies (1) n 050.3
tamales (26) n 131.8
Tamaulipas (1) 081.8
tame (16) adj 056.8
  ~ blackberries (1) n 062.4
  ~ cherries (1) n 062.1
  ~ cherry (1) n 062.1
  ~ flowers (1) n 101.4
  ~ hogs (2) n 035.5
  ~ mulberries (1) n 062.5
  ~ squirrels (1) n 059.6
  ~ tomatoes (1) n 055.3
tamed down (1) v 080.8
Tamiami Trail (1) 107A.4
Tammany (7) 087.3
Tammy (1) 125.3
Tampa (76) FL 087.3

~ Airport (1) 106.5
~ Bay (3) FL 087.8
~ Heights (2) 106.1
~ International (1) 106.5
~ International Airport (3) 106.5
~ -Saint Petersburg area (1) FL 087.2
~ -Saint Petersburg International Airport (1) 106.5
~ Street (3) 107.6
~ Terrace (2) 105.1
Tampico (2) 086.3
Tamworth (1) 035.5
tan (25) v/adj 075.8
  ~ -like (1) adj 059.7
  ~ our hides (1) v 065.5
  ~ peaches (1) n 054.3
  ~ sparrows (1) n 059.3
  ~ trough (1) n 035.8
  ~ your behind (1) v 081.3
  ~ your bottom (1) v 065.5
  ~ your breeches (1) v 080.6
  ~ your hide (5) v 065.5
  ~ your hind part (1) v 065.5
  ~ your pants (1) v 081.3
Tan (6) 033.1
tan[V-t] (1) v 065.5
Tanacrest (1) 087.4
tanagers (1) n 089.8
Tancahua (1) 115.6
tandem (3) n 033.7
tangerine (17) n/adj 055.1
  ~ trees (1) n 061.8
tangerines (13) n 055.1
Tangipahoa (9) LA 030.7
  ~ Parish (1) LA 087.5
  ~ River (2) LA 030.7
Tangi(pahoa) (1) LA 087.2
tangle (3) n/adj 045.2
  ~ breeches (1) n 045.2
  ~ face (1) n 125.2
tangled (3) v 104.2
  ~ up (1) v 102.6
tanglefoot (2) n 084.9

Tanglewood (3) 106.2
tango (14) n 083.1
tangos (1) n 083.1
tangy (1) adj 047.8
tank (78) n/adj 112.8
~ cars (1) n 023.6
~ truck (1) n 111.2
tankage (4) n 015.5
tankard (1) n 048.9
tanked up on (1) v 080.9
tanker (2) n 111.2
tankers (1) n 111.1
tanks (19) n 109.4
tanky (1) n 050.8
tanned (3) v 065.5
~ him up (1) v 065.5
~ our breeches (1) v
065.5
Tannehill Furnace (1)
106.4
tanner (2) n 088.7
tannery (2) n 080.7
tanning (12) n/v 065.5
tantrum (2) n 075.2
Tanyard Branch (1) GA
030.7
tap (82) n/v/adj 018.7
~ dance (6) n/v 083.1
~ dances (1) n 083.1
~ dancing (1) n 083.1
~ water (6) n 040.6
tapaderos (1) n S 088.7
tape (16) n/adj 057.4
~ cartridge (1) n 022.4
~ measure (1) n 070.8
~ recorder (1) n 012.2
tapeable (1) adj 080.6
taper (3) n/adj 024.3
~ cuts (1) n 123.9
tapered off (1) v 007.3
tapering (2) v 024.9
~ off (1) v 007.3
tapes (2) n 130.8
tapeworm (2) n 060.5
taping (1) n 040.6
tapioca (1) n 061.4
tapon (1) n S 020.4
tapped (1) v 040.8
tapper (1) n 067.8
tapping (1) v 097.4
taproot (19) n 061.4
taproots (1) n 061.4
taps (6) n 018.7
tar (528) n/adj 031.6
~ baby (4) n 031.6

~ belt roads (1) n
031.6
~ blocks (1) n 031.6
~ brush (2) n 038.7
~ bucket (1) n 017.2
~ covering (1) n 031.6
~ cup (1) n 017.7
~ jacket (1) n 080.6
~ jackets (1) n 061.4
~ kiln (1) n 080.9
~ lighterd (1) n 008.6
~ paper (5) n 011.2
~ -paper roof (1) n
036.8
~ pits (1) n 031.6
~ road (10) n 031.6
~ roads (3) n 031.6
~ streets (1) n 031.6
~ substance (1) n 031.6
~ surface (1) n 031.6
~ -surfaced (1) adj
031.6
~ top (1) n 031.6
tara (3) n/adj 015.9
~ leaves (1) n 104.7
~ vines (1) n 015.9
Tara Hills (1) 106.1
tarantula (6) n 066.9
tarantulas (6) n 060A.8
tardes (1) n S 002.6
tardy (1) adj 083.4
target (3) n/adj 130.6
~ practice (1) n 130.6
~ worm (2) n 060.5
Tarheel (5) LA 069.8
tarheels (1) n 069.9
Tarheels (3) 069.4
Tarkington Prairie (1)
TX 087.6
Tarmac (1) 031.6
tarnation (1) interj 092.3
tarnished (1) adj 047.5
tarp (2) n 014.7
tarpaulin (17) n 014.7
tarpaulins (3) n 014.7
tarpon (19) n 059.9
Tarpon Springs (2) FL
087.4
Tarrant (4) TX 087.4
~ City (2) AL 087.7
tarred (4) v 031.7
tart (9) n 045.2
Tart (1) 122.8
tartans (1) n 128.1
tartar sauce (1) n 048.5

tarter (1) n 078.4
tarts (22) n 048.3
Tarts (2) 044.5
Tarver (1) GA 086.4
Tarvia (1) 031.6
Tarviated (2) 031.6
~ roads (1) n 031.6
Tarzan (2) 012.8
Tascosa (1) TX 086.7
taskmaster (1) n 073.5
tassel (897) n/v/adj 056.3
~ flies (1) n 060A.8
~ out (1) v 056.3
~ pulls (1) n 056.3
tas(sel) (2) n 056.3
tassel[N-i] (1) n 035.7
tasseled (5) v/adj 009.5
~ out (3) v 056.3
tasseling (10) v 056.3
~ out (3) v 056.3
tassels (52) n/v 056.3
~ out (1) v 056.3
tasso (6) n 037.4
taste (78) n/v/adj 070.8
~ food (1) n 080.8
~ like (3) v 013.1
~ of (12) v 051.1
~ [P-0] (2) v 012.9
taste[V-p] (3) v 047.5
taste[V-r] (1) v 104.1
tasted (17) v 002.8
~ like (1) v 047.5
~ of (10) v 051.1
tastes (20) v 016.7
tastewise (1) adv 005.7
tasting (6) v/adj 048.6
~ stage (1) n 056.3
tasty (1) adj 055A.1
tat (1) n 081.9
Tataille (1) F 090.1
Tate (8) GA MS 087.8
~ County (1) MS 087.2
~ Hammock (1) AL
029.7
Tater Knob (1) AL 030.8
Tates (2) 094.8
~ Bluff (1) AR 094.8
~ Hell (1) FL 030.7
tatting (1) n 088.8
tattle (70) v/adj 101.3
~ box (5) n 101.3
~ boxes (1) n 101.3
~ butt (1) n 101.3
~ tattler (1) n 101.3
tattled (4) v 101.3

~ on (1) v 053.8
tattler (99) n 101.3
tattlers (9) n 101.3
tattles (3) v 101.3
tattletale (538) n/v/adj
101.3
~ lady (1) n 101.3
~ on (1) v 101.3
~ tit (2) n 101.3
tattletaler (2) n 101.3
tattletalers (2) n 101.3
tattletales (41) n 101.3
tattletaling (3) v 101.3
tattletelling (1) v 101.3
tattling (36) n/v/adj
101.3
~ child (1) n 101.3
tattly box (1) n 101.3
Tattnall (6) GA 087.5
~ County (1) GA 087.2
Tatum (1) TX 087.9
taught (828) v 101.1
~ at (1) v 053.4
~ by (1) v 101.1
~ in (1) v 101.1
~ to (1) v 041.1
taure (1) n F 033.8
taureau (3) n F 033.5
Tavares (2) FL 087.2
tavern (1) n 084.3
Tavern (2) 106.4
taverns (2) n 084.9
taw (7) n/adj 101.7
~ board (1) n 080.9
~ hole (1) n 093.6
Tawakoni (1) 030.7
taws (1) n 130.6
Taws Mill (1) GA 029.9
tax (10) n/adj 068.4
~ (as)sessor (1) n
068.4
taxes (1) n 024.9
taxi (37) n/adj 109.9
~ drivers (1) n 097.8
taxicab (1) n 109.9
taxicabs (9) n 109.9
taxis (15) n 109.9
taxpayers (1) n 042.7
Taylor (16) FL GA MS
TX 087.2
~ Bayou (1) TX 030.7
~ County (1) GA 085.5
~ Creek (2) FL MS
030.7
~ Mill (1) GA 087.4

~ Street (1) 107.7
Taylors Depot (1) MS 087.8
Tazewell (4) TN 087.2
TB (4) 079.6
TC-ing after (1) v 075.7
Tchaikovsky's Nutcracker Suite (1) 066.9
Tchefuncta (3) LA 030.7
   ~ River (2) LA 030.7
Tchevia (2) MS 030.7
tchi (2) n/adj 059.1
   ~ -tchi (1) n 059.1
Tchoupitoulas (3) 115.7
   ~ Street (1) 105.6
Tchoutacabouf(fa) (2) MS 030.7
   ~ River (1) MS 030.7
Tchula Vista (1) MS 087.3
TCU (1) 106.1
tea (259) n/adj 114.1
   ~ apron (1) n 026.4
   ~ boiler (1) n 017.6
   ~ box (1) n 088.7
   ~ cake (18) n 045.2
   ~ cakes (37) n 045.2
   ~ can (1) n 017.6
   ~ dance (2) n 083.1
   ~ dances (1) n 083.1
   ~ glass (7) n 048.9
   ~ glasses (3) n 048.9
   ~ gowns (1) n 084.9
   ~ olive (1) n 061.8
   ~ parties (1) n 130.7
   ~ party (1) n 048.6
   ~ sippers (1) n 080.9
   ~ towel (10) n 018.6
   ~ towels (7) n 018.4
   ~ trees (1) n 061.9
   ~ weed (2) n 015.9
   ~ weeds (5) n 015.9
teach (59) v 101.1
   ~ with (1) v 052.8
teach[V-p] (2) v 013.6
teach[V-r] (4) v 101.1
teach[V-t] (1) v 101.1
teached (10) v 101.1
teacher (572) n/adj 067.6
teacher[N-i] (2) n 067.6
teacher's (71) adj 002.6
   ~ certificate (1) n 002.6
   ~ desk (1) n 083.8
   ~ pet (68) n 125.6
   ~ pets (1) n 101.3

teachers (83) n/adj 067.6
   ~ college (1) n 083.6
   ~ normal (1) n 083.5
teaches (4) v 053.4
   ~ in (1) v 052.5
teaching (20) n/v 057.4
   ~ -school blood (1) n 067.6
Teaheads (2) TX 087.7
teakettle (191) n 017.6
teaket(tle) (1) n 017.6
teakettles (20) n 017.6
teal (1) n 081.8
team (742) n/adj 033.7
   ~ -drawn (1) adj 033.7
   ~ of goats (1) n 033.7
   ~ of good mules (1) n 033.7
   ~ of horses (25) n 033.7
   ~ of many horses (1) n 033.7
   ~ of mule[N-i] (2) n 033.7
   ~ of mules (96) n 033.7
   ~ of ox[N-i] (4) n 033.7
   ~ of oxen (29) n 033.7
   ~ of oxens (5) n 033.7
   ~ of steers (1) n 033.7
   ~ of them (1) n 033.7
   ~ of wild horses (1) n 033.7
   ~ -operated ferry (1) n 033.7
   ~ thrashers (1) n 042.1
Team (1) 033.7
team[N-i] (9) n 033.7
   ~ of steer[N-i] (1) n 033.7
teamed (2) v 101.7
teams (57) n 033.7
   ~ of mules (3) n 033.7
   ~ of oxen (1) n 033.7
teapot (41) n 017.6
teapots (1) n 017.6
tear (68) v/adj 102.6
   ~ -blank(et) (1) n 078.4
   ~ down (4) v 102.6
   ~ -down (1) adj 099.9
   ~ gas (1) n 113.3
   ~ her up (1) v 065.5
   ~ him up (2) v 065.5
   ~ me up (2) v 065.5

   ~ my ass up (1) v 065.5
   ~ them up (1) v 065.5
   ~ up (4) v 102.6
   ~ up his fanny (1) v 081.3
   ~ up on (1) v 081.8
   ~ you down (1) v 065.5
   ~ you up (3) v 102.6
   ~ your breeches (1) v 034.4
   ~ your tail up (1) v 065.5
tear[V-r] (1) v 013.6
teared (3) v 102.6
tearing (7) v 080.8
   ~ -down (1) adj 080.8
   ~ up (4) v 102.6
tearooms (1) n 116.3
tears (2) v 025.6
   ~ up (1) v 102.6
teas (3) n 130.7
tease (3) n/v 123.9
teased (7) v/adj 123.9
   ~ head (1) n 123.9
   ~ up (1) v 032.4
teaser (2) n 124.9
teasers (1) n 082.5
teasing (3) n/v 129.7
teaspoon (16) n 017.8
teaspoons (8) n 017.8
teats (1) n 046.3
tech (1) n 080.6
Tech (15) 065.9
   ~ High School (1) 065.9
Teche (4) 030.7
technical (2) adj 090.4
   ~ college (1) n 083.6
Technician (1) 080.6
Technicians (2) 111.5
technicolor day (1) n 005.4
techo (1) n S 011.4
Techwood (3) 105.4
   ~ Drive (1) 107.6
tecolote (1) n S 059.2
teddy bear (1) n 093.7
Teddy (1) 124.6
tedious (3) adj 066.9
tee (9) v/prefix 080.8
   ~ -ninesy (1) adj 080.8
   ~ -nintsy (1) adj 080.7
   ~ -niny (3) adj 071.5
   ~ -nin(y) (1) adj 002.7

   ~ off (1) v 092.8
   ~ -tottle (1) n 022.7
teed off (3) v 075.2
Teekessel (1) n G 017.6
teeky (1) adj 075.1
teenage gals (1) n 064.9
teenager (1) n 080.6
teenagers (1) n 011.9
teenages (1) n 092.7
teens (1) n 091.7
teensy (1) adj 088.9
teeny (3) adj 091.9
   ~ -niny-niny (1) adj 091.9
   ~ toes (1) n 055.3
   ~ tomatoes (1) n 055.3
teenyitis (1) adj 002.6
teeter (95) n/v/adj 022.8
   ~ horse (1) n 022.5
   ~ saw (1) n 022.5
   ~ teets (1) n 022.5
   ~ -totter (76) n 022.5
   ~ -totter thing (1) n 022.5
   ~ -tottered (1) v 022.8
   ~ -tottering (7) v 022.8
   ~ -totters (2) n 022.5
tee(ter)-tottering (1) v 022.8
teeterboard (9) n 022.5
teeterboards (1) n 022.5
teetering (11) v/adj 022.8
   ~ board (1) n 022.5
   ~ plank (1) n 022.5
teeth (1146) n/adj 071.8
teethed (1) adj 035.7
teether (1) n 022.5
teethes (19) n 071.8
teeths (2) n 071.8
teetotaled (1) adv 102.6
teetotaler (1) n 080.8
teetotally (1) adv 075.5
teets (1) n 022.5
Teflon (3) 017.7
Tehuacana Creek (1) TX 030.7
telephone (11) n/adj 130.4
   ~ booth (1) n 007A.3
   ~ booths (1) n 012.1
   ~ company (3) n 108.5
   ~ gossiper (1) n 101.3
   ~ number (1) n 102.1
   ~ post (1) n 016.5
   ~ truck (1) n 111.4

telephone[N-i] (1) n 012.9
telephones (1) n 130.6
telescopic boom (1) n 111.4
television (53) n 070.7
televisions (1) n 025.2
Telfair (3) GA 087.2
  ~ Academy (1) 106.4
  ~ County (1) GA 087.2
tell (856) v/adj 101.3
  ~ about (2) v 080.5
  ~ him no (1) v 082.1
  ~ off (1) v 081.8
  ~ on (20) v 101.3
  ~ tell (1) n 101.3
Tell (2) 067.4
tell[V-p] (4) v 080.5
tell[V-r] (2) v 080.5
  ~ about (1) v 080.5
teller (8) n 101.3
Tellico (5) TN 030.7
  ~ River (2) TN 030.7
telling (94) n/v 057.4
  ~ (a)bout (1) v 057.4
  ~ on (1) v 025.4
tells (10) v 013.8
telltale (4) n 101.3
temper (90) n/adj 051.8
  ~ tantrum (2) n 075.2
temper[N-i] (2) n 075.2
temperament (3) n 073.2
temperamental (23) adj 075.1
temperance (2) adj 093.8
  ~ lodge (1) n 093.8
  ~ sermon (1) n 089.4
temperature (38) n 066.9
temper(ature) (1) n 076.2
temperatures (1) n 070.7
tempered (261) adj 075.2
temperous (1) adj 075.1
tempestuous (1) adj 065.8
temple (3) n 071.3
Temple (18) TX 087.8
  ~ oranges (1) n 088.7
  ~ Street (1) 099.7
  ~ Terrace (2) 105.1
  ~ trees (1) n 061.9
temples (1) n 126.7
temporarily (1) adv 085.3
temporary pen (1) n 015.3
ten (3355) n/adj 001.5
  ~ -acre (1) adj 001.5

~ -by-eight (2) n 001.5
~ -by-ten (3) n 001.5
~ -by-twelve (4) n 001.6
~ -cent (5) adj 026.6
~ -cent piece (5) n 026.6
~ -cent store (3) n 026.6
~ -cent stores (1) n 026.6
~ cents (1) n 114.1
~ -dollar (1) adj 001.5
~ -feet (2) adj 007.9
~ -fifteen (2) n 004.5
~ -foot (19) adj 007.9
~ -foot-wide (1) adj 007.9
~ -forty (1) n 001.5
~ -forty-five (90) n 004.5
~ -gallon (6) adj 017.3
~ -hour (1) adj 001.5
~ -inch (3) adj 001.5
~ -mile (1) adj 001.5
~ -pound (15) adj 045.4
~ -quart (5) adj 017.3
~ -rail fence (6) n 016.4
~ -room (1) adj 001.5
~ -room house (5) n 001.5
~ ten double ten (1) n 092.8
~ -thirty (52) n 004.4
~ -thirty-five (1) n 004.5
~ till (3) n 004.5
~ -week (1) adj 080.6
~ -wheelers (1) n 109.6
~ -year-old (2) adj 012.2
~ -year-olds (1) n 001.5
Ten (27) 001.5
  ~ -Forty-Seven (1) 126.1
  ~ Street (1) 001A.3
tenable (1) adj 029.8
tenant (42) n/adj 119.4
  ~ farmer (2) n 080.6
  ~ farmers (4) n 080.8
  ~ farmhouse (1) n 011.8
  ~ flat (1) n 119.1

~ house (10) n 089.9
~ houses (16) n 118.6
~ people (1) n 069.7
~ room (2) n 007A.2
tenants (8) n 080.6
tend (13) v 049.5
  ~ to (8) v 065.4
tend[V-t] to (1) v 012.5
tendable (2) adj 016.1
  ~ land (1) n 016.1
  ~ soil (1) n 088.7
tended (3) v 065.4
  ~ to (2) v 036.1
tendencies (1) n 013.8
tender (36) adj 056.2
  ~ bean (2) n 055A.4
  ~ beans (2) n 055A.4
  ~ corn (4) n 056.2
  ~ greens (1) n 055A.5
  ~ hull (1) n 055A.3
  ~ onions (2) n 055.7
tenderer (1) adj 066.1
tenderest (1) adj 064.7
tenderfooted (3) adj 072.6
tenderfoots (1) n 080.7
Tendergreen (5) 055A.4
Tendergreens (1) 055A.4
tenderhearted (2) adj 073.2
tenderloin (46) n/adj 046.4
  ~ steak (1) n 121.1
tenderloins (7) n 121.1
tenders (1) n 080.9
Tendersweet (1) 056.9
tendonitis (1) n 079.6
tendons (1) n 013.8
tends to (1) v 010.4
tenement (41) n/adj 119.2
  ~ building (1) n 119.2
  ~ house (2) n 119.2
  ~ houses (4) n 080.6
  ~ housing (4) n 119.2
  ~ rows (1) n 108.5
tenements (4) n 119.1
Tenille (1) 115.5
Tenmile Creek (1) LA 030.7
Tenneco (1) 108.5
Tennessean (3) 084.9
Tennesseans (1) 090.8
Tennessee (1223) 086.6
  ~ ash (1) n 061.8

~ basketball (1) n 086.6
~ Central (1) 086.6
~ chicken (2) n 046.3
~ City (1) TN 087.3
~ country ham (1) n 121.3
~ Green Pod (3) 055A.4
~ Green Pods (4) 055A.4
~ hillbilly (1) n 069.9
~ line (1) n 086.6
~ Long Pod (1) 055A.4
~ Red Cob (2) 056.2
~ Red Rooter (1) 054.7
~ Ridge (1) TN 087.1
~ River (52) TN 030.7
~ Road (1) 086.6
~ State (1) 106.4
~ State Prison (1) 106.6
~ State University (1) 106.4
~ Street (1) 107.6
~ Valley (1) TN 086.6
~ Walker (1) 086.6
~ Walker[N-i] (1) 086.6
~ Walkers (2) 034.2
~ Walking Horse (2) 034.2
~ Wonders (2) 055A.3
Tenn(essee) (2) 086.6
tennies (1) n 123.8
Tennille (1) AL 075.8
tennis (113) n/adj 130.4
  ~ ball (1) n 017.1
  ~ shoe (4) n 123.8
  ~ shoes (73) n 123.8
  ~ shorts (5) n 123.4
tennises (2) n 123.8
tenny shoes (2) n 119.8
tenon (1) n 021.9
tenor (1) n 001A.3
tenpenny nail (1) n 026.6
tens (3) n 026.6
Tens (2) 001.9
Tensas (5) 087.2
  ~ Parish (2) LA 087.2
  ~ River (3) LA 030.7
Tensaw (2) AL 087.8
  ~ River (1) AL 030.7
tense (7) adj 074.2
tension (1) adj 075.1

tent (10) n/adj 014.7
~ meetings (1) n 080.7
~ plays (1) n 088.8
~ revival (2) n 080.7
~ show (1) n 088.9
~ shows (1) n 084.3
tenth (853) n/adj 001A.3
~ -grade scholar (1) n 068.7
~ -grade school (1) n 080.8
Tenth (9) 001A.3
~ District (1) 001A.3
~ Street (7) 001A.3
~ Ward (1) 105.3
tenths (12) n 016.2
tents (1) n 053.4
tenuous (1) adj 072.9
tenure (1) n 043.2
tepee (2) n/adj 014.6
~ shape (1) n 041.7
tepid (1) adj 072.9
tequila (2) n 050.9
term (38) n 076.6
terminal (30) n/adj 084.7
~ city (1) n 112.9
~ station (3) n 084.7
Terminal (2) 084.7
~ Station (1) 084.7
terminated (2) v 083.2
terminates (1) v 083.2
terminations (1) n 081.8
termite (1) n 092.7
termited (1) v 099.4
termites (16) n 065.9
terms (13) n 081.8
tern (1) n 080.7
terrace (51) n/v/adj 031.9
~ plow (1) n 021.6
Terrace (10) 007A.9
terraced (1) v 066.9
terraces (8) n 030.3
terracing (5) v/adj 030.2
~ purposes (1) n 075.8
terrapin (580) n/adj 060.7
~ hunting (1) n 060.7
~ soup (1) n 060.7
~ turtle (2) n 060.7
Terrapin (5) 030.7
~ Creek (3) AL 030.7
~ Neck (2) AR LA 087.9
terrapin[N-i] (1) n 060.7
terrapins (126) n 060.7
terrarium (2) n 017.8

terre (1) n F 060A.6
Terre (3) 087.4
~ Haute (1) IN 087.4
~ Noire (1) LA 030.7
~ Rouge (1) LA 030.7
Terrebonne (10) LA 087.3
~ Bayou (1) LA 030.7
~ Parish (3) LA 087.2
Terrell (8) GA TX 087.8
~ County (2) GA 087.1
~ Hills (2) 106.1
terrible (45) adj 066.8
~ day (5) n 005.5
~ freeze (1) n 007.5
~ -looking (2) adj 125.1
~ -looking day (1) n 005.5
~ rain (1) n 006.1
Terrible War (1) 085.8
terriblest (6) adj 064.7
~ -looking (1) adj 066.9
terribly (12) adv 091.7
terrier (23) n/adj 033.3
ter(rier) (2) n 033.3
terriers (3) n 033.3
terrific (4) adj 089.6
~ storm (1) n 006.2
terrified (1) adj 074.3
terrifying (1) adj 090.4
territorial (2) adj 088.7
~ family of Florida (1) n 088.7
~ restoration (1) n 106.4
territories (1) n 006.5
territory (3) n 093.8
Territory (3) 106.4
~ Capital (1) 106.4
terry (2) adj 018.6
~ cloth (1) n 018.6
~ dishcloth (1) n 018.4
Terry (4) MS 087.4
~ Road (1) 107.7
Terrytown (1) 105.8
Tesheva (3) MS 030.7
~ Creek (1) MS 030.7
test (14) n/v 026.2
test[N-i] (2) n 016.7
testament (1) n 066.9
Testament (1) 089.3
tested (3) v 096.8
tester (8) n/adj 060A.7

~ beds (1) n 099.6
testes (4) n/v 016.7
testicles (2) n 037.2
testify (3) v 089.3
testing (3) n/v/adj 012.8
tests (2) n 102.3
testy (9) adj 075.1
tetanus (4) n/adj 079.7
~ shot (1) n 081.8
Tete (11) 030.3
tetherball (4) n 130.4
tetrahydro(cannabinol) (1) n 114.2
tetter (1) n 077.4
Tex-Mex (5) 128.7
Texan (4) 084.9
Texans (1) 069.3
Texarkana (28) AR TX 087.6
Texas (1131) 086.8
~ Aggie (1) 069.4
~ Avenue (1) 105.1
~ City (2) LA TX 087.4
~ Company (1) 086.8
~ drawl (1) n 089.9
~ Eastern Transmission (1) 108.5
~ fever tick (1) n 081.9
~ Flat (1) 055.6
~ Giant (2) 056.9
~ grass (1) n 015.9
~ Hall of Fame (1) 106.4
~ jacks (1) n 081.8
~ League (1) 086.8
~ Longhorn (2) 033.6
~ Longs (1) 055.5
~ mosquitoes (1) n 060A.8
~ mountain laurel (1) n 062.7
~ navies (1) n 055A.3
~ northers (1) n 007.3
~ Oil Company (1) 086.8
~ onion (1) n 055.6
~ peanut (1) n 054.7
~ peanuts (2) n 054.7
~ potatoes (1) n 055.4
~ ribbon cane (1) n 051.3
~ Room (1) 086.8
~ shit (1) n 114.1

~ State Capitol (1) 086.8
~ State University (1) 065.9
~ Street (2) 107.6
~ Sweet (1) 056.9
~ Sweet Flat (1) 055.6
~ Sweet Rounds (1) 055.6
~ ticks (1) n 060A.8
~ tomato (1) n 055.3
Tex(as) (1) 107.1
Texoma (1) 086.8
text (5) n 089.4
Texter (1) 030.4
textures (1) n 013.8
TFC (1) 114.2
Thacker Mountain (1) MS 031.1
Thai (3) 114.1
~ stick (1) n 114.1
~ sticks (2) n 114.1
Thames (1) 107.7
than (1093) conj 096.9
th(an) (1) conj 043.2
(th)an (1) conj 043.2
(tha)n (56) conj 055A.3
thank (208) v 089.3
~ -you (1) n 095.7
~ -you gift (1) n 095.8
~ -you note (1) n 100.5
thankful (4) adj 093.4
thanking (1) v 088.5
thanks (47) n/interj 093.4
Thanksgiving (38) 070.7
~ Day (3) 070.6
~ Gift (1) 093.2
~ special (1) n 084.9
~ time (1) n 066.9
that (8021) adj/pron 088.3
~ way (3) adj 065.1
t(hat) (2) pron 053.1
(tha)t (3) pron 053.4
thataway (337) adv 052.3
thataways (3) adv 052.3
thatch (2) n/adj 041.5
~ chimleys (1) n 008.1
thatched roof (1) n 007A.1
that'd (4) pron 020.6
that'll (7) pron 098.6
that's (1016) pron 053.8
thaw (3) n/v 075.7
~ up (2) v 075.7

thawed up (1) v 057.8
Thayer (3) MO 087.4
THC (6) 114.2
the (31258) adj 070.9
th(e) (38) adj 031.6
t(he) (4) adj 064.2
theater (872) n/adj 084.4
~ business (1) n 084.4
thea(ter) (1) n 084.4
Theater (10) 084.4
theaters (38) n 084.4
Theatre (4) 084.4
their (470) pron 043.4
~ own self (1) pron 044.1
~ own self[M-i] (7) pron 044.1
~ own selves (2) pron 044.1
theirn (6) pron 043.5
theirs (517) pron 043.4
theirself[M-i] (171) pron 044.1
theirselves (192) pron 044.1
theirsn (2) pron 043.4
them (11077) pron 042.5
(the)m (20) pron 075.6
Them (1) 093.3
them(x2) (2) interj 033.2
them'll (1) pron 042.7
them's (66) pron 025.6
(the)m's (1) pron 098.8
thems (1) pron 060A.6
themself[M-i] (82) pron 044.1
(them)self[M-i] (1) pron 044.1
themselves (591) pron 044.1
(them)selves (1) pron 044.1
then (215) adv 065.8
Theodore (3) AL LA 105.6
there (4698) adv 052.2
th(ere) (3) adv 039.9
there(x2) (1) interj 037.5
there'd (3) adv 053.5
therefore (1) conj 013.7
there're (1) adv 025.2
there's (476) adv 025.2
(there')s (1) adv 053.5
there've (1) adv 025.2

thermal blankets (1) n 029.1
thermometer (1) n 052.6
thermos (5) n/adj 019.3
~ bottle (1) n 020.5
~ jug (1) n 017.2
thermostat (2) n 118.4
these (390) adj/pron 052.1
they (4604) pron 042.1
~ -all (1) pron 043.8
~ -all's (1) pron 043.9
th(ey) (2) pron 011.8
they[M-k] (1) pron 043.4
they'd (137) pron 095.8
they'll (41) pron 081.2
they're (191) pron 024.7
they's (62) pron 013.8
they've (69) pron 055.1
Thibodaux (7) LA 087.3
thick (208) adj 047.6
~ milk (1) n 047.6
~ rinds (1) n 056.9
~ soles (1) n 123.8
thicken (4) adj 080.7
~ gravy (3) n 080.7
thickener (1) n 048.5
thickening (9) v/adj 048.5
~ gravy (5) n 047.4
~ up (3) v 005.6
thickens (1) v 042.5
thicker (93) adj 026.3
thickest (1) adj 051.2
thicket (18) n/adj 061.6
~ whiskey (1) n 050.8
Thicket (4) 029.5
thickets (4) n 029.5
thickheaded (6) adj 074.8
thicklen (1) n 050.8
thickness gravy (1) n 048.5
thicky (3) adj 029.9
thief (10) n 073.5
thieved (1) v 100.2
thieves (9) n 059.5
thieving on (1) v 080.7
thigh (179) n/adj 072.8
~ bone (2) n 037.1
thigh[N-i] (1) n 072.8
thighs (39) n 072.8
thills (1) n 020.9
thimble (24) n/adj 065.8
~ -skein wagon (1) n 021.1
thimbles (5) n 021.8

thin (168) v/adj 072.9
~ bacon (1) n 046.5
~ ice (11) n 007.6
~ out (1) v 015.8
~ rinds (1) n 056.9
~ -shell hickor(y) nut (1) n 061.8
~ -skin (1) adj 075.1
~ -skin potato (1) n 055.4
~ -skinned (6) adj 075.1
~ soil (2) n 029.9
thin[V-s] (1) v 015.8
thing (803) n 064.4
thing[N-i] (17) n 016.7
thingamajigs (1) n 008.3
things (560) n 010.2
thingumadoogy (1) n 088.8
think (1758) v 094.1
~ about (27) v 013.5
~ like (1) v 058.3
~ of (145) v 013.5
~ on (3) v 032.8
~ over (2) v 013.5
~ through (1) v 075.3
~ up (1) v 058.7
~ [P-0] (1) v 012.8
th(ink) (1) v 062.2
think[V-p] (7) v 125.3
think[V-s] about (2) v 013.5
thinker (1) n 080.8
thinking (286) v 013.5
~ about (167) v 013.5
~ (a)bout (26) v 013.5
~ of (27) v 013.5
~ on (3) v 013.5
~ over (2) v 013.5
thinks (58) v 100.1
~ about (3) v 013.9
~ like (1) v 065.3
~ of (1) v 053.4
thinly (1) adv 007.6
thinned (9) v 015.8
~ out (1) v 015.8
thinner (8) n/adj 070.7
thinnest (1) adj 051.3
thinning (44) v 015.8
~ out (1) v 015.8
thinnings (1) n 055A.5
thins (2) v 013.9
third (1069) n/adj 001A.3
~ base (2) n 001A.3

~ -grade molasses (1) n 001A.3
~ -level roads (1) n 031.7
~ quarter (1) n 046.4
Third (32) 107.6
~ Creek (3) TN 030.7
~ John (1) 001A.3
~ Street (14) 001A.3
~ Ward (9) 001A.3
thirds (6) n 001A.3
thirsty (1) adj 026.1
thirteen (1084) n/adj 001.7
~ -minute (1) adj 001.7
~ -striped ground squirrel (1) n 059.8
Thirteen Oliver (1) 021.6
thirteenth (14) n/adj 001A.3
Thirteenth (3) 001A.3
~ District (1) 001A.3
~ Street (2) 107.8
thirties (8) n 001A.1
Thirties (22) 001A.1
thirtieth (3) n/adj 001A.1
Thirtieth Street (2) 107.7
thirty (2519) n/adj 001A.1
~ -acre (1) adj 001A.1
~ after (1) n 004.4
~ -by-forty (1) adj 009.9
~ -eight (39) n/adj 001.4
~ -eight magnum (1) n 113.1
~ -eight Remington (1) n 113.1
~ -eight Smith and Wesson (1) n 113.1
~ -eight Smith and Wesson special gun (1) n 113.1
~ -eight special (4) n 001A.1
~ -eights (1) n 113.1
~ -first (6) n/adj 001A.3
~ -five (124) n/adj 001A.1
~ -five-pound (1) adj 017.2
~ -foot (1) adj 007.9

~ -four (28) n/adj 001A.1
~ -gallon (1) adj 017.6
~ -inch (1) adj 001A.1
~ minutes after (2) n 004.4
~ minutes before (1) n 004.4
~ minutes past (7) n 004.4
~ minutes till (9) n 004.4
~ minutes to (3) n 004.4
~ -nine (33) n/adj 001A.5
~ -one (35) n/adj 001A.1
~ -second (1) n 001A.1
~ -seven (41) n/adj 001.4
~ -six (42) n/adj 001A.1
~ -some (2) adj 001A.1
~ -some-odd (1) adj 080.8
~ -something (2) n 103.2
~ -thirty (2) n 113.1
~ -three (32) n/adj 001A.1
~ -two (49) n/adj 113.1
~ -two caliber (1) n 113.1
~ -two special (1) n 113.1
~ -two water (1) n 088.9
Thirty (26) 001A.1
~ -Fifth Street (1) 001A.3
~ -Five (2) 107.1
~ -Four Street (2) 107.6
~ -Nine (1) 107.1
~ -One W (1) 107.1
~ -Second Degree Mason (1) 001A.1
~ -Six (1) 031.6
~ -Sixth Street (1) 107A.8
~ -Two (1) 031.6
this (2787) pron/adj 052.3
thisaway (323) adv 052.3

thistle (1) n 062.3
thistles (2) n 015.9
Thomas (16) GA 087.2
~ Avenue (1) 093.6
~ County (1) GA 086.1
~ Creek (2) GA TN 030.7
~ Jefferson Junior High (1) 125.8
~ melons (1) n 056.9
Thomaston (11) AL GA 087.3
Thomas(ton) (1) GA 087.2
Thomastown (2) MS 087.2
Thomasville (23) Al GA MS 087.8
~ Highway (1) 107.6
~ Road (1) 107.6
Thompson (8) 056.2
~ corn (1) n 056.2
~ Creek (4) LA TN 030.7
~ River (1) LA 030.7
~ Spring (1) AL 030.7
Thompsons (2) 056.9
~ Station (1) TN 087.1
Thomson (6) GA 087.4
thong (1) n 123.8
thongs (9) n 123.8
thorax (1) n 071.7
Thorazine (1) 114.2
thorn (6) n/adj 062.3
~ tree (4) n 062.7
~ trees (1) n 061.8
Thorn (1) MS 087.7
thornbush (1) n 061.8
thornbushes (2) n 062.2
thornless careless (1) adj 015.9
thorns (2) n 062.3
thorny (3) adj 062.2
~ ash (1) n 062.2
~ bushes (1) n 062.3
~ careless (1) adj 015.9
thornyhead (1) n 059.9
thoroughbred (2) adj 036.5
~ cattle (1) n 036.5
thoroughbreds (1) n 034.5
thoroughfare (7) n 107.5
thoroughfares (5) n 031.4
those (1442) pron/adj 052.1

though (64) adv/conj 088.3
thought (197) n/v 100.1
~ about (14) v 101.2
~ of (10) v 012.5
Thought (1) 086.2
thoughtful (1) adj 058.1
thoughtless (1) adj 074.6
thoughts (2) n 079.7
thousand (1164) n/adj 001A.2
~ -leg (1) n 060.5
~ -leg worm (1) n 060.5
~ -leg[N-i] (1) n 060A.6
~ -legged worm (1) n 060.5
~ -legs (1) n 001A.2
thous(and) (1) n/adj 001A.2
thousand[N-i] (2) n 001A.2
thousands (44) n 001A.2
thrash (343) v 042.1
~ out (1) v 042.1
thrash[V-r] (3) v 042.1
thrash[V-t] (2) v 042.1
thrashed (208) v 042.1
~ out (9) v 042.1
thrasher (51) n 042.1
thrash(er) (1) n 042.1
Thrasher Bridge (1) 106.7
thrashers (8) n 059.3
thrashes (14) v 042.1
thrashing (111) n/v/adj 042.1
~ froe (1) n 042.1
~ machine (14) n 042.1
~ machines (1) n 042.1
~ out (1) v 065.5
thread (13) n/adj 070.7
~ ball (1) n 081.8
~ follows the needle (1) n 130.3
threading (1) v 042.1
threads (30) n 123.6
threaten (3) v 005.6
~ to (1) v 100.1
threaten[V-s] (1) v 005.6
threatened (6) v 100.1
~ to (1) v 100.1
threatening (117) v/adj 005.6

~ -looking (1) adj 005.6
~ to (13) v 101.2
~ weather (8) n 005.6
threatens to (1) v 005.6
three (3279) n/adj 001.2
~ -bedroom house (1) n 014.1
~ -bottom plow (2) n 021.6
~ -car garage (1) n 007A.8
~ -cornered (1) adj 085.2
~ -cornered cupboard (1) n 010.1
~ -cornered file (1) n 077.8
~ -cornered grass (1) n 029.7
~ -door Willys Knight sedan (1) n 088.9
~ -eighty-two (1) n 001.2
~ -fifteen (1) n 004.5
~ -fifty magnum (1) n 113.1
~ -fifty-seven magnum (1) n 113.1
~ -fifty-seven magnums (2) n 113.1
~ -foot (3) n/adj 021.6
~ -foot plow (2) n 021.6
~ -forty-five (5) n 004.5
~ -gaited horse (1) n 081.9
~ -gallon (1) adj 017.3
~ -holer (3) n 012.1
~ -holers (1) n 012.1
~ -horse stag (1) n 023.9
~ -hundred-foot (1) adj 001A.2
~ -hundred-pound (1) adj 045.4
~ in the floor (1) n 110.7
~ -inch (1) adj 001.2
~ -leaf (3) adj 001.2
~ -leaf poison vine (3) n 062.3
~ -legged iron kettle (1) n 017.6

~ -legged races (1) n 088.9
~ -legged skillets (2) n 017.5
~ -minute egg (2) n 046.2
~ -minute eggs (2) n 046.1
~ -month school (1) n 080.6
~ -month summer school (1) n 083.7
~ -oh-three (1) n 001.2
~ -oh-two (1) n 001.2
~ on the column (1) n 110.7
~ on the floor (2) n 110.7
~ on the tree (1) n 110.7
~ -one-seven-seven-four (1) n 001.4
~ -packed roads (1) n 031.7
~ -path road (5) n 031.7
~ -path roads (3) n 031.7
~ -pathed roads (1) n 031.7
~ -piece bamboo couch (1) n 009.1
~ -piece suit (7) n 001.2
~ -piece suits (1) n 027.7
~ -plank fence (1) n 016.2
~ point two (1) n 121.9
~ -pound (1) adj 019.2
~ -quarter breeds (1) n 069.5
~ -quarter-mile (1) adv 088.1
~ -quarter ton (1) n 109.7
~ -quarters (4) n 004.5
~ -quarters after (1) n 004.5
~ quarters of an hour (1) n 004.5
~ -room (1) adj 001.2
~ -room box house (1) n 007A.1

~ -room house (6) n 014.1
~ -room houses (1) n 118.9
~ -room school (1) n 065.8
~ -room sharpshooter (1) n 007A.8
~ -room shotgun house (2) n 118.6
~ -room shotgun outfit (1) n 007A.5
~ -rowed turtle (1) n 060.6
~ -seed (1) adj 055A.3
~ shift (1) n 110.7
~ -six-six (1) n 001.3
~ -sixty-six (1) n 001.2
~ -speed (9) n 110.7
~ stack (1) n 045.3
~ -step (1) n 083.1
~ -story (1) n 118.9
~ -story hotel (2) n 001.2
~ -strand wire fence (1) n 016.3
~ -team crop (1) n 041.3
~ -team plow (1) n 021.6
~ -thirty (24) n 004.4
~ -three-six-oh-nine (1) n 001.2
~ -ton (1) adj 109.5
~ -track roads (1) n 031.7
~ -trail road (2) n 031.8
~ -twenty-one (1) n 001.2
~ -two (1) adj 050.9
~ -two beer (1) n 121.9
~ -up team (1) n 033.7
~ -week (1) adj 001.2
~ -wheel car (1) n 023.6
~ -year-old (2) n/adj 001.2
thr(ee) (1) adj 088.1
Three (79) 001A.1
~ Creeks (2) AR 030.7
~ -D (1) 089.8
~ -Forty-One (1) 031.7
~ -in-One oil (2) n 024.1

~ -Nineteen (1) 107.1
~ Notch Road (1) 031.9
~ -Oh-One (2) 107.1
~ Rivers (1) TX 087.9
~ Six[N-i] (1) 078.4
~ Sixes (22) 078.4
~ -Sixteen (1) 001.2
~ Sixty (2) 078.4
~ -Sixty-Sixes (1) 078.4
~ Ss (3) 078.4
~ -Thirty-One (1) 107.1
~ Trail Road (1) 031.6
Threemile Creek (1) AL 030.7
threes (1) n 001.2
threescore (1) n 001.2
threesies (2) n 130.6
thresh (116) v 042.1
~ out (1) v 042.1
thresh[V-r] (1) v 042.1
thresh[V-t] (1) v 042.1
threshed (63) v 042.1
~ out (4) v 042.1
thresher (9) n/adj 042.1
~ machine (1) n 042.1
threshhold (1) n 008.2
threshing (37) v/adj 042.1
~ machine (7) n 042.1
~ machines (1) n 042.1
~ process (1) n 042.1
threw (622) v 032.1
~ a hook (1) v 083.4
~ at (10) v 032.1
~ away (6) v 032.1
~ down (1) v 032.1
~ him back (1) v 082.1
~ him down (2) v 082.1
~ him off (1) v 082.1
~ him over (5) v 082.1
~ him overboard (1) v 082.1
~ in (1) v 032.1
~ in their cards (1) v 078.6
~ out (1) v 032.1
~ up (61) v 080.3
~ up his guts (1) v 080.3
threwed (2) v 032.1
thrift (3) adj 123.5
~ clothes (1) n 123.5
~ store (1) n 123.5

~ -store clothes (1) n 123.5
thrifty (10) adj 073.5
thrill (2) n 091.6
thrill[V-t] (1) v 054.7
thrilled (4) v/adj 032.9
thrills (1) n 114.9
thrips (1) n 080.6
throat (1098) n/adj 071.7
~ bone (1) n 061.7
~ disease (1) n 071.7
~ fever (1) n 071.7
~ trouble (1) n 076.5
throat[N-i] (1) n 071.7
throated (2) adj 059.3
throatlatch (1) n 071.7
throats (12) n 071.7
Throbber (1) 124.5
throne (1) n 012.1
throng (1) n 082.8
throttle (3) n 110.7
through (401) adj/adv/prep 032.1
~ road (4) n 031.6
~ street (3) n 107.5
~ streets (1) n 107.6
~ trains (1) n 025.2
~ with him (5) adj 082.1
throw (976) v/adj 032.1
~ at (18) v 032.1
~ away (11) v 032.1
~ back your food (1) v 080.2
~ bed (2) n 029.2
~ cover (1) n 028.7
~ off (2) v 032.1
~ off on (1) v 099.7
~ -offs (1) n 123.5
~ on (1) v 032.1
~ out (6) v 032.1
~ -out plow (1) n 021.6
~ -outs (1) n 089.8
~ pillows (1) n 028.8
~ up (383) v 080.2
~ -up (1) n 080.3
~ (u)p (1) v 053.5
throw[V-p] (2) v 013.9
throw[V-r] (6) v 032.1
~ him out (1) v 082.1
throwaway (2) n/adj 123.5
~ stuff (1) n 053.8
throwaways (3) n 010.2
throwback (2) n 055.3

throwed (382) v 032.1
~ after (1) v 032.1
~ at (3) v 032.1
~ away (17) v 032.1
~ back (1) v 032.1
~ down (1) v 032.1
~ in (1) v 040.1
~ off (7) v 034.4
~ out (1) v 032.1
~ over (1) v 032.1
~ up (31) v 080.3
~ [P-0] (1) v 057.7
throwers (2) n 129.3
throwing (93) v 032.1
~ back (1) v 032.1
~ him (1) v 082.1
~ the rope (1) v 130.6
~ up (48) v 080.3
~ up his socks (1) v 080.3
thrown (61) v 032.1
~ away (3) v 032.1
~ back (1) v 082.1
~ from (2) v 034.4
~ him over (1) v 082.1
~ off (6) v 034.4
~ out (1) v 099.4
~ up (5) v 080.3
throwned (1) v 032.1
throws (17) v 032.1
~ his toes up (1) v 080.3
~ out (1) v 059.4
~ up (4) v 080.2
thrush (7) n 079.7
thrushes (1) n 081.9
thrust (1) v 104.3
thruway (4) n 031.7
thruways (1) n 107.5
thug (2) n 113.7
thumb (39) n/adj 072.3
~ -bolt (2) n 030.8
~ -bolted (1) v 030.8
~ tomatoes (1) n 055.3
Thumb (3) 055.3
Thumbelina tomatoes (1) n 055.3
thumble-fisted (1) adj 073.3
thumbs (3) n 073.3
thump (2) n 130.5
thumper (6) n 006.1
thumpers (4) n 126.6
thumping (3) n/v/adj 093.8

~ spells (1) n 104.8
thunder (43) n/adj 006.2
~ -and-lightning storm (3) n 006.2
~ -and-lightning storms (1) n 006.2
~ cooters (1) n 060.7
~ frog (1) n 060.3
~ mug (2) n 081.8
~ oak (1) n 062.3
~ snake (1) n 092.8
thund(er) (2) n 006.2
thun(der) (1) n 006.2
thunder[V-p] (1) v 013.6
thunderation (1) interj 092.2
thunderberry (1) n 062.4
Thunderbird (4) 114.7
thunderbirds (1) n 080.7
Thunderbolt River (1) GA 030.7
thundercloud (16) n/adj 005.3
~ rain (1) n 006.1
thunderclouds (7) n 006.2
thundered (2) v 006.2
~ around (1) v 090.7
thunderhead (3) n/adj 005.3
~ clouds (1) n 005.3
thunderheads (14) n 005.3
thundering (2) v/adj 006.2
~ storm (1) n 006.2
thunders (2) v 013.1
thundershower (46) n 006.2
thundershowers (10) n 006.2
thundersqualls (1) n 006.2
thunderstorm (432) n 006.2
thunderstorms (39) n 006.2
thunderwood (28) n/adj 062.3
~ bush (1) n 062.3
~ trees (1) n 062.3
thunk (1) v 098.7
Thurber (2) TX 086.6
Thuringer (1) 121.6
Thurmond Grey (3) 056.9
Thursday (976) 002.1
~ evening (1) n 002.1
~ night (7) n 002.1

~ week (9) n 003.7
Thursdays (3) 002.1
thyroids (1) n 078.4
ti-woo(x2) (1) interj 038.3
Tibby (1) MS 030.7
tibia (1) n 072.7
Tice (1) 105.1
Tichnor (1) AR 087.1
tick (110) n/v/adj/interj 060A.9
~ bird (1) n 080.8
~ cattle (1) n 033.6
~ -eradication program (1) n 080.8
~ field (1) n 016.1
~ -tacking (1) v 093.6
~ tag (2) n 098.4
Tick (1) 030.7
ticked off (1) v 075.2
ticket (4) n/adj 093.8
tickets (2) n 103.4
Tickfaw (1) LA 030.7
ticking (7) n 080.8
tickites (1) n 069.9
tickle (6) n/adj 076.5
~ grass (2) n 015.9
tickle[V-t] (4) v 075.8
tickled (5) v 070.6
tickler (1) n 124.9
tickles (1) v 092.7
tickling (2) n 076.5
ticklish (1) adj 052.8
ticks (131) n 060A.9
ticky (2) adj 075.1
tidal (15) adj 030.3
~ area (1) n 030.3
~ basin (3) n 030.3
~ marsh (2) n 030.3
~ marshland (1) n 029.7
~ pool (2) n 030.3
~ stream (2) n 030.3
~ water (1) n 030.3
~ wave (3) n 112.2
tidbit (1) n 048.6
tide (12) n/adj 030.3
~ creeks (1) n 030.3
~ gate (1) n 030.2
~ swamp (1) n 029.7
~ wood (1) n 029.7
Tide (1) 114.7
tidelands (2) n 029.7
tides (5) n 093.9
tidewater (5) n/adj 029.7

~ creeks (1) n 030.3
tidied up (2) v 010.4
tid(ied) up (1) v 010.4
tidies (8) v 010.4
~ up (6) v 010.4
Tidwell (2) 030.7
~ Creek (1) MS 030.7
~ Thicket (1) TX 080.8
tidy (19) v 010.4
~ up (15) v 010.4
tidying (18) v 010.4
~ up (15) v 010.4
tie (46) n/v/adj 027.3
~ hacker (1) n 088.7
~ shoe (1) n 123.8
~ shoes (2) n 123.8
~ the knot (7) v 082.2
~ up (1) v 037.5
~ -up (1) n 093.9
~ -up game (1) n 130.6
~ -up shoes (1) n 123.8
tied (77) v 082.2
~ around (1) v 082.2
~ down (1) v 082.2
~ for life (1) v 082.2
~ in (1) v 041.6
~ onto (1) v 027.2
~ the knot (38) v 082.2
~ the rope (1) v 082.2
~ together (5) v 082.2
~ up (12) v 082.2
tier poles (1) n 084.8
tiered parking lot (1) n 108.4
ties (11) n/v 027.3
tievine (4) n 015.9
tievines (3) n 016.8
Tift (4) GA 087.5
~ County (2) GA 087.8
~ loam (1) n 029.8
Tifton (23) GA 087.8
~ soil (1) n 029.9
tig tag (1) n 089.8
tiger (18) n/adj 050.8
Tiger Bayou (1) LA 030.7
tigering (1) v 050.8
tigers (4) n 050.8
Tigertail (1) 106.2
tiggers (1) n 060A.8
tight (354) adj 073.5
~ ass (1) n 073.9
~ -bark hickory (1) n 061.9
~ head (1) n 073.5
~ land (1) n 029.8

~ -legged jeans (1) n 027.4
~ peach (1) n 054.3
~ salt land (1) n 029.8
~ soils (1) n 029.8
~ tongue (1) n 127.4
Tight (1) 030.8
tightening (2) v 007.2
~ on (1) v 007.2
~ up (1) v 007.2
tighter (2) adj 066.1
tightest (1) adj 095.2
tightfist (1) n 073.5
tightfisted (6) adj 073.5
tightness (1) n 128.1
tights (1) n 123.4
tightwad (396) n 073.5
tightwads (12) n 073.5
Tigre (7) 030.7
Tijuana (2) 114.1
~ Gold (1) 114.1
~ tea (1) n 114.1
tile (18) n/v/adj 030.1
~ bath (1) n 007A.6
~ floors (1) n 007A.5
tiling (2) v 030.1
till (617) v/prep 021.7
Till (1) 053.5
tillable (1) adj 029.3
Tillar (3) AR 086.2
Tillatoba (1) MS 087.3
tiller (117) n 120.4
til(ler) plows (1) n 021.6
tillers (9) n 021.7
Tillett Lake (1) TN 030.7
tilling (2) v/adj 021.7
~ plowing (1) n 021.7
Tillman (1) FL 087.2
Tillmans Corner (1) 105.1
Tilson Lane (1) 031.8
tilt (2) n/v 022.5
tilted (1) v 040.4
tilters (1) n 120.4
tilting (2) v 022.8
Tim (3) 055.3
timber (96) n/adj 029.5
~ business (3) n 065.8
~ country (1) n 061.6
~ hauling (1) n 021.4
~ holders (1) n 008.3
~ marker (1) n 080.6
~ owl (1) n 059.2
~ rattle (1) n 084.9
~ rattler (3) n 080.9
~ rattlers (2) n 088.7

~ snake (1) n 081.9
~ swamp (1) n 029.6
~ wolves (3) n 033.2
Timber (2) 106.2
~ Crest (1) 106.2
Timbercrest (1) TX 087.9
timbered off (1) v 041.4
timberland (4) n 041.4
Timberlane (1) 106.2
timberman (1) n 080.7
timbers (3) n 020.9
Timbers (1) 106.1
time (2904) n/adj 004.2
~ was up (1) v 078.5
Time (3) 088.3
~ Saver (2) 116.2
time[N-i] (24) n 071.1
timepiece (10) n 004.3
timer (2) n 115.3
timers (4) n 025.3
timers' (1) adj 048.4
times (180) n 001.2
Times (1) 086.1
timesy (1) adj 066.8
timetable (1) n 081.8
timey (63) adj 017.6
timid (9) adj 075.1
Timmons Creek (1) TN 030.7
timothy field (1) n 029.5
Timpson (2) TX 087.7
Tims (2) 055.3
tin (1261) n/adj 026.6
~ boat (1) n 024.6
~ box (1) n 028.2
~ boxes (1) n 026.6
~ bucket (83) n 017.3
~ buckets (37) n 017.3
~ building (2) n 026.6
~ can (109) n 026.6
~ -can hy spy (1) n 130.4
~ cans (65) n 019.2
~ cribs (1) n 014.3
~ cup (57) n 026.6
~ cups (21) n 026.6
~ dipper (5) n 026.6
~ dippers (2) n 026.6
~ doors (2) n 026.6
~ drinking cups (1) n 026.6
~ forks (1) n 017.8
~ funnel (1) n 019.3
~ gutter (1) n 026.6
~ gutters (1) n 026.6

~ hampers (1) n 081.9
~ heaters (5) n 026.6
~ hoop (2) n 020.3
~ hoops (2) n 020.3
~ house (3) n 011.7
~ kettle (1) n 017.6
~ lamp (1) n 026.6
~ lamps (1) n 024.3
~ lid (1) n 020.4
~ milk pail (1) n 017.3
~ pail (9) n 017.3
~ pails (7) n 017.3
~ pan (3) n 026.6
~ -pan disc (1) n 021.7
~ pans (4) n 026.6
~ peddler (1) n 026.6
~ pipe (2) n 026.6
~ pipes (1) n 026.6
~ plates (2) n 026.6
~ pots (1) n 017.6
~ ring (1) n 020.3
~ roof (35) n 014.2
~ -roof house (2) n 011.4
~ roofing (1) n 011.4
~ roofs (4) n 026.6
~ shed (1) n 026.6
~ sheets (2) n 026.6
~ skillet (3) n 017.5
~ stove (4) n 026.6
~ strips (1) n 020.3
~ syrup bucket (1) n 019.2
~ thing (1) n 026.6
~ top (6) n 020.4
~ -top house (5) n 011.4
~ -top houses (1) n 026.6
~ tops (1) n 026.6
~ tub (12) n 026.6
~ tubs (7) n 026.6
~ vat (1) n 026.6
~ vessel (2) n 017.3
~ vessels (1) n 026.6
~ wagons (1) n 026.6
Tin (9) 030.7
~ Bucket Slough (1) TX 030.7
~ Cup (1) AR 087.1
~ -Cup Alley (1) 026.6
~ Henry (1) 090.8
~ Lizzie (3) 023.6
~ Lizzies (1) 023.6
~ -Pan Lizzie (1) 023.6

tinder (11) n/adj 008.6
~ wood (1) n 008.6
tindly (1) adj 088.7
tinfoil (3) n 026.6
tinge (1) n 045.7
tingle (1) n 056.3
tinhorn (1) n 026.6
tinker (2) n 067.8
tinning (2) n 026.6
tins (7) n 019.2
tinsy (2) adj 080.7
tint (1) n 046.9
tinted (2) adj 060.3
tiny (5) adj 074.9
Tiny (5) 055.3
~ Tim (3) 055.3
~ Tims (2) 055.3
tio (1) n S 068.2
Tio Juan (1) S 068.2
Tioga (3) LA TX 070.9
tip (34) n/adj 095.7
~ steak (2) n 131.7
~ the icebox (1) n 130.2
Tiparillos (1) 057.3
Tiplersville (1) MS 087.2
Tippah (5) MS 087.2
~ Bottom (1) MS 087.2
~ River (1) MS 030.7
~ (River) (1) MS 087.3
tipped over (1) v 101.9
tipping (2) v 084.8
~ (a)round (1) v 084.8
Tippo (1) MS 087.3
tippy (1) n 130.3
tips (17) n 095.7
tipsy (1) adj 024.6
tiptoeing (1) v 057.4
Tipton (2) TN 087.1
~ County (1) TN 087.7
Tiptonville (3) TN 087.7
tire (360) n/adj 021.1
~ knocker (1) n 113.2
~ rut (1) n 030.5
~ shrinker (1) n 091.8
~ swing (11) n 022.9
~ swings (1) n 022.9
~ tools (1) n 021.2
Tire (2) 067.7
tire[V-t] (1) v 075.4
tired (1077) v/adj 075.4
~ of him (4) adj 082.1
~ out (29) v 075.5
tireless (1) adj 074.1
tires (60) n 021.1

tiresome (1) adj 075.4
tiring (1) adj 090.4
Tishomingo (6) MS 087.2
    ~ County (2) MS 070.7
    ~ Creek (1) MS 030.7
    ~ State Park (1) MS
      087.3
tissue (14) n 070.7
tisswood (1) n 061.8
tit (6) n 091.7
    ~ for tat (1) n 081.9
Titanic (2) 083.1
    ~ ship (1) n 084.8
tithe (1) v 094.8
tithes (2) n 094.8
titis (1) n 061.8
title (1) n 064.7
Title (5) 001.2
    ~ Four (1) 001.2
    ~ One (1) 001.1
    ~ Six (1) 001.3
    ~ Three (1) 001.2
    ~ Two (1) 001.1
titmouse (1) n 059.3
tittie (1) n 007.5
titties (1) n 046.3
titty part (1) n 046.4
Titus County (1) TX
    087.3
Titusville (5) FL 087.8
titzy (2) adj 085.4
Tivoli (1) TX 087.6
to (19845) prep 032.5
    ~ be husband (1) n
      081.5
    ~ -do (14) n 080.7
    ~ his stomach (39) adv
      080.4
    ~ -make-soap pot (1) n
      017.6
    ~ my stomach (4) adv
      080.4
    ~ the left (1) interj
      038.2
    ~ the stomach (5) adv
      080.4
    ~ the tummy (1) adv
      080.4
    ~ up (2) v 080.2
    ~ your stomach (1) adv
      080.4
    ~ [D-0] stomach (1)
      adv 080.4
t(o) (45) prep 082.6

    ~ his stomach (1) adv
      080.4
(t)o (1) prep 058.4
toad (909) n/adj 060.4
    ~ choker (1) n 006.1
    ~ -frog (449) n 060.4
    ~ -frog houses (4) n
      057.1
    ~ -frog stool (3) n
      057.1
    ~ -frog stools (3) n
      057.1
    ~ -frog strangler (1) n
      006.1
    ~ -frog[N-i] (1) n
      060.4
    ~ -frogs (214) n 060.4
    ~ fucker (1) n 090.6
    ~ outfit (1) n 057.1
    ~ sacks (1) n 019.7
    ~ strangler (17) n 006.1
    ~ stranglers (5) n 006.1
    ~ stringer (3) n 006.1
    ~ umbrellas (1) n 057.1
toadfish (5) n 059.9
toadies up to (1) v 125.6
toads (138) n 060.4
toadstones (1) n 057.1
toadstool (249) n 057.1
toadstool[N-i] (2) n
    057.1
toadstools (386) n 057.1
toady (20) n/adj 060.4
    ~ -frog (16) n 060.4
    ~ -frogs (3) n 060.4
toadystool (1) n 057.1
toallito (1) n S 018.5
toast (13) n/adj 044.4
    ~ bread (1) n 092.8
toasted (5) adj 044.4
    ~ biscuits (1) n 044.4
    ~ egg (3) n 046.2
    ~ egg[N-i] (1) n 046.2
toasted egg (2) n 046.2
toaster (37) n/adj 116.4
    ~ and oven (1) n 116.4
    ~ oven (16) n 116.4
    ~ -oven-type thing (1)
      n 116.4
toasters (6) n 116.4
tobacco (253) n/adj 016.1
    ~ acreage (1) n 016.1
    ~ barn (7) n 014.2
    ~ barns (4) n 014.2
    ~ base (1) n 016.1

    ~ chair (2) n 008.8
    ~ chewer (1) n 069.9
    ~ -curing barns (1) n
      014.2
    ~ factory (1) n 070.6
    ~ field (9) n 016.1
    ~ fields (1) n 025.2
    ~ ground (1) n 016.1
    ~ gum (1) n 090.8
    ~ harvester (1) n 089.8
    ~ hogheads (1) n 019.2
    ~ horses (1) n 081.9
    ~ juice (1) n 102.7
    ~ lot (1) n 016.1
    ~ patch (28) n 016.1
    ~ patches (1) n 016.1
    ~ people (1) n 013.8
    ~ plot (1) n 016.1
    ~ plow (1) n 021.6
    ~ press (1) n 084.8
    ~ sled (1) n 081.9
    ~ stick (1) n 117.7
    ~ sticks (2) n 117.7
    ~ string (1) n 088.9
    ~ tags (1) n 081.9
    ~ twist (1) n 081.9
    ~ weed (1) n 057.3
    ~ wood worm (1) n
      060.5
    ~ worm (4) n 060.5
(to)bacco (54) n/adj
    057.3
    ~ barn (4) n 014.2
    ~ beds (1) n 081.8
    ~ boxes (1) n 022.2
    ~ bundle (1) n 041.5
    ~ can (1) n 065.8
    ~ cloth (1) n 019.7
    ~ cutter (1) n 057.4
    ~ farmer (1) n 057.5
    ~ field (4) n 016.1
    ~ hills (1) n 030.8
    ~ lot (1) n 016.1
    ~ patch (6) n 016.1
    ~ sack (2) n 019.7
    ~ sacks (2) n 019.6
    ~ shed (1) n 057.3
    ~ worm (1) n 060.5
Tobacco (2) 069.7
    ~ Road (1) 069.7
    ~ -Road-type people
      (1) n 074.9
Tobannee (2) GA 030.7
    ~ Creek (1) GA 030.7
Tobesofkee (3) GA 030.7

    ~ Creek (2) GA 030.7
Tobey (1) 106.5
toby (2) n 117.7
Toby Bayou (1) MS
    030.7
Toca (1) MS 087.8
tocayo (1) n S 068.2
Toccoa (6) GA 087.3
Tocco(a) (1) GA 053.5
Toccopola (5) MS 087.1
    ~ Road (1) 031.7
today (406) n/adj 003.5
    ~ week (5) n 003.7
(to)day (1) n 024.8
Todd (1) 067.1
toddies (1) n 061.4
toddle (1) v 096.2
toddler (2) n 096.2
toddlers (1) n 064.3
toddles (8) v 096.2
toddy (11) n 050.8
toe (21) n/adj 072.6
    ~ itch (4) n 089.8
toe[N-i] (1) n 088.8
toed (8) adj 123.8
toenail (1) n 080.1
toes (23) n 070.8
tofore (1) adv 096.8
toga parties (1) n 130.7
together (208) n/adj/adv
    075.7
    ~ apartment (1) n
      119.1
togethers (3) n 130.7
togged up (1) v 028.1
Toggenburg goats (1) n
    088.9
toggery (2) n 123.6
togs (3) n 131.3
toilet (488) n/adj 012.1
    ~ articles (1) n 065.8
    ~ facilities (1) n
      007A.1
    ~ outside (2) n 012.1
    ~ paper (2) n 012.1
    ~ room (2) n 118.3
    ~ rooms (1) n 126.3
    ~ soap (1) n 080.7
toil(et) (2) n 012.1
toilets (139) n 012.1
toilette (1) n F 009.2
Tojos (1) 126.5
toke (2) n 114.1
token (20) n/adj 095.7
    ~ people (1) n 115.4

tokens (1) n 085.8
told (275) v 101.1
~ him no (3) v 082.1
~ on (3) v 101.3
~ to (5) v 058.4
tolder (2) n 080.5
Toledo (13) OH TN 087.9
~ Bend (4) LA TX 087.2
~ Bend Dam (1) LA 030.7
~ Bend Lake (1) TX 030.7
~ Bend Reservoir (1) LA 030.7
~ Lake (1) LA 087.7
(To)ledo Bend Dam (1) LA 030.5
tolerable (41) adj 079.4
toler(able) (1) adj 079.4
tolerably (4) adv 090.4
tolerate (2) v 040.6
toll (45) n/adj 019.8
~ bridge (2) n 107.5
~ bridges (1) n 077.8
~ corn (1) n 081.8
~ dipper (1) n 090.9
~ road (6) n 107.5
~ roads (1) n 107.5
Toll (1) 107.5
tollgate (1) n 092.8
tollgates (1) n 089.8
tolling (1) v 080.8
tollway (1) n 031.6
Tolomato River (1) FL 030.7
tom (16) n/adj 055.3
~ toes (2) n 055.3
~ -tom (2) n 055.3
~ -tom tomato (1) n 055.3
~ -tom tomatoes (1) n 055.3
~ tomato (1) n 055.3
~ tomatoes (2) n 055.3
~ (to)matoes (1) n 055.3
Tom (82) 069.3
~ around (1) v 068.5
~ Brown Park (1) 106.4
~ Lee Park (2) 106.4
~ Thumb (2) 055.3

~ Thumb tomatoes (1) n 055.3
~ town (1) n 105.6
~ Walkers (11) 101.8
~ Watkins (2) 056.9
~ Watson (40) 056.9
~ Watsons (1) 056.9
tomahawk outfit (1) n 020.7
Tomahawk (2) AR 087.5
tomahawks (1) n 020.7
tomate figue (1) n F 055.3
Tomates (2) 055.3
Tomatillas (1) 055.3
tomato (308) n/adj 055.3
~ can (1) n 055.3
~ cans (1) n 055.3
~ country (1) n 055.3
~ gravy (1) n 055.3
~ juice (3) n 055.3
~ patch (11) n 016.1
~ plant (2) n 055.3
~ plants (2) n 055.3
~ sack (1) n 019.6
~ sauce (6) n 048.5
~ seed (2) n 055.3
~ seeds (1) n 055.3
~ soup (4) n 055.3
tomat(o) (1) n/adj 055.3
~ worm (2) n 060.5
~ worms (1) n 060.5
(to)mato (13) n/adj 055.3
~ crops (1) n 055.3
~ plant (1) n 055.3
~ vines (1) n 055.3
Tomato (4) AR 087.3
~ Club (1) 055.3
~ Point (1) AR 087.2
Toma(to) (1) AR 087.4
tomato[N-i] (3) n 055.3
tomatoes (1368) n 055.3
(to)matoes (49) n 055.3
Tomatoes Ranch (1) 055.3
tomatoeses (3) n 055.3
tomb (18) n 078.8
Tomb (1) 106.4
Tomball (1) TX 087.4
Tombigbee (18) AL MS 030.7
~ River (8) AL MS 030.7

(Tom)bigbee River (2) AL 030.7
tomboy (65) n 124.3
tomboyish (4) adj 124.3
tomboys (1) n 124.3
tombs (5) n 117.6
tombstones (1) n 012.2
tomcat (2) n 059.5
tomcats (1) n 126.5
tomcatting (3) v 081.7
tomersault (1) n 095.5
tomfool (2) adj 073.4
~ notion (1) n 101.1
Tomisms (1) 080.9
Tomlin (1) 106.1
tommies (1) n 055.3
tommy tomatoes (1) n 055.3
tommyquat (1) n 055.3
Tommy's Rock (1) TN 101.6
tommyto (47) n/adj 055.3
~ things (1) n 055.3
~ tomato (4) n 055.3
~ (to)mato (1) n 055.3
~ tomatoes (6) n 055.3
~ (to)matoes (1) n 055.3
tommytoes (205) n 055.3
Tomoka (1) FL 030.7
tomorrow (967) n/adj 004.1
~ afternoon (1) n 002.3
~ evening (6) n 004.1
~ morning (2) n 004.1
~ night (6) n 004.1
~ week (4) n 003.7
tomor(row) (34) n/adj 004.1
~ evening (2) n 004.1
~ morning (1) n 004.1
tomo(rrow) (1) n 004.1
(to)morrow (11) n 004.1
Tompeat (1) MS 030.7
Tomrob (1) 107.8
Tom's (1) 068.2
Toms (4) 099.7
tomtit (2) n 059.3
tomtits (1) n 059.3
ton (32) n/adj 019.8
~ pickup (1) n 109.7
~ pied (1) n F 037.5
~ truck (1) n 023.6
ton[N-i] (3) n 041.7
tone (2) n/v 077.2

~ -deaf (1) adj 077.2
~ down (1) v 080.8
toney (1) adj 106.2
Toney (1) AL 087.3
tong (2) n 008.3
tongs (15) n 008.2
tongue (1006) n/adj 020.8
~ and groove (8) n 011.2
~ horse (1) n 039.4
~ -lashing (1) n 065.5
~ mules (1) n 039.4
~ side (1) n 039.4
~ steers (1) n 039.4
~ tattler (1) n 101.3
~ waggler (1) n 126.6
tongues (12) n 020.8
tonic (34) n 078.4
Tonic (1) 078.4
tonight (11) n 002.5
Tonkawa (1) 080.7
tons (4) n 019.8
tonsil[N-i] (1) n 070.9
tonsilitis (20) n 079.7
tonsils (3) n 079.7
Tontitown (1) AR 087.8
Tony Prairie (1) FL 030.7
too (1468) adv 069.1
~ -short shorts (1) n 123.4
took (1860) v 077.1
~ a liking to (1) v 081.4
~ a trip (1) v 078.6
~ after (32) v 065.3
~ aft(er) (1) v 065.3
~ and (4) v 081.3
~ away (3) v 077.1
~ behind (1) v 065.3
~ care (19) v 013.1
~ care of (34) v 077.1
~ down (4) v 077.1
~ from (1) v 077.1
~ in (12) v 083.3
~ it serious (1) v 065.1
~ off (21) v 077.1
~ on (4) v 079.3
~ on off (1) v 077.1
~ out (19) v 077.1
~ out after (1) v 092.7
~ out of (1) v 077.1
~ out to (1) v 101.2
~ over (14) v 077.1
~ the bus (2) v 078.6

~ the journey (1) v 078.6
~ to (2) v 076.1
~ up (27) v 077.1
~ up for (1) v 075.6
~ up with (1) v 088.7
~ with (1) v 076.1
~ [B-0] (1) v 052.1
tooken (17) v 077.1
~ care of (2) v 065.4
~ out (1) v 077.1
~ over (1) v 077.1
tooky (2) adj 074.7
~ -acting (1) adj 074.7
tool (258) n/adj 011.7
~ bin (1) n 011.7
~ building (2) n 011.8
~ chest (1) n 011.7
~ shack (2) n 011.7
~ shed (229) n 011.7
~ sheds (7) n 011.8
~ shelter (3) n 011.9
~ shop (1) n 011.8
tool[N-i] (1) n 013.3
toolbox (2) n 011.7
toolboxes (2) n 011.7
toolhouse (148) n 011.7
toolhouses (10) n 011.7
toolroom (15) n/adj 010.3
~ house (1) n 011.7
tools (29) n 011.7
Toone (1) TN 087.7
toot (3) n/v 125.2
~ out (1) v 027.8
tooted (2) v 077.7
~ out (1) v 077.6
~ up (1) v 077.6
tooth (894) n/adj 071.8
~ dentist (2) n 075.8
~ jostler (1) n 110.9
~ prints (1) n 071.8
~ pullers (1) n 081.9
tooth[N-i] (7) n 071.8
toothache (10) n 071.8
toothbrush (16) n/adj 071.8
~ dish (1) n 071.8
toothbrushes (3) n 071.8
toothed (1) adj 021.7
toothes (2) n 071.8
toothpaste (8) n 071.8
toothpick (3) n 071.8
toothpicks (1) n 071.8
tooths (4) n 071.8

toothy (2) n 071.8
tooting (2) v/adj 114.2
Tootsie (2) 069.4
~ Roll (1) 069.4
~ Rolls (1) 044.4
top (347) n/adj 056.3
~ buggy (1) n 095.9
~ bull (1) n 033.5
~ cover (1) n 029.1
~ cow (3) n 033.5
~ crop (2) n 042.5
~ deck (1) n 010.8
~ dirt (1) n 055.5
~ -dog horses (2) n 034.2
~ dress (1) n 081.8
~ fin (1) n 092.7
~ forty (2) n 130.8
~ -forty music (1) n 130.8
~ harrow (5) n 021.7
~ har(row) (4) n 021.7
~ harrows (2) n 021.7
~ -heavy (1) adj 065.1
~ hog (4) n 035.5
~ horse (1) n 034.2
~ husk (1) n 083.8
~ land (1) n 029.8
~ minnow (1) n 061.2
~ minnows (4) n 061.2
~ part (1) n 055A.5
~ peeling (1) n 054.8
~ people (1) n 080.8
~ porch (1) n 010.8
~ round (1) n 121.1
~ sider (1) n 122.8
~ sirloin (1) n 131.3
~ spread (1) n 029.1
~ steak (1) n 121.1
~ story (1) n 014.5
~ -water bait (1) n 061.2
~ -water minnow (1) n 061.2
~ -water minnows (2) n 061.2
~ waters (3) n 061.2
Top (4) 031.1
top[N-i] (1) n 061.4
topcoat (13) n 027.1
topcoats (1) n 027.1
Topcrop (1) 055A.5
toper (1) n 080.7
topes (1) n S 110.8
topic (1) n 053.6

Topisaw (1) MS 030.7
topknot (1) n 059.3
topless joint (1) n 114.9
topper (1) n 090.8
toppers (2) n 041.8
topping (49) n/adj 122.3
~ road (1) n 031.6
toppings (1) n 122.4
tops (75) n 055A.5
topsail (1) n 084.9
Topsiders (4) 081.9
topsoil (65) n 029.8
torch (211) n/adj 024.3
~ lamp (2) n 024.3
~ pine (1) n 008.6
Torch of Friendship (1) 106.4
torches (21) n 024.3
torchlight (2) n 024.3
tore (429) v 102.6
~ down (75) v 102.6
~ him up (1) v 065.5
~ his seat (1) v 070.2
~ in two (1) v 075.5
~ into (2) v 094.4
~ me up (2) v 065.5
~ my pants off (1) v 065.5
~ off (6) v 102.6
~ off of (1) v 102.6
~ out (2) v 102.6
~ out with (1) v 080.6
~ up (195) v 102.6
~ (u)p (1) v 102.6
~ -up (1) adj 102.6
~ us up (2) v 065.5
tored (4) v 102.6
~ up (3) v 102.6
Tories (1) 080.9
torment (2) n 090.1
torn (483) v 102.6
~ away (2) v 102.6
~ down (83) v 102.6
~ -down (2) adj 102.6
~ off (2) v 102.6
~ open (1) v 102.6
~ out (6) v 102.6
~ up (350) v 102.6
tornado (221) n/adj 112.2
~ -like (1) adj 007.2
~ season (1) n 006.3
~ storms (1) n 112.2
~ warnings (1) n 006.3
~ watch (1) n 112.2
tornadoes (95) n 112.2

toro (9) n S 033.5
Toro (3) LA 087.8
~ Creek (1) LA 030.7
Toronto (3) 087.9
torrent (7) n 006.1
torrential (9) adj 006.1
~ downpour (4) n 006.1
~ rain (1) n 006.1
~ rains (4) n 006.1
torrents (2) n 006.1
torreya tree (1) n 061.8
torso (44) n 072.4
tors(o) (1) n 072.4
tortilla (8) n 044.7
tortillas (12) n 044.6
tortoise (142) n/adj 060.7
~ turtle (1) n 060.6
tortoises (10) n 060.7
torts (1) n 048.3
Tortue (1) 030.7
Tortugas (1) 060.7
torture (1) v 065.9
Tory (1) 129.2
toss (25) n/v/adj 032.1
~ cookies (1) v 080.3
~ his cookies (2) v 080.2
~ my cookies (2) v 080.3
~ salad (1) n 055A.6
~ your cookies (2) v 080.2
tossed (15) v/adj 032.1
~ green salad (1) n 055A.5
~ his cookies (2) v 080.2
~ sallet (1) n 055A.5
~ your cookies (1) v 080.3
tossing (8) v 032.1
~ his cookies (1) v 080.3
~ watermelons (1) v 006.2
tostados (1) n S 081.9
tot (3) n 064.4
total (5) adj 088.9
totaled (1) v 089.8
tote (425) v/adj 098.1
~ around (1) v 098.1
~ bag (6) n 028.2
~ bags (1) n 098.1
~ in (3) v 098.1

~ sack (13) n 019.7
~ sacks (3) n 019.7
~ up (3) v 098.1
Tote-Sum (1) 116.2
tote[V-r] (23) v 098.1
toted (276) v 098.1
totem pole (1) n 098.1
toter (6) n 101.3
toter's (2) adj 098.6
~ license (1) n 098.6
toters (3) n 098.7
totes (4) v 098.1
toting (62) v 021.4
~ in (1) v 098.1
~ out (1) v 098.1
tots (2) n 064.4
tottering (3) v 022.8
touch (863) v/adj 098.2
~ football (9) n 098.4
~ -me-nots (2) n 089.8
~ of (1) v 098.2
touch[V-r] (3) v 098.2
touch[V-t] (1) v 098.2
touchdown (1) n 098.2
touche (1) v 084.9
touched (27) v 098.2
~ with (1) v 006.8
touches (6) v 098.2
touching (10) v/adj 098.2
touchous (86) adj 075.1
touchy (370) adj 075.1
~ -touchy (1) adj 080.8
Tougaloo (1) MS 087.9
tough (45) v/adj 073.3
~ beans (1) n 055A.3
~ gal (1) n 124.3
~ -hull beans (1) n
055A.3
~ -looking (2) adj
025.8
toughed (3) v 081.8
tougher (1) adj 090.7
toughest (2) adj 053.4
toughies (2) n 061.2
toughy (2) n/adj 061.2
~ minnows (1) n 061.2
Toulminville (5) 106.2
Toulouse (1) 089.8
tour (4) n/adj 031.7
~ guides (1) n 058.5
tourage (1) n 077.8
toured on (1) v 052.5
touring (22) n/adj 084.8
~ car (15) n 109.2
~ cars (3) n 109.1

~ Ford (1) n 023.6
tourism (1) n 080.6
tourist (11) n/adj 066.7
~ court (1) n 084.3
~ courts (1) n 084.3
~ home (2) n 084.3
~ homes (1) n 084.3
~ information center
(1) n 107.2
~ places (1) n 070.8
~ trade (1) n 080.9
tourist[N-i] (3) n 065.9
touristes (1) n 016.5
tourists (2) n 075.9
touristy (1) adj 045.2
tournament (1) n 065.9
tournaments (1) n 070.7
tours (1) n 015.5
tout (1) adj F 066.5
to've (19) v 058.1
tow (424) n/v/adj 104.5
~ bag (8) n 019.7
~ bagging (1) n 019.7
~ bags (2) n 019.7
~ boats (1) n 024.6
~ itch (1) n 080.6
~ sack (283) n 019.7
~ -sack curtain (1) n
019.7
~ -sack-looking sack
(1) n 019.7
~ -sack towel (1) n
019.7
~ -sack twill (1) n
019.7
~ sacking (1) n 019.7
~ sacks (110) n 019.7
~ truck (1) n 109.6
Towaliga Creek (1) GA
030.7
toward (481) prep 032.5
towards (428) prep 032.5
towboat (1) n 024.6
towboats (1) n 024.6
towed (6) v/adj 098.1
~ sack (1) n 019.7
towel (1492) n/adj 018.6
~ paper (1) n 018.4
~ rack (1) n 018.6
~ rag (1) n 018.3
~ sack (1) n 019.6
tow(el) (3) n 018.4
to(wel) (1) n 018.6
towel[N-i] (1) n 018.6
towels (176) n 018.6

tower (8) n/adj 014.4
~ apartments (1) n
108.5
Tower (18) TX 087.3
~ Life building (2) n
108.5
~ Mountain (1) GA
031.1
towers (2) n 119.2
Towers (12) 119.2
~ of America (1) 106.4
towhead (1) n 065.7
Towhees (1) 088.8
towing (4) v 021.4
town (496) n/adj 082.8
~ ants (1) n 060A.8
~ ball (6) n 098.4
~ ballbat (1) n 092.7
~ boy (1) n 069.9
~ boys (1) n 069.9
~ butter (1) n 089.9
~ capital (1) n 085.5
~ car (2) n 109.4
~ chickens (1) n 045.1
~ common (1) n 085.1
~ council (4) n 080.7
~ coupe (1) n 109.1
~ dude (4) n 080.6
~ dudes (4) n 069.6
~ gal (1) n 064.9
~ hall (2) n 085.1
~ house (22) n 119.1
~ houses (22) n 119.3
~ jelly bean (1) n 028.1
~ knob (1) n 030.8
~ marshall (1) n 068.8
~ park (2) n 085.1
~ part (1) n 025.4
~ people (4) n 080.6
~ person (1) n 069.9
~ schools (1) n 088.8
~ seat (1) n 085.5
~ sparrows (1) n 093.7
~ square (30) n 085.1
~ squares (1) n 085.1
~ water (3) n 080.6
~ word (1) n 010.6
Town (66) 114.8
~ Branch (2) FL TN
030.7
~ Creek (10) AL MS
TX 030.7
~ Creek route (1) n
006.4
~ East (1) 105.5

~ 'N Country (4) 105.1
towner (3) n 066.7
towners (1) n 066.7
Townley (1) AL 087.9
town's (1) adj 063.4
towns (4) n 090.8
Townsend (2) GA 087.1
township road (1) n 031.8
Township (6) 087.2
townspeople (1) n 032.3
Toxey (1) AL 087.8
toxic (4) adj 062.6
Toxish (1) MS 087.1
toy (423) n/adj 101.5
~ car (1) n 101.5
~ dog (1) n 033.3
~ dogs (1) n 101.5
~ feist (1) n 033.3
~ room (1) n 101.5
~ store (1) n 101.5
~ tomatoes (1) n 055.3
toys (388) n 101.5
~ and stick[N-i] (1) n
130.2
trace (39) n/v/adj 038.6
~ chain (6) n 021.1
~ chains (16) n 038.9
~ line (1) n 039.1
~ tree (1) n 021.2
Trace (17) 030.7
~ Creek (1) TN 030.7
trace[N-i] (2) n 038.6
traces (39) n 038.6
trachea (3) n 071.7
track (49) n/adj 031.8
~ shoes (2) n 123.8
tracking (1) v 057.4
trackless (3) adj 085.3
~ trolley (2) n 085.3
~ trolleys (1) n 085.3
tracks (21) n 031.7
tract (30) n 090.7
traction (1) n 102.7
tractor (74) n/adj 120.4
~ -drawn (1) adj 104.4
~ -driven (1) adj 011.3
~ -drove (1) v 080.6
~ harrow (1) n 021.7
~ house (2) n 011.7
~ houses (1) n 011.8
~ kind (1) n 120.4
~ mower (1) n 120.3
~ mowers (1) n 120.3
~ pens (1) n 011.7
~ plow (4) n 021.6

~ -pulled harrows (1) n 021.7
~ shed (11) n 014.2
~ sheds (4) n 011.8
~ -work (1) v 088.9
tractors (12) n 014.6
Tracy City (1) TN 087.3
trade (50) n/v/adj 094.2
~ at (1) v 094.2
~ day (1) n 080.8
~ for (1) v 094.2
~ schools (1) n 125.9
~ wind (1) n 006.5
~ with (3) v 094.2
Trade (4) 106.6
~ Mart (1) 106.6
trade[N-i] (4) n/adj 067.8
trade[V-p] (2) v 094.2
~ with (1) v 053.4
trade[V-s] (1) v 094.2
traded (17) v 094.2
~ away (1) v 053.7
~ with (1) v 094.2
trader (2) n 034.2
trades (47) n 067.8
trading (97) n/v/adj 094.2
~ center (1) n 085.5
~ in (1) v 094.2
~ post (4) n 114.6
~ with (3) v 093.4
~ with Nancy (1) v 050.9
traffic (7) n/adj 107.6
~ arteries (1) n 107.6
~ breaks (1) n 110.8
~ bump (1) n 110.8
~ bumps (1) n 110.8
~ lane (1) n 107.3
trail (163) n/adj 031.7
~ dog (1) n 033.3
~ dogs (1) n 033.1
~ riding (1) v 034.3
~ road (4) n 031.8
~ roads (1) n 031.8
Trail (19) 031.8
trailed (1) v 097.9
trailer (11) n/adj 118.6
~ house (1) n 014.1
~ load (1) n 019.8
~ parks (1) n 092.9
~ -tractor rigs (1) n 109.6
~ truck (2) n 109.7

trail(er) trucks (1) n 088.8
trailers (4) n 109.6
trailing (1) v 057.4
trails (34) n 031.8
trailway (1) n 031.8
train (237) n/adj 085.3
~ cars (1) n 085.3
~ crossing (2) n 107.8
~ depot (7) n 084.7
~ hoist (1) n 104.5
~ nurse (1) n 053.3
~ station (160) n 084.7
~ stop (1) n 084.7
~ terminal (2) n 084.7
trainasse (1) n F 030.3
traineau (1) n F 021.9
trained (8) v/adj 013.5
~ in (1) v 053.4
~ nurse (1) n 065.2
~ to (1) v 053.4
training (6) n/v 039.7
trainmen (1) n 052.1
trains (14) n 085.3
trains' overpass (1) n 107.8
trait (1) n 065.3
traits (4) n 065.3
tram (9) n/adj 085.3
~ trestle (1) n 080.9
trammel (3) n/adj 028.1
~ net (1) n 028.1
~ nets (1) n 088.8
tramp (42) n/v/adj 066.7
~ boat (1) n 080.6
~ dog (1) n 033.3
tramping (1) n 102.8
trampish-like (1) adj 073.7
trampoline (10) n 022.6
trampolines (1) n 022.6
tramps (14) n 069.7
trampy (1) adj 096.7
tramroad (1) n 031.8
tramroads (3) n 084.8
trams (2) n 085.3
tramways (1) n 085.3
Tranquility (1) VA 087.4
tranquilizers (1) n 114.2
transfer (4) n/adj 080.8
~ station (1) n 085.3
~ trucks (1) n 080.7
transferring (1) v 021.4
transformation (1) n 089.9

transient (7) n/adj 113.7
~ hotel (1) n 113.8
~ yachts (1) n 080.6
transients (2) n 066.7
transit (11) n/adj 109.9
~ buses (1) n 109.9
~ deals (1) n 085.3
~ house (3) n 113.4
Transit (4) 106.7
~ building (1) n 106.7
~ Tower (2) 108.5
transmission (14) n/adj 110.7
~ oil (2) n 024.1
Transmission (1) 108.5
transmogrified (1) v 066.8
transom (1) n 009.5
transparentes (1) n S 009.5
transpired (1) v 078.6
transplanted (1) adj 041.5
transport (3) n/v 021.4
transport[V-p] (1) v 052.5
transportation (3) n 109.9
Transportation (1) 068.9
transporting (10) v 021.4
transvestite (1) n 124.3
transvestites (1) n 124.1
Transylvania (1) LA 087.1
tranvia (2) n S 085.3
trap (17) n/v 080.7
~ [P-0] (1) v 095.9
trapdoor (2) n 110.2
trapero (1) n S 009.2
trapeze (3) n 022.9
trapped (1) v 090.9
trapping (3) n/v/adj 065.9
~ ditches (1) n 030.2
traps (8) n 123.8
trash (1137) n/adj 069.6
~ bag (5) n 116.8
~ bags (1) n 117.2
~ barrel (2) n 117.3
~ basket (2) n 117.2
~ bin (10) n 117.3
~ box (1) n 117.3
~ bucket (4) n 017.4
~ burners (1) n 008.6
~ can (57) n 117.2
~ cans (3) n 017.4
~ catcher (1) n 089.8

~ -catching place (1) n 010.3
~ collector (3) n 115.2
~ compactor (44) n 117.1
~ compactors (5) n 117.1
~ composer (1) n 117.3
~ compressor (2) n 117.1
~ compressors (2) n 117.1
~ container (2) n 117.3
~ containers (2) n 117.3
~ contractor (1) n 117.1
~ dispensers (1) n 117.3
~ disposal (1) n 117.1
~ driver (1) n 098.7
~ fish (8) n 059.9
~ lifter (2) n 006.1
~ lifters (1) n 006.1
~ liners (1) n 117.2
~ man (30) n 115.2
~ masher (10) n 117.1
~ mashers (2) n 117.1
~ men (3) n 115.2
~ mover (12) n 006.1
~ movers (1) n 006.1
~ people (1) n 115.2
~ pile (1) n 010.3
~ piles (1) n 014.8
~ presser (3) n 117.1
~ room (3) n 010.3
~ smasher (2) n 117.1
~ squeezer (1) n 117.1
~ trucks (1) n 111.3
trashy (49) adj 073.8
travel (34) n/v/adj 040.1
~ around (1) v 074.4
~ (a)round (1) v 039.8
~ bag (11) n 123.7
~ by (1) v 032.8
~ paths (1) n 031.8
travel[V-t] (1) v 011.3
traveled (8) v 090.7
traveler (6) n 021.2
Traveler (2) 024.6
travelers (1) n 080.6
Travelers' Rest (1) 106.4
traveling (22) n/v/adj 123.7
~ bag (3) n 123.7

~ men (1) n 084.9
~ preacher (2) n 067.8
~ troupe (1) n 080.9
travels (2) v 013.8
~ along (1) v 013.8
travers (1) adj F 031.7
traversin (2) n F 028.9
Travis (7) 105.1
~ County (1) TX 087.1
~ Field (1) 106.5
~ Park (2) 106.4
Trawick Creek (1) AL 030.7
trawl boats (1) n 024.6
trawler (1) n 024.6
trawlers (4) n 024.6
tray (9) n/adj 019.2
~ pea (1) n 055A.3
trays (4) n 035.8
treacherous (2) adj 065.9
tread (3) n/adj 021.1
~ -soft briers (1) n 015.9
treadle (3) n/v 023.5
Treadwell (1) 083.2
treasures (3) n 010.2
treat (17) n/v 095.7
Treat (1) 093.2
treated (8) v/adj 013.9
treating (2) v 032.3
treatment (2) n 129.8
treats (1) v 025.6
treaty land (1) n 088.7
Treaty (3) 106.4
~ Oak (1) 106.4
~ of Dancing Rabbit (1) 089.9
~ of Dancing Rabbit Creek (1) 080.6
treble block (1) n 080.8
Trebloc (1) MS 087.5
tree (2634) n/adj 061.8
~ belt (1) n 031.9
~ berry (1) n 062.5
~ climbing (1) n 096.3
~ crickets (1) n 061.1
~ farm (3) n 061.6
~ frog (231) n 060.3
~ frog[N-i] (1) n 060.3
~ frogs (199) n 060.3
~ hoe (1) n 120.7
~ house (1) n 034.5
~ houses (2) n 014.1
~ lawn (2) n 031.9
~ molasses (1) n 051.3

~ of knowledge (1) n 061.8
~ of life (1) n 098.4
~ of paradise (1) n 088.8
~ orchard (1) n 061.6
~ owl (7) n 059.1
~ post (1) n 016.5
~ root (4) n 061.4
~ roots (2) n 061.4
~ saw (3) n 120.9
~ snake (1) n 096.8
~ squirrel (18) n 059.6
~ squirrels (5) n 059.7
~ -stump preacher (1) n 067.8
~ surgeon (1) n 088.7
~ swing (8) n 022.9
~ swings (1) n 022.9
~ to tree (1) n 050.9
~ toad (5) n 060.3
~ toads (5) n 060.3
~ tomato (3) n 055.3
~ tomatoes (3) n 055.3
~ trimmers (1) n 120.4
Tree (6) 106.1
tree[N-i] (10) v 016.7
tree[N-k] name (1) n 043.9
treed (1) v 026.1
treeing dogs (1) n 033.3
trees (1569) n 061.6
tref (1) n 088.9
treize (1) n F 001.7
trellis (2) n/adj 016.2
~ fence (1) n 016.2
tremblante (1) adj F 029.6
trembles (1) n 088.9
trembling (5) adj 074.3
~ drawers (1) n 074.3
~ earth (2) n 090.2
~ prairie (2) n 029.6
tremendous (6) adj 066.8
trench (157) n/adj 030.2
~ silo (2) n 014.4
trencher (2) n 021.6
trenches (42) n 030.4
trend (3) n 052.3
trending towards (1) v 053.4
Trenton (2) MS 087.2
~ Mill (1) GA 087.1
Tres Palacios River (1) TX 030.7

trespassers (1) n 070.8
trespassing (1) v 070.8
trestle (44) n/adj 022.1
~ bench (1) n 022.1
~ horse (2) n 022.1
trestle[N-i] (1) n 008.3
trestles (13) n 022.1
trey bag (1) n 114.1
tri (4) prefix 118.7
~ -level (2) n 118.9
~ -level houses (1) n 098.9
~ -parish fair (1) n 066.8
Tri (2) 024.6
~ -Gulls (1) 024.6
~ -State (1) 108.5
trial (6) n/adj 099.2
~ bed (1) n 029.2
~ period (1) n 129.8
trials (1) n 065.8
triangle (12) n/adj 085.2
~ chimley (1) n 008.1
~ chopper (1) n 022.1
~ deal (1) n 015.5
~ mountain (1) n 031.3
~ parking (1) n 108.3
Triangle (1) 106.5
tribal (3) adj 007A.2
~ house (1) n 007A.2
~ land (1) n 088.7
~ program (1) n 080.6
tribe (5) n 055A.7
tribes (1) n 066.7
tributaries (9) n 030.6
tributary (11) n 030.3
Trichloris (1) 041.6
Trichoscat (1) 088.7
trick (13) n/v/adj 101.5
~ baby (1) n 113.3
~ shots (1) n 131.4
tricked (2) v 065.1
~ out (1) v 028.1
trickle (7) n/adj 030.6
~ toe (1) n 083.1
trickling out (1) v 102.4
tricks (2) n 113.5
trickster (1) n 125.5
tricycle (1) n 101.5
tried (19) v 057.9
~ to (13) v 074.5
tries (6) v 013.6
~ to (3) v 128.6
trifle (2) v 069.7
trifling (27) adj 069.7

trigger (3) n 097.6
Trigger Gap (1) AR 031.3
trigonometry (1) n 070.9
trigs (1) n 033.3
trilbies (1) n 093.8
trill (1) n 036.4
TRILL (1) interj 060.4
trillion (1) n 061.4
trillions (1) n 001A.2
trim (22) n/v 036.1
~ out (1) v 015.8
Trimble Creek (1) MS 030.7
trimmed (11) v 036.1
~ up (2) v 036.1
trimmer (33) n 120.8
trimmers (22) n 120.8
trimming (8) n/v 037.3
trimmings (8) n 046.8
Trinity (29) GA TX 089.3
~ Bay (1) TX 030.3
~ Church (1) 089.2
~ Park (1) 106.4
~ River (16) TX 030.7
~ River bottom (1) n 030.7
trinket (2) n 101.5
trinkets (3) n 101.5
trio (1) n 129.6
trip (44) n/v 040.1
~ around the world (1) n 029.1
~ -around-the-world parties (1) n 130.7
trip[V-r] (1) v 070.6
tripa (1) n S 037.2
tripas (3) n S 037.3
tripe (92) n 037.2
tripes (11) n 059.9
triple (16) adj 009.2
~ dresser (2) n 009.2
~ dressers (1) n 009.2
~ drives (1) n 109.6
~ hotcakes (1) n 105.7
~ hull (1) n 024.6
~ mules (1) n 033.7
~ singletree (1) n 021.3
~ tree (7) n 021.2
~ X (1) n 114.9
tripled (1) v 070.2
triplex (8) n 119.2
triplexes (1) n 119.2
tripod (3) n/adj 008.3
~ hoist (1) n 104.5

~ skiliet (1) n 017.5
Trippe Junction (1) AR 087.1
trips (3) n 016.1
Triumph (8) 055.4
~ potato (2) n 055.4
Triumphs (4) 055.4
trivet (4) n 017.5
trois (1) n F 001.1
troja (1) n S 014.3
troll (5) n 088.9
trolley (232) n/adj 085.3
~ buses (2) n 085.3
~ car (65) n 085.3
~ -car parties (1) n 081.8
~ cars (64) n 085.3
~ line (3) n 085.3
trolleys (90) n 085.3
trolling (3) n/v 059.9
~ along (1) v 080.7
tromp (2) v 097.4
tromped (1) v 097.4
tromper (1) n 071.7
tromping (1) v 097.4
tronco (1) n S 008.5
troop (3) n 129.6
trooper (2) n 111.7
trooper's car (1) n 111.7
troopers (3) n 112.5
troops (2) n 048.9
tropical (9) adj 112.1
~ depression (1) n 112.2
~ hurricanes (1) n 006.3
~ storm (3) n 112.1
~ storms (3) n 112.1
trot (41) n/v 102.3
Trot (3) 087.6
trotline (8) n/adj 080.7
~ fishing (1) n 091.9
trotlines (8) n 066.9
trots (2) n 083.1
trotters (1) n 127.9
trotting (7) v/adj 057.4
~ horse (2) n 034.2
trouble (208) n 090.8
troubled (3) adj 074.2
troublemaker (1) n 073.4
troublemakers (3) n 082.8
troubles (107) n 065.8
troubling (1) v 065.5
trough (1188) n/adj 035.8
~ concern (1) n 035.8

~ -like (2) adj 011.5
~ roof (1) n 011.6
Trough (1) 070.6
trough[N-i] (79) n 035.8
troughes (1) n 035.8
troughi (1) n 035.8
troughing (1) v 075.8
troughs (692) n 035.8
trounce (1) v 065.5
trouncing (1) n 065.5
Troup (3) GA 087.3
~ County (1) GA 087.3
troupe (1) n 080.9
Troupville (1) GA 087.7
trouser (2) adj 028.5
~ holders (1) n 028.5
~ worm (1) n 065.1
trouser[N-i] (7) n 027.4
trousers (523) n 027.4
trous(ers) (6) n 027.4
trout (439) n/adj 059.9
~ fish (10) n 059.9
~ fishing (2) n/v 059.9
~ ranch (1) n 081.8
~ season (1) n 061.2
Trout (4) 107.7
~ Bridge (1) 107.7
~ River (2) FL 030.7
~ River Bridge (1) 107.7
troutline (1) n 080.6
troutlines (2) n 080.8
trouts (22) n 059.9
trowel (51) n 120.5
trowels (2) n 120.5
Troy (41) AL MS TN TX 087.4
~ State (2) 070.6
truanc(y) (1) n 083.4
truant (22) n/adj 083.4
truck (586) n/adj 109.7
~ and ladder (1) n 111.3
~ cars (1) n 109.6
~ crop (1) n 099.5
~ crops (3) n 050.4
~ drivers (1) n 052.6
~ -driving speed (1) n 114.2
~ farm (4) n 050.4
~ farmer (3) n 050.4
~ farmers (3) n 050.5
~ farming (13) n 050.4
~ farms (1) n 093.6
~ field (1) n 016.1

~ garden (4) n 050.5
~ gardeners (1) n 050.5
~ gardening (1) n 050.4
~ gardens (1) n 050.5
~ hand (1) n 023.3
~ horn (1) n 037.5
~ patch (50) n 050.5
~ -patch vegetables (1) n 050.4
~ patchers (1) n 050.4
~ patches (16) n 050.5
~ route (1) n 106.3
~ stop (2) n 080.9
~ stops (2) n 107.2
trucker snap beans (1) n 055A.4
truckers (1) n 123.8
truckers' stop (2) n 107.2
Truckers' Favorite (1) 056.2
trucking (12) n/v/adj 084.8
~ country (1) n 088.8
~ laws (1) n 039.7
~ outfit (1) n 053.5
~ shoes (1) n 080.7
truckload (4) n 019.8
truckloads (1) n 019.8
trucks (140) n 109.6
trudging along (1) v 098.1
Trudo Creek (1) LA 030.7
true (45) adj 051.4
True South (1) 089.1
truest-shooting rifle (1) n 093.6
truie (4) n F 035.5
truly (10) adv 091.6
Trumann (2) AR 087.2
Truman's (1) 070.8
trumpet (5) n/adj 025.4
~ vine (4) n 062.3
trumpets (1) n 088.7
trundle (34) adj 029.2
~ bed (27) n 029.2
~ beds (5) n 009.3
trunk (201) n/adj 072.4
~ door (1) n 110.5
~ room (2) n 010.3
trunkback (1) n 060.6
trunks (25) n 009.2
Trussville (2) AL 086.3
trust (3) v 039.6
Trust (1) 108.5

trustee (2) n 066.4
trusting (2) adj 074.6
truth (42) n 065.8
truthful (1) adj 052.9
try (226) n/v 099.2
~ out (4) v 024.5
~ to (53) v 053.3
try[V-p] (4) v 013.6
~ to (3) v 013.6
try[V-r] to (1) v 098.6
trying (95) v 057.4
~ to (63) v 028.1
~ to make her (1) v 081.4
Ts (1) 023.6
TSC (1) 114.2
TSH (1) 114.2
tua (1) interj F 037.5
tub (182) n/adj 020.1
~ bath (2) n 018.3
~ buckets (1) n 020.1
~ butter (1) n 090.8
~ churn (1) n 081.8
~ lard (1) n 090.8
tub[N-i] (1) n 039.6
tube (882) n/adj 024.4
~ tire (1) n 024.4
tubeless (9) adj 024.4
~ tire (3) n 024.4
tuberculosis (4) n 079.9
tubes (72) n 024.4
tubing (3) n 024.4
tubo (1) n S 024.4
tubs (67) n 019.3
tubular (1) n 026.7
Tuckaleechee Pike (1) 107.8
tucked out (2) v 075.4
Tucker (2) GA 086.8
~ Road (1) 107.6
tucker (1) n 028.1
tucker[V-t] out (1) v 075.5
tuckered (68) v 075.4
~ out (65) v 075.5
Tuckerman (3) AR 087.2
Tucson (1) AZ 087.8
tudes (1) n 080.7
tudor (1) n 023.6
Tudor (3) 118.7
Tuesday (981) 002.1
~ evening (1) n 002.5
~ morning (1) n 002.1
~ night (2) n 002.1
~ week (7) n 003.7

Tuesd(ay) (1) 002.1
Tuesdays (6) 002.1
Tuffy (1) 018.3
tuft (3) n 028.8
tuft[V-r] (1) v 084.9
tufted owls (1) n 059.2
tuft(ed) spread (1) n 028.7
tufting (1) v 084.8
tug (30) n/v 098.1
~ -of-war (22) n 130.6
~ -the-war (1) n 130.6
Tugaloo River (1) GA 030.7
tugboat (4) n 024.6
tugboats (7) n 024.6
tugged (4) v 098.1
~ in (1) v 075.5
tugs (1) n 038.6
Tuinal (1) 115.7
Tuinals (1) 114.2
tuition (2) n 065.8
Tula (2) MS 087.7
Tulane (9) LA 087.3
~ Avenue (2) 107.6
~ Courts (1) 105.5
Tuleta (1) TX 087.9
tulip (13) n/adj 062.8
~ magnolia (1) n 062.9
~ poplar (3) n 061.8
~ poplars (1) n 061.8
~ tree (3) n 061.8
~ trees (1) n 062.9
Tulip (1) AR 087.5
Tull Levee (1) TN 030.4
Tullahoma (4) TN 087.2
Tulsa (20) OK 087.4
tumble (13) n/v/adj 095.5
~ over (1) v 095.5
~ turd (1) n 060A.4
~ wheel (1) n 095.5
tumblebuck (1) n 022.6
tumblebug (5) n 022.6
tumblebugs (1) n 060A.8
tumbled (6) v 095.5
~ off (1) v 034.5
~ out (3) v 034.5
~ over (1) v 095.5
tumbler (41) n 048.9
~ up (1) n 095.5
tumblers (18) n 048.9
tumblesault (37) n 095.5
tumble(sault) (1) n 095.5
tumblesaults (3) n 095.5

tumbleset (60) n 095.5
tumblesets (9) n 095.5
tumblesetting (1) v 095.5
tumbleweed (1) n 015.9
tumbleweeds (3) n 070.7
tumbling (9) v/adj 095.5
~ board (1) n 022.6
~ dam (1) n 031.5
~ weeds (1) n 095.8
Tumbling Creek (1) TN 030.7
Tumkeehatchee Creek (2) AL 030.7
tummy (11) n/adj 080.4
~ ache (2) n 080.4
~ set (1) n 095.5
~ up (2) adv 095.5
tumor (4) n 070.6
tuna (12) n/adj 060.2
~ fish (4) n 059.9
tune (11) n/v 024.3
tunes (4) n 130.8
tung (19) adj 054.9
~ nut (3) n 054.9
~ -nut field (1) n 016.1
~ nuts (2) n 054.7
~ oil (1) n 084.8
~ -oil (1) adj 088.7
~ -oil orchard (1) n 061.6
~ -oil sack (1) n 019.7
~ -oil tree (1) n 061.7
~ -oil trees (1) n 061.8
~ production (1) n 084.8
~ tree bushes (1) n 062.4
~ trees (5) n 061.8
Tunica (6) MS 030.7
~ County (1) MS 087.8
~ Hills (1) LA 030.8
tunnel (32) n 107.8
Tunnel (2) 106.6
~ Boulevard (1) 107.5
tunnels (2) n 031.3
Tunnels (1) 106.7
tupelo (15) n/adj 061.9
~ gum (10) n 062.9
~ honey (1) n 081.9
~ tree (1) n 061.8
tupel(o) gum (2) n 062.2
Tupelo (24) MS 087.8
~ River (1) GA 030.7
Tur (1) n G 011.2
turban gourds (1) n 056.6

turbines (1) n 088.7
turbot (2) n 059.9
turbulent (3) adj 005.5
~ weather (1) n 006.2
~ wind (1) n 112.1
turd (3) n/adj 006.1
~ floater (1) n 006.1
~ head (1) n 092.3
turds (3) n 039.6
tureens (1) n 088.7
turf (1) n 029.8
Turk (2) 068.2
Turkendols (2) 099.7
turkey (79) n/adj 121.5
~ barn (1) n 036.8
~ buzzard (1) n 089.8
~ drownder (1) n 006.1
~ feed (1) n 047.6
~ -gobbler's snoot (1) n 080.9
~ ham (1) n 121.3
~ hen (1) n 036.6
~ hunt (1) n 059.6
~ hunts (1) n 089.8
~ oak (4) n 061.9
~ pen (1) n 036.8
~ pens (1) n 036.8
~ stuffing (1) n 044.7
~ tails (1) n 011.5
~ track (1) n 029.3
~ trot (1) n 083.1
~ trots (1) n 056.8
~ wing (1) n 080.7
Turkey (11) 087.9
~ Creek (5) GA LA MS TX 030.7
~ Knob (3) AL AR GA 030.8
~ towels (1) n 018.6
turkeyberry (1) n 062.4
turkeys (73) n 036.6
Turkish (3) 114.1
~ hash (1) n 114.1
~ towel (2) n 018.6
Turley Street (1) 114.8
Turmans Creek (1) TN 030.7
turn (654) n/v/adj 019.8
~ around (4) v 058.6
~ back (1) v 024.7
~ basin (1) n 088.6
~ bridges (1) n 107.3
~ down (4) v 082.1
~ dry (1) v 033.9

~ him down (16) v 082.1
~ him off (1) v 082.1
~ in (1) v 024.7
~ it down (1) v 082.1
~ left (1) v 037.7
~ me down (1) v 082.1
~ milk (1) n 047.6
~ mush (3) n 044.7
~ off (2) v 005.6
~ on (1) v 019.9
~ out (46) v 083.2
~ ox (1) n 091.8
~ plow (57) n 021.6
~ -plowing (1) v 021.6
~ plows (7) n 021.6
~ right (1) v 037.7
~ road (4) n 031.7
~ roads (1) n 031.7
~ row (3) n 041.2
~ rows (2) n 031.8
~ shovel (1) n 021.6
~ to (3) v 050.3
~ under (1) v 076.7
~ up (3) v 083.2
~ your heels up (1) v 078.6
~ your legs around (1) v 037.5
turn[V-p] (11) v 005.6
~ out (9) v 083.2
turn[V-r] (18) v 082.1
~ down his offer (1) v 082.1
~ down his proposal (1) v 082.1
~ him down (10) v 082.1
~ him off (1) v 082.1
~ into (1) v 005.7
~ me down (1) v 082.1
~ to (1) v 007.6
turn[V-t] (12) v 047.6
~ around (1) v 057.8
~ down (3) v 082.1
~ out (2) v 083.2
~ to (1) v 057.8
turnabout (1) n 107.4
turnaround (2) n 022.7
Turnbo Creek (1) TN 030.7
Turnbull Creek (3) MS TN 030.7
turned (440) v 046.9
~ against (1) v 070.9

~ against him (1) v 082.1

~ down (5) v 082.1

~ down his proposal (1) v 082.1

~ her back (1) v 082.1

~ her down (1) v 082.1

~ him (1) v 082.1

~ him away (1) v 082.1

~ him down (317) v 082.1

~ him down flat (1) v 082.1

~ him off (4) v 082.1

~ him out (3) v 082.1

~ in (1) v 083.3

~ me down (2) v 082.1

~ off (7) v 096.8

~ on (1) v 052.5

~ out (34) v 083.2

~ out of (1) v 083.2

~ over (2) v 114.4

~ to (1) v 047.6

~ up his toes (3) v 078.6

~ -up stomach (1) n 080.4

~ us down (1) v 082.1

~ you down (1) v 082.1

turner (21) n/adj 021.6

~ plow (3) n 021.6

Turner (3) 030.7

~ Bend (1) AR 030.7

~ Creek (1) GA 088.7

Turner's (1) 043.9

turners (1) n 021.7

Turners Millpond (1) FL 030.7

Turnerville (1) GA 087.2

turning (402) v/adj 005.7

~ dry (1) v 033.9

~ him down (1) v 082.1

~ horse (1) n 022.7

~ lathe (2) n 080.7

~ -latheman (1) n 080.6

~ out (2) v 083.2

~ -out time (1) n 083.2

~ plow (289) n 021.6

~ plows (45) n 021.6

~ row (1) n 031.7

~ shovel (1) n 021.6

~ shovels (1) n 021.6

~ stone (1) n 023.5

~ to (2) v 007.2

turnip (718) n/adj 055A.5

~ bank (1) n 089.9

~ farmers (1) n 055A.5

~ green (15) n 055A.5

~ -green dumpling (1) n 044.8

~ -green sallet (1) n 055A.5

~ green[N-i] (13) n 055A.5

~ greens (508) n 055A.5

~ heads (1) n 055A.5

~ kiln (1) n 055A.5

~ kraut (1) n 055A.6

~ leaves (1) n 055A.5

~ patch (17) n 016.1

~ patches (1) n 016.1

~ pot liquor (1) n 080.6

~ potatoes (1) n 081.8

~ radish (1) n 055.2

~ root (3) n 055A.5

~ roots (2) n 055A.5

~ salad (48) n 055A.5

~ salads (1) n 055A.5

~ sallet (22) n 055A.5

~ sallets (1) n 055A.5

~ seed (1) n 055A.5

~ top (3) n 055A.5

~ tops (13) n 055A.5

turnip[N-i] (2) n 055A.5

turnips (248) n 055.8

turnkey (1) n 091.9

Turnmore Creek (1) AR 030.7

turnoff (19) n/adj 107.4

~ road (5) n 031.7

turnout (1) n 031.8

Turnout (1) 086.6

turnover (23) n/adj 122.2

~ bread (2) n 044.7

~ cake (2) n 044.6

~ corn bread (1) n 044.6

~ plow (1) n 021.6

turnovers (12) n 122.7

turnpike (12) n/adj 031.6

~ roads (1) n 107.1

Turnpike (2) 107.1

turnpikes (4) n 031.6

turns (129) n/v 090.4

~ him down (3) v 082.1

~ off (2) v 083.2

~ out (110) v 083.2

~ over (1) v 095.5

~ you down (1) v 082.1

turnstyle (1) n 022.7

turpentine (96) n/adj 078.3

~ barrel (3) n 019.1

~ barrels (1) n 019.1

~ business (3) n 065.8

~ chips (1) n 008.6

~ cloth (1) n 076.3

~ cutter (1) n 023.5

~ grove (1) n 061.6

~ orchard (1) n 061.6

~ still (7) n 075.6

~ stills (3) n 065.9

~ sugar (1) n 078.3

~ timber (1) n 080.6

~ tree (1) n 061.8

~ trees (2) n 061.8

~ woods (1) n 061.8

turpen(tine) (1) n 078.3

Turpentine section (1) n 106.3

turpentined (2) v 065.8

turpentining (2) n/v 080.7

turquoise rings (1) n 123.1

Turrell (1) AR 087.2

turtle (1204) n/adj 060.6

~ clouds (1) n 005.3

~ eggs (1) n 046.1

~ factory (1) n 060.6

~ head (1) n 061.3

~ meat (1) n 060.6

~ shell (3) n 060.6

~ shells (1) n 060.6

~ soup (2) n 060.6

~ squash (1) n 056.6

~ steak (1) n 060.6

~ stranglers (1) n 006.1

tur(tle) (1) n 060.6

Turtle (2) 030.7

~ Bayou (1) LA 030.7

~ Creek (2) TX 030.7

turtleback (4) n/adv 060.6

turtledoves (1) n 080.6

turtles (329) n 060.6

Tuscaloosa (71) AL 087.8

~ County (3) AL 087.2

Tuscumbia (5) AL 087.3

Tuscumbi(a) (4) AL 087.7

~ River (2) AL 030.7

tush (98) n/adj 035.7

~ teeth (2) n 035.7

tush[N-i] (58) n 035.7

tushers (1) n 035.9

tushes (395) n 035.7

tusk (136) n 035.7

tusk[N-i] (265) n 035.7

Tuskegee (16) AL 087.3

Tuske(gee) (1) AL 087.5

tuskers (1) n 035.9

tuskes (5) n 035.7

tusks (141) n 035.7

tussle (1) n 104.2

tussling (2) v 104.2

tutor (8) n 067.6

tutors (1) n 066.4

Tutt (1) 106.4

tutti-frutti (1) n 081.7

Tutwiler Hotel (1) 084.3

tux pants (1) n 027.4

Tuxachanie (1) MS 030.7

tuxedo (4) n 079.3

Tuxedo (4) 106.1

~ Junction (2) 105.4

TV (24) 066.8

~ English (1) 075.6

~ room (13) n 007.8

~ show (1) n 026.1

TVA (4) 053.4

twang (1) n 131.8

twangy (1) adj 131.3

twat (1) n 093.7

tweeds (1) n 123.6

twelfth (63) n/adj 001A.3

Twelfth (3) 107.7

~ Avenue (2) 107.7

~ Street (1) 107.7

twelve (1676) n/adj 001.6

~ -by-eighteen (1) n 001.6

~ -by-fourteen (1) n 001.6

~ -by-thirty-six (1) n 001.6

~ -by-twelve (5) n 001.6

~ -eleven (1) n 001.6

~ -fifty (1) n 001.6

~ -foot (15) adj 007.9

~ -foot-long (1) adj 007.9

~ -forty-five (5) n 004.5

~ -forty-six (1) n 004.5

~ -fourteen (1) n 001.7

~ -gauge shotgun (1) n 113.1
~ -inch (4) adj 021.9
~ -pound (3) adj 045.4
~ -quart (1) adj 017.2
~ -thirty (16) n 004.4
~ -twenty (1) n 001.6
~ -up team (1) n 033.7
~ -volt (1) adj 001.6
~ -year-old (1) adj 005.1
Twelve (12) 001.6
twelves (1) n 001.6
twenties (4) n 001.8
Twenties (9) 001.8
twentieth (8) n/adj 001A.4
Twentieth Street (3) 107.6
twenty (3059) n/adj 001.8
~ -by-twenty (2) n 001.8
~ cents (1) n 114.1
~ -dollar (3) adj 001.8
~ -eight (49) n/adj 001.8
~ -eighth (9) n/adj 001A.3
~ -eighty (1) n 001.9
~ -fifth (11) n/adj 001A.3
~ -first (13) n/adj 001.8
~ -five (235) n/adj 001.8
~ -five-cent (1) adj 033.7
~ -five-pound (15) adj 019.2
~ -five-year (1) adj 001.8
~ -four (88) n/adj 001.2
~ -four-hour (1) adj 001.2
~ -four-hour service (1) n 001.8
~ -four-pound (11) adj 019.6
~ -fourth (10) n/adj 001A.3
~ -gallon (1) adj 017.6
~ -nine (43) n/adj 001.5
~ -ninth (10) n/adj 001A.3

~ -odd (3) adj 001.8
~ -one (66) n/adj 001.9
~ -one-seventeen (1) n 001.8
~ -second (1) n 001A.3
~ -seven (855) n/adj 001.8
~ -seven flood (3) n 001.8
~ -seven overflow (1) n 001.8
~ -seven water (1) n 088.9
~ -seventh (10) n/adj 001A.3
~ -six (44) n/adj 001.8
~ -six storm (1) n 080.9
~ -sixth (5) n/adj 001.8
~ -some (3) adj 001.8
~ -some-odd (6) adj 001.8
~ -something (1) adj 001.9
~ -third (9) n/adj 001A.3
~ -three (38) n/adj 001.8
~ -three-sixty (1) n 001.8
~ -two (68) n/adj 113.1
~ -two-by-fifteen (1) n 001.8
~ -two caliber (3) n 113.1
~ -two-foot (1) adj 007.9
~ -two pistols (1) n 113.1
~ -two rifle (1) n 001.8
~ -two Saturday night special (1) n 113.1
~ -twos (2) n 113.1
~ -year (1) adj 001.8
twent(y)-five (1) n 001.8
twen(ty) (14) n/adj 001.9
~ -five (1) adj 001.9
~ -seven (11) n/adj 001.8
~ -six (1) n 001.8
Twenty (71) 107.7
~ -Eighth Street (1) 107.7
~ -Fifth (1) 107.7

~ -Fifth Street (2) 001.8
~ -First (2) 107.6
~ -First Avenue (1) 107.7
~ -First Lane (1) 107.6
~ -Five (3) 091.8
~ -Four (5) 107.1
~ Grands (1) 088.9
~ -Mile (1) MS 030.7
~ -Mule-Team Borax (1) 033.7
~ -Nine (4) 031.6
~ -Ninth (1) 107.7
~ -Second (1) 106.7
~ -Second District (1) 001A.7
~ -Second Street (4) 105.4
~ -Seven (8) 107.6
~ -Seventh (1) 001.8
~ -Seventh Avenue (1) 107.7
~ -Six (1) 107.1
~ -Sixth (1) 105.5
~ -Sixth District (1) 001A.3
~ -Third Street (3) 001A.3
~ -Three Highway (1) 001.8
twerp (1) n 125.7
twice (1123) adv 001A.5
twices (1) adv 001A.5
Twickenham (1) 106.1
twig (1) n 032.1
Twiggs (1) 107.7
twigs (7) n 008.6
twilight (19) n 003.5
Twilight (3) GA 087.9
~ Meadows (1) 105.5
twill (1) n 019.7
twin (11) n/adj 042.4
~ beds (1) n 007A.2
~ brother (2) n 078.5
~ calves (1) n 033.8
~ daughters (1) n 064.8
~ days (1) n 093.4
~ -fifty machine guns (1) n 090.9
Twin (5) 087.2
~ City (1) GA 087.2
~ Creek (1) AL 030.7
~ Sister Hills (1) TX 030.8

~ Sisters (1) TX 087.3
~ Tunnels (1) 106.7
twine mills (1) n 092.9
twins (7) n 052.9
twirl (2) n 122.7
twist (67) n/adj 083.1
~ doughnut (3) n 122.7
~ loaf (1) n 044.4
~ rolls (1) n 044.4
~ tobacco (1) n 057.3
twist[N-i] (2) n 122.7
twist[V-s] (1) v 095.9
twisted (33) v/adj 122.7
~ cinnamon rolls (1) n 122.7
~ clevis (1) n 021.9
~ doughnut (13) n 122.7
~ doughnuts (7) n 122.7
~ rolls (2) n 044.4
~ -up doughnut (1) n 122.7
twister (21) n 021.6
twisters (20) n 021.6
twistification (4) n 088.7
twisting (1) v 095.9
twists (8) n 081.8
two (4857) n/adj 001.1
~ -bedroom home (1) n 007A.2
~ -bedroom house (1) n 007A.3
~ -bit carpenter (1) n 067.8
~ -bit lawyer (1) n 067.8
~ -bit uncle (1) n 024.8
~ -bit whores (1) n 113.3
~ bits (7) n 114.5
~ bits past (1) n 004.5
~ -bottom plows (1) n 021.6
~ -bottom stuff (1) n 092.8
~ -boy swing (1) n 022.9
~ -burner oilstove (1) n 024.1
~ -bushel (3) adj 019.8
~ -by-four (5) n/adj 001.1
~ -by-four carpenters (1) n 067.8

~ -by-fours (4) n 055.5
~ -by-six (2) n 001.1
~ -by-sixes (3) n 001.3
~ -car garage (1) n 007A.7
~ -crop farmer (1) n 084.9
~ -cylinder outfit (1) n 088.7
~ -deck porch (1) n 010.8
~ -door (52) n/adj 109.2
~ -door car (18) n 109.2
~ -door cars (1) n 109.2
~ -door coupe (3) n 109.2
~ -door Cutlass (1) n 109.2
~ -door hardtop (1) n 109.2
~ -door hardtop sedan (1) n 109.2
~ -door sedan (25) n 109.2
~ -door sedans (4) n 109.2
~ -door thing (1) n 109.2
~ doors (7) n 109.2
~ -eighteen (1) n 001.1
~ -eighty-seven (1) n 001.4
~ -eleven (2) n 001.1
~ -eyed heater (1) n 095.9
~ -face (1) adj 101.3
~ -faced (1) adj 128.2
~ -fifteen (1) n 004.5
~ -fifty pump (1) n 111.2
~ -fisted (1) adj 072.2
~ -foot (4) adj 007.9
~ -forty (2) n 001A.1
~ -forty-five (2) n 004.5
~ -forty-nine (1) n 001.5
~ -fourteen (1) n 001.7
~ -furrow (1) n 089.8
~ -gallon (2) adj 017.2
~ -handed trucks (1) n 023.3
~ -holer (21) n 012.1

~ -holers (4) n 012.1
~ -horse crop (3) n 041.3
~ -horse cultivator (4) n 023.9
~ -horse disc harrow (1) n 021.7
~ -horse farm (1) n 077.8
~ -horse hay baler (1) n 080.6
~ -horse plow (20) n 021.6
~ -horse plows (1) n 021.6
~ -horse riding culti- vator (1) n 023.9
~ -horse team (1) n 033.7
~ -horse turner (1) n 021.6
~ -horse turning plow (1) n 021.6
~ -horse turning plows (1) n 021.6
~ -horse wagon (6) n 034.2
~ -horse wagonload (1) n 019.8
~ -horse wagonloads (1) n 019.8
~ -hundred-acres (1) adj 016.7
~ -hundred-pound (3) adj 001A.2
~ -hundred-proof alcohol (1) n 114.2
~ -lane (1) n 031.6
~ -lane blacktop (1) n 031.6
~ -lane highway (2) n 107.1
~ -lane street (1) n 031.6
~ -legged nuts (1) n 081.8
~ -legged sawhorse (1) n 022.1
~ -log pen (1) n 015.4
~ -man boat (2) n 024.6
~ -man crosscut saw (1) n 120.9

~ -man saw (3) n 120.9
~ -mule cultivator (1) n 021.7
~ -mule farming (1) n 033.7
~ -mule mowing mach- ine (1) n 090.9
~ -mule riding plow (1) n 021.6
~ -mule team (1) n 033.7
~ Our Father[N-i] (1) n 089.8
~ -ox team (1) n 033.7
~ -pants suit (1) n 027.4
~ -part house (1) n 118.9
~ -piece felly (1) n 021.1
~ -piece suit (1) n 027.7
~ pluck (1) n 090.8
~ -pound (8) adj 045.4
~ -room (1) adj 001.1
~ -room building (1) n 001.1
~ -room cabin (1) n 007A.3
~ -room flat (1) n 119.4
~ -room house (7) n 007A.2
~ -room school (2) n 001.1
~ -room shack (2) n 007A.3
~ -roomed house (2) n 007A.2
~ -row equipment (1) n 090.8
~ -row planter (4) n 088.8
~ -row planters (2) n 096.7
~ -row stuff (1) n 099.7
~ -row tractor (1) n 080.8
~ -rutted road (1) n 031.8
~ -seat (1) n 109.1
~ -seated car (1) n 109.3
~ -seated outfit (1) n 084.8

~ -seater (7) n 109.1
~ -seventy-eight (1) n 001A.2
~ -sixteen (1) n 001.1
~ -sixty (1) n 001.2
~ -step (35) n 083.1
~ -stepped (1) v 083.1
~ -stepping (1) v 083.1
~ -steps (3) n 083.1
~ -stirrup (1) n 039.3
~ -storied (1) adj 098.6
~ -story (11) n/adj 118.7
~ -story apartments (1) n 119.2
~ -story barn (2) n 014.2
~ -story farmhouse (1) n 014.1
~ -story frame house (1) n 014.1
~ -story garage (1) n 108.4
~ -story house (14) n 001.1
~ -story houses (4) n 118.9
~ -story log house (1) n 001.1
~ -story porch (2) n 010.8
~ -suiter (1) n 123.7
~ -teacher school (2) n 075.6
~ -team farmer (1) n 084.9
~ -ten (1) n 001.5
~ -tens (1) n 055A.4
~ -thirteen (1) n 001.7
~ -thirty (15) n 004.4
~ -thousand-pound (1) adj 001A.2
~ -timer (1) n 124.7
~ ton (1) n 109.7
~ -ton (2) adj 109.7
~ -ton pickup (1) n 109.7
~ -ton truck (1) n 109.6
~ tree (1) n 021.3
~ -twelve (1) n 001.6
~ -twenty (2) n 001.8
~ -twen(ty)-nine (1) n 001.2
~ -way flue (1) n 023.2

~ -way plow (1) n 021.6

~ -way street (2) n 107.5

~ -way tailgate (1) n 109.5

~ -week (1) adj 003.8

~ -wheel buggy (1) n 001.1

~ -wheel cart (4) n 070.6

~ -wheel dray (1) n 096.7

~ -wheel gigs (1) n 099.5

~ -wheel wheelbarrow (1) n 023.3

~ -year college (1) n 083.6

~ -year terms (1) n 001.1

Two (56) 069.3

~ Egg (1) FL 087.6

~ -Eighty Bypass (2) 107.6

~ -Eighty-Five (2) 107.5

~ -Forty (1) 107.1

~ Mile (1) AR 030.7

~ -Seed Baptist (1) 089.1

~ -Thirty-One (3) 107.1

~ -Thirty-One Bypass (1) 107.1

Twomile Creek (1) AR 030.7

twoo (1) interj 038.5

twos (2) n 113.1

twosies (2) n 130.7

Ty (8) 030.7

~ Ty (2) GA 087.3

~ Ty Creek (2) GA 030.7

Tybee (3) GA 083.9

~ Island (1) GA 083.9

~ River (1) GA 030.7

tying the knot (3) v 082.2

tyke (10) n 064.4

Tyler (15) TX 087.3

~ County (1) TX 087.6

Tylertown (2) MS 087.8

Tyndall Field (1) 106.5

type (186) n/adj 073.2

type[N-i] (7) n 042.9

typer (1) n 068.8

types (13) n 086.3

typewriter (2) n 068.8

typhoid (33) n/adj 079.7

~ fever (22) n 079.8

~ -malaria fever (1) n 088.8

typhoon (12) n 112.1

typhoons (5) n 112.1

typical (7) adj 084.8

typist (8) n 068.8

Tyrone (2) GA 087.1

Tyson (6) 106.5

~ Park (2) 106.7

U

U (4) 092.7
~ -Haul truck (1) n 109.6
Uchee (6) GA 030.7
Uchees (1) 080.6
UDC (1) 065.8
udder (2) n 042.8
udders (1) n 033.6
uglier (2) adj 026.3
ugliest (2) adj 053.6
ugly (152) adj 125.1
~ -ass (1) adj 069.4
~ -ass man (1) n 125.1
~ bitch (2) n 125.2
~ black man (1) n 125.1
~ boy (4) n 125.1
~ bugs (1) n 060A.4
~ day (12) n 005.5
~ duckling (1) n 125.1
~ dude (2) n 125.1
~ girl (1) n 125.2
~ -looking day (1) n 005.5
~ man (3) n 125.1
~ person (1) n 125.1
~ stick (7) n 051.8
~ tree (1) n 098.8
~ weather (2) n 005.5
~ -woman party (1) n 131.5
Ukran(ian) (1) 069.4
ulcer (7) n 077.4
ulcerated (1) adj 074.1
ulcers (3) n 077.4
ultra (1) n 080.7
ultraviolet (2) n/adj 116.4
~ -ray ovens (1) n 116.4
ultrawave (1) n 116.4
um(x4) (1) interj 036.4
Umbarger (1) TX 087.5
umbersol (1) n 028.6
umbrella (920) n/adj 028.6

~ china (1) n 061.9
~ Chinese (1) n 061.8
~ trees (3) n 062.9
umbrel(la) (20) n 028.6
(um)brella (1) n 028.6
umbrellas (31) n 028.6
umpteen (1) adj 055A.8
un (35) n/adj F/S 001.1
unable (3) adj 074.2
Unadilla (1) GA 075.8
unafraid (3) adj 074.2
unattractive (1) adj 125.2
unavailable (1) adj 095.2
unaware (1) adj 074.7
unbalanced (3) adj 073.4
unbeholdens (1) adj 057.5
unbeknowing (2) adj 084.9
unbeknownst (1) adj 053.7
unbelievable (1) adj 074.2
unbleached (2) adj 095.9
~ domestic (1) n 095.9
~ domestic cloth (1) n 095.9
unbreakable bean (1) n 055A.4
unbred (1) adj 051.8
unbreech (2) v 022.4
unbroke wild mustang (1) n 034.2
unbroken (1) adj 048.9
unbuttoned (1) adj 074.2
uncanny (2) adj 074.7
uncareful (4) adj 074.6
uncastrated (1) adj 034.1
uncertain (11) adj 074.2
unchangeable (4) adj 005.6
~ weather (1) n 007.1
unchoked (1) adj 074.2
uncivilize (1) adj 069.9
unclam (1) v 096.3
uncle (464) n/adj 068.2
~ general (1) n 068.3
~ pumpkin (1) n 056.5
Uncle (1267) 068.2
~ Bill (146) 068.2
~ Billy (19) 068.2
~ John (473) 068.2
~ Johnny (11) 068.2
~ John's (1) 068.2
~ John's house (1) n 068.2
~ Jonathan (1) 068.2

~ Remus's story (1) n 068.2
~ Sam (4) 089.7
~ -Sam middlebusters (1) n 021.6
~ Tom (18) 069.3
~ Tomisms (1) 080.9
~ Toms (2) 069.3
~ Will (38) 068.2
~ William (353) 068.2
~ Williams (4) 068.2
~ Willy (22) 068.2
Unc(le) (3) 068.2
~ John (1) 068.2
~ William (1) 068.2
unclean (2) adj 124.7
uncle's (11) adj 068.1
~ house (2) n 068.2
~ namesake (1) n 032.7
~ place (1) n 068.2
~ room (1) n 007A.4
~ wife (1) n 063.2
uncles (77) n 068.2
Uncola (2) 121.8
~ drink (1) n 074.2
uncomfortable (18) adj 074.2
uncommon (4) adj 074.2
unconcerned (5) adj 074.2
unconscious (1) adj 070.6
unconsciously (1) adv 074.2
uncool (3) adj 124.7
uncoordinated (10) adj 073.3
uncouth (2) adj 073.6
uncovered (3) v/adj 074.2
uncultured (1) adj 074.2
uncurable (1) adj 074.2
uncured (1) adj 055.7
uncut (1) adj 036.1
undecided (2) adj 074.2
under (125) adj/adv/prep 094.5
~ grass (1) n 092.9
~ suit (2) n 027.7
~ the cover (1) adj 072.9
~ the weather (18) adj 072.9
~ [D-0] weather (1) adj 072.9
underbit (1) n 088.7
underbits (1) n 035.6
underbraid (2) n 123.9

underbrush (4) n 022.2
underbrushed (1) v 041.4
undercoated (1) v 057.8
underdog (1) n 033.1
undergone (1) v 036.2
undergrading (1) n 080.9
underground (6) n/adj 015.5
~ cellars (1) n 015.5
~ cistern (1) n 065.9
~ garbage can (1) n 117.2
~ garbage cans (1) n 117.2
~ wash (1) n 030.4
Underground (5) 114.8
~ Atlanta (4) 106.4
undergrowth (2) n 077.9
underhanded (2) v 088.7
~ in (1) v 088.7
~ out (1) v 088.8
underneath (9) adv/prep 060.7
~ of (3) prep 075.6
underpass (89) n 107.8
underpasses (4) n 107.8
underpath (1) n 107.8
underpin (1) v 026.5
underpinned (1) v 098.7
underpinning (3) n 026.5
underprivilege (2) adj 069.7
underprivileged (1) adj 069.7
undershirt (4) n 027.3
undershirts (1) n 027.2
underskirts (1) n 026.4
understand (69) v 067.8
understand[V-p] (1) v 088.2
understand[V-r] (1) v 098.7
understanding (1) n 013.1
understood (5) v 013.4
undertake (1) n 117.4
undertaker (111) n/adj 117.4
~ school (1) n 117.4
undertaker[N-k] parlor (4) n 079.2
undertaker's (3) adj 079.2
~ parlor (1) n 079.2
~ shop (1) n 079.2
undertakers (7) n 117.4

undertaking parlor (1) n 079.2

underwear (8) n 027.4

undesirable (1) adj 052.5

undid (5) v 094.4

˜ it (1) v 082.1

undies (1) n 081.8

undo (11) v 074.2

undone (15) v 074.2

undoubtedly (2) adv 066.9

undressed (2) v 074.2

une (14) adj F 008.5

unease (1) adj 074.2

uneasiest (2) adj 064.7

uneasiness (1) n 074.2

uneasy (544) adj 074.2

uneducated (14) adj 083.5

˜ preacher (1) n 067.8

unemployed (1) adj 113.7

unexcavated (1) adj 007A.7

unexpected (4) adj/adv 074.2

unexpectedly (1) adv 074.2

unfair (3) adj 005.5

unfamiliar (2) adj 074.7

unfavorable (2) adj 005.5

unfinished (2) adj 074.2

unfold (2) v 094.4

unfolded (2) v 094.4

unfortunate (5) adj 074.2

unfortunately (1) adv 074.2

unfriendly (1) adj 074.2

ungelded (1) adj 034.1

unglazed (2) adj 122.4

unglued (1) adj 075.2

ungraded road (1) n 031.7

unhandsome man (1) n 125.1

unhang (1) v 099.7

unhappy (7) adj 074.2

unharness (1) v 038.6

unhealthiest (1) adj 064.7

unhealthy (1) adj 074.2

unheard of (2) adj 012.4

unhitch (2) v 038.6

unified (1) v 052.5

uniform (1) n 092.6

uniforms (1) n 024.7

unimproved (3) adj 031.7

˜ property (1) n 108.7

uninsane (1) adj 074.2

unintelligible (1) adj 074.2

uninteresting (2) adj 073.6

Uniolas (1) 015.9

union (7) adj 027.2

˜ suit (3) n 027.2

˜ suits (4) n 088.7

Union (74) AL AR LA MS NC TN 087.8

˜ Army (1) 085.8

˜ Bank (2) 108.5

˜ Chapel (2) GA 087.2

˜ Church (1) AR 087.8

˜ Church community (1) AR 082.6

˜ City (6) TN 087.3

˜ County (9) AR FL GA 087.1

˜ Hauls (1) 027.4

˜ Hill (1) AL 087.2

˜ Hill community (1) GA 087.6

˜ House (1) 089.2

˜ Line (1) MS 087.1

˜ Parish (2) AR LA 087.9

˜ Springs (6) AL 087.5

˜ Station (4) 084.7

˜ Street (4) 106.3

˜ Terminal (1) 084.7

Unionall[N-i] (1) 027.4

Unionalls (6) 027.4

unions (2) n 027.4

Uniontown (1) AL 087.7

Unionville (2) TN 087.8

unique (3) adj 052.8

unit (23) n/adj 118.5

˜ heaters (1) n 118.4

Unitarian (1) 089.1

united (9) v 089.2

˜ with (4) v 089.2

United (36) 108.5

˜ American Bank (1) 108.5

˜ American Bank building (1) n 108.5

˜ Daughters of the Confederacy (1) 065.9

˜ Methodist (4) 089.1

˜ Pentecost (1) 089.1

˜ State[N-i] (1) 087.8

˜ State[N-i] person (2) n 069.2

˜ Stater (1) 069.2

˜ States (18) 086.2

˜ States citizen (1) n 069.2

˜ States girl (1) n 069.2

˜ States government (2) n 085.6

˜ States of America (1) 082.8

˜ States War (1) 085.8

Unit(ed) States (1) 087.9

units (8) n 119.1

universal (1) adj 073.7

universe (2) n 002.5

university (10) n 083.6

University (41) 107.6

˜ Avenue (3) 107.7

˜ Hospital (3) 084.5

˜ Mall (1) 105.2

˜ of Arkansas (1) 086.7

˜ of Chicago (1) 083.6

˜ of Georgia (2) 083.6

˜ of Miami (1) 083.6

˜ of Missouri (1) 086.6

˜ of Paris (1) 083.9

˜ of Tampa (2) 106.4

˜ Park (8) 105.1

˜ Square (1) 105.3

Univeter Road (1) 031.7

unjointed (1) v 072.3

unknowledged (1) adj 088.7

unknown (2) adj 074.2

Unknown watermelon (1) n 056.9

unlawful (4) adj 065.7

˜ baby (1) n 065.7

˜ child (2) n 065.7

unleaven bread (3) n 044.3

(un)leaven bread (1) n 044.4

unleavened (4) adj 044.3

˜ bread (3) n 044.3

unlegal (6) adj 088.8

˜ bastards (1) n 065.7

˜ child (4) n 065.7

unlegally (1) adv 088.7

unlegitimate child (1) n 065.7

unless (600) conj 088.4

(u)nless (2) conj 088.4

(un)less (41) conj 088.4

unlessen (37) conj 088.4

(un)lessen (4) conj 088.4

unlevel (1) adj 074.2

unlike (1) prep 091.5

unlikely (2) adv 088.3

Unlimited (1) 089.3

unload (2) v 074.2

unloaded (1) v 074.2

unloading (10) v/adj 024.5

˜ dock (2) n 031.4

unloads (1) v 074.2

unlock (1) v 074.2

unlocked (1) v 074.2

unlost (1) adj 074.2

unloving (1) adj 074.2

unluckier (1) adj 074.2

unlucky (6) adj 074.2

unmad (1) adj 053.5

unmark cars (1) n 111.7

unmarked (2) adj 097.9

unmarried (1) adj 082.2

unneat (1) adj 074.2

unnecessary (1) adj 074.2

unnerved (2) v 074.2

unnerves (1) v 074.2

unopen (1) v 094.4

unordained minister (1) n 067.8

unpack (2) v 074.2

unpackaged (1) v 094.4

unpacked (1) v 094.4

unpacking (1) v 094.4

unparched (1) adj 051.5

unpave road (1) n 031.6

unpaved (6) adj 031.6

˜ road (1) n 031.7

˜ roads (2) n 031.6

unpleasant (7) adj 074.2

˜ day (3) n 005.5

Unpleasantness (2) 085.8

unpolished (1) adj 074.2

unpopular (2) adj 074.2

unpossible (1) adj 070.1

unpracticed (1) adj 074.2

unpredictable (5) adj 005.6

unprepared (3) adj 074.2

unprintable (1) adj 074.2

unravel (2) v 074.2

unraveled (1) v 094.4

unreal (1) adj 074.2

unreasonable (3) adj 074.2
unrelated (4) adj 066.6
unrestored (1) adj 108.7
unrolled (1) v 094.4
unrolling (1) v 094.4
unruly (2) adj 075.2
unsafe (2) adj 074.2
unsanitary (1) adj 074.2
unsatisfied (1) adj 074.2
unscrew (2) v 074.2
unseen (1) adj 102.5
unsettle (3) adj 005.6
~ day (1) n 005.5
unsettled (11) adj 005.5
unsexed (1) adj 036.1
unskilled (1) adj 067.8
unsleek bull (1) n 069.5
unslice bacon (1) n 046.5
unsliced (4) adj 046.5
~ bacon (2) n 046.5
unsmoked (1) adj 121.3
unsociable (1) adj 074.2
unsold (1) adj 074.2
unstable (7) adj 005.6
unstamp whiskey (1) n 050.8
unsteady (2) adj 074.2
unsterile (1) adj 029.3
unsure (3) adj 074.2
unswell (1) v 077.6
unthankful (1) adj 074.6
unthoughtedly (1) adv 103.6
unthoughtly (1) adv 103.9
untidy (1) adj 074.2
untie (5) v 094.4
untied (11) v 094.4
until (91) prep/conj 074.2
unto (1) prep 070.1
untouched (1) adj 090.4
untrained (2) adj 067.8
~ minister (1) n 067.8
~ practical nurse (1) n 051.8
untraveled (1) adj 074.2
untrue (2) adj 081.7
untwist (1) v 074.2
unusable (1) adj 074.2
unused bedroom (1) n 007A.2
unusual (28) adj 074.2
unusually (2) adv 074.2
unwanted (7) adj 074.2
~ child (2) n 065.7

~ grass (1) n 015.9
unwed (6) adj 065.7
~ child (3) n 065.7
~ mother (3) n 065.1
unwedded (3) adj 065.7
~ child (2) n 065.7
~ mothers (1) n 053.7
unwedlock child (1) n 065.7
unwelcome (1) adj 074.2
unwound (2) v 094.4
unwrap (221) v 094.4
(un)wrap (1) v 094.4
unwrap[V-r] (6) v 094.4
unwrapped (474) v 094.4
(un)wrapped (1) v 094.4
unwrapping (5) v 094.4
unwraps (3) v 094.4
unwritten law (1) n 074.2
unwrop (3) v 094.4
unwropped (8) v 094.4
unyielding (1) adj 074.8
up (15187) v/adj/adv/ prep 082.6
~ and (12) adv 078.6
~ -and-down back porch (1) n 010.8
~ -and-down front porch (1) n 010.8
~ block (1) n 039.3
~ it up (1) v 080.2
~ steps (1) n 010.7
~ -swallow (2) v 080.3
~ -to-do (1) adj 080.6
~ to par (6) adj 079.4
~ to snuff (2) adj 072.9
(u)p (5) adv 053.5
Up (6) 115.7
~ River Road (1) 115.7
~ the Hill (1) 105.1
UP (2) 108.5
~ Bank (1) 108.5
up[N-i] (1) n 050.1
Upatoi (4) GA 087.2
~ Creek (2) GA 030.7
upchoke (1) v 080.3
upchuck (111) v 080.3
upchucked (16) v 080.2
upchucking (1) v 080.3
upchucks (2) v 080.2
upcountry (1) n 082.6
updo (1) n 123.9
upgrade (2) n 030.8
uphill (3) adv 030.8
uphold (1) v 085.7

upholden (1) adj 057.5
upholstered (4) v 070.9
upholstering man (1) n 088.8
upholstery (2) n/adj 065.8
~ shop (1) n 065.8
upkeeper (2) n 119.5
upland (26) n/adj 029.4
~ blackberry (1) n 062.4
~ bottoms (1) n 029.4
~ farm (1) n 080.7
~ moccasin (1) n 081.8
uplands (1) n 029.4
upmanship (2) n 129.9
upon (38) adv/prep 032.6
(u)pon (2) prep 001A.4
upper (32) n/adj 114.2
~ barn (1) n 014.5
~ -class neighborhoods (1) n 106.1
~ gallery (1) n 010.8
~ -ground cisterns (1) n 052.5
~ -ground potato (1) n 056.5
~ -ground potatoes (1) n 055.5
~ land (2) n 029.4
~ level (1) n 014.5
~ lip (1) n 071.6
~ part (4) n 072.4
~ porch (4) n 010.8
~ rooms (1) n 009.8
~ school (1) n 125.9
~ story (2) n 007A.8
~ -story parking lot (1) n 108.4
~ teeth (3) n 071.8
~ tooth (1) n 071.8
Upper (8) 106.6
~ Garden District (1) 106.6
~ Little River (1) MS 030.7
~ Miami (1) 106.2
~ New England (1) 086.9
~ New York State (1) 086.1
~ Quihi (1) TX 087.8
~ Room (1) 106.4
~ Wetumpka Road (1) 107.7

uppers (38) n 114.2
uppest (4) adj 064.7
upping block (1) n 080.7
uppity (5) adj 073.6
~ ups (1) n 080.9
upright (2) adj 116.7
upriver (1) adv 082.6
uproar (2) n 084.8
uprooted (5) v 061.4
ups (16) n 114.2
~ and (1) adv 095.8
upset (224) adj 075.2
~ stomach (19) n 080.4
~ the fruit basket (1) n 080.7
upsets (1) v 080.4
upsetted (1) v 075.1
Upshur County (1) TX 086.8
upside (34) n/prep 092.8
~ -down (1) adj 048.3
~ -down eggs (1) n 046.2
~ -down pie (1) n 048.3
Upson (4) GA 087.1
~ County (3) GA 087.3
upstair[N-i] (21) n/adj 010.7
~ apartment (1) n 009.8
~ floor (1) n 010.8
~ part (1) n 053.5
~ porch (5) n 010.8
~ rooms (1) n 007A.4
upstairs (287) n/adj 010.7
~ apartment (1) n 007A.7
~ attic (1) n 009.8
~ back porch (2) n 010.8
~ balcony (1) n 010.8
~ bathroom (1) n 010.7
~ bedroom (4) n 009.3
~ building (1) n 009.8
~ front porch (1) n 010.8
~ hall (1) n 010.7
~ house (1) n 084.9
~ part (2) n 010.7
~ piazza (2) n 007A.3
~ porch (35) n 010.8
~ porches (1) n 010.8
~ room (5) n 007A.6
upstate (1) n 082.6

Upstate New York (1)
086.1
upstirred (1) adj 080.2
upswallow (1) v 080.3
uptight (17) adj 075.2
uptightness (1) n 093.9
uptown (72) n/adj 123.6
~ area (2) n 105.3
~ crowd (1) n 106.1
~ girls (1) n 075.8
~ people (1) n 080.6
~ section (1) n 089.9
uptownish (1) adj 080.6
upward (1) adj 080.6
upwards (1) adj 088.7
up(x2) (34) interj 038.2
up(x3) (5) interj 037.5
urban (6) adj 106.2
~ areas (2) n 106.2
~ renewal (3) n 108.7
~ -renewal area (1) n
108.7
Urbana (1) AR 087.4
urchin (3) n 064.3
urgent (1) adj 088.4
urinals (1) n 126.3
url (1) v 080.3
urn (9) n 017.2
urns (4) n 008.3
urp (30) v 080.2
~ my toes up (1) v
080.3
~ up (1) v 080.2
urped (12) v 080.2
~ up (1) v 080.3
urping (1) v 080.2
urps (1) v 080.2
us (1366) pron 044.2
(u)s (1) pron 040.8
Us (1) 129.6
US (13) 107.7
~ Four-Eleven (1)
107.7
~ Government (1)
085.6
~ Highway Number
One (1) 031.7
~ Highway Sixty (1)
107.5
~ One (7) 107.1
~ Twenty-Seven (1)
107.1
~ Two-Thirty-One (1)
107.1
us[M-k] (1) pron 043.4

usable (1) adj 052.7
usage (4) n 073.6
use (552) n/v/adj 090.5
~ -car lot (1) n 023.6
~ clothes (6) n 010.2
~ clothing (1) n 123.5
~ to (289) v 074.5
use[V-p] (2) v 013.8
use[V-r] (2) v 047.7
use[V-s] (2) v 026.1
~ [P-0] (1) v 075.2
use[V-t] (5) v 057.8
used (2489) v/adj 123.5
~ as (1) v 088.6
~ clothes (8) n 123.5
~ clothing (4) n 123.5
~ for (2) v 013.9
~ for to (1) v 081.3
~ on (1) v 095.8
~ stuff (1) n 010.2
~ to (2321) v 074.4
~ t(o) (6) v 074.4
~ to'd (1) v 074.4
~ up (9) v 075.5
~ [P-0] (24) v 025.8
useful (2) adj 053.4
useless (4) adj 033.3
~ dog (2) n 033.3
usen't (2) v 074.5
users (1) n 114.3
uses (19) v 013.7
usher (6) n 082.3
ushers (14) n 082.3
using (48) v 057.4
usn (2) pron 043.4
us's (3) pron 043.4
usual (8) adj 079.4
usually (54) adv 065.8
UT (6) 106.4
~ dormitories (1) n
108.5
~ football (1) n 084.8
~ Knoxville (1) 087.4
Utah (8) 086.1
utensil (5) n/adj 070.7
~ room (1) n 010.1
utensils (3) n 017.8
Utica (2) MS 087.1
utilities (2) n/adj 007A.8
~ room (1) n 007A.8
utility (205) n/adj 010.3
~ bill (1) n 001A.2
~ building (4) n 011.9
~ closets (1) n 009.6

~ compartment (1) n
110.2
~ house (17) n 011.8
~ man (1) n 119.5
~ pantry (1) n 010.1
~ porch (2) n 007A.1
~ room (155) n 010.3
~ rooms (1) n 010.3
~ shed (4) n 011.7
~ -storage house (1) n
011.7
~ truck (1) n 111.4
(u)tility room (2) n
007A.3
Utotem (4) 116.2
UTPN (1) 084.6
Uvalde County (1) TX
087.8

V

V (15) 024.6
  ˜ boat (1) n 024.6
  ˜ bone (1) n 037.1
  ˜ -bottom boats (1) n 024.6
  ˜ harrow (4) n 021.7
  ˜ harrows (3) n 021.7
  ˜ hull (1) n 024.6
  ˜ Schale (1) n G 024.6
  ˜ siding (1) n 011.2
  ˜ type (2) n 021.7
va (1) v F 092.6
vaca (1) n S 033.6
vacant (136) adj 108.7
  ˜ area (1) n 108.7
  ˜ field (2) n 108.7
  ˜ land (3) n 108.7
  ˜ lot (110) n 108.7
  ˜ lots (13) n 108.7
  ˜ place (1) n 108.7
  ˜ spaces (2) n 108.7
  ˜ truck (1) n 109.6
  ˜ yard (1) n 108.7
vacated (1) v 108.7
vacates (2) v 083.2
vacation (8) n/adj 091.7
  ˜ house (1) n 007A.1
vaccination (1) n 130.6
vache (4) n F 033.6
Vacherie (2) LA 087.2
vacuum (231) n/v/adj 010.4
  ˜ bag (19) n 116.8
  ˜ bags (3) n 116.8
  ˜ cleaner (138) n 116.7
  ˜ -cleaner bag (15) n 116.8
  ˜ cleaners (2) n 116.7
  ˜ sweeper (5) n 116.7
  ˜ tanks (1) n 077.8
  ˜ up (1) v 010.4
vacuuming cleaner (1) n 116.7
Vadis (1) 123.9
vagabond (2) n 113.7

vagabonds (3) n 069.6
vagrant (5) n 113.7
vagrants (6) n 069.7
vaguely (1) adv 100.3
Vaiden (5) MS 087.5
vain (2) adj 028.1
valance (2) n 009.5
Valdosta (34) AL GA 087.6
vale (4) n 030.4
valedictorian (1) n 070.6
Valencia (3) 090.8
  ˜ peanuts (1) n 054.7
Valencias (1) 090.8
Valentine (6) 055A.4
  ˜ bean (1) n 055A.4
  ˜ dance (1) n 083.1
  ˜ parties (1) n 130.7
  ˜ party (1) n 070.7
valet (1) n 009.3
Valikia (1) 056.9
valise (2) n 028.2
Valium (1) 114.2
Val(ium) (1) 114.2
Valiums (1) 114.2
Valkari(a) (2) FL 087.5
valley (668) n/adj 011.6
  ˜ puds (1) n 069.9
  ˜ rafter (2) n 011.6
  ˜ road (2) n 031.7
  ˜ roof (2) n 011.6
  ˜ stream (1) n 030.6
  ˜ tin (7) n 011.6
  ˜ trough (1) n 011.6
Valley (93) 011.6
  ˜ Brook (1) TN 030.7
  ˜ Creek (2) AL 030.7
  ˜ Creek Apartments (1) 030.7
  ˜ Mills (1) TX 087.4
  ˜ North (1) 105.1
  ˜ Park (1) MS 087.8
  ˜ Springs (2) AR 087.4
  ˜ View (2) MS TX 087.7
valleys (64) n 011.6
Valrico (1) FL 087.6
valse (1) n F 083.1
valuable (1) adj 051.4
valuation (1) n 040.5
value (2) n 048.4
values (1) n 065.8
valve (6) n 018.6
valves (1) n 018.7
vamoosed (1) v 080.9

vampires (1) n 090.2
van (121) n/adj 109.6
  ˜ truck (1) n 109.6
  ˜ trucks (2) n 111.5
  ˜ type (1) n 109.6
  ˜ -type truck (1) n 111.5
Van (15) 087.1
  ˜ Buren (12) AR TN 087.1
  ˜ Buren County (2) AR TN 087.6
  ˜ Vleet (1) MS 087.7
Vance (2) AL 087.3
Vancleave (5) MS 087.5
Vancouver (3) 087.1
Vanderbilt (7) FL 087.2
  ˜ Street (1) 031.6
  ˜ University (1) 106.4
Vandervoort (1) AR 087.1
Vandiver Boulevard (1) 107.6
Vandyke (1) 071.4
vane (1) adj 089.8
vanilla (1) n 075.8
vanish (1) v 057.6
vanishing (1) v 102.2
vanities (3) n 009.2
vanity (33) n/adj 009.2
  ˜ chest (1) n 009.2
  ˜ dresser (2) n 009.2
  ˜ dressers (1) n 009.2
  ˜ mirror (1) n 009.2
vans (20) n 109.6
vapor (3) n 006.7
Vardaman (1) MS 087.2
variable (1) adj 005.6
varied (1) adj 025.2
varies (1) v 090.1
varieties (12) n 025.2
variety (12) n/adj 065.9
  ˜ store (2) n 116.2
Variety (1) 033.3
variety[N-i] (2) n 033.3
various (6) adj 075.6
varmint (327) n 059.5
  ˜ -proof (1) adj 059.5
varmint[N-i] (3) n 059.5
varmints (489) n 059.5
varnish (2) n/adj 039.9
  ˜ tree (1) n 061.8
Varsity (2) 105.4
  ˜ Street (1) 105.4
vary (1) v 067.1

vase (850) n 017.7
vasectomy (1) n 036.1
Vaseline (2) 078.3
vases (127) n 017.7
vast (2) adj 090.7
vat (13) n 017.6
vats (4) n 019.2
vaudeville (2) n 084.4
Vaughn (2) GA 080.6
vault (73) n 117.6
vaults (13) n 079.1
vaurien (1) adj F 069.7
VC (1) 126.4
veal (18) n/adj 121.2
  ˜ calf (1) n 033.8
  ˜ chops (1) n 121.2
  ˜ cutlet (1) n 121.2
  ˜ cutlets (1) n 121.2
  ˜ liver (1) n 121.2
  ˜ steaks (1) n 121.1
veau (2) n/adj F 033.9
  ˜ boeuf (1) n F 033.8
Vedra (1) 106.1
vee (1) n 031.3
Vegas (6) 087.5
vegetable (238) n/adj 050.4
  ˜ -beef soup (1) n 050.4
  ˜ bin (1) n 015.5
  ˜ brush (1) n 022.2
  ˜ building (1) n 014.3
  ˜ dinners (1) n 050.4
  ˜ dishes (1) n 050.4
  ˜ eggs (2) n 088.9
  ˜ farm (3) n 050.4
  ˜ fat (1) n 050.4
  ˜ forks (1) n 017.8
  ˜ garden (64) n 050.5
  ˜ gardens (3) n 050.5
  ˜ greens (2) n 055A.5
  ˜ knife (1) n 088.8
  ˜ lot (1) n 016.1
  ˜ man (1) n 050.4
  ˜ matter (1) n 050.4
  ˜ oil (3) n 050.4
  ˜ oils (1) n 024.1
  ˜ patch (13) n 050.5
  ˜ peelings (1) n 050.4
  ˜ plants (1) n 050.4
  ˜ product (1) n 050.4
  ˜ production (1) n 050.4
  ˜ season (1) n 050.4

~ shortening (1) n 050.4

~ soup (10) n 050.4

~ supper (2) n 050.4

~ truck farmers (1) n 050.4

vegeta(ble) (3) n 050.4

veget(able) (1) n 050.4

vegetable[N-i] (41) n 050.4

vegetables (915) n 050.4

vegeta(bles) (1) n 050.4

vegetation (4) n 015.9

vegetations (2) n 015.9

veggie (1) n 050.4

veggies (3) n 050.4

vehicle (38) n 023.6

vehicles (12) n 111.5

veil (2) n 060A.8

veillee (2) n F 082.5

vein (10) n 065.8

velocipede (1) n 084.8

velocity (1) n 007.2

velvet (27) adj 055A.6

~ bean (3) n 055A.6

~ beans (21) n 055A.3

~ bush (1) n 088.9

~ sofas (1) n 009.1

~ -tail rattler (1) n 090.8

vending machine (1) n 032.7

vendor (1) n 114.4

veneer (5) n/adj 011.2

~ mill (1) n 080.6

veneered (1) adj 065.8

venetian (210) n/adj 009.5

~ blinds (180) n 009.5

~ shades (2) n 009.5

~ blind (26) n 009.5

(ve)netian blind (3) n 009.5

(ve)netian blind[N-i] (1) n 009.5

(ve)netian blinds (4) n 009.5

Venetian Causeway (1) 107.4

venganse (1) interj S 037.5

Venice (3) FL LA 087.3

venison (6) n/adj 121.4

~ sausage (1) n 121.6

venom (2) n 061.9

venomous (1) adj 065.8

vent (11) n/adj 008.2

~ pipe (2) n 023.2

ventilate (1) v 088.8

ventilation pipe (1) n 023.2

ventriloquist (1) n 065.8

vents (27) n 118.5

venturesome (1) adj 092.7

Venus (2) TX 087.2

vera (2) adj 061.4

Veracruz (1) 086.3

veranda (189) n 010.8

verandas (15) n 010.8

verbal exchange (1) n 129.7

Verbena (1) AL 087.1

verbs (1) n 119.8

Verdun (3) LA 087.1

Verdunville (1) LA 087.6

verger (2) n F 053.2

~ de pechers (1) n F 053.2

verify (1) v 026.2

Vermilion (11) 030.3

~ Bay (2) LA 030.3

~ Bayou (1) LA 030.7

~ Co-op (1) 081.8

~ Parish (4) LA 087.2

~ River (3) LA 030.7

vermin (6) n 059.5

Vermont (17) 065.8

~ maple (1) n 061.5

Vernia (1) 087.8

Vernon (19) AL FL LA TN 087.4

~ Parish (5) LA 087.4

~ River (2) GA 030.7

Verns Creek (1) GA 030.7

Vero (6) FL 087.8

~ Beach (4) FL 086.5

Verona (1) MS 088.7

verrat (2) n F 035.3

Verret (3) 030.7

versa (1) adj 070.6

verse (1) n 097.8

versions (1) n 089.8

vertical (10) adj 108.3

~ parking (4) n 108.3

very (770) adv 090.6

ver(y) (20) adv 091.7

vessel (10) n 024.7

vessels (9) n 017.2

vest (936) n/adj 027.3

~ -pocket (2) n 027.3

~ -pocket park (1) n 080.7

~ -pocket parks (1) n 088.7

~ -pockets (1) n 027.3

~ suit (2) n 027.7

~ watch (1) n 004.3

vest[N-i] (21) n 027.3

Vestavia (15) AL 087.7

~ Hills (1) 106.1

vestes (27) n 027.3

vestibule (6) n 010.8

vestments (1) n 080.6

vests (5) n 027.3

vet (3) n 097.5

vetch (2) n 014.4

veteran (4) n 085.8

Veteran[N-i] Hospital (1) 084.5

Veterans (2) 107.1

~ Highway (1) 107.1

~ Hospital (1) 084.5

veterans (1) n 071.2

veterinarian (3) n 084.8

veterinari(an) (3) n 077.8

veterinary (2) n/adj 065.9

~ work (1) n 036.1

veuve (2) n F 063.3

vexed (6) adj 075.2

viaduct (48) n 107.8

Viaduct (2) 107.8

viaducts (5) n 066.8

vibration (1) n 065.8

vicar-general (1) n 068.3

vice (2) n/adj 085.6

~ -president (1) n 085.6

~ versa (1) adv 070.6

vicinity (1) n 065.8

vicious (5) adj 073.2

Vicksburg (66) MS 087.7

~ Blues (1) 087.3

victim (2) n 057.9

Victoria (14) TN TX 087.6

~ County (1) TX 087.6

Victori(a) (1) TX 087.5

Victorian (13) 088.7

~ house (2) n 098.6

~ love seat (1) n 009.1

~ parlor organ (1) n 080.8

~ -shaped (1) adj 090.4

victory (2) adj 050.5

~ garden (1) n 050.5

~ gardens (1) n 050.5

Victory (4) 107.6

~ Drive (2) 107.6

~ Lake (1) GA 030.7

~ Park (1) 091.8

Victrola (3) 081.8

victual (2) n 048.4

victuals (248) n 048.4

Vida (2) LA 065.8

Vidalia (20) GA LA MS 055.6

~ onion (1) n 055.6

~ onions (3) n 055.6

Vidor (1) TX 073.8

vieille (2) n/adj F 063.2

~ truie (1) n F 093.5

vieja (1) adj S 047.4

Viejo (2) 087.1

Vienna (12) GA LA 087.2

~ bread (1) n 044.4

~ sausage (4) n 121.6

~ sausages (2) n 121.6

Vietnam (6) 065.9

~ fight (1) n 085.8

~ War (2) 038.8

Vietnamese (6) 126.4

Vietnams (1) 126.4

Vieux Carre (6) 105.1

view (2) n/v 080.6

View (27) 105.4

vigilante committee (1) n 085.7

vigor (1) n 074.1

vigorous (14) adj 002.6

~ -looking (1) adj 090.9

vigorously (1) adv 077.8

Vilano Beach (1) FL 086.3

Villa (5) 007A.6

~ Rica (2) GA 087.4

village (6) n/adj 065.8

~ green (1) n 085.1

~ shop (1) n 011.7

Village (27) 105.1

~ Creek (2) AL TX 030.7

villains (2) n 059.5

ville (1) n F 082.6

Ville (4) 109.2

~ Platte (3) LA 087.3

Villere Street (1) 070.7

Villita (5) 106.4

vim (3) n 074.1

Vina (1) AL 087.1
Vince Dooley (2) 065.5
Vincennes (1) IN 086.3
Vincent (2) 030.5
vine (125) n/v/adj 062.7
~ beans (2) n 055A.3
~ in (1) v 084.8
~ Porto Rico (1) n 055.5
~ string bean (1) n 055A.4
~ swing (1) n 022.9
Vine (7) 105.1
~ City (4) 105.1
~ Creek (1) GA 030.7
~ Street (2) 107.5
vinegar (24) n/adj 066.8
~ barrel (1) n 019.1
~ cobbler (1) n 048.3
~ cruet (2) n 051.7
~ custard (1) n 048.5
~ factory (1) n 053.7
~ keg (1) n 020.2
~ pie (3) n 048.3
~ pies (1) n 048.3
vines (19) n 062.3
Vineville (1) GA 087.9
vineyard (3) n 053.2
Vineyard (1) 067.2
vineyards (2) n 065.8
vingt (1) n F 001.8
vining (2) adj 055A.4
~ beans (1) n 055A.4
~ type (1) n 055A.3
Vinings (1) GA 087.7
vino (4) n 114.7
vinoleum (1) n 065.9
Vinton (1) 087.7
Viny Grove (1) AR 087.2
vinyl (2) adj 109.2
~ top (1) n 109.2
~ tops (1) n 109.2
viol (1) n 083.3
violated (1) v 058.3
violent (3) adj 081.2
~ storm (1) n 006.2
violet (2) n 065.9
violets (2) n 062.8
violin (4) n 070.6
violins (1) n 070.6
virgin (9) n/adj 035.6
~ ground (1) n 041.4
~ soil (1) n 029.8
~ timber (4) n 084.8
~ timbers (1) n 052.1

Virgin (6) 067.1
~ Mary (3) 067.1
Virginia (934) 086.2
~ bunch (4) n 054.7
~ coastline (1) n 086.2
~ Colony (1) TX 087.2
~ creeper (4) n 062.3
~ cure (1) n 080.9
~ drums (1) n 059.9
~ ham (2) n 121.3
~ hams (2) n 121.3
~ -Highland (2) 105.6
~ Key (1) 106.2
~ peanuts (2) n 054.7
~ reel (7) n 083.1
(Vir)ginia (4) 086.2
Virginias (2) 086.2
virile (5) adj 073.1
virtually (1) adv 099.5
virus (2) n 076.3
vision (3) n 097.2
Vision (1) 082.6
visions (2) n 097.2
visit (26) n/v 080.5
~ with (1) v 093.1
visited (1) v 052.5
visiting (10) v/adj 081.4
~ pastor (1) n 067.8
~ with (1) v 082.7
visitor (9) n 066.7
visitors (1) n 065.8
Visitors (1) 093.5
visits (1) n 093.1
Vista (11) 105.1
vitae (1) n 091.8
vitamin (1) n 082.9
vitamin[N-i] (1) n 012.4
vitamins (1) n 075.9
vitam(ins) (1) n 066.9
vitex (1) n 061.9
vitrified-brick roads (1) n 031.6
vivacious (3) adj 074.1
Vizcaya (1) 106.4
Vleet (1) 087.7
voca (1) n S 020.5
vocal (3) adj 071.7
~ cords (2) n 071.7
~ singing (1) n 089.9
vocalizing (1) v 057.4
vogue (1) n 123.6
voice (14) n/adj 071.7
~ box (8) n 071.7
voile (1) n 080.9
volador (5) n S 022.7

volatile (1) adj 075.1
Volks bus (1) n 109.6
Volkswagen (4) 109.2
~ bus (1) n 109.6
~ van (1) n 109.6
Volkswagens (1) 102.9
volleyball (22) n 126.2
volt (1) adj 001.6
volume (4) n 051.5
voluntarily (2) adv 041.5
voluntary (2) adj 041.5
volunteer (310) n/v/adj/ adv 041.5
~ babies (1) n 065.9
~ beehive (1) n 090.9
~ corn (7) n 041.5
~ cotton (1) n 041.5
~ crop (37) n 041.5
~ grass (1) n 041.5
~ hill (1) n 041.5
~ oats (2) n 041.5
~ peanuts (1) n 041.5
~ plant (1) n 041.5
~ plants (3) n 041.5
~ potatoes (2) n 041.5
~ rice (1) n 041.5
~ seed (1) n 041.5
~ stuff (2) n 041.5
~ to (1) v 041.5
~ tomato (1) n 055.3
~ tomatoes (5) n 041.5
~ (to)matoes (1) n 041.5
~ -type crop (1) n 041.5
~ vine (1) n 041.5
~ weed (1) n 041.5
~ work (1) n 041.5
volunteer[V-r] (1) v 041.5
volunteered (9) v/adj 041.5
~ crop (1) n 041.5
volunteers (16) n 041.5
Volusia (3) FL 087.9
vomir (1) v F 080.3
vomit (682) v/adj 080.2
~ wheel (1) n 022.7
vomit[V-r] (5) v 080.2
~ up (1) v 080.3
vomited (80) v 080.2
~ up (5) v 080.2
~ up your toenail (1) v 080.2

~ stomach (1) n 080.2
~ up (1) v 080.3
vomits (17) v 080.2
~ his food up (1) v 080.2
~ up (1) v 080.2
voodoo (8) n/adj 090.3
~ artist (1) n 088.8
~ medicine (1) n 061.4
~ queen (1) n 090.3
voodooism (1) n 090.3
vote (32) n/v 071.2
~ for (23) v 043.5
voted (4) v 057.9
~ for (2) v 099.1
Voters (1) 091.6
votes (3) n/v 001A.1
voting precinct (1) n 070.7
vouchered (1) v 088.7
Vowells Mill community (1) LA 087.5
vowels (1) n 066.8
voyage (3) n 089.6
Vulcan (7) 021.6
~ statue (1) n 106.4
vulcanized road (1) n 031.7
vulcanizer (2) n 088.9
vulgar (7) adj 073.6
~ pictures (1) n 114.9
vulgarity (1) n 070.7
vultures (2) n 089.8

vomiting (83) v/adj 080.2

W

W (5) 080.6
~ and A Road (1) 080.6
~ -Fourteen diversion canal (1) n 030.2
W. (2) 106.4
~ C. Handy (1) 106.4
~ C. Handy Park (1) 106.4
wa (3) interj 037.8
Wabash (3) AR 087.9
~ Cannonball (2) 087.5
Wabasso (2) FL 087.8
Wabbaseka (2) AR 087.3
~ Bayou (1) AR 030.3
Waccasassa (2) FL 030.7
~ River (1) FL 030.7
Wachee (1) 087.1
wacky (5) adj 074.7
~ tobacco (2) n 080.6
~ -wacky (1) adj 074.7
Waco (18) TX 087.4
~ Springs (1) TX 087.3
wad (9) n 073.5
wadding (1) n 022.4
waddle hogs (1) n 035.3
wade (3) v 095.6
~ out (1) v 095.7
~ [P-0] (1) v 012.8
Wade (3) MS 087.1
waders (1) n 027.4
wading (2) v 057.4
~ [P-0] (1) v 013.9
Wadley (2) AL GA 086.2
wads (1) n 114.5
waffle (12) n/adj 045.3
~ iron (2) n 116.4
~ irons (2) n 017.5
~ syrup (1) n 051.3
waffles (60) n 045.3
wag (5) v 098.1
~ with (1) v 098.1
Wagarville (1) AL 087.5
wage hand (2) n 096.7
wages (5) n/adj 080.7

~ hand (1) n 080.7
~ hands (1) n 080.7
wagged (1) v 098.1
waggle (1) v 098.1
waggler (1) n 126.6
Wagner Creek (1) TN 030.7
wagon (753) n/adj 111.8
~ axle (3) n 021.8
~ bed (4) n 020.8
~ box (1) n 019.8
~ bunk (1) n 093.7
~ chair (1) n 008.8
~ dope (1) n 021.8
~ fellies (1) n 021.1
~ felly (3) n 021.1
~ gear (1) n 038.6
~ grease (3) n 023.7
~ greasings (1) n 023.7
~ harness (3) n 038.6
~ house (2) n 014.5
~ hub (1) n 021.8
~ line (2) n 039.1
~ lines (13) n 039.1
~ path (1) n 031.8
~ rim (5) n 021.1
~ road (12) n 031.7
~ roads (5) n 031.7
~ shaft (1) n 020.9
~ shed (18) n 010.3
~ sheds (1) n 011.7
~ sheet (3) n 070.8
~ sheet stuff (1) n 019.7
~ shelter (1) n 011.8
~ shelters (1) n 014.2
~ skein (1) n 021.8
~ -tail pr(eacher) (1) n 067.8
~ tap (1) n 021.3
~ team (1) n 033.7
~ thimble (1) n 021.8
~ thimbles (1) n 089.8
~ tire (28) n 021.1
~ tires (3) n 021.1
~ tongue (119) n 020.8
~ trails (1) n 031.7
~ train (3) n 080.6
~ -train days (1) n 080.8
~ tree (1) n 021.2
~ trees (1) n 021.2
~ wheel (15) n 023.3
~ -wheel quilts (1) n 029.1

~ wheels (4) n 021.1
~ whip (3) n 019.4
~ wrench (1) n 021.9
Wagon Wheel (1) 119.8
wagonload (38) n 019.8
wagonloads (3) n 019.8
wagons (64) n 014.6
wagonyard (4) n 085.1
wagonyards (2) n 088.7
wags (1) v 013.1
wagtail (1) n 101.3
wah (2) adj/interj 037.7
~ -wahs (1) n 088.8
wahoo (3) n/adj 061.7
~ roots (1) n 061.4
Wahoo (5) GA 030.7
~ Creek (1) GA 030.7
~ District (1) GA 087.1
~ Park (1) 106.7
wahs (1) n 088.8
waif (4) n 066.3
waifs (1) n 033.8
wail (2) v 036.2
wailing (1) v 079.3
wainscoted (1) v 007A.7
wainscoting (1) n 081.8
waist (9) n/adj 072.4
~ apron (1) n 026.4
~ aprons (2) n 026.4
~ breeches (1) n 027.4
~ pants (2) n 027.4
~ trousers (1) n 017.4
waistcoat (40) n 027.3
waistcoats (6) n 027.3
wait (826) n/v/adj 099.1
~ for (405) v 099.1
~ man (8) n 082.3
~ men (1) n 082.3
~ on (163) v 988.1
~ to (1) v 082.6
~ until (1) v 099.1
~ up (1) v 099.1
waited (19) v 099.1
~ for (5) v 099.1
~ on (11) v 099.1
~ upon (1) v 082.3
waiter (29) n/adj 082.3
~ girl (2) n 082.4
waiters (10) n 082.3
waiting (80) v/adj 082.4
~ for (29) v 099.1
~ girl (1) n 082.4
~ man (1) n 082.3
~ on (28) v 099.1
~ on her (2) v 081.4

~ room (1) n 084.7
~ rooms (1) n 007A.6
~ station (1) n 084.7
~ wom(an) (1) n 082.4
~ [P-0] (1) v 099.1
waitings man (1) n 082.3
waitress (2) n 082.4
waits (3) v 013.8
~ for (1) v 099.1
~ on (1) v 065.2
Wakaya Road (1) 115.7
wake (796) n/v 079.4
~ up (345) v 076.7
~ -up (1) n 076.7
~ -up call (1) n 076.7
wake[V-r] (5) v 076.7
~ up (2) v 097.3
wake[V-s] (1) v 076.7
waked (109) v 097.3
~ up (93) v 076.7
Wakefield (1) 055A.1
wakem (1) interj 037.7
waken (10) v 097.3
waken[V-r] (1) v 097.3
wakened (3) v 097.3
wakes (9) n/v 079.3
~ up (3) v 076.7
waking (5) v 076.8
~ up (4) v 076.7
Wakulla (6) FL 087.2
~ River (1) FL 030.7
~ Springs (1) 106.4
Walden (4) 030.7
~ Creek (1) TN 030.7
~ Ridge (3) TN 031.1
Waldron (3) AR 087.9
wale (1) v 081.3
Wales (5) 087.9
Waleska (2) GA 087.9
Walhalla (1) SC 087.5
walk (481) n/v/adj 064.6
~ across (3) v 025.4
~ (a)cross (1) v 028.9
~ area (1) n 009.9
~ in (1) v 057.7
~ -in (1) n 009.6
~ -in box (1) n 052.6
~ -in closet (13) n 009.6
~ -in closets (5) n 009.6
~ -in cooler (1) n 080.7
~ -in den (1) n 007A.6
~ -in half bath (1) n 118.3

~ -in locker (1) n 007A.6
~ -in lockers (1) n 009.6
~ -in pantries (1) n 010.1
~ -in pantry (2) n 010.1
~ -in theater (1) n 084.4
~ into (1) v 053.6
~ on (1) v 057.7
~ out (2) v 099.5
~ out on (1) v 089.2
~ -out porch (1) n 010.8
~ through (1) v 058.2
~ -through (1) n 118.6
~ to (1) v 089.2
~ under (1) v 080.8
~ up (4) v 010.7
~ -up (1) n 119.2
~ -up attic (1) n 009.8
~ with (20) v 074.4
Walk (4) 106.7
walk[V-r] (4) v 066.8
~ along (1) v 039.6
~ into (1) v 032.6
walk[V-t] out (1) v 098.7
walked (20) v 102.3
~ across (1) v 085.2
~ away (1) v 082.1
~ off with (1) v 100.2
~ on (1) v 075.6
~ out (2) v 065.9
~ under (1) v 053.4
~ up (1) v 053.6
~ up on (2) v 032.6
walker (6) n/adj 064.5
~ cultivator (1) n 021.7
Walker (53) AL LA TX 033.3
~ Branch (1) TX 030.7
~ County (4) AL TX 087.1
~ dog (1) n 033.3
~ dogs (1) n 033.3
~ Drive (1) 107.7
~ Homes (1) 106.2
~ hound (2) n 033.3
~ hound dog (1) n 033.3
~ Levee (1) AR 030.7
~ Station (1) GA 087.3
Walker[N-i] (1) 086.6

walkers (1) n 052.1
Walkers (17) 033.3
walkie-talkie (1) n 113.3
walking (127) v/adj 064.6
~ along (1) v 026.1
~ (a)long with (1) v 097.5
~ around (3) v 057.4
~ away (1) v 052.2
~ catfish (1) n 059.9
~ corpse (1) n 072.9
~ cultivator (6) n 021.8
~ cultivators (2) n 021.8
~ horse (4) n 099.5
~ horse show (1) n 099.5
~ horses (5) n 034.2
~ mower (1) n 120.2
~ off (1) v 075.5
~ on (3) v 104.9
~ outfit (1) n 021.9
~ papers (4) n 082.1
~ planter (2) n 021.8
~ plow (2) n 021.6
~ shoes (3) n 123.8
~ shorts (33) n 123.2
~ size (1) n 002.8
~ stick (3) n 060A.4
~ street (1) n 031.9
~ talking Tootsie Roll (1) n 069.3
~ the dog (1) n 083.1
~ to (1) v 032.5
~ towards (1) v 032.5
~ zombi (1) n 084.9
Walking (3) 030.7
~ Hill Pond (1) AL 030.7
walks (24) n/v 013.7
~ in (2) v 053.4
~ on (1) v 025.6
~ under (1) v 053.4
walkway (56) n 031.8
walkways (1) n 031.9
wall (415) n/adj 016.6
~ bag (1) n 009.6
~ broom (1) n 010.5
~ cabinet (1) n 010.1
~ fence (2) n 016.6
~ heater (2) n 118.4
~ heaters (4) n 118.5
~ ladders (1) n 111.5
~ -to-wall cousins (1) n 080.8

~ units (1) n 118.4
Wall (2) 105.2
wall[N-i] (1) n 080.6
wallaby (1) n 123.8
Wallace (2) 068.5
Wallaceite (1) 069.3
Wallahatchee Creek (1) AL 030.7
Walland Gap (1) TN 031.3
wallboard (1) n 011.2
wallboards (2) n 011.2
Waller Creek (1) TX 030.7
wallet (61) n 028.2
wallets (2) n 028.2
walleye (4) n/adj 059.9
~ pike (2) n 059.9
walleyed (3) adj 059.1
~ owl (1) n 059.1
~ perch (1) n 059.9
~ pike (1) n 059.9
wallflower (1) n 125.2
Wallingford (1) CN 087.4
Wallisville Dam (1) TX 030.7
wallop (1) n 053.4
walloped (2) v 065.5
walloping (2) n 065.5
wallow (13) n/v 015.4
~ out (2) v 097.9
wallowed (4) v 015.4
~ around (2) v 097.1
~ in (1) v 015.4
wallows (1) n 029.7
walls (59) n 016.6
walnut (473) n/adj 054.8
~ bread (1) n 054.8
~ chest (1) n 008.8
~ dye (1) n 054.8
~ filling (1) n 054.8
~ goody (1) n 054.8
~ hull (3) n 054.8
~ hulls (1) n 054.8
~ juice (1) n 054.8
~ rind (1) n 054.8
~ roots (1) n 061.4
~ shell (3) n 054.8
~ stone (1) n 054.8
~ tree (24) n 061.9
~ trees (35) n 061.8
~ wine (1) n 114.7
Walnut (25) MS 054.8
~ Corner (1) AR 087.3

~ Creek (8) AL TX 030.7
~ Grove (7) AR GA TN 087.3
~ Grove Road (2) 106.3
~ Hill (2) LA MS 054.8
~ Mountain (1) TN 066.9
~ Ridge (1) AR 087.6
~ Street (1) 054.8
walnut[N-i] (2) n 054.8
walnuts (706) n/adj 054.8
~ trees (1) n 061.8
Waloopa Pass (1) TX 031.2
Walrus (1) 111.2
Walt Disney World (1) 106.4
Walton (28) FL GA 087.3
~ County (5) FL GA 087.1
~ Senior High (1) 125.9
waltz (80) n/adj 083.1
~ dance (1) n 083.1
waltzed (1) v 083.1
waltzes (9) n 083.1
waltzing (12) v 083.1
wamba (1) n 083.1
wan (7) adj 072.9
wand (1) n 019.4
wander (1) v 070.6
wandering (1) v 070.6
Wanians (1) 127.7
want (1385) v/adj 085.4
~ in (1) v 085.4
~ list (1) n 088.7
~ off (41) v 085.4
~ off at (3) v 085.4
~ out (3) v 085.4
~ out of (1) v 085.4
~ to (691) v 085.4
~ [P-0] (14) v 057.5
want[V-p] (18) v 052.7
~ to (7) v 013.6
~ [P-0] (1) v 085.4
want[V-r] (11) v 052.5
~ to (8) v 085.4
want[V-s] to (1) v 095.8
wanted (286) v 085.4
~ for (2) v 053.7
~ in (2) v 085.4

~ off (2) v 085.4
~ out (1) v 085.4
~ to (61) v 085.4
~ [P-0] (1) v 025.5
wanting (25) v 085.4
~ out (2) v 085.4
~ to (11) v 098.8
wanton (1) adj 073.6
wants (154) v 085.4
~ in (11) v 085.4
~ off (1) v 085.4
~ on (1) v 085.4
~ out (43) v 085.4
~ to (58) v 053.5
war (110) n/adj 085.8
~ blades (1) n 011.2
~ bonds (1) n 065.8
~ department (4) n 063.2
~ march (1) n 129.7
~ memorial (1) n 106.4
~ paint (4) n 028.1
~ soldier (1) n 092.7
~ woman (1) n 060A.5
War (1436) 085.8
~ against the State (1) 085.8
~ against the States (2) 085.8
~ among the States (1) 085.8
~ between North and South (4) 085.8
~ between the Nations (1) 085.8
~ between the North and South (9) 085.8
~ between the North and the South (15) 085.8
~ between the Northern States and the South States (1) 085.8
~ between the State [N-i] (4) 085.8
~ between the States (295) 085.8
~ between the Two States (2) 085.8
~ between [D-0] North and the South (1) 085.8
~ between [D-0] States (1) 085.8

~ betwixt the State[N-i] (1) 085.8
~ for Independence (1) 085.8
~ for Southern Independence (2) 085.8
~ for the Confederacy (1) 085.8
~ in the States (1) 085.8
~ Memorial Park (2) 106.4
~ of Eighteen-Twelve (3) 085.8
~ of Hate (1) 085.8
~ of Northern Aggression (5) 085.8
~ of Rebellion (2) 085.8
~ of Secession (2) 085.8
~ of Slavery (1) 085.8
~ of the Confederacy (2) 085.8
~ of the Divided Nation (1) 085.8
~ of the Northern Aggression (1) 085.8
~ of the Rebellion (5) 085.8
~ of the Revolution (1) 085.8
~ of the South (1) 085.8
~ of the States (7) 085.8
~ of Yankee Aggression (2) 085.8
~ One (1) 081.8
~ to Free the Slaves (1) 085.8
~ with State[N-i] (1) 085.8
~ with the Yankees (1) 085.8
ward (5) n/adj 066.3
~ heeler (2) n 115.3
~ roads (1) n 031.7
~ school (1) n 083.7
Ward (46) AL 087.5
~ Creek (2) AR 030.7
~ Lake (1) MS 030.7
~ Three (1) 001.2
warden (1) n 063.2

wardens (1) n 066.8
wardrobe (545) n/adj 009.7
~ chest[N-i] (1) n 009.7
~ closet (2) n 009.7
~ trunk (1) n 009.7
~ trunks (1) n 009.7
wardrobes (103) n 009.6
wardroom (2) n 009.7
wards (4) n 070.7
Wards (1) 105.4
ware (1) n 017.1
Ware County (6) GA 087.7
warehouse (10) n 014.4
Warehouse (1) 106.5
warehouses (1) n 014.1
Waresboro (1) GA 087.3
Warfield Road (1) 031.8
warm (96) v/adj 005.4
~ -morning (1) n 008.4
~ -morning heater (4) n 008.3
~ -morning stove (2) n 008.5
~ over (3) n/v 050.1
~ overs (6) n 050.1
~ spell (1) n 007.4
~ up (8) v 050.1
~ -up[N-i] (1) n 050.1
~ -ups (2) n 050.1
~ you up (1) v 065.5
~ your leather (1) v 065.5
Warm Springs (10) GA 087.7
warm[V-r] by (1) v 052.6
warm[V-s] (1) v 050.1
warm[V-t] (5) v 050.1
~ over (1) v 050.1
warmed (391) v 050.1
~ over (265) v 050.1
~ o(ver) (2) v 050.1
~ -over (4) adj 050.1
~ -over dinner (1) n 050.1
~ -over food (15) n 050.1
~ -over meal (2) n 050.1
~ -over stuff (1) n 050.1
~ -over supper (1) n 050.1

~ over[N-i] (4) n 050.1
~ overs (16) n 050.1
~ up (41) v 050.1
~ -up (2) adj 050.1
~ -up food (2) n 050.1
~ -up leftovers (2) n 050.1
warmer (14) n/adj 008.2
~ closet (1) n 080.6
warmers (3) n 008.2
warming (25) v/adj 080.7
~ cabinet (1) n 080.7
~ closet (13) n 049.3
~ closets (2) n 008.2
~ oven (2) n 116.4
~ up (2) v 050.1
warmongers (1) n 025.8
warmouth (18) n/adj 059.9
~ bream (1) n 059.9
~ perch (11) n 059.9
~ trout (1) n 059.9
warmth (1) n 052.6
warned (3) v 101.6
Warner (7) 030.7
~ Creek (1) AL 030.7
~ Robins (3) GA 087.7
warning (5) n/adj 110.8
~ devices (1) n 110.8
warnings (1) n 006.3
warp (3) n 065.9
~ -minded (1) adj 074.8
warrant (1) n 080.7
warrantied (1) adj 051.4
Warren (9) AR GA MS 087.1
~ County (2) MS 087.6
Warrenton (1) TX 087.3
Warrick Creek (1) AL 030.7
Warrington (1) 087.4
Warrior (17) AL 087.2
~ Creek (2) GA MS 030.7
~ River (7) AL 030.7
War's (1) 085.8
wars (13) n 085.8
warsaw (1) n 059.9
Warsaw (2) 083.6
~ College (1) 083.6
~ winner (1) n 127.4
wart (7) n/adj 078.2
~ frog (3) n 060.4
Wartburg (2) TN 087.1

warthog (3) n 035.9
wartime (1) n 085.8
Wartrace (5) TN 030.7
warts (2) n 060.3
Warwick (3) GA 087.3
  ~ mail carrier (1) n 013.1
wary (1) adj 074.2
was (5510) v 013.8
w(as) (1) v 013.5
(wa)s (5) v 013.8
Waschlappen (1) n G 018.3
Waschtopf (1) n G 017.6
wash (1785) n/v/adj 018.1
  ~ -and-iron day (1) n 010.6
  ~ and wear (1) n 103.3
  ~ arena (1) n 116.5
  ~ away (2) v 018.1
  ~ basket (13) n 020.1
  ~ baskets (1) n 020.1
  ~ boiler (5) n 017.6
  ~ bucket (1) n 017.2
  ~ buckets (2) n 017.2
  ~ down (1) v 018.1
  ~ drain (1) n 030.4
  ~ gravel (2) n 031.6
  ~ hole (8) n 030.5
  ~ holes (1) n 030.5
  ~ in (4) v 040.7
  ~ kettle (55) n 017.6
  ~ kettles (9) n 017.6
  ~ lady (1) n 093.5
  ~ machine (1) n 039.7
  ~ machines (1) n 070.8
  ~ off (4) v 018.1
  ~ out (13) v 030.5
  ~ pad (1) n 018.3
  ~ pan (9) n 020.1
  ~ pans (1) n 020.1
  ~ place (6) n 029.4
  ~ shed (5) n 011.8
  ~ shelf (1) n 010.6
  ~ shelter (1) n 011.8
  ~ skillet (1) n 017.6
  ~ table (1) n 009.2
  ~ towel (16) n 018.5
  ~ towels (1) n 018.5
  ~ up (5) v 018.1
  ~ water (5) n 010.6
  ~ with (3) v 018.1
  ~ wood (1) n 098.9
wash[V-r] (11) v 018.1

wash[V-t] (5) v 018.1
  ~ down (3) v 018.1
washamateria (1) n 010.6
washateria (56) n 116.5
washateri(a) (5) n 116.5
washater(ia) (5) n 116.5
washaterias (5) n 010.6
washaway (1) n 030.5
washbasin (5) n 080.7
washbasins (2) n 018.1
washboard (29) n/adj 010.6
  ~ road (4) n 031.8
  ~ roads (2) n 030.5
washboards (5) n 081.8
washboil(er) (1) n 017.6
washbowl (2) n 009.3
washcloth (395) n 018.5
washcloths (15) n 018.3
washday (160) n 010.6
washdays (6) n 010.6
washed (222) v/adj 010.6
  ~ away (13) v 018.1
  ~ for (1) v 010.6
  ~ in (2) v 029.3
  ~ off (3) v 030.5
  ~ out (19) v 030.4
  ~ -out (2) adj 030.4
  ~ -out area (1) n 030.5
  ~ -out creek (1) n 030.6
  ~ -out gully (1) n 030.5
  ~ -out place (5) n 030.4
  ~ place (1) n 030.4
  ~ -through (1) adj 030.4
  ~ up (6) v 075.4
  ~ with (2) v 032.4
washer (191) n/adj 006.1
  ~ bucket (1) n 017.2
  ~ carriage (1) n 010.6
  ~ -dryer (1) n 018.1
washer[N-i] (1) n 010.6
washerette (9) n 116.5
washers (35) n 034.8
washerwoman (2) n 017.6
washery (1) n 010.6
washes (54) v 010.6
  ~ on (2) v 010.6
  ~ out (1) v 012.8
washette (2) n 010.6
washhouse (39) n 011.7
washhouses (2) n 116.5

washing (677) n/v/adj 010.6
  ~ board (2) n 010.6
  ~ day (1) n 010.6
  ~ machine (20) n 010.6
  ~ machines (2) n 010.6
  ~ pot (1) n 017.6
  ~ powder (1) n 080.8
  ~ rag (2) n 018.3
  ~ rain (2) n 006.1
  ~ rains (3) n 006.1
  ~ tub (2) n 017.6
wash(ing) machine (1) n 010.6
washingmat (1) n 010.6
washings (7) n 018.1
Washings (1) DC 087.1
Washington (1033) AL AR DC FL GA LA MS 087.1
  ~ Avenue (5) 107.7
  ~ chair (1) n 008.8
  ~ County (3) MS TX 087.8
  ~ Ferry (1) TN 087.7
  ~ haircut (1) n 115.6
  ~ Heights (2) GA 087.1
  ~ Parish (1) LA 087.6
  ~ Park (3) 106.4
  ~ Square (1) 106.3
  ~ State (4) 087.1
  ~ Street (2) 087.1
  ~ Terrace (1) 106.2
  ~ worms (1) n 060.5
Washing(ton) (11) DC 087.1
  ~ Bullets (1) 086.9
Wash(ington) (1) DC 087.1
Washington's (2) 067.2
Washingtons (2) 114.5
washout (114) n/adj 030.7
  ~ place (2) n 030.4
washouts (3) n 030.5
washpot (460) n 017.6
washpots (62) n 017.6
washrag (402) n 018.5
washrag[N-i] (1) n 018.5
washrags (28) n 018.3
washroom (29) n 118.3
washstand (79) n/adj 009.2
  ~ dresser (1) n 009.2
washstands (9) n 009.2

washtub (60) n 018.1
washtubful (1) n 019.8
washtubs (17) n 017.6
washup (2) n 006.1
washwoman (15) n 010.6
washwomen (1) n 010.6
Waskom (3) TX 087.3
wasn't (2105) v 025.7
  ~ going to marry him (1) v 082.1
was(n't) (1) v 039.7
wasp (904) n/adj 060A.6
  ~ dauber (1) n 060A.6
  ~ family (2) n 060A.6
  ~ sting (4) n 060A.6
  ~ stings (2) n 060A.6
WASP (8) 126.6
wasp[N-i] (477) n 060A.6
wasp[N-k] (58) adj 060A.6
  ~ nest (52) n 060A.6
  ~ -nest bread (2) n 044.4
  ~ nest[N-i] (1) n 060A.6
  ~ nestes (2) n 060A.6
  ~ nests (1) n 060A.6
wasper (4) n 060A.6
wasper[N-i] (2) n 060A.6
waspers (10) n 060A.6
waspes (91) n 060A.6
wasps (169) n 060A.6
WASPs (4) 126.6
waspy-looking (1) adj 060A.6
Wassaw Sound (1) GA 030.7
waste (21) n/v/adj 041.5
  ~ bag (1) n 116.8
  ~ can (2) n 017.4
  ~ cans (1) n 117.2
  ~ collector (1) n 117.3
  ~ compactor (1) n 117.1
  ~ -control containers (1) n 117.3
  ~ pail (1) n 017.4
  ~ pipe (1) n 011.5
wastebasket (14) n 017.4
wasted (6) v 075.4
wasteful (2) adj 069.6
wasteland (11) n 029.7
wastepaper basket (2) n 020.1
wasting (1) v 092.8

Watauga (3) TN 030.7
~ River (1) TN 030.7
watch (873) n/v/adj 004.3
~ after (1) v 013.1
~ bracelet (2) n 028.3
~ chain (3) n 004.3
~ chains (1) n 004.3
~ fob (3) n 004.3
~ -meeting night (1) n 081.9
~ out (2) v 098.2
~ party (1) n 093.3
~ pocket (3) n 004.3
watchband (4) n 004.3
watchdog (5) n 033.1
watchdogs (1) n 033.1
watched (1) v 095.9
watchers (1) n 065.9
watches (22) n 004.3
watchful (1) adj 075.6
watching (17) v 057.4
~ for (1) v 099.1
~ his goose nest (1) v 065.1
watchmaker (2) n 004.3
water (3634) n/adj 077.7
~ bag (1) n 019.6
~ barrel (5) n 019.1
~ barrels (3) n 019.1
~ basketball (1) n 130.5
~ bench (1) n 017.2
~ blister (22) n 077.7
~ blisters (2) n 077.7
~ boats (1) n 024.6
~ bowl (1) n 048.9
~ boy (3) n 081.8
~ -boy with (1) v 032.9
~ bread (32) n 044.6
~ bucket (158) n 017.2
~ buckets (31) n 017.2
~ bug (2) n 060A.8
~ bumps (1) n 077.7
~ burn (2) n 095.4
~ can (1) n 017.2
~ carriers (1) n 111.2
~ channel (1) n 030.5
~ channels (1) n 011.5
~ closet (7) n 012.1
~ cooler (10) n 108.8
~ cotton gin (1) n 080.7
~ ditch (2) n 030.5
~ doctors (1) n 080.8

~ dog (1) n 060.8
~ dogs (2) n 060.5
~ drain (6) n 011.5
~ drainer (1) n 011.5
~ drainers (1) n 011.5
~ drinker (1) n 049.1
~ facilities (1) n 048.9
~ faucet (32) n 108.8
~ fill (1) n 031.5
~ flow (1) n 031.5
~ fountain (103) n 108.8
~ fount(ain) (2) n 108.8
~ fountains (5) n 108.8
~ frog (2) n 060.2
~ frogs (4) n 060.3
~ furrow (8) n 041.2
~ fur(row) (2) n 030.5
~ furrows (1) n 041.2
~ gaps (2) n 031.3
~ gates (1) n 016.7
~ glass (11) n 048.9
~ glasses (3) n 048.9
~ goblets (1) n 048.9
~ gourd (1) n 048.9
~ grass (16) n 015.9
~ grazing (1) n 081.8
~ -ground meal (2) n 080.8
~ gully (1) n 030.5
~ gutter (1) n 011.5
~ gutters (2) n 011.5
~ guy (1) n 115.2
~ haul (7) n 040.5
~ hole (5) n 048.9
~ house (1) n 007A.5
~ hydrant (12) n 018.7
~ hydrants (1) n 062.7
~ jug (4) n 048.9
~ jugs (3) n 017.2
~ keg (17) n 020.2
~ kegs (7) n 020.2
~ kettle (6) n 017.6
~ kettles (2) n 017.6
~ level (1) n 048.9
~ -like (1) adj 077.7
~ lilies (1) n 062.7
~ lily (1) n 062.7
~ line (2) n 048.9
~ maple (1) n 061.8
~ meter (2) n 108.2
~ mill (3) n 088.7
~ mills (2) n 088.8

~ moccasin (38) n 081.9
~ mocca(sin) snake (1) n 080.6
~ moccasins (28) n 092.7
~ -mouth moccasins (1) n 088.7
~ oak (79) n 061.9
~ oak tree (3) n 061.8
~ oak trees (1) n 061.8
~ oaks (25) n 061.8
~ pail (32) n 017.2
~ pails (7) n 017.2
~ pine (1) n 061.8
~ pipe (3) n 023.2
~ pipes (5) n 048.9
~ pitcher (1) n 053.2
~ plug (2) n 108.2
~ plugs (1) n 108.2
~ ponds (1) n 091.9
~ pot (1) n 017.6
~ purslane (1) n 015.9
~ rattle (1) n 092.8
~ rattler (1) n 081.9
~ rent (1) n 089.9
~ shelf (10) n 088.8
~ shelves (1) n 009.2
~ sinkhole (1) n 031.5
~ -ski (1) v 098.6
~ snake (2) n 088.8
~ snakes (8) n 084.8
~ -sob place (1) n 029.6
~ spaniel (1) n 033.1
~ spicket (10) n 018.7
~ spill (1) n 031.5
~ spring (2) n 030.6
~ springs (1) n 030.6
~ sprinkler (1) n 120.3
~ stream (1) n 030.6
~ system (2) n 048.9
~ tank (5) n 018.7
~ tap (2) n 018.7
~ tender (1) n 048.9
~ terrapin (8) n 060.6
~ terrapins (2) n 060.6
~ toilet (1) n 012.1
~ tower (3) n 108.5
~ trough (15) n 035.8
~ trough[N-i] (1) n 011.5
~ troughs (10) n 035.8
~ truck (7) n 111.2
~ trucks (1) n 111.2

~ trunk (1) n 111.2
~ turkey (1) n 059.6
~ turner (1) n 018.7
~ turtle (11) n 060.6
~ turtles (8) n 060.6
~ wagon (2) n 111.2
~ well (3) n 080.9
~ wells (1) n 084.8
~ willow (1) n 061.8
~ witching (1) n 048.9
~ worms (1) n 060.5
wat(er) (3) n 048.9
wa(ter) (2) n/adj 048.9
~ drains (1) n 011.5
Water (14) 030.3
~ Creek (1) FL 030.7
~ Hollow (1) AR 030.7
~ Street (1) 107.6
~ Valley (4) MS 087.5
watercress (2) n 055A.6
watercresses (1) n 015.8
waterfall (526) n 031.5
waterfalling (1) n 031.5
waterfalls (54) n 031.5
Waterford (2) 048.9
~ Road (1) 107.7
waterfront (2) n 080.6
Watergate (2) 104.6
waterhead (1) n 089.8
watering (11) v/adj 048.7
~ trough (4) n 035.8
~ troughs (5) n 035.8
waterings (1) n 080.7
waterlogged (2) adj 090.8
Waterloo (2) LA 087.7
~ Road (1) 107.7
Waterman (2) 107.6
~ building (1) n 108.5
watermelon (656) n/adj 056.9
~ capital (1) n 056.9
~ cutting (2) n 083.1
~ cuttings (1) n 091.9
~ eat (1) n 084.8
~ farm (1) n 056.9
~ feast (1) n 056.9
~ festival (1) n 056.9
~ field (1) n 016.1
~ party (1) n 130.7
~ patch (44) n 056.9
~ patches (1) n 056.9
~ pickle (1) n 056.9
~ rime (1) n 046.6
~ rind (1) n 092.7

~ -rind preserves (1) n 051.6
~ rinds (2) n 056.9
~ row (1) n 056.9
~ seed (3) n 065.1
watermel(on) (2) n 056.9
Watermelon Park (1) FL 087.3
watermelon[N-i] (9) n 056.9
watermelons (462) n 056.9
waterproof (2) adj 048.9
Waterproof (3) LA 087.7
waters (28) n 030.7
Waters (2) 107.6
~ Avenue (1) 107.6
watershed (3) n 031.3
watersheds (1) n 030.3
waterspout (30) n 006.1
waterspouting (1) n 006.1
waterspouts (11) n 112.2
Watertown (3) TN 087.2
waterway (3) n 030.3
waterways (1) n 030.6
waterwheel (2) n 088.8
waterworks (7) n 048.9
watery (23) adj 077.7
~ blister (1) n 077.7
~ -like (1) adj 077.7
~ -like substance (1) n 077.7
~ liquid (1) n 077.7
~ matter (1) n 077.7
~ part (1) n 047.7
~ stuff (1) n 077.7
~ substance (5) n 077.7
~ -type substance (1) n 077.7
Watkins (8) 107.5
~ area (1) n 105.1
~ Drive (1) 107.7
~ Greens (1) 056.9
~ Liniment (1) 088.7
~ reunion (1) n 087.1
Watley's District (1) GA 087.1
Watson (51) AL AR 106.4
~ melon (2) n 056.9
~ melons (1) n 056.9
~ Park (1) 106.4
~ watermelon (2) n 056.9
Watsons (2) 030.7

~ Creek (1) AL 030.7
watt (1) adj 019.9
Wattensaw (1) AR 030.7
wattle (1) n 071.8
wattles (3) n 035.7
watts (1) n 013.9
Watts (3) AL AR 087.4
~ Bar River (1) TN 030.7
Watula (1) AL 087.1
Watusi (1) 083.1
Wauchula (2) FL 087.8
Waukomis Creek (1) MS 030.7
Wausau (1) FL 087.1
wave (8) n/v 005.4
Waverly (15) GA MS TN TX 087.5
~ Hall (3) GA 087.1
~ Immigration Company (1) 080.6
~ section (2) n 105.6
waves (7) n 115.8
Waving Girl (1) 106.6
wax (60) n/adj 020.4
~ bag (1) n 019.7
~ bean (16) n 055A.3
~ beans (24) n 055A.3
~ museum (2) n 106.6
~ string bean (1) n 055A.4
~ tree (1) n 061.9
Wax Lake (1) GA 030.7
Waxahachie (3) TX 087.4
~ Creek (1) TX 030.7
Waxahatchee (2) AL 030.7
~ Creek (1) AL 030.7
waxed beans (1) n 055A.4
waxing (2) v/adj 010.4
~ beans (1) n 055A.4
waxwing (1) n 084.8
waxy (5) adj 029.8
~ mud (1) n 029.8
~ soil (1) n 029.8
way (2652) n/adj 040.1
~ -back-yonder stuff (1) n 093.6
~ -off kinfolk (1) n 066.5
~ -off relatives (1) n 066.5
~ station (1) n 084.8
Way (6) 107.6
way[N-i] (3) n 098.6

Waycross (32) GA 087.3
wayfar(er) (1) n 069.7
Wayne (8) GA 087.2
~ Bayou (1) LA 030.7
~ County (5) GA TN 087.5
Waynesboro (4) GA 087.4
Waynesburg (1) LA 087.7
ways (912) n 039.5
wayside (2) adj 107.2
~ park (1) n 107.2
~ parks (1) n 107.2
Wayside (2) MS 087.3
we (3264) pron 042.2
~ ones (4) pron 043.5
~ oneses (1) pron 042.7
weak (143) adj 072.9
~ beer (1) n 121.9
~ -eyed (1) adj 072.9
~ -kneed (1) adj 073.3
~ land (1) n 029.5
~ -looking (1) adj 072.9
~ -minded (1) adj 073.4
~ spell (1) n 076.1
weaked (1) adj 072.9
weaken down (1) v 007.2
weakened (1) v 072.9
weakening (4) v 007.4
weaker (18) adj 007.3
weakfish (5) n 059.9
Weakley (3) TN 087.1
~ County (1) TN 087.4
weakly (6) adj 072.9
~ -looking (1) adj 072.9
wealth (1) n 082.2
wealthier (1) adj 053.3
wealthy (47) adj 053.3
~ clothes (1) n 123.6
wean off (1) v 036.2
wean[V-t] (1) v 057.8
weaned (4) v 057.8
weaning (4) adj 035.7
~ age (1) n 035.5
~ pigs (1) n 035.5
~ size (2) n 033.3
weanlings (1) n 034.3
weapon (3) n 113.1
weapons (1) n 096.8
wear (65) v 075.5
~ him out (1) v 065.5
~ out (11) v 075.5

~ -out (2) n 075.5
~ us out (1) v 065.5
~ you down (1) v 065.5
~ you out (2) v 065.5
Wear Valley (8) TN 011.6
wear[V-p] (1) v 013.8
wear[V-r] (1) v 013.8
weared (2) v 075.5
~ out (1) v 075.5
wearers (1) n 128.1
wearied (1) adj 075.4
wearing (16) v/adj 065.1
~ a hatching jacket (1) v 065.1
~ clothes (1) n 080.6
~ out (2) n/v 065.5
~ out his welcome (1) v 081.4
wears (16) v 013.7
~ out (1) v 080.6
weary (42) adj 075.5
weasel (49) n 059.5
weaselly (1) adj 072.9
weasels (44) n 059.5
weather (471) n/adj 088.2
~ breeder (2) n 006.4
~ -breeding day (1) n 005.4
~ change (2) n 007.2
~ frogs (1) n 060.3
~ -locked (1) adj 011.2
~ reasons (1) n 052.7
~ report (1) n 066.8
~ sheds (1) n 011.9
~ siding (1) n 011.2
~ storm (1) n 006.1
~ strip (2) n 011.2
~ stripping (2) n 011.2
~ -wise (1) adv 080.7
weatherboard (119) n/adj 011.2
~ house (1) n 011.2
~ houses (2) n 011.2
weatherboard[N-i] (4) n 011.2
weatherboarded (36) v/adj 011.2
~ frame house (1) n 007A.2
~ house (4) n 011.2
~ over (2) v 011.2
weatherboarding (423) n/adj 011.2
~ strips (1) n 011.2

weatherboardings (1) n 011.2

weatherboards (54) n 011.2

weathercock (1) n 059.3

Weatherford (2) TX 086.3

Weatherly Road (1) 025.8

weatherman[N-k] prediction (1) n 006.2

weatherproof (1) adj 011.2

weathers (1) n 072.9

Weathers (1) 087.5

Weathersby (1) MS 087.1

weave (4) n/v 016.4

weaved (2) v/adj 098.6

~ fence (1) n 016.4

weaven (1) v 019.7

weaver (1) n 020.1

Weaver Chapel (1) AR 086.8

Weaverville (1) CA 087.5

weaving (10) n/v/adj 081.8

~ fence (1) n 126.1

web (663) n/v/adj 061.3

~ fences (1) n 016.3

~ up (1) v 061.4

~ wire (11) n 016.3

~ -wire (1) adj 016.3

~ -wire fence (1) n 016.3

Webb (8) AL MS TX 087.2

~ County (2) TX 087.7

~ Creek (1) TN 087.7

webbed (1) v 090.9

Webberville (1) TX 086.4

webbing (3) n/v/adj 061.3

~ -wire fence (1) n 016.3

Weber School (1) 088.5

webfeet (1) n 069.9

webs (271) n 061.2

Webster (5) FL LA 087.7

~ County (2) MS 087.5

~ Parish (1) LA 087.2

webworm (1) n 060.5

wed (9) v/adj 082.2

~ man (1) n 082.3

we'd (98) pron 040.5

wedded (3) v 082.2

wedding (73) n/adj 082.5

~ band (7) n 123.1

~ bands (2) n 123.1

~ cakes (1) n 122.1

~ dance (1) n 083.1

~ parties (1) n 130.7

~ party (23) n 082.5

~ reception (5) n 082.5

~ receptions (1) n 130.7

~ ring (22) n 123.1

~ rings (3) n 123.1

~ shower (1) n 130.7

~ supper (1) n 082.5

weddings (2) n 088.7

wedge (36) n/adj 123.9

~ cuts (1) n 123.9

~ heel (4) n 123.8

~ -heel sandals (1) n 123.8

~ heels (3) n 123.8

~ maul (1) n 081.9

wedged heel (1) n 123.8

wedges (7) n 054.6

wedgies (7) n 123.8

wedlock (64) n/adj 065.7

~ child (2) n 065.7

Wednesday (979) 002.1

~ evening (1) n 002.1

~ night (7) n 002.1

~ nights (2) n 002.1

~ week (5) n 003.7

Wednesdays (2) 002.1

Wedowee (2) AL 087.7

wee (12) adj/interj 036.4

~ hee (1) interj 038.3

~ -wee worms (1) n 060.5

Wee Willie (1) 067.4

wee(x2) (5) interj 038.5

weed (109) n/v/adj 114.1

~ coffee (1) n 048.8

~ digger (1) n 120.6

~ field (1) n 016.1

~ frogs (1) n 060.2

~ heads (1) n 114.3

~ patch (1) n 016.1

Weed (3) 120.8

~ Eater (2) 120.8

~ Eaters (1) 120.8

weed[N-i] (6) n 015.9

weeded (2) v 041.4

weeder (2) n 120.4

weeders (1) n 120.6

weeding (17) v/adj 015.8

~ down (1) v 078.6

~ hoe (1) n 084.8

~ hoes (1) n 015.8

~ out (1) v 015.8

Weedon Island (1) 106.4

weeds (305) n 015.9

Weejuns (4) 123.8

week (1281) n/adj 003.7

~ Sunday (1) n 003.7

Week (1) 080.6

week[N-i] (13) n 016.7

weekend (14) n/adj 066.9

~ bag (1) n 123.7

weekend[N-i] (2) n 025.8

Weeki Wachee Falls (1) FL 087.1

weekly wash (3) n 010.6

week's (2) adj 003.6

~ Friday (1) n 003.6

weeks (556) n 070.6

ween (1) v 033.8

weep (1) v 036.2

weeping (39) v/adj 079.3

~ widow (1) n 063.3

~ willow (20) n 061.8

~ willow tree (4) n 061.8

~ willows (6) n 061.8

weepy weather (1) n 006.6

weevil (37) n/adj 059.5

~ -eaten (2) adj 048.7

weevil[N-i] (1) n 093.5

weevils (25) n 060A.2

Wehadkee (2) GA 030.7

~ Creek (1) GA 030.7

weigh (8) v 074.5

~ up (2) v 005.8

weigh[V-p] (1) v 052.8

weighed (1) v 053.4

weighing (1) v 024.9

weight (12) n/adj 115.3

~ lifter (3) n 073.1

weights (2) n 126.2

Weimar (2) TX 087.1

Weiner (1) AR 087.8

Weinert (1) TX 087.2

Weir (2) MS 087.4

~ Lake (1) FL 087.2

weird (106) adj 074.7

~ -ass (2) adj 128.5

~ -looking (1) adj 080.7

weirdball (1) n 073.4

weirdo (12) n 074.7

weirdos (7) n 129.3

Weirgate (1) TX 087.5

Weiss Lake (1) GA 030.7

welcome (21) n/adj 070.7

~ center (2) n 107.2

~ -home parties (1) n 103.7

~ road (1) n 031.7

~ station (3) n 107.2

weld on (1) v 027.2

welded wire (1) n 016.3

Welder (1) TX 087.8

welders (1) n 032.4

welding (2) v/adj 102.2

~ torch (1) n 024.3

welfare (22) n/adj 066.9

~ building (1) n 075.6

~ Cadillac (1) n 109.4

~ cars (1) n 109.4

~ days (1) n 032.8

~ families (1) n 069.7

~ office (2) n 084.2

~ people (2) n 069.7

~ recipients (1) n 069.7

~ trade (1) n 114.8

~ trip (1) n 091.8

welfarers (1) n 069.7

Welk (4) 130.8

well (2114) n/adj/adv/ interj 091.5

~ -blessed (1) adj 074.1

~ -bred (1) adj 073.2

~ bucket (25) n 017.2

~ buckets (6) n 017.2

~ -built (10) adj 073.1

~ coop (1) n 011.9

~ -covered (1) adj 090.4

~ -digger's asshole (1) n 007.4

~ -discipline (1) adj 073.2

~ -dressed (9) adj 028.1

~ -dresser (1) n 028.1

~ drillers (1) n 081.8

~ -educated (11) adj 083.5

~ -fertilized (3) adj 029.3

~ -fitted (2) adj 027.6

~ -fixed (2) adj 080.8

~ -grease[V-t] (1) adj 023.7

~ -greased (2) adj 023.7

~ GRUNT(H)   (85) interj 091.5
~ house (16) n 015.5
~ houses (1) n 011.7
~ -kept (1) adj 074.1
~ ledge (1) n 015.5
~ light (1) n 090.9
~ livers (2) n 088.8
~ -made-up mind man (1) n 074.8
~ -off (13) adj 106.1
~ porch (2) n 010.8
~ -preserved (9) adj 074.1
~ -read (1) adj 097.1
~ shed (4) n 011.7
~ spring (1) n 030.6
~ sweep (1) n 017.2
~ -tempered (1) adj 073.2
~ -to-do (6) adj 053.3
~ -turned (1) adj 073.2
~ water (2) n 088.8
~ windlass (1) n 070.7
we'll (112) pron 081.2
well[N-i] (1) n 118.6
Wellborn (1) TX 087.4
wells (36) n 015.5
Wells (5) 087.4
  ~ Creek (4) TN 030.7
Welsh (2) LA 127.8
welt (1) n 077.6
welts (1) n 013.6
wench (7) n 124.8
wenny (1) interj 038.5
went (800) v 065.8
  ~ across (4) v 028.9
  ~ and (79) v 081.3
  ~ around (1) v 053.5
  ~ (a)round (1) v 014.8
  ~ away (4) v 078.5
  ~ back (8) v 053.7
  ~ back on him (1) v 082.1
  ~ by (1) v 053.4
  ~ courting (1) v 081.4
  ~ down (18) v 082.6
  ~ for (3) v 093.8
  ~ home to Heaven (1) v 078.5
  ~ home to Jesus (1) v 078.5
  ~ in (10) v 042.7
  ~ into (1) v 095.8
  ~ off (6) v 082.1

~ off to (1) v 053.5
~ on (16) v 078.6
~ on back (1) v 038.8
~ on by (1) v 075.9
~ on out (1) v 078.6
~ on to his reward (1) v 078.5
~ on to meet his Maker (1) v 078.5
~ on to meet their Maker (1) v 078.5
~ out (12) v 081.3
~ out with (2) v 053.5
~ out [P-0] (1) v 053.4
~ over (12) v 052.2
~ right on out (1) v 078.5
~ right on to hell (1) v 078.6
~ through (4) v 032.1
~ to (291) v 024.9
~ to Heaven (1) v 078.5
~ to hell (1) v 078.6
~ to her grave (1) v 078.5
~ to his glory (1) v 078.5
~ to his reward (3) v 078.5
~ to meet his Father (1) v 078.5
~ to meet his Maker (1) v 078.5
~ to see his Maker (1) v 078.5
~ to the great beyond (1) v 078.5
~ to the happy hunting ground (1) v 078.6
~ to their final reward (1) v 078.5
~ to their reward[N-i] (1) v 078.5
~ together (6) v 081.4
~ truant (1) v 083.4
~ under (1) v 057.9
~ up (13) v 082.7
~ with (16) v 081.4
~ with a girl (1) v 081.4
~ without (1) v 032.3
~ [J-0] (2) v 081.3
~ [P-0] (1) v 012.9
Wenzel's (1) 131.6

we're (129) pron 042.3
were (1211) v 025.5
weren't (87) v 025.7
werewolves (1) n 090.2
Werner Park (1) LA 087.1
we's (35) pron 025.5
Wesley (2) 106.4
Wes(ley) Chapel (1) GA 087.5
Wesson (8) MS 087.9
  ~ Oil (3) 023.7
Wessy (2) 035.5
  ~ hog (1) n 035.5
west (431) n/adj 006.4
  ~ bedroom (1) n 007A.6
  ~ house (1) n 007A.2
  ~ -northwest (1) n 006.5
  ~ porch (2) n 010.8
  ~ room (1) n 007A.5
  ~ shed (1) n 011.7
  ~ side (3) n 006.4
  ~ storm (1) n 006.5
  ~ wind (21) n 006.5
West (372) 105.1
  ~ Africa (1) 105.4
  ~ Alabama (1) 086.4
  ~ Bank (1) 087.8
  ~ Batesville (1) AR 086.9
  ~ Bay (1) 106.3
  ~ Birmingham (1) 105.1
  ~ Carroll (1) LA 087.1
  ~ Carroll Parish (1) LA 087.3
  ~ Coast (6) 006.5
  ~ Colyell (1) LA 030.7
  ~ Commerce (2) 105.6
  ~ Cove Bayou (1) LA 030.7
  ~ Dallas (12) 105.1
  ~ Dumas (2) 105.1
  ~ End (33) 105.4
  ~ End Boulevard (1) 107.6
  ~ End Park (1) 106.4
  ~ Feliciana (1) LA 087.4
  ~ Flagler (1) 107.6
  ~ Florida (2) 086.4
  ~ Fork (1) AR 087.1
  ~ Fulton (1) 105.1

~ Gate (1) 105.6
~ Gray (1) 107.7
~ Grove Avenue (1) 107.7
~ Harlem (1) NY 087.5
~ Haven (2) 106.2
~ Helena (3) AR 087.2
~ Huntsville (1) 106.3
~ Indies (2) 016.7
~ Jackson (8) 105.1
~ Jacksonville (2) 106.3
~ Knoxville (2) 105.3
~ Lake (1) 082.6
~ Laurel Heights (1) 106.2
~ Little Rock (1) 105.1
~ Meade (2) 105.5
~ Memphis (7) AR 105.1
~ Middle (1) LA 030.7
~ Mobile (7) 105.5
~ Monroe (4) LA 087.8
~ Montgomery (3) 106.1
~ Mountain (1) AR 031.1
~ Nashville (7) 105.1
~ Navidad (1) TX 030.7
~ Ninth Street (1) 105.4
~ Norris Cove (1) TN 030.3
~ Paces Ferry (2) 107.7
~ Palm Beach (6) FL 087.7
~ Panama City (1) 105.1
~ Pearl (1) LA 030.7
~ Plains (3) MO 087.5
~ Point (19) AR GA MS NY 087.4
~ Point Road (1) 107.7
~ Prairie (1) TX 087.4
~ Sandy (2) TX 030.7
~ Second (1) 001A.3
~ section (2) n 105.3
~ Shore (1) 105.3
~ Shore Boulevard (1) 105.8
~ Side (46) 105.1
~ Side Creek (1) TX 030.7
~ Side Park (2) 107.2

~ Side Square (1) 085.1
~ Springfield (1) 105.3
~ Street (1) 105.6
~ Tampa (11) 105.1
~ Tennessee (7) 086.6
~ Texas (10) 086.8
~ Tomlin (1) 106.1
~ Town (3) 105.1
~ Union (2) GA MS 087.4
~ Valley (1) 114.8
~ Virginia (39) 086.2
Wester (1) 073.6
westerly (10) adj 006.5
~ wind (3) n 006.5
~ winds (1) n 006.5
western (24) n/adj 130.8
~ part (1) n 105.1
~ pines (1) n 061.8
Western (17) 083.1
~ Auto (1) 070.6
~ Avenue (2) 107.6
~ Bank (1) 108.5
~ boots (1) n 123.8
~ dance (1) n 083.1
~ dancing (1) n 083.1
~ hillbilly (1) n 131.6
~ Hills Mall (1) 105.3
~ Plaza (1) 106.7
~ section (2) n 087.4
~ state (1) n 043.3
~ Tennessee (2) 086.6
~ word (1) n 015.4
westerner (1) n 006.5
Westerner (2) 066.7
westernly (1) adj 006.5
Westers (1) 088.8
Westheimer (5) TX 107.5
~ Road (1) 107.7
Westinghouse (1) 032.4
Westlake (1) LA 087.6
Westmoreland (4) 105.9
~ Park (1) 106.8
westnorth (4) n/adj 006.5
~ wind (2) n 006.5
Weston (1) TX 086.1
Westport (2) TN 087.2
Westshore (2) 105.3
westsouth wind (1) n 006.5
westward (3) adj 006.4
Westwood (5) 105.7
wet (112) adj 029.4
~ bin (1) n 080.8
~ bottom (1) n 029.6

~ bottom fields (1) n 029.6
~ bottomland (1) n 029.6
~ -cell batteries (1) n 081.9
~ day (3) n 005.5
~ dream (1) n 097.2
~ flat (2) n 029.6
~ grass (1) n 029.7
~ marsh (1) n 029.6
~ -mop (2) v 010.4
~ -natured land (3) n 029.6
~ nurse (2) n 065.2
~ place (2) n 029.6
~ places (3) n 029.6
~ roads (1) n 031.6
~ season (2) n 006.1
~ spell (9) n 006.1
~ spells (1) n 007.1
~ spot (1) n 029.6
~ time (1) n 006.1
~ weather (3) n 005.5
~ -weather branch (4) n 030.6
~ -weather branches (1) n 030.3
~ -weather creek (1) n 030.5
~ -weather pond (2) n 029.6
~ -weather rain (1) n 006.6
~ -weather spring (3) n 030.3
~ -weather springs (1) n 030.3
~ -weather stream (2) n 030.6
~ -weather streams (1) n 030.6
~ wood (1) n 008.6
Wetappo (2) FL 030.7
~ Creek (1) FL 030.7
wetback (24) n 128.7
wetbacks (41) n 128.7
wether (10) n/adj 034.9
~ goat (1) n 088.8
~ sheep (1) n 034.9
wethers (1) n 035.2
wethill (1) n 030.8
wetland (29) n 029.6
wetlands (4) n 029.5
wets (1) n 069.3

wetting on (1) v 033.6
Wetumpka (5) AL 087.7
~ Road (1) 093.8
(We)tumpka (1) AL 087.2
we've (112) pron 070.2
Wewahitchka (1) FL 087.3
whack (6) n/v 083.1
whack[V-t] (1) v 065.5
whacked (1) v 104.3
whacking (4) n/v 065.5
whale (11) n/adj 075.8
~ oil (7) n 024.2
~ -oil lamps (1) n 024.3
whaled (3) v 088.8
~ away (1) v 088.8
~ out of (1) v 065.5
whaling (1) v 065.5
wham (1) v 032.1
whang (4) n 065.5
whap (3) v 098.7
wharf (172) n/adj 031.4
~ boat (1) n 031.4
~ rat (7) n 059.5
~ rats (8) n 059.5
Wharf (2) 031.4
wharfs (13) n 031.4
Wharton (3) TX 087.6
wharves (4) n 031.4
what (3769) pron 043.8
~ -all (420) pron 043.8
~ -all's (4) pron 043.8
what'd (1) pron 052.5
whatever (37) pron/adj 052.6
whatnot (11) n/adj 084.8
~ shelf (4) n 008.4
~ stand (1) n 095.9
whatnots (2) n 080.6
what's (95) pron 039.7
~ -all (1) pron 043.8
whatsoever (4) adj 042.7
wheat (742) n/adj 044.3
~ bags (1) n 019.7
~ belt (1) n 081.8
~ bin (8) n 014.4
~ bins (3) n 014.4
~ bran (3) n 044.4
~ bread (129) n 044.3
~ cakes (9) n 045.3
~ country (1) n 041.6
~ cradle (2) n 023.4
~ crib (1) n 014.4

~ crop (5) n 041.3
~ field (10) n 016.1
~ fields (2) n 016.1
~ flour (8) n 044.3
~ garner (3) n 014.4
~ -germ bread (2) n 044.3
~ gran(ary) (1) n 014.4
~ ground (2) n 044.4
~ harvest (2) n 044.5
~ hoecake (2) n 044.4
~ house (14) n 014.4
~ houses (3) n 014.4
~ loaves (1) n 044.3
~ mills (1) n 044.6
~ pancakes (1) n 045.3
~ planters (1) n 021.6
~ sacks (1) n 019.6
~ sheaf (1) n 041.6
~ shed (1) n 014.4
~ shock (1) n 041.7
~ shocks (1) n 041.7
~ shorts (5) n 084.8
~ stack (3) n 041.7
~ stacks (2) n 041.7
~ straw (4) n 041.5
~ thrash (1) n 042.1
~ thrasher (5) n 042.1
~ thrash(er) (1) n 042.1
~ thrashing (1) n 042.1
~ -thrashing time (2) n 042.1
~ thresher (1) n 042.1
Wheat (2) 107.6
~ Street (1) 107.6
~ Street Baptist (1) 106.6
wheatmeal (2) n 044.3
whee (3) interj 036.3
wheel (347) n/v/adj 021.1
~ axle (1) n 021.8
~ casing (1) n 021.1
~ file (1) n 023.5
~ -like (1) adj 081.9
~ -looking (1) adj 080.6
~ mule (5) n 039.4
~ mules (2) n 039.4
~ plow (2) n 021.6
~ rim (2) n 021.1
~ roll (1) n 021.8
~ -shaped (1) adj 023.3
~ sow (1) n 023.3
~ team (5) n 039.4

~ tire (1) n 021.1
Wheel (1) 119.8
wheel[N-i] (3) n 023.3
wheelbarrel (10) n 023.3
wheelbarrels (1) n 023.3
wheelbarrow (773) n/adj
  023.3
  ~ car(rier) (1) n 023.3
  ~ load (2) n 019.8
wheelbar(row) (223) n/
  adj 023.3
  ~ load (1) n 019.8
(wheel)barrow (1) n
  023.3
wheelbarrowful (2) n
  019.8
wheelbarrows (32) n
  023.3
wheelchair (9) n 023.3
wheeler (3) n 109.6
Wheeler (8) 115.8
  ~ Business College (1)
    083.6
  ~ County (1) GA 087.3
  ~ Dam (1) AL 030.4
  ~ Road (1) 031.7
  ~ Street (1) 107.7
  ~ watermelon (1) n
    056.9
wheelers (6) n 039.4
Wheelers (1) 060.5
wheelhorse (23) n 039.4
wheelhorses (4) n 039.4
wheeling (11) v 064.6
Wheeling (1) WV 086.5
wheels (89) n 023.3
wheelwright (3) n/adj
  080.6
  ~ man (1) n 084.8
wheely (1) n 095.5
whees (1) v 036.4
whelp (6) n/v/adj 077.4
  ~ dog (1) n 033.3
  ~ up (1) v 062.2
when (664) adv/conj
  089.7
whenever (9) adv/conj
  053.7
(when)ever (1) conj
  024.9
whensoever (1) adv 042.8
where (459) adv/conj
  040.2
  ~ -all (4) conj 090.8

~ the green grass grows
  (1) n 130.6
whereabout (2) adv/conj
  088.7
whereabouts (5) adv/conj
  080.8
where'd (4) adv 052.4
where's (6) adv 043.6
whereupon (1) conj 053.6
where've (2) adv 090.6
wherever (3) adv/conj
  040.2
whet (14) n/v/adj 023.4
  ~ knife (1) n 023.4
  ~ wheel (1) n 023.5
whether (625) conj 088.2
wheth(er) (22) conj 088.2
whe(ther) (48) conj 088.2
whetrock (464) n 023.4
whetrocks (26) n 023.4
whets (1) v 023.4
whetstone (324) n 023.4
  ~ quarries (1) n 070.7
  ~ rock (1) n 023.4
  ~ stuff (1) n 023.4
whetstones (9) n 023.4
whetted (2) v 023.4
whetter (3) n 023.4
whetting (12) v/adj 023.5
  ~ rock (3) n 023.4
  ~ stone (6) n 023.4
whew (4) interj 092.2
whey (58) n/adj 047.6
  ~ milk (1) n 047.6
wheyed (3) v 047.6
  ~ up (1) v 047.6
wheys up (1) v 047.6
which (213) pron/adj/
  conj 052.4
  ~ way (1) n 081.8
whichaway (38) n/pron/
  conj 052.3
whichever (3) conj 042.7
whick (1) interj 084.9
whicker (48) n/v 036.4
  ~ to (1) v 036.4
whicker[V-p] (1) v 036.4
whickered (2) v 036.4
whickering (17) v/adj
  036.4
  ~ noise (1) n 036.4
whickers (23) v 036.4
whicking (1) n 036.4
Whiddons (1) GA 087.1
whiff (15) n 051.1

whiffle ball (1) n 130.4
whiffletree (12) n 021.2
whigger (2) v 036.4
whigging up (1) v 047.6
Whigham (2) GA 086.4
whigs up (1) v 047.6
while (1264) n/conj 004.6
whiles (2) n 041.9
whillikins (2) interj 092.2
whilst (2) conj 004.6
whimper (7) n/v 036.4
whimpering (2) v 036.4
whine (12) n/v 036.2
whined (1) v 036.2
whines (3) v 036.4
whining (5) v/adj 036.4
whinker (13) n/v 036.4
whinkering (3) v 036.4
whinkers (4) v 036.4
whinnied (2) v 036.4
whinnies (22) v 036.4
whinny (224) n/v 036.4
  ~ -like (1) adj 036.4
whinnying (11) v 036.4
whiny (2) adj 036.4
whip (1324) n/v/adj/
  interj 019.4
  ~ cream (13) n 048.5
  ~ handle (1) n 019.4
  ~ leather (3) n 019.4
  ~ -like (1) adj 019.4
  ~ on (1) v 088.8
  ~ over the river (1) n
    130.2
  ~ snake (2) n 093.6
  ~ the tail off (1) v
    065.5
  ~ the whip (1) n
    130A.4
  ~ ticket (1) n 092.8
  ~ topping (1) n 048.5
  ~ up (1) v 019.4
  ~ yip(x2) (1) interj
    033.3
Whip (1) 130.5
whip[V-r] (11) v 065.5
whip[V-t] (5) v 019.4
  ~ with (1) v 125.1
whiplash (2) n 019.4
whipped (106) v/adj
  065.5
  ~ cream (3) n 048.5
  ~ -cream topping (1) n
    048.5
  ~ off (1) v 042.1

~ out (7) v 075.5
~ with (1) v 125.1
whipper (1) n 113.2
whippet (2) n 080.7
whipping (657) n/v/adj
  065.5
  ~ cream (1) n 048.5
  ~ post (1) n 019.4
  ~ up (4) v 007.2
  ~ up on (1) v 080.9
whippings (11) n 065.5
whippletree (12) n 021.2
whippoorwill (31) n/adj
  059.3
  ~ pea (1) n 055A.1
  ~ pea hay (1) n 014.9
  ~ peas (6) n 055A.4
Whippoorwill Hollow (1)
  TN 030.4
whippoorwills (12) n
  059.2
whips (43) n/v 019.4
whipstock (2) n/adj 019.4
  ~ holder (1) n 019.4
whirl (4) n/v/adj 022.7
  ~ around (2) v 022.7
  ~ jenny (1) n 022.7
whirlaround (1) n 022.7
whirligig (30) n 022.7
whirligigs (6) n 022.7
whirlimajig (1) n 022.7
whirling (9) v/adj 057.4
  ~ around (1) v 022.8
  ~ dervish (3) n 022.7
  ~ horse (1) n 022.7
  ~ jenny (1) n 022.7
  ~ seat (1) n 022.7
whirliwigs (1) n 022.7
whirlwind (12) n 112.2
whirly-burly (1) n 099.5
whirlybird (13) n 022.7
whirlybirds (5) n 111.9
whisk broom (4) n 010.5
whisked (1) v 080.5
whisker (2) n 071.4
whisker[N-i] (2) n 071.4
whiskers (158) n 071.4
whiskey (495) n/adj 050.8
  ~ barrel (3) n 019.1
  ~ barrels (2) n 019.1
  ~ bottle (1) n 071.7
  ~ capital (1) n 050.9
  ~ cup (1) n 071.7
  ~ fits (1) n 104.9
  ~ kegs (1) n 020.2

~ makers (1) n 050.8
~ making (2) n 050.9
~ runners (1) n 050.9
~ still (2) n 050.8
Whiskey (5) 030.7
~ Bay (1) LA 030.7
~ Chute (1) AR 030.7
~ Creek (1) FL 030.7
~ John (1) 068.2
whisper out (1) v 047.5
whist (1) n 130.9
whistle (163) n/v/adj 037.8
~ at (6) v 037.8
~ breeches (1) n 027.4
~ for (8) v 037.8
~ owl (1) n 059.1
~ to (7) v 033.2
~ tune (1) n 080.7
Whistle Ditch (1) AR 030.4
WHISTLE (3) interj 037.8
whistled (4) v 037.8
whistler (1) n 006.4
whistles (2) n/v 065.8
whistling (14) v/adj 037.8
~ kettle (1) n 017.6
~ kettles (1) n 017.6
~ locust (1) n 061.2
~ teakettle (3) n 017.6
whistlingest (1) adj 064.7
Whitaker (1) 107.6
white (4581) adj 008.7
~ acre (1) n 055A.4
~ -acre pea (1) n 055A.7
~ Americans (1) n 069.4
~ ash (3) n 101.9
~ asphalt (1) n 031.6
~ Autaud peanuts (1) n 054.7
~ baby lima beans (1) n 055A.3
~ back (3) n 046.3
~ bacon (32) n 046.3
~ bass (7) n 059.9
~ bastard (1) n 069.4
~ bay (6) n 062.9
~ bays (1) n 029.6
~ bean (3) n 055A.3
~ bean[N-i] (1) n 055A.3
~ beans (25) n 055A.3

~ beech (1) n 061.8
~ Bermuda (1) n 055.6
~ Bermuda onion (1) n 055.6
~ Bermudas (1) n 055.6
~ birch (1) n 061.8
~ bleached (1) adj 044.3
~ blood pudding (1) n 047.3
~ board fence (1) n 016.2
~ boss (1) n 069.4
~ boudin (9) n 047.3
~ boy (7) n 069.4
~ boys (12) n 069.4
~ bread (165) n 044.3
~ brother (1) n 069.4
~ brush (1) n 062.8
~ bushy beans (1) n 055A.4
~ business (1) n 080.6
~ butter bean (4) n 055A.3
~ butter beans (1) n 055A.3
~ cabbage (1) n 055A.1
~ cases (1) n 069.4
~ cat (2) n 059.9
~ catfish (1) n 059.9
~ Caucasian people (1) n 069.4
~ cells (1) n 077.5
~ cemetery (2) n 078.8
~ center lines (1) n 107.3
~ chalk (1) n 031.6
~ cheese (11) n 048.1
~ chert (1) n 031.9
~ child (2) n 069.4
~ children (1) n 069.4
~ clay (7) n 029.8
~ clay dirt (1) n 029.9
~ clear seed (1) n 054.4
~ cling (1) n 054.3
~ cloth (2) n 019.6
~ cloth sack (1) n 019.6
~ cobblers (2) n 055.4
~ coffee (1) n 099.5
~ communities (1) n 069.4
~ community (1) n 069.4
~ corn (40) n 056.2

~ corn bread (2) n 044.7
~ corn liquor (1) n 050.8
~ corn whiskey (3) n 050.8
~ cornmeal (2) n 044.7
~ cotton bags (1) n 019.6
~ cotton sacks (2) n 019.6
~ couple[N-i] (1) n 052.7
~ cracker (7) n 069.4
~ crackers (5) n 069.4
~ crappie (1) n 059.9
~ cross (1) n 114.2
~ crosses (1) n 115.5
~ crowder (1) n 081.8
~ crowder pea (1) n 080.6
~ crowders (1) n 055A.2
~ customers (2) n 069.4
~ cymling (1) n 056.5
~ cypress (2) n 061.8
~ dirt (1) n 008.7
~ -duck trousers (1) n 027.4
~ ducks (1) n 027.4
~ dude (1) n 069.8
~ dudes (1) n 069.8
~ -eared (1) adj 059.7
~ egrets (1) n 059.3
~ elder (1) n 062.3
~ elephant (1) n 114.2
~ elephants (2) n 010.2
~ elm (2) n 061.9
~ enamel egg (1) n 017.1
~ English peach (1) n 054.4
~ eyes (3) n 069.4
~ -faced heifer (1) n 033.8
~ -faced owl (1) n 059.2
~ family (1) n 069.4
~ farmer (1) n 069.4
~ farmers (1) n 069.4
~ feed sack (1) n 019.6
~ feed sacks (1) n 019.7
~ fellow (16) n 069.4
~ fellows (2) n 069.4

~ female (2) n 008.7
~ fence (1) n 016.2
~ fig (1) n 061.4
~ flat squash (2) n 056.6
~ flesh (1) n 079.7
~ flight (1) n 093.5
~ flour (2) n 044.3
~ -flour bread (1) n 044.3
~ folk (9) n 069.4
~ folk[N-i] (3) n 069.4
~ folks (104) n 069.4
~ -folks' doings (1) n 069.4
~ -folks' stores (1) n 069.4
~ -folks's fountain (1) n 016.7
~ food (1) n 088.7
~ friend (2) n 069.4
~ friends (3) n 069.4
~ frost (10) n 007.5
~ gas (2) n 024.3
~ girl (7) n 069.4
~ girls (2) n 069.4
~ globes (1) n 055.7
~ granite (1) n 017.7
~ grape (2) n 080.7
~ grapes (1) n 062.5
~ gravel (1) n 031.6
~ gravelly ground (1) n 029.9
~ gravy (3) n 047.4
~ ground (1) n 029.9
~ gum (2) n 061.8
~ gum tree (1) n 061.8
~ guys (1) n 069.4
~ half runner (1) n 055A.4
~ half runners (7) n 055A.4
~ -headed bumblebee (1) n 060A.5
~ heath (1) n 054.3
~ help (1) n 069.4
~ herbs (1) n 061.4
~ heron (1) n 059.8
~ hick (1) n 069.9
~ hominy (1) n 050.6
~ honky (1) n 112.5
~ hoosier (1) n 069.4
~ house (1) n 069.4
~ housekeeper (1) n 069.4

~ huckleberries (1) n 062.4
~ ibis (1) n 081.8
~ iceberg radishes (1) n 055.2
~ icicle (1) n 055.2
~ Idaho (1) n 055.4
~ Irish (1) n 055.4
~ Irish potato (1) n 055.4
~ jack (1) n 050.9
~ jeans (1) n 008.7
~ jigs (1) n 061.2
~ kernel (1) n 054.2
~ kids (2) n 069.4
~ ladies (2) n 069.4
~ lady (18) n 069.4
~ land (6) n 029.8
~ laurel (1) n 062.7
~ lightning (350) n 050.8
~ lightning whiskey (1) n 092.2
~ lima beans (1) n 055A.3
~ lima butter beans (1) n 055A.3
~ limas (2) n 055A.3
~ line (8) n 107.3
~ -line squash (1) n 056.6
~ lines (11) n 107.3
~ liquor (3) n 050.8
~ -livered (2) adj 073.8
~ loaf (1) n 044.3
~ loaves (1) n 044.3
~ -looking (11) adj 008.7
~ male (1) n 008.7
~ mammy (1) n 090.2
~ man (98) n 069.4
~ man[N-i] (1) n 069.4
~ man[N-k] mule (1) n 057.8
~ mannerisms (1) n 069.4
~ man's (2) adj 069.4
~ man's bone[N-i] (1) n 069.4
~ man's nigger (1) n 069.3
~ man's place (1) n 069.4
~ man's plantation (1) n 069.4

~ maple (5) n 061.8
~ marking (1) n 107.3
~ McCaslans (1) n 055A.4
~ meal (2) n 008.7
~ meat (73) n 046.3
~ -meated (1) adj 056.9
~ melon (1) n 056.9
~ men (10) n 069.4
~ MF (1) n 069.4
~ -minded (1) adj 069.4
~ mistress (1) n 069.6
~ motherfuckers (1) n 069.8
~ mouth (1) n 101.3
~ -mouth moccasin (1) n 080.7
~ -mouth moccasins (1) n 080.8
~ muck (1) n 029.8
~ mucus (1) n 077.7
~ mud (3) n 008.7
~ mudhole (1) n 088.7
~ mulberries (1) n 062.7
~ mulberry (1) n 061.9
~ mule (17) n 050.9
~ mule whiskey (1) n 050.8
~ mush peas (1) n 099.6
~ myrtle (1) n 062.8
~ navy beans (1) n 055A.4
~ Negro (2) n 069.8
~ neighbors (1) n 069.4
~ nest onions (1) n 055.7
~ nigger (3) n 069.5
~ niggers (5) n 069.5
~ oak (142) n 061.8
~ -oak leaves (1) n 079.7
~ oak logs (1) n 061.8
~ oak sapling (1) n 061.8
~ -oak snake (3) n 088.9
~ -oak snakes (3) n 089.9
~ -oak split (1) n 061.8
~ -oak splits (1) n 084.9

~ oak timber (1) n 061.8
~ oak tree (6) n 061.9
~ oak trees (6) n 061.8
~ oak wood (1) n 008.7
~ oaks (11) n 061.8
~ onion (12) n 055.6
~ onions (13) n 055.6
~ owl (10) n 059.2
~ owls (4) n 059.1
~ paling fence (1) n 016.2
~ pan squash (1) n 056.6
~ part (4) n 045.6
~ pattypan (1) n 056.6
~ pavement (1) n 031.6
~ peach (1) n 054.3
~ peaches (1) n 054.3
~ peas (1) n 055A.3
~ peck (1) n 069.8
~ peckers (1) n 069.8
~ pecks (1) n 069.4
~ people (247) n 069.4
~ people[N-k] church (2) n 043.9
~ people's (2) adj 069.4
~ peoples (16) n 069.4
~ pepper (1) n 055.6
~ perch (66) n 059.9
~ perches (1) n 059.9
~ person (47) n 069.4
~ pers(on) (1) n 069.7
~ picket fence (5) n 016.2
~ picket fences (2) n 016.2
~ pine (15) n 061.8
~ planks (1) n 055.6
~ poor (1) n 069.8
~ poplar (3) n 061.8
~ population (1) n 069.4
~ pork (3) n 046.3
~ potato (43) n 055.4
~ potatoes (46) n 055.4
~ press (2) n 054.3
~ race (44) n 069.4
~ radish (2) n 055.2
~ radishes (1) n 055.2
~ rain (1) n 006.1
~ raspberries (1) n 062.5

~ rice (3) n 050.7
~ rind (1) n 056.9
~ -rind melon (1) n 056.9
~ round squash (1) n 056.6
~ runners (3) n 055A.4
~ russets (2) n 055.4
~ sack (5) n 019.6
~ sacks (5) n 019.7
~ salt (1) n 046.5
~ salt bacon (1) n 046.5
~ salt meat (2) n 046.3
~ salt pork (1) n 046.3
~ sand (7) n 029.8
~ sandy land (2) n 029.9
~ sassafras tree (1) n 061.4
~ sauce (4) n 048.5
~ school (1) n 069.4
~ schools (2) n 069.4
~ section (1) n 093.8
~ seed (1) n 056.9
~ settlement (1) n 069.4
~ settlers (2) n 013.8
~ sharecroppers (1) n 069.4
~ shiner (1) n 061.2
~ shinny (1) n 050.8
~ shirt (1) n 008.7
~ shit (1) n 093.6
~ shorts (1) n 088.7
~ shrimp (2) n 060.9
~ side (11) n 046.3
~ side meat (1) n 046.3
~ -skin (1) adj 055.6
~ -skinned (1) adj 069.5
~ slag (1) n 031.6
~ snake (1) n 088.8
~ soil (3) n 029.8
~ son of a bitch (1) n 069.4
~ son [P-0] [D-0] bitch (1) n 069.8
~ sop (2) n 070.7
~ sowbelly (1) n 046.3
~ squash (63) n 056.6
~ squirrel (8) n 059.6
~ squirrels (2) n 059.6
~ streak (1) n 107.3

~ string beans (1) n 055A.4
~ stripe (2) n 107.3
~ striped watermelon (1) n 056.9
~ stripes (1) n 008.7
~ stuff (2) n 077.5
~ suckers (3) n 059.9
~ sugar (3) n 051.3
~ sugar maple (1) n 061.5
~ sumac (3) n 062.2
~ sweet (1) n 056.2
~ sweet corn (1) n 056.2
~ sweet onions (1) n 055.6
~ sweet potato (3) n 055.5
~ sweet potatoes (1) n 055.5
~ sweet (po)tatoes (1) n 055.5
~ sycamore (1) n 061.7
~ teacher (2) n 069.4
~ teachers (2) n 067.6
~ tenants (2) n 069.4
~ tender corn (1) n 056.2
~ tip (2) n 055.2
~ town (3) n 069.4
~ trash (534) n 069.7
~ tree (1) n 061.8
~ trout (8) n 059.9
~ turtle (1) n 060.6
~ walnut (3) n 061.4
~ walnuts (2) n 054.8
~ wasp (1) n 060A.6
~ water (2) n 031.6
~ wedding cakes (1) n 122.1
~ wheat flour (1) n 044.3
~ whiskey (7) n 050.8
~ wine (3) n 114.7
~ wines (1) n 114.7
~ woman (13) n 069.4
~ women (6) n 069.4
~ wooden fence (2) n 016.2
~ world (1) n 069.4
~ worm (2) n 060.5
~ worms (4) n 060.5
~ yam (1) n 055.5
~ yams (2) n 055.5

~ yard (1) n 076.9
~ yard fence (1) n 016.2
~ yolk (1) n 045.6
~ young one (2) n 064.3
White (117) AR GA 087.3
~ Anglo-Saxon Protestant (1) 126.6
~ Anglo-Saxon Protestants (1) 088.7
~ Bayou (2) LA 030.7
~ Bluff (2) GA 087.5
~ Castle (1) LA 087.5
~ Chapel (1) MS 087.5
~ Church (1) AR 087.4
~ County (3) AR GA 087.2
~ Essex (1) 035.5
~ Falls (1) 087.2
~ Gold (1) 114.2
~ Haven (2) 105.6
~ Hill Lake Bottom (1) AR 092.8
~ Horse Saloon (1) 034.2
~ House (3) 085.6
~ House of the Confederacy (1) 106.7
~ House [P-0] [D-0] Confederacy (1) 106.4
~ Lake (3) LA MS 087.4
~ -Legged (1) 084.9
~ -Legged laying hens (1) n 036.7
~ Legging (1) 036.7
~ Leghorn (2) 121A.5
~ Leghorn chickens (1) n 036.6
~ Leghorn eggs (1) n 046.1
~ Leghorns (1) 036.8
~ Lightning Road (1) 031.6
~ Mountain half-runner bean (1) n 055A.4
~ Northern beans (1) n 055A.4
~ Oak (6) AR GA MS TX 087.2
~ Oak Bayou (4) TX 030.7

~ Oak Creek (7) AL GA TN TX 030.7
~ Oak Mountain (1) TN 031.1
~ Oak River (1) TN 030.7
~ Park (1) 106.7
~ Pine (1) TN 087.6
~ Plains (3) AL GA 087.1
~ Plains Road (1) 107.7
~ Plymouth Rock (1) 036.9
~ Queen (1) 055.5
~ River (20) AR TX 030.7
~ River Development place (1) n 080.6
~ Rock (8) TX 030.7
~ Rock Creek (1) TX 030.7
~ Rock Lake (1) TX 030.7
~ Rocks (3) 080.6
~ Shoe Peg (1) 056.2
~ Side (1) 105.4
~ Spring (1) TX 030.7
~ Star (1) 055.4
~ Station (1) 105.4
~ Station Towers (1) 108.5
~ Water (1) AL 030.7
~ Water Creek (1) GA 030.7
white[N-i] (4) n 069.4
whiteback (1) n 046.3
whiteberries (1) n 062.5
Whitecap (1) 069.4
Whitecaps (2) 080.6
whiteface (10) n/adj 069.4
~ bull (1) n 033.5
~ cows (1) n 033.6
~ Hereford (1) n 092.7
~ Hereford cows (1) n 033.6
~ Herefords (1) n 033.6
whitefaces (1) n 008.7
whitefish (3) n 060.2
Whitehall (4) 105.3
~ Street (1) 107.9
Whitehaven (7) TN 106.2
whitehead (8) n/adj 077.4

~ runners (1) n 055A.4
Whitehead Creek (1) GA 030.7
whiteheads (1) n 077.4
Whitehouse (3) TN 087.1
~ Church (1) 089.2
~ Fork (1) FL 087.3
Whitemarsh Island (1) GA 087.1
Whiteoak (1) TX 030.7
whiter (4) adj 008.7
White's (1) 106.4
whites (210) n 069.4
Whites (10) 069.4
~ Bayou (1) LA 030.7
~ Bay(ou) (1) LA 030.7
~ Creek (2) TN 030.7
~ Creek Pike (1) 030.7
~ Lane (1) MS 087.2
~ River (1) FL 030.7
~ Switch (2) TX 087.3
Whitesboro (1) TX 087.6
Whitesburg (2) TN 087.6
whitest (1) adj 026.3
whitetail (2) adj 008.7
~ deer (1) n 008.7
~ dove (1) n 059.2
Whitetop Mountain (1) TN 031.1
whitewalls (1) n 123.9
whitewash (9) n/v/adj 088.7
~ fence (1) n 016.2
whitewashed (5) v/adj 008.2
~ fences (1) n 016.2
~ her (1) v 082.1
whitewashing (1) n 016.8
Whitewater (5) GA 030.7
~ Creek (4) AL GA 030.7
whitewing (3) n/adj 059.3
Whitey (46) 069.4
Whiteys (14) 069.4
Whitfield (5) GA MS 087.2
whities (2) n 059.9
whiting (19) n 059.9
whitings (1) n 059.4
whitish (11) adj 008.7
~ -looking (1) adj 090.4
Whitney (2) FL 087.1
Whittington (3) 030.7

whittle (2) n/adj 031.3
~ rock (1) n 023.4
whittled (1) adj 020.4
whittler (2) n 023.5
whittling (4) adj 080.6
~ bench (1) n 080.6
~ rock (1) n 023.4
~ stone (2) n 023.4
Whitwell (1) TN 087.5
Whitworth College (1) 083.6
whiz (78) n/v/adj/interj 032.1
~ kids (1) n 125.5
whizzes (5) n 021.7
whizzing (1) v 006.2
who (1895) pron 043.7
~ -all (356) pron 043.7
~ -all[M-k] (12) pron 043.7
~ -all's (77) pron 043.7
who[M-k] (6) pron 043.7
whoa (930) interj 038.2
~ -back(x2) (3) interj 038.2
~ -calf(x2) (1) interj 037.6
~ now (2) interj 038.2
~ sook(x3) (1) interj 037.5
~ there (1) interj 037.5
~ up (1) interj 038.2
~ (u)p (1) interj 038.2
whoa(x2) (3) interj 038.2
whoa(x3) (2) interj 038.2
whoaee (2) interj 038.2
who'd (5) pron 043.7
Who'd Have Thought It (1) AR 086.2
whoever (14) pron 042.7
whole (1593) n/adj 082.8
~ bath (1) n 007A.4
~ bread (3) n 044.3
~ brothers (1) n 082.6
~ cake (3) n 044.6
~ chicken (3) n 121.5
~ chickens (1) n 121.5
~ fryer (1) n 121.5
~ grain (1) n 082.8
~ -grain black pepper (1) n 051.7
~ -grain coffee (1) n 082.8
~ -grain corn (1) n 056.2

~ -grain hominy (1) n 050.6
~ ham (5) n 121.3
~ -hog sausage (1) n 121.6
~ hominy (1) n 050.6
~ -kernel corn (3) n 056.2
~ milk (4) n 082.8
~ shovel (1) n 021.6
~ wheat (48) n 044.4
~ -wheat (1) adj 044.4
~ -wheat bread (64) n 044.4
~ -wheat cakes (1) n 044.4
~ wheat flour (1) n 044.3
~ -wheat muffins (1) n 044.4
~ -wheat pancakes (1) n 045.3
~ -wheat rolls (1) n 044.4
wholeheartedly (2) adv 091.1
wholesale (26) n/adj 051.5
~ house (1) n 014.1
wholesales (1) n 051.5
wholesome (1) adj 073.1
Wholesome (1) 045.1
who'll (1) pron 043.7
whom (19) pron 043.7
whomped on (1) v 065.5
whompy-jawed (1) adj 085.2
whoo (54) interj 092.2
~ -hee(x2) (1) interj 038.4
~ hoo(x2) (1) interj 059.2
~ -hoo(x3) (1) interj 037.5
~ -pig(x2) (5) interj 038.3
~ -pigs(x2) (1) interj 038.3
~ rump(x2) (1) interj 093.7
~ sook(x4) (1) interj 037.5
~ wa (1) interj 037.5
~ -wee(x2) (1) interj 038.3

~ whooey (1) interj 037.5
whoo(x2) (6) interj 037.5
whoo(x3) (1) interj 038.3
whoo(x4) (1) interj 038.3
whoo(x5) (1) interj 038.3
whooey (5) interj 037.5
whooey(x2) (1) interj 037.5
whooey(x3) (1) interj 038.3
whook (2) interj 037.5
whoop (13) n/v/adj/ interj 038.2
~ and hide (1) n 098.4
~ owl (1) n 059.2
~ -pig(x2) (1) interj 038.3
~ shack (1) n 113.4
whoop(x2) (3) interj 038.3
whoop(x3) (1) interj 038.3
whoopa(x4) (1) interj 038.3
whooped (1) v 037.5
whoopee (4) n/adj/interj 092.3
~ house (1) n 113.4
whooping (77) v/adj 057.4
~ cough (55) n 079.7
~ crane (2) n 059.3
~ -crane-looking (2) adj 095.8
~ owl (9) n 059.2
~ owls (4) n 059.2
whoops (3) n/interj 037.5
whop (4) n/v 095.4
whope(x2) (1) interj 038.3
whopped (19) v 065.9
whopper (1) n 121.9
~ -jawed (1) adj 085.2
Whopper (1) 121.7
whopperburger (1) n 121.7
whoppers (1) n 059.3
whore (148) n/adj 113.3
~ hopper (6) n 124.7
~ town (1) n 073.8
whorehouse (93) n 113.4
whorehouses (7) n 113.4
whoremonger (3) n 113.5
whore's baby (1) n 065.7

whores (22) n 113.3
whorish (1) adj 124.8
who's (120) pron 053.1
~ -all (1) pron 043.7
whose (457) pron 053.3
~ -all (10) pron 043.7
(who)se (2) pron 053.3
whosever (1) pron 053.3
whosoever (1) pron 042.7
who've (3) pron 053.5
whu(x2) (1) interj 037.8
whup(x2) (1) interj 037.8
why (149) adv/interj 091.5
Wichita (13) KS TX 087.5
~ Falls (9) TX 087.6
wick (30) n/adj 065.8
~ lamp (3) n 024.3
wicked (2) adj 088.6
wicker (12) adj 020.1
~ basket (2) n 020.1
~ baskets (1) n 020.1
~ chairs (1) n 008.8
~ furniture (3) n 009.4
~ rocking chair (1) n 008.8
~ rocking chairs (2) n 008.8
~ set (1) n 008.9
~ -type chairs (1) n 008.8
Wicker (1) MS 087.1
wickered suites (1) n 080.6
Wickes (1) AR 087.7
Wickliffe (1) KY 087.6
wicks (6) n 024.3
Wicks (1) AR 087.4
widdy(x2) (1) interj 038.5
wide (124) adj/adv 051.8
~ board (1) n 011.2
~ -open range (1) n 081.9
~ -tooth rake (1) n 120.7
widemouth bass (1) n 059.9
Widener (1) AR 082.6
wider (2) adj 025.7
wides (1) n 080.6
widow (1272) n/adj 063.3
~ indeed (1) n 063.3
~ lady (6) n 063.3

~ mother (1) n 063.3
~ oak (1) n 061.9
~ woman (70) n 063.3
~ -woman's daughter (1) n 063.3
~ -woman's home (1) n 063.3
~ women (8) n 063.3
~ womens (2) n 063.3
wid(ow) (1) n 063.3
Widow (2) 106.6
widowed (6) v/adj 063.3
~ daughters (1) n 063.3
~ parent (1) n 063.3
~ sisters (1) n 001.3
~ woman (1) n 063.3
widower (48) n 063.3
widow's (12) adj 063.3
~ door (1) n 063.3
~ dowry (1) n 063.3
~ perch (1) n 010.9
~ walk (5) n 010.9
~ watch (2) n 011.4
~ weed[N-i] (1) n 063.3
widows (30) n 063.3
width (5) n 070.7
widths (1) n 007.9
wiener (26) n/adj 121.6
~ pig (1) n 035.5
Wiener schnitzel (1) n 121.2
wieners (28) n 121.6
wienie (31) n/adj 121.6
~ bun (2) n 089.8
~ dogs (1) n 033.3
~ roast (2) n 130.7
~ roasts (1) n 130.7
~ rolls (1) n 044.4
~ sausage (1) n 046.8
~ wrap (1) n 044.7
wienies (28) n 046.8
Wiergate (2) TX 087.2
wife (1442) n 063.2
~ to be (2) n 081.6
Wife (1) 042.4
wife[N-i] (1) n 017.8
wife[N-k] mother (2) n 095.8
wife's (31) adj 063.2
~ age (1) n 063.2
~ allergy (1) n 063.2
~ aunt (2) n 067.9
~ birthday (1) n 052.5
~ brother (1) n 063.2

~ chair (1) n 098.7
~ cousin (1) n 063.2
~ cousin's husband's father (1) n 096.7
~ daddy (1) n 063.2
~ grandfather (1) n 063.2
~ grandmother (1) n 063.2
~ home (1) n 063.2
~ mother (1) n 063.2
~ mother's people (1) n 063.2
~ name (2) n 063.2
~ niece (1) n 063.2
~ people (1) n 066.5
~ picture (1) n 063.2
~ room (1) n 007A.3
~ side (1) n 063.2
~ sister (2) n 063.2
~ uncle (1) n 068.2
wig (2) n 123.9
wig(x2) (1) interj 038.3
Wiggins (5) MS 086.8
~ Road (1) 087.2
wiggle (21) n/adj 060.5
~ -tail (2) n 060.5
~ -tails (5) n 060A.2
~ worm (6) n 060.5
~ worms (7) n 060.5
wiggler (43) n/adj 060.5
~ worms (2) n 060.5
wigglers (133) n 060.5
wiggling (1) v 057.5
wiggly (4) n/adj 060.5
~ worm (1) n 060.5
~ worms (2) n 060.5
Wiggs (1) AR 087.6
wiggy-wig(x2) (1) interj 038.3
wiggy(x3) (1) interj 038.3
wigs (2) n 123.9
wigwags (1) v 088.7
wigwam (3) n/adj 015.5
~ shape (1) n 014.6
Wilbur D. Mills (1) 107.4
Wilcox (7) AL 087.3
~ County (2) AL GA 087.5
wild (1117) adj 035.9
~ about her (1) adj 081.4
~ animal (4) n 059.5
~ animals (6) n 059.5
~ azalea (5) n 062.7

~ azaleas (3) n 062.8
~ (a)zaleas (1) n 062.8
~ beans (1) n 055A.3
~ bee (1) n 060A.5
~ bees (1) n 060A.7
~ beet (1) n 015.9
~ berries (1) n 013.2
~ black olive trees (1) n 061.8
~ blackberries (6) n 062.4
~ blackberry (1) n 062.5
~ blueberries (1) n 062.4
~ boar (144) n 035.9
~ -boar bristle[N-i] (1) n 035.3
~ -boar crossing (1) n 035.9
~ boar hog (4) n 035.9
~ -boar hunting (1) n 035.9
~ boars (56) n 035.9
~ bull nettle (1) n 062.2
~ cattle (1) n 033.6
~ cherries (11) n 062.1
~ cherry (25) n 062.1
~ cherry tree (3) n 062.1
~ cherry trees (3) n 062.1
~ -cherry wine (1) n 114.7
~ coffee bush (1) n 062.2
~ coffeeweed (1) n 093.6
~ cow (2) n 033.6
~ cress (1) n 055A.5
~ crop (5) n 041.5
~ cucumber (2) n 062.9
~ deer (1) n 088.8
~ dewberries (2) n 062.4
~ dog (4) n 033.1
~ dogs (5) n 033.3
~ ducks (1) n 089.8
~ fern (1) n 061.4
~ flesh (3) n 078.2
~ flower (1) n 101.4
~ garlic (1) n 055.7
~ geese (1) n 059.2
~ gilt (2) n 035.9

~ gourds (1) n 056.6
~ grape (1) n 062.2
~ grapes (3) n 062.5
~ grass (8) n 015.9
~ greens (6) n 055A.5
~ hickory nuts (3) n 054.7
~ hickor(y) nuts (1) n 054.8
~ hog (331) n 035.9
~ -hog meat (1) n 035.9
~ hog[N-i] (2) n 035.9
~ hogs (210) n 035.9
~ honeysuckle (7) n 062.7
~ honeysuckles (1) n 062.7
~ horses (2) n 034.2
~ huckleberries (1) n 062.4
~ huckleberry (1) n 062.4
~ ivy (2) n 062.8
~ jackasses (1) n 065.7
~ kitty (1) n 059.4
~ land (1) n 029.5
~ lemon trees (1) n 061.8
~ magnolia (3) n 062.9
~ male (2) n 035.9
~ man (1) n 069.9
~ mango (1) n 092.7
~ maple (2) n 061.9
~ mint (1) n 061.4
~ mulberries (1) n 062.4
~ mulberry (1) n 061.8
~ mushroom (2) n 057.1
~ mushrooms (2) n 057.1
~ music (1) n 089.5
~ mustang (1) n 034.2
~ myrtle (1) n 061.4
~ oats (1) n 041.5
~ onion (9) n 055.7
~ onions (16) n 055.7
~ over her (1) adj 081.4
~ parties (1) n 130.7
~ peach tree (1) n 061.9
~ pecans (2) n 054.9
~ people (1) n 069.9

~ persimmon (1) n 062.5
~ persimmon tree (1) n 061.8
~ pig (20) n 035.9
~ pigeons (1) n 059.2
~ pigs (9) n 035.9
~ plum (1) n 061.8
~ plum trees (2) n 061.8
~ plums (3) n 062.5
~ range hogs (1) n 035.9
~ raspberries (1) n 062.5
~ rhubarb (1) n 061.4
~ rice (3) n 050.7
~ rooters (1) n 035.9
~ rye (1) n 015.9
~ sage (2) n 061.4
~ set (1) n 055A.7
~ sow (2) n 035.9
~ sows (1) n 035.9
~ squirrels (2) n 059.6
~ stag (1) n 035.9
~ stock (1) n 035.9
~ strawberries (12) n 062.4
~ strawberry (1) n 062.4
~ stuff (2) n 041.5
~ thing (1) n 013.8
~ toadstool (1) n 057.1
~ tomato (1) n 055.3
~ tomatoes (3) n 055.3
~ -turkey hunting (1) v 081.8
~ turkeys (6) n 059.7
~ up (1) adj 075.2
~ varmints (3) n 059.5
~ walnut (1) n 054.8
~ walnut trees (1) n 054.8
~ walnuts (1) n 054.8
~ wiggler (1) n 060.5
~ wigglers (1) n 060.5
Wild (2) 033.6
~ Cow (1) LA 033.6
~ Turkey (1) 050.8
wildcat (58) n/adj 059.5
~ distillery (1) n 050.8
~ liquor (1) n 050.9
~ piss (1) n 050.8
~ stuff (1) n 050.9
~ whiskey (14) n 050.9

Wildcat (2) 030.4
~ Bay (1) FL 030.4
~ Hollow (1) TN 030.5
wildcat[N-i] (1) n 059.5
wildcats (16) n 059.5
wilder (2) adj 082.8
wilderness (3) n 041.4
wildfowl (1) n 036.6
wildlife (2) n/adj 036.5
~ superintendents (1) n 115.3
wildwood (1) n 082.7
Wildwood (2) FL 075.6
~ Park Road (1) 107.7
wildwoods kid (1) n 065.7
Wiley (2) TX 087.7
~ Branch (1) AL 030.7
Wileys Cove (1) AR 087.3
Wilhelmina (3) AR 031.1
Wilkes (4) GA 087.1
~ Station (1) AL 082.6
~ Stream (1) AL 030.7
Wilkesboro (1) 086.4
Wilkinson (6) GA MS 087.3
~ County (3) GA MS 087.6
will (862) n/v 081.1
~ -o'-[D-0]-wisp (2) n 090.2
(wi)ll (1) v 013.1
Will (66) 067.4
Willacoochee (7) GA 030.7
~ Creek (1) GA 030.7
~ River (1) GA 030.7
(Willa)coochee Creek (2) GA 030.3
Willacy County (1) TX 087.7
Willard (1) 068.2
willed (8) adj 074.9
William (685) 068.2
~ Bonney (1) 068.2
~ Faulkner (1) 068.2
~ Shakespeare (1) 068.2
~ Tell (2) 067.4
William[N-k] (1) 043.9
Williams (26) MS 068.2
~ Creek (2) TN 030.7
~ Extension (1) 031.7
Williams' (2) 068.2

Williamsburg (9) VA 087.7
Williamson (10) GA TN 080.8
~ Branch (1) TX 030.7
~ County (2) TN TX 087.2
~ Creek (1) TX 030.7
~ Swamp Creek (2) GA 030.7
Williamsport (1) TN 087.4
Williamsville (1) MS 087.8
Willie (3) 067.4
willing (4) v/adj 089.3
~ her (1) v 081.4
Willingham Lake (1) AR 030.7
Willis (1) TX 087.4
Williston (5) FL 087.5
~ Creek (1) TX 030.7
Willkie (1) 107.7
Willkieites (1) 129.2
willow (141) n/adj 061.8
~ basket (1) n 020.1
~ beans (1) n 055A.3
~ branches (1) n 061.8
~ cat (2) n 059.9
~ flies (1) n 060A.1
~ fly (3) n 060A.4
~ oak (4) n 061.8
~ pole (1) n 052.5
~ swamps (1) n 029.6
~ thickets (1) n 061.9
~ tree (17) n 061.8
~ trees (23) n 061.9
~ wand (1) n 019.4
Willow (8) 107.8
~ Bayou (1) LA 030.7
~ Ford (1) AR 030.7
~ Glen (2) LA 087.2
~ Grove (2) TN 061.8
~ Wood (1) 105.4
willows (38) n 061.8
Willowwood (1) 105.4
willowworms (1) n 060.5
willy goat (1) n 067.4
Willy (123) 067.4
Willy's (2) 075.7
Willys Knight sedan (1) n 088.9
Wilmar (1) AR 087.4
Wilmington (4) AR IN 087.4

~ Island (1) 106.1
~ River (1) GA 030.7
Wilmont (1) MS 087.5
Wilshire Estates (1) 106.2
Wilson (17) LA TN 087.3
~ Branch (2) AL LA 030.7
~ chair (1) n 008.8
~ County (1) MS 087.4
~ Creek (1) TX 030.7
~ Dam (2) AL 106.8
~ Lake (1) AL 030.7
~ Park (3) 106.4
wilt (3) n/v 055.9
wilted (2) v 055.9
Wilties Creek (2) AL 030.7
Wilton Manors (1) 105.1
Wiltshire Park (1) 106.2
wily (1) adj 033.6
Wimauma Road (1) 031.7
Wimberley (1) TX 087.8
wimp (1) n 090.9
wimpy (2) adj 125.6
win (11) v 130.4
win[V-t] (1) v 013.8
Winborn (1) MS 087.1
winces (1) v 036.4
winch (11) n/v/adj 104.5
~ -type thing (1) n 104.5
winched (4) v 021.5
Winchester (5) TN 087.6
~ rifle (1) n 084.9
wincing (1) v 036.4
wind (605) n/v/adj 007.2
~ about (1) n 085.2
~ beam (1) n 081.9
~ funnels (1) n 112.2
~ harp (1) n 020.5
~ heaps (1) n 014.8
~ pile (1) n 014.8
~ rakes (1) n 014.8
~ up (3) v 053.2
~ -up stuff (1) n 080.8
Wind (1) 055.1
windblown (3) adj 123.9
~ soil (2) n 029.8
windbreaker (1) n 027.4
windbreakers (1) n 027.1
winded (1) adj 075.4
Winder (1) GA 102.4
windier (2) adj 007.2
winding (4) adj 095.5
~ staircase (1) n 010.7

~ stairsteps (1) n 010.7
~ step[N-i] (1) n 010.7
windjammer (1) n 101.3
windlass (15) n 081.8
windlass[N-i] (1) n 080.8
windlasses (1) n 080.8
windmill (10) n/adj 088.8
windmills (2) n 081.8
window (401) n/adj 118.5
~ air-conditioner (1) n 118.5
~ air-conditioners (1) n 118.5
~ blind (4) n 009.5
~ blinds (21) n 009.5
~ box (3) n 017.7
~ boxes (1) n 118.5
~ curtain (5) n 009.5
~ curtains (17) n 009.5
~ display (1) n 070.7
~ drapes (1) n 009.5
~ dresser (1) n 009.2
~ fan (3) n 118.5
~ fans (1) n 118.5
~ light[N-i] (1) n 018.8
~ mirror (2) n 009.2
~ rollers (1) n 009.5
~ safe (1) n 010.1
~ seat (1) n 080.7
~ shade (69) n 009.5
~ shade[N-i] (1) n 009.5
~ shades (188) n 009.5
~ -shop (1) v 094.2
~ shopping (3) n/v 094.2
~ shutter (2) n 009.5
~ shutters (3) n 009.5
~ sills (1) n 009.5
~ -type (1) adj 118.5
~ unit (4) n 118.5
~ units (3) n 118.5
~ weights (1) n 009.5
Window (1) 106.4
windowpane (1) n 114.2
windowpanes (1) n 098.8
windows (66) n 009.5
windpipe (28) n 071.7
windrolls (1) n 014.8
windrow (71) n/v 014.8
windrow[N-i] (1) n 014.8
windrowed (8) v 014.8
windrowing (3) v 041.9
windrows (118) n 014.8
winds (19) n 006.5

windshield wiper (1) n 110.2
Windsor (4) LA 087.2
~ Forest (2) 106.1
windstorm (23) n 006.2
windstorms (10) n 006.2
windward side (1) n 084.8
windy (33) adj 006.3
~ day (1) n 007.2
~ spell (1) n 005.5
~ weather (2) n 007.2
~ -weather thaw (1) n 053.6
wine (176) n/adj 114.7
~ and cheese (1) n 130.7
~ -and-cheese parties (1) n 130.7
~ cellar (1) n 007A.6
~ cellars (1) n 015.5
~ doctor (1) n 060A.4
~ glass (6) n 048.9
~ glasses (4) n 089.8
~ head (2) n 113.6
~ heads (1) n 089.8
~ home brew (1) n 050.9
~ keg (1) n 020.2
~ pipe (1) n 071.7
~ room (1) n 011.9
~ -tasting party (1) n 130.7
wineberries (1) n 062.4
wines (11) n 114.7
Winfield (6) AL TN 087.3
wing (53) n/adj 021.7
~ back (1) n 008.8
~ -back chair (1) n 008.8
~ -back chairs (1) n 008.8
~ chair (1) n 008.8
~ disc (1) n 021.6
~ feathers (1) n 052.1
~ jenny (1) n 022.7
~ net (1) n 080.7
~ plow (4) n 021.6
~ tip (3) n 123.8
~ -tip (1) adj 123.8
~ -tip shoes (1) n 123.8
~ tips (13) n 123.8
~ turning plow (1) n 021.6
Wing (3) AR 087.4

~ Forest (1) LA 087.2
wingding (1) n 130A.7
winged (1) adj 059.4
wings (16) n 123.9
Wings (2) 088.9
~ Park (1) 106.4
wink (2) n 012.5
winker (1) n 080.9
winkle-picker shoes (1) n 123.8
Winn (12) LA 086.5
~ -Dixie (1) 116.1
~ -Dixies (1) 116.1
~ Parish (4) LA 087.4
~ Parish cur (3) n 033.3
Winnebagos (1) 109.5
winned (1) v 080.9
winner (4) n/adj 125.4
winners (2) n 039.9
Winnetka Way (1) 107.7
Winnfield (7) LA 087.5
winnies (1) n 034.2
winning (2) n/v 099.2
Winnipeg (2) 087.2
winnow (9) v 042.1
winnowed (1) v 042.1
winnowing (3) v 042.1
Winnsboro (3) LA TX 087.1
wino (66) n/adj 113.6
~ street (1) n 114.8
~ types (1) n 113.6
winola (1) n 113.6
Winona (3) MS 087.7
winos (20) n 113.6
Winslow (2) AR 087.1
Winston (22) AL AR GA MS NC 087.3
~ County (7) AL MS 087.3
~ -Salem (5) NC 087.4
winter (66) n/adj 001A.8
~ bag (1) n 123.7
~ cabbage (1) n 055A.1
~ collards (1) n 055A.5
~ crop (1) n 041.3
~ crops (1) n 041.3
~ evening (1) n 002.5
~ green (1) n 055A.5
~ huckleberry (2) n 062.2
~ kitchen (3) n 009.9
~ onion (3) n 055.7
~ onions (8) n 055.7

~ patch (1) n 015.7
~ pear trees (1) n 061.9
~ radish (1) n 055.2
~ shallots (1) n 055.7
~ squash (8) n 056.6
~ storm (1) n 112.3
~ storms (1) n 112.3
~ turnip (1) n 055A.7
~ turnips (1) n 055A.7
~ water (1) n 081.8
~ wheat flour (1) n 088.8
Winter Park (2) 105.1
Winterboro (1) AL 087.3
wintergreen (1) n 055A.5
winters (3) n 091.7
wintertime (12) n 065.8
Winterville (1) LA 086.3
wip(x2) (1) interj 038.5
wipe (6) v/adj 018.2
~ cloth (2) n 018.4
~ towel (1) n 018.3
wipe[V-r] (1) v 095.8
wiped out (3) v 075.4
wiper (2) n 018.4
wipers (1) n 123.3
wiping (4) adj 018.3
~ cloth (3) n 018.3
~ rag (1) n 018.4
wire (1341) n/adj 016.3
~ bands (1) n 020.3
~ basket (1) n 020.1
~ broom (1) n 120.7
~ brush (3) n 022.2
~ cages (1) n 036.8
~ coop (2) n 036.8
~ edge (1) n 075.1
~ fence (204) n 016.3
~ fence[N-i] (1) n 016.3
~ fences (82) n 016.3
~ fencing (9) n 016.3
~ field fencing (1) n 016.3
~ gap (1) n 080.8
~ grass (18) n 015.9
~ -grass colt (1) n 065.7
~ -grass cows (1) n 015.9
~ iron fences (1) n 126.1
~ mesh (3) n 048.2
~ -mesh fence (1) n 126.1

~ metal fence (1) n 126.1
~ Page (1) n 126.1
~ pliers (2) n 020.7
~ rake (1) n 120.7
~ rakes (1) n 120.7
~ road (1) n 031.8
~ safe (1) n 010.1
~ strainer (1) n 048.2
~ strap (1) n 020.3
~ stretcher (2) n 016.3
~ stretchers (1) n 093.9
~ things (1) n 020.3
~ trap (1) n 084.9
~ type (1) n 040.6
wired (2) v 066.9
~ in (1) v 016.3
wireless (1) n 081.9
wires (18) n 016.3
wiring (3) n 016.3
wiry hair (1) n 035.6
Wisconsin (12) 087.3
wisdom (2) adj 071.8
~ teeth (1) n 071.8
~ tooth (1) n 071.8
Wisdom (1) 105.9
wise (12) adj/suffix 080.6
wised up (1) v 089.9
wiser (1) adj 066.1
wish (74) n/v/adj 037.2
~ to (1) v 013.9
~ -washies (1) n 067.8
wishbone (492) n 037.1
wished (7) v 103.4
wishes (1) n 081.1
Wishes (2) 093.2
wishing (4) v/adj 037.1
~ bone (3) n 037.1
wishy-washy (4) n 010.6
wising up (1) v 081.4
Wisner (2) LA 087.8
~ Boulevard (1) 070.8
wisp (2) n 053.5
wispes (1) n 060A.6
wisteria (6) n 061.8
wit (3) n 083.5
witch (38) n/adj 125.2
~ doctor (4) n 060A.4
~ doctors (2) n 090.8
~ hazel (1) n 061.4
~ house (2) n 090.3
~ story (1) n 104.8
Witch Creek (1) AL 030.7
witchcraft (2) n 088.8

witched (1) v 070.6
witches (13) n 090.2
witchified (1) adj 013.7
witching (4) n/adj 080.6
~ hour (3) n 080.6
witch's (3) adj 060A.4
~ horse (1) n 060A.4
~ tit (1) n 091.7
~ tittie (1) n 007.5
with (4025) adv/prep 032.4
~ a baby (6) adj 065.1
~ a calf (1) adj 033.9
~ a child (2) adj 065.1
~ a stomachache (1) adv 080.4
~ calf (6) adj 033.9
~ child (61) adj 065.1
~ his stomach (2) adv 080.4
~ it (1) adj 123.6
~ purpose (1) adv 103.6
~ the angels now (1) adv 078.5
~ the Lord (1) adv 078.5
~ the stomach (1) adv 080.4
(wi)th (2) prep 032.4
withdraw (1) v 104.4
withdrew (9) v 104.4
wither (28) v 055.9
~ away (2) v 055.9
~ (a)way (1) v 055.9
~ up (2) v 055.9
with(er) up (1) v 055.9
withered (16) v 055.9
~ up (5) v 055.9
withering (2) v 055.9
~ away (1) v 055.9
~ up (1) v 055.9
withers (2) v 055.9
withery-looking (1) adj 055.9
within (7) adv/prep 032.4
(with)in (1) prep 070.2
Withlacoochee (7) GA 030.7
~ River (4) FL GA 030.7
without (995) adv/prep 032.3
(wi)thout (20) adv/prep 032.3

(with)out (1) prep 032.4
witness (5) n 082.3
Witness[N-i] (2) 089.1
witness[V-t] (1) v 053.4
witnesses (2) n 082.4
Witnesses (6) 126.7
wits (1) n 012.5
Witt (2) 087.5
witted (1) adj 069.3
witty (1) adj 073.2
wives (32) n 063.2
wives' (6) adj 063.2
~ auxiliary (1) n 063.2
wizard (1) n 089.8
wo (3) interj 037.5
~ -ah co-ah (1) interj 037.5
wo(x3) (2) interj 037.5
wobbling (1) v 080.8
wobbly (3) adj 080.7
wocam (2) interj 037.7
woe (5) n/interj 081.8
~ be God (2) n 081.8
woey(x2) (1) interj 037.5
wogs (1) n 128.2
wok (2) n 116.4
woke (603) v 097.3
~ up (525) v 076.7
~ up with (1) v 076.3
woked up (2) v 097.3
woken (3) v 097.3
~ up (2) v 097.3
wolf (68) n/adj 066.8
~ across the river (1) n 130.2
~ on the river (1) n 130.2
~ over the river (3) n 098.4
~ over [D-0] river (1) n 081.8
~ tickets (1) n 096.8
Wolf (27) 030.7
~ Creek (13) Al AR GA TN 030.7
~ Lake (1) MS 030.7
~ River (13) AR GA MS TN 030.7
wolf[N-i] (2) n 055A.7
Wolfe City (1) TX 087.2
Wolftever Creek (1) TN 030.7
wolves (36) n 066.8
Wolvington Creek (1) MS 030.7

woman (684) n/adj 065.2
~ actor (1) n 069.1
~ doctor (3) n 065.2
~ educator (1) n 083.5
~ man (1) n 028.1
~ of the evening (1) n 113.3
~ of the house (1) n 063.2
~ pig (1) n 035.5
~ preacher (1) n 081.8
~ teacher (15) n 067.6
wom(an) (1) n 082.4
Woman (1) 063.2
woman[N-k] husband (1) n 002.7
womanhood (1) n 065.3
womanish (2) adj 124.1
womanizer (1) n 124.5
woman's (12) adj 065.2
~ club (2) n 063.2
~ college (2) n 083.6
~ house (1) n 070.7
~ husband (1) n 063.1
~ nose (1) n 101.7
womans (1) n 016.8
Womble (1) AR 087.5
women (124) n/adj 113.5
~ of ill repute (1) n 073.6
~ of the street (1) n 113.3
~ of the streets (1) n 098.7
~ people (1) n 084.8
~ teachers (2) n 067.6
women[N-k] night (1) n 043.9
womenfolk (2) n 096.9
womenfolks (25) n 080.7
womenkind (1) n 088.8
women's (3) adj 126.3
womens (10) n 016.8
won (6) v 053.1
wonder (10) n/v/adj 040.6
~ tree (1) n 061.8
Wonder (64) 056.9
~ bread (1) n 045.1
wondered (6) v 012.9
wonderful (30) adj 089.6
~ -tasted (1) adj 013.8
Wonderful Christmas (2) 093.2

wonderfulest (3) adj 064.7
wondering (4) v 057.4
wonders (2) n/v 013.9
Wonders (68) 055A.4
won't (1245) v 058.5
woo (70) interj 091.1
~ cow (1) interj 037.5
~ hoo (1) interj 037.5
~ hoo(x2) (1) interj 059.2
~ pig(x2) (1) interj 038.3
~ -pig(x2) (3) interj 038.3
~ -piggy(x2) (1) interj 038.3
~ sook(x5) (1) interj 038.3
woo(x2) (4) interj 037.5
woo(x3) (1) interj 038.4
wood (1795) n/adj 008.6
~ alcohol (2) n 050.8
~ ash (1) n 008.7
~ ashes (10) n 008.7
~ barrel (2) n 019.1
~ barrels (2) n 019.1
~ bats (1) n 059.1
~ -beam plow (1) n 021.6
~ bedstead (1) n 009.3
~ bee (2) n 067.8
~ bench (1) n 022.1
~ benches (1) n 083.8
~ bird (1) n 059.3
~ block (4) n 031.7
~ blocks (1) n 031.6
~ boat (5) n 024.6
~ boats (3) n 024.6
~ box (1) n 079.1
~ brace (1) n 022.1
~ buck (1) n 022.1
~ bucket (5) n 017.2
~ buckets (4) n 017.2
~ buildings (1) n 011.8
~ bunkers (1) n 059.3
~ burner (1) n 012.2
~ -burning furnace (1) n 118.4
~ -burning stove (3) n 008.5
~ -burning stoves (1) n 008.5
~ butcher (3) n 067.8
~ butcherer (1) n 067.8

~ chicken (1) n 065.7
~ child (1) n 065.7
~ chips (4) n 008.6
~ chisel (1) n 020.7
~ -chopping place (1) n 022.1
~ chunks (1) n 008.6
~ colt (7) n 065.7
~ colts (3) n 065.7
~ cookstove (5) n 008.5
~ cookstoves (1) n 118.4
~ cradle (1) n 022.1
~ crates (1) n 036.8
~ deal (1) n 118.4
~ dog (1) n 008.3
~ dogs (2) n 008.3
~ duck (2) n 059.2
~ ducks (2) n 059.5
~ egg (1) n 017.1
~ fence (17) n 016.2
~ fences (9) n 016.2
~ fireplace (1) n 008.6
~ fireplaces (1) n 065.9
~ fires (1) n 008.6
~ floor (2) n 008.6
~ frame (5) n 022.1
~ frames (1) n 022.1
~ god (1) n 059.3
~ grass (1) n 015.9
~ hammer (1) n 020.7
~ hammers (1) n 059.3
~ harrow (1) n 021.7
~ hauler (2) n 021.4
~ heat (3) n 008.5
~ heater (7) n 118.4
~ heaters (5) n 008.6
~ hen (13) n 059.3
~ hens (6) n 059.3
~ hogs (1) n 035.9
~ holders (1) n 008.3
~ hoops (2) n 020.3
~ horses (1) n 022.1
~ house (1) n 089.8
~ iron (1) n 088.9
~ irons (1) n 008.3
~ jack (1) n 022.1
~ jugs (1) n 017.2
~ kegs (1) n 020.2
~ kindling (1) n 008.6
~ kitty (1) n 059.4
~ knocker (4) n 059.3
~ lengths (1) n 019.8
~ lice (1) n 081.8
~ loggers (1) n 008.3

~ logs (1) n 008.5
~ maple (1) n 061.8
~ oak (1) n 061.8
~ owl (3) n 059.2
~ pail (2) n 017.2
~ pails (2) n 017.2
~ palings (1) n 016.2
~ paneling (1) n 011.2
~ pens (1) n 015.4
~ piece (1) n 053.4
~ planks (1) n 011.2
~ plow stock (1) n 021.6
~ post (1) n 016.5
~ post[N-i] (2) n 016.5
~ pulp (1) n 075.8
~ pussy (1) n 059.4
~ -rail (1) adj 016.4
~ railing (1) n 016.4
~ rails (1) n 016.4
~ range (4) n 008.9
~ rasp (2) n 066.9
~ rat (4) n 059.6
~ rick (1) n 022.1
~ rim (11) n 021.1
~ roaches (1) n 060A.2
~ roads (1) n 031.6
~ rooters (1) n 035.9
~ safes (1) n 010.1
~ saw (1) n 008.6
~ sawhorse (1) n 022.1
~ sawyer (1) n 060.5
~ scaffold (2) n 022.1
~ school (1) n 008.7
~ shack (4) n 011.7
~ shavings (1) n 008.6
~ shelf (1) n 081.9
~ shelter (4) n 011.7
~ shingles (6) n 011.2
~ shutters (1) n 007A.3
~ siding (2) n 011.2
~ slat fence (1) n 016.2
~ slats (2) n 008.5
~ snake (1) n 080.6
~ spokes (1) n 021.1
~ squirrel (3) n 059.7
~ stand (2) n 008.3
~ stove (80) n 009.8
~ stove[N-i] (1) n 008.6
~ stoves (21) n 118.4
~ terrapin (1) n 060.7
~ tick (1) n 060A.9
~ ticks (2) n 060A.9
~ tire (1) n 021.1

~ troughs (1) n 035.8
~ tubs (1) n 017.6
~ walks (1) n 031.9
~ water bucket (1) n 017.2
Wood (5) 107.6
~ Avenue (1) 107.6
~ County (1) TX 086.5
wood[N-i] (2) n 052.1
Woodall Mountain (1) MS 031.1
Woodard Street (1) 084.9
Woodbine (3) GA 087.2
woodbox (23) n 023.1
woodboxes (3) n 011.7
woodburning stove (1) n 080.6
Woodbury (8) GA TN 087.2
~ Elementary (1) 125.7
woodchecker (1) n 059.3
woodchuck (57) n 059.3
woodchucker (1) n 059.3
woodchuckers (1) n 059.3
woodchucks (16) n 059.3
woodcock (11) n 059.3
woodcocks (4) n 059.3
Woodcrest (1) 105.5
woodcutter (1) n 091.8
wooded graveyard (1) n 078.8
wooden (474) adj 016.2
~ barn (2) n 014.2
~ barrel (18) n 019.1
~ barrels (13) n 019.1
~ bathroom (1) n 012.1
~ -beam plow (2) n 021.6
~ -beam turning plow (1) n 021.6
~ bedstead (2) n 009.2
~ bedsteads (3) n 009.3
~ bench (2) n 009.1
~ benches (3) n 083.8
~ blinds (1) n 009.5
~ blocks (2) n 031.6
~ boat (11) n 024.6
~ boats (13) n 024.6
~ -bottom boats (1) n 024.6
~ box (17) n 079.1
~ boxes (1) n 079.1
~ bridge (1) n 031.9
~ bucket (53) n 017.2
~ buckets (36) n 017.2

~ casket (1) n 079.1
~ caskets (1) n 079.1
~ cedar buckets (3) n 017.2
~ chairs (4) n 008.8
~ churn (1) n 017.4
~ coffin (1) n 079.1
~ containers (1) n 019.2
~ crock (1) n 017.3
~ driveways (1) n 031.8
~ drum (1) n 017.6
~ egg (5) n 017.1
~ eggs (2) n 017.1
~ faucet (4) n 018.7
~ faucets (1) n 018.7
~ felly (3) n 021.1
~ fence (46) n 016.2
~ fences (17) n 016.2
~ forks (1) n 017.8
~ -frame fence (1) n 016.2
~ gutters (3) n 011.5
~ hammer (1) n 020.7
~ handle (1) n 032.4
~ handles (2) n 017.8
~ harrow (1) n 021.7
~ har(row) (3) n 021.7
~ harrows (1) n 021.7
~ horse (5) n 022.1
~ horses (9) n 022.1
~ house (5) n 011.2
~ houses (1) n 014.1
~ icebox (1) n 015.5
~ keg (9) n 020.2
~ kegs (6) n 020.2
~ log (1) n 008.5
~ mallet (4) n 089.9
~ mantel (1) n 008.4
~ maul (3) n 090.8
~ overcoat (3) n 079.1
~ pail (9) n 017.2
~ pails (3) n 017.2
~ palings (1) n 016.2
~ part (1) n 054.8
~ peg (1) n 065.9
~ -pegged houses (1) n 014.1
~ pegs (3) n 065.8
~ pen (1) n 015.4
~ piece (1) n 092.1
~ pin (2) n 026.5
~ plank (1) n 016.2
~ plug (1) n 020.4
~ pole (1) n 042.7

~ poles (1) n 016.5
~ post (3) n 016.5
~ post[N-i] (3) n 016.5
~ postes (1) n 016.5
~ range (2) n 088.7
~ rim (8) n 021.1
~ rims (1) n 021.1
~ roofs (1) n 011.4
~ runners (1) n 021.7
~ schoolhouse (1) n 014.1
~ shaft[N-i] (1) n 020.9
~ shafts (1) n 020.9
~ shed (1) n 015.3
~ shingles (2) n 011.4
~ shutter (1) n 009.5
~ -shutter windows (1) n 070.7
~ shutters (8) n 009.5
~ sides (1) n 013.1
~ siding (1) n 011.2
~ spicket (2) n 018.7
~ spoon (1) n 017.8
~ spoons (1) n 017.8
~ stand (1) n 019.2
~ steps (1) n 010.7
~ sties (1) n 016.2
~ stilts (1) n 080.6
~ stopper (5) n 020.4
~ stove (8) n 118.4
~ stoves (2) n 008.5
~ thing (1) n 035.8
~ -tie fence (1) n 016.2
~ tire (1) n 021.1
~ toilet (1) n 012.1
~ trays (2) n 019.2
~ trestle (1) n 022.1
~ trough (7) n 035.8
~ troughs (1) n 035.8
~ tub (3) n 017.6
~ tubs (4) n 019.2
~ wall (1) n 016.6
~ water bucket (3) n 017.2
~ water buckets (3) n 017.2
~ water keg (1) n 020.2
~ well bucket (2) n 017.2
~ wheel (1) n 021.1
~ wheels (1) n 021.1
~ whittled stick (1) n 020.4
~ windows (1) n 027.2

Wooden Grove Baptist Church (1) 089.2
woodfish (1) n 056.8
Woodgate (1) 105.5
Woodhaven (1) 106.1
woodhorse (7) n 022.2
woodhorses (4) n 022.1
woodhouse (146) n 011.7
woodhouses (4) n 011.7
woodland (6) n/adj 029.8
~ pasture (1) n 015.7
Woodland (8) GA TN 087.2
~ Circle (1) 107.7
~ Heights (2) 106.3
~ Mills (1) TN 087.3
Woodlawn (6) MI 106.2
~ Lake (2) TX 106.4
~ Stream (1) TX 030.7
Woodlea (1) 106.1
woodling colts (1) n 065.7
woodlot (3) n 015.6
woodman (1) n 065.7
woodmens (1) n 065.7
woodpeck (1) n 059.3
woodpecker (727) n 059.3
wood(pecker) (1) n 008.5
woodpecker's bill (1) n 059.3
woodpeckers (100) n 059.3
woodpecks (2) n 059.3
woodpile (25) n 011.7
Woodpile (1) 083.2
woodrack (85) n 022.1
woodracks (6) n 022.1
Woodrow (3) 107.7
~ Wilson (1) 107.7
~ Wilson Park (2) 106.4
Woodruff (1) AR 087.5
woods (348) n/adj 061.6
~ child (1) n 065.7
~ childs (1) n 088.9
~ colt (109) n 065.7
~ colts (13) n 065.7
~ country (1) n 088.7
~ cow (1) n 088.7
~ cows (2) n 033.6
~ creature (1) n 059.8
~ dirt (2) n 029.3
~ goat (1) n 099.5
~ herd (1) n 093.5
~ hog (3) n 035.9

~ hogs (6) n 035.9
~ land (2) n 029.6
~ lot (3) n 015.4
~ lots (1) n 016.1
~ mice (1) n 080.6
~ owl (1) n 059.2
~ road (3) n 031.7
~ roads (1) n 031.7
~ rooters (1) n 035.9
~ row patch (1) n 016.1
~ squirrel[N-i] (1) n 059.6
~ terrapins (1) n 060.7
~ wasp (1) n 060A.6
Woods (5) 030.7
Woodsboro (2) TX 087.6
woodshed (238) n/adj 011.7
~ psychology (1) n 080.8
woodsheds (10) n 011.7
Woodside (1) LA 087.2
woodsiness (1) n 069.8
woodsman (1) n 069.9
Woodstock (10) AL GA TN 087.1
woodsy (1) adj 069.9
woodturner (1) n 080.6
Woodville (16) AL GA LA MS 087.5
~ Road (1) 082.6
Woodward (3) TX 087.9
~ building (1) n 108.5
~ Mountain (1) MS 031.1
woodwork (1) n 008.5
woodworker (1) n 060A.5
woodworking machinery (1) n 042.7
Woody (4) 059.3
~ Gap (1) GA 087.8
woodyard (3) n 011.7
wooey (3) interj 038.3
woofing (1) v 025.3
wooflepoo dust (1) n 093.5
wooing (7) v 081.4
~ her (1) v 081.4
wool (993) n/adj 035.2
~ blanket (2) n 035.2
~ blankets (2) n 035.2
~ cloth (1) n 035.2
~ clothing (1) n 035.2
~ comforts (1) n 029.1

~ filler (1) n 029.1
~ goods (1) n 035.2
~ hat (1) n 035.2
~ -hats (1) n 069.9
~ hides (1) n 035.2
~ jacket (1) n 035.2
~ moth[N-i] (1) n 060A.2
~ nuts (1) n 062.3
~ pull (1) n 035.2
~ quilts (1) n 035.2
~ rolls (1) n 035.2
~ sacks (1) n 035.2
~ socks (1) n 035.2
~ thread (1) n 035.2
~ trail (1) n 035.2
~ worms (1) n 060.5
Wool Market (1) MS 087.2
Wooldridge Park (1) 085.1
woolen (8) adj 035.2
~ clothes (1) n 035.2
~ coat (1) n 027.1
~ head (1) n 099.8
~ mill (2) n 035.2
~ scraps (1) n 035.2
woolhatter (1) n 069.7
woollies (1) n 069.3
woolly (11) adj 035.2
~ -head nigger (1) n 069.3
~ heads (1) n 069.3
~ worms (3) n 060.5
wools (1) n 035.2
Woolsey (6) GA 080.7
~ Creek (2) GA 030.7
woop (8) interj 038.2
~ -piggy(x2) (1) interj 038.3
woop(x2) (5) interj 037.8
woopy(x2) (1) interj 038.3
woos her (1) v 081.4
Wooster (1) AR 087.3
woozy (3) adj 080.4
wop (31) n 127.3
wope (2) interj 038.3
wope(x2) (1) interj 037.8
woppo (1) n 127.3
woppy-jawed (1) adj 085.2
wops (49) n 127.3
Worcester (4) MA 086.9
~ sauce (3) n 048.5

Worcestershire sauce (2) n 048.5
word (112) n 051.8
Word (8) 102.8
word[N-i] (1) n 016.7
words (44) n 055A.8
wore (303) v 075.5
~ him out (1) v 065.5
~ off (5) v 075.7
~ out (248) v 075.5
~ -out (10) adj 075.5
~ -out land (1) n 029.9
~ -out points (1) n 029.9
~ -outen (1) adj 075.5
wored (6) v 075.5
~ out (5) v 075.5
~ -out (1) adj 075.5
work (589) n/v/adj 070.7
~ animals (2) n 033.7
~ around (1) v 014.1
~ at (3) v 040.6
~ boots (1) n 122.8
~ clothes (16) n 027.4
~ for (7) v 096.8
~ him over (1) v 065.5
~ in (2) v 074.4
~ jeans (1) n 027.4
~ like (2) v 088.9
~ mule (1) n 033.7
~ mules (1) n 033.7
~ off (1) v 050.9
~ on (42) v 036.1
~ out (2) v 102.8
~ over (1) n 010.4
~ overalls (1) n 027.4
~ pants (19) n 027.4
~ room (1) n 011.4
~ shed (3) n 011.7
~ shirt (1) n 027.4
~ shoe (2) n 123.8
~ shoes (4) n 123.8
~ steers (1) n 033.7
~ stock (6) n 036.5
~ (su)spenders (1) n 028.5
~ time (7) n 037.4
~ to (2) v 065.6
~ trousers (1) n 027.4
~ up (1) v 077.3
~ us over (1) v 065.5
~ with (9) v 053.4
work[V-p] (5) v 013.8
~ on (1) v 013.6
work[V-r] (15) v 040.6

~ for (6) v 053.1
~ from (2) v 003.2
~ on (1) v 053.4
~ to (1) v 032.2
~ [P-0] (1) v 012.9
work[V-s] (1) v 025.8
work[V-t] (4) v 075.5
~ down (3) v 075.4
workbench (9) n 022.1
workbenches (4) n 022.1
worked (257) v 057.8
~ around (1) v 096.9
~ at (4) v 057.8
~ down (1) v 075.4
~ for (9) v 053.4
~ in (9) v 070.6
~ like (4) v 033.1
~ on (38) v 036.1
~ out (6) v 075.5
~ up (1) v 075.2
~ with (5) v 032.4
worker (10) n 073.6
workers (17) n 091.8
workhorse (15) n/adj 022.1
~ bench (1) n 022.1
workhorses (12) n 034.2
workhouse (1) n 112.8
working (188) v/adj 065.8
~ boots (1) n 123.8
~ boy (2) n 074.1
~ for (12) v 016.7
~ in (3) v 015.8
~ lady (1) n 075.6
~ mothers (1) n 063.6
~ off (2) v 088.8
~ on (12) v 036.1
~ over (2) v 065.5
~ pens (1) n 015.6
~ shoes (1) n 123.8
~ shop (1) n 011.7
~ to (2) v 032.8
~ toward (1) v 101.2
~ up (1) v 005.6
~ -up baseball (1) n 098.4
~ with (4) v 024.9
workingest (1) adj 053.6
workmen (1) n 077.3
workmen's area (1) n 007A.2
workroom (5) n 010.1
works (55) n/v 031.6
~ at (2) v 052.5

~ for (2) v 053.6
~ from (1) v 003.2
~ in (5) v 025.2
~ like (1) v 069.3
~ on (2) v 013.8
~ with (3) v 032.4
~ [P-0] (2) v 025.2
Works (1) 087.7
workshop (20) n 011.7
worktable (1) n 009.4
worktables (1) n 009.4
world (112) n/adj 085.8
World (45) 085.4
~ War (14) 085.8
~ War One (14) 001.1
~ War Three (1) 088.7
~ War Two (11) 085.8
world[N-i] (1) n 075.7
World's (4) 092.8
~ War One (1) 043.9
worlds (42) n 081.8
worm (358) n/adj 016.4
~ bait (1) n 060.5
~ bed (1) n 096.7
~ beds (1) n 060.5
~ board (1) n 016.4
~ farm (1) n 060.5
~ farms (2) n 060.5
~ fence (14) n 016.4
~ fences (1) n 016.4
~ fuse (1) n 080.4
~ kind (1) n 016.4
~ rail (5) n 016.4
~ -rail fence (1) n 016.4
~ style (1) n 016.4
~ tree (1) n 061.8
worms (977) n 060.5
wormy (2) adj 060.5
worn (560) v/adj 075.5
~ down (3) v 075.5
~ out (522) v 075.5
~ -out (3) adj 075.5
~ -out clothes (1) n 075.5
~ -out land (1) n 075.5
~ -over clothes (1) n 123.5
worned out (3) v 075.5
worracious (1) adj 088.7
worried (337) v/adj 074.2
~ about (3) v 079.5
~ (a)bout (1) v 079.5
~ up (1) v 057.5
~ with (3) v 075.6

worries (15) n/v 079.5
~ about (1) v 079.5
worrisome (2) adj 092.8
worry (849) n/v/adj
   079.5
~ about (50) v 079.5
~ (a)bout (30) v 079.5
wor(ry) (14) v 079.5
~ about (1) v 079.5
~ (a)bout (5) v 079.5
worry[V-p] (1) v 079.5
worry[V-s] (1) v 079.5
worry[V-t] (5) v 079.5
~ about (2) v 025.3
~ with (1) v 098.7
worrying (17) v 079.5
~ about (1) v 053.1
worrywart (2) n 088.8
worse (80) n/adj 070.6
~ half (2) n 063.2
worsening (2) v 005.6
worser (37) adj 066.1
worsest (2) adj 064.7
worship (5) v 089.2
worshiper (1) n 073.5
worshipers (2) n 126.5
worst (12) n/adj 065.8
worsted (2) adj 035.2
~ serge (1) n 027.5
worstest (2) adj 002.6
worth (56) n/prep 065.8
Worth (48) 087.5
~ Circle (1) 080.6
~ County (1) GA 086.3
Wortham (1) TX 087.8
worthless (23) adj 033.3
~ land (1) n 029.8
Worthville (1) GA 087.2
worthwhile (1) adj 004.6
would (852) v 100.1
~ might (1) v 058.6
(woul)d (15) v 070.3
wouldn't (572) v 058.5
~ accept (1) v 082.1
~ have him (4) v 082.1
would've (1) v 033.4
wound (834) n/v/adj
   078.1
~ place (2) n 078.1
~ up (2) v 083.2
wounded (56) v/adj 078.1
~ place (1) n 078.1
wounds (15) n 078.1
wove (11) v/adj 025.6
~ wire (9) n 016.3

woven (73) v/adj 016.3
~ bag (1) n 019.7
~ baskets (1) n 020.1
~ fence (4) n 016.3
~ fences (1) n 040.8
~ sack (1) n 019.6
~ wire (43) n 016.3
~ -wire (2) adj 016.3
~ -wire fence (14) n
   016.3
~ -wire fences (2) n
   016.3
~ wiring (1) n 016.3
wow (31) interj 092.2
wowee (1) interj 092.3
Wowie (1) 114.1
WPA (4) 012.1
~ road (2) n 031.7
~ time (1) n 095.2
wraiths (1) n 090.2
wrangle (1) n 025.9
wrangling (1) v 104.2
wrap (325) n/v 094.3
~ around (7) v 094.3
~ up (4) v 094.3
wrap[N-i] (1) n 043.6
wrap[V-p] (1) v 094.3
wrap[V-r] (17) v 094.3
wrap[V-t] (5) v 094.3
wraparound (2) n/adj
   026.4
~ porch (1) n 010.8
wrapped (670) v/adj
   094.3
~ in (3) v 084.3
~ sausage (1) n 121.6
~ up (22) v 094.3
~ up in (3) v 094.3
~ up with (1) v 080.8
wrapper (2) n 094.3
wrappers (1) n 081.8
wrapping (13) n/v/adj
   094.3
~ paper (1) n 094.3
wrappings (1) n 094.4
wraps (55) n/v 094.3
Wray (1) GA 086.4
wreath (3) n 061.8
wreck (13) n 023.6
wreckage (1) n 108.7
wrecked (2) v 075.5
wrecking days (1) n 075.6
wren (2) n/adj 059.2
~ bird (1) n 059.2
wrench (2) n 067.8

wrenches (3) n 066.8
wrens (2) n 059.3
wrestle (14) v 104.2
wrestled (3) v 130.5
~ with (1) v 098.1
wrestling (13) n/v/adj
   130.5
~ games (1) n 130.5
wrigglers (2) n 060.5
wriggly worms (1) n
   060.5
Wright brothers (1) n
   053.4
Wrights Creek (1) FL
   030.7
Wrightsville (1) GA 087.2
wring (3) v 075.8
wringer (6) n/adj 116.9
~ -type washer (2) n
   010.6
~ washer (1) n 010.6
wringing-wet (3) adj
   077.3
wrinkle (14) v 055.9
~ up (3) v 055.9
wrinkle[V-r] up (1) v
   055.9
wrinkled (32) v/adj 055.9
~ up (4) v 055.9
wrinkledy (3) adj 090.9
~ -round (1) adj 088.9
wrinkles (2) n/v 055.9
wrinkling (1) v 055.9
wrinkly (1) adj 055.9
wrist (50) n/adj 072.3
~ bracelet (1) n 028.3
wrist[N-i] (3) n 072.2
wristband (16) n 028.3
wristbands (1) n 028.3
wristed (1) adj 124.1
wristwatch (164) n 004.3
wristwatches (8) n 004.3
writ (15) v 100.5
write (968) v 100.5
~ about (1) v 024.7
~ down (3) v 100.5
~ on (7) v 100.5
~ out (1) v 100.5
~ to (3) v 100.5
~ up (4) v 100.5
~ -up (2) n 100.5
~ -ups (1) n 100.5
~ with (1) v 100.5
write[V-r] (4) v 100.5
writer (1) n 100.5

writes (8) v 100.5
writing (57) n/v/adj
   100.5
~ desk (1) n 083.8
~ pen (9) n 026.5
~ school (1) n 080.6
~ spider (1) n 080.7
~ table (1) n 083.8
~ tablet (1) n 100.5
~ to (1) v 098.6
writings (1) n 100.5
written (477) v 100.5
~ down (2) v 100.5
~ out (1) v 100.5
~ up (2) v 100.5
wrong (148) n/adj 125.1
~ side of the bed (2) n
   065.7
~ side of the blanket
   (3) n 065.7
~ side of the cover (1)
   n 069.5
~ side of the tracks (1)
   n 075.7
~ -sided (1) adj 085.2
~ sidewards (1) adv
   080.8
Wrong Creek (1) TN
   030.7
wrop (17) v 094.3
~ up (3) v 094.3
wropped (15) v 094.3
~ up (2) v 094.3
~ with (1) v 094.3
wropping (1) v 094.3
wrops (1) v 094.3
wrote (1005) v 100.5
~ about (2) v 100.5
~ back (2) v 100.5
~ by (1) v 100.5
~ down (4) v 100.5
~ in (2) v 100.5
~ off (1) v 100.5
~ on (4) v 100.5
~ out (2) v 100.5
~ to (4) v 053.4
~ up (4) v 100.5
wroten (3) v 100.5
wrought (9) adj 016.2
~ -iron fence (3) n
   016.2
~ -iron fences (1) n
   016.6
~ -iron frying pans (1)
   n 017.5

~ -iron pot (1) n 017.6
~ up (3) adj 075.2
wrung (4) v 075.8
wu wee (2) interj 037.5
wuh (1) interj 037.6
wuh(x3) (1) interj 038.3
wup (3) interj 037.8
Wurstfest (1) n G 104.7
wus (1) n 125.6
wushel (1) interj S 033.2
Wyandottes (1) 093.5
Wyches Bay(ou) (1) LA
    030.3
wye (1) interj 037.5
Wynne (2) AR 087.8
Wynnton (1) 081.8
Wynnville (1) AL 087.9
Wyoming (11) 086.1

X

X (67) 114.9
~ -frame (5) n 022.1
~ -rated (13) adj 114.9
~ -rated cinema (1) n
114.9
~ -rated movie (4) n
114.9
~ -rated movie house
(4) n 114.9
~ -rated movie houses
(2) n 114.9
~ -rated movie theater
(5) n 114.9
~ -rated movie theaters
(2) n 114.9
~ -rated movies (13) n
114.9
~ -rated place (1) n
114.9
~ -rated shop (1) n
114.9
~ -rated theater (7) n
114.9
~ -ray (1) n 070.7
~ -ray pictures (1) n
075.7
XJ (1) 080.9
Xs (1) 126.1
XXX (3) 050.8

Y

y (1) adv F 021.6
yacht (8) n 031.4
Yacht (2) 106.4
  ~ Basin (1) 106.4
  ~ Club (1) 106.4
yachtes (1) n 024.6
yachts (8) n 024.6
Yacona (1) 030.7
Yahoo (2) 069.9
Yahoola (1) GA 030.7
Yahoos (3) 069.9
yakking (1) v 036.2
Yalaha (1) FL 087.6
y'all (616) pron 043.5
Y'all (1) 043.5
y'all[M-k] (12) pron 043.
  ~ self[N-i] (1) pron
   043.6
y'all's (144) pron 043.6
y'all'ses (12) pron 043.6
Yalobusha (5) MS 030.7
  ~ Bottom (1) MS 029.4
  ~ County (1) MS 087.1
  ~ River (2) MS 030.7
yam (247) n/adj 055.5
  ~ potato (10) n 055.5
  ~ (po)tato (2) n 055.5
  ~ potatoes (5) n 055.5
  ~ yam (1) n 055.5
yam[N-i] (2) n 055.5
Yamacraw (1) 105.4
yammy (2) n/adj 055.5
  ~ -yammy (1) n 055.5
yams (371) n 055.5
Yangs (1) 126.4
yank (3) v 104.5
Yank (1) 075.7
yank[V-r] (1) v 021.5
yanked (5) v 021.5
 . ~ up (1) v 065.6
Yankee (83) 066.8
  ~ area (1) n 080.8
  ~ Bayou (1) LA 030.7
  ~ beans (1) n 055A.4
  ~ Branch (1) AL 030.7

  ~ expression (1) n
   081.9
  ~ gal (1) n 064.9
  ~ gunboat (1) n 088.7
  ~ overseer (1) n 090.8
  ~ people (1) n 014.7
  ~ pudding (1) n 081.8
  ~ States (2) 086.9
  ~ team (1) n 088.7
  ~ War (2) 085.8
Yankeefied (2) 066.7
  ~ folks (1) n 066.7
Yankeeland (3) 080.6
Yankees (59) 066.8
Yankees' bedding (1) n
  081.8
Yankeetown (2) 080.6
Yanks (1) 085.8
yap (3) n 069.4
yap[N-i] (1) n 069.4
yapper (3) n 033.3
yappers (1) n 033.3
yapping (5) v/adj 033.3
  ~ dog (1) n 033.3
  ~ dogs (3) n 033.3
yard (516) n/adj 007A.5
  ~ ape (3) n 069.3
  ~ apes (1) n 069.3
  ~ ax (2) n 067.8
  ~ baby (1) n 080.7
  ~ bean (3) n 055A.4
  ~ beans (1) n 055A.4
  ~ boy (3) n 089.8
  ~ broom (16) n 020.7
  ~ brooms (5) n 010.5
  ~ brush (1) n 010.5
  ~ child (1) n 065.7
  ~ children (1) n 065.7
  ~ cleaning (1) n 092.9
  ~ clothes (1) n 027.7
  ~ dog (16) n 033.3
  ~ dogs (1) n 033.3
  ~ faucets (1) n 018.7
  ~ fence (44) n 016.2
  ~ fences (8) n 016.2
  ~ flower (1) n 101.4
  ~ frogs (1) n 060.4
  ~ furniture (1) n 009.4
  ~ garden (1) n 050.5
  ~ house (1) n 014.1
  ~ level (1) n 015.6
  ~ light (1) n 019.9
  ~ long (1) n 055A.4
  ~ -long bean (2) n
   055A.4

  ~ -long beans (2) n
   055A.4
  ~ -long peas (1) n
   055A.3
  ~ man (1) n 081.8
  ~ master (1) n 084.9
  ~ parties (1) n 130.7
  ~ people (1) n 015.6
  ~ pets (1) n 033.1
  ~ rack (1) n 022.1
  ~ rake (22) n 120.7
  ~ scissors (2) n 120.8
  ~ snake (1) n 080.9
  ~ spicket (1) n 018.7
  ~ -sweeping day (1) n
   002.1
  ~ swing (1) n 022.9
  ~ toad (1) n 060.4
  ~ wheelbarrow (1) n
   023.3
  ~ whip (1) n 080.9
  ~ wire (1) n 016.3
  ~ work (3) n 015.6
  ~ worm (1) n 060.5
  ~ young ones (1) n
   064.3
Yard (2) 066.9
yard[N-i] (2) n 026.6
yardbirds (1) n 130.3
yardful (2) n 055A.6
Yardley (1) 030.7
yards (31) n 015.6
yardstick (1) n 012.2
yarn (2) n/adj 089.8
  ~ piece (1) n 075.6
Yarn (1) 013.8
Yates (1) 106.3
Yatesville (1) GA 087.3
yaupon (9) n 061.9
yaw (1) interj 037.7
yawl (3) n 024.6
yawls (1) n 024.6
yawning (2) v 077.8
yawny (1) adj 076.6
yay-oo (1) interj 033.3
Yazoo (36) MS 030.7
  ~ and Mississippi Valley
   Railroad (1) 092.7
  ~ Basins (1) MS 030.7
  ~ City (9) MS 087.3
  ~ County (2) MS 087.1
  ~ Creek (1) MS 030.7
  ~ Mississippi Valley (1)
   066.8
  ~ River (10) MS 030.7

Ybor City (16) 105.1
ye (4) adj 089.3
yea (59) interj 038.2
yea(x2) (2) interj 038.2
Yeager Creek (1) GA
  030.7
yeah (1484) interj 091.3
year (2139) n/adj 005.1
  ~ -(a)round (2) adj
   050.5
Year (734) 093.3
year[N-i] (301) n 005.2
Year[N-k] (4) 093.3
yearling (95) n/adj 033.8
  ~ boy (1) n 075.9
  ~ calf (3) n 033.8
  ~ cow (1) n 033.8
  ~ hog (1) n 035.5
  ~ steer (1) n 033.5
  ~ tick (2) n 060A.9
  ~ timber (1) n 061.8
yearlings (20) n 033.8
year's (6) adj 004.7
  ~ crop (1) n 004.7
Year's (243) 093.3
years (2835) n 005.1
Years (1) 088.8
yeast (1164) n/adj 045.5
  ~ biscuits (2) n 044.4
  ~ bread (125) n 044.3
  ~ breads (3) n 044.3
  ~ cake (28) n 045.5
  ~ cakes (15) n 045.5
  ~ corn bread (1) n
   044.7
  ~ dough (1) n 045.5
  ~ doughnut (3) n 045.2
  ~ doughnuts (6) n
   045.2
  ~ light bread (1) n
   044.3
  ~ loaf (1) n 044.3
  ~ powder (2) n 045.5
  ~ powders (1) n 045.5
  ~ -rise bread (1) n
   044.3
  ~ -rising bread (2) n
   044.7
  ~ roll (3) n 044.4
  ~ rolls (7) n 044.4
yeasted (2) v/adj 045.5
  ~ bread (1) n 045.5
yeasters (2) n 044.3
yeasts (1) n 045.5
yee (8) interj 037.7

~ -hoo(x2) (1) interj 038.3
~ -wye (1) interj 037.5
yee(x2) (1) interj 038.2
yegua (1) n S 034.2
Yegua (2) TX 030.7
~ Lake (1) TX 030.7
yell (6) n 036.2
Yell (2) AR 087.5
yelling for (1) v 036.2
yellow (3549) n/adj 045.6
~ apple (1) n 045.7
~ backs (1) n 126.4
~ bean (1) n 045.7
~ beans (3) n 055A.3
~ bee (1) n 060A.7
~ -bellied (1) adj 059.7
~ -bellied bream (1) n 059.9
~ -bellied sapsucker (2) n 059.3
~ -bellied turtle (1) n 060.7
~ breast (1) n 059.3
~ -breasted sapsuckers (1) n 059.3
~ breeding (1) n 080.9
~ butter bean (1) n 055A.3
~ cat (19) n 059.9
~ catfish (3) n 059.9
~ cats (5) n 059.9
~ cheese (1) n 048.1
~ chills (1) n 079.8
~ clay (5) n 029.8
~ clay soil (1) n 029.9
~ clear seed (1) n 054.4
~ cling (2) n 054.3
~ cling peach (2) n 054.3
~ corn (50) n 056.2
~ corn bread (3) n 044.6
~ corn on the cob (1) n 056.2
~ cornmeal (3) n 044.7
~ crook squash (1) n 056.6
~ crooked neck (2) n 056.6
~ crooked-neck (2) adj 056.6
~ crooked-neck squash (2) n 056.6

~ crookneck (10) n 056.6
~ crookneck squash (5) n 056.6
~ crowder (2) n 050.4
~ cushaw (1) n 056.6
~ divider (1) n 107.3
~ dock (1) n 061.4
~ -dog Democrats (1) n 129.1
~ dogs (1) n 126.4
~ fever (63) n 079.8
~ fe(ver) (1) n 079.8
~ -fever epidemic (1) n 079.8
~ field corn (2) n 056.2
~ flies (5) n 060A.6
~ fly (9) n 060A.8
~ gal (1) n 080.7
~ garden corn (1) n 056.2
~ garden squash (1) n 056.6
~ -gold chain (1) n 045.7
~ gourd-neck squash (1) n 056.6
~ Granex (1) n 055.6
~ grass (1) n 045.7
~ grasshopper (1) n 061.1
~ grit (1) n 050.6
~ grits (7) n 050.6
~ gumbo (1) n 029.8
~ -headed woodpecker (1) n 059.3
~ -heart pine trees (1) n 061.8
~ hominy (1) n 050.6
~ honeybee (1) n 060A.7
~ hornet (1) n 060A.5
~ hornets (1) n 060A.5
~ -hull (1) adj 055A.4
~ -hull snap bean (1) n 055A.4
~ hybrid (1) n 056.2
~ jacket (390) n 060A.7
~ jack(et) (12) n 060A.7
~ jack(et) bees (1) n 060A.7
~ jacket wasp (3) n 060A.7

~ jacket[N-i] (4) n 060A.7
~ -jacket[N-k] nest (2) n 060A.7
~ -jacket's nest (1) n 060A.7
~ -jacket's sting (1) n 060A.7
~ jackets (427) n 060A.7
~ jacks (1) n 060A.7
~ jaundice (623) n 079.8
~ jaun(dice) (3) n 079.8
~ land (1) n 045.7
~ -like (3) adj 046.8
~ line (20) n 107.3
~ lines (13) n 107.3
~ liquid (1) n 077.7
~ locust (1) n 061.9
~ -looking (2) adj 045.7
~ man (1) n 126.4
~ mangroves (1) n 045.7
~ mark (1) n 107.3
~ meal (2) n 044.5
~ -meal corn (1) n 044.5
~ meat (24) n 056.9
~ -meat (1) adj 056.9
~ -meat melon (1) n 056.7
~ -meat melons (1) n 056.9
~ -meat watermelon (10) n 056.9
~ -meat watermelons (3) n 056.9
~ -meated (21) adj 056.9
~ -meated melon (4) n 056.9
~ -meated melons (2) n 056.9
~ -meated watermelon (11) n 056.9
~ -meated watermelons (1) n 056.9
~ melon (3) n 056.7
~ -mouth trout (1) n 093.5
~ mulatto (1) n 069.5
~ neck (1) n 056.6

~ -neck crookneck squash (1) n 056.6
~ -neck squash (2) n 056.6
~ Negro (4) n 069.5
~ nigger (9) n 069.5
~ niggers (5) n 069.5
~ onion (7) n 055.6
~ onions (4) n 055.6
~ pancakes (1) n 045.3
~ part (13) n 045.7
~ peach (1) n 054.3
~ peaches (1) n 054.3
~ pecan (2) n 061.4
~ people (2) n 126.4
~ perch (1) n 059.9
~ perches (1) n 084.9
~ person (3) n 069.5
~ pine (13) n 061.9
~ pines (1) n 061.8
~ poplar (5) n 061.8
~ poplar trees (1) n 101.7
~ potato (1) n 055.5
~ (po)tatoes (1) n 055.5
~ press (2) n 054.3
~ puccoon (1) n 061.4
~ puccoon root (2) n 061.4
~ race (1) n 069.5
~ rice (1) n 050.7
~ roe (1) n 045.7
~ roe mullet (1) n 059.9
~ sand (1) n 045.7
~ shells (1) n 059.9
~ skin (1) n 126.4
~ -skin onion (1) n 055.6
~ -skin yam (2) n 055.5
~ skins (1) n 126.4
~ slip (1) n 045.7
~ snap beans (1) n 055A.4
~ soap (5) n 045.7
~ squash (58) n 056.6
~ squashes (3) n 056.6
~ squirrel (2) n 059.7
~ stone (1) n 054.3
~ straight neck (2) n 056.6
~ string beans (4) n 055A.4
~ strip (1) n 107.3

~ stripe (3) n 107.3
~ stripes (1) n 045.7
~ strips (1) n 107.3
~ sucker (1) n 059.9
~ summer crookneck (1) n 056.6
~ summer squash (2) n 056.6
~ sweet corn (1) n 056.2
~ tomato (4) n 055.3
~ tomatoes (1) n 055.3
~ turnip (1) n 045.7
~ -type weed (1) n 061.4
~ walnut (1) n 054.8
~ walnuts (1) n 054.8
~ wasp (15) n 060A.6
~ wasps (1) n 060A.6
~ watermelon (3) n 056.9
~ watermelons (1) n 056.9
~ wax (4) n 055A.3
~ wax bean (1) n 055A.3
~ wax beans (4) n 055A.4
~ woman (1) n 069.4
~ worms (1) n 060.5
~ yam (19) n 055.5
~ yam potato (3) n 055.5
~ yam (po)tato (1) n 055.5
~ yams (18) n 055.5
~ yolk (2) n 045.6
yel(low) (4) n 045.6
~ jacket (2) n 045.7
Yellow (39) 045.7
~ Bayou (1) TX 030.7
~ Branch (3) LA TX 045.7
~ Cab (2) 109.9
~ Cotton (1) LA 030.7
~ Creek (5) AL GA TN 030.7
~ Danvers (2) 055.6
~ Dent (1) 056.2
~ Dog (1) 033.1
~ Golden Dent (1) 056.2
~ Jacket (1) 060A.7
~ Jacket Creek (1) GA 030.7

~ Jackets (1) 060A.7
~ River (12) AL FL GA LA 030.7
~ Shoe Peg (1) 056.2
~ Water (1) AL 030.7
yellowbellies (2) n 099.7
yellowbelly (4) n 060.7
yellowest (1) adj 064.8
yellowfish (2) n 059.9
yellowhammer (56) n 059.3
yellowhammers (8) n 059.3
yellowhandle (1) n 080.6
yellowhands (1) n 059.3
yellowhanger (1) n 059.3
yellowhead peckerwood (1) n 059.3
yellowish (9) adj 045.7
Yellowleaf Creek (2) AL 030.7
Yellowpine (1) TX 087.7
yellowroot (17) n 061.4
yellowroots (1) n 061.4
yellows (16) n 045.6
Yellowstone (2) 087.3
~ National Park (1) WY 087.3
~ Park (1) WY 045.7
yellowtail (6) n/adj 059.9
~ tarpon (1) n 059.9
yellowtails (1) n 059.9
yellowtop (3) n/adj 061.4
~ clover (1) n 045.7
yellowweed (1) n 088.8
yellowwort (1) n 062.6
yells (1) n 036.4
yeomen farmers (1) n 081.9
yep (42) interj 091.3
yes (2068) adj/interj 091.3
~ -man (1) n 125.6
~ sirree (20) interj 091.1
~ sirree bob (1) interj 091.3
y(es) (1) interj 091.4
yesterday (1137) n/adj 003.5
~ afternoon (2) n 003.5
~ evening (11) n 003.5
~ morning (3) n 003.5
~ week (1) n 003.6

yesterd(ay) afternoon (1) n 003.5
yester(day) (7) n 003.5
yesterday's paper (1) n 003.5
yet (107) adv 040.1
Yet (1) 025.3
yet(x2) (1) interj 037.5
yew (2) n/adj 061.8
~ tree (1) n 061.8
yews (1) n 061.9
Ygnacio (3) 087.9
Yid (1) 126.7
Yiddish (1) 126.8
Yids (1) 126.7
yield (17) n/v/adj 041.3
yina (1) pron 092.8
yip(x2) (1) interj 033.4
yippie (2) n 129.3
yippies (1) n 129.3
yips (1) n 126.8
Yma Sumac (1) 062.2
YMV (1) 092.7
yo (10) n/adj/interj 037.7
~ wo (1) interj 038.3
~ -yo (2) n 080.9
~ -yo bedspread (1) n 028.7
~ -yos (2) n 130.6
Yoakum (2) TX 087.6
Yockanookany (5) MS 030.7
yodel (1) n 037.5
Yoestown (1) AR 087.2
yogi (1) n 121.7
yogurt (13) n 047.6
yoke (231) n/v 033.7
~ of beeves (1) n 033.7
~ of cattle (2) n 033.7
~ of lead oxens (1) n 033.7
~ of ox[N-i] (1) n 033.7
~ of oxen (56) n 033.7
~ of oxens (12) n 033.7
~ of oxes (1) n 033.7
~ of steers (10) n 033.7
~ of twin steers (1) n 033.7
~ up (1) v 033.7
yoke[N-i] (20) n 048.8
~ of cattle (1) n 033.7
~ of oxen (3) n 033.7
~ of oxens (2) n 033.7
~ of steers (1) n 033.7

~ of them steers (2) n 033.7
~ of your oxen (1) n 052.5
yoke[V-t] (2) v 033.7
yoked (1) v 033.7
yokel (1) n 069.9
yokels (3) n 069.8
yokes (38) n 033.7
~ of cattle (1) n 033.7
~ of oxen (8) n 033.7
~ of oxens (4) n 033.7
Yokohama (1) 087.7
yolk (813) n 045.6
yolks (13) n 045.6
Yonah Mountain (1) GA 031.1
yonder (1203) adj/adv 052.2
yond(er) (2) adv 052.2
yon(der) (29) adv 052.2
Yonder (1) 052.2
yonders (2) adj/adv 052.2
~ land (1) n 052.2
yoo (3) interj 037.5
yoody-roo(x2) (1) interj 037.5
yooey (2) interj 038.3
yoogly (1) adj 125.1
York (1042) AL 087.8
~ County (1) SC 086.8
Yorker (1) 121.1
Yorkers (1) 086.1
Yorks Creek (1) TX 088.7
Yorkshire (2) 035.3
~ bread (1) n 044.4
Yosemite Valley (1) CA 087.7
you (15453) pron 043.5
~ -all (564) pron 043.5
~ -all[M-k] (4) pron 043.6
~ -all's (84) pron 043.6
~ -all'ses (3) pron 043.6
~ know what (1) n 063.1
~ old heifer (1) interj 037.5
~ ones (31) pron 043.5
~ (o)nes (1) pron 043.5
~ oneses (3) pron 043.5

~ [X-0] better stand
    still (1) interj 037.5
y(ou) (11) pron 090.6
you[M-k] (7) pron 027.5
you'd (105) pron 104.1
you'll (48) pron 081.2
young (498) adj 074.1
    ~ bull (4) n 033.8
    ~ corn (11) n 056.2
    ~ -looking (8) adj
        074.1
    ~ male (1) n 033.8
    ~ man (2) n 081.5
    ~ master (1) n 069.6
    ~ mister (1) n 080.6
    ~ Noah (1) n 006.1
    ~ one (44) n 064.3
    ~ one[N-i] (2) n 064.3
    ~ one[N-i][N-k] (1)
        adj 064.3
    ~ ones (212) n 064.3
    ~ ones' (1) adj 064.3
    ~ onion (5) n 055.7
    ~ onions (7) n 055.7
    ~ peas (1) n 055A.4
    ~ -people's parties (1)
        n 083.1
    ~ potatoes (1) n 055.4
    ~ roasting-ear corn (1)
        n 056.2
    ~ tomatoes (1) n 055.3
Young (3) 067.7
    ~ Miss (1) 067.7
    ~ Street (2) 107.7
young[A-w] (3) adj 043.2
youngberries (1) n 062.5
Youngblood (3) AL 087.3
younger (100) adj 075.7
youngest (46) adj 064.7
youngster (16) n 064.3
youngsters (29) n 064.3
Youngstown (1) 106.3
Youngsville (1) LA 087.4
your (3683) pron 043.6
    ~ -all's (12) pron 043.6
    ~ own self (13) pron
        044.2
y(our) (2) pron 016.1
Your Honor (3) 068.6
you're (176) pron 068.5
yourn (39) pron 043.4
yournses (1) pron 043.4
yours (605) pron 043.4
yourself (839) pron 044.1

yourself[M-i] (6) pron
    092.1
yourselves (16) pron
    044.1
you's (52) pron 043.5
youse (7) pron 043.5
    ~ -all's (1) pron 046.3
youth (3) n/adj 065.8
Youth Center (1) 106.4
youthes (1) n 033.8
youthful (7) adj 074.1
you've (101) pron 101.2
yucca (2) n 061.4
yucky (1) adj 080.6
Yugoslavia (1) 075.9
yuk (4) interj 049.6
yukky (2) adj 047.5
Yule (8) 093.2
    ~ log (7) n 008.5
Yuletide (3) 093.2
yum (2) adj 080.6
    ~ -yum (1) adj 080.6
Yuma (1) AZ 087.1
yup(x2) (1) interj 038.2
YW (1) 082.7
YWCA (1) 084.3

Z

Z (8) 008.9
Zachary (5) LA 087.2
zafado (2) n S 073.4
zany (1) adj 074.7
Zapata (6) TX 087.9
Zarzamor(a) 107.7
zebra (8) n/adj 059.4
~ baits (1) n 060.5
~ wasp (1) n 060A.7
zebras (1) n 069.5
Zebulon (6) GA 087.1
~ Church (3) AL 086.4
Zelda (1) 032.7
Zephiran (1) 078.3
zero (17) n/adj 007.5
~ night (1) n 075.6
~ weather (3) n 007.6
Zero Bay (1) GA 030.3
Zest (1) 088.8
zesty (1) adj 007.4
'zhe'be (2) adj F 091.9
zig (1) v 104.5
zigzag (65) v/adj/adv 016.4
~ fence (9) n 016.4
~ fences (3) n 016.4
~ kind (1) n 016.4
~ rail fence (1) n 016.4
zigzagged (5) v 016.4
zigzagging (3) v 085.2
Zilpha Creek (2) MS 030.7
Zimmer (1) n G 007A.4
zinc (50) n/adj 017.3
~ bucket (7) n 017.3
~ buckets (6) n 017.3
~ dipper (1) n 075.8
~ pan (1) n 020.1
~ tub (9) n 017.3
~ tubs (3) n 017.6
~ washtub (1) n 020.1
zinnias (1) n 101.4
Zion (10) AR 087.8
~ Hill (1) LA 030.8
zip (7) adj/adv 088.7

~ bag (1) n 123.7
~ gun (2) n 113.1
~ -up boots (1) n 123.8
~ -up shoes (1) n 123.8
ZIP Code (2) 100.8
zipper (4) n/adj 123.7
~ bag (1) n 123.7
~ bags (1) n 123.7
Zippy Mart (2) 116.2
zit (6) n/adj 077.4
~ face (2) n 125.1
~ holes (1) n 129.7
Zittle Boy (1) TX 030.7
zodiac (1) n 104.7
zombi (3) n 117.4
zombis (2) n 090.2
zone lines (1) n 107.3
Zone (1) 086.1
zonked (3) v 115.5
~ out (2) v 115.5
~ -out people n 114.3
zoo (17) n/adj 106.8
~ park (1) n 106.4
Zoo (3) 106.4
zoon bug (1) n 020.6
zoot suit (1) n 081.9
Zouave troops (1) n 075.6
Zs (2) 096.6
zu (1) adv G 011.1
zucchini (36) n/adj 056.6
~ squash (8) n 056.6
Zulu (1) 088.8
Zunge (1) n G 020.8
Zwolle (1) LA 086.1
zydeco (2) n 037.4